D1759186

MILTON KEYNES
COUNCIL

WHO'S WHO IN ART

AN APPEAL

TO

ARTISTS

AND

AGENTS

Applications for inclusion in *Who's Who in Art* are always sympathetically considered. If you know of an artist who you think should be included an entry form will be sent on request. Ten lines are inserted free of charge and there is no obligation whatsoever to purchase a copy of the book. Any information that should be added to existing entries should be sent to the Editor immediately. *Who's Who in Art* is revised every two years.

WHO'S WHO
IN ART

THIRTIETH EDITION

THE   ART   TRADE   PRESS   LTD
HAVANT   HANTS

Distributed exclusively in the United States of America, its possessions, Canada and Mexico by The Gale Group Inc. 27500 Drake Road, Farmington Hills, Michigan 48331 - 3535 U.S.A.

©

THE ART TRADE PRESS LTD., 2002

9 BROCKHAMPTON ROAD, HAVANT, HANTS

First Published *1927*
Sixth Edition (Reset) *1952*
Thirtieth Edition *2002*

ISBN 0-900083-19-0

Printed in Great Britain by
The Cromwell Press, Trowbridge, Wiltshire

CONTENTS

PUBLISHER'S NOTES

IN COMPILING *Who's Who in Art* it is our aim to produce a comprehensive list of biographical details of living artists in Britain and Ireland today.

Overseas artists are represented but we have decided not to add any new names, so that their numbers will gradually dwindle, until we are left with artists in or from the British Isles.

Who's Who in Art embraces exponents of all forms of painting and drawing, graphic art and sculpture in their widest forms and in any mediums.

One of the criticisms always levied at "Who's Who"-type publications is that many famous names are excluded. The omission of well-known names is most regrettable, but we are limited to those artists who wish their names to appear.

If by any chance there are any artists of repute in Britain today who have never been approached by us, we can only apologize for the oversight and hope that if they should read these Publisher's Notes they will inform us of the omission so that they may appear in the next edition of *Who's Who in Art*, which will be published in 2004.

All the entries in the last edition have been submitted to the individuals concerned and any corrections or additions sent in by them have been incorporated in the *Thirtieth Edition.* We have approached numerous additional artists, and many new names appear for the first time. We always welcome applicants and names of artists recommended by others.

Exactly the same procedure has been followed as in the compilation of former editions. We gratefully acknowledge the kind assistance of all who have contributed information, including the various societies, art galleries and numerous individuals who have helped us in this edition.

Unfortunately, several months must elapse between the closing dates for accepting revision of entries and final publication and we regret any late changes which are not reflected in this edition.

AIMS AND ACTIVITIES OF ACADEMIES, GROUPS, SOCIETIES, ETC.

Armed Forces Art Society

Annual Exhibition in London. All who are currently serving or have ever served in any branch of the Royal Navy, the Army or the Royal Air Force (including auxiliary, territorial, volunteer and reserve units and the Women's branches of the services) and/or their spouses, are eligible to submit works for the exhibition as Members or Associates of the Society.

Chairman: Col. C. D. A. Blessington, The Oast House, Peelings Manor, Hankham, nr. Pevensey, East Sussex BN24 5AP.

British Society of Painters
(In Oils, Pastel and Acrylics) (1987)

Formed to promote the very best in works of art in these media. Society formed of Hon. Fellows, Fellows and Members, in a very short time has become a leading Society in the field with twelve Fellows and fifty members; promoting all that is best in traditional values, allowing artists in any media to compete unrestricted in open exhibition - showing their works alongside those of the Fellows and Members - with the opportunity of being selected for Membership. (Membership on merit - restricted by selection).

Major Prize "The Old Masters Award", presented annually. Also many other prestigious prizes. Exhibitions bi-annually, Spring and Autumn at the Kings Hall/Winter Gardens Complex, Ilkley, West Yorkshire - central geographical position, equi-distant from Scotland, the South, the West Country and the East Coast. Applications for exhibition to the Director.

Hon. Fellows: David Shepherd, O.B.E., F.R.S.A., Terence Cuneo, O.B.E., Rowland Hilder, P.P.R.I., R.S.M.A., O.B.E. *The First International Hon. Fellow*: The late Pietro Annigoni. *Secretary*: Margaret Simpson, Briargate, 2 The Brambles, Ilkley, W. Yorkshire LS29 9DH.

The British Watercolour Society

Only the second major Art Society to leave London; formerly The Royal Water-colour Society Art Club, reverted its title to that of The British Watercolour Society (1911) which became defunct in 1961. The aims of The Society are to promote all that is best in the traditional values of watercolours, allowing watercolourists to compete in unrestricted open exhibition, showing their works alongside those of the Members and Associate Members - membership restricted by selection.

Several thousands of pounds in prizes annually - two Exhibitions per year, Summer and Christmas, at The Kings Hall/Winter Gardens Complex, Ilkley, West Yorkshire - central geographical position equi-distant from Scotland, the South, the West Country and the East Coast. Applications to The Director.

Hon. Members: Sir Robin Philipson, R.S., P.P.R.S.A., R.S.W., Rowland Hilder, P.P.R.I., R.S.M.A., O.B.E., Edith Hilder, W. J. L. Baillie, R.S.A., P.R.S.W., W. Heaton-Cooper, R.I. *President:* Kenneth Emsley, M.A. (Cantab), L.L.M., F.R.S.A. *Secretary:* Margaret Simpson. *Director:* Leslie Simpson, F.R.S.A., Briargate, 2 The Brambles, Ilkley, W. Yorkshire LS29 9DH.

The Chartered Society of Designers

The Chartered Society of Designers is the professional body representing the interests of designers. Its function is to promote high standards of professional practice in design, to foster professionalism and to emphasise designers' responsibility to Society, to the client and to each other.

Established in 1930 and granted its Royal Charter in 1976, it represents product, exhibition interior, fashion, textile and graphic designers, design educators and design managers.

The CSD provides a wide range of member benefits and services including events, training, seminars and information service, a wide range of specialist publications and professional services, and its journal.

The CSD is the British member of BEDA, Bureau of European Design Associations.

Address: 5 Bermondsey Exchange, 179-181 Bermondsey St., London, SE1 3UW. *Tel:* 020 7357 8088. *Fax:* 020 7407 9878. *e-mail:* csd@csd.org.uk

Chelsea Art Society

Exhibition held annually at The Main Hall, Chelsea Old Town Hall, Kings Rd., London SW3.

President: Julian Barrow. *Vice-President*: Sheila Donaldson Walters. *Hon. Secretary:* Heather Wills-Sandford. *Hon. Treasurer:* Michael Reeve. *Council:* Julian Barrow, Roger Dellar, Sheila Donaldson Walters, F.R.S.A., Dennis Gilbert, N.E.A.C., Leslie Gooday, O.B.E., John J. Petts, Ann Mavroleon Dixon, Sally McGill, James Parfitt, Marie Claire Romagny, Diana Whelan, A.R.B.S., Ann Wright, Katherine Yates. *Address:* Hon.Secretary, 50 Bowerdean St., London SW6 3TW. *Tel*: 020 7731 3121.

Federation of British Artists

The Federation of British Artists was incorporated on 13 Feb., 1961 with the following objects: (1) To provide adequate and modern facilities for art exhibitions, conferences, lectures, etc., at a reasonable cost to societies and individual artists. (2) By using the accommodation to the utmost extent, to reduce the costs to the art societies, thus enabling each society to retain its individual character and raise the standard of its exhibitions by being more selective. (3) To sponsor or help to sponsor exhibitions of work by younger or deserving painters, to enable them to become better known to the public. (4) To provide a central forum for the arts and to establish a representative body which would speak with authority. (5) To provide a central source of information on all contemporary art matters. The Federation administers The Mall Galleries, The Mall, London SW1.

The Federation is a charity and incorporates the majority of London art societies, including the Royal Institute of Oil Painters, The Royal Institute of Painters in Watercolours, The Royal Society of British Artists, The Royal Society of Marine Artists, The Royal Society of Portrait Painters, The Hesketh Hubbard Art Society, The New English Art Club, The Pastel Society (incorporating The Pencil Society), The Society of Wildlife Artists.

The Singer and Friedlander and the Laing Group Awards for the Best Watercolours and the Best Oils of the year are presented at Annual Exhibitions.

In addition, the Federation organises annually many exhibitions and important One Man Shows or group exhibitions.

No financial aid is given to the Federation which maintains itself upon the proceeds of its own activities.

Chairman of Governors: Bob Boas. *Address:* 17 Carlton House Terr., London SW1Y 5BD. *Tel:* 020 7930 6844.

Free Painters and Sculptors (F.P.S.)

This FPS was founded in 1952 when painter members of the ICA formed an individual group devoted to the principle of a 'free association of painters for mutual assistance, without regard to style, with no theory held in common, but believing in vital experiment and friendship'. Initially known as the Free Painters Group, the name was changed in the mid-Sixties to the Free Painters and Sculptors to include sculptors who had become an integral part of the Group.

In 1972 the FPS opened the Loggia Gallery in Buckingham Gate where exhibitions of members' work, either in group or one-person shows, are held throughout the year. Group exhibitions are also held in galleries out of London.

Membership is £25 annually. Persons interested in the visual arts are welcomed and applications will be submitted to the Executive Committee. Full membership is awarded to practising artists whose work is of the required standard. Fellowship is awarded to Full members solely on the quality of their work.

The Free Painters and Sculptors is an Incorporated body and is registered as an Educational Charity.

Chairman: Max Birne. *Hon. Secretary:* Owen Legg. *Address:* 15 Buckingham Gate, London SW1E 6LB. *Tel:* 020 7828 5963.

The Loggia Gallery is temporarily closed for refurbishment. An active circuit of outside exhibitions is being reintroduced.

Glasgow Art Club

This Club was formed in 1867 to advance the cause of and stimulate interest in art in all its branches by means of exhibitions of works of art, life classes, the acquisition of Publications on art, lectures on art subjects, and by such other means as the Council may decide from time to time. Consequently, the Club's Membership comprises painters, sculptors, architects and others involved in creative work as Artist Members and ladies and gentlemen interested in art as Lay Members. To be admitted to Artist membership, candidates must submit examples of their work for the approval of the Artist Members. Painters, sculptors and members pay on admission an entry fee.

Secretary: David Watson, C.A., Gillespie & Anderson, 147 Bath St., Glasgow G2 4SN. *Tel:* 0141 248 4884. *Fax:* 0141 248 5630.

Hesketh Hubbard Art Society

Founded as RBA Art Club under the auspices of the Royal Society of British Artists. Members meet on Monday or Friday evenings to draw from the model throughout the year. New members admitted any Monday or Friday after a folio of work is inspected. No tuition unless specially requested. The Mall Galleries, The Mall, SW1.

President: Simon Whittle. *Chairman:* Colin McMillan. *Address:* 17 Carlton House Terr., London SW1Y 5BD. *Tel:* 020 7930 6844.

The Hilliard Society of Miniaturists

Society founded in 1982. Membership of approximately 300 worldwide consisting of Patrons and Artists. Annual exhibition in June. Awards dinner lunch A.G.M. and workshop at that time. Two Newsletters a year. Full Exhibiting Artists entitled to use H.S. (H.S.F.- Founder member). Charter Member of the World Federation of Miniaturists.

Enquiries: The Secretary, 7 Priory Rd., Wells, Somerset BA5 1SR. *Telephone:* 01749 674472. *Fax:* 01749 672918. *e-mail:* hilliard.society @talk21.com. *website:* www.art-in-miniature.org.

The International Guild of Artists

Now exclusively restricted to 20 leading artists as Hon. Fellows and Fellows of the Society. Lesser activities have been suspended for 1992.

Principal: I.G.A., Briargate, 2 The Brambles, Ilkley, W. Yorkshire LS29 9DH.

Ultimate aim of the Guild to act as adviser to the British Watercolour Society, Society of Miniaturists, British Society of Painters, Yorkshire Artists Exhibition. The four major National Societies annually on show at The Kings Hall/Winter Gardens Complex, Ilkley, West Yorkshire, and The G-Mex, Manchester.

Ipswich Art Society

President: Jack Haste. *Chair:* Jacqueline Marks.

Ipswich Art Society, founded in 1874, put on its 124th Annual Open Exhibition in 2001. There have been held, also, a Print Fair by the society's printmakers group, the Anna Airy Award Exhibition for young artists aged 16-25, and separate exhibitions of work of full members and of friends of the society. Membership in 2001 was 214.

To join, write to the Membership Secretary, 2 Tuddenham Rd., Ipswich, IP4 2SG. For further information visit the website, www.ipswich-art-society.org.uk.

The National Acrylic Painters' Association

This Association, founded in 1985, is for all practising artists and painters, who wish to explore the potential of the acrylic medium. A person is elected into either full or associate membership. It is recognised that acrylic painting is but a medium amongst others, yet that as a painting substance it has a flexibility that renders it extremely versatile.

Founder and Director General: Kenneth J. Hodgson. *President:* Alwyn Crawshaw. *Vice-President:* Vacant. *The Association's patrons are:* Professor Brendan Neiland, R.A., Dr. Sally A. Bulgin, Kay Greenwood-Casey, Mark Golden, Dr Catherine Marcangeli, The Master of the Fine Art Trade Guild.

In 1995 the Association established an American Division. The Director is Linda S. Gunn, the President is Gerald Brommer, the Vice-President is Sandy Carpenter. N.A.P.A. also has members in Brazil, Canada, France, Germany, Greece, India, Italy, Malta, Portugal and Spain.

Further information and details of membership obtainable from: Membership Secretary, National Acrylic Painters' Association, 103 Springfield Park, Haydock WA11 0XP, or 134 Rake Lane, Wallasey, Wirral, Merseyside CH45 1JW.

National Society of Painters, Sculptors and Printmakers

The National Society was formed in 1930 to escape rigid traditionalism by allowing Member Artists to exhibit a diversity of the best of creative art with full freedom of expression. The objects of the Society are to advance the awareness of the public by promoting, demonstrating or teaching painting, sculpture and printmaking and to hold an annual exhibition in London (and secondary exhibitions from time to time) of the work of artists of every creed and outlook representing all aspects under one roof without prejudice or favour to anyone.

Membership is in two categories: Members (N.S.) and Associate Members (A.M.N.S.). Members are elected on merit from among those Associates who have had at least two works selected for the annual exhibition for three years. Application information may be requested from the Hon. Secretary.

A Newsletter is sent to Members and Associates twice a year.

President: Denis C. Baxter, U.A., F.R.S.A. *Hon. Secretary:* Gwen Spencer. *Address:* 122 Copse Hill, Wimbledon, London SW20 0NL.

Nature in Art

NATURE IN ART is a museum of fine, decorative and applied art inspired by nature. It opened to the public in May 1988 and in June 1988 HRH Princess Alexandra attended a celebration of the opening. Nature in Art is the first of its kind anywhere in the world. It is housed in a fine, early Georgian mansion set in its own grounds and is owned and managed by Nature in Art Trust, registered charity 1000553.

Nature in Art is readily accessible from M5 (J11 and 11A) and the centre of Gloucester (both 10 minutes by car). The entrance is on A38 in Twigworth, one mile North of A40.

Art inspired by nature, from all periods and parts of the world in any medium, including works by living artists, is included in the permanent collection. All aspects of nature are included (but domestic, farm and sporting animals etc. are excluded). Temporary exhibitions are held regularly and the permanent collection on show is regularly changed.

Nature in Art was twice "specially commended" in the National Heritage Museum of the Year Awards. The museum is fully registered.

Handicapped people are specially welcome. Facilities include free car parking, meals and light refreshments all day, library and reference collection of slides and other information, childrens play area, shop, studios and nature garden with open air sculptures. Different artists are in residence February/November and courses and demonstrations on a wide range of art techniques are arranged. A new conference/education centre opened in 1994.

Open Tuesday-Sunday and Bank Holidays 10am-5pm. Closed other Mondays, (except by special arrangement when the facilities of Wallsworth Hall can be privately hired), and on Dec. 24, 25 and 26. Full details are available from the Deputy Director.

Patron: H.R.H. Princess Alexandra. *President:* Lady Scott. *Director:* Simon H. Trapnell. *Address:* Wallsworth Hall, Twigworth, Gloucester GL2 9PA. *Tel:* 01452 731422. *Fax:* 01452 730937. www.nature-in-art.org.uk

Nature in Art Trust

Established as a Registered Charity (No. 1000553) in 1982, the Trust owns and manages Nature in Art. This centre has been created to exhibit, study and teach fine, decorative and applied art inspired by nature in all media from all national origins and all historical periods depicting any living (or previously living) wild thing. The facilities of Nature in Art are described under that title.

Friends of the Trust receive a regular Newsletter, *Nature in Art*, free admission to all regular activities of the Society, use of the library etc. Individual and gallery membership (for commercial and institutional galleries) is available. Further details from the Membership Secretary, Nature in Art (q.v.).

Patron: H.R.H. Princess Alexandra. *President:* Lady Scott. *Director:* Simon H. Trapnell. *Address*: Wallsworth Hall, Twigworth, Gloucester GL2 9PA. *Tel*: 01452 731422. *Fax:* 01452 730937. www.nature-in-art.org.uk

New English Art Club

The New English Art Club was founded in 1886. Its origin was a wave of foreign influence in the person of a number of students who had worked in the Parisian schools. The New English Art Club came into existence as a protest against a false concept of tradition, and it stands today against an equally false rejection of tradition. The annual exhibition is held in the Mall Galleries, The Mall, SW1, when the work of non-members is considered for display, November/December.

President: Ken Howard, R.A., R.W.S., R.W.A. *Hon. Treasurer:* David Corsellis. *Keeper:* Charlotte Halliday, R.B.A. *Assistant Keeper:* Robert Brown. *Address:* 17 Carlton House Terr., London SW1Y 5BD. *Tel:* 020 7930 6844.

Newlyn Art Gallery

Newlyn Art Gallery plays an important role in the South-West as one of the leading venues for contemporary art. The programme reflects current U.K. and international art practice and includes regular shows from locally-based artists. As an educational charity Newlyn Art Gallery aims to promote and encourage greater understanding and enjoyment of contemporary art. Throughout the year we present nine major exhibitions and associated educational events.

Director: Elizabeth Knowles. *Education Officer:* Esen Kaya. *Address:* Newlyn, Penzance, Cornwall TR18 5PZ. *Tel:* 01736 363715. *Fax*: 01736 331578.

Pastel Society

Founded 1898. Annual exhibition open to all artists who work in any 'dry" medium, i.e. pastel, pencil, charcoal, chalk, conté, sanguine, etc., at The Mall Galleries, The Mall, SW1, usually March.

President: Thomas Coates. *Vice-President:* Moira Huntly. *Secretary:* Brian Gallagher. *Treasurer:* David Danridge. *Address:* 17 Carlton House Terr., London SW1Y 5BD. *Tel:* 020 7930 6844.

Royal Academy of Arts

The Royal Academy was founded in 1768 under the patronage of George III. Sir Joshua Reynolds was the first President. It was to be a "Society for promoting the arts of design". Since that date it has fulfilled this role through promotion of the work of living artists with an unbroken series of Summer Exhibitions, held annually since 1769. It provides post-graduate training for 60 students in the Royal Academy Schools, which were established at the foundation. The Academy continues to administer trust funds for the benefit of artists and for the promotion of the visual arts, and has a distinguished Library. Loan exhibitions, of great international importance, date from the 1870's. The Royal Academy receives no direct Government subsidy. It is an independent, self-supporting institution, under the patronage of the Crown, and its activities are directed by its Members (Painters, Engravers, Sculptors and Architects) who serve in rotation on the Council. The President is elected annually.

The Royal Academy is supported by sponsorship, through the subscriptions of its 83,000 Friends, and of its Corporate Members, through an active fund-raising programme and through retail sales of art books and specially commissioned works and a fine art framing service.

President: Professor Phillip King, C.B.E. *Keeper:* Professor Brendan Neiland. *Treasurer:* Professor Paul Huxley. *Secretary:* David Gordon. *Address:* Burlington House, Piccadilly, London W1J 0BD. *Tel:* 020 7300 8000.

Royal Birmingham Society of Artists

The Royal Birmingham Society of Artists is a non-profit-making society, with its own spacious exhibition galleries in the Jewellery Quarter of Birmingham, close to St. Paul's Square which is an active restaurant/cultural centre.

The gallery has a craft area featuring the work of local craftsmen, a cafe, and two further exhibition galleries. These galleries are available for hire for exhibitions and evening meetings, when not in use by the Society - the programme for which is published early each year.

Schedules for the three Open Exhibitions may be obtained from the Secretary by sending a stamped addressed envelope six weeks before the sending in day.

A Prize Exhibition is held annually with a top prize of £1000 for Painting, donated to the R.B.S.A., and many other prizes for sculpture, ceramics, etc. that are specially donated by Birmingham industries.

The Society also holds a Members and Associates Exhibition in the Autumn, and hosts, for Birmingham, the Singer & Friedlander/Sunday Times Watercolour Competition.

There is also a flourishing Friends of the R.B.S.A., who hold two Exhibitions per year at the Gallery.

For details apply to the Hon. Secretary, The Royal Birmingham Society of Artists, 4 Brook St., St. Paul's, Birmingham B3 1SA. *Tel:* 0121 236 4353.

Royal Cambrian Academy of Art

The Royal Cambrian Academy of Art was founded in 1881, and granted its Royal Charter in 1882. The Headquarters have been in Conwy since 1886. In 1993 the Academy moved from Plas Mawr to its new purpose built Gallery, where Exhibitions are held throughout the year. The main open Exhibition is the Annual Summer Exhibition, and forms for this exhibition and membership of the Academy, may be obtained from the Gallery.

President: Kyffin Williams, O.B.E., M.A., R.A. *Vice-President:* Dr. Ivor Davies. *Hon. Treasurer:* Tom Jones. *Hon. Secretary:* Malcolm Edwards. *Curator:* Ms.Vicky Macdonald. *Address:* Crown Lane, Conwy LL32 8AN. Gallery open 11 a.m.-5p.m. daily except Monday, Sunday 1-4.30p.m. *Tel:* 01492-593413.

Royal Glasgow Institute of the Fine Arts

This Institute was founded in 1861 and has now over 1,500 Members. Its object is "to promote a taste for art generally and more specifically to encourage contemporary art, to further the diffusion of artistic and aesthetic knowledge and to aid the study, advancement and development of art in its application." Towards the attainment of this object, the Institute holds open annual exhibitions in the McLellan Galleries, Glasgow, and shows approximately 400 works in all mediums. The R.G.I. Kelly Gallery is available for hire. The Membership fee is an initial payment of £35, Annual subscription £15, Corporate membership £100.

President: Dr. Kenneth G. Chrystie, LL.B. (Hons.). *Secretary:* Gordon C. McAllister, C.A. *Address:* 5 Oswald St., Glasgow G1 4QR. *Tel:* 0141 248 7411. *Fax:* 0141 2210417. *e-mail:* enquiries@robbferguson.co.uk

Royal Hibernian Academy

The Academy was incorporated by Charter of King George IV in 1823 with the intention of encouraging the fine arts in Ireland by giving Irish artists the opportunity of exhibiting their works annually. It was reorganized under a new Charter in 1861 and enlarged to thirty Constituent Members, and up to the present time has consistently fulfilled its original aims.

The Academy has encouraged and developed art in Ireland since its foundation. It has given the Irish artist his status; and the present position of Irish Art can be said to be the outcome of the encouragement it has afforded to Irish men and women of talent and the part it has taken in art affairs generally in the country. There is hardly an Irish artist of note living or dead who has not been a member of the Academy or who has not benefited in one way or another by its activities.

President: Arthur Gibney. *Treasurer:* Carey Clarke. *Secretary:* Conor Fallon. *Keeper:* Liam Belton. *Address:* 15 Ely Place, Dublin 2.

Royal Institute of Oil Painters

Founded in 1883 as the Institute of Painters in Oil Colours. The annual exhibition, which is open to all artists, subject to selection, is held in the Mall Galleries, The Mall, SW1.

President: Olwen Tarrant. *Vice-President:* Julia Easterling. *Hon. Treasurer:* Dennis Syrett. *Hon. Secretary:* Brian Roxby. *Address:* 17 Carlton House Terr., London SW1Y 5BD. *Tel:* 020 7930 6844.

The Royal Institute of Painters in Water-colours

Formed in 1831 as the "New Society of Painters in Water-colours," a title which was afterwards changed to the "Institute of Painters in Water-colours." Shortly after the opening of the 1884 Exhibition the command of Queen Victoria was received that the Society should henceforth be called "The Royal Institute of Water-colours."

The honour of a diploma under the Royal Sign Manual was given to the members on August 29, 1884, by virtue of which they rank as *Esquires.*

Members are limited to 100. Annual Open Exhibition, March, at The Mall Galleries, The Mall, SW1.

President: Ronald Maddox, F.C.S.D., F.S.A.I. *Vice-President:* Peter Folkes, R.W.A. *Hon. Secretary:* Peter Dawson, A.R.W.A. *Exhibitions Secretary:* Tony Hunt. *Address:* 17 Carlton House Terr., London SW1Y 5BD. *Tel:* 020 7930 6844.

Royal Scottish Academy

The Academy is an independent body incorporated by Royal Charter for the furtherance of art in Scotland and for educational purposes. Annual exhibitions of contemporary art: Mid-April to July; special Festival exhibitions: August to mid-September.

President: Ian McKenzie Smith, O.B.E., D.A., R.S.A., P.R.S.W., F.R.S.A., F.S.S., F.M.A., F.S.A.Scot., LL.D. *Secretary:* Bill Scott, R.S.A., D.A., F.R.B.S. *Treasurer:* Isi Metzstein, O.B.E., R.S.A., M.A., A.R.I.A.S. *Librarian:* Peter Collins, R.S.A. *Administrative Secretary:* Bruce Laidlaw, A.C.I.S. *Address:* 17 Waterloo Place, Edinburgh, EH1 3BG. *Tel:* 0131 558 7097. *Fax*: 0131 557 6417. *e-mail:* info@royalscottishacademy.org

Royal Scottish Society of Painters in Watercolour

This Society was founded in 1878, and in 1888 Queen Victoria conferred on it the title "Royal." In its first Exhibition twenty-five artists showed their works; today there are 118 exhibiting Members. The object of the Society is to encourage and develop the art of painting in watercolour and the appreciation of this art, and toward the attainment of that object exhibitions of watercolour painting are held annually. While these are normally held in Edinburgh, they have on occasion been held in Glasgow, Aberdeen, Dundee and Perth. Candidates for Membership must be sponsored by Members of the Society, and must submit works for the consideration of the Members at an election meeting. The entrance fee is £30 and the annual subscription £45.

Secretary: Gordon C. McAllister, C.A. *Address:* 5 Oswald St., Glasgow G1 4QR. *Tel:* 0141 248 7411. *Fax:* 0141 221 0417. *e-mail:* enquiries@robbferguson.co.uk. *Website:* www.rsw-exhibitions.com.

Royal Society of British Artists

This Society was founded in 1823, incorporated by Royal Charter in 1847 and constituted a Royal Society in 1887. Membership is limited to 200. Annual exhibition held each year, when the work of non-members is admitted after selection at The Mall Galleries, The Mall, SW1.

President: Cav. Romeo di Girolamo. *Hon. Secretary:* Carol Hubble. *Hon. Treasurer:* Leigh Parry. *Keeper:* Alfred Daniels. *Address:* 17 Carlton House

Terr., London SW1Y 5BD. *Tel:* 020 7930 6844.

Royal Society of British Sculptors

The Royal Society of British Sculptors (R.B.S.) is a membership society for professional sculptors, founded in 1904. It is a registered charity which exists to 'promote and advance the art of sculpture', to ensure the continued widespread debate on contemporary sculpture and to promote the pursuit of excellence in the artform.

We provide services to subscribing members by offering advice on all technical, aesthetic and legal matters concerning the production of sculpture, which assists artists in producing excellent work and ensures that both artist and client can achieve the best results. We advocate good and fair practice in the commissioning and exhibition of work, and offer guidelines for both artists and clients to help ensure this is achieved. We actively encourage the exchange of ideas by organising workshops, lectures and exhibitions and are involved in projects which ensure the continued improvement in sculpture education.

The R.B.S. has over 350 professional members throughout the U.K. and internationally, from world acclaimed names like Sir Anthony Caro and Richard Serra. It also offers membership for recent sculpture graduates and less established artists, providing advice on the way to establishing professional practice.

The R.B.S. houses a comprehensive resource centre and library for contemporary sculpture which contains visuals and information about all members of the R.B.S. Via an easy-to-use slide library, the best of contemporary sculpture is accessible to all for commissioning, exhibiting or research purposes. The R.B.S. extends an invitation to anyone wanting to obtain a work of sculpture, source a particular artist or learn more about the artform to use the slide library.

The R.B.S. can also offer a consultancy service for large scale public commissions, providing advice and expertise from the selection of an artist right through to safe installation and the PR activities surrounding an unveiling.

The Society is run by a Council of elected sculptors. Membership of the R.B.S. is by application (submit 10 slides and an up-to-date CV). The Council meets every month to review the applications and membership when the work submitted is of a sufficiently professional criteria. The general membership meet twice a year in April and October.

Criteria for membership.

Any practicing professional sculptor over the age of 21 may apply by submitting:

(1) An up-to-date CV (to include name, address, phone/fax number).

(2) 10 x 35mm slide.

(3) Typed slide list detailing title of work, dimensions and material.

(4) A cheque for £23.50 to cover our administration costs.

President: Derek Morris, P.R.B.S., A.R.C.A. *Vice President:* Simon Stringer, V.P.R.B.S. *Hon. Treasurer:* Maurice Blik. *Address:* 108 Old Brompton Rd., S. Kensington, London SW7 3RA. *Tel:* 020 7244 7788. *Fax:* 020 7370 3721. *e-mail:* RBS@SculptureCompany.demon.co.uk

Royal Society of Marine Artists

Founded 1939, following a major exhibition entitled "Sea Power" under the patronage of King George V and opened by Winston Churchill. First exhibition was not until 1946 owing to the war. Initially known as The Society of Marine Artists, the right to use the title "Royal" was granted by H.M. The Queen in 1966.

Membership in two categories: Artist Members and Lay Members who are not necessarily painters but wish to further marine painting. The latter are admitted for a subscription of £15.00 p.a. and are given many advantages i.e. invitation to annual party, Private Views, prizes of pictures and first choice of pictures for sale. Open exhibition annually at The Mall Galleries, The Mall, SW1 Oct./Nov.

President: Bert Wright. *Vice-President:* Geoff Hunt. *Hon. Secretary:* David Howell. *Hon. Treasurer:* Alan Simpson. *Address:* 17 Carlton House Terr., London SW1Y 5BD. *Tel:* 020 7930 6844.

Royal Society of Miniature Painters, Sculptors and Gravers

This Society was founded in 1896 and its aim is to promote the fine art of minia-ture painting or any allied craft. The annual exhibition will usually be held in November (handing-in day in September) at the Westminster Gallery, Westminster Central Hall, Storey's Gate, London SW1H 9NH.

The Gold Bowl Award was established in 1985 and is one of the highest accolades for miniature art in the world. Non-members may submit work.

Membership is by selection after establishing a consistently high standard of work. (A.R.M.S. - Associate Member, R.M.S. - Full Member).

President: Suzanne Lucas, F.L.S. *Hon. Treasurer:* Alastair MacDonald. *Hon. Secretary:* Pauline Gyles.

For further information contact the *Executive Secretary:* Mrs. Pamela Henderson, 1 Knapp Cottages, Wyke, Gillingham, Dorset SP8 4NQ. *Tel:* 01747 825718.

Royal Society of Painter-Printmakers

The Royal Society of Painter-Printmakers was founded in 1880. The Society was granted a Royal Charter in 1911. Eminent Past-Presidents have been Sir F. Seymour Haden, Sir Frank Short, Malcolm Osborne and Robert Austin. All the well-known printmakers have exhibited with the Society, whose annual exhibi-tion caters for and encourages all forms of printmaking. An election of Associates is held annually.

As part of its aim to promote a knowledge and understanding of original printmaking, the Society organises courses, talks and tours.

President: Prof. David Carpanini. *Secretary:* Judy Dixey. *Address:* Bankside Gallery, 48 Hopton St., London SE1 9JH. *Tel:* 020 7928 7521. *Fax:*

020 7928 2820.

Royal Society of Portrait Painters

This Society was founded in 1891 and has for its object the promotion of the fine art of portrait painting. The annual exhibition is held during April/May in The Mall Galleries, The Mall, SW1 and non members may submit work in any medium, except miniatures or sculpture, to the Selection Committee.

President: Paul Brason. *Vice-President:* Richard Foster. *Hon. Treasurer:* John Walton. *Hon. Secretary:* David Cobley. *Address:* 17 Carlton House Terr., London SW1Y 5BD. *Tel:* 020 7930 6844.

Royal Ulster Academy of Arts

President: Joseph McWilliams, P.R.U.A. *Secretary:* Kay McKelvey, 57 Ballycoan Rd., Belfast BT8 8LL. *Treasurer:* Ken Kennedy, A.C.A. All communications to *Secretary.*

Royal Watercolour Society

The Royal Water-Colour Society, which is next in seniority to the Royal Academy, was founded in 1804. It has numbered amongst its distinguished Members John Varley, Peter de Wint, David Cox, John Sell Cotman, Samuel Prout, Samuel Palmer, Ambrose McEvoy and D. Y. Cameron to mention but a few. Two exhibitions are held annually - in the spring and autumn. These exhibitions are confined to the works of Members. An annual exhibition open to all water-colour painters is held in the summer. There is an annual election of Associates.

As part of its educational remit, the Society organises courses, talks, tours and other events on the subject of water-colour.

President: Francis Bowyer. *Secretary:* Judy Dixey. *Address:* Bankside Gallery, 48 Hopton St., Blackfriars, London SE1 9JH. *Tel:* 020 7928 7521. *Fax:* 020 7928 2820.

Royal West of England Academy

The Academy was founded in 1844. Election to Membership (R.W.A.) is by postal ballot. The Academy is an independent, self-supporting institution, founded to assist professional artists, sculptors and architects, through exhibitions and other activities. Regular and varied exhibitions are shown at its galleries. An Open Exhibition is held every autumn; open sculpture, painting and print exhibitions are held triennially; information may be obtained from the office.

President: Derek Balmer, P.R.W.A., *Academy Secretary:* Rachel Fear.

Address: Queen's Rd., Clifton, Bristol BS8 1PX. *Tel:* 0117 973 5129. *Fax:* 0117 923 7874. *Website:* www.rwa.org.uk

St. Ives Society of Artists

Holds exhibitions of new works by Members between March and November in the main body of the Old Mariners Church. Downstairs in the Mariners Gallery (the old crypt) there is a full programme of solo or group exhibitions through-out the season.

President: Lord St. Levan. *Secretary and Curator:* Judy Joel. *Address:* Old Mariners Church, Norway Sq., St. Ives, Cornwall TR26 1NA.

Scottish Artists' Benevolent Association

This Association was formed in 1889, and gives assistance to distressed deserv-ing artists, their widows and dependants. Each year it disburses over £10,000. Membership is open to anyone and the subscription payable is £25 (Life).

Secretary: Gordon C. McAllister, C.A. *Address:* Second Floor, 5 Oswald St., Glasgow G1 4QR. *Tel:* 0141 248 7411. *Fax:* 0141 248 0417.

Society of Botanical Artists

The Society of Botanical Artists is an International Society, founded in 1985. Holds an open exhibition in the Westminster Gallery, Westminster Central Hall, Storey's Gate, London SW1H 9NH each year April/May with other exhi-bitions of members' work. Combines art and science and strives to enhance botanical art by proper promotion. Newsletter and Social meetings for mem-bers.

Founder President: Suzanne Lucas, F.L.S. *Hon. Treasurer:* Pamela Davis. *Hon. Secretary:* Paula Joyce. Enquiries to *Executive Secretary:* Mrs. Pamela Henderson, 1 Knapp Cottages, Wyke, Gillingham, Dorset SP8 4NQ. *Tel*: 01747 825718.

Society of Designer Craftsmen

The Society of Designer Craftsmen was founded in 1888 as The Arts and Crafts Exhibition Society with Walter Crane and William Morris among its most promi-nent members, each of whom was to serve as President. Its aim is to strengthen the professional standards and status of designer-makers in Great Britain and to stimulate public awareness by bringing works of fine craftsmanship before the public through major comprehensive exhibitions and specialised displays. In 1960 the Society assumed its present title as representative of the largest body of independent professional crafts practitioners in Britain. It lays great emphasis on helping young graduates at the outset of their careers by arranging assessments of their work and offering Licentiateship of the Society (L.S.D.C.) to those whose work is of a high standard. Among its other activities, the society mounts an annual exhibition of work by selected fellows, members and licentiates.

Applications for election as Members (M.S.D.C.) are considered on a regular basis thoughout the year by a Selection Committee, which meets to examine the individual craft pieces submitted. Fellowship of the Society (F.S.D.C.) may be awarded by a majority vote of the Fellows on Council.

Annual subscriptions: Fellows, £50; Members, £40; Licentiates, £25; Associates, £20. *Hon. Secretary:* Alicia Merrett, M.S.D.C. and Joanna Hayes. *Address:* 24 Rivington St., London EC2A 3DU. *Tel:* 020 7739 3663.

Society of Equestrian Artists

Founded in 1978/79, the Society of Equestrian Artists exists to encourage the study of equine art and, by mutual assistance between members, to promote a standard of excellence in its practice worthy of the subject's importance in British artistic traditions.

Membership comprises Associate and Full Members, who have attained a consistently high standard in their work, as well as Friends, who may be artist or non-artist.

Annual Exhibitions, normally August/September at Christie's, St. James's, London.

President: Peter Fenwick, O.B.E. *Vice-Presidents:* Air Vice-Marshal Norman E. Hoad, C.V.O., C.B.E., John N.Thompson. *Chairman:* Caro Skyrme. *Treasurer:* John Campbell. *Secretary:* Corinne Bickford, Golf Cottages, Godden Green, Sevenoaks, Kent, TN15 0JJ. *Tel:* 01732 762908.

Society of Graphic Fine Art
(formerly Society of Graphic Artists)

The Society was founded in 1919 to promote fine drawing skills whether with brush, pen, pencil, charcoal or any of the forms of original Printmaking. Newly elected Members remain Associates for a period of three years. The Society holds Annual Open Exhibition in central London and are increasing their out-of-town Exhibitions.

President: David Brooke, U.A., N.A.P.A., B.A.(Hons.). *Vice-Presidents:* Jo Hall, Geraldine Jones, Dip.A.D., R.A.P.G.C. *Hon. Treasurer:* Roger Lewis. *Secretary:* Sharon Curtis, 15 Willow Way, Hatfield, Herts. AL10 9QD.

Society of Miniaturists
(Founded London, May 1895)

The oldest Miniature Society in existence and the first major Society to leave London - its main aim is to promote the traditional, ancient and precise art of miniature painting that goes back many centuries. The Society holds two Exhibitions per year, Summer and Christmas, at The Kings Hall/Winter Gardens, Ilkley, West Yorkshire - a central geographical position equi-distant from the South, Scotland, West Country and the East Coast.

A major prize is presented at each Exhibition for the best miniature. Non-members can exhibit alongside Members work - applications to the Director.

President: Kenneth Emsley, M.A. (Cantab), L.L.M., F.R.S.A. *Secretary:* Margaret Simpson. *Director:* Leslie Simpson, F.R.S.A., Briargate, 2 The Brambles, Ilkley, W. Yorkshire LS29 9DH.

Society of Scottish Artists

The S.S.A. was founded in 1891 to represent the adventurous spirit in Scottish art. Today the S.S.A. has over 500 members throughout Britain of which 150 are elected Professional members. Associate and Ordinary membership is also available by payment of an annual subscription.

The main focus of the Society is its Annual Exhibition which traditionally takes place in the Royal Scottish Academy in Edinburgh in the Autumn. Submission of work is open to both members and non members, who undergo the same selection procedures, ensuring that each Annual Exhibition is unique, challenging and innovative.

For details about the Annual Exhibition (available from August) or about membership, contact the Secretary.

President: Katayoun Pasban Dowlatshahi. *Secretary:* Susan Cornish, 4 Barony St., Edinburgh, EH3 6PE. *Tel:* 0131 557 2354. *Website:* www.s-a-a.org.

Society of Wildlife Artists

Founded in 1964 to foster contact and co-ordinate activities among the many wildlife artists resident in this country and to improve both the standard and recognition of their work. The Society is supported by a number of Lay Members interested in the Society's work but not necessarily artists themselves. An annual exhibition is held in The Mall Galleries, The Mall, SW1 during July/August and this is open to non-members who may submit work.

President: Bruce Pearson. *Hon. Vice-Presidents:* Robert Gillmor, Roger Tory Peterson and Keith Shackleton. *Hon. Secretary:* Andrew Stock. *Address:* 17 Carlton House Terr., London SW1Y 5BD. *Tel:* 020 7930 6844.

Society of Women Artists

This Society was founded in 1855 for the encouragement of women painters and sculptors, etc. Annual Exhibitions February/March at the Westminster Gallery, Westminster Central Hall, Storey's Gate, London SW1H 9NH. Open to all women artists.

Patron: Princess Michael of Kent. *President:* Elizabeth Meek, R.M.S., H.S., F.R.S.A. *Vice-Presidents:* Susan Millis, S.E.A., Muriel Owen, U.A., N.D.D., A.T.D., F.R.S.A., Joyce Rogerson, R.M.S., Joyce Wyatt, R.M.S., Hon. U.A., A.S.A.F.(HC). *Hon. Treasurer:* Susan Millis, S.E.A. *Hon. Secretary:* Joyce Rogerson, R.M.S. *Executive Secretary:* Pamela Henderson, 1 Knapp Cottages, Wyke, Gillingham, Dorset SP8 4NQ.

The Society of Wood Engravers

Founded in 1920 by Gibbings, Gill, Hagreen, Raverat et al., and revived, after a brief lapse, in 1984, the Society promotes the practice and appreciation of wood engraving and related relief printmaking arts through an annual, open, touring exhibition, occasional publications and a regular newsletter. It is an international contact organisation for those interested in the subject. Subscription (£25 p.a.) is open to all, artists, collectors or enthusiasts. Membership is by election.

Chairman: Hilary Paynter, R.E. *Hon. Treasurer:* Joan Deckker. *Secretary:* Geraldine Waddington, 3 West St., Oundle, Northants, PE8 4EJ.

Ulster Society of Women Artists

The Ulster Society of Women Artists was founded in 1957 by Gladys Maccabe, M.A.(Hon.), R.O.I., F.R.S.A., for which she had long felt there was a need. This was to include painting, sculpture and other visual arts.

The aims of the Ulster Society of Women Artists are: (1) To promote and encourage a high standard of art in Ulster. (2) To maintain such a standard in exhibitions that election to membership be considered a mark of distinction. (3) To seek out and encourage talent.

The Society always welcomes new members. Those interested in joining may submit work to the Election Committee. Applications to the Hon. Secretary.

Patron: Her Grace, The Duchess of Abercorn. *President:* Maureen Cashell, U.S.W.A. *Vice-President:* Sara S. McNeill, D.A., F.I.L.S., U.S.W.A. *Hon. Treasurer:* Yvonne Adams, B.A., U.W.S. *Hon. Secretary*: Elizabeth Morrow, D.A., U.S.W.A., U.W.S., 33 Kensington Gdns South, Belfast, BT5 6NN.

United Society of Artists

Founded in 1921, the aim of the Society is to exhibit work of professional quality in oils, water-colours, pastels (with particular reference to drawing) and sculpture. Venues in London and throughout Britain. Election of new members is based on work submitted. 'U.A. News and Views' is a newsletter edited and produced by the President.

President: Leo Illesley Gibbons-Smith, S.G.F.A. *Vice-Presidents:* Constance Nash, N.D.D., A.T.D., Geoffrey I. Lilley, Roy Chaffin. *Secretary:* David Headon, Holmdene, 2 Wade Court Rd., Havant, Hants. PO9 2SU.

The Wapping Group of Artists

The Wapping Group of Artists is a muster of painters dedicated to painting from nature in company with one another on Wednesdays throughout the summer months. The founding membership was drawn from the Langham Sketching Club - their chosen subject London's river.

Following the 39/45 war, the founders, meeting in the Prospect of Whitby Public House at Wapping in 1946, decided to paint the Thames from the Pool of London down the dozen reaches to the estuary.

The 21 original members decided on a limited membership of 25 and this is still so.

The first president was Jack Merriott. One founder member, Pat Jobson, still paints with them.

Annual exhibitions were first at the P.L.A. on Tower Hill, later at the Royal Exchange, and subsequently at St. Botolphs Church, Aldgate, and then many other venues.

The river has changed amazingly but todays members still have the same love of painting and the same enthusiasm for their subject. Now in its 55th year, the group looks forward confidently.

Chris Beetles, who staged our 50th annual exhibition in his gallery, wrote in his introduction to the 50th year celebration book - "The Wapping Group of Artists is the last proper artists society left in England"

President: Trevor Chamberlain, R.O.I., R.S.M.A. *Hon. Sec.:* Alan Runagall, R.S.M.A., 7 Albany Rd., Rayleigh, Essex, SS6 8TE.

Yorkshire Artists Exhibition

Now recognised as the largest event of its kind in Great Britain, with between 1,000 and 1,500 paintings by over 200 artists on show, bi-annually. Exhibitions Spring and Autumn at The Kings Hall/Winter Gardens Complex, Ilkley, West Yorkshire.

The Exhibitions attract leading artists from all over Britain and abroad. Established over ten years, it is well supported by the art-buying public and commercial galleries, etc.

Application for entry to: The Director.

Hon. Patron: David Shepherd, F.R.S.A., O.B.E. *Director:* Leslie Simpson, F.R.S.A., Briargate, 2 The Brambles, Ilkley, W. Yorkshire LS29 9DH.

Yorkshire Watercolour Society

The Yorkshire Watercolour Society was founded in 1983 by several Yorkshire artists. The membership is by election of the Y.W.S. Committee, and has now grown to 50 Members, representing some of the counties finest exponents in water-colour.

It holds three prestigious regional exhibitions each year, and has occasional London showings.

Its 'Friends of the Society' includes Sir Marcus Fox and the President is the Rt. Hon. Lord Mason of Barnsley.

The Y.W.S. permanent exhibition is housed at Cannon Hall, Cawthorne, nr. Barnsley, Yorks.

Hon. Secretary: M. Townsend. *Tel:* 01484 713694.

WHO'S WHO IN ART

A

AARONS, Andrew, N.D.D. (1958), Postgrad.Dip. Printmaking (1991); painter/printmaker etchings and mezzotints; senior lecturer, Anglia University, Cambridge; *b* London, 1 Feb., 1939. *m* Paula. one *s.* one *d. Educ:* Camberwell School of Art, Junior Dept. (1951-54). *Studied:* Camberwell School of Art (1954-58). *Exhib:* Germany, U.K., Canada and U.S.A. *Work in collections:* C.B.C. Toronto; York University, Toronto; Barclays Bank; Bank of Mexico; Cambridge University; Sternberg Centre, London. *Commissions:* Bodilly Suite; Sporting Etchings: Serigraphs of Newmarket Life; Portraits; Landscapes and Mythology. *Publications:* Two Nations in a New Land; A History of Canadian Painting; Is this Art; Journal of Progressive Judaism: Jewish Quarterly; Kettles Yard Publication. *Signs work:* "AARONS" followed by year. *Address:* 16 Huntingdon Rd., Cambridge CB3 0HH.

ABBASSY, Samira, B.A.(Hons.) (1987); painter in oil on paper, canvas and board, gouache on paper, etchings; *b* Ahwaz, Iran, 29 May, 1965. *m* Guy Buckles. *Educ:* Hillview School for Girls, Tonbridge; West Kent College of F.E. *Studied:* Maidstone College of Art and Design, Canterbury College of Art. *Exhib:* Mercury Gallery, East West Gallery London, Joan Prats Gallery, N.Y. *Work in collections:* South East Arts, Leicestershire C.C. *Publications:* book jackets: Landscape Painted with Tea by Milorid Pavich, The Ice Factory by Russell Lucas. *Clubs:* Rye Soc. of Artists. *Signs work:* "Samira Abbassy." *Address:* c/o Mercury Gallery, 26 Cork St., London W1X 1HB.

ABBOTT, Paul Philip John, B.A. (Hons.) degree in painting (1986-1989); painter in oil and teacher; currently living and working in the U.S.A.; *b* London, 1960. *m* Audrey Pietre. one *s.* one *d. Studied:* Plymouth Foundation Course, W.S.C.A.D. Farnham, Surrey under Richard Mann (1973-1978) and Robert Lenkiewicz (1979-1985). *Exhib:* 16 solo and 8 group exhibs. (1979-2001). *Work in collections:* Christian Marquant, Christopher and Dominique Brooks, and throughout Europe and U.S.A. *Commissions:* Include - Kate Mortimer, Micky Burn, Donald Martin Betts, John Ingram, Asia Tanlaw. *Signs work:* "P. Abbott." *Address:* c/o Jonathan Cooper, Parkwalk Gallery, 20 Park Walk, London SW10 0AQ. *Email:* mail@jonathancooper.co.uk

ABELL, Roy, R.B.S.A., A.R.C.A. (Silver Medal, Painting, First Class Hons. 1957); oils, water-colour, etching; Head of School of Painting, Birmingham College of Art; Course Director B.A. Fine Art, Birmingham Polytechnic (retd.); *b* Birmingham, 21 Jan., 1931. *m* Mary Patricia. two *s.* one *d. Educ:* Waverley Grammar School, Birmingham (Jack Davis). *Studied:* Birmingham College of Art (1947-52, Harold Smith, Fleetwood-Walker); Royal College of Art (1954-57, Carel Weight,

Ruskin Spear, John Minton). *Exhib:* Young Contemporaries, R.A., John Moores; one-man exhbns.: National Museum of Wales, Ikon, Oriel (Cardiff), Thackeray (London), Tegfryn (Menai), Birmingham Centenary Artist 1989. *Work in collections:* National Museum of Wales, A.C.G.B., Art Galleries of Birmingham, Bradford, Lichfield, Walsall, University of Wales, University of Central England. *Publications:* The Birmingham School – The Lavenham Press. *Signs work:* "Roy Abell." *Address:* 204 Birmingham Rd., Sutton Coldfield, Birmingham B72 1DD.

ABRAHAMS, Ivor, R.A., F.R.B.S., Sir Winston Churchill Fellow (1989); sculptor in bronze; *b* Lancs., 10 Jan. 1935. *m* Evelyne. two (one decd.) *s. Educ:* Wigan Grammar School. *Studied:* St. Martin's School of Art (Frank Martin, Anthony Caro), Camberwell School of Art (Prof. Karel Vogel). *Exhib:* One-man shows: Arnolfini Gallery, Bristol (1971), Aberdeen A.G. (1972), Mappin Gallery, Sheffield (1972), Ferens Gallery, Kingston upon Hull (1979), Warwick Arts Trust, London (1982); Kölnischer Kunstverein, Cologne (1973), Ikon Gallery, B'ham (1976), Yorkshire Sculpture Park, Wakefield (1984). *Work in collections:* A.C.G.B.; Bibliotheque National, Paris; British Council; Denver Museum, Colorado; Metropolitan Museum, N.Y.; V. & A.; Wilhelm Lembruck Museum, Duisburg; Boymans Museum, Rotterdam, etc. *Commissions:* Black Lion Home, Whitechapel Rd., E1; 39 Chancery Lane with Brian Clark; Pamshill Park, Cobham, Surrey. *Publications:* E.A. Poe (1975), Oxford Gardens Sketchbook (1976). *Clubs:* Chelsea Arts, Colony. *Signs work:* "Ivor Abrahams." *Address:* 204 Roundwood Rd., London NW10 3UG: and Royal Academy, Piccadilly, London W1V ODS.

ABRAHAMS, Ruth, N.D.D. (Painting) (1955), Cert. R.A.S. (1959), Leverhulme award; painter in oil and water-colour on canvas and paper; part-time lecturer, Loughborough College of Art; *b* London, 11 Mar., 1931. *m* formerly to David Willetts. one *s. Educ:* Dagenham Grammar School, Essex. *Studied:* St. Martin's School of Art (1951-55, Frederick Gore, Bateson Mason), R.A. Schools (1955-59, Peter Greenham, R.A.). *Exhib:* Young Contemporaries, London Group, John Moores, R.A., Middlesbrough Drawing Biennale (1980); work selected for Sunday Times water-colour competition (1990). *Work in collections:* Durham University, J. Walter Thompson. *Signs work:* "R.A." or "Ruth Abrahams." *Address:* Pear Tree Cottage, 1 Allington Rd., Sedgebrook, nr. Grantham, Lincs.

ACKROYD, Jane V.M., B.A.(Hons.), M.A., R.C.A. (Sculpture); sculptor in mild steel; *b* London, 25 Feb., 1957. *m* David Annesley, (divorced). one *s. Educ:* Godolphin and Latymer School, London. *Studied:* St. Martin's School of Art (1975-79, Adrian de Montford, David Annesley, Anthony Caro); R.C.A. (1980-83, Philip King, Bryan Kneale). *Exhib:* International Garden Festival Liverpool (1984), Serpentine Gallery (1984), Anti-Thesis Angela Flowers Gallery (1986), R.A. Summer Exhbn. (1988, 1989, 1995, 1996, 1997, 1998, 2001); one-man shows Anderson O'Day (1988), Worcester College, Oxford (1997). *Work in collections:* A.C.G.B., Contemporary Arts Soc., Leics. Educ. Authority, London Docklands Development Corp. *Commissions:* 'Herring Gull' Limehouse, 'Moonlight Ramble' Haymarket London, and others. *Signs work:* "Jane Ackroyd." *Address:* 34, Winton Ave., London N11 2AT.

ACKROYD, Norman, R.A. (1991); painter/etcher; *b* Leeds, 26 Mar., 1938.

Educ: Cockburn High School, Leeds. *Studied:* R.C.A. (1961-64). *Exhib:* extensively in Europe and U.S.A. *Work in collections:* Tate Gallery, V. & A., Museum of Modern Art, N.Y., National Galleries of Scotland, Canada, S. Africa, Norway, The Rijksmuseum and Stedelijk Amsterdam, The Albertina Vienna, Musee d'Art Historie Geneva, British Council, Leeds, Manchester, Sheffield, Hull, Glasgow, Aberdeen, Norwich, Preston, Bradford, Newcastle, and other city A.G's. *Publications:* Thirty minute film on etching for B.B.C., writing for Studio International. *Signs work:* see appendix. *Address:* 1 Morocco St., London SE1 3HB.

ADAIR: see PAVEY, Don.

ADAIR, Hilary, N.D.D. (1963), A.T.C. (1965), R.E. (1991); painter/printmaker in water-colour, acrylic, oil, etching, silkscreen; *b* Sussex, 29 May, 1943. *m* Julian Marshall. two *s. Educ:* Chichester High School for Girls. *Studied:* Brighton College of Art (1960-61; 1964-66, J. Dickson), St. Martin's School of Art (1961-63, F. Gore, A. Reynolds). *Exhib:* British Council, R.A., Sue Rankin Gallery, Jill Yakas Gallery Athens, R.W.A., Concourse Gallery, The Barbican, Bankside Gallery, Museum of Garden History, London. *Work in collections:* Arts Council, Gray's Library, Eastbourne, Lancs., Oldham and Stoke-on-Trent Educ. Authorities, Paintings in Hospitals, Royal Devon and Exeter Hospital, Ashmolean Museum. *Commissions:* Hilton and Intercontinental Hotels, Athens, P. & O.'s 'Aurora' four Edns. of etchings. *Publications:* The English Garden (Aug. '98) - Arts Review - The Athenian Magazine. *Signs work:* "Hilary Adair" on prints, "Adair" on paintings. *Address:* Halse Cottage, Winsford, nr. Minehead, Som. TA24 7JE.

ADAMS, Anna: see BUTT, Anna Theresa.

ADAMS, Ken Praveera, M.A. (1958), Dip. F.A. (1964), Dip. A.T. (1986); artist painter, sculptor and composer of music; *b* Northumberland, 1 Sept.,1933. *Educ:* Balliol College, Oxford. *Studied:* Slade School of Fine Art. *Exhib:* London, Suffolk, Amsterdam, Dusseldorf, Paris, New York, R.A. Summer Shows (intermittently). *Work in collections:* Museum Sztuki, Lodz, Poland, and private collections in Europe and U.S.A. *Commissions:* Netherhall Gardens Gable. *Publications:* Leonardo Vol. 12 (1979) Commentary on Sculptures. Dealers: Heifer Gallery, 3 Calabria Rd, London N5 1JB. Tel: 020 7226 7380. *Signs work:* "Ken Praveera Adams" or "K.P.A." or intermediate forms. *Address:* 19 Dartmouth Park Rd., London NW5 1SU. *Email:* 2000@hotmail.com

ADAMS, (Dorothea Christina) Margaret, A.R.M.S. (1990), R.M.S. (1992), Hon. R.M.S. (1997); Suzanne Lucas award H.S. (1989), Hon. Men. R.M.S. Gold Bowl award (1991); portrait miniature painter in water-colour on ivorine; *b* Haslemere, 17 Feb., 1918. *m* Stanley V. Adams, O.B.E. (decd.); Harry E. Gaze (1996). four *s.* two *d. Educ:* St. Mary's School, Colchester, The Grove School, Hindhead. *Studied:* Farnham School of Art, Bloomsbury Trade School. *Exhib:* R.M.S., H.S. *Signs work:* "Margaret Adams" and see appendix. *Address:* 2 St. Nicholas Park, Penn Hill, Yeovil, Som. BA20 1SX.

ADAMS, Marina, A.L.I. (1968); landscape architect in private practice: drawings in ink, water-colour, gouache, crayon; *b* Athens, 27 Aug., 1940. *m* (1964) Robert John Adams, dissolved (1980). one *s.* one *d. Educ:* Pierce College, Athens;

Landscape Architecture Dip. L.A. Reading University (1959-62). *Exhib:* R.A. Summer Exhbn. (1987, 1988, 1989, 1990, 1992, 1993, 1994, 1998). *Signs work:* "Marina Adams." *Address:* 3 Pembroke Studios, Pembroke Gdns., London W8 6HX.

ADAMS, Norman, A.R.C.A., R.A.; painter; Prof. of Painting and Keeper, Emeritus, Royal Academy, London; Prof. of Fine Art, Newcastle University (1981-86); *b* London, 9 Feb., 1927. *m* Anna Butt. two *s. Studied:* Harrow Art School, and R.C.A. *Exhib:* R.A., Tate Gallery, City Art Galleries of Bradford, Leeds, York; also Rome, Paris, Brussels, Pittsburgh, Glasgow. *Work in collections:* C.A.S., Arts Council, National Gallery, N.Z., Tate Gallery, Fitzwilliam; provincial galleries, education committees. Murals in public buildings. Décor for Sadler's Wells and Covent Garden. *Commissions:* 'Stations of the Cross', St. Mary's R.C. Church, Manchester. *Publications:* book 'Angels of Soho'. *Signs work:* "Norman Adams," "R.A." *Address:* Butts, Horton-in-Ribblesdale, Settle, Yorks. BD24 0HD. *Second Address:* 6 Gainsborough Rd., Chiswick, London W4 1NJ.

ADAMSON, Crawford, D.A. (1975); painter in oil and pastel; *b* Edinburgh, 24 Mar., 1953. *m* Mary Phimister. one *s.* one *d. Educ:* Royal High School, Edinburgh. *Studied:* Duncan of Jordanstone College of Art (1971-76, Alberto Morrocco, David McLure, Jack Knox). *Exhib:* 12 one-man shows since 1984 (seven in London); group shows in U.K., U.S.A., Spain, France, Japan, Monaco. *Work in collections:* Metropolitan Museum of Art, N.Y. *Publications:* exhibition catalogues (1991, 1995). *Signs work:* "Crawfurd Adamson." *Address:* c/o Jill George Gallery, 38 Lexington St., London W1R 3HR.

ADAMSON, George Worsley, R.E., M.C.S.D.; illustration, humour, design; *b* N.Y.C., 7 Feb., 1913. two *s. Studied:* Wigan and Liverpool City Schools of Art. *Exhib:* Walker A.G.; R.A.; Arts Council Exhbn.; American Inst. of Graphic Arts: covering Punch; British humour, Paris, Los Angeles; illustrations to Ted Hughes Poems Word Perfect/Ginn. *Work in collections:* V. & A., B.M., Imperial War Museum, Air Ministry Coll., Ulster Museum, Exeter Museum, Ashmolean. *Publications:* work repro.: British Airports Authority magazine, Nursing Times. Publication planned: Humour/100 illustrations on three Italian cities. *Signs work:* "Adamson" *Address:* 46 Bridge Rd., Countess Weir, Exeter, Devon EX2 7BB.

ADDYMAN, John, N.D.D. (1949), A.R.C.A. (Illustration 1952); artist in watercolour (large scale), ceramics; fired panels for architecture, printmaker; *b* Wallasey, 1929. *m* Madeline Southern. two *s.* two *d. Educ:* Wallasey Grammar School. *Studied:* Wallasey School of Art (1945-49), R.C.A. (1949-52). *Exhib:* New Art Centre, Gainsborough House, Sudbury, Minories Colchester, Christchurch Museum Ipswich, Oriel Bangor (Welsh Arts Council), '4 Artists from Britain' Antwerp (British Council, 1998), Chappel Gallery, Royal Academy. *Work in collections:* include: National Museum of Wales, Welsh Arts Council, Government Art Collection, Suffolk C.C., Christchurch Museum Ipswich, Steel Co. Wales, Flemings Investment Bank Lux., Museum Communal Lux., t'Elzenveld Antwerp, Chelmsford and Essex Museums. Republic of Ireland, Fellow of Ballinglen Arts Foundation (1994), Artists in Residence Programme, British Embassy Luxembourg (1994-98). Anglia Television "Constable Country in the 80's". *Signs work:* "John Addyman" or "J.A." *Address:* 50 St. James St., Narberth, Pembrokeshire SA67 7DA.

AIERS, Pauline Victoria, painter and printer in oil, pastel, charcoal, monoprint, collagraph; *b* Inverness, 1926. *m* David Aiers (decd.). one *s.* one *d. Educ:* West Heath School, Sevenoaks. *Studied:* Warsaw Beaux Arts (1947-48), Ju I. Hsiung, Philippines (1959-62), Morley College (1984-85), with Oliver Bevan, London (1984-89). *Exhib:* solo shows: Lionel Wendt Gallery, Colombo, Gallery 47 and Wine Gallery, London, National Museum of Fine Arts, Malta; two person: Hyde Park Gallery, London, Riverside Gallery, Richmond; others, Singapore Art Soc., Spirit of London, Royal Festival Hall, Camden Annual, Southwark Cathedral, Gallery 10, Flying Colours Gallery, International Arts Fair, Islington, Art for Sale. *Work in collections:* National Museum of Fine Arts, Malta. *Signs work:* "P.A." *Address:* 13 Harefield, Hinchley Wood, Surrey KT10 9TG.

AINLEY, John Anthony, retired Head Teacher; Diploma in Child Development; M.Sc., Diploma in the Visual Arts; water colour painter; *b* Sheffield, 1931. married. two children. *Clubs:* Secretary of Leatherhead Art Club. Convenor of "Five Surrey Painters". *Address:* Bridleside, 1A Yarm Ct. Rd., Leatherhead, Surrey KT22 8NY.

AINSCOW, George Frederick, Paris Salon gold and silver medallist (1980, 1981); textile designer, artist in water-colour and oil; *b* Manchester, 10 Feb., 1913. *m* (1) Margaret Shackleton (decd.). (2) Marjorie Standring. one *s.* one *d. Educ:* Derby St. School, Rochdale. *Studied:* Rochdale College of Art (1929-33, G.Wheeler, Principal). *Exhib:* R.A., R.I., R.B.A., N.E.A.C., Preston A.G., R.W.S. Open; one man shows, Rochdale A.G., Mall Galleries, Salford A.G., Oldham A.G. *Work in collections:* R.A.F. Museum, Hendon, Bury A.G., Rochdale A.G., work in private collections, textile designs in V.&A. and Whitworth Art Gallery, Manchester. *Signs work:* "G.F. Ainscow." *Address:* 4 Saxonholme Rd., Castleton, Rochdale, Lancs. OL11 2YA.

AITCHISON, Craigie, painter in oil; *b* 13 Jan., 1926. *Studied:* Slade School of Fine Art. *Commissions:* Four panels for Truro Cathedral. *Publications:* Art of Craigie Aitchison by Gillian Williams. *Signs work:* "Craigie Aitchison." *Address:* c/o Royal Academy of Arts, Burlington House, London W1.

AIVALIOTIS, Sharon Firth, R.E., B.A.(Hons.) (1979), Postgrad. Dip. (Printmaking) (1980); artist/printmaker in mezzotint, all intaglio processes and graphite; part-time lecturer, St. Martin's School of Art and Design; *b* Trinidad, 12 Apr., 1951. *m* Stak Aivaliotis. *Studied:* St. Martin's School of Art (1975-79, Albert Herbert), Slade School of Fine Art (1979-80, Bartolomeo Dos Santos). *Exhib:* solo shows: Jill George Fine Art London since 1985; many mixed shows nationally and internationally. *Work in collections:* V. & A., Library of Congress Washington D.C., Whitworth Gallery Manchester, Ferens A.G. Hull. *Publications:* The Mezzotint: History and Technique by Carol Wax (Thames and Hudson). *Signs work:* "Sharon Firth Aivaliotis" or "S. Aivaliotis." *Address:* 22 Brownlow Mews, London WC1N 2LA.

ALEXANDER, Elsie W. M., A.M.N.S. (1977); artist in oil on canvas; retired company director; *b* Ware, Herts., 13 Feb., 1912. *m* Herbert John Alexander, Ph.D. one *d. Educ:* Grammar School, Ware. *Studied:* pastel and abstract painting at Montclair State College, N.J. (1958); graphic art with Hyman J. Warsager; also pupil of the late Victor Askew, R.O.I., F.I.A.L. (1972-73). *Exhib:* City of London (awarded vellum and freedom, Worshipful Co. of Painters and Stainers, freedom, City of London), Leicester, Chelsea, Cornwall, Norfolk; one-man show, Mill Hill (1971). First prize winner of She comp. (Chelsea, 1968). *Clubs:* Buckingham Art Soc., Wine Trade Art Soc. *Signs work:* "ALEXANDER." *Address:* 20 Parkside Drive, Edgware, Middx.

ALEXANDER, Gregory, R.W.S. (1984), B.A. (1981); artist in water-colour and oil; *b* Ramsgate, Kent, 14 May, 1960. *m* Francesca Rigony. *Studied:* Canterbury College of Art (1976-78), W. Surrey College of Art (1978-81). *Exhib:* R.W.S., N.E.A.C., R.A. Summer shows, and over 12 one-man exhbns. in England and Australia. *Work in collections:* R.W.S. Diploma, A.N.Z. Bank Melbourne. *Publications:* Kipling's The Jungle Book (Pavilion 1991), Tales from the African Plains (Pavilion 1994), Step by Step Water-colour Painting (Weidenfeld & Nicolson 1994). *Signs work:* "Gregory Alexander." *Address:* 1/73 Abbott St., Sandringham, Melbourne, Victoria 3191, Australia. *Second Address:* U.K. Address: 1 Joann's Ct., Stephen Cl., Broadstairs, Kent CT10 1NY.

ALEXANDER, Hazel, sculptor in bronze and cold cast bronze; *b* Newcastle-on-Tyne, 1 Feb., 1912. *m* John Alexander. one *s.* three *d. Educ:* Smarts College. *Studied:* Luton Art School (1936), Camden Inst. (1970, Joan Armitage), and Fred Kormis. *Exhib:* Mall Gallery, Ben Uri Gallery, Bristol Cathedral (Amnesty), St. Paul's Cathedral, Festival Hall. *Work in collections:* Cambridge University Library, All England Lawn Tennis Club (Members Lounge), Museum of Israel Defence Forces, King Solomon Hotel, Elat, Wimbledon Museum, Wolfson-Poznansky Home, London, Ben Uri Gallery; private collections in England, France, Italy, Germany, U.S.A., Israel. *Signs work:* "Hazel Alexander." *Address:* 34 West Heath Rd., Hampstead, London NW3 7UR.

ALEXANDER, Naomi, N.D.D. (1959), R.O.I. (1982); asst. mem. British Picture Restorers; Publicity Officer, R.O.I.; Cornelissen, Stanley Grimm, Visions prize; Trustee for Paintings in Hospitals; *b* 1938. one *d. Studied:* Hornsey College of Art (1954-59), Central School of Art (1961-63). *Exhib:* R.A., Spink, Mercury Gallery, N.E.A.C., R.B.A., R.O.I., R.P., Fosse, David Messum Galleries, British municipal galleries, Richmond Gallery; one-man shows Ben Uri, Sheila Harrison, Sheridan Russell Gallery, Buxton Museum, Baker Tilly, Lambs Chambers, the Temple. *Work in collections:* V. & A.; Duke of Devonshire; Japanese Broadcasting Assoc.; Salomon Bros. Bank, Tokyo; Merryfield Gallery; Sir Richard Storey; Katharine, Viscountess Macmillan; 2nd Royal Tank Regt.; Sultan of Oman; Paintings in Hospitals; Baker Tilly. *Publications:* The Arts Review, Royal Academy Illustrated, Graves Encyclopedia of R.A. Exhbns., Observer, Artist and Illustrator, Tableaux, Mail on Sunday, Quarto Publications, Harper Collins publications, Galleries. *Signs work:* "Naomi Alexander." *Address:* 6 Bishops Ave., London N2 0AN.

ALEXANDRI, Sara, Dip. of Royal Academy of Fine Arts in Painting (Florence, Italy); art teacher; landscape, flower and figure painter in oil and water-colour; etcher; *b* Kherson, Russia, 22 Oct., 1913. *m* Michael Perkins. one *s. Educ:* High School, Palestine, and privately in Italy and Switzerland. *Studied:* Royal Inst. d'Arte, Florence, and Royal Academy of Fine Arts, Florence (1936-40, 1946-47). *Exhib:* R.A., R.B.A., W.I.A.C., R.W.A., Paris Salon, foreign and main provincial galleries.

Signs work: "S. ALEXANDRI" or "S. Alexandri." *Address:* 28 Gensing Rd., St. Leonards-on-Sea, Sussex TN38 0HE.

ALFORD, John, N.D.D., A.T.D., R.B.A., N.E.A.C.; painter in oil and water-colour; Director of Art, Shrewsbury School (retd. 1989); *b* Tunbridge Wells, 14 Oct., 1929. *m* Jean. one *s.* two *d. Educ:* Reading School. *Studied:* Camberwell School of Art (1949-53, Gilbert Spencer, Richard Eurich, Bernard Dunstan). *Exhib:* R.A., R.W.A., R.B.A., R.S.M.A., N.E.A.C.; numerous one-man shows in England, S. Africa, France, Canada. *Work in collections:* At home and abroad, Reading A.G., Shropshire C.C. *Commissions:* several for the Royal Navy and Royal Canadian Navy. *Signs work:* "John Alford." *Address:* 47 Porthill Rd., Shrewsbury, Shropshire SY3 8RN.

ALLCOCK, Annette, painter in oil and gouache, greeting card designer, illustrator; *b* Bromley, Kent, 28 Nov., 1923. *m* James Allcock. one *s.* one *d. Educ:* various private schools. *Studied:* West of England College of Art (Stanley Spencer). *Exhib:* R.A., R.W.A., Bath Contemporary Arts Fair. *Work in collections:* Japan. *Publications:* work repro.: illustrating childrens books. *Signs work:* "Annette Allcock." *Address:* 22 South St., Corsham, Wilts. SN13 9HB.

ALLEN, Barbara, A.R.U.A., B.A. (Hons.) Graphic Design, Ad.Dip.; John Ross Prize for Water-colour (R.U.A. 1992); self employed artist in water-colour; *b* Belfast, 5 Sept., 1959. *m* Paul Ferran. three *s. Studied:* University of Ulster, Belfast (1978-84, Terry Aston). *Exhib:* annually with R.U.A., regularly with Gallery 148, Holywood, Co.Down; solo shows: St. John's Arts Centre, Listowel (1998), Townhouse Gallery, Belfast (1998), McGilloway Gallery, Derry (1998), Galleri Parken, Bergen, Norway (1993). *Work in collections:* The White House, Washington D.C., Tele (Norwegian Telecom), B.P. Oil Europe, etc, and private collections throughout N.America and Europe. *Commissions:* N.I. Blood Transfusion Service, Bass Ireland Ltd., Royal Norwegian Embassy, London, etc. *Publications:* illustrations for 'Irish Shores' and 'Uster Rambles' (Greystone Press). Residencies: The Florence Trust, Islington (1991); several residencies at Tyrone Guthrie Centre since 1983. *Signs work:* "Barbara Allen." *Address:* 12 Newton Park, Four Winds, Belfast BT8 6LH.

ALLINSON, Sonya Madeleine, M.F.P.S. (1989); artist in oil, acrylic, gouache, collage, pen and wash; *b* London. *Studied:* St. Martin's School of Art; Landscape scholarship from R.A.; R.A. Schools. *Exhib:* one-man shows: Federation of British Artists, Cheltenham General Hospital, Cirencester Workshops, Everyman, Axiom Centre for the Arts, Cheltenham, Sheffield; mixed: R.A., Leicester Galleries, R.B.A., New English, Tooth's, Heal's, Brighton, Fosse, Manor House, Delahaye, Loggia, R.W.A., Bloomsbury, Anderson, Waterman Fine Art, Masters Fine Art, Bath, Gloucester City A.G., Albany, Cardiff, Stroud House Gallery. *Work in collections:* Britain, France, Holland, Israel, U.S.A., S. America. *Clubs:* Cheltenham Group, F.P.S. *Signs work:* "Allinson" or "S.M. Allinson." *Address:* 13 Cleevemont, Evesham Rd., Cheltenham GL52 3JT.

ALLISON, Jane, 1st Class B.A. Hons. (1980), Slade Higher Dip. (1982); portrait painter in oil/pastel; *b* Woking, 21 Mar., 1959. *m* John Tatchell Freeman. one *s. Studied:* Chelsea School of Art (1977-80, Norman Blamey), Slade School of Fine Art (1980-82). *Exhib:* B.P. Portrait Award, Royal Library, Windsor Castle, St. Pancras

Hospital, University of Surrey. *Work in collections:* Royal College of Surgeons, Edinburgh, University of Surrey, Royal Institute, Royal Library, Windsor Castle, Guys Hospital. *Commissions:* Sir George Edwards, O.M., F.R.S., Lord Robens, Lord Mishcon, Sir Christopher Collet, Prof. P.S. Boulter, Lord Nugent, etc. Court of Examiners, Royal College of Surgeons, London, Prof. Nairn Wilson, President of the General Dental Council. *Signs work:* "Jane Allison." *Address:* 12 Sydney Rd., Guildford, Surrey GU1 3LJ.

ALSOP, Roger Fleetwood, S.G.F.A. (1991); painter in water-colour, crayon, oil; *b* Skipton, 1946. *Educ:* Queen's Boys' Sec. Mod., Wisbech. *Studied:* Cambridge School of Art (1966-72). *Exhib:* Amalgam Gallery, Barnes, Roy Miles Gallery, Zella Nine Gallery, Old Fire Engine House, Ely. *Commissions:* Medici Soc., Mercedes-Benz, Right Now magazine. *Signs work:* "Roger Alsop." *Address:* 4 St. John's Villas, London N19 3EG.

AMBRUS, Victor Gyozo Laszio, A.R.C.A. (1960), R.E. (1973), F.R.S.A. (1978); Library Assoc., Kate Greenaway Gold Medal (1966 and 1975); book illustrator, graphic designer; visiting lecturer, Graphic Design; *b* Budapest, 19 Aug., 1935. *m* Glenys Rosemary, A.R.C.A. two *s. Educ:* St. Imre Grammar School, Budapest. *Studied:* Hungarian Academy of Fine Art, Budapest; R.C.A., London. *Exhib:* R.A., R.E., Biennale: Bratislava; Bologna, Italy, Belgium, Japan, Belgrade, New York. *Work in collections:* University of Southern Mississippi, U.S.A.; Library of Congress, U.S.A.; O.U.P., London; Prizes: R.A. Arts' Club Prize (1996) Summer Exhbn.; P.S. Prize (1995); Daler Rowney Prize; World Wildlife Prize (1994); Mall Galleries. *Publications:* The Royal Navy, British Army, Royal Air Force, Merchant Navy, Three Poor Tailors, Brave Soldier Janos, The Little Cockerell, The Sultan's Bath, Hot Water for Boris, Country Wedding, Mishka, Horses in Battle, Under the Double Eagle, O.U.P.: Dracula (1980), Dracula's Bedtime Storybook (1982), and Blackbeard (1983) author and illustrator. *Signs work:* "V.G. Ambrus." *Address:* 52 Crooksbury Rd., Farnham, Surrey GU10 1QB.

AMERY, Shenda, A.R.B.S. (1984); sculptor in bronze; Council mem. R.B.S.; *b* England, 1937. *m* Sheikh Nezam Khazal. two *s. Educ:* Municipal College, Southend-on-Sea (H.N.C. chemistry). *Exhib:* R.A., Paris Salon, Mall Galleries, Locus Gallery, Osbourne Studio Gallery, Orangery, Holland Pk., Tehran Gallery, Iran, Kessel Long Gallery, Scottsdale, Ariz. *Commissions:* Portrait bust: Rt. Hon. John Major M.P., Prime Minister, H.H. Queen Noor of Jordan, Baroness Thatcher, Prime Minister, Dr. Lee, King Hussein of Jordan, The Earl of Bessborough, Sir Francis Dashwood, President Roh Tae Woo of S. Korea, Sir John Richards, Mayor Herb Drinkwater. *Clubs:* Arts. *Signs work:* "Shenda Amery." *Address:* 25a Edith Grove, London SW10 0LB.

ANDERSON, Douglas Hardinge, R.P.; portrait painter and wildlife artist in oils; *b* 8 Aug., 1934. *m* Veronica née Markes. one *s.* two *d. Studied:* under Pietro Annigoni in Florence. *Exhib:* R.P., R.A. Paintings in private collections worldwide and National Gallery, Edinburgh. *Clubs:* Turf. *Signs work:* "Douglas Anderson." *Address:* 56036 Palaia, (Pisa), Italy. *Second Address:* Luthy, Recess, Co. Galway, Ireland.

ANDERSON, James, B.A.; East of England art show Under-30 award (1993);

printmaker, painter, writer, teacher; *b* Cambridge, 3 Mar., 1965. *Educ:* Worcester College, Oxford. *Studied:* Central School of Art and Design. *Exhib:* mixed and solo shows in Oxford, Bristol, London, Svendborg Denmark, Lvov Ukraine. *Work in collections:* Museum of History of Religion, Lvov, Ukraine. *Signs work:* "J.W. ANDERSON." *Address:* 18c Digby Cres., London N4 2HR.

ANDERSON, Wendy, M.A.; artist; visiting lecturer, Central/St. Martin's School of Art; *b* Elgin, Scotland, 10 Feb., 1961. *Studied:* Gray's School of Art (1979-83), Birmingham Polytechnic (1983-84). *Exhib:* 'British Art' Eritrea, Eagle Gallery; 'Self-Contained, The Field Institute, Dusseldorf. *Work in collections:* Arthur Andersen, The Economist, Warwickshire Museum. *Commissions:* Scottish Touring Exhbns. Consortium - Touring Exhbn. (1999-2002). *Publications:* 'Artists Now'; author: Education Guides for R.A. 'Sensation' and 'Joseph Beuys'. *Clubs:* London Group (member). *Address:* 19 Arrow Rd., London E3 3HE.

ANDERTON, Eileen, A.R.M.S., S.M., H.S., F.R.S.A.; Gold Medal (1981) Accademia Italia delle Arti e del Lavoro, Gold plaque (1986) Premio d`Italia Targa Djoro; freelance artist in body-colour, water-colour, mixed media; *b* Bradford, Yorks., 26 April, 1924. *Educ:* Bradford Girls' Grammar School. *Studied:* Bradford Art School (1939-44) under John Greenwood and Vincent Lines. *Exhib:* Cartwright Hall, Bradford, Wakefield, Halifax, S.W.A., Royal Water-colour Soc. Gallery; one-man show at Bradford Library Gallery. *Work in collections:* Bradford University. *Clubs:* Bradford Arts. *Signs work:* "E. Anderton." *Address:* 4 Braybrook Ct., Keighley Rd., Bradford BD8 7BH.

ANDREW, Keith, R.C.A. (1981); artist, painter/printmaker in water-colour, tempera, etching; elected V.P. Royal Cambrian Academy (1993); *b* London, 26 Jan., 1947. *m* Rosemary. two *s*. *Educ:* Picardy Secondary, Erith, Kent. *Studied:* Ravensbourne College of Art and Design (1963-67, Mike Tyzack, John Sturgess). *Exhib:* R.A. Summer Exhbn. (1981), Mostyn A.G., Llandudno, Oriel Cardiff (1982), Bangor A.G. (1982), Aberystwyth Arts Centre (1982), Williamson A.G., Birkenhead (1982), National Eisteddfod Swansea (1982) and Anglesey (1983), Oriel Mold (1983), Tegfryn Gallery, Anglesey (1983); group exhbn. 'Through Artists Eyes'. *Work in collections:* National Library of Wales, Contemporary Art Soc. for Wales, University of Wales, Amoco, Ocean Transport, British Gypsum, Milk Marketing Board. *Signs work:* "Keith Andrew." *Address:* Gwyndy Bach, Llandrygarn, Tynlon P.O., Holyhead, Anglesey LL65 3AJ, Wales.

ANDREWS, Carole, S.B.A.; Founder Presidents Hon. Award S.B.A. (1995); professional artist in water-colour; tutor for mid-Surrey Educ.; *b* Worcester Park, Surrey, 13 Jan., 1940. *m* Peter Leonard. two *d*. *Studied:* Sutton College of Liberal Arts (Philip Meninsky, Ken Bates). *Exhib:* Mall Galleries (1983-86), Westminster Central Hall (1986-95), The Guildhall, London, Alexandra Palace, Turner A.G., Denver, U.S.A. Work in private collections. *Publications:* work repro.: Limited edn. and volume prints, illustration for Coalport and Wedgwood porcelain. *Signs work:* "Carole Andrews." *Address:* 129 Chapel Way, Epsom Downs, Epsom, Surrey KT18 5TB.

ANDREWS, Marcia Tricker, life member I.A.A.; painter in oils; *b* London, 1923. *m* Edward Andrews. one *s*. one *d*. *Educ:* St. Andrews; New City, London. *Exhib:* London and provinces, Mexico City and Morelia, Paris, Manhattan. *Work in* *collections:* University of Surrey; Medway Council Library Loan Service; private collections at home and abroad. *Signs work:* "M. ANDREWS," "M. Andrews" or "M.A." *Address:* 40 Robin Hood La., Walderslade, Chatham, Kent ME5 9LD.

ANDREWS, Mrs. Pauline Ann, graphic artist and designer in Bournemouth; *b* Bournemouth, 4 Mar., 1968. *Educ:* Stourfield and Beaufort Schools, Bournemouth. Work includes book illustration, leaflet, poster, card and badge design and production in addition to normal commercial work. Also undertakes drawings and sketches as Fine art. *Address:* 99 Carbery Ave., Southbourne, Bournemouth BH6 3LP.

ANGADI, Patricia, artist in oil; *b* Hampstead, 23 Sept., 1914. *m* Ayana Angadi, Indian author and lecturer. three *s.* one *d. Educ:* Prior's Field, Godalming. *Studied:* Heatherleys (1933-37). *Exhib:* R.P., W.I.A.C., S.W.A., R.B.A., R.O.I., Goupil Galleries, Paris Salon, N.E.A.C., Utd. Artists, Camden Arts Centre. *Work in collections:* Portraits of James Maxton, M.P., by Glasgow People's Gallery, C. E. M. Joad by Birkbeck College, Baron Reuter by Reuter's Press Museum, Aachen. *Publications:* novels: The Governess, The Done Thing, The Highly Flavoured Ladies, Sins of the Mothers, Playing for Real, Turning the Turtle (Gollancz). *Signs work:* "Angadi" in red. *Address:* 32a Belsize Park, London NW3 4DX.

ANGEL, Marie, A.R.C.A. (1948); calligrapher, illustrator; *b* 1923. *Educ:* Croydon School of Art (1940-45), R.C.A. Design School (1945-48). *Exhib:* R.A., S.S.I., and widely in U.S.A.; one-man shows: San Francisco (1967), Casa del Libro (1975). *Work in collections:* Harvard College Library, Hunt Botanical Library, Casa del Libro, San Francisco Library and V. & A. *Publications:* A Bestiary, A New Bestiary, Two Poems by Emily Dickinson, An Animated Alphabet (Harvard); illustrated: The Tale of The Faithful Dove, The Tale of Tuppenny by Beatrix Potter; Catscript, Cherub Cat, Angel Tiger; author: The Art of Calligraphy, Painting for Calligraphy. *Signs work:* "Marie Angel," "Angel" or "M.A." *Address:* Silver Ley, 33 Oakley Rd., Warlingham, Surrey CR6 9BE.

ANNAND, David, sculptor in clay, bronze resin, bronze, mixed media; *b* Insch, Aberdeenshire, 30 Jan., 1948. *m* Jean. one *s.* one *d. Educ:* Perth Academy. *Studied:* Duncan of Jordanstone College of Art, Dundee (Scott Sutherlands). *Exhib:* Royal Scottish Academy, Open Eye, Edinburgh, etc. *Work in collections:* throughout the world, including Edinburgh, Dundee, Perth, Canberra, Wisconsin, Hong Kong. *Commissions:* "Deer Leap" Dundee Technology Pk.; "Man Feeding Seagulls" Glasgow Gdn. Festival; "Grey Heron" Edinburgh Botanic Gdns.; "Cranes" British High Commission Hong Kong; "Naeday Sae Dark", Perth; "Civic Pride" four life-size lions on pillars of steel, Barnet, London. Awards: Royal Scottish Academy: Latimer (1976), Benno Schotz (1978), Ireland Alloys (1982); Sir Otto Beit medal, R.B.A. (1987). *Signs work:* "David A. Annand," a tiny frog on a lily leaf. *Address:* Pigscrave Cottage, The Wynd, Kilmany Cupar, Fife KY15 4PU.

ANNESLEY, David Robert Ewart, F.R.B.S. (1994); sculptor in welded steel; Senior lecturer, St. Martin's School of Art (1975-95); *b* London. *m* divorced. two *s.* one *d. Studied:* St. Martin's School of Art (1958-62, Anthony Caro, Frank Martin). *Exhib:* Waddington (1966, 1968), Poindexter Gallery, N.Y. (1966, 1968). *Work in collections:* Tate Gallery, Arts Council, British Council, etc. *Commissions:* Peterborough, Orton Centre, Royal Hampshire County Hospital. *Signs work:* "David

Annesley." *Address:* 80 North View Rd., London N8 7LL.

ANSCHLEE: see SCHLEE, Anne H.

ANSELMO, (Anselmo Francesconi), painter in oil, acrylic on canvas, drawing and etching, sculptor in clay for bronze; *b* Lugo (Ravenna), Italy, 29 July, 1921. *m* Margherita Francesconi. *Educ:* Lugo. *Studied:* Liceo Artistico, Ravenna; School of Fine Art, Bologna; Brera, Milan. *Exhib:* one-man shows: Catherine Viviano, N.Y., Engelberths, Geneva, Galleria d'Eendt, Amsterdam, Musée d'Art et d'Histoire, Geneva, Fine Art Faculty, University of Teheran, Iran, Galleria Toninelli, Milan, Galleria Giulia, Rome, Bedford House Gallery, London, stained glass windows and murals for two churches - Canton de Friburg, Switzerland, Mussavi Art Center, N.Y., Fante di Spade, Milano, Museum of Bagnacavallo, Museum of Bulle, Switzerland, Palazzo Trisi - Lugo, Palazzo Corradini, Ravenna, etc. *Work in collections:* Musée d'Art et d'Histoire, Geneva; Musée Cantonale de Lausanne; Cabinet delle Stampe, Castello Sforzesco, Milan; Museum of Fine Art, N.Y.; Museum of Fine Art, Buffalo. *Signs work:* "Anselmo." *Address:* 8b Berkeley Gdns., London W8 4AP.

AP **RHYS PRYCE, Vivien Mary,** F.R.B.S.; sculptor in modelling clay and wax for bronze; *b* Woking, 1 Nov., 1937. *Educ:* Claremont School, Esher, Surrey. *Studied:* City and Guilds of London Art School. *Exhib:* R.A., R.W.A., Jonathan Poole Gallery, London, and various provincial galleries. *Work in collections:* National Gallery of New Zealand, Wellington, University of Exeter (water sculpture), Nymans Gdns., Handcross, Sussex (fountain). *Signs work:* Impress of signet ring (Lion's head). *Address:* 15 North St., Calne, Wilts. SN11 0HQ.

ARCHAMBAULT, Louis, sculptor, B.A. (1936), D.E.B.A. (1939), R.A.I.C. Allied Arts Medal (1958), O.C. (1968), R.C.A. (1968), C.C.A. Diplôme d'honneur (1982); *b* Montreal, 4 Apr., 1915. *m* Mariette Provost. four children. Teaching career: Musée des Beaux-Arts, Montreal; Ecole des Beaux-Arts, Montreal; University of British Columbia, Vancouver; Université du Québec, Montreal; Concordia University, Montreal. *Exhib:* group: Festivals Britain (1951), 10th and 11th Milan (1954-57), XXVIIIth Venice (1956), Brussels Universal (1958), Pittsburgh International (1958), Montreal Expo 67, 300 Years of Canadian Art, National Gallery, Ottawa (1967), etc.; one-man, Canada, France, England. *Work in collections:* National Gallery, Ottawa; Musée du Québec, Quebec City; Musée d'art contemporain and Musée des Beaux Arts, Montreal; Art Gallery of Ontario, Toronto; Winnipeg A.G., Winnipeg; Museo Internazionale della Ceramica, Faenza, Italy; Sun Life building, Quebec City; Place des Arts, Montreal; Malton Airport, Toronto; Scarborough College, Toronto; Macdonald Block, Queen's Park, Toronto; Federal Food and Drug building, Longueuil, Quebec; Canadian Imperial Bank of Commerce, Montreal; Canada Council Art Bank, Ottawa; Justice Court building, Quebec City, etc. *Commissions:* Canadian Pavilion, Brussels (1958), Canadian Pavilion, Expo 67, Montreal, etc. *Signs work:* "Louis Archambault." *Address:* a/s Patrice Archambault, 114, chemin Broughton, Montréal-Ouest (Québec), Canada H4X 1K1.

ARCHER, Cyril James, R.I.; self taught artist in water-colour; retd. company director; *b* London, 7 Aug., 1928. *m* Betty. two *s*. *Educ:* West Ham Municipal College. *Exhib:* numerous galleries in London, south of England, also one-man shows. *Work in collections:* England, U.S.A., Canada, Middle and Far East, Japan.

Limited Editions etc. *Commissions:* numerous. *Clubs:* Sussex Water-colour Soc. *Signs work:* "ARCHER." *Address:* 4 Willowbrook Way, Hassocks, W. Sussex BN6 8QD.

ARCHER, Patricia Margaret Alice, PhD., Dip. F.A., A.T.D., F.M.A.A., Hon. F.I.M.I.; Head of Dept. of Medical Illustration, Guy's Hospital Medical School (1964-83); *b* London. *Educ:* Convent Collegiate School, Sacred Heart of Mary, Chilton, Bucks. *Studied:* Ruskin School of Drawing, Slade School of Fine Art (1944-47), Inst. of Education, London (1947-48). *Exhib:* Medical Artists' Assoc., London (1952, 1964, 1970, 1989, 1993); one-man show, London Hospital (1955), Medical Picture Show, Science Museum (1978); "A Brush With Medicine", Barber-Surgeons' Hall, London (1993). *Publications:* illustrations for teaching the medical sciences. *Clubs:* Fellow, Medical Artists' Assoc., Hon. Sec. (1964-68), Chairman (1984-86) and (1990-93), Vice-Chairman (1986-1988) and (1993-1995), Archivist (1986-); Founder Associate, Inst. of Medical Illustrators (1968). *Signs work:* "ARCHER." *Address:* Rangemore, Park Ave., Caterham, Surrey CR3 6AH.

ARDAGH, Elisabeth (now Mrs. Tredgett), elected Hon. Senior mem. R.O.I. (1994); artist in oil, acrylic, gouache; *b* Brighouse, Yorks., 26 Mar., 1915. *m* L.V. Ardagh (decd.). one *d. Educ:* Godolphin School, Salisbury. *Studied:* Farnham (1934-36, Otway McCannel), Chelsea Polytechnic (1936-37, sculpture under Henry Moore), Wimbledon (1937-39, painting under Gerald Cooper). *Exhib:* F.P.S., N.S., R.O.I., R.A. *Clubs:* Overseas. *Signs work:* "Ardagh." *Address:* 40 Orchard Ave., Chichester, W. Sussex PO19 3BG.

ARDIZZONE, Charlotte, N.E.A.C., N.D.D., R.W.A., Byam Shaw Dip. (1st); artist in oil; oil; *b* London, 24 Oct., 1943. one *d. Educ:* Rye St. Antony School, Oxford. *Studied:* Byam Shaw Art School under Maurice de Sausmarez. *Exhib:* one-man shows: Blond Fine Art, Bohun Gallery, Curwen Gallery, Drian Gallery, Sally Hunter Fine Art, Broughton House Gallery, Albemarle Gallery. *Work in collections:* National Gallery, Australia, National Gallery, Warsaw, Dublin University, Nuffield Foundation. *Clubs:* N.E.A.C., R.W.A. *Signs work:* "Charlotte Ardizzone," and "CA" joined. *Address:* The Old School, Whinburgh, Norfolk NR19 1QR. *Email:* charlotte@ardizzone.freeserve.co.uk

ARKLESS, Lesley Graham, B.A. Hons.; painter/illustrator in oil, gouache, water-colour; M.A. Museums and Galleries in Education (1993); Head of Education, Design Museum, London; *b* Northumberland, 30 Jan., 1956. *m* John M. Butterworth. two *s.* one *d. Educ:* Church High School for Girls, Newcastle-upon-Tyne. *Studied:* West Surrey College of Art and Design (1974-78). *Exhib:* Ash Barn Gallery, Petersfield, St. Edmund's Art Centre, Salisbury, National Museum of Wales, 'Pictures for Schools', Astoria Theatre, London, Le Havre Municipal Gallery, Sanderson's Gallery, London. *Publications:* author and illustrator: 'What Stanley Knew' (Andersen Press, London). *Signs work:* "LESLEY ARKLESS." *Address:* 2 Nun's Walk, Winchester, Hants.

ARLOTT, Norman Arthur, S.WL.A.; freelance wildlife illustrator in water-colour, author; *b* 15 Nov., 1947. *m* Marie Ellen. one *s.* two *d. Educ:* Stoneham Boys School. *Exhib:* Annual S.WL.A., London, widely in U.K., also U.S.A. *Publications:* over fifty, including Norman Arlott's Bird Paintings, and many commonwealth stamp issues, i.e. Bahamas, Jamaica, British Virgin Islands. *Signs work:* "Norman Arlott." *Address:* Hill House, School Rd., Tilney St. Lawrence, Norfolk PE34 4RB.

ARMFIELD, Diana M. (Mrs. Bernard Dunstan), A.R.A. (1989), R.A. (1991), R.C.A. (Wales), M.C.S.D., Hon. P.S., N.E.A.C., R.W.A., R.W.S.; painter, retired textile and wallpaper designer; taught at Central School, and Byam Shaw Art School; *b* Ringwood, Hants, 1920. *m* Bernard Dunstan, R.A. three *s. Educ:* Bedales. *Studied:* Bournemouth Art School, Slade School, Central School. *Exhib:* Festival of Britain; one-man shows, Browse and Darby, National Eisteddfod Wales, Albany Gall. Cardiff, U.S.A. etc.; R.A. with book launch, Holland, R.A. Summer Exhbns. (1966-), Royal Cambrian Academy, Conwy. *Work in collections:* V. & A., R.W.A., Govt. picture collection, Contemporary Art Soc. (Wales), National Trust, Reuters, Yale Centre (British Art), Faringdon Collection, H.R.H. Prince of Wales, Lancaster City Gallery, Mercury Asset Management Collection, R.A. Diploma Collection. *Commissions:* H.R.H. Prince of Wales, Reuters, Contemporary Art Soc. for Wales, National Trust. *Publications:* The Art of Diana Armfield by Julian Halsby (David & Charles, 1995). Artist in Residence: Perth (1985), Jackson Hole, U.S.A. (1989). Mitchell Beazley - "Drawing', Mitchell Beazley -"Painting in Oils". *Clubs:* Arts. *Signs work:* "D.M.A." *Address:* 10 High Park Rd., Kew, Richmond, Surrey TW9 4BH.

ARMITAGE, Joshua Charles, freelance artist in black and white and colour; *b* Hoylake, Cheshire, 26 Sept., 1913. *m* Catherine Mary Buckle (decd.). two *d. Studied:* Liverpool School of Art (1929-36). *Work in collections:* twelve water-colour drawings for the United Oxford and Cambridge University Club. *Publications:* work repro.: Punch, The Countryman, etc. 100th Open Championship at Royal Birkdale and illustrations for many books for adults and for children. Many water-colour drawings with golf as the subject. Long association with Penguin Books editions of P.G. Wodehouse. *Clubs:* Royal Liverpool Golf. *Signs work:* "Ionicus." *Address:* 34 Avondale Rd., Hoylake, Cheshire L47 3AS.

ARMITAGE, Kenneth, C.B.E. (1969); sculptor; *b* 18 July, 1916. *Exhib:* works shown in North and South America, France, Italy, Germany, Austria, Yugoslavia, Malta, Cyprus, Gibraltar, Israel, Lebanon, Ethiopia, Spain, Portugal, Australia, New Zealand, Sarawak, Sebah, Malaysia, Singapore, Bermuda, Jamaica, Trinidad, Cuba, Argentina, Peru, Venezuela, Chile, Brazil, Japan, Finland, Norway, Sweden, Denmark, Poland. Works in major public collections throughout the world. *Address:* 22a Avonmore Rd., London W14 8RR.

ARN or ARNEAL: see NEAL, Arthur Richard.

ARNETT, Joe Anna, painter in oil; *b* Texas. *m* James D. Asher. *Educ:* Baylor University and University of Texas. *Studied:* Art Students' League, N.Y. (1979-83), University of Texas (1970-72). *Exhib:* Gilcrease Museum, Albuquerque Museum, Artists of America, Denver (1988, 1995), Catto Gallery, London (1987-92), Zaplin-Lampert Gallery, Santa Fe, N.M., Art Asia (1994) Hong Kong, Prix de West, National Cowboy Hall of Fame, Ok, Ok. (1996-99). *Work in collections:* Norwest Bank. *Publications:* Painting sumptuous vegetables, fruits & flowers in oil. *Signs work:* "J.A. Arnett." *Address:* P.O. Box 8022, Santa Fe, New Mexico 87504-8022, U.S.A.

ARNOLD, Gordon C., R.C.A.; artist in water-colour; *b* Sheffield, 30 Mar., 1910.

Studied: Liverpool School of Art (Will Penn, R.O.I., R.P., R.C.A., G. Wedgwood, R.E.). *Exhib:* one-man shows: Birkenhead A.G., Warrington A.G., Bootle A.G., Wrexham Library, Weaver Gallery, Weaverham, Pratts Hotel, Bath, etc. *Work in collections:* Williamson A.G., Birkenhead, Warrington A.G., Liverpool Corp. Library, etc. *Signs work:* "Gordon Arnold." *Address:* 58 Fairfield Terr., Newton Abbot, Devon TQ12 2LH.

ARNOLD, Phyllis Anne, R.M.S. (1988), A.R.M.S. (1983), S.M. (1976-86), U.S.W.A. (1982), P.U.S.W.A. (1988-91), P.U.S.M. (1987-93), U.W.S. (1984), H.S. (1985); miniaturist, artist in water-colour, ink, gouache and oils; Hunting Group finalist (1980, 1981, 1983), R.M.S. Memorial Gold Bowl (1988); *b* Belfast, 1938. *m* Michael J. Arnold, C.Eng. two *s. Educ:* Victoria College, Wallace High School. *Studied:* self taught, entered Commercial Art Dept. Short Bros & Harland (1956-58). *Exhib:* S.M., R.M.S., R.A., U.S.W.A., H.S., U.W.S., R.U.A. *Work in collections:* Ulster Museum, Belfast. *Signs work:* "P.A. ARNOLD" or "P.A.A." for miniatures, see appendix. *Address:* Phyllis Arnold Studio, Deepwell House, Lowry Hill, Bangor, Co. Down, N. Ireland BT19 1BX.

ARNUP, Sally, A.R.C.A. (1954); sculptor in bronze; *b* London, 15 July, 1930. *m* Mick Arnup, A.R.C.A. two *s.* two *d. Studied:* Kingston School of Art (1943-50, H. Parker), Camberwell School of Art (1951, Dr. Vogel), Royal College of Art (1952-55, John Skeaping). *Exhib:* Tryon Gallery (1973, 1976, 1981), U.S.A. (1977, 1980, 1986, 1987), Drobak Norway (1976), Wexford Festival (1974, 1978, 1982, 1986), York Festival (1969, 1976, 1978, 1980, 1984, 1988, 1992), Florence (1983), Edinburgh Festival (1988), Stamford Art Centre (1987, 1990), Holland & Holland (Paris, London 1994, 1995, 1997), Gainsborough's House, Suffolk (1998). *Work in collections:* H.M. The Queen, Burton Agnes, York A.G., Lord Halifax, Lord Middleton, York University. *Commissions:* Robert Fleming, Rowntree Trust, Hartrigg Oaks (1999). *Clubs:* R.B.S. *Signs work:* "ARNUP." *Address:* Studios Holtby, York YO19 5UA.

ARRIDGE, Margaret Irene Chadwick, N.S. (1988), F.S.B.A. (1988), A.R.M.S.; artist in water-colour, pastel, oil, private teacher; *b* Salisbury, Wilts., 13 Feb., 1921. *m* I.M.C. Farquharson, M.A., F.I.A. one *s. Educ:* Croydon High School. *Studied:* Chelsea School of Art (Bernard Adams, Violet Butler, miniaturist). *Exhib:* R.A., Paris Salon, Mall Galleries; one-man shows Johannesburg. *Signs work:* "M. Arridge." *Address:* 5 Dudley Rd., Parkwood, Johannesburg 2193, S.A.

ARTHUR, Harry H. Gascoign, F.L.A. (1948), F.R.S.A. (1949), F.I.Mgt. (1974), Mem. Museums Assoc. (1949); lecturer, writer and broadcaster on the arts; W.E.A. lecturer on art, architecture and art history; Director of Libraries, Museums and Arts, Wirral (1974-80); formerly held libraries and arts posts at Bath, Bristol and Blackpool; Librarian and Curator, Buxton (1949-50), Director of Libraries and Arts, Wigan (1950-68), Borough Librarian and Director, Williamson A.G. and Museum, Birkenhead (1968-74), Chairman Liverpool W.E.A. Branch (1998-); *b* Bristol, 30 June, 1920. *m* Kathleen Joan Fuge. one *s.* one *d. Educ:* Bristol Cathedral School. *Studied:* West of England College of Art. *Publications:* History of Haigh Hall; Guide to the Williamson A.G. and Museum; Guide to the Wirral Maritime Museum; Lee Tapestry Room. *Address:* 20 Christchurch Rd., Prenton, Wirral M.B. Merseyside CH43 5SF.

ASCHAN, Marit Guinness, enamellist, painter and jeweller; President, Artist; Enamellers since foundation 1968; *m* C. W. Aschan. one *s.* one *d. Exhib:* R.A., Leicester Galleries, Lincoln Center, N.Y., Worshipful Company of Goldsmiths, etc.; one-man shows, Beaux Arts, International Faculty of Arts, The Leicester Galleries, Roy Miles, Saga Gallery, London; The Minories, Colchester; Lilienfeld Gallery and Van Diemen-Lilienfeld Galleries, Bodley Gallery, N.Y.; Waldhorn Company Inc., New Orleans; Galerie J. Kraus, Paris; Inter Art Gallery, Caracas, Venezuela; Oslo Kunstforening, Galleri Galtung, Oslo; etc. *Work in collections:* V. & A., central enamel of Louis Osman Cross, Exeter Cathedral; Worshipful Company of Goldsmiths, London; Oppé Coll., Brooklyn Museum; New York University Art Coll.; Fordham University Art Coll.; Yale University A.G.; Nelson Gallery and Atkins Museum, Kansas; North Carolina State Museum of Art, Raleigh; Rochester A.G., N.Y.; University of Kansas Museum of Art, New Orleans Museum of Art; Parrish Art Museum, Southampton, N.Y.; Weatherspoon A.G., University of North Carolina; Finch College A.G.; The Housatonic Museum, Bridgeport, Connecticut; The Snite Museum of Notre Dame University; The Ian Woodner Family Collection, N.Y.; The Royal Norwegian Embassy, London; Kunstindustrimuseet, Hans Rasmus Astrup Coll. Oslo, etc. *Clubs:* Chelsea Arts. *Address:* (residence) 25 Chelsea Park Gdns., London SW3; (studio) Moravian Close, 381 King's Rd., London SW10 6AF.

ASH, Lucy, B.A. (1977), B.Tech. Dist. (1995); painter in acrylic, digital artwork; designer; creative director of lucyash.com; *b* London, 4 Feb., 1955. *Educ:* Millfield School, Somerset. *Studied:* Central School of Art and Design, Camberwell School of Art and Crafts, South Thames College. *Exhib:* Heseltine Masco, Oztenzeki, Austin Desmond, London, Mokotoff, New York, On the Wall, London, R.W.A., Cork St. Fine Art, London. *Work in collections:* private Collections, Bluedoor Ltd. *Commissions:* Bluedoor Ltd., Sony Radio Awards, Microsoft. *Publications:* 'A Taste of Astrology', pub. Alfred A Knopf, New York. (1988), written and illust.; 'The Astrological Cookbook', pub. Sainsbury (1993), written. Multimedia Digital Artwork. *Clubs:* Chelsea Arts. *Signs work:* "Ash." *Address:* 43 Honeywell Rd., London SW11 6EQ. *Email:* la@lucyash.com

ASHBY, Derek Joseph, D.A. (Edin.); artist in oil painting and steel and aluminium; lecturer in drawing and painting, Gray's School of Art, Aberdeen; *b* 24 June, 1926. *m* Mairi Catriona. one *s.* one *d. Educ:* Oldham High School. *Studied:* Edinburgh College of Art (1948-51) under Gillies, Henderson, Blyth; R.A. Schools (1953-55) under Rushbury. *Exhib:* R.S.A., Aberdeen Artists, S.S.A. *Work in collections:* Scottish Arts Council. *Clubs:* A.A.S., S.S.A. *Signs work:* "Derek Ashby." *Address:* Old Invery, Auchattie, Banchory, Kincardineshire AB31 6PR.

ASHE, Faith: see WINTER, Faith.

ASHER, James, artist in water-colour, oil, lithograph; *b* Butler, Missouri, 14 Apr., 1944. *m* Joe Anna Arnett. one *s.* one *d. Educ:* Central Missouri University. *Studied:* The Art Center College of Design, Los Angeles, Calif. *Exhib:* Catto Gallery, London, Zaplin-Lampert Gallery, Santa Fe, N.M., Artists of America, Denver (1991-1997), Gilcrease Museum, Royal Water-colour Soc., London (1992). *Work in collections:* Museum of Fine Arts, Santa Fe. *Publications:* Water-colour Magic (Summer, 1999). *Signs work:* "James Asher." *Address:* P.O. Box 8022, Santa

WHO'S WHO IN ART

Fe, New Mexico 87504-8022, U.S.A.

ASHMORE, Lady, Patricia, P.S. (1953); landscape and portrait painter in pastel, oil and water-colour; *b* Horsham, 13 July, 1929. *m* Vice Admiral Sir Peter Ashmore. one *s.* three *d. Educ:* North Foreland Lodge. *Studied:* Chelsea Polytechnic (portrait painting with Sonia Mervyn). *Exhib:* Pastel Exhbn. (annually), Women Artists, Sussex Artists Assoc. (member and exhibitor), Kentish Artists Annual Exhbn. for Charities. *Signs work:* "Patricia Ashmore." *Address:* Netherdowns, Sundridge, Sevenoaks, Kent TN14 6AR.

ASHTON-BOSTOCK, David A., F.I.A.L. (1960), N.D. (1950), intermed. (1949); artist in oil and interior decorator; Fellow of I.D.D.A. Ltd.; *b* London, 17 Feb., 1930. *m* Victoria Rosamond White (divorced). one *d. Educ:* Wellington College. *Studied:* Maidstone College of Art (1947-50) under A. G. Cary and W. Eade, Byam Shaw School of Art (1953-54) under P. E. Philips. *Exhib:* United Artists, Nat. Soc., R.B.A., N.E.A.C., R.O.I., Paris Salon, Summer Salon, Chelsea Artists, City of London Artists, Ridley Art Club, Hambledon Galleries (Blandford). *Publications:* work repro.: La Revue Moderne, Queen, Country Life, Times, Sunday Express, House and Garden, Tatler, Christmas cards, posters. *Signs work:* "Ashtock." *Address:* Danes Bottom Place, Wormshill, nr. Sittingbourne, Kent ME9 0TS. *Second Address:* Flat 1, 82 Eaton Place, London SW1X 8AU.

ATHERTON, Barry, N.D.D., D.A. (Manc.) Dist. (1965), Leverhulme Scholarship (1965-66), R.A.S.Cert. (1969); artist in mixed media; Lecturer in Fine Art, Glasgow School of Art; *b* England, 1944. *m* Linda. two *s. Studied:* Manchester College of Art and Design (Norman Adams), R.A. Schools (Edward Bawden). *Exhib:* solo shows: New Academy Gallery (1990, 1992, 1994, 1997, 1999), Mistral Galleries (1996). *Work in collections:* Aberdeen A.G., University of Strathclyde, Glasgow Caledonian University, also private and corporate collections, in U.K., Europe and U.S.A. *Commissions:* University of Strathclyde, Glasgow Caledonian University, Alexon/Vogue, The Crown Estate Millennium Exhbn. *Publications:* 'Interview with the Artist', Pryle Behrman (Artline), 'Reflections in the Glass of History', Ray McKenzie. *Clubs:* N.E.A.C., S.S.A. *Signs work:* no signature, identification on the back. *Address:* 235 Nithsdale Rd., Glasgow G41 5PY.

ATKIN, Ann (neé Fawssett), *b* Lindfield, Sussex, 1937. *Educ:* graduate of Brighton College of Art and Royal Academy Schools. *Exhib:* founded The Gnome Reserve, The Wild Flower Garden and The Pixie Kiln in N. Devon; current paintings – birds surrounded by the flow of their songs/sounds. The Gnome Reserve has been featured 55 times on TV and numerous times on radio and in newspapers, magazines and books worldwide, paintings in mixed and solo exhibitions. *Work in collections:* painting in the Dartington Hall Trust Collection. *Commissions:* many pottery landscape scenes with the people depicted as boy and girl pixies. *Signs work:* "Ann Atkin; Ann Fawssett" and see appendix. *Address:* Wild Flower Cottage, Abbots Bickington, N. Devon EX22 7LQ.

ATKIN, Peter, U.A. (1968); artist in water-colour; Past President, Northampton Town and County Art Soc; founder member Northamptonshire Water-colour Group; *b* Wallasey, 16 Aug., 1926. *m* Joyce Wood. one *s.* one *d. Educ:* Stamford School, Lincolnshire; no formal art training, instruction from the late Wilfred R. Wood of

Barnack, nr. Stamford. *Exhib:* R.B.A., R.I., U.A., Britain in Water-colour, N.S.; one-man shows, York Galleries and Municipal Gallery, Northampton, Savage Fine Art, Northampton. *Work in collections:* in U.K., Australia, Holland, U.S.A. *Signs work:* "PETER ATKIN." *Address:* 1 High St., Collingtree, Northampton NN4 0NE.

ATKIN, Ron, F.R.S.A.; painter in water-colour and oil; *b* Leics., 3 Feb., 1938. *m* Ann. two *s. Studied:* Loughborough College of Art (1954-57), R.A. Schools (1957-61). *Exhib:* regularly at R.A.; mixed shows: Roland, Browse and Delbanco. *Work in collections:* Lincoln College Oxford, Dartington Trust, Devon C.C. Schools Museum Service, Alexander Theatre, B'ham, Plymouth City Museum and A.G. Shortlisted for a Gulbenkian Printmakers award; featured in first and second edition of Dictionary of British Art Volume VI, 20th century painters and sculptors; also in Debrett's. *Publications:* Book 2001 ISBN 0-9538907-2-4. *Signs work:* "Atkin" or "Ron Atkin." *Address:* Wild Flower Cottage, Abbots Bickington, Devon EX22 7LQ.

ATKINS, David Alexander, B.A. (Hons.) Fine Art Painting; artist in oil and watercolour, lecturer in art; Course leader, Foundation Art and Design; *b* London 20 Feb., 1964. *m* Jacqueline. two *d. Studied:* St. Martin's School of Art (1982-83), Winchester School of Art (1983-86). *Exhib:* Discerning Eye, Alresford Gallery, Singer & Friedlander, R.A. Summer Show, Laing, Albermarle Gallery. *Work in collections:* Creasey Collection, Salisbury; Guildhalll, Kingston, Surrey. *Commissions:* four murals for G.L.C. *Address:* 34 Albany Rd., New Malden, Surrey KT3 3NY.

ATKINS, Ray, D.F.A. (Lond.); painter in 2D-oil, acrylic, drawing mediums, sculptor in 3D-clay, cement, wax; *b* Exeter, 9 July, 1937. *m* Geraldine. one *s.* one *d. Studied:* Bromley College of Art (1954-56, 1958-61), Slade School of Art (1961-64). *Exhib:* one-man shows: Whitechapel A.G. (1974), R.W.A. Bristol retrospective (1996), and many other one-man and group shows. *Work in collections:* B.M., British Council, Arts Council, South West Arts, Somerset C.C., and private collections Europe and America. *Publications:* 'Ray Atkins' R.W.A. (1996) ISBN No. 1899525 04 1; Ray Atkins – Paintings of the Figure, Truro (1999); 'Broken Ground' (2001). *Signs work:* "Ray Atkins," 2D work is signed on the back. *Address:* Carn Marth House, Pennance Rd., Lanner, Redruth, Cornwall TR16 5TH.

ATKINSON, Anthony, A.R.C.A. (1954); painter in oil; Dean, Colchester Inst.; *b* 1929. *m* Joan Dawson. one *s.* one s- *d. Educ:* Wimbledon College. *Studied:* Royal College of Art. *Exhib:* R.A., Leicester Galleries R.W.S.; one-man: Minories, Colchester, Leighton House, London, Gainsborough's House, Sudbury, Mercury Theatre, Colchester, British Council, Kuwait, Coach-House Gallery, Guernsey, Highgate Fine Art, Chappel Gallery, John Russell, Ipswich. *Work in collections:* Essex Museum; Ernst & Young; Essex C.C.; Colchester Hospital, etc. *Publications:* work repro.: Shell, London Transport, The Artist, Artist v Illustrators. *Clubs:* President Colchester Art Soc. *Signs work:* "ATKINSON." *Address:* Coach House, Great Horkesley, Colchester, Essex CO6 4AX.

ATKINSON, Eric Newton, N.E.A.C., R.C.A.; painter in oils and collage; Nat. Dipl. (1st hons., painting), R.A. Drawing Medal, Silver Medal for Painting; Dean, Faculty of Arts, Fanshawe College, London, Canada; *b* W. Hartlepool, 23 July, 1928. *m* Muriel H. Ross. one *s.* one *d. Educ:* Dyke House, W. Hartlepool. *Studied:* W. Hartlepool College of Art and R.A. Schools. *Exhib:* Redfern Gallery, Tate Gallery,

Austin Hayes, York, Leeds Univ., Wakefield and Middlesbrough city galleries, Zwemmer Gallery, Corcoran Gallery, Rothman Gallery, Mendelson Gallery, Capponi Gallery, Pollock Gallery, Mendel Gallery, Carnegie Mellon, U.S.A., Tate, St. Ives, Wallace Gallery, Calgary. *Work in collections:* National Portrait Gallery, Contemporary Art Soc., M. of W., Leeds, Leicester, Wakefield, Hereford and Kendal A.G., Leeds City A.G. Collection, McIntosh Gallery U.W.O., Government Art Collection, U.K. *Publications:* "The Incomplete Circle" Eric Atkinson, Art and Education. Scolar Press, 2000. *Signs work:* "Eric Atkinson." *Address:* 69 Paddock Green Cres., London N6J-3P6, Ontario, Canada. *Email:* murielatkinson@sympati-co.ca

ATKINSON, Kim, M.A. (R.C.A.) (1987); S.W.L.A. (1992); artist in water-colour, oil, printmaking, drawing; *b* Bath, 1962. *m* Gwydion Morley. one *s*. *Studied:* Falmouth School of Art (Foundation); Cheltenham College of Art (B.A. Painting); Royal College of Art (M.A. Natural History Illustration). *Exhib:* Wales, England, Europe, America. *Publications:* Birds in Wales (Poyser, 1994) (illustrations); chapter in Water-colour Masterclass by Lawrence Wood (Collins, 1993), work included in Artists for Nature Foundation; publications resulting from projects in Poland, France, Spain and India; Drawn to the Forest (SWLA and Forestry Commission proj-ect in the New Forest, pub'd, Wildlife Art Gallery, 2000). *Signs work:* "Kim Atkinson." *Address:* Ty'n Gamdda, Uwchmynydd, Pwllheli, Gwynedd LL53 8DA.

ATKINSON, Ted, D.F.A. (Lond., 1952), R.E. (1988), F.R.B.S., F.R.S.A. (1957), Slade Prize Winner (1952); sculptor; Head of Sculpture School, Coventry University (1968-83); *b* Liverpool, 21 Mar., 1929. *Educ:* Oulton School, Liverpool. *Studied:* Liverpool College of Art and Slade School, Slade Post-graduate Scholar (1952-53). *Work in collections:* Arts Council, London, Ashmolean Museum, Oxford, Dallas Art Museum, Kunst Academie, Dresden, Fitzwilliam Museum, Cambridge, Museum of Modern Art, N.Y., Seattle Art Museum, etc.; public sculptures in Coventry, Dusseldorf, Hamburg, Univ. Birmingham. One of six sculptors chosen to represent Britain at Expo 88 Brisbane. *Address:* 4 De Vere Pl., Wivenhoe, Essex CO7 9AX.

ATTREE, Jake (Jonathan), Dip.A.D. (Painting) (1972), R.A. Schools Post-Grad. Cert. (1977); Landseer prize, Creswick prize, David Murray Scholarship; painter; *b* York, 13 Oct., 1950. *m* Lindsay Knight. *Educ:* Danesmead, York. *Studied:* York College of Art (1966-68), Liverpool College of Art (1969-72), R.A. Schools (1974-77). *Exhib:* regular one person and group shows include R.A. Summer Exhbn. (1975, 1985), Serpentine Summer (1982), Maastricht, Dortmund (1992), Leeds City A.G. (1993), Michael Richardson Contemporary Art, London, Dean Clough Halifax (1994). *Work in collections:* Leeds City Council, City of Dortmund, Grays A.G. Hartlepool, Sheffield University, Nuffield Trust. *Publications:* illustrated At This Time and The Purblind Man by John Holmes. Studio: Dean Clough, Halifax HX3 5AX. *Signs work:* usually unsigned, unless requested, then "J. Attree." *Address:* 33 Titus St., Saltaire, Shipley BD18 4LU.

AUERBACH, Frank Helmut, painter; *b* Berlin, 29 Apr., 1931. *Educ:* privately. *Studied:* St. Martin's School of Art; R.C.A. *Exhib:* one-man shows: Beaux-Arts Gallery (1956, 1959, 1961, 1962, 1963); Marlborough Fine Art (1965, 1967, 1971, 1974, 1983, 1987, 1990, 1997); Marlborough, N.Y. (1969, 1982, 1994); retrospective, Hayward Gallery (1978), Venice Biennale (1986) (joint winner Golden Lion), Hamburg (1986), Essen, Madrid (1987), Rijksmuseum Vincent Van Gogh, Amsterdam (1989), Yale Center for British Art, New Haven (1991), National Gallery, London (1995). *Work in collections:* Metropolitan Museum, N.Y.; Museum of Modern Art N.Y.; Los Angeles County Museum; National Gallery of Australia; B.M.; Tate Gallery, London; and many other museums; British Council; Arts Council; Contemporary Art Society, etc. *Address:* c/o Marlborough Fine Art Ltd., 6 Albemarle St., London W1X 4BY.

AUGUST, Lillias Anne, B.A. Hons. (1978), C.N.A.A. (1979); painter in watercolour; member of management council, Bury St. Edmunds Art Gallery, Suffolk; *b* Gloucester, 5 May, 1955. *Studied:* Goldsmiths College, London (1973-1977), Birmingham Polytechnic (1977-1978). *Exhib:* Cloister Gallery, Bury St. Edmunds (1999, 2002); Hunter Gallery, Long Melford (2001); Singer & Friedlander Sunday Times Watercolour Exhib. (2001); Artworks, Rougham (2000, 2001); R.I. (2000, 2001); Cross Country, Bury St. Edmunds Art Gallery (2001); Laing Exhibs. (1992, 1995, 1998 regional prizewinner, 2000); This Flat Earth, Firstsite, Colchester (2000); Old Fire Engine House, Ely (2000), On the Border, Wolsey Gallery, Ipswich (1998); Manor House Museum, Bury St. Edmunds (1997); Heffer Gallery, Cambridge (1996); R.W.S. (1996). *Work in collections:* Hylands House, Chelmsford, Manor House Museum, Bury St. Edmunds. *Commissions:* Chelmsford Borough Council; St Edmundsbury Borough Council, Suffolk; St. Bartholomew's Hospital, London; The National Trust; project artist, Suffolk Cathedral Millennium Project (2000-2004). *Signs work:* "Lillias August" or "LA." *Address:* West Barn, Golden Lane, Lawshall, Bury St. Edmunds, Suffolk IP29 4PS. *Email:* lilliasaugust@btinternet.com

AULD, John Leslie M., D.A. Belfast, A.R.C.A., N.R.D., F.I.A.L.; art teacher, designer-craftsman in goldsmiths' work; head, Art Dept., Municipal Tech. College, Londonderry (1940-46); Senior Lecturer, Glasgow School of Art (retd. 1979); *b* Belfast, 21 Jan., 1914. *m* Doreen M. W. Auld (née Sproul). one *s. Educ:* Methodist College, Belfast. *Studied:* Belfast Coll. of Art (1931-35); Royal Coll. of Art (1935-39). *Exhib:* London, Brussels, Paris, New York, Stockholm, Arts Council, etc. *Work in collections:* Goldsmiths' Company, London; New York City Corpn.; University of Glasgow. *Commissions:* crozier: R.C. Bishopric Motherwell; font & ewer: Bearsden Parish Church; altar vases: Knightswood Parish Church, Glasgow. *Publications:* Your Jewellery. *Signs work:* "J. L. AULD," but see appendix. *Address:* Flat 20, 41 Dundas Ct., East Kilbride G74 4AN.

AVATI, Mario, Prix de la Critique, Paris (1957), Gold Medal First International Prints Exhbn., Florence (1966), Prix du Lion's Club (1972), Grand Prix des Arts de la Ville de Paris (1981); painter/printmaker in mezzotint; *b* Monaco, 27 May, 1921. *m* Helen. *Educ:* College de Grasse, France. *Studied:* Ecole des Arts Decoratifs, Nice, Ecole des Beaux Arts, Paris. *Exhib:* one-man shows worldwide. *Work in collections:* museums in Europe, America, Asia, Oceania. *Publications:* 12 'Livres de Luxe' illustrated with original prints. *Clubs:* Soc. Les Peintres-Graveurs Paris, La Jeune Gravure Contemporaine Paris, Royal Soc. of Painter-Printmakers, London. *Signs work:* "AVATI." *Address:* 12 Cite Vaneau, Paris, France F75007.

AYERS, Duffy, painter in oil; senior art teacher, Denham Coll., Nr. Oxford; *b* Bucks., 19 Sep., 1919. *m* Eric Ayers A.R.C.A. (children from prev. marriage to Michael Rothenstein). one *s.* one *d. Educ:* private boarding schools, Sussex. *Studied:* Central School of Arts and Crafts, under William Roberts, Benard Meninsky and Maurice Kestleman. *Exhib:* Fry Art Gallery, R.A., Battersea Art Fair. *Work in collections:* private collections in U.K. and U.S.A. *Commissions:* private portraits. *Signs work:* "Duffy Ayers." *Address:* 4 Regent Sq., London WC1H 8HZ.

AYERS, Eric, A.R.C.A., M.S.I.A.; consultant designer; *b* 12 Aug., 1921. *m* Duffy Rothenstein (née Fitzgerald). *Educ:* Balgowan Grammar School, Beckenham. *Studied:* The School of Photoengraving and Lithography, London, E.C.I, Beckenham School of Art, R.C.A. *Exhib:* Design in Business Printing Exhibition, Festival of Britain (Dome of Discovery); Milwaukee Library, Wisconsin (U.S.A.); C. of I.D. "100 Good Catalogues"; R.A. Summer Shows. *Work in collections:* Museum of Modern Art, N.Y., B.M. Dept. of Prints and Books, V. & A. Dept. of Prints and Books, O.U.P. Library. *Commissions:* Collaborated with David Hockney's artist's book 'Grimms Fairy Tales' (1969/1970), Henry Moore's artist's book 'W.H. Auden Poems' (1971/1972), Patrick Caulfield's artist's book 'The poems of Jules Laforge' (1972/1973), Claes Oldenburgh's Multiple, 'London Knees' 1966, etc. *Publications:* work repro.: Graphis, Graphis Annual, Design Magazine. No. I42 1960. Article, "Do Posters Work?". Taught at London College of Printing, Senior Lecturer Camberwell School of Art, Graphic Arts Department (1972-1983), Fellow, Fine Art Dept., University of Newcastle, (1966-1967), Director and Art Director, since conception, of Editions Alecto (1963-1968). *Signs work:* "ERIC AYERS." *Address:* 4 Regent Sq., London WC1H 8HZ.

AYRES, Gillian, O.B.E., A.R.A.; painter; taught at Bath Academy, St. Martin's; Head of Painting, Winchester School of Art since 1978; *b* Barnes, London, 3 Feb., 1930. two children. *Educ:* St. Paul's Girls' School. *Studied:* Camberwell School of Art. *Exhib:* group shows: Musée d'Art Moderne; Bienale de Paris, Paris (1959); Situation, London (1960-61); one-man shows, Gallery One (1956), Kasmin Gallery (1965-66, 1969), Hayward Gallery (1972), Kasmin/Knoedler (1979), Knoedler London (1979, 1982, 1985, 1987), Knoedler New York (1985), R.A. British Art (1987), London, and Stuttgart, Germany. Awarded Japan International Art Promotion Association Award (1963). *Work in collections:* Tate Gallery, Museum of Modern Art, N.Y. *Signs work:* "Gillian Ayres." *Address:* Tall Trees, Gooseham, nr. Bude, Cornwall.

B

BACK, Ken, Cert. R.A.S. (dist.) (1967), N.D.D. (1964); painter in oil and ink; part-time art lecturer; *b* Guildford, 2 Apr., 1944. *m* Corinne Jones, artist (decd.). one *s.* one *d. Educ:* Astor School, Dover. *Studied:* Dover, Folkestone and Canterbury Colleges of Art (1959-64), R.A. Schools (1964-67, Peter Greenham, Charles Mahoney). *Exhib:* R.A., Piccadilly Gallery, Park Walk Gallery, London, Chappel

Galleries, Colchester, etc. *Work in collections:* Europe and U.S.A. *Signs work:* "K.W. BACK" or "K.B." *Address:* White Cottage, Semere Green Lane, Dickleburgh, nr. Diss, Norfolk IP21 4NT.

BACKHOUSE, David John, R.W.A., F.R.B.S., F.R.S.A.; sculptor in bronze; *b* Corsham, Wilts., 5 May, 1941. *m* Sarah Barber. one *s.* two *d. Educ:* Lord Weymouth School, Warminster. *Studied:* West of England College of Art. *Exhib:* one-man shows: London, New York. *Work in collections:* R.W.A., British Steel Corp., Royal Opera House, Covent Garden, Morgan Crucible Co., Mercantile and General Reinsurance Co., Haslemere Estates, Telford Dev. Corp., City of Bristol, Tesco plc, J. Sainsbury plc., Standard Life, and private collections throughout Europe and in U.S.A. Studio: Lullington Studio, Lullington, Frome, Som. BA11 2PW. *Signs work:* "Backhouse," and see appendix. *Address:* The Old Post Office, Lullington, Frome, Somerset BA11 2PW. *Second Address:* La Chapelle Pommier, 24340 Mareuil, France.

BAFFONI, Pier Luigi, N.S. (1975), R.O.I. (1979); artist in oil, water-colour and pastel; *b* Turin, Italy, 11 Aug., 1932. *m* Mary Bainbridge. *Educ:* College of the Missioni Consolata, Turin. *Studied:* College of Art, Turin (1954-58) under Luigi Guglielmino and privately from Alessandro Pomi of Venice. *Exhib:* one-man shows, Italy, Hertford, Cambridge, Bedford, Hitchin; mixed shows, Biennale of Castelfranco Veneto, Bologna, Mall Galleries, London. *Work in collections:* Montebelluna Town Hall, Bedfordshire Educ. Art Loan Service. *Publications:* included in "Modern Oil Impressionists" by Ron Ranson – David & Charles, (1992). *Signs work:* "P. L. Baffoni." *Address:* 140 Station Rd., Lower Stondon, Beds. SG16 6JH.

BAGHJIAN, Manouk, artist in water-colour, pastel, oil; *b* Nicosia, Cyprus, 7 Jan., 1929. married. one *s.* one *d. Educ:* Armenian High School, Cyprus. *Studied:* Richmond A.E.C. *Exhib:* Gulbenkian Hall Kensington, Clarendon Gallery Holland Pk., Chiswick Library, Pinacoteca Tossa de Mar, R.S.M.A. Mall Galleries (1989, 1990, 1991, 1994, 1995, 1996), B.B.C. Bush House, Hogarth Club W4, Hertford Art Soc. (1995), Chelsea Art Soc. (1995). *Work in collections:* 8 Turnham Green Terr., London W4. *Clubs:* Ealing Art, Richmond Art Soc. *Signs work:* "Manouk." *Address:* 213 Popes La., London W5 4NH.

BAILE de LAPERRIERE, Charles, editor; *b* Le Mans (France), 17 Sept., 1939. *Educ:* Ecole Pascal (Paris), College St. Esprit (Beauvais). *Publications:* edited: Royal Academy Exhibitors 1971-89, The Royal Scottish Academy Exhibitors 1826-1990 4 Vols., The Society of Women Artists Exhibitors 1855-1996 4 Vols., The Royal Society of Marine Painters 1946-1996, Silver Auction Records. *Clubs:* Army & Navy Club, London, Scottish Arts, Edinburgh. *Address:* Hilmarton Manor, Calne, Wilts. SN11 8SB.

BAILEY, Caroline, B.A.(Hons.), M.A.; artist in water-colour, gouache, acrylic; *Studied:* Manchester Polytechnic (1972-76). *Exhib:* John Noott Galleries Worcs., City Gallery London, Thompson's Gallery Dover St. and Aldeburgh, Walker Galleries Harrogate, Clifton Gallery Bristol, Colours Gallery Edinburgh, The Gallery Manchester's Art House, Manor House Gallery Oxon, Castlegate House Cumbria, Waterford Gallery Hale Cheshire, also Open Exhbns. R.S.W., R.S.A., R.W.S. *Work* *in collections:* Irish Management Inst., Maclay Murray & Spens, Edinburgh Fund Managers, Callscan Ltd. Awards: Daler Rowney R.W.S. Open (1994), The Artist Award R.W.S. Open (1997), Glasgow Arts Club Fellowship R.S.W. (1999), N.S. Macfarlane Charitable Trust Award R.S.A. (1999). Scottish Arts Club Award. *Clubs:* Mem. R.S.W. *Signs work:* see appendix. *Address:* c/o John Noott Galleries, 14 Cotswold Ct., Broadway, Worcs. WR12 7AA.

BAILEY, Julian, B.F.A. Oxon. (1985), R.A.Dip. (M.A.) (1988); artist in oil and pastel; *b* Cheshire, 8 Apr., 1963. *m* Sophie Cullen, ceramist. one *s.* two *d. Educ:* Malvern College. *Studied:* Ruskin School of Art (1982-85), R.A. Schools (1985-88, Jane Dowling, Norman Blamey, R.A.). *Exhib:* R.A., New Grafton Gallery, Browse & Darby. *Work in collections:* National Trust (F.F.A.), New College, Oxford, Warbergs, Reed Executive, H.R.H. the Prince of Wales, Dorchester County Council. *Clubs:* Chelsea Arts. *Signs work:* "J.B." or "JULIAN BAILEY." *Address:* The Old Vicarage, Stinsford, Dorchester, Dorset DT2 8PS.

BAILEY, Terence Robert, N.D.D. (1958), A.T.D. (1962), R.B.S.A. (1991); painter in oil; Senior lecturer, Northumberland C.H.E. (1962-79); *b* Wolverhampton, 21 Dec., 1937. *m* Kate (Valerie Ann Browning). three *s. Educ:* Wolverhampton Technical High School. *Studied:* Wolverhampton College of Art (1954-58), Bournemouth College of Art (1962). *Exhib:* Northern Painters (1966), Northern Art Exhbn. (1978), prize winner R.B.S.A. Open (1986), R.P., R.O.I., regularly at R.B.S.A.; several one-man shows. Winner in Alexon "Women on Canvas" portrait competition (1990). *Work in collections:* Northumberland C.C., Northern Arts, National Library of Wales, R.B.S.A.; many private collections. *Signs work:* "Terry Bailey." *Address:* Dovey Studio, Aberdyfi, Gwynedd LL35 0LW.

BAILLIE C.B.E., William James Laidlaw, P.P.R.S.A., P.P.R.S.W., R.G.I., H.R.A., H.R.H.A., H.R.W.A., H.B.W.S., H.F.R.B.S., H.R.U.A., H.S.S.A., D.Litt., D.A.Edin. (1950); painter in oil and water-colour; Past President, Royal Scottish Academy; *b* Edinburgh, 1923. *m* Helen Baillie. one *s.* two *d. Educ:* Dunfermline High School, Fife. *Studied:* Edinburgh College of Art (1941-42); (War Service 1942-46) (1946-50, Gillies, Maxwell, Rosoman, Philipson, MacTaggart), Diploma (1950), Moray House Teaching College 1950-51. *Exhib:* one-man shows: Edinburgh, Harrogate, Newcastle, Salisbury, London, etc. *Work in collections:* Aberdeen, Edinburgh, Glasgow, Fife, Perth, Kansas, U.S.A., Australia, Canada, Germany, Greece, Sweden, U.K., U.S.A., etc. *Commissions:* several private commissions. *Clubs:* Scottish Arts and New Club. *Signs work:* "W.J.L. Baillie." *Address:* 6a Esslemont Rd., Edinburgh EH16 5PX.

BAIN, Julia Mary, M.F.P.S. (1985), Mem. Chelsea Art Soc. (1984); Woodrow Award (1986); sculptor in terracotta, wax and bronze; *b* London, 22 June, 1930. *m* David Bain, F.R.C.S. three *s.* one *d. Educ:* The Legat School of Russian Ballet. *Studied:* I.L.E.A. Chelsea/Westminster (1978-81), Sir John Cass College (1981-83). *Exhib:* F.B.A. (1983-89), R.B.A., S.W.A., N.S., F.P.S. Trends, Art of Living S.P.S., Chelsea Art Soc.; one-man shows, Windsor Festival (1981, 1986, 1989), Century Gallery, Datchet (1990, 1995), The Deanery, Windsor Castle (1993, 1995). Work in private collections. *Signs work:* "J.B." *Address:* The Studio, Holimans Platt, 31 High St., Datchet, Berks. SL3 9EQ.

BAIN, Peter, painter in oil; *b* London, 15 December, 1927. *m* Jennifer. four *s*. *Studied:* Bath Academy of Art. *Signs work:* "Bain." *Address:* Tiled Cottage, Old Bosham, Sussex PO18 8LS.

BAINES, Richard John Manwaring, M.A., Ph.D., R.O.I., R.D.S., N.D.D., A.T.D., V.P.R.O.I. (1997), P.R.O.I. (1998); painter, writer, lecturer, critic, broadcaster (radio & TV); previously Senior lecturer/Head of Academic Studies, London College of Fashion; *b* Hastings, 1940. *m* Maureen Gregory. two *s*. one *d. Studied:* Regent St. Polytechnic, Goldsmiths' College, Birmingham Polytechnic. *Exhib:* R.O.I., R.B.A., N.S., R.E., Painter-Etchers, London and provinces; one-man exhbns. Hastings (1968, 1987). *Work in collections:* County Borough of Hastings, Manx Museum, London Inst. *Commissions:* Royal Arms and mural restorations, All Saints Church, Hastings. *Publications:* Mainly design history. *Clubs:* East Sussex Arts (Past President). *Signs work:* see appendix. *Address:* Badgers End, Warren Rd., Fairlight, E. Sussex TN35 4AG.

BAINES, Valerie, A.R.M.S. (1985), founder-member of S.B.A. (1988), F.L.S. (1991), V.P.S.B.A. (1996); Botanical artist, miniature painter and natural history illustrator in water-colour and oil; *b* Romford, 1935. *m* Brian Norman. one *s. Educ:* Roxeth Mead School, Harrow on the Hill; Royal College of Music, London. *Studied:* Harrow Art School. *Exhib:* R.A., R.M.S., S.B.A., R.H.S. Westminster Galleries, Mall Galleries, Alpine Gallery, Medici Gallery, Llewellyn Alexander Gallery, 7th Exhbn. of International Botanical Art, Carnegie Mellon University, Pittsburgh, U.S.A., Memorial University, Botanic Gardens, Newfoundland, Canada, Le Jardin des Cinq Sens, Yvoire, France. *Work in collections:* Carnegie Mellon University Botanical Library, Pittsburgh, U.S.A., Port Lympne, Kent; many private collections worldwide. *Publications:* The Naturalist's Garden by John Feltwell (Ebury Press, 1987), Botanical Diary (St. Michael, 1989), The Story of Silk by J. Feltwell (Allen Sutton 1990), The Big Book (Collins, 1991), Meadows by J. Feltwell (Allen Sutton 1992), Glorious Butterflies, (Butterfly Conservation 1993), Gardens and Butterflies Calendar (Butterfly Conservation 1998), Mindful of Butterflies by Bernard S. Jackson (The Book Guild 1999). *Signs work:* "V.B." and "V. BAINES." *Address:* Shreives Oak, 16 Medway Rd., Gillingham, Kent ME7 1NH. *Website:* www.valeriebaines.com

BAKER, Christopher William, B.A.Hons. (Fine Art, 1978), P.G.C.E. (1981), R.B.A. (1981); etcher, oil on canvas, dramatic landscape paintings; Tutor, West Dean College; *b* Essex, 27 May, 1956. *Educ:* Kingham Hill School, Oxon. *Studied:* West Surrey College of Art and Design (1974-75, M. Fairclough), Glos. College of Art and Design (1975-78, D. L. Carpanini), Exeter University. *Exhib:* R.W.A., R.B.A., Mall Galleries, Phoenix Gallery, Highgate, Burstow Gallery, Brighton College, Wyckeham Gallery, Stockbridge. *Work in collections:* Coventry Adult Educ., Oundle School, Eartham House. *Publications:* work repro.: The Artist, Quattro Publications. *Signs work:* "Christopher Baker." *Address:* 110 Fitzallan Rd., Arundel, W. Sussex.

BAKERE, Ronald Duncan, M.A., F.R.S.A.; sculptor in metal and ceramic; *b* Lanark, Scotland, 7 Sept., 1935. *m* (1) Dr. Jane Earthy. (2) Macaria Saducos. three *s*. one *d. Educ:* Norwich School, Christ Church, Oxford. *Studied:* Putney School of Art, Sir John Cass Dept. of Art at London Guildhall University. *Exhib:* Arts Club, Dover

St., Brixton A.G.; South Thames College, etc. *Commissions:* churches and private. *Clubs:* sometime Chairman Brixton Art Gallery, Sussex Arts Club, London Flotilla. *Address:* 11B Sussex Heights, St. Margaret's Place, Brighton BN1 2FQ.

BALDWIN, Arthur Mervyn, N.D.D. (1955), Rome Scholarship, Sculpture, 1960; sculptor in metals and synthetics; self employed artist and restorer; 1978, retired defeated by lack of public appreciation - now restores antique watches for which service people happily pay; *b* Immingham, Lincs., 1 Feb. 1934. *m* Patrica Mary. two *s. Educ:* Humberstone Foundation School, Old Clee, Lincs. *Studied:* Grimsby School of Art, Leicester College of Art. *Work in collections:* National Museum of Wales, Arts Council (Wales); Städtischen Kunstammlungen, Ludwigshafen. *Signs work:* sculpture unsigned; drawings etc. signed "MERVYN BALDWIN." *Address:* 18 The Walk, Cardiff CF2 3AF.

BALDWIN, Gordon, O.B.E. (1992), N.D.D. (1952), Central Dip. (1953); ceramist; Hon. Dr. R.C.A.; *b* Lincoln, 1932. *m* Nancy Chandler. one *s.* two *d. Educ:* Lincoln School. *Studied:* Lincoln School of Art (1949-51, Toni Bartl), Central School of Art and Design (1951-53, Dora Billington). *Work in collections:* V. & A.; Southampton A.G.; Crafts Council; Leicester Educ. Authority; Usher Gallery, Lincoln; Abbots Hall, Keswick; Paisley A.G.: Boymans van Beuningen, Rotterdam; Bellrive Museum, Zurich; Penn. State University, U.S.A.; Gateshead A.G.; Swindon A.G.; Museum of Art, Melbourne; Museum of Art, Perth; Knukke-Heiste, Keramion, W. Germany; Octagon Centre, Idah., U.S.A. *Address:* Rylands House, Greathales St., Market Drayton TF9 1JN.

BALDWIN, Martyn John, Dip.A.D.; painter in oil; *b* Edgware, 18 May, 1959. *m* Christine Vivianne Baldwin. *Educ:* Downer Grammar School. *Studied:* Harrow School of Art (1979-83). *Exhib:* R.A., N.P.G. *Signs work:* "M. Baldwin" or "BALD-WIN." *Address:* Flat 3, 132 Headstone Rd., Harrow HA1 1PF.

BALDWIN, Nancy, painter; *m* Gordon Baldwin. one *s.* two *d. Educ:* St. Joseph's Convent, Lincoln. *Studied:* Lincoln School of Art (1949-52, Toni Bartl), Central School of Art and Design (1952-54, Dora Billington). *Exhib:* Reading Gallery, Thames Gallery, Windsor, The Gallery, Eton College, Cross Keys Gallery, Beaconsfield, Salix, Windsor, Oxford Gallery, City Museum and Gallery, Stoke-on-Trent, Midland Group, Nottingham, Ikon, Birmingham, Holsworthy, London, Carmel College Gallery, Bohun Gallery, Henley, Ellingham Mill, Bungay, prize winner Midland View (1980), Lynne Strover Gallery, Cambridge, Barrett Marsden Gallery, London. *Work in collections:* Ashmolean Museum, Oxford and private collections in U.K., Italy, Switzerland, Belgium, Hong Kong, France, U.S.A. *Address:* Rylands House, Greathales St., Market Drayton TF9 1JN.

BALFOUR, Maria, Medal Winner, Internationale Academie de Lutece, Paris (1977); painter in oil; self taught artist; *b* 27 June 1934. *m* Lord Balfour of Inchrye. one *d. Educ:* America and Great Britain. *Exhib:* Loggia Gallery (1975, 1980, 1985), Paris Salon, Galerie Internationale, N.Y., Chelsea Art Soc., Kensington & Chelsea Artists; R.I. Galleries, Medici Galleries, Lloyds Bank (Pall Mall) in aid of Mental Health Foundation (1990), exhbns. with other artists in aid of British Diabetic Assoc., Southwold, Suffolk (1995). *Work in collections:* New Zealand, S. Africa, Belgium, Holland, U.S.A., British Isles, Israel and Italy. *Commissions:* crest for

Bridal Kneeler to celebrate 250th year of founding of Guy's Hospital (1976). *Address:* 4 Marsh End Flats, Ferry Rd., Walberswick, Suffolk IP18 6TH.

BALKWILL, Raymond James, painter in water-colour and pastel; *b* Exeter, 7 Oct., 1948. *m* Jane. two *s. Studied:* Exeter College of Art. *Exhib:* Open shows including R.I., R.W.A., Bristol, South West Academy of Fine and Applied Arts. *Work in collections:* internationally. *Publications:* regular contributor of articles to 'The Artist'. *Clubs:* St. Ives Soc. of Artists. *Signs work:* " RAY BALKWILL." *Address:* 'Thistledown', Marley Rd., Exmouth, Devon EX8 4PP. *Email:* raybalkwill@eclipse.co.uk

BALL, Gerald, R.C.A. (1979); painter in water-colour and tempera; *b* Ashton-under-Lyne, 24 May, 1948. *m* Ann Mumford. *Educ:* Hartshead Comprehensive. *Studied:* Ashton-under-Lyne C.F.E. *Exhib:* R.W.S., Richard Hagen, Ltd., R.I., Manchester Academy, Agnews, Tegfryn Gallery, Bourne Gallery, Catto Gallery, David Curzon Gallery, Walker Galleries, Crossing Gate Gallery. *Work in collections:* Coleg Harlech. Work in many private collections worldwide. *Commissions:* numerous. *Signs work:* "GERRY BALL." *Address:* Old Golderwell, Golderfield, Pudleston, Leominster, Herefordshire HR6 0RG.

BALL, Robert, A.R.C.A. (1942), R.E. (1943), R.B.S.A. (1943), F.R.S.A. (1950), R.B.A. (1979), A.R.W.A. (1988); British Inst. Scholarship for Engraving (1937); teacher of painting, drawing and anatomy, Birmingham College of Art (1942); Princ. Stroud School of Arts and Crafts (Jan., 1953); teacher of painting, Glos. College of Art (1959-81); artist in oil, water-colour, drawing, etching, line-engraving, mezzotint, aquatint, and wood-engraving; *b* Birmingham, 11 July, 1918. *m* Barbara Minchin. one *s.* two *d. Studied:* Birmingham Junior School of Art (1930-33), Birmingham College of Art (1933-40); R.C.A. (1940-42). *Exhib:* R.A., R.W.A., R.E., R.B.S.A., R.B.A. *Work in collections:* V. & A., Ashmolean, Gloucester, Dudley, Hunterian, Walsall, Cheltenham and Birmingham Museums. *Publications:* illustrated Cotswold Ballads by Mansell. *Signs work:* "Robert Ball." *Address:* Bethshan, Kingsmead, Painswick, Glos. GL6 6US.

BALMER, Barbara, A.R.S.A. (1973), R.S.W. (1966), R.G.I. (1988); painter in oil and water-colour; *b* B'ham, 23 Sept., 1929. *m* George Mackie, D.F.C., R.D.I., R.S.W. two *d. Studied:* Coventry School of Art; Edinburgh College of Art. *Exhib:* one-man shows: Demarco Gallery, Edinburgh (1965-70), Scottish Gallery, Edinburgh (1975, 1980, 1985, 1988), Posterngate Gallery, Hull (1983), Stirling Gallery (1976), Usher Gallery, Lincoln (1984); Retrospective '55-'95 Touring Exhbn. (1995-96). *Work in collections:* Glasgow Kelvingrove A.G., Edinburgh City Art Centre, Aberdeen A.G., Perth A.G., S.N.P.G., S.A.C., Usher Gall. Lincoln, Coventry A.G., Dundee A.G., Leicester City Museum, Royal Bank of Scotland, Citibank. *Signs work:* "Barbara Balmer." *Address:* 32 Broad St., Stamford, Lincs. PE9 1PJ.

BALMER, Derek Rigby, R.W.A.; painter in oil; President, Royal West of England Academy; *b* Bristol, 28 Dec., 1934. *m* Elizabeth Mary Rose. one *s.* one *d. Educ:* St. Gabriel's Convent, Waterloo House, Sefton Pk. *Studied:* West of England College of Art (Dennis Darch, Derek Crowe, Paul Feiler). *Exhib:* Arnolfini (four), New Art Centre, Leicester Gallery, R.W.A. Represented by Anthony Hepworth Fine Art Bath, and Gisela Van Beers London, Dutch Dealers: Smelik and Stokking The

Hague and Amsterdam. *Clubs:* Chelsea Arts. *Signs work:* "Balmer" or "Derek Balmer." *Address:* Mulberry House, 12 Avon Grove, Sneyd Pk., Bristol 9 1PJ.

BANEY, Ralph R., F.R.B.S. (1984), M.F.A. (1973), Ph.D. (1980), A.T.C. (1962), Who's Who in American Art (1973); Professor of Art; sculptor in wood, bronze, ceramic, fibreglass; *b* Trinidad, 22 Sept., 1929. *m* Vera. one *s. Educ:* Naparima College, Trinidad. *Studied:* Brighton College of Art (1957-62, A.J.J. Ayres), University of Maryland, U.S.A. (1971-76, Ken Campbell). *Exhib:* Washington County Museum, O.A.S. Gallery, Washington D.C.; Sculpture House, N.Y.C.; Georgetown University. *Work in collections:* H.M. The Queen; Washington County Museum of Fine Arts, Hagerstown, Md.; Central Bank, Trinidad. *Clubs:* R.B.S., Sculptors Guild Inc. N.Y., Washington Sculptors Group. *Signs work:* "R. BANEY." *Address:* 5203 Talbot's Landing, Ellicott City, Md. 21043, U.S.A.

BANKS, Brian, painter in acrylic, oil, mixed media; *b* London, 21 Oct., 1939. *m* Christine, divorced 1974. two *s.* one *d. Educ:* Sir Walter St. John's Grammar School, London. *Studied:* St. Martin's (1956-57), Peter de Francia, Edward Middleditch, James Dring; privately with John Flavin, A.R.C.A. (1958). *Exhib:* one-man shows: Colin Jellicoe Gallery, Manchester; Ansdell Gallery, London; Zaydler Gallery, London; Fermoy Art Gallery, King's Lynn; Conway Hall, London; Leigh Gallery, London, (1984, 1985), Trinity Arts Centre, Tunbridge Wells. Represented by Leigh Gallery, Bloomsbury, London. *Work in collections:* Britain, Australia, France, U.S.A., Denmark. *Signs work:* "BANKS" (year). *Address:* 8 Ravenet Ct., Battersea Pk. Rd., London SW11 5HE.

BANKS, Nancy, U.A., M.F.P.S.; sculptor in bronze, direct plaster, terracotta and mixed media; *m* John Banks, M.Eng., F.Eng. two *s. Educ:* Nutgrove, Rainhill, Lancs. *Studied:* Sir John Cass College of Art, and Eltham Art Institute. *Exhib:* Mall Galleries, R.B.A., U.A., N.S., R.M.S., S.W.A., S.P.S., Barbican, Bloomsbury, Guildhall, Alpine, Weighouse galleries, I.E.E., Blackheath, Usher, Lincs., Worthing Museum and A.G., M.A.S.-F. *Work in collections:* U.K., U.S.A., Japan, Spain. *Commissions:* several private; trophy for presentation to HMS Brave. *Clubs:* L.L.L.C. *Signs work:* "N. BANKS" or "Nancy Banks" depending on size of work. *Address:* B.1. Marine Gate, Brighton, E. Sussex BN2 5TQ.

BANNING, Paul, N.D.D. (Hons.) Furniture Design (1956); painter in water-colour and oil, most subject matter; designed furniture in industry until 1986, now professional painter; *b* Port of Spain, Trinidad, 1 Aug., 1934. *m* Margaret. three *s.* one *d. Educ:* Clifton College, Bristol. *Studied:* West of England College of Art, Bristol (1953-1957), taught drawing by Victor Passmore. *Exhib:* 16 solo exhibs. in U.K., Holland, Dubai, and group exhibs. in U.K., France, and U.S.A. *Work in collections:* Freshfields. *Publications:* articles for Artists and Illustrators Magazine. *Clubs:* Member of Wapping Group of Artists. *Signs work:* Now signs work "PB." *Address:* Woodlands Corner, Redlands Lane, Ewshot, Farnham, Surrey GU10 5AS. *Email:* margaretbanning@compuserve.com

BANNISTER, Geoffrey Ernest John, served Royal Navy Minesweepers (1942-46); E.V.T. instructor in Commercial Art (Royal Navy, 1945-46); artist/designer, figure, scraper-board, water-colour, oils; *b* Birmingham, 15 Jan., 1924. *m* Beryl Parr Robinson, 1949 (deceased, 1966). one *s.* one *d.*; remarried, 1967, Susan Jennefer

Peters. three *s*. one *d*. *Educ:* St. Philip's Grammar School. Proprietor, Minster Print & Packaging. *Exhib:* Walsall Art Gallery. *Work in collections:* boardrooms. *Commissions:* chairpersons, directors, general public, portraits, animals, landscapes etc. *Clubs:* Great Barr Golf, Catenian Assoc., Walsall Society of Artists. *Signs work:* "Geoff Bannister." *Address:* Crossways, 811 Sutton Rd., Aldridge, Walsall, W. Midlands WS9 0QJ. *Email:* geoff_bannister@hotmail.com

BARANOWSKA, Janina, artist in oil; *b* Poland, 28 Oct., 1925. *m* Maksymilian Baranowski. one *s*. *Educ:* In Poland, Middle East and Scotland. *Studied:* Borough Polytechnic under Prof. Bomberg (1947-50), School of Art at the Polish University of Stefan Batory in London (1951-54). *Exhib:* One-man shows: Drian Gallery, Grabowski Gallery, Raymond Duncan Galleries, Alwin Gallery, Grand Prix Rencontre Lyon, France, Det Lille Galleri, Norway, State Galleries in Krakow and Poznan, Poland, Royal Festival Hall, London, Dixon Gallery - University of London, Bloomsbury Gallery, Woburn Fine A.G., Polish Cultural Inst. Mixed exhib.: R.A., Burlington Gallery, Cassel Gallery, R.B.A. Galleries, New Vision Centre, Walker's Galleries, Whitechapel A.G., Edinburgh. *Publications:* Editor of Contemporary Polish Artists in G.B. (1983), Form and Colour (Congress of Polish Culture). *Clubs:* W.I.A.C., Group 49, I.A.L., I.A.A. - U.K. National Com., A.P.A. in G.B. (Chairman), N.S.P.S. (Mem.). *Signs work:* "Baranowska." *Address:* 20 Strathmore Rd., London SW19 8DB.

BARBER, Raymond, A.C.F.I., A.M.II.M., City and Guilds, London Inst. (1943), E.M.E.U. (1937), S.S.I.A. (1945); Course Tutor at Footwear Dept Wellingborough Technical College; Footwear Section Head (retd.); *b* 30 Sept., 1921. *Educ:* Kettering Rd. Inst., Northampton, College of Technology, Northampton, Leicester College of Technology. *Exhib:* Walsall, London, in conjunction with "Leather, Footwear and Allied Industries" Export Corp., Ltd.; Quality Footwear Exhib., Seymour Hall, London. *Clubs:* N.C.T.S.A., N.G.C., N.S.M.E. *Signs work:* "Renny." *Address:* 10 Wantage Cl., Moulton, Northampton NN3 7UY.

BARBER KENNEDY, Mat, B.A.(Hons.) (1984), M.A. (1988), R.I. (1994); painter in mixed media collage using water based media, water-colour, acrylic, ink; *b* Hornchurch, Essex, 7 Oct., 1962. *m* Sherry Kennedy. two *s*. *Educ:* Coopers Company and Coborn School. *Studied:* Royal College of Art (Derek Walker, Kit Alsop). *Exhib:* annual Spring show at Mall Galleries, regular events at galleries in England and America. *Work in collections:* Chicago Public Library, Hertfordshire County Council. *Commissions:* The Marchday Group, Pollard Thomas & Edwards Architects. *Signs work:* see appendix. *Address:* 1906½ S. Halsted, Chicago, Illinois 60608, U.S.A. *Email:* mbkri@matbarberkennedy.com

BARCLAY, Sir Colville, Bart., M.A.; painter in oil and water-colour; *b* London, 7 May, 1913. *m* Rosamond Elliott. three *s*. *Educ:* Eton and Oxford. *Studied:* Ruskin School, Oxford. *Exhib:* R.B.A., R.A., London Group, Brighton and Bradford A.G. *Work in collections:* L.C.C. Schools, Arts Council, Bradford City Art Gallery. *Signs work:* "Barclay." *Address:* 23 High St., Broughton, Stockbridge, Hants. SO20 8AE.

BARKER, Allen, H.N.D. (1960); artist in acrylic paint; Personal tutor and Specialist lecturer, Central St.Martin's School of Art; *b* Australia, 1937. *m* Marilyn Norton-Harvey. one *s*. *Educ:* Lismore High School. *Studied:* art at National Art

School, Sydney (1995-60); lithography at Central School of Art, London (1962). *Exhib:* one-man shows: University of Kent (1967), University of Essex (1968), Galerie Junge Generation, Vienna (1969), Lucy Milton Gallery, London (1971, 1973), Galerie Van Hulsen, Amsterdam (1972), Ferens A.G., Hull (1973), City A.G. Manchester (1973), Laing A.G., Newcastle-upon-Tyne (1973), Museum and City A.G., Leicester (1974), City Museum and A.G., Portsmouth (1974), Ikon Gallery, Birmingham (1974), Park Sq. Gallery, Leeds (1974), Kinsman Morrison Gallery, London (1975), Galerie Grafica, Tokyo (1976), I.C.A. (1976), Structured Theatre Co., Nuffield Theatre, Lancaster University (1976), Galerie Grafica, Nasaka (1977), Architectural Assoc., London (1977), Coracle Press, London (1978), Galleri Morner, Stockholm (1978), Gallery Pinc Studio, London (1996), 21st Century Gallery, London (1997), retrospective exhbn. Bonham's Fine Art, London (1998), Cambridge University (1998), Carpet designed by Barker produced and made by Mike Evans and showing in London (1999). Documentation of all exhbns. held in the archives of the Tate Gallery, London (1999). Formed: Structured Theatre Co. (1976), Bassett Architectural Constructions and Designs (1984), Boreatton Bat Soc. of Fine Artists and Designers (1990). Travelling Visually - Boreatton Hall, Shrewsbury - Master Classes and Performance Workshops (1991). *Work in collections:* Sheffield Museum and City A.G., Leicester Museum and City A.G., Manchester City A.G., Galerie Orez Mobile, Den Haag, Holland, AT and T, New York, Museum Boymans Van Beuningen, Rotterdam, Cambridge University, Sir Norman Foster Bldg., Faculty of Law; numerous work in private collections. *Publications:* Two-page colour article on Boreatton Workshop, Nippon Broadcast Publications, Japan (1992), The Australian Magazine, colour article and review by Jane Cornwell titled "London Bridges", (July 2000). *Signs work:* "Barker." *Address:* 14 Bassett Rd., London W10 6JJ.

BARKER, Clive, sculptor in bronze and chrome; *b* Luton, Beds., 29 Aug., 1940. *m* Rose Bruen. two *s*. *Educ:* Beech Hill Secondary Modern. *Studied:* Luton College of Technology and Art (1957-59) under Clifford Barry, A.R.C.A. *Exhib:* Robert Fraser Gallery, Hanover Gallery, Musee d'Art Moderne, Museum of Modern Art, N.Y., Palais des Beaux-Arts, Palazzo Strozzi, etc. *Work in collections:* Arts Council of Gt. Britain, British Council, V. & A., Tate Gallery, etc. *Publications:* Pop Art Re-defined (Thames & Hudson), Image as Language (Penguin), Pop Art (Studio Vista), Art in Britain 1969-70 (Dent), Objekt Kunst (Dumont). *Signs work:* "Clive Barker." *Address:* 6 The Clocktower, Heath St., Hampstead, London NW3 6UD.

BARKER, Dale Devereux, R.E., B.A. (Hons.) (1984), H. Dip. F.A. (Slade) (1986); artist, printmaker, enamelist; *b* Leicester, 4 Feb., 1962. *m* Rebecca Weaver. *Educ:* Alderman Newton's Grammar School, Leicester. *Studied:* Loughborough College of Art and Design, Leicester Polytechnic and Slade (Stanley Jones). *Exhib:* 25 solo exhbns. *Work in collections:* Tate Gallery, V. & A., Ashmolean, New York Public Library, Harvard University, Yale University, Columbia University. *Commissions:* Clifford Chance, British Rail, Lloyds Insurance, Taylor-Woodrow, Penguin Books. *Publications:* Published own collaborative books with poets Martin Stannard (G.B.), Paul Violi (U.S.) and Kenneth Koch (U.S.). *Signs work:* "D.D. Barker." *Address:* 'Untitled', The Bungalow, Capel Grove, Capel St. Mary, Suffolk IP9 2JS.

BARKER, David, Dip. A.D. (1966), A.T.C. (1967), Hon. R.E. (1995), Prof. Lu

Xun Academy of Fine Arts, China (1997); Senior lecturer/ research translator; Senior lecturer, University of Ulster, Prof., Lu Xun Academy of Fine Arts, Mem. International Exchange Com., China National Academy of Fine Arts; drawing/silk screen; *b* Dorchester, 11 Jan. 1945. *m* Catherine Elizabeth (née Grover). one *s.* two *d. Educ:* University of London (1962-67), University of Leeds (1988). *Studied:* Goldsmiths' College, London. *Publications:* An English - Chinese Glossary of Printmaking Terms (1995), The Chinese Arts Academies Printmaking Exhibition (1993), The Techniques of the Chinese Print (in preparation), The Woodcuts of Zheng Shuang (1999), '30 Years of the Printmaking Workshop' (2001). *Signs work:* "David Barker." *Address:* University of Ulster, School of Art and Design, York St., Belfast BT15 1ED.

BARKER, Jill, B.A. (1982), S.G.F.A. (2001); wood engraver; *b* Hong Kong, 21 May, 1955. *Educ:* Durham High School. *Studied:* Newcastle-upon-Tyne (1979-1982) under Ralph Sylvester. *Exhib:* S.W.E., W.E.N., S.G.F.A. *Work in collections:* Princeton University, Graphic Arts Library, U.S.A. and private. *Publications:* Alembic Private Press Guide (1984), Holy Sonnets by John Donne (Alembic Press 1986), Black Goddess (Chiron Press 1991). *Signs work:* "Jill Barker." *Address:* 7 Church House, Churchview, Evercreech, Somerset BA4 6HX.

BARKLAM, Harold, A.R.C.A. (1936); artist in oil, water-colour; art lecturer, Derby College of Art; art teacher, Lowestoft School of Art (1946-50); *b* Tipton, Staffs., 14 Jan., 1912. *m* Marjorie Hale. one *d. Educ:* Ryland Memorial School of Art, W. Bromwich, R.C.A. and College of Art, Birmingham. *Exhib:* Birmingham A.G., Derby A.G., Norwich Castle, Nottingham Castle. *Publications:* oil paintings of Dunster Castle, Hardwicke Hall, Serlby Hall, Berkeley Castle, Blithfield Hall, Ingestre Hall; mural paintings entitled "Children's Games" painted for Lady Bagot of Blithfield Hall. *Signs work:* "H. BARKLAM." *Address:* Royal Manor Nursing Care Home, 346 Uttoxeter New Rd., Derby DE22 3HS.

BARLOW, Bohuslav, Dip.A.D.(Hons.) (1970), S.G.F.A.; artist mainly in oil, some pastel; *b* Bruntal, Czechoslovakia, 8 July, 1947. *m* Karen Barlow. *Educ:* St. Mary's Grammar School, Blackburn. *Studied:* Manchester (1966), Central School of Art, London (1967-70). *Exhib:* R.A., R.E., P.S., International Contemporary Art Fairs. Work in many Northern municipal collections, Manchester Academy. *Work in collections:* Leeds City Council, Coopers & Lybrand, N. Rothschild, Royal Family of Saudi Arabia. *Commissions:* Four large murals for M.E.P.C. plc., Bronte Soc. *Publications:* Visual Alchemy - Bohuslav Barlow. Opened own gallery in Todmorden 1997. *Clubs:* Manchester Academy. *Signs work:* "B. Barlow." *Address:* 262 Rochdale Rd., Todmorden, Lancs. OL14 7PD. *Website:* www.bohuslav.co.uk *Email:* slavo@bohuslav.co.uk

BARLOW, Gillian, B.A. (1970), M.A. (1971), P.G.C.E. (1972), R.H.S. Gold medal (1994, 1997, 1999); artist in water-colour on paper and vellum; *b* Khartoum, Sudan, 10 Dec., 1944. *Educ:* Ashford School for Girls, Kent; University of Sussex. *Studied:* Slade School (1962-63, Patrick George, John Aldridge). *Exhib:* solo shows: British Council, Bombay; Hudson View Gallery, N.Y.; Vassar College, N.Y.; Blond Fine Art, London; Spinks Fine Art, London; numerous mixed shows. *Work in collections:* Hunt Inst. of Botanical Documentation, Pittsburgh, U.S.A.; Vassar College,

N.Y.; Lady Margaret Hall, Oxford; Boscobel Restoration, N.Y.; British Council, India; Shirley Sherwood Botanical Painting Collection, London; Royal Horticultural Soc. London; Chelsea Physic Garden, London; Royal Botanic Gardens, Kew, London. *Publications:* Plantsman, (1992, 1993); New Plantsman (1994, 1997); Curtis Botanical Magazine, Kew (1998, 1999, 2000, 2001). *Signs work:* see appendix. *Address:* 33a Moreton Terr., London SW1V 2NS.

BARNARD, Roger, B.A. Fine Art (1974); artist, participatory set-ups some include video; painting, drawing, photography, holography, writing; *b* London, 4 Nov., 1951. *Educ:* Chichester High School for Boys. *Studied:* West Sussex College of Design (1970-71), North Staffs. Polytechnic (1971-74). *Exhib:* one-man shows, Tate Gallery, Air, Scottish Arts Council Gallery, Third Eye Centre, South Bank London, Truro, etc.; mixed shows, Tate, Serpentine, Hayward, Air, Holborn Underground Comp., Whitechapel, Arts Council of G.B. touring exhbn., Coventry, Chichester, Third Eye Centre, Osaka Triennale '90' (Painting), '91' (Print) Japan, etc. *Work in collections:* Royal Inst. of Cornwall County Coll., Contemporary Art Centre Osaka, Japan; private collections in U.K., U.S.A., France, Germany; U.C.H. London. *Commissions:* Organisations, incl. British Refugee Council, and private individuals. *Signs work:* paintings since 1970 unsigned, drawings dated, some signed "R. Barnard." *Address:* 151 Archway Rd., London N6 5BL.

BARNDT, Helen Grace, artist in sepia ink, oil, tempera; *b* Santa Rosa, Calif., 1928. *Educ:* S.F. Academy of Art. *Exhib:* S.F. De Young Museum, Palace Legion of Honor, San Fransisco, Calif. *Work in collections:* Dr. J. Trenton Tully, Ronald M. Tully, Victor Hansen. *Commissions:* Commissioned by: Dr. J. Trenton Tully for the Metaphysical Research Society of Denver, Colorado (1968-92) for series of religious oil paintings, ceiling murals and interior designs; paintings - Denver Museum of Natural History (1993-1998) - faux painting and murals exhibits, Denver Museum of Nature & Science (2000-), Tully Galleries. *Signs work:* "H. G. Barndt" and "H.G." *Address:* Apt 9, 940 E. 8th Ave., Denver, Colorado. 80218.

BARNES, Ann Margaret, B.Ed.(Hons.) (1973), M.F.P.S. (1974), A.M.N.S. (1978), F.R.S.A. (1995); artist in airbrush on botanical themes, head teacher; *b* London, 1951. *Educ:* Wimbledon County School for Girls; Stockwell College of Education, Bromley. *Exhib:* F.P.S., N.S., Soc. of Botanical Artists; one-man shows: London, Chiswick, Leatherhead, Henley, Croydon, Morden. *Signs work:* "A. Barnes." *Address:* 16 Mount Pleasant, Ewell, Epsom, Surrey KT17 1XE.

BARNES, Diane Stephanie, B.A.(Hons) 3-D design (Jewellery) Sheffield (1973), Leverhulme Travel Scholar (1973-74); printmaker in lino; demonstrator (Art in Action); artist in residence (Nature in Art, various schools, stately homes); part-time teacher of multiply disabled young adults; *b* London. *m* Roger (jeweller). two *s. Studied:* Sheffield Polytechnic (1970-73). *Exhib:* many, nationally and internationally including Beatrice Royal, Bankside, Mall Galleries. *Work in collections:* Gallup, Royal Marsden Hospital, Provident Bldg. Soc., National Trust, Dewsbury Hospital. *Commissions:* Year 2000 calendar for New Internationalist, which won "Best International Food Calendar 2000" Award. Appeared recently on "Handmade" for Channel 4 T.V. *Address:* 8 Moor Park Mount, Leeds LS6 4BU.

BARNES-MELLISH, Glynis Lily, B.A.Hons. Fine Art (1975), Advanced

Combined Fine Art Dip. (1983); portrait painter in water-colour; *b* Bromley, Kent, 10 June, 1953. one *d. Educ:* The William School, Letchworth. *Studied:* St. Albans School of Art (1971-72, 1981-83), W. Surrey College of Art and Design (1972-75). *Exhib:* annually R.I., S.W.A., P.S. *Work in collections:* Self portrait - Lee Valley University. *Publications:* The Artist, Hodder & Stoughton, Penguin Books. Limited Edition Prints (Solomon & Whitehead Ltd.). *Clubs:* S.W.A., Cambridge Drawing Soc. *Signs work:* "Mellish." *Address:* 16 Lytton Ave., Letchworth, Herts. SG6 3HT.

BARNS-GRAHAM C.B.E., Wilhelmina, D.A. (Edin.), D.Litt. St. Andrews (1992); D.Art Plymouth (1999); D.Litt. Exeter (2001); founder mem. Penwith Soc. of Arts (1949); painter in oil, acrylic, gouache; *b* St. Andrews, Fife, 8 June, 1912. *Exhib:* London, Edinburgh, Oxford, St. Ives, Penzance, Leeds, Cumbria, Orkney, St. Andrews, Wakefield, Perth, Kendal, Glasgow, Exeter, Tate St. Ives, Truro, Dundee, Australia, Belgium, Canada, France, Germany, Italy, N Zealand, U.S.A. *Work in collections:* English Arts Council; S.A.C.; British Council; B.M.; V. & A.; Contemporary Art Soc.; Scottish National Gallery; Government Collection; Tate Gallery; Edinburgh City Collection; New South Wales A.G., Australia; Universities of Michigan U.S.A.; Aberdeen, Cambridge, Edinburgh, Manchester; Museums of Glasgow, Ayr, Birmingham, Dundee, Hull, Hove, Kirkcaldy, Leeds, Plymouth, Sheffield; Educ. authorities of Cornwall, Herts., Leeds, W. Riding. *Publications:* W Barns-Graham – A Studio Life. ISBN 0 85331 828X. *Clubs:* Chelsea Art Club; Hon. Scottish Arts Club. *Signs work:* "W. Barns-Graham." *Address:* 1 Barnaloft, St. Ives, Cornwall TR26 1NJ *Second Address:* Balmungo, St. Andrews, Fife KY16 8LW.

BARÓN, Maite, B.A. Art and Design (Fashion), Interior Design, B.Tec., P.D.C.; Interior Decorative Applications B.T.E.C., P.D.C in Fine Art Management and Professional Practice; Teachers Training City & Guilds 7307, stages 1 & 2; teaching experience – interior design, photoshop and dreamweaver, papermaking and paper products, colour workshops, decorative paint finishes, decoupage, stencilling, drawing; designer, artist and printmaker in drypoint, collograph, etching, screen printing, acrylics, paper making, fibre art; *b* Barcelona, Spain, 10 June, 1965. *Studied:* International Centre of Art Studies Interart, Barcelona (1985-88), Art and Design School, Barcelona (1984-85), London Print Studio (1999), Kensington and Chelsea College (1999), Westminster Adult Education (1997-01). *Exhib:* R.B.A. and National Print Exhbn. at Mall Galleries, Falmouth Arts Centre; U.A. at Westminster Gallery; Walford Mill (Wimborne); New York Prestige Artists Debut (2000), Manhattan, N.Y., U.S.A.; The Laing Art Competition Exh. (2001); Saatchi & Saatchi, the Art Phoenix Art Auction for the Kosovo children; the Intrinsic Book, the Barbican Library, London; Open Biennale 1999, Whiteley's, London; Freshly Printed, Buckingham Galleries, Southwold, Suffolk; Impact at Spike Island Printmakers, Bristol; Royal Society of British Artists (1998), Mall Gallery, London; National Print Exhibition (1998 & 1999), Mall Gallery, London; The Laing Art Competition Exhibition (2001), The Mall Gallery, London. *Clubs:* N.A.A., Printmakers' Council, Paperweight, Axis, N.A.P.A., N.S.A., A.V.A. *Address:* Flat 2, 46 Chiswick Lane, London W4 2JQ. *Email:* maite@tessabaron.demon.co.uk

BARRATT, Mary H., B.A. (1969); painter in oil; part time art lecturer; *b* Annesley Woodhouse, Notts., 27 Mar., 1948. *m* Michael Ian Barratt. *Studied:* Loughborough College of Art and Design (1966-69, Philip Thompson, Colin

Saxton). *Exhib:* 359 Gallery, Nottingham, Crucible Theatre, Sheffield, Rufford Country Pk., Ollerton, Merlin Gallery, Sheffield, Pierrepont Gallery Thoresby Park, Newark. *Signs work:* "M. Barratt." *Address:* 7 Craigston Rd., Carlton-in-Lindrick, Worksop, Notts. S81 9NG.

BARRETT, Priscilla, freelance illustrator and wildlife artist in water-colour, pastels, pencil, pen and ink; *b* S. Africa, 4 May, 1944. *m* Gabriel Horn. *Educ:* Universities of Cape Town and Stellenbosch. *Exhib:* solo exhbns. in Cambridge, also exhib. London, Brighton, Lavenham. *Publications:* Collins Field Guide - Mammals of Britain and Europe; European Mammals; Evolution and Behaviour; The Domestic Dog; Running with the Fox; The Wolf; A Year in the Life: Badger; A Year in the Life: Tiger; RSPCA Book of British Mammals; Ecotravellers Wildlife Guides to Costa Rica, Belize, Tropical Mexico, Ecuador; History of British Mammals. *Clubs:* mem. S.W.L.A. *Signs work:* "Priscilla Barrett." *Address:* Jack of Clubs, Lode, Cambridge CB5 9HE.

BARRIE, Mardi, M.A., D.A. (1953), R.S.W. (1969); painter in oil, acrylic/water medium; *b* Kirkcaldy, Fife, 25 Apr., 1931. *Educ:* Kirkcaldy High School. *Studied:* Edinburgh University and Edinburgh College of Art. *Exhib:* regularly in group and solo exhbns. since 1963; private galleries including Scottish Gallery, Edinburgh, Stenton Gallery, Thackeray Gallery, London, Bruton Gallery, Leeds, Kingfisher Gallery, Edinburgh. *Work in collections:* U.K. and abroad, including H.R.H. Duke of Edinburgh, R.S.A., Glasgow A.G., E.C.C., Scottish National Gallery of Modern Art, Robert Fleming Holdings. *Signs work:* "Mardi." *Address:* Studio 5, 33 Melville St., Edinburgh EH3 7JF.

BARTH, Eunice, painter in oil and acrylic in contemporary style; *b* London, 1937. *m* Philip Barth M.A. two *d. Educ:* Neyland House, Sevenoaks; Regent Polytechnic; local Quinton and Kynaston art classes. *Studied:* in England, France and Spain; principal teacher Chris Channing. *Exhib:* F.B.A., V.A. and local venues. *Work in collections:* Stoller Household and various private collections in England. *Clubs:* United Society of Artists. *Signs work:* "Eunice Barth." *Address:* 53 Charlbert Court, Macrennal St., St. Johns Wood, London NW8 7DB.

BARTLETT, Adrian, N.D.D. (1961), A.T.D. (1962); artist in painting, etching, lithography; *b* Twickenham, 31 Mar., 1939. *m* Victoria Bartlett. two *d. Educ:* Bedales School. *Studied:* Camberwell School of Art. *Exhib:* British Council, Athens (1985), Morley College (1996), Walk Gallery (1999). *Work in collections:* B.M., Ashmolean, V. & A., Berlin Graphotek, etc. *Commissions:* mural for Anglo American (2000). *Publications:* Drawing and Painting the Landscape (Phaidon, 1982). *Clubs:* Chelsea Arts. *Address:* 132 Kennington Park Rd., London SE11 4DJ.

BARTLETT, Charles, P.P.R.W.S., R.E., A.R.C.A.; artist in oil and water-colour, printmaker; *b* Grimsby, 23 Sept., 1921. *m* Olwen Jones. one *s. Educ:* Eastbourne Grammar School. *Studied:* Eastbourne School of Art, R.C.A. *Exhib:* two one-man shows in London; major Retrospective Exhbn. (1997), Bankside Gallery, London. *Work in collections:* V. & A. Museum, National Gallery of S. Australia, Arts Council of Great Britain, numerous public and private collections in Britain and abroad. *Publications:* Monograph: Charles Bartlett, Painter and Printmaker. *Clubs:* The Arts. *Signs work:* "Charles Bartlett." *Address:* St. Andrew's House, Fingringhoe, nr.

Colchester, Essex CO5 7BG.

BARTLETT, Paul Thomas, R.B.A. (1981), R.A. Schools P.G. Cert./M.A. (1980), B.A.Hons. Fine Art (Falmouth 1976), B'ham Poly.: F.E.T.C. (1987), P.G. Dip. hist. art/design (1990), B.P.S. (1993), R.B.S.A. (1997). Prizes: Turner Gold Medal, Landseer Life Painting, Sir James Walker; scholarships: David Murray, Elizabeth Greenshield; painter/printmaker/lecturer; *b* B'ham, 7 July, 1955. *Exhib:* (major Prizes): Stowells Trophy, Royal Overseas League, Spirit of London, Mid Art, Mid 25, Hunting Group, R.B.A., R.B.S.A., Alexon Women on Canvas; other exhbns.: R.A., V. & A., N.P.G., I.C.A. *Publications:* work repro.: Alan Hutchison, Quarto, Dorling Kindersley. *Signs work:* "Paul Bartlett" or " P.T.B." *Address:* 144 Wheelers Lane, Kings Heath, B'ham. B13 0SG.

BARTLETT, Victoria Anne, N.D.D., A.T.D.; artist working in 3D mixed media and paper; Visiting Tutor, Goldsmiths' College, London University; *b* Caterham, 1940. *m* Adrian Bartlett. two *d. Studied:* Camberwell School of Art, and Reading University (1957-62). *Exhib:* solo shows: The Egg & The Eye, Los Angeles; Van Doren Galleries, San Francisco and Morley, Edward Totah, Benjamin Rhodes Galleries; Camden Art Centre, Peralta Pictures in London and Gallerie Simoncini, Luxembourg; group shows: worldwide and with Browse & Darby Gallery, London (1995-). Work in public and private collections internationally. *Signs work:* "Victoria Bartlett." *Address:* 132 Kennington Park Rd., London SE11 4DJ.

BARTOLO, Maria, painter in mixed media, including wax and varnish; *b* Cardiff, 7 Dec., 1967. *Educ:* Oaklands R.C. Comprehensive. *Studied:* City and Guilds of London Art School (Roger de Grey). *Exhib:* The Discerning Eye, Mall Galleries, Christie's, Sotheby's, R.A. Summer Show, Barbican. *Work in collections:* Art Council, De Beers. *Publications:* work repro.: R.A. magazine, C.V. magazine, Evening Standard Newspaper (four edns.). Winner of Evening Standard prize. *Address:* 23a Milner Sq., London N1.

BARTON, Patricia: see MYNOTT, Patricia.

BASIA: see WATSON-GANDY, Basia.

BASKO, Maurice P. Duviella, Dip. Salon Automne, France; Prize, Figuratif Chateau of Senaud, France; painter in oil and water-colour, art researcher; restoration of paintings; art expert; *b* Biarritz, 30 Sept., 1921. three *d. Educ:* Jules Ferry College, Biarritz. *Studied:* Academy Frochot, Paris. *Exhib:* Museum of Modern Art, Paris, Salon Automne, Salon Bosio, Grand Prix, Pont Aven, Salon Art Libre, Paris, Salon Versailles, France, Paris Gallery, N.Y., Galerie Colise, Paris, Fontainebleu Gallery, N.Y.; one-man shows: Paris, N.Y., Lyon, Mallorca, Vichy, Cannes, Biarritz. *Work in collections:* Guggenheim Museum, N.Y., Albertina Museum, Vienna, Museum of Modern Art, Miami, Public Library, N.Y.; and more than 400 works in private collections. *Publications:* 5000 painter's signatures (famous painters) all world, all periods. President of Biarritz Art Festival since 1991. *Signs work:* "BASKO" and sometimes "Duviella." *Address:* Résidence Arverna/Bloc C, 26 Ave. Lahouze, 64200 Biarritz, France.

BATCHELOR, Bernard Philip, R.W.S.; painter in water-colour and oil; *b* 29 May, 1924. *Studied:* St. Martin's and City and Guilds of London Art schools gaining

City and Guilds Painting medal and a David Murray Scholarship. Subject matter relates mainly to town or landscapes with figures, coastal scenes, etc. *Work in collections:* many in private collections here and abroad; also M.O.W., Museum of Richmond and Richmond Parish Charity Lands. *Signs work:* "B.P. BATCHELOR" or sometimes "B.P.B." *Address:* 50 Graemesdyke Ave., East Sheen, London SW14 7BJ.

BATCHELOR, Valerie, artist in water colour, acrylic and pastel; *b* 16 Mar., 1932. *m* John. one *s. Studied:* Salisbury College of Art (1947-50). *Exhib:* solo shows: Salisbury Library (1990, 1993, 1996), Salisbury Playhouse (1991- 98), R.I. since 1985, R.W.A. since 1990. *Publications:* book illustrations including Collins Artists Manual. *Clubs:* N.A.P.A. *Address:* 'Tresses', Larkhill Rd., Durrington, Wilts. SP4 8DP.

BATEMAN, Robert McLellan, O.C., R.C.A., D.Litt., D.Sc., Ll.D., D.F.A., B.A.; artist in oil and acrylic; *b* Toronto, 24 May, 1930. *m* Birgit Freybe Bateman. four *s.* one *d. Studied:* University of Toronto (1950-54). *Exhib:* major one-man shows in museums throughout Canada and U.S.A. incl. Smithsonian Institution, Washington D.C. (1987) and the Joslyn Fine Arts Museum, Nebraska (1986); Tryon Gallery, London (1975, 1977, 1979, 1985); Canadian Embassy, Tokyo (1992); Everard Read Gallery, Johannesburg, South Africa (2000). *Work in collections:* the late Princess Grace of Monaco, H.R.H. Prince Philip, H.R.H. Prince Charles, H.R.H. Prince Bernhard, Hamilton Art Museum, Canada, Leigh Yawkey Woodson Art Museum, U.S.A. etc. *Commissions:* numerous. *Publications:* numerous articles, four major books and seven films on Robert Bateman. *Clubs:* Life membership in numerous clubs and conservation organizations. *Signs work:* "Robert Bateman." *Address:* Box 115, Fulford Harbour, B.C. Canada V8K 2P2.

BATES, Joan Elliott, D.F.A. (Lond. 1952); painter, draughtsman and printmaker; *b* Sheffield, 22 Jan., 1930. *m* John F. Bates. three *s. Studied:* Sheffield College of Art (1947-49), Slade School of Fine Art (1949-52, Prof. William Coldstream). *Exhib:* R.A. Summer Exhbns., Hunting Award finalist, N.E.A.C., R.W.S., R.O.I., R.E., etc. and in numerous galleries in London and the provinces. *Work in collections:* Paintings in Hospitals, The House of Commons. *Publications:* work repro.: Harper Collins, Anness Publishing, etc. Awards: Laing Painting Competition 3rd prize (1981) 2nd prize (1984), Cornelissen award (1986). *Signs work:* "J. Elliott" or "J.E." *Address:* 17 Marlow Mill, Mill Rd., Marlow, Bucks. SL7 1QD.

BATES, Patricia Jane, B.Ed. (Lond.) (1976), M.F.P.S. (1980); artist in oil, oil collage, mixed media, sculpture, printmaking; *b* Surbiton, 8 Jan., 1927. *m* Martin Colin Bates. one *s.* one *d. Educ:* Priors Field, Godalming. *Studied:* Bartlett School of Architecture (1944-46), Epsom School of Art (1947-48), Byam Shaw (1952-53). *Exhib:* one-man shows: Loggia Gallery, London, Cranleigh Art Centre; mixed shows: Mall Galleries, London, Guildford, Westcott Gallery, Mill Gallery, Coverack, Cornwall. Work auctioned: East African Wildlife Soc. Kenya. *Work in collections:* England and many other countries. *Signs work:* "PAT BATES" or "PAT SIMON BATES." *Address:* Brackenhurst, Wonham Way, Gomshall, Guildford, Surrey GU5 9NZ.

BATT, Deborah Jane, artist in acrylic, oil and water-colour; *b* London, 12 Dec.,

1966. *Exhib:* London, Birmingham, Bath, Stratford-upon-Avon, etc. *Signs work:* "D.J.B." *Address:* 45 The Terrace, Wokingham, Berks. RG40 1BP.

BATTERBURY, Helen Fiona, self taught artist in water-colour; *b* Stockton-on-Tees, 30 July, 1963. *m* Paul Batterbury. two *s.* one *d. Educ:* Durrants School, Watford. *Exhib:* S.Eq.A., S.WL.A., S.W.A., Wildlife Art Soc., numerous mixed exhbns.: Century Gallery, Thoresby Hall, Newport Gallery. *Commissions:* Commissioned as equestrian artist primarily. *Publications:* wrote and illustrated article The Horse in Watercolour for Leisure Painter magazine (Jan. 1997); paintings reproduced in many sporting magazines as promotions for exhbns. *Clubs:* S.W.A., Wildlife Art Soc. *Signs work:* "Fergusson." *Address:* Dunham House, Dunham-on-Trent, Notts. NG22 0TY.

BATTERSHILL, Norman James, R.B.A. (1973), R.O.I. (1976), P.S. (1976), F.S.I.A.D. (1968); R.O.I. Stanley Grimm award (1989); R.O.I. Awarded Cornelissen Prize for outstanding work (1999); landscape painter in oil, pastel, acrylic and water-colour, author, tutor; *b* London, 23 Apr., 1922. two *s.* three *d. Exhib:* R.A., R.B.A., R.O.I., N.E.A.C., P.S., etc., numerous one man shows etc. *Work in collections:* work in many private collections. *Commissions:* Ciba Geigy, Beechams, Post Office, Southern Gas. *Publications:* Light on the Landscape, Draw Trees, Drawing and Painting Skies, Draw Landscape, Draw Seascapes (Pitman Publishing), Working with Oils, Painting Flowers in Oils, Painting Landscapes in Oils, Drawing for Pleasure, Teach Yourself to Draw (Search Press Ltd., London; and Pentalic Corp. U.S.A.), Painting and Drawing Water (A. & C. Black Ltd., 1984), Learn to Paint Trees (Collins, 1990), Painting Gardens (Batsford 1994), Painting Landscapes in Oils (Batsford 1997). *Signs work:* "Norman Battershill." *Address:* Christmas Cottage, Burton St., Marnhull, Sturminster Newton, Dorset DT10 1PS.

BAUMFORTH, David John, painter of seascapes and landscapes in watercolour, acrylic and oil; *b* York, 21 Oct., 1942. *m* Jenny. two *d. Educ:* Nunthorpe Grammar School. *Studied:* self taught. *Exhib:* R.W.S. open, R.A. Summer Exhib., Hunting Prizes, various national galleries. *Work in collections:* various national and international collections. *Signs work:* "D J Baumforth." *Address:* Low Garth, Snainton, Scarborough, N. Yorks YO13 9AF.

BAWTREE, John Andrew, D.Arch. (Kingston, 1977), A.R.B.A. (1982), R.B.A. (1984); Greenshield Foundation Award (1978, 1980); painter in oil on canvas; *b* Cheam, Surrey, 1 Nov., 1952. *Educ:* Bradfield College, Berks. (1966-70). *Studied:* Kingston Polytechnic School of Architecture (1970-73, 1975-77). *Exhib:* R.A., R.B.A.; one-man: Caius College, Cambridge, Christ Church, Oxford, British Council, Oman, Aldeburgh Cinema Gallery, Piers Feetham Gallery, London, Melitensia Gallery, Malta, British Embassy, Oman. *Work in collections:* Greenshield Foundation, Montreal, Foreign and Commonwealth Office, Muscat. *Clubs:* Chelsea Arts. *Signs work:* "John Bawtree." *Address:* Pine View, Peasenhall, Suffolk IP17 2HZ.

BAXTER, Ann W., N.D.D.(Hons.) (1955), S.E.A.; winner, British Sporting Art Trust Sculpture Prize (1990), joint winner (1986, 1998) and President's Medal (1994); freelance sculptor in wood, stone and bronze; *b* Leeds, Nov., 1934. *m* W.L.J. Potts (decd.). one *s. Educ:* Leeds Girls' High School. *Studied:* Leeds College of Art

(1950-55, Harry Phillips). *Exhib:* S.E.A. annually, Open exhbns.: Leeds City A.G., Cartwright Hall Bradford, Wakefield City A.G., and widely in U.K. in private and public galleries. *Work in collections:* York City A.G., and private collections in U.K., U.S.A., Europe and Australia. Breeds Arabian horses. *Signs work:* "A.W. Baxter." *Address:* Ivy Farm, Roecliffe, Boroughbridge, York YO51 9LY.

BAXTER, Denis Charles Trevor, F.R.S.A., U.A. (1986), Mem. Printmakers Council (1981), N.S. (1987), President, N.S. (1989), Society of Graphic Fine Art (2001); teacher, lecturer, artist in oil and etching; *b* Southsea, 1 Mar., 1936. *Educ:* Ryde School, I.O.W. *Studied:* Bournemouth and Poole College of Art (1964-65); Stockwell College, Bromley, Kent (1965-68). *Exhib:* R.A., R.W.A., R.E., N.E.A.C., P.S., N.S., U.A., awarded the Gold Medal for Graphic Art at the 2nd Biennale Internazionale DellArte Contemporanea in Florence (1999), awarded the Gold Medal for Graphic Art presented by the Spanish Embassy at the Kyoto International Exchange Exhibition, Japan (1999). *Work in collections:* Canada, France, Germany, Japan, Switzerland, U.K., U.S.A. *Clubs:* Chelsea Arts, Royal Over-Seas League. *Signs work:* "Denis Baxter" or "D.B." *Address:* 20 Church Rd., Southbourne, Bournemouth, Dorset BH6 4AT.

BAYLY, Clifford John, R.W.S. (1981), N.D.D. (1950); painter in oils, acrylic, water-colour, illustrator, lecturer, writer. Five times prizewinner in national competitions (1992/93, 1996, 1997); *b* London, 1927. *m* Jean Oddell. two *s.* one *d. Studied:* St. Martin's and Camberwell Schools of Art (Sir William Coldstream, Prof. Sir Lawrence Gowing). *Exhib:* R.A., R.W.S., various galleries in U.K., also Malta, Sydney, Melbourne and Adelaide, Australia. *Work in collections:* H.R.H. Prince Charles, Westpac Bank, T.V. South, Tricentrol, London, Chevron U.K. *Commissions:* Winchester Hospital, many garden portraits. *Publications:* children's educational books, books on painting and drawing techniques. *Signs work:* "CLIFFORD BAYLY." *Address:* The Stables, Oaks Farm, High St., Staplehurst, Tonbridge, Kent TN12 0BH.

BAYNES, Pauline Diana, M.S.I.A.; designer and illustrator; *b* 1922. widow of Fritz Gasch. *Studied:* Farnham School of Art and Slade. *Publications:* books illustrated include: A Treasury of French Tales, Farmer Giles of Ham and Tom Bombadil (Allen and Unwin), Arabian Nights and Fairy Tales of the British Isles (Blackie), seven Narnia Books by C. S. Lewis (Bles and Bodley Head), Sister Clare, Miracle Plays, St. George and the Dragon (Houghton Mifflin, U.S.A.), Dictionary of Chivalry (Longmans), Kate Greenaway Medal (1968), Companion to World Mythology (Kestrel Books, 1979). *Signs work:* "PAULINE BAYNES" - occasionally with a small bird - see appendix. *Address:* Rock Barn Cottage, Dockenfield, nr. Farnham, Surrey GU10 4HH.

BAYS, Jill, N.D.D. (1951), S.W.A. (1988), B.A. (Open)(1985); artist in watercolour and oil, teacher; *b* Ambala, India, 24 Nov., 1931. *m* Bernard Bays (decd.). two *d. Educ:* Sir William Perkins', Chertsey. *Studied:* Guildford School of Art (1947-51). *Exhib:* R.I., S.WL.A., S.W.A., numerous shared exhbns. with husband and others. *Publications:* The Watercolourist's Garden (David and Charles, 1993), Flowers in the Landscape (David and Charles, 1995), Drawing Workbook (David and Charles, 1998), The Watercolourist's Nature Journal (David and Charles, 2001). *Signs work:*

"Jill Bays." *Address:* Bayswater, Hamm Ct., Weybridge, Surrey KT13 8YB.

BAZAINE, Jean, painter, Commandeur des Arts et Lettres (1980); *b* Paris, 1904. *Educ:* L. ès L. *Exhib:* Galerie Carré and Maeght, Paris, retr. exhbn., Berne (1958), Eindhoven (1959), Hanover, Zürich, Oslo (1963), Paris (1965), Athènes, London, Edinburgh (1977), Oslo (1983), Maeght's Foundation (1987); repr. Biennele de Venice, São Paulo and Carnegie (member of the jury, 1952). *Work in collections:* most important museums in Europe and America. *Publications:* Notes sur la peinture d'aujourd'hui (ed. Seuil, Paris, 1948), Exercise de la peinture (ed. Seuil, 1973), Illustration de l'oeuvre de 12 poétes francais. Mombreux décors et costumes de théa-tre. Awards: Prix Blumethal (1939), Prix National des Arts (1964). Executed stained-glass windows for the church of Assy (1946), Saint Séverin, Paris (1966), Cathedrale St. Die (1986), Chapelle de la Madeleine Bretagne, Chapelle de Berlens Suisse, Chapelle St. Dominique paris; ceramic mural and windows at Audincourt (1951-54); ceramic mural at U.N.E.S.C.O. (1960); Maison de l'O.R.T.F., Paris (1963), Se'nat, Paris (1986), Subway 'Cluny' (1987). *Address:* 36 r. P. Brossolette, 92140 Clamart.

BEALE, Philippa Sally, B.A. (Hons.) 1969, A.T.D. (1970), M.F.A. (1985); sculptor, printmaker and video artist in casting, photoprint and video; P.L Central St. Martin's College of Art and Design; *b* Winchester, Hants., 17 Jan., 1946. *m* David Troostwijk, A.R.C.A. (divorced). one *s. Studied:* University of Reading, Goldsmiths' College, London. *Exhib:* widely including: Akumulatory 2 Galleria, Poznan, Poland; Richard Demarco Gallery, Edinburgh; Flowers East, Acme Gallery, Gulbenkian Gallery, Inst. of Contemporary Art, London; The Third Eye, Glasgow; Arnolfini, Bristol; Blue Coat, Liverpool. Most recently at Danielle Arnaud and The Discerning Eye, Mall Galleries, London. *Work in collections:* Tate Gallery Archive, National Art Archive, V. & A., Southampton A.G., Camden Council. *Commissions:* Southampton A.G. *Publications:* J. Moreau, The Sexual Imagination, edited by Harriet Gilbert (Jonathon Cape), Roszika Parker, Women's Images of Men, edited by S. Kent and J. Moreau (Pandora Press, Unwin Paperbacks), L. McQuiston, Graphic Agitations (Phaidon), D. Postle, The Mind Gymnasium (Gaia Books). *Clubs:* President, London Group (1995-98). *Signs work:* "P.S.B." *Address:* 1 Burnt Ash Lane, Bromley BR1 4DJ.

BEAUMONT, Sarah Elizabeth, B.A. (Hons.) (1988), FRSA (2001), N.S. (2000), N.A.P.A. (1997); painter in oil and acrylic; *b* London, 10 Sept., 1966. *Educ:* City of London School for Girls, EC1; University of Lancaster (1985-88). *Exhib:* R.A., S.W.A., N.S., group shows include Scott Gallery, Lancaster, Westminster Gallery, London, The Atrium, Whiteley's, London, Mall Galleries, London, R.A, and numerous galleries around the U.K. *Commissions:* various for public bldgs. including the Millfield Theatre, London. *Clubs:* Fine Art Trade Guild. *Signs work:* "S.E Beaumont." *Address:* 114 Colin Crescent, The Hyde, London NW9 6EX.

BECK, Stuart, R.S.M.A. (1980); artist in water-colour and oil; former technical illustrator and graphic designer; *b* London, 18 June, 1903. *m* Jane Gwendoline (decd.). one *s.* one *d. Studied:* Rochester School of Art (1919-21). *Exhib:* R.S.M.A., R.B.A., S.G.A., etc. Abroad: R.S.M.A. (Vancouver 1982), Paris (1984), New Zealand (1984), R.S.M.A. (Mystic Seaport, U.S.A. 1987), Dusseldorf (1987). *Work in collections:* National Maritime Museum, Hull, R.N.L.I. Museum, Poole.

Publications: How to Draw Fishing Craft; How to Draw Pleasure Craft; Ships, Boats and Craft; A Dash of Salt (autobiography). *Signs work:* "STUART BECK." *Address:* 22 Parish Ct., Emsworth Rd., Lymington, Hants. SO41 9BS.

BECKER, Haidee, draughtsman, painter in oil; *b* Los Angeles, Calif., 13 Jan., 1950. one *s.* one *d. Educ:* French Lycée. *Studied:* with Uli Nimptsch, R.A., Elizabeth Keys, Adrian Ryan. *Exhib:* R.P., H.A.C., R.A., Ben Uri, Roland, Browse & Delbanco, New Grafton, C.D. Soar & Son, Odette Gilbert Gallery, Timothy Tew Galerie, Atlanta, Georgia; Anne Berthoud, Redfern Gallery. *Work in collections:* N.P.G. *Signs work:* "Becker." *Address:* 46 Glebe Pl., London SW3 5JE.

BECKERLEY, Tracy, M.A. (1989), B.A.(Hons.) (1986), Higher Dip. in Visual Art (1987), Art Foundation Dip. (1983); artist in gouache, paper making, printmaking; visiting lecturer, Lincoln Art School and Brooks University; and psychotherapist; *b* Bournemouth, 10 Dec., 1963. *Studied:* Harrow C.H.E. (1982-83, Brian Pummer), Gwent C.H.E. (1983-86, Roy Ascot), Oxford Polytechnic (1986-87, Ivor Robinson), Chelsea School (1988-89, Tim Mara). *Exhib:* Whitechapel Open (1994); mixed shows in East-West Gallery, Todd Gallery, Concourse Gallery Barbican, Flowers East, Overseas League House, Whitworth Gallery, Business Design Centre. *Signs work:* "Beck." *Address:* Suite 22, Sparkford House, Battersea Church Rd., London SW11 3NQ.

BEECROFT, Glynis: see OWEN, Glynis.

BEESON, Jane, Arnolfini Open Competition prize winner, 1963; painter in P.V.A., oil and enamel; *b* Weybridge, Surrey, 10 Apr., 1930. *m* Christopher Beeson. three *s.* one *d. Studied:* Kingston School of Art, Surrey (1949-51); Beaux Arts, Paris (1951-52), under Brianchon; Slade, London (1953). *Exhib:* John Moore's (1961); London exhib., Rowan Gallery and New Art Centre; Arnolfini, Bristol. *Work in collections:* "Mauve and Yellow" bought by Director, Ferens Art Gallery, Hull, and in other private collections; also painting in Richard Demarco Gallery Collection, Edinburgh. *Signs work:* "J. Beeson." *Address:* Ford Farm, Manaton, S. Devon TQ13 9XA.

BEILBY, Pauline Margaret, N.D.D. (1950); portrait and equestrian sculptor in clay, textile designer, freelance; *b* Bramcote, Notts., 21 June, 1927. *m* Keith David Barnes, lace manufacturer. two *s. Educ:* Nottingham Girls' High School. *Studied:* Nottingham College of Arts and Crafts under A. H. Rodway, A.R.C.A., F.R.S.A., principal. *Signs work:* see appendix. *Address:* Burleigh House, 15 Albemarle Rd., Woodthorpe, Notts. NG5 4FE. *Second Address:* Flat 1, 116 Queen's Gate, South Kensington, London SW7 5LP.

BELL, Catherine, B.A. (1985), painter in water-colour; *b* Tadcaster, 30 Nov., 1951. *m* Derek Ogle. *Educ:* Wakefield Girls' High School, University of Sussex. Elected mem. S.B.A. (1995), winner Joyce Cumming Presentation Award for Botanical Painting (1994) and Cuthbert Mill Award (1998). *Exhib:* R.I., R.W.S., and many mixed exhbns., one-woman shows at Harrogate, Leeds and York. *Work in collections:* corporate collections. *Signs work:* "C. Bell." *Address:* 11 Neville Terr., The Groves, York YO31 8NF.

BELL, Stanley Fraser, D.A. (Mural Design) Glasgow (1970); artist in mixed media reliefs and painted murals; former Senior Lecturer, Glasgow School of Art; former Chairman, Glasgow League of Artists; *b* Glasgow, 12 Jan., 1928. *m* Catherine MacDonald. one *s*. *Studied:* Glasgow School of Art (1966-70). *Exhib:* Scottish Young Contemporaries (1969, 1970, 1971), The Clyde Group, Edinburgh (1971), John Player Bienalle 2 Touring Exhbn. (1971), 'With Murals in Mind' Acheson House, Edinburgh (1974), 'Un Certain Art Anglais' Paris, Brussels (1979); regular exhibitor in group exhbns. in Scotland and elsewhere. *Work in collections:* large scale exterior murals in Glasgow. *Clubs:* Glasgow Art. *Signs work:* "Stan Bell." *Address:* 419 North Woodside Rd., Glasgow G20 6NN.

BELLAMY, David, self taught artist in water-colour, writer; *b* Pembroke, 15 June, 1943. *m* Jenny Keal. one *d*. *Educ:* Narberth Grammar School. *Exhib:* Cleveland Gallery, Bath; Lincoln Joyce Fine Art, Gt. Bookham; Albany Gallery, Cardiff, and many others. *Work in collections:* Berol Ltd., Welsh Development Agency, and world-wide. *Publications:* written and illustrated: Wild Places of Britain; Painting in the Wild; Wild Coast of Britain; David Bellamy's Water-colour Landscape Course, Developing your Water-colours; Images of the South Wales Mines, Wilderness Artist; Learn to Paint Water-colour Landscapes; also fine art prints, calendars, magazines, greetings cards and films. *Clubs:* Societé des Peintres de Montagne. *Signs work:* "David Bellamy." *Address:* Maesmawr, Aberedw, Builth Wells, Powys LD2 3UL.

BELLANY, John, C.B.E. (1994), D.A. (Edin.), M.A. (Fine Arts), A.R.C.A., R.A., Hon. R.S.A.; artist in oil, water-colour, etching; Dr. Honoris Causa, Edinburgh University (1997), Dr. Lit., Heriot Watt University, elected Senior Fellow, Royal College of Art (1999); *b* Port Seton, Scotland, 18 June, 1942. *m* Helen. two *s*. one *d*. *Educ:* Preston Lodge, Prestonpans, Scotland. *Studied:* Edinburgh College of Art (1960-65), R.C.A. (1965-68). *Exhib:* one-man shows in major galleries and museums throughout the world. *Work in collections:* National Galleries of Scotland, N.P.G., Tate Gallery, V. & A., M.O.M.A. (N.Y.), Metropolitan Museum (N.Y.), etc. *Publications:* John Bellany - Retrospective (Scottish National Gallery of Modern Art), John Bellany by John McEwen (Mainstream), John Bellany as Printmaker by Prof. Duncan Macmillan. *Clubs:* Chelsea Arts. *Signs work:* "John Bellany." *Address:* c/o Royal Academy of Arts, Piccadilly, London W1V 0DS.

BELSEY, Hugh Graham, B.A. (1976), M.Litt. (1981); museum curator; Curator, Gainsborough's House; *b* Hemel Hempstead, 15 May, 1954. *Educ:* University of Manchester and The Barber Inst. of Fine Arts, Birmingham. *Publications:* articles for art periodicals and exhbn. catalogues. *Address:* Gainsborough's House, 46 Gainsborough St., Sudbury, Suffolk CO10 2EU.

BELSKY, Franta, A.R.C.A., F.R.B.S., P.P.S.P.S., Hon. Doc., Fulton, Westminster College, Missouri; *b* Brno, 1921. *m* Margaret C. Owen (d. 1989). *Studied:* sculpture: Prague Academy, R.C.A. *Work in collections:* The Queen, Queen Mother, Universities, N.P.G., Europe and U.S.A., c. councils, ind. and pte. companies, e.g., "Joy-ride," Stevenage; "Triga," Tattersalls, Knightsbridge; "Lesson," Bethnal Green; "Astronomer Herschel," Slough; "Oracle," Temple Way, Bristol; "Totem," Arndale Centre, Manchester (destroyed); Admiral Cunningham, Trafalgar Square; Mountbatten Memorial, Horse Guards Parade; Winston Churchill statue, Fulton, Missouri; Winston Churchill sculpture, Prague; Harry S. Truman, Pres. Library,

Independence; Lord Cottesloe, National Theatre; fountains: Shell Centre, London; "Leap," Jamestown Harbour, London Dockland; R.A.F. Memorial, Prague (1995). Monograph (Zwemmer, 1992). *Address:* 4 The Green, Sutton Courtenay, OX14 4AE.

BELTON, Liam, R.H.A. (1993), A.R.H.A. (1991), A.N.C.A. (1971); painter in oil, keeper of Royal Hibernian Academy (1995); *b* Dublin, 1947. *m* Sharon Lynch. two *s.* one *d. Educ:* Synge Street. *Studied:* National College of Art, Dublin (1966-72). *Exhib:* five one-man shows, various group shows throughout Ireland. *Work in collections:* Dept. of Labour, E.S.B., G.P.A., National Self-Portrait Collection, K.P.M.G., Craig Gardner, Sisks, Elm Park Hospital, An Post., A.I.B., O.P.W., Haverty Trust, Contemporary Arts Soc., Ulster Bank. Member of A.A.I. and S.S.I.; Board mem. N.S.P.C. and R.H.A. Gallagher Gallery. *Signs work:* "Liam Belton, R.H.A." *Address:* 18 Whitethorn Rd., Artane, Dublin 5, Ireland.

BELTRAN, Felix, B.A., B.Sc.; American Inst. of Graphic Arts, N.Y. (1961), Internationale Buchkunst Ausstellung, Leipzig (1971), Bienale Uzite Grafiky, Brno (1972), International Print Biennale, Listowel (1980); painter, printmaker, illustrator; Titular Prof. Universidad Autónoma Metropolitana, México; *b* Havana, 23 June, 1938. *m* Lassie Sobera. one *d. Educ:* Colegio Cubano Arturo Montori, Havana. *Studied:* School of Visual Arts, N.Y., American Art School, N.Y. *Exhib:* Rousski Gallery, Sofia; Galerie Manes, Praha; Sala Ocre, Caracas; Galería Elisava, Barcelona. *Work in collections:* Museo de Arte Contemporaneo, Panamá; Brooklyn Museum, N.Y.; Museo de Bellas Artes, Caracas; Muzeum Sztuki, Lodz; National Museum, Stockholm; Museum Narodowe, Warsaw. *Publications:* Desde el Diseño (Havana, 1970), Artes Plásticas (Havana, 1982). *Clubs:* World Print Council, San Francisco, Print Club, Philadelphia, L'Accademia d'Europa, Parma, Assoc. Internationale des Arts Plastiques, Paris. *Signs work:* see appendix. *Address:* Apartado M-10733, México 06000 DF, México.

BENDALL-BRUNELLO, Tiziana, B.A. Joint Hons. (Fine Art/Ceramics) 1994; glass/ceramic artist in glass and porcelain; *b* Turin, Italy, 8 Feb., 1959. *m* John Bendall-Brunello. *Studied:* Camberwell College of Art (1991-94). *Exhib:* Hayward, Sotheby's, Barbican, Bowes Museum, Kettles Yard, Cambridge, Kunstmuseum, Wolfsburg, Germany, National Glass Centre, C.C.A. Cambridge, Roger Billcliffe, Glasgow, Scottish Gallery, Edinburgh, The Bluecoat, Liverpool, etc. *Publications:* to be published: Fusing and Slumping (A. & C. Black). *Address:* 33 Cowper Rd., Cambridge CB1 3SL.

BENGE, Bryan Neil, B.A. (Hons.) (1977), M.A. (1994); lecturer, conceptual artist; Hon.Sec., London Group (1995-); *b* Middlesex, 16 June, 1953. *m* Maria Wasley. *Studied:* Chelsea School of Art (1973), Kingston Polytechnic (1974-77), Kingston University (1992-94). *Exhib:* Young Contemporaries, R.A., American Council for the Arts, N.Y. (Liquitex in Excellence, prize winner 1993); London: Mall Galleries, Barbican Centre, Danielle Arnaud, Morley Gallery, Westminster, Bedford Hill, St. James, Tricycle, London Inst., Central St. Martin's; Europe: Pompidou Centre, Reichstag Germany, Sarajevo, Obala Gallery. *Work in collections:* Tate Gallery London Archives. *Clubs:* London Group. *Signs work:* "BRYAN BENGE." *Address:* 51 Bramble Walk, Epsom, Surrey KT18 7TB.

BENHAM, Clive Graham, R.B.S.A., City and Guilds (1951); teacher/artist in wood (wood carving, sculpture and cabinet making), painting; Retd. Head of Dept. Careers Education; V.P.R.B.S.A. (1984-87); *b* Melbourne, Australia, 23 Sept., 1929. *m* Doreen Hazel. two *s. Studied:* Moseley Rd. School of Art, B'ham College of Arts and Crafts (A. Gregory), Aston Technical College (now Central University). *Exhib:* joint shows, lectures and demonstrations in Wales and the Midlands. *Clubs:* Chairman and organiser `Winter Salon' Group of Artists. *Signs work:* "C. Graham Benham." *Address:* 53 Spiceland Rd., Northfield, Birmingham B31 1NL.

BENJAMIN, Norman: see IBRAM, Peter B.

BENJAMINS, Paul, B.A. (1st Class Hons.), M.A. (R.C.A.); artist in oil and acrylic; *b* London, 18 Oct., 1950. *m* Jacqui. one *s.* one *d. Studied:* Camberwell School of Art (1969-73), R.C.A. (1973-75). *Exhib:* solo shows: Thumb Gallery, London (1984, 1986, 1987), Galerie Pascal Gabert, Paris (1989, 1991, 1994), Gallery Cafe Mandy, Bergenz, Austria (1990), Jill George Gallery, London (1991, 1994, 1996, 2000), Champagne Vranken, Epernay (1993), Galerie Wam, Caen (1995), Brighton University Gallery (1998); group shows: numerous including Brighton Polytechnic Gallery, John Moores W.A.G. Liverpool, Thumb Gallery, International Contemporary Art Fairs (London, Bath, Los Angeles), Galerie Pascal Gabert, Paris, Original Print Gallery, Dublin, etc. *Commissions:* Royal Princess, Rhombert Austria, Herouville-St.Clair, Normandy, France. *Address:* c/o Advanced Graphics London, B206 Faircharm Estate, 8-12 Creekside, London SE8 3AX.

BENNETT, Brian Theodore Norton, M.A. Oxon. (1954), R.O.I. (1973), P.R.O.I. (1987), N.S. (1985), Hon. U.A. (1985); landscape painter in oil; Director of Art, Berkhamsted School (1957-87), Governor, Federation of British Artists (1992-98); *b* Olney, Bucks., 1927. *m* Margrit Elizabeth Brenner. *Educ:* Magdalen College School, Oxford and Magdalen College, Oxford. *Studied:* Ruskin School of Art, Oxford (1950) part-time; Regent St. Polytechnic (1956) evening classes. *Exhib:* R.A., R.B.A., R.O.I., R.S.M.A., etc. *Publications:* Choir Stalls of Chester Cathedral (1965), Oil Painting with a Knife (1993), A Painter's Year; Twelve Months in the Chilterns (2001). *Signs work:* "BRIAN BENNETT" on reverse. *Address:* 18 Upper Ashlyns Rd., Berkhamsted, Herts. HP4 3BW.

BENNETT, David Stuart, B.A. (Hons.) (1992), M.A. (R.C.A.) (1995), S.WL.A. (1992-present); artist in water-colour and oil; *b* Doncaster, 11 Dec., 1969. *Studied:* Leeds Polytechnic (1989-92), Royal College of Art, London (1993-95). *Exhib:* one-man shows: England; mixed exhbns. America, Holland, Spain, France, Ireland. *Publications:* Artist for nature publications, Flight of Cranes to Extremadura; and Alaska`s Copper River Delta; Nick Hammond, Modern Wildlife Painting; Robin Darcy Shilcock: Pintores de la Naturaleza. *Signs work:* "David Bennett." *Address:* 16 Pearl St., Harrogate HG1 4QW.

BENNETT, June, N.D.D., A.T.D.; painter/jeweller in silver and gold; *b* Grange over Sands. *m* Michael Bennett. two *s. Educ:* Ulverston G.S. *Studied:* Lancaster and Leicester Colleges of Art. *Exhib:* Goldsmiths Hall, Midland Group Gallery, Nottingham, Park Square Gallery, Leeds, Mignon Gallery, Bath, Ashgate Gallery, Farnham; one-man shows, Castlegate House Gallery, Cockermouth (1988, 1989, 1991, 1993, 1994, 1999, 2001). *Work in collections:* Jewellery: Abbot Hall Gallery, Kendal, Shipley A.G.; Paintings: Carlisle Museum and A.G., Copeland C.C. Painting full time from 1987. *Signs work:* "June Bennett," "J.B." and Sheffield Assay Office hallmark. *Address:* The Hollies, Port Carlisle, Cumbria CA7 5BU.

BENNETT, Michael, N.D.D., A.T.D.; painter in oils; *b* Windermere, 1934. *m* June Steer. two *s. Educ:* Windermere Grammar School. *Studied:* Lancaster and Leicester Colleges of Art. *Exhib:* one-man shows: Park Square Gallery, Leeds, Mignon Gallery, Bath, Bluecoat Gallery, Liverpool, Ashgate Gallery, Farnham, Abbot Hall, Kendal, A.I.A. Gallery, London; Leeds, Birmingham, Hull and Lancaster Universities, Castlegate Gallery, Cockermouth, Broughton House Gallery, Cambridge. *Work in collections:* Abbot Hall Gallery, Wakefield City A.G., Lincolnshire Arts Assoc., John Player Collection, Leeds Educ. Authority, Kettle's Yard, Univ. of Cambridge and Northern Arts Assoc. *Signs work:* "Bennett" and date. *Address:* The Hollies, Port Carlisle, Cumbria CA7 5BU.

BENNETT, Terence, N.D.D., F.R.S.A., Yorkshire Television Fine Art Fellowship (1973-74); painter in oil on canvas and water-colour, teacher; Head of Fine Art, Thomas Rotherham College, Rotherham (1976-91); the Sidney Holgate Fellowship, University of Durham (2001); *b* Doncaster, 7 Nov., 1935. *Studied:* Doncaster School of Art (Eric Platt, T.A. Anderson). *Exhib:* R.A., R.O.I., N.E.A.C., Drian Gallery, Travelling exhbn. Yorkshire, Lincolnshire, N.S., British Painting, Mall Galleries. *Work in collections:* Nuffield Foundation, Bank of England, Yorkshire Television, Yorkshire Arts Assoc., Leeds Educ. Authority, Halifax Bldg. Soc., Sheffield University, Cambridge University, Doncaster Borough Council, I.C.I. Ltd., Durham University. Prizes: Singer and Friedlander, Sunday Times Water-colour competition. *Signs work:* "Terence Bennett." *Address:* Rambler Cottage, 43 Main St., Sprotbrough, Doncaster, S. Yorks. DN5 7RH.

BENNETT, William, R.M.S.; freelance artist of miniature portraits, still life and marine paintings in water-colour and oil; Council mem. R.M.S.; *b* London, 21 June, 1917. *m* Isabel Weaver. one *s.* one *d. Educ:* Heritage School. *Studied:* Sir John Cass College, London. *Exhib:* R.A., F.B.A. Gallery. *Work in collections:* H.M. The Queen Elizabeth II Collection, Balmoral Galleries, Geelong, Australia, Manyung Gallery, Mt. Eliza, Victoria, Australia. *Signs work:* monogram of initials - see appendix and "Wm. Bennett." *Address:* 11 St. Peter's Ct., Sidmouth, Devon EX10 8AR. *Second Address:* La Villeneuve, Caurel 22530, France.

BENNEY, Prof. Adrian Gerald Sallis, C.B.E., R.D.I. (1971), Hon. M.A. (Leics., 1963), Des. R.C.A. (1954); goldsmith and silversmith; Professor of Silversmithing and Jewellery at Royal College of Art (1974-83); *b* Hull, 21 Apr., 1930. *m* Janet Edwards. three *s.* one *d. Educ:* Brighton Grammar School. *Studied:* Brighton College of Art (1946-50); Royal College of Art (1951-54) under Prof. Robert Goodden, R.D.I. Royal Warrants of Appointment to H.M. The Queen (1974), Queen Elizabeth, The Queen Mother (1975), H.R.H. The Duke of Edinburgh (1975) and H.R.H. The Prince of Wales (1980). *Publications:* Gerald Benney 50 Years at the Bench by Graham Hughes (1998). *Signs work:* "Gerald Benney." *Address:* The Old Rectory, Cholderton, nr. Salisbury, Wilts. SP4 0DW.

BENSON, Dawn Mary, L.S.I.A. (1974), Surrey Dip. (1974); sculptor in raku fired and bronzes from clay; painter in water-colour and mixed media; *b* Montreal, Canada, 7 Dec., 1952. one *d. Studied:* Twickenham College (1970-74, Stan Smith).

Exhib: various in London area. *Work in collections:* U.S.A., London and Europe. *Commissions:* portrait sculptures in London, Amsterdam; paintings in N.Z. and U.S.A. *Clubs:* Richmond Art Soc. and U.A. *Signs work:* "D.M.B." on sculpture "D.M. Benson" on paintings. *Address:* 10 Clarendon Cres., Twickenham TW2 5LN.

BENSON, Rosemary, R.E. (1977); artist in engraving, water-colour and oil; *b* Malawi, 1948. *m* Mark Burgess, author and illustrator. *Educ:* Livingstone High School, Zambia; Cambridge High School for Girls. *Studied:* Cambridge College of Arts and Technology (1966-67), Michaelis School of Fine Art, University of Cape Town (1973-75), Slade School of Fine Art (1977-79). *Exhib:* R.A., R.E., R.W.S. *Address:* Stoke Cottage, Stoke St. Mary, Taunton TA3 5BZ

BENTON, Graham, N.D.D. (1964), A.R.B.S.A. (1986); abstract painter/illustrator in oil, gouache, collage, charcoal, pastel; part-time art tutor; Former Sec. and Chairman Walsall Arts Council and Walsall Soc. of Artists; coordinator Walsall Artists Network; Associate mem. Penwith Soc. of Arts; Mem. N.S.E.A.D.; associate mem. Royal Birmingham Soc. of Artists; *b* Birmingham, 24 Oct., 1934. *Studied:* Walsall School of Art (1952-56, George Willott, Angus Macauley), Wolverhampton College of Art (1962-64, John Finnie, Bernard Brett). *Exhib:* Stafford A.G., Lichfield A.G., Walsall A.G., Letchworth A.G., 273 Gallery, London, Keele University, Salthouse Gallery, St. Ives, Penlee House, Penzance, R.B.S.A. Galleries, Birmingham, Wednesbury A.G., Camborne School of Mines; Solihull A.G., Mid-art, Dudley, Staffordshire Open. *Work in collections:* Arthur Andersen, London. *Signs work:* "(Graham) Benton" - see appendix. *Address:* 17 Clarendon St., Bloxwich, Walsall, W. Midlands WS3 2HT.

BERESFORD-WILLIAMS, Mary E., B.A.Hons. Fine Art, Reading (1953 Class 1); Cert. Educ. (1954); painter, printmaker and photographer; Mem. Newlyn Society of Artists; Mem. Devon Guild of Craftsmen. South-West Arts Major Award (1978); Photographer in Residence, Television South-West (1986-87); First Prize (Purchase) Burton Gallery, Bideford Open Art Competition (1999); *b* London, 30 Apr., 1931. *m* David Beresford-Williams. one *s. Educ:* Watford Grammar School. *Studied:* painting: Reading University under Prof. J. A. Betts. *Exhib:* Galleries in London and the South-west; solo shows Burton Gallery, Bideford, Devon (1998), Torre Abbey, Torquay, Devon (2000). *Work in collections:* Paintings, photographs and prints in public and private collections. *Commissions:* portraits. *Publications:* Since 1970 made many screen prints, sold in limited editions. 1988 book of photographs: A Portrait of TSW. *Signs work:* "M. Beresford-Williams" or "MBW." *Address:* 11 Langdon Lane, Galmpton, nr. Brixham, S. Devon TQ5 0PQ. *Email:* mary@beresfordw.freeserve.co.uk

BERG, Adrian, R.A.; Gold medal, Florence Biennale (1973), major prize, Tolly Cobbold (1981), third prize, John Moores (1982); painter; *b* London, 1929. *Educ:* Charterhouse; Caius College, Cambridge (M.A.); Trinity College, Dublin (H.Dip.Ed.). *Studied:* St. Martin's (1955-56), Chelsea (1956-58), R.C.A. (1958-61). *Exhib:* 5, Tooth's (1964-75); 3, Waddington Galleries (1978-83), Rochdale A.G. (1980), 6, Piccadilly Gallery (1985-99), Serpentine Gallery, Walker A.G. (1986), Barbican Touring Exhbn. (1993-94), Royal Academy, 1992-94 water-colours (1999). *Work in collections:* Arts Council, British Council, B.M., European Parliament,

Govt. Picture Coll., Hiroshima City Museum of Contemporary Art, Tate Gallery, Tokyo Metropolitan Art Museum. *Signs work:* "Adrian Berg." *Address:* c/o Piccadilly Gallery, 43 Dover St., London W1X 3RE.

BERNARD, Mike, B.A. (Hons.) (1978), R.A.S.Dip. (1981), R.I. (1997); demonstrator of painting techniques to art societies; painter in mixed media, acrylics, oil, tutor; *b* Dover, 2 Aug., 1957. *m* Susan. one *s.* one *d. Studied:* West Surrey College of Art and Design (1975-78), R.A. Schools (1978-81). *Exhib:* R.A., N.E.A.C., R.I., numerous one-man and group exhbns. *Commissions:* several mural and large scale works. *Publications:* work repro.: writer for art magazine. *Address:* Old House Farm, Nursted, Petersfield, Hants. GU31 5RD.

BERRISFORD, Peter, N.D.D., A.T.D.; painter (oils, water-colours), lecturer: Arts Council, National Trust, N.A.D.F.A.S., Swans (Hellenic); *b* Northampton, 11 Feb., 1932. *m* Jacqueline. one *s. Studied:* Northampton, Chelsea, Bournemouth Art Colleges (Travelling Scholarship 1953). *Exhib:* Bear Lane, Wildensteins, Piccadilly, Trafford , Leicester, Hahn Galleries, London, R.B.A., R.A., John Moore's, regularly at Melitensia Gallery, Malta. *Work in collections:* Hertfordshire, Hull, Surrey, Leicester, Sheffield, Northampton, Wales University, East Sussex C.C. Lithographs: New York Book of Month Club, Curwen Studios. Paintings for B.B.C.'s 'The Clothes in the Wardrobe' and 'The House of Eliott' (filmed 1992 and 1993). *Signs work:* oils "Berrisford," water-colours "Peter Berrisford." *Address:* 73 Woodgate Rd., Eastbourne BN22 8PD.

BERRY, John, A.I.C.A., Soc. of Portrait Artists, U.S.; Portrait artist U.S. Gallery of Presidents; artist in oil and pastel; *b* London, 9 June, 1920. *m* Jessie. two *s.* two *d. Studied:* Hammersmith Art College; Royal Academy Schools. *Exhib:* Weighhouse one-man show; Patterson Gallery; Driffold Gallery. *Work in collections:* Imperial War Museum, Regimental H.Q. Tidsworth, Hants. *Publications:* work repro.: Esso Tiger, Ladybird Books, covers for Corgi, Four Square, Panther, Penguin and Readers Digest. U.S. Contact: Bob Mallenfant, Southwest Gallery, 4500 Sigma, Dallas, Texas. 75244 U.S.A. *Signs work:* "19 Berry 98." *Address:* Dove Cottage, 1 Scropton Old Rd., Hatton, Derbyshire DE65 5DX.

BERRY, June, D.F.A.Lond. (1948), R.E. (1986), R.W.S. (1993), N.E.A.C. (1990), R.W.A. (1993); artist in etching, oil and water-colour; *b* Melbourne, Derbyshire. *m* John Berry. one *s.* two *d. Educ:* Boston Lincs. *Studied:* Slade School of Fine Art (1941-42, 1946-49). *Exhib:* R.A., R.E., R.W.S., R.W.A., N.E.A.C., and in Germany and U.S.A. *Work in collections:* Ashmolean Museum Oxford, Royal West of England Academy, Graphotek, Berlin, National Museum of Wales, Kettering A.G., Oldham A.G., Fitzwilliam Museum, Cambridge, H.M. The Queen. *Publications:* Limited Edn. Livre d'Artiste 'Passing Days' (1984). *Signs work:* "June Berry." *Address:* 45 Chancery La., Beckenham, Kent BR3 6NR.

BERRY-HART, David James, M.A.; painter and sculptor; *b* Trinidad, 1940. *Studied:* St. Martin's School of Art (1959-1961), City of Birmingham Polytechnic (1981-83). *Exhib:* one-man shows: A.I.A. Gallery, London (1969), Herbert A.G. Coventry (1970), Camden Arts Centre (1975), University of Warwick (1977), Imperial College (1979), Royal National College for the Blind (1979), Cannon Hill Park (1979), Whitefriars Coventry (1988), mid-Warwickshire College Gallery

(1990), Worcester City A.G. (1991), Quaker Gallery, London (1994), Nuneaton A.G. (1996), Brewhouse Gallery, Taunton, (1999); group: Spectrum Central (1971), Art in Steel (1972), Gawthorpe Festival (1974), On the Town sculpture (1987), Cultural Connections (1995), Nottingham Trent University; with "The Firm" exhib. Hampshire (Touring) (1983-4), Carlisle A.G. (1984), Liverpool University (1985), Williamson A.G. (1986), Beecroft A.G. (1987), Chelmsford A.G. (1987), Nuneaton A.G. (1998). *Work in collections:* R.N.C.B. Imperial College. *Publications:* Midlands Arts Magazine, Spectrum Central Catalogue. Awards: Arts Council (1975), West Midlands Arts Association (1978). *Address:* 13 Tennant St., Nuneaton, Warwickshire CV11 4NT.

BERRYMAN, Derek James, N.D.D. (1951), A.T.D. (1955), B.Ed.(Hons.) (1977), F.R.S.A. (1960); artist in oil, water-colour, etching, lithography; Head of Art Dept., Prince Henry's Grammar School, Otley, Yorkshire (1957-1961), lecturer (retd.); London Guildhall Univ. Sir John Cass College, Leeds College of Art, Buckinghamshire C.H.E., Weston-super-Mare School of Art; Graphic Designer, Carlton Studio, London; Hydrographic Dept., Admiralty, London; *b* Chingford, Essex, 1926. *m* Irene Metzger, elder daughter of Peter Metzger, architect and lecturer, Tübingen University, Germany. one *s.* one *d. Educ:* Normanhurst School, Chingford, St Aubyn's School, Woodford, S.W. Essex Technical College. *Studied:* St. Martin's School of Art; Sir John Cass College; King's College, University of Durham; University of Bristol; also English Speaking Union Scholarship to Syracuse University, U.S.A. *Exhib:* R.A., R.B.A., R.O.I., R.W.A., Scotland, Germany, U.S.A., and provincial galleries in England. *Work in collections:* Various U.S.A. Germany and Britain. War service: 1944-48 initially R.A.F.V.R. Air Crew cadet (compulsorily transferred into Infantry); Gordon Highlanders and Indian Army. *Signs work:* "Berryman" or initial "B" with date. *Address:* The Mill House, Wester Tillyrie, by Milnathort, Kinross-shire KY13 0RW. Scotland.

BERTHOLD: see DUNNE, Berthold.

BEST, Irene, artist in acrylic; *b* Sunderland, 3 June, 1937. *m* Kenneth. one *s.* one *d. Educ:* New College, Durham. *Exhib:* Witham Hall Gallery, Barnard Castle; Westminster Gallery, London; Darlington A.G.; Durham A.G.; Bede Gallery, Jarrow; R.B.S.A. Gallery, Birmingham. *Clubs:* N.A.P.A., Soc. of Amateur Artists. *Address:* 10 Wilbore Croft, Aycliffe, Co. Durham DL5 6TF.

BEST, Ronald O'Neal, R.C.A., Dip. F.A., Post Dip.; teaches litho at Heatherley School of Fine Art, London; painter and printmaker; *b* London, 25 May, 1957. *Educ:* Sladebrook High School, London. *Studied:* Byam Shaw School of Art; Croydon College of Art; R.C.A. London; Asst. to Winston Branch, painter. *Exhib:* R.O.I., N.E.A.C., P.S., S.G.A., Salon des National, Paris, Lynn Stern Young Artists, London, Eva Jekel Gallery, Twentieth Century British Art Fair, R.C.A. London, 1492-1992 Un Nouveau Regard sur les Caraibes, Paris, Art House, Amsterdam, President Portobello Group, Pall Mall Deposit Gallery, the Portobello Group, W11 Gallery, Gallery Cafe, Portobello Printmakers. Coordinator, Visual Arts Portobello Festival. Founded the Chelsea Painters and Printmakers (1999), manager, Notting Hill Fine Art Gallery, co-ordinator, Art for the Unemployed, Portobello Academy of Drawing. *Work in collections:* R.C.A., Croydon College, Grange Museum, London.

Commissions: London Art Forms. *Clubs:* Portobello Group, Chelsea Painters and Printmakers, Portobello Printmakers. *Signs work:* "Ronald Best." *Address:* 51 Exton Cres., Stonebridge, London NW10 8DA.

BETHEL, Marion Ross, illuminator and letterer in water-colour, gold leaf, ink, parchment in illuminated books; *b* Wiesbaden, Germany, 19 Mar., 1929. *Educ:* P.N.E.U. correspondence course. *Studied:* with Gladys Best, R.W.A., and Daisy Alcock, A.R.C.A., F.R.S.A. *Exhib:* Salon de Soc. des Artistes Français. *Publications:* in Revue Moderne. *Signs work:* "M.R.B." or "Marion Ross Bethel." *Address:* 17 Strand, Topsham, Devon.

BETHELL, David, C.B.E., LL.D.(Leic.), D.Litt. (Lough), D.Ed. (U.W.E.), D.Des (Bournemouth), R.W.A., F.R.S.A., N.D.D., A.T.D., F.S.A.E., F.C.S.D.; graphic and typographic designer; Director, Leicester Polytechnic (1973-87); Chairman, CNAA Committee for Art and Design (1974-80); mem. Design Council (1980-88); Chairman, Design Council Educ. Advisory Com. (1981-88); Hong Kong University and Polytechnic Grants Com. (1982-92); Chairman, Hong Kong Council for Academic Accreditation (1990-92); Chairman, Education and Training Committee, Chartered Society of Designers (1987-90); Senior Vice-President, R.W.A. (1997); Chairman, Bursary Awards Com. Worshipful Company Framework Knitters (1994); *b* Bath, 7 Dec., 1923. *m* Margaret (decd.). one *s.* one *d. Educ:* King Edward's School, Bath. *Studied:* Gloucester College of Art (1946-48), West of England College of Art (1948-51). *Work in collections:* Gloucester and Stafford Art Galleries, R.W.A., and private collections in U.S.A. and Israel. *Publications:* A Case of Sorts, 120 Woodcuts & The Bard, An Industrious People. *Clubs:* Athenaeum, Royal Overseas. *Signs work:* "David Bethell." *Address:* 48 Holmfield Rd., Stoneygate, Leicester LE2 1SA.

BETOWSKI, Noel Jan, B.A. Hons. Fine Art Painting (1976), Central School of Art Diploma (1976), A.T.C. London University (1977); painter in mixed media, oil etc. and sound; artist and musician; *b* Essex, 11 Dec., 1952. *m* Pamela Jane Niblett. one *s. Educ:* St. Mary's R.C. School, Tilbury, Essex. *Studied:* Thurrock Technical College, Essex (1970-1972), Central School of Art and Design, London (1973-1976), London University, Inst. of Education (1976-1977). *Exhib:* N.P.G. (1983), R.A. (1976, 1984), New Grafton Gallery, London, (exhibitor since 1982), Royal Festival Hall (1983,1984), Mercury Gallery, London (1984, 1985), Worcester City Art Gallery (Cornish & Contemporary 1985), Crane Kalman Gallery, London (1986), Camden Arts Centre (John Constable Landscape Competition prize winner 1987 3rd, 1988 2nd), Walker Galleries, Harrogate (1996,1997, 2000), Highgate Fine Art (1997, 2000), John Davies Gallery, Glos. (1993), Penhaven Gallery, St. Ives, Cornwall (1999-) *Work in collections:* numerous collections worldwide. *Commissions:* Kinlet Hall School, Bewdley, Worcs. (1987), Peters and May Shipping Company, Southampton (1992). *Publications:* Noel Betowski (1998), various gallery catalogues, C.D.s including On The Water C.D. album (2000). *Signs work:* "Noel Betowski." *Address:* Tregonebris House, Sancreed, Penzance, Cornwall TR20 8RQ. *Website:* www.noelbetowski.co.uk *Email:* noel.betowski@lineone.net

BEVAN, Daniel Vaughan Gwillim, R.I., W.C.S.W.; artist in water-colour; *b* Cardiff, 8 June, 1921. *m* Betty Eileen, divorced. one *d. Educ:* Willesden and Hendon Technical Colleges. *Signs work:* "Vaughan Bevan." *Address:* Bryn Glas,

Garndolbenmaen, Gwynedd, LL51 9UX.

BEVAN, Oliver, A.R.C.A. (1964); painter in oil, pastel, monoprint; *b* Peterborough, 28 Mar., 1941. *Educ:* Eton. *Studied:* R.C.A. (Carel Weight, Colin Hayes, Leonard Rosoman). *Exhib:* Angela Flowers (1981), Odette Gilbert (1984), Gallery 10 (1991), "City/Two Views", Barbican (1986); exhib. in and curated "The Subjective City" touring exhbn. (1990-91), "Witnesses and Dreamers" touring (1993-94), "The Motor Show" touring (1996-97); solo "Urban Mirror" National Theatre (1997), Hunting Art Prizes, R.C.A. (2000, 2001). *Work in collections:* Contemporary Art Soc., Museum of London, Cleveland Gallery, Unilever, Sainsbury, Guildhall A.G. *Commissions:* four ptgs for B.A.A. Gatwick (1990), Art on the Underground (1993). *Publications:* "London in Paint" Mus. of London, Modern Paintings in the Guildhall Art Gallery. *Signs work:* canvases signed on back "Oliver Bevan" - elongated vertical in "B"; works on paper "OB '87", etc. *Address:* 5 Rue Paul Foussat, 30700 Uzès, France *Website:* www.thor-bev.dircon.co.uk *Email:* oliverbevan@wanadoo.fr

BEVAN, Tony, Dip.A.D. (1974), H.D.F.A. (1976); painter in acrylic and oil; *b* Bradford, 1951. partner: Glenys Johnson. one *d. Studied:* Bradford College of Art (1968-71), Goldsmiths' College (1971-74), Slade School of Fine Art (1974-76). *Exhib:* I.C.A. London touring Britain (1980-87), Haus der Kunst Munich (1989), Kunsthalle Kiel (1988), Whitechapel A.G. (1993). *Work in collections:* Staats Galerie Moderner Kunst Munich, Kunsthalle Kiel, Metropolitan Museum of Art N.Y., Yale University, B.M., Theo Wormland Foundation Munich, British Council, Arts Council, M.O.M.A. (N.Y.), Toledo Museum, Ohio, Wolverhampton A.G. *Signs work:* "Bevan." *Address:* Studio 2, Acme Studios, 165 Childers St., London SE8 5JR.

BEVIS, Michael John Vaughan, Cert Ed., A.I.E., A.R.P.S., F.R.S.A., M.F.P.S., M.CollP., D.F.A. (Painting); educational art consultant; artist in oil, photographer; Exam Moderator, G.C.S.E., G.C.E, G.N.V.Q., Edexcel Foundation; *b* London, 11 Oct., 1948. *m* Marie Janice Gair. two *d. Educ:* Clarks College (1960-65). *Studied:* Hornsey College of Art (Foundation, 1966-67), Walthamforest Technical College and School of Art (1967-70), Barking N.E.L.P. (1970-72), London University Inst. of Educ. (Associateship, 1980-81). *Exhib:* one-man: Loggia Gallery, London (1980); group: Mall Gallery, London. *Publications:* associateship report 'Some Art activities in Prison'. Work on file at: Art Search Ltd., Project Art Ltd., Contemporary Arts Project Ltd., The Antiques and Fine Art Location Agency. *Signs work:* "M.J.V. BEVIS." *Address:* 2 Bergen Ct., Maldon, Essex CM9 6UH.

BEWICK, Pauline, R.H.A., Áosdana; awards: U.N. Poster (1981), Irish Life Arts (1990); artist in water-colour, tapestry, sculpture, etching, ceramic, etc.; *b* Northumberland, 1935. *m* Dr. Patrick Melia, psychiatrist. two *d. Studied:* N.C.A.D., Dublin. *Exhib:* Taylor Gallery Dublin, Catto Gallery London, Odette Gilbert Gallery London, Guinness Hop Store, Irish Museums, Frank Lewis Kerry, etc. *Work in collections:* in many public and private collections worldwide. *Publications:* subject of Painting a Life by James White, former Director of the National Gallery of Ireland, (1985); author and illustrator, Ireland: An Artist's Year (Methuen, 1990); A Boy and a Dolphin (Granada, 1983); illustrated, Irish Tales and Sagas (1994); author and illustrator: The South Seas and a Box of Paints (Art Books Int. London, 1996); The Yellow Man (1996). Documentary: A Painted Diary by David Shaw-Smith, R.T.E., Channel 4, Pompidou Centre Paris, Los Angeles and Chicago film festivals (1994). Two years spent painting and writing in Polynesia. *Clubs:* Chelsea Arts, London; United Arts, Dublin. *Signs work:* see appendix. *Address:* Treanmanagh, Glenbeigh, Co. Kerry, Ireland.

BICKNELL, John, B.A.(Hons.) (1980), H.Dip.F.A.(Lond.) (1983), Slade prize (1983), Boise Scholarship (1983), Greater London Arts award (1986), John Moores prize (1987), Henry Moore Fellow, Leeds Polytechnic (1989-90); painter; *b* Surrey, 1958. *m* Christina Dorees. two *d. Educ:* Ottershaw School. *Studied:* W.S.C.A.D. (1975-77), N.E. London Polytechnic (1977-80), Slade School of Fine Art (1981-83). *Exhib:* numerous group shows, including John Moores, Whitechapel, Christie's, New Contemporaries, R.C.A., Miro Foundation, Barcelona, Monjuic, Girona, Cleveland International Drawing Biennale, Metathesis Touring Greece, Slow Burn Touring U.K.; one-man shows: Pomeroy Purdy Gallery, London. *Work in collections:* Nat. West, Reed International, Texaco. *Signs work:* "John Bicknell." *Address:* School of Art, Architecture and Design, Leeds Metropolitan University, Calverley St., Leeds LS1 3HE. *Second Address:* Iridos St., Filothei 15237, Athens, Greece.

BICKNELL, Les, B.A. (Hons.); book artist, printmaking/sculpture; visiting lecturer, Camberwell College of Art; *b* Coventry, 4 Mar., 1963. *m* Jayne Knight. two *s. Educ:* Binley Park Comprehensive. *Studied:* London College of Printing (1982-85). *Exhib:* over 20 one-man shows since 1985 including Maison du L.A.C., Domart-en-Pontenthieu, V. & A., Nigel Greenwoods. *Work in collections:* Tate Gallery, V. & A., Rijkmuseum, Bodleian Library, M.O.M.A., N.Y. Public Library. *Commissions:* Many bookworks, including Eastern Arts Board and Birmingham Libraries. *Publications:* edited: Mapping Knowledge, The Book as Art, Beyond Reading. *Address:* Eva's Place, Sibton Green, Saxmundham, Suffolk IP17 2JX.

BIDDULPH, Elizabeth Mary, R.O.I. (1952), Hon. senior mem. R.O.I. (1982), N.D.D. (1947), Hon.Cert.R.D.S. (1942); painter chiefly in oils, portraits, landscapes, still-life, flowers; judging panel, John Laing Painting Competition (1988); voluntary art teaching to small class of mentally ill patients from 2000; *b* Port Elizabeth, S.A., 17 June, 1927. *m* Nicholas Osborne John Biddulph. one *s. Educ:* Hamilton House School, Tunbridge Wells. *Studied:* Wimbledon School of Art (1944-47) under Gerald Cooper, A.R.C.A., Slade School of Fine Art (1949-51). *Exhib:* yearly at R.O.I.; one-man shows, Hornsey Library (1971), Barclays Bank, Egham (1977), Egham Library (1985), murals in shop, Virginia Water (1984). *Commissions:* repainted and designed ceiling panels for writer Ralph Dutton's home 1961-62 (original ones destroyed by fire). *Publications:* articles for Leisure Painter Magazine (1980-81, 1987). *Signs work:* "E. Biddulph." *Address:* 74 Clarence St., Egham, Surrey TW20 9QY.

BILL, Joan Ada, N.D.D. (1954), A.T.D. (1955); painter in watercolour, pastel and oil; *b* Redcar, 14 June, 1933. *m* Frank Bill. one *s.* one *d. Educ:* Saltburn High School. *Studied:* Middlesborough Art College (1950-1954); Sheffield Art College (1955). *Exhib:* British Artists (1989), United Artists (from 1994), Artists in Essex. *Commissions:* portraits in pastel and oils. *Publications:* pen and ink illus. - Farmhouses in an English Landscape by Sir William Addison; Hidden Essex by Stan

Jarvis; countryside books for F.E.W.I. *Signs work:* "JABILL." *Address:* 11 Egg Hall, Epping, Essex CM16 6SA.

BINNS, David, N.D.D. (1956), S.WL.A. (1968); R.S.P.B. Fine Art Award (1990, 1992, 1993, 1994); awarded Doctor of Letters, Bradford University (2000); freelance artist in water-colour, lino, scraperboard; teacher SP courses; with wife runs own Brent Gallery; *b* Sutton-in-Craven, 30 Sept., 1935. *m* Molly. one *s*. two *d. Educ:* Ermysted's Grammar School, Skipton. *Studied:* Skipton Art School (Dan Binns, J. C. Midgley), Leeds College of Art and Pulée. *Exhib:* S.WL.A., R.I., H.C. Dickens, Bloxham, Oxfordshire, Manor House, Ilkley, Aquarious Gallery, Harrogate, Leigh Yawkey Woodson Museum, Wisconsin, U.S.A., Northern Exh'n wildlife art (Liverpool), NEWA (ABR). *Publications:* work repro.: Dalesman, childrens animal books, circular jigsaws, print by Soloman & Whitehead, Medici cards, R.S.P.B. calendar and cards, Yorkshire Journal, Country Artists Plate Designs. *Clubs:* S.WL.A. *Signs work:* "David Binns." *Address:* Holmestead, 9 Boundary Ave., Sutton-in-Craven, Keighley, Yorks. BD20 8BL.

BINNS, Lorna, A.R.C.A. (1938), R.W.S. (1977); painter in water-colour; *b* Sheffield, 23 Oct., 1914. *m* John Dawson Binns (decd.). two *d. Educ:* Abbeydale Girls' Grammar School, Sheffield. *Studied:* Sheffield College of Art (1930-35) under Maurice Wheatley, R.C.A. (1935-39) under Prof. Tristram. *Exhib:* R.A., F.B.A. Gallery, The Guildhall, R.W.S. Gallery. *Publications:* 'Visions of Venice' by Michael Spender, (1990). Work on many tours. Featured artist R.W.S. Spring Exhibition, (1995), and in many collections at home and abroad. Interviewed as part of the Artists' Lives Collections (Nat. Sounds Archives British Library 1997). *Signs work:* "Lorna Binns." *Address:* Otterstone House, 38 Sparrows Herne, Bushey, Herts WD2 3EU.

BIRCH, David William, painter/printmaker in water-colour and wood engraving; landscape and architectural subjects; *b* 28 Jan., 1945. *m* Annabel Carey (artist and art tutor). one *s. Educ:* Wellesbourne School, Birmingham. *Studied:* mentors: water-colour - Kay Kinsman, wood engraving - William T. Rawlinson. *Exhib:* R.A., R.I., R.W.S., R.E., S.W.E., R.W.A.; one-man shows: Birmingham and Midland Inst., John Noott Gallery, Broadway, Ombersley Gallery, Worcester, Confederation Life, Bristol; regular solo shows in towns and villages of the Cotswolds, South Midlands and West Country. *Work in collections:* University of Bristol, Confederation Life Insurance Co. *Signs work:* "David W. Birch." *Address:* Croftsbrook, Blind La., Chipping Campden, Glos. GL55 6ED.

BIRD, Henry, A.R.C.A. (1933), Art Workers Guild, Civil List for Services to Art; figure draughtsman, mural decorator; *b* Northampton, 1909. *m* Freda Jackson (decd.), actress. one *s. Educ:* Northampton. *Studied:* Northampton and R.C.A. *Exhib:* many exhbns. in public and private galleries. *Work in collections:* University & Nat. Library, Wales; Carlisle; Brighton; Northampton; Theatre Museum, Covent Gdn., Drottningholm Theatre Museum, Sweden. Mural paintings in Conference Centre, Ecton, Northants.; Earls Barton Church; University Commonwealth Studies, London; Royal Theatre, Northampton; Ashcroft-Fairfield, Croydon; Drottningholm Theatre Museum, Sweden. Total decorative schemes, St. Crispin Hospital Chapel, Northants.; Daventry Hospital Chapel; Denton Church, Northants; Charwelton

Village Chapel, Northants. *Signs work:* "H. Bird." *Address:* Hardingstone House, Northants NN4 7BU.

BIRNE, Max Sidney, F.F.P.S.; landscape and abstract painter in oil, water-colour and gouache; *b* London, 12 Jan., 1927. *m* Rosemarie Kesselman. one *s. Studied:* City Literary Inst., London; Harrow School of Art. *Exhib:* one-man shows: Burgh House, Hampstead, Lauderdale House Highgate, Mandel's Gallery Goodmayes, Margaret Fisher Gallery London, Tricycle Theatre London; group shows: Loggia Gallery, Chenil Gallery, Alpine Gallery, Mall Galleries, Barbican Arts Centre, Bloomsbury Gallery, Usher Museum Lincoln, Brighton Polytechnic A.G., R.S.B.A.G. Birmingham, Boxfield Gallery, Stevenage. *Signs work:* "BIRNE." *Address:* 82 Preston Rd., Wembley, Middx. HA9 8LA.

BIRO, Val (B. S.), freelance illustrator, painter, author; assistant production manager, Sylvan Press (1945-46), production manager and art director, C. & J. Temple (1946-48), John Lehmann, Ltd. (1948-53); *b* Budapest, Hungary, 6 Oct., 1921. *m* (1) Vivien Woolley. one *d.* (2) Marie-Louise Ellaway. one s- *s.* one s- *d. Educ:* Cistercian School, Budapest. *Studied:* Central School of Arts, London. *Exhib:* Budapest, London. *Work in collections:* V. & A. Museum, British Museum. *Publications:* Author of the Gumdrop Series; Hungarian Folk Tales, Rub-a-Dub-Dub and other books for children; illustrated some 400 books, incl. My Oxford Picture Word Book, The Father Brown Stories, American Start with English, Bible Stories for Children, etc. Lecturer on Art and storytelling. *Clubs:* Vintage Sports Car. *Signs work:* "Biro" or "Val Biro." *Address:* Bridge Cottage, Brook Ave., Bosham, W. Sussex PO18 8LQ.

BISHOP, William Henry, self taught artist in water-colour and oil of seascapes and landscapes; *b* Liss, Hants., 21 June, 1942. *m* Helen Dunkerley. three *s. Educ:* King's School, Canterbury. *Exhib:* R.S.M.A., Armed Forces, Southampton Maritime Year; one-man show: Royal Exchange Gallery, London (1989). *Work in collections:* U.S.A., Australia, New Zealand, Oman, Singapore, Hong Kong, Falkland Islands, U.K., Gibraltar, Germany. *Commissions:* R.N. Museum, Portsmouth, and Mary Rose Museum, Portsmouth; HMS. Warrior Museum, The Mathew Project, City of Bristol. *Publications:* Dictionary of Sea Painters (E.H.H. Archibald). Represented in America by: Quester Gallery, Stonington, Connecticut 06378. *Signs work:* "W. H. Bishop" and "William H. Bishop" in new millenium. *Address:* West Mill, Mill Lane, Langstone, Havant, Hants. PO9 1RX.

BIZON, Edna, S.W.A. (1987); artist in oil; *b* 13 Aug., 1929. *m* Ken Bizon. *Educ:* Honor Oak School. *Studied:* St.Martin's School of Art (1943-44), Camberwell School of Art (1944-46, Lawrence Gowing, John Minton, Claude Rogers). *Exhib:* R.A. from 1974 to 1994; one-man shows: Thorndike, Leatherhead (1970, 1977), Augustine, Holt (1973), Munich, W.Germany (1982), O'Nians King St. Galleries (1987), Look of Helmsley (1988), King St. Galleries (1990), Llewellyn Alexander (1991, 1993, 1995, 1997, 1999). *Clubs:* Guild of Norwich Painters. *Signs work:* "Edna Bizon." *Address:* Drove End, West St., North Creake, Norfolk NR21 9LQ.

BLACK, Ian, Art Teaching Diploma, Bristol University (1956), R.W.A. (1978); art teacher and artist in oil, acrylic, pen and ink; Head of Art, Bristol Cathedral School; Hon. Sec. R.W.A.; *b* Bury St. Edmunds, 31 May, 1929. *m* Judith Rhiannon. *Educ:* Culford School, Bury St. Edmunds. *Studied:* Southampton College of Art

(1949), Bath Academy of Art (1952-56) under William Scott, Martin Froy, Jack Smith, Terry Frost, Peter Lanyon. *Exhib:* five one-man shows, R.W.A., R.A., travelling exhibs. *Work in collections:* R.W.A., Walsall Educ. Centre, Bath University, N.Z. Government, St. Catherine's College, Oxford, Wadham College, Oxford, Oxford Corp., Clifton High School, Redland School, Dorset House, Oxford. *Signs work:* "IB" or "Ian Black." *Address:* Blakes Farm, Englishcombe, Bath BA2 9DT.

BLACKBURN, David, artist in pastel on paper, visiting lecturer; *b* Huddersfield, 1939. *Studied:* Huddersfield School of Art (1955), Royal College of Art (1959-62, Kenneth Clark, patron and adviser). *Exhib:* solo shows include: Peter Bartlow Gallery, Chicago; Huddersfield A.G.; Kreis Unna, Germany; Charles Nodrum Gallery, Melbourne, Australia; Hart Gallery, London and Nottingham. *Work in collections:* M.O.M.A. (N.Y.), British Council, Leeds City A.G., Queensland A.G. *Publications:* 'David Blackburn and the Visionary Landscape Tradition' by Sasha Grishin, 'A Landscape Vision' by Malcolm Yorke (both Hart Gallery Publications). Lives and works in Huddersfield. *Signs work:* "David Blackburn." *Address:* c/o Hart Gallery, 113 Upper St., Islington, London N1 1QN.

BLACKBURN, Keith, full time artist in oil and mixed media, and writer; *b* Wakefield, Yorks., 2 Apr., 1943. *Exhib:* Cornwall; one-man shows: Holland. *Publications:* Between September (Book Guild, 1994), Lamentations of a Young Pig (Book Guild, 1997), Changes in a Landscape (Minerva, 1998), Feathers for Laura (Book Guild 2000), designed own covers. *Address:* c/o A.G Hoegen, Keizersgracht 42E, 1015 CR Amsterdam, Holland.

BLACKBURN, Mavis, N.D.D. (Painting), A.T.D. (1948), R.C.A. (1952), B.A. (1979); artist in oil, polymer and gouache; *b* Wallasey, Ches., 29 Oct., 1923. *Educ:* Upton Hall Convent School. *Studied:* Liverpool College of Art (1942-48, Alfred Wiffen, R.C.A., Will C. Penn, R.O.I., R.S.P. R.C.A., Martin Bell, A.R.C.A.). *Exhib:* Royal Cambrian Academy, Wirral Soc. of Art, Deeside Art Group, Atkinson Gallery, Southport, Glasgow Inst. of Fine Arts, R.B.A., R.A., etc.; one-man shows, Liverpool, R.C.A., Williamson Gallery, Birkenhead. *Work in collections:* Williamson A.G., Birkenhead, Senate House, Liverpool University. *Signs work:* "Mavis Blackburn." *Address:* The Bend, Village Rd., West Kirby, Wirral, Merseyside CH48 7EL.

BLACKLOCK, George, Dip.A.D. (1974), M.F.A. (1976); painter in oil and wax on canvas; Senior lecturer in painting, Wimbledon School of Art; *b* Durham, 11 Apr., 1952. one *s. Studied:* Stourbridge College of Art (1971-74, Barrie Cook), Reading University (1974-76, Terry Frost). *Work in collections:* A.C.G.B. *Signs work:* "George Blacklock." *Address:* 11-31 Oarsmen Rd., London N1.

BLACKMORE, Clive David, painter; *b* Kingston-on-Thames, 1940. *Studied:* Twickenham and Kingston Schools of Art. *Exhib:* regularly in the west country and New Academy, London. *Signs work:* "Clive Blackmore." *Address:* Eastcliff Farm, Rinsey, Ashton, Helston, Cornwall TR13 9TS.

BLACKWOOD, Brian, F.R.I.B.A., F.R.S.A.; painter in watercolour, line, gouache, pastel and etcher; *b* 4 Feb., 1926. *Educ:* Holmesdale School, Reigate (hons. cert. Royal Drawing Soc. 1935), Inverness High School. *Studied:* Tunbridge Wells School of Art, Chelsea College of Art. *Clubs:* Liveryman, Painter-Stainers,Co., member Soc. of Architectural Artists, Société Internationale des Artistes Chrétiens, Artworkers Guild. *Signs work:* "Brian Blackwood." *Address:* Ebony House, Whitney Drive, Stevenage SG1 4BL.

BLACKWOOD, Simon Anthony James, Dip.Ad. (1970); artist in oil; *b* Chelmsford, 17 May, 1948. *m* Laura C.M. Blackwood. one *d. Educ:* Gilberd School, Colchester. *Studied:* Colchester School of Art, Coventry School of Art (Anthony Atkinson, Don Foster). *Exhib:* Art and Mysticism (1975) I.C.A. London; one-man shows: Dundas Gallery 'Bus Stop' Series (1985), Netherbon Arts Centre 'Aquatic Light' Series (1986), Anthony Mould Ltd. London (1989), Michael Parkin Fine Art (1991, 1995), William Hardie Gallery Glasgow (1992), Brian Sinfield Gallery Burford (1992, 1994), Kusav, Istanbul (1994, 1995), Cynthia Bourne, London (1996). *Work in collections:* Flemings Collection, Nomura International. *Signs work:* "S.A.J.B." or "S.B." *Address:* 10 & 11 Bourtree Terrace, Hawick, Roxburgh, Scotland TD9 9HN.

BLAKE, Marie Dora, N.D.D. (1958), A.T.C. (1959); oil, acrylic, watercolour, pastel, printmaking; *b* London, 12 Mar., 1938. *m* Charles Calcutt Smith. two *s.* one *d. Educ:* Richmond and E.Sheen Grammar School. *Studied:* Kingston-on-Thames School of Art (1954-58), London University Inst. of Educ. (1959). *Exhib:* N.E.A.C., R.O.I., R.S.M.A., S.W.A., dfn Gallery New York. *Publications:* author – "You Can Paint Pastels" Harper Collins U.K., (2000); Watson Guptil, NY (2000); Editions Fleuris, Paris (2001); Artist & Illustrator Magazine (1996); regular contributor Leisure Painter Magazine. *Clubs:* S.W.A. '87-'97. *Signs work:* "Marie Blake." *Address:* Long Close, Clappentail La., Lyme Regis, Dorset DT7 3LZ. *Website:* www.marieblake.com *Email:* marie@marieblake.com

BLAKE, Naomi, F.R.B.S.; sculptor in bronze; *b* Czechoslovakia, 1924. one *s.* one *d. Studied:* Hornsey School of Art (1955-60). *Exhib:* Salon de Paris, R.B.S., City of Leicester Museum, R.A. International Art Fair, St. Paul's Cathedral, Barbican London, Exhbn. Gallery Swansea University. *Work in collections:* Leicester Arts Council, North London Collegiate, Oxford Synagogue, Jews College Hendon, Fitzroy Sq. London, Bristol Cathedral, Hebrew University Jerusalem, Leo Baeck College London, Tel Aviv University Israel, Yarnton Manor Oxford, Norwich Cathedral, Duai Abbey Reading, St. Botolph's Church Aldgate, St. Anthony's College, Oxford. *Publications:* contributor, Anthologies, Each in his Prison, The Bridge is Love, London Statues, The A.A. Book of London, Open Air Sculpture in Britain. *Signs work:* "N.B." *Address:* 41 Woodside Ave., London N10 3HY.

BLAKE, Pippa Jane, B.A. Hons. (1976); painter in oil and gouache; *b* Portsmouth, 6 Apr., 1954. *m* Sir Peter Blake. one *s.* one *d. Educ:* Downe House School, Berks. *Studied:* Camberwell School of Art (1972-76). *Exhib:* one-man shows: Sussex, London, Auckland, N.Z.; mixed shows: Sussex, Hampshire and London. *Work in collections:* in Gt. Britain, France, Switzerland and New Zealand. *Signs work:* "P. Blake" or P.B." *Address:* Longshore, 3 Western Parade, Emsworth, Hants. PO10 7HS.

BLAKE, Quentin, O.B.E., R.D.I., M.A., F.C.S.D.; illustrator and teacher; Head of Dept. of Illustration, Royal College of Art (1978-85), Visiting Professor (1988-), Appointed Children`s Laureate (1999); *b* Sidcup, Kent, 16 Dec., 1932. *Educ:*

Downing College, Cambridge. *Studied:* part-time, Chelsea School of Art. *Exhib:* one-man shows, Workshop Gallery, Illustrators A.G.; retrospective of illustration work, National Theatre (1983); Chris Beetles' Gallery (1994, 1996). *Commissions:* All Join In (Maschler Prize 1991); Clown (Bologna Ragazzi Prize 1996). *Publications:* illustrated over two hundred children's books, also books for adults; Mr. Magnolia (Kate Greenaway medal 1981). *Signs work:* "Quentin Blake." *Address:* 30 Bramham Gdns., London SW5 0HF.

BLAKER, Michael, Senior Fellow, Royal Soc. Painter-Printmakers; *b* Hove, 19 Jan., 1928. *m* Catriona McTurk. *Studied:* Brighton College of Art. *Exhib:* R.A., R.E., R.W.A., R.P., etc., and galleries U.K., U.S.A., Japan, widely. *Work in collections:* Tate Gallery, V. & A., Ashmolean, etc. *Publications:* The Autobiography of a Painter-Etcher (1986); M.B. Etchings (1985); M.B. Paintings (1986); A Beginner's Guide to Oil Painting (1994). Editor, Printmaker's Journal (1983-93). Contributor to Printmaking Today. Published (own Prospect Lodge Press): novels: Out of Place Angel; An Architect Unleashed; Artists at Large (1999) etc. *Signs work:* see appendix. *Address:* 122 Grange Rd., Ramsgate, Kent CT11 9PT.

BLANDINO, Betty, Dip. A.E. (London); potter in clay (stoneware/porcelain); *b* London, 12 Sept., 1927. *m* Dr. G.O. Jones, C.B.E. *Studied:* Goldsmiths' College, London (painting/pottery). *Exhib:* Over 20 solo pottery exhbns. since 1973 and many group exhbns. *Work in collections:* Fitzwilliam Museum, Cambridge; Welsh Arts Council; National Museum of Wales; Bristol Museum and A.G.; many city and county museums in U.K. and Europe. *Publications:* Coiled Pottery - Traditional and Contemporary Ways (Black/Chilton 1984); Revised edn. (1997). The Figure in Fired Clay (A. & C. Black 2001). On Crafts Council Selected Index; President, Oxfordshire Craft Guild (1989-93); exhibiting member, Contemporary Applied Arts, London. *Signs work:* Two B's impressed back to back - see appendix. *Address:* 12 Squitchey Lane, Summertown, Oxford OX2 7LB.

BLASZKOWSKI, Martin, Bronze Medal, Brussels (1958), Grand Prize, Buenos Aires (1960), First Prize, Competition: "Homage to Peace" of the City of Buenos Aires (1986); painter in oil, sculptor in wood; lecturer at Tulane University, New Orleans, U.S.A. (1976); *b* Berlin, 1920 (Argentine citizenship since 1958). *Exhib:* Brussels, Biennale Venecia, Argentine, Chile, Tate Gallery, London, Bienale de São Paulo, Brazil. *Publications:* Leonardo, 2.223 (1969) Oxford, Sculpture International 2.26 (1968) Oxford, Sculpture International 3.28 (1970) London, Sculpture of this Century, Editions du Griffon, Neuchatel, Switzerland (1959), Dictionnaire de la Sculpture Moderne, Fernand Hazan, Paris (1970). *Signs work:* "BLASZKO." *Address:* Santa Fé 3786-11-A, Buenos Aires, Argentine.

BLIK, Maurice, A.T.C. (1968), P.P.R.B.S. (1997), F.R.S.A. (1999); sculptor in bronze; *b* Amsterdam, 21 Apr., 1939. one *s.* one *d. Educ:* Downer Grammar School. *Studied:* Hornsey College of Art (1956-60), University of London (1968-69). *Exhib:* Mall Galleries, Ben-Uri Gallery, Royal Academy, Art for Offices (London, U.K.), Cavalier Galleries (Conn., U.S.A.), Museum Masters (New York), Irving Gallery (Palm Beach, U.S.A.), Blains Fine Art (London). *Commissions:* East India Dock, London; J.P. Morgan, London; Donnington Valley, Newbury, U.K.; Middlesex University, London; Jersey Museum, Jersey, C.I.; Glako Smith Kline H.Q., London;

University Hospital, Nashville, Tenn. U.S.A. Work in private and public collections. *Clubs:* Chelsea Arts. *Signs work:* see appendix. *Address:* c/o Blains Fine Art, 23 Bruton St., Mayfair, London W1X 7DA.

BLISS, Ian Reynolds, N.D.D. (1954), A.T.D. (1955), R.I. (1992); artist in water-colour and wood engraving; social worker; *b* Derby, 2 Apr., 1930. *m* Jill Michelle Cheney. one *s.* three *d. Educ:* Repton. *Studied:* Leicester (1950-55). *Exhib:* R.A., R.I., Piccadilly Gallery, Nevill Gallery Canterbury, Alex Gerard Fine Arts, Fenny Lodge Gallery. *Signs work:* "IAN BLISS." *Address:* 10 Vicarage Lane, Wing, Leighton-Buzzard LU7 0NU.

BLOCH, Gunther, F.R.A.I.; 1st prize winner of first National Crafts Competition (1948); art master of L.C.C. schools since 1948; sculptor in wood, stone, clay and ivory; *b* Dt. Krone, Germany, 24 Aug., 1916. married. one *s. Educ:* German Colleges; Leeds College of Art (John Frank Kavanagh); Regent St. Polytechnic; and in Germany under Gerhard Priedigkeit. *Exhib:* Berkeley Galleries, Cooling Galleries, Ben Uri Galleries, Leeds Art Gallery, Britain Can Make It. *Work in collections:* Denmark, France, Australia, New Zealand. *Signs work:* "Gunther Bloch" or "G. Bloch." *Address:* 88 Camden Mews, London NW1 9BX.

BLOW, Sandra, R.A. (1971), Hon. F.R.C.A. (1983); painter in acrylic on canvas; *b* London. *Studied:* St. Martin's School of Art, R.A. Schools, London, and l'Academia di Belle Arti, Rome. *Exhib:* numerous including Gimpel Fils, London; John Moores, Liverpool; Tate Gallery, London and St, Ives; M.O.M.A. (Oxford); annually R.A. Summer Exhbn.; Hayward Gallery, London; R.G.I.F.A.; Royal College of Art, London; Ozten Zeki Gallery, London; also in Italy, U.S.A., Canada, Holland, Switzerland, Germany, etc. *Work in collections:* Tate Gallery, London; M.O.M.A. (N.Y.); V. & A.; A.C.G.B.; Fitzwilliam Museum, Cambridge; Chelsea and Westminster Hospital, etc. *Commissions:* B.A.A.: Glass screen for Heathrow Airport (1995). *Clubs:* Chelsea Arts. *Signs work:* "Blow." *Address:* c/o Royal Academy of Art, Piccadilly, London W1X 0DS.

BLOXHAM, Judith Ann, B.Ed.Hons. (1985); artist, specialist in painting detailed silks, mainly ties; *b* Workington, Cumbria, 28 Jan., 1961. *m* David Gerald Bloxham. one *s.* one *d. Educ:* Whitehaven Grammar School. *Studied:* Cumbria College of Art and Design, Carlisle, St. Martin's College, Lancaster. *Exhib:* R.S.M.A. 4th International Miniatures Exhbn., Toronto, Fitz Park Museum, Keswick, St. Martin's, Lancaster, Cumberland Pencil Museum, Keswick, Wild ties V. & A., Whale tail Nairobi. *Commissions:* Mural commissions in Carlisle City. Specialist tie commissions, including B.P. and Akito Racing. Work in private collections. *Signs work:* "J.A.B." or "J.A. Bloxham." *Address:* 3 Boston Ave., Carlisle, Cumbria CA2 4DR. *Email:* judybloxham@hotmail.com

BOCKING, Helen, Harrow Dip. in Illustration (1976); artist in water-colour of wildlife, country sports, animal and equestrian portraits; *b* Gillingham, 4 June, 1954. *Educ:* Fort Pitt School, Kent. *Studied:* Goldsmiths' College (1972), Harrow School of Art (1973-76, Sam Marshall, Brian Liddel). *Exhib:* S.WL.A., R.S.P.B., B.F.S.S., Game Conservancy; various one-man shows. *Work in collections:* S. London A.G., and many private collections. *Signs work:* "H. Bocking." *Address:* 30 Town Dam Lane, Donington, nr. Spalding, Lincs. PE11 4TP.

BODEN, Margaret, P.S., S.W.A., U.A., F.R.S.A.; portrait painter; *b* Ecclesmachen, Scotland. *m* Leonard Boden (decd.). one *d. Educ:* Dowanhill. *Studied:* School of Art, Glasgow; Heatherley School of Art, London. *Exhib:* R.P., R.O.I., Royal Inst. of Fine Arts, Glasgow; National Soc.; Summer Salon; Royal B'ham Soc. of Artists; City of Bradford A.G., etc. Honourable Mention, Paris Salon. *Work in collections:* Official Portraits include: Sir Lawrence Verney, Recorder of London. *Publications:* work repro.: The Times, The Artist, many magazines and periodicals, etc. *Signs work:* "MARGARET BODEN." *Address:* 36 Arden Rd., London N3 3AN.

BOLAN, Sean Edward, G.R.A.; artist in oil and water-colour of landscapes, architecture, historical transport and military subjects; *b* Rowlands Castle, Hants., 25 May, 1948. *m* Raina Marion. two *d. Educ:* Warblington Secondary Modern School, Havant, Hants. *Studied:* Portsmouth College of Art (1965-68). *Work in collections:* private, municipal, Science Museum, S. Kensington, Guards Museum and Sgt's. Mess Grenadier Guards. Plays cornet, leader 'The Charleston Chasers'. *Signs work:* "Sean Bolan." *Address:* Drive Cottage, Campden House Estate, Chipping, Campden, Glos. GL55 6UP.

BOLTON, Janet Mary, Dip.A.D. (1970), A.T.D., S.B.A. (1992), R.H.S. Gold medallist (1994); teacher, artist in pastel and pencil specializing in botanical subjects; art teacher, Kingsmead School, Hednesford, Staffs.; *b* 26 Sept., 1947. *Educ:* Gravesend Girls' Grammar School. *Studied:* Bath Academy of Art (1968-70), Bristol University (1972). *Exhib:* R.H.S., S.B.A., Oxford University and numerous shows in Midlands. *Work in collections:* Oxford University and private collections worldwide. *Publications:* 'Fruits' design for Aynsley china 'Grande Tasse' range (1993). *Signs work:* "Janet M. Bolton," "J.M. Bolton" or "J.M.B." *Address:* 7 Raven Cl., Hednesford, Staffs. WS12 5LS.

BOLTON, Richard Marston, artist in water-colour; *b* Aberdeen, 28 June, 1950. *m* Margaret. two *s. Studied:* Shrewsbury School of Art. *Exhib:* Linda Blackstone Gallery, Pinner; Firenze Gallery, Taiwan; L'Bidi Gallery, Cambs. *Work in collections:* St. Ives Museum. *Commissions:* Views of China and Tibet by Taiwanese Collector. *Publications:* written and illustrated: Weathered Textures in Water-colour, and Weathered Textures, Workshop (Watson & Guptil), Texture and Detail in Water-colour, and Creative Drawing and Sketching (Batsford), Creative Watercolour Techniques, (Search Press). *Signs work:* "R.M. Bolton." *Address:* Granville House, 27 London Rd., St. Ives, Huntingdon, Cambs. PE27 5ES. *Email:* richardmbolton@hotmail.com

BONADA, Cinzia, R.B.A.; painter in oil, pencil and pastel; *b* Jersey, C.I., 22 Apr., 1938. *m* Johnny Bonada. one *s.* two *d. Educ:* Jersey Ladies College, Bush-Davies, Royal Ballet School. *Studied:* Richmond Adult College (1975-79, Charles Fowler) and with Peter Garrard (1982-87). *Exhib:* R.A., R.B.A., R.P., N.E.A.C., etc. Founder member of Small Paintings Group. *Work in collections:* Drapers' Hall, A.W.G., Lampeter University, Japan, New Zealand, Europe, U.S.A., Egypt, Australia. *Commissions:* Trevor Eldrid Past Master/Drapers' Hall, Sir John Hill, F.R.S., Chev. Stephen Weiss, Prof. W. Winklestein, Peter Barker, M.B.E., Valerie Guy, B.E.M., Prof. D. Cohn-Sherbok. *Publications:* 'Portraits' by Thomas Coates. Awarded first prize for Artistic Excellence (1997/1998) by Kensington/Chelsea Arts Council. *Signs work:* "Cinzia." *Address:* 9 Alexandra Rd., Twickenham, Middx. TW1 2HE. *Website:* http://home.freeuk.net/cinziabonada

BOND, Jane, R.P., N.E.A.C., City & Guilds School of Art, (Roger de Grey, Dip. F.A. 1981), R.A. Schools (Peter Greenham, Post Grad Dip. F.A. 1984); artist in oil, charcoal and pencil of portraits, still lives, interiors. Formerly theatre, film and T.V. designer; *b* Zimbabwe, 1 Apr., 1939. *Educ:* Holy Trinity Convent, Bickley; Kinnaird Park School, Bromley, Kent. *Exhib:* R.A., N.E.A.C., Hayward Gall., National Theatre, Glyndebourne Opera House, etc. *Work in collections:* private: England, Europe and U.S.A. *Clubs:* Two Brydges. *Signs work:* see appendix. *Address:* 8 Ceylon Rd., London W14 0PY.

BOND, Marj, D.A. (Glas.), S.S.W.A. (1974), R.S.W. (1989), S.S.A. (1989); artist in oil, acrylic, etching; *b* Paisley, Scotland, 23 May, 1939. *m* James A. Gray, architect. one *s.* two *d. Educ:* Paisley Grammar School. *Studied:* Glasgow School of Art (David Donaldson, Mary Armour, Benno Schotz). *Exhib:* many one-man shows, R.S.A., S.S.A., R.S.W., Scottish Soc. of Woman Artists now Scottish Artist Artist Craftsmen, R.G.I. *Work in collections:* Arts in Fife, Edinburgh University, Dunfermline Building Soc., Perth A.G. *Commissions:* Paintings in Hospitals. *Publications:* Who's Who in Scotland. *Signs work:* "Marj." *Address:* Eden Cottage, Old Town, Gateside, Fife KY14 5SL.

BONE, Charles, P.P.R.I., A.R.C.A., Hon F.C.A. (Canada); F.B.I. Award for Design; painter and designer; former Governor, Federation of British Artists (Mall Galleries); Past President, Royal Institute of Painters in Water-colour; artist in water-colour, oil, variety of mediums including ceramic and murals; *b* Farnham, Surrey, 15 Sept., 1926. *m* Sheila Mitchell, F.R.B.S., A.R.C.A., sculptor. two *s. Studied:* Farnham School of Art; Royal College of Art. *Exhib:* 39 one-man, Spain, Holland, U.S.A., Britain. *Work in collections:* many mural paintings in public buildings and water-colours and oils in private collections. *Publications:* author, Charles Bone's Waverley; Foreword by H.R.H. Prince of Wales; author, The Authors Circle, Foreword by Sir John Gielgud; Cathedrals, forward by Archbishop of Canterbury. Awarded Hunting Group prize of £5000 for a British water-colour (1984). *Clubs:* Chelsea Arts. *Signs work:* "BONE." *Address:* Winters Farm, Puttenham, nr. Guildford, Surrey GU3 1AR.

BONE, Ronald, Dip.A.D. (1972), M.A.(R.C.A.) (1976); painter and designer in acrylic and water-colour; *b* Consett, Co. Durham, 22 June, 1950. married. one *s.* one *d. Educ:* Consett Grammar School. *Studied:* Bath Academy of Art (1968-72), R.C.A. (1973-76). *Exhib:* R.A., R.W.A., C.C.A. Galleries, Linfield Galleries, John Noott, Broadway, Llewellyn Alexander. *Work in collections:* U.K., Europe and America. *Publications:* work repro.: illustrations in various books from London publishing houses. Many T.V. programmes. *Signs work:* "BONE." *Address:* Manor Farm Cottage, Pump La., Bathford, Bath, Avon BA1 7RT.

BOOTH, Rosa-Maria, R.M.S., H.S.F., M.A.S.F., Dip. Fashion (1970); painter and miniaturist in oil, acrylic, water-colour; *b* Olot, Spain, 9 Nov., 1947. *m* Peter Booth. *Educ:* Sagrado Corazón de Maria, Olot; Inst. Marti, Barcelona. *Studied:* privately and in Paris under Madeleine Scali; L'Escola Olotina, Spain (Emilio Parejo,

J.M. Agusti); Thurrock Technical College (M. Martin). *Exhib:* R.A., R.M.S., Mall Galleries, Barbican, Westminster Gallery, Llewellyn Alexander, N. Ireland, Spain, France, Sweden, Canada, U.S.A. *Work in collections:* Work in private collections. *Publications:* 100 Years of Miniatures by S. Lucas. Awards: 18 including 1st place I.M.A.S. Florida (drawing and pastel 1982; abstract 1984, 1988), Best in Mixed Media-Allegheny I.A.E. W. Virginia (1985). *Clubs:* Founder mem. H.S., R.M.S., M.A.S.-F. *Signs work:* "ROSMAR." *Address:* 36 Windsor Ave., Grays, Essex RM16 2UB.

BORCHARDT, Karolina, M.F.P.S., A.P.A., Mem. International Professional Artist (UNESCO); *b* Minsk, Lit, 26 July, 1913. *m* Karol. one *d. Educ:* Krakow, Poland. *Studied:* University of Stephen Batory in London. Diploma di Merito at Universita Delle Arti, Italy. *Exhib:* one-man shows, English Painters Art Group, London, Gallerie Internationale, New York, Richmond Gallery and Barrett Gallery, London; group shows, Barbican A.G., Bloomsbury Galleries, Mall Gallery, Weighouse Gallery, London, Salon des Nations, Paris, London Cassel Gallery, Loggia Gallery, New Vision Gallery, Centaur Gallery, and POSK Gallery, Germany Gallery P.R.O. Stuttgart, and many others. *Work in collections:* U.S.A., Poland, England, Spain and France. *Publications:* Karolina Borchardt, Introduction by Pierre Rouve, V.P. of World Art Critics Assoc. Now a British subject and lives in London. First Polish woman air pilot. *Clubs:* F.P.S. *Signs work:* "K. Borchardt." *Address:* 4 Somerset House, Somerset Rd., Wimbledon, London SW19.

BORKOWSKI, Elizabeth Irena, Dip.A.D., Prix de Rome, Feodora Gleichen award (1971) Sculpture; sculptor/painter in clay, bronze, water-colour, charcoal, pencil, art teacher; *b* Redhill, 7 May, 1949. *Educ:* Ursuline High School, Brentwood. *Studied:* Camberwell School of Art and Crafts, British School at Rome (Brian Taylor, Paul de Moncheaux). *Exhib:* R.A. Summer Show (1973), Palazzo Barberini National Museum of Rome (1973), Chelsea School of Art Rome Scholars (1986), Chelsea Harbour (1993). Elected A.R.B.S. (1992). *Signs work:* "Lissa Borkowski." *Address:* 3 High Trees Rd., Reigate, Surrey RH2 7EH.

BORRIE: see HOPE HENDERSON, Eleanor.

BOSTOCK, James Edward, R.E. (1961), A.R.C.A. (Lond.) 1939; illustrator, wood engraver, painter; formerly Academic Development Officer, Bristol Polytechnic; *b* Hanley, Staffs, 11 June, 1917. married. three *s. Educ:* Borden Grammar School, Sittingbourne, Kent. *Studied:* Medway School of Art, Rochester (1933-36), Royal College of Art (1936-39). *Exhib:* R.A., R.B.A., N.E.A.C., Crafts Centre of Great Britain, V. & A. Museum, many provincial galleries, travelling exhbns. to Poland, Czechoslovakia, S. Africa, New Zealand and the Far East. *Work in collections:* V. & A. Museum, Ashmolean Museum, British Museum, Wakefield Collection, Hunt Botanical Library, Pittsburgh, U.S.A., Hereford Museum. *Publications:* Roman Lettering for Students (Studio), 1959; wood engravings for Poems of Edward Thomas published by Folio Soc. (1988); articles in The Studio, The Artist, Guardian, Staffordshire Sentinel, Times Ed. Supp. *Clubs:* mem. Soc. Wood Engravers, East Kent Art Society. *Address:* White Lodge, 80 Lindenthorpe Rd., Broadstairs, Kent CT10 1DB.

BOSZIN, Endre, founded, Taurus Artists (1961), London; painter in oil and water-colour, sculptor in bronze; President, Sculptors Society of Canada (1971-73), (1979-83); *b* Hungary, 1923. *m* Charlotte de Sarlay. one *s.* one *d. Studied:* Budapest, R.C.A. *Exhib:* London Group; Festival of Visual Art at Harrogate, Edinburgh Festival; Grabovsky, Crane Kalman, Chiltern, Woodstock; Piccadilly Galleries, London, Gallery Raymond Creuze, Paris; International Medal Exhbns.: Madrid, Cologne, Helsinki, Prague; Sculpture Biennale: Dante Centre, Ravenna; Palace of Art, Budapest. *Work in collections:* Budapest, National Museum of Hungarian Art, Ujpest, City Collection, B.M., Pennsylvania Univ. *Clubs:* Sculptors Soc. of Canada. *Address:* 39 Gilgorm Rd., Toronto, M5N 2M4, Canada.

BOTT, Dennis Adrian Roxby, Dip.A.D. (1972), Cert.Ed. (1973), A.R.W.S. (1981), R.W.S. (1983), A.W.G. (1989); painter in water-colour and oil; *b* Chingford, 29 Apr., 1948. *Educ:* Forest School, nr. Snaresbrook, London E17. *Studied:* Colchester School of Art (1967-69), Norwich School of Art (1969-72). *Exhib:* one-man shows, Ogle Gallery, Eastbourne, Gallery 33, Billingshurst, The Grange, Rottingdean, Ogle Gallery, Cheltenham, Bourne Gallery, Reigate, Worthing Museum and A.G., Canon Gallery, Chichester, Ebury Galleries. *Work in collections:* National Trust, Towner A.G., Eastbourne, Hove Museum, Brighton Museum. *Clubs:* Arts. *Signs work:* "Roxby Bott." *Address:* Maplewood, Cherry Tree Rd., Milford, Surrey GU8 5AX.

BOTTOMLEY, Eric, G.R.A. (1985); artist/illustrator in oil and gouache; *b* Oldham, 14 July, 1948. *m* Jeanette. *Educ:* N. Chadderton Secondary Modern. *Studied:* Oldham School of Art and Crafts. *Exhib:* Omell Gallery, Shell House Gallery, Ledbury. *Work in collections:* National Museum of Wales (Industrial and Maritime Museum). *Publications:* illustrated three books, Limited Edn. prints, calendars, greetings cards, magazines and posters. *Signs work:* "Eric Bottomley." *Address:* The Old Coach House, Much Marcle, Ledbury, Herefordshire HR8 2NL. *Website:* www.eb-prints.co.uk *Email:* eb-prints@lineone.net

BOULTON, Janet, painter, water-colour and paper relief, specialising in still life and landscape gardens; *b* Wiltshire, 14 Sept., 1936. *m* Keith Baines, poet and translator. one *d. Studied:* Swindon and Camberwell Schools of Art (1953-58). *Exhib:* widely in mixed shows including Belfast Arts Council Open, Chichester National, London Group, R.A. Summer Exhbns., The Cairn Gallery, etc.; one-person shows: Mercury Gallery, 26 Cork St. W1, (1988, 1991, 1994, 1997); Redfern Gallery (2001). *Work in collections:* Southern Arts, Radcliffe Infirmar, John Radcliffe Hospital, I.O.W. Area Health Authority, National Gallery, Ottawa. *Publications:* edited and transcribed, Paul Nash Letters to Mercia Oakley 1909-1918 (Fleece Press, 1991), Monograph, Mercury Graphics (1985-91), Homage to Andre Derain, collaboration with Ian Hamilton Finlay (Wild Hawthorn Press, 1998), Monograph, Two Gardens. Residencies: Lankmead Comprehensive, Abingdon (1980), Radcliffe Infirmary, Oxford (1986). *Address:* 64 Spring Rd., Abingdon OX14 1AN.

BOURDON SMITH, Diana, R.W.A. (1990); painter in oil; *b* 16 Dec., 1933. *m* Richard. four *d. Studied:* Kingston Art School. *Exhib:* R.A., N.E.A.C., R.W.A. *Work in collections:* Royal West of England Academy. *Signs work:* "D.M.B.S." *Address:* 19 Crescent La., Bath BA1 2PX.

BOURGUIGNON, Doris (née Blair), A.R.C.A.; painter in acrylic, oil, water-colour and gouache; *Studied:* College of Art, Belfast; R.C.A., London; Wallace Harrison, N.Y.; Fernand Leger, Paris; Andre Lhote, Paris. *Exhib:* one-man and group shows: Belfast, Galerie l'Angle Aigu, Brussels; Museum and A.G., Belfast. *Work in collections:* Museum and A.G., Belfast. *Publications:* illustrated Various Verses by John O'The North. *Signs work:* "Doris Bourguignon," "Doris V. Blair" on academic work. *Address:* 8a Gunter Grove, London SW10 0UJ.

BOURNE, D. Peter, D.A. (Glasgow), R.S.W. (1982); painter in oil, gouache, water-colour; *b* Madras, India, 1 Nov., 1931. *m* Marjorie. two *s.* two *d. Educ:* Glasgow. *Studied:* Glasgow School of Art (1950-54, David Donaldson). *Exhib:* R.S.A. Edinburgh, R.G.I. Glasgow, R.S.W. Edinburgh. *Work in collections:* City Art (Edinburgh), Pictures for Schools (Edinburgh), paintings in hospitals. *Publications:* Dictionary of Scottish Painters - Paul Harris and Julian Halsby (Cannongate Publishing). *Signs work:* "Bourne." *Address:* Tressour Wood, Weem, Aberfeldy, Perthshire PH15 2LD.

BOURNE, Jean Susan, B.A.Hons. (1971), Dip.Mus.Stud. (1972), A.M.A. (1974), F.M.A. (1992); Museum curator; Curator, Towneley Hall Art Gallery and Museum, Burnley; President, North West Federation of Museums and Art Galleries (1993-94); *b* Rochdale, 23 Feb., 1950. *Educ:* Queen Margaret's School, Escrick, Lancaster University, Manchester University. *Publications:* museum guides, exhbn. catalogues, articles on oak furniture. *Address:* 94 Higham Hall Rd., Higham, Lancs. BB12 9EY.

BOWEN, Denis, A.R.C.A. (1949), Mem. A.I.C.A.; painter; directed The New Vision Centre (1956-66); Premio Internationale Europa Arte (1964) Silver Star with Antonioni Pasolini; visiting Associate Prof., University of Victoria, B.C., Canada (1969-71); elected 1994 to The Royal Cambrian Academy; *b* Kimberley, 5 Apr., 1921. *Studied:* King James I Grammar School, Almondbury; Huddersfield School of Art (1938-40); Royal College of Art (1946-49). *Exhib:* First Retrospective Bede 1300 Festival, Bede Gallery, Jarrow (1973); '50 years on', Second Retrospective Exhbn., Huddersfield A.G. (1989) and Ljubljana Municipal A.G., Slovenia (1992); exhib. The Sixties Art Scene London, Barbican A.G. London, and internationally; lecture tour Australia (1993); Skopje City Gallery (1999); Belgrave Gallery, London (2001). *Publications:* illustrated, A Concise History of English Painting by William Gaunt (Thames & Hudson, 1964), Dream of Icarus by Kenneth Coutts-Smith (Hutchinson, 1969), Etching and Engraving by John Brunsdon (Batsford, 1969), Art since 1945 by Herbert Read, Les Peintres Célèbres III Angleterre et Irlande, Alan Bowness (Mazenod, Paris 1964), L'Art Abstrait, Maeght Vols. 3.4. Michel Seuphor/Michel Ragon; critical writings in Art International Lugano, Vie des Arts, Art and Artists, D'Ars Milano, Arts Canada Toronto, R.S.A. Journal and Arts Review, London. Founder mem., Celtic Vision, co-ordinating Ireland, Wales, Scotland, Cornwall, Brittany and Galicia. Mem., Celtic League. *Address:* 4a Seymour Pl., London W1H 7NA.

BOWER, Susan, B.Sc. (1973), M.Sc. (1974), P.G.C.E. (1976), R.O.I., R.B.A; naive painter in oil; *b* Tadcaster, Yorkshire, 20 Mar., 1953. *m* Stephen Bower. one *s.* three *d. Educ:* Nottingham, Sussex and Leeds Universities. *Exhib:* R.O.I., R.B.A., N.E.A.C., R.I., R.W.S., R.A. Summer exhibitions. *Signs work:* "BOWER." *Address:* Larchfield House, Church St., Barkston Ash, Tadcaster, N. Yorks. LS24 9PJ.

BOWEY, Olwyn, A.R.C.A., R.A.; painter in oil and gouache; *b* Stockton-on-Tees, Cleveland, 10 Feb. 1936. *Studied:* West Hartlepool School of Art, Royal College of Art. *Signs work:* "Olwyn Bowey". *Address:* 4 Peace Lane, Heyshott, Midhurst, Sussex GU29 0DF

BOWNESS, Sir Alan, C.B.E., M.A.; art historian; formerly Director, Henry Moore Foundation, Director of the Tate Gallery, and Professor of History of Art and Deputy Director, Courtauld Inst. of Art, University of London; *b* London, 11 Jan., 1928. *m* Sarah Hepworth Nicholson. one *s.* one *d. Educ:* University College School, Downing College, Cambridge, and Courtauld Inst. of Art. *Publications:* William Scott: Paintings (Lund Humphries, 1964); Modern Sculpture (Studio Vista, 1965); Henry Moore: Complete Sculpture 1949-1986 (Five vols. Lund Humphries, 1965-1988); Alan Davie (Lund Humphries, 1968); Gauguin (Phaidon, 1971); Complete Sculpture of Barbara Hepworth 1960-69 (Lund Humphries, 1971); Modern European Art (Thames & Hudson, 1972); Ivon Hitchens (Lund Humphries, 1973); The Conditions of Success (Thames & Hudson, 1989); Bernard Meadows (Lund Humphries, 1994). *Address:* 91 Castelnau, London SW13 9EL.

BOWYER, Francis David, B.A. Hons. (1974), R.W.S. (1991); artist in water-colour and oil; part time teacher; *b* London, 20 May, 1952. *m* Glynis Porter. one *s.* one *d. Educ:* St. Mark's School, London SW6. *Studied:* St. Martin's School of Art (1971-75, Ken Roberts, Ken Bale), Hammersmith School of Art (1976-77, Ruskin Spear). *Exhib:* R.A. Summer Exhbn., N.E.A.C., R.W.S. *Work in collections:* Bankside Gallery. *Signs work:* "Francis Bowyer." *Address:* 12 Gainsborough Rd., Chiswick, London W4 1NJ.

BOWYER, Jason Richard, M.A., N.E.A.C.; Greenshield Foundation (1983), Daler-Rowney award R.A. Summer Exhbn. (1986), William Townesend scholarship (1987); British Council visit, Bulgaria (1991); painter in oil and pastel, draughtsman; part-time lecturer, University of Westminster; Founder, New English School of Drawing (1993); *b* Chiswick, London, 4 Mar., 1957. *m* Claire Ireland/(Bowyer). one *s. Educ:* Chiswick School. *Studied:* Camberwell School of Art (1975-79), R.A. Schools (1979-82). *Exhib:* R.A. (1980-85, 1992-01); one-man show New Grafton (1991, 1995, 1997, 2001). *Work in collections:* AA Club, Dover St.; Arthur Andersen, Warburgh; Royal Tank Regiment. *Commissions:* Royal Tank Regiment; Emmanuel School. *Publications:* Starting Drawing (Bloomsbury Press, 1988). *Clubs:* Arts, Dover St. *Signs work:* "J.R. Bowyer." *Address:* 35 Clifden Rd., Brentford, Middx. TW8 0PB. *Second Address:* Studio No.7, Kew Bridge Steam Museum, Green Dragon Lane, Brentford, Middx. TW8 0EN.

BOWYER, William, R.A. (1981), R.W.S., N.E.A.C., R.P.; artist in oil paint, water-colour; Head of Fine Art, Maidstone College of Art (1970-81); Hon. sec. N.E.A.C.; *b* Leek, Staffs., 25 May, 1926. *m* Vera Mary. two *s.* one *d. Educ:* Burslem School of Art. *Studied:* R.C.A. (Carel Weight, Ruskin Spear). *Exhib:* R.A., N.E.A.C., R.W.S., many galleries London and provinces. *Work in collections:* R.A., R.W.S., N.P.G., Sheffield City A.G., City of Stoke-on-Trent, many provincial, and private collections home and abroad. *Clubs:* Arts, Dover St. Arts. *Signs work:* "William Bowyer." *Address:* 12 Cleveland Ave., Chiswick, London W4.

BOYD, G., A.T.D. (1951); Head of Painting, University of Hertfordshire (1976-

93); *b* Bristol, 1928. *m* Pauline Lilian. one *s.* one *d. Educ:* Watford Grammar School. *Studied:* Watford School of Art and London University. *Exhib:* include London Group, R.A., John Moores, Belfast 68, Triangle Artists, N.Y., London and Barcelona, Atlantic Fusion: Lisbon, Madrid, London Docklands; one-man shows: A.I.A. (1962, 1967), Molton Gallery (1963), Oxford Gallery (1969, 1971, 1982), University of Hertfordshire (1980, 1988, 1994-2001), Spacex 1983, Sandra Higgins Fine Arts (1991), Harriet Green (1997), deli Art, Smithfield (1999). *Work in collections:* Walker Gallery, Trinity College, Oxford, City of Barcelona, Azores, University of Hertfordshire. *Publications:* 'Disruptive Tendencies' recent paintings by Graham Boyd, University of Hertfordshire. *Signs work:* "Graham Boyd" or "G. BOYD." *Address:* Blackapple, 54 Scatterdells Lane, Chipperfield, Herts. WD4 9EX.

BOYD, John G., R.P., R.G.I.; painter; *b* Stonehaven, Kincardineshire, 7 Apr., 1940. two *s. Educ:* Mackie Academy, Stonehaven. *Studied:* Gray's School of Art, Aberdeen (1958-62) under R. H. Blyth; Hospitalfield College of Art (summer 1961) under James Cumming. *Exhib:* Everard Read Gallery, Johannesburg (1997), Contemporary Fine Art, Eton (1996), Portland Gallery, London, Bourne Fine Art (1995), Wm. Hardie, Glasgow (1994), Graeme Mundy Fine Art (1991), Open Eye Gallery (1989), Present Gallery, Lanark (1975), Armstrong Gallery, Glasgow (1970), New 57 Gallery, Edinburgh (1967), R.S.A., R.G.I., R.P. *Work in collections:* Jose Berardo Collection, Portugal; Paisley; Milngavie; People's Palace, Glagow. *Clubs:* Glasgow Art. *Signs work:* "Boyd." *Address:* 21 Orleans Ave., Glasgow G14 9LA.

BOYD-BRENT, James, A.R.E. (1988), B.A.(Hons.) (1988), M.F.A. Univ. of Minnesota (1994); artist/printmaker in etching, woodcut, water-colour; Asst. Professor, University of Minnesota, Minn. U.S.A.; *b* Solihull, England, 10 Aug., 1954. *m* Mary. one *s. Educ:* Selborne College. *Studied:* Anglia Polytechnic (1984, Walter Hoyle), Central/St. Martin's School of Art (1985-88, Norman Ackroyd, Bernard Cheese, David Gluck), University of Minnesota (1991-94, Malcolm Myers). *Exhib:* U.K. and U.S.A. *Work in collections:* work in public and private collections in U.K. and U.S.A. *Publications:* "Here by Design" (pictorial survey of design) published by Goldstein Museum of Design, U.S.A. *Clubs:* A.R.E., Mem. Southern Graphic Council, U.S.A. *Signs work:* "James Boyd-Brent." *Address:* 2231 Scudder St., St. Anthony Park, St. Paul, MN 55108. U.S.A. *Email:* jboydbre@umn.edu

BOYDEN, Ann (née Cowley), S.W.A.; portrait painter in oil, water-colour, pastel, teacher; art teacher for Adult Educ.; *b* London, 1 June, 1931. *m* to the late Alan Boyden. three *s. Educ:* Godolphin School, Salisbury. *Studied:* Southern College of Art, Bournemouth (1948-52). *Exhib:* S.W.A. Nottingham Castle Gallery, Dillington House; solo shows: Ancaster Gallery, British Council, Brussels. *Clubs:* Dillington Water-colour Soc., Artists 303 Group. *Signs work:* "Ann F. Boyden." *Address:* Russets, Lopen Rd., Hinton St. George, Som. TA17 8SF.

BOYDEN, John, B.A.(Lond.), Dip.A.G.M.S.(Manc.), A.M.A.; teacher at The Old Grammar School, Lewes (1991-2001); Curator, Hove Museum of Art, Sussex (1973-86); *b* Tunbridge Wells, 1942. *m* Christine Portsmouth. two *s. Studied:* Ruskin School of Drawing. *Exhib:* Society of Catholic Artists, (2001). *Publications:* illustrations for The Farthing Press, Museum catalogues. *Address:* 3 Rosslyn Rd., Shoreham-by-Sea, W. Sussex BN43 6WL.

BOYES, Judy Virginia, S.W.A. (1984), B.W.S. (1985); self taught landscape painter in water-colour; *b* Alton, Hants., 1 July, 1943. *m* John Boyes. two *d. Educ:* Eggars Grammar School, Alton. *Exhib:* R.I., Mall Galleries, S.W.A., Westminster Gallery; one-man shows: Liverpool University, Atkinson A.G., Southport, Guildford House A.G., Forest Gallery, Guildford. *Publications:* front cover of Artist Magazine, features and articles on water-colour technique in Artist. *Signs work:* "Judy Boyes." *Address:* Town Foot, Troutbeck, nr. Windermere, Cumbria LA23 1LB.

BOYT, Judy, M.A., F.R.B.S., S.E.A.; awarded R.B.S. medal for Rebellion (1993); British Sporting Art Trust and Sladmore Awards; sculptor in bronze, resins, silver; *b* 7 June, 1954. *Educ:* Oxford High School, West Oxon. Tech. College, Henry Box, Witney. *Studied:* Oxford, Wolverhampton and North Staffs. Universities. *Exhib:* U.K., U.S.A., Jersey, Switzerland, France. *Work in collections:* Japan; East India House, London; The National Racing Museum, Newmarket; Cheltenham Racecourse; Princeton University, U.S.A.; Wildenstein, Kenya; H.M. The Queen. *Commissions:* 'Rebellion' - Standard Life; Mitsubishi Motors Trophy, Badminton Horse Trials; Golden Miller, Cheltenham racecourse; 'Up to the Line' lifesize horse, Windsor; The Working Horse Monument – Liverpool. *Signs work:* "Judy Boyt." *Address:* Westwood, Easterton Sands, Devizes, Wilts. SN10 4PY.

BRADSHAW, Bronwen Jeanette, B.A.(Hons.) (1966), R.W.A. (1988); artist in etching, silkscreen, oil, tempera, musician; *b* London, 7 Sept., 1945. divorced. one *d. Educ:* Sutton High School G.P.D.S.T. *Studied:* University of London. *Exhib:* R.A., R.W.A., R.E., New Munich Gallery, many group shows in the South-West. *Work in collections:* R.W.A. *Clubs:* Sherborne Contemporary Art; Print Europe; Spike Island Printmakers; Royal West of England Academy. *Signs work:* "Bronwen Bradshaw," "Bradshaw" or "B.B." *Address:* The Dove, Butleigh, Glastonbury, Som. BA6 8TL.

BRADSHAW, Peter, freelance artist in oils and gouache; *b* London, 23 Oct., 1931. divorced. one *d. Educ:* Kingsthorpe Grove, Bective. *Studied:* Northampton School of Art (1945-47) under F. Courtney, E. Goodson. *Exhib:* United Artists, R.O.I., Northampton Town and County and local exhbns. *Work in collections:* various U.K., worldwide. *Commissions:* various private collections. *Publications:* Railway Art; work repro.: various Christmas and greetings cards. *Signs work:* "P. Bradshaw" (cat and robin featured in work). *Address:* 4 Bective Rd., Northampton NN2 7TD.

BRAMER, William, M.A., R.C.A. (1968), gold medal, R.C.A. (1968); printmaker, etcher; visiting lecturer, R.C.A., Kingston University, head of painting, University of Northumbria, fellow in creative arts, Trinity College, Cambridge (1970-1972); *b* Nottingham, 14 May, 1943. one *s. Educ:* Loughborough Grammar School. *Studied:* Nottingham College of Art (1960-1965), R.C.A. (1965-1968). *Exhib:* numerous exhibs. internationally, including galleries in Paris, Berne, Zurich, London, New York. *Work in collections:* Arts Council, Queen Elizabeth College, London University, Trinity College, Cambridge, Leicester Education Authority, R.C.A., I.B.M., and others. Studio and editions printed at Atelier Lacourière et Frèlaut, Paris; studio in St. Ives, Cornwall. *Signs work:* "William Bramer." *Address:* 11 Maryon Mews, Hampstead, London NW3 2PU.

BRAMLEY, Victor, painter in oil, watercolour and acrylic; *b* Sheffield, 16 Nov.,

1933. *m* Jacque Moran. *Educ:* Firth Park Grammar School, Sheffield. *Studied:* self taught. *Exhib:* London, Exeter, Cornwall, Cumbria. *Work in collections:* many private collections. *Clubs:* senior member of St. Ives Society of Artists. *Signs work:* "VICTOR BRAMLEY." *Address:* 13 St. Warren St., Penzance, Cornwall TR18 2DW.

BRAND, Margaret Mary Madeleine, A.I.M.B.I. (1968), M.M.A.A. (1969); medical artist, figurative and expressionist painter in oil, water-colour and mixed media; founder associate of I.M.B.I.; *b* London, 1938. *Educ:* Stella Maris Convent, Devon. *Studied:* Reigate and Redhill School of Art; Post-grad. diploma in medical illustration, Guy's Hospital Medical School (1961); Deputy Head of Dept. of Medical Illustration, Guy's Hospital (1963-69). *Exhib:* R.A., R.M.S., London and provincial societies and galleries. *Publications:* work repro.: illustrations in medical and scientific books and journals. *Signs work:* "M. Brand" or "M.B." *Address:* 'Whitecot', Doctors Lane, Chaldon, Surrey CR3 5AF.

BRAND, Paul Benedict, N.D.D., A.T.D., A.U.A.; artist in oil paint, acrylic, watercolour, mosaic, internet online axis; *b* Glasgow, 14 Oct., 1916. *m* Barbara Meriel Newman Brand. three *s.* two *d.* *Studied:* Sir John Cass, Heatherleys and Camberwell School of Art (1948-52). *Exhib:* one-man shows: Gallery Nees Morfes, Athens (1966), Gallery Sphinx, Amsterdam (1969), Gallery Siau, Amsterdam (1970), Portsmouth County Library, Haslemere Educ. Museum; N.E.A.C., F.B.A., R.O.I., R.B.A., U.A., Laing, National Trust, Whiteley's 'Guardian' show, 'Borderlands' Meudon-Paris Exchange show, etc. *Work in collections:* private: Greece, Holland, England, U.S.A. *Publications:* two/three guides (Skye, etc.). *Signs work:* "Paul Benedict", "Paul Benedict Brand" or "P.B.B." *Address:* Ladygate Bungalow, Ladygate Drive, Grayshott, Hindhead GU26 6DR.

BRANDEBOURG, Margaret, (previously listed as M. E. Winter); part-time teacher in adult educ. for I.L.E.A.; *b* Surbiton, Surrey, 28 Apr., 1926. *m* Deryck Winter. *Educ:* Tiffin Girls' School. *Studied:* Kingston Art School and R.A. Schools. Since 1976 has worked in textiles. *Exhib:* British Crafts Centre, Seven Dials Gallery, etc. *Commissions:* in Portsmouth Museum. *Publications:* book on Seminole Patchwork (Batsford, 1987). Lectures and demonstrates on this subject. *Clubs:* Quilter's Guild (founder mem.). *Address:* 3 Cedars Rd., Hampton Wick KT1 4BG.

BRANNAN, Noel Rowston, A.T.D. (1952); painter; *b* Tynemouth, 25 Dec., 1921. *m* Mavis Annie (née Leitch). one *s.* one *d.* *Educ:* Humberstone Foundation School, Clee, Lincs. *Studied:* School of Art, Lincoln (1947-51), College of Art, Leicester (1951-52). *Exhib:* one-man: Willoughby Gallery, Corby Glen, Lincs. (1985); R.A., R.B.A., New English, A.I.A., etc. *Work in collections:* Usher Gallery, Lincoln, Riversley A.G. Nuneaton. *Clubs:* Lincolnshire Artists' Soc. *Signs work:* "Noel Brannan." *Address:* Athelstan, Hinckley Rd., Burbage, Leics. LE10 2AG.

BRANSBURY, Allan Harry, F.R.B.S., F.C.I.P.D., N.D.D., A.T.C. (Lond.); artist, designer; *b* Jersey, 1942. married. two *s.* *Educ:* Victoria College, Jersey). *Studied:* West of England College of Art, Bristol, and the University of London Inst. of Educ., followed by study-travel in Canada and U.S.A. *Exhib:* various galleries including Royal Scottish Academy (1990 and 1992). *Commissions:* in Jersey and England. Artist in Residence, University of Sussex (1976). Principal of the London Borough of Bromley Centre for Arts and Crafts (1977-80). Resident in Scotland since 1980. *Signs work:* see appendix. *Address:* Burnside, Kilmuir, North Kessock, Inverness IV1 3ZG.

BRANSCOMBE, Dianne Lois, R.M.S. (1996), A.R.M.S. (1993), S.W.A. (1994), H.S. (1991); artist in water-colour and oil, teacher; *b* Norwich, 1 Oct., 1949. *m* Robert. two *d. Educ:* Norwich City College. *Studied:* Goldsmiths' College (1969-72). *Exhib:* R.M.S., S.W.A., H.S., R.A. Summer show, Mandell's Gallery Norwich, Llewellyn Alexander Gallery London, and many mixed shows. *Signs work:* "D.L. Branscombe." *Address:* Bangala, The Green, Surlingham, Norwich, Norfolk NR14 7AG.

BRASIER, Jenny, R.H.S. Gold medals: for pencil drawing (1982, 1989), for paintings in water-colour on vellum (1988, 1994); botanical artist and illustrator in water-colour on vellum, pencil; *b* Worcs., 9 Aug., 1936. two *s. Educ:* Sir James Smith's Grammar School, Camelford; University of Nottingham, School of Agriculture. *Exhib:* R.B.G. Kew, R.H.S., S.B.A., V. & A., Natural History Museum, Hunt Inst. Pittsburgh, Smithsonian Inst. Washington. *Work in collections:* V. & A., Natural History Museum, Nature in Art (Gloucester), Hunt Inst. for Botanical Documentation, Carnegie-Mellon University Pittsburgh. *Commissions:* numerous. *Publications:* illustrated: Hosta, the Flowering Foliage Plant, Diana Grenfell; The Cyclamen Soc. Journals; illustrations included in: The Art of Botanical Illustration, Blunt and Stearn; The R.H.S. Dictionary of Gardening; An Approach to Botanical Painting, Evans and Evans; Treasures of the Lindley Library, Brent Elliott; Picturing Plants, Gill Saunders (V. & A.). *Signs work:* see appendix. *Address:* Bridge Cottage, Camelford, Cornwall PL32 9LT.

BRASON, Paul, R.P. (1994); portrait painter in oil; *b* London, 17 June, 1952. *m* Judy. two *s.* one *d. Educ:* King James I Grammar School, I.O.W. *Studied:* Camberwell College of Art (1970-74). *Exhib:* N.P.G., R.P. *Work in collections:* N.P.G., Royal Collection Windsor Castle, Government Art Collection, Eton College, Trinity and Balliol Colleges, Oxford. *Clubs:* Arts. *Signs work:* "P.B." or "BRASON" and date. *Address:* The Old Inn, Market Pl., Marshfield, Wilts. SN14 8NP.

BRAZDA, Jan, abstract painter, sculptor, stained glass artist and stage designer; *b* Rome, Vatican, 1917. *Studied:* Academy of Fine Arts, Prague, Prix de Rome, 1st Prize Triennale Milan, Gran Premio, Biennale, Venice. *Exhib:* National Museum, Stockholm, Leonardo da Vinci (1982), Centre International du Vitrail Chartres (1995); retrospective: Prins Eugen Waldemarsudde, Stockholm (1981). *Work in collections:* National Museum, Moderna Museet, Prins Eugen Waldemarsudde Stockholm, Röhsska Konstslöjdmuseum, Gothenburg, Skissernas Museum Lund University. *Commissions:* designed Thermal Bath "Giardini Poseidon", Ischia, Bay of Naples; executed stained glass windows, mosaics and bronzes Växjö Cathedral, Sankt Andreas Malmö, and other churches; scenery: Covent Gdn. London, Lyric Opera Chicago, Bayerische Staatsoper Munich, Royal Opera Stockholm, Bolshoi Moscow. *Address:* Rindögatan 44, S115 58 Stockholm, Sweden.

BRAZIER, Connie, S.W.A. (1980); artist in water-colour, and engraved glass; Glass Engraving Tutor (retd.), Sutton College of Liberal Arts; *b* Croydon. *m* Desmond Brazier. two *s. Educ:* Stamford High School for Girls, Lincs. *Studied:*

Croydon School of Art (Reginald Marlow, Frederick Hinchliffe, Michael Cadman). *Exhib:* Europa Gallery, Sutton (1977, 1979, 1981, 1983, 1984), Whitehall, Cheam (1986), Fairfield Halls (shared) (1987), Civic Centre A.G., Tunbridge Wells (1987), Playhouse, Epsom (1991), R.I., R.M.S., S.B.A. *Clubs:* Lewes Art. *Signs work:* see appendix. *Address:* 27 Sadlers Way, Ringmer, Lewes, East Sussex BN8 5HG.

BREEDEN, Keith James, R.P. (1999); self taught painter and sculptor in oil, water-colour, pencil, wood and metal; *b* Cheshire, 25 Mar., 1956. *m* Helen. one *s.* two *d. Exhib:* M.O.M.A. Wales, Hamiltons London, Arts Connection, Llanfyllin, R.P. at Mall Galleries, B.P. Awards, N.P.G., London. *Work in collections:* private collections internationally, R.L.C. Bicester, Oundle School. *Commissions:* Maj. Gen. G.W. Field, C.B., O.B.E., Resident Governor H.M. Tower of London; Jack and Morley Richards, Ty Nant; Maj. G. Crook & Smuts; H. Lloyd, Q.C.; David McMurray. *Publications:* work repro.: record sleeves for Pink Floyd, Fine Young Cannibals, ABC, The Cult, Scritti Politti, etc. *Clubs:* R.P. *Address:* Fronheulog, Llanfihangel, Llanfyllin, Powys, Cymru SY22 5HZ.

BREEZE, George, M.A., F.R.S.A., F.M.A.; museum curator; Head of Art Gallery and Museum, Cheltenham Borough Council; *b* Wilmslow, Ches., 12 Mar., 1947. *m* Rachel M. Breeze. two *s. Educ:* University of Manchester (B.A.), Barber Inst. of Fine Arts, University of B'ham (M.A.). *Publications:* include: Edith Payne (1978); Joseph Southall (1980); Arthur and Georgie Gaskin (1981) (co-author); Margaret Gere (1984) (co-author). *Address:* c/o Cheltenham Art Gallery and Museum, Clarence St., Cheltenham, Glos. GL50 3JT. *Email:* ArtGallery@cheltenham.gov.uk

BRENNAND, Catherine, B.Ed. Art and Design, R.I.; artist in water-colour, water-colour with wax resist, line and wash; specialises in paintings of buildings and abstracts; *b* Woking, 11 Oct., 1961. *m* Mark Brennand. two *s. Educ:* Dover Grammar School. *Studied:* Bishop Otter College, Chichester (1980-83, Geoff Lowe, Malcolm Norman, Alan Saunders). *Exhib:* Linda Blackstone Gallery Pinner, Stafford A.G., David Curzon Gallery, Wimbledon Village, Shell House Gallery, Ledbury, Broad Street Gallery, Wolverhampton. *Commissions:* The Crown Estate; Goodyear Plc; Stafford C.C.; Tarmac Building Materials Ltd.; Eldridge Pope & Co. Ltd.; Ivory Gate Plc. *Signs work:* "Brennand." *Address:* The Coign Studio, 1 Newbridge Ave., Wolverhampton WV6 0LW.

BRENT, Isabelle, painter/illustrator in water-colour and gold leaf; painter of commissioned portraits of animals throughout the world; *b* Caversham, 17 Mar., 1961. *Studied:* Loughborough College of Art and Design; further studies in France and Italy; research studies in the Dept. of Decorative Arts, Leicester Museum. *Exhib:* R.A., London and provincial galleries. *Work in collections:* private throughout the world. *Publications:* illustrated: The Christmas Story, Cameo Cats, Just So Stories, Oscar Wilde Fairy Tales, Fairy Tales of Hans Andersen and Grimm, also Celtic Fairy Tales. *Signs work:* see appendix. *Address:* Quarr Hill Cottage, LulworthRd., Wool, Wareham, Dorset BH20 6BY.

BRETT, Simon, S.W.E., A.R.E. (1986); wood engraver; Chairman, S.W.E. (1986-92); *b* Windsor, 27 May, 1943. *m* Juliet Wood. one *d. Educ:* Ampleforth College. *Studied:* St. Martin's School of Art (1960-64, as a painter; learned engraving from Clifford Webb). *Exhib:* S.W.E., R.E., R.A., and occasional one-man shows.

Publications: for own Paulinus Press (Francis Williams Award 1982 for 'The Animals of Saint Gregory'); Readers Digest Bible (1990); 'Clarissa', 'Jane Eyre, 'Confessions of St. Augustine', 'Amelia', 'The Folio Golden Treasury' (picture ed.), 'Fifty Love Poems', 'Middlemarch', 'The Poetry of John Keats' (Folio Soc.); edited 'Engravers' (1987, 1992), 'An Engraver's Globe' (2001); 'Wood Engraving-How to do it' (1994). *Signs work:* "Simon Brett." *Address:* 12 Blowhorn St., Marlborough, Wilts. SN8 1BT.

BRETTINGHAM, Walter David, N.D.D. (1953), A.T.D. (1954); painter in oil; *b* London, 1924. *Educ:* Marley School and Royal Navy. *Studied:* Sir John Cass College, London (1948-51), St. Martin's School of Art (1951-53), Bournemouth College of Art (1953-54). *Exhib:* one-man shows, Berystede Hotel, Ascot (1972), 3 Households Gallery, Chalfont (1973), Upper St. Gallery, Richmond (1974), Century Gallery, Henley (1979), Guildford House, Guildford (1981), Holkham Gallery, Norfolk (1982), Bloomsbury Gallery, London (1984). *Work in collections:* Deanery, Westminster Abbey, London University Educ. Inst. *Publications:* colour supplements, 'Pictorial Education' (1963-69); 'De Brethenham and Brettingham' (1971), 'Godless Waters' novel (1996), 'To Live a Lie' novel (1999). *Signs work:* "Brettingham." *Address:* 25 Cabrera Ave., Virginia Water, Surrey GU25 4EZ.

BREWSTER, Martyn Robert, B.A. (1974), Post. Grad. Dip. in Printmaking (1975), A.T.C. (1978); Eastern Arts award (1977), British Council Award (1991); painter in oil and acrylic, drawings, printmaking; *b* Oxford, 24 Jan., 1952. *Educ:* Watford Boys' Grammar School. *Studied:* Herts. College of Art (1970-71), Brighton Polytechnic (1971-75), Brighton Art Teachers' Centre (1977-78). *Exhib:* one-man shows: Jill George Gallery London since 1988. *Work in collections:* Russell-Cotes A.G. and Museum, Dorset. Many public and private collections U.K. and abroad. *Publications:* Monograph on artist by Simon Olding (Scolar Press, 1997). *Signs work:* "Brewster" either on front or back of work with date. *Address:* 15 West Rd., Boscombe, Bournemouth, Dorset BH5 2AN.

BRIDGE, Muriel Elisabeth Emily (Mrs. Millie Taylor), N.D.D.; artist in mixed media, water-colour and oils; *b* Rome, 1934. *m* John R. Taylor. one *s*. two *d*. *Studied:* (graphic design) at St. Martin's School of Art. *Exhib:* regularly with S.W.A. Westminster; R.I. exhbn. at Mall Galleries; Whiteleys, Queensway; one-man shows: West Dean College, Brighton Museum, Portsmouth Museum, Bishops Palace Chichester, Centre of Arts Chichester. Paintings in private collections worldwide. *Commissions:* 8ft. mural for travel agents in Regents St.; Brochure cover for Chichester Festivities. *Publications:* Art in Nature. Winner of national art prize 1996. Head of Art Dept. at Grammar school for 17 yrs.; Art Lecturer, Chichester College. *Clubs:* Founder mem. New Park Artists; Ridley Soc. *Signs work:* "M. Bridge." *Address:* The Mews, 22 Victoria Rd., Chichester, W. Sussex PO19 4HY.

BRIDGEMAN, John, A.R.C.A. (1949), F.R.B.S. (1960); sculptor; *b* Felixstowe, Suffolk. *m* Irene Dancyger, journalist. one *s*. one *d*. *Studied:* Colchester School of Art; Royal College of Art. Exhibited widely. *Work in collections:* sculptures at St. Helen's, Birmingham, Queen Elizabeth Hospital, Dudley Road Hospital, Keighley, Coventry Cathedral; 8ft. bronze group, St. Bartholomew's, Barking Rd., London; Mother and Child (Relief), West Bromwich; public gardens, Coventry, private gardens, private collections; font, Hillmorton Church, Rugby etc. *Signs work:* see appendix. *Address:* 27 Hyde Pl., Leamington, Warwickshire CV32 5BT.

BRIDGES, Ann Elizabeth, B.A. (Hons.) Design (1st class Hons. 1999), R.Cam. A. (2000); monoprint (printmaker); artist in residence Chester Zoo (1999-2001); *b* London, 27 Apr., 1960. one *s.* two *d. Educ:* Thomas Peacocke Comprehensive, Rye. *Studied:* Yale College, Wrexham (1995-6), North Wales College of Art and Design (North East Wales Institute) (1996-1999). *Exhib:* London, Wales (National Eisteddfod), U.K. and U.S.A. *Work in collections:* private collections, Art for Health (Glan Clwyd cancer unit). *Commissions:* Chester Zoo. *Publications:* Debretts Guides to Etiquette (1999). *Clubs:* Arts Centre Group. *Signs work:* "AB" or "Ann Bridges." *Address:* Dol Rhedyn, Llanfair Rd., Ruthin, Denbighshire LL15 1DA. *Email:* ann@bridgeprint,fsnet.co.uk

BRIERTON, Irene Annette, S.W.A. (1988), H.S. (1997); painter of wildlife in water-colour; *b* Belper, 10 Dec., 1948. *m* Robert Brierton. one *s.* one *d. Educ:* Burnham Grammar School, Bucks. *Exhib:* R.I. (1985-88), S.WL.A. (1985), S.W.A., Llewellyn Alexander (Fine Paintings) Ltd., London, R.M.S. (1996-99). *Publications:* works repro.: paintings by W.W.F. as cards. *Signs work:* "Irene Brierton." *Address:* 17 St. Michael's Cl., Crich, Derbyshire DE4 5DN. *Email:* brierton@talk21.com

BRIFFETT, Susan Joyce, painter of landscapes in pastels and murals and scenery in acrylic; *b* London, 10 May, 1960. *m* Geoffrey Hewlett. two *s. Educ:* Kingsbury High School, London. *Exhib:* Stanmore Library, Harrow Art Centre and with U.A., Westminster Central Hall, London. *Commissions:* various, locally. Briffett is the painting name of Mrs Susan J. Hewlett. *Clubs:* United Society of Artists. *Signs work:* "S.J.BRIFFETT." *Address:* 39 Wemborough Rd., Stanmore, Middx. HA7 2EA.

BRIGHT, Madge, A.R.O.I. (1990); winner, R.O.I. award Cornellissen prize; self taught artist in oil and mixed media; *b* S. Africa, 15 Feb., 1939. *m* P.S. Johnson. three *s. Educ:* Chaplin Gwelo, Rhodesia. *Exhib:* R.O.I. Mall Galleries, S.B.A., Britain's Painters, Hertford-Century Gallery Henley-on-Thames, Iwano Gallery Osaka Japan, Noor Gallery Bahrein, Look Out Gallery Plettenberg Bay S. Africa, Llewellyn Alexander Fine Art. *Work in collections:* National Gallery Zimbabwe. *Clubs:* S.B.A., Hertford Art Soc., Five Women Artists Plus. *Signs work:* "Madge Bright." *Address:* 1 Great Ash, Lubbock Rd., Chislehurst, Kent BR7 5JZ.

BRIGSTOCK, Jane Lena, A.R.E., B.A. Hons. (Painting) (1979), M.A. (Printmaking) (1980), British Institution Fund Printmakers award (1981); guest artist, California College of Art and Crafts (1981-82); painter in pastel, water-colour, printmaker; lecturer, Nene College, Northampton; Maidstone School of Art; Chelsea School of Art; *b* 28 Mar., 1957. *m* Michael Addison. one *s.* two *d. Educ:* Wellingborough County High School for Girls. *Studied:* Maidstone School of Art, and Chelsea School of Art. *Exhib:* R.A., Cleveland Drawing Bienale, Royal Overseas League, Drew Gallery, Canterbury. *Work in collections:* Northampton C.C. Mem. Soc. of Painter-Printmakers. *Signs work:* "J.L. Brigstock." *Address:* 76 West Hill Rd., St. Leonards on Sea, E. Sussex TN38 0NE. *Email:* jane.brigstock@btinternet.com

BRINDLEY, Donald, A.R.C.A. Sculpture (1951), F.R.B.S. (1973); sculptor in clay, bronze, ceramics of portraiture, equestrian subjects; Consultant to Josiah Wedgwood & Sons, Royal Worcester Porcelain Co., and continental and American businessses; *b* Penkhull, Stoke-on-Trent, 22 Feb., 1928. one *s.* one *d. Educ:* Junior Art Dept. Burslem College of Art. *Studied:* R.C.A. (1948-51, Profs. Frank Dobson and John Skeaping, R.A.). *Work in collections:* H.M. The Queen, the late Lord Mountbatten. *Signs work:* "D. BRINDLEY" and see appendix. *Address:* Fernlea, Leek Rd., Stockton Brook, Staffordshire Moorlands ST9 9NH.

BRINDLEY, Robert Edward, R.S.M.A. (1997); painter in water-colour, oil, pastel; *b* Burton on Trent, Staffs. 11 Feb. 1949. *m* Elizabeth Brindley (née Brooke). one *s.* one *d. Exhib:* Mall Galleries (R.S.M.A. and R.O.I.); Ferens Hull; Carrisbrooke Gallery; Mercer Gallery, Harrogate; Houses of Parliament. *Work in collections:* Royal Inst. of Naval Architects. *Commissions:* paintings for "Allied Breweries U.K. Ltd." Burton on Trent. *Publications:* illustrations for "Minewinding and Transport" (1988). *Signs work:* "Robert Brindley." *Address:* Sundial Cottage, Sleights, Whitby, N. Yorks. YO22 5EQ. *Email:* brindley@sundialstudio.freeserve.co.uk

BRISCOE, Michael J., B.A. (Hons.), R.Cam.A.; artist in oil and acrylic on canvas; *b* Colwyn Bay, 11 May, 1960. three *s.* one *d.* two s- *d. Educ:* Eirias High School. *Studied:* Wrexham College of Art (1978-79, David Cooper), Sheffield City Polytechnic (1979-82, Brian Peacock, Terry Lee). *Exhib:* Sheffield National (1980), Stowells Trophy (prize winner), Wales '83 Travelling Exhbn., R.A. Summer Exhbn. (1983-85), Through Artists Eyes Mostyn A.G., Paris Salon des Nations (1984), Blackthorn Galleries, Birkenhead (1998), Quay Arts, Kingson upon Hull (1999); mixed shows, Piccadilly Gallery (1984-85). *Work in collections:* Welsh Contemporary Art Soc. Produces illustrations for advertising since 1988. Selling paintings in Holland, Germany in 1995. *Signs work:* "Mike Briscoe." *Address:* 81 Coed Coch Rd., Colwyn Bay, Clwyd LL29 9UW.

BROAD, Ronald Arthur, freelance artist in oil and water-colour specialising in winter landscape and line drawing; *b* Crookham, Berks., 2 Sept., 1930. *Educ:* Newbury Grammar School, St. Aidan's College (C. of E.), Birkenhead. *Studied:* tutored by George Bissill. *Exhib:* regularly at R.A. *Clubs:* Hockley Golf. *Signs work:* "Ronald A. Broad." *Address:* Belmont, Orchard Rd., S. Wonston, Winchester, Hants. SO21 3EX.

BROBBEL, John Christopher, R.B.A., W.C.S.I., P.G.C.E., R.A.S. (Cert.); awards, R.A.S. silver medal for fig. drawing, David Murray studentship (1975-1976), British Inst. Fund award, Richard Jack prize, Landseer Scholar (1976-1977), Vincent Harris mural design prize, Painter Stainers bursary, Spirit of London prizewinner, R.U.A.William Connor award; painter in oil; teacher and author; *b* Hartlepool, 16 Dec., 1950. *m* Rosemary Stapleton. *Studied:* Byam Shaw School of Art, under Peter Garrard P.P.R.B.A., R.A. Schools, under Peter Greenham R.A. *Exhib:* R.A., R.H.A., R.U.A., R.B.A., N.E.A.C., Cleveland International Drawing Biennial; solo exhibs.: Kilcock Gallery, Kildare, Jorgensen Fine Art, Dublin, Grant Fine Art, N. Ireland. *Work in collections:* Sir Brinsley Ford, O.P.W., Dublin, Masonic Museum, Dublin, Trinity College, Dublin, St. James's Hospital, Dublin. *Commissions:* Masonic Museum, Dublin, Trinity College, Dublin. *Publications:*

'Drawing With Ink', and 'Pencil Drawing', F Warne, London (1981); articles, reviews for Artist magazine. *Clubs:* United Arts, Dublin, Friends of National Gallery, Ireland. *Signs work:* "John C. Brobbel." *Address:* 14 Lansdowne Park, Ballsbridge, Dublin 4, Eire.

BROCKWAY, Michael Gordon, N.E.A.C.; artist in oil and water-colour; *b* 11 Apr., 1919. *m* Margaret. two *s. Educ:* Stowe and Peterhouse, Cambridge. *Studied:* Farnham School of Art (1946-50), Cheltenham School of Art (1950), and Ruskin School of Drawing, Oxford (1951-54). *Exhib:* R.A., R.I., R.B.A., N.E.A.C. *Publications:* Charles Knight, R.W.S., R.O.I., 1952. *Signs work:* "MICHAEL BROCKWAY." *Address:* 1 Swan Lane Cl., Burford OX18 4SP.

BRODERICK, Laurence John, A.R.B.S., F.R.S.A., N.D.D.; sculptor in figurative art - bronze and stone, well known for otter carvings and portrait heads; *b* Bristol, 18 June, 1935. *m* Ingrid. three *s. Educ:* St. Nichol's, Clifton, Bristol; Bembridge School, I.O.W. *Studied:* Regent St. Polytechnic (1952-57), Hammersmith School of Art (1964-65). *Exhib:* Century Galleries, Henley-on-Thames; Park St. Gallery, Bristol; Belgrave Gallery, London; Gallery 1667, Halifax, Canada; City of London Festival; Rue Paradis, Monte Carlo, Monaco; Manor Gallery, Royston; Printmakers Gallery, Inverness; Malcolm Innes Gallery, Edinburgh; Phoenix Gallery, Lavenham; Chester Arts Festival; Warrington Museum A.G.; since 1980 annual sculpture exhbn. Isle of Skye; mixed shows: Keats House, Hampstead; C.P.S., London; R.W.A., Bristol; R.A., London; R.B.A., London; Art London '91; Broxbourne Festival. *Work in collections:* Crucifix, Christchurch, Hants.; Madonna of the Magnificat, Priory, Dunstable, Beds.; Elation, Mother and Child, The Otter, Cherrybank Gdns., Perth (Bell's); Teko - The Swimming Otter, The Otter Trust, Earsham, Suffolk; Leaping Salmon, Chester Business Park; Head of Philippe Chatrier (Pres. ITF), Queen's Club, London and Roland Gaross, Paris; Turtle, Prudential, London; Mother and Child, Leicester Royal Infirmary; Family of Otters, Powergen, Coventry; Trophies, International Tennis Federation. *Publications:* Life of Purcell (Chatto & Windus), Uncle Matts Mountain (Macmillan), Village life through the Ages (Evans), Soapstone Carving (Alec Tiranti). *Signs work:* "Laurence Broderick." *Address:* Thane Studios, 10 Vicarage Rd., Waresley, Sandy SG19 3DA. *Website:* www.laurencebroderick.co.uk *Email:* info@laurencebroderick.co.uk

BROGAN, Honor, B.A. (English and French), Dip.Ed. (1967 and 1968, Cardiff); artist in charcoal, oil, water-colour, clay; *b* Welshpool, 26 Jan. 1946. *m* Diarmuid Brogan (decd.). one *s. Educ:* Welshpool High School. *Studied:* Morley College (Peter Richmond and Alan Thornhill). *Exhib:* Artist in Residence, Lichfield Festival (1996); Celtic/Uzbek Exchange at Tashkent Artists Union (1995); R.A. Summer (1997); Belgravehall Painters at Pump House, Battersea Park; B.A.C.F.; Chelsea Arts Soc.; Sculpture for Rumania; G.L.C. Peace Exhbn.; Not the Royal Academy. *Work in collections:* Slaughter and May Collection. *Signs work:* "Honor Brogan," small works "H.B." *Address:* 12 Westover Rd., London SW18 2RG.

BRONDUM-NIELSEN, Birgitte, R.I., S.S.W.A.; Diplome d'Honneur, Vichy (1964); artist in water-colours; illustrator; *b* Copenhagen, 1917. *m* H. Brondum-Nielsen. *Educ:* Copenhagen. *Studied:* College of Arts and Crafts, Copenhagen. *Exhib:* group shows: R.A., R.S.A., S.S.A., R.S.W., Pitlochry Festival Theatre,

Charlottenborg (Copenhagen), Salon International de Vichy, Brighton Art Gallery, Royal Glasgow Institute of Fine Arts, English-Speaking Union Galleries (Edinburgh), The Danish Cultural Inst. (Edinburgh), The Mall Galleries, London; one-man shows: Bristol, Stirling, Edinburgh (seven), Roskilde (Denmark), Edinburgh Festival, Copenhagen. *Work in collections:* Glasgow Art Gallery, the private collection of H.R.H. The Duke of Edinburgh. *Publications:* illustrations for songbooks for children (Danish), De Smaa Synger, (Bestseller of Danish Childrens' songbooks, publ. 1948); Fairytales from many Lands; Switzerland, etc. *Signs work:* "BITTE B-N." *Address:* Tuborgvej 15 S. 3, 2900 Hellerup, Denmark.

BROOK, Peter, R.B.A.; painter in oil; *b* Holmfirth, Yorks., 6 Dec., 1927. *m* Margaret. two *d. Studied:* Goldsmiths' College, London University. *Exhib:* one-man shows: Agnews (7), Anna-Mei Chadwick (3), New Grafton (2). *Work in collections:* in many public and private collections in this country, Switzerland, U.S.A., South Africa and Australia. *Publications:* 'Peter Brook - The Pennine Landscape Painter', 'Peter Brook in the Pennines with Mary Sara', and 'Peter Brook in and out of the Pennines, Even'. Painted: West Riding; Pennine Landscapes; Oxford Almanak, Cornwall; Hannah Hauxwell (40 pictures); Scotland; Bowland; "About Peter Brook with Sir Tom Courtenay". *Signs work:* "PETER BROOK." *Address:* 119 Woodhouse La., Brighouse, W. Yorks. HD6 3TP.

BROOKE, Anne Isabella, A.T.D.; landscape painter in oil and former art teacher; *b* nr. Huddersfield, 1916. *Educ:* Downe House, Newbury. *Studied:* The Byam Shaw, Chelsea and Huddersfield Schools of Art and London University Institute of Educ. *Exhib:* R.A., R. Scottish A., N.E.A.C., Paris Salon, R.B.A., R. Cambrian A., R.O.I., W.I.A.C., R.I. Salon, United Artists, National Soc. and many provincial exhbns. *Work in collections:* Official purchases: Harrogate A.G., Wakefield A.G., Keighley A.G., The Beecroft A.G., Southend-on-Sea, the former Herts., Lincs., Bristol and Northumberland Educ. Coms. *Signs work:* "A. Brooke." *Address:* 3 Oak Terr., Harrogate HG2 0EN.

BROOKE, David, B.A.Hons. (1978), S.G.F.A. (1993), U.A. (1994), N.A.P.A. (1997); Society for Art of the Imagination (1998); artist in oil, acrylic, pen and ink; President Soc. of Graphic Fine Art; *b* Yeovil, 24 Nov., 1956. *Studied:* Yeovil School of Art (1972-75), Hull College of Art (1975-78). *Exhib:* R.O.I., U.A., S.G.F.A., R.W.A., N.A.P.A., plus twelve one-man shows and many mixed exhbns. in England. *Work in collections:* Longleat House, Wilts. Co-founder of the Mabon Fine Art Gallery, 27a Market Sq., Crewkerne, Som. TA18 7LL. *Clubs:* S.G.F.A., U.A., N.A.P.A., Society for Art of the Imagination. *Signs work:* "D. Brooke" or "David Brooke." *Address:* 18 Stiby Rd., Yeovil, Som. BA21 3EF.

BROOKE, Geoffrey Arthur George, D.S.C., R.N. (retd.); oil painter; *b* Bath, 25 Apr., 1920. *m* V.M. Brooke. three *d. Educ:* R.N. College, Dartmouth. *Studied:* under Miss Sonia Mervyn, 28 Roland Gdns., SW7 (1949-50). *Exhib:* Army Art Soc. exhbns. *Signs work:* "G.A.G.B." *Address:* Beech House, Balcombe, Sussex RH17 6PS.

BROOKES, Malcolm John, A.T.D. (1964), R.B.S.A. (1974), R.C.A (1995); teacher, painter in gouache, oil and pastel; *b* Birmingham, 11 July, 1943. *m* Norma Turner. one *s.* one *d. Educ:* Moseley School of Art. *Studied:* Birmingham College of Art and Crafts (1959-64, Gilbert Mason). *Exhib:* R.B.S.A., Worcester A.G.,

Lichfield, Malvern, Stoke-on-Trent A.G., Dudley A.G., Icon Gallery, Birmingham, Royal West of England Academy, Mall Galleries, Royal Cambrian Academy. *Clubs:* R.B.S.A., R.Cam.A., Malvern Festival Artists. *Signs work:* "M.J. Brookes." *Address:* 3 Clive Rd., Bromsgrove, Worcs. B60 2AY.

BROOKS, Brenda, self taught artist specialising in oil - beach scenes/seascapes; *b* London, 1932. *m* William. two *d. Educ:* Middleton College, Purley, Surrey. *Exhib:* Mall Galleries, various solo and mixed shows in London and South East. *Work in collections:* NatWest, Paintings in Hospitals. *Commissions:* Brighton Museum, C.D. covers for Voiceprint. *Signs work:* "B.B." *Address:* The Pointed Gable, 35 West Parade, Worthing, Sussex BN11 5EF.

BROTHERSTON, Daphne, F.S.B.A.; R.H.S. Grenfell silver gilt medal (1996); artist specializing in flower drawing with water-colour tint, and botanical painting; *b* 19 Apr., 1920. *m* Peter Brotherston, engineer. one *s.* one *d. Educ:* Sutton High School, G.P.D.S.T. *Studied:* Epsom A.E.C. *Exhib:* S.B.A. Westminster Hall, S.G.F.A. Knapp Gallery; three-man shows: Fairfield Halls, Hampton Court International Flower Show. *Publications:* work repro.: wedding cards/Christmas cards (C.C.A. Stationery Ltd.). *Clubs:* S.B.A. *Signs work:* "Daphne Brotherston." *Address:* 8 Bushby Ave., Rustington, W. Sussex BN16 2BZ.

BROWN, Bob, N.D.D. (1956), N.E.A.C. (1964); painter in oil; Assistant Keeper, N.E.A.C. (1990-); *b* London, 10 Feb., 1936. *m* Susan. two *s. Studied:* Croydon College of Art (Fred Dubury, Lionel Bulmer). *Exhib:* usual mixed and private. *Work in collections:* private/corporate. Full name is Robert Auger Brown but known as Bob Brown. *Signs work:* "Brown." *Address:* North Lodge, Hamstead Marshall, Newbury, Berks. RG20 0JD.

BROWN, Deborah, sculptor in glass fibre, papier mache and bronze; *b* Belfast, 1927. *Studied:* in Belfast, Dublin, Paris. *Exhib:* one-man shows and major group exhbns. in Ireland, Gt. Britain, France, Germany, Scandinavia, U.S.A. and Canada. *Work in collections:* in Ireland, Gt. Britain and U.S.A. *Commissions:* 1965, by Ferranti Ltd., panels for their building at Hollinwood, Manchester; 1989 and 1991, major commissions in bronze. Prizes: 1970 First Prize Carroll Open Award, Irish Exhibition of Living Art, Dublin; 1970 Prize Open Painting Arts Council of N. Ireland; 1980 Sculpture Prize Eva Limerick. Included in ROSC Dublin 1984. *Address:* 115 Marlborough Pk. Sth., Belfast BT9 6HW.

BROWN, Diana Elizabeth, S.W.L.A. (1967); painter in pen and ink, oil and watercolour; wildlife and animal artist and illustrator, specialises in deer and British wild mammals; *b* Cambridge, 16 Apr., 1929. *m* Ian Alcock. *Educ:* Perse, Cambridge. *Exhib:* S.W.L.A., P.S. *Work in collections:* private collections worldwide. *Publications:* Wildlife, deerstalking and scientific books, magazines and newspapers. *Clubs:* S.W.L.A., friend S.E.A., U.D.A.S., A.A.A. *Signs work:* "Diana E Brown" and monogram of "DEB." *Address:* Shannel, Ballogie, Aboyne Aberdeenshire AB34 5DR. *Email:* inverchat@btinternet.com

BROWN, Doris, S.W.A. (1987); freelance landscape artist in water-colour and ink, tutor and lecturer; *b* Newcastle under Lyme, Staffs., 17 Apr., 1933. *Educ:* Burslem College of Art, Stoke-on-Trent. *Studied:* Burslem and Stoke Schools of Art and privately under Reginald G. Haggar, R.I., F.R.C.A. *Exhib:* R.I., B.W.S., S.W.A., and numerous one-man shows. *Work in collections:* Hanley Museum, Stoke-on-Trent and Newcastle Fine A.G., University of Keele; paintings in private collections in England, America, Italy, S. Africa. *Clubs:* President and tutor to: Newcastle Watercolour Soc., Blythe Bridge Water-colour Soc., Oulton Water-colour Soc. *Signs work:* "Doris Brown S.W.A." *Address:* 86 Dunbrobin St., Longton, Stoke-on-Trent, Staffs. ST3 4LL.

BROWN, John Robert, F.R.B.S.; sculptor in bronze and stone; formerly Head of Art, Hampstead Garden Suburb Inst.; *b* London, 7 July, 1931. *m* Pauline Brown. one *s.* one *d. Educ:* Queen Elizabeth's, Barnet. *Studied:* Hornsey School of Art, Hampstead Garden Suburb Inst. (Howard Bate, R.A.). *Commissions:* 'Joy of the Family', Priors Court School, Thatcham (2000); BBC People's Award Trophy (2000); 'Tête à Tête', Harpenden Town Centre (2001); 2 sculptures for Jeffrey Kelson Centre, Central Middx. Hospital (2001). *Signs work:* "J.R. Brown." *Address:* The Bow House, 35 Wood St., Barnet EN5 4BE. *Website:* www.johnbrown-sculptor.co.uk *Email:* info@johnbrown-sculptor.co.uk

BROWN, Julian Seymour, A.T.D., N.D.D.; painter and graphic designer in water-colour, acrylic and oil; *b* Swansea, 3 July, 1934. *m* Gillian Thomas. two *s.* two *d. Educ:* Swansea Grammar School. *Studied:* Swansea College of Art (1950-55, Howard Martin), University College of Wales (1955-56). *Exhib:* one-man shows: W.W.A.A. Gallery, Henry Thomas Gallery, Trapp Art Centre (1989, 1990, 1991), The Session House Gallery (1991, 1992, 1993, 1994, 1995, 1996, 1997, 1998, 1999), The Abulafia Gallery (1998); work exhib. throughout the Principality. *Work in collections:* Dyfed C.C. *Signs work:* "Julian Brown." *Address:* Penyrallt, Alltycnap, Johnstown, Carmarthen, Carmarthenshire SA31 3QY.

BROWN, Lucy, M.A.(Hons.) Fine Art (1991); tutor; artist in mixed media installations and video; *b* Herts., 4 Aug., 1967. *Educ:* Haberdashers' Aske's School for Girls, Elstree. *Studied:* Edinburgh University and Edinburgh College of Art (1986-91). *Exhib:* S.S.A., group and solo shows in Scotland, U.K. and abroad. *Work in collections:* Edinburgh City Arts Centre, Glasgow Museums and Galleries. *Signs work:* "Lucy Brown" or not at all. *Address:* 48 Montrose Terr., Edinburgh EH7 5DL.

BROWN, Mary Rachel: see Marais.

BROWN, Neil Dallas, D.A. (Drawing and Painting, 1958); major prizewinner, Arts Council of N. Ireland Open Painting Exhibition (1970); painter in oil; lecturer in painting studios, Glasgow School of Art; *b* Elgin, 10 Aug., 1938. divorced. two *d. Educ:* Bell Baxter High School, Cupar, Fife. *Studied:* Dundee College of Art (1954-59, Alberto Morrocco), Royal Academy Schools (1960-61, Peter Greenham). *Exhib:* over 40 one-man shows (9 in London); work has become abstracted with a growing structuralist tendency. *Work in collections:* Scottish Arts Council, Dundee City Museum, Skopje Museum, Yugoslavia, Nottingham City Art Gallery, Scunthorpe Education Committee, Hertfordshire County Council, Schools Collection, Walker Art Gallery, Liverpool, Kingsway Technical College, Dundee. *Signs work:* see appendix. *Address:* 65 John St., Cellardyke, Anstruther, Fife KY10 3BA.

BROWN, Peter Edward Mackenzie, B.A. (Hons.) Fine Art (1990), P.G.C.E.

(F.E.) 1993, R.B.A., N.E.A.C., P.S., A.R.O.I.; Arts Club Award (Pastel Society, 2001), W. H. Patterson Memorial Award (Neal 2000), Llewelyn Alexander Award (Neal 1999), Winner, Bristol F.A. oil painting prize R.W.A. Open (1998), St. Cuthbert's Mill Award, R.B.A. Open (1997), P.S. non-members award (1996); artist in oil and charcoal; *b* Reading, 28 July, 1967. *m* Lisa Maria. two *s. Studied:* Bath C.H.E. (1986-87), Manchester Polytechnic (1987-90). *Exhib:* regularly with N.E.A.C. R.B.A., P.S. W.H. Patterson Fine Art Ltd. London, Victoria Art Gallery, Bath and Albany Gallery, Cardiff. *Work in collections:* National Library of Wales, Victoria A.G., Bath, Holburne Museum, Bath. *Clubs:* N.E.A.C., R.B.A., P.S., Associate R.O.I. *Signs work:* "Peter Brown" in handwriting. *Address:* 18 Tennyson Rd., Lower Weston, Bath BA1 3BG. *Email:* Peter@Peterbrownneac.com

BROWN, Philip, A.M.G.P., former V.P.S.I.A.C., former V.P.S.C.A.; painter, stained glass artist, author, publisher; *b* London, 4 Nov., 1925. *m* Gounil Hallin. five *d. Educ:* St. Paul's School, London. *Studied:* Slade School of Fine Art, Ateliers d'Art Sacré, Paris. *Exhib:* one-man shows: London, Brighton, Oxford, Paris, Carmargue, Madrid, Malaga, Alicante, Sweden, Japan. *Work in collections:* stained glass in St. John's Cathedral, Umtata, S.A., many churches in England. *Publications:* The Essentials of Drawing and Painting; Picture Making; A Painter in Spain; Never Mind Picasso, Create Your Own World; Pen Drawing and Art of Hatching; Life Through Eyes of the Masters; Time Travel at Ratton; Links with the Past (2000), A Strange Vehicle (2000), Conquest Country (2001), all Icon Press. *Signs work:* "Philip Brown." *Address:* 1 Huggetts La., Lower Willingdon, Eastbourne, E. Sussex BN22 0LZ.

BROWN, Ralph, R.A. (1972); sculptor in bronze and marble, draughtsman; *b* Leeds, 24 Apr., 1928. *m* Caroline Ann Clifton. two *s.* one *d. Educ:* Leeds Grammar School. *Studied:* Leeds College of Art, R.C.A. and in Paris, Italy and Greece. *Exhib:* frequent one man and group exhbns. in this country and abroad, since 1954. *Work in collections:* Tate Gallery, Rijksmuseum Kroller-Muller, Arts Council, Gallery of N.S.W., Sydney, Stuyvesant Foundation, S.A., Contemporary Art Soc., Leeds City A.G., and many other provincial and foreign museums. *Commissions:* Harlow New Town, Jersey Zoo. *Publications:* Motif 8, Ralph Brown, Sculpture and Drawings, Leeds City Art Galleries. *Signs work:* see appendix. *Address:* Southanger Farm, Chalford, Glos. GL6 8HP. *Website:* www.ralphbrown.co.uk

BROWN Robert Auger: see Bob Brown.

BROWN, Stephen Edward, R.B.A (1998); artist in oil; *b* Chard, 20 Dec., 1947. *m* Kathleen Irene. one *s.* one *d. Studied:* Somerset College of Art (1969-71), and privately with Patrick Larking, R.P., R.O.I. *Exhib:* R.W.A., R.B.A., R.O.I., R.A. Summer Exhbn., one exhbn.: Thompson's Gallery, Ainscough, Contemporary Art, Rowley Gallery Contemporary Art, all in London. *Signs work:* "S.B." *Address:* 7 Denbeigh Terrace, Sidmouth, Devon EX10 9AU.

BROWN, William McClure, artist in painting, printmaking and sculpture; *b* Sunnyside, Toronto, Canada, 11 Dec., 1953. *Exhib:* contact: Eastwest Gallery, 8 Blenheim Cr, London, U.K. www.david@ew-art demon.co.uk *Work in collections:* National Maritime Museum Greenwich, Plymouth City Museum, Peel Heritage Gallery Ontario, Newport, Gwent, City Museum, etc. *Publications:* written and illustrated: Contemporary Printmaking in Wales, Someone Stole a Bloater, Five Schools: Image and Word; The New Bestiary (Suel Publications, France); March in Welsh, Old Emulsion Customs (with Greenslade). *Clubs:* 56 Group, Welsh Group. *Signs work:* "Wm. Brown." *Address:* (studio) 31 Newcastle Hill, Bridgend, Mid Glamorgan CF31 4EY. *Email:* williammcclurebrown@hotmail.com

BROWNELL, Raymond, M.B.E. (1998), B.A. (1989), Dip. T.P.(1977), Dip. Arch. (1959); painter in acrylic - geometrical abstracts derived from mathematics; main career in architecture and project management, now painting full time; *b* Hobart, Tasmania, 27 Nov., 1934. *Educ:* Friends' School, Hobart, Tasmania. *Studied:* Hobart Technical College (1953-1959), Edinburgh College of Art (1974-1977), Open University (1984-1989). *Exhib:* various group exhibs. in London and South-East and in France and Australia (1996-2001); solo exhib.: Green Man Gallery, Eastbourne (2001). *Clubs:* associate, United Society of Artists. *Signs work:* "RB." *Address:* 32 St. Swithun's Terr., Lewes, E. Sussex BN7 1UJ.

BROWNING, Mary Helena, N.D.D. (1956), A.T.D. (1957), S.Eq.A. (1988); animal artist in pastel specializing in horses and dogs; *b* Watford, 15 Mar., 1935. *Educ:* East Haddon Hall School, Northants. *Studied:* Southampton College of Art (1953-56), Leicester College of Art (1956-57). *Exhib:* S.Eq.A. (annually since 1985); awarded President's Medal (1991). *Publications:* Coursing - The Pursuit of Game with Gazehounds (Standfast Press, 1976), Rebecca, the Lurcher. *Signs work:* "MARY BROWNING." *Address:* Parish House, Greatworth, Banbury, Oxon. OX17 2DX.

BROWSE, Lillian, C.B.E. (1998); founder partner of Roland, Browse & Delbanco, 19 Cork St. W1; editor and writer of books on art; Hon. Fellow, Courtauld Inst. of Art (1986); former ballet critic, Spectator; organized wartime loan exhbns. at National Gallery, London (1940-45); also exhbns. for C.E.M.A. and British Inst. of Adult Education; *m* S.H.Lines (decd.). *Educ:* Girl's High School (Barnato Park) Johannesburg, S.A. *Studied:* Ballet, Cechetti School Margaret Craske, London. *Publications:* Augustus John Drawings (Faber & Faber, 1941); Sickert (Faber & Faber, 1943); Degas Dancers (Faber & Faber 1949); general editor of Ariel Books on the Arts, published for the Shenval Press by Faber & Faber; William Nicholson (Rupert Hart-Davis, 1955); Sickert (Rupert Hart-Davis, May 1960); Forain - the Painter (Elek, 1978); 'Duchess of Cork Street - the Memoirs of an Art Dealer' (Giles de la Mare, 1999); contributed articles to Apollo and Burlington Magazines; Sunday Times, Country Life, etc. *Address:* 19 Cork St., London W1.

BRUCE, George J. D., elected R.P. (1959), Hon. Sec. (1970-84), Vice President (1985-90), President (1991-94); portrait painter and painter of landscapes, still life, flowers etc. in oil; *b* London, 28 Mar., 1930. *Educ:* Westminster. *Studied:* Byam Shaw School of Drawing and Painting (Brian D. L. Thomas, O.B.E., Patrick Phillips, R.P., Peter Greenham, R.A.). *Clubs:* Athenæum. *Signs work:* see appendix. *Address:* 6 Pembroke Walk, Kensington, London W8 6PQ.

BRUNSDON, John Reginald, A.R.C.A. (1958), R.E. (1995); full time artist in etching; *b* Cheltenham, 1933. *m* Ibby. one *s.* four s-*s.* one s- *d. Educ:* Cheltenham Grammar School. *Studied:* Cheltenham College of Art (1949-53, R.S.G. Dent, K. Oliver), R.C.A. (Julian Trevelyan, Alastair Grant, Edwin Ladell). *Exhib:* one-man shows, England, U.S.A., Canada, Australia, Sweden, Belgium. *Work in collections:* Arts Council, Tate Gallery, British Council, V. & A. *Publications:* Technique of Etching and Engraving (Batsford, 1964). *Signs work:* "John Brunsdon." *Address:* Old Fire Station, Church St., Stradbroke, nr. Eye, Suffolk IP21 5HG.

BRUNSKILL, Ann, Assoc. of Royal Society of Painter Etchers (1969); painter and printmaker; *b* London, 5 July, 1923. *m* John Brunskill. three *s.* one *d. Educ:* Langford Grove School. *Studied:* Central School of Arts and Crafts, Chelsea College of Art. *Work in collections:* V. & A., Bibliothèque Nationale, University College, Oxford, South London Collection of Original Prints, Lib. of Congress, Washington, U.S.A., J. Lessing Rosenwald Alverthorpe Coll., U.S.A., Universities of Princeton, Yale, U.S.A., National Library of Australia, Canberra. *Signs work:* "Ann Brunskill" and "AB" with date on paintings. *Address:* Star & Garter Cottage, Egerton, Ashford, Kent TN27 9BE.

BRUNWIN, David Martin, M.A., D.Phil.(Oxon); painter in water-colour and oil; *b* Banbury, Oxon., 27 Nov., 1939. *m* Margaret. one *s.* one *d. Educ:* Oxford University. *Exhib:* R.S.M.A., R.I. *Clubs:* Wapping Group of Artists. *Signs work:* "David Brunwin" or "DMB." *Address:* 10 Eskdale Lodge, Lexham Gardens, Amersham, Bucks HP6 5JJ. *Email:* david@brunwin.com

BRYANS, Jeremy William, artist in water-colour (landscapes); *b* Harrow, 7 Dec., 1929. *m* Rachel Jane. four *s. Exhib:* two independent exhbns., also with U.A. and other local artists. *Address:* 94 West Hill, Wembley Park, Middx. HA9 9RR.

BRYANT-DUNCAN, Enid Dena (née Bond), artist in oils, scraper-board, water-colour; retired gallery owner and restorer; *b* Gloucester, 19 Mar., 1930. three *s. Educ:* Red Maids' School, Westbury-on-Trym, Bristol. *Studied:* Royal West of England Academy of Art. *Exhib:* St. Albans Gallery (1975), St. Albans Museum (1970), Paris, Salon de Nations (Jan. 1983), R.H.S. International Exhbn. (Mall Galleries, 1984), St. Albans Gallery (1987), Paris (1987), Galerie Salammbo, Paris (1988), St. Albans Abbey (1991), Luton Hoo Station House (1996, 1998), Artists Corner, Chepstow (1999). *Work in collections:* St. Albans, South Africa, Canada, America. *Publications:* True Ghost Stories (Hamilton). TV appearances, radio, magazine articles. *Signs work:* "D.B.", "Dena" or a snail. *Address:* The Manse, The Village, Westbury-on-Severn, Glos. GL14 1PA.

BUCHANAN, Elspeth, D.A. (Edin.); painter in oil; mem. of Council of S.S.W.A. (1956-59), S.S.A.; *b* Bridge of Weir, 29 Nov., 1915. *Educ:* St. George's School for Girls, Murrayfield, Edinburgh. *Studied:* Edinburgh College of Art (1933-38) under Wellington. *Exhib:* R.A., R.Scot.A., S.S.A., S.S.W.A., G.I., N.E.A.C.; first one-man show, Great King St. Gallery; by invitation Alton Gallery, London SW13 (1990-95), R.S.A. Gallery. *Commissions:* War work from 1939: Cartographic draughtsman N.I.D (5) New College, Oxford. *Publications:* illustrated Land Air Ocean (Duckworth). *Clubs:* Soroptomist, Edinburgh. *Signs work:* "Elspeth Buchanan." *Address:* Viewpoint Residential Club, 7 Inverleith Terr., Edinburgh EH3.

BUCK, Jon, M.A., R.W.A., A.R.B.S.; sculptor in bronze; *b* Bristol, 8 Sept., 1951. *m* Jane Buck. two *d. Studied:* Trent Polytechnic (1976-79), Manchester Polytechnic (1979-80), Fellow at Cheltenham College of Art and Design (1980-81).

Commissions: 1995: John St., Porthcawl 'Street Beacon'; New Plaza, Harlesden 'On Our Heads'; 1996: British Consulate General, Hong Kong 'New Age'; 1997: Merthyr Tydfil Library, Merthyr Tydfil 'Common Knowledge'; 1998: Deal Pier, Deal, Kent 'Embracing the Sea'; 2000: 'In the Swim' West Quay shopping centre, Southampton; 2001: 'Family' Milton Keynes General Hospital, Milton Keynes. *Signs work:* see appendix. *Address:* Luther Cottage, 619 Wellsway, Bath BA2 2TY.

BUCKMASTER, Ann Devereaux, M.S.I.A. (1951-80); freelance artist in pen; *b* London, 27 Mar., 1924. *m* the late Anthony Gilbert. *Educ:* Bromley High School. *Studied:* Beckenham School of Art, Bromley College of Art. Illustration and fashion drawing for magazines and advertising. *Address:* Kimbell House, Charlbury, Oxon. OX7 3QD.

BUDD, Rachel, R.C.A., B.F.A. (Hons.), M.F.A. (Hons.); painter in oil on canvas; part-time lecturer, Cheltenham College of Art and Design, and Central St. Martin's School of Art; *b* Norwich, 6 Mar., 1960. *Studied:* University of Newcastle upon Tyne (1978-82, Prof. Rowntree), R.C.A. (1983-86, Peter de Francia). *Exhib:* one-man shows: Purdy Hicks (1991), '3 Ways' British Council travelling show, Hungary, Poland, Czechoslovakia (1990), Athena Art Awards (1987), London Group (1987), Lloyds Bldg. Art for the City (1987), R.A. Summer Exhbn. (1987), Contemporary Arts Soc. Market, Covent Gdn. (1987). *Work in collections:* County Nat.West. London, I.B.M., Contemporary Art Soc., Lloyds of London, Arthur Anderson Collection, I.C.I. *Signs work:* see appendix. *Address:* 67-71 Columbia Rd., London E2 7RG.

BUHLER, Michael Robert, A.R.C.A.; artist in oil and acrylic; *b* London, 13 June, 1940. one *s.* one *d. Educ:* Bryanston School. *Studied:* Royal College of Art (1960-63, Carel Weight, Roger de Grey, Ruskin Spear, Colin Hayes). *Exhib:* Galeria Boitata, Porto Alegre, Brazil, Museo do Estado da Bahia, Brazil, Eastern Arts Assoc., New Art Centre, R.A., England Gallery. *Work in collections:* Liverpool University, Carlisle City A.G., B.M., Arts Council, R.A., D.O.E. *Commissions:* Posters for British Museum (1979); U.F.O. illustrations, Mary Evans Picture Library. *Publications:* Tin Toys 1945-1975 (Bergstrom and Boyle). "Abductees" animated film (1994). *Clubs:* Chelsea Arts. *Signs work:* "Michael Buhler." *Address:* 6 Cavell St., London E1 2HP.

BULGIN, Sally, B.A.(Hons.), M.A., Ph.D. (History of Art); painter in acrylic; Editor, The Artist magazine; *b* Ashford, Kent, 8 Nov., 1957. *Educ:* Highworth School for Girls, Ashford. *Studied:* Reading University (1977-81, Martin Froy, Terry Frost), Courtauld Inst., London (1981-91). *Exhib:* R.A. Dip Galleries, N.A.P.A. Annual, Clare College, Cambridge. Work in private collections. *Publications:* author of Acrylics Masterclass (1994); Oils Masterclass (1996); Lucy Willis: Light in Watercolour (1997), (all Harper Collins); and Ken Howard: Inspired by Light (David & Charles, 1998). *Clubs:* Patron, National Assoc. of Painters in Acrylics; Hon. Vice-Pres., Royal Birmingham Soc. of Artists; Patron, Birmingham Pastel Society. *Signs work:* "Sally Bulgin." *Address:* 16 Blackwall Rd. North, Willesborough, Ashford, Kent TN24 0NU.

BULLIVANT, Tina, B.A.Hons.; artist in water-colour, mixed media, oil; *b* Brighton, 25 May, 1958. *m* Clive Bullivant. one *s. Educ:* Lourdes Convent. *Studied:*

Brighton University (1976-80, Luther Roberts, Robert Birch). *Exhib:* S.W.A Sussex Open, Guild of Sussex Artists Open Exhbn., many mixed exhbns. *Work in collections:* Crawley Arts Council. *Clubs:* Artists of the Weald. *Signs work:* "T. Bullivant, s.w.a." *Address:* 110 Streatfield Rd., Uckfield, E. Sussex TN22 2BQ.

BULLOCK, Hazel, M.F.P.S. (1970); painter in oil and acrylic; *Studied:* Sir John Cass School of Art (1962) under R. V. Pitchforth, Percy Horton, David Graham. *Exhib:* R.B.A., F.P.S., H.A.C., Browse and Darby, Whitechapel; one-man shows, Loggia Gallery (1973), Judd St. Gallery (1985), Phoenix Gallery, Highgate (1989), Phoenix Gallery, Lavenham (1989), dn Gallery New York (2000), Loggia Gallery, London (2001), mixed exhibitions. *Work in collections:* private collections in England and Spain. *Clubs:* Arts. *Signs work:* "H. Bullock." *Address:* 32 Devonshire Pl., London W1N 1PE.

BULLOCK, Jean, S.P.S. (1964); sculptor in clay cast in foundry bronze and poly-ester resins, occasionally wood and stone, printmaker; *b* Bristol, 27 Apr., 1923. *Educ:* Bishopshalt, Haberdasher Askes, George Watsons Ladies College, Edinburgh. *Studied:* Watford School of Art (Guido Belmonte), Camberwell School of Art (Dr. Karl Vogel). *Exhib:* R.A., S.P.S., Singapore Art Soc., Art Exhbns. Bureau Travelling Exhbns., Zillah Bell Gallery Thirsk, etc. *Work in collections:* M. of D., Central Institute, NW1, South Norwood School, Tulse Hill; stained glass window, St. Giles, Lockton. *Signs work:* "JEAN BULLOCK." *Address:* Fern Cottage, Lockton, Pickering, N.Yorks.

BUMPHREY, Nigel, schoolmaster, goldsmith, and furniture maker; Diocesan adviser to Diocese of Norwich for Church Plate; Freeman of the Worshipful Company of Goldsmiths & The City of London; Fellow of the Royal Society of Arts; *b* Norwich, 22 Feb., 1928. *m* Eileen. *Educ:* The City of Norwich School and Loughborough College (now Loughborough University). *Studied:* Central School of Arts and Crafts and Norwich Art School. *Exhib:* Norfolk Contemporary Crafts Soc., and others. Works mainly on commissions. *Work in collections:* Norwich City Collection. *Commissions:* Badges of office for various societies - British Association of Occupational Therapists, Travelling Club of Surgeons of Gt. Britain et al. *Clubs:* Royal Overseas League. *Signs work:* see appendix. *Address:* 28g Jessopp Rd., Norwich NR2 3QB.

BUNTING, John Joseph, F.R.B.S. (1972), A.R.C.A. (1954); Sir Otto Beit Bronze medal (1985); sculptor wood, stone, bronze; *b* Highgate, London, 3 Aug., 1927. two *s.* three *d. Educ:* Ampleforth College, Oriel College, Oxford. *Studied:* St. Martin's School of Art (1949-51); R.C.A. (1951-54). *Exhib:* One-man shows at Paris (1965), Billingham (1972). *Work in collections:* Churches: St. Michael and All Angels (Oxford), War Memorial Chapel (Hambledon), St. Aidan's Church (Oswaldkirk); schools: St. Wilfrid's (Featherstone), St. Thomas à Becket (Wakefield), St. Bernard's (Rotherham). *Publications:* Monthly Report (1958-60), illustrations to Partage de Midi Paul Claudel (1963), Stages of the Cross (1972), John Bunting, sculptor (Paris, 1966), Sculptor's Luck (1993), On Making Saints (1994), Stone Crosses (1995), Sculptors Log (1997). Scullion II (1998), Sculptors Story (1999), 'Sailing Bye' (2000). *Address:* Nunnington, York YO62 5UP.

BURBRIDGE, Claire-Chantal Emma, B.A. (Hons.) Fine Art and History of Art

(Oxon.), M.A. Printmaking; fine artist in sculpture, printmaking and painting; *b* London, 14 Dec., 1971. *m* Joby Talbot. *Studied:* Magdalen College, Oxford, Ruskin School of Fine Art (1990-93), Camberwell College (1993-95). *Exhib:* Coram Gallery London, Mall Galleries, Collyer Bristow, R.W.A., St. John's College Oxford, M.W. Contemporary Art, Hanging Space London, Attendi London, etc. *Work in collections:* Ashmolean Museum, Oxford, Herts. C.C. Art Collection. *Address:* 16 Denman Rd., Peckham, London SE15 5NP.

BURDEN, Daniel, A.R.C.A. (1955), R.W.A.; painter in oil, pastel, chalks, lino, collage, ceramic; *b* Paris, 20 Jan., 1928. *m* Sallie Turner. two *d. Educ:* Kilburn Grammar School, London. *Studied:* Willesden Art School (1949-52, Ivor Fox, James Neal, Francis Gower), R.C.A. (1952-55, John Minton, Rodrigo Moynihan, Ruskin Spear, Colin Hayes). *Exhib:* R.A., R.W.A., A.I.A., R.B.A., Drian Gallery, Mignon Gallery, David Durrant Gallery, London Group, N.E.A.C., Salon des Independants Bordeaux, various expos Aquitaine. *Work in collections:* Leicester University, Southend Museum, Walsall Educ. Development Centre, Avon Art and Design Loan Service, R.W.A. Collection. *Signs work:* "Burden." *Address:* Atelier Moulin A Vent, 47800 Moustier, France.

BURDETT-SOMERS, Wilhelmina Maria, A.R.M.S. (1983), H.S.F. (1983), M.A.S.-F. (1980), M.A.S.-N.J. (1985), M.A.S.-W. (1983), Mem. Min. Art of America (1990); Grumbacher Art award Gold Medal (1986); artist in miniature oil painting on copper, larger painting on canvas and board, founder mem. Hilliard Soc.; *b* The Hague, Netherlands, 23 July, 1923. *m* John Richard Burdett. *Educ:* Convent School, The Hague. *Studied:* Netherlands Royal Academie of Art. *Exhib:* all socs. annually to date, solo show: Queen's Gate, London (1981); R.A. Summer Show (1984). *Publications:* St. Pete, "Beach C/abber. U.S.A." (1997). *Signs work:* "W. Burdett-Somers, A.R.M.S., M.A.A." *Address:* 18 Hunter Pl., Louth, Lincs. LN11 9LG.

BURGESS, Peter, painter in oil and watercolour; *b* 1952. *m* Catherine. *Studied:* Wimbledon School of Art (1972-74), R.A. Schools (1974-77). *Exhib:* R.A., etc.; one-man shows: Thackeray Gallery, etc. *Work in collections:* Contemporary Art Soc., Derby City A.G., The Harborough Museum, Nottingham City Council, Leics. Educ. Authority, S. Derbyshire Health Authority, S. Nottingham College, Adam and Co., The Boots Co. plc.; many private collections in Britain, U.S.A. and Europe. *Signs work:* "Peter Burgess" on reverse of painting, "PB" on front. *Address:* 99 Ella Rd., Nottingham NG2 5GZ.

BURKE, Peter, sculptor using reclaimed materials; *b* London, 29 Feb., 1944. *m* Wendy. two *d. Educ:* Bristol Technical School and Rolls Royce Bristol. *Studied:* Bristol Polytechnic (1972). *Exhib:* one-man shows: Festival Gallery, and Cleveland Bridge Gallery Bath, New Art Centre London (1992), New Art Centre Rochecourt (1993); mixed shows: London, Chicago, New Mexico, Berlin, Basel, Miami, Madrid, Zurich. *Work in collections:* Contemporary Art Soc. *Commissions:* Installation: Hat Hill Sculpture Foundation, Goodwood. *Publications:* Internet entry for sculpture at Goodwood: www.sculpture.org.uk *Signs work:* "P. Burke," "PB." or not at all. *Address:* 9 Woolley Green, Bradford on Avon, Wilts. BA15 1TZ.

BURLEIGH, Veronica, Slade Scholarship (1927); portrait and landscape painter in oils and water-colour; *b* Hove, 17 Apr., 1909. *Educ:* Hoove Lea, Hove. *Studied:*

Brighton School of Art (1926-27), Scholarship to Slade School (1927-30). *Exhib:* 31 one-man shows in England, Rhodesia and Zambia. *Work in collections:* Worthing. *Clubs:* S.W.A., Sussex Water-colour Soc., Sussex Painters. *Signs work:* "Veronica Burleigh." *Address:* 2 Corner Cottages, Blackstone, Henfield, Sussex.

BURMAN, Chila Kumari, B.F.A.(Hons.) (1980), M.F.A. (1982); mixed media artist, printmaker, photographer; *b* Liverpool, 17 Jan., 1957. *Studied:* Southport College of Art, B.A. Leeds Polytechnic (1st Class Hons. in Printmaking and M.F.A.), and Slade School of Fine Art, University College of London. *Exhib:* Internationally and nationally - widely, e.g New York, Canada, Cuba, India, S.Africa, Europe. *Work in collections:* V. & A., Birmingham and Walsall Museums and A.G.'s, private and public collections. *Publications:* Own monograph 'Beyond two Cultures' by Lynda Nead (Kala Press); contributed to Framing Feminism, Visibly Female, Women and Self - Portraiture by Francis Barzello (Thames & Hudson). Currently represented by the Andrew Mummery Gallery, London. *Signs work:* "C.K. Burman." *Address:* 20 Woodview Cl., Hermitage Rd., London N4 1DG.

BURN, Hilary, B.Sc.Hons. (Zoology) (1967), S.WL.A. (1983); freelance wildlife artist/illustrator in gouache, specialising in birds; *b* Macclesfield, Ches., 8 Apr., 1946. *Educ:* Macclesfield High School, and University of Leeds. *Exhib:* S.WL.A. Annual, regularly with R.S.P.B., Wildfowl Trust, Wildlife A.G., Lavenham, Nature in Art, Glos. *Publications:* illustrated, R.S.P.B. Book of British Birds (1982); Wildfowl: An Identification Guide to the Ducks, Geese and Swans of the World (1987); Crows and Jays: An Identification Guide (1993); The Handbook of Bird Identification (1998); Handbook of the Birds of the World. *Clubs:* S.WL.A. *Signs work:* "Hilary Burn." *Address:* Huish Cleeve, Huish Champflower, Taunton, Som. TA4 2HA.

BURNS, William, R.I.B.A., F.S.A.I., F.R.S.A.; artist in oil; *b* Sheffield, 1923. *m* Betty. one *d. Studied:* Sheffield Art School and architecture at Sheffield University. *Exhib:* R.O.I.; Medici Galleries, Bond Street; John Campbell Galleries, Kensington; Walker Galleries, Harrogate; Hibbert Fine Art, Bakewell, Derbys. *Work in collections:* John Campbell Gallery London, Walker Galleries Harrogate, Yorks. *Signs work:* "William Burns." *Address:* 29 Newfield Cres., Dore, Sheffield S17 3DE.

BURNS McKEON, Katherine Balfour Kinnear, D.A.(Edin.) 1950; Hong Kong Urban Council painting prize (1979), 1st prize (Painting) R.S.A., W.R.N.S. Art Competition (1945); artist in oil on canvas, muralist in mosaic, fresco; *b* Edinburgh, 10 Oct., 1925. *m* Leonard J. McKeon. two *s.* one *d. Educ:* Trinity Academy, Edinburgh. *Studied:* Edinburgh College of Art (1946-50, William Gillies, Leonard Rosoman). *Exhib:* Arts Council, S.S.A., Edinburgh, East Africa, Aden, Fiji, Hong Kong, London, France, Australia. *Work in collections:* Museums: Imperial War London, Nairobi, Hong Kong, Macau, Grimaud. *Commissions:* High Court, Dar es Salaam; murals: City Bank, Fiji; Hong Kong Bank, Paris; mosaic: Queen Elizabeth Stadium, Hong Kong and Mosque Social Centre. *Publications:* Hong Kong Art 1970-80. Fus Art, France 1996. 1st Prize, St. Raphael International Exhbn. (1990) and Grimaud (1994). *Signs work:* "Kitty Burns." *Address:* Hameau de Sauve Clare, Flayosc 83780, France.

BURROUGH, Helen Mary (Mrs.), R.W.A.; artist in oil, water-colour, sepia and wash; *b* Ceylon, 17 Feb., 1917. *m* T. H. B. Burrough. two *s. Educ:* St. George's Ascot.

Studied: Miss McMuns Studio, Park Walk, Chelsea (1937), Prof. Otte Skölds' Ateljé, Stockholm (1938-39). *Work in collections:* R.W.A. Bristol. *Clubs:* Royal Commonwealth Society. *Signs work:* "Helen." *Address:* The Old House, Frenchay, nr. Bristol BS16 1ND.

BURROWS, Geoffrey Norman, painter in oil and water-colour; *b* St. Faiths, Norfolk, 16 May, 1934. *Educ:* The Paston Grammar School, N. Walsham, Norfolk. *Exhib:* R.A., R.W.A., R.B.A., R.O.I., R.M.S.A., N.E.A.C., R.I., Paris Salon, various mixed exhbns. at home and on the continent. *Work in collections:* Atkinson A.G., Southport, Norfolk C.C., Norwich Union Insurance Co. *Clubs:* Norfolk and Norwich Art Circle. *Signs work:* "Geoffrey Burrows." *Address:* 84 Crostwick La., Spixworth, Norwich NR10 3AF.

BURTON, Charles William, painter in oil and water media; *b* Treherbert, 17 Aug., 1929. *m* Rosemary (children from former marriage to Jean Francis). two *s.* *Studied:* Cardiff College of Art, Royal College of Art. *Exhib:* one-man shows: British Council Brussels, Welsh Arts Council, Cardiff, Brecknock Museum. *Work in collections:* B.B.C. Wales, Welsh Arts Council, Contemporary Arts Soc. of Wales, D.O.E., etc. *Publications:* A Taste of the Belgian Provinces. *Address:* 12 Plymouth Rd., Penarth CF64 3DH.

BURTON, Philip John Kennedy, B.Sc. (1958), Ph.D. (1967), S.W.L.A.; painter in acrylic; retired scientific civil servant, British Museum (Natural History); *b* London, 9 Jan., 1936. *m* Jennifer Mary. one *s.* one *d.* *Educ:* Finchley Catholic Grammar School, University College, London. *Exhib:* S.WL.A. *Publications:* Birds of the Western Palearctic, various field guides, Identification Guide to Raptors of the World. *Signs work:* "Philip Burton." *Address:* High Kelton, Doctors Commons Rd., Berkhamsted, Herts. HP4 3DW. *Email:* pjkburton@aol.com

BURTONSHAW, Keith, B.W.S., U.A., N.S.; artist, teacher and demonstrator in water-colour and oils; *b* Beckenham, 25 Sept., 1930. *Educ:* Beckenham and Penge County School. *Studied:* Beckenham School of Art. *Exhib:* R.I., R.S.M.A. *Work in collections:* over 5000 paintings sold in U.K. *Clubs:* London Sketch Club, Armed Forces Art Soc., Croydon Art Soc., Cantium Group of Artists, West Wickham Arts Assoc., Lewisham Soc. of Art. *Signs work:* "Keith Burtonshaw." *Address:* 150 Beckenham Rd., Beckenham, Kent BR3 4RJ.

BUSBY, George Cecil, M.C.S.D. (1970), R.B.S.A. (1971), F.R.S.A. (1970), G.R.A. (1987); painter and illustrator in water-colour, gouache, ink, acrylic; *b* Birmingham, 2 Feb., 1926. *m* Dora Snape. three *s.* one *d.* *Educ:* Montpelier College, Brighton. *Studied:* Birmingham College of Art (part time). *Exhib:* R.I., R.B.S.A., Kingsmead Gallery, Beckstone's Gallery, Cumbria, Tegfryn Gallery, Anglesey, and several Midland galleries. *Work in collections:* Warwick Castle, National Library of Wales; illustrations commissioned by: Courage Breweries, Abbey National Bldg. Soc., Amoco Oil Co., British Waterways, British Gas. *Publications:* work repro.: illustrator for Christmas cards, also included in books "To the Seaside" and "A Century of Railways.". *Signs work:* "George Busby." *Address:* 377 Lugtrout La., Solihull, W. Midlands B91 2TN.

BUSBY, John P., A.R.S.A., R.S.W., S.WL.A.; lecturer, Edinburgh College of Art

(1956-88); *b* Bradford, 2 Feb., 1928. *m* Joan. one *s.* two *d. Educ:* Ilkley Grammar School. *Studied:* Leeds Art College (1948-52), Edinburgh Art College (1952-54); Post Grad. (1954-55), major travel scholarship (1955-56). *Work in collections:* S.A.C., Flemmings Bank, Bradford, Glasgow and Wakefield A.G's., Yorks Arts Assoc.; many private collections including H.R.H. The Duke of Edinburgh. *Publications:* The Living Birds of Eric Ennion (Gollancz), Drawing Birds (R.S.P.B.), Birds in Mallorca (Helm), Nature Drawings (Arlequin), many illustrated books. *Signs work:* "John Busby." *Address:* Easter Haining, Ormiston Hall, E. Lothian EH35 5NJ.

BUSHE, Frederick, O.B.E. (1994); sculptor; *b* Coatbridge, Scotland, 1931. *Studied:* Glasgow School of Art (1949-53), University of Birmingham (1966-67). Elected R.S.A. (1986); Scottish Arts Council Awards (1971, 1973) and S.A.C. Major Bursary (1977-78). *Clubs:* Established Scottish Sculpture Workshop (1980) and Scottish Sculpture Open Exhbn. (1981). *Address:* Scottish Sculpture Workshop, 1 Main St., Lumsden, Aberdeenshire AB54 4JN.

BUSHELL, Dorothy, H.S., R.M.S., Mundy Sovereign award (1983), Hilliard Soc. awards for best portraits (1998, 1999); miniature portrait painter in water-colour; *b* Halifax, Yorks., 3 Feb., 1922. *m* Philip Bushell. two *s.* one *d. Studied:* Halifax School of Art. *Exhib:* R.A. (1974, 1983, 1984, 1989, 1990, 1991, 1997), Mall Galleries, Westminster Gallery, R.M.S. (1982-97). *Work in collections:* Comte et Comtesse de Martigny, Soc. of Apothecaries, London, The Royal Anglian Regiment. *Signs work:* "D. Bushell, 98" *Address:* 90 Fairdene Rd., Coulsdon, Surrey CR5 1RF.

BUSTIN, Jane, B.A. (Hons.) Fine Art; painter.; *b* Borehamwood, Herts., 11 May 1964. *m* David Gryn. one *s. Educ:* Nicholas Hawksmoor School, Herts. *Studied:* Hertfordshire College of Art, Portsmouth Polytechnic. *Exhib:* solo exhibs.: John Jarves Gallery (1995), Eagle Gallery (1998/2000); group exhibs. include British Abstract Painting (2000), Flowers East, Chora - touring exhib. (1999). *Work in collections:* Unilever, British Land, United Overseas, DLA Solicitors, KIAD Canterbury, V. & A. Museum, Goldman Sachs. *Commissions:* private commissions. *Publications:* "And a Year Ago, I Commemorated a Missed Encounter.", collaboration with writer Andrew Renton, pub. E.M. Arts; catalogues: Nameless Grace, Eagle Gallery; Chora, by Sue Hubbard and Simon Morley; British Abstract Painting, by Mathew Collins. *Signs work:* "Jane Bustin." *Address:* 6 Mackeson Rd., London NW3 2LT. *Email:* janebustin@hotmail.com

BUTCHER, Sue, U.E.I. Cert. A.D. (1979); artist in acrylic and plant fibres; *m* Edward Butcher. two *s. Educ:* Penarth Grammar School. *Studied:* Hereford College of Art (1977-80). *Exhib:* regular exhibitor R.A. and West of England, winner, Sainsbury's National Touring Exhib. (1982-83), Japan (1987, 1993), S.W.A. (1987), various mixed and one-man shows. *Work in collections:* Tayor Gallery, London, Hereford City A.G., Hereford Council Offices. *Publications:* poetry in various magazines. B.B.C. and I.T.V. television programmes (1990), radio broadcasts to U.S.A. and Canada. *Signs work:* "S. Butcher." *Address:* Litley Orchard, Gorsty La., Hereford HR1 1UN.

BUTLER, Anthony, R.C.A. (Cambrian, 1960), A.T.D. (1950); schoolmaster; artist in oil and gouache; head of art, Birkenhead School (retd.); *b* Liverpool, 1927.

m Jean. two *s.* one *d. Educ:* Liverpool Institute. *Studied:* Liverpool School of Art (1944-45, 1948-50) under Martin Bell, Alfred Wiffin, Alan Tankard. *Exhib:* R.A., New Burlington, Agnews, Northern Young Contemporaries. *Work in collections:* Walker Art Gallery, Liverpool; Whitworth Art Gallery, Manchester; Williamson Art Gallery, Birkenhead; and various county educational collections. *Commissions:* ceramic decoration commissioned by Dudley C.C. for new shopping precinct. *Signs work:* "BUTLER." *Address:* Otthon, Tan Yr Eglwys, Henllan, nr. Denbigh, Clwyd, Denbighshire LL16 5BD.

BUTLER, Auriol, F.R.S.A., Fellow, International Institute of Art, Associate, Société des Artistes Français; Gold and Silver medallist, Academia Internazionale, Rome; Life Fellow of the Royal Society of Arts; Gold medal and diploma from the Academia Italia (1981); artist in oil, pastel, water-colour; *b* Pitney, Somerset. *m* Richard Butler. one *s.* one *d. Studied:* Byam Shaw School, London, under Ernest Jackson, and at Slade School, pastel with Mlle. Landau in Paris. *Exhib:* Pastel Soc., London, R.B.A., S.W.A., London Group, Paris Salon, United Society, and in the U.S.A. *Publications:* work repro.: La Revue Moderne. Works include portraits of the Princess Royal, General Sir Michael Rose, etc. *Signs work:* "A. Butler." *Address:* Glebe Studio, Longham, Cornwood, Ivybridge, Devon PL21 9QZ.

BUTLER, James, R.A. (1972), R.W.A. (1980), F.R.B.S. (1981); sculptor in bronze and stone; *b* Deptford, 25 July, 1931. *m* Angela Berry. five *d. Educ:* Maidstone Grammar School. *Studied:* Maidstone School of Art (1948-50); St. Martin's School of Art (1950-52). *Commissions:* Major commissions: portrait statue of President Kenyatta of Kenya, Nairobi; monument to Freedom Fighters of Zambia, Lusaka, Zambia; sculpture of The Burton Cooper, Burton-upon-Trent; memorial statue of Richard III, Castle Gardens, Leicester; statue of Field Marshal Earl Alexander of Tunis, Wellington Barracks, London; Dolphin fountain, Dolphin Sq., London; statue of John Wilkes, New Fetter La., London; bronze sculpture of the Leicester Seamstress, Hotel St., Leicester; statue of Thomas Cook, London Rd. Leicester; memorial statue to Reg Harris, N.C.C. Manchester; statue of Billy Wright, Wolverhampton; statue, James Greathead, Cornhill, London; D-Day Memorial to Green Howards, Crépon, Normandy; statue of James Brindley, Coventry Canal Basin, Fleet Air Arm Memorial, Embankment, London, portrait statue Jack Walker, Blackburn Rovers F.C., bust of Robert Beldam, Corpus Christi College, Cambridge, Royal Seal of the Realm. *Clubs:* Arts. *Signs work:* surname and year. *Address:* Valley Farm, Radway, Warwicks. CV35 0UJ.

BUTLER, Richard Gerald Ernest, painter, graphic designer; *b* Essex, 31 Dec., 1921. *m* Mary Driscoll. three children. *Studied:* Salisbury School of Art. *Exhib:* R.A., Arts Council Touring Exhbns., etc., one-man shows: Walker Galleries. *Publications:* work repro.: book illustration (Macmillan Educ.), mural designs (Fitzroy Robinson & Partners). *Signs work:* "Richard Butler." *Address:* 32 Denne Rd., Horsham, Sussex.

BUTLER, Vincent, sculptor, figurative, bronzes; mem. Royal Scottish Academy, Royal Glasgow Inst.; *b* Manchester, 1933. *m* Camilla. two *s. Studied:* Academy of Fine Art, Milan. *Exhib:* numerous one-man shows in various parts of the country, *Work in collections:* private collections in Britain, U.S.A., Germany, Italy, Israel, etc.

Publications: Casting for Sculptors (A. & C. Black, 1997). *Clubs:* Scottish Arts. *Signs work:* see appendix. *Address:* 17 Dean Park Cres., Edinburgh EH4 1PH. *Email:* vincentbutler@msn.com

BUTT, Anna Theresa, (until 1985 Anna Adams); N.D.D. Painting (1945), N.D.D. Sculpture (1950); artist in water-colour, terracotta; *b* Richmond, Surrey, 9 Mar., 1926. *m* Norman Adams. two *s. Educ:* St. Michael's Modern School, Eastcote. *Studied:* Harrow School of Art (1939-46), Hornsey College of Art (1948-50). *Exhib:* widely in north of England as Anna Adams; R.A. Summer Show (1986-99). *Work in collections:* terracottas in Abbot Hall, Kendal, W. Yorks. Educ. Com., Moorside Mills Museum, Rochdale Museum. *Commissions:* Two angels for Habergham Parish Church, near Gawthorpe; Madonna, font panel and tabernacle panel for Our Lady of Lourdes, Milton Keynes (1975). *Publications:* several collections of poems under name of Adams; R. Wren's "Animal Forms" Batsford Book on Pottery (1977). *Signs work:* "Anna Butt" and see appendix. *Address:* Butts Hill, Horton in Ribblesdale, Settle, N. Yorks. BD24 0HD.

BUTT, Laurence Arnold, B.A. (Hons.) Fine Art (1998); artist in oil and charcoal; *b* London, 9 Sept., 1954. *m* Tatiana. two *s. Studied:* Surrey Inst. of Art and Design, Farnham. *Exhib:* Whiteley's London, R.A., Brighton, etc. *Commissions:* still life and portraits. *Signs work:* "Laurence A. Butt." *Address:* 12 Curzon House, Chichester Drive East, Saltdean, Brighton, E. Sussex BN2 8LU

BUTTERFIELD, Sarah Harriet Anne, B.Soc.Sci. Architecture Edin. (1975) 'Magna cum Laude', Cert. Fine Art Ruskin School of Fine Art, Oxford (1978), Distinction; qualified as architect 1983; self employed as artist since 1986; *b* London, 28 Aug., 1953. *Exhib:* Judd St. Gallery, London (1987), Agnew's Young Contemporaries (1988), Richmond Gallery, Cork St. (1990), Roy Miles Gallery (1991); one-man show: Cadogan Contemporary (1991, 1994, 1997), Discerning Eye (1997); dfn Gallery New York (2000); 27 Cork St., London (2001). *Work in collections:* British Airways: Terminal 4 Departure Lounge, Gatwick Airport; Jerry's Home Store, Chelsea, London; David Lloyd Slazenger Racquet Club; Trusthouse Forte Hotels in Yorkshire and Exeter; Wimbledon Lawn Tennis Museum; 'Davies', Gt. Newport St., London. Awards: Egerton Coghill Landscape prize (1977), Winsor and Newton award, Hunting Group Competition finalist, commendation Spectator Magazine Three Cities Competition, art reviewer, LBC Arts & Entertainment Sunday Program. *Clubs:* mem., Equity. *Address:* 21 Ashchurch Grove, London W12 9BT.

BUTTERWORTH, John Malcolm, M.A.(Ed.), F.R.S.A., N.D.D., A.T.D.; artist in oils, water-colour, etching, silkscreen and lithography, paper; Fine Art Degree Course Leader, Design Faculty, Southampton I.H.E. (retd. from post 1997); *b* Lancs., 16 July, 1945. *m* Lesley G. Arkless, B.A.Hons. two *s.* one *d. Educ:* Rochdale Technical School for Boys. *Studied:* Rochdale College of Art (1961-63), Newport College of Art (1965-66), Cardiff College of Art (1965-66), David Murray Scholarship (R.A.) 1965. *Exhib:* Wills Lane Gallery, St. Ives, University of Surrey, Southampton Civic A.G. (one-man shows), Pictures for Schools Exhbn., National Museum of Wales, Cardiff, Midsommergarten Gallery, Stockholm, Cleveland, Drawing Biennale, International Print Biennale, Monaco, "Outpost" Venice Biennale (1995). *Work in collections:* Bristol Educ. Authority, Kent Educ. Authority, Surrey

University, Hampshire C.C. *Signs work:* normal signature for prints, "J.M.B." monogram for paintings. *Address:* 2 Nuns Walk, Winchester, Hants. SO23 7EE.

BUXTON, Jennifer, H.R.M.S. (retd.), Hon. Sec. R.M.S. (1980-87), Hilliard Soc.; portrait, animal and landscape painter in water-colour, silverpoint, pastel, oil, gouache and acrylic; first winner of R.M.S. Gold Memorial Bowl Award for best miniature (1985); *b* Hornsey, 12 Apr., 1937. *m* Captain Vic (R.N.). two *s. Educ:* Northfield School, Watford. *Studied:* Frobisher School of Animal Painting (1948-53, Marguerite Frobisher), Byam Shaw School of Art (1954-57, Dunstan, Phillips, Mahoney). *Exhib:* Watford, Manchester, Bath, Wells, Paris Salon, Kendal, Ulverston, Ilkley, Toronto, annually R.M.S. London. *Signs work:* "jb" or "J. Buxton." *Address:* Windy Ash Barn, Ulverston, Cumbria LA12 7PB.

BUYERS, Donald Morison, D.A.(Aberdeen), R.S.W.; artist in oil and water-colour; lecturer retired; *b* Aberdeen, 1930. *m* Margaret. one *s.* one *d. Educ:* Aberdeen Grammar School. *Studied:* Gray's School of Art, Aberdeen, (1948-52). *Exhib:* Arts Council, Young Scottish Contemporaries, Contemporary Art in Scotland, Painting 70, Edinburgh Open 100, Glasgow Group, etc. *Work in collections:* Arts Council, I.B.M., Aberdeen A.G., Universities of Colorado, U.S.A., Boston, U.S.A. and Aberdeen, Dunbartonshire Educ. Trust, Schools Pictures Leeds and Midlothian, Robert Flemming, London, H.R.H. The Duke of Edinburgh, etc. *Signs work:* "Buyers." *Address:* 96 Gray St., Aberdeen AB10 6JU.

BYROM, Gillie Hoyte, R.M.S., H.S., B.S.O.E., M.Ed. (Exeter), B.Ed. (Cambridge); portrait miniaturist working in vitreous enamel on copper or gold; *b* Ceylon, 5 Nov., 1952. *m* Peter Byrom, O.B.E. *Educ:* Llotja School, Barcelona. *Exhib:* numerous. *Work in collections:* Wimbledon Lawn Tennis Museum, Diploma Collection of R.M.S. *Publications:* The Royal Miniature Society 100 Years; The Techniques of Painting Miniatures; Macmillan Dictionary of Art: Limoges. *Clubs:* Royal Society of Miniature Painters, Sculptors and Gravers, Hilliard Society, British Soc. of Enamellers, Devon Guild of Craftsmen. *Signs work:* see appendix *Address:* Barton House, Woodland, Ashburton, Devon TQ13 7LN. *Website:* www.enamelportraitminiatures.co.uk

C

CADENHEAD, William Collie Milne, D.A., cert.R.A.S., Bronze Medal R.A. Schools (1957), David Murray Landscape Scholarship (1957), elected prof. member S.S.A. (1969); painter in oil and pastels; lecturer in drawing and painting, Duncan of Jordanstone College of Art, Dundee; *b* Aberdeen, 8 Oct., 1934. *m* Violet. *Educ:* Aberdeen Grammar School; Forfar Academy. *Studied:* Dundee College of Art (1951-55); travelled Europe (1956); Hospitalfield Art College, Arbroath; R.A. Schools, London (1957-61). *Exhib:* R.S.A., S.S.A., R.S.W., Savage Gallery, Compass Gallery, Royal Overseas League, Edinburgh Festival (1968), etc., one-man shows, Woodstock Gallery (1980), The Scottish Gallery (1981, 1983), Retrospective,

Meffan Inst. (1992), Texas Touring Exhbn. (1996-97). *Work in collections:* H.M. Queen Elizabeth, The Queen Mother, Scottish Arts Council, (Stations of the Cross), St. Fergus, Forfar; Meffan Institute, Forfar; Steel Company of Wales, Dundee A.G., and private collections in U.K., Europe and U.S.A. *Signs work:* "Cadenhead." *Address:* The Rowans, Muir of Lownie, Forfar, Angus DD8 2LJ.

CADMAN, Michael Lawrence, R.I. (1970), A.R.C.A. (1944); painter in watercolour, acrylic, oil and pastel; Instructor Epsom School of Art (1947-68), Croydon College of Art (1947-53); B of E art-exams (1939-41); *b* Epsom, 1920. *m* decd. *Educ:* Glyn Grammar School, Epsom, Surrey. *Studied:* Wimbledon School of Art (1937-41), R.C.A. (1941-44, under Gilbert Spencer). *Exhib:* R.A., R.W.S., R.B.A., R.O.I., eight one-man shows. *Work in collections:* 2 large collections, Britain. *Commissions:* Protexulate Ltd. (large mural) Esher: Plant - illustrations. *Publications:* Orange Cap - Red Cap (Paul Hamlyn, 1968); four fine art prints (Cornish Harbours and Hedgerow themes, 1981). B.B.C. TV (1947, 1964). Numerous calendar illustrations. favourite subjects – jockeys, rooftops, cattle, architectural. *Clubs:* R.I., St. Ives Soc. of Artists. *Signs work:* "Michael Cadman." *Address:* Ballard Glebe, The Glebe, Studland, Dorset BH19 3AS.

CAHILL, John, B.A. (Hons.) Fine Art (1976), M.A. Painting (1980); painter in oil and water-colour, printmaker, etcher; professional artist and gallery owner; *b* 19 Nov., 1954. *m* Gillian. one *d. Studied:* Portsmouth Polytechnic (1976), Royal College of Art (1980). *Exhib:* R.A. Summer Shows; one-man shows: Harris Museum, Preston, St. David's Hall, Cardiff. *Work in collections:* Lord Bath, Longleat House. *Commissions:* many private commissions. *Publications:* work repro: fine art prints, calendars, cards. *Address:* The Harbour Gallery, 1 St. Julian St., Tenby, Pembrokeshire SA70 7AY.

CAINE, Osmund, B.A.(Hons.), M.D.C.S., A.S.M.G.P., M.S.I.A.; teacher, painter in oil, water-colour, illustrator, lithographer, artist in stained glass and mosaic; Principal Lecturer, Graphic Design, Twickenham College of Technology (1962); *b* Manchester. four *s.* one *d. Studied:* Birmingham College of Art (1930-37) and in Italy (1938). *Exhib:* R.A., N.E.A.C., R.B.A., R.B.S.A., V. & A., Craft Centre, Lambeth Palace, Guildhall, and Walker, Adams, Piccadilly Galleries, Leicester, Whitworth Gallery, R.I.B.A., Southwell-Brown Gallery, Richmond, Hampton-Hill & Ashbarn Gallery, Petersfield, and Garden Gallery, Kew, London; one-man exhbns.: Walker's Gallery; Richmond Hill Gallery (1961); Foyles A.G. (1966); Canaletto Gallery (1966, 1969); Open Studio, Kingston-on-Thames (1980); Old Bell Gallery, Chepstow (1981); Century Display Gallery, Surbiton (1982); Southwell-Brown Gallery, Richmond (1984); Garden Gallery, Kew; Merlin Theatre, Frome (1985); Duncan Campbell Fine Art, London (1986); Galerie Salammbo, Paris (1987); Questra Gallery, Kingston-on-Thames; Gallery Upstairs, Henley-in-Arden (1996); Orleans House Gallery, retrospective exhbn. (1998). *Work in collections:* Ministry of Transport; Nottingham Castle A.G.; University of London; Dorset House, London; Borough of Richmond-on-Thames; Borough of Kingston-on-Thames; Melbourne A.G.; Erdington Abbey, B'ham; V. & A.; B'ham A.G. Stained glass: St. Gabriel's Church, Cricklewood, London (N. Aisle window); St. Paul's Church, Kingston (Porch window); St. Augustine's Church, Edgbaston, B'ham (Lady Chapel); St. Cuthbert's Church, Copnor, Portsmouth (E. window); St. Luke's Church,

Wadestown, N.Z. (S. Aisle window); St. Keyne's Church, St. Keyne, Liskeard (N. Aisle window); All Saint's Church, Stechford, B'ham (S. Aisle window); All Saint's Church, Four Oaks, B'ham (four N. & three S. Aisle windows); Private Chapel, Chile, S. America (E. window); Mortuary Chapel, Erdington Infirmary, B'ham (E. window); Old Church, Smethwick (S. Aisle windows); Fourteen Stations of the Cross, St. Mary's, Hong Kong; Private House, N. Wales (Memorial window); Private House, Knowle, B'ham (Geometric window). *Publications:* The Studio, The Artist, L'Art Moderne, Careers in Art, The School Leaver, etc. Films: The Glastonbury Giants (in conjunction with Mary Caine), (1966); The Ruskin Country (1966). *Signs work:* see appendix. *Address:* 25 Kingston Hill, Kingston-on-Thames, Surrey KT2 7PW.

CAINS, F. Blanche, S.W.A., A.T.D. (1927); artist in water-colour, mixed media, fabric collage, embroidery; art teacher, Head of Dept. Grammar School (mixed); *b* Bristol, 1905. *Educ:* St. George Grammar School, Bristol. *Studied:* West of England College of Art (1922-27) Princ. R. E. J. Bush, R.E. *Exhib:* R.A., R.I., R.W.A., S.W.A., various other galleries in London, Brighton, Bristol, etc. *Signs work:* "F.B. Cains." *Address:* 99 Summerhill Rd., St. George, Bristol BS5 8JT.

CAINS, Gerald Albert, N.D.D. (Painting S.L. 1953), A.T.D. (1957), A.R.W.A. (1971), elected R.W.A. (1978), A.D.A.E. (University of Wales, 1975); painter in oil and water-colour; *b* Stubbington, Hants., 11 May, 1932. *m* Ruth Lillian Blackburn. one *s.* one *d. Educ:* Gosport County Grammar School. *Studied:* Southern College of Art, Portsmouth (1949-53). *Exhib:* mixed: R.A.; R.W.A.; R.O.I.; R.B.A.; Football and Fine Arts, London 53: Pics for Schools (Cardiff); Euro '96 London; Wessex Artists, Southampton 78 (2nd prize). Selected for Touring Exhbn. A.C.G.B., Art Federations Bureau, R.W.A. *Work in collections:* Lancashire Museum Service, R.W.A., Walsall Museum Service, Wessex Longleat House. *Commissions:* mural: Southmead Hospital, Bristol. *Clubs:* R.W.A., Bath Soc. of Artists. *Signs work:* "G. A. CAINS." *Address:* 1 Broadway Cottages, Broadway Lane, Clandown, Radstock, Somerset BA3 2XP.

CALDICOTT, Glenys Rita, C. & G. (1982), A.R.M.S. (1990), S.W.A. (1991), S.M. (1991); Margaret Ryder award, R.M.S. (1989), Dartington Rose Bowl, S.M. (1991), Llewellyn Alexander award, R.M.S. (1992); miniaturist, specialising in animal portraits in gouache on card and vellum; *b* Nottingham, 20 Aug., 1941. *m* Harvey C. Caldicott. one *s. Educ:* Mablethorpe, Highfield College, Grimsby. *Studied:* Grimsby School of Art (1958-60, Peter Todd), Bourneville College of Art (1979-82, Alex Jackson). *Exhib:* R.M.S., S.W.A., S.M. Work in private collections. *Signs work:* "G.R. Caldicott." *Address:* Rose Cottage, 16 Flaxley Rd., Stechford, B'ham B33 9AS.

CALLMAN, Jutta Gabrielle: see SAUNDERS, Jutta Gabrielle.

CALVERT, Diana, N.E.A.C. (1979); artist in oil; *b* Capel, Surrey, 7 Oct., 1941. *m* Richard Martineau. *Educ:* Benenden School, Cranbrook, Kent. *Studied:* Byam Shaw (1959-63, Charles Mahoney). *Exhib:* R.A., R.P., R.B.A., N.E.A.C. *Signs work:* "D.C." *Address:* The Lawn, Walsham-le-Willows, Bury St. Edmunds, Suffolk IP31 3AW.

CALVOCORESSI, Richard, B.A., M.A.; Keeper (now Director), Scottish

National Gallery of Modern Art, Edinburgh (since 1987) and Dean Gallery (since 1999); research asst., Scottish National Gallery of Modern Art (1977-79); research asst., Modern Collection, Tate Gallery (1979-82), asst. keeper (1982-87); member, British Council's Visual Arts Advisory Committee (since 1991), chair (since 1999); *b* 1951. *m* Francesca Temple Roberts. one *s*. two *d*. *Educ:* Magdalen College, Oxford; Courtauld Inst. of Art, University of London. *Publications:* author, Magritte (1979, 1984, 1990, 1994, 1998, 2000); exhbn. catalogues: Tinguely (1982), Reg Butler (1983), Cross Currents in Swiss Art (1985), Oskar Kokoschka 1886-1980 (1986), Early Works: Lucian Freud (1997), and catalogue essays on Miró, Klee, Penck, Baselitz, Lüpertz, von Motesiczky, Gormley, Picabia, Gabrielle Keiller Collection etc.; various articles and reviews; co-curator, 'Vienna 1908-1918', 'Century City', Tate Modern, (January-April 2001). *Clubs:* Fellow of Royal Society of Arts (2000). *Address:* Scottish National Gallery of Modern Art, Belford Rd., Edinburgh EH4 3DR.

CAMBRON, Ghislaine, Officier de l'Ordre de Léopold II (1990); artist, painter, ceramist; Directrice de L'Académie des Beaux-Arts de Molenbeek Saint-Jean (Brussels); Academie de Molenbeek, Brussels; Grand Prix de Belgique (1954), Grand Prix de Decoration (1955), Grand Prix de Belgique (1956), Prix de l'État Belge (1942), Distinction-Prix Europe Peinture (1962); *b* St. Amand-les-Eaux, 6 July, 1923 (France). *m* Mariee. *Studied:* Académie de Bruxelles. *Work in collections:* Musée Art Moderne, Brussels, Centre Culturel, Uccle, Musée de Molenbeek, Timbres-Poste du Congo (Serie Masques). *Signs work:* "Cambron, Ghislaine." *Address:* Dréve Angevine, Domaine de la Motte, Bousval 1470, Brabant, Belgique.

CAMERON, Ronald, N.D.D. (1951); sculptor in bronze, terracotta, pewter and silver; *b* London, 8 Oct., 1930. *m* Dorothy. two *d*. *Educ:* Wilson's Grammar School. *Studied:* Camberwell School of Art (1947-51). *Exhib:* bronzes at Bruton Street Gallery, Mayfair, London; also galleries in Europe and N. America. *Signs work:* "R. Cameron." *Address:* 9 Morecambe St., London SE17 1DX.

CAMP, Ann, A.R.C.A. (1946), F.S.S.I.; freelance calligrapher and lettering designer; lecturer at Digby Stuart College, Roehampton Institute; retd. from teaching (1990); *b* London, 1924. *Studied:* Hampstead Garden Suburb Inst. and R.C.A. *Work in collections:* loan collections of V. & A., L.C.C. and National Museum of Wales; Book 4, R.A.F. Book of Remembrance in St. Clement Dane's Church; lettering on stamps, murals, etc. *Publications:* Pen Lettering (first published 1958 by Dryad Press; republished by A. & C. Black, 1984). *Clubs:* Soc. of Scribes and Illuminators. *Signs work:* "Ann Camp." *Address:* 115 Bridge La., London NW11 9JT.

CAMP, Jeffery, R.A. (1984); artist; lecturer, Slade School; *Educ:* Edinburgh College of Art, D.A. (Edin.). *Exhib:* one-man, Galerie de Seine (1958), Beaux Arts Gallery (1959, 1961, 1963), New Art Centre (1968), Serpentine Gallery (1973), S. London A.G. (retrospective, 1973), Bradford City A.G. (1979), Browse and Darby (1984, 1993), Nigel Greenwood Gallery (1986, 1990); retrospective, Royal Albert Memorial Museum, Exeter, Royal Academy of Arts, London, Manchester City A.G., Laing A.G., Newcastle (1988-89); group shows: Hayward Annuals (1974, 1982, 1985), British Council Touring Exhbns. to China and Edinburgh (1982) and to India

(1985), Chantrey Bicentenary, Tate Gallery (1981), Narrative Painting I.C.A., London Arts Council Touring, The Hard Won Image Tate Gallery (1984); Twining Gallery, N.Y. (selected by William Feaver 1985), Peter Moores Liverpool Exhbn. (selected by William Feaver 1986); Athena Art Awards, Barbican Centre, London (1987), Land: Sea: Air, Herbert Read Gallery, Canterbury and tour (1987), 'The Self Portrait' Artsite Gallery, Bath and tour (1987). *Publications:* Draw (1981). *Signs work:* see appendix. *Address:* 27 Stirling Rd., London SW9 9EF.

CAMPBELL, Alex, professional artist in acrylic paint; Adviser N.A.P.A.; *b* Dukinfield, Ches., 5 Apr. 1936. *m* Anne. one *s.* one *d. Educ:* Hyde County Grammar School, Ches. Worldwide private collections and commissions. *Address:* Wern Mill, Nannerch, Mold, Flints. CH7 5RH. *Email:* huwpc@hotmail.com

CAMPBELL, Alexander Buchanan, P.P.R.I.A.S. (1979), A.R.S.A. (1972), B.Arch. (1937), F.R.I.B.A. (1955); architect; *b* Findochty, 14 June, 1914. *m* Sheila Smith. one *s.* one *d. Studied:* architecture: Glasgow School of Architecture (Strathclyde University) (1930-37) under Prof. T. Harold Hughes, Mr. J. A. Coia. *Clubs:* Glasgow Art. *Signs work:* "A. Buchanan Campbell." *Address:* 19 Lochan Ave., Kirn, Dunoon, Argyll PA23 8HT.

CAMPBELL, Huw Phillip, B.A. Graphic Art and Design (1977); artist/graphic designer in acrylic paint; *b* Madagascar, 27 Feb., 1955. *Studied:* Newport College of Art (1974-77). *Exhib:* U.K. and U.S.A. with N.A.P.A. including: Westminster Gallery, London, and the first International Open Long Beach Arts Gallery, Calif.; 'Vital Art 1993', Atlantis Gallery, London, 'Lyrical Orientations', Beatrice Royal Contemporary A.G., Eastleigh, British Work House Gallery, Dallas, Tex., Clifton Arts Club annual Open, Bristol, Cheltenham Group of Artists Summer Open. *Clubs:* N.A.P.A., Design and Artists Copyright Soc. *Signs work:* "H.P.C." and see appendix. *Address:* Middle Cottage, Little Drybrook, nr. Coleford, Glos.GL16 8LP. *Email:* huwpc@hotmail.com

CAMPBELL, James Alexander, A.R.C.A. (1964); ceramist and draughtsman in ceramic, charcoal, pastel; Crafts Council index of selected makers; *b* Cawdor, Scotland, 1942. *m* Jane U'ren. five *d. Educ:* Eton (1955-60). *Studied:* R.C.A. (1960-64 David Queensberry). *Exhib:* Oxford Gallery, Aberystwyth Arts Centre, Anderson Galleries, West Wales Arts Centre, Amalgam, London, Brewery Arts, etc. *Work in collections:* National Gallery of Victoria, Australia, Manchester City A.G., Dundee A.G., Aberdeen A.G. *Publications:* Collector's History of English Pottery by Griselda Lewis, Painted Ceramics - Colour and Imagery on Clay by Brenda Pegrum, The Potter's Dictionary of Shape and Form by Neal French. *Address:* Ashleigh House, Manorbier, Tenby, Pembrokeshire SA70 7TD.

CAMPBELL, Joan Betty, R.M.S. (1980), S.W.A. (1975), Retd. Hon.R.M.S. (1995), H.R.S.W.A. (1994); artist in water-colour, oil and acrylic; teacher of miniature painting, private tuition; *b* London, 4 May, 1923. *m* Archie Campbell. one *d. Educ:* Loughton County High School for Girls, Essex. *Studied:* Ilford Evening Institute (mostly self-taught). *Exhib:* Westminster Galleries, Llewellyn Alexander Gallery, M.A.S.-F. (Florida), Paris Salon (1973, 1974), Bilan l'Art Contemporain of Paris (1978). *Publications:* Art Editor, Hillingdon Writer. *Signs work:* miniatures "J.B.C." or "JC" entwined; larger works "Joan Campbell." *Address:* 3 Fineshade Cl.,

Barton Seagrave, Northants NN15 6SL.

CAMPBELL, Lee, B.A. (Hons) Fine Art (1991), M.A. History and Theory of Art (1993); professional artist and lecturer, painter in oil, drawings in charcoal; first Artist-in-Residence, King's School, Canterbury (1994-95), Artist-in-Residence, St. Saviour's Church, Pimlico; *b* New Zealand, 25 Feb., 1951. *Studied:* Chelsea School of Art, Canterbury College of Art, University of Kent. *Exhib:* Solo show: Fairfax Gallery, Tunbridge Wells (1997); Albemarle Gallery, London (1997 gallery artist). *Work in collections:* U.S.A., Scandinavia, Australia. *Commissions:* mural: Space Science Dept., University of Kent. Winner of Worshipful Co. of Painters Stainers Award (1993). *Clubs:* F.P.S. (Hon. Sec.). *Signs work:* "Lee Campbell." *Address:* 212 Hood House, Dolphin Square, London SW1V 3NQ.

CAMPBELL, Raymond, self taught artist in oil and acrylic, known for still life subjects; *b* Morden, Surrey, 2 Apr., 1956. *Educ:* Garth High, Morden. *Exhib:* R.A., etc. *Work in collections:* England, Germany, Austria, Australia. *Publications:* work repro.: limited edn. prints. *Signs work:* "Raymond Campbell." *Address:* 63 Courtnay Rd., Woking, Surrey GU21 5HG.

CANNING, Neil, A.R.B.A. (1983); Paris Salon (1994) bronze medal; artist in mixed media and oils, screen printing; *b* Enstone, Oxon., 28 Apr., 1960. *Educ:* Spendlove School, Charlbury, and Chipping Norton School. *Studied:* privately with Betty Bowman (1978-81). *Exhib:* numerous including: R.A. Summer Show (1981, 1983, 1984, 2000), N.P.G. (1987), Europart Geneva, London Contemporary Art Fair (1992-01), 20th Century Art Fair (1994-00). *Work in collections:* H.M. Customs and Excise, Rolls Royce, Eagle Star, Smithkline Beecham, University of Wales, NatWest Bank, London Insurance Investment Trust, I.C.I., Paintings in Hospitals, Unilever. *Publications:* illustrated Skylighters (Methuen). *Clubs:* Oxford Art Soc. *Signs work:* "CANNING." *Address:* c/o Advanced Graphics London, B206, Faircharm Estate, 8-12 Creekside, London SE8 3DX.

CANTER, Jean Mary, S.G.F.A. (1977); painter in gouache, water-colour, pencil and scraperboard; lecturer; tutor, Mid-Surrey Adult Educ.; past President S.G.F.A.; *b* Epsom, 18 Mar., 1943. *Educ:* Convent of the Sacred Heart, Epsom. *Studied:* Epsom School of Art (1956-61); Wimbledon School of Art (1961-63). *Exhib:* S.G.F.A., R.W.S., S.B.A., R.I., R.M.S., Medici Gallery etc., S.G.F.A. Prizes: Frisk (1983, 1985); Rexel (1984); Daler-Rowney (1990); Liquitex (1993, 1997); Winsor and Newton (1996); Acco-Rexel (1996). *Work in collections:* Museum Collection, Ewell. *Publications:* work repro.: Demonstrations for many art books (Quarto); articles for "Artist's and Illustrator's" and "Painting World" magazines; greeting cards etc. *Clubs:* S.G.F.A. *Signs work:* "JEAN CANTER." *Address:* 7 Cox Lane, Ewell, Epsom, Surrey KT19 9LR.

CAPRARA, Julia Rosemary, N.D.D., A.T.C. Lond. (1961), M.S.D.C., mem. 62 Group (1970); designer in embroidery, textile artist; co-principal, Opus School of Textile Arts; *b* London, 27 Feb., 1939. *m* Alex. Caprara. one *s. Educ:* Perse School for Girls, Cambridge; Henrietta Barnett School, Hampstead. *Studied:* Hornsey College of Art (1955-61). *Exhib:* one-man show of Embroidery at Commonwealth Institute A.G.; 62 Group shows: Guildford House, National Museum of Wales, Congress House, Foyle's A.G., Australia, U.S.A., Japan. *Work in collections:*

National Museum of Wales, Cardiff, Holocaust Museum, Israel; private collections. *Commissions:* Wall panel, City Technology College, Bradford, Braintree Art Collections; private commissions. *Publications:* The Magic of Embroidery (B.T. Batsford). *Signs work:* "Julia Caprara." *Address:* 20 Crown St., Harrow-on-the-Hill, Middx. HA2 0HR.

CARDEW , Sidney, R.S.M.A.; senior design engineer, Ford M.C. (retd.); self taught marine artist in water-colour and oil; *b* London, 1931. *m* Eunice. one *s.* one *d. Educ:* S.E. Essex Technical College. *Exhib:* R.S.M.A., R.W.S., London galleries. Work in collections internationally. *Commissions:* Large marine water-colour for London offices. *Publications:* article on Wapping Group, Calendar 1992. *Clubs:* Wapping Group, London Sketch, Essex Art, Chelsea Arts. *Signs work:* "Sidney Cardew." *Address:* 31 Tudor Ave., Gidea Park, Essex RM2 5LB.

CARDNELL, Delia, R.I. (2000); painter in water-colour; *b* London, 14 Oct. 1974. *Educ:* Francis Holland School (Clarence Gate), (1986-91); South Hampstead High School, (1991-93). *Exhib:* R.P., N.E.A.C., R.B.A., Laing Art Competition, Singer & Friedlander/ Sunday Times Watercolour Competition. *Work in collections:* S.W.A.; Marine House Gallery, Beer; South West Academy of Fine and Applied Arts. Awarded the Stokes-Roberts Bursary by the Worshipful Company of Painter Stainers (1995); R.I. Winsor & Newton Young Artist, 1st prize winner (1999); National Young Artist winner of the Laing Art Competition (1999); Frank Herring Award for the best Still Life at R.I. (2000). *Signs work:* "Delia Cardnell." *Address:* 26 Ockendon Rd., Islington, London N1 3NP.

CARLETON, Elyn, R.A.A., R.A.S., F.F.P.S.; creative artist, teacher and founder, Creator's A.G. (1980), Innovators (1988); Council and Publicity Officer, Ridley Art Soc. (1987-89); Council Mem. and Executive Officer, N.C.A.C. (1993-97), F.S.C.C.A.G. (1993 N.S.W.); *b* Palmyra, W.A. *m* Laurence E. Carleton. one *s.* two *d. Educ:* Australia. *Studied:* privately with Wesley Penberthy, Melbourne (1968-69); Victoria University, Wellington, N.Z. (Paul Olds, 1970-74); Dr. Desiderius Orban, O.B.E., Sydney (1975-79). *Exhib:* N.Z. Academy, Wellington, N.Z. (1973), Victoria University (1973), (In Mind) Eight Wellington Artists, N.Z. Academy, Wellington (1974), other galleries in N.Z. and Australia; U.K.: Mall Galleries, R.O.I., H.A.C., C.P.S., R.A.S., U.A., F.P.S., C.W.A.C., N.C.A.C., Bloomsbury Intaglio Crafts (Creative Images 1987), Richmond Antiquary (Two Hemispheres 1988), Chertsey Hall (Australian Paintings 1988-89), Bourne Hall (1989-97), Queensland House London (1990), Loggia (1991), Edith Grove (1993), Boxfield Stevenage (1994). *Work in collections:* B.H.P. H.Q. Sydney, N.C.R. World H.Q. Dayton, Ohio, Queensland House London, Stevenage Council; private collections in U.K., Europe, U.S.A., Singapore, N.Z., Australia. *Commissions:* B.H.P. H.Q. Sydney, others private. *Publications:* Creative Images, Art Yesterday, Today and Tomorrow, Art Appreciation, Hanging an Exhibition, Constructive Criticism, Abstract Art, Developed Unique Creative Art Teaching Method (1980). *Signs work:* "Elyn Carleton." *Address:* c/o 'Woodlands', 8 Pelling Hill, Old Windsor, Berks. SL4 2LL.

CARLINE, Nancy Mona, N.E.A.C.; artist in oil; *b* London, 30 Nov., 1909. *m* Richard Carline (decd.). one *s.* one *d. Educ:* Wycombe Abbey School. *Studied:* Slade School (1928-32, Prof. Henry Tonks, 1933-35, Vladimir Polunin). *Exhib:* R.A.,

N.E.A.C., London Group, Leicester Gallery, retrospective Camden Arts Centre (1985). *Work in collections:* Tate Gallery, Manchester City A.G. *Signs work:* "N.C."; early work "Nancy Carline." *Address:* 168 Oxford Rd., Cowley, Oxford OX4 2LA.

CARLTON, Cedric Charles, N.D.D., A.T.D., F.R.S.A., (1953), U.A., (1992); painter in oil, pastel, graphite; art teacher (1950-79); *b* London, 16, July, 1920. *m* Unity Mary. one *s.* four *d. Studied:* Hornsey (1937-39), Chelsea (1946-49), London University Inst. Educ. (1949-50). *Exhib:* Galleries: R.A., London Group, S. London, Westminster, U.A., Mall Galleries, Business Design Centre, Llewellyn Alexander, Army Museum, Chelsea Town Hall, Dyers and Painters Hall, Newport Quay I.O.W., Platform Kent; Sussex: Autumn Art Show, Neal Centre, Michelham Priory, Newtown, Sussex Artists, Gardener Centre, Brighton, Tunbridge Wells Museum Gallery, Stables Hastings, Hastings Museum A.G., Slides on View S.E.A. *Work in collections:* England, Canada, U.S.A. *Commissions:* portrait, sculpture, mural, design. *Signs work:* "C. Carlton." and see appendix. *Address:* Flat 1 Highland Mansions, 117 Pevensey Rd., St. Leonards-on-Sea, E. Sussex TN38 0LZ.

CARLTON, Unity Mary, artist in oil, pastel and pencil; *b* London, 24 June, 1918. *m* Cedric Charles Carlton. one *s.* four *d. Studied:* Hornsey School of Art. *Exhib:* Warfe Gallery I.O.W., Stables Theatre Hastings, annually: Autumn Art Show Sussex, U.A. Westminster Gallery, A.F.A.S., National Army Museum, Michelham Priory, Sussex, and Chelsea Art Soc. *Signs work:* "U. CARLTON" or "Unity Carlton." *Address:* Flat 1 Highland Mansions, 117 Pevensey Rd., St. Leonards-on-Sea, E. Sussex TN38 0LZ.

CARNIE, Andrew John, B.A. (1982), R.C.A. (1986); painter, sculptor, photographer and new media artist; *b* 8 Jan., 1957. *m* Judith Mary Wallas. two *s.* one *d. Educ:* Lakes School, Windermere. *Studied:* Goldsmiths' School of Art, London, Royal College of Art, London. *Exhib:* many mixed person shows including Whitechapel Open, Mostyn Open, John Moores; and one-person shows including Girray Gallery, London, Flowers Gallery, London, Winchester Gallery, Bracknell Gallery, Plymouth Art Centre, Tram Gallery, London, and Columbus Gallery, Georgia, U.S.A. *Work in collections:* Unilever London, Chase Manhattan Bank London, Coopers and Lybrand London, Kaempher Corp., Washington, U.S.A. *Commissions:* D.C. Dance Company. *Publications:* Andrew Carnie (Winchester Gallery). *Signs work:* "ANDREW CARNIE" or not at all. *Address:* 5 Powell Rd., London E5 8DJ.

CARO, Sir Anthony, C.B.E. (1969), Kt (1987), O.M. (2000); Chevalier des Arts et Lettres (1996), 8 Hon Doctorates, 5 Hon Degrees, 7 Hon Fellowships; Nobutaka Shikanai Prize (1991), Praemium Imperiale (1992), Lifetime Achievement Award (1997); sculptor, part-time teacher of sculpture St. Martin's School of Art (1953-81), Trustee Tate Gallery (1982-89), co-founder of Triangle Workshop, New York (1982); *b* London, 8 Mar., 1924. *m* Sheila Girling. two *s. Educ:* Charterhouse School and Christ's College, Cambridge. *Studied:* Regent St. Polytechnic and R.A. Schools. *Exhib:* hundreds of one-man shows worldwide, including retrospectives at Museum of Modern Art, New York (1975, travelled to Minneapolis, Houston, Boston), Trajan Markets, Rome (1992), Museum of Contemporary Art, Tokyo (1995). *Work in collections:* represented in over 150 public collections throughout the world.

Commissions: include National Gallery Ledge Piece, Washington (1978), Sea Music, Poole (1991), Chant des Montagnes, Grenoble (1994), Palma Steps, Mallorca (1999). *Clubs:* R.A.C. *Address:* 111 Frognal, Hampstead, London NW3 6XR. *Website:* www.barford.org/caro *Email:* sculpture@barford.org

CARPANINI, David Lawrence, Prof. , P.R.E. (1995), Dip.A.D., M.A. (R.C.A.), A.T.C., R.B.A., R.C.A., R.W.A., R.E., N.E.A.C., Hon R.W.S.; painter, printmaker; British Inst. Awards Committee Sch. Engraving (1969); *b* Abergwynfi, Glam., 1946. *m* Jane Allen. one *s. Educ:* Glan Afan Grammar School, Port Talbot. *Studied:* Gloucestershire College of Art (1964-68), Royal College of Art (1968-71), University of Reading (1971-72). *Exhib:* R.A., R.B.A., R.W.A., R.E., N.E.A.C., Bankside Gallery, New Academy Gallery, Agnews, Piccadilly Gallery, Attic, Albany, Mostyn, Fosse and Brandler Galleries, Welsh Arts Council, etc. *Work in collections:* National Library and National Museum of Wales, Contemporary Art Society for Wales, Newport A.G., Glynn Vivian A.G., Dept. Environment, R.W.A., N.C.B., A.S.T.M.S., Glam., Glos., Clwyd., Avon, Yorks. Educ. Authorities, and private collections in U.K., U.S.A., Canada, Europe Australia, etc. Television Films: C4 (1984), H.T.V. (1987, 1997, 1998). *Publications:* regular contributor to art periodicals. *Signs work:* "David L. Carpanini." *Address:* Fernlea, 145 Rugby Rd., Milverton, Leamington Spa, Warwickshire CV32 6DJ.

CARPANINI, Jane, Dip.A.D., A.T.C., R.B.A., R.W.A., R.W.S., R.C.A.; artist in water-colour and pencil; *b* Luton, 1949. *m* David L. Carpanini. one *s. Educ:* Bedford High School. *Studied:* Luton College of Art (1967-68), Brighton Polytechnic (1968-71), University of Reading (1971-72). *Exhib:* R.A., R.W.A., R.B.A., R.W.S., Bankside Gallery, Attic, New Academy Gallery, Fosse and Brandler Galleries, Welsh Arts Council, Mostyn, Albany, etc. Winner of Hunting Group prize Watercolour of the Year (1983). *Work in collections:* National Library and National Museum of Wales, Burnley Building Soc., etc., and private collections in U.K., U.S.A., Europe. TV films, H.T.V. (1997). *Publications:* regular contributor to art periodicals, reproductions; cards, prints, calendars, catalogues, etc. *Signs work:* "Jane Carpanini." *Address:* Fernlea, 145 Rugby Rd., Milverton, Leamington Spa, Warwickshire CV32 6DJ.

CARR, David James, Dip.F.A.(Lond.); fine artist in oil, water-colour, gouache, distemper; Slade School Painting prize, Steer prize, Nettleship prize, David Murray Landscape Scholarship, Boise Scholarship U.C.L.; *b* Middlesbrough, 15 Mar., 1944. *m* Marie Wylan. (from first marriage) one *d. Studied:* Slade School (1962-66), John Aldridge, Auerbach, Coldstream, Uglow). *Exhib:* R.A., London Group, London-Waterman Fine Art, Adam Butler Fine Art, The Walk SE1, Thomas Reynolds, San Francisco, Calif. *Work in collections:* London Heritage, Royal Free, U.C.L., local authorities; private collections: U.K., U.S.A., Japan. *Commissions:* Wesley Chapel, London (millennial). *Publications:* Introduction to Painting the Nude (Quarto). *Clubs:* London Group. *Signs work:* "DAVID CARR." *Address:* 22 Minton Mews, London NW6 1XX.

CARRICK, Desmond, R.H.A.; artist in sculpture, oil, water-colour and tempera, lithography, stained glass and ceramics; secretary, Royal Hibernian Academy of Arts (1971-1982 resigned); *b* Dublin, 18 Dec., 1928. *m* Deirdre Mellett. *Educ:* Synge St.

School. *Studied:* Dublin National College of Art. *Exhib:* R.H.A., Oireachtas, Waterford, Dublin Painters, Water-colour Soc. of Ireland, Living Art, Irish Contemporary Painters organized by the Cultural Relations Com. of Ireland, English and Canadian Contemporary Painters; one-man shows: Dublin (15) 1953-1992, England (1) 1989. *Work in collections:* National Self-portrait collection, National Water-colour collection. *Commissions:* Murals in Guinness Visitors' Waiting Room (Dublin). *Signs work:* see appendix. *Address:* Studio, Woodtown, Rathfarnham, Co. Dublin 16.

CARRINGTON-KERSLAKE, Lynette, Dip.A.D., S.B.A., S.M., S.L.M. (R.H.S.); water-colour artist, illustrator and tutor; *b* Bath, 9 Oct., 1946. one *s.* one *d. Educ:* Wycliffe School, Avon. *Studied:* West of England College of Art (textiles). *Exhib:* Westminster Hall (S.B.A.), Northamptonshire, U.S.A. and France. *Publications:* currently working on Rare Flora of Mt. Kinabalu, N. Borneo (Sabah); illustrator of greetings cards. *Clubs:* S.B.A. *Signs work:* "L.C.K." or "Lynette Carrington-Kerslake" and see appendix. *Address:* 35 Nightingale Drive, Towcester, Northamptonshire NN12 6RA.

CARRON, William John, W.S.I. (1977); A.R.H.A. (1996); acrylic marine and landscape painter; tutor; *b* Dublin, 28 July 1930. *m* Barbara Warren, R.H.A. one *d. Educ:* Bolton Street School of Education and Technology. *Studied:* N.C.A.D., Dublin. *Exhib:* R.H.A. and W.S.I.; one-man shows in Dublin. *Work in collections:* R.H.A. and W.S.I. collections; Nat. self-portrait (Limerick University); private collections in Ireland, U.K. and U.S.A. *Clubs:* Royal Dublin Society. *Signs work:* "W. CARRON." *Address:* "Matakana", Grey's Lane, Howth, Co. Dublin, Ireland.

CARRUTHERS, Derek William, Prof., (Emeritus), B.A.; artist in various media, mainly oil painting; *b* Penrith, Cumbria, 1935. *m* Eileen. one *s.* one *d. Educ:* Royal Grammar School, Lancaster. *Studied:* Durham University, King's College (now Newcastle University) (Victor Pasmore, Richard Hamilton, Lawrence Gowing). *Exhib:* John Moores Liverpool, 'Structure' Bradford Arts Festival, Midland View, Open Drawing Show, Cheltenham, etc. *Work in collections:* Northern Arts, Leics. Educ. Authority, Bradford A.G., Abbot Hall Gallery Kendal, Leicester University, etc. *Commissions:* Relief for Attenborough Building, Leicester University. *Publications:* Artisan (1979), Haunting Monuments (1985), Recent Paintings (1985-88). *Signs work:* "CARRUTHERS" and "Derek Carruthers." *Address:* The School House, Harston, nr. Grantham NG32 1PS.

CARSWELL, Fiona Charis, B.A. Hons. (1983); artist in water-colour, mixed media and book binding; *b* Scotland, 10 Mar., 1960. *m* Richard Hackett. one *s.* two *d. Educ:* Rugby High School. *Studied:* Oxford Polytechnic (1980-83, Ivor Robinson). *Exhib:* various exhbns. showing book work and paintings in London, Brussels, Oxford and U.S.A. *Signs work:* "Fiona Charis Carswell" or "F.C.C." *Address:* Windrush Cottage, Fulbrook, Oxon. OX18 4BL.

CARTER, Albert Henry, B.Ed. Hons. (1977), R.B.A. (1983); artist in water-colour, acrylic, etc.; Past Vice Pres., R.B.A.; former Director of Art, Oundle School; *b* Trowbridge, Wilts., 22 Feb., 1928. *m* Eunice Enfield. one *s.* three *d. Educ:* Trowbridge Boys' High School. *Studied:* St. Paul's College, Cheltenham (1973-77, Harold W. Sayer, A.,R.C.A.). *Exhib:* R.B.A., R.W.S., R.W.A., and provincial galleries. *Work in collections:* American Embassy, and many private collections in U.K., Canada, U.S.A., Russia, Germany, Hong Kong, Australia, France and New Zealand. *Signs work:* "A. H. Carter." *Address:* Haydn Studio, 27 South Rd., Oundle, nr. Peterborough PE8 4BU.

CARTER, Bernard Thomas, Hon.R.E. (1975), N.D.D. (1950), A.T.D. (1951); artist in oil; former keeper in charge of Pictures and Conservation, National Maritime Museum, Greenwich (retd. 1977); *b* London, 6 Apr., 1920. *m* Eugenie Alexander, artist (decd.). one *s. Educ:* Haberdasher Aske's. *Studied:* Goldsmiths' College of Art. *Exhib:* one-man shows, Arthur Jeffress (1955), Portal Gallery (twelve); mixed, R.A., Arts Council, British Council, galleries in Europe and U.S.A. *Commissions:* numerous. *Publications:* Art for Young People (with Eugenie Alexander). Work shown on television (BBC and ITV). *Signs work:* "Carter." *Address:* 56 King George St., Greenwich, London SE10 8QD.

CARTER, Derek Ronald, S.G.F.A., painter in black and white media, watercolour, pastel, acrylic and oil; cityscape artist; *b* London, 1930. *m* June. two *s.* one *d. Educ:* Clarks College, London. *Studied:* with Brian Gallagher P.S. (1990-1993), Slade Summer School (1991-1993) under Jo Volley. *Exhib:* R.O.I., Pastel Society and various in South East England. *Work in collections:* private collections in U.K. and U.S.A. *Signs work:* "CARTER." *Address:* 5 Park Lawn Rd., Weybridge, Surrey KT13 9EU.

CARTER, Joan Patricia, R.M.S. (1986), S.W.A. (1985); Gold medallist Paris Salon (1974), finalist Hunting Group prizes (1980), Hon. men. Gold Bowl R.M.S.; freelance portrait painter, book illuminator, illustrator and calligrapher in watercolour, pastel, acrylic and silverpoint; writer; *b* Vancouver, B.C., Canada, 11 Mar., 1923. *m* Alan Henry Carter. two *s. Educ:* Lord Selkerk School, Vancouver, Canada; C.F.E., Longbridge Rd., Ilford; Havering C.F.E., Hornchurch. *Studied:* 'A' level art and Art History. *Exhib:* Schweinfurt, Germany, Paris Salon, R.A., numerous one-man shows etc., M.A.S.-F. *Work in collections:* miniature portrait (1.5" x1") of Mrs. S. Lucas on gold bowl, R.M.S. (1985). *Publications:* Uncle Bill and Aunt Ethel, Allergy Cooking (Ian Henry Pub.), Solo Cooking on a Shoe String (Ian Henry Pub.), Illuminated Calligraphy (Search Press), Illuminated Alphabet (Search Press), Illuminated Design (Search Press), Silverpoint (Search Press), numerous Remembrance books - thirteen in England, one Normandy, France, one Tristan da Cunha, various talks and broadcasts, and articles; art work for book cover (Fowler Wright). *Signs work:* art books: "Patricia Carter"; other books: "J.P. Carter"; and see appendix. *Address:* 4 Osprey Close, Hoveton Norwich, Norfolk NR12 8DR.

CARTER, Kenneth, N.D.D. (Sculpture), A.T.D. (1955), F.R.B.S. (1970), R.W.A. (1995), Hon.D.Arts (Plymouth) 1997; sculptor in bronze and synthetic resins; *b* Hull, 16 June, 1928. *m* Brenda Hubbard. two *s.* two *d. Educ:* Kingston High School, Hull. *Studied:* Hull and Leicester Colleges of Art (1944-46, 1948-50, 1954-55). *Exhib:* Woodstock Gallery, London; various mixed exhbns. London and provinces. *Work in collections:* Exeter Cathedral Chapter House: 15 life-size niches; Ferens A.G., Hull. *Publications:* Open Air Sculpture in Britain by W.J. Strachan (1984); Images of Alban, by Eileen Roberts (1999). *Signs work:* "K. Carter." *Address:* Figgins Gallery, Church Rd., Lympstone, Devon EX8 5JT.

CARTER, Mary, painter in oil, egg tempera, gouache, water-colour; *b* Hartsdale, N.Y., 12 Apr., 1931. *m* Peter Gould, decd. one *s. Studied:* Art Students League of N.Y. (1951-55, Reginald Marsh, R.B. Hale). *Exhib:* Audubon Artists Annual N.Y. (1954, 1972), National Academy Design, N.Y. (1955, 1972), Hartford Athaneum, Conn. (1955), National Competition, Springfield Art Museum, Missouri (1966), Annual Drawings and Sculpture Show, Del Mar College, Corpus Christi, Tex. (1967), Hudson Guild Invitationals, N.Y. (1975-99), Krasdale Foods Gallery (1994). *Address:* 253 W. 16 St. New York, N.Y. 10011.

CARTER, Mary Elizabeth, M.A., A.R.C.A.; painter in oil of miniatures, portraits, rural and domestic scenes; *b* London, 1947. *m* J. B. Hiscock, painter. two *s.* one *d. Educ:* Ursuline Convent, Wimbledon. *Studied:* Kingston School of Art, Royal College of Art (Carel Weight, Roger de Grey). *Exhib:* Zaydler Gallery, R.W.A., Llewellyn Alexander Gallery, Richard Hagen Gallery, Miniaturist for New Grafton Gallery, R.A. Summer Exhbn. since 1968. *Work in collections:* Southend-on-Sea Library, R.A., Camden Council. *Publications:* The Dog Who Knew Too Much. *Signs work:* "Mary E. Carter." *Address:* 2 Hodges Cottages, Hemyock, Cullompton, Devon EX15 3RW.

CARTWRIGHT, Richard Saint George, painter in pastel and oil; *b* Epsom, Surrey, 30 Sep., 1951. *Studied:* self taught. *Exhib:* solo shows every two years at John Martin, London and Adam Gallery, Bath. *Work in collections:* private collections. *Signs work:* "Richard Cartwright." *Address:* 9 Woolcot St., Redland, Bristol BS6 6QH. *Email:* rsgcartwright@hotmail.com

CARUANA, Gabriel, sculptor, painter, ceramist; *b* Malta, 7 Apr., 1929. *m* 1980 Mary Rose Buttigieg. two *d. Exhib:* one-man shows: Malta, England, Italy, Switzerland, Germany, Holland; participated in International Exhbn. of Ceramic Art (Faenza), Lincoln Centers, New York, World Bank, Washington D.C. U.S.A., Foresteria, Venice Bn. (1995). *Work in collections:* Museum of Fine Arts, Valletta, Malta; Whitworth A.G., Manchester; City of Manchester A.G.; Museum of Ceramics, Faenza, Italy; Albert Einstein (1879-1955) International Academy Foundation, Delaware, U.S.A., Malta University Campus, Museum of Ceramics, Faenza, Deruta, and Cervara di Roma, Italy; also several private collections. Artist of the Year, Malta (1985-86); 1988, town of Faenza hosts one-man show to honour 25 Years of Artistic Activity within the City. Founder and Hon. Director, Modern Art, Culture and Crafts Centre, The Old Mill, B'kara, Malta. Artist for Porta del Terzo Milleniua, Cervara di Roma, Open Air Modern Art Museum; 1999 Medal for Cultural Activities re modern art, by the Malta Government; elected Accademico di Merito at Accademia Pietro Vannucci, Perugia Italy. Artistically active since 1953. Studio: 37, Balzan Valley, Balzan, Malta. *Signs work:* "Gabriel Caruana." *Address:* Dr. Zammit St., Balzan, Malta. *Second Address:* Res. 24 Carmel St., B'kara, BKR05, Malta. *Website:* http://www.zorin.com/gabriel/

CARVER, Margaret, R.M.S. (1995), S.W.A. (1997); artist in oil, pastel, water-colour, pencil; Chairperson, Gt.Yarmouth Soc. of Artists; *b* Caister-on-Sea, 10 Sept., 1941. *m* Richard Carver. two *s. Educ:* Caister High School; Gt. Yarmouth C.F.E. *Studied:* evening classes and part-time courses. *Exhib:* Westminster Galleries with S.W.A. and R.M.S., Norwich, Gt. Yarmouth. *Work in collections:* Gt. Yarmouth and

District. *Signs work:* "M. CARVER." *Address:* 3 Orchard Cl., Caister-on-Sea, Gt. Yarmouth, Norfolk NR30 5DS.

CARY, Caroline Anne, F.P.S.; painter in acrylic and mixed media; *b* 28 July, 1940. *m* Lucius Cary (divorced). one *s*. three (one decd.) *d*. *Educ:* Convent of the Sacred Heart, Woldingham. *Studied:* Camberwell and Chelsea Colleges of Art under Lawrence Gowing. *Exhib:* mixed shows: Clarges Gallery, Jonathon Poole, Clark Fine Art, Gallery Zol, Bruton St. Gallery, Austin Desmond Fine Art, William Desmond Fine Art, Devon, etc.; solo shows: London: Loggia Gallery, Langton Gallery, Lord Leighton's Studio, Leighton House, Sue Rankin Gallery; Watatu Gallery, Nairobi, Century Gallery Henley, Galerie Souham, Paris, Z Gallery, N.Y., The Millinery Works, London; The Royal London Hospital - Sam Pease; Corporate Connoisseurs. *Work in collections:* private collections: R. Agnew, J. Agnew, K. Shapland, M. Fisher; public collections: The Royal London Hospital, Whitechapel, London. *Clubs:* Chelsea Arts. *Signs work:* "C.A.C." *Address:* The Studio, 14 Gunter Grove, London SW10 0UJ. *Email:* caro@cacauf.freeserve.co.uk

CASDAGLI, Daphne Catherine, M.A., R.C.A. (1969-1972), A.R.E. (1999); painter, printmaker; visiting lecturer (1973-1984), head of dept. Illustration/Printmaking, City and Guilds of London Art School (1984-1998); elected associate member of Royal Society of Painter Printmakers (1999); *b* Cairo, 11 Dec., 1946. *Educ:* in Cairo and England. *Studied:* Beaux Arts de Versailles under René Aubert (1964-1965), Guildford and Farnham Art Schools, R.C.A. under Carel Weight and Sir Roger de Grey (1969-1972). *Exhib:* British Council, Athens (1977, 1982), R.A. Summer Exhib., R.W.S. open, R.E. Bankside Gallery, Mall Galleries, Jonleigh Gallery, Guildford (1983-1997). *Work in collections:* in Europe and America, Venezuela, and U.K. *Commissions:* Murals for Greek Restaurant, St. Quinteric Press portfolio. *Publications:* illus. for books on techniques. *Signs work:* "D. Casdagli." *Address:* 7 Northwood Rd., London N6 5TL.

CASE, David Charles, M.A. (1966), Hon. R.E.; publisher; *b* 18 Oct., 1943. *m* Anthea. two *d*. *Educ:* Oakham School, Oxford University. *Address:* Marlborough Fine Art Ltd., 6 Albemarle St., London W1X 4BY.

CASSELDINE, Nigel, A.R.W.A. (1985), R.W.A. (1991), Brandler Painting prize (1988); artist/painter in oil on gesso/drawing; Council mem. R.W.A. (1990-93, 1996-98); Mem. A.O.I.; *b* Havering, Essex, 1947. *m* Jenny Partridge. one *s*. one *d*. *Educ:* N. Romford Comprehensive School. *Studied:* Camberwell and Sir John Cass Schools of Art (1966-68, part-time); studio assistant to F.V. Magrath (1969-72). *Exhib:* R.A., R.W.A., Bath Festival, Edinburgh Festival, Medici Gallery, Gloucester A.G. and Museum, Bruton Gallery, Penwith Galleries (St. Ives), etc. *Work in collections:* R.W.A., Cheltenham and Gloucester, Marquis of Bath. *Publications:* 20th Century Painters and Sculptors by F. Spalding; Light by L. Willis. *Signs work:* "CASSELDINE" in red. *Address:* Mount Cottage, St. Marys, Chalford, nr. Stroud, Gloucs. GL6 8PU.

CASSON, Simon John, A.R.E. (1992), R.A.S.(M.A.) (1994), Central Printmaking Dip. (1990), B.A.(Hons.) Fine Art (1988); painter in oil, printmaker in etching; *b* York, 17 May, 1965. *Educ:* Rose Avenue School, Zambia, Cumbria, Penistone Grammar School, Sheffield. *Studied:* Barnsley College of Art (1985),

Exeter College of Art and Design (1985-87), Central St. Martin's (1988-90, Norman Ackroyd), Royal Academy of Arts (1991-94, Prof. Norman Adams). *Exhib:* Regular solo shows at Long & Ryle Gallery, London. *Work in collections:* Private collections home and abroad. *Address:* 87a Albion Rd., Stoke Newington, London N16 9PL.

CASTLE, Roger Bernard, U.A. (1988); landscape marine artist in oil; council mem. U.A.; *b* Dartford, 30 Apr., 1945. *m* Brenda. two *s.* one *d. Educ:* Dartford. *Studied:* under the late William Walden, R.B.A. *Exhib:* R.A., R.O.I., N.E.A.C., R.B.A., U.A.; gallery artist at Century Gallery Henley, Roger Freen Fine A.G. Kent, Blackheath Gallery, F. Illes, Rochester. *Work in collections:* K.C.C. Ashford. *Signs work:* "R.B. CASTLE." *Address:* 26 Harper Rd., Ashford, Kent; studio: Hales Pl., High Halden, Kent.

CATCHPOLE, Heather O., R.M.S., H.S.F., M.A.S.S.A.; National Dip. in commercial and Applied Art (1962); portrait and dog artist in water-colour on ivorine, pastel; *b* Winnipeg, Canada, 26 Aug., 1942. *m* Brian E. Catchpole, L.D.S. *Educ:* Durban Girls' High School. *Studied:* Natal School of Arts and Craft. *Exhib:* R.M.S., R.A., Hilliard Soc. M.A.S.F., M.A.S.S.A. *Work in collections:* Hilliard Soc. Permanent Collection. *Publications:* author/illustrator 'Heidi, Holly and other dogs'. In various books on techniques of miniature painting. 2001 elected President of Hilliard Society. *Signs work:* "Heather O. Catchpole," miniatures: the letter O with H inside with the year underneath it. *Address:* Heelers, Fitzhead, Taunton, Som. TA4 3JW.

CATTRELL, Annie Katherine, B.A.(Hons.) Fine Art (1984), M.A. Fine Art (1985); artist in glass, paper and mixed media; lecturer, Sculpture Dept., Cheltenham School of Art; *b* 15 Feb., 1962. *Studied:* Glasgow School of Art (1980-84, Sam Ainsley), University of Ulster (1984-85, Alistair MacLennan). *Exhib:* Collins Gallery Strathclyde University (1989), 369 Gallery 'Artist's Choice' (1990), Artist in Residence, Chessel Gallery (1991), Paperworks, Seagate Gallery (1992). *Work in collections:* S.A.C., MacManus A.G. and Museum Dundee, City Art Centre Edinburgh. *Publications:* reviews, Edinburgh Medicine vol.65, Alba (1991) Mar./Apr., etc. *Clubs:* Collective Gallery, Edinburgh. *Signs work:* "Annie Cattrell." *Address:* 10a Greenhill Park, Churchill, Edinburgh EH10 4DW.

CAUDWELL, Celia, N.D.D. (1995), S.W.A. (1993), S.B.A. (1994), A.U.A. (1994); artist in water-colour, oil, pen and ink, pottery/ceramics; gallery owner, mem. F.A.T.G.; *b* Ewell, Surrey, 11 July, 1943. *m* John Caudwell. two *s. Educ:* Upper Chine School, Shanklin, I.O.W. *Studied:* Winchester School of Art (1961-64), Goldsmiths' College School of Art (1964-65). *Exhib:* Ryde Library/Gallery I.O.W., Boldrewood Gallery, Southampton University, Seely Gallery, Newport I.O.W., Westminster Gallery, Mall Galleries, Omell Gallery, Laing Art Competition Winchester. *Publications:* A Brief History of Winkle Street I.O.W. *Signs work:* "Celia Caudwell." *Address:* Brookside Cottage, Winkle St., Calbourne, I.O.W. PO30 4JF. *Second Address:* The Afton Gallery, The Broadway, Totland Bay, I.O.W. PO39 0BW.

CAULKIN, Martin, R.I. (1983), R.B.S.A. (1983); artist in water-colour and ink; *b* B'ham, 12 Feb., 1945. *m* Anne Cherry, S.W.A. one *d. Educ:* Great Barr Comprehensive. *Studied:* B'ham College of Art (1962-65, Glyn Griffiths). *Exhib:*

R.W.S., R.B.S.A., R.I., R.A. Summer Show, Singer and Friedlander water-colour exhbn., Shell House Gallery, Ledbury, Ombersley Galleries, Worcs., Montpellier Gallery, Cheltenham, Manor House Gallery, Chipping Norton, Bill Toop Gallery, Salisbury, Barn End Gallery, Solihull. *Publications:* Landscape in Watercolours (Studio Vista); Paintings from Photographs (Harper Collins); Contemporary British water Colour Artists (Shandong Fine Arts Publishing House). *Signs work:* "Martin Caulkin." *Address:* September Cottage, Naunton, Upton upon Severn, Worcester WR8 0PY.

CAVACIUTI, Peter, painter on handmade paper from China, Korea, Japan and Nepal using Chinese ink and traditional pigments and has developed methods of mixing colours from 17thc. Chinese recipes; *b* London, 13 May, 1952. *Studied:* seven years with Prof. Fei Cheng Wu, continued with Prof. Bao at Central School of Art, Beijing. *Exhib:* Urasenke Foundation, Kyoto, Japan; Salon de l'Aquarelle de Belgique, Belgium; R.A. Summer Show, London; R.W.S.; S.G.F.A.; The Discerning Eye, London; Kettles Yard, Cambridge; recent solo shows: Daiwa Foundation, London (1999) and Galerie Leda Fletcher, Geneva (2001). *Work in collections:* Urasenke Foundation; Clare Hall College, Cambridge. *Publications:* illustrated: 'Taoist Wisdom' by T. Freke (Godsfield Press, 1999), 'The Japanese Tea Ceremony' (Element Books, Ltd.); included in 'Dictionary of Painters in Britain since 1945' (1998); work repro.: Millennium Calendar for Ikea Ltd., posters and cards Art Group Ltd, calendar for W.H.Smith Ltd, (2002). *Clubs:* Far Eastern Painting Soc., Kaetsu Chado Soc. *Signs work:* see appendix. *Address:* 2 Oxford Rd., Cambridge CB4 3PW.

CAVANAGH, John Bryan, couturier (retd. Sept. 1974); *b* Belmullet, 28 Sept., 1914. *Educ:* St. Paul's School. *Exhib:* Munich, 1954 (Gold Medal); designed Wedding Dress for H.R.H. Duchess of Kent (June, 1961); designed Wedding Dress for H.R.H. Princess Alexandra (April, 1963). *Work in collections:* V. & A., Museum of Costume, Bath. Trained: with Molyneux and Balmain in Paris. *Signs work:* "JOHN CAVANAGH." *Address:* Nazareth House, Hammersmith Rd., London W6 8DB.

CECIL, Roger, artist in oil and oil pastel; David Murray Award (1966); *b* Abertillery, 18 July, 1942. *Studied:* Newport College of Art. *Exhib:* Howard Roberts Gallery, Cardiff (1966), R.A. Summer Exhbn. (1987, 1989); one-man shows, New Academy Gallery, London (1988, 1989, 1991, 1993, 1995-97), Cleveland Drawing Biennale (1989). *Publications:* B.B.C. documentary The Gentle Rebel. *Signs work:* "Roger Cecil." *Address:* c/o The New Academy Gallery, 34 Windmill St., London W1P 1HH.

CERCI, Sharon L., F.M.A.S., A.R.M.S. (1983); scrimshander scribing on ivory with ink, lecturer; heraldic artist and designer; *b* Providence, R.I., U.S.A., 4 July, 1942. two *s.* one *d. Educ:* Brockton High School. *Studied:* B.H.P. Art School (1963). *Exhib:* I.F.M.A.S., R.M.S., International Circle of Miniature Artists, Spencer Gallery, Dunedin Fine Art Center. *Commissions:* Coat-of-Arms design: USCG cutter, Durable (1991), Dunedin Highland Games (1994), Ocala Scottish Games and Irish Feis (1996), Ye Mystic Krewe of Neptune, St. Petersburg, Fla. (1991), Neptunus Rex XIII, XIV, XV, XVI, XVII and XV111 (1991-97), Coat-of-Arms design with Expository entitled: The Trinity Arms d.b.a. the King's Crest (1993). *Publications:*

author of 'Penning Generation Around the World'. *Signs work:* S within a C, "S.Cerci," "Sharon Cerci," "Cerci." *Address:* 1358 N. Lotus Drive, Dunedin, Florida, U.S.A.

CHADWICK, Lynn, C.B.E., 1st Prize, Venice Biennale (1956); sculptor, chiefly in iron and bronze; *b* London, 24 Nov., 1914. *m* Eva Reiner. two *s*. two *d. Educ:* Merchant Taylors. *Exhib:* Stedelijk Museum (Amsterdam, 1957), Palais des Beaux Arts, Bruxelles (1957), Arts Council of G.B. (London, 1957). *Work in collections:* Tate, Museum of Modern Art (N.Y.), Allbright Art Gallery (Buffalo), The Kroller-Müler Museum (Otterlo). *Publications:* Contemporary British Art (Herbert Read), Sir Herbert Read, Lynn Chadwick (Bodensee Verlag, Amriswill, Swiss), Pelican, Lynn Chadwick (Dr. J. P. Hodin, Zwemmer), Lynn Chadwick (Alan Bowness, Methuen), Dennis Farr and Eva Chadwick, Lynn Chadwick (O.U.P.), Lynn Chadwick (Edward Lucie Smith, Lypiah). *Address:* Lypiatt Pk., Stroud, Glos. GL6 7LL.

CHAFFIN, Roy, wildlife artist in acrylic; President, Herts. Visual Arts Forum; *b* Nottingham, 22 Jan., 1948. *m* Dinah Louise. one *s*. two *d*. Founder of the PAWS (Paint a Wildlife Subject) Competition, now the major event of its kind in Europe. Nominated as 'Creative Briton' (1999). *Address:* Blackwood, 10 Nascot Wood Rd., Watford, Herts. WD17 4RS. *Website:* http://www.roychaffin.com

CHALKER, Jack Bridger-, A.R.C.A., R.W.A., A.S.I.A., Hon. F.M.A.A.; painter in oils, illustrator, medical/surgical artist, illustrator in oil, gouache, pen and wash etc.; Consultant, Birmingham University (art and design); War artist with Australian Army, Bangkok (1945); *b* 10 Oct., 1918. *m* Hélène. three *s*. one *d. Educ:* Alleyn's School, Dulwich. *Studied:* Goldsmiths' College (1936-39), R.C.A. (1946-49). *Exhib:* R.B.A., R.W.A., R.P., London galleries; mixed shows: London, Cheltenham; one-man shows: Dixon Gallery London, R.W.A., Australia and Thailand. *Work in collections:* Cheltenham, Imperial War Museum London, Army Museum London,War Memorial Canberra, Australia. *Publications:* author and illustrator: Burma Railway Artist (Leo Cooper, 1944, and Viking O'Neil Australia); wide range of surgical/medical publications, U.K., America and Australia. *Clubs:* Arts, Lansdowne. *Signs work:* "Chalker." *Address:* Bleadney Mill, Bleadney, nr. Wells, Som. BA5 1PF.

CHAMBERLAIN, Trevor, R.O.I. (1972), R.S.M.A. (1970); President of the Wapping Group of Artists; Chris Beetles award, Winner at 1987 R.W.S. Exhbn.; marine, town, figure and landscape painter in oil and water-colour; *b* Hertford, 13 Dec., 1933. *m* Elaine Waterfield. one *s. Educ:* Ware Central School. *Exhib:* London and abroad, R.A. Summer Exhbns. *Work in collections:* Guildhall A.G., London, Ferens A.G., Hull, Hertford Museum, Government Art Collection. *Publications:* The Connoisseur, Studio International, Dictionary of Sea Painters, 20th Century Marine Painting, Water-colour Impressionists; Author of 'Oils', and Trevor Chamberlain - A Personal View. *Signs work:* "T. Chamberlain." *Address:* Braeside, Goldings La., Waterford, Hertford, Herts. SG14 2PT.

CHAMBERS, Stephen Lyon, B.A.Hons., M.A., Rome Scholarship; painter in oil on canvas; *b* London, 20 July, 1960. *m* Denise de Coruova. two *s. Educ:* Holland Park Comprehensive. *Studied:* Winchester School of Art (1978-79), St. Martin's School of Art (1979-82), Chelsea School of Art (1982-83). *Exhib:* widely in Europe,

U.S.A. and U.K. Represented by Flowers East, London. *Publications:* Strange Smoke by John Gillett; Paintings 1988-89 by Gerard Wilson; Felonies and Errors by Isabella Oulton. *Signs work:* paintings on canvas only signed on reverse. *Address:* 129 Offord Rd., London N1 1PH.

CHANDLER, Cynthia Ann, landscape and coastal scene painter in water-colour and oil and portrait painter in oil, pastel and water-colour; *b* Isleworth, Middx., 1 Jan., 1937. *m* Frank Chandler. two *s.* one *d. Educ:* Hampton High School. *Studied:* Twickenham School of Art (Mr. Duffy, Mr. Kane, Miss Palby). *Exhib:* U.A., P.S., and several Midland exhbns. *Work in collections:* Nuneaton Art Gallery (3). *Clubs:* President, Rugby and District Art Soc., Coventry and Warwickshire Soc. of Artists, Banbury and District Art Soc. *Signs work:* "Cynthia Chandler," "CYNTHIA CHANDLER." *Address:* 36 Dunsmore Ave., Rugby, Warwickshire CV22 5HD.

CHANEY, Professor Judith Hilary Desforges, B.Soc.Sc., M.Soc.Sc.; Assistant Rector, Director of Academic Affairs The London Institute; *b* 31 May, 1944. *Educ:* Nottingham High School for Girls, G.P.D.S.T., University of Birmingham. Taught at University of Leicester, University of Hong Kong, Sunderland Polytechnic. Registrar, Art and Design, C.N.A.A. (1985-91). *Address:* c/o The London Inst., Davies St., London W1K 5DA. *Email:* j.chaney@linst.ac.uk

CHANG, Chien-Ying, B.A. (1935); artist in water-colour; mem. of R.I., R.W.A. and Soc. of Woman Artists; *b* 27 June, 1915. *m* Cheng-Wu Fei, artist. *Educ:* National Central University, China, and Slade School of Fine Art. *Exhib:* R.A., R.I., R.B.A.; one-man shows at Leicester Gallery (1951, 1955, 1960). *Work in collections:* London University; St. John's College, Oxford; R.W.A., Bristol; Grave's Gallery, Sheffield; Derby Art Gallery. *Publications:* work repro.: Studio, Art News and Review, Future, Picture Post, La Revue Moderne, Kunst, etc. *Signs work:* see appendix. *Address:* 27 The Fountains, Ballards Lane, London N3 1NL.

CHANNING, Leslie Thomas, A.R.I.B.A. (1941), U.A. (1973), A.N.S.P.S. (1975); artist in water-colour; architect (retd.); *b* Weymouth, 24 Apr., 1916. *m* (1st) Florence Helen (decd.). (2nd) Audrey Joan. one *s.* one *d. Educ:* The Wandsworth School and Regent St. Polytechnic Evening Inst. School of Architecture (1934-39). *Exhib:* R.I., U.A., N.S.P.S., Thames Valley Arts Club, Richmond Art Soc. *Clubs:* U.A., N.S.P.S., Thames Valley Arts, Richmond Art Soc. *Signs work:* "L. T. Channing." *Address:* 30 Fullerton Court, Udney Park Road, Teddington, Middx. TW11 9BF.

CHAO, Shao-an, M.B.E. (1980); Prof. in Art (Canton University, 1948); painter in ink and water-colour; founded 'Lingnan School of Art' in Canton (1930); Conferred the honorary degree of Doctor of Letters by University of Hong Kong (1994) in recognition of services to the Arts; *b* Canton, China, 6 Mar., 1905. *Studied:* painting at 15 under Kao Chi-feng, a key figure in the early development of 'Lingnan Painting'. *Exhib:* repeated one-man shows in major cities in China: Nanking, Shanghai, Canton, Chungking, etc. (1929-48); one man shows, in major universities and art museums and galleries in U.S.A., England, Japan, France, W. Germany, Switzerland, Italy, Canada, Australia, New Zealand, Singapore and Malaysia (1951-78); Urban Council Hong Kong Museum of Art (1979), National Museum of History, Taiwan (1980). *Work in collections:* Boston Museum of Fine Art, Washington

County Museum, Nanyang University Museum, Singapore, Hong Kong Museum of Art and National Museum of History, Taiwan, Museum für Kunsthandwerk, Übersee-Museum, Romer-Museum, Museum der Stadt Ettlingen, W. Germany (1989). *Publications:* Charming Cicadas Collection (1 vol.), Shao-an's Paintings (1 vol.), Recent Paintings by Prof. Chao Shao-an (3 vols.), Collection of Shao-an's Paintings (20 vols.), The Art of Chao Shao-an (1 vol.), The Paintings of Chao Shao-an (1 vol.). Awarded International Art Gold Medal by the Belgium Centenary Independence World Fair, Brussels; moved to Hong Kong in 1948 and re-established 'Lingnan School of Art' there. To date, he has students in many parts of the world. Lectures: at a number of universities including University of Leeds, U.K. (1954), Harvard University and Berkeley University, U.S.A. (1960). *Signs work:* "CHAO Shao-An" and see appendix. *Address:* 295A Prince Edward Rd., (2nd Floor), Kowloon, Hongkong.

CHAPLIN, Michael James, N.D.D., R.E., R.W.S.; printmaker, water-colourist; Past Vice-Pres. Royal Soc. of Painter-Printmakers; *b* St. Neots, 19 Sept., 1943. *m* Gay Lloyd. one *s.* one *d. Educ:* St. Albans Boys' Grammar School. *Studied:* Watford College of Art (1961-64), Brighton College of Art (1966-67), post-graduate. *Exhib:* R.E. Annual, R.W.S. Open (Prizewinner 1989), R.A. Summer Shows. *Work in collections:* Ashmolean and Fitzwilliam museums; public and private collections worldwide, Royal Collections. *Commissions:* mural for Express Newspaper's boardroom; United Arab Shipping. *Publications:* regular contributor to Artist Magazine. Resident art expert on Channel 4 T.V. 'Water-colour Challenge'; "Mike Chaplin's Expressive Watercolours" published Oct. 2001, Harper Collins. *Signs work:* "Michael Chaplin, R.W.S." *Address:* Suffield, Orchard Drive, Weavering, Maidstone, Kent ME14 5JG.

CHAPMAN, John Lewis, artist in water-colour, gouache, oil; *b* Blackburn, 11 Sept., 1946. *Studied:* Blackburn Art College (James Dolby). *Exhib:* R.A. Summer Exhbn., Patersons, London, Lewis Textile, Blackburn, Haworth A.G., Accrington, Jersey, Birmingham, Warrington, Newcastle, Harrods, London. *Work in collections:* Blackburn A.G. *Publications:* 22 signed Limited Editions (published by Miss Carter Publications, Bolton). *Signs work:* "J.L. CHAPMAN." *Address:* 25 Silverwell St., Bolton BL1 1PP.

CHAPMAN, June Dianne, painter in oil; *b* Ruislip, 12 June, 1939. *Educ:* St. Joan of Arc's Convent School, Rickmansworth. *Studied:* Camberwell School of Art (1955-56). *Exhib:* R.A., R.B.A., R.O.I., U.A., Blackheath Gallery, Edwin Pollard Gallery, Foyles A.G.; group show: Kingsmead Gallery; Lincoln Joyce Fine Art. *Signs work:* "J. Chapman" or "June Chapman." *Address:* 99f Mycenae Rd., Blackheath, London SE3 7SE.

CHAPMAN, Mark, B.A. (Hons.) Fine Art: 1st Class (1982), M.A. Fine Art (1983); artist in water-colour, metal and wood construction; Lecturer in Art and Design, School of Art, Weymouth College; *b* Cuckfield, Sussex, 30 Jan., 1958. *Studied:* Sunderland (1979-82), Birmingham (1982-83). *Exhib:* Leicestershire Schools Exhbn. (1983-90); Sculpture in the Garden, Deans Court, Wimborne (1991, 1993, 1995). *Signs work:* "M. Chapman." *Address:* Marnel Cottage, Church Lane, Osmington, Dorset DT3 9EW.

CHART, Helga, R.S.W. (1994), D.A. (Edin.) Post Grad.; artist in oil and mixed media; lecturer in art and design, Edinburgh's Telford College (retired); *b* Edinburgh, 31 Aug., 1944. *m* H. Robertson. one *s*. *Educ:* Edinburgh. *Studied:* Edinburgh College of Art (1962-66, Sir Robin Philipson, David Michie, John Houston). *Exhib:* mixed shows 1968-95; three solo shows Edinburgh; R.S.A., R.S.W., S.A.A.C., S.S.A. *Work in collections:* British Rail, IBM, Edinburgh schools, Pictures in Hospitals (Scotland). *Signs work:* "Helga Chart." *Address:* 19 Dalrymple Cres., Edinburgh EH9 2NX.

CHATTEN, Geoffrey, R.B.A. (1992); self taught painter of E. Anglian life and landscape, figures and marine subjects in oil; *b* Gorleston, Norfolk, 20 Sept., 1938. *m* Patricia Chatten. one *s*. one *d*. *Exhib:* R.A., R.B.A., R.O.I., Southwell Brown Gallery, Richmond, Surrey, John Noott Gallery, Broadway, Fosse Gallery, Fosse on the Wold, Waterman Gallery, London, Dassin Gallery, Los Angeles, Gt. Yarmouth Galleries. *Work in collections:* Maritime Trust, many private collections throughout Britain and overseas. *Publications:* Lydia Eva (Maritime Trust). *Clubs:* Hon. Member Gt. Yarmouth Society of Artists. *Signs work:* "Chatten." *Address:* 82 Suffield Rd., Gorleston, Norfolk NR31 7AL.

CHATTERTON, George Edward, F.I.A.L.; Accademia Italia Gold Medal (1979), Prize of Italy Distinction (1980); artist, cartoonist and photographer; *b* Kidderminster, 15 July, 1911. *m* Iris Betty Wilce. two *s*. *Educ:* Toronto. *Studied:* Kidderminster School of Art; photography at School of Photography, Farnborough. *Publications:* work repro.: since 1932 in leading London and Dundee illustrated journals, including London Opinion, Daily Mirror, Daily Sketch, Weekly News, etc. R.A.F. Artist/Photographer (1938-50). Cartoon creations include "Chad" of "Wot, No-?" fame (1938), "Sheriff Shucks" (1948), "Leo CV" mascot of Lions Clubs, G.B. (1969), etc. *Signs work:* see appendix. *Address:* Canal Cottage, Ryeford, Stonehouse, Glos. GL10 2LG.

CHAUVIN, Enid, Board of Educ. art dip. (1934), elected M.A.I.A. (1948), Hon. S.G.A. (1969); artist in oils, lithography and water-colour; art teacher; awarded Medal and Diploma of Merit, Annuale Italiana d'Arte Grafica (1968); Medal and Honourable Mention, Biennale degli Regioni, Ancona (1968); Diplome Palme d'Or des Beaux Arts (1969); Grand Prix de Bastia (1976); Mention International (1977); Fondation Michel Ange; Mention Speciale "Arts Inter" (Avignon) 1978; elected Conseiller Culturel of International Arts Guild (1969); Diplome d'Honneur I.A.G. (1984); Hon. Vice-President L'Internazionale de Centro Studi e Scambi Internazionali (1972); *b* Blackheath, 21 June, 1910. *m* Victor Patrick Law. one *s*. *Studied:* Blackheath School of Art and Goldsmiths' College. *Exhib:* R.A., R.B.A., R.O.I., A.I.A., United Artists, S.W.A., R.P., N.S., Senefelder Group, Redfern, Kensington, Mercury, Piccadilly, Curwen, and Furneau Galleries, Ganymed Editions, Exhbn. Grand Prix International de la Corse Porto Vecchio (1993); one-man exhbn. Heal's Gallery, Maison de la Culture, Ajaccio (1971, 1976, 1978, 1981), Bastia (1972, 1975, 1976), Calvi (1972, 1973, 1974), île Rousse (1978, 1979, 1980, 1986), Geneva (1980), Monaco (1985), Marseille (1986), in artist's studio Santa Reparata-di-Balagna (1987-1996). Work purchased by Southampton Education Authority and Maison de la Culture. *Publications:* Circus Horses in Children's Oxford Ency., biography and reproduction in La Femme dans L'Art Contemporain

(1972), Dix Ans d'Arts Graphiques et Plastiques (1970-80), Artistes et Modeles (1982) and Repertorium Artis (1984). *Signs work:* see appendix. *Address:* Place de L'Ormeau, 68 Santa Reparata-di-Balagna, 20220 Ile-Rousse, Corsica.

CHEEK, Carl F., A.R.C.A.; portrait painter in oil, pastel and conté; *b* Karlshamn, Sweden, 7 Mar., 1927. divorced. one *s.* two *d. Educ:* Clifton College. *Studied:* Chelsea School of Art, Royal College of Art. *Exhib:* one-man shows: London (2), Manchester (1); twice at John Moores, Liverpool. *Commissions:* Sir Clough William Ellis, Lord Eden, Lord Butterfield, Field Marshall Sir Nigel Bagnall, etc. Taught at several art schools: Heatherleys, Berkshire College of Art, Croydon College of Art, S.E. Essex School of Art. *Signs work:* "Carl Cheek." *Address:* Flat 2, 24 Ladbroke Gdns., London W11 2PY.

CHEESE, Bernard, R.E. (1988), A.R.C.A. (1950); printmaker in lithography and water-colour; *b* London, 1925. one *s.* three *d. Educ:* Beckenham Grammar School. *Studied:* Beckenham School of Art (Edward Bawden), R.C.A. (Edwin Ladell). *Exhib:* Bankside Gallery, Zwemmer Gallery (1965), R.A., John Russell Gallery, Ipswich, Thompson Gallery, Aldeburgh, Fry Gallery, Saffron Walden, Royal Academy. *Work in collections:* Library of Congress, Washington, Cincinnati Museum, N.Y. Public Library, Leeds Library, V. & A. (Print Room), Government Art Collection, University of Wales, Hunterian Museum Glasgow. *Publications:* illustrated many music books for A. & C. Black. *Signs work:* "Bernard Cheese." *Address:* 2 High St., Nayland, Colchester CO6 4JE.

CHEFFINS, Valma Maud, M.F.P.S.; artist/printmaker in etching and aquatint; former teacher; *b* Maidenhead, 18 June, 1946. *m* Frank Cheffins. *Educ:* Clark's College, Ilford; Beal Grammar School for Girls. *Studied:* St. Osyth's Training College (1964-67, Graham Eccles, Michael Kaye), Barking Technical College (1967-80, Harry Eccleston, O.B.E.). *Exhib:* Loggia Gallery, Bankside Gallery, R.E., The Barbican, International Print Triennial, Japan (2001). *Work in collections:* Britain, America and Europe. *Clubs:* Ilford Art Soc., Essex Art. *Signs work:* "VALMA CHEFFINS." *Address:* 62 Chadville Gdns., Chadwell Heath, Romford, Essex RM6 5UA.

CHEN, Chi, painter-artist; *b* Wusih, China, 2 May, 1912. *Studied:* in China; 1940-46 art instructor St. John's University. *Exhib:* first one-man show Shanghai (1940). In 1947 invited to come to U.S.A.; one-man shows at universities, museums, galleries in New York, Boston, Philadelphia, Washington, D.C., Chicago, New Orleans, Houston, Dallas, Fort Worth, San Antonio, Denver, Seattle, San Francisco, Los Angeles, San Diego, etc. Recipient numerous gold medals: 1955 A.W.S. Spl. $1000 Award for Water-colour of the Year, 1960 Nat. Inst. Arts and Letters $1500 Grant, 1961 Nat. Academy Samuel Finley Breese Morse Medal, 1969 Nat. Academy Saltus Gold Medal of Merit, 1976 A.W.S. Bicentennial Gold Medal and many others. *Publications:* Aquarelles de Chen Chi (Shanghai 1942), A Portfolio of Chen Chi Paintings, Limited Edition (Switzerland 1965), Sketchbooks of Chen Chi (New York 1969), China from Sketchbooks of Chen Chi (New York 1974), Chen Chi Watercolours, Drawings, Sketches (New York 1980), Chen Chi Watercolour (Shanghai, The People's Republic of China 1981), Heaven and Water, Chen Chi (New York 1983), Heart & Chance (New York 1993). *Clubs:* Nat. Academy of

Design, American Watercolour Society, Nat. Arts Club, Century Club, Dutch Treat Club and others. *Signs work:* "Chen Chi." *Address:* 23 Washington Sq. North, New York, N.Y. 10011; Studio: 15 Gramercy Park, New York, N.Y. 10003, U.S.A.

CHERRY, Anne, M.A. (R.C.A.) (1973), S.W.A. (1987), A.R.B.S.A. (1990); artist in water-colour; *b* Isle of Sheppey, 16 Oct., 1948. *m* Martin Caulkin, R.I., R.B.S.A. one *d. Educ:* John Willmott Grammar School. *Studied:* Sutton Art College (1967-68), B'ham College of Art (1968-71), R.C.A. (1971-73, Joanne Brogden, Zandra Rhodes). *Exhib:* R.B.S.A. Galleries, R.W.S., R.I., Shell House Gallery, Ledbury, Ombersley Galleries, Worcs., Montpellier Gallery, Cheltenham, Manor House Gallery, Chipping Norton. *Publications:* "Landscape in Watercolour", Patricia Monahan, (Studio Vista), Beginner's Guides. *Signs work:* "Anne Cherry." *Address:* September Cottage, Naunton, Upton upon Severn, Worcester WR8 0PY.

CHERRY, Norman, D.A., M.C.S.D., F.R.S.A.; designer - jeweller and silversmith, precious and non-precious metals; academic; Head, School of Jewellery, U.C.E.; *b* Airdrie, Lanarkshire, 2 Aug., 1949. *m* Kate Cherry, H.M.I. one *s. Studied:* Glasgow School of Art (1966-70, J. Leslie Auld). *Exhib:* various inc. Hipotesi, Barcelona. *Work in collections:* Dundee Museums and A.G.'s, Tennessee Technological Univ., U.S.A. and Royal Museum of Scotland. *Publications:* "Textile Techniques for Jewellers" by Arline Fisch (Lark Books). Churchill Fellow (1983). Although work is undertaken in various areas of jewellery and metalwork, a major preoccupation in recent years has been the weaving of metals. *Signs work:* Sponsors mark: N.C. inside lozenge struck on all precious metalwork and assayed and hallmarked @ Edinburgh. *Address:* School of Jewellery, Vittoria St., Birmingham B1 3PA.

CHEVINS, Hugh Terry, M.S.I.A.; artist, oil, gouache, pen and ink, commercial and book illustrator, landscape, mural painter, portrait painter; R.A. Bronze Medal (1953), Paris Salon Medaille d'Argent (1955, 1956); *b* Retford, 2 July, 1931. *m* Veronika. one *s.* one *d. Educ:* Gunnersbury Grammar School. *Studied:* Twickenham School of Art, Paris, R.A. Schools. *Exhib:* R.A., R.B.A., United Artists, Glasgow Academy, Paris, Piccadilly Gallery, Brighton Art Gallery, Bournemouth, Lincoln Joyce Art Gallery, David Curzon Gallery. *Work in collections:* Rijksmuseum, Amsterdam, Science Museum, London. *Publications:* work repro.: Imperial Chemical Industries, Shell, John Laing, John Mowlem. *Signs work:* "HUGH CHEVINS." *Address:* 'Haven', Guildford Rd., Rowley, Craileigh, Surrey GU6 8PP.

CHEYNE, Anna, Slade Dip. (1950), A.R.U.A. (1990), R.U.A. (1994); sculptor and painter in ceramic, bronze, papier mache and batik paintings; *b* London, 9 Apr., 1926. *m* Donald Cheyne. two *s.* three *d. Studied:* Kingston School of Art, Slade School. *Exhib:* Belfast, Dublin, Bristol, Bath, Sligo, Kilkenny, Limerick and Brussels. *Work in collections:* Antrim Hospital; National Portrait Collection, Limerick; Ulster Television Collection; R.U.A. Diploma Collection. *Commissions:* bronze coat-of-arms, F.A.N.I. (1991); 'Regeneration', Belfast (1993); bronze wall plaque, National Maternity Hospital, Dublin (1994); 'Centenary Sculpture' R.U.A.S., Belfast (1996); 'My Lady of the Chimney Corner', Antrim (1998). *Clubs:* Sculptors' Soc. of Ireland, Assoc. of Artists of Ireland. *Signs work:* "Anna Cheyne" and see appendix. *Address:* 30 Railway St., Lisburn BT28 1XG.

CHILTON, Elizabeth, Ruskin Cert. Fine Art and Design (1964-67); artist in oil, some etching and sculpture; *b* Darlington, 1 Mar., 1945. *m* R. G. Denning. two *s.* *Educ:* Headington School for Girls, Oxford. *Studied:* Ruskin School, Oxford University, University of Illinois, U.S.A., Mem. of the Italian Academy. *Exhib:* R.A., Paris Salon, Oxford University Colleges, N.E.A.C., R.O.I., Southwark Cathedral. *Commissions:* mostly private. *Signs work:* "Chilton." *Address:* Purlin House, Toot Baldon, Oxford OX44 9NE.

CHIPP, Beverley, artist in eclectic media, photography, paint, literary and 3D art; specialises in thought provoking pieces and propaganda; younger sister of painter Terry Chipp; *b* Yorkshire. *Studied:* self-taught. *Exhib:* "It's a Fine Line" and "Angeltoad Landing", Lauderdale House (2001), "All Stars", Union Chapel, London (2001). *Publications:* "Going to Court, Not War", an introduction to the International Court of Justice. *Signs work:* "angeltoad." *Address:* 10 Chenies St. Chambers, 9 Chenies St., London WC1E 7ET. *Email:* angeltoad@aol.com

CHIPP, Terry, M.A. (1994); painter and mixed media constructor; artist and art education adviser, tutor to individuals and small groups; *b* Yorkshire, 1949. *Studied:* Doncaster and Durham (1967-1971). *Exhib:* four solo exhibs. and many group exhibs., including Doncaster Artists, touring exhib. in Kentucky, U.S.A. *Work in collections:* private collections across U.K. and ten countries worldwide. *Commissions:* many private commissions for landscapes and house portraits. *Signs work:* "T CHIPP." *Address:* 250 Sprotbrough Rd., Doncaster, S. Yorks. DN5 8BY. *Email:* terry@chippco.co.uk

CHRISTIE, Janet Mary, D.A. (Edin.) (1961), F.S.B.A. (1986 resigned 1997); R.H.S. Silver medal (1982), Grenfell medal (1985); former founder mem. Soc. of Botanical Artists; painter in water-colour; *b* Kampala, Uganda, 12 Mar., 1939. two *s.* one *d. Educ:* Cranley, Edinburgh. *Studied:* Edinburgh College of Art (1957-61, Robin Philipson, Gillies, John Maxwell, John Houston). *Exhib:* R.S.S.W., S.A.A.C., R.H.S., also various mixed exhbns.; solo shows: Norwich, London, and Edinburgh area; Royal Academy Summer Exhibition 2001. *Signs work:* "J.M.C." *Address:* Marbert, Springhill Rd., Peebles EH45 9ER.

CHRISTOPHER, Ann, R.A., F.R.B.S., R.W.A., B.A.; sculptor; *b* Watford, Herts., 4 Dec., 1947. *m* K. Cook. *Educ:* Watford Girls' Grammar School. *Studied:* Harrow School of Art (1965-66), West of England College of Art (1966-69). *Exhib:* Redfern Gallery, London; Ann Kendall Richards Inc., New York; R.A. *Work in collections:* Bristol City A.G., Contemporary Arts Soc., Chantrey Collection, London, Glynn Vivian A.G., Royal Academy. *Commissions:* 1997 Linklaters & Paines, London, 1998 Gt. Barrington, U.S.A., 2001 Port Marine, Bristol. *Publications:* Ann Christopher 'Sculpture 1969-89'. also 'Sculpture 1989-94. *Signs work:* "AC." *Address:* Stable Block, Hay St., Marshfield, Chippenham SN14 8PF.

CHUGG, Brian J., N.D.D., A.T.D. (1951); painter in oil, etc., author; lecturer, North Devon College (1953-79); *b* Braunton, Devon, 3 Nov., 1926. *m* Mary Bryan Cooper. *Educ:* Challoners School. *Studied:* architecture: under B.W. Oliver F.R.I.B.A. (1944-46); art: Bideford Art School (1946-49), Camberwell Art School under M. Bloch and K. Vogel (1949-50). *Exhib:* Westward Ho! Art Soc., one-man exhbns., Barnstaple (1953, 1958, 1994), Bideford (2001). *Publications:* author, Devon a Thematic Study; Victorian and Edwardian Devon from Old Photographs, etc. *Signs work:* "BRIAN CHUGG" (plus date). *Address:* Crossley House, Bishops Tawton, Devon EX32 0BS.

CHUHAN, Jagjit (Ms.), D.F.A.(Lond.) (1977); artist in oil on canvas; lecturer, curator; *b* India, 10 Jan., 1955. *Studied:* Slade School of Fine Art (1973-77). *Exhib:* solo shows: Ikon Gallery, B'ham (1987), Commonwealth Inst., London (1987), Horizon Gallery, London (1987); mixed shows: Barbican Centre, London (1988), Tate Gallery, Liverpool (1990-91), Galeria Civica, Marsala, Sicily (1991), Arnolfini, Bristol (1991), Pitshanger Gallery, London (1999). *Work in collections:* Arthur Anderson & Co.; Arts Council Collection; North West Arts Board. *Publications:* Co-editor: Lines of Desire (Liverpool Art School/Oldham Art Gallery, 1998). *Address:* Liverpool Art School, John Moores University, 68 Hope St., Liverpool L1 9EB.

CINZIA: see BONADA, Cinzia.

CIOBOTARU, Gillian Wise: see WISE, Gillian.

CLARK, Bruce Michael, M.A., D.A.E., Cert. Ed.; painter in oil; *b* Bedfont, 17 July, 1937. *m* Jill Clark. two *s. Educ:* Strodes School. *Studied:* Bath Academy of Art, Corsham (1958-60) under Howard Hodgkin, Gwyther Irwin, William Crozier. *Exhib:* nine one-man shows including Chiltern Gallery, London; Compendium Galleries, Birmingham; Worcester City A.G.; One Off Gallery, Dover; Tabor Gallery, Canterbury; numerous group shows including Walker's Gallery; Woodstock Gallery; Kootenay Gallery, Canada; Festival de Provence, France; Minotaur Gallery, Toronto; Royal Academy, Rowley Gallery, London.; Cambridge Contemporary Arts. *Signs work:* "Clark." *Address:* Mingladon, Manns Hill, Bossingham, Canterbury, Kent CT4 6ED.

CLARK, John M'Kenzie, D.A. (Dundee, 1950); N.D.D. (Painting) St. Martin's (1956); artist in oil, water-colour, ink; winner of Punch scholarship; *b* Dundee, 29 Nov., 1928. *Educ:* Harris Academy, Dundee. *Studied:* Dundee College of Art (1945-50), Norwich Art College (1950-51), Hospitalfield Art School (1953), St. Martin's Art School (1955-56). *Exhib:* R.A., R.S.A., R.S.W., S.S.A., R.G.I., United Soc. of Artists, one-man shows at Dundee, Edinburgh (1960). Mem. Royal Glasgow Institute of Fine Art. *Work in collections:* City of Dundee Permanent Collection (1961). *Publications:* work repro.: in Glad Mag. *Signs work:* "J. M'KENZIE CLARK." *Address:* 2 Birchwood Pl., Dundee DD1 2AT.

CLARK, Kenneth Inman Carr, M.B.E. (1990), D.F.A. (Lond. 1948); artist in ceramics; partner with Ann Clark; *b* 31 July, 1922. *m* Ann Clark. one *s.* one *d. Educ:* Nelson College, N.Z. *Studied:* Slade School of Fine Art (1945-48) painting, Central School of Art and Design (1949) under Dora Billington, ceramics, and G. Friend, engraving. *Exhib:* one-man shows, Piccadilly Gallery, Zwemmer Gallery, and many group shows in England and abroad. *Work in collections:* Wellington, N.Z., Auckland, N.Z., Japan. *Publications:* Practical Pottery and Ceramics, Throwing for Beginners, The Potters Manual. *Signs work:* see appendix. *Address:* Merton House, Vicarage Way, Ringmer, Lewes, E. Sussex BN8 5LA.

CLARK, Norman Alexander, R.W.S.; Royal Academy Schools Gold Medallist and Edward Stott Scholar in Historical Painting (1931), Armitage Bronze Medallist in Pictorial Design (1931), Landseer prize-winner in Mural Decoration (1932),

Leverhulme Scholar (1935); painter in oil and water-colour; *b* Ilford, Essex, 17 Feb., 1913. *m* Constance Josephine Barnard. one *d. Educ:* Bancroft's School, Woodford. *Studied:* Central School, London (1929), R.A. Schools (1930-35). *Exhib:* R.A., R.W.S. *Work in collections:* Harris Museum and Art Gallery, Preston, Lancs., Imperial War Museum, and in private collections. *Signs work:* "Norman Clark." *Address:* Mountfield, Brighton Rd., Hurstpierpoint, Sussex.

CLARK, Peter Christian, Oxford University Certificate of Fine Art; professional painter of abstract paintings in oil, acrylic and gouache; hand-made prints and wallpaper, bas-relief constructions; *b* Bradford, Yorks., 19 Apr., 1950. *Educ:* Clifton House School, Harrogate, H.M.S. Conway, Anglesey, N. Wales. *Studied:* Ruskin School of Drawing and Fine Art under Richard Naish, M.A. *Exhib:* mixed shows: Ashmolean Museum, Oxford, Museum of Modern Art, Oxford, Llewellyn Alexander Gallery, London. Private commissions. *Signs work:* "Peter Clark", "Christian Clark" and "P.C.C." *Address:* 40 Delancey St., London NW1 7RY.

CLARK, Thomas Humphrey, A.C.P., A.R.D.S.; artist in black and white, water-colour, traditional canal ware painter; *b* Manchester, 30 Jan., 1921. *m* Betty Whitley Clark. two *s. Educ:* Leeds Grammar School. *Studied:* Bradford Regional College of Art under Frank Lyle, A.T.D., Fred C. Jones, A.T.D., R.B.A. *Exhib:* Royal Cambrian Academy. *Signs work:* "T. H. Clark" and see appendix. *Address:* Woodland Rise, Beemire, Windermere, Cumbria LA23 1DW.

CLARKE, Edward, M.A., R.A.S. (Cert.), B.A. (Hons.); figurative portrait and landscape artist painting in oils and drawing in charcoal; *b* Hartlepool, 1962. *Educ:* Manor Comprehensive School, Hartlepool. *Studied:* Cleveland College of Art (1980-81), Sheffield Hallam University (1982-85), R.A. Schools (1985-88). *Exhib:* R.A. Summer Exhbn. and R.A. Dip. Galleries, London (1986, 1987, 1988), N.P.G., London (1988, 1991), Agnews, London (1990), Gray A.G., Hartlepool (1994), Middlesbrough A.G. (1995). *Work in collections:* various, including National Trust's Foundation for Art. *Signs work:* "Edward Clarke." *Address:* 304 Catcote Rd., Hartlepool, Cleveland TS25 3EF.

CLARKE, Geoffrey, R.A., A.R.C.A.; artist and sculptor; *b* 28 Nov., 1924. *m* 1947, Ethelwynne Tyrer. two *s. Educ:* Royal College of Art (Hons.). *Exhib:* one-man shows: Gimpel, Redfern, Taranman, Yorkshire Sculpture Park and Travelling Retrospective, Fine Art Society. *Work in collections:* (stained glass) Coventry and Lincoln Cathedrals, Taunton, Ipswich, Crownhill Plymouth; (sculpture) Coventry and Chichester Cathedrals; Cambridge (Churchill, Homerton, Newnham), Exeter, Liverpool, Newcastle, Manchester and Lancaster Universities; Bedford, Chichester and Winchester Colleges. Other Principal Work: Castrol House, Thorn Electric, Newcastle Civic Centre, Nottingham Playhouse, Culham Atomic Energy, Guard's Chapel, Birdcage Walk, Aldershot Landscape, St. Paul Minnesota, Majlis Abu Dhabi, York House, Warwick University. *Publications:* Symbols for Man by Peter Black. *Address:* Stowe Hill, Hartest, Bury St. Edmunds, Suffolk IP29 4EQ.

CLARKE, Graham Arthur, Hon.M.A. Kent Ambassador, A.R.C.A. Chevalier de la Confrerie du Cep Ardechois, Hon. Associate K.I.A.D.; artist in etching and water-colour, author; *b* Chipping Norton, Oxon., 27 Feb., 1941. *m* Wendy. one *s.* three *d. Studied:* Beckenham School of Art, R.C.A. *Work in collections:* V. & A., British

Museum, Tate Gallery, National Libs. Scotland, Ireland and Wales, Hiroshima Peace Museum, National Lib. Congress (U.S.A.). *Publications:* Graham Clarke's History of England, Graham Clarke's Grand Tour, Joe Carpenter and Son - English Nativity, W. Shakespeare (Gent.) actual notte booke, The World of Graham Clarke (Japanese), A Norwegian Sketchbook, Graham Clarke's Kent & 'Baitboxsten' – Graham Clarke's Cornwall. *Signs work:* "Graham Clarke." *Address:* White Cottage, Green Lane, Boughton Monchelsea, Maidstone, Kent ME17 4LF.

CLARKE, Granville Daniel, F.R.S.A., Y.W.S.; professional artist in water-colour and pencil; lecturer/demonstrator combining art, poetry and music; *b* Keighley, Yorks., 26 Oct., 1940. *Studied:* Barnsley School of Art (1955-60). City & Guilds 1st Class Hons. (1957), Full Tech. Cert. (1959). Professional musician/writer/performer with 'Foggy Dew-O' (1965-76); Director, Scarlet Songs Publishing; com.mem., Yorkshire Water-colour Soc.; co-founder, Meadowlands; environmental artist: Sight Savers, Whale and Dolphin, The Countryside Commission, wild flower conservation; environmental education through The Arts, Kirklees, W. Yorks. (1992-97). *Exhib:* numerous one-man exhbns. since 1977; Westminster Gallery, London, Salford A.G., Mercer Gallery Harrogate, Doncaster A.G., Sir William Russell Flint Gallery Guildford, Laing at Mall Galleries London, Barnsley to Bombay Round the World Exhbn., Cooper Gallery Barnsley. Permanent exhibtn.: Cannon Hall, Cawthorne, Yorks; Four Seasons Gallery, Wortley, S. Yorks. *Commissions:* English Nature, P. & O. Cruise Lines, Mercedes Benz, Guardian Newspapers, Michael Stewart Fine Art, Yorkshire Electricity, Yorkshire Water, Michael Parkinson, Countess of Wharncliffe. *Publications:* 'Sketches and Expressions' (1991). Produced and presented: Clarke Colours the Lowry Trail - Art TV (1993), Clarke Colours York - Art Video (1999). 36 national TV appearances Channel 4 artist in residence/commentator 'Water-colour Challenge' (1998). *Signs work:* "Granville D. Clarke" see appendix. *Address:* Huskar Cottage Studio, Silkstone Common, nr. Barnsley, S.Yorks. S75 4RJ. *Website:* Granville D. Clarke Water-colour Gallery website: http//www.yol.co.uk.clarke *Email:* g.danny.clarke@virgin.net

CLARKE, Hilda Margery, B.A. (Hons.), F.R.S.A.; artist in oils and other media; Director, 'The First Gallery'; *b* Manchester, 10 June, 1926. *m* Geoffrey Clarke. two *s. Educ:* Eccles Secondary School. *Studied:* privately in Manchester (Master: L. S. Lowry) and Hamburg; Southampton Art College, Ruskin School Print Workshop, Oxford; B.A. Southampton. *Exhib:* Tibb Lane, Manchester, Bettles Gallery, Ringwood; London Galleries: Camden Town, F.P.S., Buckingham Gate; Southampton City A.G., New Ashgate, Farnham; one-man shows, Hamwic, Southampton, Westgate Gallery, Winchester, Southampton University; The First Gallery, Southampton, Turner Sims Concert Hall, Soton., Hiscock Gallery, Southsea, Ramsgate Library Gallery, Kent. *Work in collections:* Southampton University, Southern Arts, (RAB) St. Mary's Hospital, I.O.W. *Signs work:* "H.M. Clarke." *Address:* The First Gallery, 1 Burnham Chase, Bitterne, Southampton SO18 5DG.

CLARKE, Jeff, A.R.E., N.D.D., Rome Scholarship (1956-58), British Inst. Fund Scholarship; *b* Brighton, 1935. *Studied:* Brighton College of Art (1952-56). *Exhib:* Oxford Bear Lane Gallery, Oxford Gallery, Museum of Modern Art Oxford, Christ Church Picture Gallery, R.E., R.A. Summer shows, National Print shows Mall Galleries, London. *Work in collections:* Ashmolean Museum, Universities of Oxford,

Cambridge, Reading. Many private collections in Europe and U.S.A. *Signs work:* "Jeff Clarke". *Address:* 17 Newton Rd., Oxford OX1 4PT.

CLARKE, Pat, Surrey Dip. (1969); artist in water-colour, oil, pastel; printmaker; Adult Education teacher, and special needs teacher (1970-80); since 1984, joint owner with husband of art gallery, Oriel y Odraig, Blaenau Ffestiniog, N. Wales; *b* Banstead. *m* Peter Elliott. *Studied:* Reigate Art School (1966-69). *Exhib:* Loggia Gallery, Gallery of Modern Art, London, Hereford City A.G., Rhyl and Denbigh Arts Centres, etc; 45 one-woman shows. *Work in collections:* Hereford City A.G. *Publications:* To the Mountain (1994). *Clubs:* N.S.P.S., F.P.S., R.Cam.A.Conwy, Watercolour Soc. of Wales. *Signs work:* "Pat Clarke." *Address:* 4 Bryn Dinas, Rhiwbryfdir, Blaenau Ffestiniog, Gwynedd LL41 3NS.

CLARYSSE, Maggy, Dip. Brussels Academy of Art (1956); painter in oil, water-colour, pastels, silk-screen printing; *b* Brussels, 21 Oct., 1937. married. one *s. Educ:* Convent Sacre Coeur, Brussels. *Studied:* Brussels Academy of Art. *Exhib:* numerous exhbns. in U.K., France, Belgium. *Work in collections:* Bourne Gallery Reigate; private collections in U.S.A., Japan, Australia, S. America, France, Germany, Belgium, Italy, Switzerland, Sweden. *Publications:* The Graphic Artist (1980). *Signs work:* "M. Clarysse." *Address:* 13 The Elms, Vine Rd., London SW13 0NF.

CLATWORTHY, Robert, R.A. (1973); sculptor; mem. Fine Art Panel of National Council for Diplomas in Art and Design (1961-71); head of Fine Art, Central School of Art and Design (1970-75); *b* 1 Jan., 1928. *Studied:* West of England College of Art, Chelsea School of Art, The Slade. *Exhib:* Hanover Gallery (1954, 1956), Waddington Galls. (1965), Holland Park Open Air Sculpture (1957), Battersea Park Open Air Sculpture (1960, 1963), Tate Gallery British Sculpture in the Sixties (1965), Basil Jacobs Gallery (1972), British Sculpture '72, Burlington House, Diploma Galleries R.A. (1977), Photographer's Gallery (1981). *Work in collections:* Arts Council, Contemporary Art Society, Tate Gallery, V. & A., G.L.C.; Monumental Horse and Rider installed at 1 Finsbury Ave., EC2. (1984); portrait of Dame Elisabeth Frink purchased by N.P.G. (1985). *Address:* 1a Park St., London SE1.

CLAUGHTON, Richard Bentley, F.R.B.S.; sculptor; *b* London, 1917. married. one *s. Educ:* Woodford House School, Kent. *Studied:* Slade School (1946-49). Public commissions in London and provinces; Australia; Nigeria. *Exhib:* in galleries and open-air exhbns. in London and provinces; Holland and Lisbon. *Work in collections:* in Britain; Canada; Iraq and U.S.A. Former Director of Sculpture Studies, Slade School, University College, London. *Address:* Telham Lodge, Telham Lane, Battle, E. Sussex TN33 0SN.

CLAY, Andie Joy, B.A. (Hons.) 1975; artist in mixed media, oil; *b* Surrey, 13 Apr., 1954. *m* Dave Clay. *Studied:* London College of Printing, London (1971-75). *Exhib:* De Putron Fine Art, London; Chelsea Art Fair; Laing (97, 98); Originals Gallery, Stow on the Wold; Wexford Arts Centre, Ireland; National Botanic Garden of Wales; Oriel Plas Glyn y Weddw, N. Wales; West Wales Art Centre, Fishguard; Wales Drawing Biennale (97, 99); Washington Gallery, Penarth; Moma Wales, Machynlleth; Albany Gallery, Cardiff; Ogilvy & Estill, Conway; R.C.A., Conway; R.B.S.A. B'ham; Oriel Ceri Richards, Swansea. *Publications:* 'Paint! Landscapes

(RotoVision)'. *Clubs:* N.A.A., Permanent Waves, Axis. *Signs work:* "Andie Clay." *Address:* Porth, Blaenporth, Cardigan, Ceredigion SA43 2AP. *Website:* stdavids.co.uk/artspace/andie.htm *Email:* andieclay@blaenporth.freeserve.co.uk

CLAY, Elizabeth Hervey, S.B.A. (1998); botanical sculptures in liquid porcelain and alabaster, porcelain painter on bone china and porcelain; *b* Nakuru, Kenya, 24 Sept.,1928. *m* decd. two *s*. one *d. Educ:* Loreto Convent, Nairobi, Kenya, Rhodes University, Grahamstown, S.Africa. *Exhib:* S.B.A. Work in international and private collections. *Work in collections:* various flower sculptures. *Commissions:* various flower sculptures and painted porcelain. *Signs work:* "Sally Clay, s.b.a." *Address:* 13 Chelsea Close, Bexhill on Sea, E.Sussex TN40 1SJ.

CLEMENTS, Jeff, N.D.D. (1955), Fellow Designer Bookbinders; artist in acrylic, fine bookbinder; partner with Katinka Keus, Binderij Meridiaan, Amsterdam; formerly Dean, Faculty of Art and Design, University of the West of England (to 1988); *b* Plymouth, 23 Feb., 1934. two *s. Educ:* Devonport High School for Boys. *Studied:* Plymouth College of Art (1950-55), Central School of Arts and Crafts (1956-57). *Exhib:* from 1955 Daily Express Young Artists to recent ones in the Netherlands. *Work in collections:* fine bindings in: Royal Library, V. & A., London; Royal Library, The Hague; The Museum of the Book, The Hague; Texas University; University of Indiana; Röhsska Museum, Sweden; The National Library of Estonia, Tallin; The Keatley Trust; The John Paul Getty jr. Trust, etc.; paintings in private collections: Nice, Geneva, London, Birmingham, Bristol, Exeter, Oxford, York, The Hague, Amsterdam, Washington D.C., etc. *Publications:* Book Binding (Arco, 1963), Ambachtelijk Boekbinden (Gaade, 1991). *Signs work:* see appendix. *Address:* Jan Luijkenstraat 38II, 1071 CR Amsterdam, Netherlands.

CLEMENTS, Keith, N.D.D., A.T.D., D.A.E., Ph.D.; painter, illustrator; designer, author, lecturer; *b* Brighton, 9 May, 1931. *m* Jackie Sinclair. one *s*. one *d. Educ:* Varndean Grammar School, Brighton. *Studied:* Brighton College of Art (1947-53), Birmingham School of Art Education (1964-65). *Exhib:* Alwin Gallery, Bloomsbury Workshop, R.A., R.E., Young Contemporaries, Arts Council tours. *Work in collections:* Brighton Museum, University of Sussex. *Publications:* Henry Lamb: The Artist and his Friends (1985). *Signs work:* "Keith Clements." *Address:* 29 Meeching Rd., Newhaven, E. Sussex BN9 9RL.

CLIFTON, David James, A.R.C.A., M.A.; professor fine art; exhbn. artist, painter in water-colour and oil, mixed media; *b* Derby, 10 July, 1938. *Educ:* at private and public schools; sometime placed Truro's (Eton). *Studied:* Bournville School of Art (Ruskin Hall), Birmingham College of Art (1956-58), Royal College of Art (1958-61). *Exhib:* Bourneville, Birmingham, Young Contemporaries, Royal College of Art, and London shows. Possible retrospective hung at Tate: withdrawn. *Commissions:* private. *Publications:* Contemporary Situation; New Wave Writing; Poetry; Serious Matters; Existential Surreal Metaphysical Metaphor Ethic Image and Criterion. *Clubs:* Sometime: guest invitation National Liberal Club in London. *Signs work:* "D. J. Clifton." Ref: no third party agent. *Address:* Flat 8, 63 Fountain Rd., Edgbaston, Birmingham B17 8NP.

CLIFTON-BLIGH, Olivia, B.A. (Hons.); sculptor in bronze, plaster and paper; *b* Wroughton, 11 Oct., 1971. *m* Daniel Petkoff. one *d. Educ:* Downe House, Berks.

Studied: Goldsmiths' College, London University (1990-1993), Brighton Polytechnic (1989-1990). *Exhib:* solo and group exhibs., London and various galleries in British Isles; R.A. Summer Exhib. (1996-1998), Kings Rd. Gallery, London (2000), Merriscourt, Oxon (2000). *Signs work:* "OLIVIA CLIFTON-BLIGH." *Address:* 2 Bull Mill, Crockerton, Warminster, Wilts. BA12 8AY.

CLINE, Penelope, Cert. of Art, Cert. of Printmaking; artist in oil and acrylic; *b* London, 27 Apr., 1947. *m* Keith Richard Cline. one *s.* two (one decd.) *d. Educ:* Deepdene School. *Studied:* Brighton Polytechnic. *Exhib:* S.W.A. (1994-97), N.A.P.A. (1994-96, 1998-99), Brighton Open (1993, 1996), Chichester Open (1995); solo shows: Brighton Festival and local socs. annually. *Work in collections:* U.S.A. and S. Africa. *Publications:* contributed to 'Her Mind's Eye'. *Clubs:* N.A.P.A., Assoc. Sussex Artists. *Signs work:* "Penelope Cline" or "P. Cline." *Address:* 23 Brangwyn Drive, Westdene, Brighton BN1 8XB.

CLORAN, Julian Thomas (aka:Jules), N.A.P.A. (1998); self taught artist in acrylic and felt-tip pens; *b* Brighton, 10 Mar., 1967. *Exhib:* numerous local and national shows since 1987, including Westminster Gallery, N.A.P.A. London show (1999). *Commissions:* series of posters advertising exhbns., cabaret and other events for Brighton venues including 'One Off Gallery'. *Publications:* work repro.: line drawings in small press magazines. *Clubs:* N.A.P.A., Mensa. *Signs work:* "Jules Cloran." *Address:* 22a Loder Rd., Brighton, BN1 6PJ.

CLOSSICK, Peter, B.B.S.I. (1969), B.A. (Hons.) Fine Art (1978), A.T.C. (1979); artist in 2D painting and drawing, lecturer/fine art; *b* London, 18 May, 1948. *m* Joyce. one *d. Studied:* Camberwell School of Art (1974-78, Antony Eyton, David Hepher). *Exhib:* John Moores, London Group, R.A., Whitechapel Open, P.S., Cooling Gallery, Cork St., Gallery Duncan Terrace, London. *Work in collections:* Corpus Christi College, Oxford, private and international. *Publications:* The New Painting Course (Quarto plc). Painting Without a Brush (Studio Vista). *Clubs:* President London Group (2001-). *Address:* 358 Lee High Rd., Lee Green, London SE12 8RS. *Email:* peter@crazymoose.co.uk

CLOUDSLEY, J. Anne, M.C.S.P. (Chartered Physiotherapist 1935), L.C.A.D. (1975), Dip. B.S. (1976); artist in oil, mixed media, etcher, lithographer; *b* Reigate. Surrey, 20 Mar., 1915. *m* Prof. J. L. Cloudsley-Thompson. three *s. Educ:* St. Monica's, Reigate, Surrey, University College Hospital, London (1932-1935). *Studied:* Byam Shaw School of Fine Art (1972-1976), Goldsmiths College (1976-1977), under John Flavin, Bill Jacklin, Bernard Dunstan, Diana Armfield, Peter Gerrard. *Exhib:* Recent exhibs. include, New Burlington Gallery (1994), Atrium Gallery (1997), Pump House Gallery (1998), Curwen Gallery (1998), Barbican Centre (2000), National Theatre (2001). *Work in collections:* Statoil (U.K.) Ltd. and many private. *Commissions:* University College, London, design for Biological Council Medal. *Publications:* book illustrations for Allen and Unwin, Foulis, Crowood Press. *Signs work:* "Anne Cloudsley." *Address:* 10 Battishill St., Islington, London N1 1TE.

CLOUGH, Carolyn Stafford: see STAFFORD, C. Carolyn.

CLOUGH, Pauline Susan, P.S. (1982); artist in pastel, acrylic and oil; *b* 16 Oct.,

1943. *m* Peter Clough. one *s.* one *d. Educ:* Sharmans Cross High School. *Studied:* Bourneville School of Art, Birmingham (Phyllis Devey). *Exhib:* R.A., R.I., P.S., S.W.A., R.B.S.A. and many provincial galleries. *Work in collections:* Worthing Museum. *Clubs:* Council mem. Pastel Soc. *Signs work:* "P.S. Clough" and "Clough." *Address:* Sundown, 103 Allington Rd., Newick, Lewes, E. Sussex BN8 4NH.

CLUTTERBUCK, Jan, painter in water-colours; teacher of painting, Cassio College, Watford; Chairman, Women's International Art Club (1973-76); *b* Newton, Mass., 16 July, 1919. *m* Jeremy R. H. Clutterbuck. one *s.* one *d. Educ:* Greenbrier College, West Virginia. *Studied:* self-taught; studied printmaking at Harrow School of Art. *Exhib:* R.A., N.S., American Embassy. *Work in collections:* Gloucester Education Committee, Coventry Education Committee. *Clubs:* W.I.A.C. *Signs work:* "Jan Clutterbuck." *Address:* Penthands House, Sarratt, Herts. WD3 6BL.

CLYNE, Henry Horne, D.A.(Edin.); sculptor; Principal Lecturer i/c Sculpture Dept. (retd.); *b* Caithness, Scotland, 5 Mar., 1930. *m* Elaine Dunnett. one *s. Educ:* Edinburgh College of Art (1948-54); Harkness Fellow, U.S.A. (1959-61); IWCAT Tokoname, Japan (1986). *Exhib:* generally group shows and major Festivals (1954-66), and several one-man shows. *Work in collections:* University of Stirling (S.A.C.); University of East Anglia and Sainsbury Collection; IWCAT permanent collection (Japan); and many private collections in U.K., U.S.A., Europe and Japan. Awarded bronze medals, Bicentenaire, Haute Garonne; 1990 started "Sheepshapes", ceramic sheep individually hand-made. *Signs work:* "Henry H. Clyne" and see appendix. *Address:* Sunnymede, Horsebridge Rd., Kings Somborne, Stockbridge, Hants. SO20 6PT.

CLYNE, Thora, M.A.Hons. in Fine Art (1960); Special Prize (S.S.W.A., 1984); Anne Redpath Award (S.S.W.A., 1979); Andrew Grant postgrad. Scholarship and Travel Fellowship (1960-61); artist in oil, water-colour, pastel, pen and ink, lithography; *b* Wick, Caithness, 10 Nov., 1937. *m* G. Clemson, composer. *Educ:* Edinburgh University; Edinburgh College of Art (1955-61). *Exhib:* Lybster Gallery, Caithness (1993, 1995); group shows: Morrison Portrait Competition, Royal Scottish Academy (1991, 1995, 1997); Laing Landscape Competition (1991); Scotland's Gardens, Inverleith House, Edinburgh (1996, 1999); Braveart, Smith Gallery, Stirling (1996); 'Homage to Senefelder', Edinburgh Printmakers Workshop (1996); London Print Fair, Air Gallery (1997); S.O.F.A., Llewellyn Alexander, London (1997, 1998, 1999, 2000); Inverness Open (1998, 2001); Torrance Gallery Edinburgh Christmas Show (1998, 1999, 2000); 200 years of lithography E.P.M.W. (1999); S.O.F.A. Clifton Gallery, Bristol (1999); N.A.Y.D. (2000); dfn Gallery, New York. *Work in collections:* Edinburgh Corporation Schools, Ross & Cromarty Educ. Authority, First Scottish-American Trust Co., Ltd., Gillies Bequest, R.S.A. *Commissions:* Portraits of cats. *Signs work:* "Thora Clyne." *Address:* Tillywhally Cottage, Milnathort, Kinross-shire KY13 0RN. *Website:* www.catpawtraits.co.uk *Email:* thoracat@catpawtraits.co.uk

COATE, Peter, R.W.A., A.T.D., Chelsea Dip. (1950); painter in oil, water-colour, and teacher; Director, Mendip Painting Centre (1974-86); *b* Nailsea, Som., 9 Mar., 1926. *m* Margaret Bickerton (died 1978). Pamela Somerville (1980). one *s.* one *d. Educ:* Sherborne. *Studied:* Chelsea under Robert Medley and Claude Rogers. *Exhib:*

London Group, R.A., S.WL.A., R.W.A., R.O.I. and many exhbns. in west country galleries. Painter of wild landscape and old buildings, including churches. Early work mostly of Somerset. Later made many painting excursions to Wales - Brecon, Pembrokeshire and around Cader Idris. Also Cill Rialaig in Western Ireland. Since 1996 became increasingly interested in painting birds. *Work in collections:* R.W.A., Hertfordshire and Cumberland County Councils, Nuffield Foundation. *Signs work:* "Peter Coate." *Address:* The Manor Farm, Stone Allerton, nr. Axbridge, Somerset BS26 2NN.

COATES, Thomas J., P.R.B.A., N.E.A.C., R.W.S., R.P.; awarded De Lazlo Medal, 1st and 3rd prizes in Sunday Times Water-colour Exhbns. (1988, 1989); painter of landscapes, townscapes and portraits in oil and water-colour; *b* 1941. *Studied:* Bournville and Birmingham Colleges of Art (1956-61), R.A. Schools (1961-64). *Exhib:* R.A., R.B.A., and many one-man shows including New Grafton Gallery. *Address:* Bladon Studio, Hurstbourne Tarrant, Hants. SP11 0AH.

COBB, David, P.P.R.S.M.A., R.O.I.; self taught artist; *b* 13 May, 1921. *m* Jean Main, Associate Fellow, Guild of Glass Engravers (died 1998). one *d. Educ:* Nautical College, Pangbourne. *Exhib:* R.O.I., R.S.M.A. *Work in collections:* National Maritime Museum, Royal Naval Museum, Fleet Air Arm Museum, Army Museum, Mersey Museum, Hull Museum. *Clubs:* Royal Cruising Club (Life mem.), Royal Yacht Squadron (Hon. painter). *Signs work:* "DAVID COBB." *Address:* Woodis, Setley, Brockenhurst, Hants. SO42 7UH.

COBLEY, David Hugh, R.P. (1997), R.W.A. (2001); John Brandler prize (1993); portrait and figure painter in oil, charcoal, pencil, pen; Hon. Sec., Royal Soc. of Portrait Painters; *b* Northampton, 27 June, 1954. *m* Masami Minagawa. three *d. Studied:* Northampton and Liverpool. *Exhib:* R.A., B.P. Portrait Award, R.P., R.W.A., Hunting Art prizes, Discerning Eye, New English Art Club. *Work in collections:* throughout the U.K. and abroad. *Commissions:* English National Ballet, Royal Engineers, Royal Marines, National Soc. for Epilepsy, Westminster Abbey, etc. *Publications:* work repro.: The Artist, Artists and Illustrators, International Artist, Art Class (Harper Collins) magazines. *Clubs:* R.P., R.W.A. *Signs work:* see appendix. *Address:* 22 Linden Cres., Lower Westwood, Bradford-on-Avon, Wilts. BA15 2AN. *Website:* www.davidcobley.co.uk *Email:* mail@davidcobley.co.uk

COBURN, Ivor Basil, D.A. (1955), N.D.D. (1956), A.R.U.A., F.S.B.A.; R.H.S. six Gold and two Silver medals, two Grenfell; Royal Ulster Academy Gold medal (perpetual); artist in water-colour and oil; *b* Belfast, 10 Apr., 1934. *m* Patricia. one *s.* three *d. Educ:* Grosvenor High School, Belfast. *Studied:* Belfast College of Art, Leeds College of Art, and University. *Exhib:* one-man shows: Belfast, Dublin, Newcastle, Londonderry, Glasgow, London, Antwerp, Brussels, Paris, Annecy, Compiegne; group shows: London, Belfast, Brussels, Paris, Dublin, Rochester, Windsor. *Work in collections:* U.S.A., Canada, France, Belgium, Holland, Australia, New Zealand, Israel, Sweden, England, Ireland, Scotland, Wales, Germany. *Publications:* Flower Painting Techniques by Sue Burton. *Clubs:* S.B.A. (Founder mem.). *Signs work:* "Ivor B. Coburn." *Address:* The Springs, 50 Megargy Rd., Magherafelt, Co. Londonderry BT45 5HP, N. Ireland.

COCHRAN, Margi, C.L.W.A.C. (1976), R.M.S. (1987), M.A.A. (1989); artist in oil, pastel, water-colour and colour pencil; *b* Philadelphia, Pa., 30 Aug., 1925. *m* Arthur Oschwald, Jr. one *s.* one *d. Studied:* Philadelphia Museum School of Art (1945-47), Montclair Art Museum (1974-79). Teacher - private groups (1973-83). *Exhib:* 16 solo shows; many group shows; many juried shows, many awards, N.J., N.Y.C., Fla., Ga., Wash. D.C. International solo exhbn. (1995), Kirkleatham Old Hall Museum, Redcar, England. *Work in collections:* M.A.S.-F., Kirkleatham Old Hall Museum, Redcar, Millburn-Shorthills Collection of noted N.J. artists in area. *Publications:* American Impression of Staithes (1995). *Clubs:* C.L.W.A.C., R.M.S., M.A.A., M.A.S.-F., M.P.S.F.S. (Washington D.C.), G.M.A.S. *Signs work:* see appendix. *Address:* Box 483, Bernardsville, New Jersey 07924-0483, U.S.A.

COCKER, Doug, D.A., A.R.S.A., F.R.B.S.; sculptor; *b* Alyth, Perthshire, 1945. *m* Elizabeth. two *s.* one *d. Educ:* Blairgowrie High School. *Studied:* Duncan of Jordanstone, Dundee (1963-68). *Exhib:* R.S.A., Yorkshire Sculpture Pk., The British Art Show, Air Gallery London, Serpentine Gallery London, Fruitmarket Gallery, Edinburgh, Third Eye Centre, Glasgow. *Work in collections:* Arts Council, Scottish Arts Council, Contemporary Art Soc., Kelvingrove A.G., Glasgow, Peterborough A.G., Greenshields Foundation, Montreal, Leicester University, Hunterian A.G., Glasgow, Essex C.C., Staffs. C.C., M.M.A. Sarajevo. *Signs work:* "DOUG COCKER." *Address:* Lundie Mill, Lundie, Angus DD2 5NW.

COCKRILL, Maurice, artist in oil on canvas; *b* England, 1936; partner Helen Moslin. three *s. Studied:* Wrexham School of Art and University of Reading (1960-64). *Exhib:* one-man shows: Edward Totah Gallery (1984, 1985), Kunstmuseum, Düsseldorf (1985), Bernard Jacobson Gallery (1987, 1988, 1990, 1992, 1994, 1995), Retrospective '1974-94' Walker A.G. (1995) (illus. cat.), Galerie Clivage, Paris (1995), Annandale Galleries, Sydney (1995), Galleri Clivage, Paris (1997), Galerie Helmut Pabst, Frankfurt (1997), Royal West of England Academy (1998). *Work in collections:* A.C.G.B., Walker A.G., Unilever, B.M., Contemporary Art Soc., Centro Cultural Arte Contemporaneo, Polanco, Mexico, Kunstmuseum, Düsseldorf. *Signs work:* full signature on back. *Address:* 78b Park Hall Rd., London SE21 8BW.

CODNER, John, R.W.A. (1937); artist in oil, portrait, landscape, still lives, marine, etc.; asst. master, Sir John Cass School of Art (1947-51); *b* Beaconsfield, 1913. *m* Rachael Notley. two *s. Studied:* Regent St. Polytechnic School of Art (1930-32, Harry Watson). *Exhib:* R.A., R.P., R.W.A., most provincial galleries etc. *Work in collections:* Office of Works, R.W.A., Bristol, Gloucester Essex Corps., London Universities, Inst. of Civil Engineers, City Livery Club, Bristol Masonic Hall, R.C.G.P., many boardrooms and private collections, Belgium, Canada, Europe, America, U.K., Far East, etc. Served in H.M. Forces (1939-45) in R.E. in camouflage; Co-founder of C.A.R.E. for the Mentally Handicapped with Peter Forbes (Slade). *Clubs:* Arts Dover St., Bristol Savages. *Signs work:* "John Whitlock" until death of his father 1958, since then "John Codner." *Address:* 16 Albert Rd., Clevedon, N. Somerset BS21 7RR.

CODNER, Stephen Milton, painter in oil, pastel, portrait, landscape, still life, etcher; *b* Clevedon, Som., 1952. *m* Carolyn Hamilton. three *d. Educ:* Bryanston School Dorset. *Studied:* Camberwell School of Art and Crafts, City and Guilds Art School. *Exhib:* R.A., R.P., R.W.A., 'Discerning Eye.' *Signs work:* "S. M. CODNER" or "STEPHEN CODNER." *Address:* 23 Maplestead Rd., London SW2 3LY.

COHEN, Bernard, Slade Dip.; professional artist in painting and printmaking; Slade Professor and University of London Chair in Fine Art; Director of Slade School, U.C.L.; Emeritus Slade Professor (2000), Fellow of University College, London; *b* London, 28 July, 1933. *m* Jean. one *s.* one *d. Studied:* Slade School of Fine Art (1951-54, Sir William Coldstream). *Exhib:* Gimpel Fils (1958, 1960), Hayward Gallery (1972 touring), Waddington Galleries (1972, 1974, 1977, 1979, 1981, 1990), Flowers East (1998), Flowers West, L.A. (1999), Tate Gallery (1976), drawing retrospective Ben Uri (1994), 'Artist in focus', Tate Gallery (1995), and major group exhbns. worldwide. *Work in collections:* Arts Council, M.O.M.A. (N.Y.), Tate Gallery, V. & A., etc. *Publications:* major catalogues: Hayward Retrospective 1972 - Arts Council G.B., Waddington Galleries (1974-1990), Bernard Cohen, Paintings from the 90's - Flowers East Gallery, Flowers Central (2001). *Signs work:* "Bernard Cohen" on works on paper only. *Address:* 80 Camberwell Grove, London SE5 8RF. *Email:* bc–art@excite.co.uk

COHEN, Mary, artist in oil, pen and wash, water-colour; *b* London, 21 Nov., 1910. *m* Cdr. Kenneth Cohen, C.B., C.M.G., R.N. one *s.* one *d. Studied:* Florence, Slade under Prof. Tonks and Prof. Schwabe (1928-31), and Euston Road School. *Exhib:* Leicester Galleries Mixed Exhbns., R.A., R.B.A., N.E.A.C., London Group, Roland, Browse and Delbanco, New Grafton Gallery. *Work in collections:* National Trust, Whitworth, A.G. and private collections in Gt. Britain, France and U.S.A. *Signs work:* "Mary S. C." *Address:* 33 Bloomfield Terr., London SW1.

COKER, Norman, Richard, City & Guilds of London Inst. F.E.T.C. (1974), F.S.B.A. (1986); art teacher Adult Educ. Centres; artist in oil, lecturer; *b* Grays, Essex, 27 Jan., 1927. *m* Doreen Anne. *Educ:* Park Secondary School, Grays. *Studied:* Thurrock Tech. College. *Exhib:* Nairobi, Kenya (wild life), The McEwan Gallery, Scotland (British Flower Painters), The Veryan Gallery, Cornwall, Singapore, London, Amsterdam, The Frinton Gallery; one-man show at Beecroft Gallery, Westcliff-on-Sea (1991). *Work in collections:* many private collections worldwide including H.R.H. The Princess Anne, The Princess Royal, an equestrian portrait of H.R.H. with her horse Doublet. *Commissions:* James Last (orchestra leader) a painting of the Royal Albert Hall. *Publications:* work included in "The Encyclopedia of Flower Painting Techniques" by Sue Burton (Quarto, 1997); work in print with Rosentiel's and Chelsea, Medici, Camden Graphics. Founder mem. S.B.A. (Society of Botanical Artists); awarded the Founder President's Honour in the year 2000. *Signs work:* "Norman R. Coker." *Address:* "Tensing", Muckingford Rd., Linford, Stanford-le-Hope, Essex SS17 0RF.

COKER, Peter, A.R.C.A. (1953, A.R.A. (1965), R.A. (1972), Hon. R.E. (1998); painter in oil; *b* London, 27 July, 1926. *m* Vera Crook. one (decd.) *s. Studied:* St. Martin's School of Art (1947-50) R.C.A. (1950-54). *Exhib:* Zwemmer Gallery (1956-67), Thackeray Gallery (1970-78), Gallery 10, Grosvenor St. (1980-88), retrospective: Butcher's Shop series, R.A. and touring (1979), Fitzwilliam Museum (1989), Kendal, London (1992). *Work in collections:* Tate Gallery; Arts Council; Fitzwilliam Museum, Cambridge; N.P.G.; R.C.A.; V. & A.; R.A.; Contemporary Art Soc.; Birmingham, Sheffield and Leeds City A.G's.; National Maritime Museum;

British Museum, etc. *Publications:* Etching Techniques (1974). *Signs work:* "Peter Coker" or "P.C." *Address:* The Red House, Mistley, Manningtree, Essex CO11 1BX.

COLEBORN, Deanne, A.R.C.A., R.E.; painter/etcher; *b* Worcs., 30 Dec., 1931. *m* Keith. six *d. Studied:* R.C.A. *Exhib:* R.A., R.E. *Signs work:* "DEANNE." *Address:* Downe Hall Farm, Downe, Kent.

COLEBORN, Keith, A.R.C.A., A.T.D., F.R.S.A.; until July 1976 principal, Ravensbourne College of Art and Crafts; regional art principal, N.W. Kent; principal, Bromley College of Art (1946-62); principal, Stourbridge School of Art (1937-40); principal, Wallasey School of Art (1940-46); *b* Portsmouth. *Address:* Downe Hall Farm, Downe, Kent.

COLEMAN, Brian, Mem. Pastel Soc.; painter in water-colour; Art Director/Graphic Designer, advertising; *b* Cheam, Surrey, 3 Sept., 1935. *m* Joan Coleman. *Educ:* Stoneleigh Secondary Modern. *Exhib:* Kingsmead Gallery, Bookham, Surrey. *Signs work:* "Brian Coleman." *Address:* 2 Sheraton Drive, West Hill, Epsom, Surrey KT19 8JL.

COLEMAN, Christine, A.N.S.P.S., A.B. (University of Chicago, 1946) sculptor in stone, wood and cement; *b* Joliet, Illinois, U.S.A., 22 Dec., 1925. *Educ:* Mary Ward Centre, London (1986-). *Exhib:* group shows in London. *Signs work:* "COLE-MAN." *Address:* 24 Ladbroke Gdns. London W11 2PY.

COLLES, Dorothy Margaret Tyas, portrait painter in pastel and oil, drawings in pencil and chalk; *b* Cairo, 1917. *Educ:* Parsons Mead, Ashtead. *Studied:* Epsom Art School; Westminster Art School; St. Martin's School of Art. *Exhib:* P.S., R.P., R.A. Work in private collections. *Commissions:* mainly private families. *Publications:* Portraying Children; Christian Symbols Ancient and Modern with Heather Child. *Signs work:* "COLLES." *Address:* 70 Heath Rd., Petersfield, Hants. GU31 4EJ.

COLLETT, Paula, B.A.(Hons.); public/community artist in textile/soft sculpture; workshop leader; *b* Wakefield, 16 July, 1969. *Educ:* Woodkirk High. *Studied:* Chelsea School of Art and Design (1989-92, Roger Hoare). *Exhib:* tree art: Oakwell Hall. *Work in collections:* Huddersfield Royal Infirmary, Airville Leisure Centre. *Signs work:* "P. Collett." *Address:* 11 Boldgrove St., Earlsheaton, Dewsbury, W. Yorks. WF12 8NA.

COLLINGBOURNE, Stephen, painter, sculptor; prize winner, R.S.A., and John Moores; full time artist; *b* Dartington, 15 Aug., 1943. one *s.* one *d. Studied:* Dartington College of Art (1960-61); Bath Academy, Corsham (1961-64). *Exhib:* British Council, Malaya; Chapter, and Oriel, Cardiff; Camden Arts Centre, Zella 9, Fisher Gallery and Serpentine, London; Kettles Yard, Cambridge; MacRobert Arts Centre, Stirling; Third Eye Centre, Glasgow; City Art Centre, Edinburgh. *Work in collections:* Leicester A.G., Scottish and Welsh Arts Councils, Devon, Leicestershire and Hertford Educ. Authorities, City Art Centre, Edinburgh, Motherwell Council. *Commissions:* Welsh Arts Council, Leicester University, Livingstone, Edinburgh. *Address:* Tofts, West Linton, Peeblesshire EH46 7AJ.

COLLINGE, Robert Anthony, N.D.D. (1955), A.T.D. (1956), Blond Travelling Scholarship (1957), Slade Dip. (1959); artist in collage and construction; taught at: Canterbury College of Art (1961-63), London College of Printing (1962-63),

Goldsmiths' School of Art (1963-96, working with Anton Ehrenzweig and Harry and Elma Thubron); mem. London Group; Vice President London Group (2000-2001); *b* Cheshire, 28 July, 1934. *Educ:* King's School, Chester. *Studied:* Liverpool College of Art (1951-56), British School at Rome (1957), Slade School (1957-59). *Exhib:* Northern Young Artists; Five Painters, Sandon Studios, Liverpool; Young Contemporaries; Drian Gallery; Hope Hall Gallery, Liverpool; New Art Centre, London; London Group's 75th Anniversary Exhbn. R.C.A. (1988), Storey Inst., Lancaster, Invited Artists Exhbn. (1993), London Group's 80th Birthday Open Exhbn., Concourse Gallery, Barbican (1993), Joint exhbn. with Elma Thubron, Storey Inst., Lancaster (1994); London Group's Biennial Open Exhbn., Concourse Gallery, Barbican (1995), 'Musée Imaginaire' group exhbn. Museum of Installation, Deptford (1997); solo show: Woodlands Gallery, Blackheath (1995), The Walk Gallery, London (Mar. 2001), Stark Gallery, London (2001). *Work in collections:* Arts Council, Goldsmiths' College Gallery, Archive of the Museum of Installation; various private collections. *Publications:* in collaboration with Anton Ehrenzweig a booklet 'Towards a theory of Art Education (Goldsmiths' College, 1964). *Signs work:* "TONY COLLINGE." *Address:* 32 Prior St., Greenwich, London SE10 8SF.

COLLINGS, David, Dip. (1969), A.T.D. (1972); artist in oil on board, canvas; teacher of mentally handicapped; *b* London, 1949. *Studied:* Redruth School of Art (1965-69), Berks. College of Education (1969-72). *Exhib:* widely in S.W. England, Brittany and Ireland. *Work in collections:* Contemporary Art Soc. *Clubs:* Newlyn Soc. of Artists. *Signs work:* "David Collings." *Address:* 3 Lyn Terr., Newlyn, Penzance, Cornwall.

COLLINS, Michael, Inter.Dip.A.C., N.D.D., A.T.D., S.G.F.A., F.S.A.I., F.R.S.A.; mixed media draughtsman/painter; schoolmaster; Head of Art Dept., Emanuel School, London (1974-95) (Assistant Art Master 1967-74); *b* New Malden, Surrey, 13 Mar., 1936. *Educ:* King's College School, Wimbledon. *Studied:* under E. M. Scales; and at Wimbledon School of Art (1962-65), Swansea College of Art (1965-66). *Exhib:* S.G.F.A., S.A.I. *Signs work:* see appendix. *Address:* 53 Lauderdale Drive, Petersham, Richmond, Surrey TW10 7BS.

COLLINS, Peter Gerald, A.R.C.A. (1950); artist in oil, water-colour, pen and ink; *b* London, 11 June, 1943. *m* Georgette Andreassi 1943. *Educ:* Willesden. *Studied:* Willesden School of Art, Hornsey School of Art, Royal College of Art. *Exhib:* by appointment in own studio. *Clubs:* Chelsea Arts. *Signs work:* "Peter Collins." *Address:* 7 Stanley Studios, Park Walk, Chelsea, London SW10 0AE.

COMBES, Simon Glenton, S.WL.A. (1996); wildlife artist in oil; no formal art education. Took up painting after 14 year military career; *b* Shaftesbury, Dorset, 20 June, 1940. *m* Susan Margaret Coutts. one *s.* one *d. Educ:* in Kenya. *Exhib:* three major exhbns. in U.S.A. *Work in collections:* Nature in Art. *Signs work:* "Simon Combes." *Address:* Laburnum Cottage, Bushley, Tewkesbury, Glos. GL20 6JB.

COMPSTON, Diana Mary, retired painter in oil; *b* Brighton, 4 Dec., 1919. *m* Dr. Nigel Compston C.B.E., F.R.C.P. (decd.). two *s.* one *d. Educ:* Westcliff, Weston-super-Mare. *Studied:* Hampstead, Tunbridge Wells, and Farnham Colleges of Further Education. *Exhib:* R.O.I., S.W.A., Laing, Mall Galleries, Gallerie de Defense, private exhibs., East Grinstead, Tunbridge Wells, Winchester. *Work in collections:* Laing

Calendar (2001), Royal College of Physicians, London. *Signs work:* "D C" in red. *Address:* 6 Little Larchmount, Saffron Walden, Essex CB11 4EF.

CONLON, Elizabeth, self taught part-time painter in oil, water-colour, egg tempera and embroidery; *b* Dublin, 1938. *m* Norman Rogers. one *s.* one *d. Exhib:* annually at S.B.A., R.S.M.A., R.O.I., etc. *Publications:* author and illustrator: Learn to Paint Flower Portraits in Water-colour. *Address:* 61 Orchard Ave., Poole, Dorset BH14 8AH.

CONNER, Angela, F.R.B.S., American Inst. Architects Award; sculptor in stone, bronze, water, light, wind; competition winner, Economist Plaza, London, Aston University, de Gaulle, London, Cambridge, Lexington Airport, Kentucky etc.; *b* London. *Exhib:* solo exhibs., Lincoln Center, N. Y., Browse and Darby, and Hirschl Gallery, Cork St., London, Friends of the Tate, etc.; group exhibs., Gimpel Fils Gallery, N. Y., R.A. Summer Show, V. & A. Museum, Carnegie Museum of Modern Art, Washington Museum, etc. *Work in collections:* Arts Council G.B., National Portrait Gallery, Pittsburgh Museum of Modern Art, Jewish Museum, N. Y., Musee de l'Armee, Paris, V.&A. Museum, House of Commons, National Trust, etc.; private collections, H.R.H. Prince of Wales, Paul Mellon, Dr. Roy Strong, Lucien Freud, President Chirac, John Major, Crown Prince of Saudi Arabia, Duke of Devonshire, Lord Sainsbury, Dame Drew Heinz, Gunter Sachs, Evelyn Rothschild, Mrs. Henry Ford, Lord Cranbourne, 10 Downing St., French Embassy, etc. *Commissions:* largest outdoor sculpture in Europe, Dublin; city centre pieces for Heinz Hall Plaza, Pittsburgh, U.S.A.; Horsham, Surrey, Chesterfield, Derbyshire; largest indoor sculpture, Lovells, London. *Signs work:* "Angela Conner." *Address:* 1 George and Dragon Hall, Mary Pl., London W11 4PL. *Email:* angelaconner@which.net

CONNON, William John, D.A. (1959), post-Dip. (1960); painter in oil, draughtsman; retd. lecturer in drawing and painting at Grays School of Art, Aberdeen; *b* Turriff, 11 Dec., 1929. *m* Margaret R. Mair. one *s.* one *d. Educ:* Turriff Academy. *Studied:* Grays School of Art under R. Henderson Blyth, R.S.A., Ian Fleming, R.S.A. *Exhib:* R.S.A., S.S.A., A.A.S., McBey printroom, Aberdeen A.G., Artspace, Aberdeen, Scottish Gallery, Edinburgh. *Work in collections:* Aberdeen A.G., Scottish Arts Council, City of Edinburgh Art Centre, Royal Scottish Academy (Muirhead Bequest). *Signs work:* "wjconnon." *Address:* 8 Fonthill Rd., Aberdeen AB11 6UB.

CONSTABLE, Richard Golding, artist in gouache; *b* Lewes, 8 June, 1932. *m* Valerie Zelle. two *s.* four *d. Educ:* Marlborough College, Millfield School, Cambridge University. *Exhib:* London, Ipswich, Bath, Norwich, Lincoln, Woodbridge, Halesworth, Hereford, Spanish Biennale, Versailles, Singapore, W. Germany, Eire, Glasgow, New York, Cincinnati, Dubai, Al Ain, Abu Dhabi, Muscat. *Clubs:* Artists '303', Bruton Art Soc. *Signs work:* "R. Constable." *Address:* Courtfield, Norton sub Hamdon, Stoke sub Hamdon, Somerset TA14 6SG.

CONTRACTOR, Dorab Dadiba, N.S.; sculptor, artist, jeweller, designer; sculpture in wood, marble, stone, pottery, glass, clay, plaster, school chalkstick, avocado stone, mango stone, tafua nut, betelnut and nutmeg. Also excels in pencil, pastel, pen and ink, water-colour and scraperboard; part-time instructor for creative art, sculpting in wood and stone, and modelling at several Adult Educ. Centres and technical colleges in the U.K. Employed by the Government of India in Archaeological Dept.

to restore the famous rockcut sculptures of Ellora, Ajanta and Elephanta Caves; *b* Bombay, 13 Feb., 1929 to Parsee Zoroastrian parents (naturalised British citizen). *Studied:* Sir J.J. School of Art, Bombay, and obtained Government of India Dip. in Modelling and Sculpture (1957). Won special awards for wood sculptures, Bombay State (1958-59). *Exhib:* group: Guggenheim Gallery, London (1970); joint: Central Library, Romford (1972), Euro Arts and Crafts, B'ham (1976), Mall Gallery, London (1978-81), Le Salon des Nations a Paris (1983); one-man shows: India House, London (1972), Woodstock Gallery, London (1975), Queen's Theatre, Hornchurch (1977), Central Library, Romford (1982), Kenneth More Theatre, Ilford (1988). *Work in collections:* H.R.H. Prince Philip, Duke of Edinburgh (Windsor Castle), H.M. The Queen (Buckingham Palace), H.M. The Queen Mother (Clarence House), the late Dame Barbara Hepworth (St. Ives, Cornwall), the late Henry Moore (in his collection). His works are very widely appreciated and regarded as collectors pieces for their uniqueness. They are in private collections of art connoisseurs throughout the world, and in public libraries, schools, hospitals and Town Hall, Romford. Awards: 'Premier Award' for the most outstanding work in miniature sculpture in school chalkstick, London (1969); 'Dennis Price Challenge Trophy' for the best wood sculpture, London (1970-78); silver medal for wood sculptures, London (1985-86). *Signs work:* "DORAB" or "D.C." *Address:* 10 Elizabeth House, Elvet Ave., Gidea Park, Essex RM2 6JU.

CONWAY, Bryan, S.Eq.A.; artist in oil and water-colour; *b* Derbyshire, 3 Jan., 1932. married. four *s. Educ:* Becket School, Nottingham. *Studied:* Arthur Spooner's studio and Nottingham College of Art. *Exhib:* Christie's of London annually, and many provincial galleries. *Publications:* work repro.: calendars British Coal, British Steel publications, numerous cards. *Signs work:* "Bryan Conway." *Address:* 14 Ellesmere Drive, Trowell, Nottingham NG9 3PH.

CONWAY, Frances, R.W.A.; painter in oil, conté, water-colour, collage; *b* Bristol. married. two *s.* two *d. Studied:* West of England College of Art, Bristol, under George Sweet, Robert Hurdle, Francis Hoyland, William Townsend. *Exhib:* England and France. *Work in collections:* Lord Bath's collection of Wessex Painters at Longleat; Royal West of England Academy. *Clubs:* R.W.A. *Address:* 37 Cornwallis Cres., Clifton, Bristol BS8 4PH.

CONWAY, Jennifer Anne, R.M.S. (1979), S.M. (1981), Dip.B.C.P.E. (1957); painter and miniaturist in water-colour and oils; *b* Brecon, Oct., 1935. *m* John F. Conway. one *s.* one *d. Educ:* Brecon Girls' Grammar School; Bedford College of Physical Education (1954-57). *Exhib:* R.A., Paris Salon, R.M.S., S.W.A., Mall Galleries, Westminster Gallery, Bankside Gallery, Woburn Abbey, Miniature Art Soc. Florida, Soc. of Miniature Painters, S and G, Washington, U.S.A.; solo shows: Brecknock Museum (1980, 1989, 1993, 1998), Lion House Gallery (1988), Hay Festival (1991). *Work in collections:* Marchioness of Tavistock. *Publications:* work repro.: Welsh Crafts, Brecon 900 commemorative plate Royal Doulton, greetings cards, post cards, series of prints 'Country Collection' and 'Brecon Cathedral'; illustrated book 'A Pocketful of Posies' by J. & J. Conway. *Signs work:* "J. Conway" and see appendix. *Address:* Copper Beech, Maescelyn, Brecon, Powys, Wales LD3 7NL.

COOK, Christian Manuel, N.D.D. (1965); artist in acrylic, gouache, pastel, charcoal, collage; *b* Grossenhain, Germany, 26 June, 1942. one *s. Educ:* Kent College, Canterbury. *Studied:* Camberwell School of Art (Robert Medley, Frank Auerbach, Frank Bowling, Patrick Proctor, Charles Howard). *Exhib:* Kingsgate Gallery, Hornsey Library (New Gallery), H.A.C. (Camden Arts Centre), City Literary Inst., Loggia Gallery. *Work in collections:* Westminster City Council. *Signs work:* "Christian Cook" or "C.M. Cook" or "Chris Cook". *Address:* 77 Cumbrian Gdns., London NW2 1EH.

COOK, Ian David, R.I., R.S.W. (1978); Post. Grad. Fine Art, Glasgow; Hutcheson Drawing Prize, Cargill Travelling Scholarship to Spain/N. Africa, Arts Council Travel Award to Central Africa; artist in oil, gouache, watercolour, acrylic; *b* 1950. *m* Elaine. two *s.* one *d. Educ:* Camphill High School, Paisley. *Studied:* Glasgow (1969-72). *Exhib:* Royal Glasgow Concert Hall, (1996); major exhibition on hist./contemporary aspects of American West; Scottish Gallery ('80, '81); Scottish Contemp. shows, R.G.I., R.S.W.; various London galleries; Dublin; European and American venues; R.I. Award at Mall (2000); works in U.K. and U.S. *Work in collections:* Trainload Freight, Lloyds Bank, BBC. *Commissions:* decor. work/ Stakis PLC, Crest Hotels, Continental Hotels. *Publications:* Dorling Kindersley/ Watercolour Techniques series. *Signs work:* "Cook." *Address:* 3 Falside Rd., Paisley PA2 6JZ. *Email:* idcook@lineone.net

COOK, Jennifer Martin, N.D.D., A.T.D.; painter; *b* Preston, Lancs., 1942. *Educ:* Casterton School. *Studied:* Harris College, Preston (1960-65); Leicester College of Art (1965-66). *Exhib:* R.A. (1975, 1976, 1981, 1982, 1983); one-man shows: Mercury Gallery, London (1976, 1978), Leics. Museum and A.G. (1982), City Gallery, Leicester (1997); group shows: Yew Tree Gallery, Oxford Gallery, Gallery on the Green, Lexington, Mass., U.S.A., Shipley Art Gallery. *Work in collections:* Middlesbrough, Leics., Oxfordshire. *Publications:* work repro.: greetings cards for Aries Design and Medici Soc. *Signs work:* "Jenny Cook." *Address:* 17 Brookhouse Ave, Leicester LE2 0JE.

COOK, Richard, Dip.A.D. (Painting), M.A.(R.C.A.) Painting; artist; *b* Cheltenham, 31 Oct., 1947. one *s. Educ:* Salesian College, Oxford. *Studied:* St. Martin's School of Art (1966-70), R.C.A. (1970-73). *Exhib:* House Gallery, London (1981), Hayward Gallery, London (1976, 1980), Artists Market, London (1976-80), Serpentine Gallery, London (1987), Odette Gilbert Gallery, London (1989, 1991), Austin/Desmond (1995, 1997, 2000), "Luminous", Tate St. Ives (2001). *Work in collections:* B.M., Arts Council, Manchester City A.G. *Publications:* "Luminous", Tate St. Ives catalogue. *Signs work:* "Richard Cook." *Address:* 13 North Corner, Newlyn, Penzance, Cornwall TR18 5JG.

COOK, Richard Peter, R.B.A., Dip.A.D. Maidstone (1971), Post Grad. Royal Academy Schools (1975), A.T.C. (1977), R.B.A. (1978), E.T. Greenshield Travelling Scholarship (1972), Richard Ford Spanish Scholarship (1981); landscape and portrait painter in oil, water-colour, gouache; *b* Grimsby, 27 Feb., 1949. *m* Christine. two *d. Educ:* Grimsby College of Art, Maidstone College of Art (1968-71), Royal Academy Schools (1972-75). *Exhib:* one-man show, R.A. Schools (1980); R.B.A. (1977-); R.A. Summer Shows (1975-81, 1983, 1993); Art in Action (1988-93); N.E.A.C.; Royal Portrait Soc.; N.P.G. in 1984 John Player Award Show; Singer & Friedlander

Water-colour Exhbns. and commercial galleries. *Work in collections:* in U.K. and overseas. *Signs work:* "Richard P. Cook." *Address:* 17 Windlesham Gdns., Brighton BN1 3AJ.

COOKE, Jean, R.A., N.D.D., R.B.A.; painter; lecturer, Royal College (1965-74); *b* London, 18 Feb., 1927. *m* John Bratby. three *s.* one *d. Educ:* Blackheath High School. *Studied:* Central School of Arts and Crafts, Goldsmiths' College of Arts, Camberwell School of Art, City and Guilds, Royal College. *Exhib:* one-man show: Farnham (1962, 1964, 1973), Establishment (1963), Leicester Gallery (1964), Bear Lane, Bladon Gallery (1966), Phoenix (1970), New Grafton (1971); mixed show: R.A., Zwemmer, London Group, R.B.A., Arts Council, Young Contemporaries, Royal College of Art, Upper Grosvenor, Arundel, Furneaux (1968), Agnew (1974). *Work in collections:* R.A., R.C.A., Tate. *Signs work:* "Jean E. Cooke." *Address:* 7 Hardy Rd., Blackheath, London SE3.

COOKE, Stanley, artist in oil and water-colour; *b* Mansfield, Notts., 11 Jan., 1913. *m* Anne M. Clayton (decd.). one *s. Educ:* King Edward School, Mansfield. *Studied:* Mansfield School of Art (1924-32) and The Press Art School. *Exhib:* R.A., R.I., R.O.I., Britain in Water-colours exhbns., provinces; one-man shows at Drian Galleries, London and Mansfield Art Gallery. *Work in collections:* Quarry at Mansfield, Mansfield Art Gallery. *Publications:* work repro.: in Apollo, Arts Review and greetings cards. *Signs work:* see appendix. *Address:* Broadlands, Grasmere Cl., Guildford GU1 2TG.

COOKSON, Dawn, R.B.S.A. (1974); artist of portraiture, still-life, flower and landscape paintings in oil, tempera, pastel and water-colour; *b* B'ham, 11 June, 1925. *Educ:* Westonbirt School, Glos. *Studied:* Birmingham College of Art (1943-48, B. Fleetwood-Walker, R.A.), Accademia di Perugia, Italy (1954-56), Nerina Simi Studio, Florence (1955-58), and under Pietro Annigoni, Florence (1958-68). *Exhib:* R.P., P.S., R.B.S.A., B'ham Water-colour Soc., Fosseway Glos. bi-annually; one-man shows: Lygon Arms and Dormy House, Broadway, Worcs. (1972-82-85), Guildhouse, Stanton, Glos. (1976-79), Reade's Gallery, Aldeburgh, Suffolk (1977). *Work in collections:* throughout G.B., Europe and Overseas. *Clubs:* V.P. Birmingham Water-colour Soc. *Signs work:* "Dawn Cookson." *Address:* Quiet Place, Lifford Gdns., Broadway, Worcs. WR12 7DA.

COOKSON, Delan, F.S.D.C., Gold Medal (Vallauris, 1974), Churchill Fellow (1966); Senior Lecturer in ceramics at Buckinghamshire College of Higher Education; *b* Torquay, 13 Sept., 1937. *m* Judith. two *s. Educ:* Bournemouth School. *Studied:* Bournemouth College of Art, Central School of Arts and Crafts. *Exhib:* Oxford Gallery, British Crafts Centre, Craftsman Potters Assoc., Design Centre, Midland Group Gallery, Whitworth Art Gallery, New Craftsman, St. Ives; one-man shows: Salix, Windsor, Bohun Gallery, Henley, Peter Scott Gallery, Lancaster and Galerie an Gross, St. Martin, Cologne. *Publications:* Ceramic Review, Studio Porcelain and Studio Ceramics by Peter Lane. *Clubs:* Cornwall Crafts Assoc., C.A.C. Index of Selected Members. *Address:* Lissadell, St. Buryan, Penzance, Cornwall TR19 6HP.

COOLIDGE, John, A.B. (Harvard University, 1935), Ph.D. (New York University, 1948); director, Fogg Art Museum (1948-68); Prof. of Fine Arts, Harvard

University (1955-85); *b* Cambridge, Mass., 16 Dec., 1913. *m* Mary Welch Coolidge. one *d. Educ:* Groton School, Harvard and New York Universities. *Publications:* Mill and Mansion (Columbia University Press, 1943); Patrons and Architects (University of Texas Press, 1990). *Address:* Fogg Art Museum, Quincy St. and Broadway, Cambridge, Mass.

COOMBS, Jill, 3 Gold Medals (R.H.S.); botanical illustrator in water-colour; *b* Horsham, 1935. *m* Bernard Coombs. one *s.* one *d. Educ:* High School for Girls, Horsham. *Studied:* West Sussex College of Art (1952-55), botanical illustration under Mary Grierson at Flatford (1976-79). *Exhib:* Kew Gdns. Gallery, National Theatre, R.H.S., Broughton Gallery, Arundel Festival, Chelsea Physic Gdn., Carnegie-Mellon University U.S.A. *Work in collections:* U.S.A., Australia, Japan, U.K., Shirley Sherwood Collection, Kew, R.H.S. *Commissions:* Crabtree & Evelyn, Readers' Digest, R.H.S. Kew. *Publications:* illustrated: Plant Portraits by Beth Chatto (J.M. Dent), Herbs for Cooking and Health by C. Grey-Wilson (Collins); illustrated for: Country Life, Curtis Botanical Magazine, Flora Iraq, Flora Qatar, Flora Egypt, The Crocus, Flower Artists of Kew. *Signs work:* "Jill Coombs." *Address:* Weald House, Handford Way, Plummers Plain, Horsham, W. Sussex RH13 6PD.

COOPER, Eileen, artist in oil and works on paper, prints, ceramics; *b* Glossop, 1953. *m* M. Southward. two *s. Studied:* Goldsmiths' College and R.C.A. (1971-77). *Exhib:* numerous solo and group shows, R.A. Summer Exhib. (2001). *Work in collections:* Arts Council, various museums. *Signs work:* "Eileen Cooper" on reverse. *Address:* Art First, 9 Cork St., London W1.

COOPER, Emmanuel, potter stoneware and porcelain, writer and broadcaster; editor of Ceramic Review; member of Arts Council of England, visiting Professor, Royal College of Art; *b* Derbyshire, 12 Dec., 1938. *Educ:* Tupton Hall Grammar School, Derbyshire. *Exhib:* Contemporary Applied Arts, London, many other one-man and mixed exhbns. here and abroad. *Work in collections:* V. & A. *Publications:* A Handbook of Pottery, A History of Pottery (Longman); Taking up Pottery (Arthur Barker); New Ceramics (with E. Lewenstein); Pottery (Macdonalds); A Potters Book of Glaze Recipes (1979); A History of World Pottery (Batsford, 1980). Contributes art criticism to Time Out, Tribune, etc. *Signs work:* see appendix. *Address:* 38 Chalcot Rd., London NW1 8LP.

COOPER, Josephine Mary, S.M. (1974), R.M.S. (1983), U.A. (1975), S.W.A.(1988); Silver Medallist, Paris Salon (1974), Prix Rowland (1977); artist in oil and water-colour, also drypoint engravings and monotypes; *b* Brighton, 8 Aug., 1932. *m* Tom Cooper. one *s.* one *d. Studied:* St. Albans School of Art under Kathleen Pargiter; Mid-Herts. College of Further Education under Kenneth Haw; Hertfordshire College of Art and Design under Peter Jacques; Will Raymont, privately. *Exhib:* R.M.S., U.A., S.M., R.I., R.S.M.A., R.B.A., Laing, S.G.A., Britain in Water-colour, Bilan de l'Art Paris and Quebec, Liberty of London, Medici Gallery, R.A. Summer Exhbn. (1980-85); one-man shows throughout mid-Herts area, also Liberty of London. *Publications:* included in 20th Century Marine Paintings. *Clubs:* Welwyn Garden City Art, Hertford Art Soc. *Signs work:* "Jo Cooper" and "JMC" (miniatures dated). *Address:* 27 Parkfields, Welwyn Garden City, Herts. AL8 6EE.

COOPER, Julian, B.A.(Hons.) Fine Art; painter in oil, water-colour, pastel; *b* Grasmere, 10 June, 1947. *m* Linda. *Educ:* Heversham Grammar School. *Studied:* Lancaster Art College (1963-64), Goldsmiths' College (1964-69), Boise Travelling Scholarship (1969-70). *Exhib:* London Group, Serpentine Gallery, J.P.L. Fine Art, Paton Gallery, V. & A., Laing A.G., University of Durham. *Work in collections:* A.C.G.B., Laing A.G., Bolton A.G., Lancaster University, Northern Arts, I.L.E.A., Abbot Hall A.G., Reuters, Unilever, Pentagram, Davy Offshore Modules, Ferguson Industrial Holdings. *Publications:* work repro.: book cover for Fleur Adcock's Under Loughrigg. *Signs work:* "Julian Cooper." *Address:* 100 Lake Rd., Ambleside, Cumbria LA22 0DB.

COOPER, Paul Anthony, N.D.D. (1951), F.R.B.S.; sculptor in all traditional and modern materials including precious metals and stones; *b* Wool, Dorset, 23 May, 1923. *m* Audrey Beryl Carnaby, A.R.C.A. one *d. Studied:* Poole College of Art (1939-41), Goldsmiths' College, London (1948-51), Lincoln College (1958). *Exhib:* R.A., Covent Garden London, Scone Palace Perth, R.I.B.A. *Work in collections:* Oxford City Educ. Authority, Lincoln Educ. Authority, and places open to the public at Bond St., Westminster, City of London, Thorpe Tilney, Lincoln and Denton, Grantham; private collections in this country and in Holland, Israel, U.S.S.R.; ecclesiastical work in churches in England, Westminster Abbey, Wales and the Falkland Islands. *Signs work:* "Paul Cooper." *Address:* Quarr Hill Cottage, Wool, Dorset.

COOPER, William Alwin, R.W.A.(1973), Artist Chairman (1993-96), Sherborne School (1952-83), Lecturer, Bristol University Extra Mural Dept. (1983-86); artist in oil and collage; *b* Merthyr Tydfil, 2 June, 1923. *m* Dorothy Tustain, G.R.S.M. one *s.* two *d. Educ:* Westminster School, Corpus Christi College, Cambridge. *Exhib:* oneman shows: Drian Gallery (1971), Albany Gallery, Cardiff (1972), Hambledon Gallery, Blandford, Pentagon Gallery, Stoke on Trent (1977), St. John's, Smith Sq. (1986), Rona Gallery, R.W.A. (1988), Bloomsbury Workshop Gallery (1994); group shows include: R.A., N.E.A.C., UNESCO, New York; Westward TV Open (Prizewinner), South West Open (Prizewinner) 1991, Laing Open (Prizewinner) 1999. *Work in collections:* Royal West of England Academy, Bryanston School, Staffordshire Educ. Com., Welsh Development Corporation, Sherborne School and various public and private collections. *Publications:* illustration in History of Corpus Christi College, Cambridge. *Signs work:* "Cooper." *Address:* Elizabeth House, Long St., Sherborne, Dorset DT9 3BZ.

COOTE, Michael Arnold, painter in oils, water-colour, acrylic, oil and soft pastel, charcoal, pencil; Freeman of the City of London (1977); *b* London, 1939. *m* Anita Davies. two *s.* one *d. Studied:* mainly self taught; Sir John Cass (sculpture and life class). *Exhib:* P.S., R.O.I., Mall Galleries, Alpine Gallery, many provincial galleries including John Noott Gallery and Barry Keene Gallery, Henley on Thames. *Work in collections:* London, Bath, America, Germany, Italy. *Signs work:* see appendix. *Address:* 1 Tadlows Cl., Upminster, Essex RM14 2BD.

COPELAND, Lawrence Gill, Cranbrook Medal, U.S. State Dept. Purchase Award, Y.S.C. First Prize, National Merit Award, Craftsmen, U.S.A.; designer in metal; prof., Art Dept., City College of City University of New York (retd.); *b* Pittsburgh, Pa., U.S.A., 12 Apr., 1922. *m* Mary Cuteri. two *s.* one *d. Educ:* Ohio State

Univ., Cranbrook Academy of Art, Univ. of Stockholm, Univ. of Paris. *Studied:* Stockholm (1947-48, Baron Erik Fleming), Paris (1948-49, Emeric Gomery). *Work in collections:* National Gallery, Washington, D.C. *Address:* 5 Peach Tree La., Warwick, N.Y. 10990, U.S.A.

COPNALL, John, painter in acrylics and oils; *b* Slinfold, Sussex, 16 Feb., 1928. *Studied:* R.A. Schools (1950-55). *Exhib:* one-man shows: Piccadilly Gallery, Bear Lane (Oxford), Stone Gallery (Newcastle), I.C.A. (London), Ikon (Birmingham), Sala Vayreda (Barcelona), Wolfgang Gurlitt (Munich), Boisserée (Cologne), Universa-haus (Nüremberg), Institut für Auslandsbeziehungen (Stuttgart), Aberdeen Museum, Demarco (Edinburgh), Galeri Mörner (Stockholm), Oxford Gallery, Oxford, Windsor Art Centre, Austin/Desmond (London), Reeds Wharf London, De La Warr Pavilion Bexhill; mixed shows: John Moores of Liverpool, R.A., Art Spectrum, London, Wildenstein, Hayward 72, Whitechapel Open; Steven Lacey 99 group show. *Work in collections:* Bristol and York Universities, A.C.G.B., Aberdeen Museum, Ateneum Museum, Helsinki, Sara Hildred Museum, Tampere, Finland. *Publications:* work repro.: Studio International, Artist, Arts Review. *Signs work:* "john copnall" or "copnall." *Address:* 9 Fawe St. Studios, London E14 6PA.

COPPINGER, Sioban, B.A.Hons. (1977), A.R.B.S. (1991); sculptor in bronze, concrete and re-constituted stone; *b* 20 May, 1955. *Educ:* New Hall School, Boreham, Essex. *Studied:* Bath Academy of Art (1975-77). *Exhib:* 1993: The Bronze Bird, Gallery Pangolin, Glos.; R.B.S. Gallery, Chelsea Harbour Sculpture '93, London; 1st Royal West of England Academy Open Sculpture Exhbn. Bristol. Work in public places: Man and Sheep on a Park Bench, Rufford Country Park, Nottingham; The Gardener and the Truant Lion (Chelsea Flower Show 1986); Stoke Mandeville Station, Bucks.; Sundial (Gateshead Garden Festival 1990); Templecombe Station, Somerset; The Birmingham Man, Chamberlain Sq., Birmingham. *Signs work:* "S. Coppinger." *Address:* Riverside Works, West Mills, Newbury, Berks. RG14 5HY.

CORBETT, Peter George, B.A. Hons. (1974); artist in oil on canvas, pencil; *b* Rossett, N. Wales, 13 Apr., 1952. *Educ:* Liverpool College. *Studied:* Liverpool College of Art and Design (1970-71, Maurice Cockrill), Manchester Regional College of Art and Design (1971-74, Brendan Neiland, Keith Godwin). *Exhib:* Centre Gallery (1979), Acorn Gallery, Liverpool (1985, 1988), Major Merseyside Artists, Liverpool (1988), Marie Curie Art (Open), Albert Dock, Liverpool (1988), Surreal Objects Exhbn. Tate Gallery, Liverpool (1989), Merkmal Gallery "Alternative 17" Liverpool (1991), Manchester Academy 136th Exhbn. (Open) 1995, The Three Month Gallery, Liverpool (1996), Academy of Arts, Liverpool (1997, 1999), Academy of Arts, Liverpool St. George's Hall (Open) 1998, Walker Art Gallery, Liverpool (internet auction), (1999), dfn Gallery, New York, U.S. (2000); one-man shows: Southport Arts Centre (1980), Liverpool Playhouse (1982), Pilgrim Gallery, Liverpool (1984), Royal Institution, Liverpool (1986), Church Gallery, London (1988), Anglican Cathedral (1988), Senate House Gallery, Liverpool University (1993), Atkinson Gallery, Southport (1995), International Biennial of Visual Art, Liverpool 'A Journey of Revelation' (1999), Liverpool Biennial of Contemporary Art (1999); two-man shows: Liverpool University (1983, 1990), Acorn Gallery, Liverpool (1985), Royal Liver Bldg., Pier Head, Liverpool

(1991), Hanover Gallery, Liverpool (1999). *Work in collections:* Liverpool, London, Manchester, America and Australia, Netherlands, West Germany. Founder Mem. Chair, Merseyside Visual Arts Festival (1989-90). International German Art Prize, St. Lukas Academy, Memmelsdorf, Germany (Painting and Poetry) Grand Diploma (1998). *Publications:* Merseyside Arts Directory (2000/1), Brit Art Directory (2001), dfn Gallery write up/photo, Merseyside Arts Magazine (2000), Prestige Debut Artists NY 2000 Exhibition, dfn Gallery catalogue (2000), Liverpool Biennial of Contemporary Art catalogue (1999), 'The Pool of Life' exhibition (one-man), Senate House, Liverpool University (1993), Merseyside Visual Arts Festival, catalogue (1990). awards: 2000 – Vincent Van Gogh Award, St. Lukas Academy, Memmelsdorf, Germany; 2000 – Albert Einstein International Academy Foundation, honour in recognition of outstanding achievements; 1998 – Merseyside Contemporary Artists Exhibition, Purchase Prize, Liverpool; 1993 – Honorary Professor, Académie des Sciences Humanie Universelles, Paris, France. Galleries www.designbank.org.uk, www.newartportfolio.com/petercorbett. Silde libraries: Pompidou Centre, Paris, France; Museum of Modern Art, New York, U.S.A.; Guggenheim Museum, New York, U.S.A. *Clubs:* Design and Artists Copyright Society, London (life member), Maison Internationale des Intellectuels, Paris, France (1994). *Signs work:* see appendix. *Address:* Flat 4, 7 Gambier Terr., Hope St., Liverpool L1 7BG. *Website:* www.axisartists.org.uk/all/ref7166.htm

CORETH, Mark Rudolf, self taught sculptor in bronze (wildlife); *b* London, 5 Sept., 1958. *m* Seonaid. one *s.* two *d. Educ:* Ampleforth College. *Exhib:* Sladmore Gallery, London W1. (1986, 1990, 1992, 1994, 1996, 1998), Galerie la Cymaise, Paris (1993, 1995, 1997, 1999), Sydney (1996), Geneva (1997), New York (1999). *Commissions:* life-size Cheetah Group, Dubai; Drinking fountains at Globe Theatre and National History Museum. *Clubs:* Boodles. *Address:* Stowell House, Sherborne, Dorset DT9 4PE.

CORNELL, David, F.R.S.A. (1970), F.R.B.S. (1971), V.P.S.P.S. (1977), P.S.S.M.C.E. (1995); sculptor in bronze; *b* Enfield, 18 Sept., 1935. *m* Geraldine. four *s. Educ:* Essendene. *Studied:* Central School of Art, London and Harrow School of Art (1952-62, Friend, Fryer and Philip Turner) Engraving and Sculpture; Academy of Fine Art, University of Pennsylvania (1968-70, Robert Beverley Hale) Anatomy. *Exhib:* London: R.A., Mall Galleries, Guildhall, R.B.S. Hall Place, Pavlova Soc., Park Walk Galleries, Plazzotta Studio, Edith Grove Gallery, Harrods; Iberian Bronze Gallery, London and Dublin, Newmarket Gallery, Newmarket, Royal Fine Art, Tunbridge Wells, Armstrong-Davis Gallery, Arundel, Scone Palace Scotland, English Gallery, Beverly Hills, U.S.A., L.C.A. Chelsea, Royal West of England Academy, Bristol, Alwin Gallery, Tunbridge Wells. *Work in collections:* Wellcome Foundation, London. Recent works include portrait of Princess Diana and Queen Mother. *Commissions:* Life-size: Sir Arthur Conan-Doyle, numerous coins for world mints. *Signs work:* "David Cornell." *Address:* Barcombe Manor, Innhams Wood, Crowborough, E. Sussex TN6 1TE.

CORNWELL, Arthur Bruce, S.G.F.A.dip.(1947); illustrator in gouache, oil, water-colour, indian ink; *b* Vancouver, B.C., 11 Feb., 1920. *m* Peggy Brenda Huggins. one *s. Educ:* Palms Public School, and Page Military Academy, California. *Studied:* Art Centre School, Los Angeles, Regent St. Polytechnic, London,

Heatherley's, London, Academy Julien, Paris. *Exhib:* R.A., N.E.A.C., S.M.A., S.G.F.A., Sunderland Gallery, Bolton Gallery. *Work in collections:* Diploma Gallery, R.A. Stott Bequest, R.A., The Coaster. *Publications:* The Ship's Crew; work repro.: Yachting Monthly, Macmillan teach-visuals. *Signs work:* see appendix. *Address:* Westways, 132 Eastcote Rd., Ruislip, Middx. HA4 8DU.

CORSELLIS, Jane, N.E.A.C., R.W.A., R.W.S.; artist in oil, water-colour, etching, lithography; *b* Oxford, 1940. two *s.* *Studied:* Byam Shaw School of Art (Maurice de Sausmarez, Bernard Dunstan, R.A., Peter Greenham, R.A.). *Exhib:* R.A., R.B.A., N.E.A.C., R.W.A., R.W.S.; one-man shows: Hong Kong, Ottawa, Kuala Lumpur, Upstairs Gallery, R.A. London (1985, 1986), New Academy Gallery, London (1988, 1990, 1992, 1994, 1996, 1998, 2000), Hollis Taggart Gallery, N.Y. (1998). *Work in collections:* Canada, U.S.A., Italy, France, Malaysia, Singapore and U.K. *Commissions:* Freshfields, Capital Club London. *Publications:* Painting Figures in Light; Jane Corsellis, A Personal View (David and Charles). *Clubs:* Chelsea Arts; Arts Club, Dover St. *Signs work:* "Corsellis." *Address:* 8 Horbury Mews, London W11 3NL.

COSMAN, Milein, Slade Diploma Fine Art; painter, graphic artist; *b* Gotha. *m* Hans Keller. *Educ:* Düsseldorf; International School, Geneva. *Studied:* Slade School. *Exhib:* one man shows: Berkeley Galleries, Matthiesen, Molton Gallery, City of London Festival, Camden Arts Centre, Aldeburgh Festival, Stadtmuseum, Düsseldorf, Clare Hall Cambridge, Ambleside, Menuhin School, Dartington, Belgrave Gallery. *Work in collections:* e.g. N.P.G., R.C.M., V. & A., British Academy, Cardiff University, Britten-Pears Foundation, Clare Hall Cambridge, Stadtmuseum Dusseldorf, Lancaster University, Royal Free Hospital, McMaster University, Swarthmore College, Texas University. *Publications:* Musical Sketchbook (Bruno Cassirer, Faber & Faber, 1957), Stravinsky at Rehearsal (Dobson, 1962), Strawinsky Dirigiert (Ullstein, 1962), Stravinsky Seen and Heard (Toccata Press, 1982); books illustrated: Penguin Music Magazine, A Composer's Eleven (Cardus, Cape, 1975), etc. Work repro.: Radio Times and other national and foreign press, art and musical magazines. Series of Educational Programmes on Drawing for ITV. *Address:* 3 Frognal Gdns., Hampstead, London NW3.

COTTINGHAM, Grenville George, R.S.M.A.(1988), R.B.A.(1989); painter in oil, water-colour, acrylic; *b* Exeter, 16 Apr., 1943. *m* Lucy June. *Educ:* Exeter School. *Studied:* Exeter College of Art (1960-63), Liverpool College of Art (1963-64). *Exhib:* R.A, R.S.M.A., R.B.A., R.I., Bonhams; one-man shows, Hallam Gallery, SW14 (1989), Bruton St. Gallery (1994), Barnes Gallery (1996). *Work in collections:* P. & O., Marine Soc., 2nd Batt. Royal Fusiliers, R.N. Reserve (London Division), Royal Artillery, Woolwich, London Mutual Insurance, Securities Investment Board. *Publications:* Seafarers' Sketchbook (Bartholomew Press), You Can Paint; work repro.: various ships of the P. & O. passenger fleet. *Clubs:* Wapping Group of Artists. *Signs work:* "Grenville Cottingham." *Address:* 83 Kidbrooke Grove, London SE3 0LQ.

COTTON, Alan, P.S.W.A., N.D.D., A.T.D.(B'ham), F.R.S.A., M.Ed.; painter in oil, water-colour and pastel; works on art films for television; Executive Com., Phoenix Arts Centre, Exeter, President South West Academy of Fine & Applied Arts,

Arts Advisory Com., University of Exeter; *b* Redditch, 8 Oct., 1938. *m* Patricia Esmé. two *s.* two *d. Educ:* Redditch County High School. *Studied:* Redditch School of Art, Bournville College of Art, B'ham College of Art, Universities of B'ham and Exeter (Research Fellow). *Exhib:* over 40 one-man shows in U.K., Canada, France and the U.S.A. including Hammer Galleries N.Y. (1993). *Work in collections:* City of Exeter A.G., City of Plymouth A.G., Carlton Television, Royal Marines, Lympstone, Universities of Southampton and Exeter, etc. *Publications:* Learning and Teaching through Art and Crafts (Batsford). Represented by: David Messum Galleries since 1983: annual exhibitions. *Clubs:* Dover St. Arts, Chelsea Arts Club, University of Exeter Staff Club. *Signs work:* "Alan Cotton." *Address:* Brockhill Studio, Colaton Raleigh, nr. Sidmouth, Devon EX10 0LH.

COULING, Paula, S.W.A. (1993); landscape painter in acrylic; no formal art training; *b* Birmingham. *m* Robert H. Couling. two *s. Exhib:* S.W.A. Westminster Gallery; solo shows: Christchurch. *Publications:* greetings cards by the Medici Soc. *Clubs:* Romsey Art Group, Hengist Group of Artists. *Signs work:* "Paula Couling." *Address:* 201 Salisbury Rd., Burton, Christchurch, Dorset BH23 7JT.

COULOURIS, Mary Louise, R.E. (2000), A.R.E. (1973); Dip. A.D. (London) (1961); Post Grad. Scholarship, Slade School (1962); French Government Scholarship (1963); Churchill Fellowship in U.S.A. and Mexico (1993); artist and printmaker; *b* New York, 17 July, 1939. *m* Gordon Wallace. one *s.* one *d. Educ:* Parliament Hill School. *Studied:* Slade School, London University (1958-62) under Antony Gross; Ecole des Beaux Arts, Paris (1963-64); Atelier 17, Paris (1963-64) under William Hayter. *Exhib:* R.A. (1966, 1971, 1972, 1973); one-man shows: London, Oxford, Paris, Aberdeen, Glasgow, Athens. Artists Exchange: Athens for Glasgow Year of Culture (1990). Sainsbury Wine Label Competition Winner (1997), Purdue University, U.S.A. (1999). *Work in collections:* London Weekend TV, Bibliotheque Nationale, Paris, New York Public Library, Nuffield Trust, Trinity College, Oxford, Bank of Scotland, Edinburgh District Council, Hambros Bank, Sainsbury PLC. *Commissions:* Scottish Poetry Library 3 Carpets (1999); mural: British Rail (1985); print: British Healthcare Arts (1993). *Publications:* 'Techniques to Trigger the Mind' Printmaking Today Vol.7 No. 4 (1998). *Clubs:* Scottish Arts. *Signs work:* "Mary Louise Coulouris." *Address:* 5 Strawberry Bank, Linlithgow, West Lothian EH49 6BJ. *Website:* www.axisartists.co.uk, www.edinburgh-printmakers.co.uk, www.newmangalleries1865.com *Email:* strawberrybanks@yahoo.co.uk

COULSON, Nancy Diana (née Hibbert), sculptor stone, marble, clay, wood, bronze; subjects: animals, portrait heads in terracotta, clay for bronze; *b* Kenilworth, 1926. *m* Robert Coulson. two *s.* one *d. Educ:* Kingsley School. *Studied:* Leamington Spa, Chelsea Art School (1946-48), Chelmsford (Ivor Livi). *Exhib:* R.A., F.P.S., S.C.A., Vaughan College Leicester, Bury St. Edmunds, Aldeburgh, Chelmsford, Westcliff-on-Sea. *Work in collections:* Guy Harlings and Chapter House, Chelmsford; Mansion House, London; Broomfield Hospital; Lord St. John of Fawsley; Abe Lerner, N.Y.; Peter Rippon; Sir Alastair Stewart, Bt.; Baroness Platt of Writtle; Daniela Landschuetz; Munich; Mrs. Martin Read of Felstead; and others, St. John Baptist Church Loughton; St. Barnabas Church Woodford. *Commissions:* church sculpture: Madonna St. Barnabus; sundials: St. Mary Great Warley, and Broomfield Hospital, Chelmsford. *Signs work:* "N.C." *Address:* Medlars, Mounthill

Ave., Chelmsford CM2 6DB.

COUSENS, Ruth Margaret, F.S.A.I.; Medaille d'Or, Paris Salon (Tricentenaire 1973) T.C., Women of the Year Luncheon; artist in water-colour; art teacher of history, architecture and painting: St. George's Ramsgate, Maidstone Technical High, Sittingbourne Girls' Grammar, pupils of Wilmington Grammar Schools; Founder-Project Director, Castle Trust Arts Centre, Ramsgate; *b* London, 1930. *m* Stanley G. Cousens. one *s. Educ:* St. George's Ramsgate, and Clarendon Malvern. *Studied:* Rolle College, Exeter (1948-50, E.T. Arnold). *Exhib:* Paris Salon, R.A., R.I., R.I.B.A., etc.; one-man shows, 'Regency Ramsgate', Townley House, Ramsgate (1973), Royal Museum, Canterbury (1978), Geneva (1985), Westend, London (1986); by invitation: 'La Femme Creatrice d'Art', Monte Carlo (1976) (Brit. rep.), 'British Artists', Paris (1979), Expo Quebec, Canada (1980). *Work in collections:* Thanet Council, Ramsgate Charter Trustees; private: Sir Robert Bellinger, Rt. Hon. Edward Heath, M.P. *Publications:* work repro.: book jackets, retail postcards; booklet 'Regency Ramsgate'. *Signs work:* "R.M. COUSENS." *Address:* 17 Spencer Sq., Ramsgate, Kent.

COUTU, Jack, A.R.E., A.R.C.A.; printmaker and sculptor; etching and engraving on copper, miniature carving in boxwood and ivory; *b* Farnham, Surrey, 1924. *Educ:* Farnham Grammar School. *Studied:* Farnham School of Art (1947-51), R.C.A. (1951-54). *Work in collections:* King Gustave of Sweden, Museum of Fine Art, Boston, Mass., Bradford City Art Gallery, V. & A., Arts Council of Great Britain. *Publications:* articles in "International Netsuke Society Journal" (1996). *Signs work:* "Coutu" and see appendix. *Address:* Bramblings, 22 Quennells Hill, Wrecclesham, Farnham, Surrey GU10 4NE.

COWAN, Judith, B.A. (Hons.) Sculpture, 1st class, (1977), M.A. (1978), Gulbenkian Rome Scholarship, British School at Rome (1979); sculptor; *b* London, 8 Dec., 1954. *Studied:* Sheffield Polytechnic (1974-77); M.A. at Chelsea School of Art (1977-78). *Exhib:* recent group exhbns. in England and abroad include: Anabaleps, Stefania Miscetti, Rome; Furniture, Richard Salmon Gallery (touring) (1999); solo exhbns. include: Angel Row Gallery, Newlyn A.G (1999), Kettles Yard (1996), Stefania Miscetti, Rome (1995), Camden Arts Centre (1993), Yorkshire Sculpture Park (1992), Oriel Mostyn, Llandudno (1989-90) touring. *Work in collections:* A.C.G.B., London Borough of Tower Hamlets, Leics. Educ. Authority. *Address:* 2a Culford Mews, London N1 4DX.

COWAN, Ralph Wolfe, A.P.S., A.A.A., A.S.A., P.I.; Royal Portrait Painter to: Sultan of Brunei (1984-), Monaco (1956, 1981), Morocco (1983), Malacanang Palace, Philippines (1982, 1983); portrait painter in oil; *b* Phoebus, Va., 16 Dec., 1931. *m* Judith Page. two *s. Studied:* Art Students League (1949-50, Bouché and Frank Reilly). *Work in collections:* Royal Palace Brunei, Palace Monaco, Royal Palace Morocco, Malacanang Palace Philippines, Carter Presidential Center, Atlanta, Reagan Private Coll., Los Angeles, Graceland Coll., Memphis, Portsmouth Museum, Portsmouth Va., N.P.G. Wash. D.C. *Publications:* seven Johnny Mathis album covers; first book "A Personal Vision" collector plate of His Holiness Pope John Paul II. *Signs work:* "Ralph Wolfe Cowan." *Address:* 243 29th St. West. Palm Beach, Fl.33407 U.S.A.

and the teaching that Christ's human nature preceded His human birth were prevalent in the preaching of the Anabaptists, who stressed that those who joined their ranks must undergo a new form of baptism, whether they were already Baptists or not.

In 1536 ten basic articles of faith were agreed upon 'to stablyshe christen quietnes and unitie amongst us, and to avoyde contentious opinions.' These articles displayed more Medieval tradition than sound doctrine, so Reformers such as Cranmer and Hooper demanded 'an entire purification of the Church from the very foundation'. A letter is preserved from Hooper to Baucer (also anglicised as Bucer) dated June 25, 1549 in which the Reformer complains that the Anabaptists are flocking to his lectures denying the incarnation, affirming sinless perfection yet teaching that those who fall into sin after partaking of the Holy Ghost will be lost for ever. In the same letter Hooper complains that 'a great portion of the kingdom so adheres to the popish faction as altogether to set at naught God and the lawful authority of the magistrates'. [1]

The *Ten Articles* were quickly revised and added to until they had reached 42 in number by 1553, including those against the papists. The number was reduced to 39 in 1571 when most of the papists had separated themselves from the English Church as the result of a papal bull. Articles I, II and III were aimed at Anabaptist errors concerning the Trinity whereas Article IV defended the doctrines of the Incarnation and manhood of Christ. The main heretic in mind, here, was Casper Schwenckfeld (1489-1561) who, in 1528, contended that Christ's flesh was never that of a created human and, after the resurrection, Christ dropped all resemblance of humanity.[2] Article VI defends the canonical status of the Old Testament which was rejected by many Anabaptists. Articles VIII to X dealing with original sin, free will and grace were aimed at the Pelagian Anabaptist doctrine which taught that Adam's curse did not apply to his offspring and that man, of his own will, was able to co-operate with God in salvation. Article X attacks the Anabaptist teaching that man's sin was a fiat of God. Articles XV and XVI oppose the Anabaptist heresy that sins committed after baptism cannot be repented of and thus redeemed. Article XVIII is against the Anabaptist error that sincere followers of pagan religions will be saved even if they wilfully reject Christ. Article XXIII stresses that ministers of

---

[1] Charles Hardwick, *A History of the Articles of Religion*, Cambridge, 1859. p. 90.

[2] Schwenkenfeld's teaching is still looked upon as a 'continuation of the Reformation' by certain British Baptists and Charismatics such as the Apostolic Church and is still very widespread amongst evangelicals on the Continent.

the Gospel must be called to preach through their church, thus attacking the Anabaptist doctrine that all believers are seen as exercising a teaching and pastoral function. This was one of the major points Featley wished to clear up in the Southwark debate but the Baptists were too much on the defensive and obviously were insulted at his questions which, because of the historical circumstances, were, nevertheless, highly valid. Article XX, one of the oldest post-Reformation articles, deals with God's Word as the sole authority in decreeing rites and ceremonies and the sole authority in controversies regarding faith. This was worded against any additions to what the Church of England believed was Scriptural, whether they came from the side of Rome or from the side of too radical protestants. Thus Featley firmly believed that 'it is not lawful for the Church to ordain any-thing that is contrary to God's word written, neither may it so expound one place of Scripture, that be repugnant to another' and, as the Baptists professed to repudiate this basic Article along with the other 38 Articles, they were to be treated as enemies of the Church.

The validity of John's baptism for Christians questioned

It was Anglican practice at this time to accept a baptism in the name of the Lord or in the name of the Trinity by immersion or sprinkling but not the baptism of John. The Baptists' claim that John's baptism was Christian baptism appeared to the Anglicans to be contrary to Scripture. Thus John Newton in his famous *Apology* gives the Baptists' acceptance of John's baptism as the pattern for Christian baptism as one of the reasons why he cannot join the Baptists whom he, nevertheless, greatly respected. That is, until they started accusing him of wrong motives in remaining an Angli-can minister. This point is still a hot topic of debate not only between Baptists and non-Baptists but amongst the Baptists themselves. Article XXXVIII is a direct refutation of the view of many Anabaptists that Chris-tians should have all their goods in common.

Featley was nearer Kiffin and his friends than they were to other Baptists

After the debate, Featley, whether rightly or wrongly, concluded that the Baptists were quite unaware of the origin, teaching and purpose of the *Thirty-Nine Articles*. Furthermore, as his opponents argued dogmatically that the Articles were against the Word of God, he could only conclude that the British Baptists were thus defending the very Anabaptist heresies against which the *Thirty-Nine Articles* were drawn up.

Actually, the doctrinal gap between the British Particular Baptists and the more radical Continental Anabaptists was far, far wider than that

CREE, Alexander, D.A.(Edin.) 1950; painter in oil, pastel and water-colour; *b* 24 Feb., 1929. *Educ:* Dunfermline High School. *Studied:* Edinburgh College of Art (1946-52), Post Graduate Scholarship (1950), Travelling Scholarship (1951). *Exhib:* Scottish Lyceum Club (1957), Demarco Gallery (1968, 1976), Loomshop Gallery (1969), Shed 50 (1974), Macaulay Gallery (1990), Solstice Gallery (1991), Westgate Gallery (1991), Open Eye Gallery (1993), Ewan Mundy Gallery, Broughton Gallery, Kingfisher Gallery, Gallery 41, Edinburgh Gallery. *Work in collections:* Scottish Arts Council, Nuffield Foundation. *Signs work:* "A. Cree." *Address:* Sospiri, Braeheads, E. Linton, E. Lothian EH40 3DH, Scotland.

CREFFIELD, Dennis, *b* London, 29 Jan., 1931. *Educ:* Colfes Grammar School, London. *Studied:* Borough Polytechnic with David Bomberg (1948-51), Slade School (1957-61); Gregory Fellow in Painting at the University of Leeds (1964-67). *Exhib:* many mixed and one-man exhbns. *Work in collections:* include: Tate Gallery, Contemporary Art Soc., National Trust, House of Commons, Arts Council of Gt. Britain, Government Art Collection, Imperial War Museum, The Contemporary Art Soc. *Commissions:* include: South Bank Board – Medieval English Cathedrals (1987); The National Trust Foundation for Art – Petworth (1990); Orfordness (1994). *Signs work:* Dennis Creffield. *Address:* 45 Marine Parade, Brighton BN2 1PE.

CREME, Benjamin, artist in oil; *b* Glasgow, 1922. *m* Phyllis Power. two *s.* one *d. Educ:* Queens Park, Glasgow. *Studied:* with Jankel Adler. *Exhib:* A.I.A., London Group, Carnegie International (1952), Whitechapel (1954), Arts Council (1974), I.C.A. (1979); one-man shows: Gallery Apollinaire (1952), St. George's Gallery (1955), Bryant M. Hale Gallery (1964), Dartington New Gallery (1977), Themes and Variations Gallery (1985), England & Co. (1988); group shows: South Molton Gallery, Gimpel Fils, Redfern, Roland Browse and Delbanco, Leger Gallery, Reid and LeFevre. *Work in collections:* Pembroke College, Oxford, V. & A., B.M. *Publications:* Cage Without Grievance (W.S. Graham, Parton Press, 1942). *Signs work:* "Creme." *Address:* P.O. Box 3677, London NW5 1RU.

CRESWELL, Alexander Charles Justin, artist in water-colour, author; *b* Helsinki, 14 Feb., 1957. *m* Mary Curtis Green. one *s.* one *d. Educ:* Winchester College. *Studied:* Byam Shaw School of Art (1976), W. Surrey College (1976-78). *Exhib:* Hirschl & Adler Galleries New York; Spink & Son, Cadogan Gallery, New Academy London, also Europe, Hong Kong and S. Africa. *Work in collections:* Palace of Westminster, The Royal Collection, The Frick Museum. *Commissions:* Royal Collection, Royal Bank of Scotland, English Heritage, B.B.C., Duchy of Cornwall, HSBC Bank Middle East. *Publications:* The Silent Houses of Britain (1991), Out of the Ashes (1999). *Clubs:* Architecture, A.W.G., Arts Club. *Signs work:* "Alexander Creswell." *Address:* Copse Hill, Ewhurst, Surrey GU6 7NN.

CREW, Rowan Alexander, A.R.B.A. (1987), R.B.A. (1988); self taught artist in water-colour, acrylic and oil; *b* Woodchurch, Kent, 31 Dec., 1952. *m* Linda Bannister. three *d. Educ:* Homewood Secondary Modern. *Exhib:* R.I., R.B.A., R.O.I. *Work in collections:* K.C.C., and private collections. *Signs work:* "Rowan Crew." *Address:* Brookfarm House, Brook St., Woodchurch, Ashford, Kent TN26 3SP.

CRISFIELD CHAPMAN, June, D.A. (Glasgow) (1955); wood engraver, portrait painter (oil), illustrator (literary, theatre, plant themes in engraving, gouache); *b*

Kent, 4 June, 1934. *m* William Woodside Chapman, D.A. two *s. Educ:* Kilmarnock Academy. *Studied:* Glasgow School of Art. *Exhib:* solo shows: Royal National Theatre London, International Shakespeare Globe Centre London, Edinburgh College of Art, Royal Scottish Academy of Music and Drama Glasgow, Glasgow City A.G. Kelvingrove, etc.; group shows: Edinburgh International Festival, Royal Scottish Academy, Royal Society of Painter Printers' Open, Chaucer/Caxton, Westminster Abbey, etc. *Work in collections:* engravings in Glasgow, Edinburgh City, Ashmolean, Oxford, collections, paintings in theatres including 'Tribute to Scottish Theatre', Glasgow. *Commissions:* portraits, engraving, theatre gouaches. *Publications:* engravings Folio Book Society's Shakespeare (1988), 'The Countryman' ('87-'98). talks, demonstrations, including British Library, V. & A. Museum. *Signs work:* "CRISFIELD" or "CRISFIELD CHAPMAN." *Address:* 23 Smythe Rd., Billericay, Essex CM11 1SE.

CROFT, Ivor John, C.B.E., M.A. (Oxon. and Lond.); painter and former civil servant; *b* 6 Jan., 1923. *Educ:* Westminster School; Christ Church, Oxford; Institute of Education, University of London; London School of Economics and Political Science. *Exhib:* group shows: various, 1958 onwards including Camden Arts Centre (Survey of Abstract Painters, 1967); John Player Open Exhbn. (1968, 1969); Covent Garden Gallery (Critical Discoveries, 1973); Lorient, Brittany (Festival Interceltique, 1993); one-man shows: Gardner Centre for the Arts, University of Sussex (1970); University of Warwick (1971). *Publications:* work repro.: Art and Artists, postcard. *Clubs:* Reform. *Signs work:* "John Croft" on back. *Address:* 15 Circus Mews, Bath BA1 2PW.

CROFT, Richard John, R.U.A. (1967); artist in oils/print; President, Royal Ulster Academy of Arts (1997-2000); *b* London, 1935. *m* Helen Kerr, R.U.A. one *s.* one *d. Studied:* Bromley, and Brighton Colleges of Art. *Exhib:* Ireland, England and abroad. *Work in collections:* public and private, N.I. Arts Council, etc. *Signs work:* see appendix. *Address:* The Lodge, 187 Main St., Dundrum, Co. Down N.I. BT33 0LY.

CROKER, Valerie, S.B.A. (1987), H.S. (1994); artist in water-colour, pen and ink; *b* Cardiff, 19 Aug., 1931. one *s.* one *d. Educ:* Abbey School, Reading. *Studied:* Maidenhead Art School (1950), Reading University (1951-53, Prof. Betts). *Exhib:* S.WL.A., U.A.; solo shows: Henley, Bath, Wells, Winchester; and many other mixed shows in U.K. and abroad. *Publications:* illustrated: People and Places by J. H. B. Peel, Old Wives Tales by Eric Maple, The Secret Lore of Plants and Flowers by Eric Maple, Still Waters by Margaret Cornish. Work used for cards, tableware, etc. *Signs work:* "Valerie Croker" or "V.C." *Address:* Jessamine Cottage, 7 Lower Rd., Edington, Westbury, Wilts. BA13 4QW.

CROOK, P. J., R.W.A. (1993), M.A.F.A.; painter; *b* Cheltenham, 28 June, 1945. *m* Richard Parker Crook, painter. one *s.* one *d. Studied:* Gloucestershire College of Art (1960-65). *Exhib:* One Woman Show: Theo Waddington Fine Art, Boca Raton, Florida (2000), Theo Waddington Fine Art, London (1998), Robert Sandelson, London (1994-96), Galerie Alain Blondel Paris (1991, 1993, 1995, 1997, 1999), Royal West of England Academy (1997), Brian Sinfeld, Burford (1999), Brian Sinfeld, Compton Cassey (1997), Portal Gallery, London (1980-1994), 112 Greene

Street, New York (1989), Cheltenham A.G. and Museums (1986); retrospective (1980-1996); Cheltenham A.G. and Museums; Oriel Gallery, Theatr Clwyd, Mold; Musée Paul Valery, Séte; Rye A.G.; group shows: Royal Academy of Arts (1978-83, 1985, 1987, 1988, 1990, 1991, 1994, 1995), Royal West of England Academy (since 1978) (first prize 1984; A.R.W.A 1988, R.W.A.1993), Royal Bath and West Open, (First prize 1978), World of Newspapers, Sotheby's, R.A. Prizewinner (1982), Cheltenham Group, Purchase prize (1983), First prize (1990), Tolly Cobbold/Eastern Arts Open (1985), Athena International Arts Awards Open (1985, 1987), Five Gloucestershire Artists, Cheltenham Festival (1985), John Player Portrait Award Exhbn., National Portrait Gallery (1986), Small Pictures, Salisbury, Prizewinner, (1986), British Figurative Painting Since 1945, British Council tour of the Far East (1988-89), Friends of Carel Weight, London (1991), South West Open, Special Commendation (1992), Contemporary Icons, Royal Albert Memorial Museum, Exeter (1992), The Gift of Life, London, Prizewinner (1993), Manchester Academy of Fine Arts (since 1993), Dept. of Transport Exhbn., London, Purchase prize (1993), Reclaiming the Madonna, Lincoln Museum and A.G. tour (1993-94), Murs Peints, Mairie de Paris (1995), Salon des Independants, Paris (1995), Die Kraft der Bilder, Realismus der Gegenwart, Berlin (1996), Contemporary British Painting, Toronto (1996). *Work in collections:* Imperial War Museum; Dept. of Transport; Cheltenham A.G. and Museum; Allied Domecq plc; J.P. Morgan Inc; Ralli Institute, Geneva; University of Pennsylvania; London Business School; Cheltenham Racecourse; City of Paris; Canadian Museum of Animal Art. *Publications:* P.J. Crook: Peintures (Editions Ramsay, Paris, 1993); P.J. Crook: A Retrospective (Cheltenham A.G and Museums, 1996). *Clubs:* Arts, London. *Signs work:* "P.J. Crook." *Address:* The Old Police Station, 39 Priory La., Bishop's Cleeve, Cheltenham GL52 4JL.

CROSS, Roy, R.S.M.A. (1977), S.A.A. (1952), G.Av.A. (1998); historical marine and aviation painter in gouache, acrylic and oils; *b* London 1924. *m* Rita May (decd.). one *s. Exhib:* Malcolm Henderson Gallery, St. James's, (1973); one-man shows: Börjessons Gallery, Gothenborg, Sweden, (1975 and 1977); Marine Arts Gallery, Salem, Massachusetts (1976, 1989, 1999). *Work in collections:* National Maritime Museum; Constitution Museum, Boston, U.S.A.; Peabody Museum, Salem, U.S.A. *Publications:* many limited edition prints of marine pictures signed and numbered by the artist (1977-1999) published in Sweden (2), U.S.A. (7) and Britain (3), plus art prints by Franklin Mint, Rosenstiel's, plates by Hamilton Collection, etc. *Signs work:* "Roy Cross ©" and usually dated. *Address:* Squirrels, Hither Chantlers, Langton Green, Tunbridge Wells, Kent TN3 0BJ.

CROSS, Tom, N.D.D.(1953), Dip.(Lond.)(1956); painter in oil and gouache; Principal, Falmouth School of Art (1976-87); mem. London Group; Chairman, Penwith Soc. of Artists (1982-84); *b* Manchester, 1931. *m* Patricia. one *s. Studied:* The Slade School, Abbey Minor Scholarship, Rome, French Govt. Scholarship. *Exhib:* one-man shows, Penwith Galleries, Montpelier Studio, Charleston, S.C. *Work in collections:* Welsh Arts Council, Contemporary Art Soc. for Wales, Leicester and Glamorgan Educ. Authorities, U.S.A. and Australia, private collections. *Publications:* The Shining Sands, Artists in Newlyn and St. Ives 1880-1930; Painting the Warmth of the Sun, St. Ives Artists 1939-75. *Clubs:* Chelsea Arts; . *Signs work:* "Tom Cross." *Address:* Dinyan, Port Navas, Constantine, Cornwall.

CROSSLEY, Bob, painter, printmaker; *b* Northwich, 1912. *m* Marjorie. one *s.* two *d. Educ:* Heybrook School, Rochdale. *Exhib:* 11 one-man shows: Crane Gallery, Manchester (1959), Reid Gallery, London (1960, 1964), Gallery Bique, Madrid (1965), Reid Gallery, Guildford (1966), Curwen Gallery, London (1972), Singers Fridden Division, Stevenage (1972), John Player & Sons, Nottingham (1972), Bristol Arts Centre (1980), Penwith Galleries, St. Ives (1987, 1999), also Tate Gallery and Belgrave Gallery St. Ives (2000). *Work in collections:* Contemporary Art Society, Rochdale A.G., Durban, A.G., S.A., Winnipeg A.G., College of Advanced Education, Port Elizabeth, S.A., Hereford A.G., Open University, Sommerfield College. *Commissions:* R.A.F. Museum, Hendon (The Nimrod). *Signs work:* "Crossley." *Address:* Studio Annexe, Porthgwidden, St. Ives, Cornwall TR26 1PL.

CROSSLEY, Gordon, painter in oil; Retd. Senior lecturer in Art and Design, Barking College of Technology; *b* Surrey, 6 Dec., 1929. *m* Jo Glosby. one *s.* three *d. Educ:* Rutlish School, Merton. *Studied:* Wimbledon School of Art. *Exhib:* R.A., R.B.A., N.E.A.C., P.S., N.S., Madden Gallery; one-man shows, Phoenix Gallery (1984), Gainsborough Gallery, Beecroft Gallery. *Work in collections:* Essex Museum. *Signs work:* see appendix. *Address:* The Sanctuary, Sheering, nr. Bishop's Stortford, Herts. CM22 7LN.

CROSTHWAITE, Sally, S.B.A.; R.H.S., Silver medal (1998); botanical illustrator in water-colour; *b* Woking, Surrey, 14 Apr., 1944. *m* Patrick Crosthwaite. one *s.* two *d. Studied:* English Gardening School, Chelsea Physic Garden (Distinction, Diploma Course, Botanical illustration). *Exhib:* 1997-98: Contemporary Botanical Artists of the World, Swann and Tryon Gallery, London, Malcolm Innes Gallery, London, S.B.A. Open, etc., also in Sweden, U.S.A. *Work in collections:* Hunt Inst. for Botanical Documentation, Carnegie Mellon University, U.S.A., Library of Chelsea Physic Garden. *Commissions:* numerous private in U.K. and U.S.A. *Publications:* various illustrations in books. tulip designs on plates. *Clubs:* Chelsea Physic Garden Florilegium Soc., S.B.A., American Soc. of Botanical Artists, Soc. of Floral Painters. *Address:* Lynchmere Farmhouse, nr. Haslemere, Surrey GU27 3NG. *Email:* sallycrosthwaite@supanet.com

CROW, Kathleen Mary, R.O.I. (1988), N.S. (1983); painter in oil and water-colour; *b* Oxton, Notts., 4 June, 1920. *m* John Richard Crow. one *s.* one *d. Educ:* Ackworth; Basel, Switzerland. *Studied:* Nottingham Polytechnic (1964-76 part-time, Ronald Thursby), Leicester (1976-82 part-time, Leslie Goodwin). *Exhib:* R.A. Summer Exhbns., R.W.A., R.O.I., R.I., N.S., Nottingham, Rufford, Leicester, Oakham. *Clubs:* Nottingham Soc. of Artists. *Signs work:* see appendix. *Address:* 2 Blind La., Oxton, Southwell, Notts. NG25 0SS.

CROWE, Barbara, R.I., S.W.A., S.B.A.; painter in water-colour and oil, teacher, demonstrator; *b* Wirral, Ches. *m* Ronald Crowe. one *s.* three *d. Studied:* Bolt Court, Croydon Art School, Epsom Art School, but mostly self-taught. *Exhib:* R.I., S.W.A., S.B.A., Mall Galleries, Westminster Gallery, London. *Commissions:* numerous. *Publications:* contributor to Artist and Leisure Painter, also Water-Colour Impressionists by Ron Ranson. *Clubs:* The Dorking, Guildford and Sussex Art Socs. *Signs work:* "Barbara Crowe." *Address:* Sawyers, Peaslake Lane, Peaslake, Surrey GU5 9RL. *Website:*

CROWE, Maida, F.F.P.S.; sculptor in wood and stone; *b* Axminster, 1915. *m* Jim Crowe. *Educ:* privately. *Studied:* City and Guilds of London (1957-62). *Exhib:* R.B.A., F.P.S., A.I.R., Barbican, Surrey, Birmingham, Southampton, Lincoln and London Universities, etc.; open air, Berkeley Sq., and Brixton; one-man shows, Loggia Gallery, Cockpit Gallery, I.A.C., Bridport and Southwark Cathedral. *Publications:* First and Last - A Search for Meaning (Purzebrook Press, 1994). *Clubs:* F.P.S., I.C.A., N.F.T. *Signs work:* "MAIDA." *Address:* 906 Keyes House, Dolphin Sq., London SW1V 3NB.

CROWE, Victoria Elizabeth, N.D.D. (1965), M.A. (R.C.A.) (1968), R.S.W. (1983), A.R.S.A. (1987); artist in oil and water-colour; *b* 1945. *Studied:* Kingston College of Art (1961-65), R.C.A. (1965-68). *Exhib:* R.A., R.S.A.; solo shows, Scottish Gallery, Edinburgh (1970, 1974, 1977, 1982, 1995, 1998, 2001), Thackeray, London (1983, 1985, 1987, 1989, 1991, 1994, 1999, 2001), Mercury Gallery, Edinburgh (1986), Bruton Gallery, Bath and Leeds (1989, 1993, 1998), Scottish National Portrait Gallery (2000). *Work in collections:* R.A., R.C.A., Scottish National Gallery of Modern Art, Scottish Arts Council, N.P.G. London, Scottish N.P.G., I.L.E.A., Edinburgh Educ. Authority. *Publications:* 'Painted Insights' Victoria Crowe, pub. A.CC. (2001). *Signs work:* "Victoria Crowe." *Address:* The Bank House, Main St., W. Linton, Peeblesshire EH46 7EE.

CROWTHER, Hugh Melvill, artist in oil, pastel; *b* Newby, nr. Scarborough, Yorks., 25 June, 1914. *m* Margaret Steele Wainey. *Educ:* St. John's, Tutshill, Chepstow. *Studied:* Newport Technical College, Gwent. *Exhib:* Royal Glasgow Institute of Fine Arts, Cardiff, Newport, Monmouth, Hereford, Gloucester, London. *Work in collections:* Newport Museum, Gwent. *Publications:* work repro.: Chepstow Castle, Village Smithy, Naturalist's Collection, all in La Revue Moderne. *Clubs:* West Gloucestershire Art Soc., Wye Valley Art Soc., Gloucestershire Soc. of Artists. *Signs work:* see appendix. *Address:* Meadow End, Tidenham, Chepstow, Gwent NP16 7JG.

CROWTHER, Stephen, A.R.C.A., R.B.A. (1958); artist in oil, charcoal, conté, pastel; lecturer, drawing and painting, College of Art, Hartlepool (1950-1987); elected senior member of Royal Society of British Artists (1999); *b* Sheffield, 23 Aug., 1922. *m* Sheila Maria Higgins. two *s.* one *d. Educ:* De la Salle College, Sheffield. *Studied:* Sheffield College of Art; Royal Scholarship to Royal College of Art (1941); war service (1941-46); R.C.A. (1946-49). *Exhib:* R.A., R.B.A., R.P., Llewellyn Alexander Gallery, London, and many provincial galleries; one-man shows: Gray A.G., Hartlepool; Billingham A.G.; Zaydler Gallery, London; Green Dragon Yard A.G., Stockton; Abbot Hall A.G., Kendal; Middlesbrough A.G. *Work in collections:* Hartlepool A.G.; Derbyshire and Hartlepool Education Committees; Abbot Hall A.G., Kendal; Hartlepool, South Tees, Cleveland; Bradford General Hospitals; Yarm School, Yarm, Cleveland; Higgs and Hill; The Sultan of Oman. *Commissions:* Port Solent Marina, Portsmouth, for Higgs and Hill (1989); three oils for the Sultan of Oman (1992); and portrait commissions in oil and pastels. *Publications:* in The Complete Portrait Painting Course including front cover; Portrait, and Perspective for Artists, both by Angela Gair (Mitchell Beazley, 1990); The Oil Painter's Question and Answer Book by Hazel Harrison (Quarto Publishing), and many other books including The Reader's Digest Figure Sketching School by Valerie Wiffen (1997).

With two of my drawings on the front cover. *Clubs:* President, Hartlepool Art Club. *Signs work:* see appendix. *Address:* 5 The Cliff, Seaton Carew, Hartlepool, TS25 1AB.

CROZIER, William, Premio Lissone, Milan (1960), Visiting Fellowship New York Studio School (1979), Prof. Emeritus, Winchester School of Art (1987), Gold Medal for Painting The Oireachtas, Dublin (1994); painter in oil on canvas; *b* Glasgow, 1930. *m* Katherine. *Studied:* Glasgow School of Art (1949-53), David Donaldson, Mary and William Armour. *Exhib:* include: Serpentine Gallery, London, (1978), Scottish Gallery, Edinburgh (1985), Bruton St. Gallery, London (1995-96). *Work in collections:* National Galleries worldwide, A.C.G.B., W.A.G. Liverpool, V. & A. etc. *Signs work:* "CROZIER" lower left on canvas. *Address:* c/o Bruton St. Gallery, 28 Bruton St., London W1X 7DB.

CRYAN, Clare, A.T.C., D.A.; artist specializing in water-colour; Tutor-in-Charge, The Blue Door Studio; *b* Dublin, 1935. *Educ:* Dominican Convent, Sion Hill. *Studied:* National College of Art, Dublin; Ulster College of Art, Belfast and with Kenneth Webb in The Irish School of Landscape Painting. *Exhib:* R.H.A., R.U.A., N.S., Salon d'Automne, Festival International Paris, Osaka, Brussels, Luxembourg, Hong Kong. *Work in collections:* Killiney Castle, Dublin, H.M. Queen Beatrix of the Netherlands. *Clubs:* European Inst. of Water-colours. *Signs work:* "Clare Cryan." *Address:* The Blue Door Studio, 16 Prince of Wales Terr., Dublin 4.

CRYER, Ian David, painter in oils, visual celebrator of all things English; *b* Bristol, 1959. *m* Wendy Patricia. one *s.* one *d. Educ:* Ridings High School, Bristol. *Studied:* part-time Bristol Polytechnic (1978-82); and in Kensington under Leonard Boden, R.P. (1978-81). *Exhib:* Bristol Art Centre (1976), P. Wells Gallery (1983), Linfield Galleries (1984, 1985), R.A., R.S.M.A., G.R.A., R.B.A., R.W.A., N.E.A.C., Hunting Group finalist (1990), Discerning Eye (1991), Cooling Gallery (1992), 1st International Art Biennial, Malta (1995). *Work in collections:* many private collections including Price Waterhouse, Longleat House, Bass Museum, Burton-on-Trent, Wadworth & Co., Bristol Rovers F.C. *Signs work:* "Ian Cryer." *Address:* 93 Bath Rd., Willsbridge, Bristol BS30 6ED.

CUBA, Ivan, D.Litt.; professor extraordinary of art, proclaimed for distinguished service, Dictionary of International Biography, Vol. V (1968); elected The Temple of Arts, U.S.A. (1970); elected Fellow, Academy Leonardo da Vinci and Poet Laureate Award (1979); President, Temple of Art Academy, N.Z.; developed educational composite painting, segment painting and aluminium engravure, discovered colour-balancing by mathematics and weight changes in matter; decorations include 14 diplomas, sets of other letters and two gold medals, ten other. Awarded, International Poet Laureate (1995), India; International Man of Year (1995-97); *Studied:* University of Auckland, N.Z. *Exhib:* U.K., U.S.A., N.Z. Author of books. *Address:* P.O. Box 5199, Wellesley St., Auckland, N.Z.

CULLEN, Patrick, N.E.A.C., artist in oil, watercolour, and pastel; *b* 8 Aug., 1949. *m* Sally. two *d. Studied:* Camberwell 1973 -1976. *Exhib:* The Thackeray Gallery, Kensington, London W8. *Work in collections:* R.A., Sheffield City Art Gallery. *Clubs:* New English Art Club and Pastel Society. *Signs work:* "Patrick Cullen." *Address:* 19, Mount Pleasant Cres., London N4 4HP.

CULLINAN, Edward, C.B.E., R.A.; architect, artist; has taught and lectured in Canada, U.S.A., Australia, N.Z., Norway, Malta, Japan, Eire, etc. and many places in England, Wales and Scotland; Founder and principal architect, Edward Cullinan Architects, authors of many modern bldgs. and receivers of many awards; *b* London, 17 July, 1931. *m* Rosalind. one *s.* two *d. Studied:* architecture: Architectural Assoc., Cambridge and Berkeley, Calif. *Publications:* Edward Cullinan Architects by Kenneth Powell (Academy Editions, 1995). *Signs work:* "E.C." or "Edward Cullinan Architects." *Address:* The Wharf, Baldwin Terr., London N1 7RU.

CUMBERLAND-BROWN, James Francis, R.S.H., A.R.M.S., H.S.; self taught miniature marine artist in scrimshaw (engraving) and pencil; *b* Finsbury, 12 Apr., 1934. *m* Tamara Robertson Provis. two *d. Educ:* Kingham Hill, Oxon. *Exhib:* R.M.S., H.S., Montelimar, France, and numerous private galleries throughout Australia; received Bidder and Bourne Award for most outstanding work in sculptors and gravers, R.M.S. (1996). *Work in collections:* National Maritime Museum, Australia; W.A. Maritime Museum; Murdock University; Museum of Fine Art, Geneva; McKenzie Gallery, Perth. *Signs work:* "J.F.C." *Address:* "Mira-Near", 16 Coldwells St., Bicton, W.A. 6157.

CUMING, Fred, A.R.C.A., A.R.A. (1969), R.A. (1974), N.E.A.C., Hon. R.O.I.; painter in oil; *b* London, 16 Feb., 1930. *m* Audrey Lee. two *s. Studied:* Sidcup School of Art (1945-1949), R.C.A. (1951-1955) under John Minton, Carel Weight, Rodrigo Moynihan, Ruskin Spear, Colin Hayes, Robert Buhler. *Exhib:* U.K., U.S.A., Argentina, Ireland and Europe. *Work in collections:* R.A., Canterbury, Scunthorpe, Preston, Eastbourne, Salford, Monte Carlo. *Commissions:* Worcester Coll., Oxford, St. John's Coll., Oxford, Lloyds of London, W.H.Smith, Farendon Trust, L.W.T., Nat. Trust Foundation for Art etc., also U.S.A. and South America. *Publications:* Figure in the Landscape, Unicorn Press; video, The Art of Fred Cuming R.A., R.A. collection. *Signs work:* "Cuming." *Address:* The Gables, Wittersham Rd., Iden, Rye, E. Sussex TN31 7UY.

CUMMINGS, Albert Arratoon Runciman, U.A. (1973), F.S.A. (Scot.)(1973); painter in tempera, oil and water-colour, book illustrator, picture restorer; *b* Edinburgh, 20 Aug., 1936. *m* Marjorie Laidlaw. one *s.* one *d. Educ:* Edinburgh. *Studied:* apprentice stage designer under William Grason, Edward Bowers, painting under Charles Napier, Robert Jardine. *Exhib:* U.A., Scottish Gallery, Fine Art Soc., Edinburgh Gallery, Open Eye Gallery. *Work in collections:* Leeds Educ. authorities, Edinburgh Hospital Board. *Publications:* Dictionary of Scottish Art and Arch (Pub. Antique Collectors Club). *Clubs:* Scottish Arts. *Signs work:* see appendix. *Address:* 4 School Rd., Aberlady, E. Lothian.

CUMMINGS, Ann, painter in oil, pastel and egg tempera; *b* Edinburgh, 12 Dec., 1945. *m* Dr. Laurie Jacobs, B.Sc., M.B.Ch.B. three *s. Educ:* Stamford College (1989-91) and under Albert A.R. Cummings (1991-94). *Exhib:* Edinburgh, Glasgow, Dunkeld, Stamford and Peterborough. *Clubs:* Welland Art Soc. *Signs work:* "A.C." *Address:* Hollywell, 38 Church St., Werrington, Peterborough, Cambs. PE4 6QE.

CUMMINGS, George Reid, L. Bryne Waterman Award (1995) Boston, U.S.A. for work in preserving the history of the modern whaling industry, Lay Mem., Royal Soc. Marine Artists; artist in oil; *b* Edinburgh, 11 May, 1932. *m* Mabel A. one *s.* one *d. Studied:* studied the use of oil painting by Joan Renton, R.S.A. Edinburgh (1985). *Exhib:* R.S.M.A. (1988); permanent exhbns.: Kendall Whaling Museum, Sharon Boston, Massachusetts; Sandefjord Whaling Museum, Sandefjord, Norway; Tonsberg Maritime Museum, Tonsberg, Norway; Grytviken Whaling Museum, South Georgia, Falkland Islands; Chr. Salvesen plc., Edinburgh, Scotland. *Commissions:* from Sir Gerald Elliott, Past Chairman Chr. Salvesen plc., Sir Maxwell Harper Gow, and numerous private individuals worldwide. Specializes in recording accurate details of the modern whaling industry ships and general maritime art. Paintings are technically correct giving very accurate detail of the vessel painted for historic purposes. *Clubs:* Chairman Salvesen's ex Whalers Club, Edinburgh. *Signs work:* "George R. Cummings, Edinburgh" and year completed. *Address:* 19 Blackford Hill View, Edinburgh EH9 3HD.

CUMMINS, Gus, N.D.D. (1963), M.A. (R.C.A.)(1997), R.A. (1992); painter in oil, gouache, water-colour, etc.; *b* London, 28 Jan., 1943. *m* Angela Braven, painter. two *s.* one *d. Educ:* Sutton and Wimbledon Art School and R.C.A. *Exhib:* extensively, seven solo shows since 1990. *Work in collections:* R.A., R.C.A., Contemporary Arts Soc., Towner Coll., Hastings Museum Coll., Hastings Library, Freshfields plc., F.T. Coll. *Clubs:* Chelsea Arts. *Signs work:* "Gus Cummins." *Address:* Harpsichord House, Cobourg Pl., Hastings, Sussex TN34 3HY.

CUNNINGHAM, Anne, painter in pastel and oil; fine furniture painter;one *s.* one *d. Educ:* Welwyn Garden City Grammar School. *Exhib:* solo exhibs., London, Paris, group exhibs., New York. *Clubs:* former member of Chappaqua Artists' Guild, New York State, and Chichester Art Society, W. Sussex. *Signs work:* "Anne Cunningham." *Address:* The Studio, Uncle Dick's Cottage, Church Lane, Hayling Island, Hants. PO11 0SB. *Website:* www.artprinthouse.com *Email:* annec57@aol.com

CURMANO, Billy, M.S. (1977), B.F.A. (1973); intermedia artist; *b* U.S.A., 1949. *Educ:* Art Students League, N.Y.C.; University of Wisconsin; former director, Broadway Galleries. *Exhib:* solo shows: New Orleans, Chapel Hill, Minneapolis, Milwaukee, La Crosse, Winona; group shows: Nature Art, Korea (1999), Artpool, Budapest, Hungary (1995), Vienna Graphikbiennale, Austria (1977), International Miniprint, Ourense, Spain (1993), Franklin Furnace, N.Y.C. (1987), Small Works, N.Y.C. (1986), Public Works, N.Y.C. (1984), Metronom, Barcelona, Spain (1981), Mail Art, New Zealand (1976), # 18, N.Y.C. (1972), Paula Insel, N.Y.C. (1972), Tyler National, Texas (1972), Graphics U.S.A., Chicago (1971). *Work in collections:* Museum of Modern Art, N.Y.C. *Publications:* "The Search for the Spiritual in Art", videorecording, (2000). *Signs work:* "Billy Curmano." *Address:* Route # 1, Rushford, Mn. 55971, U.S.A. *Email:* billyx@acegroup.cc

CURRY, Denis Victor, Dip.F.A. (Slade) painting (1950) sculpture (1951), R.C.A. (1992); artist/scientist in oil, water-colour, bronze, stone, kinetic; *b* Newcastle-on-Tyne, 11 Nov., 1918. *m* Jennifer Coram. *Educ:* Durham Johnson School. *Studied:* Durham (Kremer), Slade School of Fine Art (Schwabe, Coldstream). *Exhib:* London Group, R.A., R.W.A., Slade Bi-Centenary, Oriel, Cardiff, Residency - sculpture, St. David's (1991), R.Cam.A., Sculpture at Margam, National Eisteddfod (1994); many group and one-man shows U.K. and abroad. *Work in collections:* Pembrokeshire

Museum and A.G., Tunnicliffe Museum, Anglesey, Chatsworth House, Contemporary Art Soc., Wales. *Commissions:* Numerous public and private, inc. 2 x life-size bronze eagles. *Publications:* Poetry Wales, This Land is Our Land (B.M. Nat.Hist. 1989), Laying Out the Body (Seren 1992), R.Ae.Soc. Symposium - Manpowered Aircraft Group (1975), own publication: Denis Curry Painting Sculpture Images (1985). *Signs work:* "Denis Curry," "D. Curry" or "D.C." *Address:* Fron, Llanycefn, Clynderwen, Dyfed SA66 7XT.

CURSHAM, Juliet, S.Eq.A.; self taught sculptor in bronze of equestrian subjects, animals and figures; *b* Nottingham, 23 Aug., 1960. *m* Edward Packe-Drury-Lowe. one *s.* one *d. Educ:* Ockbrook Girls' School, Derbyshire, Nottingham High School, Winkfield Place, Berks. *Exhib:* Les Hirondelles Gallery, Geneva; Van Dell Gallery, Palm Beach, Florida; Osbourne Gallery, London; Tryon Gallery, London; Compton Cassey Gallery, Gloucestershire; Osbourne Studio Gallery; Royal Hong Kong Jockey Club. *Work in collections:* Life-size horse and jockey for the Hong Kong Jockey Club at Happy Valley; collections in America, Japan, Brunei, Canada. *Commissions:* Dancing Brave, Generous, Venture to Cognac, Ryadian. *Signs work:* "Juliet Cursham." *Address:* Prestwod Hall, Loughborough, Leics. LE12 5SQ.

CURTIS, Anthony Ewart, Dip.A.E.(Lond.), R.W.A.; experimental and landscape artist; served R.N. (1946-48); *b* Wakefield, 7 July, 1928. *m* Joyce Isabel Yates. three *s.* one *d. Educ:* Kingswood Grammar School, Loughborough (1948-50); London (1974-76). *Studied:* Bath Academy, Corsham (1950-51, Potworowski, Scott, Armitage, Lanyon, Wynter). *Exhib:* (1952-): Redfern, Zwemmers, Daily Express Young Painters, London Group, R.W.A. (1952 to date), Arts Council Modern Stained Glass (1960-61), R.I. (1983), R.W.S. (1984), 'Migraine Images' at St. Martin-in-the-Fields (1993). One-man shows include Bear Lane, Oxford (1959), Reading (1961), Cookham (1964), R.W.A. (1995); ceramic sculpture: Scopas, Henley (1975), Century, Henley (1980), Recent and Retrospective Work, Bloomsbury Gallery, University of London (1987), Retrospective shows 'Recollections', Wooburn Festival (1992); Australian Works, Methuen Gallery, R.W.A. (1995), Art on Paper Fair, British Art Fair, R.C.A. (2000). *Work in collections:* R.W.A., Bristol Educ. Com., sand-blasted screen, St. Andrew's, High Wycombe. *Publications:* work repro.: Young Artists of Promise (1957); contributor: A Celebration of Bath Academy of Art at Corsham. Working visits to Australia (1988-89); Oregon, U.S.A. (1990, 1993), S.Africa (1996). *Signs work:* "Anthony Curtis," or see appendix (on small works). *Address:* Oak Tree House, 143 Heath End Rd., Flackwell Heath, High Wycombe HP10 9ES.

CURTIS, David Jan Gardiner, R.O.I. (1988), R.S.M.A. (1983); artist in oil and water-colour; *b* Doncaster, 15 June, 1948. one *s. Educ:* Doncaster Grammar School. *Exhib:* R.A., R.S.M.A., R.I., R.W.S., R.B.A., N.E.A.C. R.O.I., R.P. Singer Friedlander/Sunday Times water-colour competition 1st prizewinner (1992), 2nd prizewinner (1997). *Work in collections:* Doncaster Museum and A.G., Ferens Gallery, Hull, Sultanate of Oman, Rockefeller Institute, New York. *Commissions:* H.M. Crown Commissioners, Cavalry & Guards Club, Piccadilly. *Publications:* author, A Light Touch - The Landscape in Oils and The Landscape in Water-colour - a Personal View and films of the same titles; also 'Light effects in Water-colour' (video) 1997. *Clubs:* R.O.I., R.S.M.A. *Signs work:* "D.J. Curtis." *Address:* Gibdyke

House, Gibdyke, Misson, Doncaster, S. Yorks. DN10 6EL.

CURTIS, Joyce, Dip.A.E.(Lond.); artist and children's book illustrator in watercolour, gouache, oil, pencil; former Organiser (S.Bucks.), Bucks. Art Week Visual Images Group; *b* Sulhamstead, 5 Aug., 1934. *m* Anthony Curtis. three *s.* one *d. Educ:* Faringdon Grammar School; Post-grad. Dip., London (1985-86). *Studied:* Bath Academy of Art, Corsham (1952-54, Potworowski, Litz Pisk, Frost, Meadows, Armitage, Ellis). *Exhib:* solo shows, Dixon Gallery, University of London (1986), Corsham (1990), High Wycombe Museum (1993); three joint exhbns. with husband; mixed shows including R.W.A. *Publications:* contributor: A Celebration of Bath Academy of Art at Corsham. *Signs work:* "Joyce Curtis." *Address:* Oak Tree House, 143 Heath End Rd., Flackwell Heath, Bucks. HP10 9ES.

CURTIS, Roger, N.D.D. (1965), A.T.D. (1966); painter in oil, watercolour and acrylic; paints beaches, harbours and landscapes of the far South-West of Cornwall; *b* Birmingham, 9 Apr., 1945. *m* Christine. two *d. Educ:* George Dixon Grammar School. *Studied:* Birmingham College of Art and Design (1961-1965). *Exhib:* various group exhibs. including R.I. and R.W.A.; currently at a number of small galleries in the West country. *Work in collections:* private collections in Britain, U.S.A., Europe and Japan. *Clubs:* St. Ives Society of Artists. *Signs work:* "R Curtis." *Address:* 2 Coombe Vale, Newlyn, Cornwall TR18 5QU.

CUTHBERT, Rosalind, M.A. (R.C.A.) 1977, R.W.A. (1998); painter-engraver in gouache, oils, mixed media and wood engraving; *b* Weston-super-Mare, 1951. *m* David. one *d. Studied:* Central School of Art and Design (1971-74), R.C.A. (1974-77). *Exhib:* mainly in the South-West and London, also France and U.S.A. *Work in collections:* N.P.G., National Poetry Library, National Art Library (V. & A.), Contemporary Art Soc. *Commissions:* various portraits and other commissions. *Publications:* Founded Yellow Fox Press (1993). Publish handmade books of poetry and wood engravings: 'Islands' (1993), 'Birdsong and Water' (1994), 'Nature Studies' (1995), 'Bouncing Boy' (1999), 'HLEP!' (2001). *Clubs:* R.W.A., Fine Press Book Assoc. *Address:* Winscombe Farm Studio, Parsons Way, Winscombe, N. Somerset BS25 1BT. *Email:* roscuthbert@hotmail.com

CZERWINKE, Tadeusz, N.D.D. (1957), A.T.C. (1973), S.P.S. (1976), D.A.E. (1981); sculptor, carver, modeller and potter in stone, wood, perspex, bronze and terracotta; Head of Arts and Crafts Dept., Shoeburyness Comprehensive School; *b* Poland, 19 May, 1936. *m* Ewa. one *s.* one *d. Educ:* St. Peter's Winchester. *Studied:* Winchester School of Arts and Crafts (1957, Norman Pierce, F.R.B.S.). *Exhib:* regularly at S.P.S., Mall Galleries, Federation of British Artists, A.P.A. in G.B., Salon des Nations, Paris; one-man portrait sculpture exhbn. Posk Gallery (1987) and at the Polish Hearth, London. *Work in collections:* Church of Czestochowa, Huddersfield; Kosciuszko Museum, Rappersville, Switzerland; St. Peter's Hinkley, Leics.; Les Laurents, Dordogne, France; St. Catherine's Dock, London; Our Lady of Lourdes Convent, Kent; Town Hall, Monte Cassino, Italy; Parish Church, Devonia Rd., London; St. Sebastian & John the Baptist, Preston; Andrzej Bobola Church, London; Memorial, Eaton Pl., London; General Sikorski Museum, London; Memorial, Marshal J. Pilsudzki Inst., London; Posk (Centre of Polish Culture, London); Dom Narodowca, London; S. Michalowski, Shute House, nr. Honiton; sculptures and portraits in private collections in U.K. and overseas. *Signs work:* "Tad. Czerwinke." *Address:* 20 Whitehouse Way, Southgate, London N14 7LT.

CZIMBALMOS, Magdolna Paal, S.I. Museum, N.Y., Gold Med. (1958, 1960, 1962, 1963, 1966); personal letter from President J. F. Kennedy for portrait of Jacqueline Kennedy (1961); Italian Culture Award, N.Y. (1967); Szinyei Merse Gold Med., N.Y. (1971); several Silver Med. and Hon. Men.; artist in oil; *b* Esztergom, Hungary. *m* Kalman Sz. Czimbalmos. one *d.* *Studied:* under Prof. A. Bayor pr. Art Sch. Esztergom, Hung., Radatz pr. Art Sch. Germ. *Exhib:* Paris, Germany, Monaco, Canada, U.S.A., Budapest (1982), Esztergom, Hungary (1985); several one-man and group shows. *Work in collections:* S.I. Museum, N.Y., International Inst., Detroit, Carnegie International Cent., N.Y., Bergstrom Art Cent., Ill., City Museum, Esztergom and Budapest, Hungary. *Clubs:* S.I. Museum, N.Y., World Fed. of Hung. Artists, International Soc. of Fine Artists, U.S.A. *Signs work:* "Magdolna Paal Czimbalmos" and see appendix. *Address:* 31 Bayview Pl., Ward Hill, Staten Island, New York, 10304.

CZIMBALMOS, Szabo Kalman, Hung. Roy. Acad. Pr. (1933), S.I. Museum, N.Y., Pr. Gold Med. (1950, 1956, 1962, 1963, 1967), St. Stephen Gold Medal, N.Y. (1971), several Silver Med. and Hon. Men.; M.F.A., painter-educator, Dir. Czimbalmos Pvt. Art Sch., N.Y.; owner, Czimbalmos Fine Art Studio, S.I., N.Y.; artist in oil, water-colour, tempera; *b* Esztergom, Hungary, 1914. *m* Magdolna Paal Bohatka. one *d.* *Studied:* Royal Academy of Fine Art, Budapest (1936) under Prof. J. Harahghy, E. Domanowsky; postgrad. Vienna, Munich, Paris, Rome. *Exhib:* Munchen, Paris, Monaco, Canada, U.S.A., Budapest (1982), Esztergom, Hungary (1985); several one-man and group shows. *Work in collections:* S.I. Museum, N.Y., S.I. Com. Coll. N.Y., Bergstrom Art Center, Ill., City Museum, Esztergom, Hung., etc.; murals in churches, convents and private inst., U.S.A. *Clubs:* Bavaryan Fine Art Soc., S.I. Museum, N.Y., World Fed. of Hung. Artists, International Soc. of Fine Artists, U.S.A. *Signs work:* "K. Sz. Czimbalmos" and see appendix. *Address:* 31 Bayview Pl., Ward Hill, Staten Island, New York, 10304.

D

DACK, Tom, artist in water-colour, oils, gouache and line, specialises in marine, aviation and landscape; *b* Newcastle Upon Tyne, 26 May, 1933. *m* Catherine. one *s.* one *d.* *Educ:* Newcastle College of Art. *Exhib:* solo shows; Patricia Wells Gallery (Bristol), Oddfellows, Kendal, Darlington A.G., Trinity Maritime Centre, Newcastle. *Commissions:* Several private. *Signs work:* see appendix. *Address:* 13 Selwyn Ave., Whitley Bay, Tyne & Wear NE25 9DH.

D'AGUILAR, Michael, gold, silver and bronze medals, Royal Drawing Soc., Armitage and silver medal, R.A. (1949); artist in oil and pastels; *b* London, 11 May, 1922. *Educ:* privately and in Spain, Italy and France. *Studied:* R.A. Schools under Henry Rushbury, R.A., Fleetwood-Walker, A.R.A., William Dring, R.A. (1948-53).

Exhib: R.A., R.B.A., N.E.A.C., Irving Galleries, Gimpel Fils, Leicester Galleries, Young Contemporaries; one-man shows, Gimpel Fils, Irving Galleries, New Grafton Gallery, Bruton St. Gallery, Redfern Gallery. *Publications:* work repro.: Artist, Studio, La Revue Moderne des Arts; articles in Diario de Tarragona. *Clubs:* Chelsea Arts, Arts Dover St., London Sketch, Reynolds. *Signs work:* "M. D'Aguilar." *Address:* Studio 4, Chelsea Farm House, Milmans St., London SW10 0DW.

D'AGUILAR, Paul, artist in oil, water-colour; 1st prize for drawing at R.A. Schools (1949); gold, silver and bronze medals, R.D.S.; *b* London, 9 Sept., 1927. *Educ:* privately in Spain, Italy and France. *Studied:* R.A. Schools (1948-53) and with Prof. Barblain (Siena). *Exhib:* R.A., Redfern, Young Contemporaries, Leicester Galleries, Daily Express Young Artists, R.B.A., N.E.A.C., Sindicato de Iniciativa (Spain), Irving Gallery (1952), Temple Gallery (1960), New Grafton, Canaletto (1971), Southwell Brown Gallery (1974), Langton Gallery (1973, 1976). *Work in collections:* Lord Rothermere. *Publications:* work repro.: Artist, Studio, Collins Magazine, La Revue Moderne, Drawing Nudes (Studio Vista). *Signs work:* "P. D'Aguilar." *Address:* 11 Sheen Gate Gdns., London SW14.

DAINES, Deirdre, R.A. Silver medal, bronze medal and Greenshields Award, R.A. Cert., Eric Kennington prize for drawing, Winsor and Newton prize; painter in oil drawing and pastel, mainly figure paintings; teacher; *b* Ware, 2 May, 1950. *Educ:* Tottenham High Grammar School. *Studied:* R.A. Schools (1970-73, Peter Greenham). *Exhib:* New Grafton, R.A. Summer Exhbn., R.P., Agnew's, Watermans; one-man shows, Thos. Agnew (1988), Cale Art (1982). *Work in collections:* Guinness, Nuffield Trust, Pole Carew, Bonham Carter. *Commissions:* Studio 6D The Depot, Michael Rd., Chelsea, SW6 2AD. *Clubs:* N.E.A.C., Dover St. Art. *Signs work:* "Daines." *Address:* 34a Eardley Cres., London SW5 9JZ.

DAKEYNE, Gabriel, Membre Associé des Artistes Français; artist in collage, pen and ink, water-colour, oil; *b* Marske-by-the-sea, Yorkshire, 23 Feb., 1916. *m* Wing-Cdr. Jack Brain, Retd. two *d. Educ:* home. *Studied:* Swindon Art School, Press Art School, The Hague Holland. *Exhib:* R.A., Royal West of England Academy, Paris Salon, S.W.A., Graphic Artists, Flower Paintings, 9th Grand Prix de la Côte d'Azure Cannes, one-man show: St. Aldates, Oxford. *Publications:* work repro.: La Revue Moderne. *Signs work:* see appendix. *Address:* Sadlers Cottage, Sadlers End, Sindlesham, Wokingham RG41 5AL.

DALBY, Claire, R.W.S., R.E.; Vice-Pres. R.W.S. (1994-98); artist in water-colour drawing, wood-engraving and botanical illustration; *b* St. Andrews, 1944. *m* D. H. Dalby, Ph.D. *Studied:* City and Guilds of London Art School (1964-67). *Exhib:* R.A., R.W.S., R.E.; one-man shows: Consort Gallery, Imperial College, London (1981, 1988), Shetland Museum, Lerwick (1988, 1991, 1995). *Commissions:* four wild plants for Surrey C.C.'s Norbury Park Project (1996), "Charity" rose for National Gardens Scheme (1997). *Publications:* "Claire Dalby's Picture Book" (Carr, Kettering 1989); Designed and illustrated two wallcharts on Lichens (Natural History Museum 1981, 1987). *Signs work:* see appendix. *Address:* 2 West Park, Stanley, Perthshire PH1 4QU.

DALE, Tom, D.A. (1958), R.M.S., H.S.F.; artist in water-colour; Hon. Treasurer, Hilliard Soc. of Miniaturists; *b* Greenock, 23 June, 1935. *m* Myra. two *d. Studied:*

Glasgow School of Art. *Exhib:* House artist with Medici. *Work in collections:* private in Europe and N.America. *Signs work:* "Dale." *Address:* Woodbourne House, West Shepton, Shepton Mallet, Som. BA4 5UN.

DALE, William Scott Abell, M.A. (Toronto, 1946), Ph.D. (Harvard, 1955); Prof. Emeritus; Professor of Art History, University of Western Ontario (1967-87); Deputy Director, National Gallery of Canada (1961-67); director, Vancouver Art Gallery (1959-61); curator, Art Gallery of Toronto (1957-59); research curator, Nat. Gallery of Canada (1951-57); mem. College Art Assoc. of America, Medieval Academy of America, R.S.A.; research fellow, Dumbarton Oaks, Washington (1956-57); *b* Toronto, 18 Sept., 1921. *m* Jane Gordon Laidlaw. three *s. Educ:* University of Toronto Schools; Trinity College, Toronto; Harvard University. *Address:* 1517 Gloucester Rd., London, Ont., N6G 2S5, Canada.

DALRYMPLE, Neil, Dip. A.D. (1971), A.T.C. (1972), S.W.L.A., F.B.A.; ceramic sculptor; *b* 16 June, 1949. one *s.* three *d. Educ:* Cardiff University (1971-1972), post grad. *Studied:* Loughborough College of Art and Design (1968-1971). *Exhib:* Nigel Stacey Marks Fine Art Gallery, Perth, Henry Brett Gallery, Stow-on-the-Wold. *Work in collections:* Canada Art Bank, Greater Victoria Art Gallery, Nature in Art, Wallworth Hall. *Commissions:* numerous, incl. Salmon and Trout Assoc., Atlantic Salmon Trust, two life size salmon presented to Orri Vibusson by H.R.H. Prince Charles. *Signs work:* "Neil Dalrymple." *Address:* 20 Maes-y-Dre, Ruthin, Denbighshire LL15 1DB.

DAMINATO, Vanda, Independent professional painter 1970; works include oil paintings, collages, fine prints, art ceramics, advertising posters for industry; Accademico Accademia Arti Incisione, Pisa; *b* Mezzolombardo, Italy, 1951. *Exhib:* Palazzo Grassi, Venezia; Galerie Internationale, N.Y.; Museo Leonardo da Vinci, Milano; Villa Olmo, Como; Palazzo della Gran Guardia, Verona; Museo Arte Moderna, Malta. Creator of the Image of the Groups: Maristel - Sirti - Pirelli "Telecom '91" 6 Exposition mondiale des télécommunications, Genève; Ambroveneto-La Centrale Fondi SPA; Goglio Luigi Milano SPA; Sarplast SPA; Feltrinelli Giangiacomo Editore. *Signs work:* "DAMINATO." *Address:* Corso XXII Marzo 28, 20135 Milano, Italy. *Website:* www.daminatoarte.it *Email:* daminato@energy.it

D'AMOUR, Viola, art nouveau co-collaborator with Vlad Quigley; model and ballerina; *Educ:* Charterhouse, Orpington College. *Exhib:* pop art nouveau portraits of Viola D'Amour, Vampyria, Damned U.S. tour Ad2000, The Big Draw, Vampire Viola, Shock/ Anglo-French Aubrey Beardsley centenary. *Publications:* Viola D'Amour, Viola D'Amour's Phantom Sword, Evlalie, Vampire Viola, Varney the Vampyre, 21st. Century Ghouls, Viola and the Vampires, Crimson, Demeter, Betty and the Boobies; advertising, catwalk, films, T.V. *Signs work:* "Viola D'Amour." *Address:* c/o 276a Lower Addiscombe Rd., Croydon, Surrey CR0 7AE.

DANIELS, Alfred, R.W.S., R.B.A., A.R.C.A.; painter in oil, alkyd and acrylic; *b* London, 1924. *m* Margot Hamilton Hill. *Educ:* George Greens School. *Studied:* Woolwich Polytechnic, R.C.A. *Exhib:* R.A., Rona Gallery, Mall Gallery, Bankside Gallery, Manya Igel Fine Arts. *Work in collections:* G.L.C., Cambridgeshire Educ. Com., Leicester Educ. Com., Sheffield A.G., Leeds University, Bezalel Museum,

Israel, I.L.E.A. *Commissions:* Hammersmith Town Hall, British Rail, O.U.P., St. Fergus Gas Terminal, Shell Oil, Glaxo. *Publications:* work in repro.: Drawing and Painting (1961), Drawing Made Simple (1963), Enjoying Acrylics (1975), Painting with Acrylics (1988); Studio International, The Artist, Art and Artists, R.A. Illustrated, Arts Review. *Clubs:* Langham Sketching. *Signs work:* "Alfred Daniels." *Address:* 24 Esmond Rd., London W4 1JQ.

DANIELS, Harvey, R.E.; artist in all paints and media; *b* London, 17 June, 1936. *m* Judy Stapleton. two *d. Studied:* Willesden School of Art; Slade School of Fine Art (Ceri Richards). *Exhib:* London, U.S.A., Scandinavia. *Work in collections:* Museum of Modern Art, N.Y., V. & A., Towner A.G., Metropolitan Museum, N.Y., Bergens Kunstforening, Norway. *Commissions:* pathway/cycle way designed and made in aggregate commissioned Southampton City Council, 175 metres in length. *Publications:* Summer Psalms 10 etchings by Harvey Daniels, poems by Pacernick. *Signs work:* "H. Daniels." *Address:* 95 Springfield Rd., Brighton BN1 6DH.

DANNATT, George, lyrical abstract painter and constructivist; self-taught , his techniques and influences derived from the concentrated observation required in his other professions, Chartered Surveyor and music critic; thus his work developed "from his own personal experience of living" (Ben Nicholson); elected mem. Critics' Circle (1948) now honorary; associate Penwith Society of Arts since 1970 and mem. Newlyn Society of Artists (1973); *b* Blackheath, London, Aug., 1915. *Exhib:* has contributed to, or had one-man shows at the following galleries: Penwith, Newlyn (Cornwall), Schreiner (Basel, Switzerland), Artica (Cuckhaven, Germany), Parkin (London), New Ashgate (Farnham), Chesil (Dorset), Dorset County Museum, Reeds Wharf (London), Book Gallery (St. Ives, Cornwall), Town Mill (Lyme Regis), Russell-Cotes (Bournemouth), Broadstreet (Lyme Regis), Ditchling Museum (Sussex), New Art Centre (Basel Art Fair), Maltby Contemporary Art (Winchester). *Work in collections:* Galerie Artica and Stadt Bibliotek, Cuxhaven, Germany; R.A.F. Museum, Hendon; Russell-Cotes Gallery; Dorset County Museum; University of Southampton. *Publications:* include: 'One Way of Seeing', anthology of paintings and photographs, text in English and German; 'Three Essays' by Simon Olding, Mark Bills and the artist; A critical biography of Dannatt's work by Mark Bills is in preparation; commissions include sleeve-covers for two C.D.'s of orchestral works by Arthur Bliss; book cover for 'Je m'en Vais' by Jean Echenoz (Swedish & English publication); copies of Dannatt's books and selections of his catalogues are held by the Kunstmuseum, Basel, the Witt Library, Courtauld Institute; The National Art Library; V. & A. Museum; The Bridgeman Art Library hold a selection of transparancies of his work; in 1986 he established a Charitable Trust for the advancement of education in the visual arts. *Clubs:* The Lansdowne, The Savage. *Address:* East Hatch, Tisbury, Wilts. SP3 6PH.

DANVERS, Joan, I.A.A.; painter in oils, potter, calligrapher; *b* Diss, Norfolk, 4 Feb., 1919; married. one *s. Educ:* Diss Grammar School; Norfolk and Norwich Hospital, S.R.N. (1940). *Studied:* Chelmsford School of Art under Clifford Smith; Belstead House, Ipswich under Cavendish Morton, R.O.I., R.I.; calligraphy at Wensom Lodge under Mr. Webster, and at Belstead House with Gerald Mynott. Silver Palette award (1966) International Amateur Art Exhbn. *Clubs:* Writtle Art Group (until 1976), Norfolk and Norwich Art Circle. *Signs work:* "Joan Danvers" and see appendix. *Address:* Little Haven, Cromer Rd., W. Runton, Cromer, Norfolk.

d'ARBELOFF, Natalie, painter, printmaker, book-artist, writer; *b* Paris, 7 Aug., 1929. divorced. *Educ:* Marymount School, N.Y. *Studied:* Art Students' League, N.Y., Central School of Art, London. *Exhib:* numerous group shows; solo shows include: Museum Fine Arts, Colorado Springs, Camden Arts Centre, Victoria & Albert Museum, Rijksmuseum, Meermano-Westreenianum, The Hague. *Work in collections:* V. & A., Manchester Polytechnic Library, Library of Congress, Washington D.C., N.Y. Public Library, Harvard, Princeton, Newberry Library, Humanities Research Center, Austin, National Library, Australia, and many more. *Commissions:* murals: Asuncion, Paraguay and London. *Publications:* Creating in Collage (Studio Vista), An Artist's Workbook (Studio Vista), Designing with Natural Forms (Batsford), Livres d'Artiste (own NdA Press), Augustine's True Confession, The Augustine Adventures. *Signs work:* see appendix. *Address:* c/o Society of Design Craftsmen, 24 Rivington St., London EC2A 3DU.

DARBISHIRE, Stephen John, B.Ed. (1971), R.B.A. (1983); painter in oil, water-colour, pastel; *b* Greenodd, Cumbria, 9 Dec., 1940. *m* Kerry Delius. two *d.* *Educ:* Ulverston Grammar School, Cumbria. *Studied:* Byam Shaw School of Art (1958-59): R.A., R.B.A., R.P., R.I.O., N.E.A.C. *Signs work:* "Stephen J. Darbishire," "Darbishire" and see appendix. *Address:* Agnes Gill, Whinfell, Kendal, Cumbria LA8 9EJ.

DARBY, Philip, self taught artist in oil; *b* Birmingham, 14 June, 1938. *m* Susan. two *s. Exhib:* Newlyn Orion, Penwith Soc., Galerie Artica, Cuxhaven, Germany, R.W.A. *Work in collections:* Open University. *Signs work:* "Phil Darby." *Address:* Prospect House, Trevegean, St. Just, Penzance, Cornwall TR19 7NX.

DARTON WATKINS, Christopher, M.A.(Oxon.) (1951); painter in oil, wax, collage and mixed media; *b* Hants., 1928. *m* Torun. one *s. Educ:* Ampleforth College and Oxford. *Studied:* Ruskin School of Art, and privately. *Exhib:* Bear Lane Gallery, Oxford, Arnolfini Gallery, Bristol, Gallery Aix, Stockholm, Seifert-Binder Gallery, Munich, Alwin Gallery,London, Indar Pasricha Fine Art, Anthony Dawson Fine Art, Edwin Pollard Gallery, David Curzon Gallery, Gerard Peters Gallery, Santa Fe, Original A.G., Båstad, Sweden. *Work in collections:* Linacre and Hertford Colleges, Oxford, Liverpool University, Royal Hospital, Chelsea, S.N.E.E., Lisbon, Soc. of Apothecaries, Stockholm, Svenska Handsbanken, Stockholm, Charterhouse Bank, London. *Clubs:* Chelsea Arts. *Signs work:* "Darton Watkins." *Address:* 7 Parkstead Rd., London SW15 5HW.

DARWIN, Thomas Gerard, F.R.B.S. (1978), B.Ed. (1976); sculptor in resins and metal powders; *b* Standish, Lancs., 10 June, 1928. *m* Marie Agnes (decd.), remarried Bridget. three *s.* two *d. Educ:* St. Peter's College, Freshfield. *Studied:* St. Mary's College, Strawberry Hill (1951-53, L. de C. Bucher, K.S.S., A.R.C.A.), Wigan School of Art (1955-57, Woffenden). *Exhib:* one-man show: Rural and Industries Bank, Perth, W.A.; numerous joint shows. *Work in collections:* Monument (Warrior and Maiden) Manzini, Swaziland; several religious works in churches and schools in England and Australia, busts in private collections and public places in Swaziland and Australia; a series of historic bronze reliefs and water feature for the Memorial Walk at Armdale Memorial Hospital, Perth, Western

Australia. *Signs work:* "G. Darwin." *Address:* Ezulwini, 34 Croyden Rd., Roleystone, W.A. 6111.

DAVIDSON, Anne, D.A. (1959), A.R.B.S. (1988); sculptor in bronze, resin bronze, fibreglass; *b* Glasgow, 3 Feb., 1937. *m* James G. Davidson. one *s.* three *d. Educ:* Convent of the Sacred Heart, Aberdeen. *Studied:* Gray's School of Art (1955-59, Leo Clegg). *Exhib:* Aberdeen Artists Soc., Institut Français, London, Posk Gallery, London, Coventry Cathedral, Dundee A.G., etc. *Work in collections:* St. Mary's Cathedral, Aberdeen; St. Mary's, Inverness; Corpus Christi, St. Helens; St. Michael's, Whitefield, Manchester; Christ the King, Liverpool; and other churches, schools, etc.; public works in Edinburgh, Aberdeen and New York; portraits etc. in private collections. *Signs work:* "Anne Davidson." *Address:* 15 Redmoss Pk., Aberdeen AB12 3JF. *Email:* ajdavidsonsculptors@btinternet.com

DAVIDSON DAVIS, Philomena, P.P.R.B.S., R.W.A., F.R.S.A.; sculptor; *b* Westminster, 1949. *m* Michael Davis, sculptor/founder. two *d. Educ:* Convent of Jesus and Mary, Willesden. *Studied:* sculpture: City and Guilds, London (1967-70, James Butler, R.A.), R.A. Schools (1970-73, Willi Soukop, R.A.). *Exhib:* R.A. Summer Show, R.W.A. Bristol, sculpture at Margam, Chelsea Harbour Sculpture (1993, 1996). April 1990 elected first woman President Royal Society of British Sculptors (1990-96), Managing Director, The Sculpture Company (1995-present day). *Work in collections:* life-size bronzes Queens Ct., Milton Keynes Shopping Centre; Lady Henry Somerset Memorial, Victoria Embankment Gdns., London; "Fairway" a large outdoor sculpture for Donnington Valley. Hotel and Golf course, Newbury, Berks. *Clubs:* Chelsea Arts. *Signs work:* see appendix. *Address:* The Mike Davis, Bronze Foundry, St James St., New Bradwell, Milton Keynes, Bucks.

DAVIES, Anthony John, R.E. (1994); artist/printmaker in etching, lithography and silkscreen; currently, tutor, Unitec.Poly., Auckland, N.Z.; A.U.T. Auckland, N.Z.; *b* Andover, Hants., 14 Jan., 1947. *Educ:* Andover Grammar School. *Studied:* Winchester School of Art (1966-70), R.C.A. (1970-73), Prix de Rome, engraving (1973-75). John Brinkley Fellow (1990-91). *Exhib:* over 62 one-man shows: U.K., U.S.A., S. Africa, N.Z. Represented U.K. at numerous overseas print biennales. *Work in collections:* U.K., U.S.A., Japan, Norway, Hungary, Poland, Russia, Bulgaria, New Zealand. *Publications:* numerous exhbn. catalogues, articles and reviews. *Signs work:* "A.J. Davies." *Address:* 14 Alexander St., Kingsland, Auckland, N.Z.

DAVIES, Gareth, Hon. S.G.F.A.; artist in pencil, black ink, coloured pens; *b* St. Asaph, N. Wales, 10 Feb., 1972. *Educ:* Gogarth School/TVEI Centre Gogarth. *Exhib:* S.G.F.A., Botanical Fine Art Soc. *Publications:* Heroes All: The Story of the R.N.L.I. by Alec Beilby. *Signs work:* "G.P. Davies." *Address:* Bryn Awelon, Pentywyn Rd., Deganwy, Gwynedd LL31 9TL.

DAVIES, Gordon Lionel, A.R.C.A.; artist; *b* 14 Apr., 1926. *Educ:* Sevenoaks School. *Studied:* Camberwell School of Art (1949-50), R.C.A. (1950-53). *Exhib:* R.A. Summer Exhbns. (1953-91); one-man shows: Wye College, Kent (1964, 1967), King St.Galleries (1973, 1975, 1977, 1979, 1983, 1985); retrospective at The Royal Museum and A.G., Canterbury, Sally Hunter Fine Art (1993, 1994, 1997). *Work in collections:* mural decorations at Challock Church, Kent, Wolfson College, Cambridge, Wye College, Kent, Braxted Park, Essex, Clerical and Medical

Assurance Bldg., Bristol; shellwork decoration at Basildon House, Pangbourne for National Trust. *Publications:* botanical illustrations for House and Garden magazine (1949-70); Working with Acrylics (Search Press). *Signs work:* "Gordon Davies." *Address:* South View, Hastingleigh, Ashford, Kent TN25 5HU.

DAVIES, Iris Mary, F.S.B.A. (1986), B.Sc. (1949), Cambs. Cert. in Teaching (1950); artist in water-colour; retd. from teaching (1979); *b* Shotley, Ipswich, 4 Oct., 1919. *m* David Maldwyn Davies, B.Sc. one *d. Educ:* University College of Wales, Aberystwyth, Cambridge University. *Studied:* Cambridge University and privately. *Exhib:* R.I. (1982-89), S.B.A. (1986-95), S.W.A. (1987-93). *Signs work:* "Mary Davies." *Address:* High Trees, Minstead, Lyndhurst, Hants. SO43 7FX.

DAVIES, Ivor, N.D.D. (1956), A.T.D. (1957), Ph.D. (Edin.) (1975), V.P.R.C.A. (1993); artist/painter in oil, tempera, water-colour, gouache, crayon; *b* Wales, 9 Nov., 1935. *Studied:* Cardiff (1952-56) and Swansea (1956-57) Colleges of Art, Lausanne University, Edinburgh University. *Exhib:* over 20 one-man shows worldwide since 1963, also Multi-media Destruction in Art 1960's. *Work in collections:* Deal Coll. Dallas, A.C.G.B., W.A.C., National Museum of Wales, etc. *Publications:* articles on Modern Art History, others in Welsh language journals; illustrations: Spirit (1971), Rubaiyat (1981), Science and Art (1981). *Signs work:* "Ivor Davies." *Address:* 99 Windsor Rd., Penarth CF6 1JF.

DAVIES, Ogwyn, R.Cam.A. (1995), A.T.D. (1952), N.D.D. (Hons. Painting 1951); retd. schoolmaster; painter in various media and ceramics; *b* Swansea Valley, 29 Mar., 1925. *m* Beryl. one *s.* one *d. Studied:* Swansea School of Art (1947-52). *Exhib:* four one-man shows and many mixed shows. *Work in collections:* National Museum of Wales, National Library of Wales, Welsh Arts Council, Contemporary Art Soc. for Wales, Gwent C.C., Merthyr Borough, Wilts. C.C., City of Bath, University of Wales, Y Tabernacl, Machynlleth. *Publications:* three Welsh children's books, "Certain Welsh Artists", "Darllen Delweddau"; Radio Wales interviews; TV programmes: S4C., H.T.V., B.B.C. *Clubs:* Watercolour Society of Wales. *Signs work:* "Ogwyn" above "Davies" and date. *Address:* Ty Hir, Tregaron, Ceredigion SY25 6PR.

DAVIS, Cynthia, self taught artist in oil; *b* Allahabad, India. *m* Eric Bernard Davis. *Exhib:* St Ives Soc. of Artists, Mariners Gallery, Penwith Gallery. *Signs work:* "Cynthia Davis." *Address:* 1 Bay Villas, St. Ives Rd., Carbis Bay, St. Ives, Cornwall, TR26 2SX.

DAVIS, Derek Maynard, F.C.P.A.; Artist in Residence, University of Sussex (1967); painter, potter; Hon. Mem. International Academy of Ceramics; *b* London, 1926. *m* Ruth. one *s. Educ:* Emanuel School, Wandsworth. *Studied:* painting: Central School of Arts and Crafts, London, under Keith Vaughan, Robert Buhler. *Exhib:* Istanbul, Munich, Toronto, Zurich, Tokyo, Paris, Primavera (London and Cambridge). *Work in collections:* Paisley Museum, V. & A., Portsmouth Museum, Southampton Museum, Keramion, Frechen, Germany, University of Sussex, Bradford Museum, Garth Clark Collection, U.S.A., Contemporary Art Soc., Musee Ariana, Geneva, Switzerland. *Signs work:* "D.M. Davis." *Address:* Duff House, 13 Maltravers St., Arundel, Sussex BN18 9AP.

DAVIS, James, L.I.F.A.; Freeman the Worshipful Company Painter-Stainers (1972); Freeman of the City of London (1973); sculptor, carver and restorer in stone, marble; *b* London, 16 July, 1926. *m* Joan Davis. *Educ:* Eastbrook Boys School, Dagenham, Essex. *Studied:* Sir John Cass School of Art (1949-53) under Bainbridge Copnal. *Exhib:* Guildhall; Leighton House, Royal Exchange, Mall Galleries. *Work in collections:* Painters Hall, Chelsea and Kensington Town Hall, Community Centre, Shoeburyness, Barclay International, Gracechurch St., St. Nicholas Church, Elm Park, Essex, St. Nicholas Church, Canewdon, Essex, Hyde Park Corner, London W1, Town Centre, Chelmsford, Essex. *Signs work:* "J. Davis." *Address:* Studio Workshop, 39a West Rd., Shoeburyness, Essex SS3 9DR.

DAVIS, John Warren, M.C., A.T.D.; sculptor in wood, stone and metal; *b* Christchurch, 24 Feb., 1919. *m* Evelyn Ann. three *s.* one *d. Educ:* Bedford School. *Studied:* Westminster School of Art (1937-39), under Bernard Meninsky and Mark Gertler; Brighton College of Art (1948-52), under James Woodford, R.A. *Work in collections:* Cardiff, Leeds, Southampton, New York, Arts Council, Contemporary Art Soc., London, Houston, Texas, Fogg Art Musem, Mass., U.S.A. *Address:* Northfields Farm, Eastergate, Chichester, Sussex PO20 6RX.

DAVIS, Kate, B.A. (1982), H.Dip. (1986), M.A. (Status) Oxon. (1992), Stanley Picker Fellow (1986-87), Whitechapel Young Artist of Year (1988), Sargant Fellow, British School of Rome (1998); subject-led sculpture, video, photography and drawing; sculpture tutor, Royal College of Art; *b* Chesham, Bucks., 1960. *m* A. Ruethi. one *d. Studied:* Herts. College of Art and Design (1978-79), Falmouth School of Art (1979-82), Slade School of Fine Art (1983-86). *Exhib:* solo: Milch, London, Newlyn A.G., Penzance, University Gallery, Whitechapel A.G., group shows in Britain and abroad. *Work in collections:* National Sculpture Centre, Oronsko, Poland; British Land, Middlesborough Art Gallery. *Publications:* Kate Davis (Milch, 1997); as if (Univeristy of Essex, 2001). represented by Rhodes & Mann, London. *Signs work:* "K.A. DAVIS." *Address:* 56 Nelson Rd., London N8 9RT.

DAVIS, Michael Robert, N.D.D., M.A. (R.C.A.); artist in charcoal conté (drawing), lecturer; Principal Lecturer (Painting), Kent Inst. of Art and Design; *b* Birmingham, 11 Sept., 1943. *m* Susan Davis. one *d. Educ:* Birmingham College of Art (1959-64), Royal College of Art (1964-67). *Exhib:* R.A. Summer Exhbn. since 1986, Hayward Annual (1982), 15 British Painters, British Council, Barcelona, 5 British Artists - de Grey, Davis, Hockney, Freud, Weight, Alabama U.S.A., Mike Davis (drawings El Palau Valencia), Cassian de Vere Cole, London. *Work in collections:* Arts Council, and private. *Publications:* Guardian Arts Review, Contemporary Arts Review Guardian, Times Arts Review, 5 British Artists Honouring England, Alabama Times, Panning for Gold - George Melly (1993), Andrew Lambirth review or show at Cassian de Vere Cole (1996). *Signs work:* see appendix. *Address:* 5 Elmers End Rd., London SE20 7ST.

DAVIS, Pamela, V.P.R.M.S. (1979), F.S.B.A. (1985), S.W.A. (1977), H.S.F. (1983); miniaturist and flower painter in water-colour, acrylic, gouache; Vice-Pres. R.M.S.; *b* Molesey, 27 Aug., 1927. *m* Ronald. two *s. Educ:* Ashford County School. *Studied:* Twickenham School of Art (1942-45, Dorothy Parlbey). *Exhib:* Westminster Gallery, London: R.M.S., S.W.A., S.B.A.; Llewellyn Alexander

Gallery, London; Linda Blackstone Gallery, Pinner. *Signs work:* "Pamela Davis." *Address:* Woodlands, Pond Copse Lane, Loxwood, W. Sussex RH14 0XF.

DAVIS, Robin, self taught painter in oil; *b* Bournemouth, 28 Feb., 1925. one *s.* one *d. Educ:* St. Catherine's College, Oxford; Birkbeck College, London. *Exhib:* one-man shows: Woodstock Gallery, London (1960), New Vision Centre, London (1964), Aston University, B'ham (1965), Horizon Gallery, London (1988), Belgrave Gallery, London (1995), Bakehouse Gallery, Penzance (1996). *Signs work:* "Robin Davis." *Address:* 45 Trelissick Rd., Hayle, Penzance, Cornwall TR27 4HY.

DAWSON, Patricia Vaughan, printmaker, sculptor and writer; *b* Liverpool, 23 Jan., 1925. *m* James N. Dawson. one *s.* two *d. Educ:* Croham Hurst School. *Studied:* Croydon School of Art (1941-45) under Reginald Marlow and Ruskin Spear. *Exhib:* Bear Lane Gallery, R.A., London Group, Pastel Soc., R.S.P.A., Alchemy Gallery. *Work in collections:* B.M., Bibliothèque Nationale. *Publications:* The Artist Looks at Life (a series of books and slides published by Visual Publications introducing art to children), La Lanterne des Morts - illustrated poem (Ram Press), The Kiln and The Forge Reliquaries - collections of poetry (Hub Editions). *Address:* Flat 1, 3 Albion Villas Rd., London SE26 4DB.

DAWSON, Peter, R.I., B.Ed.; painter in water-colour, oil; Adviser for Art and Design, Hertfordshire; *b* Leeds, 19 Mar., 1947. *m* (1) Andrea Dixon. (2) Sarah Harrison. *Educ:* Roundhay School, Leeds. *Studied:* Bingley College of Educ. (1967-71). *Exhib:* R.I., Yorkshire Artists, Hitchin Museum, Luton A.G., October Gallery, San Francisco, Federation of Canadian Artists Gallery, Vancouver, Fry Art Museum, Seattle, Shell House Gallery, Attendi Gallery. *Work in collections:* Herts. Educ. Authority, Luton A.G., Winsor and Newton R.I. award (1999). *Publications:* Co-author, Albania - A Guide and Illustrated Journal; prints and limited editions. *Signs work:* "P. Dawson" or "Peter Dawson." *Address:* Little Cokenach, Nuthampstead, Royston, Herts. SG8 8LS.

DAWSON, Susan Shepherd, B.A. (Hons.) fine art (painting); painter of land-scapes and garden scenes in oil, watercolour, and charcoal drawings en plein air; also maker of silver jewellery; *b* Ponteland, Northumberland, 18 Feb., 1955. one *s.* two *d. Educ:* Church High School, Newcastle-upon-Tyne. *Studied:* Bath Lane School of Art, Newcastle, Liverpool Polytechnic. *Exhib:* St. Ives Society of Artists and various exhibs. in Cornwall. *Work in collections:* various collections in Europe and New Zealand. *Signs work:* "Sue Dawson." *Address:* Boswartha, Church Rd., Lelant, St. Ives, Cornwall TR26 3LE. *Website:* www.stivessocietyofartists.com *Email:* sues-dawson@hotmail.com

DAY, D.P.A., Prof., A.G.P.P. (1979), S.G.F.A. (1986); archivist for S.G.F.A., U.A. (1998); artist in oil and water-colour; *Exhib:* Mall Galleries, Knapp Gallery, Art Connoisseur Gallery, Westminster Gallery and Lauderdale House; one-man show: Durban and Johannesburg (1954); Heraldic portrait of Sir Winston Churchill exhib. for 6 years at Blenheim Palace from 1967. *Signs work:* "Daphne Day." *Address:* 20 The Avenue, Bedford Pk., Chiswick, London W4 1HT.

DAY, Jane, B.Ed.(Hons.) (1989); ceramist in T-material; Subject Leader (ceram-ics), City of Bath College; *b* Cambridge, 18 June, 1966. *Educ:* Bath College of

Higher Educ., but largely self taught. *Commissions:* Selfridges, London (Smokefired Vessel Forms). *Signs work:* see appendix. *Address:* 2 West Barnes, Shepreth Rd., Barrington, Cambridge.

DAY, Lucienne, R.D.I., A.R.C.A. (1940), F.C.S.D.; textile designer; Royal Designer for Industry (1962), (Master 1987-89); Hon. Doctor of Design, Southampton University (1995); Senior Fellow R.C.A.; Hon. Fellow R.I.B.A.; *b* Coulsdon, Surrey, 1917. *m* Robin Day. one *d. Educ:* Convent of Notre Dame di Sion, Worthing. *Studied:* Croydon School of Art (1934-37), Royal College of Art (1937-40). *Exhib:* London, Manchester, Zürich, Milan, Oslo, Toronto, New York, Tokyo, Kyoto, Gothenburg. *Work in collections:* V. & A., Whitworth A.G., University of Manchester, museums of Cranbrook, Michigan, Museum of Industrial Design Trondheim, Norway, Röhsska Konstslöjd Museum, Gothenburg, Sweden, Musee des Arts Decoratifs, Montreal, and Art Inst. of Chicago. *Signs work:* silk mosaic tapestries: "L." *Address:* 49 Cheyne Walk, Chelsea, London SW3 5LP.

DAY, Robin, O.B.E., A.R.C.A., F.C.S.D., R.D.I.; designer; *b* High Wycombe, Bucks., 1915. one *d. Studied:* High Wycombe School of Art and R.C.A. *Exhib:* Museum of Modern Art, New York, I.C.A., Triennale, Milan (1951), Copenhagen, Oslo, Stavanger, Bergen, Zürich, Canada. *Work in collections:* Museum of Modern Art, New York, Trondheim Industrial Art Museum, V. & A. *Publications:* work repro.: many architectural and design publications here and abroad. *Clubs:* Alpine, Eagles Ski. *Address:* 49 Cheyne Walk, Chelsea, London SW3 5LP.

DAYKIN, Michael, M.A. (R.C.A.); artist, curator; *b* Yorkshire, 1947. *Studied:* Watford School of Art (1970-71), St. Martin's School of Art (1971-74), R.C.A. (1974-77). *Exhib:* City University Gallery, Cleveland College of Art Gallery, XO Gallery, The Figure of Eight Gallery, Gallery K, Attache Gallery. *Work in collections:* Northern Arts, Brown and Wood, Musee d'Art Contemporaire, Skopje, Macedonia. *Commissions:* Benchmark Holdings, Quaglino's. *Signs work:* "Daykin." *Address:* 9 Lowder House, Wapping Lane, London E1W 2RJ.

DEAKIN, Liz (née Boatswain), S.W.A.; artist in water-colour, gouache and acrylics of landscapes, flower painting, interiors, silk painting and murals; runs painting courses and gives demonstrations to societies; *b* Dorchester, 1929. marriage dissolved. two children. *Studied:* Poole School of Art, and with Edward Wessen. *Work in collections:* many private collections throughout the world, including the Royal Family. *Publications:* "Deakin's Dorset"; designs hotel brochures. *Signs work:* "Liz Deakin." *Address:* 3 Hunters Mead, Motcombe, Shaftesbury SP7 9QG.

DEAKINS, Cyril Edward, A.R.E. (1948), A.T.D. (1947); painter in oil, tempera and water-colour, wood-engraver; *b* Bearwood, nr. Birmingham, 5 Oct., 1916. married. one *s.* one *d. Educ:* Christ's College, Finchley. *Studied:* under J. C. Moody, Norman Janes, at Hornsey School of Art. *Exhib:* R.A., N.E.A.C., R.E., R.B.A., R.I. *Work in collections:* Print Collectors' Club, presentation print, Ellingham Mill E. Anglian Artists Exhbn. (1977), Beecroft A. G., Westcliff (1986), Chelmsford and Essex Museum (1996). *Commissions:* mural, Dourdan Pavilion, Dunmow (2000), Millenium Window, Dunmow Parish Church (2000). Lindsell Prize (1999). *Signs work:* "C.D.", "Cyril Deakins" or "C. Deakins." *Address:* 1 Mill Lane, Dunmow, Essex CM6 1BG.

DEAKINS, Sylvia, A.T.D. (1946), S.G.F.A. (1986), C.D.S. (1987); painter and illustrator in oil, gouache, pastel, ink, collage; Vice-Pres. Cambridge Drawing Soc. (1997); *b* Eccleshill, W. Yorks., 18 Oct., 1924. *m* C.E. Deakins. one *s*. one *d. Educ:* Hendon County Grammar. *Studied:* Hornsey College of Art (1941-46, Douglas Percy Bliss, Russell Reeve, Francis Winter). *Exhib:* R.A., R.B.A., N.E.A.C., and numerous galleries in E. Anglia. *Publications:* illustrated many for O.U.P. Longmans, Ward Lock, including A Beginner's Bible (1958), and Listening to Children Talking (1976). *Signs work:* "Sylvia Deakins," or "S.D." *Address:* 1 Mill Lane, Gt. Dunmow, Essex CM6 1BG.

DEAKINS, Thomas William (Tom), B.A. (Hons.) (1980), A.T.C. (1982), Charles Spence Memorial prize (1977); painter in oil; *b* Barnet, 8 Dec., 1957. *m* Ann Logan. two *s. Educ:* Newport Grammar School, Essex. *Studied:* University of Newcastle upon Tyne (1976-80, Kenneth Rowntree, Derwent Wise). *Exhib:* R.A. Summer Shows since 1983, Medici Gallery (1989), William Hardy Glasgow (1991), Chappel Gallery, Colchester (1995, 2000), Bruton St. Gallery (1999). *Work in collections:* Hatton Gallery, University of Newcastle, Epping Forest District Museum, Beecroft A.G. Westcliff on Sea. *Signs work:* "T. Deakins" or "T.D." *Address:* Clock House Cottage, 79a The Causeway, Gt. Dunmow, Essex CM6 2AB.

DEAN, Dorothy, S.W.A.; artist in gouache, oil, pastel; *b* 14 May 1920. *m* K.W. Howard. one *s. Educ:* Bromley County School, Kent. *Studied:* Goldsmiths' School of Art (1936-39), Eastbourne Art School, Guildford (part-time pre war). *Exhib:* R.I., R.O.I., R.B.A., R.P.S., P.S., numerous solo and shared exhbns. in S. England and Bedford, private galleries Hampshire. *Work in collections:* private collections: France, Germany, Switzerland and Canada. *Signs work:* "Dorothy Dean" and "D. Dean." *Address:* Ashley Cottage, Bentworth, Alton, Hants. GU34 5RH.

DEAN, John H. W., R.M.S., S.M., F.R.S.A., F.S.O.A.; Fellow British Soc. of Painters; Founder Mem. and Pres., Upper-Wharfedale Museum Soc.; self taught artist in oil of large river landscapes, miniatures on ivory in oil; *b* Grassington, N. Yorks., 25 Mar., 1930. *m* Dorothy. *Educ:* Grassington C. of E. School. *Exhib:* R.M.S., U.A., S.M., Yorkshire Artists, International Art Fair, Olympia, Salon des Nation, Paris. *Work in collections:* Shell Oil International, A.E. Auto Parts, John Ward Textiles, Lord Harewood, The Earl of Burlington, etc.; and in most countries of the world. *Publications:* work repro.: Limited Edition prints by Delta Prints, Guernsey, self, Medici and Dalesman. *Signs work:* "John Dean, R.M.S." in black on oils, "J. Dean" in black on miniatures. *Address:* Norwood, 13 Southwood La., Grassington, Skipton, N. Yorks. BD23 5NA.

DEAN, Pauline Margaret, R.H.S. Gold medals (6); freelance botanical illustrator in water-colour, ink; nurse (retd.); tutor of Botanical Art Courses, R.H.S. Gdn. Wisley, Surrey; *b* Brighton, 20 Aug., 1943. *m* George. three *s*. one *d. Educ:* Brighton and Hove High School; no formal art training. *Exhib:* Kew Gdns. Gallery; R.H.S. shows Vincent Sq. London; Linnean Soc., London; Guildford House Gallery, Guildford; Chelsea Flower Show; Jardin Botanique, Geneva. *Work in collections:* Hunt Inst. for Botanical Illustration, Pittsburgh, U.S.A.; Linnean Soc. London; Lindley Library R.H.S. London; Chelsea Physic Garden, London. *Publications:* with other artists: various inc. Curtis' Botanical Magazine, R.H.S. New Dictionary of

Gardening, The New Plantsman. *Signs work:* "P.M. Dean." *Address:* 27 Poltimore Rd., Guildford GU2 7PR.

DEAN, Ronald Herbert, R.S.M.A. (1970), F.C.I.I. (1965); self taught painter in water-colour and oil; Insurance broker; *b* Farnborough, Hants., 1929. *m* Audrey Grace Payne. two *d. Educ:* Farnborough Grammar School. *Exhib:* R.S.M.A., R.I., R.B.A., Biarritz, Salem Or., U.S.A., National Maritime Museum. *Clubs:* Tonbridge Art Group. *Signs work:* "RONALD DEAN" printed. *Address:* 8 Glebelands, Bidborough, Tunbridge Wells, Kent.

DEANE, Frederick, R.P. (1972); painter in oil, gouache, pastel; *b* Manchester, 1924. *m* Audrey Craig. two *s.* one *d. Studied:* Manchester College of Art (1940-43), R.A. Schools (1946-51, Philip Connard). Served with Para Regt. 1st Airborne Div. (1943-45). Visiting tutor: Manchester College of Art (1952-60), City of London Polytechnic (1970-82). *Exhib:* R.A., R.P. *Work in collections:* Chatsworth; Oxford, Cambridge, Manchester, Rhodes, McGill and Kent Universities; Manchester City A.G. *Clubs:* Chelsea Arts. *Signs work:* "Deane." *Address:* Penrallt Goch, Llan Ffestiniog, Gwynedd LL41 4NS.

DEANE, Jasper, Cert.F.A. (Oxon.) (1971), M.A. (R.C.A.) (1978); artist in water-colour and oil; *b* Ches., 15 July, 1952. *Educ:* Bryanston School, Blandford. *Studied:* Ruskin School of Drawing (1969-71), R.C.A. (1975-78). *Exhib:* numerous exhbns. of paintings, drawings and water-colours in London & Paris, including R.C.A., Cadogan Gallery and Royal Festival Hall. *Publications:* includes work for the Folio Society and R.C.A. *Clubs:* Old Students Assoc. R.C.A., Chelsea Arts. *Signs work:* "J.D." or "Jasper Deane." *Address:* 13c St. Stephens Ave., London W12 8JB.

DEARDEN, Chris, N.D.D., A.R.U.A., U.W.S., W.C.S.I. (Ireland); painter in water-colour, art teacher; Council mem.: R.U.A., and U.W.S.; *b* Halifax, 27 Dec., 1941. two *d. Studied:* Huddersfield College of Art. *Exhib:* Mall Gallery, London (1991-1996), Royal Hibernian (1979-98), Royal Ulster (1978-99), Laings, Cavehill Gallery, Belfast, etc. *Work in collections:* B.B.C., U.T.V., D.O.E., Albert Reynolds (Irish Prime Minister), H.R.H. Prince Charles, National Trust, U.S.A. and Russia. *Commissions:* M.O.D., Palace Barracks, Belfast, B.B.C. *Signs work:* "Chris Dearden." *Address:* 4 Knockagh Terr., Greenisland, Co. Antrim, N.I. BT38 8RN.

de BURGH, Lydia, R.U.A. (Hon.), U.W.S., U.W.A., Dip.Mem. Chelsea Art Soc. (1958-65); portrait, African wildlife and landscape painter in oil and water-colour; lecturer; *b* London, 3 July, 1923. *Educ:* privately. *Studied:* under Sonya Mervyn, R.P. (1948-51), Byam Shaw School of Art (1952), Edward Wesson, R.I. *Exhib:* London, N. Ireland Office (1955), Boston, Vose Gallery (1957), R.P., R.B.A., R.G.I., R.U.A., Royal Birmingham, Wildlife Artists, etc.; retrospective exhbns. 1993 Down Museum, Belfast for 6 weeks. *Work in collections:* (personal sittings) of H.M. The Queen and the Royal Family; numerous works in public and private collections. *Commissions:* portraits and landscape. *Publications:* autobiography, "Lydia's Story" (1991), further autobiog. "Another Way of Life" (1999). *Signs work:* "L. de Burgh, R.U.A." (or earlier works A.R.U.A.) now "H.R.U.A." *Address:* 4 Church Ct., Clough, Downpatrick, Co. Down, N. Ireland BT30 8QX.

de FRANCIA, Peter, painter in oil, author; Principal, DFA, School of Art,

Goldsmiths' College, University of London; Professor, School of Painting, R.C.A. London (1972-87); *b* Beaulieu, Alpes Maritimes, France, 25 Jan., 1921. *Studied:* Academy of Brussels, Slade School. *Work in collections:* Museum of Modern Art, N.Y., Arts Council of Gt. Britain, Tate Gallery, V. & A., British Museum, National Portrait Gallery, London, National Gallery of Modern Art, Prague, Imperial War Museum; private collections in U.K., and U.S.A. *Publications:* Fernand Léger (Cassells, 1968-69); Fernand Léger (Yale University Press, London, Sept. 1983); "Untitled" 49 drawings (Brondums Forlag, Copenhagen 1989). *Signs work:* see appendix. *Address:* 44 Surrey Sq., London SE17 2JX.

DE GOEDE, Julien Maximilien, painter/sculpture in mixed media; *b* Rotterdam, Holland, 20 May, 1937. *Educ:* High School, Nijmegen, Holland. *Studied:* Academie voor Beeldende Kunsten en Kunstnijverheid, Arnhem, Holland; Eindhoven School of Art , Eindhoven, Holland; Julian Ashton and Orban Schools of Art, Sydney, Australia. *Exhib:* private galleries in Australia and London; also, Serpentine Gallery, Whitechapel Gallery, Museum of Modern Art Oxford, Aberdeen Art Gallery, Riverside Studios, London, Glasgow Institute of Fine Art, Museum of Modern Art, Belfast, Ireland. *Work in collections:* include: Arts Council of Great Britain; Laing Art Gallery, Newcastle Upon Tyne; City Art Gallery, Bristol; Australian National University; Museum Sztuki, Lodz, Poland; Deutsche Bank; Unilever; Johnson & Johnson; U.S.A. De Beers. *Publications:* nearly all main newspapers and Arts Magazines, G.B. *Signs work:* "Jules de Goede." *Address:* 71 Stepney Green, London E1 3LE.

DE LA FOUGÈRE, Lucette, R.O.I., R.B.A.; painter in oil, water-colour and pastel; *b* London. *Educ:* both in Touraine, France, and London. *Studied:* under Leopold Pascal R.O.I., R.B.A., N.E.A.C. and Krome Barratt, P.P.R.O.I., R.B.A. *Exhib:* R.A., Royal Institute of Oil Painters, Royal Society of British Artists, National Soc. of Painters, Printers and Engravers; French Institute, London; one-man show: Mall Galleries. *Work in collections:* The National Museum of Wales, Cardiff. *Clubs:* Chelsea Arts. *Signs work:* "FOUGÈRE." *Address:* The Studio, 20 Lower Common South, Putney, London SW15 1BP.

DELAHAYE, Muriel, D.A. (Manc.); teacher's certificate, University of Manchester; artist in oil on canvas, charcoal, pastel (figurative paintings, mainly local coastline, people on the beach, fishermen and folklore); *b* Lancs., 18 Feb., 1937. *Studied:* Regional College of Art, Manchester; Victoria College, Unversity of Manchester. *Exhib:* numerous including six solo shows; 1994 – 1st prize winner, Museum Modern Art, Wales; 2000 – 1st prize winner, 'Art West 2000 – Wales, Land and People'. *Work in collections:* Showcase Wales, Museum of Modern Art, Machynlleth, Wales, Paintings in Hospitals, Wales, Attic Gallery, Swansea, Wales. *Address:* 'Efailwen', High St., Borth, Ceredigion SY24 5JQ.

DELHANTY, Denys, A.T.D. (1949), R.W.A. (1963); artist in collage, oil, water-colour, gouache; past Hon. Sec. and council mem. R.W.A.; Head of Art, Cheltenham Ladies College (1951-64), Senior Lecturer, Rolle College, Exmouth and Gloucester (1964-81); *b* Cardiff, 13 Oct., 1925. *m* Kate Ormrod. three *s.* one *d. Educ:* St. Illtyd's College, Cardiff. *Studied:* Cardiff College of Art (1942-44, 1947-50, Ceri Richards).

Exhib: R.W.A., etc. *Work in collections:* R.W.A., Welsh Arts Council, Cheltenham A.G. *Clubs:* Fosseway Artists. *Signs work:* "Denys Delhanty." *Address:* Combe House, Sheepscombe, Stroud, Glos. GL6 7RG.

DELHANTY, Kate Elisabeth, D.F.A. (Slade); artist in oil; artist mem. R.W.A.; taught art at Cheltenham Ladies College (1953-60); *b* London, 8 Nov., 1928. *m* Denys Delhanty. three *s.* one *d. Educ:* Downe House, Newbury, Berks. *Studied:* Reading University, Slade School of Fine Art (1950-53, Prof. Coldstream). *Exhib:* R.A., Bristol (R.W.A.), Cheltenham A.G., Bristol Guild, etc. *Work in collections:* R.W.A., Cheltenham A.G. *Publications:* articles in Leisure Painter Magazine. *Clubs:* Fosseway Artists. *Signs work:* "Kate Delhanty." *Address:* Combe House, Sheepscombe, Stroud, Glos. GL6 7RG.

DELLAR, Roger, self taught artist in all media; *b* St.Albans, 29 May, 1949. *m* Lynda Ann Dellar. one *s.* one *d. Exhib:* R.W.S., P.S., R.S.M.A., N.E.A.C., R.I., R.O.I., R.W.A., R.B.A., R.A. *Work in collections:* internationally. *Commissions:* Sir Donald Limon, Clerk of House of Commons. *Clubs:* Royal Institute of Painters in Watercolour (R.I.), Wapping Group of Artists, Langham Sketching Club, Chelsea Arts Society. *Address:* Nutcombe Hill Cottage, Hindhead Rd., Hindhead, Surrey GU26 6AZ.

DEMARCO, Richard, O.B.E., l'Ordre des Arts et Lettres de France, Cavaliere de la Reppublica d'Italia, Gold Order of Merit Republic of Poland, Hon. F.R.I.A.S., Hon.D.F.A. (A.C.A.), R.S.W., S.S.A., R.S.A.; water-colourist/printmaker in watercolour, gouache, pen and ink, screen printing, etching; Prof. of European Cultural Studies, Kingston University; Artistic Director, Demarco European Art Foundation; *b* Edinburgh, 9 July, 1930. *m* Anne Muckle. *Educ:* Holy Cross Academy, Edinburgh. *Studied:* Edinburgh College of Art (1949-54, Sir William Gillies, Leonard Rosoman). *Exhib:* over sixty one-man shows including Third Eye Centre, Aberdeen Artspace, Editions Alecto Gallery. *Work in collections:* S.N.G.M.A., Dundee City A.G., V. & A., Aberdeen A.G., Hunterian Museum Glasgow, S.A.C., Edinburgh City A.G., Citibank, Chemical Bank, Bank of Scotland, Royal Bank of Scotland, Clydesdale Bank, H.R.H. Prince Philip, H.R.H. Prince Charles. *Publications:* The Road to Meikle Seggie - The Artist as Explorer, A Life in Pictures. *Clubs:* Scottish Arts. *Signs work:* "Richard Demarco." *Address:* (home) 23a Lennox St., Edinburgh EH4 1PY; (office) Kingston University, River House, 53-57 High St., Kingston-on-Thames, Surrey KT1 2HX.

DEMEL, Richard, Ph.D. (1981), Art Diploma (1948), F.I.L.Incorp. Linguist, F.R.S.A.; retd. art master, writer; lecturer: Univ. of Padova and Venice; stained glass artist (transparent mosaic method inventor), painter, engraver; *b* Ustron, Poland, 21 Dec., 1921. *m* Anna Parisi. one *s.* one *d. Educ:* Andrychow and Biala-Bielsko. *Studied:* Accad. d. Belle Arti (1945-47), Rome, Polish Accad. Art Centre, Rome, London (1945-49); London University Slade School (1949); LCC Central School of Art (1949-51) B.A. Lang, Venice University; M.A. Lang, Polish University, London; asst. to J. Nuttgens (St. Etheldreda's Church windows); asst. lecturer to Prof. M. Bohusz-Szyszko. *Exhib:* 26 one-man and 140 collective; ITV film (1961), BBC TV on pupils' work (with Miró 1962); Polish TV Documentary (1992); designed and exec; H.C. Comu. S.Leonards O.S. (4); Rome (1); 3 mosaic windows: Cathedral, Padua; Duomo Cittadella (4); Codevigo Church (2) Italy. *Publications:* in 68 art encyclopaedias and art publications. Biographer of Sergiusz Piasecki. *Signs work:* see appendix. *Address:* Via S. Domenico 21-35030 Tencarola, Padova, Italy.

de MEO, P. (Pamela Synge), artist in oil and water-colour; *b* London, 2 Sept., 1920. *m* Major Brian Synge. three *s. Educ:* Cheltenham Ladies' College. *Studied:* St. Martin's College of Art, Chelsea School of Art, Heatherleys (1953). *Exhib:* R.A. (1988), Paris Salon, R.B.A. Galleries, Chelsea Artists, Bankside Gallery (G.B., U.S.S.R. Assoc., 1985), Mall Galleries, Bowmore Gallery, Halkin St., W1 (1989), Charity Exhbn. for Red Cross (1991), Gagliardi Gallery, Chelsea (1993), Patterson Gallery, Albemarle St. (1994), Chelsea Arts Soc. (1993, 1994), Britain-Russian Assoc. (1995); one-man show: Tradescant Trust Museum (1988). *Clubs:* Dover St. Arts, Chelsea Arts. *Signs work:* "P. de Meo." *Address:* 4 Pembroke Cl., Grosvenor Cres., London SW1X 7ET.

DENISON, David, surrealist artist in acrylic and oil; tutor, Prison Staff College, Wakefield; *b* Wakefield, 21 May, 1939. *m* Linda. one *s.* two *d. Educ:* Snapethorpe Secondary Modern School, Wakefield. *Studied:* Doncaster College of Art (1972). *Exhib:* Wakefield, Skipton, London, Keighley, Bradford, Camden Arts Centre; one-man shows: Manor House Public A.G., Ilkley (1970, 1977), Goole Museum and A.G. (1971), Wakefield Museum and A.G. (1972, 1974), Leeds City Gallery (1973), Doncaster A.G. (1973), Arthur Koestler Exhbn. London (1977), Bradford Cartwright Hall (1980), Angela Flowers Gallery, Arts Council of Gt. Britain. *Work in collections:* Brighton Museum and A.G., Sir Roland Penrose Collection. *Publications:* illustrated The Battle of Wilderness Wood by R. Adams. *Signs work:* "D. Denison." *Address:* 58 Station Rd., Burley in Wharfedale, W. Yorks.

DENNING, Antony, C. & G. Dip. (1988); sculptor and carver in wood, stone, welded steel; *b* Berks., 1 Nov., 1929. *m* Mary Denning. three *d. Educ:* Claysmore. *Studied:* Horsham School of Art, Weymouth College (1985-86), City & Guilds Art School (1986-88). *Exhib:* Cumberland Lodge, Windsor (1965), Blythes, Edinburgh (1966), Hambledon, Blandford (1971), Nuffield, Southampton (1972), Museum, Dorchester (1977), Arts Centre, Salisbury (1979), Honiton Festival (1994), etc. *Work in collections:* Southampton University; private collections in U.K., Europe, U.S.A., Canada. *Commissions:* Fishmongers' Co., Grocers' Co., St. Peter's Boyatt Wood, All Saints' Wardour, St. Mary's School, Highgate School, and private commissions. *Publications:* The Craft of Woodcarving (Cassell, 1994), Woodcarving - Two Books in One (Sterling, U.S.A., 1999; Apple Press, U.K., 2000). *Clubs:* Soc. of Heraldic Arts. *Signs work:* "Antony Denning." *Address:* 42 Nettlecombe, Shaftesbury, Dorset SP7 8PR.

DENNIS, Christopher John, H.S., S.Lm., A.S.E.A.; artist in water-colour and oil of equestrian, countryside and dogs art, abstract and miniatures; *b* Derby, 10 Feb., 1946. three *s.* one *d. Educ:* Ushaw College. Taught by artist mother B.C. D'Oyly Aplin. *Exhib:* exhbns.: Chelsea, Mall Galleries, Alexander Llewellyn, Royal Miniature Soc., Society of Equestrian Artists, Hilliard Soc. *Work in collections:* Queen's miniatures. *Commissions:* York Race Committee, Racecourse Association. *Signs work:* see appendix. *Address:* 10 Church Lane, Knaresborough, N.Yorks. HG5 9AR.

DENTON, Kenneth Raymond, R.S.M.A., F.R.S.A., I.S.M.P.; landscape and marine artist in oil; *b* Chatham, 20 Aug., 1932. *m* Margaret Denton. three *s. Educ:* Troy Town School, Rochester. *Studied:* Rochester School of Art and Technical School, Medway College of Art for decorative design and painting, landscape painting with David Mead. *Exhib:* York, Rochester, London, Eastbourne, Thames Ditton, Stratford-on-Avon, Norwich, Los Angeles, Mystic, Vancouver, San Francisco, Pennsylvania, Washington D.C., Tunbridge Wells; 43 one-man shows, R.O.I., R.B.A., etc. *Publications:* work repro.: Medici Soc., Royles, Artists Britain, Yachting Monthly, Yachting World, Connoisseur, Guild Prints. *Clubs:* R.S.M.A. *Signs work:* "Kenneth Denton." *Address:* Priory Farm Lodge, Sporle, Kings Lynn, Norfolk PE32 2DS.

de QUIN, Robert, N.D.D. (1950); sculptor working in welded metals mainly in abstract style; retd. art teacher; *b* Namur, Belgium, 6 July, 1927. *m* Diana. two *d. Educ:* Belgium and U.K. *Studied:* Hornsey School of Art (1945-50). *Exhib:* several one-man shows including Mall Galleries (1972); numerous group shows including Berkeley Sq., London (1972), B.P. Oil sculpture, Festival Hall, London (1990), Dolphin Sq. sculpture, London (1993), Loggia Gallery, London. *Work in collections:* Britain, Belgium, S. Africa, U.S.A.; several commissioned works. *Clubs:* Fellow and Past Chairman, F.P.S. and Loggia Gallery, London. *Signs work:* "Robert de Quin." *Address:* 95 Fortis Green, London N2 9HU.

DERRY, Pamela Mary, N.S.; artist in oil; *b* Welwyn Garden City, 13 Apr., 1932. married. two *s.* two *d. Educ:* Bedford High School. *Exhib:* Mermaid Theatre, London, New Ashgate Gallery, Farnham, Century Gallery, Henley, Bladon Gallery, Andover, Fortescue Swann Gallery, London, Wold Galleries, Burton-on-Water, Cookhouse Gallery, Cumbria, Walton Gallery, Stow-on-the-Wold. *Work in collections:* Chelmsford Council, Russell Cotes Museum and Gallery, Bournemouth. *Publications:* work repro.: Leisure Painter. *Clubs:* N.S. *Signs work:* "Pamela Derry." *Address:* Whitemoor Farm, Whitemoor, Holt, Wimborne, Dorset BH21 7DA.

de SAULLES, Mary, A.R.I.B.A., (1948), A.A.dip (1947), F.C.S.D. (1959), F.R.S.A. (1981); architect and designer, interior, exhbn., display; deputy to chief officer of specialized design section, L.C.C. Architects' Dept. (1950-52); partnership with John Lunn, F.S.I.A. (1951-55); Industrial Designer, B.E.A. (1959); private practice (1960), interiors, exhbns., housing, etc. Conservation consultant; *b* Westcliff-on-Sea, 1925. *m* Patrick de Saulles, A.A.dip. (d. 1997). two *s. Studied:* architecture: Architectural Assoc. School of Architecture. *Publications:* The Book of Shrewsbury (Barracuda Books Ltd.). Designers in Britain, Nos. 4 and 5, Architectural Review. *Clubs:* Architectural Assoc. *Signs work:* "Mary de Saulles." *Address:* Watergate House, St Mary's Water Lane, Shrewsbury SY1 2BX.

DESMET, Anne, M.A.(Oxon.) (1986), R.E. (1991), Dip. (Advanced Printmaking) (1988), Rome Scholar in Printmaking (1989-90); artist in wood engraving and collage; *b* Liverpool, 14 June, 1964. *m* Roy Willingham. one *s.* one *d. Educ:* Sacred Heart High School, Liverpool. *Studied:* Ruskin School of Art (1983-86), Central School of Art (1987-88). *Exhib:* group shows: worldwide; solo shows U.K.: Ashmolean Museum, Duncan Campbell Gallery, Royal Overseas League, Godfrey & Twatt Gallery; and Ex Libris Museum Moscow, Russia. *Work in* *collections:* Ashmolean Museum, V. & A., National Art Library. *Commissions:* Sotheby's, British Museum. *Publications:* Engravers Two (Silent Books), The Times, O.U.P. *Signs work:* "ANNE DESMET" or "A.J.D." *Address:* c/o Duncan Campbell Contemporary Art, 15 Thackeray St., London W8 5ET.

DESOUTTER, Roger Charles, R.S.M.A.; painter in oil; *b* London, 21 Mar., 1923. *m* Mary Elizabeth. one *s.* one *d. Educ:* Mill Hill School and Loughborough College. *Exhib:* R.S.M.A., Stacy-Marks Galleries, R.O.I., G.Av.A., Lloyds, Mystic Seaport, Forbes Gallery, New York, Marine Arts Gallery, Salem, Kirsten Gallery, Seattle. *Work in collections:* U.S. Mercantile Marine Academy. *Commissions:* Shipping Companies, Banks, Insurance Companies, Lloyds Agents. *Publications:* 20th Century British Marine Painting, Liners in Art, A Celebration of Marine Art; paintings reproduced as greeting cards, calendars and fine art prints. *Signs work:* "ROGER DESOUTTER." *Address:* Copshrews, Amersham Rd., Beaconsfield, Bucks, HP9 2UE.

de VERE COLE, Cassian, art dealer; Director, Elgin Gallery (Cassian de Vere Cole Fine Art) (since 1993) specialist in twentieth century British and contemporary art; previously: Christie's, London (1990-92), freelance New York, Chicago (1989-90), Parkin Gallery, London (1986-88); *b* London, 17 Nov., 1966. *Clubs:* Chelsea Arts, Garrick. *Address:* c/o Elgin Gallery (Cassian de Vere Cole Fine Art), 50 Elgin Cres., London W11 2JJ.

DEVLIN, George, R.S.W. (1964); painter in oil, water-colour, etching and ceramics; *b* Glasgow, 8 Sept., 1937. *Studied:* Glasgow School of Art (1955-60). *Exhib:* many one-man shows; Belfast Open 100, 2nd British Biennale of Drawing, Contemporary Scottish Painting (Arts Council), etc. *Work in collections:* H.M. The Queen, Scottish National Gallery of Modern Art, Arts Council, Aberdeen A.G., Essex County Council, Leicester and Strathclyde Universities, Edinburgh City Collection, Argyle County Council. *Publications:* illustrations for Scotsman and Maclellan Publishers. Designed set and costumes for new ballet by Walter Gore (1973) and presented by Scottish Ballet. *Signs work:* "Devlin." *Address:* 6 Falcon Terr. Lane, Glasgow G20 0AG.

DEWSBURY, Gerald, B.A.; landscape, architecture and natural history painter in oil and water-colour; *b* Dartford, 11 Jan., 1957. *m* Kim Rolling. one *s.* one *d. Educ:* King Edward VI Grammar School, Retford. *Studied:* Falmouth School of Art (1977-80). *Exhib:* R.A., London; John Noott Gallery, Broadway; St. David's Hall, Cardiff; Theatr Clwyd, Mold; Alderley Gallery, Alderley Edge; plus numerous others. *Work in collections:* Stowells of Chelsea; Grosvenor Museum, Chester; Soc. for Contemporary Art in Wales; plus numerous private collections. *Signs work:* "Gerald Dewsbury" or "G.D." *Address:* Tyn-Y-Ffridd, Llangwm, nr. Corwen, Clwyd LL21 0RW.

DEXTER, James Henry, designer; *b* 23 July, 1912. *m* Marjorie Ellen Gurr. *Educ:* Leicester College of Art. *Exhib:* N.E.A.C., R.A., London Group, various provincial galleries. *Work in collections:* Corporation of Leicester. *Signs work:* "James Dexter." *Address:* 52 Scraptoft Lane, Leicester LE5 1HU.

DICK, Colin, N.D.D. (1951); figurative painter in oil, water-colour, stoneware sculpture, retd. teacher; former Head of Art, Campion School, Royal Leamington Spa; *b* Epsom, Surrey, 28 Feb., 1929. *m* Delia D., M.A. one *s.* two *d. Educ:* Wennington School, and Leighton Park. *Studied:* St. Martin's (1947-1951, Frederick Gore, R.A., R.V. Pitchforth, R.A.). *Exhib:* 'Romanies, Fairs and local customs' Nuneaton Riversley Gallery (1995), Herbert A.G. Retrospective, Christchurch J.C.R. Oxford, Musée Boulogne sur Mer, Biarritz Galerie Municipal, 'Coventry between Bombing and Reconstruction' Herbert A.G. (1997), R.A. Summer Exhbns. (seven oil paintings). *Work in collections:* Herbert A.G. and Museum, Coventry (35 paintings). *Commissions:* Midland waterways and traditional gatherings commissions accepted, portraits of people of ephemeral lifestyles in unusual beautiful settings, multi-cultural musicians. *Clubs:* Umbrella for the Arts, Coventry. *Signs work:* "Colin Dick." *Address:* Stoke Green Studio, 98 Binley Rd., Stoke, Coventry CV3 1FR.

DICKENS, Alison Margaret, company director; painter in oil; *b* London, 1917. *m* G.E.J. Dickens (decd.). one *s.* one *d. Educ:* Haberdasher Aske's Girls' School. *Studied:* Ealing Art School (Kenneth Procter). *Exhib:* R.A., N.S., R.P., S.W.A.; numerous one-man shows at own studio, E. Horsley, and Thorndike Theatre, Leatherhead. *Work in collections:* Japan. *Publications:* dust cover for Foyles. *Signs work:* "Alison M. Dickens" and see appendix. *Address:* Norrels Lodge North, Norrels Drive, E. Horsley, Surrey KT24 5DL.

DICKERSON, John, M.F.A., (1968), Dr.R.C.A. (1974); artist and lecturer in painting, ceramics, mixed media sculpture, drawing; subject leader for studio art, Richmond International University, London; *b* Swaffham, Norfolk, 11 Oct., 1939. *Educ:* Hammond's School, Swaffham. *Studied:* Goldsmiths' College, Art Students' League, N.Y., Pratt Inst., N.Y. (1966-68), R.C.A. (1971-74). *Work in collections:* Japan, U.S.A., U.K., Taiwan, Malaysia, Sweden, Australia, Yugoslavia, Hong Kong, Spain. *Publications:* author: Raku Handbook; Pottery Making - A Complete Guide; Aspects of Raku Ware; Pottery. *Signs work:* some ceramics and sculpture carry "JD" monogram; works on paper "John Dickerson." *Address:* 47 Creffield Rd., London W5 3RR.

DICKS, Margo, S.G.F.A.; R.H.S. medallist for Botanical Painting (1989, 1991, 1994); sculptor, potter and painter in water-colour; *b* Coventry, 1925. *m* Dr. David Dicks. two *d. Educ:* Clarence House School, Coventry, Italia Conti School, London. *Studied:* pottery with Cecil Baugh, Jamaica (1954-56), recently, sculpture with Nigel Konstam, Italy. *Exhib:* Mall and Westminster Galleries. *Clubs:* Arts. *Signs work:* "Margo Dicks" or "M.D." *Address:* Bradstones, Hewshott Lane, Liphook, Hants. GU30 7SU.

DICKSON, Evangeline Mary Lambart, B.W.S.; artist in water-colour and other media; Cert. of Merit for Distinguished Service (International Biographical Centre); *b* 31 Aug., 1922. *m* John Wanless Dickson, F.R.C.S. one *s.* two *d. Educ:* Stover, Newton Abbot. *Studied:* under Anna Airy, R.I., R.O.I., R.E. *Exhib:* solo shows: E. Anglia, London, Ipswich B.C. Museums and Galleries, Salisbury and S. Wiltshire Museum, English Heritage (Framlingham Castle); group shows include Cambridge, Hertfordshire, Yorkshire, Scotland, Paris Salon, R.W.S. Open and R.I. exhbns. (London), Ipswich B.C. Museums and Galleries, Gainsborough's House, Sudbury, Suffolk. *Work in collections:* Sheffield City A.G's (Picture lending scheme, Graves

A.G.), Ipswich B.C. Museums and Galleries. *Publications:* commissioned illustrations "In Search of Heathland", Lee Chadwick (Dobson Books Ltd.) and for Collins publishers; painting for W.S.Cowell Ltd. calendar for international distribution. At their request transparancies of six paintings sent to the Bridgeman Art Library, London. Art career entered in 1999 Dictionary of International Biograhy. *Clubs:* B.W.S., Yorks., Ipswich Art Soc., Eight Plus One Group. *Signs work:* "E.M. Dickson" and see appendix. *Address:* Stow House, Westerfield, Ipswich, Suffolk IP6 9AJ.

DICKSON, James Marshall, D.A. (Edin., 1964), R.S.W. (1972); artist in ink, gouache, P.V.A.; Head of Art, Lochgelly Centre; *b* Kirkcaldy, 31 July, 1942. *Educ:* Beath High School. *Studied:* Edinburgh College of Art (1960-64, Stuart Barrie). *Exhib:* R.S.W. (Edin.), R.G.I. (Glasgow), Kirkcaldy A.G., Perth A.G., Loomshop Gallery. *Work in collections:* Banff County, Angus County, Aberdeen, Tayside, Leeds Educ. *Signs work:* "James Marshall Dickson, R.S.W." *Address:* 44 Main St., Lochgelly, Fife.

DICKSON, Jennifer, R.A., R.E., LL.D. (1988), C.M. (1995); printmaker and photographer; *b* Piet Retief, S. Africa, 17 Sept., 1936. *Studied:* Goldsmiths' College School of Art (University of London, 1954-59) and Atelier 17, Paris, under S. W. Hayter. *Work in collections:* V. & A.; National Gallery of Canada; Hermitage, Leningrad; Cleveland Art Institute, etc. *Publications:* 30 major suites of original prints. *Address:* 20 Osborne St., Ottawa, Ontario K1S 4Z9, Canada.

DIGGLE, Philip, painter in oil on canvas; *b* 30 Dec., 1956. *Educ:* Ancoats Manchester Grammar; Trinity College, Oxford. *Exhib:* Bede Gallery, Jarrow, Warwick Arts Trust (1985), Angela Flowers Gallery (1986, 1987), Art Now, London (1986, 1987, 1988), Festival of the 10th Summer, Manchester (1986), Barcelona Workshop (1988), Flowers East (1989, 1991); one-man shows: Rochdale A.G. (1985), Angela Flowers Gallery (1985), Warwick Arts Trust (1985), Some Bizarre Gallery (1988, 1989), Barbizon Gallery, Glasgow (1989, 1990, 1991), Barcelona Workshop (1991), Flowers East (1991); Granada/LWT (1988), B.B.C. Playbus (1990). *Work in collections:* Chase Manhattan Bank, N.Y., Rockefeller Center. *Address:* 498 Archway Rd., London N6 4NA.

DI GIROLAMO, Megan Ann, M.A. Ceramics (1987), A.T.C. (Lond.) (1963), N.D.D. (1962); ceramic sculptor – stoneware and raku, casting – bronze and resin; lecturer Buckinghamshire Chilterns University College; *b* New Delhi, 13 Jan., 1942. *m* Romeo di Girolamo P.R.B.A. two *d*. *Educ:* Aylesbury Grammar School. *Studied:* High Wycombe College; Hornsey School of Art; South Glamorgan Institute of Higher Education. *Exhib:* The Mall Galleries Royal Society of British Artists (1987-2001), Royal Academy (1993, 1996), Royal West of England Academy (1996-7), Society of Portrait Sculptors (1999-2001), R.B.S. Summer Exhibition (2000), various solo and mixed exhibitions. *Commissions:* Great Missenden Church (Dunford), Villa Scalabrini (Vatican), Harris – sculpture, Bennet – sculpture, Dr. Riley – Wendover Health Centre, Trilogy – St. Mary's Church, Aylesbury (Fairclough), Patricia (Finch). awards: De Laszlo Medal (R.B.A.), 1996; Silver Medal (R.B.S.), 1997; Frink Sculpture School Award, 1999; Potclays Award, 2000. *Clubs:* elected membership: Associate Royal Society of British Sculptors, Royal Society of British

Artists, Society of Portrait Sculptors. *Signs work:* see appendix. *Address:* Bridge Bend, Nash Lee Rd., Wendover, Bucks. HP22 6BE. *Website:* www.megan-di-giro-lamo.co.uk/megan htm *Email:* megan-di-girolamo@hotmail.com

DI GIROLAMO, Romeo, R.B.A., N.D.D.; artist in oil; Bucks. Architectural Competition (1953, 1954); Bucks. Art Scholarship (1954-59); Granada Theatre National Painting Prize (1957); David Murray Travelling Scholarship awarded by R.A. (1959); formerly Head of Art Depts., Gt. Marlow Secondary, Slough Grammar for Boys, The Radcliffe Comprehensive; at present Head of Painting Dept., Amersham College of Further Education and School of Art (formerly High Wycombe School of Art); mem. of the Academic Board and Governor of the College; *b* Civitella Casanova, Italy, 1939. *m* Megan, A.T.C. *Educ:* Quainton and Waddesdon secondary schools. *Studied:* High Wycombe School of Art (1954-59). *Exhib:* R.A., R.B.A., Art Bureau Travelling exhbns. and many one-man shows. *Work in collections:* private collections in many countries. *Signs work:* "Romeo di Girolamo." *Address:* Bridge Bend, Nash Lee Rd., Wendover, Bucks.

DINKEL KEET, Emmy Gerarda Mary, A.R.C.A. (1933), R.W.A. (1987); artist in water-colour brush drawings; former teacher of art and crafts, Sherborne School for Girls; Principal Asst., Malvern College of Art; and part-time in schools in Scotland; *b* 5 Sept., 1908. *m* E. Michael Dinkel, R.W.S., R.W.A., F.S.G.E., A.R.C.A. two *s.* two s- *d. Studied:* Southend College of Art (1927-30), R.C.A. (1930-33, Sir William Rothenstein, Prof. Tristram, Prof. Osborne, Robert Austin, Edward Johnston, Eric Ravilious); studied peasant art and design in Hungary. *Exhib:* R.A., R.W.A., R.S.A., Laing A.G., Brighton A.G., many provincial art galleries. *Publications:* "Dream Children", collected works of Emmy Dinkel-Keet, recently published. *Signs work:* "E.G.M. Dinkel-Keet." *Address:* 1 The Mead, Cirencester, Glos. GL7 2BB.

DINN, Catherine Margaret, B.A. (1979), M.A. (1980), Dip. Art Gallery and Museum Studies (1981); Curator, Falmouth Art Gallery (1981-92); freelance writer and lecturer; *b* Norfolk, 4 Sept., 1957. *m* Michael E. Richards. two *d. Educ:* Walthamstow Hall, Sevenoaks. *Studied:* History of Art and English, University of Nottingham (1976-79), Courtauld Inst. of Art (1979-80), University of Manchester (1980-81). *Publications:* Co-author (with David Wainwright) of biography of Henry Scott Tuke, R.A. (Sarema Press, 1989; reprinted 1991). *Address:* Boscolla, Florence Pl., Falmouth, Cornwall TR11 3NJ.

DI STEFANO, Arturo, M.A. Fine Art (1981); painter in oil on linen, woodcuts, etchings; *b* England, 25 Feb., 1955. *m* Jan Di Stefano. one *s. Studied:* Goldsmiths' College, University of London (1974-77, Jon Thompson), R.C.A. (1978-81, Peter de Francia). *Exhib:* Kettle's Yard, Cambridge (1988), Serpentine Gallery (1989), John Hansard Gallery (1989); one-man shows, Oxford O4 Gallery, Pomeroy Gallery, London (1987), Woodlands Gallery (1987), Fasolino Gallery, Turin (1987), Pomeroy Purdy Gallery, London (1989), Purdy Hicks (1991,1993,1996), Walker A.G. (1993). *Work in collections:* Unilever, Arthur Andersen, Museum of London, N.P.G. London, Government Art Collection, Walker A.G., L'pool, Barclays Bank, Leicester Museum, Harris Museum, Preston. *Commissions:* Portrait of Sir Richard Doll for National Portrait Gallery, London. *Publications:* The School of London: A Resurgence in

Contemporary Painting (Alistair Hicks, Phaidon 1989); four catalogues: 1989, 1991, 1993, 1995. *Signs work:* "A. Di Stefano." *Address:* 92 Fairfoot Rd., Bow, London E3 4EH.

DMOCH, Paul, self taught artist in water-colour, architect; *b* Warsaw, 22 Sept.,1958. *m* Grazyna. one *d. Studied:* Polytechnic of Warsaw (architecture). *Exhib:* R.I. (1997 winner Frank Herring award, 1998-99), R.B.A. (1997-98), N.E.A.C. (1997), Singer and Friedlander/Sunday Times Water-colour Competition (1996-00), R.W.S. (1997, winner Daler-Rowney Premier and Saunders Waterford awards) (1999-00); Albermarle Gallery, London (2001). *Work in collections:* Vatican and private collections worldwide. *Signs work:* "PaDmoch" - see appendix. *Address:* 5 Cherry Close, South Wonston, Winchester, Hants. SO21 3HU. *Website:* http://www.globalart.net/dmoch.htm

DOBSON, Mary: see THORNBERY, Mary.

DOCHERTY, Michael, D.A. (Edin.) (1968), Post-Grad. Dip. (1969), A.R.S.A. (1984); artist in oil/acrylic on canvas/wood, ink/graphite on paper/card; lecturer, Edinburgh College of Art; *b* Alloa, 28 Dec., 1947. *m* Odette Dominique Vitse. one *s.* one *d. Educ:* St. Modan's High School, Stirling. *Studied:* Edinburgh College of Art (1964-68, 1968-69). *Exhib:* Richard Demarco Gallery, New 57 Gallery, Fruitmarket Gallery, French Inst., National Gallery of Modern Art, Fremantle Art Centre, Western Australia, Canabias, France, R.S.A., R.S.W., Air, London, Fine Art Soc. *Work in collections:* Contemporary Art Soc., Scottish National Gallery of Modern Art, Scottish Arts Council, Edinburgh College of Art. *Signs work:* "Michael Docherty" on reverse. *Address:* 20 Howard Pl., Edinburgh EH3 5JY.

DODD, Alan, N.D.D. (1963), Cert. R.A.S. (1966); painter, interior designer, muralist; *b* Kennington, Ashford, Kent, 23 Nov., 1942. *Studied:* Maidstone College of Art, Royal Academy Schools. *Exhib:* R.A. Bicentenary Exhibition (1968); one-man shows: New Grafton Gallery (July, 1969, Nov., 1970, Oct., 1972), 'Four English Painters' Galleria Estudio Cid, Madrid (Nov., 1970). *Work in collections:* V. & A., Sir John Soane's Museum; also in private collections in England, U.S.A., Australia, Spain, Portugal. *Commissions:* V. & A.: The Painted Room (1986), Alexandra Palace: Murals (1988), Spencer House: Trompe l`oeil work (1990), Sir John Soane`s Museum: re-created Pompeiian ceiling (1992), Home House: re-creation of three lost works by Zucchi (1998), set designs for Opera Omnibus: "Masked Ball" (2000), designed the Westminster Millenium Cross, memorial to the late Cardinal Hume (2000). *Signs work:* "Dodd" with date. *Address:* 295 Caledonian Rd., London N1 1EG; and High Hall, Weston, Beccles, Suffolk NR34 8TF.

DODDS, Andrew, F.C.S.D., N.D.D.; freelance illustrator and painter; Principal Lecturer, Suffolk College, School of Art and Design (retd. 1991); *b* Gullane, Scotland, 5 May, 1927. *Studied:* Colchester School of Art (1942-45), L.C.C. Central School of Arts and Crafts (1947-50). *Exhib:* R.A.; one-man exhbns.: Drawn from London, Mermaid Theatre (1961), Minories, Colchester (1968), Chappel Galleries (1999). *Publications:* Radio Times (1957-70) and other national publications. 'Reportage' type drawings for Eastern Daily Press, each week since 1957. Has illustrated 43 books including own books 'East Anglia Drawn' (1987), 'London Then' (1994) and 'East Anglian Sketchbook' (1999). *Signs work:* "Andrew Dodds."

Address: The Round House, Lower Raydon, Ipswich, Suffolk IP7 5QN.

DODDS, James, Shipwright (1976), B.A. (1980), M.A. (1984); artist in oil and linocut; *b* Brightlingsea, 3 May, 1957. *m* Catherine. one *s*. one *d*. *Studied:* Colchester School of Art (1976-77), Chelsea School of Art (1977-80), R.C.A. (1981-84). *Exhib:* Sue Rankin Gallery (1992), Aldeburgh Festival (1984, 1990, 1995, 1998, 2000), Bircham Contemporary Arts, Norfolk (1988, 1989, 1992, 1998), Printworks, Colchester (1989, 1990, 1992), Chappel Galleries, Colchester (1989, 1990, 1994), Simbouras Gallery, Athens (1995), Union of Artists, St. Petersburg (1997), Hitzacker, Germany (1997), R.A. Summer Show (1998, 1999, 2000), First Site, Colchester (2001). *Work in collections:* Britten-Pears Library, Ipswich and Horniman Museums. *Commissions:* Nationl Trust, Lloyds Register. *Publications:* Peter Grimes, The Wanderer, The Shipwright Trade, Wild Man Of Orford, Wild Man of Wivenhoe, On the Beach, Alphabet of Boats, Black Shuck, James Dodds paintings, ABC of Boat Bits. *Signs work:* "James Dodds" or "J.D." *Address:* Barnacle House, 20 St. John's Rd., Wivenhoe, Colchester, Essex CO7 9DR. *Website:* www.jamesdodds.co.uk *Email:* james@jamesdodds.co.uk

DOGGETT, Susan Marguerite, B.A. (Hons.); W.C.C. award for Contemporary Craft (1994); book artist and bookbinder in mixed media; Lecturer in book arts, Croydon College; M.A. (design by independent project); *b* Reading, 24 Sept., 1960. one *d*. *Educ:* Waingel's Copse School, Woodley, Reading. *Studied:* Oxford Brookes University and Brighton University. *Exhib:* Festival Hall London, Royal Library Copenhagen, Angel Row Gallery Nottingham, Crafts Council, London, American Crafts Museum, N.Y., Washington D.C. Centre for Book Arts Minnesota. *Work in collections:* Tom Phillips, private libraries U.S.A. *Commissions:* Booker Prize bindings (1996, 1998, 1999). *Publications:* 'Bookworks' (Apple Press, 1998). *Clubs:* Fellow of Designer Bookbinders. *Signs work:* "S.D." or "Sue Doggett." *Address:* 4 Lancaster Ct., Lancaster Ave., London SE27 9HU.

DONALD, George M., D.A. (1967), A.T.C. (1969), M.Ed. (1980), R.S.A. (1993), R.S.W. (1976); artist in printmaking, papermaking; lecturer in drawing and painting, Edinburgh College of Art; Director, Centre for Continuing Studies and Summer School; *b* Ootacamund, S. India, 12 Sept., 1943. one *s*. one *d*. *Educ:* Aberdeen Academy. *Studied:* Edinburgh College of Art and Hornsey College of Art; Edinburgh University. *Work in collections:* V. & A., R.S.A., S.A.C., Aberdeen A.G., S.N.G.M.A., Hunterian Museum; and in public and private collections in U.K., U.S.A., Europe, Far East. *Commissions:* worldwide. *Signs work:* "George Donald." *Address:* Bankhead, By Duns, Berwickshire TD11 3QJ.

DONNE, Leonard David, N.D.D., A.T.D. (1951); artist in oil, water-colour and etching; Head of Art, Cheshunt School; *b* Leicester, 19 June, 1926. *m* Elizabeth Donne. one *s*. two *d*. *Educ:* Wyggeston School, Leicester. *Studied:* Leicester College of Art under D. P. Carrington. *Exhib:* one-man shows: Gordon Maynard Gallery (1974), Loggia Gallery (1973), Countesthorpe College (1976), Hitchin Museum (1977), Loggia Gallery (1984), Birmingham University (1992), and various provincial and London galleries. *Clubs:* F.P.S. *Signs work:* "D.D." *Address:* 15 Church St., Leintwardine, Herefordshire SY7 0LD.

DOREY, Russell Peter, B.A. Hons. (Painting), Post.Grad.Dip. R.A. Schools;

artist in oil on canvas, pencil drawing; *b* Chelmsford, Essex, 26 Mar., 1961. one *s.* one *d. Educ:* Felsted School, Essex. *Studied:* Maidstone College of Art (1979-82, John Titchell, A.R.A.), R.A. School (1983-86, Norman Blamey, R.A.). *Exhib:* R.A. Summer Exhbns. (1985-86), Agnews Young Contemporaries (1988). *Signs work:* "Russell Dorey." *Address:* 31 St. Thomas Rd., Hastings, E. Sussex TN34 3LG.

DORMENT, Richard, B.A. (1968), M.A. (1969), M. Phil. (1975), Ph.D. (1975); art critic, Daily Telegraph; *b* U.S.A., 15 Nov., 1946. *m* Harriet Waugh. one *s.* one (by a previous marriage) *d. Studied:* Princeton University (1964-68), Columbia University (1969-75). *Publications:* Alfred Gilbert (1985); Alfred Gilbert, Sculptor and Goldsmith (exhbn. catalogue, R.A. London, 1986); British Painting in the Philadelphia Museum of Art, From the Seventeenth through the Nineteenth Century (1986). *Address:* Daily Telegraph, 1 Canada Square, Canary Wharf, London E14.

DOS SANTOS, Bartolomeu, Emeritus Prof. in Fine Art, University of London, Fellow (U.C.L.), R.E.; artist and printmaker, public art, ceramic tiles, etched stone; taught at Slade School of Art (1961-1996); *b* Lisbon, 24 Aug., 1931. *Studied:* Lisbon Art School (1950-1956), Slade School, under Anthony Gross (1956-1958). *Exhib:* 87 solo exhibs. worldwide, retrospective, Gulbenkian Foundation, Lisbon (1989). *Work in collections:* British Museum, V. & A., M.O.M.A., N. Y., Bibliotheque Nationale, Paris. *Commissions:* include, etched stone decoration for Entre Campos tube station, Lisbon, Nihonbashi station, Tokyo, Macau Museum. *Publications:* Pas Memorial, by J. Saramago, Koron Verlag, Zurich (1999). *Signs work:* "B Dos Santos." *Address:* 57 Talbot Rd., London N6 4QX.

DOUBLEDAY, John, sculptor; *b* Langford, Essex, 1947. *m* Isobel J. C. Durie. three (one decd.) *s. Educ:* Stowe. *Studied:* Goldsmiths' College (1965-68). *Exhib:* one-man shows in London, New York, Amsterdam, Cologne. *Work in collections:* include Mary and Child Christ (1980) Rochester Cathedral; Charlie Chaplin (1981) Leicester Square; Isambard Kingdom Brunel (1982) Bristol and Paddington; The Beatles (1984) Liverpool; Commando Memorial C.T.C.R.M. (1986); Sherlock Holmes (1991) Switzerland; Graham Gooch (1992) Chelmsford; J.B. Pflug (1994) Braith Mali Museum, Biberach, Nelson Mandela (1997) U.W.C. in Italy, U.K., U.S.A., Singapore; Gerald Durrell (1999) Jersey; Sherlock Holmes (1999) Baker St. Station, London; The Dorset Shepherd (2000) Dorchester. Museums include: Ashmolean Museum, B.M., V. & A., and Tate. *Address:* Goat Lodge, Great Totham, Maldon, Essex CM9 8BX.

DOUGLAS, Jean Mary, Dip.A.E. (1979), S.B.A. (1991); artist in pastel, school teacher (retd.); *b* London, 26 Sept., 1927. *m* Frank Douglas. two *d. Educ:* Loughton County High School and Teacher Training College, Portsmouth. *Studied:* London University Art Diploma (1976-79). *Exhib:* Royal Exchange, Guildhall, Mall Galleries, Central Hall Westminster, and mixed exhbns. E. Anglia, S. England and Wales, also Sweden and Austria. *Publications:* Reproduction rights of paintings sold to Royle and Medici, etc. *Clubs:* Soc. of Floral Painters. *Signs work:* "J.M.D." *Address:* Park House, Liston, Sudbury, Suffolk CO10 7HT.

DOUGLAS, Jon, F.R.B.S., F.R.S.A.; sculptor in foundered bronze and resin bonded bronze, decorative art designer; *b* London, 7 Mar., 1911. *m* Doris Helen. two *s.* one *d. Educ:* University College School, Frognal, Hampstead; Bethany College,

Goudhurst, Kent. *Studied:* Institute Quinche, Lausanne (1928-31). *Exhib:* Mall Galleries, Camden Art Centre, R.B.S. Work in permanent collections worldwide. *Signs work:* "Jon Douglas." *Address:* 47 Finchley La., Hendon, London NW4 1BY.

DOUGLAS-DOMMEN, Marguerite France, C.I.A.L.; artist in oil and watercolour; *b* 12 July, 1918. *m* John Haig Douglas. one *s.* three *d. Educ:* Cheltenham Ladies' College. *Studied:* Derby, Lausanne (1935) and R.A. Schools under Russell and Monnington (1936-39). *Exhib:* S.S.A., R.S.W., Ancona. *Publications:* work repro.: illustrated three books of James Hogg's poetry. *Clubs:* Reynolds. *Signs work:* "M.F.D." *Address:* Craigsford, Earlston, Berwickshire TD4 6DJ.

DOVER, Peter Charles, B.A. (Hons.) Graphic Design (1984), M.A. (R.C.A.) Fine Art (1988), A.R.E (1995); printmaker, painter, maker in relief printmaking on paper, found objects and materials; also musician; *b* Merseyside, 10 Apr., 1954. *Educ:* Wallasey Grammar School. *Studied:* Wallasey College of Art (1980-81), Leeds Metropolitain University (1981-84), R.C.A. (1986-88, under the late Alistair Grant). *Work in collections:* Tate Gallery, Ashmolean, Dudley Museum, Plymouth Museum, London Hospital, St.Thomas's, Estonia National Museum. *Commissions:* I.T.U. Floor of Gt. Ormond Street Hospital for Sick Children, silkscreen mural 'The Sea' (1990-91). *Signs work:* "P.C. Dover" usually verso. *Address:* 8 Betts House, Betts St., London E1 8HN.

DOWDEN, Joe Francis, painter in watercolour; *b* Wimbledon, London, 16 June, 1958. *m* Ruth. *Exhib:* Singer & Friedlander, Sunday Times watercolour competition (1998, 2000), Laing art competition (1998, 1999, 2000), R.I. (1998), R.S.M.A. (1998), Chichester Open (1998), eleven solo exhibs., yearly exhib. in Surrey. *Publications:* Water in Watercolour (Search Press), Two in One Watercolour (David & Charles), regular articles for Artists & Illustrators magazine; videos: Make it Look Real, Volumes 1&2 (Teaching Art). *Signs work:* "Joe Francis Dowden." *Address:* 91 Downlands Ave., Worthing, W. Sussex BN14 9HF. *Email:* joedowden@yahoo.co.uk

DOWLING, Jane, B.A. (Oxon.) Hons. (1946), M.A. (Oxon.) (1977); painter, etcher, engraver; tutor, Ruskin School, Oxford, formerly tutor for over 30 years at R.A. schools; *b* 1925. *m* Peter Greenham, (decd.). one *s.* one *d. Educ:* St. Anne's College, Oxford. *Studied:* Slade and Ruskin; Byam Shaw; Central School (Gert Hermes). *Exhib:* New Grafton Gallery, R.A. Summer Exhbn. since 1954; many mixed exhbns., Travelling Arts Council exhbn. with Peter Greenham (1984), 'The Glass of Vision' at Chichester Cathedral, 'The Long Perspective' Agnews (1987), 'A Personal Choice' Kings Lynn (1988), 'Art in Churches' Tewkesbury and Worcester (1991), small retrospective, Mompesson House, Salisbury (1992), Leighton House (2001) Tempera Society, Stations: The New Sacred Art, Bury St. Edmunds Art Gallery Trust, (Lent 2000). *Work in collections:* Farringdon Trust Buscot House, Southampton City A.G., John Radcliffe Hospital, Oxford, Ashmolean Museum and Churchill Hospital. *Commissions:* small mural: Edwin Abby Mural Fund for the Oxford Oratory Church (1995). *Publications:* various articles. *Clubs:* Oxford Union. *Signs work:* "J.D." and see appendix. *Address:* The Old Dairy, Charlton-on-Otmoor, nr. Islip, Oxon. OX5 2UQ.

DOWLING, Tom, artist in oil; *b* Dublin, 23 June, 1924. *Educ:* Royal Naval College, Dartmouth. *Studied:* City & Guilds of London Art School (1963-67, Gilbert

Spencer, Rodney Burn, Bernard Dunstan). *Exhib:* R.A., R.B.A., N.E.A.C., R.O.I., R.P., R.E., Richard Allen Gallery, New Grafton Gallery, Pictures for Schools exhbn. *Clubs:* Emsworth Sailing. *Signs work:* "TOM DOWLING" or "T.B.D." (on small paintings). *Address:* 31 Slipper Rd., Emsworth, Hants. PO10 8BS.

DOWNIE, Kate, D.A., Post Dip.F.A.; artist/lecturer in acrylic, collage, printmaking, photography; part-time tutor, Fine Art Dept., Edinburgh College of Art; *b* N. Carolina, U.S.A., 7 June, 1958. *m* Peter Clerke. one *d. Educ:* Ellon Academy, Aberdeenshire. *Studied:* Gray's School of Art, Aberdeen (1975-80, Alexander Fraser, Francis Walker). *Exhib:* Collins Gallery, Glasgow (1991), Talbot-Rice Gallery, University of Edinburgh (1992), Amsterdam, Brussels, Utrecht, Cardiff, Aberdeen. *Work in collections:* Aberdeen A.G., Aberdeen University, Edinburgh University, Kelvingrove A.G., Peoples Palace Glasgow, Allied Breweries, Cleveland A.G., S.A.C., B.B.C. Scotland. *Clubs:* Scottish Arts, Edinburgh. *Signs work:* "Kate Downie." *Address:* 12 Iona St., Edinburgh EH6 8SF.

DOWSON, Sir Philip Manning, C.B.E., P.P.R.A., M.A., A.A.Dip., R.I.B.A., F.C.S.D., Hon. F.A.I.A., Hon. F.R.C.A.; architect; Founder architectural partner, Arup Associates, and a senior partner, Ove Arup Partnership (1969-90), Consultant (1990-), President, Royal Academy of Arts (1993-99); *b* Johannesburg, 16 Aug., 1924. *m* Sarah. one *s.* two *d. Educ:* Gresham's School, University College, Oxford University (1942-43), Clare College, Cambridge University (1947-50). *Studied:* Architectural Assoc. (1950-53, Arthur Korn, Ernesto Rogers, Edwardo Catalano). *Exhib:* Arup Associates: R.A. Summer Exhbns., R.I.B.A. Anthology of British Architecture (1981), Venice Biennale (1982), R.I.B.A. Architecture Now (1983), R.I.B.A. The Art of the Architect (1984). *Clubs:* Garrick. *Signs work:* "Philip Dowson." *Address:* Royal Academy of Arts, Piccadilly, London W1V 0DS.

DOYLE, John, M.B.E. (1994), R.W.S.; 3rd prize Singer & Friedlander; artist in water-colour and aquatint; past President, Royal Water-colour Soc. (1996-2000); *b* London, 15 Feb., 1928. *m* Elizabeth. two *s.* two *d. Educ:* Sherborne School. *Exhib:* Canterbury Cathedral (1973, 1976), R.A., R.W.S., Spinks (1981, 1983, 1990), Catto Gallery, Hampstead (1989), exhibition to mark 1400th anniversary of Foundation of Cantebury Cathedral (1997). *Work in collections:* The Vatican. *Publications:* An Artist's Journey down the Thames (Pavilion Books, 1989). *Clubs:* Garrick. *Signs work:* "J.D." on small works, "John Doyle" on large works either pencil or water-colour. *Address:* Church Farm, Warehorne, Ashford, Kent TN26 2LP.

DRAGER, Bertha, artist in water-colour and oil; teacher of art, Washington Junior High School, Honolulu (1930-33); fashion: Okla. City University (1940), Cornell Extension, N.Y. (1962); *b* Moorefield, W.Va., U.S.A., 29 Dec., 1905. *m* John C. Drager. *Educ:* B.F.A. University, Okla. (1930), Art Students' League, N.Y. (1940), Traphagen School of Fashion, N.Y. (1941), Kokoschka's School, Salzburg (1960). *Exhib:* National, Manila, Philippines, Okla. Museum of Art, Crespi A.G., N.Y.C. (1960), Art's Place II Okla. City A.G. *Work in collections:* University of Okla. Museum of Art. *Publications:* author and illustrator, Hat Tactics (and film 'Hat Tactics'), 'Hat Patterns' and 'Hat Trimming'. *Signs work:* "BRETT DRAGER." *Address:* Quail Plaza Apts., Apt. 112, 11002 N.May Ave., Oklahoma City 73120, U.S.A.

DRAGER, Brett: see DRAGER, Bertha.

DRAPER, Kenneth, M.A. (1969), R.A. (1992); artist/sculptor and painter in resins, pigments for sculpture and paintings, and pastel on paper; *b* Killamarsh, Sheffield, 19 Feb., 1944. *m* Jean Macalpine, photographer. one *s. Educ:* Killamarsh Secondary Modern. *Studied:* Kingston College of Art and R.C.A. (Profs. Bernard Meadows, Bryan Kneale, Ralph Brown, Elizabeth Frink). *Exhib:* one-man shows: Redfern Gallery, Royal Academy, Hart Gallery, Islington, Peter Bartlow Gallery, Chicago, Adelson Gallery, N.Y. *Work in collections:* A.C.G.B., Contemporary Arts Soc., Fitzwilliam Museum, Ashmolean Museum Courtauld Inst. *Publications:* The Life and Art of Kenneth Draper by Roger Bertoud. *Signs work:* "Kenneth Draper." *Address:* Hart Gallery, 113 Upper St., Islington, London N1 1QN.

DREISER, Peter, artist glass engraver; copper-wheel technique; Founder Mem. and Fellow, Guild of Glass Engravers, Fellow, Soc. of Designer Craftsmen, ex-Vice President, Royal Miniature Soc.; mem. The Contemporary Glass Soc.; for 25 years was part-time tutor Morley College, London; *b* Cologne, 11 June, 1936. *Studied:* School for Art Glass, Rheinbach, Bonn (1951-54). *Work in collections:* City of Portsmouth Museum, Northampton Museum, V. & A., Corning Museum of Glass, Fitzwilliam Museum Cambridge, Ulster Museum Belfast, Castle Museum Nottingham. *Publications:* Engraving and Decorating Glass by Barbara Norman; Modern Glass by R. Stennett-Wilson; International Modern Glass by Geoffrey Beard; Glass Engraving Lettering and Design by David Peace; Glass a Contemporary Art by Dan Klein; Engraved Glass by Tom and Marilyn Goodeart; co-author of The Techniques of Glass Engraving. *Signs work:* "P. Dreiser." *Address:* 18 Rowland Ave., Kenton, Harrow, Middx. HA3 9AF.

DREW, Joanna Marie, C.B.E. (1985), Officier, l'Ordre des Arts et Lettres, 1988 (Chevalier, 1979); Director, Hayward and Regional Exhbns., South Bank Centre, (1987-92); *b* Naini Tal, India, 28 Sept., 1929. *Educ:* Dartington Hall; Edinburgh University (M.A.Hons. Fine Art); Edinburgh College of Art (D.A.). Arts Council of G.B. 1952-88: Asst. Director of Exhbns. (1970), Director of Exhbns. (1975), Director of Art (1978-86), Mem. Council, R.C.A. (1979-82). *Address:* Lloyds Bank, Wallingford, Oxon. OX10 0EH.

DRING, Melissa Jane, B.Sc. (Hons.) (1989), I.A.I., P.S., F.B.I.Dip. (1988); police forensic artist, portrait painter in pastel and oil, freelance courtroom artist; *b* Winchester, 1 Apr., 1944. *m* Michael Little. two *s. Educ:* St. Swithun's, Winchester. *Studied:* Winchester School of Art, R.A. Schools. *Exhib:* R.A., R.P., R.B.A., P.S. *Work in collections:* Northampton Central Museum and A.G. *Commissions:* portraits in private and public collections in oil and pastel. *Publications:* articles on forensic artwork in Police Review, and The Journal of Audiovisual Media in Medicine. *Signs work:* "Melissa Dring." *Address:* 10 St. George's Pl., Northampton NN2 6EP.

DRLJACHA, Zorica, A.R.B.S.; awarded First Prize British Institute in Sculpture (1961), anatomy drawing competition (1962), Landseer Scholarship, first prize and silver medal (1963), Catherine Adeline Sparkes prize; sculptress in bronze, aluminium, resin, ciment fondu; *b* Yugoslavia, 14 July, 1942. *m* Mladen. two *d. Educ:* Grammar school (Yugoslavia), Luton College of Technology. *Studied:* Goldsmiths'

College under H. W. Parker, F.R.B.S., R. Jones, R.A.; R.A. Schools under C. Mahoney, R.A., Sir Arnold Machin, O.B.E., R.A., Sir Henry Rushbury, K.C.V.O., C.B.E. *Exhib:* R.A. summer exhbns., R.B.S., Alwyn, Chelsea, Forty Hall, Portrait Society, open-air Holland Park, Davies St., Ealing, Chiswick, etc. *Work in collections:* England, U.S.A., Yugoslavia, Germany, Italy, France. *Commissions:* figures for "Battle of Trafalgar" at Madame Tussauds (1966), Expo '67 (Canada). *Address:* 152 Sutton Ct. Rd., Chiswick, London W43HT.

DRURY, Christopher, Dip.A.D. (1970); sculptor, land artist, works on paper, photography; *b* Colombo, Ceylon, 1948. two *d. Educ:* Canford School. *Studied:* Camberwell School of Art (1966-70, Paul de Moncheaux, Brian Taylor). *Exhib:* one-man shows: London, Los Angeles, Leeds, Dublin, Edinburgh; mixed shows: Europe, America and Japan. *Work in collections:* British Museum, C.A.S., Leeds City A.G., Whitworth A.G. Manchester, Henry A.G. Seattle, Towner A.G. Eastbourne, Cheltenham A.G. *Commissions:* Site specific works and cloud chambers in Britain, Europe, America and Japan. *Publications:* The Unpainted Landscape, Medicine Wheel, Shelters and Baskets, Amanita Muscaria, Stones and Bundles, Vessel, Silent Spaces (Thames & Hudson) Chris Drury, Journeys on Paper. *Signs work:* "Chris Drury." *Address:* 18 Eastport La., Lewes, E. Sussex BN7 1TL.

DUBERY, Fred, A.R.C.A.; painter in oil, illustrator; Prof. of Perspective, Royal Academy; *b* Croydon, 12 May, 1926. *m* Joanne Brogden. *Educ:* Whitgift School, Croydon. *Studied:* Croydon School of Art, and R.C.A. *Exhib:* Leicester Gallery, Rowland, Browse and Delbanco, R.A., N.E.A.C., New Grafton Gallery, Trafford Gallery, Markswood Gallery, Patterson Fine Arts, Waterman Fine Art, Alresford Gallery. *Work in collections:* Brighton City A.G., Huddersfield City A.G., Nuffield Foundation, Arts Club Dover St., Worcester College, Oxford, Warburg Inst., London University. *Publications:* Drawing Systems, Dubery and Willats (Studio Vista); Perspective and other Drawing Systems, Dubery and Willats (Herbert Press). *Clubs:* N.E.A.C. *Signs work:* "Fred Dubery." *Address:* Buxhall Lodge, Gt. Finborough, Stowmarket, Suffolk IP14 3AU.

DUCHIN, Edgar, M.A. (Oxon.), B.A. (O.U.); artist in oil and gouache; consultant solicitor; founder chairman, Solicitors Art Group; *b* 3 Sept., 1909. *m* Betty Margaret Bates. two *s.* two *d. Educ:* St. Paul's School; Brasenose College, Oxford. *Exhib:* Margaret Fisher Gallery, Hesketh Hubbard Art Soc. (prize winner). *Work in collections:* Prof. Dr. Paul Hodin, Dr. M. Altmann, Mr Nigel Wray, Mrs Alice Schwab. *Clubs:* Savile. *Signs work:* "Edgar Duchin." *Address:* 16 West Heath Drive, London NW11 7QH.

DUCKER, Catherine, B.A. (Hons.) Fine Art, R.W.S.; painter in water based and oil paints: subject focus is colour and abstracted forms from flowers and the natural landscape; *b* Wallingford, 24 Apr., 1973. *Studied:* Central St. Martin's (1990-91, 1992-96). *Exhib:* Contemporary Art Soc. (1996), Royal Water-colour Soc. (1997), Henley Festival (1997), Royal Academy Summer (2001), Singer and Frielander (2000/2001). *Work in collections:* private collections. *Commissions:* Henley Festival, and various private garden commissions. *Address:* Littlestoke Farm, Littlestoke, Wallingford, Oxon. OX10 6AX. *Email:* catherineducker@hotmail.com

DUCKWORTH, Barbara, F.M.A.A., A.I.M.B.I., S.R.N.; medical artist, artist in water-colour, conté, black and white, pastel and acrylic; *b* Wallasey, Ches., 31 Oct., 1913. *Educ:* Sandford Private School, Blundellsands. *Studied:* Liverpool College of Art (1934-38). *Exhib:* Walker Art Gallery, Liverpool; Liver Sketching Club; medical work at B.M.A. House, London, and Med. Institution, Liverpool. *Work in collections:* Fundus and eye paintings, St. Paul's Eye Hospital, Liverpool. *Publications:* many illustrations in medical journals; medical text-books. *Signs work:* "Barbara Duckworth." *Address:* 131 Milner Rd., Heswall, Wirral, Ches. CH60 5RX.

DUDLEY NEILL, Anna, D.F.A. (Lond., 1957), R.I. (1980); artist in water-colour and oil; *b* Merton, London, 26 July, 1935. *m* Michael A. Neill. two *s. Educ:* Tolworth Secondary School. *Studied:* Winchester School of Art (1950-54), Slade School of Fine Art (1954-57). *Exhib:* Deist, Belgium (1977, 1979), R.I., Cahors, France (1992). *Work in collections:* R.I. *Clubs:* R.I. *Signs work:* "Anna Dudley." *Address:* 15 Putney Heath Lane, London SW15 3JG.

DUFFIN, Stuart, R.E., A.R.S.A.; artist in etching and mezzotint; Studio Manager, Glasgow Print Studio; active musician; *b* Windsor, 13 June 1959. *Studied:* Grays School of Art, Aberdeen (Dip.Fine Art Printmaking). *Exhib:* U.S.A., Europe, Israel, Russia. *Work in collections:* Scottish Arts Council, Jerusalem Foundation, Glasgow City Council, Karkov Museum. Artist and writer with 'The Moors' multi-media projects. *Commissions:* "Last Supper" oil on canvas for Langside Parish Church, Glasgow. *Address:* 40 Cromarty Ave., Glasgow G43 2HG.

DUFFY, Stephen James, artist, potter, printmaker in linocuts, screen-print, lithography, water-colour, ceramics; *b* Winchelsea Beach, E. Sussex, 5 Feb., 1962. *Educ:* Rye Comprehensive. *Exhib:* Rye Soc. of Artists, Fremantle Print Biennial, W.A., Farnham Maltings Gallery, Modern Print Gallery, Wirksworth, Ormond Rd. Printmakers, Grundy A.G., Blackpool, Rye A.G. Easton Rooms, U.A., various mixed exhbns. *Publications:* Rye Nature Reserve, Irish Folk Tales (to be published). *Clubs:* Printmakers Council, U.A., Rye Fishheads. *Signs work:* see appendix. *Address:* 88 New Winchelsea Rd., Rye, E. Sussex TN31 7TA.

DUFFY, Terry, B.A.Hons., M.A.; painter of abstract art in oils on canvas/paper, also photography and glass; Chair: British Art and Design Assoc.; Founder: Arena Studios, Liverpool; Dean/Head of Faculty Art & Design, Liverpool (1986-91); 1992 British Council visiting Professor of Fine Art: Hungarian Academy, Budapest; *b* Liverpool, 25 Mar., 1948. *m* Angela. one *s.* one *d. Studied:* Liverpool Art College (1972-75), Liverpool University (1995-97). *Exhib:* one-man shows: Acme London (1976), Air London (1981), Harris Preston (1984), Blom & Dorn, N.Y. (1984), Laing Newcastle (1989), Merkmal Liverpool (1993), New Millennium St. Ives (1997); group shows: New Contemporaries (1976), Sotheby's Fine Art prize Chester (1980), European Artists Stuttgart (1981), Contemporary Arts Soc. (1991-93), John Moores Liverpool (1991), Stroud House Gallery (1998), New Millennium Gallery, St. Ives (1996-2000), International Art Consultants, London (1998-2000). *Work in collections:* many corporate and private collections in Europe and U.S.A., including Sainsbury, Bosch, Panasonic, B.B.C., A.O.N., Welsh National and many others. *Publications:* "Her Revealing Dress" illustrations, Quartet London (1986), cover Collins "Chopin" concertos (1992), cover for Edmund White's "States of Desire" (Penguin 1984). Reviews, media coverage: Studio International, The Guardian, Time

Out, Art Scene U.S.A., B.B.C. World News, Art Review, Art World U.S.A., The TUBE, The Independent, Granada T.V., B.B.C. T.V., Artists Newsletter, etc. *Signs work:* see appendix. *Address:* Studio: 47 Warren Drive, Wallasey CH45 0JP.

DUFORT, Antony, M.A. (1975), Dip.A.D. (1974) Chelsea School of Art; sculptor, painter and portrait painter; *b* Belfast, 12 June, 1948. *Educ:* Ampleforth College, New College Oxford. *Studied:* Central School of Art (1971) under Norman Ackroyd, Winchester School of Art (1971) under John Bellany, Chelsea School of Art (1972-74) under Norman Blamey, painting; (1974-75) under Dick Hart, printmaking. *Exhib:* R.A., N.E.A.C., R.W.S., R.O.I., R.B.A., R.P.; one-man shows: St. Catherine's College, Oxford (1971), Arts Theatre, London (1981), Leighton House Museum (1988), Maas Gallery (1990), Artbank Gallery, Glasgow (1993), Knöll Gallery, Basel (1994), Milne & Moller, London (1997). *Work in collections:* Eton College, Brooks' Club, Hard Rock Cafe, Los Angeles, M.V.E.E. Chobham, Oriel College, Oxford, London Oratory School (bronze Virgin and Child) (1995), 'Miner's Memorial', Cinderford Triangle, Forest of Dean Glos. (monumental bronze) (2000), Cardinal Basil Hume (sculpture) Ampleforth College, Yorks, M.C.C. at Lords ground, monumental bronze of fast bowler (2001). *Publications:* wrote and illustrated: Ballet Steps, Practice to Performance, Clarkson N. Potter, N.Y. (1985), paper back edition, Hodder & Stoughton (1993). *Signs work:* "Antony Dufort" or "Dufort." *Address:* 69 Streatham Hill, London SW2 4TX.

DUGDALE, Mary, Distinction Adv. Art (Leeds), Dip. U.S.W.A., U.W.S.; painter in pastel, oil, water-colour; art teacher, Girls' Schools, Burnley; Past President, U.S.W.A., Com., U.W.S.; *b* Burnley, Lancs., 15 July, 1921. *m* Dr. N. Dugdale (decd.). *Educ:* Burnley High School for Girls. *Studied:* Burnley College of Art, Belfast College of Art, City of Leeds Training College. *Exhib:* Five solo exhbns., many group shows, R.U.A., Laing, London. *Commissions:* portraits of many public figures, including Lord Eames, Archbishop of Armagh. *Publications:* book cover for husband's last book (1997). *Clubs:* local art. *Address:* 16 Massey Park, Belfast, BT4 2JX.

DULEY, Helen Elizabeth, B.A., A.S.G.F.A.; painter of Australian wildlife and birds in watercolour and mixed media collage; imaginative art in oil and mixed media; drawing tutor, Morley College, London; *b* Bairnsdale, Australia, 18 Sep., 1949. *m* John. one *s. Educ:* La Trobe University, Australia (1971). *Studied:* Mongoong Darwung, with the Miriwong (traditional Aboriginal group), Western Australia. *Exhib:* U.A., S.G.F.A., various galleries in London, Great Britain, Australia, and New Zealand (solo shows). *Work in collections:* nationally and internationally, Japan, Middle East, Australia, New Zealand, Brazil, Poland and Russia. *Commissions:* nationally and internationally. *Signs work:* "HD" or "H Duley." *Address:* 12 Ann Moss Way, London SE16 2TL. *Email:* heduley@hotmail.com

DUNBAR, Lennox, A.R.S.A. (1990); artist in drawing, painting and printmaking; Lecturer in Charge of Printmaking, Grays School of Art, Aberdeen; *b* Aberdeen, 17 May, 1952. *m* Jan Storie. two *s.* one *d. Educ:* Aberdeen Grammar School. *Studied:* Grays School of Art, Aberdeen (1969-74). *Exhib:* New Scottish Prints (1983, N.Y. and touring U.S.A.), Bradford Print Biennale (1984), Cleveland Drawing Biennale (1989), Intergrafik, Berlin (1990), International Print Biennale Cracow Poland

(2000), and many group exhbns. national and international. *Work in collections:* Aberdeen, Paisley, Middlesbrough A.Gs., Portland Museum, Oregon, U.S.A., B.B.C., Mobil Oil, Royal Scottish Academy, Contemporary Art Soc., etc. *Signs work:* "Dunbar" or "L.R. Dunbar." *Address:* West Denmore, Auchnagatt, Ellon, Grampian AB41 8TP. *Email:* l.dunbar@rqu.ac.uk

DUNCAN, Clive Leigh, F.R.B.S. (1983), R.B.A. (1984), N.D.D. (1966); sculptor; Principal lecturer and Head of Sculpture, London Guildhall University, Sir John Cass Faculty of Art (1973-93); President, Thomas Heatherly Educational Trust (1974-94); *b* London, 1944. *m* Janet McQueen, painter. one *s.* one *d. Educ:* John Colet School, Wendover. *Studied:* High Wycombe College of Art (1961-64), Camberwell School of Art (1964-66 under Sidney Sheppard), City and Guilds School of Art (1966-68 under James Butler, R.A.). *Exhib:* R.A., R.B.A., Guildhall, London, G.I., Nicholas Treadwell, Portland Sculpture Pk., Playhouse Gallery, Harlow. *Work in collections:* Britain, Spain, U.S.A. *Signs work:* "DUNCAN." *Address:* Holme Cottage, Shiplake, Henley on Thames, Oxon. RG9 3JS.

DUNCAN, Jean, R.U.A., U.S.W., D.A. (Edin.) 1955, Advanced Dip. printmaking University of Ulster (1981); artist in painting and printmaking; Hon. Director, Seacourt Print Workshop; *b* Edinburgh, 27 Dec., 1933. *m* Roderick. two *s.* two *d. Studied:* Edinburgh College of Art (William Gillies, Leonard Rosoman), University of Ulster (David Barker). *Exhib:* solo shows: Guiness Gallery, Dublin, One Oxford St. Gallery, Belfast, Waterfront Hall, Belfast, Hillsboro Fine Art, Dublin. *Work in collections:* Arts Council of N.I., U.C.D. Dublin, U.T.V. Belfast, Northern Bank, A.I.B. Bank, Dept. of Arts, Culture and the Gaeltacht, Irish National Self-portrait collection, Office of Public Works, Dublin, Limerick University, Dundee City A.G. *Clubs:* Artists Assoc. of Ireland. *Address:* 15 Rugby Court, Belfast, N.I. BT7 1PN. *Email:* jeaniduncan@hotmail.com

DUNCAN, Terence Edward, artist in oil and water-colour; specialist in display service for museums and personal collections; *b* Harpenden, Herts., 17 Aug., 1947. *Educ:* Manland Secondary Modern, Harpenden. *Studied:* St. Albans School of Art; Harpenden Art Centre. *Exhib:* St. Albans Gallery (1971), Amateur Artists' Exhbn., London (1967), Batchwood Hall, St. Albans. *Publications:* article, Hertfordshire Countryside; woodwork projects Guild of Mastercraftsmen; Traditional Woodworking Tools (Eddington Press, 1989). Lecturing on: woodwork, Oaklands College, Harpenden (1993-97), picture framing, Oaklands College Hatfield Campus (1993-98), antique furniture restoration, Stanmore College, Middx. (1996-98). Teaching own workshop. *Signs work:* "Terry" with date. *Address:* The Manse, The Village, Westbury-on-Severn, Gloucs. GL14 IPA.

DUNCE, Brian Redvers, P.S. (1992); painter and draughtsman in all media; assoc. senior lecturer, Middlesex University, Heatherley School of Fine Art, the Yehudi Menuhin Music School; *b* Godalming, 29 Apr., 1937. *m* Veronica. one *d. Studied:* Guildford School of Art, Salisbury School of Art, Reading University, under Jack Rodway, John Kashdan, Peter Startup. *Exhib:* major galleries in U.K., France, Germany, Switzerland, U.S.A. *Work in collections:* Royal Brunei Collection, V.& A. Prints and Drawings, McColls, Price Waterhouse, English Trust. *Signs work:* "Brian Dunce." *Address:* The Studios, Wonersh Court, The Street, Wonersh, Guildford,

Surrey GU5 0PG. *Email:* b.dunce@mdx.ac.uk

DUNHAM, Susan, Curator, Doll Museum of Oregon, Mem. U.F.D.C., Mem. O.D.A.C.A.; artist, designer and doll maker in porcelain buisque; Owner, Dunham Arts, designer of artist original dolls; *b* Portland, Oregon, 6 Aug., 1943. *m* Jack Dunham, Jr., D.M.D. two *s. Educ:* Grants Pass, Oregon High School. *Studied:* University of Oregon (1983-85, Paul Buckner). *Exhib:* U.F.D.C. National Doll Convention (1983), Convention of Dolls, Victoria, Australia (1985). *Work in collections:* Ruth Doll Museum, China; Favel Museum, Klamath Falls, Oregon; Doll Castle Museum, N.J.; Jimmy Carter Library Collection, Ga.; Yokohama Doll Museum, Japan. *Clubs:* Eugene Doll, O.D.A.C.A. *Signs work:* "SUSAN Dunham" hand printed. *Address:* 36429 Row River Rd., Cottage Grove, Oregon 97424.

DUNLOP, Alison M., B.A.(Hons.) (1980), R.S.W. (1990); Greenshield Foundation award (1982, 1986); painter in water-colour, oil; President, S.A.A.C.; *b* Chatham, Ontario, Canada, 24 Mar., 1958. *m* R.F. Hood. *Studied:* University of Western Ontario, London (1976-78), L'Ecole des Beaux-Arts, Besançon, France (1978-79), University of Guelph, Canada (1979-80), Edinburgh College of Art (1982-83). *Exhib:* Canadian Soc. of Painters in Water-colours, Gallerie Rochon, Toronto, R.S.W., S.A.A.C., Scottish Gallery, Thackeray Gallery, Kingfisher Gallery, Bruton Gallery. *Work in collections:* Canada, U.S.A., G.B. *Signs work:* "DUNLOP" and year. *Address:* Croft Cottage, Crichton, By Pathhead, Midlothian EH37 5UZ.

DUNN, Alfred, A.R.C.A. (1961); artist; *b* Wombwell, Yorks, 4 Oct., 1937. *Educ:* Wath-upon-Dearne Grammar School. *Studied:* Royal College of Art (1959-61). *Exhib:* Galerie Buchhandlung Claus Lincke, Dusseldorf (1976), Monika Beck Gallery, Hamburg (1976, 1993), Redfern Gallery, London (1965, 1966, 1969, 1971, 1975, 1978, 1983, 1993), L'Umo del Arte, Milan (1971), Atlantis Gallery (1982), Galarie Julia Philippi, Heidelberg (1994); Das Druckgraphisce work retrospective 70er bis 90er Jahre (1944). *Work in collections:* Manchester City A.G., Cadillac Co., Houston, General Hardware Manufacturing Co., New York, Monika Beck Gallery, Germany, L'Umo del Arte, Milan, Yorkshire Sculpture Park, V. & A., Arts Council, London. *Commissions:* Concourse - Macau Ferry Terminal, Hong Kong; Hotel Victoria, Hong Kong; 574nd Dorothy Weinstein, New York, U.S.A. *Signs work:* "Alf Dunn." *Address:* Little Moss Farm, Trawden, nr. Colne, Lancs. BB8 8PR.

DUNN, Anne, painter, all mediums; *b* London, 4 Sept., 1929. *m* (1) Michael Wishart, 1950. one *s.* (2) Rodrigo Moynihan, 1960. one *s. Studied:* Chelsea, Academie Julian, Paris. *Exhib:* one-man shows, Leicester Galleries (8); Redfern Gallery, London; Fischbach Gallery, N.Y.(8); Philadelphia; Ville de Paris (2); Gallery 78, Federicton, Canada (2); many group shows worldwide, R.A. (1978-93). *Work in collections:* Arts Council, M. of W., Carlisle City A. G., Columbus Gallery of Fine Arts, U.S., Beaverbrook A.G., N.B., Financial Times Inc. G.B., Commerce Bankshares, Kansas City, Mo., Amerada Hess Corp. N.Y., Xerox Corp. N.Y., Chemical Bank N.Y., Bank of Nova Scotia, Canada, New Brunswick Provincial Art Bank, Canada, The Art Centre, University of New Brunswick, Canada. *Commissions:* numerous, portraits, book illustrations, book jackets. *Publications:* Editor, Art and Literature (1964-68). *Clubs:* W.I.A.C. *Signs work:* "Anne Dunn." *Address:* Domaine de St. Esteve, Lambesc, B.D.R. 13410, France.

DUNN, Philip, Dip.A.D. (Fine Art) (1968), A.T.C. (1969); painter/printmaker in acrylic, oil, gouache, screenprinting; Mem. Fiveways Artists' Open House since 1990; *b* London, 26 May, 1945. *m* Carole-Anne White. *Educ:* Chiswick Grammar School, London. *Studied:* Twickenham College of Technology (1964), Hornsey College of Art (1964-68), Brighton College of Art (1968-69). *Exhib:* many including London, N.Y., Brighton, Bath, Cheltenham, also twenty solo exhbns. since 1968. Exhib. exclusively through Window Gallery, Brighton since 1982. *Work in collections:* Brighton Centre. *Clubs:* Sussex Arts. *Signs work:* "Philip Dunn." *Address:* c/o Window Gallery, 59 Ship St., Brighton, E. Sussex BN1 1AE.

DUNNE, Berthold, Mem. Water-colour Soc. of Ireland (1951), Member Artists Association of Ireland; artist in water-colour; *b* Dublin, 21 Sept., 1924. *m* Barbara Kelly. two *d. Educ:* Christian Brothers Schools, Synge Street. *Studied:* National College of Art, Dublin, under John Keating, P.R.H.A., and Maurice MacGonigal, R.H.A. (1946-51). *Exhib:* R.H.A., Oireachtas Art Exhbn., Water-colour Soc. of Ireland. *Work in collections:* Self-portrait in the National Self-Portrait Collection; one painting in Water-colour Soc. of Ireland Coll.; University of Limerick; water-colour "Low Tide Howth" acquired by Office of Public Works, Dublin. *Signs work:* "Berthold," see appendix. *Address:* Goa, 29 Shrewsbury Rd., Shankill, Co. Dublin, Ireland.

DUNSTAN, Bernard, R.A. (A.R.A. 1959: Trustee 1990-95), N.E.A.C., R.W.A. (President 1980-84); painter in oil and pastel; *b* 19 Jan., 1920. *m* Diana Armfield, R.A. three *s. Educ:* St. Paul's School. *Studied:* Byam Shaw School, Slade School of Fine Art. *Exhib:* R.A., etc., one-man exhbns. at Roland Browse & Delbanco, Agnew's, etc. *Work in collections:* Bristol, Rochdale, Coventry, National Gallery of New Zealand, London Museum, National Portrait Gallery, Royal Collection, Contemporary Art Soc., Arts Council, etc. *Commissions:* many portrait commissions. *Publications:* Painting Methods of the Impressionists, The Paintings of Bernard Dunstan (1993), ed. Ruskin's Elements of Drawing. *Clubs:* Arts. *Signs work:* "B.D." *Address:* 10 High Park. Rd., Kew, Surrey TW9 4BH.

DURANTY, Charles Henry, artist in water-colour; *b* Romford, Essex, Feb., 1918. *m* Vivian Marguerite. *Educ:* St. Lawrence College, Ramsgate Kent. *Exhib:* Leicester Galleries, Roland, Browse & Delbanco, New Grafton, Mercury, Heal's, Zwemmers, Medici, Thackeray Gallery, London; outside London: Ashgate, Farnham, Rye Art Gallery, Sussex, Brighton Art Gallery, Sussex, Guildford House and Reid's Gallery, Guildford, Westgate Gallery, Winchester, Phoenix Gallery, Lavenham, Blakesley Gallery, Northamptonshire; abroad: Johannesburg, S.A., Galerie Racines, Brussels. *Publications:* Audition (poetry). *Signs work:* "Charles Duranty." *Address:* Blue Horses, Levylsdene, Merrow, Guildford, Surrey GU1 2RT.

DURBIN, Eleanor Mary, B.A. (Hons.) (1972), M.Phil. (1984); artist/teacher in painting in acrylic, gouache, water-colour, printmaking: etching, woodcut; Head of Art Dept., Guildford High School; *b* London, 11 June, 1949. *m* Martin Henley. one *s.* one *d. Educ:* Twickenham County School, Middx. *Studied:* Hornsey College of Art (1967-68), Leeds University (1972) B.A. Hons., (1984) M. Phil. Fine Art. *Exhib:* Cleveland Drawing Biennale (1975, 1977); Chenil Galleries, Young British Printmakers (1978); Printmakers Council National Touring exhbn. (1979); R.W.S.,

Bankside Gallery, Contemporary Water-colours (1983); Tradescant Museum of Garden History (1986); National Print Exhbn. Mall Galleries (1999, 2000). *Signs work:* "Eleanor Durbin." *Address:* 89 Park Rd., Teddington, Middx. TW11 0AW.

DURBIN, Leslie, C.B.E. (1976), L.V.O. (1943), Hon. LL.D. (Cambridge) 1963; silversmith; liveryman of Worshipful Company of Goldsmiths (1943); *b* Fulham, London, 21 Feb., 1913. *m* Phyllis Ginger, R.W.S. one *s*. one *d. Commissions:* Altar plate for Guildford Cathedral (1938); principal part in making Stalingrad Sword to Prof. R.M. Gleadowe's design (1943); R.A.F. (1941-1945); Regional variants of £ coin design (1983); Coventry Cathedral; Smithsonian Institution, Washington D.C.; St. George's Chapel, Windsor. Apprenticeship and journeyman with late Omar Ramsden (1929-1938). *Address:* 298 Kew Rd., Richmond, Surrey TW9 3DU.

DURRANT, Roy Turner, N.D.D. (1952), F.R.S.A. (1953), F.F.P.S., N.E.A.C. (1985); painter; *b* Lavenham, Suffolk, 4 Oct., 1925. *m* Jean, née Lyell. four *s. Educ:* Camberwell School of Art (1948-52); served in Suffolk Regt. (1944-47). *Exhib:* R.A., Artists of Fame and Promise (Leicester Galleries), London Group, N.E.A.C., etc.; about thirty one-man exhbns. in London and provinces including: Beaux Arts Gallery (1950), Artists' International Assoc. Gallery (1953, 1957, 1969), Roland, Browse and Delbanco (1954), Grabowski Gallery (1959), Loggia Gallery (1973, 1975, 1981, 1984), Galerie of M.A. Lausanne (1988), Belgrave Gallery, London (retrospective) 1991. *Work in collections:* Impington Village College, Cambs.; Sirrell Collection, C.W.A.C.; City Museum and A.G., Gloucester; Leeds University; Linton Village College, Cambs.; Leicester Educ. Dept., Grammar School, Ashby-de-la-Zouch; Tate Gallery, London; Museum and A.G., Luton; Graves A.G., Sheffield; Dept. of Biochemistry, Cambridge University; British Rail (Sealink); Usher Gallery, Lincoln; Imperial War Museum, London; Bury St. Edmunds Town Council; City of Bradford A.G.; Southampton A.G.; Carlisle A.G.; Kettles Yard Collection, Cambridge University; Holywell Manor, Oxford; Bertrand Russell Foundation, Nottingham; Castle Museum, Norwich; University of Adelaide, Australia; Western Australia A.G., Perth; University of Mass., Amherst, U.S.A.; Beecroft A.G., Westcliff-on-Sea, Essex; G.M.A., Rio de Janeiro; Worthing A.G.; Museum of Art, Hove; R.A.F. Museum, Hendon; 8th Air Force Museum, Barkside, Louisiana, U.S.A. Work in many private collections. *Publications:* A Rag Book of Love, poems (Scorpion Press, 1960). *Signs work:* see appendix. *Address:* 38 Hurst Pk. Ave., Cambridge CB4 2AE.

DU TOIT, Susanne, B.A.F.A., M.F.A.; artist in oil, etching; *b* S. Africa, 5 Mar., 1955. *m* Pieter. two *s.* two *d. Studied:* University of Pretoria, Massachusetts College of Art. *Exhib:* S. Africa, U.S.A., England. Work in collections internationally. *Address:* Le Bosquet, Wellingtonia Ave., Crowthorne RG45 6AF. *Email:* susannedt@hotmail.com

DUVAL, Dorothy Zinaida, mem. U.A. (1962), F.B.A. (1963-78); gold medal, Accademia Italia (1980); silver medal, Paris Salon (1959), art merit, Stock Exchange Art Soc., (1969, 1973, 1981, 1986); oil painter, teacher of art; *b* Ipplepen, Newton Abbot, Devon, 26 Sept., 1917. *Educ:* Bedford Park High School. *Studied:* Slade School. *Exhib:* R.A., R.P., N.E.A.C., R.B.A., R.O.I., R.Scot.A., U.A., R.S.M.A. (1987, 1990), Paris Salon, Galerie Vallombreuse, Biarritz (1976) awarded Dip. of

Merit (1986); one-man shows: Saffron Gallery, Saffron Waldon, Broadstairs Library (1978), Margate Library (1979), Westminster Gallery U.A. exhbn. annually (1962-97). *Work in collections:* Grenadier Guards, H.Q., (Harry Nicholls, V.C.). *Signs work:* "D. Z. Duval." *Address:* 166 Percy Ave., Kingsgate, Broadstairs, Kent CT10 3LF.

DYNEVOR, Lucy (née Rothenstein), painter and formally conservator of works of art; *b* Sheffield, 1934. *m* Lord Dynevor; (divorced). one *s.* three *d. Educ:* The Old Palace, Mayfield, Sussex. *Studied:* Ruskin School of Fine Art in Oxford and conservation of art with Dr. Helmuth Ruhemann. *Exhib:* one-man shows: University College of Swansea, New Grafton Gallery, London (1991); mixed shows include Crane Kalman Gallery (1995). *Signs work:* "L.D." or "Lucy Dynevor." *Address:* Beauforest House, Newington, Oxon. OX10 7AG.

DYRENFORTH, Noel, artist in batik; *b* London, 17 June, 1936. one *s. Educ:* St. Clement Danes, London; C.A.C. Bursary (1977); Craftsmen-in-residence Arts Victoria '78, Toorak State College; study/travel in U.S.A., Indonesia, India, China. *Studied:* Goldsmiths' College of Art, University of London, Central School of Art, London. *Exhib:* one-man shows: 1965-90: Cambridge, London, Coventry, Bradford, Loughborough, Oxford, Nottingham, L.A. (U.S.A.), Lincoln, Hull, Halifax, Melbourne (Australia), Bremen and Cologne (Germany), Banbury, Tokyo (Japan), Indonesia, Guizhou University, China (1990), over 100 mixed exhbns. *Work in collections:* V. & A., and six others. *Publications:* Batik with Noel Dyrenforth by J. Houston (Orbis Publications, London); The Technique of Batik by Noel Dyrenforth (Batsford Publishing Co. 1988), new paperback issue (1997). *Address:* 11 Shepherds Hill, Highgate, London N6 5QJ.

DYSON, Douglas Kerr, A.R.C.A. (1949); painter and draughtsman; lecturer (retd.), Department of Visual Studies, Faculty of Art and Design, Manchester Polytechnic; *b* Halifax, 11 Dec., 1918. *m* Sylvia Varley. one *s. Educ:* Royds Hall Grammar School, Huddersfield. *Studied:* Huddersfield School of Art (1935-39), R.C.A. under Gilbert Spencer and Rodrigo Moynihan (1946-49). *Exhib:* R.A., Manchester Academy. *Work in collections:* Manchester Education Committee, Manchester City Art Gallery; Co-operative Insurance Society; private collections. *Signs work:* "Dyson." *Address:* 32 Broomfield La., Hale, Cheshire WA15 9AU.

E

EAMES, Angela, B.A.Hons., H.D.F.A., M.A.(Computing in Art and Design); artist/lecturer in drawing/electronic media; *b* Malmesbury, Wilts., 28 May, 1951. *m* Bill Watson. *Educ:* Woking County Grammar School. *Studied:* Bath Academy of Art (1971-74, Michael Kidner), Slade School of Art (1974-76, Tess Jaray, Noel Forster), Middlesex University (1991-92, John Lansdown). *Exhib:* widely, including London, Berlin, Linz, Bratislava and the U.S.A. Work commissioned and in private collections. Lectures: Associate Senior Lecturer in Computer Aided Studies, University of

Wolverhampton. *Signs work:* "A. Eames." *Address:* 15 Chapter Rd., Kennington, London SE17 3ES.

EARLE, Donald Maurice, A.T.D., D.A.E., M.Phil., Ph.D., F.R.S.A.; artist; taught art in variety of secondary schools (1951-88); *b* Melksham, Wilts., 15 Aug., 1928. *m* Jennifer Mary Isaac. one *s.* one *d. Educ:* Trowbridge (Wilts.) Boys' High School. *Studied:* W. of England College of Art, Bristol (1944-47, 1949-51). *Exhib:* N.E.A.C., R.W.S., R.W.A., R.B.S.A., Eastern Arts, Artists in Essex, Colchester Art Soc., Gainsborough House Print Workshop, and one-man shows in public galleries. *Work in collections:* work in private and public collections in Britain and France. *Signs work:* "D. M. Earle." *Address:* 50 Maltese Rd., Chelmsford, Essex CM1 2PA.

EASTON, Arthur Frederick, Surrey Dip. (1964), R.O.I. (1979), N.S. (1980); Dip. of Merit for Painting, University of Arts, Italy (1982); Pres. Reigate Soc. of Artists; artist in oil and water-colour, art teacher; *b* Horley, Surrey, 9 Feb., 1939. *m* Carolle. three *d. Studied:* Reigate School of Art and Design (1961-64). *Exhib:* R.A., R.O.I., R.B.A., N.S., R.P., N.E.A.C.; 20 one-man shows; 14 shared shows; 36 mixed shows. Prize winner Upper St. Gallery (1973), Hunting Art Prize exhbn. (1990), International Arts Fair, Olympia (1991). *Work in collections:* Museum of British Labour. *Publications:* work repro.: The Artist, Quarto Publishing, Leisure Painter; posters, Ikea of Sweden; greetings cards, Les Editions Arts et Images du Monde. *Clubs:* Reigate Soc. of Artists. *Signs work:* "A. Easton." *Address:* 4 Winfield Grove, Newdigate, Surrey RH5 5AZ.

EASTON, Bella, Postgraduate Diploma (2000), B.A. (Hons.) (1993), Fine Art painting; B.Tec. Nat. Dip. (1990) Art and Design; painting in oil, printmaker in etching and silkscreen; *b* Epsom, Surrey, 28 Dec, 1971. *m* Daniel Wray. two *s. Studied:* Suffolk C.F.E. (1988-90), Winchester School of Art (1990-93), Fellowship in Printmaking, City & Guilds of London Art School (2000-02), Royal Academy of Art (1997-2000). *Exhib:* Panter & Hall, London (2002), Japan (2001), event; John Russell Gallery, Suffolk (2002), 401½ Open Studio (2001), Curwen Gallery, London (2001), Summer Show (2001, 2000, '99, '98), Thompson's Gallery, London ('99), N.E.A.L, London ('98, '97), Discerning' Eye, London ('98). *Work in collections:* M. & G. Ltd., R.W.A., Tesco's, San-Ei Gen F.F.I. (U.K.), B.M.W. (G.B.) Ltd., Rover Group. *Commissions:* Tesco's 'a bag for life'; Rover Group Motor Show. *Publications:* limited edition books: English Fish in Foreign Lands, Japan (2001), Alf'n'Betty, (1998), Royal Academy Summer Exhibition illustrated catalogue (2001), R.A. Magazine (June 2000 issue), Royal Academy greeting card published by Canns Down Press. Awards: Japan 2001 subsidy (2000), R.O.S.L. Arts travel scholarship (2001), MacFarlane Walker Trust (2000), David Murray Prize (2000), The Gen Foundation for research in Japan (2000), The Worshipful Company of Painters/Stainers ('97-'00), Lever Hulme Scholarship, ('97-'00), M&G Purchase Prize, ('98), R.W.A. – Bursary, ('98), etc. *Signs work:* "Bella Easton." *Address:* 33 Jansen Walk, Battersea, London SW11 2AZ. *Email:* bella.easton@virgin.net

EASTON, David William, R.I. (1985), N.D.D. (1956), B.Ed. (1976); painter in water-colour, pastel, acrylics, gouache; *b* Leicester, 29 Aug., 1935. *m* Shirley. two *s.* one *d. Educ:* Wyggeston School, Leicester. *Studied:* Leicester College of Art (1952-56). *Exhib:* R.A., P.S., R.I., and many galleries throughout the U.K. *Publications:*

Watercolour Flowers (Batsford, 1993), and Watercolour Inspirations (Batsford, 1997), both re-issued in paperback (2001). *Signs work:* "David Easton." *Address:* 9 Evington La., Leicester LE5 5PQ.

EASTON, Frances, 1st Class Dip. (Florence, 1960); painter of landscapes, nudes and still life in oil; *b* Kenya. *m* Keith Stainton. three s- *s.* three s- *d. Educ:* Wycombe Abbey. *Studied:* Accademia di Belle Arti, Florence (1957-60, Prof. Giovanni Colacicchi). *Exhib:* one-man shows: London, Paris, Rome, most F.B.A. socs., Paris Salon (1977), Laing Competition (1986), Venice - Treviso (award). *Work in collections:* U.K., France, Canada. *Commissions:* Kennedy Inst., London (Founder's portrait); Suffolk/W. Germany 'Twinning' landscape of Gainsborough's birthplace. *Clubs:* Hesketh Hubbard Art, Hurlingham, The Arts. *Signs work:* "Frances Easton (Stainton)." *Address:* 5 Chelsea Studios, 410 Fulham Rd., London SW6.

EASTON, Shirley, S.W.A. (1988-92), N.D.D. (1956), A.T.D. (1957); painter in water-colour and acrylic; *b* Leicester, 28 Apr., 1935. *m* David Easton, R.I. two *s.* one *d. Educ:* Gateway Girls' School, Leicester. *Studied:* Leicester College of Art (1952-57, D.P. Carrington). *Exhib:* R.A. (1986), R.I. (1985-2001), S.W.A. (1988, 1990, 1991). *Signs work:* "Shirley Easton." *Address:* 9 Evington La., Leicester LE5 5PQ.

EASTON, Timothy, Heatherley's Scholarship, London (1966), Elizabeth Greenshields Memorial Award, Montreal (1973); Winston Churchill Travelling Fellowship (1996); painter in oil on canvas, sculptor in bronze; *b* 26 Aug., 1943. *m* Christine Darling. two *d. Educ:* Christ College, Brecon. *Studied:* Kingston School of Art (1960-64), Heatherley School of Art (1966-67). *Exhib:* Chicago, Kansas, Los Angeles, Washington, New York and various Art Expos in America between 1968 and 1987; London and provinces from 1970 onwards; Germany, Luxembourg and Jersey 1984-1987. *Work in collections:* Hereford City A.G. *Publications:* John Hedgecoe's Nude Photography (Ebury Press, 1984), Timothy Easton, Oil Painting Techniques (Batsford, 1997). *Signs work:* "Timothy Easton" or "Easton." *Address:* Bedfield Hall, Bedfield, Woodbridge, Suffolk IP13 7JJ.

EASTOP, Geoffrey Frank, N.D.D. (1951), A.T.D. (1952), F.S.D.C. (1979); lecturer, potter; *b* London, 16 Jan., 1921. *m* Patricia Haynes. three *s.* one *d. Educ:* St. Olave's Grammar School. *Studied:* Goldsmiths' College (1949-52); Academie Ranson, Paris (1952-53). *Exhib:* V. & A., London (1983-95), Stuttgart (1982), Cologne (1983), International Ceramics, Holland (1990), Contemporary Ceramics, London (1991) (solo); Touring retrospective: Portsmouth City Museum, Newbury Museum, Holburne Museum, Bath (1992-93), Berkeley Sq. Gallery, London (1995, 1998-99, 2001). *Work in collections:* V. & A., National Museum of Wales, Fitzwilliam Museum, Cambridge, Southampton Museum A.G., Reading Museum, B'ham City Museum, Portsmouth City Museum. *Publications:* 'The Hollow Vessel' (1980), 'Forty years of change in Studio Pottery' (1993), 'Geoffrey Eastop A Potter in Practice' (1999). *Clubs:* Craft Potters' Assoc. of Gt. Britain, S.D.C. *Signs work:* see appendix. *Address:* The Pottery Ecchinswell, Newbury, Berks. RG20 4TT.

EATWELL, David, painter in oil, landscape, abstract and cubism; *Educ:* Hereford High School. *Studied:* self taught. *Exhib:* Lower Nupend Gallery, one man shows - Wood for the Trees, Lees (1996), Recent Paintings (1997, 1998), Recent Paintings - Christmas (1998), 5th Exhibition (1999). His paintings are on permanent exhibition at the Lower Nupend Gallery. *Signs work:* "DAVID EATWELL." *Address:* c/o Lower Nupend Gallery, Cradley, Nr. Malvern, Worcs. WR13 5NP. *Website:* www.gallery-modern-art.com

EAVES, John, A.T.C. (1952); *b* Bristol, 10 Nov., 1929. *m* Cecily Edith. two *s.* two *d. Educ:* Bembridge School, Bembridge, I.O.W. *Studied:* Bath Academy of Art, James Tower (ceramics), William Scott (painting) (1949-52). *Exhib:* throughout G.B., Germany and U.S.A. *Work in collections:* Arts Council of G.B.; City A.G., Bristol; Royal West of England Academy; South West Arts; Victoria A.G., Bath; University of Bath; Prediger, Schwäbisch Gmünd, G.; City of Braunschweig, G.; private collections in G.B., Germany and U.S.A. *Commissions:* mural entitled "Horizons" completed January 2001 for Hotel Barcelona, Exeter. *Publications:* in Henry Cliffe's Lithography (Studio Vista, 1965). Awarded Winston Churchill Travelling Fellowship to U.S.A. (1966), Print and Water-colour Prizes, Westward T.V. Open Competition (1973, 1975), Leverhulme Emeritus Fellowship (1986) to study painter Emil Nolde, 'A Cast of Stones' by Philip Gross 1996 (drawings). *Signs work:* "Eaves '98." *Address:* 2 Belgrave Pl., Bath, Avon BA1 5JL.

ECCLESTON, Harry Norman, O.B.E., P.P.R.E. (1975-89), Hon. R.B.S.A. (1989), R.W.A. (1991), P.R.E. (1975), R.W.S. (1975), R.E. (1961), A.R.E. (1948), A.R.C.A. (1950), A.T.D. (1947), A.R.W.S. (1964), Hon. N.E.A.C. (1996); engraver in all processes; artist in oil and water-colour; artist designer at the Bank of England Printing Works (1958-83); *b* Bilston, Staffs., 21 Jan., 1923. widower. two *d. Educ:* Wednesbury County Commercial College. *Studied:* Birmingham College of Art (1939-42) and R.C.A. (1947-51). *Exhib:* R.E., R.W.S., N.E.A.C., R.B.S.A., etc. *Clubs:* Arts. *Signs work:* "H. N. Eccleston." *Address:* 110 Priory Rd., Harold Hill, Romford, Essex RM3 9AL.

ECCLESTON, Margaret, N.D.D. (1954), A.T.D. (1955), B.A. Hon. Ed. (1955); painter in oil, pastel and watercolour; retired from full time education, now giving private workshops, demonstrations etc.; *b* Worcestershire, 30 Mar., 1934. two *d. Educ:* Holy Trinity Convent, Kidderminster, Worcs. *Studied:* Birmingham College of Art, under Marion Mackay (textile design). *Exhib:* recent exhibs. include - Contemporary Print Show, Barbican Centre, London; Mariners Gallery, Penhaven Gallery, The New Craftsman, Printmakers Gallery, all St. Ives; St. Ives Soc. of Artists, Penwith Printmakers Exhib., St. Ives; solo exhib., Gordes, Provence, France. *Work in collections:* New York and Paris. *Commissions:* private in England and U.S.A. *Publications:* History of Moseley, Birmingham. *Clubs:* Porthmeor Printmakers, St. Ives, Dartmouth Art Soc., St. Ives Soc. of Artists. *Signs work:* "Margaret Eccleston." *Address:* 16 Mount View Terr., Totnes, Devon TQ9 5EB.

EDEN, Max Nigel Byron, N.D.D. (1950), A.T.D. (1951); painter in oil, acrylic, water-colour; *b* St. Helens, Lancs., 12 Nov., 1923. *m* Valerie Currie. one *s.* one *d. Educ:* Cowley School, St. Helens (1928-41), Borough Rd. College, London (1942-43, 1947-48). *Studied:* Liverpool College of Art (1948-51), Ecole des Beaux Arts de Paris (1951-52), Copenhagen Academy (1954-55). *Exhib:* In France, Denmark, England, U.S.A., Canada and Spain. Recent, "View" Liverpool (1999). *Work in collections:* Southport Atkinson Gallery; private collections: Leo and Jilly Cooper, also in Europe, U.K., U.S.A., and Canada. *Signs work:* "Eden." *Address:* 36 Ash St.,

Southport, Merseyside PR8 6JE. *Email:* max.eden@btinternet.com

EDGERTON, Charmian, B.A. (Hons.) (Graphic Design), S.B.A., S.W.A.; painter in pastel; *b* 16 Sept., 1944. *m* Nick Edgerton, psychologist. one *d. Educ:* Hillcourt School, Dublin. *Studied:* Zurich Kunstgeverbe Schule (1961), Dublin (1962, K. McGonigal), Stoke-on-Trent Polytechnic (1967, graphic design/illustration). *Exhib:* Medici (1991), Alresford Gallery (1993), Gallery Artist of John Thompson Gallery and Alresford Gallery, Aldburgh and Albemarle St., assorted Opens, Barry Keene Gallery, Henley, Blackheath Gallery SE3, John Noott Gallery, Broadway, Pheasantry Fine Arts, Headcorn, Kent, 20th Century Gallery, Windsor, John Falle, Jersey. *Publications:* Pastel Painting, and Flowers and Plants Ed. Jenny Rodwell (Cassell, 1993); author, Learn to Draw Flowers (Harper Collins); regular contributor to Leisure Painter magazine, and demonstrator for Rowney's Pastels. *Signs work:* "Charmian" and "C.P.E." *Address:* 13 Camden Row, London SE3 0QA.

EDMONDS, Angela, B.A. Hons. Fine Art (1990), M.A. (1997); artist in mixed media drawing, assemblage, photoworks; part-time lecturer; *b* London, 26 Nov., 1946. *m* Brian. one *s.* one *d. Educ:* Hendon County Grammar School. *Studied:* Watford College of Art (1985-86), University of Herts. (1986-90), Middlesex University (1995-97). *Exhib:* solo shows: Moor Park Mansion (1989), Flower Gallery, London (1991), Harlequin Centre (1992); 'Landmarks', Cyberaxis, curator (2000); The Bull Gallery, Barnet (2001); two-person show: Knapp Gallery, London (1995); group shows: 1988: Camden Art Centre, Wexner Center, U.S.A., R.A.; 1991: Ikon Gallery, B'ham, Conference Centre, Brighton, Business Design Centre; 1994: Arts - Fife Touring; 1995: Leicester City Gallery, Kettles Yard, Cambridge; 1996: Stoke Newington Gallery; 1997: Contact Gallery, Norwich; 1999: Bilston Gallery, Osterley Park (2001); Ferens Gallery, Hull, Maragaret Harvey Gallery (2000). *Work in collections:* Glaxo Plc., Aldenham School, Watford Museum, Capital & Counties Plc., Bushey Museum, Ruskin Museum, and many private collections. *Commissions:* 1989-92: drawings on site - The Harlequin Centre Development. Prizes: 1989: 1st Prize 'Hertfordshire Open' touring, 'Hunting Group Art prizes' touring; 1992: 1st Prize 'Drawings for All' Gainsborough House, touring. *Publications:* awards: Paul Hamlyn 1997, Year of the Artist 2000. *Signs work:* "Angela Edmonds" or not at all. *Address:* 102 Oaklands Ave., Oxhey, Watford, Herts. WD19 4LW.

EDWARDS, Alan C.L., B.A. (Hons.) (1982), P.G.C.E. (1983), A.T.D. (1983), M.Ed. (1990); painter/teacher; Chair N.A.P.A.; *b* 1947. *m* Carmel Wood. two *s.* two *d. Studied:* Laird School of Art (1965-67), Liverpool Polytechnic (1979-83), Liverpool University (1986-90). *Exhib:* Five Artists, Unity Theatre, Liverpool (1981), School of Architecture, Liverpool (1982), Stowells Trophy, R.A. Galleries London (1982), Artists of Wirral, Williamson A.G., Birkenhead (1984), Merseyside Artists 3, Touring Exhbn. (1986-87), N.A.P.A. Annual Exhbn. (1988-01), Theatre Clwyd (1995), Grosvenor Open (2001). *Work in collections:* England, N.Z. and Ireland. *Publications:* Visual Resource Packs for Teachers. *Signs work:* "Alan Edwards." *Address:* 6 Berwyn Boulevard, Bebington, Wirral, Merseyside CH63 5LR.

EDWARDS, Benjamin Ralph, C. & G. Dip. (1972), R.A.S. Cert. (1977), A.T.C.

P/G Goldsmiths' College (1978); painter/etcher in black and white etching, drawing, charcoal and pencil, lecturer; painting tutor P/T City and Guilds Art School, London; *b* London, 11 Dec., 1950. *m* Ylva. one *s. Educ:* St. Christopher School, Letchworth, Herts. *Studied:* pre college with Capt. P.J. Norton, D.S.O., R.N.; City and Guilds Art School (1968-72, Eric Morby), Atelier 17, Paris (1972-73, S.W. Hayter), R.A. Schools (1973-77, Roderick Barret). *Exhib:* R.A. Summer Exhbn. (1977 onwards), Kanagawa Prints, Okohama, Japan (1982-84), R.E. (1969-75). *Work in collections:* V. & A., Wellesley College Library, Mass., Newberry Library, Chicago, Bridwell Library, Dallas, Texas. *Publications:* illustrated, The Four Seasons at Parkgate Cottages (Parkgate Press), A Fox under my Bed (Macmillan). *Signs work:* see appendix. *Address:* The Parkgate Press, 7 Argyle Rd., N. Finchley, London N12 7NU.

EDWARDS, Brigid, B.Sc. (Hons.); artist in water-colour on vellum; *b* London, 16 Feb., 1940. *m* R.J. Edwards. *Educ:* Our Lady of Sion, London, University College, London. *Studied:* Central School of Art (1960-63). *Exhib:* R.H.S., R.B.G. Kew, R.A., Thomas Gibson Fine Art, Beadleston, N.Y., S. H. Ervin, Sydney, Yasuda Kasai Museum of Art, Tokyo. *Work in collections:* Hunt Inst., Carnegie Mellon University, Penn., R.B.G. Kew. *Publications:* illustrated: 'Primula' monograph (Batsford). *Signs work:* "Brigid Edwards" or not at all. *Address:* c/o Thomas Gibson Fine Art Ltd., 44 Old Bond St., London W1X 4HQ.

EDWARDS, John, A.R.B.S.; painter and sculptor; Head of Painting, Sculpture, St. Martin's School of Art (1980-88); *b* London, 3 Mar., 1938. *Studied:* Hornsey School of Art, Leeds University Inst., and L'Cambre Brussels. *Work in collections:* Arts Council, British Council, Belgian Government, C.A.S., C.N.A.A., Govt. Art Collection, Gulbenkian Foundation, Solomon R. Guggenheim Museum, N.Y.C. *Commissions:* Southampton University, Hackney Council, etc. Fellowships: British Council Scholarship Brussels, Winston Churchill Fellowship, Leverhulme Fellowship, London Arts Board, Pollock-Krasner Foundation Grant. *Signs work:* "John Edwards." *Address:* (studio) 52 Isledon Rd., London N7 7LD. *Website:* www.johnedwards-artist.com *Email:* johnedwards@bun.com

EDWARDS, John Colin, R.P., Cert. R.A. Schools; portrait, nude and wildlife painter in oil, pencil, chalk, etc.; *b* Kidderminster, 23 Aug., 1940. *m* Patricia Rose, M.Sc. two *d. Educ:* Sladen School, Kidderminster (1951-53), Stourbridge Art School (1953-55). *Studied:* Pietro Annigoni in Florence; R.A. Schools; E.T. Greenshields Foundation award, Canada (1970, 1972); Silver and Bronze Medallist R.A. Schools; W.W.F. Art Award (1986). *Exhib:* Tate Gallery, N.P.G., R.A., R.P., Windsor Castle. *Work in collections:* H.M. The Queen; Baroness Thatcher, O.M.; Royal Collection, Windsor; Adjutant General's Corps; Royal College of Radiologists; The Law Society; Carpenters Company; Cambridge, Oxford, Birmingham (Aston), Leicester universities, etc. *Commissions:* Rt.Hon. William Hague, M.P.; House of Commons. *Publications:* Tate Gallery, Mitchell Beazley, Collins Publications, etc. *Signs work:* "John Edwards" and "Edwards." *Address:* Chesterville Gallery and Studio, Chester Rd. North, Kidderminster, Worcs. DY10 1TP.

EDWARDS, Sylvia, artist, printmaker, painter in water-colour, oil, acrylic; *b* Boston, Mass. *m* Sadredin Golestaneh. one *s.* two *d. Educ:* Boston public schools. *Studied:* fine art at Massachusetts College of Art, Boston, Mass. (1956-60, Prof.

Lawrence Kupferman), Boston Museum of Fine Arts. *Exhib:* consistently in one-woman and mixed shows and international art expositions; London: Berkeley Sq. Gallery, C.C.A. Gallery and Christopher Hull Gallery; Tokyo, Bankamura, Mitsukoshi Mihonbashi Branch; Osaka, Nii Gallery (1989); Alexandria, Egypt, Alexandria Museum of Fine Arts (1980); Mediterranean Biennale (1980); Munson Gallery, Chatham, Mass. (1992); Morehead Planetarium, Chapel Hill, N.C.; Natalie Knight Gallery, Johannesburg, S.A. (1991); Singapore, Art Base Gallery (sponsored by Citibank, 1989); Bankamura, Tokyo (1991); C.C.A. Gallery Oxford (1996); The Galleria, Boca Grande Florida (2000). *Work in collections:* Tate Gallery, London; Boston University Special Collections; National Museum of Women in the Arts, Washington, D.C.; Alexandria Museum of Women in the Arts; Alexandria Governorate, Egypt; Cape Museum of Fine Arts, Dennis, Mass.; Midwest Museum of American Art, Elkhart, Indiana. *Publications:* 'The Nucleus' narrative book of drawings; 'The Undoing of the Square' 'Painters' Wild Workshop'; Sylvia Edwards 'Works on Hand Cast Paper'; work widely published by U.N.I.C.E.F., Coriander Studios and C.C.A. Galleries, London for limited editions in silkscreen, and the London Art Group for prints and Bruce McGaw graphics; numerous gallery handbooks and catalogues; articles and television talks 'Sylvia Edwards Talks with Mel Gooding'. *Signs work:* "Sylvia Edwards." *Address:* 14 Cadogan Sq., London SW1X 0JU.

EDWARDS, Yvonne Sylvia, S.B.A., C.B.M. (1997) and (2000), S.F.P.; artist in water-colour; *b* S. Australia, 26 Nov., 1942. *m* Malcolm Edwards. two *s. Exhib:* S.B.A. since 1994. *Address:* Lodge Farm, Moot Lane, Dowton, Wilts. SP5 3LN. *Email:* yvonneedwards@totalise.co.uk

EICHLER, Richard W., Professor, holder of "Schiller-Preis" (1969); art writer and critic; *b* Liebenau, Bohemia, 8 Aug., 1921. *m* Elisabeth Eichler (née Mojr). one *s.* six *d. Educ:* Gymnasium at Reichenberg. *Studied:* Vienna, Munich (history of art). *Publications:* Könner-Künstler-Scharlatane (Munich, 1960; 7th ed., 1970), Künstler und Werke (Munich, 1962; 3rd ed., 1968), Der gesteuerte Kunstverfall (Munich, 1965; 3rd ed., 1968), Verhexte Muttersprache (1974), Wiederkehr des Schönen (Tübingen, 1984; 2nd ed. 1985), Unser Geistiges Erbe (1995), Baukultur gegen Formzerstörung (1999) and many papers. *Address:* Steinkirchner Strasse 16, D-81475 München, Bundesrepublik Deutschland.

EISELIN, Rolf, Architect SIA dipl.EPFZ, reg. arch. State of Illinois, U.S.A. and Switzerland; *b* Zürich, 6 Nov., 1925. Architect with Skidmore, Owings & Merrill, Chicago (in team for U.S. Air Force Academy design). *Exhib:* individual show, prints: San Francisco Museum of Modern Art; group shows: architecture: Univ. Zürich; sculpture: Oakland Art Museum; painting: Univ. California; prints: U.S. National Museum, Washington; photography: Musée d'histoire naturelle, Fribourg; Honour Medal, Nat. Exhbn., Jersey City Museum; hon.mention, Photography USA 88, 89. *Work in collections:* San Francisco Museum of Modern Art, Graphik-Sammlung ETH Zürich. *Address:* Rés. La Côte 60, 1110 Morges, Switzerland.

ELDRIDGE, Harold Percy, A.R.C.A. (1950), artist in oil, mural painter; *b* London, 8 June, 1923. one *s.* two *d. Studied:* Camberwell School of Arts and Crafts and R.C.A. (Items of work in Camberwell Book, 1995). *Exhib:* R.A., R.B.A.,

London Group. *Publications:* work in repro.: in The Sketch. Also illustrations, scale models and historical reconstructions for Schools Television Programmes. Taught art at school in Coventry, but now retired. *Address:* 42 Beechwood Ave., Coventry CV5 6QG.

ELFORD, Norman, N.D.D., A.T.D., G.R.A.; artist in oil, acrylic, alkyd; *b* Portsmouth, 6 July, 1931. *m* Dorothy. one *s.* one *d. Educ:* Portsmouth Northern Grammar School. *Studied:* Southern Colleges of Art, Portsmouth (1947-51), Bournemouth (1951-52). *Exhib:* N.R.M. York; Hexagon, Reading; two one-man shows: Stroud Festival, Gloucs.; regular exhbns. G.R.A. Work in private collections. *Commissions:* designs for Royal Doulton and Spode Fine China plates; calendars and greetings cards, fine art marine prints. *Clubs:* G.R.A., President, Portsmouth & Hampshire Art Soc. *Signs work:* "NORMAN ELFORD." *Address:* 36 Torrington Rd., North End, Portsmouth PO2 0TP.

ELGAR, Juliet Jane, B.A. (Hons.) Art/Teaching; painter; arts crafts tutor in drawing and painting, now independent; *b* Wiltshire, 18 Mar., 1942. three *s.* two *d. Educ:* La Retraite Convent, Salisbury, Wilts. *Studied:* Bath Academy of Art under J. Hoskin sculptor, H. Hodgekin and M. Hughes, painters. *Exhib:* Westminster Gallery, London, Arthouse, Richmond, Gallery at Dauntsey's School, Wilts. *Commissions:* various landscape, portrait and design. Would like to be commissioned in aid of environmental charities on 50/50 profit. *Signs work:* "Jane Elgar." *Address:* 22 St. Mary's Grove, Richmond, Surrey TW9 1UY. *Email:* j-elgar@hotmail.com

ELIAS, Ken, B.A. Hons. Fine Art (1969), M.A. Fine Art (1987), R.C.A.; painter in acrylic on paper; Royal Cambrian Academician; *b* Glynneath, West Glamorgan, 9 Nov., 1944. *Studied:* Cardiff College of Art (1965-66, 1985-87), Newport College of Art (1966-69), University of Wales, Cardiff (1969-70). *Exhib:* regularly in solo and group shows in U.K. and abroad. *Work in collections:* National Museum of Wales, National Library of Wales, Arts Council of Wales, Brecknock Museum & Art Gallery and private collections U.K. and abroad. *Clubs:* Welsh Group, R.Cam.A. Watercolour Soc. of Wales. *Address:* 29 Park Ave., Glynneath, West Glamorgan SA11 5DP.

ELLIOTT, J.: see BATES, Joan.

ELLIOTT, Mary E.: see BERESFORD-WILLIAMS, Mary E.

ELLIOTT, Walter Albert, F.B.I.S., L.F.I.B.A., S.G.F.A., P.S., U.A.; artist in pastel, oil, water-colour, acrylic; mem. Academy of Italy, Pres. Ilfracombe Art Soc., mem. International Assoc. of Art; *b* Wembley, 24 Oct., 1936. *m* Beryl Jean (decd.). one *s.* one *d. Educ:* Pinner Grammar School; de Havilland Aero College. *Studied:* Hammersmith Polytechnic, Harrow College of Art. *Exhib:* annually: P.S., S.G.F.A., U.A. (Mall Galleries), Pilton Arts Exhbn., Ilfracombe Art Soc.; Burton Gallery, Bideford (1976), Salon de Paris (1984), Torbay Guild of Artists. Permanent exhbn. of artwork at the Elliott Gallery, Hillsview, Braunton, N. Devon. EX34 9NZ. *Work in collections:* 'The Ascent of Man' (N. Devon Atheneaum 1970-81); Europe, Geneva, Canada, Australia, U.S.A. *Publications:* articles, Spaceflight, British Interplanetary Soc. *Signs work:* "Walter A. Elliott." *Address:* Sollake Studio, Warfield Villas, Ilfracombe, N. Devon EX34 9NZ.

ELLIS, Christine Elizabeth, A.D.B. (1960), A.O.I (1990); landscape and portrait artist in pencil, ink, water-colour, acrylic and oil; illustrator; writer; *b* London, 10 Sept., 1939. *Educ:* Sacred Heart High School. *Studied:* Maria Assumpta College, Kensington (1957-59), Theatre Arts at Rose Bruford College, Kent (1959-60), part-time at Regent St. Polytechnic, Richmond and Putney Schools of Art. *Exhib:* in mixed gallery exhbns. including R.I., R.B.A, Discerning Eye, Pastel Soc., and S.W.A. *Work in collections:* life-size, paper based, illustrative sculpture at Bursledon Brickwork's Museum. *Commissions:* Cover illustrations 1997 Egon Ronay Guides. Landscapes and portraits: Martina Navratilova; All England Club, Wimbledon; Equitable Life, and for private individuals in many countries. Illustrations: St. George's; La Prairie; Keymer Tiles; Wates; Squires. *Publications:* illustrations for "Pull`s Ferry" (Norwich, 1998), B.B.C. short stories for children broadcast (1979-82). Limited edition prints: National Trust Enterprises Chartwell. *Clubs:* mem. F.B.A. *Signs work:* "C.E. Ellis." *Address:* North Cottage, 6 High St., Hampton on Thames, Middx. TW12 2SJ.

ELLIS, Edwina, R.E. (1987), S.W.E. (1984); wood engraver; *b* Sydney, Australia, 14 May, 1946. *m* P.J.N. Ellis. *Educ:* Manly Girls, Sydney. *Studied:* John Ogburn, and National Art School, Sydney. *Exhib:* R.A., R.E., Duncan Campbell (1988-97), Godfrey and Watt (1987-2001), N.S.W. State Library, Australia, Fine Art Soc., London, Ashmolean Museum, Redfern Gallery London. *Work in collections:* V. & A., University Library of California, Australian National Library Canberra, Ashmolean Museum Oxford, Fitzwilliam Museum Cambridge, Art Gallery of N.S.W. Australia, London Transport Museum, Museum of London. *Commissions:* London Transport: 'Art on London Transport' poster (1996). *Publications:* Prigs Seven Virtuous Lady Gardeners (Smith Settle, 1997). *Clubs:* Chelsea Arts. *Signs work:* "E.N. Ellis." *Address:* Rhyd Goch, Ystrad Meurig, Ceredigion SY25 6AJ.

ELLIS, Harold, draughtsman and artist in oil, water-colour, line; *b* Baildon, 10 Apr., 1917. *m* Margaret Lovatt. one *s.* one *d. Educ:* Bradford Grammar School. *Studied:* as apprentice in commercial art studio, Messrs. Field, Sons & Co., Lidget Green, Bradford (1933-39). *Exhib:* Bradford City A.G. *Publications:* work repro.: cartoons, general anonymous commercial work. *Signs work:* "H. Ellis" or "ELLIS." *Address:* 5 Whitelands Cres., Baildon, Shipley, Yorks. BD17 6NN.

ELLIS, John Colin, U.A. (1988), M.B.I.A.T. (1971), M.I.P.D. (1973); artist/architectural illustrator in water-colour, oil, acrylic; artist working mainly on architectural subjects, plus land and town scapes developing into abstract art; design-er/illustrator within retail commercial and residential sectors; *b* Fleetwood, Lancs., 1945. *m* Penny. one *s.* one *d. Educ:* Bailey Secondary, Fleetwood. *Studied:* Blackpool School of Art (1961-67). *Exhib:* one-man shows: N.Wales, Stamford, Peterborough, London. *Publications:* work repro.: housing sale illustration and brochure design. *Clubs:* U.A. *Signs work:* "John C. Ellis." *Address:* The Gallery, Braceborough, Stamford, Lincs. PE9 4NT.

ELLIS, Noel, A.R.C.A. (1948); painter and printmaker; *b* Plymouth, 25 Dec., 1917. *m* Linda Zinger. *Educ:* Sutton High School, Plymouth. *Studied:* Plymouth School of Art, R.C.A. *Exhib:* R.A., R.O.I., R.B.A., N.E.A.C., London Group, Grundy A.G., Blackpool, Plymouth A.G., Works in public and private collections. *Signs work:* "Noel Ellis" (cursive script). *Address:* 95 Bennerley Rd., Battersea,

London SW11 6DT.

ELLIS, Robert, O.N.Z.M. Officer of the N.Z. Order of Merit; Professor Emeritus, Aukland University; *b* Northampton, 2 Apr., 1929. *m* Elizabeth. two *d. Studied:* Northampton School of Art (1943-47), R.C.A. (1949-52). *Exhib:* 50 one-man shows in N.Z., Australia and U.S.A.; group shows in Australia, Canada, Malaysia, India, Japan, England, U.S.A., etc. *Work in collections:* all major N.Z. public collections, National Gallery of Australia, British Foreign Office, N.Z. Arts Council, etc. *Signs work:* "Robert Ellis." *Address:* 23 Berne Pl., Auckland 1310, N.Z. *Email:* robellis@akc.quik.co.nz

ELLIS, William John, F.R.S.A.; artist in oil, water-colour, crayon; author/artist; *b* Rhyl, 21 Sept., 1944. *m* Gaynor Ellis. one *s.* one *d. Educ:* Glyndwr Secondary Modern, Rhyl. *Studied:* Glyndwr Secondary and later under Robert Evans Hughes R.A. *Exhib:* Rhyl Town Hall and Holywell Library. *Publications:* author of Seaside Entertainments 100 Years of Nostalgia; Rhyl in old Picture Postcards; Entertainment in Rhyl and N. Wales (published July 1997). *Clubs:* Clwydian Art Society, Clwyd Assoc. for the Visual Arts, Mem. of Rhyl Liberty Players, Abergele Players, British Music Hall Soc., Manchester Music Hall Soc., Derbys. and Notts. Music Hall Soc. *Signs work:* "B. Ellis." *Address:* 2a Carlisle Ave., Rhyl, Clwyd LL18 3DU.

ELMORE, Pat, R.B.A. (1996); sculptress in stone and wood, also portraits and ceramics; *b* Rugby, 10 Sept., 1937. four *s.* two *d. Exhib:* solo shows, Bampton Arts Centre, Bedford Central Library, Swindon Links Library, Wantage Museum, The Stable Gallery at Green College Oxford; group shows: R.B.A., Mall Galleries, R.W.A., Cheltenham Art Soc., Syon Lodge London, Salammbo Galerie Paris, Gloucester Museum, Jersey (Village Gallery). *Work in collections:* Thamesdown Arts, Abingdon Town Council, The Church Army Exeter, Magdalen College Oxford. Permanent sculpture garden and gallery, and ongoing sculpture tuition at Nutford Lodge. *Address:* Nutford Lodge, Longcot, nr. Faringdon, Oxon. SN7 7TL.

ELPIDA, née Georgiou, B.A.Hons. (1986), M.A. (1990); artist in oil on canvas; *b* London, 23 Sept., 1958. *Educ:* St Marylebone School for Girls. *Studied:* St Martin's School of Art (1983-86), R.A. Schools (1987-90). *Exhib:* R.O.I. at Lloyd's, Royal Overseas League (prizewinner), 'New Generation' Bonham's, R.A. Summer Show (1991) (prizewinner, Guinness award), R.A. Premium Show (Winsor and Newton award), Berlin Academy of Art; one-man shows: Christopher Hull Gallery, Lynne Sterne Gallery, 'The Leicestershire Collection', Leicester, 'East End Open Studios', Acme Studios, London, Whitechapel Open. *Work in collections:* Unilever plc, Guinness Collection. *Signs work:* "Elpida." *Address:* 65 Ellesmere Rd., Chiswick, London W4 3EA.

ELSTEIN, Cecile, M.A., F.R.S.A.; sculptor, bronze, wood, printmaker, screen-print, environmental artist, rope, video; N. W. Arts Bursary Award (1983), 9th British International Print Biennale (1986) prize winner; *b* 8 Feb., 1938. *Educ:* South Africa and U.K. *Studied:* self-directed art education (1958-69), (Catherine Yarrow: ceramics 1965-69), sculpture/printmaking, West Surrey College Art Design (1975-1977), M.A. Manchester Metropolitan University (1996). *Exhib:* internationally. *Work in collections:* private and public collections, e.g. Clare Hall Cambridge, Whitworth Art

Gallery, Manchester, U.K. *Commissions:* portrait sculpture/sculpture in Landscape. *Publications:* Design for Physical Variety, EcoDesign, 111, (3). video – collaborative project with Maureen Kendal. *Clubs:* Landscape and Art Network, M.A.F.A., P.M.S.A., F.R.S.A. *Signs work:* see appendix. *Address:* 25 Spath Rd., Didsbury, Manchester M20 2QT. *Email:* cecile.elstein@talk21.com

EMERY, Edwina, A.R.B.S. (1984); Freeman of Worshipful Company of Goldsmiths (1986); sculptor and designer in chalk, oil and acrylic; retained exclusively by Garrard, the Crown Jewellers, animalier, portrait and design since 1982; *b* Huntingdonshire, 10 May, 1942. divorced. two *s.* two *d. Educ:* Grammar School and privately. *Exhib:* permanently at Garrard, Regent St., Oscar and Peter Johnson Gallery. Work collected by Royalty and Heads of State worldwide, also private collectors. *Commissions:* include prestigious confidential commissions, also racing, polo, portraits Lester Piggott and Willie Shoemaker, many for industry and commerce. *Publications:* Commercial Art in Youth. *Clubs:* The Farmers, Whitehall Court. *Signs work:* see appendix. *Address:* Little Manor, Ibberton, Dorset DT11 0EN.

EMMERICH, Anita Jane (née POLLOK), International member and exhibitor: R.M.S., S.W.A., M.P.S.G.S., M.A.S.F., W.F.M.; miniature painter specializing in contemporary and historical portrait silhouettes in oil on vellum or old ivory, and fine modern abstract oil canvases; the President's Special Commendation Award for all miniature paintings submitted, R.M.S. Exhibition, London (1998), the Master's Award for the Most Outstanding Set of Miniatures at The Llewellyn Alexander Gallery, London (1996), Judges Choice, G.M.A.S., Atlanta, U.S.A. (1997). Individual Member's Award Cerificate, W.F.M., Tasmania (2000), plus numerous awards U.K. and U.S.A.; *b* London, 3 Feb., 1938. *m* W. M. Ernst. two *s. Educ:* Sydenham High School for Girls (G.P.D.S.T.), London. *Studied:* self taught miniature painter. *Exhib:* London, the South East, and various overseas galleries; England, Jersey, N. Ireland, France, Germany, U.S.A., Australia, Japan. *Work in collections:* Work in private collections, R.M.S.Diploma collections, can be seen at the Llewellyn Alexander Gallery, London. *Commissions:* for collectors and private requests. *Publications:* 'R.M.S. 100 Years', work reproduced in Art Magazines. 1993 Contemporary Art Consultant, Diocese of Rochester Kent. Previously mem. of S.M., S.Lm., H.S.F., A.S.M.A. (Q). (T). (N.S.W.)., G.M.A.S. *Signs work:* see appendix. *Address:* The Penthouse, 16 Stonegate, Wye, Ashford, Kent TN25 5DD.

EMSLEY, Kenneth, M.A. (Cantab.), LL.M. (Newcastle), A.C.I.S., F.R.Hist.S., F.R.S.A.; artist in water-colour, pen and ink, author, retd. lecturer, President, Soc. of Miniaturists, President, British Water-colour Soc.; former chairman, Bradford Arts Club; *b* Shipley, 7 Dec., 1921. *m* Nancy Audrey Slee, B.Sc., Dip. Ed. *Educ:* Loughborough College, St. John's College, Cambridge. *Studied:* various schools under Edward Wesson, Arnold Dransfield. *Exhib:* Mall and Bankside galleries, London, Florida, U.S.A., Cartwright Hall, Bradford. *Publications:* Northumbria, Tyneside, Historic Haworth Today, etc. *Signs work:* "K.E." or "K. EMSLEY." *Address:* 34 Nab Wood Drive, Shipley, W. Yorks. BD18 4EL.

ENGLAND, Frederick John, N.D.D., A.T.C. (Lond.), I.A.G., M.F.P.S., Norwegian Scholarship (1960), Medaille d'Argent, Paris Salon (Gold Medal, 1975), Diploma d'Honneur, International Arts Guild, Monte Carlo; painter in oil, lithograph, etching, water-colour; ex-lecturer in painting and design at Leek School of Art; ex Pres. Soc. of Staffordshire Artists; director, England's Gallery, Leek; *b* Fulham, London, 5 Mar., 1939. *m* Sheelagh Jane. *Educ:* Deacons School. *Studied:* Brighton College of Art and Crafts (1956) under Sallis Bonney, R.O.I., R.W.S., Charles Knight, R.O.I., R.W.S., R.T. Cowen, Principal; Hardanger Folkschule, Norway (1960) under Oddmund J. Aarhus; London University (1961) under Ronald Horton. *Exhib:* Paris Salon, Arts Council of N. Ireland, R.B.A., R.I. Summer and Winter Salon, R.B.S.A., Manchester Academy, Bradford Open Exhibition, Trends Free Painters and Sculptors, R.W.A., S.I.A. (travelling shows included). Open Exhibition Stafford, Society of Staffordshire Artists; one-man shows: Galerie Helian, Montreux, England's Gallery, Burlington Gallery, Buxton Schaffer Gallery, Market Drayton, Galerie für Zeitgenössische Kunst, Hamburg, Galerie Bernheim-Jeune, Paris, I.A.G. Monte Carlo, Zilina, Czechoslovakia, Octagon Gallery, Bolton, University of Keele, Gallerie Helion, Montreux, Hüstebro, Denmark. *Work in collections:* Nicholson Institute, Goritz Coll., Fenning Coll., Geneva, City of Stoke-on-Trent Art Gallery. Reviewed work in La Revue Moderne, Les Journal des Jeunes, Boomerang (Paris Salon Edition of One Hundred Young European painters), Dictionnaire des Artists, Repertorium Artis, Dictionnaire International d'Art Contemporain. *Signs work:* "England." *Address:* Ball Haye House, 1 Ball Haye Terr., Leek ST13 6AP Staffs.

EUSTACE, Eric George, H.S. (1991), A.R.M.S. (1993); painter in water-colour and acrylic; *b* Dunstable, 14 Jan., 1925. *m* Edna Roberts. *Studied:* art at Luton College (1953-55). *Signs work:* "Eric G. Eustace." *Address:* 28 Buttercup Close, Dunstable, Beds. LU6 3LA.

EVANS, Bernard, N.D.D. (1954), A.T.D. (1955); artist in oil, water-colour, pastel; Tutor/Director, Mounts Bay Art Centre, Newlyn, Penzance; Chairman, Newlyn Soc. of Artists; *b* Liverpool, 6 July, 1929. *m* Audrey M. Evans. three *s*. two *d*. *Educ:* St. Francis Xavier's Grammar School, Liverpool. *Studied:* Liverpool College of Art, Camberwell School of Arts and Crafts (Martin Bloch, Richard Eurich, R.A.). *Exhib:* Darlington Nottingham, Lincoln, Newlyn, Penzance, London. *Publications:* Drawing Towards the End of a Century. *Clubs:* Penzance Arts. *Signs work:* "Bernard Evans" or "B. Evans" or "B.E." *Address:* Trevatha, Faugan La., Newlyn, Penzance, Cornwall TR18 5DJ.

EVANS, Brenda Jean, B.A.Hons. (1976), R.A.S. (1979), S.W.A. (1986); artist in water-colour; *b* Birmingham, 6 June, 1954. *Educ:* Aldridge Grammar School. *Studied:* Sutton Coldfield School of Art, Loughborough College of Art, R.A. Schools. *Exhib:* R.A. Summer Shows, Highgate Gallery, Tenterden, S.W.A., Grape Lane Gallery, York, Edinburgh, New Grafton Gallery, Business Art Galleries, Singer and Freidlander. *Work in collections:* H.R.H. Princess Michael of Kent, Mr. and Mrs. Ronnie Corbett. *Signs work:* "Brenda Evans." *Address:* 61a Beulah Rd., Walthamstow, London E17 9LG.

EVANS, David Pugh, A.R.C.A. (1965), R.S.W. (1975), R.S.A. (1989); artist in oil and acrylic; *b* Abercarn, Gwent. *Educ:* Newbridge Grammar School, Gwent. *Studied:* Newport College of Art (1959-62, Thomas Rathmell), R.C.A. (1962-65, Prof. Carel Weight). *Exhib:* Fruit Market Gallery, Edinburgh, University of York, Mercury Gallery, London. *Work in collections:* Carlisle A.G., S.A.C., Hunterian

Museum, Glasgow, Glasgow A.G., Royal Scottish Academy, R.A., City A.G., Edinburgh, Aberdeen A.G., Scottish Television. *Signs work:* "D.P. Evans." *Address:* 17 Inverleith Gdns., Edinburgh EH3 5PS.

EVANS, Eurgain, N.D.D. (1958), R.A. Schools Cert. (1961); painter in oil and water-colour; retd. lecturer, Faculty of Art and Design, W. Glamorgan Inst. of Higher Educ., Swansea; *b* Betws y Coed, Gwynedd, 28 Mar., 1936. *Educ:* Llanrwst Grammar School. *Studied:* Wrexham College of Art; R.A. Schools. *Exhib:* Pritchard Jones Hall, Bangor University Wales, London Welsh Assoc. Young Contemporaries, R.A., F.P.S., etc. *Work in collections:* National Museum of Wales, Aberystwyth, and many private collections. *Signs work:* "Eurgain." *Address:* 14 Valley View, Sketty, Swansea SA2 8BG, S. Wales.

EVANS, Garth, sculptor and draughtsman; *b* Cheadle, Ches., 23 Nov., 1934. *m* Leila Philip. one *s. Studied:* Regional College of Art, Manchester, and Slade School. *Work in collections:* Metropolitan Museum, N.Y.; Museum of Modern Art, N.Y.; Tate Gallery; V. & A.; Power Gallery of Contemporary Art, Sydney; Manchester City A.G.; Portsmouth City A.G.; Bristol City A.G.; Contemporary Arts Soc. of G.B. Lives and works in both London and New York. *Signs work:* " Garth Evans." *Address:* 106 North 6th St., Brooklyn, N.Y.11211.

EVANS, Margaret Fleming, D.A., A.T.C., U.A.; portrait painter in oils and pastels, art tutor; teacher in adult education in Kent; *b* Glasgow, 9 Apr., 1952. *m* Malcolm William Evans. one *s. Educ:* Whitehill Senior Secondary School, Glasgow. *Studied:* Glasgow School of Art (1970-74, Dr. David Donaldson, R.P., A. Goudie, R.P., L. Morocco, J. Robertson, A.R.S.A.). *Exhib:* London and S.E. England. *Signs work:* see appendix. *Address:* Larasset, High Halden, Ashford, Kent. TN26 3TY.

EVANS, Marlene Elizabeth, S.W.A. (1990), A.B.W.S. (1987), A.Y.A. (1989); artist of botanical studies and landscapes in water-colour, ink, mixed media; *b* Barking, Essex, 17 Feb., 1937. *m* Lyn Evans (decd.). one *s.* one *d. Educ:* Racecommon Rd. School, Barnsley. *Studied:* Barnsley School of Art (textile design, L.H.H. Glover, A.R.C.A., A.T.D., R. Skinner, A.T.D.). *Exhib:* one-man shows: Cawthorne S.Y. (1990), Ossett, W. Yorks. (1991), annually S.W.A. and B.W.S., also various mixed exhbns. *Signs work:* "M.E. Evans." *Address:* 14 Spencer St., Barnsley, S. Yorks. S70 1QX.

EVANS, Nicholas, R.C.A. (1981); Welsh Arts Council award; self taught artist in oil on board and canvas, and water-colour, sculptor and lecturer; *b* Aberdare, S.Wales. *m* Annie Maud Lambert. two *s.* one *d. Educ:* Junior and Secondary schools. *Exhib:* R.A.; R.C.A.; National Eisteddfodau; N.E.A.C.; Oriel, Cardiff; Browse & Darby; Herbert, Coventry; National Gallery, Bulgaria; Rechlingshausen, Germany; Turner Gallery, Penarth; Bury St. Edmunds; Swansea University; Glynn Vivian, Swansea; York University; Barbican; Chapter Arts; Doncaster A.G. (purchased by Contemporary Art Soc., Tate); MacRoberts Arts Centre; Hayward Gallery; Bede, Jarrow; R.W.A. *Work in collections:* National Museum of Wales, Arts Council of G.B., Welsh Arts Council, Sir Richard Hyde-Parker, Duke of Devonshire, Dept. of Environment, Contemporary Art Soc., National Library of Wales, Aberystwyth, West Wales Assoc. for Arts, New York, California, Alberta.

Publications: Symphonies in Black (Y Lolfa, Wales, 1987). *Signs work:* "NICK EVANS." *Address:* Shalom, 16 College St., Abernant, Aberdare, Rhondda Cynon Taff CF44 0RN.

EVANS, Ray, R.I., R.C.A.; painter, writer and illustrator; *b* 1920. one *s.* one *d. Educ:* Altrincham Grammar School. *Studied:* Manchester College of Art (1946-48), Heatherleys under Iain Macnab (1948-50). *Exhib:* worldwide. *Work in collections:* Gulbenkian Foundation; Nat. Library of Wales; Winchester Guildhall Gallery and many private collections in Europe, Britain, U.S.A. and Canada. *Commissions:* Illustration work accepted. *Publications:* Many books written and illustrated for John Murray, Consumers Assoc., Harper Collins, Batsfords. Illustrated entry in new 20th Century Painters and Sculptors, pub. by Antique Collectors Club. *Signs work:* see appendix. *Address:* New House, Eversglade, Devizes Rd., Salisbury, Wilts. SP2 7LU.

EVELEIGH, John, Dip. F.A. (Lond.) (1951), F.R.S.A. (1965), elected Fellow (W,gong) (1988), D.C.A. (W,gong) (1991), Aust. W.C.I. (1991), S.W.L.A. (1995), Professorial Fellow James Cook (1992-1994); practicing artist using mixed media; Hon. Founder Arts Director, New Metropole Arts Centre (1961), Hon. Founder Arts Director, The Long Gallery University of Wollongong, Australia (1984); *b* London, 15 Dec., 1926. *m* Margaret. three *s. Educ:* Clayesmore School, Dorset (1940-44). *Studied:* Canterbury College of Art (1944-45), The Slade - London University (1948-52), University of Wollongong (1986-90). *Exhib:* one-man shows include: Wildenstein, Piccadilly, South London, Nevill, Abbot Hall, Morley College, Posk, Drew & Marsh Galleries, Metropole Arts Centre (6), University of Wollongong and Perc Tucker - Australia. *Work in collections:* Camberwell, Herts. and Kent County Councils, Welsh Contemporary Arts Soc., Wollongong City Gallery, Wollongong University, James Cook University, Metropole Arts Centre. Private collections: Australia, Austria, China, South Africa, U.K., U.S.A. *Commissions:* public and private, portrait, landscape and wildlife. *Publications:* work repro.: books, magazines. Published 150 catalogues. Directed video art documentaries (Carel Weight/ Fred Cuming). *Signs work:* " John Eveleigh." *Address:* 4 Broadfield Rd., Folkstone, Kent CT20 2JT.

EYTON, Anthony, R.A. (1986), R.W.S., R.W.A., R. Cam. A., Mem. London Group, N.D.D., Abbey Major Scholarship in Painting (1950); prize winner, John Moore's Exhbn. (1972), awarded Grocer's Co. Fellowship (1973), 1st prize, Second British International Drawing Biennale, Middlesbrough (1975), Charles Wollaston Award, R.A. (1981), British Painting 1952-77, R.A. (1977); artist in oil; *b* Teddington, 17 May, 1923. three *d. Educ:* Twyford School (1932-37), Canford School (1937-41). *Studied:* Reading University (1941); Camberwell School of Arts and Crafts (1947-50). *Exhib:* London Group, R.A.; one-man shows: Browse and Darby (1981, 1985, 1987, 1990, 1993, 1996, 2000); Retrospective: South London A.G. (1980). *Work in collections:* Arts Council, Tate Gallery, Imperial War Museum, Govt. Picture Collection, Plymouth A.G. *Address:* 166 Brixton Rd., London SW9 6AU.

F

FABER, Rodney George, self taught artist in water-colour and pen and ink drawing; *b* Liverpool, 8 June, 1935. *m* Asne Wainer. *Educ:* Hasmonean Grammar School. *Exhib:* S.G.F.A. Annual exhbns. and mixed exhbns. in various galleries in London and the Home Counties. Commission and other works in numerous private collections both in U.K. and abroad. Rexel prizewinner S.G.F.A. (1992). *Signs work:* "FABER." *Address:* Studio: 37 Darwin Ct., Gloucester Ave., London NW1 7BG.

FAILES, Colin Michael, City & Guilds Dip. (Sculpture) (1972), Beckworth travel scholarship to Egypt (1972), Postgrad. (Sculpture) Cert. R.A. Schools, Silver medal (Sculpture) (1975), bronze medal (Sculpture) (1976); mural artist and sculptor in acrylic, wax modelling; *b* Farnborough, Kent, 2 Oct., 1948. *Educ:* Arle School, Cheltenham. *Studied:* City & Guilds of London Art School (1969-72, James Butler, R.A.), R.A. Schools (1973-76, Willi Soukop, R.A.). *Exhib:* R.A. Summer Exhbns. (1976, 1980, 1987, 1988). *Work in collections:* London, Monaco, Luxembourg. *Commissions:* murals: "Oriana" P. & O.; Vintners' Hall, City of London; Bridge Housing Assoc., London. *Publications:* work repro.: in "Painting Murals" (MacDonald Orbis), and "Murals" (New Holland). *Clubs:* R.A. Schools Alumni Association. *Signs work:* "COLIN FAILES" or "C.M. Failes." *Address:* 6 Elfindale Rd., London SE24 9NW.

FAIRCLOUGH, Michael, R.E. (1964), Rome Scholar in Engraving (1964-66), N.E.A.C. (1995); painter/printmaker; lecturer, Belfast College of Art (1962-64); West Surrey College of Art (1967-79); *b* Blackburn, 16 Sept., 1940. *m* Mary Malenoir. two *d. Studied:* Kingston School of Art (1957-61); British School at Rome, (1964-67); Atelier 17, Paris (1967). *Exhib:* one-man shows Henley-on-Thames, Farnham, Toronto, Auckland, Berkeley Square Gallery, London (2000). *Work in collections:* V. & A., Ashmolean, Usher Gallery, Bowes Museum, Royal Albert Museum, New York Public Library. *Commissions:* mural, Farnham Post Office (1970), Post Office 'National Trust' issue of five stamps (1981). *Signs work:* "Michael Fairclough." *Address:* Tilford Green Cottages, Tilford, Farnham, Surrey GU10 2BU.

FAIRFAX-LUCY, Edmund, N.E.A.C.; painter of interiors, still-life and landscapes in oil; *b* 1945. *Studied:* City & Guilds of London Art School, and R.A. Schools (1967-70) winning David Murray Travelling Scholarship (1966, 1967, 1969). *Exhib:* R.A. since 1967, New Grafton Gallery since 1971. *Work in collections:* Brinsley Ford. *Address:* Charlecote Park, Warwick.

FAIRGRIEVE, James Hanratty, D.A. (Edin.), R.S.W., A.R.S.A.; Gillies award, R.S.W. (1987); retd. lecturer, painter in acrylic; *b* Prestonpans, E. Lothian, 17 June, 1944. *m* Margaret Fairgrieve. two *s.* one *d. Educ:* Preston Lodge Senior Secondary School. *Studied:* Edinburgh College of Art. *Exhib:* Hawarth A.G. (1974), Triad Arts Centre (1974), Scottish Gallery (1974), Scottish Arts Club (1973), New 57 Gallery (1969, 1971); one-man shows: Edinburgh University (1975), Scottish Gallery (1978), Mercury Gallery, London (1980, 1982, 1987), Macauley Gallery (1983),

Mercury Gallery, Edinburgh (1984), Stichell Gallery (1990), Fosse Gallery (1992), Pontevedra, Spain (1995), Roger Billcliffe (1997), Edinburgh City Art Centre (1998), Portland Gallery (1999), Albemarle Gallery (1999). *Work in collections:* Edinburgh Corp., Scottish Arts Council, National Bank of Chicago, Milngavie A.G., H.R.H. The Duke of Edinburgh, Argyll Schools, R.C.P., Perth A.G., Lord Moray, Leeds Schools. *Publications:* 'Eye in the Wind' - Edward Gage; 'Scottish Watercolour Painting' - Jack Firth; 'A Picture of Flemings' - B. Smith; 'Dictionary of Scottish Art and Architecture' - P. McEwan. *Signs work:* "J. Fairgrieve." *Address:* Burnbrae, Gordon, Berwickshire, Scotland TD3 6JU.

FAIRHURST, Miles Christopher, painter in oil; painter of East Anglian landscape in tradition of Edward Seago and Arnesby-Brown; former owner of Fairhurst Gallery, London; *b* Norwich, 3 Dec., 1955. *Educ:* Gresham's School, Holt, Norfolk. *Studied:* largely self taught; studied under father, Joseph Fairhurst and at University of Aix-en-Provence, France. *Exhib:* R.S.M.A., Mall Galleries, Park Grosvenor Galleries, London, Barnes Gallery, London, and various London and provincial galleries. *Work in collections:* private collections in U.K., U.S.A., Australia, New Zealand, Europe. *Commissions:* oil painting for T.V. commercial for Volkswagen (1987). *Publications:* illustrations for Millers Picture Price Guide (1994 onwards). *Signs work:* "M. Fairhurst." *Address:* Turkey Hall, Metfield, Suffolk IP20 0JX.

FAIRMAN, Sheila, R.M.S., S.W.A., F.S.B.A.; awarded R.M.S. Gold Bowl (1989), Hunting Group art prize, runner up (1982); painter in oil and water-colour and miniaturist; *b* Benfleet, Essex, 18 Aug., 1924. *m* Bernard Fairman, F.A.P.S.A. one *s*. *Studied:* Southend-on-Sea College of Art (1938-41). *Exhib:* R.A., R.M.S., R.S.M.A., R.P., R.I., R.O.I., S.W.A., S.B.A. *Work in collections:* Beecroft A.G., Southend-on-Sea. *Signs work:* "SHEILA FAIRMAN" or "S.F." *Address:* 39 Burnham Rd., Leigh-on-Sea, Essex SS9 2JT.

FAIRS, Tom, N.D.D. (1950), A.R.C.A. (1953); painter in oil paint, oil pastel, stained glass designer; Senior lecturer, Theatre Dept. Central School of Art and Design (retd.); *b* London, 3 Oct., 1925. *m* Elisabeth Russell Taylor, author/academic. *Studied:* Hornsey School of Art (1948-50), R.C.A. (1950-54). *Exhib:* Arts Council Travelling Exhbns., Beaford Centre, Dartington Hall, Covent Garden Gallery, Roland, Browse & Delbanco, Hambledon Gallery, Illustrators Art, Rooksmoor Gallery, Leeds Playhouse, Stables Folkestone, The Thackeray Gallery, Ombersley Gallery, R.A. Summer Exhbns. *Commissions:* stained glass in Britain and Bahrain. *Signs work:* "FAIRS." *Address:* 21 Steeles Rd., London NW3 4SH.

FAIRWEATHER, Dorothy, painter/etcher; *b* 4 Aug., 1915, married. one *s*. *Educ:* privately. *Studied:* Folkestone School of Art (1930-34), Liverpool School of Art (1942-44). *Exhib:* leading London galleries including R.A., Barbican, Paris (1983-84), Germany (1989). *Work in collections:* Britain and abroad. President Soroptimist Club of Sevenoaks (1973-74, 1984-85). *Address:* Lanterns, 4 Cade La., Sevenoaks, Kent TN13 1QX.

FAKHOURY, Bushra, B.A., M.A., Ph.D. (Lond.); sculptor in bronze, stone; *b* Beirut, 1 Apr., 1942. two *s*. *Educ:* St. Paul's, Wimbledon School of Art and Emanuel. *Studied:* Beirut University College, American University of Beirut, University of London. *Exhib:* Bloomsbury Galleries (1986), Mall Galleries (1986), Jablonski

Gallery (1987), Ashdown Gallery (1988), Kufa Gallery (1989). *Publications:* Art Education in Lebanon. *Signs work:* see appendix. *Address:* 57 Madrid Rd., Barnes, London SW13 9PQ.

FALCONBRIDGE, Brian, Dip. A.D. (Fine Art) (1973), H.D.F.A. (Slade) (1975), elected F.R.B.S. (1997); Head of Visual Arts Dept., Goldsmiths'; sculptor in bronze; *b* Fakenham, 1 May, 1950. one *s.* one *d. Educ:* Fakenham Grammar School. *Studied:* Canterbury College of Art (1968-69), Goldsmiths' College School of Art (1970-73), Slade School of Fine Art (1973-75). *Exhib:* numerous mixed and solo exhbns. in Europe and Far East. *Work in collections:* A.C.G.B., Contemporary Arts Soc., University of East Anglia, British Council and numerous private collections in U.K. and abroad. *Clubs:* Chelsea Arts. *Signs work:* "Brian Falconbridge." *Address:* c/o Visual Arts Dept., Goldsmiths' University of London, New Cross, London SE14 6NW.

FALLA, Kathleen M., F.F.P.S (1985); relief printmaker and sculptor in wood; *b* Guernsey, C.I., 25 Jan., 1924. *m* Kenneth R. Masters. one *s.* one *d. Educ:* Ladies College, Guernsey. *Studied:* Guildford School of Art and Morley College, London. *Exhib:* solo shows: Lauragais, France, University of Surrey, Godalming Museum; shared shows: Loggia Gallery, Farnham Maltings; group shows: Barbican, West of England Academy, Brighton Polytechnic Gallery, Bloomsbury Galleries, etc. *Signs work:* "Kit Falla." *Address:* Old Barn Cottage, Church La., Witley, Surrey GU8 5PW.

FALLSHAW, Daniel, artist in oil, acrylic, pastel charcoal, ink, pencil, sculptor in various media; Past M.D. of C.M.C design consultants; *b* London, 17 Nov., 1946. *m* Elizabeth. two *d. Educ:* Broxhill, Romford and privately. *Studied:* art under the late Leonard Boden, F.R.S.A.; sculpture under Jack Gillespie and Edmund Holmes; graphic design, the London College of Printing (Leonard Cusdens and Don Smith). *Exhib:* Mall Galleries, N.S., U.A., numerous London and provincial galleries. *Publications:* "Art of Creation – inspired images'. *Clubs:* Folkestone Art Soc. *Signs work:* "Fallshaw" – sculpture "DF." *Address:* Woodside Cottage, Maydensole, Nr. West Langdon, Dover, Kent CT15 5HE. *Email:* daniel@fallshaw.freeserve.co.uk

FARLEY, James Osmer, A.R.B.S. (1990), A.N.S.S. (1985); portrait and architectural sculptor in clay, wax, direct metal, steels, bronze, copper; *b* Cleveland, Ohio, 10 Apr., 1935. *m* Gillian Lewin. one *d. Studied:* Pennsylvania Academy of Fine Art (1952-56, Walker Hancock, Harry Rosin, Andrew Wyeth), Chicago Art Inst. (1957-59, Edvard Chaisang). *Exhib:* Art and the Corporate Image (1981). *Work in collections:* Arizona: Bell Center, Sun City; City Hall, Glendale; Centennial Hall, Mesa; St. Luke's Hospital, Phoenix; Hanna Boys Center, Sonoma, Calif. *Clubs:* F. & A. Masonic Lodge. *Signs work:* "James Farley." *Address:* 150 Scott Ellis Gdns., St. John's Wood, London NW8 9HG; 4718 E. Portland, Phoenix, AZ. 85008, U.S.A.

FARQUHARSON, Alex, M.A. (Dist.) Arts Critic, B.A. English/Art Comb. Hons.; curator; Exhbn. Officer, Spacex Gallery, Exeter; *b* Chalfont St. Giles, 26 Sept., 1969. *Educ:* Exeter University, City University, London. *Studied:* Exeter College of Art and Design (now Plymouth University) (1988-91). *Publications:* numerous catalogue texts. *Address:* c/o Spacex Gallery, 45 Preston St., Exeter EX1 1DF.

FARQUHARSON, Andrew Charles, artist in water-colour; *b* Johannesburg, S. Africa, 14 Dec., 1959. *Educ:* St. John's College, Johannesburg. *Studied:* under his mother. *Exhib:* group show Johannesburg. Lectured: University of Wales, Anglo Spanish Soc., Inst. of Spain. *Signs work:* "A.C. Farquharson." *Address:* 80b Naylor Rd., Peckham, London SE15.

FARR, Dennis Larry Ashwell, C.B.E., M.A., Hon.D.Litt., F.R.S.A., F.M.A.; Director, Courtauld Institute Galleries (1980-93); Director, Birmingham Museums and Art Gallery (1969-80); Senior Lecturer in Fine Art, University of Glasgow (1967-69); Curator, Paul Mellon Collection, Washington, D.C. (1964-66); Asst. Keeper, Tate Gallery, London (1954-64); *b* 3 Apr., 1929. *m* Diana Pullein-Thompson, writer. one *s*. one *d*. *Educ:* Luton Grammar School. *Studied:* Courtauld Inst. of Art, University of London (1947-50). *Publications:* William Etty (1958), Catalogue of the Modern British School in the Tate Gallery (with M. Chamot and M. Butlin, 1964-65), English Art 1870-1940 (1978), Lynn Chadwick, Sculptor (with Eva Chadwick, 1990), etc. *Address:* Orchard Hill, Swan Barn Rd., Haslemere, Surrey GU27 2HY.

FARRELL, Alan Richard, painter in water-colour and oil, miniaturist and member of R.M.S., H.S., C.M.S., M.P.S.G. and M.A.S.F.; chartered engineer and member of Institution of Electrical Engineers; *b* London, 17 May, 1932. married. two *d*. *Studied:* S.E. Essex Technical College and School of Art (1953-56). *Exhib:* R.M.S., R.I., R.S.M.A., R.B.A., U.A., International Boat Show, Britain in Water-colours, and several international exhibitions overseas. Has received several awards in U.K. and overseas including 1st in international category in Washington and Gold for best painting in any traditional medium in Ottawa. *Signs work:* "ALAN FARRELL" printed bottom right or left-hand corner; paintings dated on reverse; and see appendix. *Address:* The White House, Whitesmith, nr. Lewes, E. Sussex BN8 6JD.

FARRELL, Anthony, N.D.D. (1965), R.A.Dip. (1968); artist in oil, etching; *b* Epsom, 28 Mar., 1945. *m* Sarah. one *s*. three *d*. *Educ:* Belfairs High School. *Studied:* Camberwell School of Art (1963-65), R.A. Schools (1965-68). *Exhib:* R.A. Common Room, Minories, Colchester, R.A. Summer Exhbns., Serpentine Gallery, Christchurch Mansions, Ipswich, Gainsborough House, Sudbury, Arts Space, London. *Work in collections:* A.C.G.B., The Minories, Colchester, Epping Forest Museum, Manchester City A.G., Beecroft A.G., Westcliff-on-Sea, Borough of St. Edmundsbury and Suffolk C.C., Essex Health Authority, Ipswich Borough Council. *Signs work:* "Anthony Farrell." *Address:* 6 Avenue Rd., Leigh-on-Sea, Essex SS9 1AX.

FARRELL, Don, R.I. (1984), R.B.A. (1985), S.F.C.A.; R.I. medal (1984); Daler Rowney award R.B.A. Exhbn. (1992); painter in water-colour and mixed media; *b* Vancouver, B.C., 3 Oct., 1942. *m* Margaret. two *s*. *Exhib:* annually at R.I. (1984-01), R.B.A. (1983-01). *Work in collections:* H.R.H. The Prince of Wales; private and corporate collections: Britain, Canada, U.S.A. and Europe. *Signs work:* "Don Farrell." *Address:* 521 Maquinna Place, Qualicum Beach, B.C., Canada V9K 1B3.

FARROW, Kieron, B.A. (Hons.) Fine Art (1982); artist, painter and printmaker in oil, monoprints; *b* Barnsley, Yorks., 25 Aug., 1949. *m* Megan Farrow. two *s*. *Studied:* Middlesex University. *Exhib:* group shows: Ikon Touring Exhbn. (1985, 1986), Present Prints, Royal Festival Hall London; one-man shows: Curwen Gallery

(1999), Museum of Archaeology, Valletta, Malta (1985). *Work in collections:* J.P. Morgan, Wall St., N.Y.; Lake Point Tower, Chicago; Royal British Legion, Malta; Royal Borough of Kensington and Chelsea, London; Norwich Castle Museum; Scarborough A.G. *Address:* c/o Curwen Gallery, 4 Windmill St., London W1P 1HF.

FASTNEDGE, Ralph William, D.F.C., B.A.; formerly curator, The Lady Lever Art Gallery, Port Sunlight, Merseyside; *b* London, 16 Apr., 1913. *Educ:* University College School; Worcester College, Oxford; Courtauld Inst. of Art. *Publications:* English Furniture Styles (1500-1830), Penguin Books, 1955; Sheraton Furniture, Faber; Shearer Furniture Designs, Tiranti; Regency Furniture (revision), Country Life. *Address:* 15 Maes Dinas, Llanfechain, Powys SY22 6YR.

FAULDS, James Alexander, D.A.; artist in water-colour and oil; art teacher; *b* Glasgow, 15 Jan., 1949. *Educ:* Knightswood Secondary School. *Studied:* Dundee College of Art (1968-72). *Exhib:* Dundee under 30's, R.S.A., S.S.A., Colquhoun Memorial, Group 81, Glasgow, Eden Court Gallery, Contemporary British Water-colours, Festival Theatre, Pitlochry, R.S.W., John Laing, London, Nürnberg, Germany. *Clubs:* Glasgow Art; founder mem., Group 81, Glasgow. *Signs work:* see appendix. *Address:* 3 Camphill Ave., Glasgow G41 3AV.

FAULKNER, Amanda, B.A.(Hons.) Fine Art (1982), M.A. Fine Art (1983); artist in charcoal and pastel on paper, acrylic on canvas, lithography and etching; Senior lecturer in Fine Art, Chelsea School of Art; *b* Poole, 5 Dec., 1953. one *s. Educ:* St. Anthony's, Leweston, Dorset, and Canford School, Dorset. *Studied:* Bournemouth College of Art (1978-79), Ravensbourne College of Art and Design (1979-82), Chelsea School of Art (1982-83). *Exhib:* regularly at Angela Flowers Gallery and Flowers East since 1983; and in U.K. and internationally. *Work in collections:* including A.C.G.B., Unilever plc, V. & A., Contemporary Art Soc., Whitworth A.G., Silkeborg Kunstmuseum, Denmark. *Signs work:* "Amanda Faulkner." *Address:* 131 Listria Pk., London N16 5SP.

FAULKNER, Robert Trevor, A.R.C.A. (1955), F.R.B.S.; figurative sculptures in bronze, terracotta, ciment-fondu and direct metal; specialist in polychrome metal wild-life and aeronautical subjects; *b* 17 Sept., 1929, married. one *d. Educ:* Penistone Grammar School. *Studied:* Sheffield School of Art (1946-50); R.C.A. (1952-55). *Exhib:* Moorland, Alwin (London). *Work in collections:* Ulster Museum, Derbys.; Oxford, Lancs., and Sheffield Educ. Authorities; Pewterers Company, London. *Commissions:* medals for Virginia Air and Space Museum; trophy, Royal Aero Club; medals for B.M.F.A. *Publications:* Manual of Direct Metal Sculpture (Thames & Hudson, 1978). Gallery: John Noott, Broadway, Worcs., S10 Gallery, Sheffield. *Signs work:* "TREVOR FAULKNER" or "T.F." *Address:* 4 Birchitt Cl., Bradway, Sheffield S17 4QJ.

FAUST, Pat, artist in oil, water-colour, pastel, theatrical designs, murals; *b* Lancs. *Educ:* Culcheth Hall, Ches. *Studied:* Manchester Regional College of Art; Crescent Theatre, Birmingham. *Exhib:* R.G.I., Manchester Academy, Birmingham A.G., Sewerby Hall, Bridlington, Scarborough A.G. and Town Hall, Ferens A.G., Hull, Beverley, Cartwright Hall, Bradford, Pannett, Whitby, R.A., R.B.A., S.W.A., R.Cam.A., U.A.S., Leeds City A.G., Paris Salon, Gallery Vallombreuse Biarritz, Brye A.G., Glaisdale, City Gallery, Darlington, Francis Phillips Gallery, Sheffield,

Northern Academy of Art, Harrogate A.G., Guildhall, York, Yorkshire Artist Biennal, City A.G. York, Yorkshire Pastel Soc., Haworth, Cliffe Castle Museum and A.G. Keighley, Yorks.; one-man shows: Marshalls, Scarborough, Hull University, Yorkshire Pastel Soc., Dewsbury A.G. and Museum, Scarborough Scene, Scarborough Art Gallery (2001); joint exhbn. March-May 1998 Sewerbury Hall, Bridlington. *Work in collections:* Scarborough A.G., Scarborough Town Hall, Menston Hospital and private collections. Official purchases: painting of Scarborough A.G. (hung R.A.) by Scarborough Corp. Winner shield best medium (1992) and award (1993, 1994) Sewerby Hall, Bridlington. *Clubs:* Leeds Fine Art, Scarborough Arts Soc. *Signs work:* "Pat Faust." *Address:* 25 Sea-Point, Flat Cliffs, nr. Filey, Yorks. YO14 9RD.

FAWLEY, Charlotte Audrey, N.D.D. Illustration (1957); painter/designer in oil, pastel, water-colour; *b* Blackpool, 6 Dec., 1934. *Educ:* Arnold High School, Blackpool. *Studied:* Blackpool School of Art (1953-57), Camden Arts Centre, London (1964-66, Aubrey Williams). *Exhib:* Royal Opera House, Covent Garden, Royal National Theatre South Bank, Primrose Hill Gallery, Soar Gallery Kensington, etc. Work in collections internationally. *Commissions:* Design of backcloth and costumes for ballet 'Serpentime' for Royal Ballet tour Kenya (1996). BBC2 Series 'Making their Mark' (R. Foster) 6 artists on drawing in different mediums. BBC2 Newsnight - graphics for Falklands War (1981) and Gulf War CNN. *Publications:* illustrated: 'Thinking About God' (HarperCollins). *Clubs:* Chelsea Arts, BAFTA, Piccadilly, London. *Signs work:* "CHARLOTTE FAWLEY." *Address:* 56 Holley Rd., Wellington Court, London W3 7TS.

FAWSSETT, Ann: see ATKIN, Ann.

FEASEY, Judith Mary, Cert. R.A.S. (1976), A.T.C. (1977); painter/etcher in oil on canvas, water-colour, etching; *b* Southgate, 3 Sept., 1945. *Educ:* St. Maurs Convent, Weybridge, Surrey. *Studied:* Guildford School of Art (1965-69), R.A. Schools (1973-76) Turner gold medal for landscape painting. *Exhib:* R.A. London and Scotland, G.L.C. Spirit of London; four-man show, Alfred East Gallery, Kettering, and Mall Galleries, London, etc. *Signs work:* "J. Feasey" or "J.M.F." *Address:* 90 Webster Rd., London SE16 4DF.

FEDDEN, Mary, R.A.; Slade Diploma of Fine Arts; teacher of painting at Royal Coll. of Art (1958-64); Yehudi Menuhin School (1965-70); President, Royal West of England Academy (1983-88); Hon. D.Litt. Bath Univ.; *b* Bristol, 14 Aug., 1915. *m* Julian Trevelyan (decd.). *Educ:* Badminton School, Bristol. *Studied:* Slade School of Art. *Exhib:* Leicester Gallery, Gimpel Fils, R.W.A., London Group; solo shows: Christopher Hull, Bohun Gallery (4), Redfern Gallery (6), New Grafton Gallery (6), Beaux Arts Gallery (3), Provincial Galleries and R.W.A., *Work in collections:* H.M. The Queen, Prince Hassan of Jordan, Tate, Hull, Carlisle, Melbourne, National Gallery of N.Z., Bristol, Bath, Durham,York, Chichester. Official purchases: murals, Charing Cross Hospital, Contemporary Arts Soc., Yorkshire C.C., Leicestershire C.C., Hertfordshire C.C., Min. of Works, Orient Line, Bristol Educ. Com., Barnet Hospital, Cambridge Colleges of New Hall and Lucy Cavendish. *Signs work:* "Fedden." *Address:* Durham Wharf, Hammersmith Terr., London W6 9TS.

FEENY, Patrick A., F.M.G.P.; ecclesiastical artist and watercolourist; *b* Harrow,

Middx., 30 Nov., 1910. *Educ:* Stonyhurst College. *Signs work:* see appendix. *Address:* Enstone Cottage, High St., Feckenham, Worcs. B96 6HS.

FEI, Cheng-Wu, painter; Prof. (1941-46), College of Fine Art, National Central University, China; *b* China, 30 Dec., 1914. *m* Chien-Ying Chang, artist. *Studied:* National Central University, China (1930-34), Slade School of Fine Art (1947-50). *Exhib:* R.A., R.I., R.W.A., R.W.S., N.E.A.C.; one-man shows at Leicester Galleries. *Work in collections:* Royal West of England Academy, Universities' China Committee, Grave's Gallery, Sheffield, Derby A.G., etc. *Publications:* Brush Drawing in the Chinese Manner (Studio); work repro.: Studio, Art News & Review, La Revue Moderne, Kunst, etc. *Signs work:* see appendix. *Address:* 27 The Fountains, Ballards Lane, London N3 1NL.

FEILER, Paul, painter; *b* 30 Apr., 1918. *m* Catharine Armitage. three *s*. two *d*. *Educ:* Canford School, Dorset. *Studied:* Slade School of Fine Art. *Exhib:* one-man shows since 1953; Redfern Gallery, Grosvenor Gallery, Warwick Arts Trust, Austin/Desmond, London, Tate Gallery, St. Ives, Hong Kong. *Work in collections:* Tate Gallery, Arts Council, British Council, Universities of London, Oxford, Cambridge, Warwick, Newcastle. Liverpool; galleries in England, U.S.A., France, Austria, Canada, New Zealand, Australia. *Address:* Kerris, nr. Penzance, Cornwall TR19 6UY.

FELL, Michael Anthony, F.S.D.C., L.R.E.; painter/printmaker; former Head of Foundation, City & Guilds London; visiting tutor, Prince of Wales Inst., London; *b* London, 31 Jan., 1939. *m* Maureen. two *s*. *Educ:* St. George's, Weybridge. *Studied:* St. Martin's, City & Guilds London. *Exhib:* Jordan Gallery (1972-84), Halesworth Gallery (1972-85), Mall Galleries, Clementi House Gallery (1991), Gallery Renata, Chicago, Belanthi Gallery, New York, Chappel Galleries, Essex (1993, 1999), Comteroux Perpignan (1993), Flaran, France (1996), Grosvenor Gallery, London (1996). *Work in collections:* B.M.; Arts Council; Victoria National Gallery University Melbourne, Australia; Churchill Library, Massachusetts; Michael Estorick Collection. *Clubs:* Asylum, Charlotte St. *Signs work:* "Michael Fell." *Address:* 17 Fonnereau Rd., Ipswich, Suffolk IP1 3JR. *Second Address:* Vic Fezensac, 32190 France.

FELLOWS, Elaine Helen, B.A.(Hons.) (1981), H.S. (1987), S.W.A. (1988), R.M.S. (1992), U.S.M. (1990); professional painter of portraits and still life in miniature in water-colour on vellum or ivorine; *b* Walsall, 27 Nov., 1959. one *s*. *Studied:* Walsall College of Art (1977), Wolverhampton Polytechnic (1978-81). *Exhib:* R.M.S. (Hon. mention 1989, 1991), S.W.A., Hilliard Soc. (Bell award 1990), Ulster Soc. of Miniaturists (Madam MacCarthy Mór Memorial Award 1991), Llewellyn Alexander Award (1993), Suzanne Lucas Award (1995), Llewellyn Alexander Gallery, Linda Blackstone Gallery, France, Hong Kong, U.S.A. *Work in collections:* G.B., U.S.A., France, Germany. *Publications:* The Techniques of Painting Miniatures; contributor to The Magic of Miniatures. *Signs work:* see appendix. *Address:* Bwlch House, Beguildy, Knighton, Powys LD7 1UG.

FENNER, Michael James, B.A. (Hons.), A.T.D. (Dist.); painter in acrylic, art teacher; Head of Art, West Kirby Grammar School for Girls; *b* Liverpool, 5 Jan, 1952. *m* Alison. one *s*. two *d*. *Studied:* Laird School of Art, Newport College of Art.

Exhib: group and one-man shows: Birkenhead, Liverpool, Durham., U.S.A., Ireland, London. *Work in collections:* Williamson A.G., Birkenhead, Dee Fine Art, private collections in Britain, Ireland and Europe. *Commissions:* portraits, England and Holland. *Publications:* magazine articles. *Clubs:* N.A.P.A. *Signs work:* "M.J. Fenner." *Address:* la Charlesville, Oxton, Birkenhead CH43 1TP.

FEREDAY, Joseph, R.E.; Diploma in Fine Art, Slade School; *b* Dudley, 9 Feb., 1917. *Studied:* Wolverhampton and Birmingham College of Art, Slade School (1946-48). *Work in collections:* Portsmouth A.G., Southampton University, De Witt Gallery, Holland, Michigan, Plymouth A.G., Bilston A.G., St. Mary's College, Twickenham, Portsmouth Corp., Seely Library, Ryde, I.O.W., British Embassy, Helsinki, Galerie Alphonse Marré, Chartres; one-man shows: Woodstock Gallery, London, Hiscock Gallery, Portsmouth, Galerie de Vallombreuse Biarritz, Southampton University, Vectis Gallery, Bembridge. *Address:* Yarborough House, New Rd., Brading, I.O.W. PO36 0AG.

FERGUSON, George, B.A., B.Arch., R.I.B.A., R.W.A., Hon. M.A. Univ. of Bristol; architect and Hon. architect to R.W.A.; on R.I.B.A. council; *b* Winchester, 22 Mar., 1947. one *s.* two *d. Educ:* Wellington College. *Studied:* University of Bristol and R.W.A. *Exhib:* R.W.A. *Commissions:* various architectural. *Publications:* Races against Time (1984). *Address:* 18 Great George St., Bristol BS1 5RH. *Email:* george@acanthusfm.co.uk

FERGUSON, Malcolm Alastair Percy, R.W.A., D.F.A.(Lond., 1950); religious landscape and portrait painter; visiting teacher; *b* Blackwater, Hants., 19 Dec., 1913. *m* Rosemary J.M. Holdsworth (decd.). one *s.* one *d. Educ:* Durham School, R.M.A., Sandhurst 1932 (invalided shortly after). *Studied:* Portsmouth and Croydon Schools of Art (1935-38), Slade School (1939, 1948-51, under Schwabe, Coldstream Monnington). *Exhib:* R.A., N.E.A.C., R.P., R.W.A., R.B.A., Paris Salon, Nat. Gall. of Wales, Bradford City A.G., etc.; one-man shows: London, provinces and Port Elizabeth, S.A. *Work in collections:* Plymouth City A.G., R.W.A., Talbot Bequest Bristol, Somerset Museum Service. Official purchases: Sponsored by Anglo American and De Beers, to paint 'True Fresco' (1982, 1985), domed apse, St. Cuthbert's, Transkei. 1985-89, four altar panels and 30 ft. choir balustrade in egg tempera St. Augustine's Church, Penhalonga, Zimbabwe; various portraits, Chairman Cecil Whiley of George. M. Whiley Ltd; Gold Beaters Ltd., etc. *Commissions:* Triptych, High Altar, St. Marks 12thC Lord Mayor's Chapel, Bristol (1992). *Publications:* work repro.: various magazines. *Signs work:* "Malcolm A.P. Ferguson." *Address:* 7 Mill St., North Petherton, Som. TA6 6LX.

FERGUSON, Mary, F.F.P.S.; painter in oil, charcoal, pen and wash; *b* 6 May, 1919. *m* E.A. Ferguson. two *s. Educ:* Friends School, Ackworth. *Studied:* The Gallery Schools, Melbourne, Australia (1953-55, Charles Bush), Reigate School of Art (1957-60, Denis Lucas, Walter Woodington). *Exhib:* one-man shows: London including Loggia Gallery, F.P.S.; mixed shows: London and provincial galleries. *Work in collections:* Australia, Canada, Mallorca, Hong Kong and U.K. *Clubs:* F.P.S., Reigate Soc. of Artists. *Signs work:* "Ferguson" or "MF" joined. *Address:* Bayhorne Lodge, 164 Balcombe Rd., Horley, Surrey RH6 9DS.

FERGUSSON: see BATTERBURY, Helen Fiona.

FERRAN, Brian, B.A., D.B.A., H.R.H.A., H.R.U.A.; painter in acrylic and oil; artist and former chief executive of the Arts Council of N. Ireland; *b* Derry, Ireland, 19 Oct., 1940. *m* Denise. one *s.* one *d. Studied:* Courtauld Inst., London University, Brera Academy, Milan, Queens University, Belfast. *Exhib:* regularly in Ireland, U.S.A., Switzerland and Mexico. *Work in collections:* Ulster Museum, Arts Council of N. Ireland, Arts Council of Republic of Ireland, Allied Irish Bank, Gordon Lambert Collection, Crawford Municipal Gallery, Cork, . *Publications:* exhib. catalogues and Basil Blackshaw - painter, a monograph published 1995. *Signs work:* "Brian Ferran." *Address:* 46 Myrtlefield Park, Belfast BT9 6NF. *Email:* brian.ferran@ntlworld.com

FERRIAN, Marie, sculptor in wood, terracotta, stone; *b* Hummelstown, Pa., 1 Jan., 1927. *m* George Ferrian. one *s. Educ:* S.T.H.S. *Studied:* Corcoran School of Art (painting: 1945-47, Eugene Weisz; sculpture: 1963-65, Heinz Warneke). *Exhib:* St. Camillus, Women's National Bank, Firenze House, Corcoran Gallery, Art Barn (2). *Work in collections:* National Museum of Women in the Arts. *Publications:* three children's books; featured in American Craftsmen (1975). *Signs work:* "M.F." *Address:* 4230 Silverwood La., Beth, M.D. 20816, U.S.A.

FERRY, David Dawson, B.A. (Hons.) (1979), H.D.F.A. (Lond.) (1981); printmaker/painter/collagist; lecturer, Camberwell/Canterbury Art Schools; 1993, appointed Head of Printmaking, Winchester School of Art; 1996, appointed Head of Fine Art, University of Southampton; *b* Blackpool, 5 Feb., 1957. *Studied:* Blackpool College Tech. (1975-76), Camberwell School of Arts and Crafts (1976-79, Mario Dubsky, Agathe Sorell), Slade School of Fine Art (1979-81, Stanley Jones). *Exhib:* Contemporary Printmaking Air Gallery, R.A., S. London A.G., Ferens A.G., Hull, Offenbach, Germany, Paris 'Trace' Biennale; one-man shows, first and second International Contemporary Art Fairs at Barbican A.G., London Olympia, 5 Contemporary Printmakers, National Museum of Wales British Tour, The Star Chamber, Herbert Read Gallery, Canterbury, Kent University, Drew Gallery Canterbury, Boundry Gallery, London, Fachhochschule, Düsseldorf, Germany, Photomontage exhbn. in Dresden. *Work in collections:* Grundy A.G., Blackpool, University College and St.Thomas Hospital, London, Maidstone A.G., Nuclear Electric, Marconi Instruments U.K. *Commissions:* G.E.C. U.K. (1997). *Publications:* author, Painting Without a Brush, U.K. (1991), U.S.A. (1992), France (1994); 'Aspects of our National Heritage', exhbn. catalogue (1999). Full mem. Rossetti Soc. Formed video production titled 'Lost Shoe Productions.' *Signs work:* "D.D. Ferry" or "D.D.F." *Address:* c/o Winchester School of Art, Hants. SO23 8DL.

FESTING, Andrew Thomas, R.P. (1992); portrait painter in oil; *b* Chalford, 30 Nov., 1941. *m* Virginia Fyffe. one *d. Educ:* Ampleforth College. *Exhib:* R.P. *Work in collections:* National Gallery Dublin, Royal Coll. *Signs work:* "A.T. Festing." *Address:* 3 Hillsleigh Rd., London W8 7LE.

FFYFFE, Terrance Michael, Winner, Discerning Eye (1995), Eastern Open (1997); artist, figurative painter of nudes, religious paintings and portraits in oil; *b* Melbourne, Australia, 21 Dec., 1957. *m* Joan. *Studied:* Prahran College now Swineburne University (1975-77). *Exhib:* numerous selected exhbns. Represented now by Lamont Gallery, London. *Work in collections:* internationally, mainly

Australia and U.S.A., *Signs work:* see appendix. *Address:* 6 Kingsley Gdns., Hornchurch, Essex RM11 2HZ.

FIELD, Peter L., A.T.D., F.R.S.A.; artist, teacher and lecturer; Head of Faculty of Art and Design, City of Birmingham Polytechnic (retd. 1982); *b* Winson, Glos., 7 Feb., 1920. *m* Cynthia G. Barry. two *d. Educ:* Rendcomb College. *Studied:* Cheltenham School of Art (1937-39) under A. Seaton-White, Goldsmiths' College School of Art (1946-49) under Clive Gardiner. *Exhib:* London and provincial exhbns. *Work in collections:* Swindon Art Gallery, Swindon Corporation. *Signs work:* "Peter L. Field." *Address:* 264 Mary Vale Rd., Bournville, Birmingham B30 1PJ.

FILIPE, Paulo D, N.A.P.A.; writer and painter in acrylic; *b* Portugal, 3 Sep., 1962. one *d. Exhib:* Teatro Lethes, Faro, Portugal (1990); Galeria "O Arco", Faro, Portugal (1991); 2nd Forum, da A.M.I., Lisbon, Portugal (1997); I.P. 3, Faro, Portugal; Vilamoura Marinotel, Portugal (1998); Centro Cultural, Lagos, Portugal (1998); Black Sheep Gallery, Hawarden, N. Wales (1999); Westminster Gallery, London (1999); Art Show, Manchester; Art Centre, Los Angeles, U.S.A.; Galerie Not, London (1999), Art Expo, New York (2000). *Clubs:* Bromley Art Society. *Signs work:* "P D Felipe." *Address:* 4 Bracken Hill Lane, Shortlands, Bromley, Kent BR1 4AJ. *Email:* paulodfilipe@hotmail.com

FINCH, Michael, B.A.(Hons.) (1980), M.A.(R.C.A.) (1986); painter in mixed media; Senior tutor, Parsons School of Art, Paris; *b* London, 6 July, 1957. *m* Bridget Strevens. one *d. Studied:* Ravensbourne College of Art (1976-80, Brian Fielding), R.C.A. (1982-86, Peter de Francia). *Exhib:* one-man shows: City Museum, Peterborough (1983), Groucho Club (1987, 1988), Pomeroy Purdy (1990, 1992), Purdy Hicks (1994), Le Carré, Lille, Art et Patrimoine, Paris. *Work in collections:* Unilever, T.I. Group Coll., Deutsche Bank. *Publications:* Sodium Nights (1990), 'N17', Closer than You Think (1998). *Clubs:* Groucho. *Signs work:* see appendix. *Address:* 59 rue de Meaux, 60300 Senlis, France. *Website:* www.mickfinch.com *Email:* mick@mickfinch.com

FINCH, Patricia, F.R.B.S., S.W.A., S.P.S., F.S.N.A.D., C.P.S., A.W.G., F.R.S.A.; sculptor; *b* London, 1921. two *d. Educ:* King's College, London, West London Hospital. International Grollo d'Oro Silver medal (1976), Silver cups (1981, 1983). *Exhib:* London, New York, Geneva, Glasgow, Venice, Malta, Le Touquet; mixed annual exhbns.: Mall Galleries, Westminster Galleries, R.A. Summer exhbn. (1979), FIDEM XIII British Museum, XXIV Budapest. Demonstrator, Tate Gallery Sculpture Course (1983). *Work in collections:* B.M. Coins and Medal Dept., Bank of England Museum: two busts, Royal Academy of Dancing, Musée Quentovic, Le Touquet, Museum of Fine Arts, Malta, Town Hall, Rhodes. Private collections: in U.K., various European countries, Canada, U.S.A., S. America, Japan, Australia, Nigeria. Over 140 portrait commissions carried out. Tutor, Hulton Studio for Visually Handicapped (1986-90). Demonstrator/lecturer portrait bust, Islington etc. Finalist L.D.D.C. (1988, 1989). Life-size figurative bronze Golders Hill Park unveiled 1991. *Commissions:* Goldsmiths' Hall London, Prime Warden Medal, silver (1996), Bronze bust Glenn Miller 1½ life-size for Corn Exchange, Bedford (1994). 1997: Institute of Child Health, Gt. Ormond St. Hospital, bronze bust of their Chairman, Leolin Price, C.B.E. Q.C. Queens Club, London "SPARKS" Children's

Medical Charity Real Tennis trophies for annual tournament. 1999: Shakespeare's Globe, London, bust of founder Sam Wanamaker. *Signs work:* "P. Finch." *Address:* 851 Finchley Rd., London NW11 8LY.

FINCH, William Robert, F.I.A.L. (1953), freelance journalist; artist various media, etcher; lecturer art country life; late head art dept. Beal Grammar School, Ilford; Chigwell School, Essex; founder-tutor, Over 40's Art Groups; lecturer Extra Mural Dept., Cambridge and London Universities; *b* Lowestoft, 6 Apr., 1905. *m* Peggy Doreen Hill. two *s*. *Educ:* Lowestoft Grammar School, College St. Mark and St. John, Chelsea. *Studied:* self taught. *Exhib:* R.A., East End Academy, Reading Art Guild, Assembly Rooms, Norwich, Southwold and Ilford, etc.; one-man show, Starston Gallery, Norfolk. *Work in collections:* Bury St. Edmund's Cathedral; Mrs. Lewis L. Douglas, New York; R. Hone, Esq.; Chigwell School, private Germany, France, Canada, Australia, U.S.A., Italy, etc. Official purchases: Ilford Libraries, Boy Scouts' Assoc., Westminster Bank, "Snowdrift" Lubricants. *Publications:* East Anglian Magazine, Review Assoc. Agriculture, Essex Countryside, Y.H.A. publications, etc.; author/illustrator: Journeying into Essex, In and Around Folkestone, Introducing Essex to America, Country Buildings, 100 years of Snowdrift Lubricants, The Sea in My Blood. *Signs work:* "Finch." *Address:* Waveney Cottage, Weybread, Diss, Norfolk IP21 5UA.

FINDLAY, Sheila Anne Macfarlane, R.W.S., D.A.(Edin.), Post-Grad.(1950), Travelling Scholar (1951); artist and illustrator in water-colour and oil; *b* Auchlishie, Kirriemuir. *m* Alfred Hackney, R.W.S., A.R.E., D.A.(Edin.). two *d*. *Educ:* Webster's Seminary. *Studied:* Edinburgh College of Art (1945-51) under John Maxwell, Penelope Beaton, Sir William MacTaggart, Leonard Rosoman. *Exhib:* R.A., R.W.S., Catto Gallery, R.A. Prizewinner (1993). *Work in collections:* Department of the Environment, MacFarlanes, Alan Howarth C.B.E. M.P. *Publications:* children's books illustrated for Faber & Faber, Adprint, Harrap, Odhams, Medici Soc. *Signs work:* "Sheila Findlay." *Address:* Barnside, Lodge La., Cobham, nr. Gravesend, Kent DA12 3BS.

FINEGOLD, Stephen M., B.A. (Hons.) 1st class, Postgrad. (Dip.); artist in oil, acrylic, pastel, collage, print; Artistic Director, F.C.A. Gallery; *b* London, 17 June, 1959. *m* Josephine. two *s*. *Educ:* Beal Grammar School, Ilford. *Studied:* Bradford College, Croydon O.C.A. (1988), Central School. *Work in collections:* F.C.A. Gallery, U.K., Spain, France, Australia, South Africa, U.S.A. *Signs work:* "Finegold." *Address:* Chantry House, Warley Town Lane, Warley, Halifax, W. Yorks. HX2 7SA.

FINER, Stephen, artist in oil on canvas; *b* London, 1949. *Studied:* Ravensbourne College of Art (1966-70). *Exhib:* one-man shows: Four Vine Lane, London (1981, 1982, 1985), Anthony Reynolds Gallery (1986, 1988), Berkeley Sq. Gallery (1989), Bernard Jacobson Gallery (1992, 1995), Woodlands A.G. (1994), Agnew's (1998), 'About the Figure' Six Chapel Row, Bath (1999), Pallant House Gallery (2001), Charleston (2002); mixed shows: British Art 1940-1980, from the Arts Council Coll., Hayward Gallery (1980), Collazione Ingleze 2, Venice Biennale (1984), The Portrait Now, N.P.G. (1993), Men on Women (1997-98), '50 Contemporary Self-Portraits', Six Chapel Row, Bath (1999), 'British Art 1900-1998' Agnews (1998), 'Painting the

Century' N.P.G. (2000-01). *Work in collections:* A.C.G.B., British Council, Contemporary Arts Soc., Southport A.G., N.P.G. (David Bowie), Pallant House Gallery, Sussex. *Signs work:* "S.A. Finer" on reverse. *Address:* 20 Kipling St., London SE1 3RU.

FINLAY, Ian, C.B.E., M.A. (Hons.), H.R.S.A.; Liveryman, Worshipful Company of Goldsmiths, London; Professor of Antiquities to Royal Scottish Academy; formerly Director, Royal Scottish Museum and Secy. Royal Fine Art Commission, Scotland; *b* Auckland, N.Z. *m* Mary Scott Pringle. two *s.* one *d. Educ:* Edinburgh Academy, University of Edinburgh. *Publications:* Scotland (O.U.P.), Art in Scotland (O.U.P.), Scottish Crafts (Harrap), History of Scottish Gold and Silver Work (Chatto), The Lothians (Collins), The Highlands (Batsford), The Lowlands (Batsford), Celtic Art (Faber), Priceless Heritage: the Future of Museums (Faber), Columba (Gollancz). *Address:* Currie Riggs, Balerno, Midlothian EH14 5AG.

FIRMSTONE, David James, N.D.D., A.T.D., M.B.E.; landscape painter in water-colour, tempera, acrylic, oils and mixed media; *b* Middlesbrough, 28 Apr., 1943. *m* Jean Gilbert-Firmstone. one *s. Studied:* Middlesbrough College of Art, Birmingham University. *Exhib:* Galleries 1995-99: The Piccadilly, Waterman Fine Art, Warrington Art, Manchester Art, Royal College Open, The Mall, British Art Show, Gallery 27, International Art Show, R.A; one-man show: Gallery 27, Cork Street June 2000. *Work in collections:* The Grosvener Collection. *Commissions:* Est, est, est Restaurants: Chester, Alderley Edge, Edinburgh, Formby, Knutsford, Shrewsbury, Newcastle, Harrogate, Chiswick, Notting Hill Gate, Liverpool, Glasgow. Recent prizes: Hunting Art Prize, short listed for 1st prize (1993), St. Helens Open, prizewinner (1994), St Helens Open, prizewinner (1995), Manchester Academy, painting prize (1996), Hunting Art Prize, prizewinner (1998), Chichester Open, prizewinner (1998), Hunting Art Prize, prizewinner (1999), Chester Open, 1st prize (1999), Laing Open, prizewinner (1999), Water-colour: Century 21: Daler Rowney 1st prize/The Artist Prize/The Ashdown Gallery prize, for best landscape (1999). *Publications:* Cheshire in Tuscany. *Signs work:* "David J. Firmstone," "David Firmstone," "D.Firmstone," "Firmstone." *Address:* Larkton Hall Studio, Goldford Lane, Bickerton Malpas, Ches. SY14 8LL.

FIRTH, Annette Rose, N.D.D., F.S.B.A.; botanical artist and china decorator in water-colour and on-glaze colours; Tutor at The Niccol Centre, Cirencester, Flatford Mill and Missenden Abbey; *b* Portsmouth, 21 May, 1921. widow. two *d. Educ:* home and Lewes, Sussex. *Studied:* in Florence (1938-39, Aubrey Waterfield), Central School, London, Whiteland College, Putney (Mary Yules). *Exhib:* S.B.A. and S.W.A., Central Hall Westminster, R.H.S., Fossewerg Artists, Glos. Soc. of Botanical Illustrators. *Commissions:* various miniature portraits. *Publications:* The Alphabet of Roses, and Mary's Flowers. *Signs work:* "A.F." *Address:* 29 Coxwell St., Cirencester, Glos. GL7 2BQ.

FIRTH, Sir Raymond William, M.A. (N.Z.), Ph.D.(Lond.), F.B.A., Emeritus Prof. of Anthropology, University of London; field research in Solomon Islands, 1928-29, 1952, 1966; Malaya, 1939-40, 1963; *b* Auckland, N.Z., 25 Mar., 1901. *m* Rosemary Upcott. one *s. Educ:* Auckland University College, London School of Economics. *Publications:* Art and Life in New Guinea (Studio, 1938); The Social

Framework of Primitive Art (ch. in Elements of Social Organization), (Watts, 1951), Tikopia Woodworking Ornament, (Man 40, 27), Tikopia Art and Society in Primitive Art and Society (ed. A. Forge) O.U.P. (1972), Art and Anthropology in Anthropology Art and Aesthetics (ed. J. Coote & A. Shelton) Clarendon (1992). *Address:* 33 Southwood Ave., London N6 5SA.

FISHER, Don Mulready, M.C.S.D., M.F.P.S.; portrait and landscape painter in oil and gouache; TV film and theatre designer; writer; *b* Finchley, 27 Apr., 1923. *m* Lyliane Guelfand (decd. 1992). one *s.* one *d. Educ:* Golders Hill School and Ravensfield College. *Studied:* Hampstead Garden Suburb Institute, Art Class (1940-41); St. Martin's School of Art under Ruskin Spear, R.A. (1943-46). *Exhib:* London Group, R.O.I., R.B.A., N.E.A.C., N.S., Berkeley Galleries, New Burlington Galleries, Piccadilly Gallery, Salon des Nations, Paris (1984), Trends (1984), Barbican Centre, Paris Salon (1985-87); one-man shows, Dowmunt Gallery (1980), Cork St. Fine Arts Gallery (1983). *Work in collections:* Britain, France, Sweden, Spain, Canada, Australia, Italy, Belgium, Poland. *Publications:* Designers in Britain Nos. 6 & 7. *Clubs:* Chelsea Arts. *Signs work:* see appendix. *Address:* 26 Rue Monsieur le Prince, 75006 Paris.

FISHER, Isabelle Diane Mulready, Diplomee Beaux Arts, Paris; stained glass artist; *b* Hampstead, 10 Dec., 1954. one *s. Educ:* Lycee Français de Londres. *Studied:* Sir John Cass College (1973-74), Wimbledon School of Art (1974-77), Beaux Arts, Paris (1978-82, Allain, Master of stained glass). *Exhib:* U.F.P.S. Luxembourg Museum, Paris (1981), Chartres Stained Glass Museum (1982), Sacred Art, le Salon des Nations (1984), Homage to Joan Miro Exhbn., Barcelona (1985). *Commissions:* window, 'Noah after the flood' l'Eglise de Ligny le-Ribaut, Loiret, France (1981); four windows, Hotel le Kern, Val d'Isere; six memorial windows for the St. Martin's Chapel (Benedictine Monastery) Monte Cassino, Italy (1989-91). *Address:* Rue de la Halle, Martel, Lot, 46.600 France. *Second Address:* 26 Rue Monsieur le Prince, 75006, France.

FISHER, Reginald Stanley, S.G.F.A. (1991); artist in oil, line and wash, pencil; retd. technical graphics illustrator and designer; Com. mem. S.G.F.A., Assoc. mem. Armed Forces Art Soc.; *b* London, 9 Nov., 1926. *Studied:* weekend courses at Heatherley School S.E. Federation of Art Socs. (Carl Cheek, Patrick Larking, Alfred Noakes). *Exhib:* S.G.F.A., U.A., R.B.A., R.I. Summer Show, Wardour Gallery, S.E.F.A.S., Int. Amateur, Wembley Art Soc., Armed Forces Art Soc., Blickling Hall, Norfolk; two one-man shows, Wembley. *Commissions:* several private commissions. *Publications:* illustrated technical books for B.P. Oil. *Signs work:* see appendix. *Address:* 36 Aldbury Ave., Wembley, Middx. HA9 6EY.

FITZGERALD, Susan Margaret, B.A. (1978), M.A. (1988); full-time painter in water-colour and oil; *b* Linc., 8 Jan., 1946. *m* Edward Michael Fitzgerald. two *s. Educ:* Boston Girls' Grammar School. *Studied:* York School of Art (1962-64), Sunderland College of Art (1964-67). *Exhib:* Chris Beetles Ltd., London; The Catto Gallery, London; World of Drawings and Water-colours, London; Adam Gallery, Bath; Bourne Gallery, Reigate; Medici Gallery, London; Nevill Gallery, Canterbury. *Commissions:* Medici Gallery, London, Nevill Gallery, Canterbury. Much time spent painting in France in her studio nr. Montpellier. Has lived/worked in Middle East and

Far East. *Signs work:* "Sue Fitzgerald." *Address:* Paragon House, 3 Stone Rd., Broadstairs, Kent CT10 1DY.

FLATTELY, Alastair F., D.A. (Edin.) 1949, Andrew Grant Fellowship (Edin.) 1953, R.W.A. (1963); painter in oil and water-colour, draughtsman in black and white; Professor and retd. Head of Grays School of Art, Aberdeen; *b* Inverness, 1922. *m* Sheila Houghton. *Studied:* Edinburgh College of Art (1945-50, Sir William Gillies). *Exhib:* London: Wildensteins, Roland Browse & Delbanco; Edinburgh: Aitken Dotts; Aberdeen: Rendezvous Gallery; R.A., R.S.A., R.W.A., R.G.I., etc. *Work in collections:* H.R.H. Duke of Edinburgh, The late President Eisenhower, Aberdeen Hull, Cheltenham, Dundee and Glasgow A.G's, R.S.A., R.W.A., Nuffield Foundation, Fleming Holdings, Grampian TV and Shell; private collections: worldwide. *Commissions:* Special artist Illustrated London News in early fifties. *Signs work:* "Flattely." *Address:* Braeside, 5 Windy Ridge, Beaminster, Dorset DT8 3SP.

FLEMING, James Hugh, B.A.Hons. (1987); printmaker, painter, illustrator, lecturer, poet; *b* Barrow in Furness. *m* Norma. one *s.* one *d. Studied:* Open University, Liverpool Polytechnic. *Exhib:* Acorn Gallery, Bluecoat Gallery, Hanover Gallery, Davey Gallery, Williamson A.G., Dee Fine Arts, Marie Curie Foundation, Merseyside Artists Touring Exhbn., Heffers, Oriel Mostyn, Cadaques Mini Print, Intaglio Mini Print, Manchester Academy, Humberside Printmaking Exhbn., Theatre Clwyd, Ruthin Craft Centre, Broekman A.G. *Clubs:* N.A.P.A., Wirral Soc. of Arts, A.B.W.S., Bluecoat Studio Printmakers' Group. *Signs work:* "Jim" and see appendix. *Address:* 19c Church Rd., West Kirby, Wirral, Merseyside L48 0RL.

FLETCHER, Adelene, N.D.D. (1960), S.B.A. (1989); artist in water-colour; *b* Stockport, 6 Aug., 1940. *m* A.J. Fletcher. one *s.* one *d. Educ:* Fylde Lodge High School. *Studied:* Stockport Art School (1956-58), Manchester Regional College of Art (1958-60). *Exhib:* R.I., R.W.S., S.B.A., and many mixed exhbns. *Publications:* author of books on flower painting, work is published in print, including limited editions. *Signs work:* "A. Fletcher." *Address:* 20 Alexandra Rd., Warlingham, Surrey CR6 9DU.

FLETCHER, Alan, A.R.C.A. (1956), M.F.A. (1957); *b* Nairobi, 27 Sep., 1931. *m* Paola. one *d. Educ:* Christ's Hospital. *Studied:* R.C.A. (1953-1956), Yale School of Design and Architecture (1957). *Exhib:* R.A. Summer Exhib., V.&A. Museum. *Publications:* Beware Wet Paint, Phaidon Press, The Art of Looking Sideways, Phaidon Press. *Clubs:* Chelsea Art Club. *Signs work:* "Alan Fletcher." *Address:* 14B, Pembridge Cres., London W11 3DU. *Email:* bwp@lavoro.u-net.com

FLETCHER, Alistair Richard, B.A.Hons. (1985), A.R.E. (1985), British Inst. award (1983), Commendation Stowells Trophy (1984), Garton and Cook award (1985); teacher, artist in etching, drawing and painting; *b* Gosforth, Northumberland, 25 Jan., 1963. *m* E.M. Fletcher. two *s.* two *d. Educ:* Henry Smith School, Hartlepool. *Studied:* Cleveland College of Art and Design (1981-82), Kingston Polytechnic (1982-85), Bretton Hall (1986-87). *Exhib:* R.E., Lowes Court Gallery, Egremont. *Clubs:* R.E. *Signs work:* "Alistair R. Fletcher." *Address:* 8 John St., Moor Row, Cumbria CA24 3ZB.

FLETCHER-WATSON, James, R.I. (1952), R.B.A. (1957); painter in water-colour; *b* Coulsdon, Surrey, 25 July, 1913. *Educ:* Eastbourne College. *Studied:* R.A. School of Architecture (silver medal for design, 1936). *Exhib:* R.A., R.I., R.B.A., Paris Salon, Stockholm, Windrush Gallery (annually). *Publications:* British Railways carriage posters; written instruction book on watercolour painting (Batsford, 1982, second book 1985, third book 1988, fourth book 1993, fifth book 1997), third video painting instruction (1993). *Signs work:* "J. Fletcher-Watson." *Address:* Windrush House, Windrush, nr. Burford, Oxford OX18 4TU.

FLOWER, Rosina, M.F.P.S., S.A.F.; painter; *b* London. one *s.* one *d. Educ:* London and Headley. *Studied:* 1971-75, P.D. Dennis Syrett, Bassetsbury Manor (Tom Coates), Burleighfield House (Anne Bruce). *Exhib:* R.B.A., R.O.I., P.S., R.I., Britains Painters, Medici Gallery, Roy Miles Gallery, Waldorf Hotel, London; Originals Gallery, Glos.; Paris Salon, France; dfn Gallery, New York; solo shows: Loggia Gallery, Roy Miles Gallery, Talent Store, Marks & Spencers, London; Henley Management College, Oxon.; Boxfield Gallery, Stevenage. *Work in collections:* in hospitals and private collections in many countries around the world. *Publications:* work repro.: greetings cards, limited edition prints. *Clubs:* F.P.S., B.A.S. *Signs work:* "Flower," "R. Flower" or "Rosi." *Address:* 132 Roberts Ride, Hazlemere, Bucks. HP15 7AN. *Email:* rosina@rosinaflower.co.uk

FLUDGATE, Rodert, artist in oil, pen and ink, pastel; specialising in pictures inspired by music and musicians; lovers and flowers; still life, portraits; also writes plays, poems, short stories; *b* Islington, London, 18 Oct., 1950. one *d. Educ:* Highbury Grove Grammar School. *Work in collections:* Channel Islands and London. *Signs work:* "Bob Fludgate," "R.E.G. Fludgate" or "R.E.G." *Address:* c/o Nevill Gallery, 43 St. Peter's St., Canterbury, Kent CT1 2BG.

FLYNN, Dianne Elizabeth, Dip. A.D. (1973), A.T.C. (1974); artist in oil and water-colour; *b* Yorkshire, 11 Oct., 1939. *m* Paul Hedley. *Studied:* Manchester School of Art (1970-73), Leeds Polytechnic (1973-74). *Exhib:* Bourne Gallery, Reigate, Priory Gallery, Cheltenham, Walker Galleries, Harrogate, Galerie Chaye, Honfleur, MacConnal-Mason Gallery, London (1981-95). *Publications:* 'Portrait Drawing Techniques' (Batsford, 1979). *Address:* 6 Powderham Cres., Exeter EX4 6DA.

FLYNN, Mary Theresa, R.S.W. (1969), D.A. (1951); landscape, figurative and still life freelance artist in water-colour, acrylic and oil; former principal teacher of art, John Paul Academy, Glasgow; *b* Selkirk, 30 Nov., 1923. *Educ:* Galashiels Academy. *Studied:* Edinburgh College of Art (1946-51, Sir Robin Philipson, P.P.R.S.A., R.A., R.S.W., Leonard Rosomon, O.B.E., R.A., R.S.W., Derek Clarke, A.R.S.A., R.S.W., J. Kingsley Cook). *Exhib:* R.S.W., R.S.A., R.G.I., S.S.W.A., S.A.A.C.; one-man shows: B.B.C. Club, Blythswood Gallery, R.S. Acad. of Music and Drama, Galashiels Scott Bi-centenary show, Gallery Paton, E.S.U. Gallery; numerous shared exhbns. *Work in collections:* Lillie A.G., S.A.C., Leeds Museum Service. *Signs work:* "Theresa Flynn." *Address:* 6 Rosebery Cres., Edinburgh EH12 5JP.

FOLKES, Peter Leonard, A.T.D., R.W.A., V.P.R.I., Hon. F.C.A., Hon U.A.; painter in oil, water-colour and acrylic; Demonstrator, Tutor and Lecturer; *b* Beaminster, 3 Nov., 1923. *m* Muriel Giddings. two *s. Educ:* Sexey's School Bruton.

Studied: West of England College of Art, Bristol (1940-42 and 1947-50). *Exhib:* R.A., R.W.A., R.I.; one-man shows: Crespi Gallery, New York (1965), University of Southampton (1965, 1973), Barzansky Gallery, New York (1967), Alwin Gallery, London (1970), Gainsboroughs' House Gallery, Sudbury (1977), R.W.A. Galleries, Bristol (1986), Guildhall Gallery, Winchester (2001). *Work in collections:* Arts Council of Great Britain, R.W.A. *Signs work:* "Folkes." *Address:* 61 Ethelburt Ave., Swaythling, Southampton SO16 3DF.

FONTAINE, Fleur', S.A.I. (1998); writer, painter in oil; *b* Denmark, 25 May, 1941. *m* John Warren (divorced). one *s.* one *d. Studied:* Hørsholm Højskole (1959-60, Helge Ernst) and Skoulunde Stage Art (Knud Hegelund), Sorø Ungdom Skole (1958-59), South France (1995-97 Pierre and Michel Mira). *Exhib:* The Mall Gallery, Orland House Gallery, Quaker Gallery, and others. *Work in collections:* throughout the world. *Commissions:* Euston Sq. Hotel. *Publications:* The Book of Life (1995); work repro.: cards, booklets, teeshirts. *Clubs:* Danish Club (part of Dover St. Arts), Soc. for Arts of The Imagination. *Signs work:* "FLEUR' FONTAINE." *Address:* 6 Pointers Cottages, Wiggins Lane, Ham, Richmond, Surrey TW10 7HF. *Website:* website: www.artmadness.co.uk

FOORD, Susan, B.A. (Hons.) Fine Art (1983), R.W.A. (1997); painter in mixed media; *b* London, 9 July, 1945. two *s. Educ:* Manchester High School of Art (1958-60). *Studied:* Jacob Kramer College of Art, Leeds (1997-80), Leeds Metropolitan University (1980-83). *Exhib:* solo: Adam Gallery Bath (1998), R.W.A. (1999), Adam Gallery London (2000, 2001); mixed: include R.A. Summer Show (1993-2001), R.W.A. Autumn Exhbn. (1993-2000). *Work in collections:* R.A., Arts Club, R.W.A., Bristol, Provident Financial, Bradford, private collections U.K., Europe, U.S., Asia. *Address:* 17 Downfield Rd., Clifton, Bristol BS8 2TJ.

FORBES, Roger David, R.B.S.A.; artist in oil, pastel, etching; Curator, Royal B'ham Soc. of Artists; *b* Smethwick, 15 Dec. 1948. *m* Andrena Patricia. two *d. Studied:* Bourneville School of Art, B' ham College of Art and Design. *Exhib:* regularly with R.B.S.A., one-man and small group exhbns. throughout Midlands, Laings (1991), National Print Exhbn. (1997). *Work in collections:* private internationally. *Clubs:* R.B.S.A. *Signs work:* "R. Forbes" (prints), "R. FORBES" or "RDF" (paintings and pastels). *Address:* 176 Poplar Ave., Edgbaston, Birmingham B17 8EP.

FORBES COLE, Joy, N.D.D., Kingston (1958); landscape painter in oil; tutor in painting at Chiswick and Isleworth Polytechnics; *b* London, 19 Dec., 1934. *m* Alban Clarke. *Educ:* Northlace School, Cheam. *Studied:* Sutton School of Art (1950-1953), Kingston School of Art (1956-1958) under Reginald Brill. *Exhib:* solo and group exhibs., London, Surrey, Hampshire and Kent. *Work in collections:* Lord Beaumont of Whitley, Dr. G.V. Planer. *Commissions:* C.I.B.A. (Arl) Ltd., G.V. Planer Ltd., Jermyn Industries. *Signs work:* "J Forbes Cole." *Address:* Flat 1, 24 Lambert Ave., Richmond, Surrey TW9 4QR.

FORD, Jenifer, V.P.N.S., F.R.S.A., Cert. Fine Art (University of Cape Town) (1953); portrait, landscape and still-life painter; *b* Cape Town, 25 June, 1934. *m* His Hon. Judge Peter Ford. one *d. Educ:* Rustenburg School, Cape Town. *Studied:* Michaelis Art School and under Bernard Adams, R.P. *Exhib:* R.P., R.O.I., N.S., C.P.S., Arts Exhbn. Bureau, Painting South East (1975), Haus der Kunst, Munich

(1988-89), Kunst in Giesing (1985-90), European Patent Office, Munich (1980-89), S.W.A.; solo shows in England and Germany. *Work in collections:* European Patent Office, Bayern Versicherung, Munich, Patents Appeal Court, Stockholm. *Signs work:* "Jenifer Ford." *Address:* 59 Lancaster Ave., Hadley Wood, Barnet EN4 0ER.

FORD, Michael, freelance artist in oils, water-colour, black and white; *b* 28 July, 1920. *Educ:* privately. *Studied:* London University; Goldsmiths' College Art School (Clive Gardiner, 1937-40). *Exhib:* R.A., R.P., N.E.A.C., R.B.A., United Soc., P.S., Paris Salon, Russell Cotes Gallery, Towner Art Gallery, also touring exhbns. on loan, etc. *Work in collections:* Three oil paintings by M. of I. (War Artists' Exhbn.). *Publications:* work repro.: Two paintings bought by M. of I.; portraits commissioned by magazines and newspapers. *Signs work:* "Michael Ford." *Address:* Studio Cottage, Winsor Rd., Winsor, Southampton SO40 2HP.

FORD, Olga Gemes, M.S.I.A. graduated in arch. (Techn. University, Berlin); lecturer, The City of Leicester Polytechnic and School of Architecture; traveller and freelance photographer, works for distinguished art publishers here and abroad (Photographic Illustrations); *m* Oliver E. Ford, B.Sc. (London), Ph.D. (Zürich), F.R.I.C. (decd.). *Educ:* Realschule, Vienna. *Studied:* architecture: Vienna, Dresden, Berlin, Paris; under Prof. Poelzig. *Exhib:* Britain Can Make It, Cotton Board, Manchester. *Publications:* work repro.: in Architectural Review, L'Architecture d'Aujourd'hui, La Construction Moderne, Design, 46 Designers in Britain 2 and 4, Decoration, etc. *Signs work:* "OLGA GEMES FORD" or "OLGA FORD." *Address:* 12 Highgate Spinney, Crescent Rd., London N8 8AR.

FORD, Peter Anthony, Sen. Fellow R.E. (1990), R.W.A. (2000); artist, independent exhibition organiser and writer; co-proprietor of Off-centre Gallery, Bristol. Designer of bookplates (ex libris); *b* 17 Apr., 1937. *m* Christine Higgott (partner). one *s.* one *d. Educ:* Hereford High School, St. Mary's College, Twickenham, Brighton College of Art, London University (Diploma in special education). *Studied:* Brighton College of Art (1960-1961) under Michael Chaplin R.E., R.W.S. (tutor in etching). *Exhib:* Create Centre Gallery, Bristol (2001), Daiwa Anglo-Japanese Foundation, London (2001) *Work in collections:* Tate Gallery (Artists' Books Collection), Nat. Art Library at V. & A. Museum, Bibliotheque National, Paris, Ashmolean Museum, Oxford, Bristol City Museum; also public collections in Poland, Russia, Spain etc. *Publications:* A Time of Transition - Contemporary Printmaking In Russia and Ukraine; articles in A.N. (Artists' Newsletter); Printmaking Today; Grapheion. *Clubs:* member of The Bookplate Society. *Signs work:* "Peter Ford." *Address:* Off-Centre Gallery, 13 Cotswold Rd., Bristol BS3 4NX. *Email:* offcentre@lineone.net

FOREMAN, William, painter in oil on canvas; *b* London, 1939. *m* Lesley. one *s.* two *d. Studied:* self taught, but encouraged by Scottish painter Angus McNab. *Exhib:* British Arts Council (1965), Galerie Daninos, Paris (1971); one-man shows: Richmond Gallery, London (1982-93), Bruton St. Gallery (1994-99), Wally Findlay Galleries, New York, Chicago, Palm Beach (2000), permanent. *Work in collections:* private: U.K., Europe, U.S.A, Canada, Middle East, Far East and Singapore. *Publications:* William Foreman Paintings 20 Years in London, (published 2000). *Clubs:* Chelsea Arts Club. *Signs work:* "FOREMAN" lower right of canvas. *Address:*

c/o Bruton St. Gallery, 28 Bruton St. London W1X 7DB.

FORREST, Martin Andrew, B.A. (Hons.), Dip. Hist. Art, F.S.A. (Scot.); artist in oil, art dealer, art historian; Com. Mem. 'Galleries and Visual Arts Committee of the Saltire Soc.'; *b* Musselburgh, E. Lothian, 7 Jan., 1951. *m* Helen Forbes. one *s*. one *d*. *Educ:* Musselburgh Grammar School. *Studied:* Wimbledon School of Art (Maggie Hambling) and post graduate Birmingham Polytechnic. *Exhib:* Royal Scottish Academy, R.G.I., Open Eye Gallery Edinburgh, Kemplay and Robertson, Edinburgh. *Work in collections:* private: U.K., U.S.A., University of Surrey, Serres Castet, France (public). *Publications:* numerous publications and exhbn. catalogues; Introduction to 'The House that Jack Built' by Robert Burns; contributor to Grove's Dictionary of Art. *Clubs:* Haddington R.F.C. *Signs work:* see appendix. *Address:* Martin Forrest Gallery, 63a Market St., Haddington, E. Lothian EH41 3JG.

FORTNUM, Peggy, book illustrator and designer; *b* Harrow-on-the-Hill, 23 Dec., 1919. *m* Ralph Nuttall-Smith, painter and sculptor (decd.). two s- *s*. *Educ:* St. Margaret's, Harrow. *Studied:* Central School of Arts and Crafts. *Exhib:* V. & A., (children's books), Public Libraries (Britain and America), British Museum (children's book show), Regional Book Show, I.C.A., Minories Colchester. *Work in collections:* The Dromkeen Collection of Australian Children's Literature. *Publications:* textile designs, magazines, illustrations for eighty books, which include The Happy Prince and Other Stories (Oscar Wilde), The Reluctant Dragon (Kenneth Grahame), A Bear Called Paddington, 12 Books (Michael Bond), Thursday's Child (Noel Streatfield), Robin (Catherine Storr), Little Pete Stories (Leila Berg), A Few Fair Days (Jane Gardam), Running Wild (Autobiography) (Chatto & Windus); drawings for television: Playschool, Jackanory. *Signs work:* "PEGGY FORTNUM" or "P.F." *Address:* 10 Hall Barn, West Mersea, Essex CO5 8SD.

FOSTER, Christine, painter in water-colour; *b* Winsford, Ches., 16 July, 1947. *m* Stuart. *Exhib:* local and London. *Clubs:* S.B.A. *Signs work:* C and F intertwined. *Address:* 133 Swanlow Lane, Over, Winsford, Ches. CW7 1JB. *Email:* fostatwins@aol.com

FOSTER, Judith, N.D.D., A.R.C.A.; painter/printmaker in oil, water-colour, pastel, etching; *b* 19 Oct., 1937. *m* Richard Pinkney. *Educ:* Bath High School G.P.D.S.T. *Studied:* Ipswich School of Art (1955-59, Philip Fortin, Colin Moss), R.C.A. (1959-62, Carel Weight, Ruskin Spear, Ceri Richards), Abbey Minor Scholarship (1962). *Exhib:* one-man shows: Ipswich, Bath, Peterborough, Edinburgh, Northampton; group shows: U.K., Belgium, Finland, and R.A., R.C.A. *Work in collections:* local authority collections; private collections U.K., U.S.A., Europe. *Clubs:* Suffolk Group, Ipswich Art Soc., Bearing 0900. *Signs work:* "J. Foster" or initials on small works. *Address:* 10 The Street, Bramford, Ipswich, Suffolk IP8 4EA.

FOSTER, Lord Norman Robert (Foster of Thames Bank), Baron 1999 (Life Peer), Kt. 1990, O.M., R.A., R.D.I. Dip.Arch. (Manc.), M.Arch. (Yale), R.I.B.A., F.C.S.D., Hon. F.A.I.A., Hon. B.D.A.; Chairman, Foster and Partners Ltd.; *b* Reddish, 1 June, 1935. four *s*. one *d*. *Educ:* Burnage Grammar School, Manchester. *Studied:* architecture: Manchester University School of Architecture and Dept. of Town and Country Planning, Yale University School of Architecture. *Exhib:* R.A., London, Paris, Bilbao, Barcelona, Seville, Tokyo, Florence, Nimes, Norwich,

Manchester, Milan, New York, Zürich, München, Madrid, Hong Kong. *Work in collections:* Museum of Modern Art, N.Y., Centre Georges Pompidou, Paris. *Publications:* Norman Foster: Buildings and Projects Vols. 1, 2 & 3 (1990), Vol. 4 (1996). *Signs work:* see appendix. *Address:* Foster and Partners, Riverside Three, 22 Hester Rd., London SW11 4AN.

FOSTER, Richard Francis, R.P.; Lord Mayor's award for London Views (1972); painter in oil; *b* London, 6 June, 1945. *m* Sally Kay-Shuttleworth. one *s.* two *d. Educ:* Harrow and Trinity College, Oxford. *Studied:* Signorina Simi, Florence (1963-66), City and Guilds, London (1967-70). *Exhib:* R.A., R.P.; one-man shows, Jocelyn Feilding Gallery (1974), Spink & Son (1978, 1982, 1984, 1991, 1997); Portrait Retrospective " So Far" with Rafael Valls (1999). Vice President R.P. (1991-1993). *Clubs:* A.W.G., Chelsea Arts. *Signs work:* "Richard Foster." *Address:* 5a Clareville Grove, London SW7 5AU.

FOUNTAIN, Desmond Hale, F.R.B.S. (1986), Pre-dip. (Stoke-on-Trent 1966), Dip.A.D. (Exeter), A.T.D./Cert.Ed. (Bristol 1970); sculptor, female nudes and life-size children, bronze editions of nine; *b* Bermuda, 29 Dec., 1946. divorced. one *s.* one *d. Educ:* Normanton College, Buxton, Derbys. *Exhib:* one-man shows (1980-96): Alwin Gallery, London; Coach House Gallery, Guernsey; Sally le Gallais, Jersey; Windjammer Gallery, Bermuda; Renaissance Gallery, Conn., U.S.A.; Cavalier Galleries, Conn., U.S.A.; The Sculpture Gallery, Bermuda; Falle Fine Art, Jersey; Bermuda National Gallery, The Desmond Fountain Gallery, newly opened in Hamlton, Bermuda. *Work in collections:* throughout U.S.A., Canada and Europe, numerous hotels, banks, public sites, corporations and Bermuda National Gallery. Founded the vehicle for Bermuda National Gallery (1982). *Signs work:* "Desmond Fountain" or "Fountain." *Address:* P.O. Box FL317, Flatts FLBX, Bermuda. *Website:* www.desmondfountain.com *Email:* sculpture@ibi.bm

FOWKES, David Reeve, B.A.; *b* Eastbourne, 15 Dec., 1919. *m* Lorna Fowkes. one *s.* one *d. Educ:* Eastbourne Grammar School; Reading University (1938-40, 1946-48). *Exhib:* Scottish Gallery Edinburgh (1973, 1976, 1980), Aberdeen University (1974, 1983), Peter Potter, Haddington (1979), Manor House, Ilkley (1984), Stonegate Gallery, York (1984, 1985, 1988, 1990, 1993, 1995, 1997), Towner, Eastbourne (1985), York University (1987), Abbot Hall, Kendal (1989), Charlotte Lampard, London (1989), Dean Clough, Halifax (1999). *Work in collections:* H.M. The Queen, Aberdeen A.G., Angus County, Towner, Eastbourne, N. of Scot. College of Agriculture, Rowett Inst., Rowntree, Scottish Arts Council. *Publications:* A Gunner's Journal (1990). *Signs work:* "FOWKES." *Address:* 75 Bishopthorpe Rd., York YO23 1NX.

FOWLER, Ronald George Francis, S.G.F.A. (1982); Mem. of Council (1985-94), Hon. Member (1999); printmaker in etching, aquatint, drypoint and wood engraving; *b* London, 15 Apr., 1916. *m* Elizabeth Jean Stewart. one *s.* two *d. Educ:* Strand School, London, and Birkbeck College, University of London. *Studied:* Glasgow School of Art, Warrington School of Art, and Chester C.F.E. *Exhib:* R.S.B.A., N.S.P.S., S.G.F.A., Mall Prints and numerous one-man shows in N.W. England. *Work in collections:* Buxton Museum and A.G., Derbyshire. *Signs work:* "FOWLER." *Address:* Yew Tree Cottage, Lower Whitley, Ches. WA4 4JD.

FRAME, Roger Campbell Crosbie, C.A. (1973); Secretary of: R.S.W.; Chartered Accountant; *b* Glasgow, 7 June, 1949. two *s.* one *d. Educ:* Glasgow Academy. *Clubs:* Glasgow Art. *Address:* 29 Waterloo St., Glasgow G2 6BZ.

FRANC, Babara, sculptor in wire; *b* London, 27 Oct., 1954. *m* Philip Sindall. one *d. Studied:* Morley College of Art (John Bellany, Maggie Hambling). *Exhib:* Phillips International Auctioneers, Molesey Gallery, Roy Miles Gallery, Fitch's Ark, Usiskin Contemporary Art, Worthing Museum; Sculpture Prize, Chelsea Art Soc., Linley & Co., Pimlico. *Commissions:* d.p.ua advertising agency - 6' fish for their offices, group of birds for L.C.A. *Publications:* Garden Crafts by Geraldine Rudge, Country Living, Homes & Gardens, Painting World, Country Homes & Interiors magazines. *Clubs:* Nine Elms Group of Artists. *Signs work:* "Babara Franc." *Address:* 11 Queen's Gdns., Ealing, London W5 1SE. *Email:* barbara.franc@btinternet.com

FRANCESCONI, Anselmo: see ANSELMO (Anselmo Francesconi).

FRANCIS, Audrey Frances, R.I. (1994); painter in gouache, oil and acrylic; *b* 5 Oct., 1931. *m* O.R. Francis. *Educ:* PND Malaya, MLC Perth, W.A., Girdlers School, Kent. *Studied:* Wimbledon School of Art (1948-52), Central School of Arts and Crafts (1953). *Exhib:* R.I., R.W.S. Open, N.E.A.C., and mixed exhbns. *Signs work:* "F. Francis." *Address:* Grove Cottage, Waldron, nr. Heathfield, E. Sussex TN21 0RB.

FRANCYN, (Dehn Fuller), F.F.P.S., W.I.A.C., N.S.; painter in oils and gouache; *b* Portsmouth. *m* Curt Dehn. one *s.* one *d. Educ:* at home. *Exhib:* one-man shows: Paris, The Hague, Utrecht, Sydney, London; group shows: Free Painters and Sculptors, W.I.A.C., Hampstead Artists, N.S., etc. *Work in collections:* Holland, Germany, U.S.A., Australia. *Publications:* Poems, Man's Moment (U.S.A.), portfolio of folk-songs, collection of poems. *Clubs:* I.C.A., Hampstead Artist. *Signs work:* see appendix. *Address:* 6 Elsworthy Ct., Elsworthy Rd., London NW3.

FRANKENTHALER, Helen, B.A. (1949); First Prize, Paris Biennale (1959); painter in oils, acrylic, on unsized cotton-duck; *b* New York, 12 Dec., 1928. *m* Stephen M. DuBrul. *Educ:* Bennington College, Vermont, (B.A.). *Exhib:* numerous throughout America including M.O.M.A. (N.Y.), Andre Emmerich N.Y., Guggenheim Museum N.Y., Knoedler Gallery N.Y., Neuberger Museum of Art, Purchase College, N.Y. (1999-2000); also France, Italy, Sweden, Canada, Korea, Japan, Spain, Germany, Singapore, etc. *Work in collections:* includes, N.Y.C.: Guggenheim Museum, M.O.M.A., Whitney Museum, Metropolitan Museum of Art; Washington D.C.: National Gallery of Art, Corcoran Gallery of Art, Hirshhorn Museum and Sculpture Garden, etc; also many museums and art galleries worldwide. *Publications:* Monographs and exhbn. catalogues; films and videos. *Signs work:* see appendix. *Address:* c/o Knoedler Gallery, 19 E. 70th St., New York, N.Y 10021.

FRANKLAND, Eric Trevor, R.W.S., R.E., R.B.A.; mem. of The London Group and Art Workers Guild, Leverhulme Fund award, Landseer Scholarship, R.A. Silver Medal for Drawing; painter and printmaker; lectured at Medway College of Art, Hornsey College of Art and Middlesex University as an associate senior lecturer; Hon. Curator, Royal Watercolour Soc.; *b* Middlesbrough, 1931. *m* Dorothy Southern, artist. *Studied:* Laird School of Art, Birkenhead; Royal Academy Schools, London. *Exhib:* many solo shows, and most major group exhbns. Work in public and private collections. Domestic landscape construction, "Summer River Bed Winter Flood Plain", show on television, four short films, Channel Four TV (1988), B. Sky B. TV (1990), London Weekend TV (1992), Carlton TV (1999). *Signs work:* "Trevor Frankland" on prints, "FRANKLAND" on other works, sometimes "T.F." *Address:* 13 Spencer Rd., London SW18 2SP.

FRANKLIN, Annette Winifred, artist in water-colour, oil, pastel, pen and ink, and gouache; miniature portraitist, Poole Pottery paintress (1945-50); *b* 28 Jan., 1932. *m* Stanley Franklin. *Educ:* St. James and Henry Harbin Schools, Poole. *Studied:* mainly self taught, some tuition - pottery painting: (John Adams, Ruth Pavley); oil painting: (Leonard and Margaret Boden). *Exhib:* R.M.S. & R.W.S. at Mall Galleries., Westminster Hall, Hilliard Society, Gatcombe Farm, Royal School of Needlework, Foyles London, College of Fashion and Design, Wallsworth Hall. *Work in collections:* U.K., U.S.A., Australia, Bahrain, Abu Dhabi, N.Z., The Princess Royal & Capt. Mark Phillips. *Publications:* Quilting and Design by M. McNeal; articles for Poole Pottery Collectors Club and Hilliard Society Magazine. *Clubs:* H.S., Fine Art Promotions, Poole Pottery Artist Collectors Club, Lansdown Art. *Signs work:* see appendix. *Address:* 'Sunnymead', 15 Marsh Lane, Leonard Stanley, nr. Stonehouse, Glos. GL10 3NJ.

FRANKLIN, Ellen, F.P.S.; Mem. Ben Uri Gallery; painter in oil; *b* Berlin, 18 Aug., 1919. *Studied:* Reiman School of Art, Berlin (1936-38), Morley College, London. *Exhib:* Gladstone Pk. Gables Gallery (1980, 1995, 1997), Loggia Gallery (1985, 1991), Trends (1987, 1989), Ben Uri (1988, 1992), Cardiff (1988), Morley Gallery (1991, 1993, 1994, 1995, 1996, 1997). Work in private collections. *Signs work:* "E. Franklin." *Address:* 44 Beechcroft Gdns., Wembley, Middx. HA9 8EP.

FRASER, Donald Hamilton, R.A.; painter; *b* London, 30 July, 1929. *m* Judith Wentworth-Sheilds, 1954. one *d. Studied:* St. Martin's School of Art, London (1949-52) and in Paris (French Gov. Scholarship). Tutor, Royal College of Art (1958-84); Hon. Fellow R.C.A. (1984); Hon. Curator, Royal Academy (1992); Trustee, Royal Academy (1993); Vice-Pres. Royal Overseas League since 1986; Vice-Pres. Artist's General Benevolent Inst.; mem. since 1986 of Royal Fine Art Commission. *Exhib:* Over 70 individual exhbns. in Europe, N. America and Japan. Work in public collections throughout the world. *Publications:* 'Gauguin's Vision after the Sermon' (Cassell, 1968), 'Dancers' (Phaidon, 1988). *Clubs:* Arts. *Signs work:* see appendix. *Address:* c/o Royal Academy of Arts, London W1V 0DS.

FRASER, Elizabeth Bertha, Mem. Society of Portrait Sculptors; sculptor in wax, plaster, bronze, painter in oil; *b* Teddington, London, 1914. *m* Lindley Maughton Fraser. *Studied:* Birmingham School of Art, Central School of Art, London, Westminster School of Art, London, Edinburgh College of Art. *Exhib:* R.A.; one-man shows, London and Edinburgh, Tour of Britain Sculptors Society, Society of Portrait Sculptors Yearly Exhbn., Edinburgh Younger Academy. *Commissions:* portrait heads. *Publications:* work repro.: television talks, theatrical designs. *Clubs:* Chelsea Arts. *Signs work:* "Liz Fraser," "Elizabeth Scott-Fraser" or "Elizabeth Fraser." *Address:* The Studio, 7 Ridgway Gdns., London SW19 4SZ.

FREEMAN, Janet A., B.Ed. (Hons.), B.S.A.; painter in oil; *b* Bedford, 5 Dec., 1933. *m* Richard Freeman. three *s.* one *d. Studied:* Goldsmiths' College, London,

Bath Academy of Art, Bath C.H.E. *Exhib:* N.E.A.C. London, Millfield Open, R.W.A., Annual Bristol, School House Gallery Bath, Laing Open, Handel House Gallery Devizes, Black Swan Guild Frome, Bath University, Ron Whittle Fine Art, Birmingham, Inoccent Fine Art, Bristol, R.A. Summer Exhib. (2001). *Clubs:* Bath Soc. of Artists. *Signs work:* "J.A. Freeman." *Address:* 27 Northampton St., Bath BA1 2SW.

FREEMAN, Lily, F.B.S., B.A. Hons. (1978); painter in oil and water-colour; lecturer on Modern Art, University of 3rd Age; *b* Vienna, 7 Feb., 1920, widow. one *d.* *Educ:* Realgymnasium, Vienna. *Studied:* Vienna, Arthur Segal School, Hampstead (A. Segal, Marianne Segal). *Exhib:* N.Y. Expo (1985), Barbican (1982), Orangery, Holland Pk. (1979, 1981-85), Alicante, Spain (1983), Loggia Gallery (1978, 1982, 1984), Cockpit Theatre, Odeon Marble Arch, Hampstead Town Hall, New Art Theatre, Alpine Club, Hampstead Art Centre, Ben Uri Gallery, Royal Overseas League, Guildhall, London, Tradescant Trust, Leighton House, Burgh House. *Work in collections:* Dr. Lansky, Vienna. *Address:* 65 Dunstan Rd., London NW11 8AE.

FREEMAN, Richard, M.Ed., R.W.A.; Morris Singer Award, R.W.A. (1997); sculptor in clay, plaster, bronze; *b* Windsor, 12 Apr., 1932. *m* Janet Freeman. three *s.* one *d. Studied:* Bognor Regis Training College, Goldsmiths' College, London, Chelsea Art School, London, University of Bristol. *Exhib:* recent shows include McHardy Sculpture Co. London, Wills Lane Gallery St. Ives, Anthony Hepworth Fine Art Bath, School House Gallery Bath, R.W.A. Annual Bristol (1992-2001), Gumstool Gallery Tetbury, etc. Work in collections internationally. *Signs work:* "FREEMAN" or "R.F." *Address:* 27 Northampton St., Bath BA1 2SW.

FREER, Roy, N.D.D., A.T.D., R.O.I., R.I.; artist in oil and water-colour; art course tutor and organiser, demonstrator, lectures on appreciation of painting and drawing.; *Studied:* Bournville School of Art, and Birmingham College of Art. *Signs work:* "ROY FREER" dated. *Address:* Flat 12, 14 Deparys Ave., Bedford MK40 3TW.

FREETH, Peter, Dip. Fine Art Slade School (1960), A.R.A., (1990), R.A. (1992), R.E. (1991); printmaker in etching, aquatint, water-colour, teacher; Tutor of Etching, R.A. Schools, London; *b* B'ham, 15 Apr., 1938. *m* Mariolina. two *s. Educ:* K.E.G.S. Aston, B'ham. *Studied:* Slade School of Fine Art (1956-60, Antony Gross, William Coldstream). *Exhib:* R.A., R.E., Christopher Mendez, London SW1, Bankside Gallery (2001), London SE1, Beardsmore Gallery, London NW5, City Gallery, EC3, Mary Kleinman Gallery, N1. *Work in collections:* V. & A., B.M., Arts Council, Fitzwilliam Cambs., Metropolitan Museum, N.Y., National Gallery, Washington, Ashmolean, Oxford, Govt. art collection. *Signs work:* "P. Freeth." *Address:* 83 Muswell Hill Rd., London N10 3HT.

FREUNDLICH, Grace Ruth, Travelling Fellowship, Scottish Arts Council (1979), Fellowship, Provincetown Workshop (1976); artist in acrylic, ink, oil, graphite; instructor; exhbn. com., Provincetown Art Assoc. and Museum; *b* New York, 6 May, 1939. two *s. Educ:* University of Wisconsin, Madison (1964), art & art history; C.U.N.Y. (N.Y.); H.S. of Music & Art, N.Y.C. *Studied:* Hunter College Graduate School (Bob Swain), Provincetown Workshop (Leo Manso, Victor Candell). *Exhib:* Gallery Matrix, Provincetown (1993, 1994), Foundry Gallery,

Washington, D.C. (1981), Demarco Gallery, Edinburgh (1980), Provincetown Workshop (1976), Provincetown Art Assoc. and Museum (1986-96); solo show, Roosevelt House of Hunter College, N.Y. (1975), Galerie Henri, Boston, Mass. (1961). *Work in collections:* University of Wisconsin, Hunter College, Histadrut, Israel, American Forum, National Press Bldg., Washington D.C.; and Ilana Soesman, Israel, Marion Namenwirth, St. Paul, Minn., A. & S. Hoffman, Jerusalem, Israel. *Commissions:* The Land meets the Sea, The Sea meets the Land, American Forum, Washington D.C. *Publications:* Precis, with Robert E. Miller on exhbns. at Gallery Matrix, Provincetown. Scottish Arts Council fellowship/travelling, through Richard Demarco. *Clubs:* College Art Assoc., National Women in the Arts Museum, Washington, D.C. Provincetown Art Assoc. and Museum. *Signs work:* "G.F." or "G. Freundlich." *Address:* 200 W. 93rd St. 4J, New York, N.Y. 10025 U.S.A. *Email:* graciousf@earthlink.net

FREW, Hilary, F.R.B.S. (1960), R.B.A. (2000), Cert R.A.S., A.T.D., P.G.C.E.; Elizabeth Frink Sch. of Sculpture Award (2000), Leverhume Award (1961); sculptor in Portland stone; design technology teacher (1979-1993), now freelance sculptor; Mem. Sec. R.A.S.A.A./Reynolds Club at R.A.; *b* Essex, 30 Mar., 1934. *m* G.R. Bonye. one *s.* one *d. Educ:* convents in Buckingham, Felixstowe, Bedford, and St. Andrews University. *Studied:* S.E. Essex School of Art (1954-1957), Royal Academy Schools (1957-1961), Stockwell College (1972-1973), Goldsmith's College (1978-1979) under T.B.Huxley Jones, Maurice Lambert, and Arnold Machin. *Exhib:* numerous group society exhibs. and garden galleries, Bruton St., Gallery, London. *Work in collections:* Bromley Educ. Authority and private collections. *Commissions:* Harlow Town Park Paddling Pool. *Signs work:* "HF." *Address:* Dees Holt, Raggleswood, Chislehurst, Kent BR7 5NH.

FRIEDEBERGER, Klaus, painter; *b* Berlin, 1922. *m* Julie. *Educ:* Quakerschool Eerde, Netherlands. *Studied:* E. Sydney Tech. College. *Exhib:* one-man shows: Belfast (1963); London (1963, 1986, 1990, Retrospective 1992); group shows since 1944. Europe Prize, Ostende 1964 (Gold Medal), National Gallery of Australia, 'Surrealism' (1993), 'The Europeans' (1997). *Work in collections:* private: Australia, England, Europe, U.S.A. Official purchases: Mosman Art Prize 1949, National Gallery of Australia, British Museum, University of Wollongong. *Publications:* Arts Review, Art and Australia, Twenty Five Years Annely Juda Fine Art (London 1985), Surrealism (Canberra 1993), The Dictionary of Art (Macmillan 1996), The Europeans (Canberra 1997), etc. *Signs work:* "Friedeberger." *Address:* 16 Coleraine Rd., London SE3 7PQ.

FRÖHLICH-WIENER, Irene, sculptress in bronze, stone, wood, fibreglass, cement; *b* Luzern, Switzerland, 26 Aug., 1947. *m* Josef Fröhlich. two *d. Educ:* Kantons-Schule, Luzern (Matura), Institut Maïeutique (Art-therapy). *Studied:* Centre de la gravure Contemporaine, Geneva (1969), Marylebone Inst. (1973-74, carving under E. Mehmet), H.G.S. Inst. (John Brown), Sir John Cass School of Art (Clive Duncan). *Exhib:* R.B.A., Royal Festival Hall, Camden Art Centre, Woodstock Gallery, Smee Gallery, Norfolk, Ben Uri Gallery, Mall Galleries, Old Bull Art Centre, Draycott Gallery, Blenheim Gallery, Cecilia Coleman Gallery, October Gallery, dfn Gallery, U.S.A. (New York). *Work in collections:* Helmut Stern Collection, Michigan, McHardy Sculpture Co., London, Gold Art, Haifa.

Commissions: Rank Xerox (1996) award. Hertsmere: Bushey Park (1998), 'Tree of Life' Finchley Synagogue (1999), Florida Parc, Lugano (2001). *Clubs:* H.V.A.F. and Royal Soc. of Sculptors, F.P.S. *Signs work:* "Irène." *Address:* 53 Oakleigh Ave., London N20 9JE. *Website:* www.breakingart.com.//:irene

FROST, Anthony, D.F.A. (1973); artist in acrylic paint on canvas; *b* St. Ives, Cornwall, 4 May, 1951. *m* Linda Macleod. two *s. Educ:* North Oxon. Technical College and School of Art, Banbury. *Studied:* Cardiff College of Art (1970-73). *Exhib:* Four Young Artists, Penwith Gallery, St. Ives; John Moores, Liverpool; Public Hanging, St. Ives; Dangerous Diamonds, Hull; Anthony Frost - on Colour, Newlyn Gallery; "Viva Blues" Newlyn Gallery (1996), touring Birmingham, Darlington and London (1997); The Belgrave Gallery, London (1997); King's University, Cambridge (1998); Corporate Connoisseurs, London (1999); Jersey Arts Centre, Jersey (1999), Hilsboro Fine Art, Dublin (2001); Corporate Connoisseurs, London (2001); Advanced Graphics, London (2001); The Original Print Gallery, Dublin (2002). *Work in collections:* Littlewoods Organisation, Liverpool, Nuffield Trust, Contemporary Arts Soc., Cornwall C.C., Kasser Foundation, New York. *Clubs:* Subbuteo Football, Petangue, Boule. *Signs work:* "Anthony Frost." *Address:* Rosemergy Cottage, Morvah, Penzance TR20 8YX.

FROST, Michael John, L.L.C.M. (1947), B.A. English Hons. (1951), M.A. Politics (1969), U.A.; painter in oil and pastel, retired; *b* Burton-on-Trent, 8 Apr., 1930. *Educ:* Burton Technical High School, Leeds University, Lancaster University. *Studied:* Glasgow School of Art, part time (1963-1966), more recently taught by Rod Williams, Victor Ambrus and Brian Gallagher. *Exhib:* Mall Galleries, Westminster Gallery, London and with various societies. *Clubs:* Armed Forces Art Society. *Signs work:* "FROST." *Address:* 2 Bedford Ave., Frimley Green, Surrey GU16 6HP.

FROST, Terry, R.A.; painter in oil, acrylic, collage; *b* Leamington Spa, 1915. *m* Kathleen. five *s.* one *d. Educ:* Central School, Leamington Spa. *Studied:* Stalag 383, Camberwell School of Art and St. Ives. *Exhib:* numerous one-man and mixed shows from 1944 to the present. *Work in collections:* Tate Gallery, B.M., V. & A., and many other public and private collections in Great Britain, U.S.A., Canada and Europe. *Commissions:* British Airways. *Publications:* 'Terry Frost' (Scolar Press, 1994). *Clubs:* Chelsea Arts. *Signs work:* "Terry Frost" on verso. *Address:* c/o The Royal Academy, Piccadilly, London W1V 0DS.

FROY, Martin, D.F.A. (1951); Emeritus Professor of Fine Art, Reading University; *b* London, 9 Feb., 1926. *Studied:* Slade School. Gregory Fellow in Painting, Leeds University (1951-54); Trustee, National Gallery (1972-79), Tate Gallery (1975-79); Fellow U.C.L. (1978). *Work in collections:* Tate Gallery, Museum of Modern Art, N.Y., Chicago Art Institute, Arts Council, Contemporary Art Society, Royal West of England Academy, Leeds University, Art Galleries of Bristol, Carlisle, Leeds, Reading, Southampton, Wakefield. *Commissions:* Artist Consultant for Arts Council to City Architect, Coventry (1953-58); mosaic decoration, Belgrade Theatre (1957-58); two murals in Concert Hall, Morley College (1958-59). *Address:* University of Reading, RG1 5AQ.

FRY, Minne, B.A. (1953); painter and printmaker in oil, water-colour, etching; *b*

Johannesburg, 20 Dec., 1933. *m* Lionel Fry. one *s.* two *d. Educ:* University of the Witwatersrand. *Studied:* Central School of Art (1955, Cecil Collins, Mervyn Peake), Morley College (Adrian Bartlett, Jennie Bowen). *Exhib:* New Vision Centre (1958), Camden Galleries (1989), Green Room (1995), Coningsby Gallery (2000). *Work in collections:* C.A.S. *Clubs:* Printmakers Council, National Society of Painters & Sculptors. *Signs work:* "Minne Fry." *Address:* 16 Caroline Pl., London W2 4AN. *Email:* britart.com

FRYER, Katherine Mary, A.T.D. (1932); Princess of Wales Scholarship for wood engraving (1932), Hoffmann Wood (Leeds) gold medal for painting (1968); artist in oil and water-colour; 1937-47 taught at Bath School (later Academy) of Art Corsham; lecturer in School of Painting, B'ham College of Art (retd.); Professor of Painting, Royal Birmingham Soc. of Artists; *b* Roundhay, Leeds, 26 Aug., 1910. *Educ:* Roundhay High School, Leeds. *Studied:* Leeds College of Art (1926-32, E. Owen Jennings). *Exhib:* R.A., R.B.S.A., etc. *Work in collections:* R.A., B'ham Register Office, Leeds, Wakefield and Harrogate Art Galleries Permanent Collections and University of Birmingham. *Publications:* book of wood engravings "Before the War and Long Ago", published by Old Stile Press Llandogo. Retrospective, exhibition, Royal Birmingham Soc. of Artists, June 2000. *Signs work:* "K.M. Fryer" or "K. FRYER." *Address:* 47 Moor Pool Ave., Harborne, Birmingham B17 9HL.

FULLER, Peter Frederic, R.A.I. (1976), A.A.H. (1976), F.P.S. (1991); Whatman prize; painter in water-colour; art historian; *b* Ramsgate, 10 Apr., 1929. *m* Rosemary Blaker. one *d. Educ:* John Hezlett School. *Studied:* Maidstone College of Art. *Exhib:* R.A., R.B.A., R.P.S., R.W.S. (Open), R.I., N.E.A.C., F.P.S., R.S.M.A., K.C.C. 'Kent Artists', Britain in Water-colours, Towner A.G., E. Stacey-Marks Gallery Eastbourne, Arts Centre Folkestone, Arune Arts Centre Arundel, Roger Green Fine Art High Halden, Bakehouse Gallery Sevenoaks, Cloisters Gallery Canterbury, Leeds Castle, etc. *Work in collections:* America, Australia, Canada, France, Germany. *Clubs:* Maidstone Art, Maidstone Archaeological Group. *Signs work:* "Peter Fuller." *Address:* 31 Sandling La., Penenden Heath, Maidstone, Kent ME14 2HS.

FULLER, Violet, F.F.P.S.; artist in water-colour, oil, pastel; *b* Tottenham, 26 July, 1920. *Studied:* Hornsey School of Art (1937-40) under Russell Reeve, R.B.A., A.R.E.; Stroud School of Art (1942-44) under Gwilym E. Jones, A.R.C.A. *Exhib:* Paris, R.A., R.I., R.B.A., N.E.A.C., W.I.A.C., Whitechapel A.G. (1967), 9 painters of East London, Bath Festival (1967), Brighton Festival (1988, 1989, 1991, 1993); one-man shows: Woodstock Gallery (1958, 1959, 1961, 1963, 1967, 1970), Old Bakehouse Gallery, Sevenoaks (1968, 1970), Hornsey Library (1968, 1973), New Gallery, Hornsey (1975), Forty Hall, Enfield (1974, 1984), Bruce Castle, Tottenham (1980), Loggia Gallery (1983, 1986, 1991), The Grange, Rottingdean (1997, 2000). *Work in collections:* London Borough of Haringey, London Borough of Enfield. *Clubs:* Soc. of Sussex Painters. *Signs work:* "VIOLET FULLER." *Address:* 1 Helena Rd., Woodingdean, Brighton, Sussex BN2 6BS.

FURNIVAL, John P., A.R.C.A.; artist in pen and ink and mixed media; retd. lecturer, Bath Academy of Art; editor, Openings Press; *b* London, 29 May, 1933. *m* Astrid Furnival. two *s.* two *d. Studied:* Wimbledon College of Art; Royal College of

Art. *Exhib:* Biennale des Jeunes, Paris; one-man show: Thumb Gallery, London; retrospective: Laing Gallery, Newcastle, Arnolfini, Bristol, plus various international exhbns. of visual and concrete poetry. *Work in collections:* Arts Council of Gt. Britain, Arnolfini Trust, Munich Pinakothek. *Publications:* The Bang Book (Jargon Press), The Lucidities (Turret Books). *Clubs:* Dorothy's Umbrellas Dining Society (DUDS). *Signs work:* "John Furnival." *Address:* Rooksmoor House, Woodchester, Glos. GL5 5NB.

G

GAGE, Anthea Dominique Juliet, S.S.A., R.S.W.; art teacher, artist in gouache and water-colour; full time teacher, Royal High School, Edinburgh; *b* Edinburgh, 21 Mar., 1956. *Educ:* John Watsons School, Stevenson's College of Educ. *Studied:* Edinburgh College of Art (Dip. 1974-78, Post. Dip. 1978-79, David Michie, George Donald). *Exhib:* annually at S.S.A., R.S.W.; various mixed exhbns. *Signs work:* "Anthea D.J. Gage." *Address:* 15 Craighouse Gdns., Edinburgh EH10 5LS.

GAINSFORD, Sylvia Petula, N.D.D., A.T.D.; painting and illustrating; co-Proprietor, Gallery One, Fishguard, Pembrokeshire, Wales; *b* 1942. *m* Leon Olin. *Studied:* Royal Tunbridge Wells (1962, painting and wood engraving). *Exhib:* numerous. Permanent: Gallery One, Fishguard. *Work in collections:* Webber Coll. Ontario, Kallis Foundation, Beverly Hills. *Commissions:* numerous. *Publications:* Food from the Countryside (Leon and Sylvia Olin); Just Like You and Me by Johnny Morris; Tarot of the Old Path published and commissioned by A.G. Müller (4th world best seller), also Tarot of Northern Shadows; Rune Vision published by Chrysalis. *Signs work:* "Sylvia P. Gainsford." *Address:* Fron Haul, Rhos-y-Caerau, Goodwick, Pembrokeshire SA64 0LB. *Email:* Gallery One (49 page website) sylvia@abergwaun.com

GALE, Martin, A.N.C.A.D. (1973), R.H.A. (1996); full time painter in oil and watercolour; represented by Taylor Galleries, Kildare St., Dublin; *b* Worcester, 20 Mar., 1949. two *s.* one *d. Educ:* Newbridge College, Co. Kildare. *Studied:* National College of Art and Design, Dublin. *Exhib:* numerous solo and group exhibs. in Ireland, group exhibs. in Britain and U.S.A., XI Biennale de Paris (1980-1981). *Work in collections:* numerous public and private collections in Ireland and Britain. *Commissions:* National Self Portrait Collection, European Parliament, Strasburg, E.S.B. Municipal Gallery, Waterford, and others. *Publications:* Exhib. catalogues, catalogue essays. *Clubs:* member of A.O.S.D.A.N.A. *Signs work:* "Martin Gale." *Address:* Coughlanstown, Ballymore Eustace, Co. Kildare, Ireland. *Email:* martin-gale@oceanfree.net

GALE, Raymond David George, N.D.D. (1958), A.T.C. (Lond.1959); printer, teacher; *b* Hanwell, London 25 June, 1937. *Studied:* Ealing School of Art (1953-58), Hornsey College of Art (1958-59). *Clubs:* Richmond Printmakers. *Signs work:* "Ray Gale." *Address:* 283 Hounslow Rd., Hanworth, Middx. TW13 5JQ.

GALE, Richard John, Dip. A.D. (1968), M.A. (R.C.A., 1973); artist in oil; *b* Bristol, 8 Feb., 1946. *m* Francis Joan. *Educ:* Weston-super-Mare Grammar School. *Studied:* Kingston upon Thames School of Art (1965-68), R.C.A. (1970-73). *Signs work:* "R. Gale." *Address:* 5 Hillside Rd., Clevedon, Avon.

GALES, Simon, B/Tec.Dip. (Dist.) (1985), B.A. (First Class Hons.) Fine Art (1988); painter in oil on linen or canvas; *b* 1964. *m* Susanne. one *s.* *Studied:* Ipswich School of Art (1983-85), Goldsmiths' College, London (1985-88). *Exhib:* Christie's (1989), Jill George Gallery London and Los Angeles (1990), Christie's, S. Kensington (1991), Bruton St. Gallery (solo: 1999, 2001). *Work in collections:* London Underground Museum, Covent Gdn., Robert Holmes à Court Museum, Perth, Australia. *Signs work:* "SIMON GALES" on back of painting. *Address:* c/o Bruton St. Gallery, 28 Bruton St., London W1X 7DB.

GALLAGHER, Brian, artist in water-colour, pastel and pencil; Secretary and Council mem. Pastel Soc; tutor to painting courses; *b* Chester, 31 May, 1935. *m* Rosemary June Webb. one *s.* *Studied:* Portsmouth College of Art, privately under Herbert Green. *Exhib:* P.S., S.WL.A., Porthill Gallery London, Anna-Mei Chadwick Gallery, London, R.B.S.A. Galleries, Birmingham, John Nevill Gallery, Canterbury, Cowleigh Gallery, Malvern, and many provincial galleries. *Publications:* work repro.: contributor to art magazines. *Clubs:* London Sketch. *Signs work:* "Brian Gallagher." *Address:* 99 Gilmore Cres., Ashford, Middx. TW15 2DD.

GALVANI, Patrick, painter in water-colour and oil, journalist, author; *b* Bures, Suffolk, 11 Sept., 1922. *m* Madeleine. one *s.* *Educ:* University College School. *Studied:* U.C.S. and self-taught. *Exhib:* London, Florida and Mandell's Gallery, Norwich, various galleries in East Anglia and Sussex, four in Florida. *Commissions:* various houses. *Clubs:* Ipswich Art. *Signs work:* "PATRICK GALVANI." *Address:* 53 Beach Cres., South Terrace, Littlehampton, W. Sussex BN17 5NT.

GAMBLE, Tom, R.W.S.; painter in oil and water-colour; Mem. A.W.G.; senior lecturer, Art and Design, Loughborough College of Art (1952-84); Freeman of City of London, Gold Medallist and Liveryman of the Worshipful Company of Painter/Stainers; *b* Norton-on-Tees, 6 Feb., 1924. married. one *s.* *Studied:* Constantine College, Middlesbrough. *Exhib:* R.A., R.W.S., Bankside Gallery London, Royal Festival Hall, Mall Galleries, Hunting Group Prizes, Brian Sinfield, Milne & Moller, Woodgates Gallery, East Bergholt, Leicester A.G., Middlesbrough A.G., Exposicion International de Acuarela Barcelona, American and Canadian Water-colour Socs., and various provincial galleries. *Work in collections:* Lloyds of London, University of Loughborough, Notts. C.C., Leics. C.C., Crathorne Collection; private collections in Europe, U.S.A., Canada. *Clubs:* Arts. *Signs work:* "Tom Gamble." *Address:* 10 Blythe Green, East Perry, Huntingdon, Cambs. PE28 0BJ.

GAMLEN, Mary, A.T.D. (Lond. 1936), Hon. U.A.; sculptor in wood and terra-cotta, painter in oil and water-colour; *b* London, 1913. *m* Alan Somerville Young (decd.). one *s.* two *d.* *Educ:* Student at Hornsey School of Art; on staff there (1937-1945). *Exhib:* R.A., R.B.A., N.E.A.C., R.W.S., Edinburgh R.A., Fermoy Gallery, Kings Lynn, Premises, Norwich, Mall Galleries. *Work in collections:* Museum of the Royal Marines (Lying-in-State of Sir Winston Churchill), Belize Cathedral (reredos),

Norfolk (village signs), Holt Church (carving of St. Andrew), Thorpe Market Church (restoration work). *Signs work:* "GAMLEN" or "Mary Gamlen" and see appendix. *Address:* Ham House Pottery, Southrepps, Norwich, Norfolk NR11 8AH.

GANLY, Rosaleen Brigid, A.R.H.A. (1928), R.H.A. (1935), H.R.H.A. (1983); artist in oil, water-colour, egg-tempera, pastels, pen and ink, etc.; *b* Dublin, 29 Jan., 1909. *m* Andrew Ganly. one *s.* one *d. Studied:* Dublin School of Art under Sean Keating, Patrick Tuohy, Oswald Reeves, Oliver Sheppard and George Atkinson, and at R.H.A. School under D. OBrien, Sean O'Sullivan, Richard Orpen, etc., Cubism under André L'hote, Paris. *Exhib:* R.H.A. (yearly since 1928), yearly with Watercolour Soc. of Ireland, Limerick, Galway, Cork, Berlin, America, Canada, Dublin Municipal Gallery of Modern Art, Royal Dublin Soc., Waterford, Blackrock (All Saints Church, murals in egg-tempera), murals in church, Ennis, Co. Clare; one-man shows, Dublin Painters Gallery (1936), Dawson Gallery (1965), Lincoln Gallery, Dublin (1980); two-man shows with B. M. Flegg, Wexford and Dunlaoghaire; retrospective exhbn. Gorry's Gallery, Dublin (1987), Hugh Lane Municipal Gallery of Modern Art, Dublin (1998). *Work in collections:* Haverty Trust, National Self Portrait Gallery, Limerick, Royal Dublin Soc. of Ireland. *Publications:* work repro.: numerous book illustrations and dust jackets. *Signs work:* Early work, up to 1936, two capital B's within a circle or "Brigid OBrien"; all works, from 1936 signed "RBG." *Address:* 6a Laurel Hill, Upper Glenageary Rd., Dunlaoghaire, Co. Dublin.

GARDINER, Vanessa, B.A. (Hons.) (1982); painter in acrylic, collage on plyboard; *b* Oxford, 7 Apr., 1960. partner: Mr. A. Lowery, painter. one *d. Studied:* Oxford Polytechnic (1978-79), Central School of Art and Design (1979-82, David Haughton). *Exhib:* solo shows: Duncan Campbell, London (1991, 1992, 1996, 1998 (twice), Gordon Hepworth, Exeter (1993), Mill Lane Gallery, Lyme Regis, Dorset (1997); recent group shows: Merriscourt Gallery, Oxfordshire (1999), Six Chapel Row, Bath (1999), Duncan Campbell London (2000), now represented by Hart Gallery, London, exhibition (Oct. 2001). *Work in collections:* Bournemouth University. *Publications:* work repro.: Modern Painters Magazine, Summer 1996 - review by Elizabeth James. *Signs work:* "Vanessa Gardiner." *Address:* Lilac Cottage, Fernhill, Charmouth, Dorset DT6 6BX.

GARDNER, Annette, Diploma Di Merito, Universita Della Arti, Italy (1982); painter in oil; Principal and Teacher, Wood Tutorial College; Founder and Director, New End Gallery; *b* 11 June, 1920. *m* C. J. Wood, M.A., (decd.1972). one *s.* one *d. Studied:* Twickenham Art School (1952-54); Hampstead Garden Suburb Institute (1954-56) under Mr. Gower; St. Martin's (1960-63) under David Tindle; principal teacher Walter Nessler. *Exhib:* Numerous group shows and travelling exhbns.; finalist, Woman's Journal Painting of the Year (1961). *Work in collections:* Australia, England, U.S.A., Israel, Hungary. *Clubs:* F.P.S., Ben Uri. *Signs work:* "A. Gardner." *Address:* The Studio, 18 Canons Drive, Edgware, Middx. HA8 7QS.

GARDNER, Derek George Montague, V.R.D., R.S.M.A., Commander R.N.V.R.; Hon. vice-president for life R.S.M.A.; marine artist in oil and watercolour; Rudolph Schaefer award at International Exhbn. of Marine Art, Mystic, U.S.A. (1984); *b* Gerrards Cross, Bucks, 13 Feb., 1914. *m* Mary née Dalton. one *s.* one *d. Educ:* Monkton Combe Junior School and Oundle School. *Exhib:* R.S.M.A.,

United Artists; one-man shows, Polak Gallery, London (1972, 1975, 1979, 1982, 1987, 1990, 1995, 1998). *Work in collections:* National Maritime Museum, Greenwich; Bermuda Maritime Museum; Tenerife Museum; R.N. College, Dartmouth. Mentioned in Despatches, H.M.S. Broke (1942). *Clubs:* Naval Club. *Signs work:* "Derek G. M. over Gardner." *Address:* High Thatch, Corfe Mullen, Wimborne, Dorset BH21 3HJ.

GARDNER, Judith Ann, B.A. Hons. Fine Art (1974); painter in oil; art tutor; *b* Welling, Kent, 15 Apr. 1952. *m* Colin. two *d. Educ:* Maryville Convent, Welling, Kent. *Studied:* Maidstone College of Art under principal, William Bowyer R.A., tutor, Frederick Cuming R.A. (1970-1974). *Exhib:* R.A., R.B.A., N.E.A.C., R.O. I., R.S.M.A., and other galleries. *Work in collections:* private collections in U.K., U.S.A. and Australia. *Clubs:* member of R.B.A. *Signs work:* "J Gardner." *Address:* 72 Gladstone Rd., Broadstairs, Kent CT10 2JD.

GARDNER, Peter Colville Horridge, R.O.I. (1977), A.T.D. (1951), F.R.S.A. (1969); artist in oil; *b* London, 25 Oct., 1921. *m* Irene. *Educ:* St. Matthias C. of E. School, London SW5. *Studied:* Hammersmith School of Art (1935-38, 1946-50), London University Inst. of Educ. (1950-51). *Exhib:* R.A., R.B.A., R.O.I., N.E.A.C. *Work in collections:* Nuffield Foundation, York University. *Signs work:* "Peter Gardner." *Address:* 11 Pixmead Gdns., Shaftesbury, Dorset SP7 8BZ.

GARFIT, William, R.B.A.; I.L.E.A. Dip with hon., Byam Shaw School Cert. with Distinction, R.A.S. Cert.; artist in oils, specialising in River Landscapes and pen and wash illustration work; *b* Cambridge, 9 Oct., 1944. *m* Georgina Joseph. one *s.* two *d. Educ:* Bradfield College. *Studied:* Cambridge School of Art (1963), Byam Shaw (1964-67), R.A. Schools (1967-70). *Exhib:* one-man shows, Waterhouse Gallery (1970, 1972, 1974), Mall Galleries (1976), Stacey Marks, Eastbourne (1978), Tryon and Moorland Gallery, London (1981, 1983, 1985, 1988, 1991), Holland & Holland Gallery (1994). *Publications:* illustrated, Dudley worst dog in the World, Amateur Keeper, Your Shoot, The Woods Belong to Me, The Fox and the Orchid, Prue's Country Kitchen, Cley Marsh and its Birds, The Game Shot, How the Heron got Long Legs, The Woodpigeon, author of Will's Shoot (1993). *Signs work:* "William Garfit." *Address:* The Old Rectory, Harlton, Cambridge CB3 7ES.

GARMAN, Evelyn Daphne, N.S. (1980), S.W.A. (1985); sculptor in clay, wax, bronze, resin bronze; *b* Beaconsfield, 6 Apr., 1913. *m* R. C. Garman, artist. three *d. Educ:* Convent of the Holy Child Jesus, Sussex. *Studied:* London studio of A. Acheson, A.R.A. privately (1933-38). *Exhib:* S.W.A., N.S., S.P.S., Winchester, Andover, and two private shows with husband. *Work in collections:* Heads of Founders in Winsor and Newton Museum, Wealdstone, Harrow. *Clubs:* Cheltenham and Cotswold. *Signs work:* "E.D.G." or "D. GARMAN." *Address:* Ashburnham, 8 Charnwood Cl., Cheltenham, Glos. GL53 0HL.

GARRARD, Peter John, P.P.R.B.A., R.P., N.E.A.C., R.W.A.; painter in oil; *b* 4 Jan., 1929. *m* Patricia Marmoy. one *s.* two *d. Educ:* Magdalen College School, Brackley. *Studied:* Byam Shaw School of Drawing and Painting. *Work in collections:* public and private collections in England, America, Australia, Canada, Germany, etc. *Signs work:* "P.J.G." *Address:* 340 Westbourne Park Rd., London W11 1EQ.

GARRETT, Roger MacLean, artist in oil; University Lecturer; Senior Lecturer, University of Bristol; *b* Nairn, Scotland, 10 Feb., 1942. *m* Bertha Garrett. one *s*. one *d*. *Exhib:* R.W.A. (1995, 1997, 1998), R.A. (1997, 1998), School House Gallery, Bath (1997), R.B.S.A. (1998), Chichester, Open Exhbn. (1998). *Signs work:* "R.G." and "Roger Garrett." *Address:* 38 Holmes Grove, Henleaze, Bristol BS9 4EE.

GARTON, Michael, N.D.D. (1956), D.F.A. (1959), R.W.A. (2000); painter in oil; retired lecturer in painting; *b* Reading, Berks., 5 June 1935. *m* Antonia. one *s*. four *d*. *Educ:* Reading, Berks. *Studied:* Guildford (1950), Exeter (1956), Slade School (1959). *Exhib:* R.A. Summer Exhib. (1977, 1987, 1997), R.W.A. (1997-2001). *Work in collections:* private collections. *Publications:* Landscape Research (1984), Art in Nature (1996). *Signs work:* "M Garton." *Address:* 5 Silver Terr., Exeter, Devon EX4 4JE.

GATTEAUX, Marcel, landscape and still-life artist in oil; *b* Mitcham, Surrey, 1 Oct., 1962. *Studied:* Camberwell School of Art (1980-81, Dick Lee, Sargy Mann); then studied restoration for a number of years before redirecting his attention to painting. *Exhib:* one-man shows, Caelt Gallery (1997, 1998, 1999, 2000, 2001). *Work in collections:* Churchill Hotel, London; Cliveden and private collections in the U.K. and U.S.A. *Signs work:* see appendix. *Address:* 182 Westbourne Grove, London W11 2RH.

GEARY, Robert John, F.C.S.D. (1980), F.R.S.A. (1981), Hon S.G.F.A. (1994); graphic artist and illustrator in ink, water-colour and drypoint; *b* London, 15 Jan., 1931. *m* Hazel Mair Plant. one *d*. *Studied:* Hammersmith School of Arts and Crafts (1945-48). *Exhib:* S.G.F.A. *Work in collections:* work in private collection: The Saatchi Gallery. *Publications:* work repro.: drawings in several children's books, The Folio Soc., humorous illustrations for: New Statesman, Punch (1978-81), The Oldie, The Sunday Telegraph, The Times Supplements, The Independent, Private Eye. *Signs work:* "Robert Geary" or "R.G." *Address:* 70 Felton Lea, Sidcup, Kent DA14 6BA.

GEDDES, Stewart John, M.A. Arts Criticism (1997), B.A. (Hons.) Fine Art (1983), R.W.A. (1996); landscape painter in oil, tutor; *b* Aylesford, Kent, 4 Mar., 1961. *m* Juliet Simmons. *Educ:* Maidstone School for Boys. *Studied:* Canterbury College of Art (1979-80, Eric Hurran), Bristol Polytechnic (1980-83, Alf Stockham), City University, London (1996-97, Dr. Eric Moody). *Exhib:* R.A., R.W.A., Waterman Gallery, Cadogan Contemporary, London. *Work in collections:* House Of Commons. *Signs work:* "S.J. Geddes" on back of work. *Address:* 49 Noyna Rd., Tooting Bec, London SW17 7PQ.

GEDEN, Dennis John, D.Litt (Hons); painter; *b* Ontario, Canada, 25 Apr., 1944. *m* Sandie. *Studied:* Sir George Williams', Montreal. *Exhib:* exhibits internationally. *Work in collections:* Tate, London, MacLaren Art Centre, Barrie, Canada, Simon Fraser University, Vancouver, Canada, Anderson Collection, Buffalo, U.S.A., Government of Ontario Art Collection, Canada, Bibliotheque Nationale, Paris. *Signs work:* "D Gedden." *Address:* c/o Redfern Gallery, 20 Cork St., London W1X 2HL. *Email:* gedensan@vianet.on.ca

GEE, Arthur, S.WL.A. (1969-1999), N.A.P.A. (1993); painter/printmaker, wildlife and landscape; Cert. of Merit, University of Art, Salsomaggiore, Italy (1982); Purchase prizewinner (1990), Mini-print International, Barcelona; Finalist, Laing Competition (1991, 1994), Manchester/London; Artists award, N.A.P.A. Exhbn. B'ham (1993, 1997, 1998, 1999); Invited Member, Sefton Guild of Artists (1997); Founder Com. Mem. National Exhibition of Wildlife Art, Liverpool (1994); Millenium Artists Index (2001); *b* Latchford, Warrington, 10 Jan., 1934. *m* Margaret Ray Robinson. one *s*. one *d*. *Educ:* Penketh and Sankey Sec. School, Warrington (1945-49). *Studied:* St. Helen's College of Art and Design (1983-84). *Exhib:* throughout U.K. and abroad, S.WL.A. annually (1965-1999), Mall Galleries, London (F.B.A.). *Commissions:* F.B.A. and B.A.S.C., plus private commissions. *Publications:* Three poems illustrated in "Flights of Imagination" (Blandford Press, 1982). *Signs work:* "Arthur Gee." *Address:* 31 Karen Cl., Burtonwood, Warrington, Ches. WA5 4LL.

GELDART, William, artist/illustrator in pencil, pen and ink, scraperboard, pen and wash, water-colour; *b* Marple, Ches., 21 Mar., 1936. *m* Anne Mary. one *s*. one *d*. *Educ:* Hyde Grammar School. *Studied:* Regional College, Manchester (1956-57). *Exhib:* R.A., Manchester Fine Arts, Chris Beetles and various others. *Work in collections:* worldwide. *Commissions:* Hallé Orchestra, Manchester International Airport, Ciba Geigy, I.C.I., Rolls Royce, C.J.S., I.C.L., Reynolds Chains, Manchester Grammar School, Chetham School of Music, Astra Zeneca, Hodder & Stoughton, Gallimard (Paris), and others. *Publications:* written and illustrated: Geldart's Cheshire; illustrated many books for leading publishers. *Address:* Geldart Gallery, Chelford Rd., Henbury, nr. Macclesfield, Ches. SK11 9PG.

GELLER, William Jasper, F.R.S.A., S.G.F.A.; artist in pen and ink, gouache, egg tempera; designer; Past Pres., Soc. of Graphic Fine Artists; *b* London, 21 Dec., 1930. *m* Olive. two *d*. *Educ:* Loughton School. *Studied:* City of London, Apprentice in Art, Central School, Regent Polytechnic (1947-52). *Exhib:* R.S.M.A. Annual show, S.G.F.A. Annual show, F.B.A. Touring Exhbn. *Work in collections:* Port of London Authority and private collections. *Publications:* 20th Century British Marine Painting. *Clubs:* Rotary International, R.Y.A. *Signs work:* "William Geller." *Address:* 17 Silver St., Maldon, Essex CM9 4QE.

GENTLEMAN, David, R.D.I. (1972); artist and designer: water-colour, lithography, wood engraving, illustration, stamps, posters, etc.; *b* London, 11 Mar., 1930. *m* Susan Evans. one *s*. three *d*. *Educ:* Hertford Grammar School. *Studied:* St. Albans School of Art (1947-48), R.C.A. (1950-53, Edward Bawden, John Nash). *Exhib:* solo exhbns. at Mercury Gallery, London (1970-2000). *Work in collections:* B.M., V. & A., Tate Gallery, National Maritime Museum, Murals at Charing Cross Underground Station. *Publications:* David Gentleman's Britain, - London, - Coastline, - Paris, - India, - Italy and many illustrated. *Signs work:* "David Gentleman." *Address:* 25 Gloucester Cres., London NW1 7DL. *Email:* d@gentleman.demon.co.uk

GEORGE, Brian, R.B.A., F.R.S.A., M.Phil. (Loughborough), M.Ed. (Nottingham), Hons. B. Ed. (Loughborough); painter in oil and acrylic; hard edge abstracts based on decay, dereliction and Suffolk coast sea defences; part-time lecturer at Nottingham University; *b* Ripley, Derbyshire, 7 June 1945. *m* Joan nee Smith. *Educ:* Queen Elizabeth's Grammar School for Boys, Mansfield;

Loughborough and Nottingham Universities; Cambridge Institute of Education. *Exhib:* R.B.A., R.O.I., Laing; exhibited one-man and with groups throughout Great Britain and Europe. *Work in collections:* Nottinghamshire Library Service, Herligenhaus Civic Collection, and numerous private collections. *Clubs:* President, Mansfield Society of Artists. *Signs work:* "B GEORGE." *Address:* Westfield House, 251 Alfreton Rd., Blackwell, Alfreton, Derbyshire DE55 5JN. *Email:* beageart@aol.com

GEORGE, David, wood sculptor, mostly fine-finished for interior display, abstract, curvacious beautiful woods; walnut, yew, cherry, etc.; *b* Winchester, 20 Feb., 1952. *Educ:* Andover Grammar School, Salisbury College. *Exhib:* various shows, galleries, South England. *Commissions:* oak troll for Test Valley Borough Council, depicting "Billy Goats Gruff" story. *Signs work:* Unsigned. *Address:* Little Park Studio, Little Park, Andover, Hants. SP11 7AX. *Website:* www.sculptor.freeserve.co.uk *Email:* davidgeorge@sculptor.freeserve.co.uk

GEORGE, Patrick, artist; *b* Manchester, 1923. *m* 1st 1955 June Griffith (dissolved 1980). four *d.* 2nd 1981 Susan Ward. *Educ:* Edinburgh College of Art, Camberwell School of Art; taught, Slade School, University College London (1949-88); Prof. of Fine Art (1983); Slade Prof. (1985-88). *Exhib:* retrospective, Serpentine Gallery (1980). *Work in collections:* Arts Council, Tate Gallery, etc. Dealers: Browse and Darby. *Address:* 33 Moreton Terr., London SW1 2NS.

GEORGIOU, Elpida: see ELPIDA.

GETHIN, Jackie, C.I.C., S.B.A.; artist in water-colour; mem. Soc. of Botanical Artists; *b* Brikendon, Herts., 14 May, 1949. *m* Richard. three *d. Educ:* Effingham House School, Cooden, Sussex. *Studied:* Southampton College of Art, Bournemouth and Poole College of Art (Keith Rennison). *Exhib:* numerous mixed shows including S.B.A. *Work in collections:* Francis Iles, Rochester, Beaulieu Fine Arts, Beaulieu, Hants. *Signs work:* "Jackie Gethin." *Address:* Trotts Ash, Sole Street, nr. Gravesend, Kent DA12 3AY.

GIARDELLI, Arthur, M.B.E., M.A. (Oxon); President, 56 Group Wales; painter and sculptor in mixed media (wood, brass, burlap, oil, etc.) for wall panels, water-colour, and lecturer; *b* London, 11 Apr., 1911. married. one *s.* one *d. Educ:* Alleyn's School, Dulwich, Hertford College, Oxford. *Studied:* Ruskin School of Art, Oxford. *Exhib:* Amsterdam, Paris, Chicago, Washington, Bologna, Bratislava, London, New York, Cardiff, Edinburgh. *Work in collections:* Arts Council of Great Britain, Welsh Arts Council, National Museum of Wales, National Library of Wales, Museum of Modern Art, Dublin, National Gallery Slovakia, National Gallery Prague, Musée des Beaux Arts, Nantes, Estorick Collection, Grosvenor Gallery, London, Tate Gallery, England & Co. *Commissions:* wall panel: Argus Newspaper; door: Grosvenor Gallery, and Brook St. Gallery. *Publications:* work repro.: The Delight of Painting (University College, Swansea); art magazines. *Signs work:* see appendix. *Address:* Golden Plover Art Gallery, Warren, Pembroke SA71 5HR.

GIBB, Avril V.: see WATSON STEWART, (Lady) Avril Veronica.

GIBBONS, Jeff, B.A. (Hons.), M.A.; painter; *b* London, 9 Nov., 1962. *m* Joanna Melvin. one *s.* one *d. Educ:* Crown Woods School. *Studied:* Ravensbourne (1980-

1981), Middx. Polytechnic (1981-1984), London University (1989-1991). *Exhib:* various exhibs including, Morley Gallery, London (1994), Bede Gallery, Jarrow (1996), John Moores (1995 - prizewinner & 1999), Natwest Gallery (1997 & 1998). *Publications:* catalogues, John Moores (19 & 21), Natwest (1997 & 1998), British Library Report (2000-2001). *Signs work:* "Jeff Gibbons." *Address:* c/o Eagle Gallery, Emma Hill Fine Art, 159 Farringdon Rd., London EC1R 3AL. *Email:* emmahilleaglc@aol.com

GIBBONS, John, B.A. Hons. (Sculpture); Head of Sculpture, Winchester School of Art, elected Prof. (1995); *b* Ireland, 1949. *Educ:* Ireland. *Studied:* sculpture: St. Martin's School of Art (1972-75, David Anneley, William Tucker). *Exhib:* one-man shows: International Arts Centre, London (1975), Project Gallery, Dublin (1979), Nicola Jacobs Gallery, London (1981), Triangle Center, N.Y.C. (1984), Serpentine Gallery (1986), John Hansard Gallery, Southampton University (1986), Galerie Wentzel, Köln (1987), Madeleine Carter Fine Art, Boston, Mass. (1988), Flowers East (1990, 1992, 1994, 1997, 1999), Flowers Graphics (1996), Butler, The Castle, Kilkenny Ireland (1996), Whitworth A.G. Manchester (1997), Kettles Yard, Cambridge (1997), Lothbury Gallery, London (1998), Temple Bar Gallery, Dublin (1998), Crawford Municipal A.G., Cork (1998), Nograd History Museum, Salgotorjan, Hungary (1999), Endre Horvath Gallery, Balassagyarmat, Hungary (1999), Taylor Galleries, Dublin (1999), Flowers Central (2001). *Work in collections:* A.C.G.B., Syracuse University, N.Y., Edmonton A.G., Alberta, Gulbenkian Foundation, Comino Foundation, Museum of Contemporary Art, Barcelona, Tate Gallery; private collections: U.K., U.S.A., Germany, Ireland, Canada, Japan, France. *Publications:* Gonzalez: A Legacy; Introduction to catalogue, South Bank Centre, Whitechapel. *Signs work:* "J.G." welded on. *Address:* 14 Almond Rd., London SE16 3LR.

GIBBS, Timothy Francis, M.A. (Oxon., 1948), C.F.A. (Oxon, 1949); painter in oils, acrylic and water-colour; deputy Ruskin master (1974-80), Ruskin School, Head of Fine Art Oxford University (1976-80); *b* Epping, Essex, 21 Aug., 1923. *m* Bridget Fry. one *s.* two *d. Educ:* Trinity College, Oxford (1946-48). *Studied:* Ruskin School (1947-49). *Exhib:* one-man shows: Piccadilly Gallery (1955), Leicester Galleries (1962, 1963, 1966, 1969), Ashmolean Museum (1981), Rockefeller Art Collection, New York (1986), Clarendon Gallery (1987, 1990), Cadogan Contemporary (1993), Gallery 28, Cork St. (1998). *Work in collections:* Government Art Collection, Atkinson A.G., Southport, Financial Times, Royal College of Music, Nottingham, Hertfordshire Educ. Authority. *Signs work:* "T. F. Gibbs." *Address:* 55 Hardinge Rd., London NW10 3PN.

GIBILARO, Jason, painter in oil and acrylic; *b* London, 25 Aug., 1962. *Studied:* St. Martin's School of Art and Design (1980-81), Brighton School of Art and Design (1981-84). *Exhib:* R.A. Summer Show, Peterborough Museum and Gallery, Christopher Hull Gallery London. *Work in collections:* University of London Picture Club. *Commissions:* Hazard Evaluation Laboratory. *Address:* 62 Kemble House, Barrington Rd., London SW9 7EF.

GIBSON, Jane Barr, B.A., A.R.M.S., H.S.; artist in oil, pastel, water-colour of miniatures and larger works; Artist in Residence, Dorothy L. Sayers Soc.; *b*

Smithton, Tasmania, 14 Sept., 1954. *Studied:* Carlisle College of Art and Design, Norwich School of Art. *Exhib:* R.M.S. Westminster Gallery London, H.S. Wells, Medici Gallery London, Polak Gallery London, Malcolm Innes Gallery, London and Edinburgh, Samap, France (miniature soc.). *Work in collections:* Capitol Hill, Washington D.C. U.S.A. *Commissions:* "Lockerbie Remembered" (commissioned by Dumfries & Galloway Constabulary). *Publications:* illustrated: To Those Who Love - poetry book by Jo McNaught. *Clubs:* R.M.S., H.S. *Address:* 'Cornerways', 7 Selkirk Rd., Kirkcudbright DG6 4BL.

GIBSON, Jean, awarded minor travelling scholarship to Italy; sculptor in hardboard, fibreglass, resin, herculite; *b* Staffs., 17 Dec., 1935. *m* Anthony Whishaw. two *d. Educ:* Abbots, Bromley. *Studied:* Royal College of Art. *Exhib:* Leicester Gallery, London (1968, 1969), Oxford Gallery (1974), Metropole A.G. and Centre, Folkestone (1973), Nicola Jacobs Gallery, London (1981). *Work in collections:* U.S.A., London, Israel, private collections. *Signs work:* "J. Gibson." *Address:* 7a Albert Pl., Victoria Rd., London W8.

GIBSON, Veronica, B.A. (Hons.); painter in oil, private teacher; *b* St. Albans, Herts., 15 Apr., 1954. *Educ:* Loretto College. *Studied:* Hertfordshire College of Art (1972-73), Canterbury College of Art (1978-81, Thomas Watt, D.A. Edin.). *Exhib:* R.A., N.E.A.C., R.O.I., R.W.A., Cardiff. *Work in collections:* S. Glamorgan; private: France and Sweden. *Signs work:* see appendix. *Address:* Ty Coed, Chapel St., Bedlinog, Mid Glamorgan CF46 6TS.

GIFFARD, Colin Carmichael, M.A. Cantab., Dip.Arch. London (A.R.I.B.A. 1947-57), R.W.A.; R.I.B.A. Schools Drawing Prize (1932), Rome finalist (Arch.) 1939; painter in oil, acrylic; lecturer, Bath Academy of Art, Sydney Place (1951-68); *b* London, 1915. *Educ:* Charterhouse, Clare College, Cambridge; University College, London. *Studied:* painting: Bath Academy of Art (1948-51). *Exhib:* R.A., R.W.A., London Group, Bristol City A.G., Salon des Nations, Paris; one-man shows, Woodstock Gallery, London (3). *Commissions:* murals in schools for Herts., Wigan Educ. Coms. Work purchased: R.W.A., Newton Park Coll., Bath, Bristol, Walsall Educ. Coms. *Address:* Little Mead, Freshford, Bath BA3 6DH.

GILBERT, Dennis, N.E.A.C.; portrait and landscape painter; formerly senior lecturer, Chelsea School of Art; *b* London, 7 Jan., 1922. *m* 1st Joan Musker; 2nd (2000) Ann Kodicek. three *s.* one *d. Educ:* Weston-super-Mare. *Studied:* St. Martin's School of Art (1946-51). *Exhib:* R.A., Paris Salon, R.P., R.B.A., N.E.A.C., Soc. of Landscape painters, Browse & Darby, Leicester Galleries, Redfern, W.H. Patterson Fine Art, Thompsons Gallery, Duncan Miller and Zwemmer Galleries, etc.; one-man shows: F.B.A. Gallery (1968), Langton Gallery (1982), Gill Drey Gallery (1989), Highgate Fine Art (1997). *Clubs:* Arts, Chelsea Arts. *Signs work:* "Dennis Gilbert." *Address:* Top Studio, 11 Edith Gr., Chelsea, London SW10 0JZ.

GILBERT, George, R.S.W. (1973), D.A. (Glasgow) 1961, Post. Dip. (1962); artist in water-colour, acrylic, pen and wash; *b* Glasgow, 12 Sept., 1939. *m* Lesley. three *s. Educ:* Glasgow. *Studied:* Glasgow School of Art (1957-61): Guthrie Book Prize (portraiture). *Exhib:* one-man shows: Kelly Gallery, Glasgow (1967), Byre Theatre, St. Andrews (1979), Loomshop Gallery, Lower Largo (1981, 1988, 1990), Torrance Gallery, Edinburgh (1991); several joint shows in Glasgow and Edinburgh;

regular exhibitor at R.S.A., R.S.W., etc., also Commonwealth Arts Festival, Bath Art Fair, Cleveland International Drawing. *Work in collections:* Nuffield Foundation, Fife Regional Council; many private home and abroad. *Signs work:* "George Gilbert." *Address:* 44 Marketgate South, Crail, Fife KY10 3TL.

GILDEA, Paul Rudolph, B.A. Hons. Fine Art; artist in oil on canvas; part time tutor, Fulham and Chelsea A.E.I.; *b* London, 3 Jan., 1956. *Educ:* Dulwich College. *Studied:* Camberwell School of Arts and Crafts (1975-76), Middlesex Polytechnic (1976-79). *Exhib:* Serpentine Summer Show (1982), Whitechapel Open (1987), Riverside Open (1987), R.A. Summer Show (1987). *Signs work:* "Gildea." *Address:* 41 Ballater Rd., Brixton, London SW2 5QS.

GILES, A. Frank Lynton, Médaille d'Argent, Paris Salon (1948), A.R.W.A. (1970), R.W.A. (1978); artist in oil, acrylic, water-colour, pastel and graphics, etc.; Finalist Sunday Times water-colour competition (1990), Mem. Advertising Association, Royal Soc. of Arts; *b* London. three *s. Studied:* Goldsmiths', St. Martin's. *Exhib:* R.A., and most other societies including R.S.A., R.Cam.A. (Eminent Artists Eastbourne), Bradford, R.P., R.B.A., R.I., R.W.S., N.E.A.C., Alresford Gallery, Bertrand Russell Centenary, Arts Council, C.E.M.A., Worthing A.G. (1996), Sheffield Open, Chesterfield, R.W.A. Sunday Times tours, toured by R.A. with C.E.M.A. in 1944, and Arts Council in 1949, *Work in collections:* Sheffield, Bristol, Worthing, Canada and private collections. *Commissions:* Portraits. *Publications:* R.A. Illustrated, R.W.A. 150th Anniversary Illustrated, Sussex Arts Publications. *Signs work:* "FRANK LYNTON GILES" or "Lynton Giles." *Address:* 19 Browning Rd., Worthing, W. Sussex BN11 4NS.

GILES, Peter Donovan, Ph.D. (Middx) (2000), N.D.D. (Special level Illustration) (1959), A.T.C. (Lond.) (1960), F.R.G.S.; painter, illustrator and sculptor; counter-tenor; teaches part-time, Manwood Grammar School, Sandwich; *b* Perivale, Middx., 15 Feb., 1939. *m* Elizabeth Ann Broom. one *s.* one *d. Educ:* Castlehill College, Ealing. *Studied:* Ealing School of Art (1954-59), Hornsey College of Art (1959-60). *Exhib:* All Hallows on the Wall, EC2; provincial one-man shows; lecture tours, U.S.A. and Canada (1973, 1975, 1978, 1996). *Work in collections:* Lichfield City A.G., War Memorial Ely Cathedral. *Publications:* novels, non-fiction, cartoon collection, board games. *Signs work:* "Peter Giles." *Address:* Filmer House, Bridge, Canterbury, Kent CT4 5NB.

GILI, Katherine, B.A. (1970); sculptor in steel; *b* Oxford, 6 Apr.,1948. *m* Robert Persey. one *s. Studied:* Bath Academy of Art (1966-70), St Martin's School of Art (1971-73). *Exhib:* Tate Gallery, Hayward Gallery, Serpentine Gallery, R.A., Conde Duque Centre Madrid, Salander / O'Reilly, N.Y. *Work in collections:* Arts Council of England, and private collections in Britain, Spain and U.S.A.; City of Lugano Switzerland, Dumfries and Galloway, General Electric, U.S.A., Railtrack. *Publications:* numerous exhbn. catalogues, reviews, articles. *Clubs:* F.R.B.S. *Signs work:* see appendix. *Address:* 7 The Mall, Faversham, Kent, ME13 8JL.

GILLESPIE, Michael Norman, A.R.B.S.; sculptor in bronze; *m* Lesley Todd. two *s.* one *d. Educ:* St. Paul's School. *Studied:* Hammersmith College of Art (1952-56). *Exhib:* nineteen plus mixed shows. *Work in collections:* Cambs. C.C., Herts. C.C. *Publications:* Studio Bronze Casting (Batsford, 1969). *Signs work:* "M.

Gillespie." *Address:* 53 Cottenham Rd., Histon, Cambridge CB4 9ES.

GILLICK, James Balthazar Patrick, B.A. (Hons.); painter in oil, drawings, drypoint, portraits, still lifes, figures; *b* Kings Lynn, 8 Feb., 1972. *m* Miriam. one *s.* one *d. Educ:* Ratcliffe College, Wisbech Grammar School. *Studied:* C. & G.C.H.E. *Exhib:* numerous exhibs., London and nationally. *Work in collections:* Baroness Thatcher. *Commissions:* portraits: Baroness Thatcher (1998), Rt. Rev. M. Couve de Murville, Archbishop of Birmingham (1999). *Signs work:* Monogram - G bisected by J - see appendix. *Address:* c/o Jonathan Cooper, Park Walk Gallery, 20 Park Walk, London SW10 0AQ. *Email:* mail@jonathancooper.co.uk

GILLIMAN, Tricia, B.A. (Hons.) Fine Art, M.F.A. Fine Art; artist in oil on canvas; Senior lecturer, Central/St. Martin's School of Art, London Inst.; *b* 9 Nov., 1951. *m* Alexander Ramsay. one *s. Studied:* Leeds University, Newcastle University. *Exhib:* Benjamin Rhodes (1985, 1987, 1993), Arnolfini (1985), Gardner Centre, Brighton (1993), Jill George (1997-99), John Moores (1983, 1985, 1989, 1991), etc. *Work in collections:* Contemporary Art Soc., Unilever PLC., New Hall Cambridge, University of Liverpool, Herbert A.G. Coventry, University of Leeds, Stanhope Properties Ltd., Television South West, The Stuyvesant Foundation. *Commissions:* B.B.C. Film: The Colour Eye: The Dynamics of Paint. *Address:* 149 Algernon Rd., London SE13 7AP.

GILLISON TODD, Margaret, M.C.S.P., Dip.Ed.Lond.; painter and illustrator; Keeper of Display, Grosvenor Museum, Chester (1966-77); *b* Warwick, 1916. *m* Hugh Michael Todd. *Educ:* Howell's School, Denbigh. *Exhib:* R.Cam.A., N. Wales Group, S. Wales Group, S.E.A. Pictures for Schools, National Eisteddfod, Royal Horticultural Soc. (Silver Gilt and Silver Medals), Alpine Garden Soc. (Gold Medal), etc. *Publications:* illustrations for "The Flora of Flintshire" by Goronwy Wynne (1993); A Histology of the Body Tissues, illustrated (E. & S. Livingston, Edinburgh); Louise Rayner (Grosvenor Museum, Chester); work repro.: medical and botanical publications, etc. *Signs work:* "MARGARET GILLISON," "MARGARET GILLISON TODD," or initials. *Address:* Pen-y-Llwyn, Llanarmon-yn-lâl, Mold, CH7 4QW.

GILLMOR, Robert, N.D.D. (1958), A.T.D. (1959); freelance illustrator, designer, painter in water-colour, black and white, lino-cut prints; Director Art and Craft, Leighton Park School (1959-65); President, S.WL.A.(1984-94), President, Reading Guild of Artists (1969-84); *b* Reading, 6 July, 1936. *m* Susan Norman, painter. one *s.* one *d. Educ:* Leighton Pk. School, Reading. *Studied:* School of Fine Art, Reading University (1954-59, Prof. J.A. Betts, William McCance, Frank Ormrod, Hugh Finney). *Exhib:* S.WL.A. *Work in collections:* Ulster Museum and A.G., Belfast, Reading Museum and A.G. *Publications:* 100 books illustrated. *Signs work:* "R.G." or "Robert Gillmor." *Address:* North Light, Hilltop, Cley, Norfolk NR25 7SE.

GILLMORE, Olwen Nina, S.W.A.; sculptor in clay and bronze; *b* Zimbabwe, 19 Mar., 1936. *m* Charles Gillmore. two *s.* three *d. Educ:* U.S.A. (1980-82), London Karin Jonzen (1983-90). *Exhib:* Chelsea; S.W.A. London; Chichester Cathedral; U.S.A.; Guernsey, C.I. *Commissions:* Several (private). *Signs work:* "Olwen." *Address:* Sarnesfield, Lurgashall, Petworth, W. Sussex GU28 9EZ.

GILMORE, Sidney, sculptor in steel, wood, stone and glassfibre; *b* London, 3 June, 1923. *Educ:* Willesden Grammar School. *Studied:* Willesden College of Technology. *Exhib:* R.A., F.P.S., Chicago British Fortnight, U.S.A., Bradford A.G., Heals, London, City of Westminster, etc. *Clubs:* F.P.S. *Signs work:* "Sidney Gilmore." *Address:* 111 Sudbury Ave., N. Wembley, Middx. HA0 3AW.

GILMOUR, Albert Edward, artist in oil, pen and ink; sec., Gateshead Art Club (1950-51); retd. B.R. train driver; *b* W. Hartlepool, 31 May, 1923. *m* Elaine Bolton. one *s.* one *d. Educ:* Heworth and Felling Elementary Schools. *Studied:* courses at Gateshead Technical College, King's College, Newcastle. *Exhib:* Federation of Northern Arts Socs. Exhbns., Artists of the Northern Counties Exhbns., Artists of Durham Exhbn., Gateshead Art Club Exhbns. *Publications:* Locomotive Express, British Railways Magazine, N.E. Region. *Clubs:* Park Rd., and West End Group, Newcastle; Gateshead Art. *Signs work:* "GILMOUR." *Address:* 11 Limewood Grove, Woodlands Pk., North Gosforth, Newcastle upon Tyne NE13 6PU.

GILMOUR, Judith, D.A. (Glas.); ceramist in stoneware and porcelain thrown and assembled; *b* Edinburgh, 2 Oct., 1937. one *d. Studied:* Edinburgh College of Art, Glasgow School of Art. *Exhib:* Art Monsky London, Roger Billcliffe Glasgow, Scottish Gallery and Open Eye Gallery, Edinburgh, R.A. Summer Show. *Work in collections:* Royal Museum Edinburgh, Art Galleries Glasgow and Aberdeen, Wustum Museum Wisconsin, Graz Museum Austria. *Commissions:* wall panel: Diaspora Museum, Tel Aviv; entry hall: Canada Life Assurance Head Office. *Clubs:* Chelsea Arts. Selected makers Inex Crafts Council, Mem.: Contemporary Applied Arts, Assoc. of Applied Arts (Scotland). *Signs work:* see appendix. *Address:* 52 Bronsart Rd., London SW6 6AA.

GILMOUR, Pat, B.A.(Hons.); Editorial Board, Print Quarterly, Founding Curator of Prints, Tate Gallery (1974-77) and National Gallery of Australia, Canberra (1982-89); *b* Woodford, Essex, 19 Mar., 1932. *m* Alexander Gilmour. two *d. Educ:* Glasgow Art School, Sidney Webb College, London University. *Publications:* author: Modern Prints (1970); Tate: Henry Moore, Graphics in the Making (1975), Artists at Curwen (1977); A.C.G.B.: The Mechanised Image (1978); B.B.C.: Artists in Print (1981); N.G.A.: Ken Tyler Master Printer (1985) and Lasting Impressions: Lithography as Art (ed.) (1988); Hayward Gallery: Shiko Munakata (1991); New Orleans Museum of Art (1997) Hockney to Hodgkin: British Master Prints; Buckinghamshire County Museum (1999), 'Great Prints of the Century'; Sotheby's New York (2000), essay and entries for sale of 'The Kenneth Tyler Collection'; Manchester University Press (2000), essay in 'Critical Kitaj'. *Address:* 25 Christchurch Sq., London E9 7HU.

GINESI, Edna, A.R.C.A.; figure draughtsman and painter in oil; Mem. London Group, Mem. Chiswick Group; *b* Leeds, 15 Feb., 1902. *m* Raymond Coxon. *Educ:* privately. *Studied:* Leeds College of Art, R.C.A. *Exhib:* London and provinces, Canada and U.S.A. *Work in collections:* Tate Gallery (2); Nat. Gallery of Wales, Leeds, Wakefield, Bradford and Manchester City Art Galleries. *Signs work:* "E. Ginesi" or "E. GINESI." *Address:* Rowfant Mill Studio, Old Hollow, Pound Hill, Crawley, W. Sussex RH10 4TB.

GINGER, Phyllis Ethel, R.W.S. (1958); freelance illustrator and water-colour artist; *b* London, 19 Oct., 1907. *m* Leslie Durbin. one *s*. one *d*. *Educ:* Tiffin's Girls' School, Kingston-on-Thames. *Studied:* Richmond School of Art (1932-35), Central School of Arts and Crafts (1937-39) (John Farleigh, William Robins, Clark Hutton). *Work in collections:* water-colours, Pilgrim Trust Recording Britain Scheme; drawings and lithographs in Washington State Library, Victoria and Albert Museum, London Museum, South London Art Gallery. *Publications:* Alexander the Circus Pony (Puffin Book); London and The Virgin of Aldermanbury, by Mrs. Robert Henrey. *Signs work:* "Phyllis Ginger." *Address:* 298 Kew Rd., Kew, Richmond, Surrey TW9 3DU.

GIRVIN, Joy, B.A. Hons. Fine Art (1984), Post Grad. Dip. in Painting (1987); artist in oils and pastels; Art Tutor; *b* Herts, 15 Nov., 1961. *Educ:* University of Northumberland (1984), Royal Academy Schools of Art (1987). *Exhib:* regularly at Cadogan Contemporary Gallery, London. *Work in collections:* Barings Bank, National Trust Foundation for Art, Paintings in Hospitals, London Weekend T.V., Manchester City A.G., Exeter Museum and A.G. *Commissions:* Gardens, Italian landscape. *Clubs:* A.C.G and Sailing, member of Chisendale Studios. *Signs work:* " Joy Girvin." *Address:* 133a Friern Park, London N12 9LR.

GLANVILLE, Christopher, R.W.A.; David Murray Landscape Scholarship (1968, 1970); landscape painter in oil on canvas, oil on panel; Vice-President R.W.A. (1992-97); *b* London, 10 Aug., 1948. *m* Zelda Glanville, potter. one *s*. *Educ:* St. Clement Danes Grammar School, London. *Studied:* Heatherley School of Art (1965), Byam Shaw School of Art (1967-70, B. Dunstan, M. de Sausmarez), R.A. Schools (1970-73, P. Greenham). *Exhib:* R.A., R.W.A., Bruton Gallery, Kaplan Gallery, Woburn Abbey, Sandford Gallery, National Museum of Wales., N.E.A.C., Alresford Gallery, Sinfield Gallery. *Work in collections:* R.W.A., Richmond Museum, Kingston Museum. *Clubs:* Arts Club. *Signs work:* "GLANVILLE." *Address:* 8 Mill St., Kingston-upon-Thames, Surrey KT1 2RF.

GLASS, Margaret, Mem. Pastel Soc., Associate Société des Artistes Français, Membre Société des Pastellistes de France, F.R.S.A.; landscape and marine artist in pastel and oil; *b* Chesham, Bucks., 1950. *Signs work:* "M.R.G." *Address:* 48 The St., Melton, Woodbridge, Suffolk IP12 1PW.

GLAZEBROOK, Christina Fay, S.G.F.A. (1987); artist in pastel, water-colour; teacher of art for Herts. C.C., and Watford Borough Council; *b* Watford, 1 Apr., 1934. *m* Charles Michael Glazebrook. two *s*. *Educ:* Watford Technical College of Art. *Studied:* Cassio College, Watford (1976) and St. Alban's College of Art (1981). *Exhib:* P.S. (1980-81), Liberty's (1982), S.G.A. (1985, 1987), Herts. in the Making (1986-87), U.A. (1998), Mall Galleries, Knapp Gallery, London, and many one-man shows. *Signs work:* "Fay Glazebrook." *Address:* 10 Monkshood Cl., Highcliffe, Christchurch, Dorset BH23 4TS.

GOAMAN, Michael & Sylvia, banknote and stamp designers; *b* East Grinstead, 14 Feb., 1921. *m* Sylvia Priestley. b London, 30 Apr., 1924. three *d*. *Studied:* (Michael) at Reading University (1938-39); (Sylvia) at Slade (1940-41); (Michael and Sylvia) at London Central School of Arts and Crafts (1946-48). *Exhib:* similarly. *Publications:* work repro.: U.K. and widely overseas. *Signs work:* see appendix. *Address:* 91 Park Rd., Chiswick, London W4 3ER.

227

GOBLE, Anthony Barton, painter in oil; Director, Oriel Llanover, National Eisteddfod prize winner (1974); Artist in Residence, Llanover Hall, Cardiff (1979); W.A.C. grants/burseries, including award to visit artists/galleries, U.S.S.R. (1982); Oppenheim/John Downes award (1984); national chairman, A.A.D.W. (1985); president, Artists Benevolent Soc. (1986-87); *b* Oct., 1943. *m* Janice Anne Morgan. two *s.* two *d. Educ:* St. Mary's College, Rhos-on-Sea, Wrexham School of Art. Numerous exhbns. and permanent collections. *Commissions:* Church in Wales/W.A.C. mosaic commission (1985); St. Saviours, Cardiff High Altar reredos painting commission (1988). *Clubs:* R.Cam.A., Welsh Group, Penwith Soc. *Signs work:* "Goble." *Address:* 10 Cyril Cres., Cardiff CF2 1DQ.

GOELL, Abby, B.A., M.F.A.; painter in oil, acrylic, lithography, assemblage; Sen. Mem., Appraiser's Ass'n. of America; *b* U.S.A. one *s. Educ:* Syracuse Univ.; Columbia Univ. (M.F.A. 1965); Art Students' League, N.Y. (Life Mem.). *Studied:* Pratt Graphic Arts Centre, N.Y.C., Attringham Adult College, Shropshire, U.K. *Exhib:* Childe Hassam Purchase Exhbn. N.Y.C. (1977), Amer. Acad. and Inst. of Arts and Letters (1977), U.S. Dept. of State, Havana (1979-82), many invitational shows in U.S. *Work in collections:* M.O.M.A. (N.Y.), Yale Univ. A.G., Grafisches Kabinet, Munich, Chase Manhatten Bank, N.Y., Atlantic-Richfield Oil Co., Sloane-Kettering Memorial Center, N.Y., N.Y. Public Library Print Coll., Neuberger Mus., Purchase N.Y. Smith College. Founder/Publisher Arcadia Press, N.Y. (1980). *Publications:* editor, English Silver 1675-1825 Ensko & Wenham rev. ed. 1980 (Arcadia Press). *Clubs:* Columbia Univ. Club, N.Y. *Signs work:* "Goell" and date. *Address:* 37 Washington Square West, New York, N.Y. 10011-9181, U.S.A. *Email:* abbygoe@att-global.net

GOLDBACHER, Fiona C., water-colourist, sculptress in marble; *b* London, 1935. *m* Rodolfo Goldbacher. one *s.* one *d. Educ:* Iona College, N.Z. *Studied:* under Ruth Liezman. *Exhib:* Chiba Museum,Tokyo; Tanja Flandria, Morocco; Blackheath, Bow House, Heiffer, Thompsons, Gagliardi Galleries, London; Turtle Gallery, Sussex. *Work in collections:* Sanyu Art Japan, Blackheath, Gagliardi, Thompsons Galleries, London, John Noott, Broadway, Cotswolds, Turtle Gallery, Sussex. *Publications:* work repro.: various cards and prints. *Signs work:* "Fiona C. Goldbacher." *Address:* 14 Edmunds Walk, London N2 0HU; and 43 via Borgo 2, Strettoia (Lucca), Tuscany.

GOLPHIN, Janet, R.W.S. (1992), V.P.R.W.S. (1998), R.B.A. (1993); artist in water-colour, oils, mixed media; *b* Pontefract, 7 Nov., 1950. one *s. Exhib:* Bankside Gallery, London, Medici Soc., London, Thompsons Gallery, London, Mall Galleries, Richmond Hill Gallery, Richmond, Surrey, R.A. Summer Exhbn., Manor House Gallery, Chipping Norton, Oxon, Ashdown Gallery, Haywards Heath, Albany Gallery Cardiff. *Work in collections:* H.M. The Queen, Provident Financial, Brodsnorth Hall, M. Doncaster, Johnson and Johnson, John Lewis Partnership. *Commissions:* John Lewis Partnership. *Clubs:* R.W.S., R.B.A., Manchester Academy of Fine Art, Leeds Fine Art. *Signs work:* "Janet Golphin." *Address:* 25 Carleton Crest, Pontefract, W. Yorkshire WF8 2QP.

GOODAY, Leslie, O.B.E., R.I., F.R.I.B.A., F.C.S.D., F.R.S.A.; painter in acrylic and collage; architect and designer; *b* Croydon, 1921. *m* Poppy. *Educ:* Stanley

Technical Trade School. *Studied:* Articled to P.A. Robson F.R.I.B.A. *Exhib:* Expo '70 Japan, B.N.F.L. Nuclear visitors centre, Cumbria, British Golf Museum, St. Andrews, Scotland, and numerous solo and group exhibs. in galleries, London and countrywide. *Publications:* The Artist. *Clubs:* The Arts Club, Chelsea Art Society. *Signs work:* "Leslie Gooday." *Address:* 5 River Bank, Hampton Court, Surrey KT8 9BH.

GOODE, Mervyn, landscape painter best known for his oil paintings of the English countryside – featuring mainly the landscape close to his main home in Hampshire, as well as seascapes/estuary subjects inspired to the landscape close to his second home in South Devon, and also known for his landscapes produced from his travels in the South of France; *b* 1948. *m* Stephanie. *Educ:* Gloucestershire College of Art. *Exhib:* has exhib. widely through the U.K. and also in the U.S.A.; one-man exhbns.: Highton Gallery, EC4 (1970), Alpine Gallery, W1 (1970, 1971), King St. Galleries, SW1 (1974), Furneaux Gallery, SW19 (1975), Southwell Brown Gallery (1976, 1984), Fraser Carver Gallery (1977), Reid Gallery (1978, 1981, 1983, 1985, 1987, 1989, 1991, 1993), Windsor and Eton Fine Arts (1978, 1980), Century Gallery (1982, 1984, 1985), David Messum (1982), Medici Gallery, W1 (1983, 1985, 1990), H.C. Dickins, W1 (1987, 1989), Arun Art Centre (1987), Bennet Galleries, U.S.A. (1988), Bourne Gallery (1992, 1994, 1995, 1996, 1998), David Messum W1 (1993, 1994), John Noott (1995, 1997), Nevill Gallery (1998), Jerram Gallery (1999); mixed exhbns.: Medici Gallery, W1; H.C. Dickins, W1; Mall Galleries (R.O.I.); Royal Academy Business Art Galleries, W1; Southampton A.G.; Bruton Gallery, Somerset; Southwell Brown Gallery, Richmond; Bourne Gallery, Reigate; David Curzon Gallery, London SW19; Century Galleries - Hartley Wintney and Henley-on-Thames; Nevill Gallery, Canterbury; Omell Galleries - London W1 and Ascot; Kingsmead Gallery, Bookham; Wykeham Gallery, Stockbridge; H.C. Dickins, Bloxham; David Messum, Cork St. W1; Burlington Paintings, W1; John Noott, Broadway, Worcs.; Ashgate Gallery, Farnham; Jerram Gallery, Salisbury; D'Art Gallery, Dartmouth; Walker Gallery, Honiton; Alexanfer Gallery, Bristol; W.H. Patterson, London, W1. *Work in collections:* private collections in U.K. and world-wide. *Commissions:* not accepted. *Publications:* work repro.: by the Medici Society, Kingsmead Publications, Bucentaur Gallery, Royle, Rosenstiel's, Almanac Gallery and Country Cards; in numerous periodicals and books; on I.T.V. and B.B.C. TV, etc. *Signs work:* "Mervyn Goode." *Address:* Lane Copse, Hawkley, Hants. GU33 6NS.

GOODWIN, Leslie Albert, R.I., R.O.I., R.W.A.; artist in oil, water-colour, pastel, book illustrator; Chairman, Leicester Soc. Artists; *b* Leicester, 13 June, 1929. *m* Elizabeth Whelband. *Studied:* Leicester College of Art (1949-55). *Exhib:* R.A., R.W.A., R.I., P.S.; six one-man shows, Vaughan College, Leicester University; mixed shows, Leicester A.G. *Work in collections:* English Electric - Nuclear Power Division; Bristol Old Vic Co.; Leicester Royal Infirmary; various public collections; N.H.S. Founder `Asterisk' Soc. of Artists; broadcaster/art critic for B.B.C. *Publications:* work repro.: The Artist, Artist and Illustrators. *Signs work:* see appendix. *Address:* The Studio, 28 Lubbesthorpe Rd., Braunstone, Leics. LE3 2XD.

GOOSEN, Frederik Johannes, V.B.K.H'sum (1981), R.S.M.A. (1990), E.K.C. (1992), K.V. Gooi & Vechtstreek (1993); artist in oil and water-colour; *b* Hilversum,

13 Dec., 1943. *m* M.R. Bekenkamp. two *s. Exhib:* one-man shows: Netherlands: Wassenaar, s'-Hertogenbosch, Enschede, Alkmaar, Nieuwkoop; Bale, Geneva, New York, Washington D.C., Mystic and Westport U.S.A., London, Edinburgh, Mönchengladbach. *Work in collections:* Mystic Seaport Museum, C.T., and several public bldgs. in Holland. *Signs work:* "F.J. Goosen." *Address:* Waterschapslaan 14, Blaricum, Netherlands.

GORALSKI, Waldemar Maria, sculptor in silver and amber, jewellery designer, architect; *b* Lwow, 2 Jan., 1942. *m* Agnieszka, M.Sc. *Studied:* Faculty of Architecture and Dept. of Sculpture and Painting, Gdansk Polytechnic (1962-68). Artistic acknowledgement, Fachhochschule Köln, Dept. of Art and Design (1981). *Work in collections:* Arts Gallery Centre, University of London; Polish Culture Inst., London; Sac Freres, London; Museum Zamkowe, Malbork; Galerie Walinska, Arnhem; Galerie Konstrast, Nijmegen; Kunst-Treff Galerie, Worpswede; Old Warsaw Galleries, Alexandria, Virginia; Aleksander Galleries, St. Petersburg, Florida; Amber Gallery, Skodsborg, Copenhagen. *Signs work:* "W. Goralski" or "W.G." *Address:* Einigkeitstr. 34, D-45133 Essen.

GORDON-LEE, Michael, A.L.I. (1977); landscape architect and garden designer, works in pastel, pencil, oil, water-colour, and sculpts in wood; *b* Harrow, 1943. widower. one *s.* one *d. Educ:* Whitehawk Boys School. *Studied:* Hammersmith College of Art and Building, Chester Art College, Liverpool, and Montmiral, France. *Exhib:* Manchester Academy, Pastel Soc. (Mall Galleries), R.W.A., Theatr Clwyd, Mold, Cheshire Artists, Finalist Look North TV painting competition (1984), Merseyside Artists, Frodsham Arts Centre, Black Sheep Gallery, Hanover Gallery. *Work in collections:* Grosvenor Museum, Chester; and public and private collections. *Commissions:* Grosvenor Museum, Chester; Rexel Ltd.; private. *Signs work:* "GORDON-LEE" and "LEE" (in France). *Address:* 2 Orchard Cottages, Eaton Rd., Tarporley, Cheshire CW6 0BP. *Second Address:* 32100 Larressingle Au Village, Gers, France.

GOUGH, Paul James, M.A. (1985), Ph.D. (1991), R.W.A. (1998); artist in pastel and chalk; Dean, University of West of England, Bristol; Head of Painting, Bristol Polytechnic; *b* Plymouth, 27 Mar., 1958. *m* Kathleen. one *s.* two *d. Studied:* Wolverhampton Polytechnic (1976-79), R.C.A. (1980-85). *Exhib:* Watermans Centre, Solomons, London; Bristol, Lancaster, Swindon, Manchester, Harlech biennale, Ottawa, Paris. *Work in collections:* Imperial War Museum, Royal Marines, Royal Artillery, Pirelli, Lord Rothermere. *Publications:* articles and chapters in numerous academic journals. Television presenter: Art Show (BBC2 1998), Canvas (HTV 1995-99). *Signs work:* "P.J. Gough." *Address:* 136 Stackpool Rd., Southville, Bristol BS3 1NY. *Website:* www.amd.uwe.ac.uk

GOURDIE, Thomas, M.B.E., D.A.(Edin.); Soc. of Scribes and Illuminators; calligrapher and handwriting consultant; *b* Cowdenbeath, 18 May, 1913. *m* Lilias Taylor. one *s.* two *d. Studied:* Edinburgh College of Art. *Work in collections:* Imperial War Museum; Kirkaldy A.G. *Publications:* Puffin Book of Handwriting (Penguin Books); Handwriting For Today, Improve Your Handwriting and Calligraphy for the Beginner (A. & C. Black); Handwriting Made Easy (Taplinger, U.S.A.); Mastering Calligraphy (Pitman, Australia); Mastering Calligraphy (Search

Press); The Simple Modern Hand (Blackie and Son); The Sonnets of Shakespeare (Cassell). *Address:* 3 Douglas St., Kirkcaldy, Scotland.

GOW, Neil, sculptor in wood, small and large scale (outdoor). Abstract and semi figurative; *b* Greenford, Middx., 22 Mar., 1940. *m* Jean Evans. one *s.* one *d. Educ:* Fitzgeorge, Malden, Kingston Technical College. *Exhib:* R.W.A., S.W.A., Amnesty International Sculptures (Bristol and London), Henry Brett Gallery, 5D Gallery, Kennys Galway, etc. *Clubs:* Glos. Soc. of Artists, Sculptree (Large Tree Carvers). *Signs work:* see appendix. *Address:* Brownshill Cottage, Brownshill, Stroud, Glos. GL6 8AG.

GRAA JENSEN, Lisa, B.A. (Hons.) (1978), R.I. (1996), A.O.I. (1994); illustrator and painter in water-colour, pen and ink; *b* Copenhagen, Denmark, 2 Mar., 1953. *m* J.A. Hendrich, M.A. one *s.* one *d. Studied:* Sir John Cass School of Art (1974-75), Camberwell School of Art (1975-78, John Lawrence). *Exhib:* R.I., Mall Galleries mixed shows, C.C.A. Galleries, numerous exhbns. in South East, work available at Forest Gallery, Guildford, Shellhouse Gallery, Ledbury, Herefordshire. *Commissions:* Fine Art prints for Rosenstiels and C.C.A Galleries, cards for Royle, Paperhouse, Kingsmead, Royal Academy Enterprises. *Publications:* work repro.: Kestral Books, Hamlyn, BBC Publications, Radio Times, Heinemann Macmillan. *Signs work:* "GRAA JENSEN." *Address:* 45 Wodeland Ave., Guildford, Surrey GU2 5JZ. *Email:* lisa@jollypix.co.uk

GRACIA, Carmen, R.E.; etcher and engraver in colour, painter in oil; *b* Mendoza, Argentina, 18 May, 1935. *m* E.T. Rockett (decd.). one *s. Educ:* Escuela de Bellas Artes, Mendoza, Argentina. *Studied:* L'Atelier 17, Paris, under Stanley Hayter (1960-1964), Slade, London, under Anthony Gross (1965-1966). *Exhib:* 32 solo, and 250 group exhibs. *Work in collections:* 30 in museums and public collections. *Clubs:* Greenwich Printmakers Assocn. *Signs work:* "Carmen Gracia." *Address:* 65 Westover Rd., High Wycombe, Bucks. HP13 5HX.

GRADIDGE, Daphne, painter in water based media; *b* Salisbury, 19 Sep., 1953. *Studied:* theatre design at Nottingham School of Art and at The Slade. *Exhib:* London, Hampshire and Dorset. *Work in collections:* private collections in England, Ireland and Australia. *Commissions:* mural paintings for the Chelsea and Westminster Hospital and other hospitals in London and Hampshire. *Signs work:* "DG." *Address:* c/o Jonathan Cooper, Park Walk Gallery, 20 Park Walk, London SW10 0AQ. *Email:* mail@jonathancooper.co.uk

GRAHAM, Brian, Kenneth, Frederick, inaugural Bournemouth International Festival Artist (1994); first prizewinner, Royal West of England Academy's annual exhibition (1992); painter in oil/acrylic; *b* 26 Aug., 1945. *m* Carol. two *s. Educ:* Poole Grammar School. *Studied:* part time at Bournemouth College of Art (1960-1962), but mainly self taught. *Exhib:* over twenty solo exhibitions, (two in Cork Street); many group shows. *Work in collections:* Dorset County Museum; Skandia Life Assurance Company; Poole Borough Council; Parnham House. *Publications:* in preparation. Represented by Hart Gallery, Islington, Cornwall and Nottingham. *Signs work:* "Brian Graham." *Address:* Central House, Mount Pleasant Lane, Swanage, Dorset BH19 2PN.

GRAHAM, Carol, Dip.A.D.; artist in oil; Council mem. R.U.A.; *b* Belfast, 17 Apr., 1951. one *s*. one *d. Studied:* Belfast College of Art and Design (1969-74). *Exhib:* Ulster Museum, N.I. Arts Council, Tom Caldwell, The Engine Room, The Guinness Hopstore Gallery, Elaine Somers Hollywood. *Work in collections:* Trinity College Dublin, National Self-portrait Collection Limerick, Ulster Television, Ulster Museum, Belfast City Council, D.o.E., N.I.E. Veridian. *Commissions:* portraits: Dr. Mary Robinson (President), James Galway (Flautist), Lord Grey (Governor N.I.), Lord Lowry, Sir Ian Frazer. *Publications:* cover, Bernard McLaverty Secrets; cover, The Blue Globe (poetry). *Clubs:* R.U.A. *Signs work:* "CAROL GRAHAM." *Address:* 1 Glenmore Terr., Lisburn, N.I. BT27 4RW.

GRAHAM, David, R.P., A.R.C.A.; painter in oil; *b* London, 20 May, 1926. *m* Martha Luz. *Studied:* Hammersmith School of Art, St. Martin's School of Art, R.C.A. (1948-1951). *Exhib:* Retrospective at Herbert Art Gallery and Museum, Coventry - 100 Paintings of Israel (1987). *Work in collections:* London Museum, Barbican, Guildhall Art Gallery, Arts Council, Belgrave House Art Collection, Coca Cola Ltd, etc. *Publications:* video - A Painters View. *Clubs:* Chelsea Arts. *Signs work:* "David Graham." *Address:* 2 Curran Studios, Lucan Pl., Chelsea, London SW3 3PG.

GRAHAM, Peter, B.A. Hons. (1980), R.O.I.; *b* Glasgow, 17 Feb., 1959. *Studied:* Glasgow School of Art (1976-80). *Exhib:* Bourne Gallery Reigate, Llewellyn Alexander Ltd, London, many mixed shows including R.S.A., R.O.I., R.S.M.A., and R.I. *Work in collections:* British Council, Nan Yang Academy, Singapore, Lord Morton, Lord Max Rayne, Lady Graham, Lady Nairn, Ernst & Young, Glasgow. *Signs work:* "Peter Graham" or "Graham." *Address:* 57 Kirklee Rd., Glasgow G12 0SS, Scotland.

GRANGER-TAYLOR, Nicolas, artist in oil; *b* London, 18 June, 1963. *Educ:* Latymer Upper School, Hammersmith. *Studied:* Kingston Polytechnic (1981-82), Bristol Polytechnic (1982-85), R.A. Schools (1987-90). *Exhib:* Royal Festival Hall (1986, 1987, 1988), N.P.G. (1987, 1990), R.A. Summer Exhbn. (1987, 1989, 1992), Cadogan Contemporary (1989, 1990); one-man shows Cadogan Contemporary (1988), Waterman Fine Art (1991, 1993). *Signs work:* "N. Granger-Taylor" or "N.G.T." *Address:* c/o Waterman Fine Art Ltd., 74a Jermyn St., London SW1Y 6NP.

GRANT, Keith Frederick, A.R.C.A.; landscape and portrait painter; *b* Liverpool, 10 Aug., 1930. *m* Hilde Ellingsen-Grant. one (decd.) *s*. two *d. Educ:* Bootle Grammar School, Lancs. *Studied:* Willesden School of Art, Royal College of Art. *Exhib:* Fitzwilliam Museum, Cambridge and elsewhere. *Work in collections:* Mural/mosaics, Charing Cross Hospital, London (1979), Gateshead Metro Station (1981/83), Beaverbrook Foundation, Peter Stuyvesant Coll., Arts Council of G.B., Contemporary Art Soc., V. & A., Fitzwilliam Museum, Cambridge, Manchester City A.G., National Gallery of N.Z. and other public and private collections at home and abroad. *Commissions:* paintings and stained glass – Charing Cross Hospital, London (2000). Agents: Cadogan Contemporary Gallery, No. 9 The Gallery, Birmingham. *Clubs:* Garrick. *Signs work:* "Keith Grant" or "K. F. Grant." *Address:* Gamlegata P.B. 107, 3810 Gvarv, Norway. *Email:* kefreg@frisurf.no

GRANT, Marianne, N.S. (1977), F.R.S.A. (1975); painter in oil; *b* St. Gallen,

Switzerland, 1931. widowed. one *s.* one *d. Educ:* High School, Zürich. *Studied:* Art Colleges in Zürich and Geneva. *Exhib:* one-man shows B. H. Corner Gallery, Cooling Gallery, Century Galleries, Henley-on-Thames, East London Gallery, El Greco Gallery, Royal Northern College of Music, Debenhams of Romford, Austria, Germany, Switzerland. *Work in collections:* Ernst Waespe (Zürich), Standard Telephone and Cables Ltd., Arts Centre Hornchurch. *Publications:* work repro.: Fine Art Prints for 'Prints for Pleasure' and Peinture. *Clubs:* N.S., Essex Art. *Signs work:* "Marianne Grant." *Address:* Erlenwiesenstrasse 18, 8152 Glattbrugg (Zürich), Switzerland.

GRANVILLE, artist in acrylic; *b* Liverpool, 12 July, 1945. *Studied:* Northwich College of Art (1961-65), Southport College of Art (1980-82). *Exhib:* Over sixty exhbns. in England and Spain since 1967. *Work in collections:* Museo de la Real Academia de Bellas artes de San Fernando, Madrid. *Publications:* work repro.: various exhbn. catalogues, articles and reviews; painting reproduced as cards and prints around the world. Work inspired by Spain and all things Spanish. *Signs work:* see appendix. *Address:* 14b Derwent Ct., Troutbeck Rd., Liverpool L18 3LF.

GRAVETT, Guy Patrick, photographer and painter; *b* Wye, Kent, 2 Nov., 1919. *Educ:* Lewes County Grammar School. *Studied:* Brighton College of Art (1937-39) under Sallis Benney, Laurence Preston and Walter Bayes. *Exhib:* various. *Clubs:* Royal Ocean Racing. *Signs work:* "Gravett" or "Guy Gravett" followed by year. *Address:* Hope Lodge, 41 Hassocks Rd., Hurstpierpoint, Sussex BN6 9QL.

GRAY, Elizabeth, L.R.A.M.; self taught painter in water-colour; *b* Scarborough, Yorks, 1928. *m* Dr. David Trapnell. two *s. Educ:* Queen Margaret's School, Yorks. *Exhib:* one-man shows, Tryon Gallery, London; Sportsmans Edge Gallery, N.Y.; Old Amersham, Bourton-on-the-Water, etc. *Work in collections:* Nature in Art, Gloucester; The Bank of England; Leigh Yawkey Woodson Art Museum, Wausau, Wisconsin, U.S.A. *Commissions:* Nature in Art, Gloucester, Leigh Yawkey Woodson Art Museum, Wausau, WI, U.S.A. *Publications:* The Wild and the Tame by H. Beamish (1957). *Signs work:* "Elizabeth Gray." *Address:* Wallsworth Hall, Twigworth, Gloucester GL2 9PA.

GRAY, Jane Campbell, A.R.C.A., F.M.G.P.; stained glass artist; Liveryman, Worshipful Company of Glaziers (1983); *b* Lincoln, 1931. *m* Kiril Gray. two *d. Studied:* Kingston School of Art (1949-52); Royal College of Art (1952-55) under Lawrence Lee and assisted him with Coventry Cathedral nave windows (1955-58). Examples of work: Uxbridge - St. Margaret's; Civic Centre entrance screen and Alphabet of Flowers in Marriage Room; Hillingdon Hospital Chapel (26 panels); St. Peter's, Martindale, Cumbria (15 windows); Pitminster, Somerset (East window, 1989); Shrewsbury Abbey (1992, 1997); Apothecaries' Hall; Glaziers Hall, London Bridge; Christchurch Priory (1999). Over 150 lights in 60 churches; coats-of-arms, domestic windows. *Signs work:* "Jane Gray," and see appendix. *Address:* Ferry Cottage, Shrawardine, Shrewsbury SY4 1AJ.

GRAY, Stuart Ian, lithographer, painter in water-colour; water-colour officer, N.S.; *b* 19 Apr., 1925. *Educ:* Streatham Grammar School. *Exhib:* R.S.M.A., R.I., Mall Galleries, Guildhall. *Publications:* work repro.: British Marine Painting by Denys Brook-Hart. *Signs work:* "Stuart Gray." *Address:* Osborne Cottage, York Ave.,

E. Cowes, I.O.W. PO32 6BD.

GREAVES, Derrick, A.R.C.A. (1952): painter and printmaker; *b* Sheffield, 5 June, 1927. *m* Mary Margaret (divorced 1991); two *s*. one *d*.; Sally Butler 1994. *Studied:* R.C.A. (Carel Weight, John Minton) and in Italy. *Exhib:* Contemporary Art Soc., Venice Biennale, Pushkin Museum Moscow, John Moores, Carnegie International Pittsburgh, R.A., Mall Galleries; one-man shows: Beaux Arts, Zwemmer, Inst. of Contemporary Arts, Bear Lane Oxford, Belfast and Dublin, Whitechapel Gallery, Cranfield Inst. of Technology, Monika Kinley, City Gallery Milton Keynes, Hart Gallery London, Galerie Daniel Wahrenberger, Zurich. *Work in collections:* A.C.G.B.; Bank of Ireland, Dublin; N.Y. Public Library; Leeds, Reading, Sheffield, Southampton and Walker A.Gs.; Wesleyan University, Chicago; Tate Gallery; British Museum, etc. *Publications:* folios and books: Also (with Roy Fisher) 1971; Songs of Bilitis (1977); Sanscrit Love Poems (1987). *Signs work:* "Derrick Greaves." *Address:* The School, Weston Longville, nr. Norwich, Norfolk NR9 5JU.

GREAVES, Jack, A.R.C.A., R.W.A., Rome Scholar; sculptor in bronze, painter in oil; Visiting Prof. O.S.U.; *b* Leeds, 24 Sept., 1928. *m* Mildred Place. four *s*. *Studied:* Leeds College of Art, R.C.A. (A.B. Rome). *Exhib:* Zwemmer, R.A., O.S.U. Gallery, Bruton Gallery, Vorpal, N.Y. and San Francisco, Gallery 200, Columbus, Ohio. *Work in collections:* Coventry A.G.; Bristol A.G.; Arts Council; R.W.A.; National Revenue Corp., U.S.A.; Columbus Museum, State Saving, U.S.A.; Sirak Collection, U.S.A.; Children's Fountain Cols., Ohio, U.S.A. *Commissions:* Naiad Fountain, Capital Sq. Columbus, Ohio; The Guardian, Police Memorial Gdn., Toledo; Christ Teaching, Cols., Ohio; Family Planning Bldg., Tucson, Arizona; Children's Fountain, Cols., Ohio, U.S.A. *Signs work:* "Greaves." *Address:* The Long House, Snainton, Scarborough, N.Yorks. YO13 9AP.

GREEN, Alan, A.R.C.A.; painter; *b* London, 22 Dec., 1932. *m* June Green. two *d. Studied:* Royal College of Art (1955-58). *Exhib:* Documenta VI Kassel (1977), 'British Art Now' Guggenheim Museum, N.Y. (1979), 'British Contemporary Art' Japan (1982). *Work in collections:* includes Arts Council of Gt. Britain; British Council; Guggenheim Museum, N.Y.; McCrory Corp., N.Y.; Tate Gallery, London; Kunstmuseum Hannover; National Museum of Art, Osaka, Japan; Power Gallery, Sydney, Australia; Kunsthalle Bielefeld; Musee d'Ixelles, Brussels. Agents: Annely Juda Fine Art London. *Address:* c/o Annely Juda Fine Art, 23 Dering St., London W1R 9AA.

GREEN, Alfred Rozelaar, R.W.A. (1994); Mem. Paris Salon, Comparaisons Nationale Beaux Arts; painter in oil, pastel, charcoal; *b* London, 14 July, 1917. *m* Betty Marcus. three *s. Educ:* Uppingham, Cambridge (two years engineering). *Studied:* Central School of Arts and Crafts (1937, Meninsky, Roberts); Academie Julian, Paris; Atelier Marcel Gromaire (1938-39). *Exhib:* London, Whibleys, Paris, Brussels, The Hague, Bale, Lyon, Marseille, New York, Strasbourg, Cannes, Le Havre, Bath, Bristol. *Work in collections:* Musee d'Art Moderne, Paris, Strasbourg, Prefecture Vaucluse, Musee d'Orange, Ashmolean, Oxford. *Publications:* 40 years of Painting (Ed. Dragger, 1988). Founded and directed Anglo-French Art Centre, St. John's Wood, London. In 1946 combined art school and 'Académie Libre' with gallery showing works of artists from Paris (André Lhote, Lurcat, Germaine Richier, Saint-Saens, Couturier, Domginuez, etc.) who taught and lectured during their exhbns. Centre closed 1951. *Signs work:* "A. Rozelaar Green." *Address:* 11 Rue de Savies, 75020 Paris.

GREEN, Anthony, R.A. (1977), Dip.F.A. Slade (1960), Harkness Fellow (1967-69); elected Fellow of University College, London (1991); painter in oil; *b* London, 30 Sept., 1939. *m* Mary Cozens-Walker. two *d. Educ:* Highgate School, N.6. *Studied:* Slade School of Fine Art. *Exhib:* over 100 one-man shows worldwide since 1962. *Work in collections:* Tate Gallery, Arts Council, museums and art galleries in U.S.A., Japan, Brazil, etc. *Publications:* A Green Part of the World (Thames and Hudson). *Signs work:* "Anthony Green," "A. Green," "Anthony," "A.G." or not at all. *Address:* 40 High St., Little Eversden, Cambs. CB3 7HE.

GREEN, David John, R.O.I.; landscape painter in water-colour and oil; *b* London, 23 Feb., 1935. *m* Eileen Ann. two *s. Educ:* Goldington Rd. Secondary Modern, Bedford. *Exhib:* R.I., R.B.A., R.O.I.; one-man shows: London, Cambridge, Bedford. *Work in collections:* Luton Museum, Boston English Gallery. *Signs work:* "DAVID GREEN." *Address:* The Wilden Gallery, Wilden, Beds. MK44 2QH.

GREEN, Gerald, Dip.Arch. (1978); freelance artist and architectural illustrator in water-colour, oil, acrylic; *b* Nuneaton, 22 June, 1947. *m* Diana. one *s.* one *d. Educ:* King Edward VI Grammar School, Nuneaton. *Studied:* Leicester Polytechnic. *Exhib:* Singer & Friedlander/Sunday Times Water-colour Exhbn., Laing, Mall Galleries, Fosse Gallery Stow-on-the-Wold, Glos. City A.G., Loggia Gallery London. *Commissions:* over 900 architectural illustration commissions undertaken for both national and international clients. *Publications:* regular contributor to The Artist magazine; work featured in three books. *Clubs:* F.P.S. *Address:* 211 Hinckley Rd., Nuneaton, Warwickshire CV11 6LL. *Email:* Gerald@ggarts.demon.co.uk

GREEN, Lorna, B.A. Hons. (1982), M.Phil. (1991), F.R.B.S. (2001); site specific environmental sculptor; permanent and temporary projects using varied relevant materials; *b* Manchester. *m* David Rose F.R.C.S. (Ed.). two *d. Studied:* Manchester Polytechnic, Leeds University. *Exhib:* throughout U.K., Australia, Austria, Bosnia, China, Germany, Hungary, Ireland, Israel, Japan, Korea, New Zealand. *Commissions:* Leed University, Cribb's Causeway Shopping Centre, Bristol, Kraftplatzroas, Irdning, Austria, Rochdale Partnership/Canalside S.R.B., Changchun, China, Beer-Sheva, Israel, Monash University, Melbourne, Australia. *Signs work:* "Lorna Green." *Address:* Mount Pleasant Farm, 105 Moss Lane, Bramhall, Cheshire SK7 1EG. *Website:* www.lornagreen.com *Email:* lg@lorna-green.com

GREEN, Richard, Dip.A.D. (1968), M.A. (1970), F.R.S.A. (1988); Curator, York City Art Gallery (since 1977); previously Keeper of Fine Art, Laing Art Gallery, Newcastle upon Tyne (1971-77); *b* 12 Oct., 1946. *Educ:* Palmer's School, Grays. *Studied:* S.W. Essex Technical College and School of Art; Bath Academy of Art; Goldsmiths' College School of Art (1964-68) studied history of art at University of London, Courtauld Inst. of Art (1968-70). *Publications:* numerous exhbn. catalogues, articles and reviews. *Address:* c/o York City Art Gallery, Exhibition Sq., York YO1 2EW.

GREENBURY, Judith Pamela, R.W.A. (1979); painter in oil, water-colour; *b* Bristol, 17 Feb., 1924. *m* C. L. Greenbury, M.D. three *s. Educ:* Badminton School, Westbury-on-Trym, Bristol. *Studied:* West of England College of Art (1943-46) under George Sweet, Slade School (1946-47) under Prof. Schwabe. *Exhib:* R.A., R.W.A., R.S.P.P., N.E.A.C., Bear Lane Gallery, Oxford, Mall Galleries, London, Alpine Gallery, London, Phyllis Court Club, Henley-on-Thames. *Work in collections:* R.W.A., and many private collections. *Publications:* "Spey Portrait: A Memoir of Fishing and Painting on the Spey 1974-1989"; "George Sweet, Painter, Teacher and Friend"; "Piers and Seaside Towns An Artist's Journey", (published June 20 2001). *Signs work:* "J.G." *Address:* Clarence House, 11 New St., Henley-on-Thames, Oxon. RG9 2BP.

GREENHALF, Bette, B.Sc. (Econ.) Hons. Lond., M.A. Multimedia (computer); Postgraduate Printmaking; Dip. Higher Education Fine Art; artist, writer; *b* London, 28 Dec., 1932. *m* Tom Greenhalf (decd.). *Studied:* Central/St. Martin's and London University. *Exhib:* R.A., Festival Hall, Mall Galleries, Camden Art Centre, Chaucer Festival, Barbican, Artists for Nuclear Disarmament, Gallery of the Future, Loughborough University. *Work in collections:* Nelson Mandela, John Major, Chaucer Heritage Trust, War Child Bosnia. *Publications:* Who's Who in International Art, British Contemporary Art (1993); artist's books: Punch and Judy; Venice Biennale 1895-1995 (a socio-political history); Etchings & poems: World War I, Tiananmen Square, Chaucer, Hampstead. *Signs work:* "Bette Greenhalf." *Address:* 91 Greenhill, Hampstead High St., London NW3 5TY.

GREENHALF, Robert Ralph, R.B.A. (1982), S.WL.A. (1981), Dip. A.D.(Graphics) (1971); artist in etching, woodcut, water-colour and oil; *b* Haywards Heath, 28 June, 1950. *m* Sally Grace. one *s. Educ:* Haywards Heath Secondary Modern School. *Studied:* Eastbourne School of Art (1966-68), Maidstone College of Art (1968-71). *Exhib:* R.A., R.B.A., S.WL.A., many mixed exhbns. and one-man shows London, England and Wales, Switzerland, Holland, U.S.A., France, Spain, Germany. *Work in collections:* South East Arts, Hastings Museum. *Publications:* "Towards The Sea" (Pica Press, 1999). *Signs work:* "Robert R. Greenhalf." *Address:* Romney House, Saltbarn La., Playden, Rye, E. Sussex TN31 7PH.

GREENMAN, Edwin, A.R.C.A., R.P., F.R.S.A.; artist in oils; head of dept., drawing, painting and design, Guildford School of Art; head of Sir John Cass School of Art, London; elected to Royal Society of Portrait Painters (1968), Hon. sec. (1984-85), Hon. treasurer (1985-89); *b* Beckenham, Kent. *m* Freda Johns. one *s. Studied:* Beckenham School of Art (1926-29) under Henry Carr, R.A.; R.C.A. (1929-33) under Rothenstein, Spencer, Tristram and Malcolm Osbourne. *Exhib:* engravings at World's Fair, New York (1938), and at Prague; paintings at R.A. *Work in collections:* V. & A.; Contemporary Art Fund; Travelling Art Exhbns., Bureau Collections. *Commissions:* Portrait commissions include Windsor Herald, Moderator of Church of Scotland, Lord Northbrook, Dame Sheila Quinn, Sir Lynton White, Sir John Harvey Jones, Mrs André Previn. *Clubs:* Chelsea Arts. *Signs work:* "Greenman." *Address:* 1 Griffin Ct., Griffin Way, Great Bookham, Surrey KT23 4JQ.

GREENSMITH, John Hiram, N.D.D. (1955), A.T.D. (1956), A.R.W.S. (1976), N.E.A.C. (1978), R.W.S. (1983), A.R.Cam.A. (1986), R.C.A. (1996); painter in water-colour; former Head of Fine Art, All Saints School, Sheffield; *b* Sheffield, 22 Apr., 1932. *m* Janet. one *s.* (by previous marriage) one *d. Educ:* De la Salle College, Sheffield. *Studied:* Sheffield College of Art. *Exhib:* R.A., R.W.S., R.B.A., R.C.A., N.E.A.C., M.A.F.A. *Signs work:* "John Greensmith." *Address:* 77 Whirlowdale Cres., Sheffield S7 2ND.

GREENWELL, Patricia K., B.A. (1960); artist in water-colour, acrylic, pastel; *b* Liverpool, 5 July, 1937. *m* Alan. three *s. Studied:* Durham University (1956-60, Pasmore, Gowing, Stephenson, Hamilton). *Exhib:* local and regional. *Work in collections:* several in national and international private collections. *Clubs:* N.A.P.A. *Address:* 3 The Mews, Cherry Orchard, Highnorth, Wilts. SN6 7TL.

GREENWOOD, Eileen Constance, A.R.C.A. (Design) 1935-38 F.B.I. award, Pedagogic Dip. (1939), R.E. (1975); printmaker: etching/aquatint, mixed media computer graphic; Lecturer/Founder Principal, Sittingbourne College of Educ. (retd.); *b* Middx., 26 May, 1915. *m* Ernest Greenwood, A.R.C.A., P.P.R.W.S. one *d. Educ:* Camden School for Girls, Frances Mary Buss Foundation. *Studied:* R.C.A., Courtauld Inst., Goldsmiths' College. *Exhib:* R.A., Bankside Gallery, many London and provincial galleries; four solo shows, three with husband. *Work in collections:* G.B., France, Germany, Japan, America, Australia. *Signs work:* "Eileen Greenwood" (all prints with 'cat' logo in margin). *Address:* Brushings Farm House, Broad St., nr. Hollingbourne, Kent ME17 1RB.

GREENWOOD, Ernest, P.P.R.W.S. (1976), A.R.C.A. (1931-35), F.R.S.A.; artist in oil and water-colour; Inspector of Art Educ. for K.E.C.; guest lecturer for W.F. & R.K. Swan (Hellenic) Ltd.; since 1977 on "Art Appreciation" - Art and Architecture of Greece and Rome; *b* Welling, Kent, 12 Feb., 1913. *m* Eileen C. Greenwood. one *d. Educ:* Gravesend School of Art. *Studied:* Royal College of Art, British School, Rome. *Exhib:* R.A., N.E.A.C., R.I., R.B.A., etc.; lectures and exhbns. given annually since 1985 in U.S.A. Exhbn. with wife at Tubac Arts Centre, Arizona, Nevill Gallery, Canterbury, Bankside Gallery, London (Sept., 1991), Musselwhites Gallery, Southampton; Retrospective exhbn.: 1934-97 County Gallery, Maidstone. *Work in collections:* Preston, Southend, Tate Gallery, Middlesbrough A.G., Lannards Gallery Billingshurst, Wenlock Fine Art; private collections, U.S.A., Municipal Galleries of Brighton, Hastings, Hull; "Holcaust" painting now in Ben-Uri collection, London. *Commissions:* Decorations for Judges chambers, Canterbury Crown Court. Guest at the feast of St. Catherine, St. Catherine's College, Oxford. Portraits in private collections. *Signs work:* "Ernest Greenwood." *Address:* Brushings Farm House, Broad St., nr. Hollingbourne, Kent ME17 1RB.

GREENWOOD, Maurice Arthur, R.C.A. (1996), Associats (1988); artist in water-colour and oil; art tutor; part-time lecturer, Dept. of Continuing Education, University College, N. Wales since 1982; *b* Rochdale, 12 Dec., 1930. *m* Joan. two *s. Studied:* part-time Rochdale Art School (1946-48) (Peter Burgess Shorrock, 1960-65). *Exhib:* R.Cam.A., and many open and one-man shows. *Work in collections:* Gwynedd Library Services; private collections in U.S.A., British Columbia, Australia, U.K. *Signs work:* "Maurice A. Greenwood, R.C.A." *Address:* Woodlands, 12 Shaftesbury Ave., Penrhyn Bay, Llandudno, N. Wales LL30 3EH.

GREENWOOD, Philip John, N.D.D. (1965), A.T.C. (1966), R.E. (1982); printmaker in etching and painter; *b* Dolgellau, N. Wales, 20 Nov., 1943. *m* Valery Ratcliff (decd.). four *s*. *Educ:* Dolgellau Grammar School. *Studied:* Harrow College of Art (1961-65), Hornsey Teachers Training College (1965-66). *Exhib:* R.A., R.E., Tate Gallery, R.G.I., 'Printmaking in Britain', Sydney; British Council Gallery, Athens; British Printmakers, Melbourne; Galerie Tendenz, Germany; J. One Fine Arts, Tokyo; Galerie Deux Tetes, Canada; 'Overseas Printmakers', Auckland, N.Z.; Galerie Beumont, Brussels. *Work in collections:* Tate Gallery, Arts Council, British Council, Derby Museum, Greenwich Museum, Oldham A.G., Graves A.G., Warwick Museum and A.G., Lincoln A.G. and Museum, etc. *Clubs:* Arts. *Signs work:* "Greenwood." *Address:* 30 Leigh Hill Rd., Cobham, Surrey KT11 2HX.

GREIG, Donald, R.S.M.A. (1967), Gold Medal Paris Salon (1967); painter in water-colour and oil, printmaker; *b* London, 1916. *m* Rita Greig, R.W.A., R.O.I., N.E.A.C. one *s*. *Studied:* Southend College of Art (Charles Taylor, R.W.S). *Exhib:* R.A., R.W.A., R.B.A., N.E.A.C., R.I., R.S.M.A., and various one-man shows. *Work in collections:* National Maritime Museum, Greenwich, Municipal Gallery, Scunthorpe. *Signs work:* "DONALD GREIG." *Address:* Tor Brook Studio, Woodleigh, Kingsbridge, S. Devon TQ7 4DF.

GREIG, Rita, R.W.A. (1983), R.O.I. (1974), N.E.A.C. (1974), Silver Medal Paris Salon (1974); painter principally in oil, also water-colour and pastel, printmaker; *b* Norwich. *m* Donald Greig, R.S.M.A. one *s*. *Educ:* Selhurst Grammar School, Ware Grammar School. *Studied:* privately. *Exhib:* R.A., R.W.A., R.O.I., N.E.A.C., R.B.A., various one-man shows in Britain and abroad, also shared shows with husband, Donald Greig. *Work in collections:* Royal West of England Academy, Chase Manhattan Bank Collection, Bishop Otter College. *Signs work:* "R.G." *Address:* Tor Brook Studio, Woodleigh, Kingsbridge, S. Devon TQ7 4DF.

GRESTY, Kenneth H., F.R.S.A. (1971), F.I.A.L. (1966), A.T.D. (1951), D.A., Manc. (1950), N.D.D., painting (1950); Head of Faculty, North Bolton Sixth Form College; Mem. Manchester Academy (1954); *b* Manchester, 17 May, 1928. *m* Marjorie Ingred Smith. four *s*. *Educ:* Sale Grammar School. *Studied:* Manchester Regional College of Art under H. Williamson, R.W.A. (1944-46, 1948-51). *Exhib:* R.A., Manchester Academy of Fine Arts. *Work in collections:* Rutherston Collection. *Publications:* work repro.: in Cheshire Life, Lancashire Life, and local press. *Signs work:* "K. H. Gresty." *Address:* 5 Ivy Terr., Borth-Y-Gest, Porthmadog, Gwynedd LL49 9TS.

GREY, Jenni, B.A. (Hons.), M.A., Fellow, Designer Bookbinders; fine binder and book artist; part-time tutor, University of Brighton; *b* London, 3 July, 1950. *Educ:* Bexley Grammar School. *Studied:* Brighton Polytechnic. *Exhib:* regularly since 1982 in England, Europe and America. *Work in collections:* National Poetry Library (England), Koninklijke Bibliotheek (Holland), University of Georgia and Wellesley College (U.S.A.), Les Amis de la Reliure d'Art (France), Biblioteca Wittockiana (Belgium). *Address:* 26 St. Lukes Rd. Brighton BN2 2ZD.

GRIBBIN, Launcelot Benedict, A.T.D. (1949); B.A. (Hons.) Hist. of Art (1953); painter in oil, photographer; lecturer, Victoria and Albert Museum; former principal lecturer, London College of Printing; visiting lecturer, Messrs. Sotheby's Institute; International freelance lecturer in History of Architecture and Decorative Arts; *b*

Gateshead-on-Tyne, 7 Nov., 1927. *m* Joanna Mary Satchell. two *s.* two *d. Educ:* Dartford Grammar School. *Studied:* Sidcup School of Art under Ruskin Spear, A.R.A., Robin Guthrie, William Clause; Courtauld Inst. of Art. *Exhib:* R.A., N.E.A.C., London Group, National Soc.; one-man shows, Artists' House, Manette St., etc. *Signs work:* "L. B. GRIBBIN" (written with brush). *Address:* 8 Mile House La., St. Albans, Herts. AL1 1TB.

GRICE, David, painter, sculptor, maker of constructions and mixed media artist; winner, national prizes for painting from age 6; teacher, Bradford School of Art (1971-72); *b* Saltaire, 1 Oct., 1946. *m* Carol Ann. two *d. Studied:* Bradford School of Art (1962-66). *Exhib:* I.C.A. (1969), Angela Flowers Gallery (1970); group shows: worldwide; one-man shows: Titus Gallery, W.Yorks. annually. *Work in collections:* private, corporate and institutional collections. *Signs work:* see appendix. *Address:* The Penthouse, Brialmontlei – 53, 2018 Antwerpen, Belgium. *Website:* artbydavid-grice.com *Email:* david.grice@pandora.be

GRICE, Sarah, P.S., S.Eq.A.; Hon. mention Paris Salon; artist in pastel and oil specializing in animals; *b* Bootle, Cumbria, 1913. *m* Richard Grice (decd.). *Educ:* private schools in Cumbria. *Studied:* in Paris with Roger Marx, animal sculptor (1927-29), in London (1934-37). *Exhib:* R.A., R.S.A., Paris Salon, and six solo shows. *Signs work:* "Sarah Grice." *Address:* Well Cottage, Cottesmore, Oakham, Rutland LE15 7DH.

GRIERSON, Janet (Deaconess), B.A. Hons. (Lond.) (1934), M.A. Lambeth (1982); painter in oil and water-colour; *b* Dublin, 10 Apr., 1913. *Educ:* Westfield College (1931-34), King's College, University of London (1934-36). *Studied:* (part time) at N. Worcs. College (1978-82), Malvern Hills College (1984-89). *Exhib:* galleries in Malvern, including one-man shows. *Signs work:* "Janet Grierson." *Address:* Flat 8 Parkview, Abbey Rd., Malvern, Worcs. WR14 3HG.

GRIFFIN, Alison Mary, B.A. Art and Design (1974); minature painter, and landscape and interior artist in water-colour and acrylic; *b* Sutton Coldfield, 23 May, 1953. *m* Charles Griffin (divorced). one *s.* one *d. Educ:* Boldmere High School for Girls, Sutton Coldfield. *Studied:* Sutton College of Art (1969-71, H. Muskett), Bath Academy of Art (1971-74, M.Flinn). *Exhib:* Francis Iles Gallery, Rochester, Westminster Gallery, London, Mall Galleries, London. Work in private collections. *Publications:* work repro.: Limited Edition Prints, Rosenstiels. *Signs work:* "Alison Griffin." *Address:* Wisteria House, 68 North St., Barming, Maidstone, Kent ME16 9HF.

GRIFFIN, David Brian, graphic designer painter in oil and water-colour, subject matter mainly nautical; Council mem. Chelsea Art Soc. since 1974, Vice-Pres. (1991-96); *b* Brighton, 15 Feb., 1927. *m* Kathleen Martin. one *s.* one *d. Educ:* Central School, Catford and Sayers Croft, Ewhurst. *Studied:* Camberwell, Northampton and St. Martin's Schools of Art (1940-43 under Roland Vivian Pitchforth, R.A., R.W.S.). *Exhib:* R.S.M.A., Armed Forces, Omell Galleries, Piccadilly. *Work in collections:* Europe, U.S.A., and Far East. Listed in "20th Century British Marine Painting". *Commissions:* include Eagle Star and British Petroleum. Served R.A.S.C. (maritime) and R.N.V.R. *Publications:* six page contribution in 1999 Collins publication "Art Class". *Clubs:* Wapping Group of Artists,

Chelsea Art Soc., Armed Forces Art Soc. *Signs work:* "David Griffin." *Address:* 19 Ross Rd., Wallington, Surrey SM6 8QN.

GRIFFITH, David Lloyd, R.Cam.A. (1996), Associate (1988); artist in oil, water-colour, gouache; teaching experience: life drawing, Conwy (1992-96), basic art, W.E.A., U.C.N.W., Bangor (1998-); *b* Colwyn Bay, 30 Mar., 1956. *Educ:* Ysgol Emrys Ap Iwan, Abergele, Clwyd. *Studied:* N.E. Wales Inst. (1975-76, N.D. Mackinson, R. Hore), Open College of the Arts (1989-93, E. Williams, H. Bowcott, N. Griffiths). *Exhib:* Rhyl Arts Centre (1997), "Land of my Fathers", Oglivy & Estil (1998), Rhyl Arts Centre (1999); selected group shows Royal Cambrian Academy, "I Know what I like, or do I?", Kings College, Cambridge (1997), The Pure Landscape, John Davies Gallery, Stow on Wold (2001). *Work in collections:* Hospitals in Wales, "Moments", Denbigh Museum & Gallery (2001). *Signs work:* "D.L.G." *Address:* 35 Glan y Fedw, Betws Yn Rhos, Abergele, Clwyd LL22 8AP.

GRIFFITHS, David, D.F.A. (Slade); portrait painter in oils; *b* Liverpool, 1939. *Educ:* Pwllheli Grammar School (1951-57). *Studied:* Slade School of Fine Art (1957-61, Sir William Coldstream). *Exhib:* Royal National Eisteddfod; retrospective exhibition, National Library of Wales (2002). *Work in collections:* City Hall, Cardiff; Museum and A.G., Newport; Croydon Town Hall; House of Lords; Eton College; R.C.S.; National Library of Wales; University of Wales, Cardiff, Swansea and Aberystwyth; Llandovery College; Trinity College; Assoc. of Anaesthetists; Speaker's House, Westminster; H.T.V. Television; Waverley School; Liverpool University; Assoc. of Chartered Surveyors; University of Indianapolis; several public and private collections throughout the country. *Signs work:* "David Griffiths." *Address:* Westville House, 49 Westville Rd., Cardiff CF2 5DF.

GRIFFITHS, Michael, A.R.E., B.A. (Hons.), Post Grad. Cert. in Printmaking; painter and printmaker; assoc. lecturer, The Arts Inst., Bournemouth; director of The Badger Press, open access printmaking studio; *b* London, 27 Sep., 1951. *m* Sally James. two *s. Studied:* Brighton Polytechnic (1973-1977). *Exhib:* 20 solo exhibs. throughout U.K., and numerous group exhibs., U.K. and abroad. *Work in collections:* numerous private and public collections, including Ashmolean Museum, Oxford, South East Arts, University of Kent. *Clubs:* Newlyn Society of Artists. *Signs work:* "Michael Griffiths" or "MG." *Address:* 4 Nuns Rd., Winchester, Hants. SO23 7EF. *Email:* mikegriffithsis@hotmail.com

GRIFFITHS, Tom, painter, designer and illuminator on vellum; Senior lecturer, Norwich School of Art (1942-49); chairman, Norfolk and Norwich Art Circle (1957, 1958, 1978), President (1983-); *Educ:* City of Norwich School. *Studied:* Norwich School of Art, Heatherleys' and The Grosvenor (London). *Exhib:* R.A., R.O.I., N.S., and provincial art galleries; one-man shows of townscapes (Norwich). *Work in collections:* many illuminated vellums include Loyal Address (Norwich); Freedom Scrolls for H.M. Queen Elizabeth the Queen Mother, Sir John Barbirolli (King's Lynn); the Royal Air Force and Regimental presentations and the County War Memorial Book of Remembrance, Norwich Cathedral. *Signs work:* "Tom Griffiths." *Address:* 15 Essex St., Norwich.

GRIGSBY, John Higham, N.D.D., A.T.D., A.R.E. (1973), R.E. (1978); *b* Staffs., 18 Dec., 1940. *Studied:* Stoke and Leicester Colleges of Art. *Exhib:* Young

Contemporaries, R.A., N.E.A.C., R.W.A., R.W.S. Galleries, Mall Galleries, F.B.A. Touring Exhbns., Woburn Abbey, Glasgow Institute, London Group, Buenos Aires Print Biennale, Bankside Gallery; solo shows: Hampstead, Exeter, Henley, Beckenham, Bedford School. *Work in collections:* Reading Museum; Whitgift Foundation; Graves Gallery, Sheffield; Open University; National Museum of Wales; Williamson Gallery, Birkenhead; Portland State University (U.S.A.); Camden and Greenwich Councils; Hertfordshire, mid-Glamorgan and Sheffield Education Authorities; Exeter University; Bedford School; Fylde Arts Assoc; Imperial College; Fitzwilliam Museum. *Commissions:* Two murals for Trust Houses (1962); Limited edition etching for Unistrut U.K. (1978) and the P.C.C. (1982). *Signs work:* "John Grigsby." *Address:* 152a Mackenzie Rd., Beckenham BR3 4SD.

GROARKE, Michael, M.A., M.C.S.D., chartered designer; B.E.D.A. Cert. (Registered European designer); wallpaper/textile/ceramics designer, painter in water-colour and oil; *b* Manchester, Oct., 1943. *m* Prudence J. Hyde. two *s. Educ:* Manchester High School of Art. *Studied:* Calico Printers Assoc. Design School, Manchester Polytechnic Faculty of Art and Design, Rochdale College of Art. *Exhib:* R.A., R.W.S., R.I., R.Cam.A.; design work/exhb. Britain, Europe and America. *Signs work:* "M.G." or "Michael Groarke." *Address:* Fourways, 2 Grovesnor Rd., Marple, Stockport SK6 6PR.

GROSVENOR, Stella Athalie (Mrs.), R.B.S., Slade Dip. Fine Art (1937); sculptor in bronze, resin, stone, wood, painter in oil; *b* Beaconsfield. *m* Hugh N. W. Grosvenor, A.R.I.B.A. *Educ:* St. Margaret's School, Hampstead. *Studied:* Slade School under Prof. Schwabe and Prof. Gerrard. *Exhib:* group shows, Society Portrait Sculptors, Hampstead Artists Council, R.A., Travers Gallery, Erica Bourne Gallery; one-man show, Foyles, London (1968). *Work in collections:* Dixons. *Publications:* Art Editor, National Trade Press; Illustrated, Caxton Publishing Co. *Clubs:* Hampstead Artists Council, R.B.S. *Signs work:* "A. Grosvenor." *Address:* 35 Flask Walk, London NW3 1HH.

GROVES, John Michael, R.S.M.A. (1977), N.D.D. (Illustration, 1957); artist in pastel, oil, pen and ink; *b* Lewisham, London, 9 Mar., 1937. *Educ:* Kilmorie Secondary School, London. *Studied:* Camberwell School of Arts and Crafts (1953-57). *Exhib:* R.S.M.A., Mall Galleries, London. *Commissions:* five (3'x 5') historical oils for this country and abroad, commiss. by Shell. *Publications:* The Tall Ship in Art – Cassell. *Signs work:* "J. Groves." *Address:* 114 Further Green Rd., Catford, London SE6 1JQ.

GRUFFYDD, Pegi, B.A. (Hons.) (1982), A.R.C.A. (1985), Dip.R.A. (1986); painter/printmaker in oil, water-colour, etching, lithography; *b* Pwllheli, N. Wales, 28 Apr., 1960. *Educ:* Ysgol Glan-y-Môr, Pwllheli. *Studied:* Manchester Polytechnic (1978-79), Wolverhampton Polytechnic (1979-82), R.A. Schools (1983-86). *Exhib:* R.A. Summer Exhbn. (1984-85), Royal National Eisteddfod of Wales (1980-88), Young Artists Forum, Cardiff University, Wales '83, the Welsh Group Touring Exhbn., Midwales Open, Aberystwyth, North Wales Open, Llandudno; one-man show, Theatre Gwynedd, Bangor; group show, Oriel, Bangor. Gallery: Oriel Glyn-y-Weddw, Llanbedrog. *Signs work:* "Pegi Gruffydd" or "P.G." *Address:* Llymgwyn Farm, Chwilog, Pwllheli, Gwynedd LL53 6HJ.

GRÜNEWALD, Eleanor Mavis (née Wilson), N.D.D. (Painting), A.T.D. (Leeds); artist in oil, acryl, aquarelle; teaches art at Kronberg Art School, Germany; *b* Stockton-on-Tees, 2 Mar., 1931. *m* Karl-Heinz Grünewald. one *s*. two *d. Educ:* Richard Hind School, Stockton. *Studied:* Middlesbrough School of Art, Leeds College of Art. *Exhib:* Frankfurt, Wiesbaden, Marburg, Paris, Le Salon, Grand Palais des Champs-Elysees, China: Peking, Shanghai; Egypt: Cairo, Alexandria, with the Frankfurt Union of Professional Artists. *Work in collections:* Cities of Frankfurt, Wiesbaden, Marburg, Middlesbrough. *Clubs:* Berufsverband Bildender Künstler. *Signs work:* "Mavis Wilson-Grünewald." *Address:* Fahrgasse 21, 60311 Frankfurt/Main.

GUARNORI, (TRUELOVE), Jacky, F.S.B.A. (1985), S.Lm. (1986); self taught flower painter in water-colour; *b* Surrey, 1943. *m* Peter Truelove. two *s* one s- *s*. two s- *d. Educ:* Grey Coat Hospital, London. *Exhib:* S.B.A.; solo shows: Bromley (4), Croydon (2), Cranbrook (1), Francis Iles Fine Art, Sevenoaks Wildfowl Trust, Soc. of Limners, Samlesbury Hall, The Lake Artists, North Wales Soc. of Botanical and Fine Watercolour Artists. *Work in collections:* Orpington Library, Shell U.K. *Commissions:* Shell U.K., Dr. Barnados. *Publications:* work repro.: greetings cards and calendars. *Clubs:* Ambleside Art Society, N.W.S.B. & F.W.A. *Signs work:* "Jacky Guarnori" or "J.G." *Address:* Oak Bank, Hill Top, Windermere, Cumbria LA23 2HG. *Email:* petert@freeuk.com

GUEST, Alan Sexty, artist in oil; teacher, private tutor, lecturer, autodidact; teacher, Coventry City Council; *b* 11 Dec., 1920. *m* Kathleen Guest. two *s*. five *d. Educ:* Woodlands, nr. Doncaster. *Exhib:* Nuneaton A.G., Coventry, Chalk Farm; two paintings selected by BBC Search for an Artist; TV appearances. *Commissions:* by owner of L'escargot, now hanging in the Curragh. *Clubs:* Unicorn. *Signs work:* "A. Guest." *Address:* 19 Sharp Cl., Holbrooks, Coventry.

GUISE, Christopher John, M.A., R.M.S.; marine painter in oil on wood panels, miniaturist in oil on ivorine; formerly on staff, Hurstpierpoint College; *b* Darjeeling, India, 19 June, 1928. *m* Phyllis Gibson. one *s*. one *d. Educ:* Charterhouse and Brasenose College, Oxford. *Exhib:* R.M.S. since 1983, Brighton, Washington, N.Y., Boston, Toronto, Maritime and Sailing Centres. *Signs work:* "C.J. GUISE." *Address:* Carys, West Furlong La., Hurstpierpoint, W. Sussex BN6 9RH.

GUMUCHIAN, Margaret, D.A. (Manc.), A.T.D., F.R.S.A.; artist in oil, gouache and lithography; *b* Manchester, 8 June, 1927. *m* Ian MacDonald Grant. one *d. Studied:* Regional College of Art, Manchester. *Exhib:* R.A., R.B.A., M.A.F.A., S.M.P. regional galleries, Paris, and Biarritz. *Work in collections:* School Loans Collection, Salford, Salford Art Gallery, Rutherston Loans Collection, Manchester City A.G. and various private collections, Arctophile. *Signs work:* "Mgt. Gumuchian." *Address:* Barrachnie, Aldersgreen Ave., High Lane, Stockport, Cheshire SK6 8EB.

GUNN, James Thomson, F.I.A.L., A.I.P.D., D.A., R.I.Dipl; artist in oil, water-colour, gouache, mixed media and designer; Letter of Commendation from H.M. The Queen (R.A.F. 1957); Diploma of Merit conferred by University delle Arti (1982); Highland Society of London award, R.S.A. (1985); *b* Gorebridge, 9 Apr., 1932. *m* Mary Lang (née Linton). one *d. Educ:* Dalkeith High School. *Studied:* Edinburgh

College of Art (1956), Diploma (Travelling Scholar). *Exhib:* R.S.A., R.S.W., R.I., S.S.A., R.G.I., City Art Centre (1983). *Work in collections:* Royal Collection, Argyll Educ. Com.; represented in private collections. *Clubs:* I.A.L., I.P.D. *Signs work:* see appendix. *Address:* 3 Park Cres., Easthouses, Dalkeith, Midlothian EH22 4EE, Scotland.

GWYNNE-JONES, Emily, A.R.C.A. (1970); Mem. Contemporary Portrait Soc.; painter in oil and water-colour; *b* 7 July, 1948. *m* M. Frank Beanland, painter. one *s.* two *d.* *Studied:* R.A. Schools, R.C.A. (1966-70), N.E. London Polytechnic (textiles), Central School (etching) (1977-78). *Exhib:* R.A. (1966-90), Mayor Gallery, New Grafton Gallery, Pigeon Hole Gallery, Brotherton Gallery, Discerning Eye, Mall Galleries (1991-92), N.E.A.C.; one-man show, Michael Parkin (1977). John Player Award N.P.G. (1987-88). *Work in collections:* R.A., Nuffield Trust, National Trust, Eton College, Paintings for Hospitals, B.S.I. *Publications:* illustrated, Pavane for a Dead Infanta by Hugh Ross Williamson. *Signs work:* "E.G.J." or "E. Gwynne-Jones." *Address:* Metfield Lane Farm, Fressingfield, Eye, Suffolk IP21 5SD.

GYLES, Pauline Yvonne, A.R.M.S. (1981), R.M.S. (1985), F.S.B.A. (1986); self taught miniature painter in water-colour; Hon. Sec., Royal Miniature Soc.; *b* Bournemouth, 31 Aug., 1931. *m* Brian Gyles. *Educ:* private schools England and Switzerland. *Exhib:* Medici, Liberty's, Llewellyn Alexander, London, Linda Blackstone, Pinner, Peter Hedley, Wareham, S.B.A., R.M.S. *Work in collections:* Russell Cotes A.G. and Museum, Bournemouth, Soc. of Apothecaries. *Signs work:* "Pauline Gyles." *Address:* 3 Old Coastguard Rd., Sandbanks, Poole, Dorset BH13 7RL.

H

HABGOOD, Yvonne Veronica, M.F.P.S. (1981); painter in oil and alkyd on canvas, pastel on paper; *b* Lincoln, 2 Oct., 1954. *m* David James Yates (partner). *Educ:* St. John's School, Episkopi, Cyprus. *Exhib:* Mall Galleries, F.P.S., Loggia Gallery, N.S.P.S. (1982), Manchester Academy, Commonwealth Inst.; one-man shows: Bagazzo Gallery Marlborough, Loggia Gallery, etc. *Work in collections:* Bath Rd. Gallery, Old Town, Swindon and numerous private collections including Jamaica, Canada and Japan. *Signs work:* "Habgood." *Address:* 24 Hill Cres., Finstock, Oxon. OX7 3BS. *Email:* Yvonneartist@amserv.net

HACKNEY, Arthur, V.P.R.W.S. (1973-76), R.E., A.R.C.A.; etcher; painter in oil and water-colour; Head of Dept., West Surrey College of Art and Design (retd. 1985); Mem. Fine Art Board, Council for National Academy Awards (1975-78), Hon. Ret. R.W.S. (1996), Hon. Ret. R.E. (1990); *b* Stainforth, Yorks., 13 Mar., 1925. *m* Mary Hackney. two *d.* *Educ:* Stoke-on-Trent. *Studied:* Burslem School of Art and R.C.A. (travelling scholarship). *Exhib:* R.A., R.E., R.W.S. *Work in collections:* V. & A. Museum; Bradford City A.G.; Nottingham Castle A.G.; Keighley A.G.; Wakefield City A.G.; Graves A.G. (Sheffield); Wellington A.G. (N.Z.); Stoke-on-Trent A.G.;

Ashmoleon. *Publications:* in 20th Century Painters and Sculptors, Who's Who. *Clubs:* Chelsea Arts. *Signs work:* see appendix. *Address:* Woodhatches, Spoil Lane, Tongham, Surrey GU10 1BP.

HACKNEY, Isla Katrina, M.A. Hons. (Edin.) (1985), R.W.S. (1993); artist in water-colour, acrylic, oil, lecturer in art and visual theory; *b* Wrotham, Kent, 6 June, 1962. *Educ:* Gads Hill Place School, Kent, and Gravesend Grammar School. *Studied:* Edinburgh College of Art (Elizabeth Ogilvie, Robert Callender, William Baillie), Edinburgh University (specialized in British art (Martin Hammer) and Scottish art (Duncan MacMillan)). *Exhib:* R.W.S., regularly at Bankside Gallery, London; Lynne Strover Gallery, Cambridge. *Work in collections:* Freshfields, Fleet Street, Lord & Lady Sainsbury. *Publications:* author: 'Charles Rennie Mackintosh' and 'A History of Water-colour Painting'. *Signs work:* "Isla K. Hackney." *Address:* 5 Randolph Cres., Edinburgh EH3 7TH.

HACKNEY, Mary, A.R.C.A., P.S.; painter in oil, pastel, water-colour; teacher of life painting and portrait; *b* Coventry, 28 Nov., 1925. *m* Arthur. two *d. Educ:* Sacred Heart, Coventry. *Studied:* Birmingham College of Art, R.C.A. (1946-49). *Exhib:* R.A., P.S., Mall Galleries, New Ashgate, Farnham, and provinces. *Work in collections:* Leicester City (Pictures for Schools), many private collections. *Signs work:* "Mary Hackney." or "M.H." *Address:* Woodhatches, Spoil Lane, Tongham, Surrey GU10 1BP.

HAGUE, Jonathan, N.D.D., A.T.D., Netherland State Scholarship; *b* Llandudno, 18 Nov., 1938. *Studied:* Liverpool College of Art (1957-63), Royal Academy of Fine Art, The Hague (1964-66). *Exhib:* one-man shows: The Germeente Museum, The Hague; The Royal Institute Gallery, Piccadilly; sponsored John Lennon. *Signs work:* "HAGUE." *Address:* 2 Regent St., Leamington Spa, Warwicks CV32 5HW.

HAIG, George Douglas (The Earl Haig), Associate Royal Scottish Academy; painter in oil and water-colour; *b* London, 15 Mar., 1918. *m* (2nd) Donna Geroloma Lopez y Royo. one *s.* two *d.* by 1st marriage. *Educ:* Stowe and Christ Church, Oxford. *Studied:* Camberwell School of Art (1945-47) under Victor Pasmore, other members of Euston Rd. School and privately with Paul Maze. *Exhib:* Redfern Gallery, The Scottish Gallery and elsewhere. *Work in collections:* paintings: Arts Council and Scottish National Gallery of Modern Art. *Signs work:* "Haig." *Address:* Bemersyde, Melrose TD6 9DP.

HAINAULT, June, essentist painter in oil, acrylic, water-colour, printer of aquatints - movement, space, time; *m* H.J. Mundy (decd.). two *s. Studied:* Regent St. Polytechnic; Heatherley School of Art. *Exhib:* solo shows: The Gallery, Cork St., London (1994), Hanover Galleries, Liverpool (1986), Fitzroy Gallery, London (1980), Carnival '75, University of Manchester (1975), Loggia Gallery (1972, 1975), Upper St. Gallery, Islington (1972, 1975), Cockpit Theatre (1970), Old Bakehouse, Sevenoaks (1970), New Town Gallery, Uckfield (1969, 1976), Lightning Mark, Rye (1967), Il Traghetto Gallery, Venice (1966), St. Martin's Gallery, London (1965), Congress Theatre, Eastbourne (1998, 1999). *Publications:* cover on book "Cultural Policy" for Council of Europe (2000). *Clubs:* F.P.S. Eastbourne Group. *Signs work:* "Hainault." *Address:* The Oast House, Five Ashes, Horleigh Green, nr. Mayfield, E. Sussex TN20 6NL. *Second Address:* Kinkwall, Walls, Shetland ZE2 9PD.

HAINES, Nick, L.S.I.A. (1974); Artist and Illustrators prize N.A.P.A. (1997), Fine Art Trade Guild prize N.A.P.A (1999); artist in acrylic, oil and mixed media; *b* Essex, 1952. *m* Diane. two *s*. four *d*. *Studied:* Somerset College of Art. *Exhib:* anually with N.A.P.A., Birmingham, Bath, N.A.P.A. (U.S.A.), London, Bath Fringe Festival, regularly at Millfield Summer Show, etc. *Work in collections:* many private throughout Britain and Europe, including Lord Bath, Longleat House. *Clubs:* Fine Art Trade Guild, Chairman of Northeast Somerset Arts, National Acrylic Painters Association, Bath Area Network for Artists, Old Bakery Artists. *Signs work:* see appendix. *Address:* Laburnham Cottage, Little Green, Mells, Som. BA11 3QW. *Email:* nick-haines@fsmail.net

HAINSWORTH, George, Slade Dip., Gulbenkian Scholar (Rome); artist in oil paint, variety of sculptural media; retired Prof. of Fine Art, Leeds Metropolitan University; *b* Leeds, 15 Dec., 1937. *m* Lucy M. Rogers. one *s*. one *d*. *Studied:* Leeds College of Art (1955-60), Slade School of Fine Art (1960-62, William Coldstream), British School at Rome (1962-63). *Exhib:* one-man shows: Serpentine Gallery, Ikon Gallery B'ham, Spacex Gallery Exeter, Sue Rankin Gallery, Ainscough Contemporary Art, London; two-person (with Lucy): Cartwright Hall Bradford, Dean Clough Halifax, Doncaster City A.G., ongoing display at Biemen de Haas Gallery, Amsterdam. *Work in collections:* Leeds University, Hammond Suddard, Baring Investors, Provident Financial Group plc, many private collections. *Clubs:* Yorkshire Sculptors Group, Leeds Fine Art. *Signs work:* "G. Hainsworth." *Address:* Otter House, Hunsingore, nr. Wetherby, W. Yorks. LS22 5HY.

HALE, Helen Margaret, R.O.I., N.S., S.W.A., F.P.S.; painter and sculptor; *b* Harpenden, 18 Apr., 1936. *m* Horne Shepherd (decd.). *Educ:* St. George's School, Harpenden. *Studied:* St. Martin's School of Art and Sir John Cass School of Art. *Exhib:* group shows: London, Edinburgh, Paris, Munich. *Signs work:* "HALE." *Address:* Atheldene, Loxwood Rd., Rudgwick, Horsham, W. Sussex RH12 3DW.

HALES, Gordon Hereward, R.S.M.A. (1981), R.B.A., F.R.S.A., M.Cam.; painter in water-colour, pastel and oil; *b* Matlock, Derbys., 24 Feb., 1916. *m* Margaret Lily Adams. two *d*. *Educ:* Avenue Road School and The Gateway School, Leicester. *Studied:* Leicester College of Art, Northampton School of Art. *Exhib:* R.I., R.O.I., P.S. *Clubs:* Wapping Group of Artists (president), London Muster of Artists (founder), The Artists Soc., and Langham Sketching Club, Armed Forces Art Soc. *Signs work:* "GORDON HALES." *Address:* 11 Rosecroft Drive, Watford, Herts. WD1 3JG.

HALFORD, Hilary, A.T.D. (1942), A.U.A. (1992); artist in oil, water-colour, pen and coloured pencils; Curator, William Morris Gallery Walthamstow (1950-52), Slide Librarian, Dept. of Art History, University of Essex (1979-81); *b* London, 13 Apr., 1920. divorced. three *s*. *Educ:* Tottenham County School. *Studied:* Hornsey College of Art (1935-42), Oxford University (1947-49). *Exhib:* Digby Gallery, Mercury Theatre, Colchester (1985). *Clubs:* U.A., Colchester Art Soc., Reading Guild of Artists. *Address:* 63 Lower Henley Rd., Caversham, Reading RG4 5LD.

HALL, Christopher Compton, R.B.A. (1988), D.F.A. (1954), R. Cam. A. (1994); painter in oil; *b* Slaugham, Sussex, 25 Dec., 1930. *m* Maria Galassi. three *s*. *Educ:* Bedales School. *Studied:* Slade School of Fine Art (1950-54). *Exhib:* Portal

Gallery, New Grafton Gallery, R.A., Waterman Fine Art, Lynne Stern Assoc., Rona Gallery. *Work in collections:* London Museum, National Library of Wales, Reading A.G., Arts Council, O.U.P. *Signs work:* "C.C. Hall." *Address:* Catherine Villa, Station Rd., Newbury, Berks. RG14 7LP.

HALL, Dennis Henry, A.R.C.A. (1955); graphic designer and producer/publisher of Illustrated Limited Edition Books; *b* Caterham, 1927. *m* Sylvia Stokeld, A.R.C.A. *Educ:* Lancing College. *Studied:* Chelsea School of Art (Brian Robb), R.C.A. (John Lewis). Taught design: Norwich, Leeds and Oxford Schools of Art or Polytechnica. Founded and ran The Inky Parrot Press at Oxford Polytechnic (1981-87) and now runs the Previous Parrot Press. Books in: V. & A., Cambridge University Library, National Library of Scotland, Rijksmuseum, Columbia and Harvard Libraries, full set (44 vols.) in Brookes Oxford University Library. *Address:* The Foundry, Church Hanborough, nr. Witney, Oxon. OX8 8AB.

HALL, Jo, B.Sc. (Hons.) Botany (1967), P.h.D. (1971); painter in pastel, watercolour, acrylic; freelance artist and illustrator; formerly biologist in water industry; *b* Sidcup, Kent, 31 Jan., 1946. *m* Geoffrey Hall. two *s. Educ:* Exeter University, Imperial College, London. *Exhib:* S.G.F.A. members and open (1996-2001), Not the Royal Academy (1997-1998), Medici Miniatures (1997-1998); solo exhib. by invitation of the European Space Agency's Fine Art Club (2001). *Work in collections:* E.S.A.'s fine art collection, Noordwijk, Holland. *Commissions:* corporate including, Southern Electric, Gardens of Woolley Hall, Assoc. Aviation Inc. (Space Division), The Creation Portfolio, a series of impressions of four galaxies; also private commissions, landscape and portrait. *Clubs:* V.P. Society of Graphic Fine Art, Assoc. of Illustrators. *Signs work:* "Jo Hall." *Address:* Morar, Altwood Close, Maidenhead, Berks. SL6 4PP. *Email:* johall@mhstudios.co.uk

HALL, Nigel John, M.Art R.C.A.; sculptor; *b* Bristol, 30 Aug., 1943. *m* Manijeh (née Yadegar). *Educ:* Bristol Grammar School. *Studied:* West of England College of Art (1960-64), Royal College of Art (1964-67), Harkness Fellowship (1967-69). *Exhib:* one-man shows, Galerie Givaudan, Paris; Wilder Gallery, Los Angeles; Galerie Neuendorf, Hamburg and Cologne; Serpentine Gallery, London; Juda Rowan Gallery, London; Nishimura Gallery, Tokyo; Elkon Gallery, N.Y., Galerie Maeght, Paris. *Work in collections:* Tate Gallery, V. & A., Arts Council of Great Britain, National Galerie, Berlin, Dallas Museum of Fine Art, Tokyo Metropolitan Museum, Chicago Art Institute, Kunsthaus, Zurich, Museum of Modern Art, N.Y. *Signs work:* "NIGEL HALL." *Address:* 11 Kensington Pk. Gdns., London W11 3HD.

HALL, Pauline Sophie, B.Sc. (1938); artist in woodcut, wood engraving, linocut; ex-mem. S.WL.A.; *b* Birmingham, 23 June, 1918. *m* Prof. K. R. L. Hall (decd.). *Educ:* Birmingham University, Oxford University. *Studied:* Michaelis School of Art, Cape Town (1955-60). *Exhib:* R.E., S.WL.A. (Mall Galleries); one-man shows, Cape Town (1973), The Shakespeare Centre, Stratford-on-Avon (1984), Coleg, Harlech (1992). *Work in collections:* Nature in Art, Wallsworth Hall, Glos. *Signs work:* "Pauline S. Hall." *Address:* Park View Flat, Church Rd., Snitterfield, Warwickshire CV37 0LE.

HALLIDAY, Charlotte Mary Irvine, R.W.S. (1976), N.E.A.C. (1961); topographical artist; Keeper, New English Art Club since 1989; *b* Kensington, 5 Sept.,

1935. *Educ:* Wester Elchies, Francis Holland. *Studied:* R.A. Schools (1953-58). *Exhib:* R.W.S., R.B.A., N.E.A.C., etc. *Commissions:* Salisbury Cathedral, Selfridges, Lord's Pavilion, the Monument, London Clubs, City Banks and many private houses. *Publications:* Illustrations for Dictionary of Edwardian Architecture by A. Stuart Gray (1985) and co-author, with him, of "Fanlights", a visual architectural history (1990). *Signs work:* "Charlotte Halliday" or "CMIH." *Address:* 36a Abercorn Pl., London NW8 9XP.

HALLIDAY, Irene, D.A. (1952), Scholarship (1953), Travelling Scholarship (1954), R.S.W. (1955); artist in gouache, acrylic, oil paint; *b* Kingsmuir, Angus, Scotland, 26 Sept., 1931. *Educ:* Arbroath High School. *Studied:* Dundee College of Art (1948-53, Alberto Morrocco, R.S.A., R.S.W.). *Exhib:* 42 one-man shows, Arbroath, Dundee, Edinburgh, Manchester, Salford, New York State. *Work in collections:* art galleries of Arbroath, Bolton, Dundee, Glasgow, Greenock, Salford; education authorities of Dundee, Dunbartonshire, Edinburgh, Fife, Manchester, Wigan; Granada TV., British National Oil Co., Shell Centre, London, Manchester Ship Canal Co., Pilkingham Glass plc. St. Helens, Bowrings and Co. London. *Commissions:* Aumbry Door, St. John's Church, Moston, Manchester (1992), Reredos Wall, St. Christopher's Church, Withington, Manchester (1999), Reredos Wall, St. Chad's Church, New Moston, Manchester (2000). *Signs work:* "Halliday." *Address:* 46 Highfield Dene Rd., Didsbury, Manchester M20 2ST.

HALLOWES, Veda Nanette, sculptor in bronze and teacher; also porcelain (mainly) and stoneware potter (1974-1999); *b* Johannesburg, 16 Jan., 1941. *m* George Richard Hallowes. two *d. Educ:* Waverley Girls High School, Johannesburg. *Studied:* Wandsworth Adult Educ. under Molly Ruddle (1988-1999), Wandsworth Adult College (1992-1994). *Exhib:* Peru, Hong Kong, Pakistan, London; two pieces in R.A. Summer Exhib. (2001). *Work in collections:* Charing Cross Hospital, London. *Commissions:* various, local. Has lived in England since 1971. *Signs work:* see appendix. *Address:* 27 Westleigh Ave., Putney, London SW15 6RQ. *Email:* veda@hallowes.demon.co.uk

HALSBY, Julian, M.A. (Cantab.), R.B.A. (1994), F.R.S.A. (1997); painter in oil, art historian, critic; Mem. International Assoc. of Art Critics; *b* London, 1948. *m* Miranda Halsby, printmaker. one *s.* one *d. Studied:* Emmanuel College, Cambridge (art history). *Exhib:* R.B.A., N.E.A.C., R.O.I., many mixed exhbns. in the U.K. and France, Patterson Fine Art, New Grafton, Wykeham, Century Gallery, Datchett; one-man show: Abbott and Holder (1998). *Publications:* include: Scottish Watercolours 1740-1940 (Batsford, 1986), Dictionary of Scottish Painters 1600-2000 (with Paul Harris) (Canongate, 1995), Venice: The Artists' Vision (Batsford, 1990), The Art of Diana Armfield, R.A. (David & Charles, 1995); plus exhbn. catalogues and articles for "The Artist." . *Signs work:* "Halsby." *Address:* 44 Claremont Rd., Highgate, London N6 5BY.

HAMBLING, Maggi, Boise Travel award, N.Y. (1969), Arts Council award (1977), Artist in Residence, National Gallery (1980-81); artist in oil on canvas, water-colour, drawing, sculpture in bronze, printmaking; *b* Suffolk, 1945. *Studied:* Camberwell School of Art (1964-67), Slade School of Fine Art (1967-69); studied with Lett Haines and Cedric Morris (1960). *Exhib:* solo shows: National Gallery

(1981), Serpentine Gallery (1987), Arnolfini Gallery, Bristol (1988), Bernard Jacobson Gallery (1990), Yale Center for British Art (1991), Northern Centre for Contemporary Art (1993), Marlborough Fine Art (1996), National Portrait Gallery (1997), Yorkshire Sculpture Park (1997). *Work in collections:* Tate Gallery, Whitworth A.G., A.C.G.B., National Gallery, British Museum, N.P.G., Gulbenkian Foundation, Australian National Gallery. *Commissions:* Public statue for Oscar Wilde, London (1998). Jerwood Painting Prize (1995). *Clubs:* Chelsea Arts. *Signs work:* surname on back. *Address:* c/o Marlborough Fine Art, 6 Albemarle St., London W1X 4BY.

HAMILTON, Katherine, Dip. (Byam Shaw) (1974), Dip. Dance and Choreography (1977); painter in oil on canvas, pastel; *b* 1954. divorced. two *s. Educ:* Dartington Hall School. *Studied:* Byam School of Art (1971-74, Diana Armfield); London School of Contemporary Dance (1974-77). *Exhib:* solo shows: Christopher Hull Gallery, Sue Rankin Gallery (1993), Thackeray Gallery (1994), Chappel Galleries (1998), Chappel Gallery (2001); mixed exhbns.: Piccadilly Gallery, New Academy Gallery (1996), Chappel Gallery (1997), R.A. Summer Show (1997), Cambridge Contemporary Art (1998), Woodgates Gallery East Bergholt (1999). *Commissions:* fourteen portraits (1996-97). *Publications:* British Artists – Francis Spalding, feature in Pastel International 'Artist' magazine. previously known as Katherine Gault. *Signs work:* "Katherine Hamilton." *Address:* Hill House, 61 Covert Rd., Reydon, Southwold, Suffolk IP18 6QE.

HAMILTON, Thomas Gottfried Louis, B.A.Hons.(Arch.); architect, artist in pen, pencil and water-colour; *b* Berlin, 29 Mar., 1930. *m* Georgina Vera Craig. one *s.* one *d. Educ:* King's School, Canterbury; U.C.L. *Studied:* architecture: Bartlett School of Architecture (1949-55, Prof. A.E. Richardson). *Exhib:* private galleries. *Clubs:* The Arts, Dover St. *Signs work:* "Thomas Hamilton." *Address:* 55 Addison Ave., London W11 4QU.

HAMMICK, Tom Henry Heyman St. Vincent, B.A. (Hons.) Ist Class (1990), M.A. Printmaking; Winston Churchill Fellow (1998), Robert Frazer Award (1998); artist in painting/printmaking; Visiting lecturer, Nova Scotia College of Art; *b* Tidworth, 6 Sept., 1963. *m* Martha Theis. one *s. Educ:* Camberwell School of Art (1987-92). *Work in collections:* B-Museum, Yale Center British Art, Arts Council of N.I., Deutsche Bank, Arthur Anderson, British Midland. *Publications:* "Lido" (1998) with poems by Maureen Duppy. *Clubs:* Groucho. *Signs work:* see appendix. *Address:* 10 Elwin St., London E2 7BW.

HAMMOND, Hermione, Rome Scholar (Painting, 1938); *Studied:* Chelsea Polytechnic, R.A. Schools (Dip.). *Exhib:* one-man exhbns.: Bishopsgate Institute (1956); Colnaghi's (1957); Arthur Jeffress (1961); All Hallows, London Wall (1965); New Grafton (1970); Great King St. Gallery, Edinburgh (1972); Six Portfolios, Chelsea (1973); Hartnoll & Eyre Iran & Cyprus (1978), Michael Parkin and University of Hull (1993); Michael Parkin (2000). *Work in collections:* ceiling decoration, University of London, Guildhall collection, Museum of London, Fondation Custodia, Institut Néerlandais, Paris, Fitzwilliam Museum, Hunterian A.G., Glasgow, Brymor Jones Library, University of Hull, Whitworth, Manchester. *Publications:* Oxford Almanack, Arts Review, R.I.B.A. Journal, Country Life. *Signs* *work:* "Hermione Hammond." *Address:* 2 Hans Studio, 43a Glebe Pl., London SW3 5JE.

HAMPTON, F. Michael, wildlife artist in water-colour, scraper-board and acrylic; S.WL.A.-W.W.F.N. Fine Art award (1988); *b* Croydon, 29 May, 1937. one *s.* *Studied:* Croydon Art School. *Exhib:* R.S.P.B., Sandy, Arnhem Gallery, Croydon, Blackheath Gallery SE3, Mall Galleries, London, Port Lympne Zoo Park, Hythe, Kent, Ringstead Gallery, Hunstanton, Cotswold Wildlife Gallery, Lechlade, Glos. *Commissions:* Mr. John Aspinall. *Publications:* work repro.: three jackets of 'British Birds', two jackets of R.S.P.B. 'Birds', (1980-1983), Calendar for Sussex Fine Arts, S.WL.A. Calendars (1987, 1988), S.WL.A.-R.S.P.B. Calendar (1990, 1991, 1992), B.B.C. Wildlife Magazine (Aug. 1992). *Clubs:* S.WL.A., Croydon Art. *Signs work:* "M" and "H" with grebe's head, see appendix. *Address:* 13 Sandy Way, Shirley, Croydon, Surrey CR0 8QT.

HANCERI, Dennis John, R.S.M.A. (1970); graphic designer, water-colour and gouache; *b* London, 7 June, 1928. *m* Jill. one *s.* one *d.* *Studied:* St. Martin's School of Art. *Exhib:* one-man show, Denver, Colorado, U.S.A., Centaur Gallery, Dallas, Texas, Southport, Connecticut, U.S.A.; also shows at Mystic Seaport, Connecticut. *Clubs:* Wapping Group of Artists. *Signs work:* "Dennis John Hanceri RSMA." *Address:* 97 Horncastle Rd., London SE12 9LF.

HANDLEY, Paul, B.A. (Hons.) 1987, A.T.C. (1991); painter in oil, lecturer; Art History lecturer, Itchen College, Soton; *b* Newark, Notts., 29 June, 1964. *Studied:* Norwich School of Art (1984-87), John Wonnacott, John Lessore), Goldsmiths' College (1990-91). *Exhib:* Spectator 1st prizewinner (1992), Hunting Group, N.E.A.C., Discerning Eye, R.P., Royal Overseas League, New Grafton Gallery, Alresford Gallery, Quantum Contemporary, Rowley Gallery London, etc. Work in private collections internationally. *Clubs:* N.E.A.C. *Signs work:* "P.H." *Address:* Brook House, 58 Upper Brook St., Winchester, Hants. SO23 8OG.

HANLEY, Liam Powys, self taught painter in oil on board, gouache and tempera; *b* S. Kensington, 4 Apr., 1933. *m* Hilary Hanley, etcher. one *s.* one *d.* *Educ:* Wrekin College, Salop. *Exhib:* Stone Gallery, Newcastle, Mermaid Theatre, Thackeray Gallery, London, R.A., Abbot Hall A.G., Kendal, Phoenix Gallery, Lavenham, Suffolk, Beardsmore Gallery, London. *Publications:* The Face of Winter by James Hanley. *Signs work:* "Hanley, L." *Address:* 21 Woodsome Rd., London NW5 1RX.

HANLY, Daithi Patrick, B.Arch., F.R.I.A.I., F.R.I.B.A., F.R.T.P.I.; architect, planner, landscaper, sculptor in stone; former Dublin City Architect; Advisory consultant architect, National College of Art and Design; *b* Cavan, 11 Mar., 1917. *m* Joan Kennedy. one *s.* one *d.* *Studied:* National University, College of Art, Dublin. *Exhib:* R.H.A., Oireachtas, sculpture in stone, architectural drawings; won competition Garden of Remembrance, Dublin (1966); Custom House Memorial to John Kavanagh, sculptor, (1950) and Altar Candlesticks (1951). *Commissions:* trustee for erection of 18ft (5.48 m) bronze monument of Christ the King, (Dec. 1978); designed church at Knock for 7,500 pilgrims which was granted the title of Basilica by H.H. Pope John Paul II on his visit there (Sept. 1979). Architect to Royal Dublin Society for Simmonscourt Pavilion large exhibition complex, seaside garden village in

Blainroe, Wicklow with golf clubhouse, on 550 acres. Designed Basilica at Knock for 7,500 pilgrims. *Signs work:* "D. P. Hanly" or "D.P.H." *Address:* San Elmo, Vico Rd., Dalkey, Dublin, Ireland.

HANN, Priscilla, B.A., S.Eq.A.; sculptor; *b* Pattingham, nr. Wolverhampton, 11 Oct., 1943. *m* Patrick Kennedy (decd.). *Educ:* Downe House, Newbury. *Studied:* Wolverhampton College of Art (1961-65, Ron Dutton), Tyler School of Art, Philadelphia (Dean Le Clair). *Work in collections:* 'Natives of Furlong', Ringwood, Hants. *Clubs:* S.Eq.A., Friend of R.A., British Sporting Art Trust, Public Sculpture and Monuments Assoc. *Signs work:* "P. Hann." *Address:* Tetstill, Neen Sollars, Cleobury Mortimer, Worcs. DY14 9AH.

HANSCOMB, Brian, R.E. (1997); self taught artist in pastel, acrylic, drawing and copperplate engraving; *b* Croxley Green, Herts., 23 Sept., 1944. *m* Jane Wilkins, née Hunt. two *d. Educ:* Rickmansworth Grammar School. *Exhib:* R.A., R.W.A., R.E., N.E.A.C., Clarges Gallery, Crane Kalman Gallery, Beaux Arts Gallery; one-man shows: England and Germany. *Work in collections:* D.O.E., V. & A. National Art Library, Science Museum, Royal Cornwall Museum and A.G., Bodleian Library. *Publications:* On the Morning of Christ's Nativity (Folio Soc., 1987); Sun, Sea and Earth (Whittington Press, 1989); Cornwall-An Interior Vision (Whittington Press, 1992), Matrix (Whittington Press, 1995). *Signs work:* "B. Hanscomb" or "B.H." *Address:* Tor View, Limehead, St. Breward, Bodmin, Cornwall PL30 4LU.

HARCUS, Robert, painter in oil; *b* 1 Sep., 1939. *m* Ethna. *Educ:* St. Vincent's C.B.S., Glasnevin. *Studied:* completely self-taught. *Exhib:* R.H.A., the Oireachtas, S.Eq.A.; annual solo exhibs. at Kilkenny Arts Festival since 1981. *Work in collections:* corporate collections in Ireland and U.S.A., including banking institutions and embassies. *Clubs:* Artists Assoc. of Ireland. *Signs work:* "Robert Harcus." *Address:* St. Endas, South Quay, Arklow, Co. Wicklow, Ireland.

HARDAKER, Charles, A.R.C.A. (1958), N.E.A.C. (1969), R.B.A. (1984); painter in oil and pastels; tutor in painting and drawing; *b* Oxford, 1 May, 1934. *m* Annick née Pouletaud. *Educ:* Wellesbourne School, B'ham. *Studied:* B'ham College of Arts and Crafts (1949-53), R.C.A. (1955-58). *Exhib:* R.A., N.E.A.C., R.B.A., R.P., five one-man shows, San Francisco (2), London (3). *Work in collections:* Tate Gallery (Chantrey Bequest), Guildhall of London, National Library of Wales, Northumbria Water, B.P., I.C.E. *Signs work:* "Hardaker." *Address:* Studio 1, St. Oswald's Studios, Sedlescombe Rd., Fulham, London SW6 1RH.

HARDIE, Gwen, Richard Ford award, R.A. (1982), Hons. Degree (1983), Daad Scholarship, W. Berlin (1984), Edward 7th British-German Foundation, W. Berlin (1986); painter in oil, sculptor in cement, plaster; *b* Newport, Scotland, 7 Jan., 1962. *Educ:* Inverurie Academy. *Studied:* Edinburgh College of Art (1979-84, John Houston), H.D.K., W. Berlin (1984-85, Baselitz). *Exhib:* solo shows: Fruitmarket Gallery, Edinburgh (1987), Fischer Fine Art, London (1989), S.N.G.M.A. (1990), Talbot Rice A.G., Edinburgh, Annely Juda, London (1994), Jason & Rhodes, London (1996), Peterborough Museum and Fine A. G. (1997); group shows: Vienna (1986), American tour (1989-92), Frankfurt (1993), Jason & Rhodes, New Artists: Hardie Colvin & Boyd (1995). *Work in collections:* S.N.G.M.A., Metropolitan Museum N.Y., Gulbenkian Museum Lisbon, Arts Council, etc. *Commissions:* Portrait of Jean

Muir (1985). *Signs work:* "G. HARDIE" or "G.H." *Address:* c/o Jason and Rhodes, 4 New Burlington Place, London W1X 1FB.

HARDING, Jane Mary, S.W.A. (1982); artist in line and water-colour; *b* London. *m* David Harding. *Educ:* Haberdashers' Aske's Girls' School. *Studied:* Lytham St. Annes School of Art (1940-41). *Exhib:* S.W.A. annually, Britain in Water-colour, Ealing Art Group. *Work in collections:* London Borough of Ealing Central Library and in private collections in the U.K. and abroad. *Publications:* editorial illustrations for Amalgamated Press, Odhams, Franey's London Diary, Grolier Press, Sunday Times, Ward Gallery. *Clubs:* Ealing Arts. *Signs work:* "Jane Harding." *Address:* Melvin House, 13 Hartington Rd., Ealing, London W13 8QL.

HARDY, (Rev) Paul Ernest, M.A., M. Arch., R.I. Dip. (Dist.), F.Ph.S., F.R.S.A., N.A.P.A., P.S.A.; artist in pastel and water-colour, demonstrator, author; Official demonstrator for Art Profile (National) & Unison Pastels; *b* 25 Sept., 1924. *m* May. one *s.* two *d. Studied:* Bath School of Art; Royal West of England School of Architecture. *Exhib:* Westminster Gallery, R.H.S., R.B.S.A., Victoria A.G. Bath, Bishops Palace Wells, Royal Albert Memorial Museum Exeter, R.W.A., Laing Open, University of Exeter, etc. *Work in collections:* private: U.K., S. Africa, U.S.A., Spain, Australia, N.Z. *Publications:* Exeter, Profile of a City; and Bath, Profile of a City (Redcliffe Press, 1982), The Care and Preservation of English Medieval Cathedrals and Churches (Longmans, 1985) also videos, Starting to Draw & Paint with Pastels (Teaching Art Ltd), book: Landscapes in Pastels, Search Press Ltd. *Clubs:* Exeter, Honiton, Exmouth Art Group, Meirionnydd Artists Soc., Wales, Armed Forces Art Society, Sidmouth, Dulverton, Otter Vale. *Signs work:* "PAUL HARDY." *Address:* 'Pandy Gader', 66 Whipton Lane, Heavitree, Exeter, Devon EX1 3DN.

HARDY HENRION, Daphne, sculptor in clay for terracotta or bronze; *b* 20 Oct., 1917. *m* F.H.K. Henrion. two *s.* one *d. Educ:* The Hague, Holland. *Studied:* R.A. Schools (1934-38). *Exhib:* Beaux Arts Gallery (1946), A.I.A. Gallery (1966), Old Fire Engine House, Ely (1975, 1979), Bury St. Edmunds (1981), Churchill College (1993), Lynn Strover Gallery, Fen Ditton (1996). *Work in collections:* bust of Arthur Koestler at N.P.G. and Edinburgh University, sculpture in relief on Addenbrooke Hospital, Cambridge. *Signs work:* "Daphne Hardy Henrion," "Daphne Henrion," "D.H." or "D.H.H." *Address:* 13 Owlstone Rd., Cambridge CB3 9JH.

HARGAN, Joseph R., D.A. (1974), P.P.A.I. (1989); elected, Glasgow Group (1996), Stirling Smith award (1978), Cargill award (1980), Torrance award (1982), Meyer Oppenheim prize R.S.A. (1985), Hunting Group prizewinner, London (1988), Paisley Art Inst. award (1993), C.F.A.G. Award (2001); Founder Mem. and Chairman of Group 81; elected Pres. P.A.I. (2001), elected P.A.I. (1996); *b* Glasgow, 23 Jan., 1952. *m* Anne Louise Clarke. two *s.* one *d. Studied:* Glasgow School of Art (1970-74, Danny Ferguson, Drummond Bone, David Donaldson). *Exhib:* R.S.A., R.G.I., R.S.W., Art Club, Group 81, R.A., P.A.I., B.W.S., S.S.A., etc. *Work in collections:* New Zealand, Brazil, U.S.A., Europe and S. America. *Clubs:* Glasgow Art. *Signs work:* "Hargan." *Address:* 40 Oakshaw St., Paisley PA1 2DD.

HARLE, Dennis F., artist in oil and gouache, naturalist; *b* Sandwich, 26 May, 1920. *m* Heather Harle. three *d.* from first marriage. *Educ:* Sandwich. *Studied:* Ramsgate and Canterbury Schools of Art (Evening classes). *Exhib:* Reading

Museum and A.G., S.WL.A.; one-man shows, Deal (1978), Maidstone (1963), Sandwich (1960). *Clubs:* S.WL.A. (founder mem.). *Signs work:* "Dennis F. Harle" or "D." *Address:* The Studio, No 72 Strand St., Sandwich, Kent CT13 9HX.

HARPER, Charles, A.O.S.D.A.N.A., A.R.H.A.; painter; head of fine art department, Limerick School of Art and Design; *b* 30 July 1943. one *s.* one *d. Educ:* Crescent College, Limerick. *Studied:* Limerick School of Art, National College of Art, Dublin. *Work in collections:* Arts Council of Ireland, P. J. Carroll & Co., Irish Museum of Modern Art, Hugh Lane Municipal Gallery, San Francisco Museum of Modern Art, Limerick City Gallery of Art. *Publications:* Profile: Charles Harper, Gandon Editions. *Signs work:* "Charles Harper." *Address:* Woodstown House, Ballyvara Rd., Lisnagry, Co. Limerick, Ireland. *Email:* charper@gofree.indigo.ie

HARRIGAN, Claire, B.A. Hons. (1986), R.S.W. (1992); painter in water-colour, acrylic, gouache and pastel; *b* Kilmarnock, 8 Nov., 1964. *Educ:* Sacred Heart Academy, Girvan. *Studied:* Glasgow School of Art (1982-86, Peter Sumsion, Neil Dallas-Brown, Barbara Rae). *Exhib:* solo shows: Christopher Hull Gallery, London; Gatehouse Gallery, Glasgow; Open Eye Gallery, Edinburgh; Macaulay Gallery, Stenton; Bruton St. Gallery, London; Flying Colours Gallery, London. *Signs work:* "Claire Harrigan." *Address:* 53 King St., Crosshill, By Maybole, Ayrshire KA19 7RE.

HARRIS, Alfred, A.R.C.A., F.R.S.A.; artist in acrylic and oil; Chairman (retd.), Dept. of Art & Design, University of London Inst. of Educ.; Mem. London Group; *b* London, 21 July, 1930. *m* Carmel. one *s.* two *d. Studied:* Willesden School of Art (1952), R.C.A. (1955). *Exhib:* numerous group exhbns. and 14 one-man shows in U.K. and abroad. *Work in collections:* 56 in public and corporate including: Ben Uri A.G.; Bradford University; Sweden: Dalarnas Konstnamind, Dalarnas Museum, Falun Museum, Gothenburg Hospital, Konsthallen Uppsala, Ministry of Culture, Scania Valis, Sodertalje Town Council, Uppsala Museum; G.L.C.; Leics. Educ. Authority; London University; Oxford University; R.C.A.; St. Thomas' Hospital, London; Tate Gallery; Tel Aviv Museum, Israel; Tokai Bank, Japan; Warwick University. *Publications:* "Portrait of the Artist" edited by Sarah Fox-Pitt, Tate Gallery Publications (1989); "Modern British Painters 1900-1980" edited by Alan Windsor, Scolar Press (1992); "Dictionary of British Artists Since 1945" edited by David Buckman, Art Dictionaries Ltd (1998). *Signs work:* see appendix. *Address:* 66-70 Camden Mews, London NW1 9BX.

HARRIS, Geoffrey, A.R.C.A. (1954); sculptor; Senior lecturer, Ravensbourne College of Art and Design (1960-86); Assistant to Leon Underwood (1954), Assistant to Henry Moore, O.M., C.H. (1957-60); *b* Nottingham, 1928. *m* Gillian Farr, M.S.I.A., textile designer. two *s. Educ:* Leeds Modern School. *Studied:* Leeds College of Art (1948-51), Royal College of Art (1951-54). *Exhib:* one-man shows: Leicester Galleries, London (1964), Queen Square Gallery, Leeds (1964). *Work in collections:* in Britain, Europe, U.S.A. *Commissions:* Baildon Primary School, Yorkshire, L.C.C. Maitland Park Housing Scheme, St. Pancras, Eurolink Industrial Centre, Sittingbourne, Kent. *Signs work:* "Harris." *Address:* 5 Queen's Rd., Faversham, Kent ME13 8RJ.

HARRIS, Jennifer Joy, N.D.D. (1955), R.W.A. (1981); etcher and painter in water-colour; display designer (1957-1965), art technician in college of education (1966-1977), and faculty of education, Bristol (1977-1978); *b* Bristol, 8 Apr., 1935. *m* Cyril Cave. *Educ:* Duncan House School, Clifton, Bristol. *Studied:* West of England College of Art, Bristol (1951-1955). *Exhib:* R.A., R.W.A., Nat. Exhib. of Modern British Prints, Blackpool (1979 & 1986); Internat. Mini-Print Exhib. (1997); Nat. Print Exhib., London (1997); and many other exhibs. nationwide and in Paris and New York. *Work in collections:* Print Archive, Scarborough Art Gallery. *Clubs:* member of Printmakers Council. *Signs work:* "J.J.Harris." *Address:* Berry House, Cheriton Fitzpaine, Nr. Crediton, Devon EX17 4HZ. *Website:* www.axisartists.org.uk

HARRIS, Josephine, R.W.S., N.E.A.C., F.G.E.; artist in water-colour, drawing and engraved glass; *Educ:* privately. *Studied:* Plymouth College of Art (1948-52) under William Mann, A.R.C.A., gained N.D.D. *Work in collections:* Plymouth A.G., Graves A.G., Sheffield, South London A.G., I.L.E.A., K.C.C. Work to commission for public companies and private individuals in engraved glass. *Signs work:* "Josephine Harris" or "J.H." *Address:* Workshop No. 2, 46-52 Church Rd., Barnes, London SW13 0DO.

HARRIS, Lyndon Goodwin, R.I., R.S.W., R.W.A., Dip. Fine Art (Lond.), A.T.D., Courtauld Certificate, Leverhulme, Pilkington, and Slade Scholar; Slade Anatomy Prizeman, Gold Medal Paris Salon (painting, 1956), Hon. Men. (painting, 1948) and Hon. Men. (etching, 1949); artist in oil, water-colour, stained glass; etcher; *b* Halesowen, Worcs., 25 July, 1928. *Educ:* Halesowen Grammar School. *Studied:* Birmingham College of Art, L.C.C. Central School of Art and Crafts, Courtauld Inst., Slade School (Profs. Randolph Schwabe and Sir William Coldstream) and University of London Institute of Education. *Exhib:* Paris Salon, R.A. (first exhib. at age of 13), R.S.A., R.I., N.E.A.C., R.B.A., R.S.W., R.G.I., R.W.A., Britain in Water-colour, Birmingham, Bradford, Wolverhampton, Bournemouth, Blackpool, Southport and other principal provincial galleries. *Work in collections:* University College, London; Government Art Collection; Birmingham and Midland Inst.; City of Worcester; stained glass window, Gorsty Hill Methodist Church, Halesowen. *Publications:* Masters of Water-colour and Their Techniques (The Artist), Young Artists of Promise, Souvenir Handbook of Halesowen, Birmingham Post, etc. *Signs work:* "Lyndon G. Harris." *Address:* c/o Lloyds Bank, 23 Hagley St., Halesowen, W. Midlands B63 3AY.

HARRIS, Phyllis, S.W.A., N.D.D., S.G.F.A., A.U.A.; artist in water-colour and pen, lithography, linocut, school teacher (retd.); *b* London, 3 Aug., 1925. *m* David Harris. one *s.* one *d. Educ:* Brondesbury High School, London and Abbey School, Reading. *Studied:* Reading University School of Art, Brighton and Camberwell, Harrow School of Art (lithography). *Exhib:* S.W.A., Brent and Harrow, S.G.F.A., London. *Clubs:* S.W.A., Wembley Art Soc., Harrow Art Soc., S.G.F.A., U.A. *Signs work:* "Phyl Harris." *Address:* 55 Slough Lane, Kingsbury, London NW9 8YB.

HARRIS, Rosemary, M.A. (Hons.) History of Art; Curator, NatWest Group Art Collection; *b* Guildford, Surrey, 1 Dec., 1962. *m* Paul Moorhouse. *Studied:* University College, London. *Address:* Royal Bank of Scotland Group Art Collection,

12 Throgmorton Ave., London EC2N 2DL.

HARRISON, Christopher David, B.A. (Hons.), A.T.C.; artist in water-colour, collage, oils; Director, Bircham Art Gallery; *b* Gt. Yarmouth, 21 Oct., 1953. *m* Deborah Margaret. two *s*. *Educ:* Bromley Grammar School, Kent, Boston Grammar School, Lincs. *Studied:* Jacob Kramer College of Art, Leeds (1973-74), Reading University (1974-78), London University Inst. of Educ. (1978-79). *Exhib:* R.B.A., R.A., R.I., R.W.S.; many mixed exhbns. throughout England; regular one-man shows Norfolk. *Signs work:* "Christopher Harrison." *Address:* 49 Church La., Bircham, King's Lynn, Norfolk PE31 6QW.

HARRISON, Claude, (Hon.)R.P., A.R.C.A.; artist in oil, oil and tempera, pen and wash, etc.; primarily a painter of conversation pieces and imaginative landscapes; *b* Leyland, Lancs., 31 Mar., 1922. *m* Audrey Johnson, painter. one *s*. *Educ:* Hutton Grammar School, Lancs. *Studied:* Preston (1938-40), Liverpool (1940-41), R.C.A. (1947-49). *Exhib:* R.A., R.P., R.S.A., R.B.A., etc. *Work in collections:* Harris A.G., Preston, Abbott Hall, Kendal, Lancaster City Museum, Bournemouth A.G., etc. *Publications:* The Portrait Painters' Handbook (Studio Vista, 1968); Book of Tobit (1970). *Signs work:* "CLAUDE HARRISON." *Address:* Barrow Wife, Cartmel Fell, Grange over Sands Cumbria LA11 6NZ

HARRISON, Margot, artist in water-colour, oil; *b* 2 Jan., 1915. *m* George Francis Harrison, M.B.E. two *d*. *Educ:* Queen Anne's, Caversham. *Studied:* privately under Prescoe Holeman (1938), and Kingsley Sutton, F.R.S.A. (1965); Farnham School of Art, part-time (1966-69, John Wilkinson, A.R.C.A.). *Exhib:* Paris Salon (1972, 1973); one-man shows: Alpine Gallery (1975), Bradshaw Room F.B.A. (1978), Mall Galleries (1974), Bradshaw Room F.B.A. (1982), R.O.I., Britain in Watercolours, R.B.A. *Work in collections:* B.P. (1974), National Trust (1980). *Signs work:* "Margot Harrison." *Address:* Stoney Cottage, The Bury, Odiham, Hants. RG29 1LY.

HARRISON, Marguerite Hazel, National Froebel Foundation Diploma in Art; artist in oil, pen and wash, and pastels; *b* Llandudno, N. Wales, 7 Oct., 1927. *m* Michael Harrison (decd.). three *s*. two *d*. *Educ:* Royal Masonic School, Rickmansworth, Herts. *Studied:* mainly self-taught; tuition for a period under Kenneth A. Jameson. *Exhib:* R.A., R.Cam.A., Grosvenor Art Soc., Wirral Soc. of Art, National ex. wildlife. *Signs work:* "Marguerite Harrison" and see appendix. *Address:* 2 The Courtyard, Poulton Hall, Bebington, Merseyside CH63 9LN.

HARRISON, Stephanie Miriam, N.D.D., R.M.S.; painter, book illustrator, graphic designer; *b* Kings Lynn, 10 Dec., 1939. *m* John Harrison. *Studied:* Medway College of Art, Rochester (1955-60). *Exhib:* Westminster Gallery, Mall Galleries, Linda Blackstone Gallery, The Headcorn Gallery, Rye A.G., and galleries throughout the U.K.; several one-woman shows. *Work in collections:* Science Museum, B.M. (Natural History), and private collections. *Publications:* Wild Flowers of Britain, Marine Life, Handbook of British Mammals, Private Life of a Country House, greetings cards. *Signs work:* "Stephanie Harrison," "S. Harrison" or "S.M.H." *Address:* Iden Cottage, Wittersham Rd., Iden, nr. Rye, E.Sussex TN31 7XB.

HART-DAVIES, Christina Ann, B.A. Hons., F.S.B.A.; botanical artist and illustrator in watercolour; *b* Shrewsbury, 1947. *Studied:* fine art, typography at Reading

University (1966-70). 5 R.H.S. Gold medals. *Exhib:* Brisbane, London, R.B.G. Kew, U.S.A. *Work in collections:* Hunt Inst. Botanical Documentation, Pittsburgh, Shirley Shirwood Collection Contemp. Botanical Artists. *Signs work:* "CHRISTINA HART-DAVIES," "CH-D" (miniatures). *Address:* 31 Shaftesbury Rd., Poole, Dorset BH15 2LT.

HARTAL, Paul, Ph.D.; artist and theorist, originator of Lyrical Conceptualism (1975); founder of the Centre for Art, Science and Technology; oil and acrylic paintings, works on paper, concrete poetry, various writings (fiction and non-fiction); *b* Hungary, 1936. *Studied:* M.A. Concordia University, Montreal; Doctoral Dissertation: The Interface Dynamics of Art and Science, Columbia Pacific University, California. *Exhib:* selected list: Musée du Luxembourg, Paris (1978), Véhicule, Montreal (1980), Montreux Centre, University of Lausanne (1983), OURS, Montreux (1990), Milan Art Centre, Italy (1993), Musée de la Poste, Paris (1994), Space Center, Houston (1994), Centre Cultural d' Alcoi, Spain (1996), Seoul International Fine Art Centre (1998), Galerie Alef, Montreal (1999), University of Oregon (2000), Lincoln Centre, New York (2001). *Work in collections:* Museum of Civilisation, Ottawa; Musee De La Poste, Paris, and many others. *Commissions:* Seoul Olympic Games; Orbitor U.S.A.; Book and record illustrations. *Publications:* Encyclopedia of Living Artists; Olympic Catalogue, Seoul; Artists/USA, Phil., The Brush and the Compass (1988); The Kidnapping of the painter Miró (illustrated novel, 1997); articles: Leonardo, Pulsar, Contemporary Philosophy, poetry. Awards include: Prix de Paris; Rubens; National Library of Poetry; Poetry Canada, University of Toledo. *Signs work:* "Hartal." *Address:* Box 1012, St. Laurent, Quebec H4L 4W3, Canada.

HARTILL, Brenda, R.E., Dip.F.A. Hons. (1964); artist/printmaker in etching, collagraph, (previously theatre design); *b* London, 27 Feb., 1943. *m* Harold Moores. one *s.* one *d. Educ:* Kings School, Ottery St. Mary; Kelston High, Auckland, N.Z. *Studied:* Elam School Fine Art, N.Z.; Central School of Art (theatre design, Ralph Koltai). *Exhib:* R.A. Summer Show, R.E. Bankside Gallery, over 50 galleries worldwide; solo shows: New Academy Gallery and galleries in Australia, N.Z., U.S.A., Barbican Centre. *Commissions:* Morgan Stanley, BP Amoco, Bank of England, B.T., The Independent. *Publications:* Printmaking Today. *Clubs:* R.E. *Signs work:* "Brenda Hartill." *Address:* Globe Studios, 62a Southwark Bridge Rd., London SE1 0AS.

HARVEY, Jake, D.A. (1972), R.S.A. (1989); sculptor, carver of limestone/granite, and forger of iron/steel; Professor, Head of Sculpture, Edinburgh College of Art; *b* Yetholm, Kelso, Roxburghshire, 3 June, 1948. *m* Penny Harvey. one *s.* two *d. Educ:* Kelso High School. *Studied:* sculpture: Edinburgh College of Art (1966-72) Postgraduate (1971-72), Travelling Scholarship to Greece (1971-72), William Gillies Bursary Research Travel in India (1989). *Exhib:* R.S.A., Talbot Rice A.G., City Art Centre (Edinburgh), Third Eye Gallery (Glasgow), Camden Arts Centre, Leinster Gallery, Houldsworth F.A., Art First (London), Pier Art Centre (Stromness), Aberdeen A.G., Seagate (Dundee), Maclaurin (Ayr), Stavanger (Norway), Lulea (Sweden), Kemi (Finland), Morioka (Japan), National Museum of Scotland (Edinburgh). *Work in collections:* Scottish Arts Council, Edinburgh Museums and Galleries, University of Edinburgh, Contemporary Art Soc., Aberdeen Art Gallery,

Hunterian Museum, Kulturoget, Lulea Sweden. *Commissions:* Hugh MacDiarmid Memorial, Langholm; Compaq Computers Commission, Glasgow; Newcraighall Mining Commission, Edinburgh; Poachers Tree, Maclay, Murray and Spens; Motherwell Heritage Centre; Hunterian A.G., Glasgow; Aberdeen City. *Signs work:* "Jake Harvey" and see appendix. *Address:* Maxton Cross, Maxton, St. Boswells, Roxburghshire TD6 0RL.

HARVEY, Michael Anthony, N.D.D. (1957), F.R.S.A. (1972), Linton prize (1973); artist in oil, pastel; journalist and art critic; mem. S.G.F.A., Reigate Soc. of Artists, life mem. I.A.A. (Unesco); *b* Kew. divorced. one *s. Educ:* Bryanston. *Studied:* Wimbledon School of Art (1955-57). *Exhib:* Whibley, Rutland, Fine Arts, Qantas and Connoisseur Galleries W1., Brighton Pavilion, Portsmouth Museum, and Melbourne, Oslo, Dortmund; fourteen one-man shows. *Work in collections:* Johns Hopkins University, Camden Council, E. Sussex Council. *Publications:* work repro.: B.B.C. TV, The Times, Standard, Artist. *Clubs:* Royal Society of Arts, London. *Signs work:* "Michael" or "Michael A. Harvey." *Address:* 15 Waterloo Sq., Bognor Regis, W. Sussex PO21 1TE.

HARVEY, Pat: see YALLUP, Pat.

HAWDON, Paul Douglas, B.A. (Hons.) (1982), Dip. R.A. Schools, R.E.; painter/printmaker in oil, gouache, etching; *b* Manchester, 13 Oct., 1953. *m* Helena Earl. one *d. Educ:* Hyde County Grammar School. *Studied:* St. Martin's School of Art (1978-82), R.A. Schools (1982-85), Rome Scholar, British School (1988-89). *Exhib:* R.E., London Group, Twelve Contemporary Figurative Artists, R.A., Christie's Print prize (1985, 1990), 11th International Print Biennale, Bradford. *Work in collections:* Metropolitan Museum of Fine Art, N.Y. *Publications:* Printmaking Today Vol.4 No.2. *Clubs:* Chelsea Arts. *Signs work:* "Paul Hawdon" or "P.D.H." *Address:* 62 Marshall Rd., Cambridge CB1 7TY.

HAWES, Meredith William, A.R.C.A., R.W.S., F.R.S.A., A.S.I.A.; Freeman of the City of London; artist in water-colour, oil, gouache; College of Art Principal (retd.); tutor (P.T.), Exeter University (Extra-mural Dept.); *b* Thornton Heath, Surrey, 17 Apr., 1905. *m* Margaret Charlotte. one *s.* six *d. Educ:* Selhurst Grammar School, Croydon. *Studied:* Croydon School of Art (1922-24), R.C.A. (1924-28). *Exhib:* R.A., R.W.S., N.E.A.C., Paris, U.S.A. and many provincial galleries. *Publications:* illustrations for John Murray, Jonathan Cape, V. & A. Museum, O.U.P. *Signs work:* "M.W. HAWES." *Address:* Emslake House, 2 Anderton Villas, Millbrook, Torpoint, Cornwall PL10 1DR.

HAWKEN, Anthony Wellington John, A.R.B.S. (1979), Cert. R.A.S. Sculpture (1971); sculptor in plastics and stone, etcher; *b* Erith, Kent, 4 July, 1948. *m* Deirdre Bew. two *s. Educ:* Northumberland Heath Secondary Modern School. *Studied:* Medway College of Art (1965-68, John Cobbett), R.A. Schools (1968-71, Willi Soukop). *Exhib:* Hammersmith Summer Exhbn., R.B.S., Chichester, Stratford upon Avon; one-man show, Blackheath Gallery. *Signs work:* "A. Hawken." *Address:* 1 Chevening Rd., Greenwich, London SE10 0LB.

HAWKINS, Barbara, ceramics painter and artist; *b* Yorks., 18 Oct., 1952. *m* Michael Hawkins. two *d. Studied:* St. Albans and Bristol. *Exhib:* Open Eye,

Edinburgh, Simon Drew Gallery, etc. Work in collections internationally. *Clubs:* Fellow, Craft Potters Assoc. *Signs work:* " MBH." *Address:* Port Isaac Pottery, Roscarrock Hill, Port Isaac, Cornwall PL29 3RG.

HAWKINS, Diana, F.R.S.A., N.S., N.A.P.A., Euro-Art; Stephen Martin Award; landscape painter, oil, acrylic and water-colour – work inspired by light and atmosphere; council member N.S. (1999); *b* Ireland, 1936. *Educ:* Sisters of Mercy Convent, Ireland. *Exhib:* R.W.A., S.W.A., National Society of Painters & Printmakers & Sculptors; Salon des Refusés; Llewellyn Alexander Gallery, London; Bath Society of Artists; Victoria Gallery; National Acrylic Painters Asscoiation; Royal Birmingham Society Gallery; Westminster Gallery; Euro-Art, Barbizon, France; La Défense – Paris; Munich, Brussels; Winchester Art Gallery, Southampton Art Gallery. *Work in collections:* U.K., Germany, France, Australia, Japan, Switzerland, Ireland. *Commissions:* for private collectors. *Publications:* Royal Publications. National Trust Workshops for school children, fellow of the Royal Society of Arts (2000). *Clubs:* Royal Overseas, London. *Signs work:* see appendix. *Address:* Leafy Screen Cottage, Cott Lane, Burley, Hants. BH24 4BB.

HAWKINS, Michael, potter; *b* 2 Aug., 1950. *m* Barbara. two *d. Studied:* Cornwall. *Exhib:* London, Edinburgh, Bath, etc. Work in collections internationally. *Clubs:* Fellow, Craft Potters Assoc. *Signs work:* " MBH." *Address:* Port Isaac Pottery, Roscarrock Hill, Port Isaac, Cornwall PL29 3RG.

HAWKINS, Philip Dennis, F.G.R.A.; artist in oil, pencil; President, Guild of Railway Artists (1988-98); *b* B'ham, 26 Sept., 1947. *m* Sonya. one *s.* one *d. Educ:* Lordswood Boys' Technical School, B'ham. *Studied:* B'ham College of Art (1964-68). *Exhib:* N.R.M. York, Science Museum, B'ham, Festival Hall London, regularly with G.R.A. *Work in collections:* B'ham Post and Mail Ltd., Bristol United Press, B.B.C., Docklands Light Railway, European Passenger Services, Railfreight, Freightliner, Midland Metro, Royal Mail. *Publications:* Fine art prints, work featured in calendars, greetings cards, magazines, books, etc.; book: (autobiography and paintings, etc.) Tracks on Canvas (1998). Co-director, Quicksilver Publishing. *Signs work:* "Philip D. Hawkins." *Address:* 112 Chaffcombe Rd., Sheldon, Birmingham B26 3YD.

HAY, Ian, N.D.D. (1960), A.R.C.A. (Painting 1963); awarded the Andrew J. Lloyd prize for landscape painting; artist in pastel, water-colour, etching, art lecturer; Senior Lecturer in drawing, Colchester School of Art, retired from teaching (2000); *b* Harwich, 25 Jan., 1940. *m* Teresa Sliska. two *s. Educ:* Harwich School. *Studied:* Colchester School of Art (1955-60, Hugh Cronyn), R.C.A. (1960-63, Ruskin Spear). *Exhib:* Craftsman Gallery and Minories, Colchester, Sandford Gallery, London, Phoenix Gallery, Lavenham, Wivenhoe Arts Centre, Patisserie Valerie, London SW3, Highgate Fine Art, London N6, Digby Gallery, Colchester. *Work in collections:* Doncaster City A.G., The Guildhall A.G., Graves A.G., Sheffield, Essex University, Essex County Council, Colchester Borough Council. *Commissions:* A series of paintings commissioned by Ernst & Young for their office space in Birmingham (1996). *Clubs:* Colchester Art Soc., Chairman of Select Committee. *Signs work:* "Ian Hay." *Address:* 32 Tall Trees, Mile End, Colchester, Essex CO4 5DV.

HAYDEN, Toni, S.B.A. (1985), F.L.S. (1995), A.S.B.A. (1995), St. Cuthbert's Mill Award (1995), R.H.S. medals: S.G.M. (1981), G.R.M. (1982), S.M. (1984, 1995); artist and calligrapher, graphite figure drawings, animal and flower paintings in gouache, pencil portraits; professional artist and tutor; *b* Woodbridge, Suffolk, 22 Aug., 1938. *m* Anthony Hayden (divorced). two *s. Educ:* Notre Dame High School. *Studied:* Norwich School of Art (1954-55, Noel Spencer, Alan Webster). *Exhib:* Yasuda Kasai, Tokyo, R.H.S. Westminster, S.B.A. Mall Galleries, Hunt, U.S.A. *Work in collections:* Hunt Inst. for Botanical Documentation, B.M. (N.S.), V. & A., London University (Q.M.C.) Shirley Sherwood, John Innes Centre. *Commissions:* Specialises in magnolia paintings. *Publications:* in progress: 'How to Paint Flowers' and 'San Francisco to Go'. *Clubs:* Assoc. of Illustrators. *Signs work:* "Toni Hayden". *Address:* 6 Belvedere Pl., Norwich NR4 7PP.

HAYES, Colin Graham Frederick, R.A., M.A.(Oxon), Hon.A.R.C.A., Hon. F.R.C.A., President R.B.A (1993-98); painter in oil and water-colour; reader, Royal College of Art (1949-84); *b* London, 17 Nov., 1919. *m* (1) Jean Westbrook Law (d. 1988). three *d.* (2) Marjorie L. M. Christensen. *Educ:* Westminster School; Christ Church, Oxford. *Studied:* Bath School of Art; Ruskin School of Drawing. *Exhib:* Marlborough, Agnews, Search, New Grafton. *Work in collections:* Arts Council, British Council, Carlisle A.G. and others. *Publications:* Stanley Spencer, Renoir, Rembrandt, A Grammar of Drawing. *Clubs:* Arts, Chelsea Arts. *Signs work:* "Hayes." *Address:* Ground Floor Flat, 2 Annandale Rd., London W4 2HF.

HAYES, Georgia, painter in oil; shortlisted for Wollaston Prize (2000); *b* Aberdeen, 1946. *m* Robert. one *s.* two *d. Educ:* privately, Brondesbury, Tring (1959-1962), and Madrid (1962-1964). *Studied:* Tunbridge Wells, under Roy Oxlade (1977-1982). *Exhib:* Trinity Arts, Tunbridge Wells (1984-1988); Riviera, Hastings (1995); Harriet Green, London (1997); Sevenoaks Library Gallery (1998); Maidstone Library Gallery (1999); Aberdeen Art Gallery (2000); East Gallery (1992); John Moores (1993); R.A. (1987-2001). *Publications:* Art Directions Book (1996), R.A. Illustrated (1998-2001), Not the Turner Prize, C.4 T.V. (2000). *Signs work:* "Georgia Hayes." *Address:* Diamonds, Bells Yew Green, E. Sussex TN3 9AX. *Website:* www.georgiahayes.theseed.net *Email:* cclhayes@aol.com

HAYNES, Alexandra, B.A.; artist in oil and water-colour; *b* 17 Mar., 1966. *Educ:* New Hall, Boreham, Chelmsford, Essex. *Studied:* Shrewsbury Foundation Course, Cheltenham Art College (Michael Hollands, Leslie Prothero). *Exhib:* Mail on Sunday, Dover St. (1988), Contemporary Fine Art Gallery, Eton; one-man shows: Soloman Gallery, London (1988), Mistral Gallery, London (1989, 1990, 1991), Flying Colours Gallery, Edinburgh (1990), Bruton Street Gallery (1992). *Publications:* A Life with Food, Peter Langan by Brian Sewell. *Signs work:* "A. Haynes." *Address:* Edgcote, Banbury, Oxon. OX17 1AG.

HAYWARD, Timothy John, painter in water-colour and gouache; freelance illustrator (1975-2000); *b* Weybridge, Surrey, 24 Dec., 1952. *m* Catherine. three *d. Educ:* King's College, Taunton. *Studied:* Somerset College of Art. *Exhib:* solo exhib. Park Walk Gallery, London (2001), Fine Art Fair, Olympia (2002). *Publications:* many natural history books and publications. *Signs work:* "Tim Hayward." *Address:* c/o

Jonathan Cooper, Park Walk Gallery, 20 Park Walk, London SW10 0AQ. *Email:* mail@jonathancooper.co.uk

HAYWARD-HARRIS, Martin John, artist and sculptor of wildlife subjects in oil, water-colour, etchings, bronze; *b* Reading, 28 Oct., 1959. *Educ:* Maiden Erlegh Comprehensive. *Studied:* Berks. College of Art and Design (1978-84). *Exhib:* S.WL.A., B.T.O., R.S.P.B., W.T.N.C.; one man show: Phyllis Court Club, Henley-on-Thames (1990, 1993), East African Wildlife Soc. *Work in collections:* Natural History Museum London, Zoologisk Museum, Copenhagen. *Publications:* work repro.: etchings published by H.C. Dickins, auctioned at Sotheby's; Birding World; cover illustration 'In Search of Stones' M. Scott Peck, M.D. auctioned at Christie's. *Signs work:* "Martin Hayward-Harris." *Address:* 47 Clarendon Rd., Earley, Reading, Berks. RG6 1PB.

HAZZARD, Charles Walker, B.A. (Hons.) Fine Art (1987), Sir Henry Doulton School of Sculpture (1988-90), Postgrad. H.Dip. Sculpture (1991), A.R.B.S. Dip. (1992); Director and Trustee, Royal Soc. of British Sculptors; sculptor and fabricator in wood; Brother, Art Workers' Guild (1996); Henry Moore sponsored Sculpture Fellow, Loughborough College of Art and Design (1996-98); *b* B'ham, 5 Feb., 1964. *Studied:* Cheltenham University (1984-87, Roger Luxton), Sir Henry Doulton School of Sculpture (1988-90, Colin Melbourne), City and Guilds of London (1990-91, Alan Sly). *Exhib:* national shows. *Publications:* books illustrated: British Contemporary Art (1993), Encyclopedic Techniques of Sculpture (1995), British Artists since 1945. *Signs work:* "C.W.H." or not at all. *Address:* 19 Steward St., Spitalfields, London E1 6AJ.

HEADON, David John, B.W.S. (1993), U.A. (1996), F.I.G.A. (1999); self taught artist in water-colour; *b* Bideford, N.Devon, 9 July, 1933. *m* Hilary. two *s*. *Educ:* Kingswood, Bath. *Exhib:* several one-man shows; Laing, R.I., galleries in Lake District, South Shields, Ilkley and Chester. *Work in collections:* worldwide, including Patricia Routledge, Dinah Sheriden and Sir Harry Secombe. *Clubs:* Fellow International Guild of Artists, member British Watercolour Soc., United Soc. of Artists, Petersfield Arts and Crafts and Portsmouth and Hampshire and Chichester. *Signs work:* "HEADON." *Address:* Holmdene, 2 Wade Court Rd., Havant, Hants. PO9 2SU.

HEALER, George, A.R.B.S. (1974); sculptor in clay, plaster, wood, cast aluminium, brass and bronze; *b* 25 Sept., 1936. *m* Brenda Maureen Healer. one *s*. two *d*. *Educ:* Bullion Lane School. *Studied:* Sunderland College of Art (1952-56) under Harry Thubron, A.R.C.A., and Robert Jewell, A.R.C.A. *Exhib:* R.A., R.G.I., Commonwealth Institute, Woolgate House, London, D.L.I. Durham City, Gulbenkian Gallery, Newcastle-upon-Tyne. *Work in collections:* life-size figures of John and Josiphe Bowes, Bowes Museum, Barnard Castle, Co. Durham. *Publications:* article, Aluminium for Schools for the British Aluminium Federation. *Signs work:* "HEALER" hammered into metal with flat chisel. *Address:* 12 Melville St., Chester-le-Street, Co. Durham DH3 6JF.

HEALER, Reuben John, H.N.D. (1984); graphic designer/illustrator; *b* Gateshead, 17 Dec., 1963. *Educ:* Hermitage Comprehensive. *Studied:* graphic design: New College, Durham (N.D.A.D. 1980-82); Cumbria College of Art and

Design (H.N.D. 1982-84). Graphic designer for: Newcastle Architecture Workshop (1984-85), Pendower Hall, E.D.C. (1985-88), By Design, Seaham, Co. Durham (1988). *Address:* 21 Bede Terr., Chester-le-Street, Co. Durham.

HEARSON, Susan: see VOGEL, Suzi.

HEAT, Ann Olivia, artist in oil; *b* Esher, Surrey, 30 July, 1945. *m* Trevor Harvey Heat. *Educ:* Waynfleet, Surrey. *Studied:* The Kathleen Browne School under Kathleen Browne and her Polish husband Marian Kratochwil. *Exhib:* R.A. , R.B.A., R.P., R.O.I., N.E.A.C. *Clubs:* R.B.A. *Signs work:* "A.H." *Address:* Stumps Grove Farm, Whitehill La., Ockham, Ripley, Surrey GU23 6PB.

HECHLE, Ann, F.S.S.I.; calligrapher in vellum, water-colour, gold leaf; *b* 31 Dec., 1939. *Studied:* Central School of Art and Crafts (1957-60, Irene Wellington). *Exhib:* many group exhbns. *Work in collections:* Minnesota Manuscript Initiative, U.S.A., V. & A., Crafts Study Centre, Bath. *Commissions:* 19 calligraphic panels for St. Mary's Hospital, Isle of Wight. *Publications:* co-author: More than Fine Writing (Life and work of Irene Wellington). Film: In the Making (B.B.C. 1979). *Address:* The Old School, Buckland Dinham, Frome, Somerset BA11 2QR.

HEDLEY, Paul, Dip. A.D. (1971); artist in oil, acrylic and chalks; *b* 19 Dec., 1947. *m* Dianne Flynn. *Studied:* Medway and Maidstone. *Exhib:* Nevill Gallery Canterbury, Priory Gallery Cheltenham, Clifton Gallery Bristol, John Davies Gallery, Stow-on-the-Wold, etc. *Work in collections:* London Borough of Camden, Queen Mary College. *Signs work:* "Paul Hedley." *Address:* 6 Powderham Cres., Exeter EX4 6DA.

HEINDEL, Robert, self taught artist; Director, The Obsession of Dance Co; *b* Toledo, Ohio, 1 Oct., 1938. *m* Rosalie. three *s. Educ:* St. Angus Grade School, Central Catholic High School. *Exhib:* Atlanta, Georgia; American Artists Gallery; Kansas City A.G.; Dallas, Texas - The Vineyard Gallery; San Francisco Gallery One; Royal Festival Hall, London; New London Theatre; Hotel de Paris, Monte Carlo. *Work in collections:* Smithsonian Inst., Washington D.C.; Caltex Corp., Dallas; Chrysler Corp., Detroit; Columbia Pictures, Los Angeles; Ford Motor Co., Detroit; Goodyear Rubber Co., Akron; The Grace Co., N.Y.; The Ladd Co., Los Angeles; Manufacturers Hanover Bank, N.Y.; Phillips Petroleum, Dallas; Quasar Oil Corp., N.Y.; Readers' Digest Inc., N.Y.; Time Inc., N.Y.; United Artists, Los Angeles; United Energy Resources Corp., Houston; Coca Cola; Champion Paper. *Publications:* illus. The Complete Phantom of the Opera (Pavilion Books); J. Steinbeck - The Grapes of Wrath; All the Kings Men. *Clubs:* Mortons, London. *Signs work:* "R. Heindel." *Address:* 140 Banks Rd., Easton, Connecticut 06612, U.S.A.

HEINDORFF, Michael, M.A. (1977), Fellow, R.C.A. (1988), Hon. Fellow R.C.A. (2001); painter in oil, water-colour, pencil, print; senior tutor, R.C.A. (1980-99); *b* Braunschweig, Germany, 26 June, 1949. *m* Monica Buferd. one *s.* one *d. Educ:* Wilhelm Gymnasium, Braunschweig. *Studied:* Braunschweig University (1970-75), R.C.A. (1975-77, Peter de Francia, Philip Rawson). *Exhib:* Bernard Jacobson Gallery, London, New York, Los Angeles (1978-92), R.A. (1988, 1989, 2001), and others internationally. *Work in collections:* Herzog Anton Ulrich Museum, A.C.G.B., Museum of London, Imperial War Museum, Museum of Modern Art, N.Y., Tate Gallery. *Commissions:* Imperial War Museum (1986); Designers Guild (1992).

Publications: CD-ROM (IBM Compatible PC) of drawings (1995) and others (1996, 1998, 1999). *Clubs:* Chelsea Arts. *Signs work:* "M. HEINDORFF." *Address:* 2 Shrubland Rd., London E8 4NN.

HEINE, Harry, R.S.M.A., F.C.A., C.S.M.A., N.W.S.; self taught artist in watercolour; *b* Edmonton, Alberta, Canada, 24 July, 1928. *m* Teresa. one *s.* two *d. Exhib:* R.I., R.S.MA., F.C.A., Mystic International (U.S.A.), Northwest Marine exhbn. (U.S.A.), and one-man shows in Canada and U.S.A. *Work in collections:* U.S.A.: Washington State Arts Commission, Mystic Seaport Museum, Conn.; Canada: Legislative Bldgs., Victoria, Mendel Gallery, Saskatoon, Maritime Museum, Victoria, Government House, Victoria, Alberta Art Foundation; England: Capt. Cook Museum, Middlesbrough, National Maritime Museum, Greenwich. *Publications:* Pacific Salmon (Govt. of Canada, Dept. of Fisheries and Oceans). *Signs work:* "HEINE." *Address:* 7059 Brentwood Dr., Brentwood Bay, B.C. V8M 1B6, Canada.

HELD, Julie, B.A. (Hons.) (1981), R.A. Schools Postgrad. Dip. (1985); painter in oil on canvas and water-colour on paper; part-time curator and tutor/lecturer; *b* 25 Mar., 1958. *Educ:* J.F.S. Comprehensive School. *Studied:* Camberwell School of Art (1977-81, Philip Mathews), R.A. Schools (1982-85, Peter Greenham). *Exhib:* Piccadilly Gallery, Boundary Gallery, Frank Kafka Gallery (Prague), Leipzig, Hayward Gallery, Royal Overseas League, Cheltenham International Music Festival, Cheltenham Open Drawing Exhbn., R.A. Summer Shows. *Work in collections:* Nuffield College, Oxford University, New Hall Cambridge University, Usher Gallery (Lincoln), L.S.E. Open University, Ben Uri Art Soc. *Signs work:* "J. HELD" or "J.H." on small works. *Address:* 48 Barrington Rd., London N8 8QS.

HELLEBERG, Berndt, sculptor; *b* Stockholm, 17 Dec., 1920. *m* Margareta Kinberg. two *s.* one *d. Educ:* High School, Härnösand. *Studied:* Stockholm (1945-48), Konstfackskolan, Stockholm (1947-49), France (1950-52). Prize, The Unknown Political Prisoner, London (1953), first prize winner, competition of modern medals (Stockholm 1955), first prize winner 20,000 Sw. crowns, competition of underground station decoration (Stockholm 1960). *Exhib:* Tate Gallery, London, Stockholm, Paris, U.S.A., etc. *Work in collections:* The underground station, Hornstull, Stockholm; Cathedral Window, Baptist Church, Stockholm; several playground sculptures in Sweden; several sculptures in Stockholm and Sweden; Sculpture 9m high in Riyadh, Saudi Arabia (1981). *Signs work:* "Berndt Helleberg." *Address:* Saturnusu 7, 18450 Akersberga, Sweden.

HELLER, Rachel Pearl, painter in oil, pastel, charcoal; *b* London, 15 Sep., 1973. *Studied:* Byam Shaw School of Art, Slade, Prince's Foundation, Hammersmith and W. London College. *Exhib:* John Jones Art Centre (1997), Flowers East Gallery (1998-2000). *Work in collections:* various, private. *Signs work:* "Rachel Heller." *Address:* 53 Fitzroy Park, London N6 6JA.

HELLMAN, Louis Mario, B.Arch. (1962), M.B.E. (1993); architect, designer, cartoonist, painter in acrylic, water-colour and collage; *b* 19 Mar., 1936. *m* Maria. one *s.* one *d. Studied:* Bartlett School of Architecture, University College, London, Ecole des Beaux Arts, Paris. *Exhib:* Architectural Assoc. (1978), Interbuild (1991-1993), Cambridge (1996), Sir John Sloane Museum (2000). *Work in collections:* R.I.B.A. Drawings Collection, V. & A., London. *Publications:* Architecture for

Beginners (1986), Archi-Têtes (2000), Architecture A to Z (2001). *Clubs:* Architectural Foundation. *Signs work:* "L Hellman." *Address:* 6 Montague Gardens, London W3 9PT. *Email:* louis.hellman@virgin.net

HEMBLEY, Stephen James, S.G.F.A.; painter in oil, water-colour, pen and ink; Founder of Shire Studios; part-time tutor; *b* Bournemouth, 21 July, 1957. *m* Rachel Crawford. *Educ:* Winton School. *Studied:* under George Denham at Bournemouth. *Exhib:* one-man shows: London, Telford, Shrewsbury, N.E.C. Birmingham; numerous group shows. Work in private collections worldwide. *Publications:* books illustrated for Tamarisk. *Signs work:* "S.J. HEMBLEY." *Address:* c/o Shire Studios (Telford), 25 Bishopdale, Telford, Shropshire TF3 1SA.

HEMMANT, Lynette, N.D.D. (1958); landscape, gardens and still-life painter in oil, mixed media, black and white drawing, etching and general illustration; Director of Dedalus (Publishers); *b* London, 20 Sept., 1938. *m* Jüri Gabriel, literary agent. *Studied:* St. Martin's School of Art (1954-58, Roger Nicholson, Bernard Cheese, Vivian Pitchforth). *Exhib:* R.O.I., and various solo and mixed shows in London, Home Counties, Italy and Australia since 1984. *Commissions:* large pieces for private clients. *Publications:* work repro.: Heinemann Group, Hamish Hamilton, Random House, O.U.P., I.P.C. magazines. *Clubs:* S.G.F.A. *Signs work:* "HEMMANT." *Address:* 35 Camberwell Grove, London SE5 8JA.

HEMPTON, Paul Andrew Keates, M.A., R.C.A.; artist in oil paint, water-colour, and etching; assoc. lecturer, University of Wolverhampton; Fellow in Fine Art, University of Nottingham (1971-73); *b* Wakefield, Yorks., 3 Oct., 1946. *m* Margaret Helena. one *s*. two *d. Educ:* King's School, Chester. *Studied:* Goldsmiths' College School of Art (1964-68), R.C.A. (1968-71) under Prof. Carel Weight. *Work in collections:* Arts Council, British Council, V. & A., Contemporary Arts Soc., Arnolfini Trust, South West Arts, Leicester Educ. Authority, Nottingham University, Bury, A.G., Newport A.G., Wakefield A.G., Whitworth A.G., Nottingham Castle A.G., Wolverhampton A.G., Wiltshire C.C., Arthur Andersen, London. *Signs work:* "P.H." *Address:* 9 West End, Minchinhampton, Stroud, Glos. GL6 9JA.

HEMS, Margaret, F.S.B.A., S.F.P.; Royal Drawing Soc. (1940-43), Grenfell Medal R.H.S. (1984-86), Founder mem. F.S.B.A. (1985); botanical artist in water-colour and pencil; *b* Fyfield, Essex, 1 Jan., 1931. *m* John Hems. one *s*. one *d. Educ:* Clark's College, Ilford. *Studied:* a period of art classes at Minehead (1981, Sylvia Cave), botanical illustration under Mary Grierson at Flatford. *Exhib:* S.B.A., H.S., Westminster Gallery, Mall Galleries, galleries, West Country, East Anglia, and other mixed exhbns. in England and Wales. *Work in collections:* private: Britain, Europe, U.S.A., Australia. *Publications:* greetings cards for Medici and Parnassus Gallery, numerous exhbn. catalogues. *Signs work:* "M. Hems" or "M.H." joined. *Address:* Daubeney Cottage, Water St., Barrington, Somerset TA19 0JR.

HEMSLEY, George Philip, R.A. Schools cert. (1958), N.D.D. (1954), British Institution award (1958), R.A. Silver medal, Landseer Scholarship, Leverhulme Scholarship, David Murray studentships; painter in oil and water-colour; teacher; *b* Stocksbridge, Yorks, 9 Dec., 1933. *Educ:* Surbiton Grammar School. *Studied:* Kingston School of Art, R.A. Schools (Henry Rushbury, Peter Greenham). *Exhib:* R.A., R.B.A, N.E.A.C., R.P., Redfern, Guildhall. *Work in collections:* Guildhall,

London, Boroughs of Camden, Hackney, Kingston-upon-Thames, Weybridge Museum, Ashford Hospital, Dept. of Educ. and Science, Leicester Educ. Authority. Work loaned to Inst. of Practitioners in Advertising. *Commissions:* Camden Council, Traylens Amusements. *Publications:* work repro.: T.E.S. *Signs work:* "Philip Hemsley." *Address:* 18 Ellis Farm Cl., Mayford, Woking, Surrey GU22 9QN.

HEMSOLL, Eileen Mary, A.T.D. (1946), R.B.S.A. (1978); artist in enamel on earthenware, oil, oil pastels, water-colour; retd. art teacher; *b* West Bromwich, 4 Feb., 1924. *m* Eric Hemsoll. one *s.* one *d. Educ:* Queen Mary's, Walsall. *Studied:* B'ham College of Art (1941-46, Eggison, Fleetwood Walker). *Exhib:* R.A., R.A. Travelling Exhbn., Local Artists, B'ham A.G., Artists for Art, R.B.S.A. Paint the City (1989), Mall Gallery Pastels Today (1994, 1995); one-man shows: Worcester College (1978), Flint Gallery, Walsall (1984), Summer Show Sally Hunters, Belgrave Sq. (1986); Retrospective: R.B.S.A. (1998). *Signs work:* "Eileen Hemsoll." *Address:* 18 Mead Rise, Edgbaston, Birmingham B15 3SD.

HENDERSON, Jacqueline Kelso, Dip. A.D. (1973), A.T.L. (1974); painter in oil and pastel; tutor of equestrian art; *b* Belfast, 29 June 1952. *m* Eyre Maunsell (partner). one *s.* two *d. Educ:* Downe House, Newbury, Berks. *Studied:* Belfast Art College (1969-1973), Goldsmiths College, London University (1974). *Exhib:* Christies with S.E.A.; Westminster with U.A. and S.W.A.; Arts Club, Dover St., London; galleries in Britain and New York. *Work in collections:* private collections worldwide. *Signs work:* "Jackie Henderson." *Address:* Hastog Farm Studio, Church Lane, Hastog, Tring, Herts. HP23 6LU. *Email:* eyremaunsell@hotmail.com or jackie.henderson@equestrianartists.co.uk

HENOCQ, Ron, Slade Dip. (1973), San Carlos Escuela del Arte M.A. (1976); artist, Gallery Director, Cafe Gallery since 1984; *b* 22 Mar., 1950. *Signs work:* "R.Henocq." *Address:* Cafe Gallery, Southwark Park, London SE16.

HENRI, Adrian, Hons. B.A. Fine Art (1955), Hon. D. Litt. (1990); artist in acrylic/canvas; author; President, Liverpool Academy of Arts (1972-81); *b* Birkenhead, 1932. *Studied:* Dept. of Fine Art, King's College, Newcastle. *Exhib:* one-man shows: Walker A.G., Liverpool (2000) Thomas Zander Gallery, Köln (1998), Stockport A.G. (1998), Whitford Gallery, London (1997), Storey Inst., Lancaster (1994); Touring Retrospective (1986); Wolverhampton City A.G. (1976), Williamson A.G. (1975), Art Net, London (1975), I.C.A. (1968); other shows: John Moores Liverpool (1962, 1966, 1968, 1974, 1978, 1980, 1989), John Moores £2,000 Prize (1972), murals, Royal Liverpool Hospital (1980 and 1983). *Work in collections:* Walker A.G., Williamson A.G., and A.C.G.B. Collection. *Publications:* poetry books. *Clubs:* Chelsea Arts. *Signs work:* "Adrian Henri." *Address:* 21 Mount St., Liverpool L1 9HD.

HENRIQUES, Benedict James, B.A. Hons. Fine Art (1986-1990); painter in oil; *b* 14 Oct., 1967. *Studied:* Newcastle -upon-Tyne University. *Exhib:* William Hardie, Glasgow; Browse and Darby, London; National Portrait Gallery (1993, 1998, 1999); Jonathan Cooper Gallery (2001). *Work in collections:* numerous. *Commissions:* assorted. *Signs work:* "B Henriques." *Address:* 160-162 Old South Lambeth Rd., London SW8 1XX. *Email:* ben.henriques@virgin.net

HENRY, Bruce Charles Reid, B.D. (Lond.) (1943), S.WL.A. (1982); painter in water-colour, pastel, oil, retd. school teacher; *b* nr. Kandy, Sri Lanka, 22 July, 1918. *m* Joyce M. Henry. one *s*. one *d*. *Educ:* Colchester Royal Grammar School, Tettenhall College, Staffs. *Exhib:* Mall Galleries (annually), S.WL.A., Budleigh Salterton, Newport, I.O.W., Sladmore Gallery, London, Northern Exhbn. of Wildlife Art, Chester. *Work in collections:* Nature in Art, Gloucester. *Publications:* Author/illustrator, Highlight the Wild - The Art of the Reid Henrys (Palaquin Publishing, 1985). *Signs work:* "Bruce Henry." *Address:* 90 Broomfield Ave., Worthing, W. Sussex BN14 7SB.

HENTALL, Maurice, F.R.S.A. (1951), S.B.A. (1987), C.B.M. (1997); retd. 22 years Managing Director of London Studios; part-time Art Tutor, painter in water-colour, acrylic, oil; several years Easter tutorial at Pendley Manor; *b* Hornsey. *m* Nora Nelson. *Studied:* Hornsey College of Art. R.A.F.V.R. from 1940, injured March 1942. Whilst convalescent official War Publication artist: encouraged by R. Stanton, Sir Alfred Munnings, Sir James Gunn. *Exhib:* R.A., Mall Galleries, Westminster Central Hall, Llewellyn Alexander - portraits, wildlife, botanical, including miniatures. *Commissions:* motif Golden Jubilee of Sperry Gyroscope Co. (unveiled by Earl Mountbatten of Burma 1963). *Publications:* Royal Manor of Hanworth; repros. Gordon Fraser, Medici, etc. *Signs work:* "MAURICE HENTALL." *Address:* 42 The Broadway, Wheathamstead, St. Albans, Herts. AL4 8LP.

HENTHORNE, Yvonne, Professor, N.D.D. (Painting 1965), A.T.C. (1966), F.R.S.A. (1967), Italian Government Bursary (1969), Brazilian Government Scholarship (1971), W. German Research Grant (1974-75); constructed painting; Head of Foundation Studies Dept., Wimbledon School of Art; *b* Wetherby, Yorks., 1942. *m* Gary Crossley, Professor, Surrey Institute. one *d*. *Educ:* Grey Coat Hospital, Westminster. *Studied:* London University Goldsmiths' College of Art (1961-66, Patrick Millard, Albert Irwin, Andrew Forge). *Exhib:* open, Young Contemporaries, Tate, Birmingham Festival, Midland Group Gallery, Sheffield Open National, S.W.A., R.B.A.; one-man shows, Ikon Gallery, Birmingham; Belgrade, Coventry; Laing Gallery, Newcastle-on-Tyne. *Work in collections:* U.K., Europe, U.S.A. *Signs work:* "Yvonne Crossley." *Address:* The Chestnuts, Bishops Sutton, Hants. SO24 0AW.

HENTY-CREER, Deirdre, F.R.S.A.; Utd. Artists Council (1947-1955); F.C.I.A.D. (1945); Artists of Chelsea (1961); Com. Chelsea Art Soc.; Com. Armed Forces Art Soc.; artist in oil; *b* Sydney, Australia. *Educ:* privately. *Exhib:* R.A., R.O.I., R.B.A., N.E.A.C., N.S., U.A., Towner A.G. Eastbourne, Russell-Cotes, Bournemouth, Williamson A.G. Birkenhead, and other municipal galleries, Submarine Museum, Gosport, Victory Museum, Portsmouth, etc. One-man shows, Fine Art Soc., Frost & Reed, Cooling, and Qantas Galleries, Bond St., Upper Grosvenor Gallery, Harrods; Nice XIV Olympiad Sport in Art at V. & A., R.N. College, Greenwich. *Work in collections:* H.R.H. the Prince of Wales, Lord Rank, Lord Rootes, Ronald Vestey, Esq. *Publications:* work repro.: The Artist, Cover of Studio, Medici Soc., T.A.V.R. Mag., Royal Sussex Regt. Mag., Poster for Municipality of Monaco, The Sphere, Stanton Corp., N.Y., Chrysons of California, U.S.A., Gruehen of Innsbruck. Portraits include: H.R.H. Prince Michael of Kent; Governor-Gen. of Australia, Sir John Kerr; Mayor of

Kensington, Sir Malby Crofton, Bt.; Prime Minister of Malta, Dr. Borg Olivier; First Sea Lord, Sir Henry Leach, etc. *Address:* 5 St. Georges Ct., Gloucester Rd., London SW7 4QZ.

HEPPLEWHITE, Val, figurative painter in oil and printer; *b* Rotherham, 4 May, 1938. *m* Chris Morgan Smith. two *s.* one *d. Educ:* Oakwood High School, Rotherham. *Studied:* R.W.A., Bristol. *Exhib:* throughout U.K. and abroad incl. R.W.A., W.G.A., S.W.A., S.G.F.A. *Work in collections:* Patrick Nicholls M.P., Prof. Robin Stowell, Bruton School, Judge Joseph, Sir Matthew Thorpe. *Signs work:* "Val Hepplewhite." *Address:* The Studio, Goosebutt Barn, Spout Lane, Seend, Melksham, Wilts. SN12 6PE.

HERBERT, Albert, A.R.C.A.; painter of mainly religious or symbolic subjects in oil and etching; ex Princ. lecturer, St. Martin's School of Art; *b* London, 10 Sept., 1925. *m* Jacqueline. three *d. Studied:* R.C.A. (1949-53), British School at Rome (1953-54). *Exhib:* R.A., Poetry Soc., University of California, Westminster, Norwich, Winchester and St. Paul's Cathedrals, Castlefield Gallery, England and Co., Lancaster University, etc. *Work in collections:* Contemporary Art Soc., Coventry Training College, Methodist Educ. Com., Shell, Stoke-on-Trent A.G., Glamorgan, Herts., Notts. and Somerset C.C's. *Publications:* "Albert Herbet" retrospective (England and Co. 1999). Agent: England and Co., London, W11. *Clubs:* Chelsea Arts. *Signs work:* "Albert Herbert." *Address:* 4 Clifton Terr., Cliftonville, Dorking RH4 2JG.

HERBERT, Barry, artist/printmaker, drawings and prints; Head of Fine Art Dept., University of Leeds (1985-92); *b* York, 19 Mar., 1937. *m* Janet. one *s.* one *d. Educ:* Archbishop Holgate's School, York. *Studied:* James Graham College. *Exhib:* 39 one-man shows include: Serpentine Gallery, London (1971), Mappin Gallery, Sheffield (1972), Galerie Brechbühl, Switzerland (1972, 1976, 1979, 1982, 1984), Galerie Steinmetz, Bonn (1979, 1984, 1993, 1995), Karl-Marx-Universität, Leipzig, (1980), Gilbert Parr Gallery, London (1982), Richard Demarco Gallery (1992). *Publications:* 30 editions of prints published in Germany, Switzerland and England; "Barry Herbert - Künstler-Grafiker" (1979); "Barry Herbert" - Drawings and Etchings (1997). *Signs work:* "Barry Herbert." *Address:* 43 Weetwood Lane, Leeds LS16 5NW.

HERICKX, Geoffrey Russell, A.R.M.S., H.S.; painter in oil and water-colour; teacher, specialist in painting miniatures – all subjects; *b* Birmingham, 1939. *m* Maureen. one *s.* one *d. Studied:* Birmingham College of Art (1956-58). *Exhib:* three one-man shows in Leicester, work in many private collections, annually at Royal Miniature Soc. and Hilliard Soc. exhibitions, 'Best in Exhibition' at 2000 Hilliard Soc. Exhibition. *Publications:* illustrated: Naturalist Summers. *Signs work:* "G.R. HERICKX." *Address:* 33 Ash Tree Rd., Oadby, Leicester LE2 5TE. *Email:* geoff@herickx.freeserve.co.uk

HERIZ-SMITH, Bridget, B.F.A. (Hons.); award with commendation, History of Art (1977), prizewinner S.G.A. (1985); sculptor in stone, cement and bronze; administrator, Clock House Studios (1979-86); *b* Hamburg, 13 Dec., 1949. one *s.* one *d. Educ:* Framlingham Mills Grammar School. *Studied:* Goldsmiths' College, Ravensbourne College (1974-77, Eric Peskett). *Exhib:* Sculpture in Anglia (1978,

1981, 1989), R.A. Summer Show (1988, 1992), Musée Lanchelevici, Belgium, Gallerie Alinna, Finland, Mercury Gallery London, Discerning Eye (1997); groups: Young Blood, Suffolk Group, Bearing 090°. *Work in collections:* Women's Art, New Hall, Cambridge. *Signs work:* "B.Heriz." *Address:* 1 Allums Yd., Low Rd., Badingham, Suffolk IP13 8JS. *Email:* b.heriz@cwcom.net

HERON, Susanna, B.A. (Hons.), F.R.S.A., Hon. F.R.I.B.A.; sculptor; *b* England, 22 Sept., 1949. *Exhib:* solo shows since 1985 include Whitechapel A.G., Camden Arts Centre, Newlyn A.G. *Work in collections:* Stedelijk Museum, Arts Council, V. & A., C.A.S., etc., museums in Europe and Australia. *Commissions:* Major public commissions: Consilium European Union, Brussels (1995), sole British representative; front British Embassy, Dublin (1995); Shoreditch Campus, Hackney Community College (1997); Phoenix Project, Priory Place, Coventry City Council (2002); Arnolfini Gallery Bristol (2003); Marunouchi Building, Mitsubishi, Tokyo (2002), Millbank Place, a new pedestrian street for City Inn, Westminster (2001-2003). *Publications:* photographs/text: Shima: Island and Garden (Abson, 1992); Stills from Sculpture (Abson, 1999), distibutor Art Books International. *Signs work:* see appendix. *Address:* 39 Norman Gr., London E3 5EG.

HERRIOT, Alan B., artist/sculptor in cold cast GRP, painting in oil, acrylic and water-colour; Proprietor, Endeavour Art Studios, Edinburgh; *b* 20 Feb., 1952. *Studied:* Duncan of Jordanstone, Dundee (1969-74, Scott Sutherland, James Morrison). *Exhib:* Aros Centre Skye, Whisky Heritage Centre Edinburgh, Inverary Court House. *Work in collections:* Miner's Monument, Newtongrange, Horse and Figure, Loanhead; 51st Highland Division Liberation Monument, Schijndel (Holland) and Perth (Scotland). *Publications:* The Foundling; Christmas is Coming; Travellers Tales; Broonies, Silkies and Fairies; Quest for a Kelpie. *Signs work:* "Alan B. Herriot" and see appendix. *Address:* Endeavour Art Studios, 75 Trafalgar La., Leith, Edinburgh EH6 4DQ.

HESELTINE, John Robert, B. of E. Drawing (1941), B. of E. Pictorial Design T.D. (1941), scholarship, Royal College (1942); artist in oil and water-colour, portrait artist; leading name in British illustration (1950s-1970s); descendent of John Postle Hestletine, artist, famous collector, early trustee of National Gallery, a founder of R.C.A. and friend and student of James McNiell Whistler; also related to Peter Worlock, composer; *b* Ilford, Essex, 14 Sept., 1923. *m* Pam Masco. one *s.* one *d.* *Studied:* S.E. Essex College of Art (Francis Taylor, A.R.C.A., Allen Wellings, A.R.C.A.). *Exhib:* V. & A., R.W.S., R.P.S., London galleries, including David Messum and W. H. Patterson, and U.S.A. Studio and Gallery at East House Petworth. *Work in collections:* Dartmouth Naval College and Museum, Fleet Air Arm Officer's Mess,Yeovilton; private and corporate collections. *Commissions:* many portraits including H.M. Queen Elizabeth and H.R.H. Duke of York for Royal Naval Air Station, Yeovilton, officers mess, investiture of H.R.H. the Prince of Wales, Bernard Gallagher, Ryder Cup captain for Wentworth golf club. *Publications:* Odhams Press, Fleetway, I.P.C., London Times, London Standard, Harpers & Queen, Wentworth Magazine, Surrey Magazine, Twentieth Century Artists by Frances Spalding, Dictionary of British Artists since 1945 by David Buckman. *Clubs:* Wentworth. *Signs work:* "John Heseltine." *Address:* East House, East St., Petworth, W. Sussex GU28 0AB.

HEWISON, William, N.D.D., painting (1949), A.T.D. (1950), M.S.I.A. (1954); illustrator in ink; line and line and wash, and colour; Art Editor, Punch (1960-1984); *b* South Shields, 15 May, 1925. *m* Elsie Hammond. one *s.* one *d. Educ:* South Shields High School; London University. *Studied:* South Shields Art School (1941-43), Regent St. Polytechnic Art School (1947-49). *Exhib:* Four one-man shows, National Theatre; drawings permanently in V. & A. and B.M. *Publications:* work repro.: illustrations and cartoons; Press advertisements, Punch, The Times; book jackets; books, Types Behind the Print, Mindfire, The Cartoon Connection, How to Draw and Sell Cartoons. *Signs work:* "Hewison" or "H." *Address:* 5 Southdown Drive, London SW20 8EZ.

HEWLETT, Francis, R.W.A. (1979), D.F.A. (1955), N.D.D. (1952); painter in oil paint, also worked in polychrome ceramic (1967-76); Painter in Residence: Gregynog Hall, Powys (1977), Newlyn Soc. of Artists; Head of Painting, Falmouth (1963-81); *b* Bristol, 26 Sept., 1930. *m* Elizabeth Allen. one *s.* two *d. Educ:* Fairfield Grammar School, Bristol. *Studied:* West of England College of Art (1948-52, George Sweet), Ecole des Beaux Arts, Paris (1953, Ateliers of Legeult and Brianchon), Slade School (1953-54, W. Coldstream, C. Rogers). *Exhib:* shown since 1958, Newlyn, R.W.A., R.A., Dublin, Belfast, Browse and Darby, London (1993), Falmouth, Plymouth (2000, 2001) retrospective exhibition (painting, drawing, ceramic). *Work in collections:* Belfast, Plymouth, Leicester, Portsmouth, Southampton, Aberystwyth, Gregynog Hall, Duisburg (Germany). *Commissions:* Peter Nichols, Tom Stoppard. *Signs work:* "Francis Hewlett" or "F.H." *Address:* 21 Penwerris Terr., Falmouth, Cornwall TR11 2PA.

HEYWORTH, James Charles, L.D.A.D. distinction University of London (1982); illustrator/painter in gouache, water-colour, pen and ink, airbrush; *b* London, 28 Feb., 1956. *Educ:* Wandsworth School. *Studied:* Putney School of Art (1975), Byam Shaw School of Drawing and Painting (1976, D. Nixon), Goldsmiths' College (1979-82, Bernard Cheese). *Exhib:* Battersea Arts Centre, Ripley Arts; one-man Bury Metro Arts Assoc. Work in private collections. *Clubs:* Assoc. of Illustrators. *Signs work:* "James Heyworth." *Address:* 99 Sutton Common Rd., Sutton, Surrey SM1 3HP.

HICKEY, Michael, F.L.S. (1979), F.S.B.A. (1986), M.I.Hort. (1987), Silver Lindley Medal (1978), Silver Gilt Lindley medal (1980); artist in pen and Indian ink for scientific botanical illustration; part-time lecturer, author; Vice-Pres. Soc. of Botanical Artists (1988-97); Chairman, Glos. Soc. for Botanical Illustration; Hon. Mem. Chelsea Physic Garden, Florilegium Soc.; President, Cambridge University Botanic Garden Assoc. in the year 2000-01; *b* Seaford, E. Sussex, 10 Mar., 1930. *m* Robin Florence Petersen. two *d. Educ:* Eastbourne College; Plumpton Agricultural College; University of Botanic Gdn., Cambridge (qualified 1954). *Studied:* St. Paul's Teacher Training College (qualified as a teacher 1957). *Exhib:* Botanical Soc. of the British Isles, R.H.S., S.B.A. (Mall Galleries, Westminster Gallery), Cheltenham and Glos. C.H.E., Linnean Soc., Glos. Soc. for Botanical Illustration. *Work in collections:* Hunt Inst. for Botanical Documentation, Carnegie Mellon University, Pittsburgh. *Publications:* over 20 books illustrated and some as author or co-author, including '100 Families of Flowering Plants' with Clive King (C.U.P. 1981), illustrated 'A New Key to Wild Flowers' by John Hayward (C.U.P. 1987), author/artist

'Drawing Plants in Pen and Ink' (Cedar 1994), co-author 'Common Families of Flowering Plants' by M.H. & C. King (C.U.P. 1997), co-artist 'The Shaping of Cambridge Botany' by Dr. S.M. Walters (C.U.P. 1981), co-artist 'Secondary Pollen Presentation' by P.F. Yeo (Berlin 1993), co-artist 'Wild and Garden Flowers' by Max Walters (Harper Collins 1993), co-author/artist 'Illustrated Glossary of Botanical Terms' (C.U.P. 2000), co-author with Clive King. Launched Certificate Course in Botanical Illustration with Cheltenham and Glos. C.H.E. (1998). *Signs work:* see appendix. *Address:* Hamlyn Cottage, France Lynch, Stroud, Glos. GL6 8LT. *Email:* michael@hickey.plus.com

HICKS, Anne, R.W.A., Slade Dip.; artist in oil and gouache of portraits, murals, costume design, environmental design; Adult Education Avon and Visiting Lecturer, University Architects Dept., Bristol (1976-84); *b* London. *m* Jerry Hicks. one *s.* one *d. Educ:* Hampstead and Minehead. *Studied:* Slade School under Profs. Schwabe and Coldstream. *Exhib:* R.W.A., British Women Painters Musée de l'Art Moderne, Paris (1967); two-person shows with husband: Bristol, Cardiff, Dorchester, etc. (1954-90). *Work in collections:* England, France, America, New Zealand, Australia. *Commissions:* S.S. Great Britain mural (with husband) 1997. *Signs work:* "Anne Hicks." *Address:* Goldrush, Gt. George St., Bristol BS1 5QT.

HICKS, Jerry, M.B.E., A.T.D., R.W.A., Slade Dip., Judo 7th Dan; painter including portraits, murals; environmentalist; *b* London, 12 June, 1927. *m* Anne Hicks (née Hayward), painter. one *s.* one *d. Educ:* Actors' Orphanage, Rishworth, Sandhurst. *Studied:* Slade under Coldstream, Freud and with Stanley Bird and Walter Bayes. *Exhib:* R.A., R.W.A., R.B.A., two-person shows with wife: Bristol, Cardiff, Dorchester, etc. (1954-90). Winner of Bristol 600 Competition (1973), Queen's Jubilee Award (British Achievement), Olympic Painting prize (1984). *Work in collections:* Britain, U.S.A., Canada, St. Lucia, Germany, Italy, France, Australia, Japan. *Commissions:* SS. Great Britain mural (with wife) 1997. Numerous national portraits incl. H.M. The Queen. *Publications:* 'Judo: Through the Looking Glass'. *Clubs:* Bristol Civic Soc. *Signs work:* "Hicks." *Address:* Goldrush, Gt. George St., Bristol BS1 5QT.

HICKS, June Rhodes, B.A. (Hons.) (1956), M.A. (1960); printmaker in etching; former teacher; *b* Yorks., 5 June, 1935. *m* J. Michael Hicks. two *s.* one *d. Educ:* Universities: Leeds, Belfast. *Studied:* Penzance School of Art (Bouverie Hoyton, John Tunnard, Joan Whiteford). *Exhib:* solo shows in Cornwall. *Work in collections:* galleries in Cornwall and elswhere; and in private collections. *Publications:* co-editor Ten Penwith Printmakers (1998). *Clubs:* Founder mem. Penwith Printmakers, mem. St. Ives Soc. of Artists. *Signs work:* "June Hicks." *Address:* Vingoe Cottage, Travescan Sennen, nr. Penzance, TR19 7AQ.

HICKS, Nicola, M.B.E, R.W.A., F.R.B.S., M.A., R.C.A.; sculptor in plaster and straw, bronze; *b* London, 1960. *m* Daniel Flowers. one *s.* one *d. Studied:* Chelsea School of Art (1978-82), Royal College of Art (1982-85). *Exhib:* numerous solo exhbns. in U.K. and abroad. *Commissions:* monument to the Brown Dog, Battersea Park, London. *Publications:* 'Nicola Hicks' (Momentum, 1999). *Signs work:* "HICKS." *Address:* c/o Flowers East, 199-205 Richmond Rd., London E8 3NJ.

HICKS, Philip, Dip. R.A.S.; painter in oil, acrylic and water-colour; Past

Chairman, Vice Pres. A.G.B.I.; *b* England, 1928. *m* Jill. one *s.* one *d. Educ:* Winchester College. *Studied:* Chelsea School of Art and R.A. Schools. *Exhib:* one-man shows, Marjorie Parr, Robert Self, Hoya, New Art Centre Galleries, Gallery 10, London, Oxford Gallery, V.E.C.U. Antwerp, Engström Galleri, Stockholm; retro-spective, Battersea Arts Centre, London, Bohun Gallery, Henley, 1977 British Council award, David Messum Fine Art, London. *Work in collections:* Tate Gallery, V. & A., Contemporary Art Soc., Imperial War Museum, Nuffield Foundation, R.C.M., De Beers, Mirror Group, Wates Ltd., NatWest. Bank, B.P., APV Holdings, Chandris Shipping. *Commissions:* Wates Ltd., Control Data Corporation, Chandris Shipping. *Clubs:* Chelsea Arts and Arts Club. *Signs work:* "Philip Hicks" (often on reverse) or "HICKS." *Address:* Radcot House, Buckland Rd., Bampton, Oxon. OX18 2AA.

HIGGINS, John, self taught artist in water-colour and drawing, mixed media; private tuition, tutor for H. F. Holiday Group, Peligon Painting Holidays and others; *b* Carshalton, 10 July, 1934. *m* Nicola. two *s. Exhib:* various exhibitions: solo exhi-bitions; St. Ives "In All Directions". *Work in collections:* various private buyers. *Publications:* article for Artist magazine Oct. '99 "Mixing the Media", BBC televi-sion short film on Godrevy Lighthouse, April 2000. *Signs work:* "J D Higgins." *Address:* 6 Richmond Place, St.Ives, Cornwall TR26 1JN.

HIGGINS, Nicola, artist in water-colour; private water-colour tutor, tutoring for H. F. Holiday Group, Pengoni Holidays Greece, and others; *b* Rustington, Sussex, 1 Mar., 1943. *m* John. one *s. Educ:* City and Guilds teachers certificate. *Exhib:* various exhibitions and galleries. *Publications:* article for Artist magazine Dec. '99 "Adventures in Watercolour", short film for BBC Pebble Mill "Which Craft" on water-colour painting Sept. '99. *Signs work:* "Nicola H." *Address:* 6 Richmond Place, St. Ives, Cornwall TR26 1JN.

HIGSON, John, M.F.P.S.; self taught sculptor in wood and ceramic, painter in water-colour and pastel; *b* 30 Oct., 1936. *Educ:* Malden West County Secondary. *Exhib:* one-man shows: Bourne Hall, Ewell, Russell Studio, Wimbledon, Malden Centre, New Malden. *Address:* 22 Croxton, Burritt Rd., Kingston upon Thames, Surrey KT1 3HS.

HILL, Anthony, artist, plastician and theorist: works in industrial materials; awarded Leverhulme Fellowship, Hon. Research Fellow, Dept. Mathematics, University College, London (1971-73); currently visiting research associate (Maths. Dept. UCL); *b* London, 23 Apr., 1930. *m* Yuriko Kaetsu, ceramicist. *Educ:* Bryanston. *Studied:* St. Martin's (1947-49), Central School (1949-51). *Exhib:* Kasmin Gallery (1966, 1969, 1980); retrospective exhbn. Hayward Gallery (1983), I.C.A. (1958); Mayor Gallery (1994). *Work in collections:* Tate Gallery, V. & A., British Museum, provincial galleries; Museum of Modern Art, Grenoble, Tel Aviv and Santiago, Louisiana Museum Denmark, Gulbenkian Museum Lisbon, Stuki Museum, Lodz (Poland), Kroller-Muller (Holland). *Publications:* edited Data Directions in Art Theory and Aesthetics (Faber, 1986), Duchamp-Passim (Gordon and Breach 1995); articles and work repro.: in English, Continental and American publications since 1950. *Signs work:* "Anthony Hill." and see appendix. Since 1975 has made works signed "Rem Doxford", and "Redo." *Address:* 24 Charlotte St., London W1T 2ND.

HILL, Charles Douglas, artist in oil; *b* Dewsbury, W. Yorks., 16 June, 1953. *m* Jennifer Haylett, singer. *Educ:* Dewsbury, England, and Sqaumish, Canada. *Exhib:* worldwide; and Longships Gallery, St. Ives. *Publications:* work repro.: book cover (Black Swan Pub.), articles 'Cornish World', 'Inside Cornwall'. *Clubs:* St. Ives Soc. of Artists. *Address:* Longships Gallery, St.Andrew's St., St. Ives, Cornwall TR26 1AN.

HILL, Francis, Cert. Criminology (1959); self taught painter in oil; retd. police chief inspector; formerly Head of Security, National Gallery and N.P.G.; *b* Barnsley, 11 Sept., 1917. *m* Barbara Heward. two *s.* two *d. Educ:* Leeds University. *Exhib:* R.A. (1982, 1984, 1992, 1993), National Gallery (staff), Sotheby's, Royal Exchange London, Hertfordshire Artists. *Publications:* chapter with illustration: A World of Their Own (Pelham); Royal Academy Exhibitors 1971-1989. Work in private collections. *Signs work:* "Francis Hill." *Address:* 6 Asquith House, Guessens Rd., Welwyn Garden City, Herts. AL8 6QA.

HILL, Reginald H., S.G.F.A.; artist in oil, water-colour, pastel and pencil of portraits, landscapes, figure; President, Croydon Art Soc.; *b* London, 26 Feb., 1919. *m* Jean Hill (decd.). one *s.* one *d. Educ:* Vauxhall Central School, London. *Studied:* City & Guilds Art School (1969-72, Middleton Todd, R.A., Robin Guthrie, R.P.; 1972-75, Rodney Burn, R.A.). *Exhib:* R.A., R.S.P.P., N.E.A.C., S.G.F.A. *Commissions:* Numerous. *Publications:* illustrated 'Scorched Earth' by 'Detonator' (Col. Brazier). Work in private collections worldwide. *Clubs:* Chelsea Arts. *Signs work:* "Reg. Hill," "R. Hill" or "R.H.H." *Address:* "Raffaello", 54 Hermitage Rd., Kenley, Surrey CR8 5EB.

HILL, Ronald James, U.A., S.G.F.A., F.S.A.I.; freelance artist in oil, water-colour, pen and ink; *b* London, 19 Oct., 1933. *m* Betty Bunn (decd.). *Educ:* Willesden Technical College. *Studied:* Heatherley's School of Art (1958-65, Jack Merriot, Patrick Larkin, Harry Riley). *Exhib:* Paris Salon (1966-69), R.B.A., U.A.; one man shows, Brent, Wantage. *Commissions:* Landscapes and architectural subjects in all media. *Signs work:* "RONN." *Address:* Orpheus Studio of Fine Art, Pound Cottage, Kingston Lisle, Wantage, Oxon. OX12 9QL.

HILL, Sonia Geraldine, painter in oil; *b* London. *Educ:* Dorchester Abbey School, Oxon. *Studied:* Maidenhead Art College, Berks.; Zambia (pupil with Andrew Hayward). *Exhib:* R.A. (1993) (two), and two further works accepted by Selection Com. (1997), R.A. (2000). *Publications:* R.A. Illustrated (1993) Jack the Lad. *Signs work:* "S.G. Hill." *Address:* 6a Warfield Rd., Hampton, Middx. TW12 2AY. *Website:* www.artserve.net/s.g.hill.2000

HILLHOUSE, David, B.A. (1969), A.T.D. (1971), R.C.A. (1979), A.M.A. (1982); artist in water-colour and egg tempera; *b* Irby, Wirral, 19 June, 1945. *m* Paula Lane. two *s. Educ:* Birkenhead Institute. *Studied:* Laird School of Art (1964-66), Liverpool College of Art (1966-69). *Exhib:* Merseyside, Wales and Bristol, U.S.A., Germany. *Clubs:* Hon. R.Cam.A., Wirral Soc. of Arts, Deeside Art Group. *Signs work:* "David Hillhouse." *Address:* 49 Cortsway, Greasby, Wirral CH49 2NA.

HILLI: see THOMPSON, Hilli.

HILLIER, Matthew, S.WL.A., S.A.A. (U.S.A.); wildlife artist in acrylic, pastel and water-colour; Council mem. S.WL.A.; *b* Slough, 7 May, 1958. *Studied:* Dyfed College of Art. *Exhib:* Christie's Wildlife Auction (1994-97), Pacific Rim Wildlife Art Expo (1994,1995) Tacoma, Vancouver, Soc. of Animal Artists (1995, 1996), Birds in Art, Wisconsin (1993, 1994, 1996), Florida Wildlife Art Expo (1997), Friends of Washington Zoo Wildlife Art Show (1996, 1997). *Commissions:* Ambleside Studio, Michigan. *Publications:* Fine Art Limited Edition prints (Millpond Press, Florida); illustrated: The Rhinocerous, a Monograph (Basilisk Press Limited Edition book). *Signs work:* "Mathew Hillier." *Address:* 166 ELMER RD., Middleton-on-Sea, W. Sussex PO22 6JA.

HILLS, Peter Faber, N.D.D., R.A.Cert., F.R.B.S., Past Secretary of the 65 Group (Public School Art Masters); Churchill Fellow in Sculpture (1972); sculptor in clay, stone, wood; schoolmaster; Director of Art, Tonbridge School (1963-79), retd. from Tonbridge School (1988); *b* Bearsted, Kent, 4 Dec., 1925. *m* Ann-Mary Ewart (née Macdonald). two *s.* one *d. Educ:* Tonbridge School. *Studied:* Bromley College of Art (1948-50), R.A. Schools (1950-55); assistant to Maurice Lambert, R.A. (1955-60), and worked for Sir Henry Rushbury, R.A., Sir Albert Richardson, P.R.A. *Work in collections:* Lord Leighton Museum, Kensington, Skinner's Library, Tonbridge School. *Signs work:* "HILLS." *Address:* 33 Yardley Park Rd., Tonbridge, Kent.

HILTON, Bo, M.A. Print (1998), B.Sc. Biology (1984); artist in oil on canvas; *b* London, 9 Nov., 1961. *m* Alice. one *s.* one *d. Studied:* Brighton (1985-88). *Exhib:* Cassian de Verre Cole (1995-96), Arthur Anderson (1998). *Clubs:* N.E.A.C. *Address:* 23 St. Luke's Terr., Brighton BN2 2ZE.

HINCHCLIFFE, Michael, artist in water-colour, designer; *b* London, 25 Apr., 1937. *m* Gillian. two *d. Educ:* St. Marylebone Grammar School. *Studied:* St. Martin's School of Art. *Exhib:* R.I., U.A.; many one-man shows. *Work in collections:* Weybridge Museum. *Signs work:* see appendix. *Address:* 37 The Furrows, Walton on Thames, Surrey KT12 3JG.

HIND, Margaret Madeleine, R.M.S., H.S., S.Lm., M.A.S.-F., Froebel Cert.; miniaturist working mainly in water-colour with gold leaf on ivorine/vellum; *b* Minera, N. Wales, 1927. *m* Lt. Col. J.G. Hind, O.B.E. (retd.). three *d. Educ:* Woodford House School, Croydon, Coloma Froebel College (1945-48). *Studied:* art: privately under C.S. Spackman, R.B.A. (1943-45), Helen Gaudin (Washington D.C., 1976-78); started miniature painting (1986). *Exhib:* R.A., R.M.S., Llewellyn Alexander Gallery (awarded Cert. of Excellence, 1994), Medici Gallery London, Hilliard Soc., Soc. of Limners, Miniature Soc. of Florida. Awarded Historical, Mythological prize M.A.S.-F. (1995). Paints stories from Chaucer/King Arthur, etc. in the medieval manner. *Work in collections:* around the world and in private collections. *Clubs:* R.M.S., H.S., M.A.S.F. *Signs work:* see appendix. *Address:* 27 Birch Cl., Send, nr. Woking, Surrey, GU23 7BZ.

HINKS, Thomas, N.D.D. (1951), F.R.S.A. (1981); lecturer-demonstrator, artist in water-colour, oil, acrylic; demonstrator, Daler Rowney; visiting lecturer at res. colleges and art societies; *b* Newcastle, 26 Apr., 1930. *m* Vera. one *s.* one *d. Educ:* Newcastle School of Art, Stoke-on-Trent College of Art. *Studied:* under Arthur Berry. *Exhib:* 15 one-man shows in Midlands. *Work in collections:* Stoke-on-Trent City A.G., Newcastle Museum and A.G., Keele University, W.E.A. Centre; paintings in America, Canada, Spain, Greece, France, Norway, and many private U.K. collections. *Publications:* author of New Methods and Techniques in Art - for schools. *Clubs:* Chairman, Unit Ten Art Soc., N.A.P.A., Soc. of Staffs Artists. *Signs work:* "Tom Hinks." *Address:* Fairways, High St., Caverswall, Stoke-on-Trent, Staffs. ST11 9EF.

HINWOOD, Kay, P.S., U.A.; painter in oil, pastel, etc.; *b* Bromley, 26 Nov., 1920. *m* (1) the late George Hinwood. (2) the late Lt. Cdr. Douglas Zeidler, R.N.V.R. one *s.* one *d. Educ:* Stratford House School, Bickley. *Studied:* first Paris, with Edouard MacAvoy, later privately with Sonia Mervyn; City and Guilds Art School, London; Kathleen Browne Studios, Chelsea under Marian Kratochwil and Kathleen Browne. *Exhib:* R.P., R.B.A., R.O.I., P.S., U.A., S.W.A., Mall Galleries. *Work in collections:* England, U.S.A., Canada, France, Spain, Australia, Holland. *Clubs:* Chelsea Arts. *Signs work:* "K. Hinwood." *Address:* 27 Edward Rd., Bromley, Kent BR1 3NG.

HIPKINS, Michael William, N.D.D. (1964), A.T.D. (1976); artist in oil and water-colour, sculptor in alabaster and marble; *b* Blackpool, 21 June, 1942. *m* Pauline Hipkins. two *s.* one *d. Studied:* Blackpool College of Art, S.W. Hayter's Studio 17, Paris. *Exhib:* Blackheath Gallery, The Gallery Manchester's Art House, R.S.A., Colours Gallery, Warstone Gallery. *Work in collections:* Grundy A.G. Blackpool, Lancaster A.G. *Commissions:* series of murals: Blackpool Zoo, several stone carving commissions. *Publications:* included in British Contemporary Art (1993); work repro.: greetings cards and prints. *Signs work:* "Michael Hipkins." *Address:* Driftwood, Ash Rd., Elswick, Preston, Lancs. PR4 3YE.

HIPKISS, Percy Randolph, R.B.S.A. (1971); freelance artist in oil, water-colour and pastel; jewellery designer; *b* Blackheath, Birmingham, 8 Aug., 1912. *m* Dorothy Alice Boraston. one *s.* one *d. Educ:* at Blackheath. *Work in collections:* Dudley A.G., and in private collections throughout U.K., America, Australia, Belgium. *Clubs:* past-president, Birmingham Water-colour Soc.; President, Dudley Society of Artists. *Signs work:* "Hipkiss." *Address:* 18 Lewis Rd., Oldbury, Warley, W.Mid. B68 0PW.

HIPPE ASGFA, Susan Kerstin, B.A. (Hons), Roehampton Inst. University of Surrey; drawing combined with mixed media; tutor; *b* Johannesburg, S. Africa, 28 Nov., 1966. *Educ:* schools in Denmark, Germany and France. *Studied:* art schools in France (Troyes, Le Havre, Mulhouse), and London (Roehampton Inst.). *Exhib:* solo exhibs. in London and group exhibs. in U.K., London, Paris, New York. *Clubs:* E.W.A.C.C. *Signs work:* "SUSAN HIPPE" or "S.H." *Address:* 68 Stroud Rd., Wimbledon Park, London SW19 8DG. *Website:* www.picassomio.com/susanhippe/ *Email:* s-hippe@excite.co.uk

HIRST, Barry Elliot, N.D.D. Painting (1956), D.F.A. (Lond.) (1958), F.R.S.A. (1989); painter; Emeritus Prof. of Fine Art, University of Sunderland; *b* Padstow, Cornwall, 11 June, 1934. *m* Sheila Mary. one *s.* two *d. Educ:* Alleyns School, Dulwich. *Studied:* Camberwell School of Art (1950-52, 1954-56), Slade School (1956-58, Keith Vaughan, Claude Rogers). *Exhib:* over fifteen one-man shows, London, Sydney, N.Y., Glasgow, Edinburgh, Newcastle upon Tyne, Riga, Atlanta. *Work in collections:* Contemporary Arts Soc., British Council, Sunday Times, Croydon Educ. Com., Northern Arts Assoc., Tyne & Wear Museums, University of

Sunderland, Darlington Memorial Hospital, Olinda Museum Brazil, Derby Museum and A.G., H.R.H. Duchess of Kent, Latvian National Museum Riga, Latvian Academy of Art Riga, R.A.C., Sunderland and Portsmouth Newspapers, Sao Paulo Museum Brazil, B.P., A. & M. Univ. Texas. *Publications:* 'From a Painting by Masaccio' with C. Day-Lewis, 'The Way of It' with R.S. Thomas, 'Waiting for the Barbarians' with Roy Fuller, 'An Ill-Governed Coast' with Roy Fuller, 'Kisses' with Alistair Eliot. *Clubs:* Sunderland Assoc. Football. *Signs work:* "BARRY HIRST" or "B.E. HIRST." *Address:* 12 Bondgate Without, Alnwick, Northumberland NE66 1PP.

HIRST, Derek, A.R.C.A.; artist; *b* Doncaster, 11 Apr., 1930. *Studied:* Doncaster School of Art (1946-48), R.C.A. (1948-51). *Exhib:* Drian Galleries (1961), Tooth's Gallery (1962-63), Stone Galleries, Newcastle upon Tyne (1962), University of Sussex (1966), Towner A.G. (1966), Angela Flowers Gallery (1970, 1972, 1975, 1979, 1984, 1987, 1989), Victorian Centre for the Arts, Melbourne, Australia (1980), Pallant House Gallery, Chichester (1987, 1991), Flowers East (1991, 1995), Flowers East at London Fields (1993, 1999), Flowers West, Santa Monica, U.S.A. (2001). *Work in collections:* Tate Gallery, V. & A., National Gallery of Canada, A.C.G.B., Contemporary Art Soc., D.O.E., Fundaçao dos Museus Regionaise de Bahia, Brazil, Bank of Ireland, Dublin, Universities of Sussex and Southampton, Art Inst. of Detroit, Brooklyn Museum, N.Y., Arizona State University, Phoenix Art Museum, etc. *Signs work:* "Derek Hirst." *Address:* 3 The Terrace, Mill La., Sidlesham, Chichester, W. Sussex PO20 7NA.

HISLOP, Helga, Cert.A.D. (Dist.) (1962), Dip.A.D. (graphics) (1964), F.S.B.A. (1986), Exhibit. A. (2000), F.L.S. (2001); botanical artist in water-colour; *b* London, 18 Jan., 1941. *m* Julian Terence Crouch M.I.L.T. one *d. Educ:* Willoughby H.S. High School, Sydney, Australia. *Studied:* Cardiff College of Art (1959-62, A.T. Kitson), Central School of Arts and Crafts (1962-64, P. Kitley). *Exhib:* mixed shows: Mall Galleries, Westminster Gallery, Linnean Soc., R.H.S., Hunt Inst. Botanical Documentation, Pittsburgh. *Work in collections:* The Shirley Sherwood Collection of Contemporary Botanical Art. *Publications:* Botanicus Publishing Limited, Talents Publishing, Kew Magazine, Harmony Prints Limited. *Signs work:* "Helga Hislop-Crouch" hidden in work. *Address:* The Mill House, Little Sampford, nr. Saffron Walden, Essex CB10 2QT.

HITCHCOCK, Harold Raymond, F.R.S.A. (1972); Hon. Col. of State of Louisiana U.S.A. (1974); artist in water-colour and oil; *b* London, 23 May, 1914. *m* Rose Hitchcock. two *s.* one *d. Studied:* Working Mens College, Camden Town (1935-36) under Percy Horton, Barnett Freedman. *Exhib:* one-man shows: Hanson Gallery, New Orleans (1990), M.K. Vance Gallery, Chicago (1992), Campbell & Franks (Fine Art) Ltd. (1975), Pilkington Glass Museum (1973), Hilton Gallery (1970), Upper Grosvenor Gallery (1969), Woburn Abbey (1967), Walker Gallery (1956); retrospective shows: R.I. Galleries (1967), Philadelphia Art Alliance, U.S.A. (1982), Phillips Gallery of Fine Art, Carmel, California, U.S.A. (2001); touring exhbn. in U.S.A.: New Orleans, Huntsville, Atlanta City, Daytona Beach, Corpus Christi and Winston Salem (opened by the Duke of Bedford, 1972); R.S.A., London (1984), Gallery 106, Perrysberg, Ohio (1984), Clossons Gallery, Cincinnati (1985), Christopher Wood Gallery, London (1986), Phillips Gallery of Fine Art, Carmel Calif. (1999). *Work in collections:* V. & A., Rowntree Memorial Trust, Hunterian

A.G. of University of Glasgow, Lidice Memorial Museum, Czechoslovakia, Museum of Fine Art, N. Carolina, University of Louisiana, Hannema-de Stuers Foundation, Nijenhuis Castle, Netherlands, New Orleans Museum of Fine Art, Paul Mellon Collection, Yale Centre for British Art. *Publications:* Harold Hitchcock: A Romantic Symbol in Surrealism (1982) by Dr. Ian Williamson; Harold Hitchcock – 'Life in Light', Phillips Gallery of Fine Art (2000). *Signs work:* see appendix. *Address:* Hood Barton Farmhouse, Dartington, Devon TQ9 6AB.

HITCHENS, John, aerial landscape painter and wood sculptor; *b* Sussex, 1940. *m* Rosalind. two *s. Educ:* Bedales School. *Studied:* Bath Academy of Art. *Exhib:* Regular London exhbns. since 1964. *Work in collections:* public and permanent collections U.K. and abroad. 1979: 52ft. mural, "A Landscape Symphony". *Signs work:* "John Hitchens." *Address:* The Old School, Byworth, Petworth, Sussex GU28 0HN.

HO, Dr. Kok-Hoe, D.Sc. (Hon.), P.B.M., M.S.I.A., F.R.A.I.A., F.R.I.B.A., A.P.A.M., A.R.A.S., A.R.P.S.; awarded St. Andrew's Gold (1935) and Bronze (1937); 2nd Inter-School Art gold medal (1939); architect; artist in oil and water-colour painting, pen and pencil drawing; art-photographer; president-director, Ho Kwong-Yew & Sons, Architects, Singapore; Chairman, Singapore Art Soc. (1953-70); *b* Singapore, 14 July, 1922. *Educ:* St. Andrew's School, Singapore. *Studied:* graduated N.S.W. College of Architecture, Sydney. *Exhib:* Sydney (1948-49); Singapore (1954-62); Kuala Lumpur (1960-62), etc. Photo salons: London (1957); La Coruna (1958); Hongkong (1958), etc. Architectural Work: National Museum, Kuala Lumpur, etc. *Publications:* Travel Sketches and Paintings, etc. *Clubs:* Royal Art Soc.; Royal Institute of Australian Architects; R.I.B.A.; Royal Photographic Soc. of Great Britain; Singapore Art Soc. *Signs work:* "Ho Kok-Hoe." *Address:* 9 Camden Park, Singapore 1129.

HOARE, Diana C., B.A. Hons.; lettering designer, calligrapher, letter carver, carving on stone and slate, calligraphy; *b* London, 10 Feb., 1956. *m* William Taunton. one *s.* two *d. Educ:* Godolphin and Latymer; University of Kent, Canterbury. *Studied:* privately with Vernon Shearer, Ievan Rees, Heather Child, Sam Somerville. *Exhib:* solo exhbns. in Dorset, London and B'ham. *Work in collections:* two MS. books at University of Austin, Texas. *Publications:* Advanced Calligraphy Techniques (Cassells), Everybodys Wine Guide (Quarto). *Signs work:* see appendix. *Address:* Upper House Farm, Dilwyn, Hereford HR4 8JJ.

HOBART, Lady Caroline Fleur: see LEEDS, Caroline.

HOBART, John, B.Sc. (Lond.), R.C.A.; self taught artist in oil and water-colour; past Vice-Pres. Royal Cambrian Academy; Fellow, University College of N. Wales, Bangor; *b* London, 27 May, 1922. one *s.* two *d. Educ:* University College, London. *Exhib:* one-man, Theatre Gwynedd; group shows, Plas Mawr, Conway, Tegfryn Gallery, Cambrian Academy, R.I., N.Wales Group, Newlyn, Penwith, Kings College, Cambridge. *Work in collections:* University College of N.Wales, Bangor; private collections in U.S.A., Canada, Australia, G.B., Holland, Germany. *Signs work:* "J. Hobart." *Address:* Buswisnan, Ludgvan, Penzance, Cornwall TR20 8BN.

HOCKIN, Julie, S.O.F.A. (1996); self taught professional artist working in water-colour, graphite and coloured pencils. Her pictures range from botanical and wildlife subjects to very detailed cat paintings and drawings; Creative Director, Hockin and Roberts Ltd, St Austell; *b* St. Austell, 3 Feb., 1937. one *d. Educ:* St. Austell Grammar School. *Exhib:* National Trust Cotehele, Marwell Zoological Pk. Winchester, Carlyon Bay Hotel, St. Austell, Llewellyn Alexander Gallery, London, R.M.S., H.S. Gives talks and classes. *Signs work:* "Julie Hockin" or "JH" joined. *Address:* Cedar Lodge, Trevarth, Mevagissey, St. Austell, Cornwall PL26 6RX.

HODGES, Cyril Walter, Hon. D.Litt. (Sussex) 1979; author, mural painter, illustrator, stage designer; *b* Beckenham, 1909. *m* Greta Becker (decd.). two *s. Educ:* Dulwich College. *Studied:* Goldsmiths' College. *Publications:* work repro.: advertisements, books, magazine illustrations in England and U.S.A. Special subjects: Shakespearean Theatres. Co-designer of Mermaid Theatre (1951), Lloyd's 1951 Exhbn. Mural painting U.K. Provident Inst. (1957). Retrospective exhbn. Folger Library, Washington D.C. (1988), Shakespeare Inst. Stratford-upon-Avon (1999). Reconstructional designs Rose Theatre excavation (1989). Columbus Sails, The Globe Restored, The Namesake, The Marsh King, Shakespeare's Theatre, The Overland Launch, Shakespeare's Second Globe, Playhouse Tales, The Battlement Garden, Enter The Whole Army. Awarded Kate Greenaway Medal for Illustration (1964). *Signs work:* "C. Walter Hodges." *Address:* 36 Southover High St., Lewes, Sussex BN7 1HX.

HODGES, Gillian Mary, S.W.A. (1987), S.Lm. (1997); portrait painter in oil, pastel and water-colour; portraits in miniature, oils and water-colour; *b* Twickenham, Middx. *m* Peter Steer Hodges. two *s. Educ:* Richmond School of Art under Jack Fairhurst, A.R.C.A., Salisbury School of Art and Heatherley School of Art (part time). *Exhib:* S.W.A., various societies in S. and S.W. of England, Northern Ireland. *Work in collections:* 'The Pageant' in Farnham (Surrey) Public Library; Officers' Mess QARANC, Aldershot; Inst. of Aviation Medicine, Farnborough. *Signs work:* "G. M. Hodges." *Address:* 2 Abbey Mill, Church St., Bradford-on-Avon, Wilts. BA15 1HB.

HODGKINS, Barbara, sculptor in marble, bronze; *b* U.S.A. *Educ:* Wellesley College, Columbia University, U.S.A. *Studied:* Chelsea School of Art, London. *Work in collections:* Sculpture in corporate collections: Prudential, Bank of China, Bank of Denmark, B.P., Reynolds, Hewlett-Packer, Foote, Cone, Belding, MCL (Art and Work award 1987) and in private European, Asian and American collections. *Clubs:* Mem. Royal Soc. of British Sculptors. *Address:* 5 Hurlingham Ct., Ranelagh Gdns., London SW6 3SH. *Second Address:* C.P.200, Pietrasanta (Lucca) 55045, Italy.

HODGSON, Carole, F.R.B.S., H.D.F.A. (1964); sculptor in cement, bronze, wax, ceramics, lead; Principal lecturer, Kingston University; *b* London, 1940. *Studied:* Wimbledon School of Art (1957-62), Slade U.C.L. (1962-64). *Exhib:* Angela Flowers Gallery, Flowers East, A.C.G.B., W.A.C., Wustum Museum, U.S.A., Whitefriars Museum, Coventry, New Ashgate, Farnham, Llanelli Festival, Christie's Fine Arts, Buenos Aires, Argentine, Santiago, Chile, Haggerty Museum, U.S.A., Flowers West, L.A., U.S.A. *Work in collections:* Welsh Contemporary Arts, A.C.G.B., W.A.C., British Council, D.O.E., Contemporary Arts, Unilever House, Universities of Wales, London, Wisconsin U.S.A., British Medal Soc., Manpower. *Publications:* From the Sea to the Wall (Kingston U. Press), Carole Hodgson by

Mary Rose Beaumont (Momentum). *Signs work:* "Carole Hodgson." *Address:* Flowers East, 199-205 Richmond Rd., London E8 3NJ.

HODGSON, Josanne, S.B.A.; botanical artist/etcher in water-colour, pastel, etching; *b* Blundellsands, Liverpool, 26 May, 1932. *m* Barrie B. one *s.* two *d.* *Studied:* Southport School of Art. *Exhib:* two solo, many shared in London, the North-West, N.Wales and the North-East. *Publications:* work repro.: greetings cards. *Clubs:* S.B.A., N.Wales Soc. of Botanical and Fine Water-colour Artists. *Signs work:* "Josanne Hodgson." *Address:* 5 The Shires, King St., Lach Dennis, Ches. CW9 7SE.

HODGSON, Kenneth Jonah, B.A., G.O.E. Dip. S.W. C.Q.S.W., P.T.A.; artist in acrylic, oil and water-colour; Exec com. mem., Merseyside Arts (1985-87); Steering com. sec., Merseyside Contemporary Artists (1988-89); *b* Liverpool, 2 Aug., 1936. two *d. Educ:* Liverpool, Herts, Oak Hill College, London, The Open University, N.E.W.I. Wrexham Cymru, Liverpool John Moore's University. *Exhib:* R.Cam.A., Williamson A.G.,various Liverpool and Chester galleries; collective exhbns. in Newcastle-Staffs, Ludlow, Crosby, R.B.S.A. Gallery B'ham and N.A.P.A., U.S.A.; individual exhbns. on Merseyside and Wirral. Daylight Group - a Tate Liverpool/Metropolitan Borough of Wirral S.S.D. Arts Project, Art Forum - M.B.W. - S.S.D. (1993). *Work in collections:* Paintings in private and public collections in U.K. and other countries. *Clubs:* Sec., Wirral Soc. of Arts (1983-87); Founder, National Acrylic Painters' Assoc. (1985). *Signs work:* "Kenneth J. Hodgson." *Address:* N.A.P.A., 134 Rake La., Wallasey, Merseyside CH45 1JW.

HODIN, Josef Paul, L.L.D. (Prague), Ph.D. (Hon., Uppsala), D.S.M., 1st Class, Czech; Commander order of merit, Italian; St. Olav Medal, Norwegian; Grand Cross, order of merit, Austrian; Grand Cross, order of merit, German; Silver Cross of Merit, Vienna; Prof. Art History h.c.(Vienna); author, art historian, critic; press attaché to the Norwegian Govt. (1944-45); director of Studies, I.C.A. (1949-54); co-editor of Quandrum, Brussels; mem. executive comm. British Society of Aesthetics; hon. mem. Editorial Council J.A.A.C., Cleveland; awarded intern. 1st prize for art criticism, 1954 (Biennale, Venice); *b* Prague, 17 Aug., 1905. *m* Doris Pamela Simms. one *s.* one *d. Educ:* Realschule, Realgymnasium, and Charles University, Prague. *Studied:* Dresden, Berlin, Paris, Stockholm, and Courtauld Inst. of Art, London University. *Publications:* numerous. *Address:* 12 Eton Ave., London NW3 3FH.

HODSON, John, sculptor in stone and bronze; *b* Oxford, 19 Aug., 1945. *Educ:* Willesden R.C. *Studied:* Courtauld Inst. of Art, London. *Exhib:* one-man show Woodstock Gallery, London (1973), Paris Salon, Salon des Independants, Haas Gallery, Albemarle Gallery, Galerie Modern, Berlin, and other international exhbns. *Work in collections:* Berlin Kunst Haas. *Commissions:* Dancing Girl, Midland Bank (large bronze). *Publications:* work repro.: Modern Art Revue, Witt Library Courtauld Inst. of Art, London, The Dictionary of Artists in Britain since 1945. *Signs work:* "Hodson." *Address:* 40 Clement Cl., London NW6 7AN.

HOFFMANN, Edith, Ph.D., Munich, 1934; art historian and critic; editorial asst. Burlington Magazine (1938-46); asst. editor of the Burlington Magazine (1946-50); Lecturer, Hebrew University of Jerusalem (1960-61); art editor of the Encyclopaedia Hebraica (Jerusalem, 1953-65); *m* Dr. E. Yapou. one *d. Educ:* in Berlin, Vienna,

Munich. *Publications:* Kokoschka: Life and Work (1947); Chagall: Water-colours (1947); contributions to the Burlington Magazine, Apollo, Art News (New York), Phoebus (Basle), Studio, Manchester Guardian, Listener, New Statesman, Twentieth Century, Neue Zürcher Zeitung, etc. *Address:* 52 Bethlehem Rd., 93504 Jerusalem, Israel.

HOFLEHNER, Rudolf, skulpturen and painter; Professor an der Akademie der bildenden Künste, Stuttgart; skulpturen in Eisen, massiv; *b* Linz, 8 Aug., 1916. *m* Luise Schaffer. *Studied:* Akademie der bild. Künste, Vienna. *Signs work:* see appendix. *Address:* Italien, Val d'Elsa, Podere Pantaneto, Provincia Siena. *Second Address:* Ottensteinstrasse 62, 2344 Maria Enzersdorf-Südstadt, Österreich.

HOGAN, Prof. Eileen, M.A. (R.C.A.), R.W.S.; painter; *b* London, 1 Mar., 1946. *m* divorced. *Educ:* Streatham Hill and Clapham High School. *Studied:* Camberwell School of Art and Crafts (1964-67), British School of Archaeology at Athens, Royal College of Art (1971-74, Carel Weight). *Exhib:* regularly at the Fine Art Soc., numerous one-man shows in Europe and America. *Work in collections:* V. & A., Imperial War Museum, R.A., and overseas museums and galleries. *Publications:* Under The Influence: catalogue to accompany retrospective, 1997, and numerous others. *Clubs:* Chelsea Arts, Double Crown. *Signs work:* "Eileen Hogan." *Address:* 13 Wythburen Place, London W1H 7BU.

HOLCH, Eric Sanford, artist in oil, printmaker of limited edition serigraphs; *b* Andover, Mass., 17 Sept., 1948. *m* Elspeth R. Holch. one *s.* one *d. Educ:* Trinity-Pawling School. *Studied:* Hobart College (1969-70), mostly self taught in serigraphy, Eric Holch Gallery, Nantucket (1997-). *Exhib:* one-man shows: Geary Gallery, Connecticut (1996), Gallery 39, Osaka, Japan (1990, 1994), Martha Lincoln Gallery, Florida (1987), The Little Gallery, Nantucket (1986), D. Christian James Gallery, N.J. (1985), Portfolio Gallery, C.T. (1982-87). *Work in collections:* Champion International, Chesebrough-Ponds, E. F. Hutton, First National Bank of Boston, Merrill Lynch, Societé General, Bermuda National Gallery. *Signs work:* "Eric Holch." *Address:* 5 Pine St. Nantucket, M.A. 02554, U.S.A. *Website:* at URL: www.ericholch.com

HOLD, William Ashley, B.A. Hons. Fine Art; painter in oil; *b* Cornwall, 1964. *Educ:* Truro School. *Studied:* Falmouth School of Art. *Exhib:* B.P. Portrait Award (1994 and 1999), Hunting Art Prizes (1996 and 1998) *Work in collections:* Truro School. *Commissions:* Grand Sec. General for the Freemasons. *Address:* 1 Trelawney Ave., Falmouth, Cornwall TR11 4QT. *Email:* ashleyhold@hotmail.com

HOLISTER, Frederick Darnton, M.A. (Cantab.) (1957), M.Arch. Harvard (1953), A.R.I.B.A., Wheelwright Fellowship, Harvard (1952), Doc. U. (Buckingham) 1998; Fellow, Clare College, Cambridge; Director of Studies in Architecture, Clare College, Cambridge; University Lecturer, Department of Land Economy, Cambridge University (retd. 1994); architect in private practice; Consultant Architect to Clare College, Cambridge, Consultant Architect to University of Buckingham (retd. 1997); *b* Coventry, 14 Aug., 1927. *m* Patricia Ogilvy Reid (marriage dissolved). two *s.* two *d. Educ:* Bablake School. *Studied:* Birmingham School of Architecture under A. Douglas Jones (1944-46, 1948-51), Harvard University under Prof. Walter Gropius (1951-53). *Clubs:* Harvard Club of London. *Signs work:* "Darnton Holister." *Address:*

Clare College, Cambridge CB2 1TL.

HOLLAND, Claerwen Belinda, N.D.D. (1964); David Murray landscape studentship (1963); artist in ink, water-colour, pastel and oils; Principal's Prize Byam Shaw; *b* Cwmdauddwr, 4 Mar., 1942. *Educ:* Miss Lambert's School, Queens Gdns., London. *Studied:* Byam Shaw School of Art (1960-64, Maurice de Sausmarez). *Exhib:* R.A., N.E.A.C., Bath Contemporary Art Fair (1991); one-man shows: Sue Rankin Gallery, Countryworks Gallery, Montgomeryshire, Thackeray Rankin, Thackeray Gallery. *Work in collections:* The Library, University College, Cardiff. *Commissions:* various. *Publications:* illustrations to A Year and a Day by J.L.G. Holland (Hodder and Stoughton). *Signs work:* "C.B. Holland." *Address:* Dderw, Cwmdauddwr, Rhayader, Powys LD6 5EY.

HOLLAND, Frances, H.S., S.Lm.; self taught artist in all media; *b* Petworth, Sussex. three *s.* one *d. Exhib:* Llewellyn Alexander, London, R.A. Summer Show (1997, 2001), R.M.S. Westminster, all local venues. Work in collections internationally. *Clubs:* H.S., S.Lm., Royal Tunbridge Wells Art Soc., Tonbridge Art Group. *Signs work:* see appendix *Address:* 107 London Rd., Southborough, Kent TN4 0NA.

HOLLAND, Harry, artist in oil on canvas, printmaking; *b* Glasgow, 11 Apr., 1941. *m* Maureen. two *d. Educ:* Rutlish School, Merton. *Studied:* St. Martin's School of Art (1964-69). *Exhib:* extensively in Britain, France, Belgium, U.S.A.; one-man shows: Jill George Gallery (1988, 1990, 1992, 1994, 1996); retrospective travelling Britain Nov. 1991- Jan. 1993. *Work in collections:* Newport Museum and A.G., National Museum of Wales, Tate Gallery Print Coll. *Commissions:* portrait of Lord Callaghan (1990). *Publications:* Painter in Reality (1991). *Clubs:* Chelsea Arts. *Signs work:* "Harry Holland." *Address:* c/o Jill George Gallery, 38 Lexington St., London W1R 3HR.

HOLLEDGE, Bryan Raymond, A.R.C.A., F.R.S.A., A.F.B.A.; part-time lecturer, Hammersmith School of Art (1949); part-time teacher, St. Hubert's Special School, Brook Green; lecturer, London School of Printing and Graphic Arts; part-time teacher, Chelsea School of Art; graphic designer, Metal Box (1955); Head of Graphics, Swiss Co. Sulzer Bros. (1958); freelance corporate design/mural, Chelsea Arts Club (1950); *b* Ealing, Middx., 1919. *m* Maria Haid. two *d. Educ:* Ealing College. *Studied:* Ealing College of Art (1937-40); H.M.F. 1940-46; Royal College of Art (1946-49). *Exhib:* painting in National Gallery Exhbn. for Young Artists, Whitechapel Gallery (1953), Arts Council U.K. tour, Mural painting, Shipping Co. and Theatres joint exhbn., London (1984); one-man show, London (1955) in assoc. with Atomic Energy Soc. Exhib. regularly at London galleries for painting/etching/wood engraving; recent exhbn. of wood engraving at Syon House, Isleworth. A Companion of Western Europe Dip., Certificate of Merit, Biographical Centre Cambridge (1998). *Publications:* poems. Graphic Consultant to Science (education) Company (2000), wood engraving for Country Life. *Signs work:* "Bryan R. Holledge." *Address:* 5 The Green, Feltham, Middx. TW13 4AF.

HOLLICK, Kenneth Russell, F.C.S.D.; designer; *b* Essex, 5 Jan., 1923. *Studied:* Central School of Arts and Crafts, London. *Publications:* work repro.: trade marks, symbols, logotypes, corporate identity programmes, vehicle livery, booklets. Designs shown in books on graphic design published in Japan, Italy, Switzerland and Britain. *Address:* 4 Knighton House, 102 Manor Way, Blackheath, London SE3 9AN.

HOLLIDAY, S. J., R.B.A.; sculptor, ceramicist and muralist; *b* Portsmouth, 10 Apr., 1955. *Studied:* Portsmouth Polytechnic & E.C.A.T. *Exhib:* Kutani Decorative Ceramics Exhib., Japan; Keramion, Keramik 25th Exhib., Frechen, Germany; European Ceramics, Germany; Westerwald Kreis Exhib., Germany; solo exhib. "Look and Like", Bern, Switzerland. *Work in collections:* Kaufmann Collection, Bern, Switzerland. *Signs work:* "SJH" (sculpture) and "S J Holliday" (mural). *Address:* 11 The Down, Trowbridge, Wilts. BA14 8QN. *Email:* usram@freenet.co.uk

HOLLOWAY, Douglas Raymond, A.R.I.B.A., R.W.A.; architect retd.; artist in water-colour, pen and wash; *b* W. Hampstead, London, 25 Aug., 1923. *m* Marjorie Cynthia. three *s. Educ:* Haberdashers Aske's Hampstead, and Reading School. *Studied:* Royal West of England Academy School of Architecture. *Exhib:* R.Cam.A., various mixed and one-man exhbns. in England and Wales. *Work in collections:* R.W.A. *Signs work:* "D.R. Holloway." *Address:* Longton Forge, 61 Liverpool Rd., Longton Preston, Lancs. PR4 5HA.

HOLLOWAY, Edgar, R.E., R.B.A.; painter, etcher; *b* 6 May, 1914. *m* (1) Daisy Hawkins. three *s.* one *d.*; (2) Jennifer Boxall. *Educ:* Doncaster Grammar School (1926-28). *Studied:* Slade School (1934). *Exhib:* one-man shows, London (1931, 1934, 1979, 1993), Brighton and Oxford (1980), Doncaster (1982), Edinburgh (1986), Abergavenny (1989), U.S.A. (1972, 1973, 1974, 1975); retrospective Ashmolean (1991-92). Touring exhbn. at 80 (1994) National Library of Wales, Hove A.G., Abbot Hall A.G., Kendal, Graves A.G., Sheffield and London (Cork St.). Wolsely Fine Art W11 (1996). 'Edgar Holloway & Friends', touring exhbn. Prints from the Thirties (1999-2001), 'Capel-y-Ffin to Ditchling', watercolours, Ditchling, Nat. Library of Wales, Brecon, Tunbridge Wells, Bankside Gallery, S.E.1 (2001-2002). *Work in collections:* Official purchases: B.M., V. & A., Ashmolean, Fitzwilliam, New York Public Library, Birmingham City A.G., Scottish Gallery of Modern Art, Scottish National Portrait Gallery, National Museum of Wales, National Library of Wales, University College of Wales, Oxford and Cambridge colleges. *Publications:* book launch, "The Etchings & Engravings of Edgar Holloway" (Scolar Press), 1996; work repro.: Dictionary of 20th Century British Art (1991), British Printmakers, 1855-1955. *Signs work:* "Edgar Holloway." *Address:* Woodbarton, Ditchling Common, Sussex BN6 8TP.

HOLLOWAY, Laura Ellen, S.W.A. (1994), Post.Dip.F.A. (R.A.), S.B.A. (1999); painter in water-colour and tempera; *b* Worcester, 1960. *Educ:* Worcester Girls' Grammar School. *Studied:* Glos. College of Art (1978-82), R.A. Schools (1985-88, Norman Blamey, R.A., Jane Dowling). *Exhib:* solo shows at Mason-Watts Fine Art, Warwick (1992); mixed shows in London and Birmingham. *Publications:* Medici Soc. Ltd. (greetings cards). *Signs work:* "L.H." *Address:* 404 Wyld's Lane, Worcester WR5 1EF.

HOLMES, Walter, artist/illustrator in oil, acrylic, pastel and water-colour; *b* Wallsend on Tyne, 21 Aug., 1936. *m* Helen. two *s. Studied:* Newcastle University Evening School, Beamish College, Durham. *Exhib:* Gulbenkian Gallery Newcastle,

Queen's Hall Hexham, Moya Bucknall Solihull, Solent Gallery Lymington, Mall Galleries London, The Art Connection, Eton. *Work in collections:* Price Waterhouse, Coopers, Bank of England. *Commissions:* Swan Hunter Shipbuilders, N.E. Shipbuilders, Northern Sinfonia, Marie Curie. *Publications:* calendars for English Estates, Newcastle Breweries, Laing Calendar Competition 2nd prize, greetings cards for Oakwood Cards and 4C, Quarto Publishing plc. *Address:* Eastern Way Farm, 4 Queensway, Darras Hall, Ponteland, Newcastle NE20 9RZ.

HOLTAM, Brenda, R.W.S., B.F.A.Hons. (1983), R.A. Schools Postgraduate Dip. (1986); painter in oil, gouache, water-colour; figurative painter of still life, interiors, portraits and landscape; Tutor in water-colour; *b* Whiteway, Glos., 2 Oct., 1960. *m* Howard Vie. two *s.* one *d. Educ:* Stroud Girls' High School. *Studied:* Glos. College of Art and Design (1979, T. Murphy), Falmouth School of Art (1980-83, F. Hewlett), R.A. Schools (1983-86, Peter Greenham, C.B.E., R.A.). *Exhib:* R.A. Summer Exhbn., N.E.A.C. Annual Exhbn., R.P., R.W.S. Members Exhbn. Bankside Gallery; two-person exhbn. Cadogan Contemporary (1994). Elected A.R.W.S. (1987), elected to full membership (1992). *Signs work:* "Brenda Holtam" or "Holtam." *Address:* 39 Ashburnham Rd., Richmond, Surrey TW10 7NJ.

HOMES, Ronald Thomas John, D.F.C., F.C.S.D.; artist/industrial designer; winner of R.S.A. industrial design bursaries (1948-49); Central School of Arts and Crafts Dip for Industrial Design; Associate, Guild of Aviation Artists; *b* London, 3 Oct., 1922. *m* Ione Winifred Amelia. two *d. Educ:* Willesden Technical College. *Studied:* Central School of Arts and Crafts. *Signs work:* see appendix. *Address:* 69 Linden Pk., Shaftesbury, Dorset SP7 8RN.

HOMESHAW, Arthur Howard, R.W.A., A.T.D.; artist in water-colour, pastel, colour prints; *b* 27 Nov., 1933. *m* Wendy Bennetto. two *s. Educ:* Chipping Sodbury Grammar School. *Studied:* West of England College of Art (1951-54, 1956-57). *Exhib:* R.A., R.W.A., R.E.; one-man show, Patricia Wells Gallery (1981), Exeter Arts Centre (1992). *Work in collections:* R.W.A., Bristol Educ. Com., Devon County Hall, Stoke-on-Trent Educ. Com., B.P. International, South Glamorgan Educ. Authority, Walsall Educ. Authority, Avon Schools Service, Exeter University. *Signs work:* "HOMESHAW." *Address:* Arwen, Alexandra Rd., Crediton, Devon EX17 2DH.

HONE, David, P.P.R.H.A., Hon. R.A., H.R.S.A.; portrait and landscape painter in oil; *b* Dublin, 1928. *m* Rosemary D'Arcy. two *s.* one *d. Educ:* St. Columba's College; Univ. College, Dublin. *Studied:* National College of Art, Dublin (1947-50), under J. Keating and M. MacGonical. *Work in collections:* Portrait Collection, National Gallery, Dublin, Cork Municipal Gallery. *Signs work:* "D. Hone." *Address:* 25 Lr. Baggot St., Dublin, 2.

HOOKE, Robert Lowe, Jr., sculptor of figures, wild animals and birds in bronze; art dealer; investment adviser; Managing Director: Research Vision Ltd; *b* Canton, Ohio, 12 Sept., 1942. *Educ:* Bowdoin College, Brunswick, Maine (B.A.); Columbia University, N.Y. (M.B.A.). *Studied:* N.Y. School of Visual Arts (1973-75, Herbert Kallem). *Exhib:* one-man shows: London, Geneva, Basel, Baden-Baden, Sydney, Johannesburg, Cape Town; group shows: Paris, Zurich, Amsterdam, San Francisco. *Work in collections:* Compton Acres, Poole; Oppenheimer Collection, S. Africa. *Commissions:* various private, Bowdoin College (U.S.A). *Clubs:* Hurlingham, Royal

Ocean Racing, Ascot Park Polo, Annabels. *Signs work:* see appendix. *Address:* 61 Holland Pk., London W11.

HOPE HENDERSON, Eleanora, D.A., S.S.A., Post Grad. Scholarship, then Highest Travelling Award (1940); artist in oil; *b* Edinburgh, 1917. *m* David Hope Henderson. two *s. Educ:* St. George's, Edinburgh. *Studied:* Edinburgh College of Art under Sir William Gillies, Sir W. MacTaggart, Westwater, Maxwell. *Exhib:* S.S.A., R.S.A., R.A., R.P., Dumfries Art Soc., McGill Duncan Gallery and Harbour Gallery, Kircudbrightshire; one-man shows: Chelsea A.G., Kirkcudbright Harbour Gallery, Woodstock Gallery, Pittenweem A.G. Fife, Coach House, Norwich, Ropner Gallery, London. *Work in collections:* including Germany, Portugal, Canada and America. Work in private collections. *Signs work:* "E. Hope Henderson", before marriage "BORRIE." *Address:* Achie, New Galloway, Kircudbrightshire DG7 3SB.

HOPE-KING, Christopher Stewart, A.R.M.S. (1993), R.M.S. (1998), S.M. (1991), H.S. (1994), Gold Bowl Hon. mention R.M.S. (1993), Fairman Members subject miniature award (1995); miniaturist in water-colour and acrylics (paints unique duck miniatures) of still life and landscapes; *b* Leeds, Yorks., 16 Sept., 1951. *Educ:* Homefield School, Bournemouth. *Studied:* with grandfather, Hector King. *Exhib:* R.A. Summer Show, Mall Galleries, British Painters, Westminster Gallery (R.M.S.); many one-man shows. *Publications:* included in: Techniques of Miniature Painting (Sue Burton, Batsford), R.M.S. One Hundred Years (Suzanne Lucas, Lucas Art). *Signs work:* "H.K." *Address:* Staddle Cottage, 1 Mill St., Corfe Mullen, Wimborne Minster, Dorset BH21 3RQ.

HOPKINS, Clyde David F., B.F.A.(Hons.) (1969); painter; Professor; Head of Painting, Chelsea College of Art; *b* Sussex, 24 Sept., 1946. *m* Marilyn Hallam. *Educ:* Barrow-in-Furness, Cumbria. *Studied:* University of Reading (Claude Rogers, Terry Frost). *Exhib:* Serpentine Gallery, Hayward Gallery, Ikon Gallery, Francis Graham-Dixon Gallery, Joan Prats Gallery, N.Y.C., U.S.A. etc. *Work in collections:* A.C.G.B., etc. Studio: London and Hastings. *Clubs:* Chelsea Arts. *Signs work:* "Clyde Hopkins." *Address:* 55 Marischal Rd., London SE13 5LE.

HOPKINS, Peter, painter, teacher, writer; Dean of Men, Emeritus, New York-Phoenix School of Design; Lecturer, Art Students League of New York; grantee, American Academy and National Institute of Arts and Letters (1950); Correspondent, Christian Science Monitor; *b* New York, 1911. *m* Gertrude L. Beach. *Educ:* Art Students League of New York. *Work in collections:* Museum of City of New York. *Publications:* work repro.: The American Heritage History of the 1920s and 1930s; The USA, a History in Art; The Complete Book of Painting Techniques; National Museum of American Art, Smithsonian Institution. *Address:* 36 Horatio St., New York, N.Y. 10014, U.S.A.

HORE, Richard Peter Paul, A.R.C.A. (Painting 1959, Mural Painting, Silver Medal 1960), N.D.D. (Illustration 1955), F.R.S.A. (1964), R.C.A. (Cambrian 1978); painter in gouache and mixed media; *b* Clacton-on-Sea, 1935. *m* Janice Hart. one *s.* one *d. Educ:* Colebaynes High School, Clacton. *Studied:* Colchester School of Art (1951-55, John O'Connor), R.C.A. (1956-60, Carel Weight, Ruskin Spear, Leonard Rosoman). *Exhib:* R.A.; Welsh Arts Council; W.A.G., Birkenhead; Mostyn, Llandudno; Mall Galleries; Oriel, Theatre Clwyd; Muse, Philadelphia, U.S.A. *Work* *in collections:* R.C.A., Cheshire County and Chester City Councils, Dept. of the Environment, various private collections. *Commissions:* Chester City Council. *Publications:* Picturesque Chester by Peter Boughton (illustrations). *Signs work:* "RICHARD HORE." *Address:* 65 Parkgate Rd., Chester CH1 4AQ.

HORNER, Michael Julian Alistair, U.A. (1999); painter in soft pastel; Council mem. U.A.; *b* Amersham, Bucks., 1 July, 1975. *Educ:* Egerton-Rothesay School, Berkhamsted. *Exhib:* U.A. Annual, East Grinstead Art Show, Lingfield Surrey, Penhurst Place Kent, Cowden Kent. *Signs work:* "MICHAEL HORNER." *Address:* The Rectory, Church St., Cowden, Edenbridge, Kent TN8 7JE.

HOROVITZ, Isabel, B.A.(Hons.) (1978), Dip.Cons. (1982); paintings conservator; freelance conservator and consultant to Royal Academy of Arts; *b* London, 1957. *m* Jonathan Blake. three *s.* one *d. Educ:* St. Paul's Girls' School. *Studied:* University of London (History of Art), Courtauld Inst. of Art (Conservation of Easel Paintings). *Exhib:* Conservator for R.A. Loans Exhbns. *Publications:* contributions to various catalogues and conservation literature. Special interest in history, techniques and conservation of paintings on copper supports. *Address:* The Painting Conservation Studio, Belgravia Workshops, 157-163 Marlborough Rd., London N19 4NP.

HORSBRUGH, Patrick B., A.A. (Hons.) Dipl., C.D. Dipl. (London), F.A.I.A., A.C.I.P., A.P.A., F.R.G.S., F.R.S.A., F.B.I.S.; Hon. Mem. A.S.L.A.; Hon. Mem. A.S.I.D.; architect; town planner and artist in ink, water-colour, gouache, etc.; Visiting Prof. of Architecture, Universities of Nebraska and Texas; organized Texas Conference on Our Environmental Crisis (1966) and International Conference, Cities in Context; Cultural, Ethical and Natural (1968); Founder and Chairman of the Board, Environic Foundation International Inc; V.P., Channel Tunnel Assoc. (1975-91); Co-chairman, Earthday (International); Prof. Emeritus of Architecture, Former Director of Graduate Programme in Environic Design, University of Notre Dame; Member, American Association for the Advancement of Science (2000); *b* Belfast, 21 June, 1920. *Educ:* Canford and A.A., School of Architecture, Dept. of Civic Design, University of London. *Studied:* Accademia Britannica, Rome (1950), Bernard Webb Scholarship. *Work in collections:* Capesthorne Hall, Cheshire. *Publications:* 'High Buildings in the United Kingdom' (1954), Texas Conference on our Environmental Crisis, (edited 1965). *Clubs:* Cosmos Club, Washington D.C. *Signs work:* "Patrick Horsbrugh." *Address:* 916 St. Vincent St., South Bend, Indiana 46617-1443, U.S.A. *Email:* environics@aol.com

HORTON, Antony Brian, landscape painter in oil and gouache; *b* Birmingham, 21 Aug., 1933. *m* Sheila Horton. three *d. Educ:* Shrewsbury School and Exeter College, Oxford. *Studied:* Cheltenham College of Art (R.S. Dent). *Exhib:* R.A., David Messum Gallery, and local exhbns. *Clubs:* M.C.C. *Signs work:* "A. B. Horton" or "Brian Horton." *Address:* The Old Rectory, Taplow, Bucks. SL6 0ET.

HORTON, James Victor, M.A. (R.C.A.) (1974), R.B.A. (1979); artist in oil, water-colour and pastel; *b* London, 24 July, 1948. *m* Rosalind. two *s. Studied:* Sir John Cass School of Art (1964-66), City & Guilds Art School (1966-70), Royal College of Art (1971-74) . *Exhib:* widely in Britain and abroad, ten-one man shows. *Work in collections:* Girton, Newnham and Trinity Colleges, Cambridge. *Commissions:* extensive portraits. *Publications:* seven books on painting and drawing; numerous articles for art magazines. Taught in art schools and summer schools in Britain and abroad. *Address:* 11 Victoria Rd., Cambridge CB4 3BW.

HORWITZ, Angela Joan, N.S. (1982), R.A.S. (1983); Associated Academician (Arts) Accademia Internationale Greci-Marino, Italy (1999); sculptress in stone, bronze, painter in oil and pastel; steward, A.G.B.I. (1985-86); Member Beaux-Arts, Cannes, South of France (1996-2001); *b* London, 14 Oct., 1934. two *s.* one *d. Educ:* Colet Court Girls' School, Rosemead Wales, Lycée Français de Londres. *Studied:* Marylebone Inst. (1978), Sir John Cass College (1983), Hampstead Inst. (1990-92). *Exhib:* Grand Palais, Paris (1985, 1986), R.B.A., N.S., S.W.A. (Mall Galleries), Civic Centre, Southend, City of London Polytechnic, Whitechapel, (1985), S.E.F.A.S., Guildhall, Ridley Soc., City of Westminster Arts Council, Alpine Gallery, Smiths Gallery Covent Gdn., Wintershall Gallery, nr. Guildford, The Orangery, Holland Pk. W8, Hyde Park Gallery (Winchester Cathedral, 1993), Beaux Arts, South of France (1997), Salon International du Livre et de la Presse à Genèva (1997), Miramar Hotel Beaux Arts (1998) Association Beaux Arts (1999), Antrum Gallery Bayswater (2000), Carre D'Or Gallery, Paris (2000), Association des Beaux-Arts, Cannes (2000). *Work in collections:* Sculpture in stone for Winchester Cathedral; Well Woman Centre, The United Elizabeth Garrett Anderson Hospital for Women, London; Zurich Switzerland private collection, London private collection, France. Listed Who's Who in International Art, Dictionary of International Biography. *Clubs:* Lansdown. *Signs work:* "A.H." or "Angela Horwitz" see appendix. *Address:* 6 Wellington House, Aylmer Drive, Stanmore, Middx. HA7 3ES.

HOSKINS, Stephen, M.A. (1981), A.R.E. (1989), R.E. (1995), B.A. (Hons.) (1977); printmaker in silkscreen, lithography and drawing; *b* Eastleigh, Hants., 31 Aug., 1955. *m* Barbara Munns. one *s. Educ:* Barton Peveril Grammar School. *Studied:* W. Surrey College of Art and Design (1974-77), R.C.A. (1978-81). *Exhib:* R.A., R.E., mixed exhbns. worldwide. *Work in collections:* V. & A., Tate Gallery. *Publications:* A pop-up book (5^3), Water-Based Screenprinting, A&C Black (2001). *Signs work:* "S. Hoskins." *Address:* 62 Monk Rd., Bishopston, Bristol BS7 8NE. *Email:* Stephen.Hoskins@vwe.ac.uk S.Hoskins@netgates.co.uk

HOUSE, Ceri Charles, artist in oil; gilding restorer; *b* London, 20 Mar., 1963. partner: Amanda Wainwright. one *d. Educ:* St. Christopher School, Herts. *Studied:* with father, Gordon House. *Exhib:* N.P.G., B.P. Portrait awards (1994), R.A. Summer Shows (1992, 1993, 1995). *Commissions:* Numerous private commissions. *Publications:* R.A. Illustrated catalogue (1993). *Signs work:* see appendix. *Address:* 109 Highbury New Park, London N5 2HG.

HOUSTON, Ian, A.R.C.M., President, East Anglian Group of Marine Artists, Member of Guild of Norwich Painters, Associate, French Soc. of Artists, F.R.S.A.; Silver medal, Paris Salon, Gold medal, F.N.C.F.; artist in gouache, oil and water-colour; *b* Gravesend, Kent, 24 Sept., 1934. *m* Angela Adams. one *s.* one *d. Educ:* St. Lawrence College, R.C.M., London. *Exhib:* over 60 one-man shows U.K., U.S.A., Australia. *Work in collections:* U.K. and abroad. Official artist to "Young Endeavour"; limited edition prints, 15 signed by Premiers Thatcher and Hawke, sold to raise funds for project, 3 times solo judge for Camberwell Rotary Art Show (Melbourne, Australia). *Signs work:* "Ian Houston." *Address:* c/o Portland Gallery, 9

Bury St., St. James's, London SW1Y 6AB.

HOWARD, Ian, M.A. (Hons.), R.S.A.; artist in acrylic, oil, mixed media, print-making; Prof. and Principal of Edinburgh College of Art; *b* Aberdeen, 1952. *m* Ruth D'Arcy. two *d. Educ:* Aberdeen Grammar School. *Studied:* Edinburgh University, Edinburgh College of Art (1970-76). *Exhib:* numerous one-man and group exhbns. *Work in collections:* S.A.C., A.C.G.B., Aberdeen A.G., Dundee A.G., Hunterian A.G., City Art Centre Edinburgh, Contemporary Art Soc., Warwick University Art Centre. *Publications:* Ian Howard, Painting, Prints and Related Works (Third Eye Centre Glasgow/Peacock Printmakers, Aberdeen), Heretical Diagrams (Peacock Printmakers, Aberdeen 1997). *Signs work:* "I.H." or "Ian Howard." *Address:* c/o Edinburgh College of Art, Lauriston Place, Edinburgh EH3 9DF.

HOWARD, Ken, R.A. (1992), Hon. R.B.S.A. (1991), R.W.S. (1983), R.W.A. (1981), R.O.I. (1965), N.E.A.C. (1961); Appointed Official Artist Northern Ireland Imperial War Museum (1973-78); President, New English Art Club (1998); *b* London, 26 Dec., 1932. *m* Dora Bertolutti. *Educ:* Kilburn Grammar School. *Studied:* Hornsey College of Art (1949-53), Royal College of Art (1955-58). *Exhib:* New Grafton Gallery (1971, 74, 76, 78, 81, 83, 86, 88, 90, 93, 95), Manya Igel Fine Art (1987-97). *Publications:* 'The Paintings of Ken Howard' (David & Charles, 1992), 'Ken Howard, A Personal View' (David & Charles, 1998). *Clubs:* Chelsea Arts. *Signs work:* "Ken Howard." *Address:* 8 South Bolton Gdns., London SW5 0DH.

HOWARD-JONES, Ray, Fine Art Dip. University of London, Slade Scholar; 1st class Hons. History of Art; painter, poet, mosaics; *b* Lambourne, Berks., 30 May, 1903. *Educ:* London Garden School. *Studied:* Slade School, University of London (1921) under Henry Tonks, Wilson Steer, Elliot-Smith (anatomy), Tancred Borenius (History of Art); Postgraduate School of Painting, Arbroath. *Work in collections:* National Museum of Wales, National Museum of S. Australia, Glynn Vivian Gallery Swansea, Contemporary Art Society, Museum and Gallery Glasgow, Imperial War Museum, Arts Council for Wales, M. of W., City Art Galleries of Aberdeen, Glasgow, Burton-on-Trent, large mosaic exterior Thomson House Cardiff and Grange Church Edinburgh. *Publications:* various contributions to The Anglo-Welsh Review. Heart of The Rock Poems 1973-92 (Rocket Press, 1993). *Signs work:* "Ray." *Address:* Studio House, 29 Ashchurch Park Villas, London W12. *Second Address:* St. Martin's Haven, Marloes, W. Wales. Agents: Rocket Gallery, 13 Old Burlington St., London W1X 1LA.

HOWARTH, Constance M., B. of E. intermed. (1946), N.D.D. (1947); winner, Vogue Cotton Design Competition 1960 designer hand painted dresses; *b* Rochdale, Lancs., 14 May, 1927. *Educ:* Merchant Taylors' School for Girls, Crosby; Bolton School. *Studied:* Manchester Regional College of Art. *Exhib:* Rayon Design Centre, London. *Work in collections:* V. & A. New works: mixed media abstract mirror windows, ornamental flower trees, decoupage furniture. *Signs work:* "Constance Howarth" and "Constanza." *Address:* 2 Upper Wimpole St., London W1G 6LD.

HOWELL, David, self taught painter in water-colour, oil and pastel; *b* Markyate, 14 July, 1939. *m* Jenny. one *d. Educ:* St. Albans Grammar. *Exhib:* R.S.M.A., S.Eq.A., many mixed and one-man shows in London and the U.K., Middle East, U.S.A., Hong Kong and Japan. *Work in collections:* United Biscuits, Provident Financial,

Charterhouse Bank, Albank Alsaudi Alhollandi, H.R.H. Sultan Qaboos of Oman. *Publications:* City of the Red Sea (Scorpion, 1985). *Signs work:* "David Howell." *Address:* Court Barn, High Ham, Langport, Som. TA10 9DF. *Email:* davidhowell@cwcom.net

HOWSON, Peter, D.Litt., Honoris Causa, Strathclyde University, B.A. (Hons.), G.S.A.; painter in oil; *b* London, 27 Mar., 1958. *m* Terry (divorced). one *d. Educ:* Prestwick Academy. *Studied:* Glasgow School of Art (1975-77 and 1979-81, Alexander Moffat). *Exhib:* widely in Europe and the U.S.A. *Work in collections:* Tate Gallery, V. & A., Metropolitan Museum of Modern Art, N.Y., M.O.M.A., N.Y., Oslo Museum of Modern Art, Glasgow Art Galleries. *Commissions:* Official war artist, Bosnia (1993). *Publications:* many publications. *Clubs:* The Glasgow Art Club, The Caledonian Club. *Signs work:* "Howson." *Address:* c/o Flowers East, 199-205 Richmond Rd., London E8 3NY.

HOYLAND, John, R.A. (1983), artist; Professor of Painting, R.A. (1999); *b* Sheffield, 12 Oct., 1934. divorced. one *s. Studied:* Sheffield College of Art (1951-56, Eric Jones), R.A. Schools (1956-60). *Exhib:* numerous exhbns. including one-man: Royal Academy of Art (1999), Marlborough New London Gallery, Whitechapel A.G., Waddington Galleries, Robert Elkon Gallery N.Y., Nicholas Wilder Gallery, Los Angeles, Andre Emmerich Gallery, N.Y., Austin Desmond Fine Art, London, also in Canada, Germany, Italy, Portugal, Australia, Sweden; two-man shows: Brazil, London, U.S.A.; group shows: R.A. Summer Exhbns., R.B.A. Gallery, John Moores, Liverpool, Ulster Museum, Belfast, Edinburgh Open, Chichester Natural Art, Barbican A.G., Francis Graham-Dixon Gallery, R.C.A., McLellan Galleries, Glasgow, etc. *Publications:* John Hoyland (1990). Television and radio broadcasts. *Signs work:* see appendix. *Address:* 41 Charterhouse Sq., London EC1M 6EA.

HUBBARD, Deirdre, B.A. (Summa cum Laude) (1957), A.R.B.S. (1981), F.R.B.S. (1999); Sohier prize (1957), Wapping Arts Trust 'Art and Work' (1987); sculptor in bronze; *b* N.Y.C., 1935. *m* Dr. John L. Wilson. three *s.* one *d. Educ:* Radcliffe College, Harvard University (1953-57). *Studied:* painting with Andreas Feininger (1954-55), Chelsea Art School (1957-61, sculpture with Willi Soukop and Bernard Meadows), Studio Elisabeth Frink (1963-65). *Exhib:* R.A., R.B.S., R.W.A., Essex University, Bristol Cathedral, Camden Arts Centre, National Museum of Wales, Bloomsbury Gallery, Barbican Centre, etc. *Work in collections:* Royal Free Hospital, Inst. of Educ. London University, Towner A.G., Usher Gallery, Lincoln, Bryn Mawr College, Bryn Mawr, P.A., U.S.A., Radcliffe Inst., Cambridge, Mass., U.S.A. *Signs work:* "D.H." *Address:* 101 Woodsford Sq., London W14 8DT.

HUCKVALE, Iris, R.M.S., S.B.A., S.M.; miniaturist in oil on wood and polymin; Silver Gilt Medalist R.H.S., Certificate of Botanical Merit S.B.A.; *b* Northampton, 27 Sept., 1930. *m* John Huckvale, O.B.E. one *s.* one *d. Educ:* Northampton Grammar School for Girls. *Studied:* Nottinghamshire Evening Inst., but mainly self taught. *Exhib:* R.A., R.M.S., S.W.A., S.B.A., S.WL.A., Medici, S.M., M.A.S.-F., M.A.S.-N.J.; one-man show, Coach House Gallery, Guernsey. *Publications:* work repro.: Medici greetings cards. *Signs work:* see appendix. *Address:* 4 Heath Green, Heath and Reach, Leighton Buzzard, Beds. LU7 0AB.

HUDSON, Eleanor Erlund, A.R.C.A. (1937); graphic artist, portraitist, figure subjects, water-colourist; costume designer, artistic adviser to former Brooking Ballet School of Marylebone; *b* S. Devon. *Educ:* Wentworth Hall, Surrey. *Studied:* R.C.A. (School of Engraving) under Professors Malcolm Osborne, R.A., R. S. Austin, R.A., Drawing Prize, 1936, Continuation Schol. (4th year) 1938, Travelling Schol. 1939. *Exhib:* R.A., Bankside Gallery, London and international. *Work in collections:* Boston Pub. Library, Fogg Museum, U.S.A., Imperial War Museum, London, War Artist's Advisory Comm. *Signs work:* "ERLUND HUDSON." *Address:* 6 Hammersmith Terr., London W6 9TS; and Meadow House, Old Bosham, Sussex PO18 8JF.

HUDSON, Thomas Roger Jackson, Teachers' Cert. (1951), Teachers' Dip. (1961), M.Coll.H. (1962), Mem. A.W.G.; self employed furniture maker and designer; *b* Bicester, Oxon., 24 July, 1929. *m* Ragnhild Ann Schanche. one *s.* two *d. Educ:* Bicester Grammar School. *Studied:* Oxford School of Art (1947), Shoreditch College (1949-51), Camberwell School of Art (1961), Goldsmiths' College (1962). *Publications:* Wheelstocks and Ploughshares (Tabb House, 1988), Gunstocks and Dovetails (Tabb House, 2000). *Signs work:* carved into all major works (cow), see appendix. *Address:* The Barn, 117 High St., Odell, Bedford MK43 7AS.

HUGHES, Christine, Dip.Ed. (1968), Dip.F.A. (1994); painter in oil, printmaker, teacher; *b* London, 20 Feb., 1946. *m* D.C.C. Hughes. two *d. Educ:* Homerton College, Cambridge. *Studied:* Southampton College of Art (1989-94). *Exhib:* many mixed and solo shows in S.W. England and Cumbria. *Signs work:* "C. Hughes" or H within a C. *Address:* Linmoor Cottage, Highwood, Ringwood, Hants. BH24 3LE. *Website:* www.users.waitrose.com/~cchughes *Email:* cchughes@waitrose.com

HUGHES, Jim, D.A. (1954), S.G.A. (1972), A.T.C. (1955), T.G.C. (1956); artist/designer/calligrapher; former teacher of art and design, Adult Educ. Dept., University of Glasgow; *b* Glasgow, 1934. *Educ:* Ayr Academy. *Studied:* Glasgow School of Art (1950-54); Jordanhill College (1954-56) under Sam Black, D.A., R.S.W. *Work in collections:* Glasgow Art Gallery, other work in private collections throughout the world. *Publications:* Graphic Design for S.S.A.E. and Ayr Adult Educ. Booklets. Work featured in B.B.C. TV series "The Quest"(1989). *Signs work:* initials on work, name on back, see appendix. *Address:* 32 Macadam Pl., Ayr KA8 0BZ.

HUGHES, Kevin Michael, B.Sc. (1969), A.L.A. (1971), R.I. (2000); artist in water-colour, oil and pastel; *b* Colwyn Bay, 4 Sept., 1947. *m* Kate Skillington. one *s.* one *d. Educ:* Reading University, Polytechnic of N. London. *Exhib:* R.I., N.E.A.C., Discerning Eye, R.W.S., R.W.A.; one-man shows: many since 1980 including three at the Alresford Gallery. *Work in collections:* Wessex Collection, Longleat. Prize for Best Water-colour in 1997 Discerning Eye Exhbn., Benton/Humphries Prize in 1999 Discerning Eye. *Clubs:* Royal Institute of Painters in Watercolour. *Signs work:* "Kevin Hughes." *Address:* Edge Hill, Helscott Rd., Marhamchurch, Bude, Cornwall EX23 0JE.

HUGHES, Robert, H.S. (1986), R.M.S. (1989), S.Lm. (1993); artist in oil and gouache; *b* London, 5 Nov., 1934. *Exhib:* R.M.S., H.S., S.Lm. *Publications:* co-author of How to Paint Miniatures. *Signs work:* "Robert Hughes" or "R. HUGHES." *Address:* Easton Barns, Easton Royal, Pewsey, Wilts. SN9 5LY.

HULME, Ursula, M.B.E., N.R.D., F.P.S., B.A.A.T.; artist in oil, water-colour, pastel, felt pen and collage; textile designer; art therapist; Founder of 'Conquest' The Society for Art for the Physically Handicapped (1979); *b* Cottbus, 5 Mar., 1917. *m* Ernest Hulme. *Educ:* Berlin. *Studied:* Reimann School, Berlin under Maria May. *Exhib:* one-man shows: Woodstock Gallery, London (3), Talent Store, London (1990); group shows: F.P.S., Mall Galleries, Loggia Gallery, Nimes, France, Leatherhead Theatre, Richmond Art Group, etc. *Publications:* entries in London Diary in book form from 1970-72. ABC book, and three videos on Conquest Teaching Methods produced 1988-96; book, Guide for Group Leaders. *Signs work:* "Ursula Hulme." *Address:* 3 Beverley Cl., E. Ewell, Epsom, Surrey KT17 3HB.

HUMPHREYS, David, B.A. (Dunelm); Thomas Penman Scholar and State Scholar at Durham University (1958-62); painter and constructor; *b* London, 27 Oct., 1937. *Educ:* Battersea Grammar School and King's College, Durham University (Dept. of Fine Art). Elected mem. Royal Cam. Academy (1994). *Work in collections:* Arts Council, Leicester, Newcastle, London Universities, Ministry of the Environment, Bishop Otter College, Ashridge College, Nuffield Foundation, I.C.I., J. Sainsbury, Shell, American Express Bank (London and N.Y.), P. & O., Financial Times, H.M. the Queen Mother, H.R.H. the Prince of Wales, National Library of Wales. *Publications:* 'A Painter's Notes'(1999). *Signs work:* "Humphreys." *Address:* Maudlin Hill House, Sopers La., Steyning, W. Sussex BN44 3PU.

HUMPHREYS, Ian, B.A. (Hons.); painter; *b* St.Albans, 30 July, 1956. *Studied:* Berkshire College of Art and Design (1972-74), Exeter College of Art and Design (1976-79). *Exhib:* Bath Art Fair, Beaux Arts, Bohun Gallery, Budapest Art Fair, Contemporary Art Soc. Dublin Art Fair, Eton A.G., Exe Gallery, Glyndebourne Opera House, Houldsworth Fine Art, Hunting Art Prize (97, 98 {prize winner} 99, 01), London Art Fair, John Martin of London, London Group, Long & Ryle, Lynne Strover Gallery, Penwith Gallery, Raw Gallery, N.Y., Redfern Gallery, Ridley Art Soc., R.A. Summer Show (1997-99), Solomon, Dublin, Southampton Museum, Stockholm Art Fair. *Work in collections:* Burmah Castrol, British Rail Board, Coopers & Lybrand, James Capel, Reading Museum and A.G., Tate & Lyle Sweeteners. *Address:* Freke's Cottage, Cunnamore Point, Church Cross, Skibbereen, Co. Cork, Eire.

HUMPHREYS, John Howard, R.O.I.(1977, resigned 1992; elected Hon. Senior Mem. 1994); artist in oil; Press Officer, R.O.I. (1978-81); Winner of Stanley Grimm Prize (1981); *b* Bethlehem, S. Africa, 20 Oct., 1929. *m* Mary Mack. one *s*. one *d*. *Educ:* King Edward VII School, Johannesburg. *Studied:* Heatherley's Art School (Iain Macnab), and privately under Stanley Grimm (1953-57). *Exhib:* R.A., R.O.I., R.B.A., R.I., R.S.M.A., S.WL.A., Paris Salon, etc.; also in the U.S.A. and Japan. *Signs work:* "J. Humphreys." *Address:* 94 Kings Ave., Greenford, Middx. UB6 9DD.

HUNDLEBY, A. R., designer-packaging and graphics, artist in water-colour; *b* 1923. *m* Marion Smallshaw, A.T.D. one *s*. two *d*. *Studied:* Lincoln and Leicester. *Signs work:* "HUNDLEBY." *Address:* 35 Kelross Rd., London N5 2QS; and Hill House, Binham, Norfolk NR21 0DW.

HUNKIN, Sally Elizabeth, artist in etching, water-colour and oils, gardener; Organizer and teacher at Kew Studio; *b* Herts. 1924. *m* Oliver Hunkin, ex-TV producer. one *s.* one *d. Educ:* St. Mary's Calne; Dartford College. *Studied:* Richmond Adult College. *Exhib:* solo shows locally and in Suffolk and Manchester; group shows include Royal Soc. of Artist Printmakers, and R.A. *Work in collections:* St. Thomas's Hospital. *Commissions:* two friezes for St. Thomas's Hospital. *Publications:* work repro.: posters and cards for Kew Gdns. *Signs work:* "Sally Hunkin." *Address:* 31 Leyborne Pk. Kew, Richmond, Surrey TW9 3HB.

HUNT, Emma, B.A. (Hons.), M.A.; Sen. lecturer, Art and Design History; Course Director, Cultural Studies, Bournemouth and Poole College of Art; adviser to Southern Arts; *b* Bideford, 27 July, 1962. *m* Martin. two *s. Educ:* Leicester and Birmingham. *Exhib:* curated small college exhbns. and at Russell-Cotes Museum. *Publications:* contributor to design history articles. *Signs work:* "E.F. Hunt." *Address:* Shepherds Cottage, Henfords Marsh, Warminster, Wilts. BA12 9PA.

HUNT, Geoffrey William, R.S.M.A. (1989); marine artist and illustrator in oil, acrylic, water-colour; *b* Twickenham, 11 Mar., 1948. *m* Vivienne Anne Hobbs. two *s. Educ:* Hampton Grammar School. *Studied:* Kingston School of Art (1966-67), Epsom School of Art (1967-70). *Exhib:* R.S.M.A. since 1977; Solent Gallery, Lymington; Mystic Seaport Gallery, U.S.A.; also Oliver Swann Gallery SW3. *Work in collections:* Royal Naval Museum, Portsmouth; R.N. Submarine Museum, Gosport; H.M.S. Neptune, Faslane; Ferens A.G., Hull; Mariner's Museum, Newport News, U.S.A. *Publications:* illustrated many book covers including complete series of Patrick O'Brian's Aubrey/Maturin novels; 'The Tall Ship in Art' (Blandford, 1998). *Signs work:* "Geoff Hunt." *Address:* 66 South Park Rd., Wimbledon, London SW19 8SZ.

HUNT, Georgina, D.F.A. (Lond.); painter; mem. London Group; *b* Reading, Berks. 15 June, 1922. one *s.* one *d. Educ:* Bishop Otter College, Chichester. *Studied:* Slade School of Fine Art (1945-50, William Coldstream), Hunter College, New York (Research 1970-71). *Exhib:* solo shows: Drian Gallery, London (1967, 1969), Gallery 66, London (1968), Pientrantonio Gallery, N.Y. (1970), Hunter College, N.Y. (1971), Space Studios, London (1974, 1975, 1976 (Major Award), 1978), Hounslow Civic Centre (1981), Camden Arts Centre, London (1982), Camden Studios (1984, 1986, 1988, 1990, 1992, 1994, 1996), Chelsea Arts Club (1993), Barbican Conference Suite - London Group (1998-99), Winchester Cathedral (1999); group shows: 1966: Blackheath Art Soc.; 1967: City A.G. Bath, City A.G. Bristol, University of Surrey; 1968: Goethe Inst., Norway, Drian Gallery, Blackheath Art Soc.; 1969: F.B.A. Gallery London, Bexley Arts Festival, Galerie Jules Salles, Nimes, France; 1972: Hunter College, N.Y.; 1980: Hounslow Civic Centre; 1981: Royal Academy, Camden Arts Centre; 1982: F.B.A. Mall Galleries, London; London Group Exhbns: Barbican, London (1992, 1994, 1996), Maltings Gallery, Farnham (1999), Lethaby Gallery, London (2000), The Walk Gallery, London (2001); Chelsea Arts Club; 1993: represented Great Britain in Osaka International Triennale, Japan (Award); 1994: United Abstract Artists Mall Galleries, Stephen Bartley Gallery, London, Chelsea Town Hall (Chelsea Arts Club), United House, Islington; Atrium Gallery, London (1995, 1996); 1996: represented Great Britain in Florence International Biennale, Logos Gallery, London (Prize in National Art Competition), The Arts Club, London, New English Arts Club London; 1999: Hunting Prize Exhbn. London and Bath, London Group, Farnham, represented Great Britain in Florence

International Biennale (Award); 2000: Hunting Prize Exhbn. London, 2001: Hunting Prize Exhbn, London. *Work in collections:* public and private: U.K., U.S.A. and Japan. *Publications:* Herbert Read, Letter to the Artist, 1967; Studio International, June 1967; Arts Review, June 1967, Sept. 1968, July 1969 (Marina Vaizey); South London Press, July 1967; Bergens Tidende, Norway, Jan. 1968; South East London Mercury, Apr. 1968; Apollo, July 1969 (James Burr); Studio International, May 1974; Hampstead and Highgate Express, June 1975; Art Monthly, July 1978 (Guy Brett); Art International, July 1978 (Malcolm Quantrill); Hounslow Art Review, May 1981 (Roger Jones); City Limits, Nov. 1981 (Guy Brett); Clement Greenberg, Letter to the Artist, 1989; 20th Century Painters and Sculptors, 1991 (Frances Spalding and Judith Collins); University College London Alumni Magazine, 1994; Financial Times, Dec. 1995 (William Packer); Press Release, 1996 (William Packer); Whistler Magazine, 1997; Winsor & Newton: Acrylic Colour, 1997; The Dictionary of Artists in Britain since 1945 (David Bickman) 1998; Camden Journal, Apr. 1999; Meridian Line Magazine, June 2001. Awards: 1976: Major award, Greater London Arts Assoc.; 1993: 21st Century prize, Osaka International Triennale; 1997: Prizewinner in Logos Gallery National Art Competition, London; 1999: Lorenzo Magnifico Prize, Florence International Biennale. Work can be seen on: www. thelondon-group.com and at the Artist's studio: 2 Camden Studios, Camden St., London NW1 0LG. *Clubs:* Chelsea Arts. *Signs work:* "Georgina Hunt." *Address:* 11b Burton St., Bloomsbury, London WC1H 9AQ.

HUNT, Susie, B.A. (Hons.) Fine Art (1980); artist in water-colour and mixed media, and framer; *b* Fareham, Hants., 18 Dec., 1957. *m* Anthony Paul Duley. one *s.* one *d. Studied:* Canterbury College of Art (1976-77), West Surrey College of Art (1977-80). *Exhib:* many mixed and solo shows in London and Home Counties, R.W.S. Awards (1997), R.I. Open (1997, 1998, 2000), Aberdeen Artists (2001). *Commissions:* Wallace City Training. *Clubs:* Reigate Soc. of Artists. *Signs work:* "Susie Hunt." *Address:* Mill Farm, Aquhythie, Invervrie, Aberdeenshire AB51 5NY.

HUNTER, Alexis, Dip.F.A. (Hons. in Painting and Art History), Teaching Dip. (1971), Computer Systems Design (2000), Multimedia (2001); painter, filmaker, photographer, writer; *b* Auckland, N.Z., 1948. *m* Baxter Mitchell, B.I.M. *Educ:* Auckland Girls Grammar. *Studied:* Elam, Auckland (Colin McCahon), Central Graphics Academy, London, (Rhys Webber). *Exhib:* Hayward Gallery, Whitechapel, Serpentine, Musee d'Art Moderne, Auckland City Gallery, etc. *Work in collections:* Imperial War Museum, Scottish National Gallery, Zurich Museum, Te Papa National Gallery N.Z., etc. *Publications:* Essays on feminism and art, theory and psycho-analysis published. N.Z. Film Archive, M.A.K.E. *Clubs:* London Arts Cafe, N.Z. Artists Assoc., S.L.A.G.S. (Soho). *Signs work:* "Alexis Hunter." *Address:* 13 Hillier Ho., 46 Camden Sq., London NW1 9XA. *Website:* www.alexishunter.net www.axis-artists.org.uk *Email:* hunteralexis@hotmail.com

HUNTER, Christa, S.W.A.; sculptor in terracotta, porcelain, bronze resin, bronze; *b* Stuttgart, Germany, 18 Aug., 1943. *m* Robin Hunter. one *s.* one *d. Educ:* Ostheim Stuttgart. *Studied:* Sculpture course by Major Tugwell/Judy Cousins (1983). *Exhib:* regularly with art socs. in Berks. and Surrey, annually S.W.A. at Westminster Hall, Medici Gallery (1994), annually Surrey Sculpture Soc. Sculpture Trail Wisley, Chelsea Flower Show (1998), Sausmarez Manor Guernsey (1999,

2000, 2001), Belvoir Castle (2001), Druidstone Wildlife Park (2001), Saville Gardens (2001), Kingsmead Gallery Great Bookham and Century Gallery Datchet. *Work in collections:* Holme Grange A.G., Wokingham, Harrods Picture Gallery, The Gallery Virginia Water. *Commissions:* several private Foundry Bronze. *Signs work:* "C.H." or "Christa." *Address:* 26 Cavendish Meads, Sunninghill, Berks. SL5 9TD.

HUNTER, Henry Hay, U.A. (2000); artist in oil; *b* Beal, Northumberland, 4 Mar., 1934. *m* Kathleen. *Educ:* St. Peter's School, York. *Studied:* Buckinghamshire College (1995-97). *Exhib:* R.D.S. (1949, 1950), U.A. (1994-2000). *Work in collections:* private: England, S. Africa, N.Z., Germany. *Publications:* Fine art prints. *Clubs:* Southwold Art Circle, Beccles Soc. of Artists. *Signs work:* "Henry Hay Hunter" or monogram of three H's. *Address:* 11 Fairmile Close, Worlingham, Beccles, Suffolk NR34 7RN.

HUNTER, Janet Claire (Jan), S.W.A. (1997), F.E.T.C. (1987), Dip. in Advertising and Design (1965); artist in water-colour, dry and acrylic media; lecturer in drawing and water-colour, Surrey Adult and Continuing Educ. Service; *b* Reading, Berks., 2 July, 1946. *m* Ian Hunter. one *s.* one *d. Studied:* Berks. College of Art, Reading (1962-65). *Exhib:* S.W.A, Guildford Art Soc., Woking Soc. of Arts and other local venues *Clubs:* Chertsey Arts. *Signs work:* "Jan Hunter" and date. *Address:* Greatwood, 209 Brox Rd., Ottershaw, Surrey KT16 0RD.

HUNTINGTON-WHITELEY, James, B.A. (Hons.) Manchester (1985); Modern British and Contemporary Art Exhbn. Organizer; *b* 14 Aug., 1963. *m* Magdalen Evans. one *s.* one *d. Address:* 38 Hopefield Ave., London NW6 6LH.

HUNTLEY, Dennis, N.D.D. (1951), A.T.C. (1952), F.R.B.S. (1970); sculptor in bronze, plastics, stone, wood; educationalist; Head of Sir John Cass School of Art; Governor, City of London Polytechnic; *b* Weybridge, Surrey, 6 Dec., 1929. *m* Gillian Huntley. one *s.* two *d. Educ:* Wallington Grammar School for Boys. *Studied:* Wimbledon School of Art (1947-51), Gerald Cooper (principal), London University Senior House (1951-52). *Exhib:* several galleries. *Work in collections:* 6 major works (4 stone, 2 wood) Guildford Cathedral, 7ft. metal fig. for L.C.C. Patronage of the Arts Scheme at Henry Thornton School, Clapham, life-sized wood fig. of Anne Boleyn, London Borough of Sutton, awarded Sir Otto Beit medal in open competition for best work, 1967, in United Kingdom and Commonwealth. *Publications:* book reviews for L.C.C. and Studio Vista and various articles for Education. *Clubs:* Arts, Chelsea Arts. *Signs work:* "D. W. Huntley" on prints and drawings, "D. HUNTLEY" on sculptured work. *Address:* The Studio, 30 Hawthorn Rd., Sutton, Surrey.

HUNTLY, Moira Gay, A.T.C. (Lond.), P.S. (1978), R.I. (1981), R.S.M.A. (1985), R.W.A. (1995); artist in acrylic, oil, pastel, water-colour; Vice-Pres., Pastel Soc.; *b* Motherwell, Scotland, 7 Nov., 1932. *m* Ian E. Buchanan Huntly. one *s.* two *d. Educ:* Wirral County School for Girls, Harrow Weald County School. *Studied:* Harrow School of Art (1948-53), Hornsey College of Art (1953-54). *Exhib:* Young Contemporaries, R.O.I., N.E.A.C., R.I., P.S., R.W.A., R.S.M.A., F.C.A., Pastellistes de France; numerous solo shows, Mystic Maritime Museum, U.S.A. *Work in collections:* Ferens A.G., Hull (R.S.M.A. Coll.). *Commissions:* for international companies. *Publications:* 'Imaginative Still Life', 'Painting and Drawing Boats', 'Painting in Mixed Media', 'Learn to Paint Gouache', 'Learn to Paint Mixed Media', 'The Artist's Drawing Book', 'Learn to Draw Boats'. *Signs work:* "Moira Huntly." *Address:* "Alpha", Collin Cl., Willersey, Broadway, Worcs. WR12 7PP.

HURDLE, Robert Henry, painter; senior lecturer until 1981, Faculty of Fine Art, Bristol Polytechnic; *b* London, 1918. two *s.* one *d. Studied:* Richmond School of Art (1935-37), Camberwell School of Arts and Crafts (1946-48) under Coldstream. *Exhib:* one-man shows, University College of Swansea (1973); Albany Gallery, Cardiff (1974); New Ashgate Gallery, Farnham (1977); City A.G., Bristol (1977); Pao Sui Loong Galleries, Hong Kong Arts Centre (1978); King St. Gallery, Bristol (1982); Farnham Maltings (1983); Pelter/Sands Gallery (1988); Cleveland Bridge Gallery, Bath (1989); Retrospective exhbn. R.W.A. (1995), Robert Hurdle at 80, R.W.A. (1998). *Work in collections:* University College, Swansea; R.W.A.; City Art Gallery, Bristol; Bath University; Hong Kong Arts Centre; Wessex Collection, Longleat and various private collections. *Signs work:* signature or seal. *Address:* 14 Oxford St., Kingsdown, Bristol BS2 8HH.

HURN, J. Bruce, A.T.D. (1946), F.R.S.A. (1966), P.P.R.B.S.A. (President 1973); painter/designer in oils, acrylic, gouache; teacher, lecturer, examiner and H.M.I. (Art and Design); *b* Spalding, 18 May, 1926. *m* June. one *s.* three *d. Educ:* King Edward's, Camp Hill, B'ham. *Studied:* Birmingham College of Art (1942-46). *Exhib:* numerous exbhns. including one-man: Universities of B'ham, Aston, Keele, Oxford, Leicester, Kent, Brunel; Compendium Gallery, B'ham and London; group shows: municipal art galleries, R.B.S.A., R.A. *Work in collections:* private, colleges, universities, schools, industrial collections in U.K., private collections in U.S.A., Europe, Australia, N.Z. *Commissions:* T.C. Kemp Memorial Crucifixion, B'ham. *Publications:* Practical Biology (Dodds and Hurn). *Signs work:* see appendix. *Address:* Hawks Wing Harkwood Lane Chislehurst, Kent. BR7 5PW.

HURST, Stephanie, Dip. in illustration (1974), R.A. Dip. of advanced studies - B.A. equivalent (1984); painter in oil on board with gesso ground; *b* Wimborne, Dorset, 3 July, 1952. *Educ:* Convent of the Sacred Heart, Weymouth. *Studied:* Bournemouth and Poole College of Art (1970-71), Hornsey College of Art (1971-74), Byam Shaw School of Painting and Drawing (1976-77), R.A. Schools (1981-84). *Exhib:* R.A., Royal Festival Hall, Spirit of London Competition (awarded prize), South Bank Show, Camden Arts Centre - Druce Competition (awarded prize), Bath Contemporary Arts Fair, Elgin Fine Art, Bath, Jonathan Poole Gallery, London. *Signs work:* "S. Hurst" on back of painting. *Address:* 3 King's Ave., Muswell Hill, London N10 1PA.

HUSON, Cedric Nigel, Dip.A.D. Painting/Printmaking (1973), R.A. Schools Post. Grad. Cert. (1978); painter; *b* Salop, 1 June, 1951. *m* Kitta Potgieter. *Educ:* Marlborough Grammar School, Wilts. *Studied:* Salisbury School of Art (1967-68), Swindon School of Art (1968-69), Winchester School of Art (1970-73), Royal Academy Schools (1975-78). *Exhib:* group shows: Piccadilly Gallery (1987-99), Lamont Gallery (1994-95), R.A. Summer Exhbn. (1988-94, 1997-98, 2000), Hunting Group Open (1989, 1990, 1994), Cleveland Bridge Gallery, Bath (1990), The London Group Open (1990, 1992, 1993), The Discerning Eye (1992, 1995, 1999, 2000), National Trust Centenary Exhbn. (1995), Everard Read Gallery, Cape Town

(1997), Southwark Festival (1997), Everard Read Gallery, Johannesburg (1998). *Clubs:* Reynolds. *Signs work:* "Cedric Huson." *Address:* 11b Camberwell Green, London SE5 7AF. *Email:* cedric@kitked.demon.co.uk

HUSSEY, Audrey, graduate in Fine Art and Theatre Design, West Country Award (1972); F.P.S. (2000), N.A.P.A. (2001); painter in acrylic, theatre design, scenic painting; *b* Kent, 24 Nov., 1945. *Educ:* Maidstone Grammar School, Kent. *Studied:* St. Martin's and Chelsea, London, under Michael Browne, and Alan Cooper (1968-1972). *Exhib:* various galleries in London and elsewhere. *Work in collections:* private. *Commissions:* nationally and internationally. *Signs work:* "Hussey." *Address:* 25 Brent Lea, Brentford, Middx. TW8 8JD. *Email:* acavstudio@talk21.com

HUSSEY, John Denis, F.R.B.S., R.W.A.; sculptor of assemblages; principal lecturer, Director of Studies, Fine Art Dept., Bristol Polytechnic (retd. 1983); *b* Slough, 26 Apr., 1928. *m* Katherine Hiller. two *s. Educ:* Slough Grammar School. *Studied:* Goldsmiths' College (1946-49); research Diploma in Fine Art/Sculpture at Bristol Polytechnic (1969-70). *Exhib:* R.A., R.W.A. *Work in collections:* Tallboys, R.W.A. *Signs work:* "J. Hussey." *Address:* Sanderling, 21 Colne View, Point Clear, St. Osyth, Essex CO16 8LA.

HUSTON, John I., History's Most Significant Artist; in oil, egg tempera, pastels, sculptures, landscapes, figures, abstracts, upon canvas, wood, masonite; writer; scientist; artist; planner; Finance Innovate: Supreme Super Soul of the Universe and yourself are ready for the coming millennium(s) with the perfect calendar; *b* Saltillo, Penna., U.S.A., 22 Jan., 1915. *Educ:* Juniata College and University Special Studies; completely self-trained in art via Commercial Art, Industrial Art, Cinema Art, Fine Art. Work in private collection. *Publications:* The Art of Life as permanent. *Clubs:* International Directory of Arts, Who's Who World Wide. *Signs work:* see appendix. *Address:* 1215 Jackson Tower, Harrisburg, Pa. 17102.

HUTCHESON, Tom, D.A. (1949) R.G.I.; artist in mixed media; principal art lecturer; *b* Uddingston, Lanarkshire, 13 Nov., 1922. *m* Mary McKay. *Educ:* Motherwell. *Studied:* Glasgow School of Art (1941-49) under Hugh Adam Crawford, R.S.A., David Donaldson, R.S.A. *Exhib:* R.S.A., G.I., R.S.W., Moores; three one-man shows, Arts Council. *Work in collections:* H.M. the Queen, H.R.H. Prince Philip, Arts Council, Liverpool and Glasgow Universities, Scottish Educ. Authorities, Leeds Local Authority, Paisley A.G., Glasgow A.G., Kelvingrove, British Embassy Collection. *Clubs:* Art, Glasgow. *Signs work:* "Tom Hutcheson." *Address:* 73 Woodend Dr., Glasgow G13.

HUXLEY, Paul, R.A., Cert.R.A.S. (1960), Harkness Fellow (1965-67); painter in acrylic, oil, printmaking; Professor Emeritus, Royal College of Art; *b* London, 12 May, 1938. *m* Susie Allen. two *s. Studied:* Harrow School of Art (1951-56, Edward Middleditch), R.A. Schools (1956-60, Peter Greenham). *Exhib:* numerous solo exhibitions, represented Britain internationally in Biennales and many major group shows. *Work in collections:* Tate Gallery, V. & A., plus various museums in the U.K., Europe, U.S.A. and Australia. *Publications:* Exhibition Road - Painters at the Royal College of Art. *Clubs:* Chelsea Arts. *Signs work:* "Paul Huxley" in bottom margin of prints and small works on paper, verso on larger works on canvas. *Address:* 2 Dalling Rd., London W6 0JB.

HYATT, Derek James, A.R.C.A.; painter/writer; *b* Ilkley, Wharfedale, Yorkshire, 1931. *Educ:* Ilkley Grammar School. *Studied:* Leeds College of Art (1948-52), Royal College of Art (1954-58). *Exhib:* London one-man shows include Austin Desmond/Gillian Jason Gallery (1987, 1989), Waddington Galleries (1974, 1977), New Art Centre (1960, 1961, 1963, 1966); group shows include John Moores, Cincinnati Bienniale, Arts Council Travelling Exhbns., and two Critics Choice exhbns., Meetings on the Moor (70 paintings), retrospective Bradford Art Gallery (Spring 2001). *Work in collections:* Museum of Modern Art, New York, Contemporary Art Soc., Carlisle, Hull, Bradford, Sheffield and Bootle Art Galleries and Nuffield Foundation. *Publications:* Edited ARK (1958); articles Modern Painters (1987-99); Alphabet Stone (1997). Video "Circles on the Dark Rock" Mappin Gallery, Sheffield (1995). *Address:* Rectory Farm House, Collingham, Wetherby LS22 5AS.

HYMAN, Timothy, painter in oil, pastel and drawing, writer; *b* Hove, 17 Apr., 1946. *m* Judith Ravenscroft. *Educ:* Charterhouse. *Studied:* Slade (1963-67). *Exhib:* Narrative Paintings (I.C.A., Arnolfini, 1979), Blond Fine Art (1981, 1983, 1985), Austin Desmond (1990), Manchester Castlefield (1993), Gallery Chemould (Bombay 1994), Flowers East (1994), Austin Desmond (2000). *Work in collections:* Arts Council, British Museum, Museum of London, Contemporary Art Soc., Government Art Collection, Los Angeles County Museum, etc. *Commissions:* Lincoln Cathedral, Sandown Racecourse. *Publications:* Bonnard (Thames & Hudson, 1998); Bhupen Khakhar (Bombay, 1999); Carnivalesque (2000); Spencer (Tate 2001). *Signs work:* "Timothy Hyman," "T.H." or "HYMAN." *Address:* 62 Myddelton Sq., London EC1R 1XX.

I

I'ANSON, Charles, F.R.B.S. (1967), F.R.S.A. (1956), R.B.S.A. (1966), M.Sc. (1980), O.L.J. (1981); sculptor in steel; *b* Birmingham, 1924. *Studied:* Birmingham College of Art. *Exhib:* F.P.S., London Group, Commonwealth Inst., New Vision and Alwyn Galleries, London; "Sculpture 1971", York, etc. *Work in collections:* Cardiff Civic Centre, Midlands Art Centre, Bristol and Leeds Universities, Trinity and All Saint's College, Leeds; Birmingham, Bradford and Wakefield A.G.'s, R.D.C., Walmley, Bristol, Minard Castle, Inveraray, Argyll; R.A. Gamecock Barracks, Nuneaton; Dore School, Sheffield; Windmill Hill School, Stourport; St. Paul's Church, Doncaster; St. Winefrid's Church, Wibsey, Bradford, etc. *Signs work:* "I'AN-SON." *Address:* April Cottage, 9 Mount Pleasant Rd., Morcott, Oakham, Rutland LE15 9DP.

I'ANSON, Mari, U.A. (1999); artist and tutor in watercolour, oil and acrylic; *b* London, 5 Sept., 1932. one *s.* one *d. Studied:* School of Science and Art, Weston-super-Mare (1947-1950), (now Technical College); St. Martins and Chelsea, London. *Exhib:* over 30 solo shows - St. John's , Smith Sq., Lauderdale House N6, Burgh House NW3, Foyles Art Gallery, Bridgwater Art Centre, Bull Gallery, Barnet; mixed shows - Central Hall, Westminster, Swiss Cottage Library NW3, Alexandra

Palace, etc. *Commissions:* Octavia Hill Museum, Wisbech, London Borough of Barnet, The Finchley Society, Isgara Restaurant N3. Artist in residence at Bangkok Patana International School four times (1994-1997), Deansbrook Junior School, Mill Hill (1999 - 2001). *Signs work:* "Mari I'Anson" or "Mari." *Address:* The Studio, 5 The Grove, Finchley, London N3 1QN. *Website:* www.mari-artist.com

IBBETT, Vera, R.M.S. (1990), Grenfell Silver medal-botanical illus. (1970), F.S.S.I. (1970), R.H.S. Lindley Silver Gilt Medal (2000); painter and illustrator in oil, water-colour, pastel; *b* Kingswood, Surrey, 30 May, 1929. *m* Raymon Strank. *Educ:* Banstead Central School. *Studied:* City and Guilds of London Art School (1955-63, Innes Fripp, John Nash, R.A.), Reigate School of Art (1968-70). *Exhib:* R.A., R.M.S., S.W.A., R.H.S. *Work in collections:* R.A.F. Chapel of Remembrance, Biggin Hill. *Publications:* Flowers in Heraldry (Alcuin Soc. Vancouver B.C., 1977), La Revue Moderne (1960), European Illustrators (1974-75). *Signs work:* "Vera Ibbett" and see appendix. *Address:* 89 Chipstead La., Lower Kingswood, Surrey KT20 6RD.

IBRAM, Peter B., artist in oil and water-colour; *b* Manchester, 15 Dec., 1937. *m* Carole. one *d. Educ:* Burnage Grammar School. *Exhib:* mixed shows: Chenil Gallery London, Leslie Jones Gallery St. Albans, Stockport A.G., Oldham A.G., Buxton A.G., Ross Gallery Manchester, Salon des Independentes Paris; one-man show: Portico Gallery Manchester, Museum Modern Art Wales. *Work in collections:* private: America, France, Spain, Italy, Germany, Portugal, Switzerland, Portico Gallery, Art in Hospital, Wales. *Commissions:* Portico Library, Art Gallery, Manchester; Paintings in Hospitals, Wales. *Signs work:* "Norman Benjamin." *Address:* c/o 24 Prestwich Hills, Prestwich, Manchester M25 9PY.

INCHBALD, Michael, F.C.S.D.; Architectural and Interior Designer; twice married.; one *s.* one *d. Studied:* A.A. *Commissions:* include: 1st Class Lounge "Queen's Room" and Library on Q.E.2, and other Liners, Ballroom, banquet areas and suites at Berkeley Hotel, Post House, Heathrow, Claridges' Penthouse, Savoy's River Room and Lincoln Room, Crown Commissioners' H.Q., Carlton House Terr., Banks of America and Trust Hanover, Player's and Plessey's H.Q. Offices, Justerini and Brooks, Boardroom etc. for Imperial Group, Law Society's Lady's Annexe, Dunhill's, Jermyn Street and Worldwide; Residential: Duc de la Rochefoucauld, Duke of St. Albans, Marquess of Ailesbury, Earls of Dartmouth and St. Aldwyn, Countess of Lonsdale, etc. *Address:* 10 Milner St., London SW3 2PU.

IND, John William Charles, F.R.S.A.; painter in oil, water-colour, sculptor in wood, designer, illustrator; *b* London, 1927. *m* Greta Bambridge-Butler. two *s. Educ:* London and Cambridge. *Studied:* in London and Oslo. *Exhib:* Royal Exchange, Madden Gallery, Barle Gallery, Harrods Gallery; one-man shows: Halford House, Newton Gallery, Kensington Ct. Gdns. *Work in collections:* Harris Bank, Barclays Bank, Hays Allan, Ind Coope, Texaco London, Taylor Hall; private collections in France, Germany, U.S.A., Britain, N.Z., Scandinavia. *Commissions:* 1994, painting commissioned for 105th Regiment, Royal Artillery. *Clubs:* Somerset Society of Artists. *Signs work:* "Ind." *Address:* Atelier; Aller, Som. TA10 0QN.

INGHAM, Alan Everard, Lt. Cdr. R.N. retd. (1965), A.R.I.C.S. (1971); painter of landscapes in water-colour; *b* Skipton, 25 Oct., 1932. *m* Rose. one *d. Educ:*

Ermysteds Grammar School, Skipton; Royal Naval College, Dartmouth. *Exhib:* R.I., R.B.A., Harrods, Selfridges, etc.; one-man shows: Granby Gallery, Bakewell (1980-90), Halcyon Gallery Birmingham, etc. *Work in collections:* Rolls Royce Motor Co., Rank Hovis McDougall, Ind Coope, etc. *Publications:* Under a Water-colour Sky (Washington Green, 1996); work repro.: work published extensively as fine art editions, calendars, etc. *Signs work:* "ALAN INGHAM" mid horizontal strokes of letters extended. *Address:* Farthings, The Cherry Orchard, Staverton Village, Cheltenham GL51 0TR. *Email:* aeingham@lineone.net

INGHAM, George Bryan, A.R.C.A.; artist; *b* Preston, Lancs., 11 June, 1936. *Studied:* St. Martin's School of Art; R.C.A.; British Academy, Rome. *Exhib:* Francis Graham-Dixon Gallery, London. *Work in collections:* V. & A., Ashmolean, Kunsthalle, Bremen, etc. *Publications:* illustrated catalogue Anthony Gross. *Clubs:* Blue Anchor, Helston. *Signs work:* "B. Ingham" on back. *Address:* c/o Francis Graham-Dixon Gallery, 17-18 Gt. Sutton St., London EC1V 0DN.

INGLIS, John, R.S.W. (1984), F.S.A. (Scot.) (1983), D.A. (1974), Post. Grad. (1975), Travelling scholar (1976); painter in water-colour, oil, lecturer; *b* Glasgow, 27 July, 1953. *m* Heather Binnie. two *s*. two *d. Educ:* Hillhead High School, Glasgow. *Studied:* Gray's School of Art, Aberdeen (1970-75, William Littlejohn, Frances Walker, Alexander Fraser). *Exhib:* R.S.A., R.S.W., R.G.I.F.A., S.S.A., Compass Gallery, Glasgow, Edinburgh, Leeds, Venice, Rome, Canada, Regensberg, Illinois, U.S.A., London. *Work in collections:* Aberdeen A.G., University of Aberdeen, Argyll and Bute Educ. Authority, Scottish Television, Inst. for Cancer Research, Aberdeen Hospitals Collection, Clackmannan District Council Collection, Royal Scottish Academy, Clackmannan College, Scottish Arts Club, Heartland College, Ill., McLean County Arts Centre, Bloomington, Ill., Scottish Arts Club, Edinburgh. *Signs work:* "John Inglis" usually on back. *Address:* 84 Burnhead Rd., Larbert, Stirlingshire FK5 4BD.

INSALL, Donald W., C.B.E., F.S.A., R.W.A., F.R.I.B.A., F.R.T.P.I., S.P.Dip. (Hons); architect; Founder-Director, Donald Insall Assocs. (Architects and Planning Consultants), London SW1; Founder-Commissioner, English Heritage, Visiting Prof. University of Leuven, Service as Consultant to City of Chester in National Pilot City Conservation Programme, Architects for post-fire Restoration of Windsor Castle; awarded the Medal of Honour (2000) by Europa Nostra; *b* Clifton, Bristol, 1926. *m* Amy Elizabeth. two *s*. one *d. Exhib:* R.A., R.W.A., R.I.B.A. *Publications:* The Care of Old Buildings Today (Architectural Press); 'Architectural Conservation' Encyclopaedia Britannica; Conservation in Action. Consultancy has received over 90 Conservation and Craftmanship Awards/Commendations. *Clubs:* Athenaeum. *Address:* 73 Kew Green, Richmond, Surrey TW9 3AH.

INWARD, Jean Mary, M.B.B.S., M.R.C. Psych., A.U.A.; painter in oil and acrylic; psychiatrist; *b* Bromley, Kent, 9 Sep., 1939. two *s*. one *d. Educ:* Guy's Hospital, London University. *Studied:* evening classes. *Exhib:* U.A, S.W.A. *Work in collections:* private. *Commissions:* private. *Clubs:* U.A. *Signs work:* "Jeanie." *Address:* 5 Birchdale, Gerrards Cross, Bucks. SL9 7JA.

IRENE: see FRÖHLICH-WIENER, Irene.

IRVIN, Albert, R.A.; painter, printmaker; Mem. London Group; *b* London, 21 Aug., 1922. *m* Beatrice Nicolson. two *d*. *Educ:* Holloway County. *Studied:* Northampton and Goldsmiths' School of Art; taught at Goldsmiths' College School of Art (1962-82). *Exhib:* one-man shows at Gimpel Fils, London, and at galleries throughout Europe and internationally. *Work in collections:* include: Tate Gallery; Arts Council; British Council; other British and international public collections. *Commissions:* Homerton Hospital, Hackney (1987), Chelsea and Westminster Hospital (1995). *Publications:* Albert Irvin Life to Painting by Paul Moorhouse (Lund Humphries, 1998). *Clubs:* Chelsea Arts. *Signs work:* see appendix. *Address:* c/o Gimpel Fils, 30 Davies St., London W1Y 1LG.

IRVIN, Magnus, Dip.F.A. (1973), R.E. (1993); artist in woodcuts, etching, mixed media, shoes made from bananas and ectoplasm sculptures; *b* London, 6 Dec., 1952; partner: Chris Stubbs. one *s*. *Educ:* Creighton School, Muswell Hill. *Studied:* Hornsey Art College (1970), N.E.L.P. Walthamstow (1971-74). *Exhib:* Redfern Gallery, Whitechapel Open, Cleveland Drawing Biennale, Bradford Print Biennale, Ljubljana Print Biennale, Xylon Museum Germany, Art Cologne. *Work in collections:* A.C.G.B., B.M., V. & A., International Centre of Graphic Art, Slovenia. *Commissions:* Tunstall Western Bypass, Stoke on Trent - concrete aeroplanes to bypass environment. *Publications:* 'Bananas at War' and 'Chairs and Fleas' - Limited Edition Books, Daily Twit newspaper (for 25 yrs). *Signs work:* "M. Irvin." *Address:* 11 Lancaster Rd., London N4 4PJ. *Email:* magno@obe.abelgratis.com

IRWIN, Flavia, R.A.; artist in acrylic on canvas, mixed media on paper, tutor; Head of Decorative Arts Dept., City & Guilds of London Art School; *b* London. *m* Roger de Grey, K.C.V.O., P.P.R.A. two *s*. one *d*. *Educ:* Hawnes School, Ampthill. *Studied:* Chelsea School of Art (Graham Sutherland, Henry Moore, Robert Medley). *Exhib:* Zwemmers, London Group, R.A., Ansdell Gallery, Gallery 10 Grosvenor St., Phoenix Gallery, Curwen Gallery, Peoples Theatre, Newcastle, Arts Council Gallery, Bury St. Edmunds, Taranman Gallery. *Work in collections:* Carlyle A.G., D.O.E., Chelsea & Westminster Hospital. *Commissions:* Daniel Galvin, George St., London. Dealers: Studio 3, 75 Leonard St., London EC2A 4QS. *Signs work:* "Flavia Irwin" back of canvas, signed in pencil on drawings. *Address:* Camer Street, Meopham, Kent DA13 0XR.

IRWIN, Gwyther, painter: oil paint, water-colour and acrylics; *b* Cornwall, 7 May, 1931. *m* Elizabeth. two *s*. one *d*. *Educ:* Bryanston. *Studied:* Central School of Art (1952-55). *Exhib:* Redfern Gallery, London. *Work in collections:* Tate Gallery, British Council, Arts Council, Contemporary Art Soc., Arts Council of N. Ireland, Calouste Gulbenkian, City Art Gallery, Bradford, Albright-Knox, Yale University, Peggy Guggenheim, Peter Stuyvesant. *Signs work:* "Gwyther Irwin." Studios in London and Cornwall. *Address:* 21 Hillbury Rd., London SW17.

ISITT, Samuel John, B.A., M.B.I.M., M.Inst.M., I.P.M.; painter in oil; retired educationist/actor; *b* Newport, Mon., 9 Feb., 1935. *m* Ann (divorced). three *s*. one *d*. *Educ:* Newport High School. *Studied:* Chelsea . *Exhib:* recent exhibs. at Mary Magdalene's Church, Oxford (1997), Oxford Playhouse (1998), Oxford University Club (2001). *Work in collections:* Drs. T. and K. Isitt, Vera Chock and others. *Commissions:* Shirley Knowlton, Hayley Bentley, Sue Walker and others.

Publications: Mary's Song , and The 7 Deadly Sins (both illustrated by Tania Holland). *Clubs:* Newport R.F.C., Royal Overseas League, Writers' Guild, U.K. Calligraphers, member of Equity (TV and Films). *Signs work:* "John Isitt." *Address:* 24 Jericho St., Oxford OX2 6BU. *Email:* taff.isitt@hot-toast.com

ISOM, Graham Michael, N.D.D. (1965), A.A.E.A., S.E.A.; equestrian artist in oils; *b* Kent, 5 Mar., 1945. married. one *s.* two *d. Educ:* Dartford. *Studied:* Ravensbourne College of Art (1961-65). *Exhib:* worldwide. *Work in collections:* Kentucky Derby Museum of Racing, Churchill Downs, Louisville. *Commissions:* Household Cavalry (Officer's Mess); large calendar of 12 paintings, 12 Limited Edition equestrian beakers, several Christmas cards. *Publications:* Racing in Art/ John Fairley; numerous Limited Edition Prints. *Signs work:* see appendix. *Address:* 5 Neville Pk., Baltonsborough, Som. BA6 8PY.

IZZARD, Pam, artist in oil, acrylic and mixed media, etching, water-colour and pastel; *b* London, 1926. *m* (1) K.Lucas. two *s.* one *d.* (decd). (2) Jack Millar. *Educ:* Old Palace School, Croydon, Torquay Grammar School. *Studied:* Beckenham, Bromley and Croydon Schools of Art. *Exhib:* R.A., London Group, N.E.A.C., R.B.A., Curwen Gallery, Linton Ct. Gallery, Ashgate Galleries and various provincial galleries. One-man shows, Ashgate Galleries, Abbot Hall, Kendal, Duncan Campbell Gallery, London, Chelsea & Westminster Hospital. Has taught in art schools in London and the provinces. *Work in collections:* local authorities and private collections in this country and abroad. *Signs work:* "P. Izzard" or "Izzard" on back. *Address:* 10 Overhill Rd., Dulwich, London SE22 0PH.

J

JACK, Kenneth William David, A.M. (1987), M.B.E. (1982), R.W.S. (1977), A.W.I. (1955), A.T.D. (1951), A.T.C. (1949); landscape and architectural painter and printmaker in water-colour, acrylic, pastel and most drawing media, lithography, silk-screen; Patron, Water-colour Soc. of Victoria; *b* Melbourne, 5 Oct., 1924. *m* Betty Dyer. one *s.* two *d. Educ:* Melbourne High School. *Studied:* R.M.I.T. (John Rowell, Harold Freedman). *Exhib:* R.W.S. twice annually at Bankside Gallery, Leicester Galleries (1975), Fine Art Soc. London, A.W.I.; many one-man shows in Australia. *Work in collections:* National Galleries of all Australian capital cities; 500 works Australian War Memorial, Canberra. *Publications:* many folios and large reproductions of paintings; Kenneth Jack by L. Klepac; Kenneth Jack-World War II Paintings and Drawings (text, K.J.); Kenneth Jack by D. Dundas; The Flinders Ranges (paintings, text by K.J.); The Melbourne Book by C. Turnbull; Charm of Hobart by C. Turnbull; Queensland Paintings and Drawings, Kenneth Jack (Boolarong Press, Brisbane, 1994); Kenneth Jack - Printmaker (Beagle Press, Sydney, 1998). *Clubs:* W.S. of V. *Signs work:* "Kenneth Jack." *Address:* P.O.Box 1, Doreen 3754, Victoria, Australia.

JACKLIN, Bill, M.A., R.C.A. (1967), A.R.A. (1989); artist in oil paintings, etching; *b* London, 1 Jan., 1943. *m* (1) Lesley (divorced). (2) Janet Russo. one *d. Educ:* Walthamstow Technical College. *Studied:* Walthamstow School of Art (1962-64), R.C.A. (1964-67, Carel Weight). *Exhib:* one-man shows, London: Nigel Greenwood (1970, 1971, 1975), Hester Van Royen Gallery (1973, 1977), Marlborough Fine Art (1980, 1983, 1988, 1992, 1995, 1997, 2000), Marlborough Gallery, N.Y. (1985, 1987, 1990, 1997, 1999, 2002), M.O.M.A. Oxford (1992), Museo de Pobo Galego, Santiago de Compostela, Spain (1993), University of Northumbria, Newcastle upon Tyne, England (1994), Hong Kong Arts Centre, Hong Kong (1995), l'Ecole de Londres Museé, Maillol, Paris (1998-99); numerous group shows. *Work in collections:* A.C.G.B., British Council, Government Arts Coll., Metropolitan Museum, N.Y., M.O.M.A. (N.Y.), Museum Boymans-Van Beuningen, Rotterdam, Tampa Museum, Museum of N.S.W., V. & A., Tate Gallery, Yale Centre for British Art. *Commissions:* by Bank of England for painting (Futures Market, London) (1988); Ivy Restaurant in London for painting (The Ivy) (1988); De Beers for Tapestry - "The Park" - 6ft. x 17ft. (1993); Metropolitan Washington Airport Authority for new terminal at Washington National Airport (1994-97); Design Architect, Cesar Pelli & Ass.; mural - "The Rink" - 6ft. x 25ft. (1997). Artist in Residence, British Council Hong Kong (1993-94). *Publications:* Monograph: Bill Jacklin by John Russell-Taylor (Phaidon Press, London, 1997); gallery catalogues and numerous articles and broadcasts. *Clubs:* Chelsea Arts. *Signs work:* "Jacklin." *Address:* Goose House, 62 Bank St., N.Y.C., N.Y. 10014, U.S.A.

JACKSON, Ashley, F.R.S.A., U.A.; artist in water-colour; lecturer and demonstrator in w/c throughout Britain, U.S.A., Valencia, Milan and Madrid; *b* Penang, Malaysia, 22 Oct., 1940. *m* Anne. two *d. Educ:* St. Joseph's, Singapore, Holyrood, Barnsley. *Studied:* Barnsley School of Art (1955-60). *Exhib:* R.I., R.B.A., R.W.S., Britain in Water-colour, U.A.; one-man shows: including Upper Grosvenor Gallery, Mall Galleries, Cartwright Hall, Bradford (1998), Armouries, Leeds (2000), etc. *Work in collections:* Royal Navy, Sir Harold Wilson, Sir Yehudi Menuhin, Lord Mason of Barnsley, Rt. Hon. Edward Heath, Yorkshire Bank, Yorkshire Television, N.C.B., Rt. Hon. John Major, Sir Bernard Ingham, President Bill Clinton. *Publications:* numerous including: autobiography "My Brush with Fortune" (Secker and Warburg, 1982); "Ashley Jackson's Yorkshire Moors – A Love Affair (Dalesman, 2000) etc. Featured on Y.T.V. documentary – Some Days are Diamond; 2001 – New T.V. series "In a Different light'; 10 series of "A Brush with Ashley" Y.T.V. (1990-2001); own series on B.B.C., Channel 4, Y.T.V. Founder Mem. Yorkshire Watercolour Soc. *Signs work:* see appendix. *Address:* Ashley Jackson Galleries, 13-15 Huddersfield Rd., Holmfirth, Huddersfield HD9 2JR. *Website:* www.ashley-jackson.co.uk *Email:* ashley@ashley-jackson.co.uk

JACKSON, H. J., R.E., S.W.E., N.D.D.; full time printmaker using lino etc.; *b* Kings Lynn, Norfolk, 7 Dec., 1938. married. one *d. Educ:* Melton Constable. *Studied:* Norwich School of Art (1954-58) under G. Wales, R.E. *Exhib:* Touring Print Exhbns. America and United Kingdom; one-man and mixed group shows throughout East Anglia, and print shows in London. Work included in a number of public collections, and private collections worldwide; and various educational authorities. *Signs work:* "H. J. Jackson." *Address:* 12 Whitehall Rd., Norwich NR2 3EW. *Second Address:* 167 Hall St., Briston, Melton Constable, Norfolk NR24 2LQ.

JACKSON, Maz, B.A.(Hons.) (1976); artist in tempera, water-colour, drypoint, charcoal and line; *b* Norwich, 6 Aug., 1953. *m* Paul Hill. two *s.* one *d. Educ:* Notre Dame High School, Norwich. *Studied:* Norwich School of Art (1972-76, Edward Middleditch). *Exhib:* dfn Gallery, Manhattan, New York; MONA Fund Raiser, Detroit; Royal Academy, London; Mall Galleries, London; Llewellyn Alexander Gallery, London; Art Connoisseur Gallery, London; Birmingham Art Centre, Hotbath Gallery, Bath, Stroud House Gallery, Stroud; Fermoy Art Centre, Kings Lynn; Primavera Gallery, Cambridge; Chimney Mill Gallery, West Stow; Thompson's Gallery, Aldeburgh, Assembly Rooms, Norwich; Gissing Hall Art Centre, Norfolk; Grapevine Gallery, Norwich. *Work in collections:* Permanent Public Archive Collection, Museum of New Art, Detroit. *Publications:* Painting World magazine. 1998 Artist in Residence at Bressingham Gardens. *Clubs:* S.G.F.A., E.W.A.C.C. Artworks. *Signs work:* "MAZ." *Address:* Friends House, Church Rd., East Harling, Norwich NR16 2NB. *Email:* mazjackson@aol.com

JACKSON, William Alexander, A.T.D., P.P.R.B.S.A. (President R.B.S.A. 1983-87); President B'ham Pastel Soc. (2000-1); artist in pastel, oil, acrylic; retd. Principal, Bournville College of Art (1964-81), teacher of drawing and painting since 1947; *b* B'ham, 11 Sept., 1919. *m* Mary Elizabeth. one *s.* one *d. Educ:* W. Bromwich Grammar School. *Studied:* Ryland Memorial School of Art (1936-40), B'ham College of Art (1946-47), Art Teacher's Diploma. *Exhib:* R.B.S.A, Mall Galleries, Perugia, Alexandria; private galleries: Worcester, Malvern, Broadway, Nottingham. *Work in collections:* Dudley A.G., various private collections. *Commissions:* portraits/various. Prizewinner Mid-Art Dudley, R.B.S.A. *Clubs:* President, Redditch Art Circle, R.B.S.A. Committee (Ex Officio), Principal's Professional Council (life member). *Signs work:* "Alex Jackson." *Address:* 18 Moss Lane Cl., Beoley, Redditch B98 9AU.

JACOB, Wendy, painter and printmaker in water-colour, gouache, etching; *b* Wigan, 1941. *m* Robin Jacob. three *s. Educ:* North London Collegiate School. *Studied:* Hammersmith College of Art. *Exhib:* R.W.S. Open, N.E.A.C., Singer & Friedlander, R.A., Laing. *Publications:* illustrated: English Bread and Yeast Cookery by Elizabeth David; North Atlantic Seafood by Alan Davidson. *Address:* 8 Ripplevale Grove, London N1 1HU.

JACOBSON, Ruth Taylor, D.F.A.Lond. (1963); 1st prize, figure drawing at the Slade (1961); painter/printmaker/stained glass artist; *b* London, 1941. *m* U. Jacobson, F.R.C.S., M.R.C.O.G. two *s.* one *d. Studied:* Slade School of Fine Art (1959-63, Peter Brooker, Andrew Forge). *Exhib:* Agnews, Wildenstein, Royal Festival Hall, Barbican Centre; one-man shows: Camden Arts Centre, Poole Arts Centre, Zionist Confederation House, Jerusalem. *Work in collections:* Panstwowe Muzeum Oswiecim Brzezinka, Poland, Yad Vashem Museum, Israel, Ben Uri Gallery, London. *Commissions:* portrait of H.M. Queen Elizabeth the Queen Mother for the Museums Association. *Clubs:* British Soc. of Master Glass Painters. *Signs work:* "Ruth B. Jacobson." *Address:* 25 Holne Chase, London N2 0QL.

JACZYNSKA, Marysia, N.D.D. (1960), A.T.C. (1961); sculptor in wood and stone, models in clay; *b* Warsaw, Poland, 30 Sept., 1937. *m* Kazimierz Jaczynski. one *s.* one *d. Studied:* St. Martin's School of Art (1956-60, Anthony Caro), Hornsey

College of Art (1960-61), Academie Julien, Paris (1963-64). *Exhib:* regularly in England; solo shows: Poland, France, England. *Work in collections:* private: England, France, Switzerland and Poland. *Clubs:* U.A., C.A.S., A.P.A. *Address:* 27 Cascade Ave., London N10 3PT. *Email:* jaczynski@hotmail.com

JAFFE, Harold, A.S.A. (1973), F.S.V.A. (1978); artist in acrylic and mixed media; interior designer and muralist, teacher and antiquarian; certified fine arts appraiser; President, Louis Comfort Tiffany Soc.; Past President, L.I. Chapter, American Society of Appraisers; Faculty, New York University, George Washington University; *b* New York City, 26 Mar., 1922. *m* Gisèle Jaffe. one *s. Educ:* Pratt Institute, Parsons School. *Studied:* Cape Ann, Gloucester under Maxwell Starr. *Work in collections:* Denton Greens Housing Development Dr. C. MacCormick, Mr. and Mrs. S. Berman, Dr. D. Bernstein, Mr. and Mrs. A. Adler. *Publications:* work repro.: Interiors Magazine, Years Work. *Signs work:* "Harold." *Address:* 5 Devon Rd., Great Neck, New York 11023, U.S.A.

JAFFE, Ilona Lola Langdorf, artist in monotype (oil), tapestries; *b* Krakow, Poland. *Studied:* P.F. Art College, S. Africa under Joan Wright. *Exhib:* solo shows: Orchid Fine Arts, Lymington, Swanage, Berlin, Johannesburg, Munich, Boston, Freising, Cape Town Eching, Sasolburg, Rustenburg, Antwerp, Van Eck Gallery; group shows: Johannesburg, Paris, London. *Work in collections:* King George VI A.G. and Museum, Port Elizabeth, Pretoria A.G. and Museum, Pretoria, R.A.U. Johannesburg, Dom Gymnasium, Freising, Franz Mark Gymnasium, Markt Schwaben, Germany; also private collections and institutions. *Address:* Flat 3, 5 St. Winifred's Rd., Meyrick Pk., Bournemouth BH2 6NY

JAGO, Joan E., F.R.S.A. (1989), F.F.P.S. (1992), Wilfred Sirrell Award (City of Westminster Arts Council) 1989, Dip. in Creative Textiles (1985); fibre artist/paper maker; *b* Leeds, 22 Mar., 1930. *Educ:* Aireborough Grammar School, W.Yorks. *Exhib:* solo show: Marks & Spencer plc H.Q. Bldg., London (1993); group shows in London, Hong Kong and the U.S.A. *Signs work:* "Joan Jago." *Address:* 606 Nelson House, Dolphin Sq., London SW1V 3NZ.

JAKOBER, Ben, sculptor in stone, iron, bronze; winner of Miro Foundation Prize (1993); *b* Vienna, 31 July, 1930. *m* Yannick Vu, with whom he now works and signs jointly. one *s. Educ:* Mill Hill School; La Sorbonne, Paris. *Exhib:* 1982: Fundación March, Palma; 1984: Palais des Beaux Arts, Brussels; Louisiana Museum, Humlebaek; Städtische Kunsthalle, Mannheim; Museum Moderner Kunst, Vienna; 1985: Recklinghausen Museum; 1986: XLII Biennale di Venezia; 1988: Olympiad of Art, Seoul; 1990: Jeune Sculpture, Paris; 1991: MVSEV, Palma; Musée d'Art Moderne, Pully (VD); 1992: EXPO 92, Seville; 1993: Arnolfini, Bristol; Museum Moderner Kunst Stiftung Ludwig Palais Liechtenstein, Vienna; "MEDIALE", Hamburg; XLV Biennale di Venezia; 1994: Fundació Pilar i Joan Miró a Mallorca, Palma de Mallorca; 1995: Salle delle Reali Poste, Gli Uffizi, Firenze; 1996: Istituto Italiano di Cultura, Paris; Galerie Pièce Unique, Paris; XXIII Bienal International de São Paulo, Brazil; 1998: "Disidentico" Palermo, Mücsarnok Budapest; 2001: Bienal of Valencia. *Work in collections:* Museo Nacional Centro de Arte Reina Sofía, Madrid; Musée d'Art Moderne, Brussels; Museum of Modern Art, Palais Liechtenstein, Vienna; Museum of Austrian Art of the XIX and XX Centuries,

Vienna; Kunsthalle Bremen; Kunsthalle, Hamburg; Musée d'Art Moderne F.A.E., Pully (VD); Colombe d'Or, St Paul de Vence; Fattoria di Celle, Pistoia; E.P.A.D., Paris; Seoul Olympic Park; Fondation Vincent Van Gogh, Arles; Fundació Pilar i Joan Miró a Mallorca, Palma de Mallorca; Gabinetto Disegni e Stampe degli Uffizi, Firenze; Museum Beelden aan Zee, Scheveningen; Ludwig Museum Budapest; Museum Fine Arts Budapest; Macba Barcelona. *Signs work:* "B.J." *Address:* 205 St Ursula St., Valletta 06, Malta. *Email:* jakobervu@kemmunet.net.mt

JAMES, Donald, painter, designer; exhibits internationally; P.E., Commonwealth of Massachusetts; M.I.E., Australia; *b* New York, 1932. *Educ:* San Francisco Art Institute, California School of Fine Arts, San Francisco State College, American University, Cocoran School of Art, Union University, Union College. *Signs work:* "Don Ald," earlier "James." *Address:* The Studio, 47 Chelsea Manor St., London SW3 5RZ.

JAMES, Kim, M.A.(R.C.A.), M.Sc., Ph.D., N.D.D., A.T.C.; Consultant to the French National Inst. for training psychiatric personnel, Dijon, France; Director P.S.I. International Ltd; *b* Wollaston, Northants, 31 July, 1928. married. two *d. Educ:* Wellingborough Grammar School. *Studied:* Borough Polytechnic under David Bomberg and Tom Eckersley; Royal College of Art; Brunel University, School of Applied Biology; and Division of Cybernetics; Special research field psychology of perception. *Exhib:* R.A., Scottish Arts Council; Middleheim Biennale, Antwerp. *Publications:* Writings include critical essays and reviews on current theories of Perception and Philosophy (Leonardo, vols. 8, 9, 10, 11, 13, 14). Gallery: Grosvenor Gallery, London. *Signs work:* "Kim James." *Address:* Hickmire, Wollaston, Northants NN29 7SL.

JAMES, Simon, M.A.(R.C.A.) (1989); artist in oil, charcoal and printmaking; *b* 22 Jan., 1965. *Educ:* Northampton School for Boys. *Studied:* R.A. Schools (1984-87), R.C.A. (1987-89). *Exhib:* R.A., N.E.A.C., Marks and Spencer Young Artist award (1992), prizewinner in the 10th Cleveland International Drawing Biennale (1991), numerous exhbns. in England, U.S.A., and Berlin. *Work in collections:* Lloyd's of London, Cleveland C.C., The Foreign Office. *Signs work:* "SIMON JAMES" or "S.J." *Address:* Houseboat Clifton, Blomfield Rd., London W9 2PB.

JAMESON, Norma Marion, R.B.A., R.O.I., N.D.D., A.T.D., Goldsmiths' Advanced Dip.; painter, lecturer; *b* Burslem, 18 Jan., 1933. *m* Kenneth Ambrose Jameson (decd.). *Educ:* Thistley Hough Grammar School, Stoke-on-Trent. *Studied:* Bath Academy of Art (1951-55); Liverpool University (1955-56); Goldsmiths' College (1978). *Exhib:* R.A.; various one-man shows in London and the South East. Mem. Royal Society of British Artists and The Royal Inst. of Oil Painters. *Work in collections:* private in the U.K. and abroad. *Publications:* articles on drawing for "Canvas" and "Leisure Painter", "Batik for Beginners" – Studio Vista. *Signs work:* "Norma Jameson." *Address:* 111 Hayes Way, Beckenham, Kent BR3 6RR.

JAMIESON, Susan Mc. Donald, painter in oil and acrylic; *b* Newbury, 1942. *m* Andrew. two *s.* one *d. Exhib:* R.A. Summer Show, R.O.I., New English, Britain's Painters, Medici Gallery, Thomson's Gallery, Dover Street, Wykeham Gallery, Stockbridge. *Clubs:* Arts, Dover St. *Address:* Minstrel House, The Croft, Kintbury, Nr. Newbury, Berks. RG17 9TJ.

JAMILLY, Victor, painter, oil and water-colour; art gallery director; *b* 31 May, 1927. *m* Audrey. two *s.* one *d. Educ:* Highgate and Cranleigh Schools. *Studied:* St. Martin's School of Art. *Exhib:* New English Art Club, R.S.B.A., various group and gallery shows. *Work in collections:* Euston Gallery, London. *Signs work:* "V. Jamilly." *Address:* Wendover, 13 Hampstead Way, London NW11.

JAMISON, Paul, B.A.Hons. (1979), P.G.C.E./A.T.D. (1982); artist in oil and water-colour; *b* Middlesbrough, 16 Sept., 1954. *Educ:* St. Mary's College, Middlesbrough. *Studied:* University of Newcastle upon Tyne (1975-79), University of Bristol (1981-82). *Exhib:* Hatton Gallery, Newcastle (1979), Alpine Gallery, London (1980, 1983), Bayswater Gallery (1987, 1989, 1991). Work in private hands throughout the world. *Signs work:* "Jamison" with year, i.e. '98. *Address:* 16 Cosway St., London NW1 5NR.

JAMMET, Lin, painter in gouache on paper, oil on canvas; *b* 22 May, 1958. *m* Valerie Jammet. two *s. Educ:* French Lycée, London; C.E.G. d'Anduze, France; Millfield, Somerset. *Studied:* Chelsea School of Art (sculpture course 1976). *Exhib:* one-man shows: Beaux Arts Gallery, Bath, St. Jude's Gallery, London, Contemporary Fine Art Gallery, Eton, Bohun Gallerie Henley, Beaux Arts Gallery, London. *Clubs:* Chelsea Arts. *Signs work:* "Lin Jammet." *Address:* Woolland House, Woolland, Blandford Forum, Dorset DT11 0EP.

JANACEK, Mirice: see MATTAROZZI DI THARASH, Mirella.

JANES, Violeta, portrait painter, still-life, artist in oil, pastel and water-colour; Directed art studies at Alma College, Ontario, Canada; *b* Buenos Aires, Argentina. *Educ:* Giffen School, Viña del Mar, Chile. *Studied:* Regent St. Polytechnic School of Art under S. Tresilian, Middleton Todd, E. Osmond. *Exhib:* R.A., R.O.I., S.W.A., R.S.A., N.E.A.C., R.P., Paris Salon and the provinces; two-man show in the West End, one-man, Broomfield Museum. Member United Society of Artists. *Signs work:* "Violeta Janes." *Address:* 2 Salisbury Ave., Harpenden, Herts AL5 2QQ.

JAQUES, Norman Clifford, D.A. (Manc., 1941), M.S.I.A. (retd.); Sen. Lecturer, Manchester Polytechnic (1950-82); President, Manchester Academy of Fine Art (1984-90); Visiting Lecturer, Cleveland, U.S.A. (1979); freelance artist; *b* 23 Apr., 1922. *m* Marjorie Hovell. two *s. Educ:* Manchester College of Art (J. M. Holmes, P. W. Keen, 1937-42); R. M. I. Heywood Prize; Proctor Travelling Scholarship (1948) Italy, France. *Exhib:* London, Manchester, Glasgow, Edinburgh, U.S.A. and Canada, etc. *Work in collections:* V. & A. Museum, M/Cr City A.G., Westminster Bank, Rochdale, Stoke, Manchester, Newcastle Education Committees, Cleveland Tric. U.S.A., etc. *Commissions:* United Steel Co., Post Office, B.B.C., British Transport, Odhams, Macmillan, etc. Agents: R.P. Gossop, London (1946-89). *Address:* 6 Wardle Rd., Sale, Ches. M33 3BX.

JARAY, Tess, D.F.A. (Lond., 1960), F.R.I.B.A.; painter and etcher, environmental artist; Reader in Fine Art; *b* Vienna, 31 Dec., 1937. two *d. Educ:* Alice Ottley School, Worcester. *Studied:* St. Martin's School of Art (1954-57), Slade School of Fine Art (1957-60). *Exhib:* solo exhbns.: Whitworth A.G., Manchester, Ashmolean Museum, Oxford, Serpentine Gallery, London. *Work in collections:* Stadtisches Museum, Leverkusen, Walker Art Gallery, Liverpool, Arts Council of Gt. Britain,

Tate Gallery, Graves Art Gallery, Sheffield, Warwick University. *Commissions:* Floor for Victoria Station, London, Centenary Square, Birmingham, Cathedral Precinct pedestrianisation, Wakefield. *Signs work:* "Tess Jaray." *Address:* 29 Camden Sq., London NW1.

JARMAN, Anne Nesta, H.R.M.S. (1981), Hon. R.M.S (retd.); prizewinner for miniature portrait, National Eisteddfod of Wales; artist of miniature portraits in water-colour and pastel; *b* Sutton, Surrey. *Educ:* Penarth County School, Bedales School, Petersfield. *Studied:* Cardiff School of Art; Heatherley's, London; privately with the late Alfred Praga in miniature painting. *Exhib:* R.A., Paris Salon, R.M.S., R.W.A., R.C.A., S. Wales Art Soc., etc. *Work in collections:* Apothecaries Hall, London; bronze portrait, lifesize, at St. Denoils Library, (Gladstone's old home), of Thomas Leckie Jarman M.A. A.M. B. Litt. (brother). *Signs work:* "Nesta Jarman." *Address:* 4 Ellenborough Ct., 17 Ellenborough Park N., Weston-super-Mare, Somerset BS23 1XQ.

JARVIS, Gloria, N.D.D.; Médaille d'Argent Paris (1976); artist in oil, water-colour, pastel, ink, gouache; lecturer on historic costume and instructor in costume drawing, Polytechnic, Regent St. (1950-63); *m* Raymond Smith, B.A. (1964). *Educ:* Heathfield School, Harrow; Aylesbury Grammar School. *Studied:* St. Martin's School of Art, London, under James Bateman, R.A., the history of art at Florence University. *Exhib:* R.A., N.E.A.C., Leicester Galleries; one-man show, Brussels (1970 .). *Work in collections:* Abbot Hall A.G., Kendal; Museum of the Dynasty, Brussels; International Museum of Carnival and Mask, Binche, Belgium; and private collections. *Commissions:* numerous portraits and genre paintings, Brussels. *Publications:* work repro.: Macmillan, Brussels Times. Short stories published; broadcast by B.B.C. *Clubs:* Soc. of Women Writers and Journalists. *Signs work:* "Gloria Jarvis." *Address:* The Bungalow, Tyler Cl., Canterbury, Kent CT2 7BD.

JASINSKI, Alfons B., R.S.W. (1978), Latimer award R.S.A. (1975), D.A. Travelling scholar (1969); artist in oil, acrylic, water-colour, pastel (seashore/fig-ure/landscape); *b* Falkirk, 1945. *m* Ann Conlan. one *s.* two *d. Studied:* Edinburgh College of Art (1964-68, Philipson, Houston, Blackadder, Cumming). *Exhib:* Loomshop Gallery, Lower Largo, Scottish Gallery, Kirkcaldy A.G., Artis: Flying Colours, Stenton, Peter Potter, Haddington. *Work in collections:* S.A.C., Edinburgh Schools Collection, Aberdeen City A.G., Duke of Devonshire, P.I.H. Scotland. *Signs work:* "A. B. Jasinski." *Address:* 15 Normand Rd., Dysart, Fife KY1 2XN.

JASON, Gillian, Art Gallery Director, Gillian Jason, Modern & Contemporary Art, London, 40 Inverness St., London NW1 7HB; *b* U.K., 30 June, 1941. *m* Neville. one *s.* one *d. Educ:* Royal Ballet School/London Opera Centre. Director of Gillian Jason Gallery, London, (1981-1994); Jason & Rhodes, London, (1994-1999); private dealer representing artists, (1999 onwards). *Address:* 40 Inverness St., London NW1 7HB. *Email:* art@gillianjason.com

JEFFERSON, Annelise, M.A. (1990), A.R.O.I. (1993); fine art painter in oil on canvas; *b* Pembury, 1965. *Educ:* Chichester High School. *Studied:* West Surrey College of Art and Design (Stephen Farthing), Royal Academy (Norman Adams). *Exhib:* R.A. Summer Exhbn. (1988, 1989, 1990, 1991), Bonhams: The New Generation (1990), Royal Overseas League (1990), Rubicorn Gallery, Dublin (1991),

The Hunting Art Prizes finalist (U.K. and Paris, 1991), N.E.A.C., Mall Galleries (1991-92). *Work in collections:* South East Arts, Lloyds of London, Leics. C.C.; also private collections in U.K., Eire, Canada. *Signs work:* see appendix. *Address:* Maycotts Lodge, The Green, Matfield, Tonbridge, Kent TN12 7JU.

JEFFERY, Juliet, N.D.D., F.S.S.I., A.C.L.A.S., S.E.A.; President's medal S.Eq.A. (1993); artist in water-colour and gouache, and calligrapher; *b* Bognor Regis, 5 Mar., 1943. *Educ:* Warren, Worthing. *Studied:* Brighton College of Art and Crafts (Dennis Flanders, R.W.S.). *Exhib:* S.Eq.A. Annual, R.W.S. Open, locally and Cumbria, S.S.I. (1996). *Publications:* Gypsy Poems and Ballads by Lavengro; Appley Fair; Bender Tents; and Sarah's Tales (Dragon Press). *Clubs:* S.Eq.A., Fellow S.S.I., Assoc. C.L.A.S. *Signs work:* "Juliet Jeffery." *Address:* The Providence, Compton, Chichester, Sussex PO18 9HD. *Email:* julietjohn@diamond63.freeserve.co.uk

JEFFREY, Jill, A.R.B.S.A. (1996), P.S. (1997); painter in oil and pastel; designer (theatre) retd. 1991; *b* Chesterfield, 30 July, 1940. *m* Peter (decd.). one s-*s*, one *s*. four s-*d*, one *d*. *Studied:* Coventry College of Art (1957-59, David Bethel), B' ham College of Art (1959-61, Roy Abel). *Exhib:* solo shows: Solihull, Chipping Norton, also Mall Gallery, London, Stour Gallery, Shipston. *Work in collections:* U.K., Europe, U.S.A., Canada. Artist on Tour – National Theatre (1991 world tour), Artist in Residence R.S.T. Stratford Upon Avon (1993). *Clubs:* Fosseway Artists. *Address:* The Pippins, Oxhill, Warwick CV35 0QR. *Email:* jillfjeffrey@aol.com

JELLICOE, Colin, painter in oils and acrylics; art gallery director; *b* 1 Nov., 1942. *Educ:* Heald Place School. *Studied:* Manchester Regional College of Art. *Exhib:* one-man shows: Monks Hall Museum, Eccles (1970), Stockport A.G. (1981), Salford A.G. (1981), Jellicoe Gallery (1974, 83, 84, 85, 90, 95, 00), Buxton Museum and A.G. (1997); group shows: Northern Images Manchester (1974), North West One Chenil Galleries, London (1976), North West Two National Theatre, London (1979), Contemporary Art Fair, Bath (1981, 82, 83), with Michael Goddard Royal Exchange Theatre Manchester (1985), Edinburgh Festival Fringe (1983, 84, 85), Contemporary Art Fair, London (1984, 85, 86); Open shows: Manchester Academy City A.G. (1970, 73, 75, 76, 81, 84, 85, 88, 92, 95), R.A. Summer Exhbn. (1981); many others in Preston, Accrington, Bolton, Southsea, Wimbledon and Manchester. *Signs work:* see appendix. *Address:* 82 Portland St., Manchester M1 4QX.

JENKINS, Christopher, Slade Dip. (Painting) (1957), A.T.C. (1958); potter in thrown and glazed oxidised stoneware and wood fired domestic ware, artist in water-colour; Mem. C.P.A., N.P.A.; *b* B'ham, 1933. divorced. one *s*. one *d*. *Educ:* Harrogate Grammar School. *Studied:* Harrogate School of Art (1949-52), Slade School of Fine Art (1952-54 and 1956-57), Central School (ceramics, 1957-59). *Exhib:* V. & A., Crafts Centre, C.P.A., York, Scarborough, Kendal, Nottingham, Manchester, Liverpool, Tokyo, Copenhagen, Paris. *Work in collections:* North West Arts, L.E.A's: London, Leicester, Bucks., N. Yorks, Kirklees, Hanley. *Signs work:* see appendix. *Address:* 19 Towngate, Marsden, Huddersfield HD7 6DD. *Email:* chris@19towngate.fsnet.co.uk

JENKINS, Heinke, R.B.S.A. (1967), R.B.A. (1977); printmaker in linocut, art teacher; *b* Heilbronn, W.Germany, 2 Jul., 1937. one *s*. *Educ:* Heilbronn Grammar

School. *Studied:* Stuttgart Academy of Arts (Prof. Henninger), Stuttgart College of Graphic and Illustration (Prof. Leo Schobinger). *Exhib:* Germany, U.S.A., England, Printmaker of the Month, Leicester (1997), Tanner Charitable Trust Prize (1998), Colex and Tilley Prize (2000). *Work in collections:* Heilbronn A.G., Stuttgart A.G. *Commissions:* 1993: drawings and linocuts by B'ham University Maternity Hospital in Memory of the old Sorrento Maternity Hospital, B'ham. *Publications:* illustrated, Arts Review, 'Ambit' poetry magazine, 'Circle' poems, M. Armstrong. *Clubs:* R.B.S.A., R.B.A., Heilbronn Kunstler Bund. *Signs work:* "HEINKE." *Address:* 26 Allesley Cl., Sutton Coldfield, Birmingham B74 2NF.

JENKINS, Thomas Raymond, artist in water-colour; Chairman: Assoc. of Civil Service Art Clubs, and Boreham Art Circle; Mem. Hilliard Soc., and Islington Art Circle; *b* London, 24 June, 1928. *m* Margaret. one *s.* one *d. Studied:* Chelmsford, and St. Ives School of Painting under Roy Ray. *Exhib:* Council of Europe Exhbn., Strasbourg (1979, premier prize), H.S. Annual at Wells, Montelimar Festival, Barbican Arts Centre 10th Anniversary Exhbn. *Work in collections:* private: U.S.A., Canada, Europe, N.Z., Australia, Scandinavia, Russia and Japan. *Signs work:* "Ray Jenkins". *Address:* 28 Butterfield Rd., Boreham, Chelmsford, Essex CM3 3BS.

JENNINGS, Walter Robin, artist in oil; portraits, landscape, and equestrian pictures; *b* Old Hill, Staffs., 11 Mar., 1927. *m* Barbara Wilkinson. *Educ:* Macefields Secondary School. *Studied:* Dudley and Staffordshire Art School, Brierley Hill School of Art, Birmingham School of Art. *Exhib:* R.B.S.A., R.W.A., R.Cam.A., Royal Institute Galleries, Utd. Soc. of Artists, N.E.A.C., etc. *Work in collections:* Allison House, Mr. H. Woodhouse; Enville Hall, Mr. and Mrs. J. Bissel; Brierley Hill A.G. *Publications:* work repro.: Royle, Medici, Solomon and Whitehead, etc. *Signs work:* see appendix. *Address:* Kestrels, Caunsall, Cookley, nr. Kidderminster, Worcs. DY11 5YJ.

JENNISON, Robert William, R.W.A., N.D.D. (1954), A.T.D. (1958); painter in oil, occasional printmaker, lecturer; *b* Grantham, 8 June, 1933. *m* Angela Cook. one *s.* two *d. Educ:* Grammar School, Weston super Mare. *Studied:* West of England College of Art, Bristol (1950-54, 1957-58, Paul Feiler). *Exhib:* frequent solo and group shows since 1962: London, Wales, South-West, N. Ireland, including R.W.A., R.U.A., Milan, Italy. *Work in collections:* public and private collections in Britain, Europe, U.S.A. etc. *Signs work:* "Robert Jennison," "R. Jennison" or "R.J." *Address:* The Old Church School, Talaton, E. Devon EX5 2RQ.

JERVIS, Sharon, Dist. Wildlife Illustration (1978), M.A. Graphic Design (1982), M.S.I.A.D. (1980), A.R.S.M. (1996); artist in water-colour and gouache; M.D. Sharon Jervis Ltd; *b* Leicester, 5 May, 1956. one *s.* one *d. Studied:* Dyfed College of Art (Wildlife Illustration), Leicester Polytechnic (now De Montfort University). *Commissions:* Many varied license contacts for a variety of publishers and manufacturers in the U.K. and worldwide. My paintings are used on a diversity of products including diaries, cards, framed and limited edition prints, table top products, mugs, rugs, tapestries, pillows, trays, flags, ceramics, giftware, stationery items and fabrics. *Address:* Farndon Grange, East Farndon, Market Harborough, Leics. LE16 9SL.

JESTY, Ronald, artist in water-colour and acrylic, part-time lecturer; Pres.

Somerset Soc. of Artists, elected mem. R.B.A. (1982) resigned (1990); *b* Weymouth, Dorset, 7 May, 1926. *m* Margaret Johnson. *Educ:* Weymouth Grammar School; no formal art training. *Exhib:* R.I., R.W.A., R.W.S., R.B.A., R.A., Singer & Friedlander/Sunday Times water-colour competition; nine one-man shows. *Work in collections:* Somerset C.C. *Publications:* "Learn to Paint Seascapes" (Harper Collins, June 1996). *Clubs:* Artists 303, Somerset Soc. of Artists. *Signs work:* "R. Jesty" and year. *Address:* 24b Brunswick St., Yeovil, Som. BA20 1QY.

JIANG HUANG, Limin, M.A.; artist in oil and water-colour, designer; *b* 14 Aug., 1952. *m* Gouping Jiang. *Studied:* St. Martin's School of Art and Design. *Exhib:* International Maritime Organization Art Soc., London, Arts and Science Form, Wells, America, France, Swiss, Manchester, Australia, Japan, Belgium, China. *Work in collections:* B.M., V. & A., National Galleries of Canada and Australia, Museum of Western Art, Japan, Art Modern of City of Paris, Association of China Art, Swiss Art, Japan Fan Art. *Publications:* Taiwan Art Almanas (1994, 1995), International Fan Art (1989-96), Dictionary of International Biography - 28th, Century Appreciate - Chinese Artists Works, The Radiance of Oriental-Chinese Artist in 21st Century, New Century Contemporary Artist Biography, China Contemporary Artist Works Appreciate, Dictionary of China Outstanding Artist, Dictionary of World Calligrapher-Painter 3rd edition, World Outstanding Specialists, Brilliant Accomplishment Century Light of Dawn (1999), Huaxia Chinese Outstanding Talents, China Famous Brush and Ink Artists Works Show. Awarded the Gold Cup Award (2000) China, the World Gold Award (2000) Hong Kong. *Clubs:* Honorary President of China Huaihai Calligraphy & Painting Institute. *Signs work:* "LIMIN J.H." *Address:* P.O. Box 4595, 9 Howick Pl., London SW1P 1AA.

JOBSON, Patrick, landscape and marine painter and draughtsman in oil, water-colour and pastel; illustrator in black and white; heraldic artist and designer; Signs for many of princ. London brewers; *b* 5 Sept., 1919. *m* Lillias Bettina. one *s. Educ:* Sir George Monoux Grammar School, Walthamstow. *Studied:* Under my father, Frank Mears Jobson, and Sir Frank Brangwyn. *Exhib:* generally. *Commissions:* mural panels "The Arts" in Harrow Art Centre. *Publications:* "A Celebration of Marine Art" (Blandford), "20th Century British Marine Painting", "Dictionary of British Book Illustrators", illustrations (O.U.P., Blackie, Macmillan), etc. "The Wapping Group of Artists" (Heron Press). *Clubs:* Langham Sketch (Past President), Wapping Group (Past President). *Signs work:* see appendix. *Address:* 117 Eton Ave., N. Wembley, Middx. HA0 3BA.

JOEL, Alan Alfred, B.Sc., B.D.S.; portrait painter in oil and pastel; retired dental surgeon; *b* Dunedin, N.Z., 27 Oct., 1921. *m* Kay Cooper. one *s.* two *d. Educ:* Kings High School, Dunedin and Otago University, N. Z. *Studied:* for fifteen years had one to one tuition with Ken Paine and Dennis Syrett. *Exhib:* Salisbury Libraries, Riverbank Gallery, Port Solent, and solo exhib. N.Z. House, London (2001). *Clubs:* London Sketch Club. *Signs work:* "Joel." *Address:* 66 St. Edmunds Church St., Salisbury, Wilts. SP1 1EQ. *Email:* aajoel1066@aol.com

JOEL, Judy, self taught artist in gouache and acrylic; Curator St. Ives Soc. of Artists, Hon. Sec., Molesey Art Soc.; *b* London, 30 Aug., 1946. *m* Paul Joel. one *s.* one *d. Exhib:* solo shows: London, Surrey, Sussex and Cornwall. *Commissions:*

Simon Weston, Nerys Hughes, etc. *Signs work:* "J.S Joel." and a little mouse. *Address:* Noah's Ark Studio, Abbey Pl., Mousehole, Cornwall TR19 6PQ.

JOHANNESON, Steven Thor, artist of land/sea-scapes and nature in most painting mediums, but especially in water-colour; has work published including several Limited Edition Prints; *b* Minneapolis, Minn., 16 June, 1948. *Educ:* Menominee High School, Michigan; Bethel College, St. Paul, Minn. *Studied:* Heatherley School of Art, London (1970-73). *Exhib:* R.S.M.A., S.WL.A., several mixed and one-man shows; galleries include St. Ives Gallery; Mid-Cornwall Galleries; Gallerie Marin Appledore; Arty Crafts, Wadebridge; St Breock Gallery; Chagford Gallery; Higher Street Gallery, Dartmouth and Grasslands Gallery, Mall of America, Minneapolis. Recipient of "St. Cuthbert's Mill Award", at R.S.M.A., (1999). *Signs work:* "S.T. Johanneson" in vermilion. *Address:* Flat 4, Brentwood Ct., Treyarnon Bay, nr Padstow, Cornwall PL28 8PL.

JOHN, Samuel, B.A. (Lond. 1958), M.B.I.M. (1968), I.P.M. (1960), M.Inst.M. (1970), M.Inst.Ex., former Overseas Marketing Manager, Glaxo Group (1972), R.L.S.S.Inst. (1953); artist in oil, pastel, water-colour, writer, former medical student, business entrepreneur; *b* Newport, Mon., 9 Feb., 1935. *m* Anne Drummond-Leigh, actress. three *s.* one *d. Educ:* Newport High School; London University; Ashridge and Sundridge Management Colleges (Marketing). *Studied:* Chelsea (St. Mark and St. John College) (1955-58, P. G. Roberts, R.A.); qualified as teacher (1957). *Exhib:* Thames Gallery (1978), Chenil Galleries (1956), The Clement, Oxford (1977-79), Oxford Art Soc. (1977-78), Barclay Gallery, Chester (1980), St. Martin's, London (1983), Royal Overseas League, London (1983). *Work in collections:* St. Helen's Convent, Oxford; Blackfriars, Oxford; Mr. R. Bradon, Australia. *Commissions:* Films: (Equity Mem.) Coronation Street, Pardon the Expression, The Jewel in the Crown, The Man in Room 17, etc. *Publications:* The Sacred and The Profane (1980), The Proitiation (1980), The Act of Love (1983); awarded Koestler Prize for Verse (1980). Literary Agent: Curtis Brown, London. Theatrical: Joan Reddin, London. *Clubs:* Royal Overseas, Oxford and Cambridge. *Signs work:* "John." *Address:* c/o Browse Darby, 19 Cork St., London W1X 2LP.

JOHNS, Phil, artist in water-colour and oil; Director of Art Publishing Co.; *b* Brentwood, Essex, 15 Feb., 1950. one *s.* one *d. Studied:* Southend Art School, Royal Wanstead School. *Exhib:* over six one-man shows since 1989 worldwide. *Work in collections:* British Petroleum; Forest Healthcare Trust; Intercontinental Hotel, Park Lane. *Commissions:* numerous. *Publications:* work repro.: Limited Editions. *Address:* Nevill Gallery, 43 St. Peter's St., Canterbury, Kent CT1 2BG.

JOHNSON, Annette, S.W.A. (1987), N.S.; painter-etcher in water-colour, oil and etching; mem. National Soc. of Painters, Sculptors and Printmakers, and Soc. of Women Artists; *b* London, 24 March., 1943. *m* Alan. one *s.* one *d. Studied:* etching at Morley College; painting at Sir John Cass College of Art. *Exhib:* N.S.P.S. (1985), R.S.M.A. (1985), R.I. (1981), R.A. (1985), S.W.A. annually, N.S. annually. *Signs work:* "Annette Johnson." *Address:* 24 Kellerton Rd., Lee, London SE13 5RD.

JOHNSON, Ben, painter/sculptor collaborating with architects; *b* Llandudno, 24 Aug., 1946. *m* Sheila Johnson. two *s. Studied:* R.C.A. (1965-69). *Exhib:* one-man shows: New York, London, Dublin, Edinburgh, Bradford; group shows: England,

Scotland, Ireland, Belgium, U.S.A., Poland, Yugoslavia, Spain, Australia, France, Germany, Switzerland, Portugal, Italy. *Work in collections:* Boymans-van Beuningen Museum Rotterdam, British Council, Tate Gallery, Contemporary Art Soc., De Beers/CSO Coll., R.I.B.A., Glasgow City A.G., Whitworth Gallery Manchester, Centre Georges Pompidou Paris, V. & A., B.P., Deutsche Bank, British Museum. *Commissions:* For last 10 years has worked exclusively to commission for both public and private collections. Numerous publications. *Signs work:* "Ben Johnson." *Address:* 4 St. Peter's Wharf, Hammersmith Terr., London W6 9UD.

JOHNSON, Brian Robert, R.I. (1988) Bronze Medal Award (1987), Hon. Citizen, Victoria B.C.; Graduated with distinction from The Art Center College of Design, Los Angeles, Calif. with a Bachelor of Professional Arts (1962); artist in water-colour; *b* Victoria, B.C., Canada, 4 Apr., 1932. married. two *s.* one *d. Educ:* Victoria High School, Victoria College; Art Center College of Design, Los Angeles. *Exhib:* R.I., R.B.A., A.W.S., F.C.A, C.S.P.W.C., N.W.W.S., C.S.M.A., numerous one-man and group exhbns. in Canada and U.S. *Work in collections:* Canada, U.S., Australia, U.K. and Europe. *Signs work:* "Brian R. Johnson." *Address:* 1766 Haultain St., Victoria, B.C., V8R 2L2, Canada.

JOHNSON, Carl, B.A. (1971), Post grad. Ateliers 63 Holland (1973), A.T.C. (1975); painter in oil, pastel, drypoint, etching; *b* Warwickshire, 5 Dec., 1946. *m* Miranda. one *s.* one *d. Studied:* B'ham College of Art (1964-65), Solihull Technical College (1965-68), Newport College of Art (1968-71), Ateliers 63, Haarlem, Holland (1971-73), Goldsmiths' College (1974-75). *Exhib:* R.A. Summer Show (1998, 1999), R.W.A., Cuprum, Poland, Produzenten Galerie, Germany, Xtreme Art, Leicester City A.G., National Print, Mall Galleries, Kunsthalle Giessen, Germany, Guildhall Gallery, Winchester, National Theatre Printmakers Council. *Work in collections:* N.Y., Texas, U.K., Amsterdam, Germany, Australia, Poland. *Clubs:* Member of Printmakers Council. *Address:* 8 Highcliffe Rd., Winchester, Hants. SO23 0JE.

JOHNSON, Colin Trever, M.A.F.A.; artist in oil, collage, water-colour and inks, principal themes: coastline, harbours, Venice, street markets, windows studio still-life; *b* Blackpool, 11 Apr., 1942. *Studied:* Salford School of Art, Manchester College of Art. *Exhib:* one-man shows: City of London Festival, Liberty's London, Barbican Art Centre London; Derby, Oldham, Bolton, Harrogate, Salford, Scarborough, Buxton, Falmouth, Blackburn, Ayr, Bideford, Margate, Blackpool and Bury Public A.Gs.; Winchester, Manchester and Leicester Cathedrals; Salford, Manchester and Exeter Universities; Taunton and Bridgewater Arts Centres; National Touring Exhibition (1995-97). *Work in collections:* Salford, Southport, Manchester, Derby, Torquay and Worthing Public A.Gs., B.B.C. Artist in Residence: Manchester (1980), City of London (1984) and Wigan International Jazz (1986, 1987) Festivals. Directed Festivals of: Bolton (1979), Swinton (1973), Teignmouth (1996). *Commissions:* Granada Television, B.B.C. North West, Royal Exchange Theatre, Manchester. *Clubs:* Manchester Academy. *Signs work:* "Colin T. Johnson." *Address:* 27 Bedford Rd., St. Ives, Cornwall TR26 1SP.

JOHNSON, Joy Alexandra, B.F.A. (Hons.) (1980), Higher Dip. (Lond.); artist in oils, water-colour; *b* Hull, 26 Aug., 1958. *Educ:* Hatfield High School, Yorks. *Studied:* Newcastle upon Tyne Polytechnic (1977-80), Slade School of Fine Art

(1982-84, Lawrence Gowing). *Exhib:* Northern Young Contemporaries (1979), Sainsbury Centre (1980), Mappin Gallery Open Art (1984, 1985), R.A. Summer Exhbn. (1985), several solo exhbns. in London. Received award from Swiss based Vordemberge Gildewart Foundation (1986). *Signs work:* "J.A. Johnson." *Address:* 17 Bempton La., Bridlington, E. Yorks. YO16 5EJ.

JOHNSTON, Brenda, painter in oil and scraperboard; *b* London, 8 Dec., 1930. *m* David Johnston. two *s.* one *d. Educ:* Rosebery Grammar School, Epsom. *Studied:* Epsom School of Art (1948-49, 1955-60) under Michael Cadman, Leslie Worth; Reigate School of Art (1961-65) under Eric Waugh. *Exhib:* R.A., R.B.A., Nimes and Avignon, Arts Council Exhbn. Midlands and East Anglia; nine one-man shows. *Work in collections:* Ryder Memorial Bequest. *Clubs:* F.P.S., Thames Valley Art, Leatherhead Art. *Signs work:* "Brenda Johnston" or "BJ." *Address:* Russells, 36 Oakfield Rd., Ashtead, Surrey KT21 2RD.

JOHNSTON, George Bonar, D.A. (Edin.), R.S.W.; artist in oil, gouache and water-colour; formerly adviser in art, Tayside Region Educ. Authority; *b* Edinburgh, 14 June, 1933. one *s.* one *d. Educ:* Bathgate Academy. *Studied:* Edinburgh College of Art (1951-56) under William Gillies, P.P.R.S.A., R.S.W., and Robin Philipson, P.P.R.S.A., A.R.A., R.S.W. *Exhib:* regular exhibitor R.S.A., R.S.W., R.G.I.; one-man shows: Perth, Kirkcaldy, Glasgow, Dundee; mixed shows: Edinburgh, Aberdeen, London, Paris, Toronto, New York. *Work in collections:* Glasgow, Strathclyde, Edinburgh, Dundee, London, Toronto, U.S.A., France, Australia. *Signs work:* "Johnston." *Address:* 10 Collingwood Cres., Barnhill, Dundee DD5 2SX.

JOLL, Evelyn, B.A. (Oxon.) (1949); art dealer, Agnew's (retd. 1994); *b* London, 6 Feb., 1925. *m* Pamela. one *s.* three *d. Educ:* Dragon School, Oxford; Eton College; Magdalen College, Oxford. *Publications:* The Paintings of J.M.W. Turner (with Martin Butlin) Yale U.P. 2 vols. 1977; awarded Mitchell Prize for History of Art (1978), Revised Edn. (1984). *Clubs:* Boodle's, Hurlingham. *Address:* Flat 3, 42 Tregunter Rd., London SW10 9LQ.

JONCZYK, Prof. Dr. Leon, painter, graphic artist, art historian, author of publications about theory of art, experimental printing; Memb., National and International Academies for Arts, Sciences and Humanities, Paris, Bordeaux, Naples, Rome; JSAST, San Francisco; Prof. of Academia Polona Artium and of Polish University of London; Dean of Faculty of Fine Arts, Munich; President, Assoc. of Graphic Artists, W. Germany; *b* Katowice, Poland, 25 July, 1934. *Educ:* High School, Poland. *Studied:* in Poland, Netherlands, Gt. Britain. *Exhib:* Czechoslovakia, France, Italy, E. and W. Germany, Gt. Britain, Netherlands, Poland, Sweden, Switzerland, Tasmania, Turkey, Yugoslavia, U.S.A. *Work in collections:* more than 30 galleries and museums in Europe, public and private collections in Europe, Australia, U.S.A. *Publications:* illustrated monographs in different languages. *Signs work:* "L. Jonczyk." *Address:* Franz-Joseph-Str. 30/IV, 80801 München, Germany.

JONES, Allen, N.D.D. (1959), A.T.D. (1960), R.A. (1984); painter, sculptor, printmaker; Trustee, British Museum (1990-99); *b* Southampton, 1 Sept., 1937. *m* Deirdre Morrow. two *d. Studied:* Hornsey College of Art (1955-59), R.C.A. (1960-61). *Exhib:* since 1961 numerous museum and group shows. *Work in collections:* public museums and private collection worldwide. *Commissions:* public sculpture commissions in the U.K. and Hong Kong. Represented by Thomas Levy, Hamburg; Charles Cowles, N.Y.C.; Ernst Hilger, Vienna; Kaj Forsblom, Helsinki. *Signs work:* "Allen Jones." *Address:* 41 Charterhouse Sq., London EC1M 6EA.

JONES, Aneurin M., N.D.D. (1950), A.T.D. (1955); artist in oil, acrylic, mixed media; retd. Head of Art Dept., Preseli Comprehensive School, N. Pembrokeshire; *m* Julie Jones. one *s.* one *d.* *Studied:* Swansea College of Art (Principal: Kenneth Hancock, A.R.C.A., Head of Fine Art: William Price, A.R.C.A.), Prix de Rome Scholar. *Exhib:* numerous one-man and mixed shows England and Wales. Welsh representative at the Celtic Festival, Lorient, Brittany. *Work in collections:* National Library of Wales, Aberystwyth; Welsh Arts Council; West Wales Assoc. for the Arts; Dyfed County Council; Ceredigion County Council; The Welsh Office, Cardiff. *Commissions:* three full-length studies of Welsh Archdruids for Gorsedd of Bards permanent collections; mural to commemorate 'Owain Glyndwr' the last native Prince of Wales's struggle for independence in the 13th Century. *Publications:* numerous Welsh/English periodicals, magazines and books. *Clubs:* lecturer for various clubs, societies and educational establishments. *Signs work:* "ANEURIN M. JONES"; 1993 onwards "ANEURIN." *Address:* Heulwen, Aberystwyth Rd., Cardigan, Ceredigion SA43 1LU.

JONES, Barry Owen, R.W.S., R.E., N.D.D.; artist in water-colour, etching/aquatint; Gallery Director; *b* London, 11 Sept., 1934. *m* Alexandria Virginia, née Parsons. one *s.* one *d.* *Educ:* Friern Barnet Grammar School. *Studied:* Hornsey College of Art (1950-55). *Exhib:* R.W.S., R.E., Coach House Gallery, Guernsey, Bankside Gallery. *Work in collections:* Guernsey Museum and A.G., South London A.G. *Commissions:* National Grid Calendar (1993). *Signs work:* see appendix. *Address:* Les Douvres Vineries, La Fosse, St. Martin, Guernsey C.I. GY4 6EF.

JONES, Edward Scott, R.C.A. (1964); artist in oil, water-colour, gouache, acrylic; *b* Liverpool, 6 June, 1922. *m* Althea. one *s.* one *d.* *Educ:* Anfield Road Elementary School. *Studied:* Liverpool College of Art. *Exhib:* R.C.A., Williamson A.G., Bluecoat A.G., R.I., R.S.M.A. *Work in collections:* Merseyside Council Libraries, Blackpool Corp. A.G., Salford A.G., Bolton A.G., Williamson A.G., Birkenhead, also works in private collections. *Signs work:* "E. Scott Jones." *Address:* 18 The Fairway, Knotty Ash, Liverpool L12 3HS.

JONES, Geraldine M.L., Dip.A.D.(Hons.) (1972), Post Grad. Cert. R.A. Schools (1975); freelance artist and illustrator in water-colour, oil, pencil, charcoal; *b* Ampleforth College, Yorks., 23 Nov., 1949. *m* Nigel Jones. *Educ:* The Bar Convent, York. *Studied:* Hull Regional College of Art (1969-72, John Clarke, Michael Chiltern), R.A. Schools (1972-75, Peter Greenham, Anthony Eyton). *Exhib:* York, Hull, Peterborough, Oxford, London, Norwich. *Work in collections:* Bradford Cathedral Chapter House. *Commissions:* Bradford Cathedral. *Publications:* 'Stories from Yorkshire Monasteries' (J. & B. Spence). 'The Yorkshire Journal', 'Against the Tide', Marjorie Bourne. *Clubs:* S.G.F.A. *Signs work:* "G. Jones." *Address:* Fleet House, Hoffleet Stow, Bicker, Boston, Lincs. PE20 3AF.

JONES, Heather Edith, artist in water-colour, silver point, pencil; tutor (retd.); specialises in miniature portraits; *b* Cardiff, 23 May, 1930. *m* Ivor Jones (decd.). one *s.* one *d.* *Studied:* Newport School of Art. *Exhib:* R.A. Summer Show, R.M.S., H.S.,

L.A. Gallery, Glyn Vivian Gallery, Swansea, Barbican and Pall Mall Galleries, and privately owned galleries in England, France and U.S.A. Work in private collections. *Publications:* illustrations for book of ghost stories. *Clubs:* H.S. *Signs work:* "H" and "J" joined see appendix. *Address:* 25 Spencer Gdns., London SE9 6LX.

JONES, Helen Coline, H.N.D. (natural history illustration), 1st prize M.A.S.-F. (animal and birds category), 2nd Prize M.A.S.-F. (2001); illustrator/artist in water-colour; *b* Hereford, 18 Feb., 1971. *Studied:* Bournemouth and Poole College of Art and Design (1990-92). *Exhib:* H.S., R.M.S., M.A.S.F., Canada, Marches Artists, international miniature exhibition Tasmania, Llewellyn Alexander Gallery, London. Work in collections internationally. *Publications:* illustrated: An Identification Guide to Dog Breeds by Don Harper; work repro.: greetings cards and wrapping paper. *Clubs:* Marches Artists, H.S., A.R.M.S., M.A.S.F. *Address:* The Croft, 96 Penn Grove Rd., Hereford HR1 1BX.

JONES, Hywel Wyn, B.A. (Hons.) 1979, M.A. (1980); sculptor; *b* Aberystwyth, 17 Nov., 1956. *Studied:* Central School of Art, Chelsea School of Art. *Signs work:* "Hywel Wyn Jones." *Address:* Flat 3, 47 Union Rd., London SW4 6JG.

JONES, Ian, B.F.A.(Hons.) (1979), M.F.A. (1982); artist; lecturer in Fine Art; *b* B'ham, 3 July, 1947. *m* Carole A. Jones. two *s. Educ:* Queensbridge Secondary Modern, Moseley. *Studied:* B'ham Polytechnic School of Fine Art (1975-78, Roy Abel, Trevor Halliday), R.C.A. (1979-82, Peter de Francia). *Exhib:* regular exhbns. since 1981, group and individual shows. *Work in collections:* Britain, Europe, America. *Signs work:* "Ian Jones." *Address:* Anderson O'Day Gallery, 255 Portobello Rd., London W11 1LR.

JONES, Joan, A.R.B.S.A. (1970); painter in oil and water-colour, also paper col-lage; painting instructor in still life, portraits, flowers and landscape; *b* Solihull, 16 Apr., 1924. married. one *s. Educ:* Malvern Hall, Solihull. *Studied:* Sutton Coldfield, Bourneville, Birmingham (1950-60, Dennis Greenwood, A.T.D., Alex Jackson, A.T.D., R.B.S.A.). *Exhib:* B'ham, Sutton Coldfield, Worcester, etc. *Signs work:* "Joan Jones" sloping upwards towards right hand side. *Address:* Elms Cottage, Grafton Flyford, Worcester WR7 4PG.

JONES, John Edward, N.D.D. (1951), A.T.D. (1952), Dip.F.A. (Slade 1954), R.W.A.; painter in oil, pen, etc.; University senior lecturer (retd.); Regional Director of Open College of the Arts (retd.); London University Moderator G.C.E. 'O', 'A' level and G.C.S.E. Art; Past President, Leeds Fine Art Club; *b* Bristol, 19 Aug., 1926. *m* Gabriela Jones. two *d. Educ:* Winterbourne Elementary; Colston's School, Stapleton. *Studied:* West of England College of Art (1942-44 (army intervened) 1948-52, George Sweet), Slade School (1952-54, Rogers, Coldstream, Wittkower). *Exhib:* R.W.A., Leeds Fine Art, etc. *Work in collections:* University of Leeds, R.W.A. *Commissions:* Communication Dept., University of Leeds. *Publications:* 'Wonders of the Stereoscope'. *Clubs:* Chelsea Arts. *Signs work:* "J.E. Jones" or "Jones" (and date). *Address:* 20 Hollin La., Leeds LS16 5LZ.

JONES, Joyce Margaret Farrall (née Mellor), R.Cam.A.(1997); illustrator, miniature painter of portraits, animals, floral; *b* Bangalore, India. *Studied:* Regional College of Art, Manchester (1954-57), St. Martin's School of Art (1957-59), Italy

(1959-60). *Publications:* illustrated books for Longmans, University of Wales Press, Cambridge School Classics, N.W. Arts Assoc., Thames and Hudson, Encyclopedia Britannica, Nature Conservancy. Work purchased: by Indian Army (portraits), miniature collectors, commercial dealers in U.K., U.S.A., S. Africa, Australia. *Address:* 3 Queens Park, Colwyn Bay LL29 7BG.

JONES, Karen, S.Eq.A.; equine water-colourist; *b* 11 Aug., 1942. *m* Mike Eaton. two *d*. *Educ:* Godolphin and Latymer. *Exhib:* R.A., England, Wales and U.S.A. *Work in collections:* England, Wales, Scotland, Ireland, U.S.A., Canada, France, Italy, Germany, Portugal, Holland, W.I., New Zealand, Spain, Australia. Gallery at home: open Summer. *Signs work:* "K.J.'98." *Address:* Blaenllyn, Llangolman, Clunderwen, Pembs. SA66 7XR.

JONES, Lee, self taught fine artist in acrylic; *b* Liverpool, 26 Aug., 1968. *m* Denise. one *s*. *Exhib:* England, America, etc. *Work in collections:* England, America, Canada, Australia. *Clubs:* N.A.P.A., South Sefton Artists. *Address:* 18 College Rd., Great Crosby, Merseyside L23 0RW.

JONES, Leslie, A.R.E., A.R.C.A., D.A.(Manc.), H.R.Cam.A., Rome Scholar; painter, printmaker, illustrator; taught at Hornsey, Kingston, St. Martin's Schools of Art (1961-67); H.M.I. (1967-83); Bangor (1987-89); *b* Tremadoc, 26 June, 1934. *Studied:* Regional College of Art, Manchester (1951-55), Royal College of Art (1955-58), British School at Rome (1958-60); visitor at Belgrade Academy (1959). *Exhib:* London, Rome, U.S.A., Austria. *Work in collections:* V. & A., Arts Council, University of Oregon, University of Wales, National Library Wales, L.E.As., Church in Wales. *Publications:* illustrated books for Lion & Unicorn, Longmans, University of Wales Press, Cambridge School Classics Project. *Address:* 3 Queens Park, Colwyn Bay LL29 7BG.

JONES, Lucilla Teresa, Cert.F.A. (Oxon.); painter in oil, water-colour, mixed media; *b* Exmouth, 30 June, 1949. divorced. one *s*. *Educ:* St David's Ursuline Convent, Brecon. *Studied:* Ruskin School of Fine Art and Drawing (1968-71). *Exhib:* many solo and mixed shows including Ashmolean Museum, Monaco Fine Arts Monte Carlo, Chapter Gallery Cardiff, Upton Lodge Galleries, Tetbury, Weatherall, Green & Smith, London, Osborne Studio Gallery, London, Julian Davies Gallery, San Diego, Louis C. Morten Gallery, Mexico City, Capriole Gallery, Virginia, Mall Galleries, Inst. of Contemporary Arts, Warwick Arts Trust Galleries, London, Roy Miles Gallery, London. *Work in collections:* Royal Artillery and Royal Marines, Brecknock Museum and A.G.; private collections in U.K., U.S.A., Singapore, S. Africa, Holland and Ireland including those of Prince Kais al Said and Ravi Tikoo. *Publications:* Horse Breeding in Ireland, Horses, Hounds and Hunting Horns by Dr. Colin Lewis (Allen, 1980). *Signs work:* "L.T.J." or "Lucilla Jones." *Address:* Dan-y-Parc, Llandefalle, Brecon, Powys. LD3 0UN.

JONES, Lucy, B.A. 1st class B.A. Hons., Fine Art, M.A. (R.C.A.); painter in oil; *b* 1955. *Studied:* Camberwell School of Art, R.C.A. *Exhib:* over 16 solo exhibs. at Flowers East Gallery, London, and many group exhibs. including Whitechapel Art Gallery, Camden Arts Centre, R.A., Metropolitan Museum of Art, New York. *Work in collections:* Arts Council, Deutsche Bank A.G., London, Government Art Collection, Sheffield City Art Gallery, Usher Gallery, Lincoln. *Signs work:* "Lucy Jones." *Address:* c/o Flowers East, 199-205 Richmond Rd., London E8 3NJ. *Email:*

gallery@flowerseast.com

JONES, Malcolm, H.Dip.A.D. (1973), B.A. (Hons.) (1971); artist in painting, installation, construction; *b* Merseyside, 12 May, 1949. *Studied:* Chelsea School of Art (1972-73), University of Reading (1967-71). *Exhib:* ten solo shows in London public galleries since 1980, internationally in group exhbns. since 1972. Work reviewed in The Architects Journal, The Times, Neue Bildende Kunst, Neues Deutschland, The Guardian, Artscribe, BBC Critics Forum, Arts Review, NRC Handelsblad, Der Tagesspiegel, Frankfurter Rundschau, Het Parool and TV Times. *Commissions:* performance: Live Art 1909 to the Present, T & H (1979), Tolly Cobbold Eastern Arts 4 (1983). *Address:* 64 Chisenhale Rd. London E3 5QZ.

JONES, Mary Lloyd, N.D.D. (1955), A.T.D. (1956); artist in water-colour and oil; Chairman, Wales Artists Development Centre Assoc.; External examiner; B.A.(Ed.) Art & Design, Trinity College, Carmarthen; *b* Devil's Bridge, Ceredigion, Wales, 21 Aug., 1934. *m* John Jones. two *d*. *Educ:* Ardwyn Grammar School, Aberystwyth. *Studied:* Cardiff College of Art (1951-56, Eric Malthouse). *Exhib:* Montserrat Gallery, N.Y., Martin Tinney Gallery, Cardiff, Gallery of Modern Art, London, John Martin Gallery, Albemarle St., London. *Work in collections:* Tabernacle Museum of Modern Art, Wales, W.A.C., Crawford Museum and Gallery, Cork, Tyrone Guthrie Centre, Ireland, B.B.C. Wales, Ceredigion C.C., S4C Centre, Cardiff Arena/World Trade Centre. *Commissions:* Earth Works, Wales Garden Festival, Ebbw Vale. *Publications:* The Mountains of Wales (Univ. of Wales Press), Our Sisters Land (Univ. of Wales Press). First Prize, Wales Open Exhbn., Aberystwyth Arts Centre (1997). *Clubs:* Gweled (Welsh Artists Assoc.), Water-colour Soc. Wales, R.Cam.A. *Signs work:* "Mary Lloyd Jones." *Address:* Yr Hen Ysgol, Aberbanc, Llandysul, Dyfed,vWales SA44 5NP.

JONES, Megan, N.D.D. (1956), (A.T.D.) B.A. (1957); artist in oil, mixed media, gouache, charcoal, conté; Arts Council of Wales travel grant, Newfoundland (1994); *b* Neath, S. Wales, 6 July, 1936. *m* Derrick Jones. two *s*. *Studied:* Swansea College of Art (1952-57, Alfred Janes). *Exhib:* widely solo and group shows in Britain and abroad. *Work in collections:* Brecknock Museum and Gallery, Brecon; University of Newfoundland, Canada; Nippon-Sieke, Japan; County Hall, Carmarthen; Prince Philip Hospital, Llanelli; British and Continental Fuels, Belgium; Rhondda Heritage Park Gallery; Lidice Community, Czechoslovakia. *Publications:* Essay 'Ceri Richards' (University of Wales Press, 1999), cover 'Songs of Silence' by Patricia Barrie (Honno Press, 1999). *Clubs:* The Welsh Group. *Signs work:* "Megan Jones." *Address:* 9 Heol Derwen, Ystradgynlais, S. Wales SA9 1HL.

JONES, Olwen, R.A.S. (1968), R.E. (1978), R.W.S. (1989); painter in oil and water-colour, printmaker in relief and etching; *b* London, 1 Mar., 1945. *m* Charles Bartlett. *Educ:* Harrow School of Art (1960-65). *Studied:* Royal Academy Schools (1965-68), engraving under Gertrude Hermes. *Exhib:* first one-man: Zaydler Gallery, London (1971). *Work in collections:* National Museum of Wales, Norwich Castle Museum, Reading Museum, Nuffield Foundation. *Signs work:* "Olwen Jones." *Address:* St. Andrews House, Fingringhoe, nr. Colchester, Essex CO5 7GB.

JONES, Philip Charles, painter in oil; Arts Council of Great Britain (1953-1956); *b* London, 1 Apr., 1933. *m* Frances. two *s*. two *d*. *Educ:* Malvern College. *Studied:*

Slade (1953-1956). *Exhib:* Grabowski, Louise Hallet, Vanessa Devereux, M. Parkin, Ainscough Contemp. Art Galleries, London, R.A. Summer Exhib. (1990-2001). *Work in collections:* British Transport, Newport and Plymouth Art Galleries, Texaco Oil Co., T.V. West. *Signs work:* "Philip Jones." *Address:* Clermont Hall, Little Cressingham, Thetford, Norfolk IP25 6LY. *Email:* philip@clermonthall.com

JONES, Robert William, N.D.D., A.T.C.; painter in oil; full-time artist; former lecturer, Falmouth College of Art; *b* Newquay, Cornwall, 22 Mar., 1943. *m* Susie Jackson. three *s.* two *d. Educ:* Tretherras School, Newquay. *Studied:* Falmouth Art School. *Exhib:* numerous throughout S. West, London, Cotswolds etc. *Work in collections:* mainly private, museums, S.W. Arts, Plymouth Museum. *Publications:* 'Robert Jones' by Jenny Pery, pub. Halsgrove Press, forthcoming, 'Alfred Wallis Artist & Mariner' by Robert Jones (2001). *Signs work:* "Robert Jones" on back or "R.J." usually in red on painting. *Address:* Bodrigey Farm, 23 Sea Lane, Hayle, Cornwall TR27 4LQ. *Email:* robertjonesfirstlightstudio@btinternet.com

JONES, Rosamund, R.E., Painting N.D.D.; artist in etching, water-colour; shepherd; original work of wildlife, countryside scenes, cockerels and animals; *b* Harrogate, 1944. married. one *s.* three *d. Educ:* Harrogate. *Studied:* Harrogate, Leeds Colleges of Art. *Exhib:* Cartwright Hall Bradford, Edinburgh, London, Scottish Royal Academy, Royal Academy, London. *Work in collections:* Bankside Gallery, London, Oxford Gallery, Oxford, Zilla Bell, Thirsk, Yorks., Printmakers Workshop, Edinburgh. *Signs work:* "Rosamund Jones." *Address:* New Bridge Farm, Birstwith, Harrogate HG3 2PN.

JONES, Royston, Dip. A.D. (1968), M.F.A. (Illinois, 1971); photographer; human interface design; computer art and design; National Co-ordinator – Artist Teacher Scheme, N.S.E.A.D.; *b* Wolverhampton, 15 Jan., 1947. one *d. Studied:* Birmingham College of Art and Design (1965-68, John Walker, Trevor Halliday), University of Illinois (1969-71, Jerome Savage, Art Sinsebaugh, Bart Parker). *Exhib:* regularly in Britain and U.S.A. *Address:* 12 Norwood Ave., Southport, Merseyside PR9 7DT. *Email:* pd@pacificstream.com

JONES, Stanley Robert, A.T.D. (1950), F.S.A.; printmaker and archaeologist; *b* Birmingham, 9 June, 1927. *Educ:* Elementary School; Yardley Grammar School, Birmingham. *Studied:* Birmingham College of Art under Harold Smith, B. Fleetwood-Walker, A.R.A. (1942-45, 1948-50), R.A. Schools under B. Fleetwood-Walker, A.R.A., Henry Rushbury, R.A. (1950-55). *Exhib:* R.A., R.B.S.A., Printmakers' Council Venues, South Yorkshire Open. *Work in collections:* Graves Art Gallery, Sheffield. *Signs work:* see appendix. *Address:* 118 Totley Brook Rd., Sheffield S17 3QU.

JONES, Steven, Dip. in Illustration (1981); artist/illustrator in oil; *b* Chester, 5 Apr., 1959. *m* Sian. one *s.* two *d. Educ:* Colwyn High School, Colwyn Bay. *Studied:* Wrexham College of Art (1976-81, Keith Bowen). *Exhib:* one-man show: Oriel Môn, Anglesey (1996), Penrhyn Castle, Bangor (1998). *Publications:* Specialises in figures in landscape scenes particularly beach scenes, golf scenes and views of Snowdonia. Many paintings sold through auctions in Britain including Christies, Bonhams and Chrystals. Limited Edition Prints and greetings cards sold throughout Britain and the U.S.A. *Signs work:* "Steven Jones." *Address:* The Steven Jones

Gallery, The Bulkeley Hotel, Castle St., Beaumaris, Anglesey, N. Wales LL58 8AW.

JONES, Trevor, N.D.D. (1953), A.T.C.(Lond.) (1954), Fellow, Designer Bookbinders, Founder Mem. and President (1983-85); artist craftsman in bookbinding; on Crafts Council Index of Selected Makers; *b* Wembley, 15 July, 1931. *m* Pauline Jones. two *d. Studied:* Harrow School of Art (1947-49, 1952-53), Hornsey College of Art (1953-54). *Exhib:* Britain and internationally with Designer Bookbinders since 1956. *Work in collections:* British Library, V. & A., Royal Library Copenhagen, University of Texas, Pierpoint Morgan Library N.Y., Lilly Library Indiana, Keatley Trust Collection of 20c. British Art, Shipley A.G. Gateshead. *Publications:* articles in The New Bookbinder, Bookbinder, Crafts, Fine Print, Magnus. *Signs work:* "T.R.J." or "Trevor Jones." *Address:* 48 Burton Stone Lane, York YO30 6BU.

JONES, Trevor Grenville, N.D.D. (1965), M.A. (1968); painter/printmaker in oil, wax, ink; *b* 4 Feb., 1945. one *s.* one *d. Studied:* Stourbridge College of Art (1960-63), B' ham College of Art (1963-65), R.C.A. (1965-68). *Exhib:* numerous including solo shows: Flowers Graphics, London (1992, 1993), Flowers East, London (1995), Glass Mountain Gallery, Connecticut, U.S.A.; group shows: '30 Years of Printmaking' Advanced Graphics London Anniversary Show, Berkeley Sq. Gallery, London (1997), Original Print Gallery, Dublin (2000). *Work in collections:* Scottish National Gallery of Modern Art, Unilever, V. & A., B.P. Group, Johannesburg A.G. and Melbourne A.G., Office of National Statistics, Lasmo U.K. *Address:* c/o Advanced Graphics London, B206 Faircharm, 8-12 Creekside, London SE8 3AX.

JONES, Yvonne, B.A.Hons.F.A.; painter; *b* Holywell, N. Wales, 9 Oct., 1946. *m* Peter M. Jones. two *s. Educ:* Holywell Grammar School. *Studied:* Liverpool College of Art. *Exhib:* mixed: Mall Gallery, Liverpool Festival of Arts, Wrexham Arts Centre, R.A. Summer Exhbns. (1989, 1990), Portsmouth City Gallery, Doncaster City Gallery; European tour: one-man shows: Bridewell Studios Liverpool (supp Eastern Arts), Quay Arts Centre (supp Southern Arts). *Work in collections:* Welsh Arts Council, Merseyside Arts Trust, New Hall, Cambridge, Contemporary Women Artists; private collections: U.K. and Germany. *Address:* Hazelwood, Waters Green, Brockenhurst, Hants. SO42 7RG.

JONES, Zebedee, B.A (Hons.) Fine Art (1992), M.A. (Hons.), Fine Art (1993); painter in oil on canvas and board; *b* London, 12 Mar., 1970. *Studied:* Norwich School of Art and Design, Chelsea College of Art and Design. *Exhib:* Arts Council, Southampton City A.G., Leeds City A.G., Unbound at the Hayward Gallery (1994), Real Art (Southhampton 1995, Leeds City A.G. 1996); two solo exhbns. (1995, 1997). *Publications:* 'Affective Light' Rear Window (1994), Unbound Possibilities in Painting, Hayward Gallery (1994), From Here Exhbn. Cat., Essay by Andrew Wilson, Waddington Galleries (1995), Foundations for Fame, The London Inst. (1997). *Address:* 1 Albert Bridge Rd., London, SW11 4PX; and c/o Waddington Galleries, 11 Cork St., London W1 2LT.

JONES-ROWE, Avril, N.D.D., D.F.A.(Slade), M.F.P.S.; painter in oil and acrylic, sculptor in bronze, landscape gardener, teacher, art historian; *b* New Forest, Hants., 1934. *Studied:* Southampton Art College (1951-55), Sander Theatre School, Southampton (1952-54), Slade School (1955-57), Perugia University (1959). *Exhib:*

group shows: Young Contemporaries, London Group, Loggia Gallery, Trends, Bloomsbury Gallery, Bougton Aluph Church, Stroud Festival; one-man shows: Bailey House, Canterbury (Artist in Residence, 1965), B'ham University (1967), St. Pancras Hospital (1975), Loggia Gallery (1987). *Signs work:* "Jones-Rowe." *Address:* 25 Station Rd, Alderholt, Fordingbridge, Hants. SP6 3AF.

JOPE, Anne, B.A.Hons. (1970), A.R.E. (1979), R.E. (1984), Central Postgrad. Printmaking Dip. (1981), S.W.E. (1984), A.O.I. (1994); painter in oil paint and water-colour, printmaker in wood engraving, woodcut and linocut, illustrator; *b* Corfe Mullen, Dorset, 31 Jan., 1945. *Studied:* Ealing Art College (1966-67), Central School of Art and Design (1967-70, 1980-81). *Exhib:* twelve one-man shows, R.A., N.E.A.C., R.B.A., Camden Arts Centre, Ferens A.G., Graffiti, Morley Gallery, Royal Western Academy, St. David's Hall, Cardiff. *Work in collections:* Liverpool public libraries, B.M., Malcolmson Collection at Hereford City A.G., Ashmolean Museum, Leics. Educ. Com., N.P.G. *Publications:* The Song of the Reeds and Rushavenn Time, The Honey Gatherers, Animals at the Table, Nightlife Poems. *Signs work:* "Anne Jope." *Address:* 14 Millwood End, Long Hanborough, Witney, Oxon. OX29 8BX.

JORDAN, Maureen Ann, S.B.A., U.A.; artist in pastel, water-colour, acrylic; *b* 14 Apr., 1941. *Educ:* Escourt High School, Kingston upon Hull. *Studied:* Kingston upon Hull College of Art and Crafts. *Exhib:* P.S., S.B.A., U.A., New Trends Hong Kong, Art Mart; one woman show New York, annual show at Llewellyn Alexander Gallery, London; also in many galleries mainly in the London area. *Work in collections:* around the world. *Publications:* art magazines, art books, greetings cards, prints and limited editions, calendars, stationery products and cards printed in the U.S.A. *Address:* 26 Manor Gdns., London SW20 9AB. *Email:* maureen.jordan@btinternet.com

JOSEPH, Jane, painter, draughtsman, printmaker; *b* Surrey, 7 June, 1942. *Studied:* painting: Camberwell School of Art and Crafts (1961-65, Robert Medley, E. Uglow, F. Auerbach, R. Kitaj, R.D. Lee, F. Bowling). *Exhib:* solo shows: Morley Gallery (1973, 1997, 2000), Minories, Colchester (1982), Angela Flowers (1987), Flowers East (1989, 1992), Edinburgh Printmakers (1994), Worcester City Art Gallery (2001). *Work in collections:* Arts Council of Wales, Government Art Collection, Castle Museum, Norwich, Unilever House, Imperial College, London, University of Northumbria, Chelsea and Westminster Hospital, British Museum, Paintings in Hospitals, New Hall, Cambridge, Fitzwilliam Museum, Cambridge, Ben Uri Art Society. *Commissions:* Chelsea and Westminster Hospital, drawings (1994); The Folio Society, etchings to accompany "If This is a Man" by Primo Levi (1999). *Signs work:* "Jane Joseph" or "JEJ." *Address:* 105 Cambridge Gdns., London W10 6JE.

JOWETT, Jenny Ann, N.D.D. (Drawing, 1957), (Lithography, 1982), S.B.A. (Founder mem.), A.S.B.A.; botanical painter in water-colour, teacher; Tutor, Flatford Mill; *b* 15 Mar., 1936. one *s.* one *d. Educ:* Bromley High School, G.P.D.S.T. *Exhib:* West Mills Newbury, Bladon Gallery, Packhouse Bath, John Magee Belfast, The Chelsea Garden London, Interiors of Ascot, Ewhurst Park Hants., Kew Gardens Gallery, Tryon Gallery London, Dr. Shirley Sherwood's Travelling Exhbn. *Work in* *collections:* Lindley Library, London, Hunt Inst. for Botanical Documentation Pittsburgh, U.S.A., Dr. Shirley Sherwood. *Commissions:* Chelsea Plate, Shell U.K. *Publications:* Limited edn. prints, cards, calendars; White Garden R.H.S. Plantsman, Curtis Magazine Kew. *Signs work:* "JENNY JOWETT." *Address:* West Silchester Hall, Silchester, nr. Reading, Berks. RG7 2LX.

JOYCE, Paula, botanical artist in water-colour; Founder Mem. The Society of Botanical Artists; *b* Hong Kong, 1 Sept., 1939. *Exhib:* solo and group shows including S.B.A. Annual. *Publications:* work repro.: greetings cards, notelets, wild flower books. Teaches botanical painting at venues throughout the country. *Address:* Bishopsgarth, Brede Hill, Brede, East Sussex TN31 6HH. *Email:* paulajoycesba@aol.com

JUKES, Edith Elizabeth, F.R.B.S., A.R.C.A. (1932), S.R.N. (Bart's, 1945); sculptor in clay, wood, stone; teacher of sculpture, Sir John Cass School of Art, City of London Polytechnic (1946-75); *b* Shillong, Assam, 19 Dec., 1910. *Educ:* Norland Pl. School, Kensington. *Studied:* R.C.A. (1928-32) under Profs. Richard Garbe, R.A., Henry Moore, and Herbert Palliser. *Exhib:* R.A., etc. *Signs work:* see appendix. *Address:* The Studio, 347 Upper Richmond Rd., London SW15 6XP.

K

KALASHNIKOV, Anatoly Ivanovich, Hon. R.E. (1988), Hon. S.W.E. (1993); Russian wood engraver; *b* Moscow, Russia, 5 Apr., 1930. *m* (1) Iulia Borisovna 1957 (died 1980). (2) Ludmila Nikolaevna 1980 (died 1994). (3) Ludmila Ivanovna 1994. *Educ:* Moscow Art Inst. (formerly Stroganoff Art School), disciple of Academician Ivan Pavlov; Freelance designer for many Soviet publishing houses and Ministry of Communications (postal designs) 1960-80; created over 100 postage stamps and 500 commemorative envelope designs, more than 900 bookplates. *Exhib:* more than 160 solo exhbns. worldwide. Academician, International Academy of the Book and Art of the Book, Moscow (1992); Merited Artist of Russian Federation; first prizes in international bookplate design competitions: Barcelona, Budapest, Kronach (Germany), Como, Genoa, Pescara, San Vito al Tagliamento (Italy), Helsingor (Denmark), Carlisle (USA). *Work in collections:* B.M., London; Cabinet of Engraving, Biblioteque Nationale, Paris; National Museum, Prague. *Publications:* Anglo-Russian Relations (1983); War and Peace: A suite of Wood Engravings, based on the novel by Leo Tolstoy (1991); 500 Exlibrisis (1993); The Dostoyevsky Suite (1994); Omar Khayam in xylographies by A. Kalashnikov (1994); Golden Ring of Russia (1995); many other albums and suites. Leisure interest: travelling, bookplate design. *Clubs:* Lions Club, Moscow. *Signs work:* see appendix. *Address:* Leninsky prospect 44, Apt.124, 117334 Moscow, Russian Federation.

KALKHOF, Peter Heinz, painter, lecturer in fine art; *b* Stassfurt, Germany 20 Dec., 1933. *m* Jeanne The (decd.). one *s. Educ:* Germany. *Studied:* School of Arts and Crafts, Braunschweig; Academy of Fine Art, Stuttgart; Slade School of Fine Art,

London; Ecole des Beaux Art, Paris (1954-62). *Exhib:* Annely Juda Fine Art (1970-79, 1990, 1997), Scottish Arts Council, Edinburgh, Glasgow, Juda-Rowan Gallery (1983), Landesmuseum Oldenburg (1988), Camden Arts Centre (1989), Galerie Rösch, Neubrunn (1993)/Karlshruhe (1994), Germany, St. Hugh's College, Oxford (1998), Gallery Roech, Houston/Texas (2000), Annel Juda Fine Art (2002). *Work in collections:* Northern Ireland Trust, Arts Council of Gt. Britain, Leics. Educ. Authority, European Parliament, Landesmuseum Oldenburg, Ostpreussen Museum, Lüneburg. *Commissions:* 1987 Treaty-Centre: Mural (Taylor Woodrow), Hounslow, London. *Signs work:* "Peter Kalkhof." *Address:* c/o Annely Juda Fine Art, 23 Dering St., London W1R 9AA. *Email:* p.kalkhof@virgin.net

KANE, Martin, B.A.(Hons.) (Edin. 1987); artist in oil on canvas, pastel; *b* Cardiff, 3 June, 1958. *Educ:* St. Andrew's High School, Clydebank, Glasgow. *Studied:* Glasgow School of Art (1981-82), Edinburgh College of Art (1982-87, David Michie). *Exhib:* Angela Flowers Gallery (1988), Jill George Gallery (1990), Thumb Gallery, Atlanta, U.S.A. (1990), Kasen Summer Coll., N.Y.; one-man shows: Jill George Gallery (1992, 1993), Beaux Arts, London (1996). *Work in collections:* Cleveland, Middlesbrough; Cleveland, Ohio; Glasgow Museums and A.Gs.; Unilever PLC; Gartmore Investments; Harry Taylor of Ashton, Kasen Summer New York. *Signs work:* "Martin Kane." *Address:* Dovehill Studios, 15 East Campbell St., Glasgow G1 5DT; and Beaux Arts Gallery, 22 Cork St., London W1X 1HB.

KANG, K.S., portrait painter in oils and sculptor; *b* India. *Studied:* Leicester University. *Exhib:* John Noott Galleries, Broadway. *Signs work:* "NICKS." *Address:* c/o John Noott Galleries, 58 High St., Broadway, Worcs. WR12 7DP.

KANIDINC, Salahattin, awarded High Moral Prize (1954); artist in pencil, pen, brush, ink, oil, polymer; letterer, calligrapher, designer, expert on historical writing systems (hieroglyphs to Roman alphabet) and modern letter forms; owner-creative director, Kanidinc International; and consultant designer for major corporations; *b* Istanbul, Turkey, 12 Aug., 1927. *m* Seniha Kanidinc. two *s*. *Educ:* 22nd Elementary School of Uskudar, Uskudar 1st High School, Istanbul, Turkey. *Studied:* Defenbaugh School of Lettering, Minn. (1954), Zanerian College of Penmanship, Ohio (1963), State University of Iowa (1963), University of Minnesota (1964), University of California (1963-64). *Work in collections:* Peabody Inst. Library, Baltimore; W.C.C., N.Y.C.; and in private collections. *Publications:* participant designer, Alphabet Thesaurus, Vols. 2-3. Listed in 'Who's Who' publications throughout the world. *Clubs:* S.S.I., W.C.C., International Assoc. of Master Penmen and Teachers of Handwriting, American Inst. of Graphic Arts, International Center for the Typographic Arts, National Advisory Board of the American Security Council. *Signs work:* see appendix. *Address:* 33-44 93rd St., Jackson Heights, New York 11372, U.S.A.

KANTARIS, Rachael Anna, Foundation Dip. Falmouth School of Art (1986), B.A. Hons. visual and performing arts, Brighton University (1989), M.A. Printmaking, Brighton University (1992); artist and freelance tutor in printmaking and colour etching; currently running Porthmeor Print Workshop, St. Ives, Cornwall; *b* Brisbane, Australia, 19 May, 1967. one *d*. *Educ:* Helston School, Cornwall. *Studied:* Falmouth School of Art (1985-1986), Brighton University degree course (1986-1989) and M.A. course (1990-1992). *Exhib:* British Council Exhib., Ayala

Museum, Manila, Philippines (1997); regular exhibs. throughout Britain, supplies twenty five galleries in U.K. *Work in collections:* British Council, Hong Kong and Manila; Bank of England; Allner Castle, Bonn, Germany. *Publications:* various - most recent, 'Behind the Canvas', by Sarah Brittain and Simon Cook, published by Truran (2001). *Signs work:* "Rachael Kantaris." *Address:* 1 Mount Pleasant, St. Ives, Cornwall TR26 1JW. *Email:* rachael@ffc.prestel.co.uk

KAPOOR, Anish, 'Premio Duemila' award Venice Biennale (1990), Turner Prize award (1991), Hon. Fellow, London Inst. (1997); *b* Bombay, 1954. *Studied:* Hornsey College of Art (1973-77), Chelsea School of Art (1977-78). *Exhib:* numerous solo shows including Patrice Alexandre, Paris (1980), Lisson Gallery (1982-), W.A.G. Liverpool, Barbara Gladstone Gallery, N.Y., Tate Gallery London, Tel Aviv Museum of Art, Scai The Bathhouse, Tokyo, Baltic Centre for Contemporary Art, Gateshead, etc. *Work in collections:* Tate Gallery, London; Hirshhorn Museum and Sculpture Garden, Washington D.C.; M.O.M.A., (N.Y.); Weltkunst Foundation, Zurich; Rijksmuseum Kroller-Muller, Holland; Auckland City A.G. (N.Z.); Vancouver A.G., Canada, etc. *Publications:* many including Breaking the Mould, British Art of the 1980s and 1990s (Weltkunst Coll., London 1999), Vision - 50 years British Creativity (Thames & Hudson, 1999), etc.; numerous exhbn. catalogues. *Address:* c/o Lisson Gallery, 67 Lisson St., London NW1 5DA.

KAUFFMANN, C. Michael, PhD. (1957), F.B.A. (1987), F.M.A., F.S.A.; Art historian and museum curator (formerly V. & A.); Emeritus Prof. of the History of Art, and former Director; Courtauld Inst., University of London; *b* Frankfurt a/M, 5 Feb., 1931. *m* Dorothea. two *s. Educ:* St. Paul's School; Merton College, Oxford (1950-53); Warburg Inst., London (1953-57). *Publications:* The Baths of Pozzuoli: medieval illuminations of Peter of Eboli's poem (1959); An Altarpiece of the Apocalypse (1968); V. & A. Catalogue of Foreign Paintings; British Romanesque Manuscripts 1066-1190 (1975); Catalogue of Paintings in the Wellington Museum (1982); John Varley (1984); Studies in Medieval Art (1992). *Address:* 53 Twyford Ave., London W3 9PZ.

KAVANAGH, Paul, B.Ed. (1975); painter in oil on canvas; freelance lecturer at The National Gallery, London; *b* Liverpool, 8 Jan. 1947. one *s. Educ:* Nottingham University. *Studied:* Folkestone, under Fred Cuming R.A. (1980). *Exhib:* London, Linda Blackstone Gallery, Pinner; various galleries in U.K. *Work in collections:* in U.S.A., Germany and France. *Commissions:* various nationally and internationally. *Signs work:* "Paul Kavanagh." *Address:* 26 Auckland Rd., Ilford, Essex IG1 4SD. *Website:* www.paul.kavanagh.cwc.net. *Email:* paul-kavanagh@cwcom.net

KAY, Nora, A.R.C.A., M.C.S.D.; decorative studio pottery, lino-cuts, book jackets; designer for Yardley's, Jenners Ltd.; teacher at St. Martin's School of Art, Newland Park College, Maltman's Green School; *Educ:* Wycombe High School, St. Martin's School of Art, R.C.A. *Exhib:* R.B.A., N.E.A.C. *Publications:* children's books; work repro.: general advertising work, London Transport posters, Christmas cards, book jackets. *Signs work:* "N.K." *Address:* Flat 5, Ethorpe Cres., Gerrards Cross, Bucks. SL9 8PW.

KEANE, John, B.A. (1976); painter in oil and mixed media on canvas, P.V.A. and mixed media on paper; Official War artist, Gulf (1991); *b* Herts., 12 Sept., 1954. *m*

Rosemary McGowan. one *d. Studied:* Camberwell School of Art (1972-76). *Exhib:* twenty five one-man shows in U.K., Europe and U.S.A. since 1980. *Work in collections:* Imperial War Museum, Contemporary Art Soc., Rugby Museum, Cleveland Gallery, Harris Museum, Preston, Glasgow Museum and A.G., Aberdeem A.G., Wolverhampton Museum and A.G., Christies Corporate Collection, British Coal, Financial Times, Unilever PLC, Detroit Art Inst. *Publications:* Conflicts of Interest by Mark Lawson (Mainstream Pub. 1995). *Clubs:* Groucho, Chelsea Arts. *Signs work:* "John Keane." *Address:* c/o Flowers East, 199-205 Richmond Rd., London E8 3NJ.

KEANY, Brian James, R.S.W. (1977), D.A. (Edin. 1967); artist in oil, acrylic, water-colour; art teacher; *b* Forfar, Scotland, 16 Jan., 1945. *m* Christina Nicol Herd, D.A.(Edin.). one *s.* two *d. Educ:* Brechin High School. *Studied:* Edinburgh College of Art (1963-67, Sir William Gillies, Sir Robin Philipson, William J. L. Baillie). *Exhib:* R.S.A., R.S.W., R.G.I., and several one-man shows and group exhbns. *Work in collections:* Carnegie Trust, Dunfermline (large tapestry design - 'History of Dunfermline', on public display since 1989. Designed by me, woven by a group of volunteers, led by Erica Betty, tapestry artist. *Signs work:* "BRIAN KEANY." *Address:* 27 Solway Pl., Glenrothes, Fife KY6 2NS.

KEARNEY, Joseph, D.A.Glas. (1961); painter in various media, sculptor, poet; *b* Glasgow, 14 Sept., 1939. *Educ:* St. Aloysius' College, Glasgow. *Studied:* Glasgow School of Art. *Exhib:* several one-man shows in Glasgow. *Work in collections:* Glasgow A.G. and Museum and in many private collections. *Commissions:* Portrait of Most Rev. J.D.Scanlan, Archbishop of Glasgow, and many other private commissions. *Clubs:* Glasgow Art. *Signs work:* "Kearney." *Address:* 97 Elmore Ave., Glasgow G44 5BH.

KEAYS, Christopher, N.D.D. (1960), R.A. Cert. (1966); landscape painter in oil; *b* Caterham, Surrey, 26 May, 1937. *m* Mary. two *d. Studied:* Wimbledon School of Art (1957-60, sculpture: Elisabeth Frink), Chelsea School of Art (1960-62, painting: Robert Buhler, Ruskin Spear), R.A. Schools (1962-66, Peter Greenham, Charles Mohoney). Work in collections internationally. *Clubs:* Reynolds. *Address:* 21 Cope Place, Kensington, London W8 6AA.

KEIR, Sally, B.A.(Hons.) (1984), M.S.B.A. (1989), M.S.F.P. (1998); designer jeweller/botanical artist in gouache; *b* Guildford, 29 Sept., 1938. *m* Peter Benson. two *d. Educ:* Sydenham School, Devon. *Studied:* Hereford College of Art (1979-81), Duncan of Jordanstone College of Art (1981-84). *Exhib:* R.H.S. gold, silver gilt and silver medals, S.B.A. (1989-97), Linnean Soc. (1990-91), Discerning Eye (1991), Del Bello Gallery, Toronto (1988-90), R.S.M. (1990), Tregaquelle (1994), S.W.A. (1991), Tryon Gallery (1998). *Work in collections:* Hunt Inst. of Botanical Art, Chicago, Shirley Sherwood Coll. *Publications:* Collin's Artists Manual, Contemporary Botanical Artists, Drawing and Painting Course. *Signs work:* "S.A.K." *Address:* "Maes Yr Haf", 8 Gorlan, Conwy LL32 8RS.

KELLY, Deirdre, B.Ed.(Hons.) (1984), M.A. (1987), R.E.; printmaker; *b* London, 1 May, 1962. *Studied:* Wimbledon School of Art. *Exhib:* B.P. International, Contemporary Art Soc., Galerie Luc Queryel, Harriet Green Gallery. *Work in collections:* Sedgewick Gp. International, Atlantis Paper Co., King's College School,

Museuda Gravura, Brazil. *Publications:* work repro.: Big Issue (1995). *Signs work:* "Deirdre Kelly" or "D.K." *Address:* c/o Hardware Gallery, 162 Archway Rd., London N6 5BB.

KELLY, Fowokan George, sculptor in resins, bronze and wood; trying to recapture lost African elements through art; *b* Kingston, Jamaica, 1 Apr., 1943. *m* Margaret Andrews. one *d. Educ:* East Queen St. Elementary Baptist School, Kingston, Jamaica. *Studied:* self taught. *Exhib:* Brixton Art Gallery (1983), Black Art Gallery (1983), Harley Studio Museum (1997), Assoc. Portrait Sculptors (1999), R.A. (1991, 2000, 2001). *Work in collections:* London Borough of Hammersmith and Fulham, W.E.B. Du Bois Institute, Harvard University, Unilever, University of West Indies, and private collections. *Commissions:* African People's Historical Foundation, London Borough of Hammersmith and Fulham and private portraits. *Signs work:* "F G Kelly." *Address:* 20 Veda Rd., Ladywell, London SE13 7JF. *Email:* fowokan@hotmail.com

KELLY, John, B.A. (1985), M.A. (1996); artist in oil on linen, bronze, mixed media; *b* Bristol, 12 Apr., 1965. *m* Christina Todesco. *Studied:* Rmit University, Melbourne, Australia, (1983-85, 1992-96), Slade School of Art, London (1996-97). *Exhib:* ten one-man shows with Niagara, Melbourne, and Piccadilly Galleries, London. Work in collections internationally. *Clubs:* Colony Room, London. *Signs work:* "Klly" and year. *Address:* Flat 1/10 Lewes Cres., Brighton BN2 1FH.

KELLY, Victor Charles, R.B.S.A. (1983), R.C.A. (1991); painter in watercolour, acrylic, pastel, lecturer, teacher; Past Hon. Sec. Royal Birmingham Soc. of Artists, Past Vice President R.B.S.A.; *b* B'ham, 6 Sept., 1923. *m* Sylvia. two *s. Educ:* B'ham Teachers Training College. *Studied:* Liverpool College of Art (1949-50). *Exhib:* R.B.S.A., R.I., Manchester Academy of Art, Chelsea Art Soc., R.Cam.A., Dudley Mid Art, Laing, London, New York. *Work in collections:* R.B.S.A. *Clubs:* Past Pres. B'ham Water-colour Soc., Easel Club, B'ham Art Circle. *Signs work:* "Victor C. Kelly." *Address:* 90 Sandringham Rd., Perry Barr, B'ham B42 1PH.

KELSO, James Philip, painter in acrylic; *b* London, 6 Jul., 1934. *m* Marianne. one *s.* one *d. Educ:* Sloane School, Chelsea. *Studied:* self taught. *Exhib:* R.A. Summer Exhibs. *Work in collections:* private collections in U.K., U.S.A., Sweden. *Signs work:* "James Kelso." *Address:* The Well House, Christmas Common, Watlington, Oxon. OX9 5HJ. *Email:* jim@kelso.co.uk

KEMPSHALL, Kim, R.B.S.A. (1985), A.R.C.A. (1960); painter/printmaker oil, acrylic, water-colour, etching, lithography; *b* 1934. *m* Sylvia. one *s.* one *d. Studied:* Manchester College of Art (1951-55); Royal College of Art (1957-60). *Exhib:* R.A., Scottish Royal Academy, Arts Council, one-man shows. *Work in collections:* Edinburgh City Coll., Scottish Modern A.G., Aberdeen A.G., Dundee A.G., Arts Council, V. & A., Herbert A.G., Whitworth A.G., Birmingham A.G., Wolverhampton A.G., Bradford A.G., City of Lyon, City of Frankfurt, Ecole de Beaux Arts, Toulouse; many private collections worldwide. *Signs work:* "K.K." *Address:* Mere House, 49 Henley Ave., Iffley, Oxford OX4 4DJ.

KENDALL, Alice R., D.A. (Edin.), F.R.Z.S. (Scot.), F.R.S.A., P.P.S.W.A. (1977-82); artist in oil, water-colour, pen and ink, writer; *b* N.Y.C. *Educ:* New York and

Edinburgh. *Studied:* Edinburgh under Sir Wm. Gillies, Sir Wm. MacTaggart. *Exhib:* R.A., Paris Salon, R.B.A., N.E.A.C., R.I., etc. and with the late Alice Kendall (Mother) at Cooling Galleries (1948, 1956) and Chelsea Gallery (1949). *Work in collections:* The Royal Society of Edinburgh: 1956 Official portrait of Prof. J.P. Kendall, P.R.S.E. (Father). *Publications:* children's book 'Funny Fishes'; articles and poems, many illustrated, in Punch, Poetry Review, The Artist, The Voice of Youth, etc. *Signs work:* "A.R. Kendall." *Address:* 35 Beaufort Gdns., London SW3 1PW.

KENDALL, Kay Thetford, R.M.S., S.W.A.; sculptor and portrait sculptor in bronze, bronze resin, and miniature sculpture; *b* Manchester. *Educ:* Cheadle Hulme Schools. *Studied:* Malvern College of Art; Hertfordshire College of Art and Design. *Exhib:* Mall Galleries, London; S.W.A., R.M.S.; one man shows, Welwyn Garden City, Hatfield, Knebworth, Wembley, Bishop's Stortford. Awards: 1st Prize for sculpture, Grolla d'oro, Venice (1981); Bidder & Borne award for sculpture R.M.S. (1986). *Clubs:* R.M.S., S.W.A. *Signs work:* see appendix. *Address:* The Studio, 45 Orchard Rd., Tewin, Welwyn, Herts AL6 0HL.

KENNEDY, Cecil, flower and portrait painter in oils; *b* Leyton, Essex, 4 Feb., 1905. *m* Winifred Aves. one *s. Studied:* in London, Paris, Antwerp, Zürich. *Exhib:* R.A., R.S.A., R.H.A., Doncaster, Oldham, Bradford, Southport, etc., and many London galleries; also U.S.A. and S. African galleries. Awarded Silver Medal, Paris Salon (1956) and Gold Medal, Paris Salon (1970). *Work in collections:* H.M. Queen Mary, Merthyr Tydfil Art Gallery, Rochdale Art Gallery. *Publications:* Numerous. *Signs work:* see appendix. *Address:* Manor Garden House, 135 Fishpool St., St. Albans, Herts. AL3 4R7.

KENNISH, Jenny, R.M.S. (1985), S.W.A., F.S.B.A.; self taught sculptress in porcelain of wild flowers and animals; school teacher; *b* England, 11 Mar., 1944. one *s.* one *d. Educ:* Nonsuch County Grammar School for Girls; Whitelands Teacher Training College. *Studied:* Zoology, botany and art. *Exhib:* Westminster Galleries with the R.M.S., S.B.A., S.W.A. and local societies. *Signs work:* "J.K." *Address:* Kinghern, Silchester Rd., Little London, nr. Basingstoke, Hants. RG26 5EX.

KENT, Colin, R.I. (1971); self taught painter in water-colour, acrylic, mixed media; *b* 10 Feb., 1934. *m* Joan. *Educ:* Romford County Technical School; S.W. Essex Technical College and School of Art. *Exhib:* R.A., R.I., Mall Galleries, Shell House Gallery, Ledbury, Adam Gallery, Bath, London, Blackstone Gallery, Pinner, Manor House Gallery, Chipping Norton, Geneva, New York. *Work in collections:* in Britain, U.S.A., France, Germany, Finland. *Signs work:* "Colin Kent." *Address:* 64 Forest Rd., Romford, Essex RM7 8DT.

KERN, Doreen, sculptor in bronze; consultant to B.M. Replica Dept.; *b* 9 Aug., 1941. divorced. two *s. Educ:* Hampstead Garden Suburb Institute; studio assistant at the Morris Singer Art Bronze foundry. *Studied:* under Howard Bates, R.A. *Exhib:* Waterloo Fine Arts, Talma Gallery, Tel-Aviv, Ryder Gallery, L.A., Galerie Nichido, Tokyo, London University, Bath Festival, National Museum of Archaeology, Valletta, Malta, Design Centre, St. Paul's Cathedral, Edinburgh Festival (1995). *Work in collections:* Dr Kwame Nkrumah, Guyana, Emperor Haile Selassie (Palace of Addis Ababa), Anne Frank for Anne Frank house, Amsterdam also British Library, Clint Eastwood, Ariel Sharon, Alistair McLean, Miss Bluebell, Chaim Topol. *Signs* *work:* see appendix. *Address:* The Studio, 38 Canons Drive, Edgware, Middx. HA8 7QT.

KERR, Janet, R.W.S. (1997); painter in water based mixed media on paper, semi abstract work mainly concerned with W. Yorkshire landscape; *b* Hornchurch, Essex, 20 May, 1947. *m* divorced. one *d. Educ:* Palmers Girls School, Barking Regional College (Graphics). *Studied:* privately with Charles Bartlett P.P.R.W.S. *Exhib:* Bankside Gallery, London, and throughout Britain. *Work in collections:* Museum of Foreign Art, Japan. *Signs work:* "JanetKerr." *Address:* 11 New Longley, Norland, Sowerby Bridge, W. Yorks. HX6 3RR. *Email:* jkerr@tinyonline.co.uk

KERSHAW, Walter, B.A. Hons. Fine Art (Dunelm); mural painter and freelance artist in oil, water-colour, mosaic; occasional visiting lecturer in Environmental Art at Universities in the U.K., Brazil and W. Germany; *b* Rochdale, 7 Dec., 1940. *Educ:* De la Salle College, Salford. *Studied:* Durham University (1958-62). *Exhib:* Large scale, public, external murals in Manchester, Trafford Park and N.W. Museum of Science and Industry; Norwich; Brazil, Sao Paulo and Recife. Internal murals for British Aerospace, Manchester United F.C., P. & O., Sarajevo International Arts Festival, Salford University, the C.E.G.B., Hollingworth Lake Visitors Centre and Italian Consulate Manchester, Airtours cruise ship 'Sunbird'. Photos of murals at the Serpentine, Whitechapel and Tate galleries. *Work in collections:* V. & A., British Council, Arts Council, Gulbenkian Foundation, 'Cultura Inglesa', Museum of Art, São Paulo, and other public galleries in the U.K. Films: 'Terra Firma' BBC 2 (1976), 'First Graffiti Artist' (1977), 'Nationwide' (1982), '5 x 5' W. Germany (1984), 'Folio' Anglia TV (1987), Bosnia T.V. (1996). International Arts Festival. Recorded: 'Conversation Piece' with Sue MacGregor, Radio 4 (1983), 'Kaleidoscope' Radio 4 (1986). *Signs work:* "Walter Kershaw." *Address:* 193 Todmorden Rd., Littleborough, Rochdale OL15 9EG.

KETCHER, Jean, B.A.Hons. Fine Art Painting (1976); painter in oil, water-colour, etc.; art teacher, Copleston High School, Ipswich; *b* 6 July, 1955. *Studied:* Ipswich School of Art (1971-73), Maidstone College of Art (1973-76). *Exhib:* Halesworth Gallery, Ellingham Mill, Bungay, Corn Exchange, Ipswich. *Signs work:* "Jean Ketcher." *Address:* 46 Sandown Rd., Ipswich IP1 6RE.

KEY, Geoffrey, D.A. (1960); painter in oil, sculptor; *b* Manchester, 13 May, 1941. *Educ:* High School of Art, Manchester. *Studied:* Regional College of Art, Manchester (1958-61), under Harry Rutherford, William Bailey. *Exhib:* Salford A.G., Clermont Ferrand France, London, Nancy France, Germany, Madison Ave., N.Y., Lausanne Switzerland, Dublin, Saint Ouen France, Hong Kong, Moret-sur-Long France, Barbizon France, Harrods Knightsbridge, Oriel Dublin. *Work in collections:* Salford A.G., Manchester City Gallery, Bolton A.G., Granada Television, Wigan Corp., Manchester University, North West Arts, Jockey Club of Hong Kong, Perrier, Society Roquefort, Manderin Hotel, Hong Kong, Chateau de St. Ouen, Chataux Relais. *Publications:* G.Key: Drawings (Margin Press), Dictionary of British Art (Collectors Club Press), European Painters (Clio Press). *Clubs:* Manchester Academy, Portico Manchester. *Signs work:* see appendix. *Address:* 59 Acresfield Rd., Pendleton, Salford M6 7GE.

KHALIL: see NORLAND (NEUSCHUL), Khalil.

KHAN, Keith Ali, B.A.(Hons.); sculptor in large scale exterior/interior constructions, using fabric and many people; Director, Carnival Designer; *b* Trinidad, 4 Dec., 1963. *Educ:* King's College, Wimbledon. *Studied:* Wimbledon School of Art, Middlesex Polytechnic (Dante Leonelli), The Street, Port of Spain, Trinidad. *Exhib:* Houston International Festival, Harris Museum, Preston, Arnolfini, Bristol; one-man shows: Bluecoat Gallery, Liverpool, Greenwich Citizen Gallery; on the streets of Notting Hill, as well as numerous designs on TV and stage. *Signs work:* "Khan." *Address:* 79 Grand Drive, Raynes Pk., London SW20 9DW.

KHANNA, Balraj, M.A. (1962); awarded Winnifred Holtby prize by R.S.L. (1984); painter in acrylic and oil, novelist; *b* 4 Oct., 1940. *m* Francine Martine. two *d. Educ:* Punjab University, Chandigarh. *Exhib:* fifty one-man shows including Ashmolean Museum, Oxford (1968), City A.G., Bristol (1969), Galerie Transposition, Paris (1966, 1968, 1974, 1975), Herbert Benevy Gallery, N.Y. (1971, 1972), Serpentine Gallery (1979), Richard Demarco (1986), Royal Festival Hall (1990), Arnolfini (1991). M.O.M.A. Wales (1993), Berlin and Frankfurt (1994), De La Warr Pavilion (1996), Oldham Gallery, M.A.C. Birmingham. *Work in collections:* Arts Council; Musee d'Art Moderne, Paris; Ville de Paris; Ashmolean Museum; National Gallery of Modern Art, New Delhi; City A.G., Bristol; City A.G., Bradford; V. & A.; Calouste Gulbenkian Foundation, Lisbon. *Publications:* Nation of Fools (Michael Joseph and Penguin), Sweet Chillies (Constable), Kalighat, Popular Indian Painting, 1800-1930 (Redstone Press), Krishna - The Divine Lover (South Bank Centre Publication), Art of Modern India (Thames & Hudson, 1998), Human & Divine – 2000 Years of Indian Sculpture. *Signs work:* "Khanna." *Address:* 3a Pindock Mews, London W9 2PY.

KIANUSH-WALLACE, Katy, self taught professional artist and illustrator in acrylic, water-colour, pen and ink, pencil, pastel; Owner of Art Gallery and Cultural Website Art Arena; Member of the Executive Council of N.A.P.A., directed the first London exhibition of N.A.P.A. at Westminster Gallery, July/Aug. 1999; *b* Tehran, Iran, 12 Apr., 1964. *m* Jim Wallace. *Educ:* Acton, London. *Exhib:* over sixty solo and group shows during last eight years: Westminster Gallery; R.B.S.A. (winner, Royal Sovereign (Rembrandt) Award 1998); Victoria A.G., Bath; Black Sheep Gallery, Hawarden (winner, Daler-Rowney International Award 1999); Handel House Gallery, Devizes; The Guildhall, Salisbury; Crosfield Hall, Romsey; Wyvern Theatre, Swindon; BBC World Service, London; National Power, Swindon, etc. Work on permanent exhbn. on Internet galleries worldwide. *Work in collections:* private collections: U.K. and abroad. *Publications:* illustrated children's poetry books, published in Iran, at age ten; cover, book of poems, 'Closed Circuit' by Shadab Vajdi (Forest Books). *Clubs:* N.A.P.A., Wessex Artists. *Signs work:* see appendix. *Address:* 4 Bennett Hill Close, Wootton Bassett, Wiltshire SN4 8LR. *Website:* http://www.art-arena.com

KIDNER, Michael, B.A. (Cantab); paintings and constructions; *b* Kettering, 1917. *m* Marion Frederick. *Educ:* Bedales School. *Studied:* self-taught. *Exhib:* widely. *Work in collections:* Tate Gallery, Arts Council of G.B., British Council, W.A.G., Huddersfield A.G., Manchester City A.G., Contemporary Art Soc., London, Sussex University, University of Wales, Gulbenkian Foundation, V. &. A., Museum Sztuki, Lodz, and Poznan Museum, Poland, Museum of Modern Art, N.Y., Southampton

City A.G., Anios Anderson Museum, Helsinki, Norrkopings Konstmuseum, Malmo Konsthall, National Gallery, Canberra, Australia, Moderna Museet, Stockholm, Henry Moore Sculpture Trust, University of East Anglia, Norwich, England, Pfalzgalerie, Kaiserslautern, Germany. *Publications:* Elastic Membrane. *Signs work:* "Michael Kidner." *Address:* 18 Hampstead Hill Gdns., London NW3 2PL.

KILLEEN, Bruce, M.A. Oxon. (1950), R.W.A. (1963), A.I.A. (1964); self taught painter in oil; formerly, senior lecturer, Colchester School of Art, tutor, R.A. Schools; Art Correspondent, The Guardian; *b* Warwickshire, 22 Jan., 1926. *m* (1) Angela Fry, artist/potter (died 1997). (2) Julie Wroughton, A.R.C.A., R.W.A. painter. one *s.* two *d. Educ:* Merton College, Oxford. *Exhib:* one-man: A.I.A. Galleries, Drian Galleries, London; Minories, Colchester; Chappel Galleries, Essex; Alpha House, Sherborne; Malcolm Innes Gallery, Edinburgh; mixed: R.A., R.W.A., Bruton Street Gallery, Penwith Gallery, St. Ives, etc. *Publications:* Arts Council Art Films (1978-80). *Signs work:* "B.A. KILLEEN" or "B.K." *Address:* Balmeanach, By Tiroran, Isle of Mull PA68 6EH.

KINAHAN, Lady Coralie, U.S.W.A., U.W.A., R.U.A. (resigned); artist in oil and water-colour; Lady Mayoress of Belfast (1959-62); President, Co. Antrim Red Cross (1955-67); *b* Surrey, 1924. *m* Sir Robin Kinahan. two *s.* three *d. Educ:* by 14 governesses and 4 schools. *Studied:* John Hassall, and Chelsea Schools of Art (1943-46); private portrait classes under Sonia Mervyn, A.R.A. (1946-49). *Exhib:* R.A., R.P., R.O.I., S.WL.A., R.S.A., R.U.A.; solo exhbns. annually, Belfast, Dublin, Wexford, Galway, Bristol and London (1964-85). Opened own gallery (1985) Templepatrick, exhibiting landscapes, wildlife, horses and portraits. *Commissions:* include Lord Bishop of Durham, Rt. Hon. Humphrey and Mrs. Atkins, Rt. Hon. James Prior, General Sir Ian Freeland, Capt. Torrens-Spence, D.S.O., R.N. (H.M. Lord Lt. for Armagh), Lord Cooke of Islandreagh, Gen. Sir John and Lady Waters and many children's portraits; Army commissions for The Black Watch Regt., The Grenadier Guards, Imperial War Museum, The Royal Highland Regt., The 2nd Parachute Regt., The 9/12th Royal Lancers and the Ulster Defence Regt.; Sporting pictures for Mr. Victor McCalmont and The Master Beagler, Terence Grainger. *Publications:* historical novels: You can't shoot the English (1982), After the war, came Peace? (1987), Memoirs: Behind every great man - ? (1998); work repro.: limited edns. 200 prints of Belfast Harbour; and Patrol looking over Belfast. Husband made H.M.'s Lord Lieut. for Belfast (1985). *Signs work:* "C. de B.K." oils; "Coralie Kinahan" water-colours. *Address:* 19 Abbey Mews, Amesbury, Wilts. SP4 7EX.

KINDER, Joan, S.G.F.A. (1965), F.F.P.S. (1960); painter and printmaker in ink and water-colour of mono prints in abstract expressionism; *b* Yorkshire, 19 June, 1916. *m* K.J. Kinder. two *d. Educ:* Bridlington High. *Studied:* Scarborough School of Art (1932-36, Edward and Ethel Walker) specialising in textile. *Exhib:* S.G.F.A., Mall Galleries, C.W.A.C., and solo shows. *Work in collections:* U.K. and U.S.A. *Signs work:* "(Joan) Kinder." *Address:* 8 Upper Woodcote Village, Purley, Surrey CR8 3HE.

KING, Andrew Norman, B.F.A. (Hons.) (1978), N.S. (1984), R.O.I. (1992); David Murray Scholarship, R.A. Schools (1978); landscape and marine artist in oil and water-colour, interested in light and atmosphere in landscape; *b* Bedford, 1956.

Educ: Barnfield College, Luton. *Studied:* Hornsey College of Art. *Exhib:* Britain in Water-colour, R.I., N.E.A.C., N.S., R.S.M.A., R.O.I., R.W.S., R.P., Laing; one-man shows, Luton, Hitchin, Linslade, Stowe, London and Aldeburgh, 'Discerning Eye' (1999). *Work in collections:* Luton Art Council, Beds. C.C., Eagle Star Offices, and in private and royal collections in Britain and abroad. Finalist, Winsor and Newton Young Artists award (1985). *Clubs:* East Anglian Group of Marine Artists. *Signs work:* "Andrew King." *Address:* Pond Cottage, Long Rd., Colby, Norwich NR11 7EF.

KING, Christabel Frances, B.Sc.Hons.(Lond.) (1971), F.S.B.A.; Linnean Society Jill Smythies Award (1989); botanical artist in water-colour; part-time lecturer, Capel Manor College, Enfield, tutor to scholars of Margaret Mee Fellowship Program, R.B.G. Kew, since 1990; *b* London, 1950. *Educ:* Sherborne School for Girls. *Studied:* scientific illustration: Middlesex Polytechnic (1973-74). *Exhib:* Messrs. Agnew (1980), Kew Gdns. Gallery (1993). *Work in collections:* R.B.G. Kew, Hunt Botanical Institute, Shirley Sherwood. *Publications:* illustrations in Curtis's Botanical Magazine since 1975; also Flowering Plants of the World, ed. V.H. Heywood (Elsevier 1978); Kew Magazine Monographs: The Genus Pleione, The Genus Echinocereus, The Genus Lewisia, The Genus Galanthus; Africa's Mountains of the Moon by Guy Yeoman (Elm Tree Books 1989); Flowering Plants of the Falkland Islands by R.W. Woods (Falklands Conservation 2000). *Clubs:* S.B.A. (Founder mem. 1985). *Signs work:* "C.F.K." or "C.F. King." *Address:* 149 Fulwell Park Ave., Twickenham, Middx. TW2 5HG.

KING, Gordon Thomas, F.A.T.G. (Guild published Artist of the Year 1999-2000); artist in water-colour, oil; Chairman, F.A.T.G. Artist Com.; *b* London, 6 June, 1939. *m* Mary. two *s.* one *d. Studied:* Carlton Studios, Reading University. *Exhib:* R.A. Summer Show, R.I., Halcyon Gallery (I.C.C., Birmingham), Singer & Friedlander/Sunday Times, retrospective exhibition at Halcyon Gallery (London) March 2002. *Publications:* 'Romance with Art', 'Drawn to Life'; over 60 limited edn. prints published; 3 special limited edition prints of Darcey Bussell, signed by both dancer and artist, published in aid of Alzheimer's Society. *Clubs:* Fine Art Trade Guild. *Signs work:* see appendix. *Address:* The Hollies, 21 Copthall Lane, Chalfont St. Peter, Bucks. SL9 0BY.

KING, John Gregory, S.E.A.; artist in oil, water-colour, bronze; *b* West Tytherley, 16 Apr., 1929. *m* Mary Rose. one *s.* one *d. Educ:* Canford School. *Studied:* briefly at Salisbury Art College. *Exhib:* ten one-man shows in London and Alnwick Castle, Goodwood House. *Work in collections:* Gordon Highlanders Museum, Perth, Royal Fusilier Museum, Tower of London. *Commissions:* Royal Tournament, Sheik Mohamod, Tattersalls, Ironmongers Co., Royal Bodyguard, etc. *Publications:* illustrated: They Meet at 11, They Still Meet at 11, The Golden Thread, The Fox and the Orchid, Gallant Horses and Horsemen. *Clubs:* The Arts, The Farmers. *Signs work:* "John King." *Address:* Church Farm House, West Tytherley, Salisbury, Wilts. SP5 1LB.

KING, Mary, A.T.C. (1947), S.W.A. (1979), N.S. (1984), F.R.S.A. (1988); artist in mixed media, water-colour and collage; lecturer, North East Surrey College of Technology (1968-80) and Surbiton Adult Education Centre; *b* London, 17 Oct.,

1926. *m* Ralph King. one *s*. three *d*. *Educ:* Wallington Grammar School. *Studied:* Chelsea College of Art (1946, painting, Ceri Richards; 1948-49, stained glass, Francis Spear), Central School of Arts and Crafts, London, Whitelands College, Putney. *Exhib:* Fairfield Halls, Croydon, Bourne Hall, Ewell, F.B.A., S.W.A., R.B.A., Mall Galleries, Westminster Gallery (1988-97 annually), R.A. Summer Exhbn. (1981, 1982), Bankside Gallery, London (1985, 1986, 1996, 1997), National Soc., Whiteleys Atrium (1995-98), Munich (1997), solo shows, Farnham Maltings (1983, 1985, 1987, 1990), Epsom Playhouse, Ashley Gallery, Epsom, Conway Hall, London (1984), Loggia Gallery (1983, 1984, 1986), many London exhbns. including Heifer Gallery, Islington (1990-96), Hyde Park Gallery, Fine Arts, Bond St. (1991, 1998), Bonhams Knightsbridge, Smiths Galleries, Covent Gdn. (1990-93), Windsor (1997), Alchemy Gallery, London (1999), Marketsmühle Gallery, Schwindegg, Germany. *Signs work:* "Mary King" or "M. King." *Address:* 42 Reigate Rd., Ewell, Epsom, Surrey KT17 1PX.

KING, Phillip, C.B.E. (1974), P.R.A., R.A.; sculptor in steel, bronze, fibreglass; Prof. of Sculpture, Royal Academy of Art, Prof. Emeritus, Royal College of Art; *b* Tunis, 1934. married. one *s*. (decd.). *Educ:* Mill Hill School; Christ College, Cambridge. *Studied:* St. Martin's School of Art. *Exhib:* Rowan Gallery London, Richard Fergen Gallery N.Y., Venice Biennale, Whitechapel Gallery London, Kunsthalle Mannheim. *Work in collections:* Tate Gallery, M.O.M.A. (N.Y.), National Gallery of Australia, Kroller Muller Museum, New Museum of Contemporary Art Hiroshima, Yorkshire Sculpture Pk., Kunsthalle Mannheim, etc. *Publications:* The Sculpture of Phillip King by Tim Hilton. *Signs work:* see appendix. *Address:* c/o New Rowan Gallery, 25 Dover St., London W1X 3PA.

KING, Robert, R.I. (1970); Mem. Leicester Soc. of Artists (1960); painter in oil, water-colour; etcher and lithographer; *b* Leicester, 28 June, 1936. *m* Christine James. *Educ:* Fosse Boys' School, Leicester. *Studied:* Leicester College of Art (1956-58). *Exhib:* one-man shows, six at Gadsby Gallery, Leicester (1970-80) and Medici Gallery (1980-89); three with Burlington Paintings (1989-97); annually with R.I., R.A., R.S.M.A., Leicester Soc. of Artists. *Work in collections:* Nottingham Educ. Com., Leicester Royal Infirmary, Leicester University, Fishmongers Hall London, Royal Yacht Squadron, Cowes, I.O.W. *Publications:* illustrated Denys Brook-Hart's 20th Century British Marine Painting. *Signs work:* "ROBERT KING." *Address:* 2 Coastguard Cottages, Lepe, nr. Exbury, Hants. SO45 1AD.

KINGS, Tarka Huxley, M.A.; painter/printer in oil, silkscreen; *b* London, 24 May, 1961. *Educ:* St. Paul's Girls School. *Studied:* City and Guilds, R.A. Schools (1982-87, Peter Greenham, Norman Adams). *Exhib:* Creative Salvage (1985), R.A., Gallery 24, Phoenix Gallery, Langton Gallery, St. Paul's, Cadogan Contemporary (1988), Bill Thomson Gallery, Rebecca Hossack Gallery (1991, 1993, 1994, 1995). Asst. to Leonard Rosoman, Lambeth Palace Chapel ceiling. *Work in collections:* private collections in U.S.A. and England. Artwork for films: 'Secrets' (Dir. Phillip Savile), 'The Dream' (Dir. Con Mulgrave). *Clubs:* Congress. *Signs work:* "THK." *Address:* 35 Beethoven St., London W10.

KINGSTON, Angela Hoppe, painter; Chairman, Water-colour Soc. of Wales; Lectures and Workshops; *b* Mumbles, nr. Swansea, 1936. *m* Dr. Gordon (Ph.D.).

three *s.* two *d. Educ:* Llwyn y Bryn High School, Swansea. *Studied:* Bath Academy of Art, Corsham, Wilts. (1955-58, Adrian Heath, Martin Froy, William Scott), University College, Cardiff (1979). *Exhib:* solo shows: Mistral Gallery, London (1992), St. David's Hall, Cardiff (1991), etc.; group shows: W.A.C. Touring (1993-95), St. Donats Arts Centre, Wales (1992), A.A.D.W. Cardiff Arts Festival (1988-89), S.B.A., W.S.W., Welsh Group. *Work in collections:* Glynn Vivian A.G., Swansea, Cork University. *Clubs:* W.S.W. (Chair), S.B.A., The Welsh Group. *Signs work:* "A. Hoppe Kingston." *Address:* Monks, Dimlands Rd., Llantwit Major, Vale of Glam. CF61 1SJ, Wales.

KINGSTON, Richard, R.H.A.; painter in oil, water-colour and pastel; founded the Wellington Gallery, Ballsbridge, Co. Dublin; governor of National Gallery of Ireland (1982-1989); *b* Ireland, 22 Mar., 1922. *m* Jennifer. three *s.* two *d. Educ:* National School, Dublin. *Studied:* Trinity College, Dublin. *Exhib:* solo exhibs. at Wellington Gallery, Ballsbridge (numerous); Hendricks Gallery (1958-1964); retrospective at R.H.A. (2001); group exhibs. at Irish Exhib. of Living Art, Dublin (1957-1960); Guggenheim Internat. Award Exhib. (1960); Salzburg Biennial Exhib. of Modern Sacred Art (1960 & 1962); Eight Irish Painters, Savage Gallery, London (1961); Artists of Fame and Promise, London (1961-1962); Exhib. of Irish Art, Greenwich, Connecticut, and San Francisco, U.S.A. (1960, 1961); R.H.A. Annual Exhib. (1964-); 21st. Ann. Exhib., Douglas Hyde Gallery, Dublin (1980); Oireachtas Exhib. (1980-1982); R.H.A. Banquet Exhib., Dublin (1990-). *Work in collections:* public and private collections world wide including, Ireland, U.K., Canada, Japan, Australia, U.S.A.; major public and corporate collections. *Signs work:* "Kingston." *Address:* 19 Heytesbury Lane, Ballsbridge, Dublin 4.

KINMONT, David Bruce, Was Senior member of the University of Bristol where, in 1971, he delivered the George Hare Leonard Memorial Lecture. Visiting professorships: George Washington University, Washington D.C. (1974); universities in Beijing, Shanghai (1986), and Hebei (1989), in China; and at the University of St. Petersburg in 1990, and the Gulbenkian Museum, Lisbon (1996); oil paintings, drawings and silk screen prints; sole dealer: J. K. Contemporary, 3 Cheyne Walk, London; *b* Kent, 1932. *Educ:* St. John's College, Cambridge. *Exhib:* one-man shows include, Ferens City A.G., Hull (1963); City A.G., Bangor (1960); St. John's College, Cambridge (1969); Churchill College, Cambridge (1976); University of Durham (1981); University of Exeter (1986); Georges, Bristol (1987). *Address:* The Lent House, Clevedon Rd., Flax Bourton, Bristol BS48 1NQ. *Email:* andlent@btinternet.com

KIRBY, Michael, M.F.P.S.; fine art restorer, artist in oil; *b* Farnham Common, Bucks., 30 Dec., 1949. married. two *s.* two *d. Studied:* High Wycombe School of Art (1967-71) under G. G. Palmer, Romeo Di Girolamo, R.B.A., Eric Smith, R.B.A., R.W.S., Henry Trivick, R.B.A. *Exhib:* R.B.A., Open Salon, F.P.S., H.U.A.S. *Signs work:* "M. Kirby." *Address:* 30 Sycamore Rise, Bracknell, Berks. RG12 3BU.

KIRK, Barry, N.D.D. (1954), A.R.C.A. (1959), F.R.S.A. (1989); Travelling scholarship R.C.A. (1959); painter, draughtsman; Canterbury College of Art 1959-1988 (Vice-Principal 1974-87, Principal 1987-88); thereafter full-time art practice; *b* Deal, Kent, 17 Feb., 1933. *m* Pleasance Kirk, A.R.C.A., M.S.D.C. two *s. Educ:*

Westminster School. *Studied:* Canterbury College of Art (1950-54), R.C.A. (1956-59). *Exhib:* R.A., Francis Kyle Gallery; one-man shows, Alwin Gallery, etc. *Work in collections:* V. & A., Kent C.C., Canterbury C.C., Glasgow C.C. *Signs work:* "Barry Kirk." *Address:* 13 High St., Bridge, Canterbury, Kent CT4 5JY.

KIRK, Douglas William, painter in oil and water-colour; lecturer, City of London Polytechnic (1976-89); *b* Edinburgh, 22 Feb., 1949. two *s.* two *d. Educ:* George Heriot's School, Edinburgh. *Studied:* Duncan of Jordanstone College of Art, Dundee (1967-71), Royal College of Art, London (1971-74). *Exhib:* S.S.A., Compass Gallery, Glasgow, Fine Art Soc., 57 Gallery, Edinburgh, Fruit Market Gallery, Edinburgh, Leonie Jonleigh Gallery, Guildford, Kunsthaudlung Jouiskeit, Stuttgart. *Work in collections:* Carlisle Museum and Gallery. *Signs work:* "douglas kirk." *Address:* 221 South Oak Knoll Avenue 305, Pasadena, CA91101, U.S.A. *Email:* dw_kirk@hotmail.com

KIRK, Robert Joseph, B.A. (1973), M.Sc. (1978), N.A.P.A. (1988); painter in acrylic and pastel; *b* Walsall, 7 Jan., 1932. *m* Sheila M. two *d. Studied:* Walsall and Stafford Schools of Art (1955, Angus Macauley, David Bethel). *Exhib:* N.A.P.A. Annual, (1989-1993). Digital images and graphic design for internet. *Clubs:* N.A.P.A., Ludlow Art Soc. *Signs work:* "Robert Kirk." *Address:* West Fortune, Ashford Carbonell, Ludlow, Salop. SY8 4DB. *Website:* www.robertkirk.co.uk *Email:* robertkirk@rkstudio.demon.co.uk

KIRKWOOD, John Sutherland, artist, mixed media, photography and etching; *b* Edinburgh, 6 Apr., 1947. *m* Ines Santy. *Educ:* George Watson College, Edinburgh. *Studied:* Dundee College of Art. *Exhib:* one-man shows: 57 Art Gallery, Edinburgh Printmakers Workshop, A.I.R. Gallery, Talbot Rice Art Centre, Demarco Gallery, "Scottish Art Now". *Work in collections:* S.A.C. Loan, Hunterian Museum, University of Glasgow, Scottish Museum of Modern Art, Imperial War Museum, Edinburgh City Arts Centre. *Publications:* Contemporary Paintings in Scotland (1995) - Bill Hare. *Signs work:* "J. S. Kirkwood." *Address:* 15 Leopold Pl., Edinburgh EH7 5LB.

KITSON, Linda Francis, B.A. (1967), M.A., R.C.A. (1970); official war artist, Falkland Islands Task Force (1982); artist/tutor; Pres. Army Arts and Crafts Soc. (1983); *b* London, 17 Feb., 1945. *m* Hon. Barnaby Howard (1996). *Educ:* Tortingdon Pk., nr. Arundel, Sussex. *Studied:* St. Martin's School of Art (1965-67), R.C.A. (1967-70). *Exhib:* Workshop Gallery, Illustrators A.G., Imperial War Museum (Falkland's War Exhbn. U.K. tour), National Theatre, R.A. *Work in collections:* Imperial War Museum. *Publications:* Picnic (Jill Norman); The Falklands War, a Visual Diary (Mitchell Beazley); The Plague; Sun, Wind, Sand and Stars (Folio Soc.). *Clubs:* Chelsea Arts. *Signs work:* "Linda Kitson." *Address:* Flat 3, 25 Onslow Sq., London SW7 3NJ.

KITTS, Barry Edward Lyndon, N.D.D. (1964), F.R.S.A. (1972); landscape painter and writer on art; visiting lecturer at Central St. Martin's College of Art and Design; *b* Bath, 18 Oct., 1943. *Educ:* Sutton East County Secondary School (Surrey Special Art Course under George Mackley, M.B.E., R.E.). *Studied:* Kingston School of Art (1959-61) under J. D. Binns, A.R.C.A., D.A. Pavey, A.R.C.A., Wimbledon School of Art (1961-64) under Gerald Cooper, A.R.C.A. *Exhib:* N.E.A.C., R.B.A.,

Wessex Artists' Exhbn. *Publications:* Co-author of a Graphic Design Sourcebook (1987). *Signs work:* "Barry Kitts." *Address:* 500 Kingston Rd., London SW20 8DT.

KLEIN, Anita, B.A.Hons. (1983), M.A. (1985), R.E. (1991); painter/printmaker in drypoint, woodcut, oil on board; *b* Sydney, Australia, 14 Feb., 1960. *m* Nigel Swift. two *d. Educ:* Hampstead School. *Studied:* Chelsea School of Art (1978-79), Slade School of Fine Art (1979-83, Mick Moon, Paula Rego; 1983-85, Barto dos Santos). *Exhib:* I.C.A., Hayward, R.I., Blond Fine Art; one-man shows: Creaser Gallery, Leigh Gallery, Tall House Gallery, Wilson Hale; Cambridge Contemporary Art, Beaux Arts, Bath, C.C.A. Oxford, Boundary Gallery, London (main dealer), Advanced Graphics, London. *Work in collections:* A.C.G.B., R.E., Ashmolean Museum. *Clubs:* Greenwich Printmakers, Royal Soc. of Painter Printmakers. *Signs work:* see appendix. *Address:* 82 Tressillian Rd., London SE4 1YD.

KNAPP-FISHER, John, R.C.A. (1992); painter; *b* London, 2 Aug., 1931. *m* Sheila Basset (divorced). one *s.* one *d. Educ:* Eastbourne College. *Studied:* Maidstone College of Art (1951-53), Designer in Theatre. *Exhib:* R.A., Business Art Galleries, Oriel, Welsh Arts Council, Upper Grosvenor, Agnews, Fry, Marjorie Parr, Johannesburg, Toronto, N.Y., Pembrokeshire Museums Touring (1984), Beaux Arts, Bath (1986), Henry Thomas Gallery, Faculty of Art and Design, Carmarthan (1989), National Museum of Wales, Lichfield Festival (1995), Attic, Swansea, Martin Tinney, Albany, Cardiff, Pump-House, London (1999), R.Cam.A. (1999), New Academy (2001). *Work in collections:* B.B.C. Cardiff, National Museum of Wales, National Library of Wales, Beecroft A.G., W. Wales Assoc. for the Arts, Swansea University, Haverfordwest Museum, prize winning panel, Withybush Hospital Haverfordwest, Contemporary Art Soc. for Wales. *Publications:* illustrated Pembrokeshire Churches (1989); included in: Cymru'r Cynfas by Hywel Harries (Lolfa Press, 1983); wrote and illustrated John Knapp-Fisher's Pembrokeshire (Senecio Press, 1995), 'Welsh Painters Talking' by Tony Curtis (Seren Books, 1997). Films: Anglia T.V. The Artist and his Work (1963), H.T.V. (Merlin T.V.) 'A Word In Your Eye' (1997), 'Movers and Shakers' B.B.C. Radio Wales (1997), 'On the House' B.B.C. Wales (1999), 'River Patrol', H.T.V. (2000), Twrio S4C TV. (2001); featured: Planet Magazine (Oct./Nov. 1998), Cambria Magazine (Winter 1998/9). *Signs work:* "John Knapp-Fisher." *Address:* Trevigan Cottage, Croesgoch, Haverfordwest, Pembrokeshire SA62 5JP.

KNEALE, Bryan, R.A. Rome Scholar; sculptor in steel and all metals, wood, etc.; Mem. C.N.A.A. Fine Arts Panel, Royal College of Art, Professor of Sculpture, Royal Academy (1980-83), Head of Sculpture R.C.A. (1985-90), Professor of Drawing (1990), Chairman A.S.G.; *b* Douglas, I.O.M., 19 June, 1930. *m* Doreen Kneale. one *s.* one *d. Educ:* Douglas High School. *Studied:* Douglas School of Art (1947) under W. H. Whitehead; R.A. Schools (1948-52) under Philip Connard, Henry Rushbury. *Exhib:* John Moores, Art d'aujourd'hui, Paris, Battersea Park, Whitechapel Retrospective, Cardiff, Leics. Educ. Com., Whitechapel, City of London, Peter Stuyvesant, Southampton, British Sculptors, R.A. Holland Park, Royal Exchange Sculpt., Hayward Gallery, R.A., London Group, Redfern Gallery, New Art Centre. *Work in collections:* Tate, Arts Council, C.A.S., W.A.G., Fitzwilliam Museum, B.M., City Art Galleries of Manchester, Birmingham, Sheffield, Bradford, Wakefield, Leicester, York and Middlesbrough, Sao Paulo,

Brazil, Museum of Modern Art, N.Y., National Galleries of N.Z., Queensland and S. Australia, Manx Museum and A.G., Abbot Hall Gallery, Cumberland, Beaverbrook Foundation, Frederickton, Bochum Museum, W. Germany, Bahia Museum, Brazil. *Clubs:* Chelsea Arts. *Signs work:* "BRYAN KNEALE" (die stamp), "Bryan Kneale" (drawings, etc.). *Address:* 10a Muswell Rd., London N10 2BG.

KNIGHT, Clifford (Edgar Levi), V.P.U.A., F.R.S.A.; painter in oil, water-colour and mixed media, lecturer/demonstrator; *b* Kempston, Beds., 8 Mar., 1930. *m* Sherri. three s- *s.* two s- *d. Educ:* Kempston Secondary Modern School. *Studied:* under William Twybel, A.R.C.A. (1948-54), L.C.C. Central School (1955-57, William Roberts, Merlyn Evans, Paul Hogarth, S.R. Badmin). *Exhib:* U.A., N.E.A.C.; one-man shows, Upper St. Gallery (1973), Carlton House Terr. (1983), Bedford, Luton, Letchworth, Northampton, Retford, Wellingborough, Welwyn Garden City, Abbotsholme School, Bedford School. *Work in collections:* Northampton, Luton and Letchworth A.Gs, Crown Commissioners, Texas Instruments, Beds. C.C.; private collections: U.S.A., S.Africa, Paris, Canada. *Commissions:* Bedford, U.S.A., Paris, London. *Publications:* work repro.: Leisure Painter; London Today, T.V. *Clubs:* Armed Forces Art Soc. *Signs work:* "Clifford Knight." *Address:* 222 Shelley Rd., Wellingborough, Northants. NN8 3DS.

KNIGHT, Sophie, R.W.S. (1992), A.R.W.S. (1990), B.A.(Hons.) Fine Art (1986), Post Grad. Dip. (1989); Ian Tragarthen Jenkins award (1986), David Murray Scholarship (1988), Erik Kennington award (1989), Hunting Group Student prize (1989), R.W.S. award (1989); painter in water-colour and acrylic; *b* London, 20 Mar., 1965. *Educ:* The New School, Kings Langley. *Studied:* Herts. School of Art, St.Albans (1982), Camberwell School of Art and Design (1983-86), R.A. Schools (1986-89). *Exhib:* numerous exhbns. including R.A. Summer Exhbn. (1988), R.W.S. Bankside Gallery S.E.1 (1988), Mall Galleries (1989), Whitechapel Open (1994); solo shows include Cadogan Contemporary (1991, 2000), Waterman Fine Arts (1993), The Unicorn Gallery, London S.W.10, Reutlingnen Gallery, Germany (1996). *Work in collections:* B.M., The House of Lords, The New Parliamentary Building W1, T.S.B. Bank. *Signs work:* "Sophie Knight." *Address:* 36 Ivinghoe Rd., Bushey, Herts., London WD2 3SW

KNOWLER, Ann Patricia, S.W.A. (1993); artist in oil and soft pastels; member of Council S.W.A.; *b* Pinner, 3 June, 1940. *m* Jonathan Knowler. one *s.* one *d. Educ:* Northwood Secondary Modern School. *Studied:* F.E. classes and privately under Claude Murrills. *Exhib:* S.W.A. Westminster Gallery, David Curzon Gallery. *Work in collections:* several private collections. *Clubs:* Weald of Sussex Art, The Adventurers Art, Assoc. of Sussex Artists. *Signs work:* "Ann Knowler." *Address:* Sundown, 7 Western Rd., Newick, E. Sussex BN8 4LE. *Email:* aknowler@talk21.com

KNOWLES, Arthur Morris, Dip.P.W. (1952), R.C.A., A.R.S.A.; landscape painter/poster artist in pencil, pastel, oil, design crafts, and professional poster writer and sketch artist; *b* Wolverhampton, 1923. married. two *s. Educ:* Graiseley (Sen. Boys) School. *Studied:* Wolverhampton School of Art and Crafts (1937-39, A. Willetts), Holborn (1948-52, E. Oldham), E.M.I. Inst., Chiswick (1952-54, J.M. Higginson). *Exhib:* Wolverhampton, Dudley, Bridgnorth, Norwich, Tettenhall and Wolverhampton stores, Moxley-Darlaston. *Commissions:* Local posters and sign boards - church posters, small paintings. Artist in Residence, St. Thomas's Church, Wednesfield, W/M. (1987). *Clubs:* Member Free Painters & Sculptors, F.P.S., (London), Dudley Soc. of Artists (West Midlands). *Signs work:* "Knowles" or "M.K." joined. *Address:* 48 Bromford Rise, Oaklands Rd., Penn, Wolverhampton WV3 0ES.

KNOX, Jack, R.S.A. (1979), R.G.I. (1981), R.S.W. (1987), Hon. R.I.A.S. (1997); painter in oil, acrylic, pastel; Head of Painting, Glasgow School of Art (1981-92); *b* Kirkintilloch, 1936. *m* Margaret. one *s.* one *d. Educ:* Lenzie Academy. *Studied:* Glasgow School of Art (1952-58, William and Mary Armour). *Exhib:* one-man shows: Scottish Gallery (1966, 1989), Demarco Gallery, Edinburgh (1969), Serpentine, London (1971), Glasgow School of Art (1982), Retrospective (1983), Glasgow A.Gs. (1990), Open Eye Gallery, Edinburgh (1991), Festival Exhbn., Open Eye Gallery, Edinburgh (1993, 1999). *Work in collections:* Scottish National Gallery of Modern Art, Manchester City A.G., Scottish National Portrait Gallery, Glasgow A.Gs., Arts Council, Otis Art Inst., Los Angeles. *Publications:* The Scottish Bestiary by George Mackay Brown (Charles Booth-Olibborn/Paragon Press, 1986), Lapotiniere and Friends by David and Hilary Brown (Century Editions/Random Century Group Ltd., 1990). *Signs work:* "Jack Knox." *Address:* 31 North Erskine Pk., Bearsden, Glasgow G61 4LY.

KOLAKOWSKI, Matthew Edmund Czeslaw, B.A. (1978), M.A. (1979); artist/painter in oil, sculptor mixed media; Foundation tutor, Woolwich College, and Central St. Martin's; visiting lecturer, Ravensbourne College; *b* Ruislip, Middx., 12 Mar., 1956. divorced. one *s. Educ:* Douay Martyrs School, Ickenham. *Studied:* Watford School of Art (Michael Werner, Peter Schmidt, Charles Harrison), Ravensbourne College of Art (Brian Fielding, Victor Kwell, Kit Twyford), Chelsea School of Art (Anthony Wishaw, Ian Stevenson). *Exhib:* London Group since 1989; one-man show: Duncan Campbell Gallery (1993, 1995), Mid Pennine Art Centre (1997). *Clubs:* London Group (Vice-Pres. since 1996), elected President (1998). *Signs work:* "M" in circle or triangle, and see appendix. *Address:* Brightside Studios, 9 Dartford St., London SE17 3UQ.

KONDRACKI, Henry Andrew, artist in oil on canvas; *b* Edinburgh, 13 Feb., 1953. *m* Sara. three *s. Educ:* Bellevue School, Edinburgh. *Studied:* Slade School of Fine Art (Ron Bowen, Jeffrey Camp, Jock McFadyen, Patrick George). *Exhib:* Vanessa Deveureux Gallery (1987, 1989), William Jackson Gallery (1991, 1994), Flowers East Gallery (1995, 1996, 1998, 2001), Flowers West Gallery, California (1998, 2000), Royal Academy Summer Exhibition (1989, 1990, 1993, 1994, 2000, 2001). *Work in collections:* British Council, A.C.G.B., Guildhall, London, Granada Foundation, Manchester, University College London, Manchester A.G., City Art Centre, Edinburgh, Glasgow Museums. *Publications:* Contemporary Scottish Painting by Bill Hare, Paint by Jeffrey Camp. *Signs work:* "H. Kondracki." *Address:* 20 Marchmont Cres., Edinburgh EH9 1HL.

KOPEL, Harold, R.O.I. (Hon. Treasurer, 1984-94); painter in oil, acrylic and pastel; art master, lecturer, Further Education I.L.E.A.; *b* Newcastle upon Tyne. *Educ:* Rutherford Grammar School, Newcastle; University College, London. *Studied:* Central School of Arts, London. *Exhib:* several one-man shows, numerous mixed shows including R.A., R.B.A., N.E.A.C., R.W.A., Paris Salon (Silver medal), Barcelona biennial, R.G.I., Contemporary Art International, Olympia (1989), many private galleries; Cornelissen prize. *Work in collections:* University College, London, Nuffield Foundation, I.L.E.A. *Signs work:* "Kopel." *Address:* 13 Hampstead Gdns., London NW11 7EU.

KORALEK, Paul George, C.B.E., R.A.; architect; Director, Ahrends Burton and Koralek; *b* 7 Apr., 1933. *m* Jennifer Chadwick. one *s.* two *d. Educ:* Aldenham. *Studied:* architecture: Architectural Assoc. *Exhib:* Heinz Gallery, R.I.B.A. (1982), R.A. Summer Show (annually since 1987). *Publications:* Monograph "Ahrends Burton and Koralek". *Address:* Unit 1, 7 Chalcot Rd., London NW1 8LH. *Email:* abk@abklondon.com

KOSTER, David, D.F.A. (Lond.), N.D.D., A.T.D., S.WL.A.; printmaker and painter; *b* London, 5 Nov., 1926. *m* Katherine Macrae. one *d. Educ:* Clayesmore. *Studied:* Slade School. *Work in collections:* Aberdeen City A.G., Royal Ulster Museum, Belfast, Berliner Graphothek, U.C.L., Dept. of Environment, All Soul's College, Oxford, Hokin Gallery, U.S.A., Hamilton Public Library, Canada, University New South Wales, S. London Gallery, Towner A.G., Eastbourne, numerous County Council and Educ. Com. Collections, Ministry of Agriculture, S.W.A.N. *Publications:* Wood engraved illustrations 'Down to Earth', drawings 'Fellow Mortals'. *Signs work:* "David Koster." *Address:* 5 East Cliff Gdns., Folkestone, Kent CT19 6AR.

KOWALSKY, Elaine Gloria, Dip. of Art, M.A.; artist in relief, litho, ceramics; Henry Moore Fellow in Printmaking, Leeds Polytechnic; *b* Winnipeg, Manitoba, 24 Sept., 1948. *m* Elton Bash, painter. *Educ:* Charleswood Collegiate, Winnipeg. *Studied:* University of Manitoba, St. Martin's School of Art, Brighton Polytechnic; M.A. Visual Theory University of East London. *Exhib:* R.A., and numerous one-man shows. *Work in collections:* V. & A., Birmingham A.G., Worcester A.G., Leeds A.G., Manchester A.G., Canada Council Art Bank, University of Manitoba, National Gallery of Australia, Smithsonian Inst. *Commissions:* banners, Dover Castle. *Publications:* Wood engraving and the Woodcut in Britain c.1890-1990, J. Hamilton (Barrie & Jenkins Ltd. 1994). *Signs work:* "Elaine Kowalsky." *Address:* 27 Aberavon Rd., London E3 5AR.

KOZARZEWSKA, Magda, L.C.A.D. (1977), S.I.A.D. (1977), B.A.Hons. (1981); artist in oil, charcoal, pencil; *b* Warsaw, 7 Oct., 1952. *m* Jonathan Goldberg. one *s. Educ:* Grammar School, Warsaw. *Studied:* Chelsea School of Art (1974-77), Slade School of Fine Art (1977-81, Prof. Sir L. Gowing, Patrick George, Euan Uglow). *Exhib:* solo shows: Polish Cultural Inst. (1975), Sue Rankin Gallery (1988), Thackeray Gallery (1991); major retrospective, Polish Cultural Inst. (1991), Thackery Gallery (1993), Duncan Campbell Fine Art (1995, 1997), Konrad Bayer Gallery, Munich (1996); group shows: Hayward Gallery (1982), N.P.G. (1986), Zacheta Gallery, Warsaw (1991), R.A. (1995), Konrad Bayer Gallery, Munich (1995), Polish Cultural Inst., London (1996). *Work in collections:* U.K., Europe, U.S.A., Canada, S. Africa. *Signs work:* "M.K." or "Kozarzewska." *Address:* 15 Woodlands Ave., New Malden, Surrey KT3 3UL.

KRUT, Ansel Jonathan, M.A. (1986), B.F.A. (1982); painter in oil; awarded

Rome prize (1987); *b* Cape Town, 1959. *m* Felicity Powell. two *d. Studied:* University of the Witwatersrand (1979-82), R.C.A. (1983-86). *Exhib:* R.A., John Moores, London Group, Cité des Arts, Paris; one-man shows Fischer Fine Art (1989, 1990), Gillian Jason Gallery (1994), Jason and Rhodes Gallery (1995, 1996). *Work in collections:* Arts Council London, British Council, Government Art Collection, Harris Museum of Art Preston, Mercer A.G. Harrogate, Ben Uri Collection, Johannesburg A.G. *Signs work:* "A. Krut." *Address:* Jason and Rhodes Gallery, 4 New Burlington Pl., London W1X 1FB.

KUELL, Victor John, A.R.C.A. (1950), Hon. Mem. London Group (1998); artist in acrylics and water-colour; *b* Andover, Hants. *m* Margaret. one *s.* one *d. Studied:* Bromley School of Art (1938-42), R.C.A. (1947-50). *Exhib:* London Group (1977-2001), R.A. (1987-95), Galerie Espace Laser, Paris (1990), Galerie Metropolis, Geneva (1985), Société de l'Art Contemporain, Paris (1984), International Biennale of Malta (Award winner, 1995), Galerie Carre D'Or Paris (2000). *Work in collections:* James Capel, N.Y., Mitsui London. *Publications:* Les Editions Art et Image du Monde. *Signs work:* "Vic Kuell." *Address:* 45 Hever Rd., Edenbridge, Kent TN8 5DH.

KUHFELD, Peter, B.A., R.P., N.E.A.C.; artist in oil and pencil; *b* Glos., 4 Mar., 1952. *m* Cathryn Showan, artist. two *d. Educ:* Gateway School, Leicester. *Studied:* Leicester College of Art (1972-76), R.A. Schools (1977-80, Peter Greenham, Jane Dowling, Norman Blamey). *Exhib:* R.A., N.E.A.C., R.P., R.B.A., R.W.A., N.P.G., Windsor Castle, Hampton Court Palace, Accademia Italiana, New Grafton Gallery, Agnews, W.H. Patterson, Christie's, Fine Art Soc., National Gallery of Wales, Cardiff. *Work in collections:* H.M. The Queen, H.R.H. Prince of Wales, Baring Bros., Lazards, Cable and Wireless, Hammerson Group, National Trust, Elizabeth Greenshield Foundation, Hambros, Mercury Asset Management, Sabanci Bank. *Signs work:* "Kuhfeld." *Address:* The Corner House, Upper Bridge St., Wye, nr. Ashford, Kent TN25 5AW.

KUMMEREHL, Colleen, R.B.A., B.A. Hons. Fine Art (1982), winner of R.B.A. De Lazlo Medal (1999); sculptor in clay, plaster, wax, bronze and polychrome; lecturer in Fine Art and consultant for the patination and colouring of bronze casts; tuition given at artist's home in Perigord, France; *b* England, 22 Apr., 1944. one *s.* one *d. Educ:* Cathedral School and Fort St. Girls School, Sydney, Australia. *Studied:* De Montfort University, Leicester (1979-1982), under Stephen Cohn, Kenneth Ford, Lee Orton, Sydney Harpley R.A., Wili Soukop R.A., Robert Adam R.A. *Exhib:* Leicester Museum and Art Galleries (1984 & 1985), Yarrow Gallery (1994 & 1995), Alfred East Gallery (1995), R.W.A. (1997), Langham Fine Art (2000 & 2001), Waterman Fine Art (1998-2000), Dolby Gallery (2001), Mall Galleries (since 1995). *Signs work:* "C. Kummerehl." *Address:* c/o Royal Soc. of British Artists, 17 Carlton House Terr., London SW1Y 5BD. *Website:* http://web.ukonline.co.uk/smcfoundry *Email:* smcfoundry@ukonline.co.uk

KUO, Nancy, director, choreographer, dancer, actress, designer, authoress, art critic and painter, gold medallist; visiting lecturer to universities, art colleges, art societies, women's societies, clubs and museums; *b* Shanghai, China. *m* Guy Davies D.A. (Edin.). *Studied:* western painting in Hanzhou National Art Academy and

Shanghai Art Academy, traditional Chinese painting under Chen Shu-ren, a founder of the Lingnan School. *Exhib:* in China, Hong Kong, Gambia, Burma, Afghanistan, France, Norway, Argentina and England. *Work in collections:* private collections all over the world, National Museums of Burma and National Museum of Ethology, Leyden. *Publications:* author of "Chinese Paper-cut Pictures", "The Sky is Singing", "Dream Valley", "Rolling and Folding", etc., catalogue, "Arts from China". Work repro.: numerous newspapers and journals of various countries; contributions: poems, essays, plays, art reviews, etc. in Chinese and English to newspapers and journals in China, Hong Kong, Burma, Afghanistan, Italy and England; scripts for B.B.C. Radio; T.V. apperances: I.T.V., B.B.C., France T.V., Monte Carlo T.V. and China T.V. Fellow International P.E.N.; mem. of International Assoc. of Art Critics, International Assoc. of Art, and British Actors' Equity; Director of Chinese Arts Inst.; Adviser to the Chinese writers in Britain, Adviser to the Hainan Poetry Soc., Adviser to the Qing Yuan City Government on Culture and Arts. *Signs work:* "Nancy" in Chinese; see appendix. *Address:* No.1 Block, 5th Fl.(Post Box 5) Riverside Residence, Bei Jiang Yi Road, New Town, Qing Yuan City, Guang Dong, P.R. China. Postcode 511515.

KYNOCH, Kathryn Marie, R.G.I. (1994); artist in oil and pastel; *b* Portobello, Midlothian, 18 Aug., 1941. *m* Michael Andrew Tribe. *Studied:* Glasgow School of Art (1959-64). *Exhib:* R.G.I., R.S.A., S.S.A. *Work in collections:* Glasgow A.G's, Kelvingrove, Hunterian Art Gallery, Glasgow University, Dover House, Whitehall; private collection in Britain and U.S.A. *Commissions:* include R.S.A. Music and Drama, Glasgow, Edinburgh, Stirling, Strathclyde and Leicester Universities. *Clubs:* Glasgow Art. *Address:* 35 Kelvinside Gdns., Glasgow G20 6BG.

L

LABAN, Keith Maurice, Surrey Dip. (1970); artist in water-colour; Sir Alec Issigonis Prize for Art (1969); *b* London, 22 May 1949. *m* Vivienne Jane Laban (née Ferne). *Studied:* Reigate College of Art (1996-70). *Exhib:* mixed exhbns. London, U.K., Holland. *Signs work:* "Laban." *Address:* 2 Bolsover Grove, Merstham, Redhill, Surrey RH1 3NU.

LACEY, Mary Elliot, A.T.D., S.WL.A.; wildlife painter and illustrator in oils, water-colour and conté chalk; *b* Birmingham, 26 Sept., 1923. one *s.* two *d. Educ:* Birmingham. *Studied:* Birmingham College of Art (1939-44). *Exhib:* Tryon Gallery, Birdland Wildlife Gallery, S.WL.A., Mall Galleries. *Work in collections:* Sultan of Oman, Miss Eleanor MacDonald, Rolf Harris, Fiona Fullerton. *Publications:* book illustrations for Hamlyn Publishing, South Leigh Press, Balberry Publishing, Royle and Medici. *Signs work:* "Mary Elliot Lacey." *Address:* Meadowbank, Snape Rd., Sudbourne, Woodbridge, Suffolk IP12 2BA.

LACKNER, Suzanne O., F.Z.S.L., F.F.P.S.; sculptor in marble, onyx, alabaster, soapstone, portland stone, etc. and recently bronze and wood; *b* Berlin, 10 Feb.,

1908. widow. one *d. Educ:* Berlin Technical University (architecture), in France since 1933. *Studied:* Camden Main Institute. *Exhib:* Camden Institute (1975), Camden Arts Centre (1976), City of Westminster Arts Council (1976), Burgh House (1992), Loggia Gallery (1999, 2001). *Work in collections:* England, France, Germany, U.S.A., Japan. *Signs work:* see appendix. *Address:* 49 Eton Hall, Eton College Rd., London NW3 2DR.

LA FONTAINE, Thomas Sherwood, painter in oil, water-colour and black and white of portraits and animal subjects; *b* 21 Dec., 1915. *Educ:* Rottingdean and Tonbridge School. *Studied:* Regent St., Polytechnic (Harry Watson, S. Tresilian, since 1934); City and Guilds, Kennington (Innes Fripp, James Grant, Middleton Todd, since 1936); Spenlove School (Reginald Eves, since 1939). *Signs work:* in printed capitals. *Address:* East Cottage, Burton Hill, Malmesbury, Wilts. SN16 0EL.

LAGO, Darren, B.A. (Fine Art), M.A. (Fine Art); sculptor in installation and object based artworks; Tutor, Kingsway College, London; *b* 22 Sept., 1965. *Educ:* King Edward VI School, Lichfield. *Studied:* Portsmouth University (Don Hopes), Chelsea School of Art and Design (Shelagh Cluett). *Exhib:* New Contemporary I.C.A. London, Annely Juda Gallery. *Work in collections:* Annely Juda Fine Art Gallery, Unilever House, Unilever plc. *Signs work:* see appendix. *Address:* 23b Lonsdale Rd., London NW6 6RA.

LAIN, Graham E.W., S.G.F.A.; architectural technician and self taught artist in water-colour, pen and ink; *b* Wymondham, Norfolk, 18 Sept., 1938. *m* Betty. one *d. Exhib:* one-man shows biennially. *Signs work:* "G.L." *Address:* Nesbit Cottage, 2 Granary Loke, Spooner Row, Wymondham, Norfolk NR18 9JW.

LAING, Gerald Ogilvie-, N.D.D. (1964), F.R.B.S. (1994); artist: figurative (Pop) painting (1962-65), highly finished abstract painting/sculpture (1966-69), abstract 3-dimensional sculpture in the landscape (1970-72), formal figurative sculpture (1973-82), figurative sculpture (1983-to date); Commissioner, Royal Fine Art Commission for Scotland; *b* Newcastle-upon-Tyne, 11 Feb., 1936. four *s.* one *d. Educ:* Berkhamsted School; R.M.A. Sandhurst. *Studied:* St. Martin's School of Art. *Exhib:* more than 30 one-man shows worldwide. Major retrospective, Fruitmarket Gallery, Edinburgh (1993). *Work in collections:* National Gallery, Tate Gallery, V. & A., N.P.G., S.N.G.M.A., S.N.P.G., M.O.M.A., N.Y., Whitney Museum, N.Y., Smithsonian, Washington D.C., and many others. *Commissions:* 'Callanish' Glasgow, 'Fountain of Sabrina' Bristol, 'Wise and Foolish Virgins', 'Axis Mundi', 'Conan Doyle Memorial' Edinburgh and 'Ten Dragons', Bank Underground Station, London, 'Four Rugby Players' Twickenham, 'Sir Paul Getty', National Gallery, London, 'Batsman', M.C.C. Lord's Ground, London. *Publications:* Kinkell: The Reconstruction of a Scottish Castle. Represented by The Fine Art Soc., London. *Clubs:* Chelsea Arts. *Signs work:* "Gerald Laing." *Address:* Kinkell Castle, Ross-shire IV7 8AT, Scotland.

LAING, Gordon James, I.S.O., Ph.D., M.Sc.; painter in acrylic and oils (or crayon, chalk, pastels for small sketches); *b* Oldham Lancs., 12 Jan., 1923. divorced. one *s. Educ:* Eltham College and Oldham Hulme Grammar School, Manchester University, Sussex University and London University. *Exhib:* R.A., Paris Salon, International Centre in Washington, also Hong Kong and New York. *Signs work:*

signs on canvas on rear of painting, and sometimes on front also. *Address:* Senlac House, 42 York Way, Fort George, St. Peter Port, Guernsey, GY1.

LAKE, C. Elisabeth Matheson, R.M.S. (1989), F.H.S. (1982-95); miniature painter in water-colour (interiors); *b* Norwich, 12 Apr., 1939. *m* Geoffrey N. Lake. one *s.* three *d. Studied:* West of England College of Art (1957-60). *Exhib:* H.S. (1982-95), R.A. Summer Exhbn. (1986), R.M.S. (1984-), many N. American and Canadian exhbns. (1985-89). *Work in collections:* England, N. America and Europe. *Publications:* Books, magazines. *Signs work:* see appendix. *Address:* Hollow End, Hollow Marsh, Farrington Gurney, Somerset BS39 6TX.

LALLY, Richard, painter in oil, pastel and water-colour; *b* London, 2 Oct., 1928. *Educ:* Brixton College of Building and Architecture (1942-45). *Studied:* Hammersmith School of Art (1955-59, Leon Underwood, Dennis Gilbert). *Exhib:* one-man shows, Real Club Nautico, Tenerife (1961), Manolette Gallery, Richmond (1977); R.O.I., N.S., U.A., S.WL.A. *Signs work:* "LALLY." *Address:* Strathcroy Studio, Drumbeg, Lairg, Sutherland, Scotland IV27 4NG. *Email:* richard.lally@tiny-world.co.uk

LAMB, Elspeth, D.A. (Glas.) (1973), H.Dip.A.D. (Manc.) (1974), A.R.S.A. (1990); lecturer/printmaker in printmaking, papermaking, drawing; Lecturer in drawing and painting, Edinburgh College of Art; *b* Glasgow, 28 Mar., 1951. *Educ:* Kings Pk. Senior Secondary School, Glasgow. *Studied:* Glasgow School of Art (Philip Reeves), Manchester Polytechnic, The Tamarind Inst. of Lithography, University of New Mexico, U.S.A. (Lynn Allen). *Exhib:* Mercury Gallery (1988, 1990), Conservative Management (1990), Marlborough Graphics (1991), Glasgow Print Studio (1990). *Work in collections:* S.A.C., British Council, Japanese Consular Coll., Perth A.G., Glasgow A.G., City Arts. *Address:* Bon a Tirer Editions, 15 E. Campbell St., Glasgow G1 1DG.

LAMBERT, Colin Joseph, sculptor in bronze and stone; *b* Guantanamo Bay, Cuba, 17 Jan., 1948. *m* Catherine Finn. *Studied:* Chouinard Art Inst., Los Angeles (1966-68); apprenticed with Karl Gomez in Amsterdam (1980-83). *Work in collections:* Stamford Forum, Stamford, Conn.; London United Bldg., London; Renaissance Vineyard and Winery, Calif.; Warminster Market Centre, Warminster, Wilts. *Signs work:* see appendix. *Address:* Flint Barn Studio, West End, nr. Essendon, Hatfield, Herts. AL9 5RQ.

LAMBIRTH, Alan, R.B.A. (1986), R.A. Gold medal (1982), R.A. Schools Advanced Dip. (1983), Higher Surrey Dip. A.D. (1980), De Laszlo medal awarded by R.B.A. (1991); artist in oil, pastel, gouache and water-colour; *b* Cuckfield, 19 Feb., 1959. *Educ:* Hazelwick School, Crawley. *Studied:* W. Sussex College of Design (1975-77), Epsom School of Art (1977-80, Peter Peterson), R.A. Schools (1980-83, Peter Greenham, R.A.). *Exhib:* R.A., R.B.A., N.E.A.C., Soc. of Landscape Painters; one-man shows: Odette Gilbert Gallery (1984, 1986), Solomon Gallery (1988), Sheila Harrison Fine Art (1989, 1991), Enid Lawson Gallery (1997); four-man show: Hallam Gallery (1990). *Address:* 22 Brushwood Rd., Roffey, Horsham, W. Sussex RH12 4PE. *Website:* www.lambirth.fsnet.co.uk

LAMONT, Ian James, painter in oil; *b* Carshalton, 16 May, 1964. *Educ:* Nork Pk. School; N.E. Surrey College of Technology; Sutton College of Liberal Arts. *Studied:* Kingston Polytechnic School of Art and Design; also portrait painting under Ronald Benham, N.E.A.C., R.B.A. (1982-86). *Exhib:* R.A., N.E.A.C., R.B.A., R.O.I. (Winsor and Newton Young Artist award finalist 1983-88), Royal Portrait Soc. *Work in collections:* United Racecourses. *Signs work:* "Ian Lamont." *Address:* 25 Woodgavil, Banstead, Surrey SM7 1AA.

LANCASTER, Brian Christy, R.S.M.A. (1997), F.R.S.A. (1995), G.R.A. (1990); artist in water-colour, illustrator (mainly architectural); *b* Atherton, nr. Manchester, 3 Aug., 1931. *m* Pauline Carol Wheler Lancaster. *Educ:* Lee St. School, Atherton. *Studied:* Bolton College of Art (1946-49), Southport College of Art (1949-52). *Exhib:* Atkinson A.G., Southport, Bristol Savages, R.W.A., R.I., R.B.A., R.W.S., G.R.A., R.S.M.A. *Work in collections:* Duke and Duchess of Beaufort, Badminton, Glos., Sir William McAlpine, Bt., Bristol Savages. *Commissions:* Second Severn Crossing Bridge Under Construction painting, Sir Charles Halcrow Co. Ltd., Nuclear Electric (Calendar), Grant Thornton, calendars. R.N.L.I. Napier Brown, Canadian Pacific Ships. *Publications:* work repro.: two art books (David & Charles), Countryside Commission annual report '94 & '95 illustrations, Post Office commemorative cover: Forth Bridge Centenary, reproductions in several magazines and books including GRA Publication '100 Years of Railways'; book jacket for Scottish Steam in the 1950's and 60's (OPC); articles in 'The Artist' magazine and 'International Artist' magazine. *Clubs:* Bristol Savages. *Signs work:* "Brian C. Lancaster." *Address:* Galloway, Waterley Bottom, N. Nibley, Glos. GL11 6EF.

LANCASTER, John Maurice, N.D.D., M.Phil., Ph.D.; painter, calligrapher, heraldic artist; *b* Wigan. *m* Janet Lancaster. *Studied:* Leeds College of Art (1946-51), advanced painting with Victor Pasmore. *Exhib:* sixteen one-man shows: Leicester, Nottingham, London, Keele, Bristol, Decatur, U.S.A., Columbus, U.S.A., Thatcher, Az., U.S.A., Cheltenham, Stowe, Wadhurst; three two-man shows; R.W.A., R.B.A., Hesketh Hubbard, Mod. Art in Yorkshire, W. Riding Artists, John Noott 20th C. Gallery, Kenulf Galleries, Bristol, and other galleries. *Work in collections:* worldwide. *Commissions:* private, public bodies, London institutions, the Church. *Publications:* 16 books. Visiting Prof. U.S.A.; Gila Valley Arts Council Visiting artist, Az., U.S.A. *Clubs:* Naval and Military, S.S.I., S.H.A. Liveryman Worshipful Company of Gardeners of London. *Signs work:* "John Lancaster." *Address:* 10 Walnut Cl., Cheltenham, Glos. GL52 3AG. *Email:* johnmlanc@aol.com

LANDAU, David, M.D. (1978), M.A. (1980); Editor, Print Quarterly; Trustee: National Gallery and N.A.C.F.; Treasurer, Venice in Peril Fund; *b* 22 Apr., 1950. *Publications:* Georg Pencz (1978); Federica Galli (1982); The Renaissance Print (with P.Parshall) (1994). *Address:* 80 Carlton Hill, London NW8 0ER.

LANDERS, Linda Anne, B.A.(Hons.) (1986), A.R.E. (1995); painter/printmaker/writer, oil, etching, wood engraving, hand-made books; *b* Herts., 27 Dec., 1959. two *s. Studied:* Central School of Art (1979-86, Cecil Collins). *Exhib:* 'Fine Press' book fairs and exhibitions. *Work in collections:* British Art Library, V. & A., Ashmolean Museum, R.C.A., Musuem Van Het Boek, Netherlands, University of California L.A., University of Plymouth. *Commissions:* wood engraving for Circle

Press, and for Delos and Redlake Press. *Publications:* published eight Limited Edn. artists books under imprint: Spoon Print Press; one under imprint: 'Merlin's Grail'. Printmaking prize at Mall Galleries (2001). *Signs work:* "Linda Anne Landers" and see appendix. Signature varies according to size of work. *Address:* 12a Tadema Rd., London SW10 0NU.

LANE-DAVIES, Hugh John, Dip. Arch. (Dist. in Thesis) R.I.B.A. (1951); architect/artist in water-colour; *b* Ramsgate, 20 Dec., 1927. *m* Wendy Isabel (née Pierce). one *s. Educ:* King's College, Taunton, and (now) University of Westminster. *Studied:* architecture. *Exhib:* numerous exhbns. in London and Home Counties, including R.I.B.A., Cider House Gallery Bletchingley, Llewellyn Alexander Fine Art, Bourne Gallery Reigate, World of Drawings and Water-colours, London, Fine Art and Antiques Fair, London. *Work in collections:* private and corporate collections world wide, including Tokai bank of Japan, I.B.M., Price Waterhouse, Trafalgar House, W.S. Atkins. *Publications:* work repro.: Christmas cards, calendars and limited edition prints. *Signs work:* "H.L.D." *Address:* White Rose Cottage, White Hill, Bletchingley, Surrey RH1 4QT.

LANG, Wharton, R.S.M.A. (1948), now Hon. Mem., F.R.S.A. (1983); sculptor in wood; ex Mem. S.WL.A.; *b* Oberammergau, Bavaria, 13 June, 1925. *m* Ingrid. *Educ:* Newquay Grammar School. *Studied:* Leonard Fuller School of Painting (1946) and privately under Faust Lang (1946-49). *Work in collections:* Ulster Museum, Belfast, R.S.M.A. Diploma Collection, National Maritime Museum, Greenwich, Carving in Relief 'Castle of Mey' presented to H.M. Queen Mother (1967). *Signs work:* "W. LANG," "Wharton Lang" and see appendix. *Address:* Fauna Studio, Mount Zion, St. Ives, Cornwall TR26 3HA.

LANGFORD, Martin James, A.R.E. (1996); artist in mezzotint; *b* Kingston upon Thames, 2 June, 1970. *m* Therese Langford. *Studied:* University of Plymouth (B.A. (Hons.) Fine Art 1993; Post Grad. Advanced Printmaking, Central St. Martin's College of Art (David Gluck, R.E.). *Exhib:* National Print (1995, 1996, 1997); one-man shows, 'A Trifle Greedy' through Alternative Arts (1995), The Mansion House, Hackney (1996-97), Cupola Gallery, Sheffield (1998), Bow House Gallery, Barnet, Herts. (1999). Selected entry in March 2000 Taipei Print Biennal. *Work in collections:* For Art's Sake, Ealing, W. London; Will's Art Warehouse, Parson's Green, London; Cupola Gallery, Sheffield; Bankside Gallery, London. Awards: Gwen May R.E. Student Award - National Print (1995), Gwen May R.E. Commemorative Award for outstanding printmaking - National Print (1996), Leeds City H.G. *Publications:* Selected for Best of International Printmaking book, whole page coverage (Rockport Publishers, U.S.A., 1997). Represented in U.S.A. by Hoorn Ashby Gallery, N.Y. and Nantucket, and Davidson Galleries, Seattle, Washington, and Derby Fine Arts, Chicago. *Address:* 2 Norfolk House, The Farmlands, Northolt, Middx. UB5 5EU.

LANGLEY, Siddy, blown glass; *b* Withnell, Lancs., 2 Feb., 1955. *m* Michael Crane. one *d. Studied:* Apprenticed to Peter Layton at London Glassblowing Workshop (1979-81). *Exhib:* Rosengalerie, Amsterdam; 'Glaskunst aus Grossbritannien' Lucerne and Frankfurt; Broadfield House Glass Museum, Dudley; Coleridge of Piccadilly, London and Edinburgh; Musée des Beaux Arts, Rouen;

Kringel Gallery, Switzerland; Museu de Arte de São Paulo, Brazil; Neville Pundole Gallery, Canterbury, etc. *Work in collections:* Musée du Verre, Liege, Belgium and Sars Poteries, France; Turner Glass Collection, Sheffield; Norwich Castle Museum; B'ham Museum and A.G.; Leics. Collection for Schools and Colleges; The Glass Museum, Ebeltoft, Denmark. *Commissions:* font for Methodist Church, Winchester. *Signs work:* "Siddy Langley" and year. *Address:* The Longhouse, Plymtree, nr. Cullompton, Devon EX15 2JW. *Email:* mail@siddy.com

LARGE, George Charles, R.I. (1986), A.T.C., R.B.A. (1997); artist in oil and water-colour; *b* London, 20 Jan., 1936. *m* Pamela Parkinson-Large. one s-*s* two *s*. one s-*d* one *d*. *Educ:* Downhills Central School, Tottenham. *Studied:* Hornsey College of Art (1958-63, Maurice de Sausmarez, John Titchell, Alfred Daniels). *Exhib:* R.I., R.B.A., S.W.E.; one-man shows, Mall Galleries, National Gallery Malta, Duncan Campbel Fine Arts, Melitensia A.G., Malta, Llewellyn Alexander, Goldmark Gallery. *Work in collections:* Ralli Foundation, British Rail, National Gallery Malta, British Consulate Malta, Cranfield Inst., I.C.I. *Publications:* illustrated, Laughter in the Kitchen, and various magazines, Taste of History, Food of the Knights of Malta, Pamela Parkinson-Large; The Cartographer, David Mackenzie. Awards: Winsor Newton Award, R.I. Singer Friedlander/Sunday Times, Llewellyn Alexander Award R.I. St. Cuthbert's Mill Paper Award. *Signs work:* "LARGE 98." *Address:* 13/14 Market Pl., Woburn, Beds. MK17 9PZ.

LARMONT, Eric, N.D.D., A.T.C.; painter in oil, etcher; part-time art lecturer; *b* South Shields, 27 Sept., 1943. *Studied:* Sunderland College of Art (1963-65); Goldsmiths' School of Art (1965-66), Post-grad. Belgian Scholarship (1968-69). *Exhib:* one-man shows, London: 273 Gallery (1969), Scribes Cellar (1978), Holsworthy Gallery (1981), Galerie Blankenese, Hamburg (1983), Pump House Gallery, London (1997); two-man show, Jonathan Poole Gallery (1986); 3 man show; Studio Gallery, London (1999). *Work in collections:* Carlisle Corporation; private collections: various. Prizes and awards: Reeves Bi-centenary Premier Award (1966); Second Non-purchase Prize, Northern Painters Exhibition (1966). *Signs work:* see appendix. *Address:* 20 Rainville Rd., London W6 9HA.

LARUSDOTTIR, Karolina, R.E., R.W.S., N.E.A.C.; painter in oil and water-colour, etcher and printmaker; *b* Reykjavik, Iceland, 1944. *Studied:* Ruskin School of Art, Oxford University and Barking College of Art. *Exhib:* Bankside Gallery, R.E., R.A., R.B.A.; one-man shows: Kjarvalsstadir Reykjavik (1982, 1986), Gallerie Gammelstrand, Kobenhagen, Gallery 10 (1984, 1987, 1991), Cambridge Contemporary Art (from 1994), John Brandler Galleries, Brentwood. *Work in collections:* Cartwright Hall Musuem, Bradford; The Vatican Collection, Rome; Nelson Atkin Museum, Kansas City, U.S.A.; British Musuem, London; Ashmolean Museum, Oxford; Fitzwilliam Museum, Cambridge; Pompidou Museum, Paris. Prizes: The Dicks and Greenbury Award, Bankside Gallery (1989). Special award: Premio Internazionale Biella per l'incisione, Italy. *Signs work:* "LARUSDOTTIR." *Address:* 71 Petersfield Mansions, Cambridge CB1 1BB.

LAUCHLAN, Anya, M.A., F.F.P.S.; painter/illustrator in oil, acrylic, water-colour; *b* 6 Apr., 1948. *m* Peter Rolland Lauchlan. one *s*. two *d*. *Studied:* Pushkin Museum of Fine Art, and Moscow Polygraphic - Art and Design (1963-75, Basov,

Goncharov, Chazanov, Burdjelian). *Exhib:* Loggia Gallery, Westminster, Leighton House Museum, Pera Arts Centre Istanbul, various commercial London galleries. *Work in collections:* work in private collections internationally. *Commissions:* Painting scenes from English National Ballet (1998-2000). *Publications:* illustrator of more than 50 books. *Clubs:* F.P.S. *Signs work:* "Anya Lauchlan," "A. Lauchlan" or "Anya" and dated. *Address:* The Studio, 2 Grovehill Rd., Redhill, Surrey RH1 6PJ.

LAUDER, Kenneth Scott, A.R.C.A. (1939); painter in oil and water-colour; *b* Edinburgh, 1916. *m* (1) Sylvia Morgan (1946) (m dissolved). one *s.* (2) Marian Mills (1966). two *s. Educ:* King Alfred's Grammar School (Albert Rutherston). *Studied:* Chelsea School of Art (1933-36, H.S. Williamson, G. Sutherland, R. Medley), R.C.A. (1936-39, P.H. Jowett, Gilbert Spencer, Percy Horton). *Exhib:* R.A., Agnews, Scottish Gallery London and Edinburgh, Liverpool Academy, Newcastle Laing Gallery, Bristol R.W.A., Stratford-on-Avon Ruskin Gallery, Bear Lane Gallery Oxford, William Jackson Gallery London, Galeries Cloots Brussels. *Work in collections:* The School of Design in Providence, Rhode Island, U.S.A. *Signs work:* see appendix. *Address:* Moreton Lodge, Eye, Leominster, Herefordshire HR6 0DP.

LAW Enid: see CHAUVIN, Enid.

LAWRENCE, Gordon Robert, Dip.A.D. (1951), Teacher's Cert. (1952), 1st Class Hons. Rome Accademia de Belle Arte (1962), M.Ed. Liverpool (1975), Ph.D. (1979); painter/sculptor in acrylic, water-colour, stone; *b* Glasgow, 1930. divorced. three *s. Educ:* Hillhead High School, Glasgow. *Studied:* Glasgow School of Art, Accademia de Belle Arte, Rome. *Exhib:* Britain, France, Germany, Spain, Ireland and U.S.A. *Signs work:* see appendix. *Address:* Camboulit, 46100 Figeac, France.

LAWRENCE, John, winner, Francis Williams Book Illustration award (twice); freelance illustrator in wood engraving and water-colour; part time lecturer, Camberwell School of Art (1960-93); external assessor, Bristol College of Art, Exeter College of Art, Duncan of Jordanstone College of Art, Brighton College of Art, Edinburgh College of Art; Kingston School of Art (various appointments between 1978-94); Visiting Professor in illustration at the London Inst.; *b* Hastings, 15 Sept., 1933. *m* Myra. two *d. Educ:* Salesian College, Oxford. *Studied:* Hastings School of Art and Central School of Art and Design. *Exhib:* R.E., S.W.E. *Work in collections:* V. & A., Ashmolean Museum, National Museum of Wales, several provincial galleries, and in several collections in U.S.A. *Publications:* over 120 books. *Clubs:* A.W.G., S.W.E., Double Crown. *Signs work:* "John Lawrence." *Address:* 6 Worts Causeway, Cambridge CBI 8RL.

LAWRENCE, Mary R., painter in oil and water-colour; *b* Wimbledon, 17 June, 1922. *m* F.R.M. Lawrence. one *s.* two *d. Educ:* Downe House, Cold Ash, Newbury. *Studied:* Epsom School of Art and Design (1970-80, John Morley, Alan Dodd, Leslie Worth). *Exhib:* R.A. Summer Shows (1974-87), N.E.A.C. (1972-76). *Address:* 15 Jackson Cl., Epsom, Surrey KT18 7RA.

LAWRENSON, Diane M., R.C.A. (2000); sculptor in bronze, resin; *b* Liverpool, 5 Sep., 1946. two *s.* one *d. Studied:* West Yorkshire. *Exhib:* Royal Cambrian

Academy, various. *Signs work:* "LAWRENSON." *Address:* Barker House, Winton, Kirkby Stephen, Cumbria CA17 4HS.

LAWSON, Gillian, painter in water-colour and oil, printmaker in etching; *b* 6 May, 1936. married. one *s*. two *d*. *Educ:* Parliament Hill Grammar School. *Studied:* Camden Institute (silkscreen printing, Ingrid Greenfield), Camden Art Centre (1971-75, etching, Dorothea Wight). *Exhib:* Cape Town, S.A., Georgetown, Washington, U.S.A., R.A., Halesworth Gallery, Burgh House, Hampstead, The Ice House, Holland Park, Hinton Gallery, nr. Horley, Ninth British International Print Biennale. *Signs work:* "Gillian Lawson." *Address:* 7 Oak Hill Way, Hampstead, London NW3 7LR.

LAWSON, Simon Nicholas, B.A. Hons. (1985), R.A. Post Grad. Dip. (1998); artist in oil, etching, photography; *b* Waltham, Lincs., 2 Aug., 1964. partner Ann Lansfield Hobson. one *d*. *Educ:* Waltham Toll Bar Comprehensive. *Studied:* Grimsby School of Art (1980-82, Peter Todd), Wimbledon School of Art (1982-85, Bernard Cohen), R.A. Schools (1985-88, Norman Adams). *Exhib:* Royal Festival Hall (1986), Mall Galleries (1985), R.A. (1986-89, 1991, 1998-2001). *Signs work:* "S. Lawson." *Address:* Flat One, 20 Allfarthing Lane, Wandsworth, London SW18 2PQ.

LAWSON, Sonia, R.A., R.W.S., R.C.A., M.A.(1st) (1959); artist in oil, water-colour, etching; visitor R.A. Schools; *b* Wensleydale, Yorks., 2 June, 1934. *m* Charles Congo. one *d*. *Studied:* Royal College of Art (1956-59, Prof. Carel Weight), Post-graduate year (1959-60), Travelling Scholarship, France. *Exhib:* retrospective tour, Leicester Polytechnic, Mappin Gallery Sheffield, Ferens Hull, Cartwright Bradford, Central Gallery Milton Keynes (1982-83); selected solo exhbns. Kirklees (1985), Manchester (1987), Wakefield (1988), Bradford (1989), London, Boundary Gallery (1989, 1995, 1998), retrospective, Dean Clough Gallery (1966-96), Halifax, R.W.A. Bristol (2000); mixed shows, New York, Fragments against Ruin tour, China, British Council tour, Arts Council, Tolly Cobbald, John Moores, Edinburgh, R.A. London, Haywards Annual London, Subjective Eye, Midland Group Nottingham. *Work in collections:* Arts Council, Sheffield, Carlisle, Belfast, Bradford, Middlesbrough, Bolton, Harrogate, Rochdale, Wakefield and Huddersfield A.G.'s, Open University, M. of W., Leeds University, R.C.A., Nuffield, Cranfield, Imperial War Museum, R.A., Vatican, Chatsworth. *Commissions:* Imperial War Museum (1984). *Publications:* Modern Painters, Summer '96; Art Review, July '96. *Clubs:* Overseas League. *Signs work:* "S. Lawson," "Sonia Lawson" or "Lawson." *Address:* c/o Royal Academy of Arts, Piccadilly, London W1V 0DS. *Website:* www.sonialawson.co.uk *Email:* art@sonialawson.co.uk

LAWSON-BAKER, Auriol, muralist, sculptor in bronze; Director, L.B.P. Sculpture and Design; owner "Scene Inside" Mural Co.; *b* 7 Sept., 1963. *m* Neil Lawson-Baker. one *s*. *Educ:* Ditcham Park, Petersfield, Hants. *Exhib:* R.A., sculpture project managed throughout U.K. and Europe including Houses of Parliament Arts Com.; London International Financial Futures Exchange; British Gas plc., etc. *Signs work:* "A. Lawson-Baker." *Address:* Graingers, West Ashling, W. Sussex PO18 8DN.

LAWSON-BAKER, Dr. Neil, M.B., B.S. (Lond.), B.D.S., L.D.S. (Lond.), L.D.S.,

R.C.S. (Eng.); dental surgeon and sculptor in bronze; Director, L.B.P. Sculpture and Design; *b* Watford, 8 Nov., 1938. *m* Auriol Lawson-Baker. one *s. Educ:* Merchant Taylors and London University. *Exhib:* one-man show: Watermans Gallery, London (1991). *Commissions:* Sterling House, Albert Bridge, London, SW11; Entrance and trading floor at London International Financial Futures Exchange; British Gas plc, 7 metre bronze flame, Reading and Loughborough; Entrance Hall, 1 Parliament Street, London SW1; Entrance Gibran Library, Beirut University, Lebanon; Inauguration Sculpture for Channel Tunnel, Eurotunnel plc; Magna Carta Fountain, Runnymead Borough Council, Egham; 14 metre Keris, National Stadium, Kuala Lumpur, Malaysia. *Publications:* Visual Times, a private Journal of sculpture. *Clubs:* Arts, R.A.C. *Signs work:* "Neil Lawson-Baker." *Address:* Graingers, West Ashling, W. Sussex PO18 8DN.

LAYCOCK, Allan Bracewell, A.T.D. (1951), F.S.A.I. (1975), R.W.A. (1986); landscape painter in acrylic, in situ; lecturer in graphics and illustration; *b* Sutton-in-Craven, 4 June, 1928. *Educ:* Keighley Grammar School. *Studied:* Keighley School of Art (1945-46, 1948-50), Sheffield College of Art (1950-51), Norwich School of Art (1951). *Exhib:* one-man and group shows in eastern and S.W. England. Work in private collections in U.K. and overseas. *Signs work:* "Allan Laycock." *Address:* Tararua, Broad St., Hartpury, Glos. GL19 3BN.

LAYZELL, Peter, B.A.(Hons.) Fine Art; artist in oil; part-time lecturer in art at Blackpool College and Lancaster University; *b* Hitchin, Herts., 1962. *m* Jean Palmer. one *s.* one *d. Studied:* Mander College, Bedford and Coventry Polytechnic (1981-84). *Exhib:* R.A. Summer Exhbn. from 1986-'00 (prizewinner, 1990); various group exhbns. in London etc. *Work in collections:* Morgan Grenfell, St. Martin's College, Lancaster, Warrington Arts Council. Dealers: Portal Gallery, London. *Signs work:* "P. Layzell" on reverse. *Address:* 72 Vale Rd., Lancaster LA1 2JL.

LEACH, D., potter in stoneware and porcelain; *b* Tokyo, 7 May, 1911. *m* Elizabeth Mary. three *s.* (all potters). *Educ:* Dauntsey's School. *Studied:* with Bernard Leach. *Exhib:* numerous in U.K., Germany, Japan, Australia, Turkey, Belgium, U.S.A., Craftsmans Art at V. & A. (1973), British Crafts Centre (1979); one-man, Craftsmen Potters Assoc. (1966, 1981, 1990, 1994). *Work in collections:* V. & A., Exeter Museum and A.G., Wakefield Museum, Liverpool Museum and A.G., Craft Study Centre, Dartington Hall Elmhirst Collection; Extensive lecture tours in U.S.A., Canada, Japan, Germany, Spain, Italy and Greece. *Commissions:* numerous. *Clubs:* Soc. Designer Craftsmen, Craft Potters Association, Devon Guild of Craftsmen. *Signs work:* seal in foot of pots, see appendix. *Address:* Lowerdown Pottery, Bovey Tracey, Devon TQ13 9LE.

LEACH, Mark Alan, P.S. (1994); self taught artist in pastel, charcoal, acrylic; *b* Bromley, Kent, 10 Apr., 1952. *m* Gabrielle Janice. three *s. Educ:* Dulwich College; Bromley Grammar School. *Exhib:* P.S., Mall Galleries, various one-man and mixed shows London and U.K. *Signs work:* "Mark LEACH" see appendix. *Address:* The White House, Pannel Lane, Pett, Hastings, E. Sussex TN35 4JB.

LEACH, Ursula Mary, A.R.E. (1996), B.A. (Hons.) (1992); printmaker/painter in etching and oil paint; *b* Woking, 14 May, 1947. *m* John Leach (separated). one *s.* one *d. Studied:* Winchester, Wimbledon and Farnham Schools of Art. *Exhib:* Attendi,

London W4, Mall Galleries, London, Redfern, London, Southampton City A.G. *Work in collections:* Diploma Collection, Ashmolean, Oxford, Royal Hospitals N.H.S.Trust, Dorset County Hospital. *Commissions:* Worthing Hospital Postgraduate Medical Centre. *Publications:* work repro.: review: Contemporary Art Vol. 2. No.3., Art on Paper Fair catalogue (1999). *Signs work:* "U.Leach." *Address:* 14 The Square, Cranborne, Dorset BH21 5PR.

LEAPER, Landreth Francis, R.W.A.; self taught artist in water-colour and mixed media; *b* Horsham, 22 Dec., 1947. *Exhib:* numerous in South and S. West England. *Signs work:* "LEAPER" or "L. LEAPER" or double LL within a circle, sometimes above the year. *Address:* 28 Gerald Rd., Ashton, Bristol BS3 2DN.

LE BAS, Rachel Ann, R.E., N.E.A.C.; Mem. A.W.G., Somerset Guild of Craftsmen; painter, line-engraver, etc.; *b* 9 Apr., 1923. *Educ:* W. Heath School, Sevenoaks. *Studied:* City and Guilds of London Art School (A.R. Middleton Todd, R.A., R.W.S., R.E., N.E.A.C.). *Exhib:* R.A., N.E.A.C., R.E., etc. *Work in collections:* Ashmolean Museum, Exeter Museum, Southampton Civic Centre, R.A. Graphics. *Clubs:* Arts, Dover St. *Signs work:* "R. A. LE BAS." *Address:* Winsford, nr. Minehead, Som. TA24 7JE.

LE BROCQUY, Louis, H.R.H.A. (1983), F.C.S.D. (1960), Hon. Litt.D., Dublin (1962), Hon. Ll.D. National University of Ireland (1988), Hon. Ph.D. Dublin City University (1998), Chevalier de la Légion d'Honneur (1975), Officier, l'Ordre des Arts et des Lettres (1996); *b* Nov., 1916. *m* Anne Madden le Brocquy. two *s.* one *d.* *Studied:* self taught. *Exhib:* Gimpel Fils (London, N.Y.), Galerie Jeanne Bucher (Paris), Taylor (Dublin), Agnexis (London). Retrospective exhbns.: Municipal Gallery of Modern Art, Dublin (1966, 1978), Ulster Museum, Belfast (1967, 1987), Fondation Maeght, St. Paul (1973), Arts Council, Belfast (1975, 1978), Musée d'Art Moderne, Paris (1976), New York State Museum (1981), Palais des Beaux Arts, Charleroi (1982), Festival Centre, Adelaide (1988), Westpac, National Gallery of Victoria, Melbourne (1988), Museum of Contemporary Art, Brisbane (1988), Musée Picasso, Antibes (1989), Museum of Modern Art, Kamakura (1991), Itami Museum of Art, Osaki (1991), City Museum of Contemporary Art, Hiroshima (1991), Irish Museum of Modern Art, Dublin (1996), Chateau Musée de Tours (1997), Municipal Gallery of Modern Art, Ljubljana (1998), Museum of Modern Art, Oaxaca (2000). *Address:* c/o Gimpel Fils, 30 Davies St., London W1Y 1LG. *Website:* www.le-brocquy.com *Email:* info@le-brocquy.com

LE BROCQUY, Melanie, Taylor scholarship (1938, 1939); California gold medal of the R.D.S. (1939); member of A.O.S.D.A.N.A. (1981); H.R.H.A.; sculptor in bronze; *b* Dublin, 1919. *m* the late Professor F.S. Stewart, T.C.D. (Dublin University). two *s.* two *d.* *Educ:* Chiefly in Dublin. *Studied:* National College of Art, Dublin; Ecole des Beaux Arts, Geneva; Royal Academy School of Art, Dublin. *Exhib:* R.H.A. (1938, 1939, 1941, 1974, 1982-2001); joint exhib. with her brother Louis Le Brocquy (1942); I.L.A. (1943, 1965, 1967, 1971); Biennale Christlicher, Salzburg (1962); 'Melanie Le Brocquy/William Scott (1973); (prints) Dawson Gallery, Dublin. *Work in collections:* Arts Council; Hugh Lane Municipal Gallery; Allied Irish Bank; Aer Kiantha; National Self-Portrait collection; 'St. Patrick'

(1941), installed in St. Patrick's cathedral (2001). *Commissions:* "The Arts Reflected", eight small sculptures commissioned by the Bank of Ireland for the Art Show Awards (1990). *Publications:* weekly illustrations for gardening articles in the Irish Times, (from 1980 to 1988). Large catalogue for retrospective in R.H.A. (1999). Solo exhibitions, or retrospectives, Taylor Galleries, Dublin (1986), Bell Gallery, Belfast (1989), Austin Desmond Fine Art, London (1990), Taylor Galleries (1991), Bell Gallery (1992); also, bust of Oscar Wilde purchased for T.C.D. (1996), the American College, Dublin, for Oscar Wilde House (1997), Magdalen College, Oxford (1997) and the Irish Embassy in Washington D.C. (2000). *Clubs:* Royal Dublin Society. *Signs work:* "M le B." *Address:* c/o The Taylor Galleries, Dublin 2, Ireland.

LE BRUN, Christopher Mark, Dip. F.A. Slade (1974), M.A. Chelsea (1975), R.A. (1996); painter, printmaker, sculptor; Trustee National Gallery (since 1996), Trustee Tate Gallery (1990-95), Trustee Dulwich Picture Gallery (2000), Profesor of Drawing, R.A. (2000); *b* Portsmouth, 20 Dec., 1951. *m* Charlotte Verity. two *s.* one *d. Studied:* Slade School of Fine Art, Chelsea School of Art. *Exhib:* numerous mixed exhbs., one-man shows worldwide since 1978. *Work in collections:* Tate, V. & A., B.M., M.O.M.A. New York, Arts Council, Fitzwilliam Museum, Courtauld, Oslo, Sydney, Yale, S.N.G.M.A., Edinburgh, Whitworth, Southampton, etc. *Commissions:* The Parables, Liverpool Cathedral (1996). *Clubs:* Groucho, Chelsea Arts. *Address:* Marlborough Fine Art, 6 Albemarle Street., London W1X 4BY.

LEDER, Carolyn, M.A. (1968); Curator, Old Speech Room Gallery, Harrow School (1989-); Trustee, Stanley Spencer Gallery, Cookham (1978-90); formerly Lecturer in History of Art, University of London, Dept. of Extra-Mural Studies (1972-88); *b* Melbourne, 5 Mar., 1945. *m* Professor Malcolm Leder. two *s. Studied:* Courtauld Inst. of Art, University of London. *Publications:* book, Stanley Spencer: The Astor Collection (1976); articles; numerous catalogues including 'Victor Pasmore', 'John Piper', 'English Watercolourists'. Historical Adviser, BBC 2 Television, 'Stanley', drama-documentary on Stanley Spencer (1988). Specialist commentator in Stanley Spencer Gallery's video 'Stanley Spencer: A Painter in Heaven' (1996). *Address:* The Steps, Hill Close, Harrow on the Hill, Middx. HA1 3PQ.

LEDGER, Janet, Hon. Citizen of Dallas; painter in oil of landscapes, townscapes, beach scenes; *b* Northampton, 22 July, 1931. *m* H.E. Clements. two *d. Studied:* Northampton School of Art. *Exhib:* Dallas Texas, R.A. Summer Show, Mall Galleries, S.W.A., Century Gallery, Henley, Medici Gallery, London, Edwin Pollard Gallery, Linda Blackstone Gallery since 1985. *Work in collections:* H.R.H. Princess Margaret, Tate Gallery, National Westminster Bank, Marks & Spencer Plc, National Coal Board, McDonalds Plc. *Address:* c/o Linda Blackstone Gallery, Old Slaughterhouse, R/O 13 High St., Pinner, Middx. HA5 5QQ.

LEE, Christine Mary, B.A. (Hons.) Fine Arts, Sculpture (1981); sculptor in various medias; Artistic Director, Ragley Hall Sculpture Park, Warwickshire (1994-95), Artistic Director, Westonbirt Arboretum Sculpture Park, Glos. (1996); *b* Bucks. *m* Douglas May. one *s.* one *d. Studied:* privately under Ulrica Seaton-Lloyd, Oxford; Banbury Art College (1977-78); St. Martin's School of Art (1978-81); Central

School of Art (1981-83, painting and drawing: Cecil Collins). *Exhib:* Spain, U.S.A., U.K., Channel Islands. Work in collections worldwide. *Commissions:* numerous including 17 ft. fountain, Stratford-upon-Avon, inaugurated by H.M. The Queen. *Clubs:* F.P.S., Fountain Soc. *Signs work:* "Lee." *Address:* Beechwood House, High Bickington, Devon EX3 9BQ.

LEE, Rern, painter in oil colour; *b* Jakarta, Indonesia, 19 Sept., 1938. *m* Siew Pui-Sam. two *d. Educ:* Singapore and Jakarta. *Studied:* Nanyang Academy of Fine Arts, Singapore. Trainee for several years in father's studio, then travelled and worked in England, France, Italy, Holland, Germany and Singapore (1969-72); Australia and New Zealand (1976); U.S.A. and Canada (1981). *Exhib:* one-man shows: Singapore (1970) and Jakarta (1980), etc. *Work in collections:* Nanyang University Museum, Singapore; Indonesia Palace Museum, Jakarta; The Asia and Pacific Museum, Warsaw, etc. Awards: Academic of Italy with Gold Medal; International Parliament U.S.A. Gold Medal of Merit; conferred Honorary Prize with Memorial Medal of Golden Centaur 1982; Diploma of Honoris Causa "Master of Painting" from the International Seminar of Modern and Contemporary Art and Diploma of Merit from Italian University of Arts. *Signs work:* "R. Lee." *Address:* Jalan Gedong 11-A, Jakarta Barat, Indonesia.

LEE, Sidney Edward, graphic artist and painter in oil and charcoal/chalks; *b* London, 22 Nov., 1925. *m* Amy Gwendoline Aston (decd.). *Studied:* Harrow School of Art, Willesden School of Art. *Exhib:* R.W.A., R.O.I., R.S.M.A., Guildhall and Mall Galleries London; International Boat Show Earl's Court, London; Royal West of England Academy, Bristol; Norway Gallery and Mariners Gallery, St. Ives; exhib. marine paintings regularly with the R.S.M.A. (1979-85) - see 20th Century British Marine Painting by Denys Brook-Hart. Recent work includes charcoal and conté drawings of the Cornish landscape. *Clubs:* St. Ives Soc. of Artists. *Signs work:* see appendix. *Address:* Rose Lea, Rose Hill, Marazion, Cornwall TR17 0HB.

LEE, Terry Glyn, D.F.A. (Lond.), 1957; artist in oil; *b* Sheffield, 28 Oct., 1932. four *s. Educ:* King Edward VII School, Sheffield. *Studied:* Sheffield College of Art; Slade School of Fine Art (1955-58); Sir William Coldstream. *Exhib:* New Art Centre, Agnews, Piccadilly Gallery, Wildenstein, R.A., Van Rijn Maastricht, Bühler Gallery Stuttgart. *Work in collections:* Liverpool Art Gallery, Ferens Art Gallery, Hull, Coventry Art Gallery, Oldham Art Gallery, The Arts Council, Financial Times, Contemporary Art Soc., Sheffield Art Galleries, Duke of Devonshire, Government Art Collection. *Signs work:* "Terry Lee." *Address:* Calton Houses, Calton Lees, Beeley, nr. Matlock, Derbyshire DE4 2NX.

LEECH, Raymond Ian, R.S.M.A. (1986), L.S.I.A.D. (1969); mem. E.Anglian Group of Marine Artists; landscape and seascape painter in oil and water-colour; partner in a design group, Pencil Point Studio; *b* Gt.Yarmouth, 1949. *Educ:* Edward Worledge School, Alderman Leach High School. *Studied:* Gt.Yarmouth College of Art and Design (1965-69). *Exhib:* R.S.M.A., Hunting Group, Mystic U.S.A., Assembly Rooms Norwich, Ladygate Gallery, and other provincial galleries. *Work in collections:* National Maritime Museum, The Sheik of Oman, Mystic Maritime Gallery U.S.A., etc. *Publications:* represented in Tonal Painting (Quarto). *Signs work:* see appendix. *Address:* 1 The Staithe, Oulton Broad, Lowestoft, Suffolk.

LEEDS, Caroline (Lady Hobart), portrait and landscape painter in oil, water-colour, pastel, silverpoint and conté; *b* Jersey, C.I., 17 May, 1931. *m* Lt. Comdr. Sir Robert Hobart, Bt. (decd.). *Studied:* under Bernard Adams, R.P., R.O.I., and Philip Lambe, R.P. *Exhib:* over forty exhbns. in London, Paris, New York, Zurich and Palm Beach including Wildenstein London, Galerie M.B. Paris, Sotheby Zurich. *Work in collections:* Moët and Chandon, Epernay, Citi Bank, Lord and Lady Montagu of Beaulieu, The Royal Hospital Chelsea. *Commissions:* H.R.H. Prince Andrew, The Duke and Duchess of Bedford, Christine Mrs. Henry Ford, Sir John Nicholson, Bt. former Commodore of the Royal Yacht Squadron, I.O.W. *Clubs:* Arts Club Dover St., Royal Yacht Squadron, I.O.W. *Signs work:* "Leeds." *Address:* Flat 14, 42 Egerton Gdns., London SW3 2BZ.

LEES, Stewart Marshall, D.A. (Edin.) (1952), R.O.I. (1987), R.S.W. (1992), R.W.S. (1991); *b* Auchtertool, Fife, 15 Jan., 1926. *Educ:* Edinburgh College of Art (1947-52). *Exhib:* R.A. Summer Exhbn., Royal Scottish Academy, R.S.W., R.W.S., and privately. *Work in collections:* Glenrothes New Town, Liverpool Educ. Com., Fife Educ. Com., University of Glasgow, University of Nottingham, Nuffield Foundation, Imperial Tobacco Co., Sheffield City A.G., Leverhulme Foundation, Scottish Arts Council, Esso Ltd., Leeds Educ. Com. *Clubs:* Arts, London. *Signs work:* "Stewart Lees." *Address:* Southlands, Arlington Drive, Mapperley Pk., Nottingham NG3 5EN.

LEES, Susan Jane, artist in gouache, acrylic, pastel, oil; Wildlife illustrator at Bristol Zoo; *b* Bristol, 23 June, 1961. *Educ:* Hengrove Comp. Bristol. *Studied:* Glos. College of Art and Design (1980-82). *Exhib:* Soc. of Amateur Artists, Soc. of Women Artists, British Soc. of Painters, The Wildlife Art Soc., and local exhbns, Northern Exhbn. of Wildlife Art. Christies Wildlife Art. *Clubs:* Soc. of Amateur Artists '93, Wildlife Art Soc. '94, Soc. of Women Artists '95-'96, British Soc. of Painters '94-'95, Whitchurch Art Club '92. *Signs work:* "Susan Jane." *Address:* 163 Avonvale Rd., Redfield, Bristol BS5 9RY.

LEGG, Owen, F.P.S.; printmaker and artist in oil on board, lino-cut prints, abstract constructions; *b* London, 1 Aug., 1935. *Educ:* Alleyns School, Dulwich. *Studied:* Tunbridge Wells Adult Education Centre. *Exhib:* York University, Tunbridge Wells Library, Loggia Gallery. *Work in collections:* Greenwich Library, Graphotek, Berlin. *Publications:* Cut in the Chalk, Rubaiyyat of Omar Khayaam; The Garden by V. Sackville West (1989), On First Seeing Iceland (1992), Christmas letters from a Friend (1997), Advice to a Young Explorer (1999). *Clubs:* Secretary to Free Painters & Sculptors, Treasurer to South East Open Studios. *Signs work:* "Owen Legg." *Address:* Woodcraft Press, 152 Hadlow Rd., Tonbridge, Kent TN9 1PB. *Email:* owen@legg152.freeserve.co.uk

LE GRICE, Jeremy Day, B.A. Slade; painter in oil; *b* Penzance, 17 Sep., 1936. *m* Lyn. two *s.* two *d. Educ:* Eton College. *Studied:* Guildford College of Art, Slade School, London University. *Clubs:* Penwith Soc., St. Ives, Newlyn Soc. of Artists. *Signs work:* "Jeremy Le Grice." *Address:* Flower Loft Studio, Trereife, Penzance, Cornwall TR20 8TJ.

LEHMANN, Olga, S.G.F.A., N.S., F.R.S.A.; painter; designer; *b* Catemu, Chile, 1912. *m* Carl E.R. Huson (decd.). one *s. Educ:* Santiago College, Chile. *Studied:*

Slade School of Fine Art (Prof. Schwabe, Alan Gwynne Jones, V. Polunin). In 1941 joined the film industry as scenic artist, later became a designer of sets and costumes. Credits include "Tom Thumb", "Guns of Navarone", "Man in the Iron Mask", "Kidnapped", " Master of Ballantrae". *Exhib:* London Group, N.E.A.C., S.G.F.A., N.S., Suffolk Art Soc., Gainsborough House, Wright Hepburn Webster Gallery, New York, Fry Gallery, Saffron Walden, and many others; one-woman shows: John Whibley Gallery, A.I.A. Gallery, London, Rushmore Rooms, and Heffer's Gallery, Cambridge, Guildhall, Finchingfield, County Library, Saffron Walden, Augustine Gallery, Holt, Guildhall Thaxted, Dunmow Art Group, Barnsdale Gallery, Yoxford, Canning House, London. *Work in collections:* Imperial War Museum; R.A.F. Museum. *Commissions:* Portraits include: Prince Harry, Faucigny Lucinge, Vice Admiral Sir Gilbert Stephenson, Sir Vivian Fuchs, Mrs Parker-Bowles, Dame Betty Paterson, C.B.E., Sir Dirk Bogarde. *Signs work:* "Olga Lehmann." *Address:* 1 Artisans Dwellings, Saffron Walden, Essex CB10 1LW. *Email:* pahuson@pacbell.net

LEIGH, David Roy, M.A.(Oxon.) (1972), F.S.B.A. (1986); botanical artist in water-colour; former official artist to the Orchid Com. of the R.H.S.; *b* Leeds, 2 June, 1945. *m* Vaila Mary Eastabrook. one *s.* one *d. Educ:* City of Leicester Boys' School, and Oxford University (Worcester College). *Exhib:* S.B.A. at Mall Galleries, R.H.S. *Publications:* illustrated Aroids (Century, 1988), author: Orchids (Cassell, 1990). *Signs work:* "David R. Leigh" or more often "D.R.L." with year. *Address:* West Hill House, Plush, Dorset DT2 7RQ.

LEK, Karel, R.C.A., A.T.D.; artist in oil, water-colour and graphic media; *b* Antwerp, 7 June, 1929. married. one *s.* one *d. Studied:* Liverpool College of Art. *Exhib:* National Museum for Wales, R.A., R.C.A., Cardiff, Albany Gallery, Cardiff, Arts Council, Bangor Gallery, Mostyn Gallery, Llandudno, Retrospective (1994) Oriel Ynys Môn, Anglesey, Breknock Museum Brecon (1997). *Work in collections:* University Coll. of N. Wales, Contemporary Art Soc. for Wales, National Library of Wales, Anglesey C.C. Welsh Collection, Michael Forte Collection, Breknock Museum, Brecon. Half hour documentary "Prime Time" H.T.V. (9 May & 9 Oct. 1994). *Address:* Studio House, Beaumaris, Anglesey LL58 8EE.

LEMAN, Martin, artist in oil; former graphic design teacher, Hornsey College of Art (1961-77); *b* London, 25 Apr., 1934. *m* Jill. *Educ:* Royal Masonic School. *Studied:* Worthing School of Art, and Central School of Arts and Crafts. *Exhib:* twenty exhbns. *Commissions:* many cat portraits. *Publications:* twenty-four books, mainly cat paintings. *Signs work:* "Leman." *Address:* 1 Malvern Terr., London N1 1HR.

LENEY, Sheila, S.B.A. (1987); floral artist in water-colour and embroidery; *b* London, 23 Nov., 1930. *m* Edward W. Leney (decd.). two *s.* one *d. Educ:* St. Helen's School, Streatham. *Studied:* Croydon School of Art (1947-49), Epsom A.E.C. (1982). *Exhib:* Mall Galleries; Outwood Gallery, Surrey; Linnean Soc.; Lannards Gallery, Sussex; Westminster Gallery, Knapp Gallery, London; McEwan Gallery, Scotland; work in private collections. *Publications:* greetings cards for Medici Soc. *Signs work:* "Sheila Leney." *Address:* Invermene, 107 Newton Wood Rd., Ashtead, Surrey KT21 1NW.

LENG-SMITH, Barbara, Hon. Mention, Paris Salon, Silver Medal; portrait painter in oil, water-colour and pastel specialising in children; *b* Isle of Man, 7 Mar.,

1922. *m* Ralph Leng-Smith. one *s.* four *d. Educ:* Sheffield. *Studied:* Manchester under Harry Rutherford. *Exhib:* one-man show: Tib Lane Gallery, Manchester; Royal Society of Portrait Painters, London; Paris Salon; R.S.A., Edinburgh. *Signs work:* "Leng-Smith." *Address:* Miramar, Arthog Rd., Hale, Altrincham, Cheshire WA15 0LS.

LENNON, Stephen, F.I.G.A. (1995), B.W.S. (1994), Y.W.S. (1997); artist in water-colour and mixed media; *b* Burnley, Lancs., 10 Mar., 1953. *m* Laila (née Wesenlund). one *s.* one *d. Studied:* mostly self taught, life classes in Burnley in the 1970's. *Exhib:* Laing Finalist (1989); one-man show: Bradford University (1990); mixed shows: Mercer Harrogate, Ginnel Manchester, Salford City A.G., Chantry House Gallery, Ripley, many private collections. *Commissions:* eight paintings for the Marquess of Hartington. *Publications:* work repro.: B.W.S. catalogue (1997), articles in the Yorkshire Journal. *Clubs:* Yorkshire Water-colour Soc., Leeds Fine Art Club. *Signs work:* "Stephen Lennon." *Address:* 24 Ickornshaw, Cowling, nr. Keighley, W. Yorks. BD22 0DE. *Website:* www.stephenlennon.co.uk *Email:* ste@stephenlennon.co.uk

LEONARD, (Douglas) Michael, painter and illustrator; *b* Bangalore, India, 25 June 1933. *Educ:* Stonyhurst College. *Studied:* St. Martin's School of Art (1954-57). Worked as an illustrator from 1957-72 and subsequently as a painter. *Exhib:* one-man shows: Fischer Fine Art London (1974, 1977, 1980, 1983, 1988), Harriet Griffin, New York (1977), Gemeentemuseum, Arnhem (1977-78) (retrospective), Artsite, Bath (1989) (retrospective), Stiebel Modern New York (1992), Thomas Gibson Fine Art, London (1993, 1997), Forum Gallery, New York (1999); mixed shows: "Realismus und Realitat" Darmstadt (1975), John Moores, Liverpool (1976, 1978), "The Craft of Art" Walker A.G. (1979), "Nudes" Angela Flowers, London (1979/80), "The Real British", Fischer Fine Art (1981), "Contemporary British Painters", Museo Municipal, Madrid (1983), "Self Portrait: A Contemporary View", Artsite, Bath (1987), "In Human Terms", Stiebel Modern, New York (1991), 'Its Still Life', Forum Gallery, New York (1998), 'Between Earth and Heaven', Museum of Modern Art, Ostend (2001). *Work in collections:* The Boymans Van Beuningen Museum Rotterdam, De Beer/C.S.O., N.P.G., V. & A., Fitzwilliam Museum Cambridge, Ferens A.G., Hull, Arnot Art Museum, Elmira, N.Y. *Commissions:* Painted H.M. Queen Elizabeth II for Readers Digest (1986) now in N.P.G. *Signs work:* "Leonard" or "ML." *Address:* 3 Kensington Hall Gdns., Beaumont Ave., London W14 9LS.

LEONARD, Patrick, A.R.H.A. (1942), H.R.H.A. (1980); painter in oil and pastel; *b* Rush, C. Dublin, 11 Oct., 1918. *m* Doreen. two *d. Educ:* O'Connell Schools, Dublin. *Studied:* Metropolitan School of Art, Dublin, under John Keating R.H.A. and Maurice MacGonigal R.H.A. *Exhib:* R,H.A. (1941-2001), solo exhibs. in Dublin, Irish Art in U.S.A. and Canada. *Work in collections:* Hugh Lane Gallery, Dublin; Cork Municipal Gallery, Waterford; Wexford Corporation Galleries. *Publications:* Exhib. catalogue, Gorry Gallery, Dublin (1990). *Signs work:* "P. Leonard" or "P. LEONARD." *Address:* 19 Dublin Rd., Skerries, Co. Dublin, Ireland.

LESTER, James Richard, N.D.D. (1955), S.B.A. (1986); artist in water-colour, oil, pastel; *b* Dover, 18 Dec., 1932. *m* Margo. one *s.* three *d. Studied:* Dover School of Art (1951-53), Canterbury College of Art (1953-55). *Exhib:* R.A., R.W.A., R.B.A.,

R.I., S.B.A.; one-man show: Tenterden and Otterton. *Publications:* co-author and illustrator: 'Painting the Secret World of Nature'. *Clubs:* S.B.A. *Signs work:* "James Lester." *Address:* Rydon Farm, Ottery St., Otterton, Devon EX9 7HW.

LETTS, John Barry, sculptor in clay for casting in bronze; *b* Birmingham, 20 Aug., 1930. *m* Patricia Letts. two *s.* one *d. Educ:* Sharman Cross Senior School, Birmingham. *Studied:* Birmingham College of Art (1945-49) under William Bloye. *Exhib:* London, Birmingham, Nuneaton, Solihull, Stratford-upon-Avon, Stoke-on-Trent. *Work in collections:* Nuneaton and Stratford-upon-Avon galleries. *Commissions:* one and a half times life-size statue of George Eliot (authoress) for Nuneaton Town Centre (1985); 1994: portrait bust of H.M. The Queen, unveiled by Her Majesty 8 Dec. 1995, commissioned by Warwickshire Health Authority. *Signs work:* "John Letts." *Address:* 160 Tilehouse, Green Lane, Knowle, Solihull, W. Midlands B93 9EJ.

LEVEE, John, B.A., Grand Prix, Academie Julian (1951), Biennal de Paris (1959); Ford Fellowship (1969); Grand Prix, Wodmark Foundation (1975); painter in oil, gouache, crayon; visiting Professor of Art, University of Illinois (1965), N.Y. University (1967-68), University Southern Calif. (1970-72); *b* Los Angeles, 10 Apr., 1924. *Educ:* University Calif., New School for Social Research, N.Y. *Studied:* New School; Academie Julian, Paris (Grand Prix 1952). *Exhib:* numerous one-man shows in U.S.A. and Europe. *Work in collections:* Kunst Museum, Basle; Smith College Museum; Museum of Modern Art, N.Y.; Stedelijk Museum, Amsterdam; Musée du Havre; Towner A.G.; Baltimore Museum; Columbus Gallery of Fine Art, Guggenheim Museum, N.Y.; and others. *Publications:* 16 Painters of Young, School of Paris, Abstract Art, Dictionary of Abstract Art, Concise History of Modern Art, L'École de Paris 1945-1965 Harumbourg. *Signs work:* "Levee." *Address:* 119 rue Notre Dame des Champs, Paris 75006.

LEVEN, Marian, D.A. (1966), R.S.W. (1993); artist in water-colour, acrylic; *b* Edinburgh, 25 Mar., 1944. *m* Will MacLean. two *s.* one *d. Educ:* Bell-Baxter, Cupar, Fife. *Studied:* Gray's School of Art, Aberdeen (1962-66). *Exhib:* R.S.A., R.S.W., R.G.I., Aberdeen Artists. *Work in collections:* Arts in Fife, Paintings in Hospitals, Lillie Gallery, Milngavie, Kirkcaldy Museum and A.G. Winner, Noble Grossart/ Scotland on Sunday Painting Prize (1997). *Signs work:* "Marian Leven." *Address:* Bellevue, 18 Dougall St., Tayport, Fife DD6 9JD.

LEVENE, Ben, A.R.A. (1975), R.A. (1986); painter (genre) in oils, water-colours; Curator, Royal Academy Schools (1995-98); *b* London, 23 Dec., 1938. *m* Susan. one *s.* two *d. Studied:* Slade School of Fine Art (1956-61), Boise Scholarship (1961-62). *Exhib:* regularly at R.A., and Browse and Darby Gallery, London; work in many private and public collections. *Commissions:* several landscape commissions especially "tree portraits" Lydham Oak (1997) and Mulberry Tree, Lindsay House (1998). *Publications:* Oils Masterclass by Sally Bulgin. *Signs work:* Usually signed on back; since 1975 with monogram "B.L." *Address:* c/o The Royal Academy, Burlington House, Piccadilly, London W1V 0DS.

LEVI, Edgar: see KNIGHT, Clifford.

LEWIS, Ann, Royal Cambrian Academician, B.A.; artist/illustrator in gouache, water-colour, mixed media, pencil, ink; *b* St. Asaph, N. Wales, 29 Aug., 1962. *Studied:* Exeter College of Art and Design (1985-88). *Exhib:* Royal Cambrian Academy - Conwy, W.A.C., National Library of Wales, Mostyn Gallery, Wales Open, Clwyd Open, Mercier Gallery, Albany Gallery - Cardiff, Tegfryn Gallery - Anglesey, Hanover Galleries - Liverpool, Royal Exchange Theatre - Manchester. *Work in collections:* National Library of Wales. *Publications:* books illustrated: eight children's books, one collection of poetry, numerous illustrations for published articles. *Clubs:* R.Cam.A. *Signs work:* "Ann Lewis." *Address:* 6 Well St. 2, Gerlan, Bethesda, Gwynedd LL57 3TW. *Website:* http://www.oriel - cambria.co.uk *Email:* ann@oriel-cambria.co.uk

LEWIS, Charles Walter Edward, A.R.C.A., F.R.B.S., A.W.G., Royal Exhibition and Continuation Scholarship (1946); sculptor in stone and wood; Head of Sculpture, Kingston College of Art (1947-78); *b* Southsea, 18 July, 1916. *m* Margaret Parkinson. two *s.* one *d. Educ:* Portsmouth Southern Secondary School. *Studied:* Portsmouth College of Art (1932-36), Royal College of Art, under Prof. Richard Garbe (1936-39). *Exhib:* retrospective, Weston Press Gallery, New York (1983). *Commissions:* sculpture commissioned by the Ministry of Public Building and Works, The G.L.C. and several private architects. *Address:* 4 Ancien Chemin D'Agel, 11120 Bize-Minervois, France.

LEWIS, Christopher Conrad Strafford, N.D.D. (1950), A.T.D. (1951), R.C.A. (1964); sculptor in clay, woodcarver and printmaker; lecturer in art history & drawing, Chester School of Art, visiting lecturer; *b* Woodford, Essex, 15 Jul., 1922. *m* Marjory Rae. two *s.* three *d. Educ:* Epsom College. *Studied:* Ealing (1946-1950) under Tom Boyley, Hornsey (1951). *Exhib:* Chester, Liverpool, London, St. Albans, Amsterdam, Wales. *Work in collections:* many private collections. *Commissions:* various. *Publications:* songs of William Shakespeare. *Signs work:* "CONRAD LEWIS." *Address:* Appletrees, 19 Fish St., Redbourn, Herts. AL3 7LP.

LEWIS, Dennis, R.W.A. (1979), F.C.S.D. (1986); artist in oil, acrylic, water-colour; Design Group Chairman (retd.); *b* Bristol, 2 Apr., 1928. *m* Irene Margaret. one *s.* two *d. Educ:* F.A.S. Bristol. *Studied:* No. 3 Army College (1948, Mervyn Levy), West of England College of Art (1948-52). President, Bristol Savages (1972, 1979, 1989). *Signs work:* "Dennis Lewis." *Address:* 4 Redcliffe Parade E., Redcliffe, Bristol BS1 6SW.

LEWIS, John, A.K.C., B.Sc. (1950), ex F.L.S., M.F.P.S. (1974), Dip.V.A. (Lond.) (1980); phanerogamic taxonomist, poet and amateur artist in oil; *b* Chingford, 25 Nov., 1921. *Educ:* City of London School, Kings College, London. *Studied:* Richmond Adult College and Field Studies Council. *Exhib:* F.P.S. and privately. *Publications:* numerous scientific papers and one poem. *Signs work:* uses ideogram, a rhomboid with two verticals included. *Address:* Applefield, North Street, South Petherton, Somerset TA13 5DA.

LEWIS, Sanchia, Cert. Printmaking and Cert. Advanced Printmaking (Distinction 1982); etcher and painter in oil, pastel, pigment stick; *b* London, 31 Mar., 1960. *m* Jeremy Youngs. *Educ:* Crown Woods Comprehensive, Eltham, London. *Studied:* City and Guilds School of Art, London. *Exhib:* Affordable Art Fair,

Battersea Park (2000), Art on Paper Fair, R.C.A. (2001), Honor Oak Gallery, London (2000); 1st prize Portobello Open Exhib. (1993), Marlborough Gallery prize at National Print Exhib. (1995). *Signs work:* "Sanchia Lewis." *Address:* 50 Cheltenham Rd., Peckham Rye, London SE15 3AQ.

LEWIS, Stephen, B.F.A.(Hons.); sculptor in steel; *b* 11 Jan., 1959. *Educ:* Deyes High School, Maghull, Merseyside. *Studied:* Southport College of Art (1976-77), Manchester Polytechnic (1977-80), Jan van Eyck Academie, Maastricht, The Netherlands. *Exhib:* New Contemporaries, I.C.I. London (1979), Kunst Europa, Germany (1991); one-man shows: Francis Graham-Dixon Gallery (1988, 1990, 1993), Holden Gallery, Manchester (1990). *Signs work:* "Stephen Lewis." *Address:* 76 Royal Hill, Greenwich, London SE10 8RT.

LEYDEN, John Michael, hon. mem., S.A. Assoc. of Draughtsmen; cartoonist in black and white; artist in water-colour and etching; staff cartoonist, Daily News, since 1939; S.A. Cartoonist of the Year (1981); awarded Papal Cross, "Pro Pontifice et Ecclesia" (1986); *b* Grangemouth, Scotland, 21 Nov., 1908. *m* Annabel Eugenie Wishart. one *s.* three *d. Educ:* St. Aloysius College, Glasgow. *Studied:* Durban School of Art, Heatherley's, Central Schools of Arts and Crafts. *Exhib:* Natal Soc. of Artists, Durban Art Gallery (one-man shows). *Work in collections:* Africana Museum, Johannesburg, Durban A.G. and University of Natal (cartoons and caricatures). *Publications:* thirteen books of cartoons. *Clubs:* Patron, Natal Motorcyle and Car Club. *Signs work:* see appendix. *Address:* 233 Nicholson Rd., Durban, Natal, S.A.

LEYGUE, Louis, Président de l'Académie des Beaux-Arts (1976 and 1982); Membre de l'Institut; sculptor; Prof., head of studio, L'École Nationale Supérieure des Beaux-Arts since 1945; *b* Bourg-en-Bresse, Ain, 25 Aug., 1905. *m* Marianne Cochet, painter. two *s. Educ:* Lycée Charlemagne, Paris. *Studied:* L'École Nationale des Arts décoratifs, Paris, L'Ecole Nationale des Beaux-Arts, Paris, Villa Medicis, Rome. *Work in collections:* Museum of Modern Art, Paris, Phenix Université de Caen, Auditorium Maison de la Radio, Paris, French Embassy, Ottawa, Fontaine des Corolles, Paris la Défense, Palais de Justice, d'Abidjan, Piave, Nantua, "Le Soleil" Autoroute Nancy-Dijon (1983). *Signs work:* "LOUIS LEYGUE." *Address:* 6 rue de Docteur Blanche, Paris XVIe.

LEYSHON-JONES, Steffan, B.A. Hons. Design Illustration (1997); painter in oil and ink; designer, Icon & Hurst; *b* Slough, 3 Aug., 1975. *Educ:* Windsor Boys School. *Studied:* Bath College of Higher Education, Central, St. Martin's, (Foundation). *Exhib:* Laing, Mall Galleries, (2000 national under twentyfive winner, 2001), various smaller exhibs. *Work in collections:* Beckford's Tower Trust, Bath, Great Western Trains, regional poster winner (2001). *Commissions:* Beckford's Tower Trust, Bath, expedition artist, Chile (2002), Raleigh International, Bath and West (1998). *Clubs:* Professional Photographers File, Bath Area Network for Artists, Axis Artists. *Signs work:* "S L Jones." *Address:* 7 Colenorton Cres., Eton Wick, Windsor, Berks. SL4 6NW. *Email:* colenorton@yahoo.co.uk

LIDDELL, John, A.T.D. (1946), D.A.E. (1974); art lecturer, printmaker in relief print, woodcut, lino, wood engraving; part-time lecturer, Bournemouth and Poole College of Art; *b* London, 6 July, 1924. *m* Jo Witchalls. two *s.* one *d. Educ:*

Minchenden School, London N14. *Studied:* Hornsey College of Art (1941-46, Russell Reeve, Norman Janes, D.P. Bliss). *Exhib:* R.A., R.W.A., Scribes, London EC4, Dorset Galleries. *Work in collections:* Print Club, Philadelphia, U.S.A., Poole Art Centre, Dorset (mural). *Publications:* work repro.: for own press, Onzello Press. *Clubs:* N.S.E.A.D., S.W.E., Founder, Poole Printmakers (1990). *Signs work:* "John Liddell" with date. *Address:* 90 Richmond Pk. Ave., Bournemouth BH8 9DR.

LIDZEY, John, B.A. (1975), M.S.C.D. (1970), F.R.S.A. (1980); artist in water-colour; formerly Senior lecturer Typographic Design, Camberwell School of Art; *b* London, 1935. *m* Elsie. one *s.* one *d. Studied:* Camberwell School of Art, Hornsey College of Art - part time. *Exhib:* one-man shows: John Russell Gallery, Ipswich; Burford Gallery, Burford, Oxon.; Linda Blackstone Gallery, Pinner, Middx. Work in collections worldwide. *Work in collections:* Europe, U.S.A., Australia. *Publications:* 'Water-colour Workshop' , and 'Paint Light in Water-colour' (Harper Collins) plus two associated videos; 'Mix Your own Water-colours' (Apple Press); regular contributor to Artist magazine. *Clubs:* President, Falcon Art Soc. *Address:* The Dell, Flixton, Bungay, Suffolk NR35 1NP.

LILLEY, Geoffrey Ivan, V.P.U.A.; painter in oil, author and illustrator in line; seascapes, still life, wildlife and animal portraits; experimental work; *b* Cambridge, 1 May, 1930. *m* Marguerite E. one *d. Educ:* Cambridge. *Studied:* Cambridge Technical College. *Exhib:* regularly at major London exhbns., including R.O.I., R.S.M.A., N.S., and U.A., etc., St. Ives, Cornwall, and major galleries in Sussex; one-man shows at London, Oxford, Bourton-on-the-Water. *Publications:* Artist, Art Review, Leisure Painter, etc.; author of several books and over 250 articles on art and craft subjects; over 1,000 drawings published. *Signs work:* see appendix. *Address:* Roosters at Golden Cross, Chiddingly, Lewes, Sussex BN8 6JE.

LILLFORD, Ralph, Ph.D., A.R.C.A., N.D.D.; Principal Lecturer in Art, Richmond University (1983-98); *b* 6 Nov., 1932. two *s.* three *d. Studied:* Doncaster Coll. of Art & R.C.A. *Exhib:* Houses of Parliament, European Parliament, Science Museum, St. Lawrence University, U.S.A., Schick Gallery, Saratoga, U.S.A., Channel Tunnel Exhbn., Universities of Bradford, Durham, Brunel and Imperial College. Retrospective Exhbn. Doncaster (1972-92). *Work in collections:* R.C.A., R.A., B.M., V. & A., Nat. Science Museum, Nat. Army Museum, Pushkin, Moscow, State Heritage, St. Petersburg, Dunedin, N.Z., Imperial War Museum; private collections in China, Japan, Australia, Sweden, Holland, France, Spain, Hungary. Taught: Richmond University (1983-98), and in U.S.A., Russia, Holland, France, Italy, Aborigine Centres in Australia. Published by catalogues. *Signs work:* see appendix. *Address:* 47 Creffield Rd., Ealing, London W5 3RR.

LILLINGSTON, Joyce Olive Mary, A.R.M.S. (1972), H.S.F. (1983); artist in water-colour and acrylic; *b* India, 11 Mar., 1922. *m* Leslie James Kastner (decd.). *Studied:* Byam Shaw School (B. Thomas, P. Greenham, B. Dunstan). *Exhib:* Walker Gallery (1959), Eastbourne Art Soc., R.A. (1950, 1965); solo show: Michelham Priory (1966). *Commissions:* five miniature portrait commissions (1997, 1998(2), 1999, 2000). *Clubs:* Campden Hill, Eastbourne Art Soc. *Address:* Moor Cottage, Belstone, Okehampton EX20 1QZ.

LIMBREY, John Nigel Stephens, N.D.D. (1953), M.C.S.D. (1969); Freeman of the Worshipful Company of Goldsmiths, City of London; silversmith and product designer; artist in water-colour and oil; landscape, architectural and marine subjects; *b* Hatfield, 2 Feb., 1933. *Educ:* King Edward's School, B'ham. *Studied:* B'ham College of Art (1949-53). *Exhib:* R.I., R.W.S., R.S.M.A. *Signs work:* "Limbrey." *Address:* Silk Mill Cottage, Chipping Campden, Glos. GL55 6DS.

LINDGREN, Carl Edwin, M.Ed., Ed.S., F.C.P., D.Litt., D.Ed., F.R.S.A., F.R.A.S., F.Coll.P. (Essex), A.S.I.I.P.C. (New Delhi); Faulknerian landscape photographer, art historian, antiquarian; *b* 20 Nov., 1949. *m* Penni Bolton, M.I.Sc.T. (Lond.), Senior Research Technician. *Educ:* University of Mississippi, College of Preceptors (Essex), U.N.I.S.A. *Exhib:* Center for Faulkner Studies, Center for the Study of Southern Culture, The Cossett Gallery, Northwest College Art Gallery, The University of Mississippi, India Intl. Photographic Council (New Delhi), Manipur University Museum, etc. *Publications:* over 200. *Signs work:* "C.E. Lindgren." *Address:* London (occasionally) or 10431-Hwy 51, Courtland, MS. 38620, U.S.A.

LINDSAY, Rosemary, S.B.A.; botanical illustrator in water-colour, pen and ink; *b* Croydon, 22 June, 1939. *Educ:* Croydon High School. *Studied:* Kingston School of Art (1957-60, architecture: Eric Brown), Morley College (botanical illustration: Margaret Merrett). *Exhib:* S.B.A. yearly, British Council Travelling Exhbn., Morley College, Horniman Museum, Battle Gallery, The Other Dulwich Picture Gallery, Limpsfield Gallery, Art in Action at Waterperry, Oriel Ynys Môn Anglesey, Everard Read, Johannesburg, S.A. Many private collections. *Publications:* illustrations in R.H.S. Journals and Herb Soc. Journals. *Signs work:* "Rosemary Lindsay." *Address:* 5 Burbage Rd., London SE24 9HJ.

LINFIELD, John Leslie, R.W.S. (1988), N.E.A.C. (1982), A.R.C.A. (1953); painter in oil and water-colour; *b* Carshalton Beeches, Surrey, 5 Jan., 1930. *Educ:* Sutton County School. *Studied:* Wimbledon School of Art, R.C.A. *Exhib:* R.A., R.B.A., R.P., N.E.A.C.; one-man shows, Trafford Gallery (1961, 1963), Ditchling Gallery (1964, 1965), Halifax House, Oxford (1972), Waterman Fine Art (1991), "Venice in Peril" W.H. Patterson since 1992. *Commissions:* Spink & Sons Ltd., Milton Abbey School, Dorset, Hove Museum and A.G., John Dickinson Ltd., Winsor and Newton Ltd. *Signs work:* "JOHN LINFIELD." *Address:* The Old Armoury, Court Barton, Crewkerne, Somerset TA18 7HP.

LISTER, Caroline Nicola Josephine, B.A.Hons. (1980), A.R.B.A.; painter and printmaker; printmaking tutor, Guildford College of Art (1980); Director and tutor, Tyger, Tyger Printmaking, Cambridge (Intaglio Printmaking Workshop); Steering Group mem. Cambridgeshire Regional College (1989); *b* Cambridge, 30 Mar., 1958. *Educ:* Perse School, Cambridge. *Studied:* Cambs. College of Arts and Technology (1976-77), W. Surrey College of Art and Design (1977-80). *Exhib:* R.B.A., R.E., R.I., P.S., R.W.S., S.W.A., C.D.S. *Signs work:* "Nicola Lister." *Address:* 79 St. Philips Rd., Cambridge CB1 3DA; studio: Tyger, Tyger Printmaking, Studio One, 37 City Rd., Cambridge CB1 1DP.

LISTER, Raymond George, P.R.M.S. (1970-80), M.A., Litt.D. (Cantab.); Governor, Federation of British Artists (1972-80); Fellow, Wolfson College, Cambridge; a syndic, Fitzwilliam Museum Cambridge (1981); painter; author; *b* Cambridge, 28 Mar., 1919. *m* Pamela Brutnell. one *s.* one *d. Educ:* Cambs. High

School; St. John's College School, Cambridge. *Studied:* privately. *Publications:* Raymond Lister, by C. R. Cammell and others (1963). Edward Calvert (1962); William Blake (1968); Samuel Palmer and His Etchings (1969); The Letters of Samuel Palmer (1975); George Richmond (1981); The Paintings of Samuel Palmer (1985); Catalogue Raisonné of Samuel Palmer (1988); With my Own Wings: Memoirs (1994). *Address:* 9 Sylvester Rd., Cambridge CB3 9AF.

LITTLEJOHN, William Hunter, D.A., R.S.A., R.S.W., R.G.I.; painter in oil and water-colour; former Head of Fine Art Dept., Gray's School of Art, Aberdeen; retd. from teaching 1986; *b* Arbroath, Angus, Scotland, 16 Apr., 1929. *Educ:* Arbroath High School. *Studied:* Dundee College of Art. *Work in collections:* National Gallery of Modern Art, Edinburgh, Arbroath Art Gallery, Aberdeen Art Gallery, Arts Council Collection, Abbot Hall Art Gallery, Kendal, Edinburgh Civic Collection, Edinburgh Education Authority, Paisley Art Gallery, Perth Art Gallery, Towner Art Gallery, Eastbourne. *Signs work:* see appendix. *Address:* 43 Viewfield Rd., Arbroath, Angus DD11 2DW. Scotland.

LITTLER, Ken, landscape and seascape painter in pastel; *b* Liverpool, 15 Aug., 1925. *Exhib:* Sarah Samuels Fine Paintings, Chester; Waterman Fine Art, London; Burford Gallery, Cotswolds; Datchet Gallery, Windsor, as guest of the Pastel Soc. *Work in collections:* England, Japan, Australia, U.S.A., Saudi Arabia. *Signs work:* "K. Littler." *Address:* 172 Booker Ave., Liverpool L18 9TB.

LLOYD, Reginald, R.I.; self taught artist in water-colour, oil, acrylic; *b* Hereford, 21 Dec., 1926. *m* (1) Diana van Klaveren (decd.) (2) Louise MacMillan. four *s.* three *d. Educ:* Dawlish Boys and County Senior School. *Exhib:* 'Portrait of the Artist' Tate Gallery, etc. *Work in collections:* Tate Gallery, V. & A., National Maritime Museum, Hatton Gallery Newcastle, Burton Gallery Bideford. *Publications:* illustrated: What is the Truth by Ted Hughes, The Cat and the Cuckoo by Ted Hughes, The Mermaid's Purse by Ted Hughes. *Signs work:* "R.J. LLOYD," "R.J.L." or "R.J. Lloyd." *Address:* Iffield, North Rd., Bideford, Devon EX39 2NW.

LLOYD-JONES, Pamela, Dip.Art Ed. (Sydney) 1968, B.A. Fine Art (Sydney); artist in mixed media and acrylic; *b* Australia, 4 Jan., 1947. *m* Nigel. one *s.* one *d. Exhib:* Sydney, Wollongong, London. Work in private collections. *Signs work:* "P. Lloyd-Jones." *Address:* 30 Avenue Gdns., London W3 8HB.

LOBANOV-ROSTOVSKY, Princess Roxane, S.W.A.; water-colourist sculptor in alabaster, marble; *b* Athens, 3 Oct., 1932. two *s.* one *d. Educ:* St. George's Ascot, Pretoria Girls High School. *Studied:* Carlton University, Ottawa; Brighton Polytechnic (Norma Weller, Norman Clarke, R.W.S.). *Exhib:* numerous exhbns., one-man show: The Grange, Rottingdean (1987), etc. *Work in collections:* in U.S.A., Austria, U.K., France, Italy. *Commissions:* Dream of Gerontius for P. Foss Esq., Standing Stones for B. White Esq. *Signs work:* "R. Lobanov-Rostovsky." *Address:* Swallowdale, 67 Woodruff Ave., Hove, E. Sussex BN3 6PJ.

LOCHHEAD, Thomas, D.A.; potter; *b* Milngavie, Glasgow, 28 Nov., 1917. *m* Anne T. Wilson. three *s.* two *d. Educ:* Dumfries Academy. *Studied:* Edinburgh College of Art under Princ. Wellington, A.R.C.A., and Alick Wolfenden, A.R.C.A. *Exhib:* S.S.A. *Work in collections:* Glasgow Art Gallery, Paisley Art Gallery. *Signs* *work:* "Lochhead." *Address:* Ashbank, Kirkcudbright.

LOCKHART, David, R.S.W. (1969), D.A. (Edin.) (1944); artist in acrylics, oil and water-colour; *b* Leven, Fife, 4 Nov., 1922. *m* Jean Lockhart. one *s.* two *d. Educ:* Beath High School, Cowdenbeath (1934-40). *Studied:* Edinburgh College of Art (1940-46). *Exhib:* Carnegie Dunfermline Trust Festival of Arts (1972), Byre Theatre (St. Andrews) (1996), Richmond Hill Gallery (1997), Billcliffe Gallery Glasgow (1997), 'Loomshop' Gallery, Lower Largo Fife (1988), 'Frames' Gallery Perth (1994); one-man show: Opening of Byre Theatre, St. Andrew's (June 2001). *Work in collections:* Scottish Committee of the Arts Council, W. Riding of Yorkshire Educ. Authority, Carnegie Dunfermline Trust, Fife County Council, Dunbartonshire Educ. Authority, Harry Cruden Coll. (Pitlochry Festival Theatre), E.I.S. award, R.S.W. (1984). *Commissions:* 19 x 12ft. mural "Many Mansions" Benarty Primary School, Fife (1963); commemorative painting – Moss Moran Pit Disaster 1901. *Signs work:* "David Lockhart" (paintings), and see appendix. *Address:* 2 Burnside North, Cupar, Fife KY15 4DG.

LODGE, Jean, R.E., B.A. (Miami), M.A. (Oxon.); painter/printmake; Emeritus Fellow of New College, Oxford; *b* U.S.A., 1941. *Educ:* Miami University, Ohio, Oxford University. *Studied:* Beaux Arts de Paris, Atelier 17 with S.W. Hayter. *Exhib:* solo shows: Europe, Japan, India, Argentina, Venezuela, U.S.A., etc.; numerous international print shows. *Work in collections:* Museums in Europe and N. and S. America; Galerie Beguin, Paris; Galerie Schweitzer, Luxembourg; Broughton House Gallery, Cambridge; Bankside Gallery, London. *Address:* 52 Granville Ct., Cheney Lane, Headington, Oxford OX3 0HS.

LOFTHOUSE, Hermione Thornton, U.A. (1975), N.S.; painter in water-colour, oil and pastel; tutor, Moor Park College (1968-82); Master Classes for Richmond-upon-Thames Arts Council (1982, 1983), Adult Educ.; V.P., Ridley Art Soc.; *m* F.H. Lockyer. three *s. Educ:* St. Paul's Girls' School. *Studied:* Heatherleys' (1946-50) under Iain Macnab, Académie Julian and La Grande Chaumière (1950); cert. History of Art, Courtauld Inst. *Exhib:* Paris, Germany, N.Z. Academy, Bombay Museum, W.A.G., Artists of Chelsea, R.B.A., R.O.I., etc.; eleven solo shows, Upper St. Gallery, Mall Galleries, Ice House - Holland Park, Surrey Univ. *Work in collections:* Richmond Parish Charity Lands, R.A.M., Surrey Univ., Guildford House Museum etc. *Publications:* The Art of Drawing and Painting. *Signs work:* "H. Thornton Lofthouse." *Address:* 48 Compton Way, Farnham, Surrey GU10 1QU.

LOGAN, Andrew, Dip.Arch.(Oxon.); sculptor in glass; *b* Witney, 11 Oct., 1945. *Educ:* Lord Williams' Grammar School; Burford Grammar School. *Studied:* architecture: Oxford School of Architecture (1964-70). *Exhib:* numerous exhbns. including I.C.A. (1970), Whitechapel A.G., Beverly Hills, L.A., Ebury Gallery, Space Gallery, Faerie Fair, Norfolk, Crafts Council, Sandbeck Hall, Yorks., Sculpture Pk., Portland Bill, Commonwealth Inst., German Film Museum, Frankfurt, Hotel Meridian, Singapore, Botanical Gdns., Rome, Angela Flowers (Ireland) Inc., Flowers East (1991), Old Library, Cardiff (1991); first one-man show: New Art Centre, London (1973); retrospective: Museum of Modern Art, Oxford (1991), 'The Happy Heart show', Manchester City Art Galleries (1995), Moscow Art Fair (1996), 'Reflections of the Heart' Show, Monterrey, Mexico (1997), 'Love' A.V.A.M.

Baltimore, U.S.A., 'Magic Moments' Ruthin, British Figurative Art, Flowers East, 'Britain in Russia', Ekaterinburg, Russia (1998). *Work in collections:* Andrew Logan's Museum of Sculpture, Berriew, Powys, 'Decadence', Crafts Council British Council Show, Vilnius, Lithuania, British Museum, 'Sweet Sounds', Paris, France (1999), installation, Expo 2000 Hanover, 'Glittering Glass', Cheltenham (2000), Summer Exhibition, Royal Academy (2001). *Commissions:* 'Millenium Pegasus', Dudley Council. *Signs work:* see appendix. *Address:* The Glasshouse, Melior Pl., London SE1 3QP.

LOIZOU, Renos, painter in oil on canvas, oil on paper and board; *b* Cyprus, 24 Jan., 1948. *m* Susan. one *s.* two *d. Educ:* Shrubbery School, Cambridge. *Studied:* Cambridge School of Art (1963-66, Alec Heath). *Exhib:* Kettles Yard, Cambridge (1974, 1981), I.C.A. (1975), Orangerie, Cologne (1976), Peterborough Museum of Art (1982), Christopher Hull Gallery, London (1982, 1985, 1987, 1989, 1991), Fine Art Soc. (1990), Fitzwilliam Museum, Cambridge (1990); many mixed shows and overseas exhbns. *Work in collections:* Kettles Yard, Fitzwilliam College, Gonville and Caius College, Magdalene College, Cambridge, M. of E. Cyprus, Arts Council Denmark, University of Surrey, B.P. Coll., Baring Bros., W.H. Smith plc. *Publications:* book cover, Voices of Czechoslovak Socialists. *Clubs:* Chelsea Arts, National Arts N.Y. *Signs work:* "Renos Loizou." *Address:* Girton Gate, Cambridge CB3 0LH.

LOKER, John Keith, D.A. Graphic Design (1958), A.R.C.A. Fine Art (1963); painter in oil; *b* Leeds, 15 Sept., 1938. *m* Emily Mayer, sculptor. two *s. Studied:* Bradford Regional College of Art (1954-58), Royal College of Art (1960-63). *Exhib:* over 30 one-man exhbns. in U.K. and abroad. *Work in collections:* Tate, Arts Council, Power Inst., etc. *Commissions:* Watmough Holding, Bradford, Essex General Hospital, I.T.N. Building (Norman Foster). *Clubs:* Chelsea Arts. *Signs work:* "John Loker," occasionally "J.L." *Address:* Union Workhouse, Guilt Cross, Kenninghall, Norfolk NR16 2LJ.

LONG, John Cecil, B.A. Slade (1988), Higher Dip. Slade (1990), Artist in Res., Byam Shaw (1990-1991), A.R.H.A. (1995); painter in oil; lecturer at N.C.A.D., Dublin (1994-1995), lecturer at Canterbury, Christchurch U.C. (1998 -); *b* Portadown, N. Ireland, 30 Aug., 1964. *Educ:* St. Patrick's Boys Academy, Dungannon. *Studied:* Slade School of Fine Art (1984-1990) under Euan Uglow. *Exhib:* European Modern Art, Dublin (1993); Twentieth Century British Art Fair, London (1996); Theo Waddington Fine Art, London (1998); Jorgensen Fine Art, Dublin (1999); London Contemporary Art Fair (2001). *Work in collections:* Haverty Trust. *Publications:* exhib. catalogue, Jorgensen Fine Art (1999), Prints and Posters. *Signs work:* "J. Long." *Address:* c/o Theo Waddington Fine Art, 6 Masons Yard, St. James's, London SW1Y 6BU.

LONGUEVILLE, James, P.S. (1983), R.B.S.A. (1989); landscape painter in oil, pastel and water-colour; lecturer and demonstrator; *b* Waverton, Chester, 22 Sept., 1942. *m* Elizabeth Mary Smith. two *s.* one *d. Educ:* Sedbergh School, Cumbria. *Exhib:* R.O.I., P.S., R.I., R.C.A., R.B.S.A., galleries in U.K., Eire, Australia, Canada. *Clubs:* R.B.S.A., P.S. *Signs work:* "James Longueville." *Address:* The Studio, Shocklach, Malpas, Cheshire SY14 7BW.

LOPEZ-REY, Jose, Ph.D. (Madrid, 1935); Doctor of Humane Letters (honorary, Southern Methodist University, 1979); art historian; Prof. Emeritus, New York University; Prize, Elie Faure, Paris, 1981; *b* Madrid, 14 May, 1905. *m* Justa Arroyo López-Rey. *Educ:* Universities of Madrid, Florence, and Vienna. *Publications:* Antonio del Pollaiuolo y el fin del Quattrocento; Realismo é impresionismo en las artes figurativas españolas del siglo XIX; Goya y el mundo a su alrededor; Goya's Caprichos; Beauty, Reason and Caricature; A Cycle of Cycle of Goya's Drawings: The Expression of Truth and Liberty; Velázquez: A Catalogue Raisonné of his oeuvre; Velázquez' Work and World; Velázquez: The artist as a maker. With a catalogue raisonné of his extant works (1979);. Vélasquez, artiste et créateur. Avec un catalogue raisonné de son oeuvre intégral (1981); Views and Reflections on Murillo (1987). *Address:* Callejón Sierra, 3, 28120 Ciudad Sto. Domingo (Madrid), Spain.

LOUDON, Irvine, R.E. (1995) R.E. (1999), B.M.B.Ch. (1951), D.M.(Oxon.) (1973), D.R.C.O.G. (1961), F.R.C.G.P. (1976); medical practitioner, medical historian, artist in etching and drawing; *b* Cardiff, 1 Aug., 1924. *m* Jean Loudon. two *s.* three *d. Educ:* Dauntseys School, Oxford University. *Studied:* Oxford Printmakers Co-operative (1983). *Exhib:* mixed shows with Oxford Art Soc., Oxford Printmakers Co-operative, Bankside Gallery, London; one-man shows in Oxford and London. *Work in collections:* Ashmolean Museum, Oxford. *Publications:* Medical Care and the General Practitioner 1750-1850 (O.U.P. 1986), Death in Childbirth (O.U.P. 1992), Western Medicine: An Illustrated History (O.U.P. 1997). *Clubs:* Oxford Art Soc., Royal Society of Painters - Printmakers (member of council). *Signs work:* see appendix. *Address:* The Mill House, Locks Lane, Wantage, Oxon. OX12 9EH.

LOVELL, Margaret, Dip. F.A. (Slade, 1962), F.R.B.S. (1973), R.W.A. (1972); sculptor in bronze, marble, slate; *b* Bristol, 1939. married. two *s.* two *d. Studied:* West of England College of Art, Bristol, Slade School of Fine Art, Academy of Fine Art, Florence (Italian Scholarship 1962-63), Greek Government Scholarship (1965-66). *Exhib:* City Art Gall., Bristol, Arts Council of G.B., Marjorie Parr Gall., London (4 one-man shows), also one-man shows inc. Park Square Gall., Leeds, Fermoy A.G., King's Lynn, Univ. of Bath , Bruton Gall., Somerset, 1st retrospective Plymouth City A.G. (1972), Adam Gallery, Bath, McHardy Sculpture Co. London, Bruton St. Gallery, London (1995-99). *Commissions:* Barclays Bank, Bristol; Grafham Water, Hunts. *Signs work:* "M. Lovell." *Address:* Greenlane Farm, Compton Dando, Bristol BS39 4JU.

LOW, Bet, A.R.S.A., R.S.W., R.G.I., Hon. D.Litt. Glasgow University; artist in oil and water-colour; *b* Gourock, Renfrewshire, 27 Dec., 1924. *Educ:* Greenock Academy. *Studied:* Glasgow School of Art. *Exhib:* regularly at Royal Scottish Academy, Water-colour Soc., Royal Glasgow Inst., Fine Art Soc., and widely in U.K. and Europe. Retrospective exhbn. 1945-'85, Third Eye Centre, Glasgow (1985), retrospective exhbn. Art Club (1999). *Work in collections:* Scottish Arts Council, Glasgow, Aberdeen, Abbot Hall, Hunterian, Lillie, Perth, Waterford A.G.'s, Fife and Dunbarton Educ. Authorities, Glasgow and Strathclyde Universities, Cruden Collection, Britoil, Clyde Shipping Co., Clydesdale Bank, Flemings, London. *Clubs:* Glasgow Art. *Signs work:* "LOW." *Address:* 53 Kelvinside Gdns., Glasgow G20 6BQ.

LOWE, Adam, M.F.A. (Oxon.), M.A. (R.C.A.); artist in oil, printmaking; *b* Oxford, 18 Feb., 1959. *m* Yuka. *Studied:* Ruskin School of Drawing, Oxford; R.C.A. (Peter de Francia). *Exhib:* regularly at Pomeroy Purdy Gallery, also exhbns. in England and America. Commissioned work in Japan. *Work in collections:* Contemporary Art Soc., Atkinson A.G. *Publications:* A Resurgence in Contemporary Painting (Alistair Hicks, Phaidon 1989). *Signs work:* "ADAM LOWE." *Address:* Reeds Wharf, Mill St., London SE1.

LOWE, Ian, M.A., Hon.R.E, (1975); Museum Curator, Ashmolean Museum (1962-87); *b* London, 18 Apr., 1935. *m* Mary Howard. one *s. Educ:* Oriel College, Oxford. Laurence Binyon prize (1958). *Publications:* author: The Etchings of Wilfred Fairclough (1990). *Address:* Spring Ford, Newton Reigny, Penrith, Cumbria CA11 0AY.

LOWRY, Peter William, R.B.A.; painter in water-colour; *b* London, 28 Oct., 1914. *m* Sandra. one *d. Educ:* Highgate, London. *Studied:* St. Martin's School of Art, London. *Exhib:* Batsford; tours of annual exhibs. R.A., R.B.A. *Clubs:* The Reform Club. *Signs work:* "Peter Lowry." *Address:* Le Petit Gaillard, 24500 Eymet, France.

LOXTON PEACOCK, Clarisse, painter in oil; *b* 7 May, 1926. *m* (1st) G. Loxton Peacock. one *s.* one *d.* (2nd) Sir Anthony Grover. *Educ:* Budapest University. *Studied:* Chelsea School of Art (Dip. course); Central School of Arts and Crafts (Post. Grad. course); St. Martin's School of Art. *Exhib:* one-man shows, Walker Gallery, London, Grosvenor Gallery, O'Hana Fine Art (two), Bodley Gallery, N.Y., Frost and Reed, Gallerie des Arts, Düsseldorf (three), Salisbury Arts Festival, Fox Gallery, London, Wylma Wane Fine Arts, Old Bond St., London (1982), Petöti Museum, Budapest (1988 - sponsored by Hungarian Government), Cadogan Contemporaries, London (1989), Makepiece Art Centre, Dorset (1989), King's Lynn Art Festival (1994), Osborne Studio Gallery (1994), University of East Anglia, John Innes, Exhbn. Centre (1996). *Work in collections:* V. & A. (Directors' Room), U.S.A., Spain, Germany, England, S. Africa (Queen's Gallery), France, Japan. *Publications:* Handbook of Modern British Painting 1900-1980. *Clubs:* Arts, London. *Signs work:* "C. Loxton Peacock." *Address:* 85 Bedford Gdns., London W8 5EQ.

LUCAS, Suzanne, F.L.S., Médaille de la France Libre, R.H.S. Gold Medal (1975, 1976, 1977, 1978, 1979, 1980, 1982, 1983, 1984, 1985, 1986, 1987, 1988); painter and miniaturist in water-colour; President, Royal Society of Miniature Painters, Sculptors and Gravers; Founder-President, Society of Botanical Artists; Vice President, Dorset Arts and Crafts Soc.; Hon. Mem. Women Artists Soc.; Hon Mem. Miniature Artists of America and Miniature Art Soc. of Florida; Hon. Director American Society of Botanical Artists, Winner R.M.S. Gold Bowl (2000); *b* Calcutta, 10 Sept., 1915. *m* Admiral Louis Lucas, C.B.E., Commander Legion of Honour. *Educ:* Roedean School, Edinburgh University; Munich and Grenoble Universities; Berlin School of Art with Professor Schmidt. *Exhib:* R.A., Paris Salon, R.I.; one-man shows in London: Cooling Galleries (1954), Sladmore Gallery (1973), Mall Galleries (1975, 1979), Liberty's (1977). *Publications:* author and illustrator of large art volume "In Praise of Toadstools" Vol. 1 (1992) and Vol. 2 (1997), a botanical work; author and editor of highest quality art book "The Royal Society of Miniature Painters, Sculptors and Gravers - One Hundred Years" the official celebratory volume. *Clubs:* Royal Automobile, Overseas League. *Signs work:* see appendix. *Address:* Ladymead, Manor Rd., Mere, Wilts. BA12 6HQ.

LUCKAS, Joy Heather, S.B.A. (1991); botanical artist in water-colour; *b* Cambridge, 1926. *m* John Richard Ainley Luckas. one *s.* two *d. Educ:* Perse Girls' School, Cambridge. *Studied:* Cambridge College of Art (1943-46, G. Stevenson, Mr. Huffer). *Work in collections:* Hunt Inst. for Botanical Documentation, Pittsburg, R.H.S. Library, London. *Publications:* illustrated: Introduction to Drawing Flowers by Margaret Stevens. *Signs work:* see appendix. *Address:* Ty'n Rhos, Llydan Rd., Rhosneigr, Anglesey, N. Wales LL64 5JE.

LUMLEY, Alexandra Mary, B.A. (Hons.) 1980, A.R.B.A. (1997); painter in water-colour, pastel, acrylic, collage; partner: Lumley White Art and Design; principal lecturer, Camberwell College of Art; *b* Essex, 15 Aug., 1958. *m* Philip White. one *d. Studied:* Camberwell College of Art (1977-80). *Exhib:* regularly at New Grafton Gallery since 1984, and in many group shows nationally. *Work in collections:* Herts. C.C., The London Inst. *Signs work:* "Alex Lumley" (occasionally "A. Lumley or "A.M.L."). *Address:* 9 Tabard St., London SE1 4LA. *Email:* lumley.white@virgin.net

LUNCH, John, C.B.E. (1975), V.R.D. (1965), F.C.A. (1946), F.R.S.A. (1976); artist in water-colour and oil; retd. Director General, Port of London Authority; Hon. Art Adviser to R.N.L.I.; Life V.P. R.N.L.I. (1994); *b* Eastbourne, 11 Nov., 1919. *m* (1st) Joyce Barbara Clerke (decd.). two *s.* (2nd) Fiona Charis Elizabeth Fleck. *Educ:* Roborough School, Eastbourne. *Exhib:* Mall Galleries. *Work in collections:* R.N.L.I. Collection (170 Years of Lifeboat History). *Clubs:* Army and Navy. *Signs work:* "John Lunch." *Address:* Martins, East Ashling, Chichester, W. Sussex PO18 9AX.

LUPTON, Lewis F., preacher, writer, historian, painter in oil and water-colour; *b* London, 18 July, 1909. *Studied:* Sheffield College of Arts (1923-30). Practised commercial art in Strand advertising agency before the war. Freelance since 1940. Exhibition designer during and just after the war. Many paintings in the R.A. at this period. Then turned to the illustration of Christian literature. Numerous exhibitions of own, and wife's work held in recent years. Publisher under the Olive Tree imprint of own History of the Geneva Bible (25 vols.) and other related literature. *Address:* 2 Milnthorpe Rd., London W4 3DX.

LYELL: see ROBINSON, Peter Lyell.

LYNCH, James, Greenshield Foundation Award (1983), Pimms Prize, R.A. (1986), Spectator prizewinner (1993); *b* Hitchin, 12 July, 1956. *m* Kate Armstrong. two *s.* one *d. Educ:* Devizes School. *Exhib:* R.A., R.W.S., Portal, Bath Festival Art Fairs; one-man shows: Linfields, Bradford-on-Avon (1982-83), Nevill, Bath (1984), Odette Gilbert, London (1988), Maas Gallery, London (1991, 1993, 1995, 1997, 1999, 2001). *Work in collections:* Longleat House, Chatsworth House, National Trust. *Publications:* illustrated "Wind in the Willows" (Folio Soc., 1995). *Signs work:* "J. Lynch." *Address:* Four Chimneys, High Ham, Langport, Som. TA10 9BB.

LYNCH , Kathleen (Kate) Mary nee Armstrong, B.A. Hons. History of Art, Essex University (1975), P.G.C.E. / A.T.D. Bristol University(1976), Post Grad. Diploma in Fine Art, University of West of England, R.W.A.; painter in oil; art teacher; *b* London, 17 Aug., 1949. *m* James Lynch. two *s*. one *d. Educ:* St. Mary's Grammar School, Northwood Hills, Middx. *Studied:* University of West of England. *Exhib:* Beaux Arts, Bath (1993, 1996, 1998), Alpha House, Sherborne, Dorset (1998, 2000). *Work in collections:* Wessex Collection and many private collections. *Commissions:* private and public commissions for community-based projects. *Signs work:* "K. Lynch" or "Kate Lynch." *Address:* Four Chimneys, High Ham, Langport, Somerset TA10 9BB. *Email:* kate@lynchmail.fsnet.co.uk

M

McADAM CLARK, Caroline, M.A. (Hons.) Dip.A.D.; painter in oil, watercolour, printmaking; co-Director, Piers Feetham Gallery; *b* London, 18 Jan., 1947. *m* Piers Feetham. one *s*. one *d. Studied:* Edinburgh College of Art, Edinburgh University (1965-70). *Exhib:* Thackeray Gallery, Highgate Fine Art, Lena Boyle Fine Art and various London art fairs. *Work in collections:* private: France, U.K., U.S.A. *Publications:* co-author with P. Feetham 'The Art of Framing' (1997). *Clubs:* Chelsea Arts. *Signs work:* "McAdam Clark." *Address:* 49 Larkhall Rise, London SW4 6HT.

McADAM FREUD, Jane, M.A. (1995), F.R.B.S.(1994), F.S.N.A.D. (1991), Freedom of the City of London (1991); sculptor in bronze; *b* London, 24 Feb., 1958. *Studied:* Central School of Art (1978-81), Scoula De l'Arte Della Medaglia, Rome (1986-89), R.C.A. (1993-95). *Exhib:* solo shows: Yorkshire Museum (1997), Fitzwilliam Museum (1997), Hunterian Museum, Glasgow (1997), Simmons Gallery, London (1998), Marishal Museum Aberdeen (1998), Inst. of Contemporary Art, St. Louis, U.S.A. (1999), University College Cork (2001). *Work in collections:* B.M., Berlin State Museum, Rijksmuseum, Leiden, Goldsmiths' Hall. *Commissions:* J.P. Getty, All Souls College, Simmons Gallery. *Publications:* Sculpture: On the Edge; Forms of Relief La Medailles (1995), Resonating: The Medal (2000). *Signs work:* "J.Mc.A.F." or "J. McA. Freud." *Address:* 116 Wendover, Thurlow St., London SE17 2UE. *Email:* jmca.freud@virgin.net

MACALPINE, Jean, Fine Art photographer of hand toned photographs; *b* Ribble Valley, Lancs., 1953. *m* Kenneth Draper, R.A. *Studied:* Bristol College of Art (1973-76), Camberwell College of Art (1976-77). *Exhib:* R.A. Summer Show; Hart Gallery, Nottingham and London; Flowers East, London; solo show: Leeds University A.G. *Publications:* Jean Macalpine: 'Intervals in Light' by Mary Rose Beaumont (Hart Gallery). *Signs work:* photographs signed on back "JEAN MACALPINE." *Address:* c/o Hart Gallery, 113 Upper St., London N1 1QN.

MACARA, Andrew, R.B.A. (1983), N.E.A.C. (1984); self taught figurative painter in oil; *b* Ashbourne, Derbyshire, 4 Apr., 1944. *m* Ann. two *s. Educ:* Derby College of Technology. *Exhib:* New Academy Gallery, London, Contemporary Fine Art Gallery, Eton, Fosse Gallery, Stow-on-the-Wold. *Work in collections:* Derby Museum and A.G. *Commissions:* Palace of Westminster (Paintings for Members

Dining Room). *Signs work:* "Andrew Macara." *Address:* Aberfoyle, 32 Farley Rd., Derby DE23 6BX.

MACARRÓN, Ricardo, R.P. (1962); 1st prize National Fine Art Exhbn. (1962), Prize Direction of Fine Art (1954); artist in oil of figures, dead nature, landscapes, portraits; *b* Madrid, 9 Apr., 1926. *m* Alicia. two *d. Studied:* Fine Art School of San Fernando, Madrid (1942); scholarship to study in France by French Institute (1950). *Work in collections:* Contemporary Art Museum, Madrid, University of Oslo, National Gallery (Cape Town), Güell Foundation (Barcelona), and several private collections. *Signs work:* see appendix. *Address:* Augustin de Bethencourt 5, Madrid 3, Spain.

McARTHUR, Christine Louise, R.S.W. (1995), R.G.I. (1990), artist in oil, acrylic, watercolour and collage; Hon. Sec. Royal Glasgow Institute of the Fine Arts (2000-2002); *b* Kirkintilloch, 14 Mar., 1953. *m* divorced. two. *d. Educ:* Lenzie Academy, Glasgow. *Studied:* Glasgow School of Art (1971-1976). *Exhib:* several, principally with Fine Art Society, Glasgow; Roger Billcliffe Gallery, Glasgow; John Martin, London. *Work in collections:* Royal Bank of Scotland, Clydesdale Bank, John Lewis Partnership, Amerada Hess. *Commissions:* murals for John Lewis Partnership, Glasgow and Peter Jones, London. Also working from a studio in St. Ives, Cornwall. *Signs work:* "Christine McArthur." *Address:* 17 Grosvenor Terr., Glasgow G12 0TB. *Email:* clmi@appleonline.net

MacARTHUR, Ronald Malcolm, R.S.W. (1982), D.A. Painting (1937); painter in water-colour and oil; Principal teacher of Art, Portobello High School, Edinburgh (1952-79); *b* Edinburgh, 1914. *m* Dorothy Stephenson. *Educ:* Royal High School of Edinburgh. *Studied:* Edinburgh College of Art (1933-37, William Allison, R.S.A., David Foggie, R.S.A., William MacTaggart, R.S.A.). *Exhib:* R.S.W. (1948-60 and 1976 onwards). *Work in collections:* Lothian Schools Collection, Strathclyde Schools Collection, and private collections. *Signs work:* "Ronald MacArthur, R.S.W." *Address:* Morden, 1 Duddingston Rd., Edinburgh EH15 1ND.

MACCABE, Gladys, M.B.E., H.R.O.I., M.A.(Honoris Causa), F.R.S.A.; Founder and Past-Pres. Ulster Society of Women Artists; Academician with gold medal Italian Academy; Diploma of Merit, University of Arts, Parma; Hon. Academician, Royal Ulster Academy; Hon. Mem. Ulster Water-colour Soc.; Hon. Mem. Ulster Soc. of Miniaturists, Mcm. Water-colour Soc. of Ireland; painter in oil and water-colour and various other media; art lecturer, writer and broadcaster; pianoforte soloist; *b* Randalstown, N. Ireland. *m* Max Maccabe. two *s. Educ:* Brookvale Collegiate School, Ulster College of Art, France and Italy. *Exhib:* London, Dublin, U.S.A., Canada, Belfast, Scotland, France, etc. *Work in collections:* Irish National Self-portrait Collection, Limerick University (3 works), Imperial War Museum, Ulster Museum, Arts Council of Northern Ireland, The Queen's University, Belfast, Ulster Office, London, Longford County Library, Thomas Haverty Trust, County Dublin Educ. Authority, B.B.C., Cyril Cusack, Esq., Miss Beatrice Lillie, Lady Wakehurst, the late Adlai Stevenson, Esq., Dr. James White, Director, National Gallery of Ireland, B.B.C. (N.I.), Royal Ulster Academy, Crawford Municipal A. G., Cork. *Commissions:* numerous. *Publications:* Many important publications; T.V. programmes at home and abroad. *Signs work:* "GLADYS MACCABE." *Address:* 1a Church Rd., Newtownbreda, Belfast BT8 7AL.

McCANN, Brian, B.A. Sculpture (1980), M.A. (R.C.A.) (1983), Picker Fellow (1983), Rome Scholar (1984-86); sculptor in bronze, mixed media, installations; part-time lecturer in sculpture, Royal College, Chelsea College, Kingston University, Royal Academy Schools; External examiner, sculpture, University of Hull; British School at Rome Assoc. Mem.; *b* Glasgow, 2 July, 1955. *Studied:* Duncan of Jordanstone, Dundee (1977-80), R.C.A. (1980-83). *Exhib:* Serpentine Gallery Summer Show (1983), Hilderbrandtstrasse, Dusseldorf (1982), Salo Uno, Rome (1988), Tate Gallery, Liverpool (1989), William Jackson Gallery, London (1992), Coexistence Gallery, London (1992), Museum of St. John, London (1995). *Work in collections:* Arts Council, Government Collection. *Publications:* 'Sojourn' poetry (1980), 'Plumage of Recognition' catalogue (1991). *Signs work:* "Brian McCann." *Address:* 11 Chandlers House, 38 London Rd., Kingston, Surrey KT2 6QF.

McCARTER, Keith, D.A.(Edin.) (1960), F.S.I.A. (1968), F.R.S.A. (1969), A.R.B.S. (1991); sculptor in bronze, stainless steel, concrete; *b* Edinburgh, 15 Mar., 1936. *m* Brenda Schofield. one *s.* one *d. Educ:* Royal High School, Edinburgh. *Studied:* Edinburgh College of Art (1956-60, Eric Schilsky, Helen Turner). *Exhib:* R.A., Monaco, Burleighfield Gallery, Alwin Gallery, Berkeley Sq. Gallery, Blains Fine Art. *Work in collections:* Numerous countries worldwide. *Commissions:* many public sited sculptures in U.K., U.S.A., Europe, Africa. *Clubs:* Farmers, London. *Signs work:* "McCarter"; small works, see appendix. *Address:* Ottermead, Church Rd., Gt. Plumstead, Norfolk NR13 5AB.

McCLOY, William Ashby, Henry B. Plant Emeritus Prof., Connecticut College; painter, sculptor, printmaker; *b* Baltimore, Md., 2 Jan., 1913. *m* Patrica C. *Educ:* Phillips Academy, Andover, Mass., University of Iowa. *Studied:* University of Iowa. *Exhib:* N.A., Whitney Museum of American Art, Pennsylvania Academy of Fine Arts, Chicago Art Inst., Carnegie Inst., Walker Art Centre, Kansas City Art Inst., Cincinnati Art Museum, Joslyn Mem. Art Museum, Library of Congress, Milwaukee Art Inst. *Signs work:* "WILLIAM A. McCLOY." *Address:* 376 Kitemaug Rd., Uncasville, Connecticut.

McCOMB, Leonard William, R.A., R.E. (1993), Slade Dip. (1960); artist-painter, sculptor, printmaker; visiting teacher: R.A. Schools; *b* Glasgow, 3 Aug., 1930. *m* Barbara Elenora. *Studied:* Manchester School of Art (Harry Suttcliffe), Slade School (Sir William Coldstream, Prof. A.H. Gerrard). Removed Golden Man sculpture - Lincoln Cathedral Travelling Exhbn. *Work in collections:* Tate Gallery, Arts Council Collection, V. & A., B.M., Towner A.G., Belfast A.G., B'ham, Manchester, Sheffield, Swindon and Worcester city galleries. *Commissions:* commemorative plaque bronze gold leaf Brookes University, Oxford (1993); tapestry 'Fishes and Invertebrates in the Sea' Boots plc (1994). *Publications:* Arts Council Catalogue (1983), Painting from the South Catalogue (1989), Catalogue Drawings and Paintings, Browse and Darby Gallery (1993), Gillian Jason Gallery; Video Film Arts Council 'Flow of Life' (1983). *Signs work:* "McCOMB" and "L.M" within circle and date. *Address:* 6 St. Saviours Rd., Brixton Hill, London SW2 5HD.

McCOMBS, John, N.D.D., R.O.I., R.B.A., F.R.S.A., M.A.F.A.; landscape artist in oil; *b* Manchester, 28 Dec., 1943. *Educ:* Manchester High School of Art (1957-62). *Studied:* St. Martin's School of Art (1962-67) under F. Gore, Reynolds, Kossoff.

WHO'S WHO IN ART

Exhib: R.A., Mall Galleries, Manchester City A.G., Saddleworth Museum, John McCombs Gallery. R.A. Scholarship and 'College prize' St. Martin's (1966); Stanley Grimm prize R.O.I. (1990); 'People's prize' Manchester Academy (1991). *Work in collections:* Manchester, Salford, Oldham A.G.'s, Saddleworth Museum. *Publications:* articles for 'Leisure Painter' magazine. *Clubs:* R.O.I., R.B.A., M.A.F.A. *Signs work:* "J. McCombs," sometimes "J.Mc." *Address:* 12 King St., Delph, Oldham OL3 5DQ.

McCRUM, Bridget, sculptor in stone, bronze-abstracted figurative; *b* Yorks., 27 Apr., 1934. *m* Robert McCrum. three *d. Studied:* painting at Farnham (1951-55, Musjynski; 1980-82 stone carving). *Exhib:* solo shows: Vanessa Deneveux, Phoenix, Plymouth School of Architecture, Dartington Hall Gdns., Wattis Fine Art, Hong Kong, Messums Fine Art; mixed shows: R.A., R.S.A., R.W.A., New Art Centre at Roche Court, Bohun, Deans Court, University of Surrey, Chelsea Harbour. *Work in collections:* Frink, Golden Door Foundation, National Trust, Charterhouse Bank, Lismore Castle, Priors Court, Spencer Stuart. *Commissions:* Hambledon Church, Dittisham; The Homewood, Greenway. *Clubs:* R.B.S. *Signs work:* "Bridget McCrum" or "McC." *Address:* Hamblyns Coombe, Dittisham, Dartmouth, Devon TQ6 0HE.

McCULLOCH, Ian, D.A. (1957), S.S.A. (1964), A.R.S.A. (1989); painter, printmaker; Fine Art Fellow, Strathclyde University (1994-); *b* Glasgow, 4 Mar., 1935. *m* Margery Palmer. two *s. Educ:* Glasgow School of Art (1953-57), Artist in Residence University of Sussex (1976). 1st prize Stirling Smith Biennial (1985), painted murals Italian Centre, Glasgow (1989), winner Glasgow Concert Hall murals competition (1990), Gillies Award R.S.A. (1999). *Exhib:* recent one-man exhbns.: Peacock Printmakers, Aberdeen (1995), Aberdeen A.G. (1992), Aberystwyth Arts Centre (1991), Glasgow Print Studio (1989), Odette Gilbert Gallery, London (1987), Camden Arts Centre (1986); group exhbns. including New North, Tate Gallery Liverpool (1990), John Moores, Liverpool (1989), Liberation and Tradition: Scottish Art 1963-1974, Aberdeen A.G. and McManus Galleries Dundee (1999), Expressions: Scottish Art 1975-1989 Aberdeen A.G., McManus Galleries Dundee and Dundee Contemporary Arts (2000), Leabhar Mòr, book exhibition and tour Stornoway (2001/2), Anxiety – The Drawn Figure, Ivan Dougherty Gallery, University of New South Wales, Sydney, Australia (2001). *Work in collections:* Saatchi Collection, Glasgow A.G., Dundee A.G., Edinburgh City A.G., Sterling Smith A.G., Sterling, R.S.A. Collections, Glasgow, Strathclyde and Liverpool Universities. *Publications:* The Artist in his World (Prints, 1986,1997) with descriptive poems by Alasdair Gray (Argyll Publishing, 1998). *Signs work:* "Ian McCulloch." *Address:* 51 Victoria Rd., Lenzie, Glasgow G6 65AP.

McCULLOUGH, George, M.S.Exc., hons. M. of E. dipl.; artist in oil, watercolour, gouache, pastel; Founder and Tutor, Donegal School of Landscape Painting, Dunfanaghy, Co. Donegal, Rep. of Ireland; *b* Belfast, 2 Oct., 1922. married. two *d. Educ:* Belfast College of Technology and Belfast College of Art (1940-47). *Studied:* as above. *Exhib:* R.U.A., United Nations, N.Y., Oriel Gallery, Dublin, Cambridge Gallery, Dublin, Eaton Gallery, Toronto, Flowerfield Art Centre, Portstewart, Yonge Gallery, Chicago, Bell Gallery, Belfast. *Signs work:* see appendix. *Address:* 20 Joanmount Drive, Carrs Glen, Belfast BT14 6PB.

MACDONALD, Alan, B.A. (Hons.) Fine Art 1984, Post Dip. (1985); painter in oil on linen and board; *b* Malawi, 1962. *m* Carol Lynda. one *s. Studied:* Duncan of Jordanstone College of Art, Dundee; Cyprus College of Art, Paphos. *Exhib:* 1987: Stirling Biennale, Scotland; 1992: 'Far Horizons' Kyoto, Japan; 1995: Hunting Group prizes competition exhbn. R.C.A. London, Leeds Educ. Com., Kailey, Hong Kong; 1994-99: Bruton St. Gallery. *Signs work:* "Alan Macdonald" and dated on back. *Address:* c/o Bruton St. Gallery, 28 Bruton St., London W1X 7DB.

MacDONALD, Alastair James Henderson, R.M.S., A.S.M.A. (Vic.), M.A.S.F., F.R.S.A., H.U.A.; Gold Bowl Hon. Men. (1991, 1992, 1993, 1998); Llewellyn Alexander Masters Award (1995); miniature painter; elected Hon. Treas. R.M.S. (1981); *b* Tighnabruaich, Argyll, 5 July, 1934. *m* Juliet Anne Mead. two *s.* three *d. Educ:* Pope Street School, New Eltham. *Studied:* Woolwich Polytechnic School of Art and Crafts. *Exhib:* R.M.S., U.A., M.A.S.F., A.S.M.A. (Vic.), NSW., QLD., TAS. *Signs work:* see appendix. *Address:* 63 Somers Rd., North Mymms, Herts. AL9 7PT.

MACDONALD, Robert James, M.A., R.C.A. (1976-1979), Dip. L.C.S.A.D. (1982); printmaker and painter in oil, acrylic, water-colour; trained as a journalist before studying art; *b* Spilsby, Lincs., 1935. *m* Annie Merrill. two *d. Educ:* Te Awamutu College, N.Z. *Studied:* R.C.A. (1976-1979), London Central School of Art (Special Advanced Printmaking Studies 1981-1983). *Exhib:* prizewinner Singer and Friedlander Watercolour Exhibs. (1994 & 1998); exhibits widely in Wales and London. *Work in collections:* V. & A. Print Collection, Ferens Gallery, Hull, Brecknock Museum and Art Gallery. *Commissions:* private. *Publications:* author and illustrator 'The Fifth Wind' (Bloomsbury 1989). *Clubs:* Welsh Group, and Watercolour Society of Wales. *Signs work:* "Macdonald" or "Macd" on early pictures. *Address:* The Lodge, Penpont, Brecon, Powys LD3 8EU.

McDOWELL, Leo, B.A.Hons., C.Ed., R.I.; Winsor and Newton R.I. award Mall Galleries (1990); self taught artist in water and acrylic colour; Council Mem. R.I.; *b* 19 Jan., 1937. *Educ:* Keighley Grammar School; Manchester University; Innsbruck University; Cambridge University. *Studied:* Modern Languages, History of Art. *Exhib:* Shell House Gallery, Ledbury, Blackstone Gallery, Pinner, Albemarle Gallery, London, The British Gallery, Los Gatos, Calif., La Difference Gallery, Dinslaken, Germany, Lisette Alibert Gallery, Paris. *Work in collections:* H.R.H. The Prince of Wales, Hertfordshire C.C., Reuters. *Signs work:* "Leo McDowell." *Address:* Craigleith, Hanbury La., Essendon, Hatfield, Herts. AL9 6AY.

McENTAGART, Brett, B.A. (1961), M.F.A. (1963), R.H.A. (1980), W.C.S.I. (1974); artist in oil, water-colour, etching, pastel; Head of Printmaking, National College of Art and Design, Dublin; Board Mem. National Gallery of Ireland; Council Mem. Royal Hibernian Academy; *b* Dublin, 27 May, 1939. *m* Miriam O'Hara. two *s.* one *d. Educ:* St. Columba's College, Rathfarnham, Dublin. *Studied:* Dartmouth College, N.H., U.S.A., University of Colorado, U.S.A., Salzburg Academy, Austria. *Exhib:* R.H.A., W.C.S.I., R.W.A., R.U.A.; one-man shows Dublin. *Work in collections:* Board of Works Dublin, H.E.A. Dublin, W.C.S.I. Collection, Limerick, National Self Portrait Collection, Limerick. *Publications:* covers for: 'Blooms' - Joyce anthology, 'At Europe's La Terrasse' by Gerard Duffy. St. Columba's College, Rathfarnham, Dublin; *Signs work:* "B.McE." *Address:* 5 Sandycove Ave. West,

Sandycove, Co. Dublin, Ireland.

McEWAN REID, Marjorie, M.A. (1942), B.A. (Oxon.) Hons. Zoology (1939), Dip.Ed. (1940), S.W.A. (1994); winner, Seifas Cup (1991); artist in oil; immunologist in medical research (retd.); *b* Uckfield, Sussex, 1917. *m* Robert. one *s.* two *d. Educ:* Talbot Heath, Bournemouth; Somerville College, Oxford. *Studied:* Bletchingley A.E.I. (1977-80, Arthur Easton, R.O.I., N.S.), Elmers End Art Centre (1992-97) and at Edinburgh College of Art (1994, George Donald); also privately (1980-86) with the late Edmond Perini and (1987-97) with Richard Walker, S.G.F.A., U.A. *Exhib:* S.W.A., F.P.S.; many mixed shows; three two-man shows with husband. *Clubs:* F.P.S., The Croydon, Tandridge and Old Coulsdon Art Socs. *Signs work:* see appendix. *Address:* 21 Byron Ave., Coulsdon, Surrey CR5 2JS.

McEWAN-REID, Robert, U.A., F.F.P.S. (2001); painter in oil and gouache; retd. lecturer in engineering; Hon. Treasurer, F.P.S.; *b* Lanarkshire, 10 Dec., 1917. *m* Marjorie McEwan-Reid. one *s.* two *d. Studied:* Heriot Watt College, Edinburgh; Edinburgh College of Art. *Exhib:* one-man shows: M. & S. Baker St. London, F.P.S. London (1998). *Work in collections:* Knox Grammar School, Sydney, N.S.W. *Commissions:* Posters for Coulsdon Millennium Festival. *Publications:* Abstract Art in Britain (in preparation). *Clubs:* Croydon Art Soc., Tandridge Art Soc., Old Coulsdon Art Soc., U.A. *Signs work:* see appendix. *Address:* 21 Byron Ave., Coulsdon, Surrey CR5 2JS.

McEWEN, Elizabeth Alexandra, N.D.D. (1960), A.T.D. (1961), U.S.W.A. (1980), U.W.S., R.U.A. (1990), S.B.A. (1987); R.U.A. Gold medallist (1991); painter in water-colour, gouache and acrylic; *b* Belfast, 13 Dec., 1937. *m* James A. Nelson. *Educ:* Belfast Royal Academy. *Studied:* Belfast College of Art (1956-60), Reading University (1960-61). *Exhib:* many mixed and solo shows throughout N. Ireland, S.B.A. London, Laing London. *Work in collections:* Royal Ulster Academy, National Self Portrait Collection, Limerick University. *Signs work:* "E.A. McEwen." *Address:* 18 Lambert Ave., Dundonald BT16 1LE.

MACEY, Julian Bernard, R.M.S. (1995); retired Divisional Youth and Community Officer; self taught artist in oils, water-colour, pastel, pencil; Hon. Life Mem. (1991) and President Gt.Yarmouth and District Soc. of Artists (1994-); *b* Minehead, Som., 13 Apr., 1920. widower. one *s. Educ:* Duke of York's Royal Military School, Dover. *Exhib:* Westminster and Mall Galleries with R.M.S. and Tasmania. *Work in collections:* Gt. Yarmouth and District Soc. of Artists. *Publications:* R.M.S. Centenary Book "One Hundred Years". *Address:* 119 Beccles Rd., Bradwell, Gt. Yarmouth, Norfolk NR31 8AB.

MACEY, Leo, C.B.E. (1979), H.S. (1988); picture restorer, painter of miniatures in oil on ivorine and board; painter of oleographs; *b* Minehead, 23 Feb., 1922. *m* Isabella. two *s.* one *d. Educ:* English Military School, Cairo and D.Y.R.M.S. *Studied:* Frobisher School of Painting (1964-66, Lucy Frobisher). *Exhib:* R.W.A., H.S., Armed Forces Art Soc. *Work in collections:* Sultan of Negri Sembilan, Malaysia; Officers' Mess C.P.O. Detmold; and others. *Clubs:* Professional/Businessmen, Warminster. *Signs work:* see appendix. *Address:* 56 Upper Marsh Rd., Warminster, Wilts. BA12 9PN.

McFADYEN, Jock, B.A., M.A.; artist in oil on canvas, plaster, wax and bronze; *b* Paisley, 1950. *m* (1) Carol (divorced). one *s*. (2) Susie. one *s*. one *d*. *Educ:* Renfrew High School. *Studied:* Chelsea School of Art (1973-77, Anne Rees Mogg, Ron Bowen, Ian Stephenson). *Exhib:* 36 one-man shows including Blond Fine Art, Imperial War Museum, William Jackson Gallery, Camden Arts Centre, Talbot Rice, Agnew's (2001). *Work in collections:* 28 public collections including British Council, Imperial War Museum, Kunsthalle Hamburg, National Gallery, V. & A. *Commissions:* Designed sets and costumes for Sir Kenneth McMillan's last ballet 'The Judas Tree', Royal Ballet, Royal Opera House, Covent Gdn. (1992). *Publications:* 'Jock McFadyen – A Book about a Painter' monograph by David Cohen, published by Lund Humphries (2001). *Clubs:* Vintage Japanese Motorcycle. *Address:* 284 Globe Rd., Bethnal Green, London E2 0NS.

McFALL, David, R.A.; sculptor in stone and bronze; *b* Glasgow, 1919. *m* Alexandra Dane, actress. one *s*. one *d*. *Educ:* English Martyrs, Spark Hill. *Studied:* Birmingham, R.C.A. and Lambeth. *Work in collections:* Bullcalf (Tate), Churchill (Burlington House), Balfour (House of Commons), Vaughan Williams (Royal Festival Hall), Lord Attlee (Imperial War Museum), bronze study of Prince Charles (Buckingham Palace), Oedipus and Jocasta (W. Norwood Library), Pocahontas, Sir Godfrey Allen (bust) in crypt of St. Paul's Cathedral, 'Son of Man', Canterbury Cathedral. *Signs work:* see appendix. *Address:* 10 Fulham Park Gdns., London SW6 4JX.

MacFARLANE, Sheila Margaret, D.A. (Edin.) 1964; artist, printmaker and engraver; lecturer in printmaking, Duncan of Jordanstone College of Art, Dundee (1970-76); founder and director, Printmakers Workshop at Kirkton of Craig (1976-90); *b* Aberdeen, 2 May, 1943. one *d*. *Studied:* Edinburgh College of Art; Atelier 17 Paris. *Exhib:* 'The Finella Prints' and 'Tangleha to Bars Nab' touring exhbn. (1999-2001). *Work in collections:* national and private collections in U.K. and private collections Overseas. Presently working with children with special needs and as a freelance artist. *Signs work:* "Sheila M. MacFarlane." *Address:* 1 Tangleha', St. Cyrus, Montrose DD10 0DQ. *Email:* sheila-macfarlane@hotmail.com

McGOOKIN, Colin Trevor, B.A. (Hons.), A.R.U.A.; artist/administrator; Administrator, Queens Street Studios; *b* Belfast, 4 June, 1958. *m* Punam. one *d*. *Educ:* Belfast. *Exhib:* U.K., Ireland, Europe, N.America. *Work in collections:* Ireland, U.K., U.S.A. *Publications:* 'Beyond the Partitions', 'From Tradition into the Light', 'Works on Paper', 'Glimpse', 'Thinking Long'. *Signs work:* see appendix. *Address:* 28 Belmont Ave., Belfast BT4 3DD.

MacGREGOR, David Roy, M.A. (Cantab). 1948, F.S.A., F.R.Hist.S.; architect, ship draughtsman, author, artist in oil, water-colour and pen; *b* Fulham, 1925. *m* Patricia M.A.P. Gilpin. *Educ:* Eton and Trinity College, Cambridge. *Studied:* under Julius Olsson, R.A., R.O.I. and Cdr. G. F. Bradshaw, R.S.M.A. *Exhib:* R.O.I., N.E.A.C., R.B.A., R.S.M.A.; one-man shows: Woodstock Gallery, London (1974), Digby Gallery, Mercury Theatre, Colchester (1976), Old Butchers Bookshop, Cley (1994). *Publications:* illustrations to his own books. *Signs work:* "D. R. MacGregor." *Address:* 12 Upper Oldfield Park, Bath BA2 3JZ.

MacGREGOR, Robert Neil, M.A., Ll.B.; Director, The National Gallery; *b* 16

June, 1946. *Educ:* New College, Oxford, University of Edinburgh, Courtauld Institute of Art. *Signs work:* "Neil MacGregor." *Address:* National Gallery, Trafalgar Sq., London WC2N 5DN.

McGUINNESS, Michael, R.W.S. (1993); painter in water-colour and oil; Senior typographic and book designer with Readers Digest and, subsequently, Art Editor of The Independent and The Independent on Sunday (1986-91); *b* Essex, 20 Mar., 1935. *Studied:* S.E. Essex Technical College (illustration and typography, Harry Eccleston, O.B.E.), Royal Academy Schools (painting, Fleetwood Walker, R.A.), Walthamstow School of Art (Stuart Ray). *Publications:* The Encyclopaedia of Water-colour Techniques (two paintings), Einstein for Beginners (illustration), Jung for Beginners (illustration). *Clubs:* Wynken de Worde Soc. *Signs work:* "McG." *Address:* 4 Denmark Rd., London W13 8RG.

McINTOSH, Iain, A.R.S.A.; sculptor; *b* Peterhead, 4 Jan., 1945. *m* Freida. two *d.* *Educ:* Peterhead Academy. *Studied:* Gray's School of Art (1962-67). *Signs work:* "I.M." plus year. *Address:* 53 Kilrymont Rd., St. Andrews, Fife, Scotland KY16 8DQ.

McINTYRE, Donald, R.I., R.C.A.; landscape painter in acrylic, oil and water-colour; *b* Yorkshire, 1923. *m* Lauren Lindee. *Educ:* Scarborough College, Skipton Grammar School. *Studied:* studio of James Wright, R.S.W. *Work in collections:* H.R.H. Duke of Edinburgh, National Library of Wales, Welsh Arts Council, Robert Fleming Holdings plc, Birkenhead A.G., Newport (Gwent) A.G., Merthyr Tydfil Gallery, Welsh Contemporary Art Soc., Atkinson Art Gallery, Southport, St. Andrew's University. *Signs work:* see appendix. *Address:* 3 Waen-y-Pandy, Tregarth, Bangor, Gwynedd LL57 4RB.

MACKAY, Arthur Stewart, R.O.I. (1949); artist in oil; former lecturer, Hammersmith College of Art and Building; *b* Dulwich, London, 25 Feb., 1909. *Educ:* Wilson's Grammar School, Camberwell, Regent St. Polytechnic School of Art. *Studied:* Regent St. Polytechnic School of Art. *Exhib:* R.A., R.S.A., Paris Salon and London galleries. *Work in collections:* Imperial War Museum (2 paintings), and many private collections in Britain and Australia. *Publications:* articles on figure painting and outdoor sketching written for the publication, Artist. *Signs work:* "A STEWART MACKAY" or "STEWART MACKAY." *Address:* 4 Dog Kennel Hill, East Dulwich, London SE22 8AA.

MACKAY CLARK, Deirdre, N.D.D.; painter in gouache, oil, mixed media; tutor; *b* Ilford, 18 Sept., 1937. *m* John Clark. three *s.* one *d. Educ:* Copthall Grammar. *Studied:* Hornsey College of Art (1954-59, Alfred Daniels, Colin Sorensen). *Exhib:* Minories, Colchester, R.A. Summer Exhbns., R.W.S., Chris Beetles, R.I., M.O.M.A. (Wales). Work in private and business collections. Designed/painted ceramics (1977-82). *Publications:* Artists Cards (1984), R.A. Pubs. (1985), card and print; Pimms Prize for Drawing R.A. (1985), book jackets (1988), range of Fine Art cards and prints (1989-90). Family ran BOURLETS -1965. *Signs work:* "D.M." or "Deirdre Mackay." *Address:* Brierley Cottage, Brierley, Leominster, Herefordshire HR6 0NT.

McKEAN, Lorne (Miss), F.R.B.S.; sculptor; silver medal for sculpture combined with architecture; Feodora Gleichen and Leverhulme Scholarships; *m* Edwin Russell,

F.R.B.S. *Exhib:* four one-man shows, London W1. Portrait sculptures include: the late Marquess of Salisbury, Hatfield House; H.R.H. Prince Philip on polo pony 'Portano', H.M. The Queen's personal Silver Wedding gift to her husband; the late Prince William of Gloucester, Kensington Palace; Earl of Lichfield for BBC programme 'Portrait'; Prince Charles on 'Pans Folly'. Public works: A.A. Milne public memorial of bear cub at London Zoo; Shearwaters, Shearwater House, Richmond Green; Girl and Swan 17 ft. bronze in Reading; 'Galoubet' French show jumping stallion; H.M. The Queen, Drapers Hall. *Signs work:* "Lorne McKean." *Address:* Lethendry, Polecat Valley, Hindhead, Surrey GU26 6BE.

McKELLAR, Robert, painter in oil and acrylic specialising in abstract and still life with a predominant interest in colour; nine years teaching experience; *b* Gravesend, 2 July, 1945. one *s. Studied:* Medway College of Art, Camberwell School of Art. *Exhib:* R.A., Hong Kong, London, Singapore, Los Angeles. The Netherlands, New York. Works with Northcote Gallery, 110 Northcote Rd., London SW11. *Commissions:* British Consulate. *Signs work:* "R. McKellar." *Address:* The Stable, Chart Hill Rd., Staplehurst, Kent TN12 0RW.

McKENNA, Laurence, artist in oil, water-colour, pastel and pencil; *b* 20 Nov., 1927. *m* Carmel Beattie. two *s.* one *d. Educ:* St. Kevin's, Belfast. *Studied:* 1965-68 under John Luke, R.U.A. *Exhib:* Belfast, Dublin, Cork, London, U.S.A. *Work in collections:* private collections: Ireland, Gt. Britain, Italy, U.S.A. *Publications:* work repro.: Revue Moderne, Paris (drawing, 1947), Sunday Independent, Dublin (drawing, 1956), Irish News (drawing, 1958), Ulster Illustrated (drawing, 1958), Sunday Independent (drawing, 1965), Ulster Tatler (pastel, Jan'01). *Signs work:* "LAURENCE McKENNA." *Address:* 23 Grangeville Gdns., Belfast BT10 0HJ.

McKENZIE SMITH, Ian, O.B.E., D.A., P.R.S.A., Hon. R.A., Hon. R.H.A., Hon. R.U.A., H.R.W.A., P.P.R.S.W., R.G.I., LL.D. (Aberdeen University, 1991), D.Art (Robert Gordon University 2000), F.R.S.A., F.S.S., F.M.A., F.S.A. Scot; artist in oil and water-colour; Commissioner, Museums and Galleries Commission; Trustee, National Galleries of Scotland; *b* Montrose, 3 Aug., 1935. *m* Mary Rodger Fotheringham. two *s.* one *d. Educ:* Robert Gordon's College, Aberdeen. *Studied:* Gray's School of Art (1953-59) under Ian Fleming and R. Henderson Blyth; Hospitalfield College of Art, Arbroath (1958 and 1959). *Exhib:* Royal Scottish Academy, Fine Art Soc., Royal Glasgow Inst. *Work in collections:* Scottish National Gallery of Modern Art, Scottish Arts Council, Abbot Hall Gallery, Kendal, Aberdeen A.G., Glasgow A.G., City Arts Centre, Edinburgh, Perth A.G., Royal Scottish Academy, Arts Council of Northern Ireland, Contemporary Art Soc., IBM, Robert Fleming Holdings, Deutsche Bank. *Clubs:* Royal Northern, Scottish Arts, Caledonian, Royal Overseas League. *Signs work:* normally unsigned, labelled on reverse. *Address:* 70 Hamilton Pl., Aberdeen AB15 5BA.

MacKEOWN, James Martin, B.A. (Open Univ.); painter in oil, acrylic, water-colour and pastel; *b* London, 3 Nov., 1961. *m* Marie Lestang. two *s.* three *d. Educ:* Gresham's School, Norfolk; left school at 14, painting full time since. *Studied:* self taught, first one-man show (1977). *Exhib:* one-man shows in London, Paris, Rouen, Belfast and Dublin. Works permanently on show at: Galerie Rollin, Rouen; Galerie Alfa, Le Havre, Galerie Colette Dubois, Paris; West Wales Art Centre, Fishguard;

Bank Street Gallery, Sevenoaks; Bell Gallery, Belfast; Solomon Gallery, Dublin; represented by the Bruton St. Gallery in London. *Signs work:* "James MacKeown." *Address:* Clos Saint-Pierre. Vattetot s/Mer, 76111 Yport, France. *Email:* james.m.mackeown@wanadoo.fr

MacKEOWN, Martin Graham Clarke, D.A. (Edin.) (1952); painter in oil; *b* Belfast, 14 May, 1931. *m* Ann Carr. four *s*. two *d. Educ:* Campbell College, Belfast. *Studied:* Belfast College of Art (1948-50), Edinburgh College of Art (1950-52). *Exhib:* numerous. *Work in collections:* National Self-Portrait Collection of Ireland, Clare College Cambridge, Arts Council (N. Ireland), Ulster Television. *Publications:* illustrated several, including ten of his wife's cookery books, e.g. 'Ann Carr's Recipe Collection' (1987). *Signs work:* "M. MacKeown." *Address:* Manor House, Itteringham, Norfolk NR11 7AF.

McKIVRAGAN, Terrence Bernard, R.I., N.D.D.; artist in water-colour and acrylic; *b* Wallasey, 22 July, 1929. two *s. Educ:* Wallasey Grammar School. *Studied:* Wimbledon School of Art (1947-51). *Exhib:* R.I. annually, Laing, Hunting Group, R.A. Summer Show, R.B.A., R.S.M.A; galleries: Albemarle, Llewellyn Alexander, Moreton Ct., London, David Curzon Wimbledon, Shell House Ledbury, Manor House Chipping Norton, Alresford Hants., K.D. Fine Art, Guildford. *Commissions:* Baltic Exchange, Daily Express, Samsung, British Medical Assoc., Abbey National, Deutsch Financial, R.A.C. Pall Mall. *Publications:* Acrylic Masterclass - one of nine featured artists. *Clubs:* Chelsea Art Soc. *Address:* The Old Pottery Bldg., Down Lane, Compton, Guildford, Surrey GU3 1DQ.

McLAREN, Sally, R.E.; *b* London, 1936. *Studied:* Ruskin School of Art, Oxford University (1956-59), Central School of Art, London (1959-61), French Government Scholarship: Atelier 17, Paris (1961, S.W.Hayter). *Exhib:* worldwide including U.S.A., Europe, Russia, S.Korea and S.America and the R.A.; solo shows: Bear Lane Gallery, Oxford (1964), Hambledon Gallery, Blandford Forum (1971, 1993), Wessex Craft Centre (1980), Salisbury Festival, Cranborne Gallery (1995), Edwin Young, Salisbury (1996), 107 Workshop, Shaw, nr. Bath (1997), Devizes Museum (1998). *Work in collections:* N.Y. Public Library, S.A.C., Ashmolean, Fitzwilliam and Devizes Museums, Scarborough Museum and A.G., Edwin Young Collection, Skopje Museum of Modern Art, Macedonia, Greenwich Library, Musee Russe en Exile, Montgeron, France, Bradford City Council, Huddersfield Gallery, Universities of Glasgow, Oxford and Fordham (N.Y.), Reed College, Oregon, Cabo Frio Print Collection, Brazil, Olivetti, J. Walter Thompson, City of Norwich Museum. Prizewinner, Mini Print Exhbn., Orense, Spain. *Commissions:* P. & O. Oriana, National Grid, Printmakers Council Print Club, Print Collectors Club. *Publications:* Printmakers Journal (1989), Water-colours, Drawings and Prints Magazine (1992), Printmaking Today (1996). Featured Artist, Art for Sale in The Guardian. *Signs work:* "Sally McLaren" or "McLaren." *Address:* Clouds Cottage, E. Knoyle, Wilts. SP3 6BE.

McLEAN, John, self taught painter in acrylic; *b* Liverpool, 10 Jan., 1939. *m* Janet. *Educ:* St. Andrews University and Courtauld Institute. *Exhib:* over twenty one-man shows worldwide. *Work in collections:* Tate Gallery, Scottish National Museum of Modern Art, Hunterian Collection, Glasgow University, Swindon,

Southampton and Glasgow A.G's., and Edinburgh City Art Centre. *Signs work:* "John McLean" or "J.M." *Address:* c/o. Angela Flowers Gallery, 199-205 Richmond Rd., London E8 3NJ.

McLEAN, John, painter in acrylic; *b* Liverpool, 1939. *m* Janet. *Exhib:* over thirty solo exhibs. worldwide. *Work in collections:* Tate Gallery, Museum of Modern Art, Edinburgh, Glasgow Museum, Hunterian Collection, Glasgow, Edinburgh City Art Centre. *Commissions:* Hairmyres Hospital, East Kilbride; Scottish Equitable H.Q., Edinburgh; Broadgate Centre, London. *Signs work:* 'John McLean." *Address:* c/o Flowers East, 199-205 Richmond Rd., London E8 3NJ.

McLEAN, Mary, R.M.S. (1994), H.S. (1990); miniature painter in water-colour; Gold Bowl Hon. Mention (1997); Llewellyn Alexander Award (2000); *b* Farnborough, Kent, 1944. *m* John S. McLean. two *s.* one *d. Educ:* Marion Vian School, Beckenham. *Studied:* privately with Ronald Jesty, A.R.B.A. *Exhib:* R.A., R.M.S., Llewellyn Alexander (Fine Arts), The Market Cross Gallery, Sturminster Newton, Dorset, Japan and U.S.A., Lannards Gallery, Billingshurst, Sussex, Hilliard Soc. Work in private collections. *Publications:* front cover illustration for specialist poultry magazine, Artist and Leisure Painter magazines, Royal Miniature Society, 100 years book. *Signs work:* "Mary McLean." *Address:* 35 Old Station Gdns., Ashvale, Henstridge, Templecombe, Som. BA8 0PU.

MACLEAN, W.J., D.A., R.S.A., R.G.I., R.S.W.; Professor, fine art, Dundee College, Univ. of Dundee; *b* Inverness, 12 Oct., 1941. *m* Marian Leven. two *s.* one *d. Educ:* Inverness Royal Academy, H.M.S. Conway, N. Wales. *Studied:* Grays School of Art, Aberdeen (1961-66); British School at Rome (1966). *Exhib:* one-man shows: Edinburgh, New 57 Gallery, Richard Demarco Gallery, R.H.W. London; group shows: Scottish Arts Council, Art First, London, 3rd Eye Gallery. *Work in collections:* Aberdeen A.G., Scottish Arts Council, Contemporary Art Society, Scottish National Gallery of Modern Art, Hull A.G., Fitzwilliam Museum, Cambridge, B.M. *Signs work:* "W. J. Maclean." *Address:* 18 Dougall St., Tayport, Fife DD6 9JD, Scotland.

MacLENNAN, Alastair MacKay, M.F.A. (1968), D.A. (1965); intermedia artist in mixed media installations, actuations, time-based work, conceptual orientation; Prof. of Fine Art, University of Ulster (1992-); *b* Blairatholl, Scotland, 3 Feb., 1943. *m* Hilary Robinson. *Educ:* Perth Academy, Scotland. *Studied:* School of the Art Institute of Chicago, U.S.A. (1966-68), Duncan of Jordanstone College of Art, Dundee, Scotland (1960-65). *Exhib:* national and international festivals of performative and time-based work throughout America, Canada, Britain, E. and W. Europe. *Work in collections:* British Arts Council; private collections in Britain, America, Canada, Germany, Switzerland and Poland. *Commissions:* Representing Ireland at the Venice Biennale (1997), with 'Body of (D) Earth'. *Publications:* reviews and interviews in art publications and periodicals. MacLennan has lived in Belfast since 1975. He is known for long, durational performances, and performance/installations, or 'actuations'. From the seminal work 'Days and Nights' (1981), a 144 hour non-stop actuation, to 'No Nemesis' (2000), his Zen-informed practice has been constant. His concerns include ethics, aesthetics, religious/political bigotry, inclusive tolerance, oppositional or concensus means of political/social improvement, death, decay, new life and transformation. An enthusiastic and influential artist and educator, he has exhibited extensively nationally and internationally. In 1989 he joined the innovative European performance art group, Black Market International. *Address:* c/o University of Ulster, Faculty of Art and Design, York St., Belfast BT15 1ED, N. Ireland. *Website:* http://art.ntu.ac.uk/liveart/maclennan

MACLEOD, Duncan, D.A. (1974), R.S.W. (1980); artist in mixed media, watercolour, school teacher; S.A.C. Lecturers Panel; *b* Glasgow, 5 Apr., 1952. *m* Maretta Macleod, artist (divorced). one *s.* one *d. Educ:* Clydebank High School. *Studied:* Glasgow School of Art (1970-74, David Donaldson). *Exhib:* R.S.A., R.S.W., R.G.I., and many mixed and one-man shows in Britain. *Work in collections:* U.K., U.S.A., France, Sweden, and the Far East. *Signs work:* "Duncan Macleod." *Address:* 13 Miltonhill, Milton, By Dumlarton.

MACLEOD, Flora, B.W.S. (1951-56), S.S.W.A. (1955-67), S.W.A. (1960-78); *b* Forres, 24 Mar., 1907. *Educ:* privately. *Exhib:* R.B.A. (Open Assembly), R.I., R.S.W., S.S.W.A., S.W.A., R.G.I., R.W.S. Art Club, Ridley Art Club, R.B.S.A., Paisley Art Inst., Aberdeen Artists, Britain in Water-colours. *Signs work:* "FLORA MACLEOD." *Address:* Meadowlark Nursing Home, Manachie Rd., Dalvey, Forres, Morayshire IV36 0JT.

MACLUSKY, Hector John, Slade Dip. (London); painter; illustrator; lecturer, Stevenage College; art master, Highgate School (1948-50); *b* Glasgow, 20 Jan., 1923. *Educ:* Roundhay and Warwick Schools. *Studied:* Leeds College of Art (1939-40) and Slade School (1945-48). *Exhib:* R.A., R.B.A., London and provinces, Barbican Foyer Exhbn., The Face of Bond (1996). *Work in collections:* America and Australia. *Publications:* freelance cartoonist and illustrator for Press and television. *Signs work:* "John McLusky." *Address:* Hollybush Studio, Baines Lane, Datchworth, Herts. SG3 6RA.

MACMARTIN, John Rayment, D.A., F.R.S.A.; Diploma of Merit, Italy; D.M.D.A.; F.S.A.(Scot.); Industrial Design Consultant and Architectural Designer; Director (Tackle & Guns); artist in oils; inventor; *b* Glasgow, 3 Oct., 1925; Creamola Kid (1936-37). *m* Evelyn Margaret Lindsay Macmartin, embroideress. two *s.* one *d. Educ:* Allan Glen's School, Glasgow. *Studied:* Glasgow School of Art (A past president of the Graduate Association). *Exhib:* oil paintings - Product design, Scottish Inventions of the year - (finalist). *Work in collections:* throughout the world. Structural Building MODULE, designed after a visit to Pompeii; invited to Leningrad, Moscow (1985), U.S.A. (1987), China (1988), Florida (1988), France (1989, 1994) and Norway (1991). National Trust for Scotland: V.P., Lanarkshire (1992-99), Probus Mem. (1992-99). Scottish Core of Retired Executives. *Address:* Rosebank, 2 Markethill Rd., East Mains, East Kilbride G74 4AA.

MACMIADHACHÁIN, Pádraig, R.W.A.(resigned 1996); artist, Travelling Prize to Moscow (1957), winner, Laing National Painting Competition (1991), winner Daler Rowney award in Royal West of England Academy (1992), Polish Govt. to Poland (1961); *b* Downpatrick, Ireland, 2 Mar., 1929. *m* Hazel McCool. two children. divorced. *m* Ann Slacke. one child. divorced. *m* Charlotte Kockelberg (T.A. Charlotte Kienitz). divorced. *m* Bonnie Brown, painter. divorced. *m* Jane Hobday, painter. *Educ:* Bangor Grammar School; Portora Royal School, Enniskillen. *Studied:*

Belfast College of Art (1944-48), National College of Art, Dublin (1948-49), Academy of Art, Krakow, Poland (1960-61). *Exhib:* one-man: Belfast, Dublin, London, Madrid, Krakow, Seattle, Los Angeles, Vancouver, Las Palmas; group shows: R.A., R.W.A., R.U.A., Gorky Park, Moscow, Irish Exhbn. Living Art, Discerning Eye, Thompson Gallery, Crane Kalman, Cadogan Contemporary City Gallery - all London, Penwith Soc. of Art, St. Ives. *Work in collections:* Arts Council, Ireland, Ronald Alley, Bob Monkhouse, Sam Wanamaker, Peter Sellers collection, Lord Briggs, King Carlos of Spain, the late President Chernenko of the U.S.S.R., Hertford College, Oxford, Sussex University, The Bank of China, Irish Allied Bank, S.G. Warburg, Kobe Steel, West Merchant Bank, Sun Oil International. *Publications:* three collections of poems. *Signs work:* see appendix. Work always in New Academy Gallery, 34 Windmill St., London, New Craftsman, St. Ives and The Molesworth Gallery, Dublin. *Address:* Wharf House Studio, 4 Commercial Lane, Swanage, Dorset BH19 1DE.

McMULLEN, Sue, R.A.S. Turner Gold Medal for Painting; painter in oil and draughtsperson in pen and ink; lecturer at Salisbury College of Art (1974-1988); Eric Kennington drawing prize Claire Fontaine-Rhodia prize for an imaginative work (2000); freelance artist since 1996; *b* Yorks., 7 Oct., 1948. *m* Andrew. one *s.* one *d.* *Studied:* Hornsey, Loughborough College of Art, R.A. Schools, P.G.C.E. Manchester Victoria University, under Peter Greenham. *Exhib:* The Athenaeum, Loggia Gallery, London; R.A. Summer Exhibs. (1980, 1982, 1986, 2000); Upstream Galleries, London; Cathedral Church of St. Nicholas, Newcastle; Ferens Art Gallery, Hull; The Mall; Crook, Co. Durham; Art Exhib. 2001 Grenville Court, Burnham, Bucks. *Work in collections:* slide collection Staffordshire University. *Commissions:* Cedric Messina (B.B.C. producer) painting of London home, Sq. Ldr. Revd. Davies painting of Hove Church, Dr. R. Langford drawing of London home. *Publications:* images for Thea P. Hilcox, Inspirational Art Books pub. Ava/Rotovision (2001). *Clubs:* R.A.S.A.A., S.G.F.A., F.P.S., A.S.A.I., Y.A.W.A. *Signs work:* "Sue Mc." *Address:* 36 Whenby Grove, Huntington, York YO31 9DS. *Website:* www.suemcmullen.com *Email:* sue-mcmullen@hotmail.com

McPAKE, John A., N.D.D., A.T.D., R.E., M.A.F.A.; painter/printmaker working in various drawing and painting media in addition to etching, relief and mixed media printmaking; *b* Lancs., 1943. *m* Anne Genner Crawford. *Educ:* St. Anselm's College, Birkenhead. *Studied:* Wallasey School of Art and Crafts (1961-65), Liverpool Polytechnic (1965-66), Birmingham Polytechnic (1966-67), Leeds Polytechnic (1977-78). *Exhib:* various group shows including R.E's, R.A. Summer shows, Seoul Print Biennale (1986, 1988), etc. *Work in collections:* Bankside Gallery (R.E's.); Colin Jellicoe Gallery, Manchester; Leeds Craft and Design Gallery; various public and private collections in the U.K. and abroad. *Commissions:* various, including etching for Wakefield in the '80's. *Signs work:* "John A. McPake." *Address:* 21 Ingbirchworth Rd., Thurlstone, nr. Sheffield S36 9QN.

MACPHAIL, Ian S., F.I.P.R.; artist in typography and print design; European Co-Ordinator, International Fund for Animal Welfare and editor; asst. music controller, E.N.S.A., specializing in publicity; asst. music director, Arts Council of Gt. Britain, responsible for all printing and publicity design; *b* Aberdeen, 11 Mar., 1922. *m* Michal Hambourg. one *s.* one *d.* *Educ:* Aberdeen Grammar School. *Studied:* with

Charles W. Hemmingway. *Exhib:* Exhbns. of posters, Council of Industrial Design. *Publications:* You and the Orchestra (McDonald & Evans), editor and designer of Dexion News, Good Company and The Griffith Graph, designed literature for the first world conference on gifted children (1975); work repro.: British Printer. *Clubs:* Savile. *Signs work:* "Ian Mac. Phail." *Address:* 35 Boundary Rd., St. John's Wood, London NW8 0JE.

MACPHERSON, Hamish, A.R.B.S.; sculptor; teacher, Central School of Arts and Crafts, London (1948-52), Sir John Cass School of Art, London (1948-53); *b* Hartlepool, 20 Feb., 1915. *Educ:* New Zealand. *Studied:* Elam School of Art, Auckland, N.Z. (1930-32), Central School of Arts and Crafts, London (1934-39). *Exhib:* one-man exhbns., Picture Hire, Ltd., London (1938), Chelsea Gallery, London (1947), Apollinaire Gallery, London (1950, 1952), Alwin Gallery, London (1968), London Group, N.S., New York, Paris, the Colonies and provinces; work for Festival of Britain (1951). *Signs work:* "Hamish Macpherson." *Address:* Casa Mia, Mitchel Troy Common, Monmouth, Gwent NP5 4JB.

MACQUEEN, Charles Thomas Keane, D.A. (1962), R.G.I. (1985), R.S.W. (1984); painter in water-colour, acrylic and oil; lecturer in Art Education at Moray House Inst. of Educ. - retired; *b* Glasgow, 23 Feb., 1940. *m* Christine Woodside R.S.W., R.G.I., (partner). two *d. Educ:* St. Aloysius College. *Studied:* Glasgow School of Art. *Exhib:* numerous exhibs. including R.S.A., R.S.W., R.G.I. *Work in collections:* Royal Scottish Academy, Paisley Museum and Art Gallery. *Clubs:* Scottish Arts club. *Signs work:* "MACQUEEN." *Address:* Tower View, 1 Back Dykes, Auchtermuchty, Fife KY14 7AB.

MacSWEENEY, Dale Pring, Dip.A.D.; painter in oil on canvas and water-colour on paper; *b* London, 1949. divorced. *Educ:* Burlington Grammar, W. London; Greycourt Secondary School, Ham, Surrey. *Studied:* Wimbledon School of Art (1966), Waltham Forest College (1967-70). *Exhib:* R.A., N.E.A.C., Piccadilly Gallery, London; Jorgensen Fine Art, Dublin; Hammer Galleries, N.Y.; Montgomery Gallery, San Francisco; Gerald Peters Gallery, Santa Fe, New Mexico, Riverside Museum, Calif. *Work in collections:* H.M. Ministry of Arts, London; Chelsea Arts Club, London; Dallas Museum of Art, Texas; U.N. New York; Inland Revenue and Customs and Excise U.K., private collectors. *Commissions:* Princess Cruise Lines; private galleries. *Publications:* American Artists Magazine. *Clubs:* Chelsea Arts. *Signs work:* "Dale Pring MacSweeney" or "Dale MacSweeney." *Address:* 2 Benhall Lodge, Benhall, Saxmundham, Suffolk IP17 1JD.

MADDISON, Eileen, N.D.D. (1955), A.T.D. (1956), S.B.A. (1998); botanical artist in water-colour; *b* Lancs., 22 Aug., 1934. *m* Colin Maddison. one *s.* two *d. Studied:* Central School of Art (1953-55), Liverpool College of Art (1955-56). *Exhib:* S.B.A., Westminster Gallery, Guildford House Gallery, American Daffodil Soc., Pashley Manor, work in private collections internationally. *Signs work:* "Eileen Maddison" or "E.M." *Address:* Cedar Cottage, Cedar Rd., Woking, Surrey GU22 0JJ.

MADDISON, John Michael, B.A. (1974), Ph.D. (1978), F.S.A. (1991); painter in oil, distemper, gouache; former architectural adviser to Victorian Soc. (1979-81), and Historic Buildings Representative, National Trust East Anglia (1981-92); *b* St.

Andrews, Fife, 17 Nov., 1952. *m* Jane Kennedy. two *s. Studied:* University of Manchester. *Exhib:* R.A., R.I., many mixed exhbns. and one-man shows in London, Norfolk, Cambridge, Salisbury and Bury St. Edmunds. *Commissions:* distemper panels for National Trust restaurant Felbrigg Hall. *Publications:* articles and books on medieval architecture and books on country houses. *Signs work:* "J.M." *Address:* 88 St. Mary's St., Ely, Cambs. CB7 4HH.

MADDISON, Robert, S.G.F.A. (1985), M.E.N.S.A. (1987); painter in water-colour, pastel, graphite; *b* Newcastle upon Tyne, 6 May, 1946. *m* Elizabeth Finch. one *s.* one *d. Educ:* Heaton Grammar School. *Studied:* Newcastle College of Art (1962-64, John Crisp), Manchester College of Art (1964-65). *Exhib:* S.G.F.A., N.S.; numerous one-man shows. *Work in collections:* Durham University; numerous private collections including H.R.H. The Prince of Wales. *Publications:* The Northern Pennines - An Artist's Impressions; articles; television broadcasts. Artist in residence "Prudhoe Community Arts". *Signs work:* "R. Maddison." *Address:* Spring Cottage Studio, Dovespool, Allenheads, Northumberland NE47 9HQ.

MADDOX, Ronald, P.R.I., Hon. R.W.S., F.C.S.D., F.S.A.I., F.R.S.A.; illustrator, consultant designer, artist in water-colour, line, gouache, specialising in architecture and landscape; *b* Purley, Surrey, 5 Oct., 1930. *m* (1st) Camilla Farrin. 1958 (decd. 1995); two *s.* (2nd) Diana Goodwin (1997). *Studied:* St Albans School of Art, Hertfordshire College of Art and Design, London College of Printing and Graphic Arts. Design/art direction 1951-61; freelance from 1962. *Exhib:* R.A., R.I., F.B.A. galleries, national and provincial exhbns., one-man shows. *Work in collections:* Britain, U.S.A., Canada, Germany. Elected President R.I. (1989) re-elected (1999), Governor F.B.A. (1989). Designer, British Commemorative stamps (1972/78/84/89); Design Council award (1973); Isle of Man Europa stamps, Prix de l'Art Philatelique (1987); Winsor & Newton R.I. Award (1981, 1991); finalist Hunting Group Art Prizes (1980-81-83); R.I. Rowland Hilder Award (1996, 2000). *Publications:* national and international publications. *Signs work:* "RONALD MADDOX." *Address:* Herons, 21 New Rd., Digswell, Welwyn, Herts. AL6 0AQ.

MADERSON, Arthur Karl, N.D.D. (1964); painter in oil, pastel, acrylic and water-colour; *b* London, 27 Dec., 1942. *m* Verlayne Maria Maderson. three *s.* three *d. Educ:* Battersea County Comprehensive. *Studied:* Camberwell School of Art (1960-64, Robert Medley). *Exhib:* regularly at R.W.A. (Cornelissen prizewinner 1986), R.A., R.H.A. (Abbey Studio prizewinner 1992), viewing of recent work at the Artists Studio Gallery, Derriheen House, by appointment. *Work in collections:* Europe and abroad. *Publications:* work repro.: contributor to many journals and art publications including The Artist. Mem. Cork Arts Soc. *Signs work:* "A.K. Maderson," or "A.K.M" on picture and reverse. *Address:* Derriheen House, Cappoquin, Waterford, Rep. of Ireland. *Second Address:* Mas Fadat, Mandagout, Le Vigan 30120, Gard, France. *Email:* maderson@gofree.indigo.ie

MADGWICK, Clive, S.E.A. (1991), R.B.A. (1983), U.A. (1976); self taught artist in oil, acrylic and water-colour; *b* London, 31 Oct., 1934. *m* Joan Patricia. one *s.* one *d. Educ:* Epsom College and London University. *Exhib:* 32 one-man shows; R.A., R.B.A., R.O.I., U.A., Royal Soc. of Miniature Artists and Sculptors. Winner Royle Landscape Prize (1978), Higgs & Hill Bursary F.B.A. (1986), Daler Rowney

Award Equestrian Soc. (1987), specializing country sports, Britain Painters Royle Landscape prize (1991), Liquitex Award U.A. Exhbn. (1996). Works in public and private collections throughout the world. *Signs work:* "C. MADGWICK" and see appendix. *Address:* Newton House, Newton Rd., Sudbury, Suffolk CO10 2RS.

MAER, Stephen, F.S.D.C.; Chairman of Soc. of Designer Craftsman, Designer Jewellers Group: Founder-Member and Chairman (1980-83, 1992-95), Crafts Council, Index; designer jeweller; *b* London, 1933. *m* Janet Eddington. two *d. Educ:* Clayesmore School. *Studied:* jewellery design at R.C.A. under Prof. R. Goodden. *Exhib:* group shows: British Crafts Centre, R.S.A., Design Centre, Goldsmiths Hall, Barbican Centre, Chelsea Crafts Fair, Mall Galleries. *Signs work:* "SM" (hallmark). *Address:* 18 Yerbury Rd., London N19 4RJ. *Email:* stephen.maer@btinternet.com

MAGIS, Pascal, Dip. National des Beaux Arts (1976); abstract artist in acrylic and oil and tapestry designer; *b* Aurillac, France, 1 Apr., 1955. *m* Lilou Magis. *Educ:* Ecole St. Joseph de Sarlat, France. *Studied:* Ecole Nationale des Arts Decoratifs de Limoges, France. *Exhib:* Wimbledon Fine Art, Galerie Lewis Guy, Holland, Galerie Inuit, Denmark, Galerie Briand, France. *Work in collections:* Glaxo Smith Kline, Rabo Bank, A.M.B. Amro. *Commissions:* R.A. Christoforides collection. *Signs work:* see appendix. *Address:* c/o Wimbledon Fine Art, 41 Church Rd., Wimbledon Village, London SW19 5DQ. *Email:* magis.art@wanaddo.france

MAGOR, William Laurence, A.R.C.A. (1939), A.T.D. (1940); Principal, Berkshire College of Art (1960-74); artist in water-colour; *b* Mountain Ash, S. Wales, 30 Apr., 1913. *m* Marie Alexander. one *s.* two *d. Educ:* Crypt Grammar School, Gloucester. *Studied:* Gloucester Art School (1932-36) and R.C.A. (1936-39) under E. Bawden, Paul Nash. *Exhib:* R.A. *Signs work:* "W. L. Magor." *Address:* Gwenville, Sellars Rd., Hardwicke, Glos.

MAI, Jinyao: see MAK, Kum Siew.

MAK, Kum Siew, (Mai, Jinyao), A.R.C.A. (1967); full-time artist in Chinese and Western media; *b* Singapore, 21 Apr., 1940. two *s. Educ:* Singapore. *Studied:* St. Martin's School of Art (1961-64) under Frederick Gore, R.C.A. (1964-67) under Carel Weight. *Exhib:* R.A., I.C.A., R.C.A., Serpentine Gallery, Tate Gallery, Whitechapel Gallery. *Work in collections:* Tate Gallery, London; National Gallery, Singapore; Museum of Modern Art, Hyogo, Japan; Arts Council of G.B. *Publications:* Talking Pictures, The Best of Friends. *Address:* Derrylehard, Ballydehob, Co. Cork, Ireland.

MAKEPEACE, John, O.B.E. (1988), F.C.S.D., F.I.Mgt., F.R.S.A.; designer and furniture maker since 1961; Founder and Director: The Parnham Trust (1977-2000); *b* 6 July, 1939. *m* 1983 Jennie Moores. two *s. Work in collections:* Cardiff; Fitzwilliam; Leeds; Frankfurt; Art Institute, Chicago; Lewis Collection, Richmond,Va.; V. & A.; Royal Museum of Scotland. *Commissions:* Furniture commissions for Nuffield Foundation; Post Office; Royal Society of Arts; Boots plc; Banque Generale du Luxembourg. *Publications:* "A Spirit of Adventure in Craft and Design" by Jeremy Myerson. Study/Consultancy Tours: Scandinavia; N.America; W.Africa; Australia and Japan. Featured in numerous books, articles and films internationally. *Clubs:* The Athenaeum, London. *Address:* Parnham House, Beaminster, Dorset DT8 3NA.

MAKLOUF, Raphael, sculptor in bronze; painter; *b* Jerusalem, 10 Dec., 1937. *Studied:* Camberwell School of Art (1953-58) under Dr. Karel Vogel. *Work in collections:* Life-size bronze bust of H.M. Queen Elizabeth II for Royal Society of Arts, John Adam St., London (1986); life-size bronze bust of General Sir John Mogg for Army Benevolent Fund (1987); Tower of London; Carnegie Hall, N.Y., etc. New portrait effigy of H.M. The Queen on all U.K. coinage from 1985; bronze of H.M. The Queen, National Theatre; 15 Stations of the Cross, for Brentwood Cathedral (architect Quinlan Terry). *Signs work:* see appendix. *Address:* 3 St. Helena Terr., Richmond, Surrey TW9 1NR.

MALCLES, Jean-Denis, Mem. Salon d'Automne, Salon des Artistes Décorateurs, Salon de l'Imagerie, Officier ordre des Arts et Lettres; Chevalier de la Légion d'honneur; painter in oil, gouache and pastel; lithographer; stage and costume designer; *b* Paris, 15 May, 1912. *m* Janine Malcles. *Educ:* École Boulle and Académies Peinture. *Studied:* under Louis Sognot and Rulhmann. *Work in collections:* Musée d'Art Moderne, City of Paris, French Government. Theatre decor: Opéra de Paris, Comedie-Francaise, Scala de Milan, Opéra de Hambourg, Cie Renaud-Barrault, Festival musique d'Aix en Provence, Le Théâtre de Jean Anouilh, Covent Garden. *Publications:* Bel Ami, Lettres de Mon Moulin, La Muse au Cabaret, Affiches, Expositions Galerie des Orfèvres, Paris; work repro.: Vogue, Femina, Plaisir de France, Graphis, Ballets des Champs-Elysées, Art et Style, Style en France. *Signs work:* see appendix. *Address:* 152 rue L. M. Nordmann, 75013 Paris, France. *Email:* jdmalcles@aol.com

MALCOLM, Bronwen, B.A. Hons. Fine Art; painter in oil; *b* London, 31 Jul., 1963. *m* Stephen Ackhurst. one *s.* one *d. Studied:* Wimbledon School of Art (1981-1982), St. Martins School of Art (1982-1985) under Eileen Cooper and Albert Herbert. *Exhib:* R.A., and various, New York and London. *Work in collections:* Unilever. *Commissions:* Merrill Lynch, U.K. *Publications:* Arts Review, (Oct. 1987, Dec. 1988), Company, (Jan. 1989). *Clubs:* Chelsea Arts. *Address:* Flat 11, 51 Drayton Gardens, London SW10 9RX. *Email:* bronny@waitrose.com

MALCOLM, Ellen, R.S.A. (1976), Guthrie Award (1952); artist in oil; teacher; *b* Grangemouth, 28 Sept., 1923. *m* Gordon S. Cameron, R.S.A. *Educ:* Aberdeen Academy. *Studied:* Gray's School of Art, Aberdeen (1940-44) under Robert Sivell, R.S.A., and Dr. D. M. Sutherland, R.S.A. *Work in collections:* Perth City Gallery, Art Gallery, Southend, Lillie Gallery, Milngavie, Edinburgh City Collection, Palace of Holyrood House, Thorburn-Ross and Dr. Arnott Hamilton Collections, Edinburgh. *Signs work:* "E. Malcolm." *Address:* c/o 4 Deemount Gdns., Aberdeen AB11 7UE.

MALCOLMSON, Joe, artist in oil and gold leaf, water-colour; *b* Lanarkshire, 28 June, 1932. *m* Joyce Franklin. *Studied:* Medway College of Art (1959-61). *Exhib:* R.A., R.W.S., R.I., R.O.I., N.E.A.C., N.S. *Signs work:* "J.L. MALCOLMSON." *Address:* The Cottage, Woodland Way, Kingswood, Surrey KT20 6NU.

MALENOIR, Mary, R.E. (1984); R.A. Schools Dip. (1964), Rome Scholar in Engraving (1965-67); artist in mixed media; *b* Surrey, 29 July, 1940. *m* Michael Fairclough, artist. two *d. Studied:* Kingston School of Art (1957-61), R.A. Schools (1961-64), S.W. Hayter's Atelier 17, Paris (1967). *Exhib:* Prizewinner in:- P.M.C. National Print Competition (1987), Hunting Group Competition (1987), Humberside

Printmaking Competition (1987), Bankside Gallery Open Print Competition (1989), Arts Club Prize (1998), R.A. Summer Exhbn. *Work in collections:* Ashmolean Museum, Ipswich Museum, Graves A.G. Sheffield. *Signs work:* "MALENOIR." *Address:* Tilford Green Cottages, Tilford, Farnham, Surrey GU10 2BU.

MALIN, Suzi, Slade Post. Grad. (1975); painter in tempera; *m* David Hames. one *s.* one *d. Educ:* Badminton, Bristol. *Studied:* Slade School of Art (1969-75, John Aldridge, R.A.). *Exhib:* one-man shows, J.P.L. Fine Arts, London (1977), Achim Moeller, London (1978), Coe Kerr, N.Y. (1978), Galerie d'Eendt, Amsterdam (1983), Gimpel Fils, London (1982). *Work in collections:* N.P.G.; Raby Castle; Gt. Hall, Christchurch, Oxford; Hull University; East Anglia University; Midland Bank. *Commissions:* Lord Home, Alistair Morton, Queen of Greece, Elton John. *Clubs:* Chelsea Arts. *Signs work:* "S. Malin." *Address:* The Meeting Hall, 158a Mill La., London NW6.

MANCHOT, Melanie, M.A. Fine Art (Photography) (1992); artist/part-time lecturer/photographer; works with video, photography and text; *b* Germany, 7 July, 1966. *Studied:* Royal College of Art (1990-92). *Exhib:* England and abroad, regularly, solo and group shows. *Work in collections:* Saatchi, National Art Collection, The Head Gallery Collection, University of Warwickshire, DG Bank Collections, Germany. *Publications:* Love is a Stranger, Prestel Verlag; Look at You Loving Me, Friedrich Reinhardt Verlag, Zurich. *Address:* 33 Dunloe St., London E2 8JR.

MANDL, Anita, R.W.A. (1978), F.R.B.S. (1980), Ph.D. (1951), D.Sc. (1960); sculptress, formerly University Reader, Medical School, Birmingham; carvings in wood and stone (alabaster, soapstone); also bronzes made from original carvings; *b* Prague, 1926. *m* Dr. Denys Jennings (decd.). *Studied:* part-time at Birmingham College of Art. *Exhib:* R.A., R.B.A., R.W.A., R.G.I.F.A., R.S.M.A., New Academy Gallery, Llewellyn-Alexander Gallery, Alresford Gallery, Falle Fine Arts, etc. and U.S.A. *Work in collections:* Ulster Museum; Royal West of England Academy; National Maritime Museum. *Signs work:* Mostly unsigned. (Highly polished carvings are marred by signature). Bronzes marked A.M. *Address:* 21 Northview Rd., Budleigh Salterton, Devon EX9 6BZ.

MANIFOLD, Debra, P.S.; artist in pastel, oil, water-colour, acrylic; urban landscape and interiors; Council Mem. Pastel Soc.; *b* London, 28 Aug., 1961. *Studied:* Harrow School of Art (1978-83), Central School of Art and Design (1983-84), Advanced Printmaking Postgrad. Dip. *Exhib:* P.S., R.I., Mall Galleries, R.W.A., Barbican Centre, Société des Pastellistes de France; widely exhib. in and around London including Linda Blackstone Gallery, Bank Street Gallery, Orleans House, Edward Day Gallery, Ontario, Canada. *Publications:* Pastels Masterclass; Encyclopedia of Pastel Techniques; articles in 'The Artist'. Lectures throughout U.K. and in Canada. *Signs work:* "Manifold." *Address:* 8 Spring Gdns., E. Molesey, Surrey KT8 0JA.

MANLEY, Jim, A.R.U.A.; Patron's prize, E.V.A. Limerick (1984), Elmwood, Belfast Smallworks (1997) Painting Prize, Iontas (1999); painter in water-colour, pastel, collage; *b* St. Helen's, 1934. *m* Margaret. three *s. Educ:* West Park Grammar School, St. Helen's; De La Salle College, Middleton. *Exhib:* over twenty exhbns. in Ireland and England, including London Gallery, Duncan Campbell Fine Arts, Dublin,

Solomon Gallery. *Work in collections:* Abbot Hall Kendal, U.T.V. Belfast, Walker Liverpool, Bank of Ireland Dublin. *Clubs:* United Arts, Dublin. *Signs work:* "J. Manley." *Address:* Coastguard Cottages, Killough, Downpatrick, Co. Down BT30 7QS, N. Ireland.

MANN, Alex, painter of 'visual-sound' (music) - portraits, landscapes, castles, homes; *b* Ayr, Scotland, 26 Feb., 1923. *m* Joyce. four *d.* *Studied:* Sidcup School of Art, Fine Art (paintings and sculpture). *Exhib:* London, Birmingham, Edinburgh, Germany, U.S.A., Work in collections worldwide. *Commissions:* worldwide. *Signs work:* "Alex Mann." *Address:* Braemar Studio, 3 Chapel Brae, Braemar AB35 5YT.

MANN, Caryl J., S.W.A. (1994), N.D.D. (1960); artist in water-colour, pastel, acrylic; *b* London, 31 Mar., 1938. *m* Christopher Mann. one *s.* *Educ:* Eastbourne High School. *Studied:* Eastbourne School of Art (1956-60). *Exhib:* S.W.A. annually since 1991, David Curzon Gallery since 1988; various mixed and solo shows in Sussex. *Signs work:* "C. Mann." *Address:* Six Birches, Upper Hartfield, Hartfield, E. Sussex TN7 4DT.

MANN, Sargy, H.N.D. Mech. (1958), N.D.D. (1964); landscape painter; *b* Hythe, Kent, 29 May, 1937. *m* Frances Carey. two *s.* two *d.* *Educ:* Dartington. *Studied:* Camberwell School of Arts and Crafts (1960-64, Frank Auerbach, Euan Uglow, Francis Hoyland) (1967, Dick Lee). *Exhib:* R.A., Hayward Annual (1983), London Group, International Drawing Biennale; one-man shows, Salisbury Festival of Arts, Cadogan Contemporary. *Work in collections:* Arts Council of G.B., Contemporary Art Soc., Cleveland C.C. *Publications:* Drawings by Bonnard (Arts Council, 1984), Pierre Bonnard Drawings (J.P.L. Fine Art, 1981), Pierre Bonnard Drawings Vols. 1-2 (J.P.L. Fine Art, 1987), Raoul Dufy (J.P.L. Fine Art, 1987), Pierre Bonnard (Nottingham Castle Museum, 1984), Introduction Past and Present (Arts Council, 1987), Bonnard Drawings (John Murray J.P.L. Fine Arts, 1991). *Signs work:* "Sargy Mann" or "Sargy." *Address:* Lawn Meadow, Bridge St., Bungay, Suffolk.

MANOUK: see BAGHJIAN, Manouk.

MANSER, Michael John, C.B.E., R.A., P.P.R.I.B.A., R.W.A. Dip.Arch., Hon. F.R.A.I.C.; architect; Chairman, Manser Assoc.; *b* 23 Mar., 1929. *m* José Manser, journalist. one *s.* one *d.* *Educ:* Polytechnic Regent St. School of Architecture (now Westminster University). *Exhib:* R.A., R.W.A., Japan, Hong Kong, U.S.A., Singapore, Canada, Italy. *Publications:* Planning Your Kitchen, co-author with wife José Manser (C.I.D.); part author: Psychiatry in the Elderly (O.U.P.), House Builder Reference Book (Newnes), The Nature of Architecture (Routledge), Innovative Trends in Psychogeriatrics (Karger, Switzerland). *Clubs:* Brooks's. *Signs work:* "Michael Manser." *Address:* Bridge Studios, Hammersmith Bridge, London W6 9DA.

MANTLE, Ruth, S.G.F.A. (1984), C.F.A. (Oxon.) (1949); artist in pencil, ink, water-colour of buildings and botanical subjects; illustrator and teacher of drawing; *b* Newbury, Berks., 27 Aug., 1925. *m* Ian Mantle, M.A. two *s.* one *d.* *Educ:* St. Catherine's School, Bramley, Surrey. *Studied:* Ruskin School of Drawing, Oxford (1946-50, Albert Rutherston, Percy Horton; History of Art, Sir Kenneth Clark). *Exhib:* S.G.F.A. Annual, provincial exhbns. Work mainly in private collections, in

Britain and abroad. *Publications:* illustrated, The Necklace Villages, Cambridge Itself, My Cambridge (Robson Books). *Clubs:* S.G.F.A., Shropshire Art Soc., Ludlow Art Soc., The Marches Artists. *Signs work:* "Ruth Mantle." *Address:* 35 Central Ave., Church Stretton, Shropshire SY6 6EF.

MANUEL, Sylvia, artist in water-colour, acrylic, pastel; tutor; *b* London. *Exhib:* England, France, Jersey C.I. *Commissions:* B.B.C., etc. *Signs work:* "Sylvia Manuel" or "S. Manuel." *Address:* Wall Cottage, Leicester Sq., Penshurst, Kent TN11 8BJ.

MAPP, John Ernest, A.R.C.A. (1948); artist in oil, acrylic, illustrator, etc.; *b* Northampton, 26 Mar., 1926. *m* Margaret Trayler. one *s.* one *d. Educ:* Eaglehurst College, Northampton. *Studied:* Northampton School of Art (1941-45), R.C.A. (1945-48) under Barnett Freedman and Gilbert Spencer. *Exhib:* Various galleries. *Signs work:* see appendix. *Address:* 64a Vineyard Hill Rd., Wimbledon Pk., London SW19 7JJ.

MARA, Pam, M.C.S.D. (1970), N.D.D. (1958), F.F.P.S. (1997); illustrator, designer, painter, printmaker in oil, pastel, acrylic, water-colour, lithography; *b* London, 12 May, 1928. *Educ:* Henrietta Barnett School, London. *Studied:* Willesden School of Art, Central School of Art. *Exhib:* mixed shows: Mall Galleries, Barbican, National Theatre, Bloomsbury Gallery, Loggia Gallery, St. Martin in the Fields Gallery, Royal Festival Hall, Holland Park Orangery. *Publications:* illustrated over 100 books, work published in England, America, several European countries, W. Africa, Near and Far East, South Africa and Australasia. *Signs work:* "Pam Mara." *Address:* 5 Gloucester St., London SW1V 2DB.

MARAIS, (Mary Rachel Brown), Mem. Visual Artist and Gallery Assoc.; self taught artist in oil; *b* New York City, 24 Sept., 1921. *Educ:* New York University. Lived in Paris several years and painted warm, charming nostalgic scenes of Paris completely capturing the ambiance in a very personal style. *Exhib:* Paris, New York, Switzerland; Centre d'Art Contemporain, Paris (1984); Galerie Chantepierre Auboune, Switzerland; Soho-20 Gallery, 545 Broadway, New York (2000); seen on NYC Channel 13 TV (1979, 1980). *Work in collections:* Jean Aberbach, Theodora Settele, Hugo Perls, Dr. M. Reder, Jacques Bellini. *Signs work:* "Marais." *Address:* 33 W. 67th St., New York 10023, N.Y.

MARDEL-FERREIRA, Elizabeth Gilchrist, painter in acrylic, ink and wash, printmaker; *b* Nottingham, 5 May, 1931. *m* Joseph Charles Mardel-Ferreira. one *s.* two *d. Educ:* Headington School, Oxford. *Studied:* Nottingham College of Art (1949-53). *Exhib:* R.A. (1978); S.W.A. Work in private collections. *Publications:* Illustrations for Warblington Church guide. *Signs work:* "E. Mardel" or "Elizabeth G. Mardel.' *Address:* 15 Warblington Ave., Havant, Hants. PO9 2SD.

MARDI: see BARRIE, Mardi.

MAREK, Jerzy, self taught primitive painter in oil; *b* Poland, 1925. *m* Margaret Baird. one *s. Exhib:* Portal and Grosvenor Galleries, London, also in a number of International and Arts Council Exhbns. for primitive painters. *Work in collections:* Salford A.G., Bolton A.G., Abbott Hall Museum, Kendal, Lancaster Museum, Glasgow Gallery of Modern Art, Sydney Janis Coll., N.Y., Salford City Art Gallery, Manchester City Art Gallery. *Publications:* Naive Kunst by Ida Niggli, The Rona

Guide to the World of Naive Art, Twentieth Century British Naive and Primitive Artists by E. Lister and S. Williams, A World of Their Own by J and M Leman; many postcards. *Signs work:* "J. Marek." *Address:* 7 Pittville St., Portobello, Edinburgh EH15 2BZ.

MARGRIE, Victor, C.B.E., F.C.S.D.; potter; Associate Editor, Studio Pottery (1993-2000), Ceramics in Society (2000-); Visiting Prof. University of Westminster (1992-96); Director, Crafts Council (1977-84); Mem. of Board of Studies in Fine Art, University of London (1989-1994); Mem. UK National Commission for UNESCO (1984-85); Fine Art Advisory Committee British Council (1983-86); *b* London, 29 Dec., 1929. *Work in collections:* V. & A., and private collections. *Publications:* contributed to: Oxford Dictionary of Decorative Arts (1975); Europaischt Keramik Seit (1950, 1979); Lucie Rie (1981); contrib. specialist publications and museum catalogues. *Signs work:* see appendix. *Address:* Bowlders, Doccombe, Moretonhampstead, Devon TQ13 8SS.

MARINKOV, Sasa (Alexandra), R.E.; artist in printmaking, lecturer, teacher, sculpture in schools; *b* Belgrade, Yugoslavia, 12 Jan., 1949. *m* Michael Jones. one *d.* *Studied:* Fine Art: Leeds University (1967-71), Advanced Dip. printmaking: Central St. Martin's. *Exhib:* Biennales at Cleveland, Bradford, Brazil, Korea, Spain, Xylon 13, Whitechapel and Riverside Open, London Group, Kunsthaus Zug, Prints from Wood (Arts Council). *Work in collections:* Leeds University; London University; Brazil; Skopje; Clare College, Cambridge; London Hospital; British Rail Freight; Bank of China; Winchester Hospital; Dept. of Transport; Arts Council/South Bank Centre; Ashmolean. Awards: G.L.C., South Bank picture show, R.A. Summer Show (twice), Ministry of Transport, London Arts Board, British Council. *Signs work:* "S. Marinkov." *Address:* Woodcut, Riverside, Twickenham TW1 3DJ.

MARJ: see BOND, Marj.

MARKEY, Danny, R.W.A.; painter; *b* Falmouth, 9 June, 1965. *Educ:* Falmouth School. *Studied:* Falmouth School of Art and Camberwell School of Art. *Exhib:* Redfern Gallery, London Group, R. A., R.W.A., South Bank Picture Show (First Prize) Discerning Eye, Newlyn Gallery, Royal Overseas League, Charleston Farmhouse Sussex. *Work in collections:* various private and Old Jail House Museum and Gallery, Texas. *Signs work:* "Danny Markey." *Address:* c/o Redfern Gallery, 20 Cork St., London W1X 2HL. *Website:* www.redfern-gallery.com *Email:* art@redfern-gallery.com

MARKS, Laura Anne Celia, Greenshields Foundation award (1982, 1983); artist in oil, water-colour and pencil; *b* Toronto, Canada, 1954. *Educ:* Forest Hill Collegiate, Toronto. *Studied:* Central Technical School, The Three Schools of Art, Art's Sake, and Ontario College of Art (1971-80, Paul Young). *Exhib:* one-man shows: Evans Gallery, Toronto (1973), Prince Arthur Gallery, Toronto (1980), October Gallery, London (1982), Alberta House, London (1982), Gallery Gabor, Toronto (1984), International Exhbn., Monte-Carlo (1985), John Denham Gallery, London (1991). *Work in collections:* Ontario House, London. *Signs work:* "MARKS." *Address:* 26 West End La., London NW6.

MARR, Leslie, M.A. (1947); painter and draftsman in oil, water-colour, etc.;

Secretary, Borough Group (1947-49); *b* Durham, 14 Aug., 1922. *m* Lynn Marr. two *d. Educ:* Shrewsbury, Cambridge. *Studied:* Borough Polytechnic under David Bomberg. *Exhib:* one-man shows: Everyman Gallery, Drian Galleries, Laing A.G., Newcastle upon Tyne, Woodstock Gallery, Maddermarket Norwich, Fermoy Gallery, Kings Lynn, "Bomberg and the Family" exhbn. Ben Uri Gallery, London, Catto Gallery, London; major retrospective, Durham City. *Work in collections:* Laing A.G., Newcastle upon Tyne, University of Haifa, Graves A.G., Sheffield. *Publications:* From My Point of View (Acorn Editions 1979). *Signs work:* see appendix. *Address:* 20 Gordon Rd., Melton Constable, Norfolk NR24 2BW.

MARRIOTT, Michael, F.R.B.S. (1974), N.D.D. (1960); sculptor in stainless steel, glass, G.R.P., stone, clay, plaster, bronze; *b* London, 3 May, 1940. *Educ:* Latymer Foundation and Christopher Wren Secondary. *Studied:* St. Martin's School of Art (1956-60, Elizabeth Frink, Anthony Caro, Edward Paolozzi). *Exhib:* one-man shows: Cockpit Theatre, London (1971), Alwin Gallery, London (1976); two-man show: Europa Gallery, Surrey (1978); group exhbns.: annually all over U.K. since 1960, Margam Park, S. Wales, Barbican Centre, Hannah Peschar Gallery, Surrey; also in U.S.A. and Europe. *Work in collections:* I.B.M. Cosham, Hunting Engineering Bedford, Heron House London, Crown House London. *Signs work:* see appendix. *Address:* 16 Seymour Rd., London SW18 5JA.

MARSHALL, Dunbar: see MARSHALL MALAGOLA, Dunbar.

MARSHALL, Joan, S.W.A. (1994); equestrian and portrait artist in oils; *b* Yorks., 8 Jan., 1931. *Studied:* Hull Art School. *Exhib:* S.W.A., S.Eq.A. *Signs work:* "Joan Marshall." *Address:* The Studio, Treskerby Lodge, Treskerby, Redruth, Cornwall TR16 5AG.

MARSHALL, John, landscape painter in water-colour; *b* Colchester. *Educ:* Rugby School. *Studied:* pupil of Cedric John Kennedy (1898-1968). *Exhib:* British Art Centre, New York, Leicester Galleries, London; one-man exhbns.: Leicester Galleries WC2 (1956-59-62), Anthony Reed's Gallery W1 (1981). *Work in collections:* Wadsworth Atheneum, U.S.A., Columbia Museum of Art, U.S.A., Norwich Castle Museum, Hull Education Committee. *Publications:* Cedric Kennedy memorial Catalogue and Monograph (1969 and 1972); work repro.: The Studio (July, 1956, Feb., 1960); monographs: Arts Review (June, 1956), The Studio (Feb., 1960). *Signs work:* "John (J) Marshall." *Address:* 41 Campden Hill Rd., London W8.

MARSHALL, Maria Heléne, B.A.Hons. (1986); sculptor in steel, stone, wood and canvas; *b* India, 14 Feb., 1964. married. *Educ:* Millfield School, Somerset, Ardingly College, Sussex. *Studied:* Chelsea Foundation (1982), Wimbledon School of Art (1986, Glyn Williams), Ecole des Beaux Arts, Geneva. *Exhib:* Gallerie Eric Frank (Geneva, Chicago, Basel); one-man shows: Odette Gilbert Gallery (London and Madrid), Crucral Gallery. Public sculpture 'Goddess' Princes Ct., Brompton Rd. *Signs work:* "Maria Marshall." *Address:* The Workshops, 23 Theatre St., London SW11.

MARSHALL, Richard, P.S. (1983); painter in oil, pastel, gouache, part-time lecturer; *b* Goring, Sussex, 29 Jan., 1943. two *d. Educ:* West Sussex College of Art. *Studied:* under William Cartledge, R.I., R.S.M.A. (1969-72), Gyula Sajo (1973-89).

Exhib: internationally; mixed shows, France, London and Sussex; one-man show, Croydon; two-man show, Arundel and Worthing. *Work in collections:* U.K., Europe and North America. *Publications:* Pastel Artist International. *Clubs:* Worthing Atelier Art Group. *Signs work:* "R. Marshall." *Address:* 17 Harsfold Cl., Rustington, W. Sussex BN16 2QQ.

MARSHALL, Steven, B.A. Hons. Fine Art; painter in oil and enamels on glass; *b* Dover, 10 Apr., 1967. *m* Michèle. *Educ:* Kings School, Wessex. *Studied:* Wolverhampton University. *Exhib:* Future Famous, London; Modern Art and Modernisms, London; View of the New, London; Contemporary Art Soc.; R.A. *Work in collections:* Ernst and Young, Unilever, Eversheds, Manorca Services. *Publications:* co producer of film for Picasso Pictures, 'In Flight', Readers Digest Award (1990). *Signs work:* "S.M." or "Steven Marshall." *Address:* c/o Wimbledon Fine Art, 41 Church Rd., Wimbledon Village, London SW19 5DQ. *Email:* steven-marshall@virgin.net

MARSHALL MALAGOLA, Dunbar, R.B.A.; painter; mem. Salon d'Automne, Paris; former Sec.-General International Assoc. of Art, UNESCO; *b* Florence, 1918. *m* Daphne Chart. *Studied:* Westminster and Chelsea Schools of Art under Gertler, Meninsky, Robt. Medley, Ceri Richards. *Exhib:* one-man shows, Grabowski, London (1961, 1964), UNESCO House (1985), Prévôt Gallery, Paris IV (1986, 1989). *Work in collections:* Museums of Contemporary Art: Skoplje and Bihac (former) Yugoslavia; Lodz, Poland; Baghdad, Iraq; Pori, Finland; Academy Savignano, Italy; University of Liverpool; Japan Artists' Centre, Tokyo; Imperial War Museum, Lambeth. *Signs work:* "D M" or "Marshall Malagola." *Address:* 14 Cross Hayes, Malmesbury, Wilts. SN16 9BG.

MARTIN, Barry John, Intermediate exam. Arts & Crafts (1963), N.D.D. Painting (1965), Post Dip. (1966), Post Grad. (1967); painter, sculptor, draughtsman, printmaker, acrylic, stainless steel, bronze, electricity, charcoal; former lecturer numerous colleges; *b* Amersham, Bucks., 20 Feb., 1943. *m* Sarah Anne. one *d.* *Studied:* University of London Goldsmiths' College (1961-66), St. Martin's School of Art (1966-67). *Exhib:* one-man shows: Arts Council, Serpentine Gallery (1970), Richard Demarco Gallery (1971), Newcastle upon Tyne Polytechnic A.G. (1977), Goya Gallery, Zaragosa, Spain (1980), 'Look - Reflections on Structure and Meaning' Olympia (1999), etc.; group shows: Northern Young Contemporaries, Whitworth A.G. (1965), Young Contemporaries, London (1966), Manifestation of Light - Light Artist's, Bromsgrove Festival, B'ham (1968), Gelsen Kirchen Museum, Berlin (1969), Onnasch Gallery, Berlin (1970), A.C.G.B. Hayward Gallery Kinetics (1970), I.C.A. Electric Theatre (1971), Arts Council, Spectrum, Alexandra Palace (1972), Harlow, Essex Movements (1973), 12 British Painters, Arts Council and British Council Exhbn. for Iceland (1977), Beaux Art Gallery, Brussels (1995), Mus. of Modern Art, Paris (2000), Tate Gallery 'New Acquisitions' (2000). *Work in collections:* numerous public and private including Science Museum, Tate Gallery, N.P.G., B.M., A.C.G.B., Mus. of Modern Art, Paris. *Commissions:* Howard Staunton Memorial, Kensal Green Cemetery; Mr. Resistor, New King's Rd. London. *Publications:* Light and Movement (1985); Comp. with Red, Mondrian (1986); Chess for Absolute Beginners, with Keene; The 'G' Spot, Lord Burlington (1998); '. au pied de la lettre' (2001); 'Movement Meaning Movement' (2001). *Clubs:* A.R.B.S.,

Athenaeum, London. *Address:* 98 Cole Park Rd., Twickenham, Middx. TW1 1JA; Studio: South Lodge, Chiswick House Grounds, Chiswick, London W4 2RP.

MARTIN, David McLeod, R.S.W., R.G.I., D.A. (Glasgow) (1948), Hon. Professional Mem. S.S.A. (1949), Past Vice-Pres. R.S.W.; *b* Glasgow, 30 Dec., 1922. *m* Isobel A.F. Smith (decd.). four *s. Educ:* Glasgow. *Studied:* Glasgow School of Art, 1940-42 (R.A.F. 1943-46), 1946-48. *Exhib:* R.A. (1984), Bath Contemporary Art Fair (1987), numerous group shows; one-man shows in Glasgow, Edinburgh, Perth, Greenock, Stone Gallery, Newcastle and London. Work in numerous public and private collections. Special Award of merit, Robert Coloquhoun memorial art prize exhbn., Kilmarnock (1974); prizewinner, Friends of the Smith Art Gallery, Stirling (1981); May Marshall Brown award, R.S.W. Exhbn. (1984); Mabel McKinlay award, R.G.I. (1990); prizewinner, Laing Exhbn., Mall Gallery, London (1990, 1993); featured artist, Perth Festival (1999), Perth Museum & Art Gallery Retrospective; 'Themes & Variations', John Martin of London (2000). *Signs work:* "DAVID M. MARTIN." *Address:* The Old Schoolhouse, 53 Gilmour St., Eaglesham, Glasgow G76 0LG.

MARTIN, John, R.B.A., B.A.(Hons.), R.A. Post Dip. (1983); painter in oil, gouache and water-colour; *b* London, 25 Jan., 1957. *Educ:* Houndsfield School, London. *Studied:* Exeter College of Art (Micheal Garton, Alexander MacNeish), R.A. Schools (Peter Greenham). *Exhib:* numerous one-man shows in England; mixed shows in France and Canada. *Work in collections:* Norfolk County Collection, Art in Hospital Fund. *Signs work:* "J.M." *Address:* 70 Florence Rd., Brighton BN1 6DJ.

MARTIN, Marie-Louise, D.F.A. (1982), B.F.A. (1983); artist printmaker in etching; Director, Black Church Print Studio, Dublin; *b* Dublin, 29 Mar., 1960. *Studied:* National College of Art, Dublin (1978-83). *Exhib:* R.A. (1987, 1988), R.H.A. (1985-99), R.U.A. (1987-99), An tÓireachtas (1984-01), E.V.A. (1984, 1986, 1988); print exhbns. in Ireland, England, Japan, America, Germany, Spain, Taiwan; exchange print exhbns. to China, Finland, Cuba. Print prizewinner R.H.A. (1989). *Work in collections:* B.P. Oil (Brussels); Kilkenny Castle; Guinness Peat Aviation; National Self portrait Coll.; Contemporary Arts Soc.; Office of Public Works; Stormont Castle, Belfast; Microsoft. *Clubs:* United Arts, Dublin. *Signs work:* see appendix. *Address:* 9 Estate Cottages, Shelbourne Rd., Dublin 4. *Email:* marielouisemartin@101free.ie

MARTIN, Nicholas Gerard, B.A. (Hons.) (1980); artist in oil-stained acrylics, paper collage and paper mosaics, mural mosaics; educational project artist, Glyndbourne Touring Opera (1987): music and composition for four part choirs; *b* Edinburgh, 5 July, 1957. *m* Marion Brandis. two *s. Educ:* Edinburgh Academy. *Studied:* Edinburgh College of Art (1975-80, Ian Davidson). *Exhib:* R.S.A., Traverse Theatre, Gardner Art Centre, Brighton Polytechnic A.G., Royal Pavilion A.G., Brighton, Dryden St. Gallery, Horsham Arts Centre, Royal Festival Hall A.G., Ramsgate Library Gallery, Booth Natural History Museum, Brighton. *Work in collections:* S.E. Arts, Royal Pavilion A.G., Forestry Commission, Edinburgh, Royal Festival Hall, Towner A.G., mosaic mural for Channel Tunnel, Ashford Library (1990), Herne Bay Sea Front Mosaic Fountain (1993), Govan Shipyard Mural, Glasgow (1993), Queen Elizabeth Queen Mother Hospital Mural (1996), Maps for

Rochester City Council. Educational residencies with: Glyndebourne Touring Opera, Destafford School, Hextable School, Spinney School; programme convenor for 'Art for Public Space' degree course at University of Roehampton, Surrey. Since 1999, has combined composition for voices with visual art. *Signs work:* "Nicholas Martin." *Address:* The Shieling, Kingstonridge, Kingston, nr. Lewes, E. Sussex BN7 3JX. *Email:* n.martin@roehampton.ac.uk

MARTINA, Toni, B.A. (Hons.) (1978), Prix de Rome scholar (1987), R.E. (elected 1992); many prizes and awards including 1st prize Dept. of Transport National Art Competition (1992), Christie's Contemporary Art award at R.A. (1987), N.Y. National Academy of Design Summer Exhbn. (1986), Lloyds Bank Printmakers award at R.A. (1986), prize, London Print Fair, Air Gallery London (1997); painter/printmaker; *b* London, 7 Mar., 1956. *m* Tessa. two *d. Studied:* Harrow College of Art (1974-75), Kingston Polytechnic (1975-78), Central School of Art (1986). *Exhib:* Europe and the U.K. including R.A. Summer Show, R.E., Rome, New York, Florida, Czech Republic, India. *Work in collections:* Cambridge libraries, Plymouth Museum, Rochdale Museum, Oldham Museum, Dept. of Transport, Museum of London, The London Hospital, Ashmolean Museum, New York Public Library. *Publications:* "Citybites" (TNT Publications). *Signs work:* "T. Martina." *Address:* 48 Elphinstone Rd., Hastings, East Sussex TN34 2EQ.

MASCO, Pam, artist in oil and water-colour, mixed media; *b* Springfield, Mass., 19 Mar., 1953. *m* John Heseltine. *Studied:* School of the Boston Museum of Fine Art, U.S.A. (Grad. Dip.) 1976. *Exhib:* Clarendon Gallery, London (1986), David Messum, London (1990), R.B.A. (1992), R.W.S. (1992), Sunday Times Singer & Friedlander Water-colour (1992), W.H. Patterson, London. Studio and Gallery at East House, Petworth., U.S. galleries. *Work in collections:* private and corporate collections; other collections Wentworth Club, Barings Bank. *Commissions:* portrait painting commissions. *Publications:* Dictionary of British Artists Since 1945 by David Buckman. *Signs work:* "P. MASCO." *Address:* East House, East St., Petworth W. Sussex GU28 0AB. *Email:* pm.hestletinemasco@virgin.net

MASON, Cyril Harry, M.C.S.D. (1966), F.C.S.D. (1979), M.S.T.D. (1966), A.R.B.S.A. (1983), R.B.S.A. (1986); landscape and marine painter in water-colour and oil; chartered designer; *b* Halesowen, Worcs., 30 May, 1928. *m* Barbara Hill. one *s.* one *d. Educ:* Halesowen Grammar School. *Exhib:* R.I., R.W.S., R.S.M.A., R.B.S.A., R.C.A., R.W.A., Clarges Gallery and Llewellyn Alexander, London and midland galleries. *Work in collections:* Wyre Forest (Kidderminster), Wychavon, Marks & Spencer. *Clubs:* B'ham Water-colour Soc. *Signs work:* until 1986 "Mason"; after 1986 "Cyril H. Mason." *Address:* Bank Cottage, Shenstone, nr. Kidderminster, Worcs. DY10 4DS.

MASON, Michael, A.T.D., D.A. (Manc.) (1956), Fellow in Sculpture British School at Rome (1976), F.R.B.S. (1992); sculptor in ceramics/bronze; former PR/lecturer sculpture, Manchester University; *b* Lancs., 1 June, 1935. *m* Barbara. one *s.* one *d. Studied:* Manchester College of Art, British School, Rome. *Exhib:* Whitworth A.G., Serpentine Gallery, Yorkshire Sculpture Park. *Work in collections:* V. & A., A.C.G.B., Zagreb A.G., A.V.A.F. Caracas. *Commissions:* Manchester Business School, Hackney Empire. *Publications:* Art International, Ceramic

Review. *Signs work:* "Michael Mason" or "M.M." in rectangle. *Address:* 89 Park Rd., Hale, Altrincham, Ches. WA15 9LE.

MASON, Richard, sculptor of constructions in metals, wood and perspex, painter in oil and acrylic; *b* Ipswich, 20 June, 1931. *Educ:* Ipswich Grammar School. *Exhib:* one-man show: Woodbridge A.G. (1967); regular exhib. with Ipswich Art Club and Felixstowe Art Group. *Clubs:* Ipswich Art, Felixstowe Art Group. *Signs work:* "Richard Mason." *Address:* Upland Gate, 39 Bishops Hill, Ipswich 1P3 8EW.

MASSEY, Carole Margaret, Dip. A.D; painter/illustrator in acrylic, water-colour, pastel, pencil; art tutor; *b* Hertford, 8 Jan., 1948. *m* Eric. one *s*. one *d. Educ:* Welwyn Garden City Grammar School, Leicester School of Art. *Studied:* St.Albans (John Brunsden), Leicester School of Art (Edward Bawden, David Howells). *Exhib:* Cambridge, Stevenage, Hong Kong. *Commissions:* portraits. *Publications:* prints, cards, brochures; book – Water-colour Pencils (Search Press); video – Water-colour Pencils (Teaching Art series). *Clubs:* Herts. Visual Arts Forum, N.A.P.A., P.A.S.A.A., Royston Art Society. *Signs work:* "CAROLE MASSEY." *Address:* 60 High St., Guilden Morden, Royston, Herts. SG8 0JS. *Email:* massey@cwcom.net

MASTER, Jean, R.O.I. (1987); painter in oil and acrylic; *b* London. married. two *s*. one *d. Educ:* St. Joan of Arc Convent, Rickmansworth, Herts. *Studied:* St. Martin's School of Art (Kenneth Martin), also in Hamburg under Prof. Karl Kluth. *Exhib:* Royal Academy, London, Royal West of England, Bristol, Mall Galleries London and other mixed exhbns. *Signs work:* see appendix. *Address:* 16 Hillside Rd., Redcliffe Bay, Portishead, N. Somerset BS20 8EW.

MATANIA, Franco, U.A., S.G.F.A., S.E.A.; First prize 'Talens' award Mall Galleries (1984), Soc. Equestrian Art prize for drawing (1986, 1988), United Soc. of Artists award (1993); artist in all media; *b* Naples, 1922 (British subject 1935). *Educ:* Salesian College. *Studied:* at studio of artist relative, the late Fortunino Matania, R.I. (Chevalier): distinguished artist (Imperial War Museum: Benizet, etc.); student apprentice 1947-55 after military service. *Exhib:* mixed shows, R.I., R.O.I., N.S., P.S., U.A., S.G.A., S.E.A.; one-man shows, Campbell and Franks Fine Art, Bajazzo Gallery, Marlborough, Alpine Gallery, Guild Fine Arts; (abroad 1980's), Galleria Maitani, Orvieto, Italy, Galleria Treves, Milan, Italy, Galleria Alandaluz, Granada, Spain, Tanisia Gallery, N.Y. Galleria Toison, Madrid. *Work in collections:* Centro Hogar, Granada, Knight Inc. Conference Centre, Boston, Industria Marmo Design of Italy. *Signs work:* see appendix. *Address:* Little Venice Studio, 20 Clarendon Gdns., Maida Vale, London W9 1AZ.

MATHESON, Andrew Kenneth Mackenzie, D.A., R.B.S.A., Cert. Ed.; artist/potter and teacher works mainly in stoneware/porcelain - from, Rose House Pottery, Lichfield, Staffs.; *b* Edinburgh, 22 July, 1949. *Educ:* Riland Bedford High School, Sutton Coldfield. *Studied:* Madeley College of Education (1968-71), Grays School of Art, Aberdeen (1974-79), Dip. in Art (1978), postgrad. Dip. in Art (1979). *Exhib:* in Scotland and England. *Clubs:* Mem. of R.B.S.A., B'ham Art Circle, Midland Potters Assoc. *Signs work:* "Andrew K.M. Matheson" and see appendix. *Address:* 7 Driffold, Sutton Coldfield, W. Midlands B73 6HE.

MATHEWS, Alister, B.Sc,; botanical painter in water-colour; *b* Prestbury, 25

Feb., 1939. *m* Carl Mathews, Ph.D. one *s.* one *d. Educ:* James Allen's Girls' School, Dulwich; University of Wales. *Exhib:* S.B.A., S.W.A., Malcolm Innes; solo show: Hitchin Museum, Westminster Gallery annually. *Work in collections:* Hunt Inst. for Botanical Illustration, Carnegie Mellon University, Pittsburg, Shirley Sherwood Collection. *Signs work:* "Alister Mathews." *Address:* 4 Bramshott Close, London Rd., Hitchin, Herts. SG4 9EP.

MATHEWS, Binny, Elizabeth Greenshield Foundation Award (1989); painter in oil, specialising in portraiture, tutor; *b* Dorset, 25 June, 1960. *m* Stuart Martin, archi-tect. two *s. Studied:* Bournemouth and Poole College of Art (1977-78), West Surrey College of Art (1978-81), Brighton Polytechnic (1981-82). *Exhib:* N.E.A.C., Hunting Award, R.P., Mall Galleries, N.P.G. (1981, 1982 1985, 1988, 1990, 1993), R.A., etc., numerous one-woman shows in the provinces and London. *Work in col-lections:* La Sainte Union College, Southampton; National Trust, Castle Drogo; Seagrams; British Gas; Carpenters Hall; American Embassy. *Clubs:* Chelsea Arts. *Signs work:* "Binny Mathews." *Address:* 13 Crescent Pl., Brompton Rd., London SW3 2EA. *Website:* www.hereasel.com

MATTAROZZI DI THARASH, Mirella (Mirice Janàcêk), artist-painter, fine arts professor, writer; Diploma, Istituto Belle Arti di Bologna, Accademia di Belle Arti di Bologna; *b* Bologna. *Exhib:* Italy, Europe, South America. *Work in collec-tions:* museums, Palazzo Vecchio, Firenze, Castello Sforzesco, Milano, Museo S. Matteo, Pisa, etc. Associate of Incisori d'Italia (I.D.IT.), Ex Libristi d'Italia (E.L.D.IT.). *Publications:* Il Comanducci, Annuario Internazionale di Belle Arti (Berlin), Guida all'arte Italiana, Who's Who in Europe, ed. Feniks, etc., Knight of the Tommaso da Vico Order; Academician of the Accademia dei 500, Rome. Lady-in-waiting of the Corporazione Internazionale della Stella Croce d'Argento (C.I.S.C.A.) dei Cavalieri del Bene. *Address:* via Sigismondo no33, Cattolica Forlì, Italy.

MATTHEWS, Anton, R.C.A., (1960) N.D.D., A.T.D., artist in oil, teacher (retired); *b* 5 Dec., 1925. *m* Janet. three *s. Studied:* Cheltenham College of Art, University of Reading. *Exhib:* R.A., R.B.A., R.W.A., R.C.A., and many mixed exhb-ns. and one-man shows. *Work in collections:* Pictures for Schools and Welsh Arts Council. *Signs work:* "Anton Matthews" or "AM" *Address:* 8 Elizabeth Way, Chard, Som. TA20 1BY.

MATTHEWS, Peter Jeffrey, N.D.D. (1962), R.E. (1983); artist/printmaker in water-colour, etching and lithography; Senior Lecturer in Printmaking, Wimbledon School of Art (retired); *b* London, 29 July, 1942. *m* Caroline Moore. one *s.* one *d. Studied:* Ealing School of Art (1958-62). *Exhib:* numerous mixed shows in G.B. and abroad. *Work in collections:* V. & A., Bibliotheque Royal, Brussels, Albertini Museum, Vienna, Morandi Museum, Bologna, Italy. *Signs work:* "Peter Matthews." *Address:* 1 Manor Rd., London SW20 9AE.

MATTHEWS, Sharyn Susan, S.W.A.; self taught artist in water-colour, acrylic, gouache, oil; *b* Bristol, 13 Jan., 1951. one *s.* one *d. Exhib:* numerous one-man shows at home and abroad, including Mall Galleries. Work permanently on show Park Lane Fine Arts, Ashtead, Surrey. *Signs work:* "Sharyn Matthews." *Address:* 19 Longdown La. North, Ewell, Surrey KT17 3HY.

MATTHEWS, Zara, M.A., R.C.A. (1999); painter in oil, artist printmaker, digital artist; part time fine art tutor; *b* London, 6 Jun., 1960. *Educ:* St Paul's Girl School, Hammersmith, London. *Studied:* Goldsmiths College (1979-1980), Kingston Polytechnic (1980-1983), Royal College of Art (1997-1999). *Exhib:* Flowers East (1991), Eagle Gallery, London (1992, 1996, 2001), Harewood House, Leeds (1996). *Work in collections:* D.L.A. Art Collection, British Land, R.C.A. Print Archive, V. & A. Print Collection, British Museum. *Signs work:* "Zara Matthews." *Address:* 73-75 Cressy Court, London E1 3JQ. *Email:* zaram@talk21.com

MAYER, Charlotte, A.R.C.A. (1952), F.R.B.S. (1980); sculptor in bronze, steel and wood; *b* Prague, 4 Jan., 1929. *m* Geoffrey Salmon. one *s.* two *d. Studied:* Goldsmiths' College School of Art (1945-49, Wilson Parker and Roberts Jones), R.C.A. (1949-52, Frank Dobson). *Exhib:* R.A., R.W.A., V. & A.; Selected Galleries: Belgrave, Bruton, Hagen, Pangolin, Sladmore, Berkeley Sq., Ashbourne, Sculpture at Goodwood. *Work in collections:* Wadham College Oxford; Merseyside C.C.; Basingstoke and N. Hants. Health Authority; Cement and Concrete Assoc.; British Petroleum; Banque Paribas; Bledlow Manor. *Commissions:* Tree of Life, North London Hospice; Ascent, Barbican, City of London; Journey 2 Nene College, Northants.; Wind and Fire, Marylebone Gate, London; Sea Circle, Liverpool; 'Lunearc', Prior's Court School, Berkshire. *Publications:* illustrated, The Mystery of Creation by Lealman and Robinson; Patronage and Practice, Tate Gallery Liverpool; Liverpool Seen by Peter Davis; The Alchemy of Sculpture by Tony Birks. *Signs work:* "C.M." or "Mayer." *Address:* 6 Bloomfield Rd., Highgate, London N6 4ET.

MAYES, Emerson, B.A. Hons., Graphic Arts, Leeds Metropolitan University (1994); painter/printmaker and draughtsman of British landscapes; *b* Harrogate, N. Yorks., 22 May, 1972. *m* Melanie Wilkins, (partner). *Educ:* St. Aidans C. of E. High School, Harrogate. *Studied:* Harrogate College, Leeds Metropolitan University. *Exhib:* N.E.A.C., Discerning Eye, Laing Landscape prize, numerous solo exhibs. including London and Edinburgh, represented by Gascoigne Gallery, Ilkley. *Work in collections:* N. Yorks. County Council, Harrogate Borough Council, Provident Financial Plc and numerous private collections. *Signs work:* "Emerson Mayes." *Address:* Garden Flat, 9 Rutland Rd., Harrogate, N. Yorks. HG1 2PY. *Email:* emerson.mayes@virgin.net

MAZ: see JACKSON, Maz.

MAZZOLI, Dino (Leopoldo), artist in oil and water-colour; *b* Terni, Italy, 10 May, 1935. *Educ:* Oriani College, Rome. *Studied:* Villa Massimo, Rome (1953-54, Renato Guttuso), Villa Medici, Rome (1954-56), Eastbourne College of Art, and with Dorothy Swain, R.C.A. *Exhib:* Don Orione, Farnesina, Rome, Heathfield A.G., E. Grinstead Autumn Show, Towner Museum and A.G., Eastbourne, Brighton Museum and A.G., Star Gallery, Lewes, Blackheath Gallery, London; also in Dusseldorf, Germany, St. Laurent en Grandvaux, France, Birmingham, Alabama U.S.A., etc. *Work in collections:* La Charbonniere, St. Laurent en Grandvaux 39150 France. *Signs work:* "D. Mazzoli." *Address:* 33 Cavalry Cres., Eastbourne, E. Sussex BN20 8PE.

MEACHER, Neil, N.D.D. (1955), A.R.C.A. (1960), R.I. (1981); artist and teacher in inkline and water-colour; visiting Professor in Illustration,

Buckinghamshire Chilterns University College; *b* Sandwich, Kent, 20 Dec., 1934. *m* Margaret Joyce. one *s*. one *d*. *Educ:* Sir Roger Manwood's Grammar School. *Studied:* Canterbury College of Art (1951-55), R.C.A. (1957-60, Humphrey Spender, Julian Trevelyan, Alistair Grant, Edward Ardizzone). *Exhib:* Shell Gallery, Mall Galleries, Campion Gallery, Alresford Gallery, Linda Blackstone Gallery, Medici Gallery, Walker Galleries. Work in numerous private collections. *Publications:* joint author 'Mastering Water-colour' (Batsford, 1994). *Clubs:* Royal Inst. of Painters in Water-colour. *Signs work:* "NEIL MEACHER." *Address:* Warehouse Studio, Apartment No. 2, The Corn Exchange, Strand Quay, Rye, E.Sussex TN31 7DB.

MEADOWS, Anthony William, A.R.M.S. (1984); self taught painter and illustrator in oil, wood engraving; *b* Aldershot, 28 Aug., 1957. *m* Dawn Hardy (jeweller). *Educ:* Fanshawe School, Ware. *Exhib:* R.A., R.I., R.M.S. and several one-man shows. *Work in collections:* Hertford Museum. *Signs work:* "A. W. Meadows". *Address:* 27 Victoria Rd., Oswestry, Salop. SY11 2HT.

MEDHURST, Doreen, R.M.S. (1993), S.B.A. (1989), S.W.A. (1989); self taught painter in acrylic and oil; *b* London, 5 Aug., 1929. *m* Cyril Medhurst. two *s*. *Educ:* Sydenham High School. *Exhib:* R.M.S., S.B.A., S.W.A., Llewellyn Alexander Gallery, Alfriston Gallery, Elan Art Centre, Limpsfield Gallery and several one-man shows. *Publications:* Greetings cards, Lings, "Penshurst, Kent". *Signs work:* "D. Medhurst." *Address:* 45 Blenheim Rd., Orpington, Kent BR6 9BQ.

MEEK, Elizabeth R., P.S.W.A., R.M.S., F.R.S.A., H.S.; portrait artist; President of Society of Women Artists (2000-), Officer of Royal Miniature Society (2000-); *b* London, 7 May, 1953. two *d*. *Educ:* Beaconsfield High School. *Exhib:* R.M.S., Hunting/Observer, Mall Galleries, Smith Gallery, Yorks., L'Espace Pierre Cardin, Paris, British Painters, Barbican Centre, S.W.A., H.S., Llewellyn Alexander Gallery, R.A. Summer Exhbn.; one-woman show in Valletta, Malta, Africa '97 London, Soc. of French Miniature Artists, France, Jersey Arts Centre, Australia. *Work in collections:* National Museum of Fine Art, Valletta, Malta. *Publications:* 'The Techniques of Painting Miniatures' by Sue Burton; '100 Years of Miniatures' by Suzanne Lucas. Awards: winner, R.M.S. Gold Memorial Bowl (1995); The Bell Award (1992, 1997) (best portrait in exhbn.); H.S. (1993, 1994) (best in exhbn. twice); R.M.S. (1992, 1994) (runner-up for Gold Memorial Bowl, twice); R.M.S. (1993) Gold Bowl hon. mention, The Mundy Sovereign Award (1995, 1999), Best Set R.M.S. (1999). *Clubs:* Fellow Royal Society Arts. *Signs work:* "E.R. Meek." *Address:* 482 Merton Rd., Southfields, London SW18 5AE. *Email:* elizabethmeek@email.msn.com

MELAMED-ADAMS, Alicia, U.A. (1965), Gold medallist, Academie Italia belle arti el Lavore (1981), Art in Edinburgh (1984), Gallery Internationale, Paris (1984); artist in oil; *b* Borystaw, Poland, 26 Sept., 1927. married. one *s*. *Studied:* St. Martin's School of Art (1960-63); Academie Chaumiere, Paris; Sir John Cass College of Art. *Exhib:* Foyles A.G., R.B.A., Augustine Gallery, Flower Paintings of Today, Flower Paintings of the World, 100 Years of British Drawing, Galerie Solombo, Paris (1987-89), Crypt Gallery, London, R.A. (1988), Hunting Group, Mermaid Theatre (1991), Real Art Gallery (1992), Intaglio Gallery, Manchester (1993), Crocodile Gallery (1993), Leicester City Gallery (1993), Laudersdale House (1994); two artists, two views, Bird and Davis Ltd. (1996); Sackville Gallery mixed (1996, 1997), Artbook

Chelsea Harbour mixed (1998), one-woman show (1998), Patron, Exh. Ark T Centre Oxford, Patron, Bishop Harris of Oxford, Holocaust exhibition, St. Luke's Church, Holloway, London (27 Jan.); mixed pottery exbn. Morley College Art Gallery (2001). *Work in collections:* Brazil, Paris, London; permanent collection, Ben Uri. *Publications:* British Contemporary Art (1993), Editions Arts et Image du Monde (1989), Britt Art 2000. *Signs work:* "Alicia Melamed." *Address:* 17 Edmunds Walk, London N2 0HU.

MELLAND, Sylvia, R.E.; painter-etcher; *b* Altrincham. *m* Brian Mertian Melland. one *s. Educ:* Altrincham Grammar School. *Studied:* Manchester College of Art, Byam Shaw, London, Euston Road, Central School (Graphics). *Exhib:* one-man shows, Wertheim and Jackson's Galleries, Manchester, Zwemmer Gallery, London, Galleria S. Stefano, Venice, Galerie Maurice Bridel, Lausanne, Galerie Bürdeke, Zürich, Agi Katz Fine Art, London. *Work in collections:* Rutherston Collection, S. London A.G., N.Y. Library, Leeds A.G., Brighton Museum, Coventry Educ. Council, Twickenham Educ. Council, Greenwich Library, Ferens A.G., Hull, V. & A., R.A. (Stott Foundation), Talmuseum des Münstertals, Switzerland, New Hall College, Cambridge and in private collections here and abroad. *Signs work:* prints, "Sylvia Melland," oils, "S.M." *Address:* 68 Bedford Gdns., London W8.

MELLOR, Mary, LL.B., A.K.C. (1961), Called to Bar (1962), B.A. Graphics (1984); artist in oil and mixed media; teacher; *b* Swansea, 1939. *m* His Hon. Judge David Mellor. two *d. Educ:* King's College, London, Inner Temple. *Studied:* Norwich School of Art and Design (1979-84). *Exhib:* Norwich Castle Museum, Advice Arcade Gallery etc. King's Lynn Eastern Open, Figurative Painting Prize (1996), Mall Galleries, N.E.A.C. (1998), New York Expo. (1999), Sheringham Little Theatre (1999); solo exhbn. Bergh Apton Sculpture Trail, Norfolk (3-Dimensional work). *Signs work:* "Mary Mellor." *Address:* The Old Hall, Mulbarton, Norwich NR14 8JS.

MELLOR, Pamela, F.R.S.A.; painter in oil, writer; Hon. Sec., Chelsea Art Society (1971-1978); Com., Armed Forces Art Society; *b* Sydney, Australia. *m* Lt.Col. Gerard Mellor, Royal Signals, retd. *Educ:* at home and abroad. *Exhib:* U.A., R.W.S., R.M.S., Artists of Chelsea, Chelsea Art Soc., Leighton House, Ridley Art Soc., Armed Forces Art Soc., Dowmunt Gallery, Qantas Gallery. *Work in collections:* H.R.H. The Prince of Wales, The Agent General of N.S.W., The Agent General of Queensland and other private collections. *Publications:* author, The Mystery of X5 (pub. William Kimber). *Signs work:* "Pam Mellor." *Address:* 44 Stanford Rd., Kensington, London W8 5PZ.

MENDEL, Renée, sculptor and potter; *b* Elmshorn, 22 Sept., 1908. *Educ:* Lichtwark School, Hamburg; universities of Berlin, Frankfurt, Paris. *Studied:* Berlin under Ernest de Fiori, Paris under Pablo Gargallo. *Exhib:* Salon d'automne, Paris, R.A., Hertford House; one-man show at Royal Copenhagen Porcelain Co., 6 Bond St., Heal & Son Exhbn. Sculpture for the Home, Camden Arts Centre, Royal Exchange (1977). *Work in collections:* sculpture (wood carving) of James Joyce, National Portrait Gallery. *Commissions:* Dm. H. Winsley-Stolz, S.P. (bronze portrait 1989). *Publications:* work repro.: The Studio, Evening Standard, Semaine à Paris, Artistes d'aujourd'hui, Hampstead and Highgate Express and News, Hornsey

Journal. Sculpture of 'Beatles' sold by Sotheby's (21 May 81), Sculpture of James Joyce, N.P.G. (Feb. 1987). *Signs work:* "Renée Mendel." *Address:* 27 Onslow Gdns., London N10 3JT.

MENDELOW, Anne, artist in oil and pastel; gallery owner promoting Scottish artists; *b* Johannesburg, 1 Apr., 1947. divorced. two *s.* one *d. Educ:* in S.Africa. *Exhib:* R.G.I., S.A.A.C., and galleries in Edinburgh and Glasgow. *Work in collections:* private galleries in Edinburgh and Glasgow. *Signs work:* "Anne Mendelow." *Address:* Park Cottage, The Gatehouse Gallery, Rouken Glen Rd., Glasgow G46 7UG.

MENDOZA, Edwin, portrait and muralist painter in oil and water-colour, interior designer; *b* Alexandria, Egypt, 11 Jan., 1936. *m* Katherina. two *d. Educ:* Victoria College, Alexandria. *Studied:* St. Martin's School of Art. *Signs work:* see appendix. *Address:* 59 The Ridgeway, London NW11 8QL.

MENDOZA, June, R.P., R.O.I.; portrait painter; *b* Melbourne, Australia; musician parents. *m* Keith Mackrell. one *s.* three *d. Educ:* Lauriston Girls' School, Australia. *Studied:* St. Martin's School of Art. *Work in collections:* government; H.M. Forces; industry; commerce; medicine; academic and legal professions; theatre; sport, and private collections internationally. Portraits include: H.M. The Queen; H.R.H. Prince Charles; H.R.H. Princess of Wales; H.M. Queen Mother; Baroness (Margaret) Thatcher; Mr John Major; Prime Ministers of Australia and Fiji; Presidents of Philippines and Iceland; series of musicians inc. Sutherland, Solti, Menuhin. Group portraits include: House of Commons in Session; Council of Royal College of Surgeons; House of Representatives, Canberra. Hon. D.Litt. Bath University; Hon.D.Litt. Loughborough University; A.O.(Australia); lectures; T.V. *Signs work:* "MENDOZA" and see appendix. *Address:* 34 Inner Pk. Rd., London SW19 6DD.

MENZIES, Gordon William, D.A.; Josef Sekalski Award for Printmaking; Head of Pottery Dept., Community Centre, Edinburgh; established Iona Pottery, 1982 (Workshop/Gallery) with own ceramics, engravings, landscapes; *b* Motherwell, Scotland, 9 Jan., 1950. *Educ:* Dalziel High School, Motherwell. *Studied:* Duncan of Jordanstone College of Art, Dundee (1969-73) under Sheila Green, Ron Stenberg; Atelier 17, Paris (1974) under S. W. Hayter. *Exhib:* Edinburgh, Printmakers Workshop, Compass Gallery, Glasgow, Montpelier Art Institute, France, R.S.A., S.S.A., Edinburgh, many others within Edinburgh and surrounding area. *Publications:* books illustrated mainly within Children's Educational area. *Address:* Lorne Cottage, Isle of Iona, Argyll PA76 6SJ.

MEREDITH, Julian Nelson, artist and printmaker; *b* Bath, 4 Mar., 1952. *m* Jane. three *d. Educ:* Clifton College. *Studied:* Exeter College of Art (1972, 1974). *Exhib:* R.A. Summer Exhbn. (1989), Henry Brett Galleries (1989), Natural History Museum London (1995), Cartwright Hall (1993), Mead Gallery (1984). *Work in collections:* V. & A. Museum, London, Birmingham University, Teesside Airport, Deutsche Bank. *Commissions:* R.V.I. Hospital Newcastle, Ross-on-Wye Hospital. *Signs work:* "J.Meredith." *Address:* Avondale House, Polmont, Falkirk FK2 0YF.

MEREDITH, Norman, A.R.C.A.; illustrator; tutor University of Aberystwyth

(1935) and St. Martin's School of Art; war service M. of A.P. (Farnborough); *m* Violet Mary Brant. *Studied:* Liverpool College of Art and R.C.A.; travelling scholar. *Exhib:* frequently at Chris Beetles Gallery, London SW1, since 1984. *Work in collections:* H.R.H. The Duke of Gloucester, etc. Textiles for Moygashel, Crowson Fabrics; designs for Metal Box Co., greetings cards, gift wraps, nursery pictures for Brunott of Holland; nursery china. *Publications:* work repro.: Punch, Tatler, Bystander; books illus. most British publishers, strip cartoonist. Hobbies: Recording piano music, photography, travel, (two world tours). *Signs work:* "NORMAN MEREDITH." *Address:* The Elders, Epsom Rd., Ewell, Surrey KT17 1JT.

MERRYLEES, Andrew, R.S.A., B.Arch., Dip. T.P., R.I.B.A., F.R.I.A.S., F.C.S.D., F.R.S.A., hon. Prof. of Arch. University of Dundee; architect, Hypostyle Architects; *b* 13 Oct., 1933. *m* Maie. two *s.* one *d. Studied:* Glasgow. *Commissions:* University Bldgs. at Edinburgh, Heriot-Watt, Dublin, Liverpool, Newcastle and Aston, Birmingham, Scottish H.Q. for Automobile Association, sorting office for Post Office, National Library of Scotland, British Golf Museum at St. Andrews, Motherwell Heritage Centre, and Dundee Science Centre. Awards: Student Senior Prize, Student Life Drawing Prize, R.I.B.A. Bronze Medal, Saltire Award, Civic Trust Award, Art in Architecture Award, R.S.A. Gold Medal, Concrete Award, Sconul Award. *Clubs:* Scottish Arts. *Address:* 204 Bonkle Rd., Newmaws, Lanarkshire ML2 9AA. *Email:* amer@hypostyle.co.uk

MERTON, John Ralph, M.B.E. (1942); painter; *b* 7 May, 1913. *m* 1939 Viola Penelope von Bernd. two (and one decd.) *d. Educ:* Eton; Balliol Coll. Oxford. Served War of 1939-45 (MBE); Air Photo reconnaissance research, Lieut.-Col. 1944. *Studied:* Ruskin Art School, Oxford. *Work in collections:* The National Portrait Gallery, Buckingham Palace. *Publications:* A Journey Through an Artist's Life. Works include Mrs Daphne Wall (1948); The Artist's daughter Sarah (1949); altar piece (1952); The Countess of Dalkeith (1958); A Myth of Delos (1959); Clarissa (1960); Mrs Julian Sheffield (1970); Sir Charles Evans (1973); Iona Duchess of Argyll (1982); Sir David Piper (1985, N.P.G.); H.R.H. The Princess of Wales in Cardiff City Hall (1987); Professor James Meade, Nobel Prize Winner (1987); H.M. The Queen (1989) as head of the Order of Merit; Head Master of Eton (1990); Triple portrait of The Duke of Grafton for the National Portrait Gallery (1992); Paul Nitze (1992); Legion of Merit (USA) 1945. Recreations: music, making things, underwater photography. Lord & Lady Rounsey with Broadlands reflected in 18th century mirror between them. *Address:* Pound House, Oare, nr. Marlborough, Wilts. SN8 4JA.

MEYER, Mary Elizabeth Anne, A.S.G.F.A.; sculptor; fine art tutor; trained as printmaker and painter; *b* London, 27 Jun., 1942. *m* Peter Meyer (divorced). three *s.* one *d. Educ:* Queensgate School. *Studied:* Regent St. Polytechnic, Central School of Art. *Exhib:* Atrium Library, Cork St., London (1999), Workhouse Gallery (2000). *Commissions:* Carnavalle Restaurant. *Clubs:* Chelsea Arts. *Signs work:* "Elizabeth Duncan Meyer." *Address:* 59 Britannia Rd., London SW6 2JR.

MICAH, Lisa, M.F.P.S. (1989), N.A.P.A. prize (1988); artist in acrylic; Council mem. Cambridge Drawing Soc. (1988-91), Consultant, Galeries d'Attente, London (1989-91); *m* M.J. Chapman. four *d. Educ:* in Europe and Africa. *Exhib:* solo-shows:

Cambridge (1987, 1988), London (1991), Lyon (1992, 1993, 1994), Château du Cingle (1994). Artiste invitée d'honneur, St.Galmier (1996). *Work in collections:* private: Austria, Belgium, England, Finland, France, Germany and Switzerland; public: England, France, United States. *Clubs:* Farmers' London. *Signs work:* "L. Micah" and see appendix. *Address:* B.P.3, F-01350 Culoz, France.

MICHIE, Alastair Milne, R.W.A., F.R.B.S., Hon. D. Arts; painter in acrylic and mixed media, sculptor in bronze; *b* St. Omer, France, 9 Dec., 1921 (eldest son of Anne Redpath, O.B.E.). *m* (1) Hazel Greenham. three *d.* (2) Sally Gaye. one *s.* one *d. Educ:* France; Hawick High School. *Studied:* Edinburgh University. *Exhib:* in Europe, North and South America, Middle and Far East. *Work in collections:* M.O.M.A., São Paulo; Robert Fleming Holdings; M.O.M.A., Rio de Janeiro; B.P. International; Mitsui Banks; British Aerospace; City A.G. Cleveland, etc. *Commissions:* numerous private commissions, British Aerospace, etc. *Address:* The Manor House, Wareham, Dorset BH20 4LR.

MICHIE, David Alan Redpath, O.B.E. (1997); painter; Prof. Emeritus, Heriot Watt University (1991); Head, School of Drawing and Painting, Edinburgh College of Art (1982-90); *b* St. Raphael, Var, France, 1928. *m* Eileen Michie. two *d. Educ:* Hawick High School. *Studied:* painting: Edinburgh College of Art (1946-1953), Italy (1953-1954). *Exhib:* one-man shows, Mercury Gallery, London (1967, 1969, 1971, 1974, 1980, 1983, 1992, 1996, 1999), Mercury Gallery, Edinburgh (1986), Lothian Region Chambers (1977), The Scottish Gallery, Edinburgh (1980, 1994, 1998), Kasteel de Hooge Vuursche, Netherlands (1991). *Work in collections:* Scottish National Gallery of Modern Art, Royal Scottish Academy, Royal West of England Academy. *Signs work:* "David Michie." *Address:* 17 Gilmour Rd., Edinburgh EH16 5NS.

MICHNA-NOWAK, Krysia, B.A. Gen. London University (1970), Post Grad. Cert. Ed. London University (1973), John West prize, Letchworth (2000); painter on paper, canvas, board; art education officer, Sheffield Art Galleries (1975-1987), exhibs. organiser, Salama Caro Gallery, Cork St., (1987-1988), art consultant, Northern General Hospital, Sheffield (1992-1994); *b* Halesworth, 18 Mar., 1948. *Educ:* Ealing College, and Garnett College, London University. *Studied:* London University under Prof. Bohusz-Szyszko (1967-1970), Marek Zulawski (1972-1973), Felix Topolski (1972-1973). *Exhib:* solo exhibs., Air Gallery, Dover St., London (2000); Thomas Plunkett Fine Art, St. Albans (2000); Seven Springs Gallery, Ashwell (2000); St. Raphael Gallery, London (2001). *Work in collections:* Worksop Town Hall, Greys College, Durham. *Commissions:* three paintings for Northern General Hospital, Sheffield. *Publications:* illustrated 'The Planet of the Towers', Sheffield (1981). *Clubs:* Printmakers Council, Polish Assoc. of Artists, Herts. Visual Arts Forum. *Signs work:* "Krysia D. Michna-Nowak." *Address:* 309 Wedon Way, Bygrave, Nr. Baldock, Herts. SG7 5DX.

MICKLEWRIGHT, Robert Flavell, D.F.A. (London), R.W.S.; illustrator, painter in oil, water-colour; *b* Staffordshire, 1923. *Studied:* Wimbledon School of Art (1947-49), Slade School (1949-52). *Exhib:* regular exhibitor in London, provinces and U.S.A. *Work in collections:* pictures in public and private collections. *Publications:* illustrated numerous books. Work reproduced in the following reference books: Artists of a Certain Line (Bodley Head), Designing a Book Jacket (Studio), Designers in Britain, 5, 6, 7 (Andre Deutsch), Drawing for Radio Times (Bodley Head), Illustrators at Work (Studio), Royal Academy Illustrated, Underground Art (Studio Vista), Dictionary of 20th Century British Book Illustrators (Antique Collectors Club). *Address:* Mount Hill, Mogador, Tadworth, Surrey KT20 7HZ.

MIDDLETON, Michael, A.R.E. (1981), R.E. (1986), Dip.A.D. (1971), H.D.A. (1974); lecturer/painter/printmaker in oil, water-colour, etching, woodcut; teaches printmaking, art history, Colchester Inst. School of Art and Design; *b* Louth, Lincs., 25 June, 1950. four *s. Educ:* Heron Wood, Aldershot. *Studied:* Farnham School of Art (1966-68), Sheffield Polytechnic (1968-71), Chelsea School of Art (1973-74). *Exhib:* R.A., R.E., and several one-man shows. *Work in collections:* Harlow Town Corp., R.E., Ashmolean Museum Oxford, Fitzwilliam Museum Cambridge. *Commissions:* Print Collectors Club. *Signs work:* "M. Middleton." *Address:* 104 Maldon Rd., Colchester, Essex CO3 3AP. *Email:* mike.middleton@btinternet.com

MIDDLETON, Michael Humfrey, C.B.E., Hon. F.R.I.B.A., Hon. F.L.I.; Assistant Editor/Editor of Picture Post (1949-53); Lilliput (1953-54); House and Garden (1955-57); Deputy Director, the Civic Trust (1957-69), Director (1969-86); art critic, Spectator (1946-56); *b* London, 1 Dec., 1917. *m* Julie Harrison. one *s.* two *d. Educ:* King's School, Canterbury. *Studied:* Heatherley's. *Publications:* Group Practice in Design; Man Made the Town; Cities in Transition; contributor to many periodicals, etc., on art, design and environment. *Address:* 84 Sirdar Rd., London W11 4EG.

MIDDLETON, Renée, S.G.F.A., S.B.A., S.W.A.; Rexel prizewinner (1984), Rotring prizewinner (1994); artist in pen and ink specialising in natural forms of stipple and/or line; *b* 19 Mar., 1920. married. one *s.* one *d. Educ:* Old Palace School for Girls, Croydon. *Exhib:* R.B.A., S.W.A., S.G.F.A., S.B.A., 'Flowers and Gardens' Mall Galleries and Central Hall, Westminster; three-man show, Fairfield Halls, Croydon. *Clubs:* S.G.F.A., S.B.A., S.W.A., local Sussex Socs. *Signs work:* see appendix. *Address:* Merryhill Corner, Thakeham, W. Sussex RH20 3HB.

MIDGLEY, Julia, A.R.E. (2001), Dip.A.D. (1969); mem.: P.M.C., Manchester Academy of Fine Arts (Vice President, 1994-96); Reader, Liverpool John Moores University; *b* 1948. *m* J. Godfrey. two *s. Studied:* Northwich School of Art and Design (1965-66), Manchester College of Art and Design (1966-69). *Exhib:* Manchester Academy annually since 1979, R.A. (1983, 1986, 1987, 1997), R.E. (1987, 1990), Business A.G's. (1981, 1982, 1983, 1985), New Academy (1987-94), Chelsea Arts Club, P.M.C. Exhbns. (1984-97). *Work in collections:* national, international, public and private. *Commissions:* corporate and public. *Publications:* 'Drawn from Experience', 'Granada Sketchbook'. *Clubs:* Chelsea Arts. *Signs work:* "Julia Midgley." *Address:* 79 School Lane, Hartford, Ches. CW8 IPG.

MIERS, Christopher John Penrose, R.B.A. (1986); artist in oil and water-colour; Secretary, The Arts Club (1986-90); Trustee, The Water-colour Foundation (1988-91); Trustee, R.B.A. (1999-); *b* 26 Sept., 1941. *m* (1) 1967 Judith Hoare. one *s.* one *d.*; (2) 1993 Liza Thynne. *Educ:* Wellington College and R.M.A. Sandhurst. *Exhib:* R.A., R.B.A., N.E.A.C., The Minories, Colchester (1964), Ansdell Gallery, Kensington (1967, 1968), Fortescue Swann, Brompton Rd. (1976), C.D. Soar & Son,

Launceston Pl. (1986, 1988), Sally Hunter Fine Art (1990, 1993, 1995), Mall Galleries (1991), Jerram Gallery (1994, 1996), Grosvenor House (1996), Tryon & Swann Gallery (1998). *Work in collections:* Imperial War Museum, House of Commons, Sultanate of Oman. *Clubs:* Arts, Chelsea Arts, Fadeaways. *Signs work:* "C. MIERS." *Address:* 114 Bishop's Mans., Bishop's Park Rd., Fulham, London SW6 6DY.

MILES, Arran Elizabeth, B.A. (Hons.) 1973; artist in charcoal, pastel and inks (drawings); *b* Southampton, 28 Mar., 1951. *m* Steve Tapper. one *s.* one *d. Studied:* Leicester School of Art (1969-70), St. Martin's School of Art (1970-73). *Exhib:* regularly with Jelly Leg'd Chicken, Reading; Handel Gallery Devizes; S.W.A. Westminster Gallery; Aberdona Gallery, Scotland; Marlborough Festival Open Studios; Newbury Open Studios; Corn Exchange, Newbury; Mosaic Garden, Buxton. *Publications:* work repro.: greetings cards, postcards. *Address:* 5 Forge Cottages, Froxfield, Marlborough, Wilts. SN8 3LE.

MILES, June, R.W.A., Slade diploma for Drawing; painter in oil; *b* London, 4 Jul., 1924. *m* Paul Mount, sculptor. one *s.* two *d.* by previous marriage. *Educ:* Portsmouth High School. *Studied:* Slade, under Prof. Randolp Schwabe (1941-1943), West of England College of Art (1945-1947). *Work in collections:* Nuffield Foundation for paintings in hospitals, Plymouth City Art Gallery, Bristol City Art Gallery, Sussex Education Committee, R.W.A. *Clubs:* Penwith Society, Newlyn Society. *Signs work:* "June Miles" on back of paintings. *Address:* Nancherrow Studio, St. Just, Penzance, Cornwall TR19 7LA.

MILLAR, Jack Ernest, A.R.C.A. (1950), R.B.A. (1954); artist in oil; former Head of Fine Art, Kingston Polytechnic (retd. 1986); *b* London, 28 Nov., 1921. *m* (1) Pauline Sawyer one *s.* two *d.*; (2) Pamela Izzard. *Studied:* Clapham School of Art (1939), St. Martin's School of Art (1941), Royal College of Art (1947-50, 1st Class Dip., awarded Andrew Lloyd Scholarship for landscape painting). *Exhib:* Odette Gilbert Gallery; one-man shows, Linton Court Gallery, Duncan Campbell Fine Art, Mason-Watts Fine Art, Ashgate Galleries. *Work in collections:* Royal Academy (work purchased for Korean Embassy by Ambassador. Shown at London Group), Leicester Galleries, Piccadilly Gallery, Trafford Gallery, Brighton Art Gallery, Roland, Browse and Delbanco, Royal Glasgow Inst. of Fine Arts. *Clubs:* Arts. *Signs work:* "J. Millar." *Address:* 10 Overhill Rd., East Dulwich, London SE22 0PH.

MILLAR, Sir Oliver Nicholas, G.C.V.O., F.B.A., F.S.A.; Director of the Royal Collection and Surveyor of H.M. The Queen's pictures (retd. 1988); Surveyor Emeritus of The Queen's Pictures; *b* Standon, Herts., 26 Apr., 1923. *m* (1954) Delia Dawnay C.V.O. one *s.* three *d. Educ:* Rugby, Courtauld Inst. *Publications:* English Art (1625-1714), with Dr. M. D. Whinney; Abraham van der Doort's Catalogue; Tudor, Stuart and early Georgian Pictures in the Collection of H.M. the Queen; Zoffany and His Tribuna; Later Georgian Pictures in the Collection of H.M. the Queen; Inventories and Valuations of the King's Goods; The Queen's Pictures; Victorian Pictures in the Collection of H.M. the Queen; catalogues; articles in various journals. *Clubs:* Brooks, M.C.C. *Address:* The Cottage, Rays Lane, Penn, Bucks. HP10 8LH.

MILLER, David, R.B.A. (1994), N.D.D. (1958); artist in oil; I.L.E.A. Head of

Dept. for Art in A.E.I. (1971-87); *b* Belfast, 25 Feb., 1931. *m* Monica A. Miller. one *s*. one *d*. *Educ:* Trinity College, Glenalmond, Perthshire. *Studied:* Polytechnic School of Art, Regent St. London (1954-60, Norman Blamey, R.A.). *Exhib:* R.A., R.B.A., R.P., New Soc. of Portrait Painters, and other mixed exhbns. *Signs work:* "DAVID MILLER." *Address:* Flat 2, 76 Auckland Hill, London SE27 9QQ.

MILLER, David T., D.A. (Edin.)., F.R.B.S., Latimer Award, R.S.A. (1961); sculptor in wood, stone, bronze, steel, fibreglass resin; lecturer, Moray House College (1962-81); *b* Bo'ness, 1931. *m* Morag Macmurray. one *s*. one *d*. *Studied:* Gray's School of Art, Aberdeen, Edinburgh College of Art (Eric Schilsky), Paris, Vallauris. *Work in collections:* public sculpture in Edinburgh, Selkirk, Dalkeith, Alyth, Linwood, Moray House, Scottish Arts Council. *Publications:* Sculptures 1941-1991; Behind The Geranium. *Signs work:* see appendix. *Address:* 13 Crichton Village, Pathhead, Midlothian EH37 5UZ.

MILLER, Ingrid, printmaker, painter in etching, drypoint, oil, acrylic, water-colour; *b* Copenhagen, 1940. *m* R.G. Miller, printmaker. *Educ:* Copenhagen University. *Studied:* Malmö Printmaking School. *Exhib:* R.A., R.S.A., Mall Galleries, Leighton House Gallery, Guildhall Gallery, R.A. Copenhagen, National Museum Gdansk, Wainö Aaltonen Museum Finland, Liljevalchs Stockholm, Print Triennales Malmö and Gothenburg. International Print Biennales: Cracow, Ljubljana, Rockford, Horgen, Cadaques, Varna, Maastrich, Biella, Berlin, Fredrikstad; Museums: Kalmar, Eksjö, Kristianstad, Vetlanda, Växjö. *Work in col-lections:* Cabo Frio, Brazil; Swedish States Arts Council; Kalmar Museum. *Clubs:* Swedish and Danish Federations of Printmakers, G.S., D.G. and K.R.O., S.K., K.K.S., F.S.K., Grant Swedish State. *Signs work:* "Ingrid Miller." *Address:* Bolmen, 34194 Ljungby, Sweden.

MILLER, Ronald George, printmaker, painter in etching, mezzotint, engraving, acrylic; sculptor in wood; *b* London, 1938. *m* Ingrid, printmaker. *Educ:* Haverstock Hill Secondary School. *Studied:* Ingrid Miller's Print Workshop, Ljungby, Sweden. *Exhib:* R.A., R.S.A. Edinburgh, International Print Biennales in Ljubljana, Krakow, Grenoble, Cadaques, Varna, Biella, Maastrich, Majdanek, Frechen, Berlin, Fredrikstad; museums in Kristianstad Vetlanda, Kalmar, Växjö, Liljevalchs, 4th National Exhbn. of British Prints, Grundy Gallery, Blackpool. *Work in collections:* Majdanek Museum Poland, Museums in Växjö, Vetlanda, Swedish Arts Council. *Clubs:* Federation of Swedish Printmakers, G.S., K.R.O., S.K., Grant Swedish State. *Signs work:* "Ronald Miller." *Address:* Bolmen, 34194 Ljungby, Sweden.

MILLINGTON, Terence, painter/printmaker in oil, water-colour, etching; *b* B'ham, 20 Oct., 1942. *m* Patricia. one *s*. *Educ:* Moseley Secondary School of Art. *Studied:* painting: B'ham College of Art (1958-63), and printmaking at Manchester College of Art (1965-66). *Exhib:* many group and one-man exhbns. throughout Europe and the U.S.A. *Work in collections:* various private and public including Tate Gallery, and V. & A. *Commissions:* Royal Mail stamp commission 1997 (100th Anniversary of sub post offices). *Publications:* Editions of etchings regularly pub-lished by C.C.A. London and Behr-Thyssen Ltd. New York. *Signs work:* "Terence Millington." *Address:* 'Oakridge', Plymouth Rd., Kingsbridge, Devon TQ7 1AT.

MILLIS, Susan M., S.W.A. (1987), S.E.A. (1995), A.R.M.S. (1997), M.A.S.F.

(1998); pyrographic artist specializing in wildlife, equestrian and pictorial subjects on hand turned wooden paper-weights, pomanders, plaques, jewellery, paper and now blowtorch fire paintings, also works in other media; Vice-Pres. Soc. of Women Artists; *b* Tidworth, Hants., 14 Nov., 1953. *m* Gareth Hughes Millis. one *s*. one *d*. *Educ:* Upbury Manor, Gillingham. *Exhib:* R.M.S., S.W.A., S.E.A., M.A.S.F. annually. Work in private collections worldwide. *Publications:* A Burning Art (Popular Crafts, May 1989). *Signs work:* "S.M. Millis," "Millis" on pastels. *Address:* 26 Doglands Farm, Newtoft, Faldingworth, Lincs. LN8 3NG.

MILLMORE, Mark Alexander, R.E., B.A. (Hons.) Fine Art; artist in etching, painter in oil and water-colour - computer art; *b* Shanklin, I.O.W., 13 Jan., 1956. *m* Catherine de Angelis. *Studied:* Falmouth School of Art (1977-80, Prof. Lionel Miskin). *Exhib:* C.C.A. Galleries, and around the U.K. (1990-95); mixed shows: Japan, U.S.A., Sweden, Taiwan, Australia, Spain, Canada, Kenya and the U.K. *Work in collections:* Ashmolean Museum, Habikino City Hall Japan, Crown Court, Bristol, Victoria A.G. Bath, Kanagawa Prefectural Gallery Japan, Auburn University Contemporary Art Collection U.S.A., International Centre for Wildlife Art Gloucester. *Publications:* 1990: 'Working with Etching' Artists& Illustrators Magazine; 1992: 'Ideas for Images' The Magazine for The International Collector of Water-colours, Drawings & Prints; 1996: 'Medi8or Magic' Pc Answers, 'Birds, Beasts & Fish' Multimedia Cd Rom, 'From Paint to Pixels' Pc Answers; 1997 & 98: Monthly column in Web Masters (Paragon Publishing); Editor of 'Printworks Magazine'. http://eyelid.ukonline.co.uk/print/works.htm Mark Millmore's Ancient Egypt, http://eyelid.ukonline.co.uk/ancient/egypt.htm. Theatre designer: Stinkfoot, a comic opera by Vivian Stanshall (Bristol 1985, London 1988); Rawlinson Dogends, starring Vivian Stanshall (London 1991). *Clubs:* Fellow, Royal Soc. of Painter-Printmakers. *Signs work:* "Millmore." *Address:* Sunnycrest, Abbey Dore, Herefordshire HR2 0AL.

MILLNER, Etienne Henry de la Fargue, figurative sculptor in plaster and clay for bronze; *b* Penang, Malaysia, 15 Jan., 1954. *m* Mary Castle. one *s*. two *d*. *Educ:* Stowe School. *Studied:* Goldsmiths' College (Michael Kenny, R.A., Ivor Roberts-Jones, C.B.E., R.A.), R.A. Schools. *Exhib:* R.A. Summer Shows (1979, 1982, 1984, 1985, 1986, 1988), N.P.G. 'New Faces' (1987), 'Art for Sale' Whiteleys (1992), Chelsea Harbour (1993), Cadogan Gallery Summer Show (1993); one-man show Cadogan Contemporary (1994). S.P.S. Annual Exhbn. (1995-2001), People's Portraits (April 2000 - July 2001). *Work in collections:* N.P.G., Wellington College, Harris Manchester College, Oxford, Goodwood House. *Commissions:* Field Marshal Sir Claude Auchinleck for Wellington College (1992), Capt. Charles Harris, M.C., Statue for Harris Manchester College, Oxford (1997), Rumer Godden (1996), Lord Thurlow (1996), Sir Derek Alun-Jones (1997), Lord Settrington (1999), Hope Pleydell-Bouverie (1999), Count Jules Dembinski (2000). *Clubs:* Chelsea Arts. *Signs work:* see appendix. *Address:* The Barton, West Buckland, Barnstaple, North Devon EX32 0SE. *Email:* etienne@millner.fsnet.co.uk

MILLS, Clive, B.A.Hons. (1987); painter in oil on canvas; *b* Shoreham, Sussex, 7 Mar., 1964. *Educ:* Portslade College. *Studied:* Brighton Polytechnic (1984-87), R.A. Schools (1987-90). *Exhib:* Mall Galleries (group show 1988; Post Grad. show 1989), R.A. Summer Exhbn. (1989). *Work in collections:* South East Arts and private collections including Switzerland. *Signs work:* "Clive Mills." *Address:* 22 Easthill Drive, Portslade, Brighton, E. Sussex BN4 2FO.

MILLS, John W., A.R.C.A., F.R.B.S.; sculptor in bronze; *b* London, 1933. *m* Josephine Demarne. one *s.* one *d. Educ:* Bec School, Tooting. *Studied:* Hammersmith School of Art (1947-54), R.C.A. (1956-60, John Skeaping). *Exhib:* Arts Council, R.A., Alwin Gallery London, Simsar Gallery Michigan, Beaux Arts Gallery Bath. *Work in collections:* Wellcome Foundation, Chicago Inst. of Fine Art, University of Cambridge, University of Michigan, Orient Express, City of London. *Commissions:* Memorials to William Blake and National Firefighter, plus various Royal Mint coins and medals. *Publications:* 8 books on sculpture techniques, recent - Encyclopedia of Sculpture Technique. *Clubs:* Chelsea Arts. *Signs work:* "John W. Mills." *Address:* Hinxworth Pl., Hinxworth, Baldock, Herts. SG7 5HB.

MILLWARD, Michael, M.A., A.M.A.; museum curator; Curator and Museum Manager, Blackburn Museum and Art Gallery; *b* Oldham, 9 Nov., 1944. *m* Dorothy. one *s.* one *d. Educ:* King George V Grammar School, Southport; St. John's College, Cambridge. *Publications:* Victorian Townscape (with Brian Coe) 1974. *Address:* Blackburn Museum and Art Gallery, Museum St., Blackburn, Lancs. BB1 7AJ.

MILNE, Judith Erica, N.D.D. (1965), A.T.D. (1966); painter of botanical, landscape and garden scenes in water-colour; publisher; tutor; *b* Malvern, 30 Oct., 1943. *m* J.A.S. Milne. one *s.* one *d. Educ:* St. Mary's Convent, Worcester. *Studied:* B'ham College of Art and Crafts. *Exhib:* London and various galleries in British Isles. *Commissions:* nationally and internationally. *Publications:* Flowers in Water-colour (B.T. Batsford); Wildflowers in Water-colour (B. T. Batsford, 1995); greetings cards and prints, regular articles for Leisure Painter magazine. *Clubs:* S.F.P. *Signs work:* "Judith Milne." *Address:* 20 Colemans Moor Rd., Woodley, Reading RG5 4DL.

MINERS, Neil, artist in oil, water-colour; *b* Redruth, Cornwall, 19 June, 1931. *m* Wendy Noak. two *d. Studied:* Falmouth School of Art under Jack Chalker (1948) drawing only. *Exhib:* R.I., R.O.I., and Britain in Water-colours; one-man shows and various in Cornwall. *Work in collections:* R.N.L.I., Trinity House and H.R.H. Prince Charles. Official designs and medals, illustrated book and Flags for Tall Ships start from Falmouth (1966). *Signs work:* see appendix. *Address:* 6 Chy Nampara Trevethan Rd., Falmouth, Cornwall TR11 2AH.

MIRECKI, Wladyslaw, painter in water-colour; co-Proprietor of Chappel Galleries; *b* Chelmsford, 1956. *m* Edna Church, née Battye. *Educ:* Kingston Polytechnic (B.Sc. Applied Sciences, 1975-78). *Exhib:* N.E.A.C. (1988), Epping Forest District Museum 'Artists in Essex' (1989), Southend-on-Sea 31st Open (1989), Foyles A.G. (1991), Dept. of Transport Art Competition (1992), Deuxième Salon Biennale de L'Aquarell, Hirson, France (1992), Singer & Friedlander/Sunday Times Water-colour Competition (1997), Beecroft A.G. Open (1997); solo shows: Chappel Galleries (1990, 1996, 1998, 1999), Nanjing, China, Jiangsu Art Museum (1999). *Work in collections:* Essex C.C., Ipswich Museum and Art Gallery, Chelmsford Museum and Art Gallery, Dept. of Culture, Jiangsu, Jiangsu Art Museum, PR China. *Commissions:* Essex C.C., Deputy Lord Lieut. of Essex. *Signs work:* "Mirecki." *Address:* 15 Colchester Rd., Chappel, Essex CO6 2DE.

MISTRY, Dhruva, R.A., M.A. (1981), M.S. University, M.A. (R.C.A. 1983), F.R.B.S. (1993); artist in Residence, Kettle's Yard, Cambridge (1984-85); sculptor in plaster, bronze, stone; Prof. of Sculpture, Faculty of Fine Arts, M.S. University of Baroda (1999); *b* Kanjari (Gujarat) India, 1 Jan., 1957. *Exhib:* over 15 one-man shows worldwide, U.K., India, Japan. *Work in collections:* Tate Gallery, National Museum of Wales, Fukuoka Art Museum, British Council, etc. *Publications:* exhbn. catalogues: Kettle's Yard (1985), Nigel Greenwood Gallery (1990), Fukuoka Art Museum (1994). *Signs work:* "Dhruva Mistry" or "D.M." *Address:* c/o Royal Academy, Burlington House, Piccadilly, London W1V 0DS.

MITCHELL, Brian, R.S.M.A.; painter in oil, water-colour, acrylic; *b* St. Ives, Cornwall, 12 Oct., 1937. *m* Marion. one *s*. *Educ:* Penzance Grammar School. *Studied:* Penzance (1958-60, Bouverie Hoyton), Falmouth (1960-62), Inst. of Educ. London University (1962-63). *Exhib:* R.W.A., R.W.S., R.I., R.B.A., R.S.M.A. *Signs work:* "MITCHELL." *Address:* Gwaynten, Porthrepta Rd., St. Ives, Cornwall TR26 2NZ.

MITCHELL, Enid G. D., F.R.B.S.; Dip.A.D. (Ceramics), Visual Arts Diploma, London University; Ghilchrist Prize; sculptor of portraits and figures cast in bronze, cement and resin, art ceramics in porcelain and stoneware;one *s*. two *d. Educ:* Lady Eleanor Holles School, Hampton, Middx. *Studied:* Ealing School of Art (sculpture tutors, Tom Bailey and Robert Thomas, A.R.C.A.). *Work in collections:* Leamington Spa, Islip Manor and Drayton Green Primary Schools and private collections: England, Holland, Israel, Denmark, U.S.A., etc. *Clubs:* Royal Society of British Sculptors. *Signs work:* "MITCHELL" or "Enid G. D. Mitchell." *Address:* 'Medmenham 2', 32 Stanier St., Swindon, Wilts. SN1 5QX.

MITCHELL, Gordon Kinlay, Dip.Art (Edin.), awarded Post.Dip. Scholarship and Travelling Scholarship; surrealist artist in water-colour, acrylic, oil; full-time professional artist; *b* Edinburgh, 16 Nov., 1952. *m* Catriona A.C. Mitchell. one *s*. one *d. Studied:* Edinburgh College of Art (Sir Robin Philipson, David Michie). *Exhib:* many major exhbns. in the British Isles; one-man shows, Henderson Gallery, Edinburgh (1978, 1981), Open Eye Gallery, Edinburgh (1992), Roger Billcliffe Fine Art, Glasgow (1993). *Work in collections:* Scottish Arts Council, Kansas City Art Inst., Educational Inst. for Scotland, Old City A.G., Jerusalem, Paisley Art Inst., Teachers Whiskey, Scottish Brewers, Alliance & Leicester Bldg. Soc. *Signs work:* "Gordon K. Mitchell." *Address:* 10 Argyll Terr., Haymarket, Edinburgh EH11 2BR.

MITCHELL, John, R.S.W., Mem. S.S.A.; lecturer and writer; works in all media; *b* Glasgow, 21 Dec., 1937. *m* Isabel. two *s*. one *d. Educ:* Glasgow Academy, Royal High School. *Studied:* Edinburgh College of Art, The Open University. *Exhib:* Royal Scottish Academy, Royal Scottish Soc. of Painters in Water-colours, Royal Glasgow Fine Arts Inst., Soc. of Scottish Artists, many one person and group exhbns. *Work in collections:* Fife Council. *Publications:* illustrated: 'Scottish Hill and Mountain Names', 'The Bothy Brew', 'The Cairngorms Scene and Unseen'. *Signs work:* "John Mitchell." *Address:* West Gowanbrae, 4 The Temple, Lower Largo, Fife KY8 6JH.

MITCHELL, S. M., P.P.S.P.S., F.R.B.S., A.R.C.A., N.D.D.; sculptor in clay, wood, stone, fibreglass, resins, concrete, bronze; *b* Farnham. *m* Charles Bone, artist. two *s*. *Educ:* Seager House School, Farnham G.G.S. *Studied:* Farnham School of Art (1946), under Charles Vyes, Guildford School of Art (1947), under Willi Soukop, R.A., Royal College of Art (1948-51), under Frank Dobson, R.A., John Skeaping, R.A., Edward Folkard, F.R.B.S. *Exhib:* R.A., S.P.S., N.E.A.C., W.I.A., Ashgate Gallery, Furneaux Gallery, Canaletto Gallery, Chenil Gallery; 20 one-man exhbns., Medici Gallery, Ashgate Gallery, Gainsborough's House, University of Surrey, Guildford House, Malta, G.C., Tarrystone Gallery, Majorca, Spain, Pasadena, U.S.A. *Commissions:* portrait commissions in bronze, terracotta. Recent portraits: H.R.H The Duchess of Kent, Sebastian Coe, Robert Bolt, Sarah Miles, Sir Edward Tuckwell, Sir George Edwards, and over 200 bronze portrait sculptures. Two 9ft. sculptures for Majorca Legend of Chertsey, forecourt of Thorn PLC, bronze 11ft. high, etc. Designer: ceramic sculpture, including Royal Worcester Porcelain. Elected first woman president Society of Portrait Sculptors (1977). *Signs work:* "S. Mitchell." sometimes (B) after signature. *Address:* Winters Farm, Puttenham, nr. Guildford, Surrey GU3 1AR.

MOCKFORD, Harold, self taught artist in oil; *b* 25 Jan., 1932. *Exhib:* one-man shows: Towner A.G. (1970, 1987), Hove Museum (1980, 1985), Thackeray Gallery, London (1978); R.A. Summer Exhbns., London Group, Newport (Gwent) A.G. (1995). *Work in collections:* Tate Gallery, Chantry Bequest, Towner Gallery, Hove Museum of Art, Government Art Collection. *Signs work:* "H. Mockford" on back of board. *Address:* 45 Hillcrest Rd., Newhaven BN9 9EE.

MOGER, Jill, S.W.A. (2001), S.WL.A. (1999); ceramic sculptor (wildlife) in stoneware, porcelain clay; Council mem. S.WL.A. (1999); *b* London, 1946. *m* Dr. Philip Moger. two *s*. two *d*. *Educ:* Ursuline High School, Ilford, and Saffron Walden County High. *Exhib:* S.W.A., Llewellyn Alexander, 'Nature in Art' Wallsworth Hall, Wildlife A.G. Lavenham, S.WL.A., Bonham's "Art of Living World", Singapore, Yorkshire Sculpture Park; many mixed and two solo exhbns. *Work in collections:* Stoke on Trent City Museum and A.G. *Commissions:* Leeds Playhouse, Yorkshire Museum of Farming. *Publications:* included in 'Drawn to the Forest' by Robert Burton and the S.W.L.A. Awards: S.W.A. President's and Vice President's Award 2001 (Best in Exbn.). *Signs work:* "Jill Moger" (and date) etched into clay. *Address:* The Studio, 75 Millfield Lane, Nether Poppleton, York YO26 6NA.

MOLLOY, Sylvia, M.A.; painter in oil and other media; *b* 27 Mar., 1914. *m* Patrick Molloy. two *s*. *Educ:* Durham, M.A. (English and Art). *Studied:* Johannesburg College of Art (1949-52). *Exhib:* R.A., R.B.A., R.O.I., S.W.A., W.S.; solo shows, six in London, Letchworth, Hitchin, Lavenham; retrospective: 27 Cork St., London (Sept. 1998). *Work in collections:* stained glass in Johannesburg and Pretoria, paintings in East London, Bloemfontein, Pretoria; U.K.: Letchworth A.G., Sax House, Heritage Foundation. *Commissions:* Archbishop Edinburgh, other portraits. *Publications:* autobiography 'Burma Bride' (1995) illustrated with own pictures. Entry in Dictionary of S. African Painters and Sculptors. *Clubs:* N.S., F.P.S. (Fellow). *Signs work:* "Sylvia Molloy." *Address:* 41 Field Lane, Letchworth, Herts. SG6 3LD.

MONCHER-DUNKLEY, Anthea, Mem. S.B.A., S.F.P.; scientific illustrator (botanical and geological) in oil; University illustrator/cartographer and muralist and botanical painter; *b* Isle of Wight, 10 Oct., 1945. *Educ:* private school. *Studied:* Southampton College of art (part-time). *Exhib:* commissioned paintings: Dept. of Geology, Southampton University, and educational establishments; commissioned work in private collections: Egypt, Japan, India, Syria, U.S.A., France and Australia. *Commissions:* private collections worldwide. *Publications:* scientific journals. *Signs work:* "Anthea Moncher Dunkley" and see appendix. *Address:* 'The Studio', 7 Lawn Rd., Portswood, Southampton, Hants. SO17 2EX.

MONTAGUE, Lucile Christine, L.C.A.D. (1974); painter; *b* London, 1950. *m* (1) Michael Montague (divorced). (2) David Greene. one *s. Educ:* Fyling Hall School, Yorks. *Studied:* Plymouth College of Art (1967-69), Byam Shaw School of Art (1971-74). *Exhib:* R.A., Whitechapel Open, London Group, Spirit of London, South Bank Show, Thumb Gallery; group shows: Ikon Gallery touring, 'Ways of Telling' Mostyn Gallery, Llandudno, 'Subjective City' touring, 'Witnesses and Dreamers' touring; 'A Century of Art' Herbert Museum, Coventry; one-man shows, Mario Fletcher Gallery, London; Clayton Gallery, Newcastle; The Studio Gallery, London; Riverside Studios, London. *Work in collections:* Bankers Trust, Coopers and Lybrand, Herbert Museum and A.G., Coventry. *Signs work:* "L.C. Montague." *Address:* 47 Hargrave Pk., London N19 5JW. *Website:* www.axisartists.org.uk *Email:* lucearts@hotmail.com

MONTANÉ, Roger, painter in oil; Prix Bethouard (1948); President, Groupe 109 (1982); *b* Bordeaux, 21 Feb., 1916. married. two *s. Educ:* Toulouse. *Studied:* self-taught. *Exhib:* Chicago (1964), New York (1965), Musée de Toulon (1965). *Work in collections:* Musée d'Art Moderne (Paris), Musées de la ville (Paris), de St. Denis (Paris), de Toulouse, d'Albi, Ishibashi (Tokyo), Groupe International d'Art Figuratif (Japan, 1960), Exposition Particulière la Maison de La Pensée Française, Paris (1961), Aberdeen Museum and Art Gall., Musées de Valence, de Rodez, de Sete, de Bagnols s/Cèze, Wellington Museum (N.Z.), de Grenoble. President, Salon d'Automne (1966-68), Musées de Narbonne, Prague, du Sport (Paris). *Signs work:* see appendix. *Address:* 33 rue Charcot, Paris 13.

MONTGOMERY, Iona Allison Eleanor, B.F.A.(Hons.) (1987), Post.Grad. D.F.A. (1988), R.S.W. (1991); Alexander Graham Munro travel award (1990), Lauder award (1991); artist in painting and printmaking; *b* Glasgow, 14 Apr., 1965. *Educ:* Boclair Academy, Bearsden, Glasgow. *Studied:* Glasgow School of Art (Philip Reeves), Tamarind Inst., Albuquerque, U.S.A. *Exhib:* one-man shows including Galerie Seghaier, Vienna, Ancrum Gallery, Edinburgh Gallery, Lillie A.G., various group shows including R.S.A., R.S.W., R.G.I., G.P.S., Consument Art, also U.S.A. Europe, U.S.S.R., and Japan. *Work in collections:* Lillie A.G., Milngavie, B.B.C., Hilton Hotels, etc. Various teaching including part-time lecturer Edinburgh College of Art. *Clubs:* R.S.W., G.P.S., G.S.W.A., S.A.C. *Signs work:* "Iona A.E. Montgomery." *Address:* 171a Maryhill Rd., Flat 2/3, Glasgow G20 7XL.

MONTGOMERY, James Alexander, artist in water-colour, pen and ink, oil; Leader of Complex of Rehabilitation Units, including Art Therapy; *b* Glasgow, 3 Oct., 1928. *m* Isabelle, artist. two *s.* one *d. Educ:* Woodside School, Glasgow.

Studied: Glasgow School of Art (David Donaldson, Edward Powell), apprenticed to industrial artist. *Exhib:* Columbus City Museum, U.S.A., Carrollton Nova Lomason A.G., Atlanta. *Clubs:* Glasgow Art. *Signs work:* "Hamish Montgomery." *Address:* 13 Avon Ave., Bearsden, Glasgow G61 2PS.

MONTGOMERY, Kate, B.F.A. (Oxon.) 1988, M.A. Fine Art (1992); painter in casein; *b* Wokingham, 5 Nov.,1965. *m* Jonathan Warner. two *d. Educ:* Oxford High School for Girls. *Studied:* Ruskin School of Drawing and Fine Art (1985-88), R.C.A. (1990-92, Prof. Keith Critchlow). *Exhib:* Cadogan Contemporary London, Piccadilly Gallery London, R.A. Summer Show, The Discerning Eye. *Work in collections:* internationally including H.R.H. The Prince of Wales. *Publications:* illustrations for children's book 'Razia, Queen of India' (Hood Hood Books). *Clubs:* London Group. *Signs work:* "Kate Montgomery" on back of work. *Address:* 18 Farm Rd., Hove, East Sussex BN3 1FB

MOOD, Kenneth, B.A. (Hons,); artist/writer, actor (equity member); *b* Gateshead, 24 Nov., 1950. *m* Margaret. one *s.* one *d. Educ:* Gateshead. *Studied:* Sunderland Art College. *Exhib:* Mail Art shows worldwide. *Work in collections:* Arts Council, Whitney Museum (N.Y.), sixty-five U.K. art galleries and museums. *Address:* 1 Burns Cres., Swalwell, Tyne and Wear NE16 3JE.

MOODIE, Stuart, artist-designer in pen and ink, water-colour, acrylic and mixed media; *b* Aberdeen, 7 Apr., 1922. *m* Christiane Bou. two *d. Educ:* Robert Gordon's College, Aberdeen; autodidactic in painting but greatly influenced by Robin Philipson. *Exhib:* Douglas and Foulis Gallery, Edinburgh, Pitlochry Festival Theatre, Craon, La Mayenne, France. *Work in collections:* Britain, America, Canada, Denmark, Spain, France. *Publications:* in the course of a career in architecture has worked on technical illustrations, drawings for architectural submissions, reports and competitions. With his wife, co-owned and ran two private art galleries in Scotland. Taught art to adults in the artists' town of Altea on Spain's Costa Blanca. *Signs work:* "Stuart Moodie" and see appendix. *Address:* 4 rue de la Grotte, Bourg de Coesmes, 35134 France.

MOODY, Catherine Olive, A.T.D. (1944), P.S. (1960), R.B.S.A. (1965), Exhbn. Scholarship R.C.A. (1941); painter in oil and pastel, writer, designer; Head of School of Art, Malvern Hills College (1962-80); President, Malvern Art Club, Editorial Consultant, Leisure Painter periodical; *b* London, 27 Nov., 1920. *Educ:* Stroud High and Thornbank Schools. *Studied:* Malvern School of Art (1935-41, Victor Moody), Royal College Art (1941), Birmingham School of Art (1944, Fleetwood-Walker). *Exhib:* R.A., P.S., R.P., R.B.S.A., R.I.B.A. *Work in collections:* Worcester City A.G., British Rail Archives. *Publications:* Silhouette of Malvern; Painter's Workshop, and articles. *Clubs:* Malvern Art. *Signs work:* "C.O. MOODY" or "C.M." *Address:* 1 Sling La., Malvern, Worcs. WR14 2TU.

MOON, Liz, B.A./M.A. Oxon. (Engineering) 1964, S.W.A. (1987); painter in acrylic, water-colour; Artist Residency, John Innes Centre, Norwich (1997-98), Downing College Cambridge (1999-2000); *b* India, 4 Oct., 1941. *Educ:* Sherborne Girls' School; St. Hugh's College, Oxford; Redlands College, Bristol. *Studied:* San Francisco Art Inst. *Exhib:* R.S.M.A., R.W.A., R.B.A., R.I.; solo shows: Barbican Level 5 West, Royal Opera House, Covent Gdn., John Russell Gallery, Ipswich, and

Clare Hall, Cambridge. "Liz Moon paints the world she knows with amused intensity. Her everyday scenes of people in action are infused with energy and humour." *Work in collections:* John Innes Centre, Norwich; Downing College and Clare Hall, Cambridge. *Publications:* article in The Artist (1987). *Address:* 21 Bermuda Terr., Cambridge CB4 3LD.

MOON, Michael, First prize, John Moores Liverpool Exhbn. (1980), print award, Gulbenkian (1984); painter in mixed media; *b* Edinburgh, 9 Nov., 1937. *m* Anjum Moon. two *s. Educ:* Shoreham Grammar School, Sussex. *Studied:* Chelsea School of Art (1958-62), R.C.A. (1963). *Exhib:* one-man shows in U.K., Australia and U.S.A. including Tate Gallery (1976); numerous group exhbns. worldwide. *Work in collections:* Tate Gallery, Arts Council, Saatchi Collection, provincial and overseas. *Signs work:* "Mick Moon." *Address:* 10 Bowood Rd., London SW11 6PE.

MOON, Tennant, A.R.C.A. (1936), F.S.E.A.D., F.R.S.A., Principal, Cumbria College of Art and Design (1957-78); Principal, Gravesend School of Art and Crafts (1949-57); Lecturer, Leicester College of Art (1946-49); President, National Society for Art Education (1972-73); Chairman, Association of Art Institutions (1976-77); Chairman, Standing Advisory Committee for Art & Design, Associated Examining Board (1970-86); *b* Penarth, Vale of Glamorgan, 12 Nov., 1914. *m* (1) Barbara Ovenden (decd.). one *s.* one *d.*; (2) Joan Whiting. *Studied:* Cardiff School of Art, Royal College of Art under Sir William Rothenstein. *Exhib:* R.A., Leicester Galleries, National Museum of Wales, South Wales Group, Newport (Gwent) A.G., Leicester A.G., etc. *Work in collections:* Cumbria Educ. Com. and private collections. *Clubs:* The New (Cheltenham). *Signs work:* "TENNANT MOON." *Address:* 15 Lansdown Parade, Cheltenham, Glos. GL50 2LH.

MOORE, Bridget, R.A.S.Dip., R.B.A., Greenshield Foundation (1985); painter in oil, gouache and mixed media; *b* Whitstable, 2 Aug., 1960. *m* Alistair Milne. one *s.* one *d. Educ:* The Sir William Nottidge School, Whitstable. *Studied:* Medway College of Design, Epsom School of Art, R.A. Schools. *Exhib:* R.A., R.B.A., numerous mixed shows, London; Enid Lawson Gallery. *Clubs:* Reynolds. *Signs work:* "BRIDGET MOORE" on back. *Address:* 29e Sylvan Rd., Upper Norwood, London SE19 2RU.

MOORE, Gerald John, N.D.D. (1958), A.T.C., A.T.D. (Manc.) (1959), B.A.(Hons.Theol.) (1969), F.R.S.A. (1985); traditional painter in water-colour and oil: landscapes, animals, birds, buildings, historical genre and portraits; *b* Ratby, Leics., 1938. *Educ:* Broom Leys School, Leics. *Studied:* Loughborough (1955-58), Manchester Regional College of Art (1958-59), University of Exeter (Theology 1966-69; History of Art 1974-75). *Exhib:* Teignmouth, Tiverton, Taunton, Widecombe-in-the-Moor, Braunton, Bournemouth, Salisbury and Bristol. *Signs work:* "G.J.M." or "G.J. MOORE." *Address:* Lower Huntham Farm, Stoke St. Gregory, Taunton, Som. TA3 6EY.

MOORE, Heather Ruth, ex S.B.A.; botanical painter in water-colour and oil; now Hon. Lay Mem. S.B.A.; *b* Scarborough, 9 May, 1925. *m* James K.L. (decd.). three *s. Studied:* Scarborough School of Art (1939-41), A.E.C. Tunbridge Wells (Maurice Weidman). *Exhib:* Mall Galleries, Westminster Gallery, Camden Arts Centre, Linnean Soc., Burlington House, etc. *Signs work:* "H.R. MOORE" (initials H.R. linked).

Address: 2 Newlands, Langton Green, Tunbridge Wells, Kent TN3 0BU.

MOORE, Jean Marigold, R.M.S. (1993); Hon. Mention R.M.S. (1995); painter in oil and water-colour, writer; *b* Valletta, Malta, 24 Nov., 1928. divorced. three *s.* *Educ:* privately. *Studied:* Lowestoft School of Art. *Exhib:* Mall, Westminster and Llewellyn Alexander Galleries; also in Brussels at the American Embassy; solo shows in Sussex. *Signs work:* "J.M. MOORE" (oils), "J.M.M." (water-colours and miniatures). Also painted under Dunbar (maiden name) and Seabrook (1st married name). *Address:* 17 Garrod House, 12 Charles Rd., St. Leonards, Sussex TN38 0QD.

MOORE, Ken, painter in oil; director, Commonwealth Biennale of Abstract Art London (1963); *b* Melbourne, Australia, 1923. *Studied:* St. Martin's School of Art under Derrick Greaves, Kenneth Martin, Russell Hall. *Work in collections:* New Britten Museum, Connecticut, Phoenix Art Museum Arizona, Cedar Rapids Art Museum, Iowa, Keppe Gallery, Denmark, Lynam Allen Museum, Connecticut, Finch College Museum, N.Y., Tweed Gallery, Minneapolis, Witchita University, Kansas, Bertrand Russell Foundation, The Australian Ballet, University of Sydney, University of Melbourne, University of New England Armidale, H.R.H. Princess Margaret, King George VI and Queen Elizabeth Foundation, Windsor, The American Legation Museum, Tangier. *Signs work:* "Ken Moore." *Address:* 33 Vicarage Ct., Vicarage Gate, London W8 4HE.

MOORE, Sally, B.A, Fine Art (1984), M.A. Fine Art (1987); prizewinner, Discerning Eye, Mall Galleries, London (1996), Abbey Memorial Scholarship at British School in Rome (1992-1993), Residency at Delfina Studios Trust (1988-1990); painter in oil, self-employed artist; *b* Barry, S. Wales, 7 Apr., 1962. *m* Brendan Hansbro. *Studied:* South Glamorgan Institute, Cardiff (1980-1981), Ruskin School of Drawing and Fine Art (1981-1984), City of Birmingham Polytechnic (1986-1987). *Exhib:* solo exhibs. include Martin Tinney Gallery (1995, 1997, 2000), Long and Ryle Art International, London (1991); group exhibs. include R.A. Summer Exhib. (2000, 2001), Art '94-'99 London with Martin Tinney Gallery. *Work in collections:* National Museum of Wales, Cardiff; Newport Museum and Art Galleries, Wales; Contemporary Art Society U.K.; Contemporary Art Society, Wales; Sunderland Art Gallery; private collections worldwide. *Signs work:* "Sally Moore." *Address:* c/o Martin Tinney, Martin Tinney Gallery, 6 Windsor Pl., Cardiff CF10 3BX. *Email:* mtg@artwales.com

MORAN, Carolyne Sandra Anne, Dip. A.D., A.T.C. (Fine Art); painter in gouache, some oils; formerly head of Art: Queensmount Bournemouth, and Knighton House, Durweston; *b* Trowbridge, Wilts., 27 Dec., 1946. *m* James. two *s.* *Studied:* Bournemouth College of Art, Exeter College of Art, Cardiff Post. Grad. College of Art *Educ. Exhib:* 1989 onwards: R.W.S., Bankside Gallery, London (Open), R.I., Mall Galleries, London (Open), Jerram Gallery, Salisbury, Four Seasons Gallery, Wimborne. *Publications:* The Encyclopedia of Water-colour Techniques, Texture, Houses and Buildings, Water-colour Still Life, The Art of Drawing and Painting, A Compendium of Water-colour Techniques; 'Step by Step' demonstrations for publications - images taken from works for greetings cards. *Address:* Cleohill Cottage, 27 Blandford Rd., Corfe Mullen, Wimborne, Dorset BH21 3HD.

MORESCHI, Maria, A.B.A., F.P.S.; art teacher, portrait artist in oil, pastel and water-colour; art teacher The American School, Cobham; *b* Florence, 18 July, 1949. married. one *s.* two *d. Educ:* SS. Ma. Annunziata. *Studied:* Academia delle Belle Arti; taught portraiture by Annigoni in Florence. *Exhib:* America, Italy, Holland, England. *Work in collections:* La Loggia, Oxshott, Walton, Epsom, Studio 54 Cobham, The Investment Gallery. *Publications:* in the process of illustrating an animal and wildlife drawing book. *Clubs:* Epsom, Oxshott, Walton, Mosley, Cobham, London. *Signs work:* "M. Moreschi." *Address:* A.C.S. Middle School, Heywood, Portsmouth Rd., Cobham, Surrey.

MORETON, Nicolas, B.A.(Hons.) (1985), A.R.B.S. (1995); fine art sculptor in English stones, plaster, clay, bronze, pencil drawing; Resident Sculptor, Manorbier Castle; *b* Watford, Herts., 22 Oct., 1961. *m* Julie Rose Bills. *Educ:* Weston Favell Upper School, Northampton. *Studied:* Nene College, Northampton (1981-82, Frank Cryer), Wolverhampton Polytechnic (1982-85, John Paddison, R.C.A.). *Exhib:* The Discerning Eye; Young Sculptors, Beaux Arts; British Art Fair ('95-2001); Conversation, Milton Keynes Gallery; Sherborne Festival; one-man shows: Mall Galleries (1989, 1991), Lamont Gallery (1992), Hunt Jennings (1993), Goldmark Gallery (1995, 1997, 1999), Peter Gwyther Gallery (2001). *Commissions:* Double public commission, Milton Keynes (1995), Millenium Sculpture, University College Northampton (2001). *Signs work:* drawing "Nicolas Moreton"; sculpture see appendix. *Address:* 4 West Lodge Cottages, London Rd., Courteenhall, Northampton NN7 2QA.

MORGAN, Geri, painter in oil; part time teacher at Hornsey College of Art (1958-1968), Camberwell College of Art (1962-1970), Principal of Byam Shaw School of Art (1970-1991); *b* London, 19 Mar., 1926. three *d. Educ:* The Bec School, Tooting, London. *Studied:* St. Martin's School of Art (1944), Camberwell School of Art (1948-1951). *Exhib:* R.A. Summer Exhibs. regularly since mid 1960s; recent solo exhibs., Duncan Campbell Gallery (1998, 1999). *Work in collections:* private collections in U.K., U.S.A., and Canada. *Commissions:* portrait of President of Institution of Civil Engineers (1991). *Clubs:* Chelsea Arts. *Signs work:* "GERI MORGAN" on verso. *Address:* 7 Mildmay Grove North, London N1 4RH.

MORGAN, Glyn, painter in oil, water-colour, collage; *b* Pontypridd, 16 July, 1926. *m* Jean Bullworthy. *Educ:* Pontypridd Grammar School. *Studied:* Cardiff School of Art (1942-44, Ceri Richards), Camberwell School of Art (1947), East Anglian School (1944-82, Cedric Morris). *Exhib:* one-man shows: Gilbert Parr, London (1978, 1980), Alwin, London (1982, 1983), Richard Demarco Gallery, Edinburgh (1973), Minories, Colchester (1971, 1981), Archway Gallery, Houston, Texas, Chappel Gallery, Essex (1991, 1996, 2001), Rhondda Heritage Park, Y Tabernacl, Wales (1997), 'The Observant Eye' (botanical studies) Chappel Gallery, Essex (1998), oil paintings (1946-98), John Russell Gallery, Ipswich (1998); organised 'The Benton End Circle' exhbn. of work by pupils of Cedric Morris and Lett Haines, Bury St. Edmunds Gallery (1985). *Work in collections:* Auckland and Brisbane A.G's, Derbyshire, Monmouthshire, Oxford and West Riding Educ. Coms., Welsh Arts Council, Contemporary Art Soc. for Wales, Ipswich Borough Museum and A.G., Newport Museum and A.G., National Museum of Wales. *Commissions:* Brecknock Museum, Nat. Library of Wales, Glynn Vivian Art Gallery, Swansea.

Publications: 'A Vision of Landscape', The Art of Glyn Morgan (Chappel Galleries). *Signs work:* "MORGAN." *Address:* Hunters, 120 High St., Hadleigh, Suffolk IP7 5EL.

MORGAN, Helena Frances, Dip. in Textiles (1985), F.F.P.S. (1997), L.C.G.I. (1992); fibre artist; *b* Mountain Ash, Mid Glam., 11 Feb., 1938. *m* Hugh. one *s.* two *d. Educ:* Mountain Ash Grammar School. *Studied:* Gloucs. College of Art (1957-61), Regent St. Polytechnic (1963-64), London College of Furniture (1983-85). *Exhib:* group shows in France, Hong Kong, Hungary, London, and throughout Britain. Work in private collections. *Signs work:* "Helena Morgan." *Address:* Lansbury, 51a High St., Langford, Beds. SG18 9RU. *Email:* hugh@hmorgan.fsnet.co.uk

MORGAN, Howard James, M.F.A., R.P.; painter in oil, water-colour, casein; *b* 21 Apr., 1949. *m* Susan Ann (divorced). two *s.* one *d. Educ:* Fairfax High School. *Studied:* Newcastle-upon-Tyne University (Ralph Holland, Charles Leonard Evetts). *Exhib:* Anthony Mould, Claridges, Agnews, Richmond Gallery. *Work in collections:* N.P.G. *Commissions:* numerous Royal and private commissions. *Clubs:* Chelsea Arts, Beefsteak. *Signs work:* roman numerals of month, followed by arabic year and surname, i.e. "MORGAN II 98." *Address:* (studio) 4011/2 Wandsworth Rd., London SW8; (home) 12 Rectory Grove, Clapham, London SW4.

MORGAN, Jennifer Frances, N.D.D. (1962), A.R.S.M.A.; freelance artist-painter, mostly in oil/gouache, specializing in marine painting, ships, sailing craft, etc.; *b* Woolwich, London, 22 June, 1942. *Studied:* Camberwell School of Art (1960-64, Robert Medley). *Exhib:* various exhbns. in U.K. including Mall Galleries, London, Ferens Gallery, Hull; one-man show: Waterman Fine Art, London (1998), Exhibited Mystic, U.S.A. (1999). *Commissions:* several private commissions over years, including works in Australia, Switzerland, Ireland. *Publications:* catalogues, book illustrations, calendar publications, Ltd. Ed. prints. Finely detailed work sold Sotheby's, London. *Clubs:* R.S.M.A., elected Associate (1996). *Address:* The Nest, Highgate lane, Sutton-on-sea, nr. Mablethorpe, Lincs. LN12 2LH.

MORGAN, Dr. Michael, M.Phil., D.Litt., Hon.LL.D., F.R.S.A., R.I.; artist in water-colour; Trustee and Founding Academician, South West Academy of Fine and Applied Arts; Member Royal Institute of Painters in Watercolours; Founding Trustee, American International University in London; Chairman, Richmond Foundation; Trustee Emeritus, New English College, New Hampshire, U.S.A.; President, Honiton Art Society; *b* 2 June, 1928. *m* Jill. two. *s. Studied:* University of Southampton (M.Phil), Exeter School of Art. *Exhib:* R.I., (winner 1998 R.I., medal), Marine House at Beer, Devon. Work in private collections internationally. *Work in collections:* R.I., Kingsmead Publications/Rowland Hilder Award (2001). *Publications:* featured in 'The Artist' magazine (1992, 1993), 'Art Review' (1999), 'Contemporary Art' (1997, 1998) (Allan & Bertram Ltd.), 'Galleries' (2000). *Clubs:* The Arts Club, Dover St. W1. *Signs work:* "Michael Morgan." *Address:* Valley House, Churchill, Axminster, Devon EX13 7LZ.

MORGAN, Ronald, R.B.A. (1984), R.O.I. (1984); draughtsman, painter in water-colour, black and white, oil and pastel, illustrator, teacher; Mem. Chelsea Art Soc.; *b* Landywood, Staffs., 28 Feb., 1936. *Educ:* Landywood Junior School, Great Wyrley Secondary School, Staffs. *Studied:* Walsall School of Art (1951-53). *Exhib:*

R.A., R.I., R.B.A., N.E.A.C., S.G.A., R.W.A., R.B.S.A., R.S.M.A., R.O.I., Paris Salon, Britain in Water-colours and touring exhbns., etc. *Work in collections:* London Boroughs of Islington, and Tower Hamlets, Graves A.G., Sheffield, Sultan of Oman. *Publications:* work repro.: Leisure Painter, La Revue Moderne (Paris, 1963, 1965), Royal Academy Illustrated. *Signs work:* "R. MORGAN. 1990." *Address:* 8 Marina Ct., Alfred St., Bow, London E3 2BH.

MORGAN, Tina, L.S.I.A.D., A.S.W.A.; painter in oil; art director (1973-1983); *b* Linton, Devon, 1952. *m* Roger. three *s. Studied:* Cornwall College of Art and Design. *Exhib:* R.W.A., R.S.M.A., R.B.A., S.W.A., Southwest Academy, Discerning Eye, Exeter University; solo exhibs. at Albemarle Gallery, Walker Galleries, First Sight Gallery, Marine House at Beer Gallery. *Work in collections:* national and international. Awards: Silver Award, Cannes Film Festival (1980), Campaign Press Award (1980), two awards London Designers and Art Directors Assoc. Gold Award, Cannes (1981), Irish Advertising Award, British Television Award (1982). *Signs work:* "Tina Morgan." *Address:* Woods Cottage, Farringdon, Exeter, Devon EX5 2HY. *Email:* solaris@eclipse.co.uk

MORLEY, John, wood engraver and painter in oil and pastel; *b* Beckenham, Kent, 12 Sep., 1942. *m* Diana. one *d. Studied:* Beckenham Art School, Ravensbourne College of Art, R.A. Schools. *Exhib:* R.A. Summer Exhibs. (1962-2001), Piccadilly Gallery (1977-2001), Brotherhood of Ruralists, International Art Fair, Basle, Cologne, Dusseldorf, London. *Work in collections:* Museum of Modern Art, Wales, Arts Council of Great Britain, Ashmolean Museum, Glasgow City Art Gallery, National Trust, V. & A. Museum. *Clubs:* Soc. of Wood Engravers. *Signs work:* "John Morley." *Address:* North Green Only, Stoven, Beccles, Norfolk NR34 8DG.

MORPETH, Vivienne Helen Bland (née Totty), B.A. Hons. Fine Art (1984), A.M.A. (Art) (1990); curator/fine art; Fine Arts Officer, Middlesbrough Art Gallery (1985-88), Exhbns. Officer, Scunthorpe Museum (1989-92), County Arts and Museums Officer, Cleveland C.C. (1992-95), freelance curator (1995-); *b* Edinburgh, 16 Feb., 1962. *Educ:* The Rudolph Steiner School, Edinburgh. *Studied:* history of art and architecture: University of E. Anglia, Norwich (1981-84). *Exhib:* curated numerous exhbns. at Middlesbrough A.G. and Scunthorpe Museums, local, national, international art and artists tours. *Publications:* exhbn. catalogues. *Address:* 28 Westfield Rd., Barton-upon-Humber, South Humberside DN18 5AB.

MORREAU, Jacqueline, artist in oil; Prof. of Art, Regent's College, London; lecturer, Royal College of Art; *b* Wisconsin, U.S.A. *m* Patrick Morreau. two *s.* two *d. Educ:* Chouinard Art Inst., L.A.; Jepson Art Inst., L.A., (Rico Lebrun); University of California Medical School, San Francisco. *Exhib:* one-person shows: Odette Gilbert (1989, 1990), Art Space, London (1986, 1988), Ferens A.G. (1997), retrospective, one person Ferens A.G., Hull (1988); group shows: Museum of Modern Art, Oxford, 'Women's Images of Men' I.C.A. London and tour, Rochdale A.G., Lamont Gallery, London (1997), Cleveland Drawing Biennial (1996), Cheltenham Drawing Show (1999). *Work in collections:* A.C.G.B., B.M., V. & A., Open University, Nuffield College Oxford, City Art Galleries, Hull, Rochdale A.G., Cleveland A.G. *Publications:* Women's Images of Men with Sarah Kent (1985, 1989), Bibliography Jacqueline Morreau, Drawings and Graphics (1985), From the Interior (Kingston U.

Press, 1997), Themes and Variations (Artemis Press, 1996), Print series, U. of Northumbria (1999), illustrations, Odysseus Poems (Cargo Press). *Signs work:* "J. Morreau." *Address:* 40 Church Cres., London N10 3NE.

MORRELL, Peter John, N.D.D. (Painting, 1956), A.R.C.A. (Painting, 1959), Rome Scholar in Painting (1959), R.W.S. (1983), Mem. London Group (1990); painter in oil and water-colour, lecturer; *b* Newton Abbot, 28 Feb., 1931. divorced. one *s.* one *d. Educ:* Worthing High School for Boys. *Studied:* Kingston-upon-Thames College of Art (1952-56), R.C.A. (1956-59, Ruskin Spear, Carel Weight, John Minton, Colin Hayes). *Exhib:* R.A., John Moores, Grabowski Gallery, New Art Centre, London Group, Beaux Arts Gallery, Arnolfini Gallery, Six Young Painters, Gimpel Fils, R.W.S., Arts Council Touring Exhbns., Gallery Appunto Rome. *Work in collections:* Arts Council, L.C.C., Charterhouse Boys' School, Science Museum. *Commissions:* P. & O. Shipping. *Signs work:* "MORRELL." *Address:* 19 Tremeadow Terrace, Hayle, Cornwall TR27 4AF.

MORRIS, Anthony, R.P., N.D.D. (1958), R.A.S. (1961), N.E.A.C. (1995); painter/illustrator in oil and water-colour; *b* Oxford, 2 Aug., 1938. *m* Aileen. *Studied:* Oxford School of Art, R.A. Schools (Peter Greenham). *Exhib:* R.A., R.P., Medici Gallery. *Work in collections:* Bodleian Library, Open University, King's College Hospital. *Publications:* B.B.C. and major publishers. *Signs work:* "MORRIS." *Address:* Church House, Cloduck, Longtown, Herefordshire HR2 0NY.

MORRIS, Caroline Nova, Dip. in Fashion; fashion designer; *b* Dewsbury, 31 Oct., 1965. *m* Christopher Thomas Morris. one *s. Educ:* Stourfield and Beaufort Schools, Bournemouth, and the School of Fashion, Bournemouth and Poole College of Art and Design. Practices as Caroline Nova Fashions. *Address:* 99 Carbery Ave., Southbourne, Bournemouth BH6 3LP.

MORRIS, James Shepherd, R.S.A., M.L.A., F.R.I.A.S., A.R.I.B.A.; Mem. Arts Council of Gt. Britain (1973-80), Vice-Chairman, Scottish Arts Council (1976-80), Arts Council Enquiry into Community Arts (1974), Trustee, Nat. Mus. of Antiquities (1980-86), Past Chairman, Scottish Arts Council Art Com.; Convenor Fellowship Com. R.I.A.S. (1982-87); Mem. Council R.S.A., Hon. Treasurer R.S.A. (1990, 1999); Partner, Morris and Steedman, Architects and Landscape Architects, Edinburgh; *b* St. Andrews, Fife, 22 Aug., 1931. *m* Eleanor Kenner Smith. two *s.* one *d. Studied:* Edinburgh College of Art, University of Pennsylvania. R.I.B.A. Award (1974), European Heritage Award (1975), Nine Civic Trust Awards (1962-90), two highly commended Geraldine Scott Design Awards (1995), two R.I.B.A. awards for Scotland (1989, 1974), three A.P.R.S. Awards (1977-89). *Exhib:* R.S.A. *Work in collections:* R.S.A. *Clubs:* New (Edinburgh), Philadelphia Cricket (Philadelphia), Valderrama (Spain). *Address:* Woodcote Pk., Fala, Midlothian, Scotland EH37 5TG.

MORRIS, John, Mem., Water-colour Soc. of Wales; painter in water-colour; *b* Deiniolen, N. Wales, 27 Sept., 1922. *m* Eluned Mary. one *s.* one *d. Educ:* Brynrefail County School, Bangor Normal College. *Studied:* Bangor Normal (1955-57, H. Douglas Williams), Press Art School, London (1958-60, Percy V. Bradshaw). *Exhib:* Williamson A.G. Birkenhead, Oriel Theatre Clwyd Mold, Wrexham Arts Centre, Albany Gallery Cardiff, R.I., N.S., Royal National Eisteddfod of Wales, Water-colour Soc. of Wales. *Work in collections:* Royal Welsh Agricultural Soc., National

Library of Wales, Midland Bank Ltd., Burnley Building Soc., Clwyd C.C., Shotton Paper Co. *Publications:* Newid Aelwyd, Newid Bro. *Signs work:* "John Morris." *Address:* Elidir, 46 Bryn Awelon, Yr Wyddgrug (Mold), Clwyd CH7 1LU, N. Wales.

MORRIS, John Meirion, N.D.D. (1959), A.T.D. (1961), M.Phil. (1989), R.C.A. (2000), Glyndwr Award (2001); sculptor in bronze; lecturer at University of Kumasi, Ghana (1966-1967), Aberystwyth University (1968-1981), Bangor University (1985-1990); *b* Wales, 14 Mar., 1936. *m* Gwawr. two *s.* one *d. Educ:* Bala Boys Grammar School. *Studied:* Liverpool College of Art (1955-1961). *Exhib:* Piccadilly Gallery, Cork St., London, National Museum Galleries of Wales, Cardiff (1999), Glynn Vivian Art Gallery, Swansea (2000); solo exhibs. Y Tebernacl Museum of Modern Art, Wales (2000), Bangor Museum and Art Gallery, Wales (2001). *Work in collections:* five portrait heads in bronze at National Library of Wales, Aberystwyth, portrait head of Lord Hooson (2001), memorial to the celtic scholar Edward Lhuyd at Aberystwyth (2001), designed cross to commemorate the poet R.S.Thomas (2001). *Signs work:* "J.M.M." *Address:* Griolen, Erwnant, Brynrefail, Caernarfon, Gwynedd LL55 3PB.

MORRIS, Mali, B.A. (1968), M.F.A. (1970); artist in acrylic on canvas, watercolour etc. on paper; Senior lecturer, Chelsea School of Art; *Studied:* University of Newcastle upon Tyne (1963-68), University of Reading (1968-70). *Exhib:* 17 solo shows since 1979, including Ikon Gallery, Serpentine Gallery and Saoh Gallery, Tokyo; many group shows worldwide. *Work in collections:* A.C.G.B., British Council, Contemporary Arts Soc., Eastern Arts Assoc., Lloyds of London, National A.G., Botswana, Northern Arts, W.A.C., Whitworth Gallery, Manchester, etc. and private collections. Many awards, including Lorne Award. *Signs work:* "Mali Morris." *Address:* 76 Royal Hill, Greenwich, London SE10 8RT.

MORRIS, Stanley William, M.Ed. (1976), A.T.D. (1951), A.R.B.S.A., M.F.P.S.; *b* 1922. *Studied:* Birmingham College of Art, University of Manchester. *Exhib:* Paris Salon, R.O.I., N.E.A.C., U.A.S., R.B.S.A., Birmingham University, Keele University. *Work in collections:* Midlands Arts Centre, wood carving for Prince of Wales Regt., Leeds Permanent Building Soc., Alexander Ross. *Address:* Bromley Cottage, Ashbrook La., Abbots Bromley, Staffs. WS15 3DW.

MORRIS-JONES (née TURNER), Muriel (Moo), R.D.S. Hons.; no formal art education; City & Guilds 'Post graduate' painting prize, prizes for water-colours, drawings and prints; portrait painting;one *s.* one *d. Exhib:* U.S.A. (1963-69), Belgium, London. *Work in collections:* U.S.A., Belgium. *Commissions:* bronze bust of Princess Diana at Gt. Ormond Street Hospital. Intellectual Property, patents granted U.S.A. and U.K. *Publications:* cartoons 'Women Draw 84' and Sunday Times; 'Science and Public Affairs' (Christmas 1999). *Signs work:* early work: "MURIEL TURNER," now "M. Morris-Jones." *Address:* 26 Old Gloucester St., Bloomsbury, London WC1N 3AF.

MORRISON, James, R.S.A., R.S.W., D.Univ., D.A.; painter in oil and water-colour; paints extensively in the high Arctic; *b* Glasgow, 1932. married. one *s.* one *d. Educ:* Hillhead High School, Glasgow School of Art. *Exhib:* Edinburgh, London, Glasgow, New York, Toronto, Florence, Dusseldorf, The Hague, Johannesburg, Tokyo. *Work in collections:* Glasgow, Dundee and Aberdeen Art galleries, Arts

Council, Argyll, Dundee and Edinburgh Educ. Committees, Glasgow, Edinburgh, Strathclyde and Stirling Universities, H.R.H. the Duke of Edinburgh, Dept. of the Environment, various embassies, Kingsway Technical College, Vaughan College, Leicester, Municipality of the Hague, Earls of Dalhousie, Moray, Airlie, Robert Fleming, Merchant Bankers, BBC, Grampian Television, General Accident, Scottish Amicable, Life Assoc. of Scotland; Banks: Royal, Scotland, Clydesdale, T.S.B. *Commissions:* numerous private and public. *Publications:* author, Affthe Squerr. *Signs work:* "Morrison" and date. *Address:* Craigview House, Usan, Montrose, Angus DD10 9SD.

MORROCCO, Leon, D.A., (Edin.), A.R.S.A., R.G.I.; painter in oil and mixed media; *b* Edinburgh, 4 Apr., 1942. *m* Jean Elizabeth Selby. two *s. Educ:* Harris Academy, Dundee. *Studied:* Duncan of Jordanstone College of Art, Dundee (1960, Alberto Morrocco, R.S.A.), Slade School of Fine Art (1960-61, Sir William Coldstream), Edinburgh College of Art (1961-65, Sir Robin Philipson, R.S.A.). *Exhib:* 20 one-man shows since 1966, Scotland, London, Melbourne, Sydney. *Work in collections:* U.S.A., Britain, Australia, etc. *Clubs:* Chelsea Arts. *Signs work:* "Leon Morrocco." *Address:* c/o Royal Scottish Academy, The Mound, Edinburgh EH2 2EL.

MORROW, Elizabeth Eleanor, D.A. (Belfast, 1954), U.S.W.A. (1961), U.W.S. (1967); housewife, painter in water-colour; Hon. Sec. Ulster Soc. of Women Artists; *b* Enniskillen, Co. Fermanagh, 14 Apr., 1926. *m* T.A. Morrow (decd.). one *s.* two *d. Educ:* Enniskillen Collegiate Grammar School. *Studied:* Belfast College of Art. *Exhib:* R.I., R.U.A., U.S.W.A., U.W.S., S.WL.A. *Clubs:* U.S.W.A., U.W.S. *Address:* 33 Kensington Gardens South, Belfast BT5 6NN, Northern Ireland.

MORSE, Colin Benjamin Scale, Dip.A.D. (1982); illustrator in water-colour and mixed media; *b* Pembrokeshire, 6 Aug., 1942. *m* Roberta Wilson. one s- *d. Educ:* Haverfordwest Grammar School. *Studied:* Dyfed College of Art, Carmarthen (1978-82); work on display in various commercial galleries throughout U.K. *Publications:* limited edition prints – images of the coast, countryside and people of Wales. *Signs work:* "Colin Morse." *Address:* Priskilly Fawr Farm, Hayscastle, Haverfordwest, Pembrokeshire SA62 5QF. *Website:* www.bestofruralwales.co.uk / www.welshpictures.co.uk

MORTIMER, Justin Roger, B.A. Fine Art (1992); painter in oil; *b* U.K., 6 Apr., 1970. *Educ:* Wells Cathedral School. *Studied:* Slade School (1988-1992). *Exhib:* solo exhibs., Beaux Arts, Bath (1993), Blue Gallery, London (1995, 1997, 1998), Lefevre Contemporary (2000). *Work in collections:* National Portrait Gallery, NatWest Collection, Henley River & Rowing Museum, Royal Collection, R.S.A. *Commissions:* portraits of Harold Pinter (N.P.G. 1992), David Bowie & Iman (1994), H.M. The Queen Elizabeth (R.S.A. 1998), Lord Chamberlain (Airlie, R.C.A. 1998), Steve Redgrave (1998). *Signs work:* "J Mortimer." *Address:* 165 Victoria Rd., London NW6 6TE. *Email:* justinmortimer@hotmail.com

MORTIMER, Martin Christopher Fortescue, Consultant, Delomosne & Son Ltd. Specialist in English Porcelain, English and Irish Glass, particularly English glass lighting fittings, and articles on these subjects in various art journals; *b* London, 4 July, 1928. *m* Sara Ann Proctor. *Educ:* Shrewsbury School. *Publications:* author,

The English Glass Chandelier (Antique Collectors' Club, 2000). *Address:* Court Close, North Wraxall, Chippenham, Wiltshire SN14 7AD.

MORTON, Cavendish, R.I., R.O.I., Hon. S.G.A., Hon. N.S.; painter of landscape, marine, in oil, water-colour, black and white; Vice Pres., Gainsborough's House Society, Vice-Pres., Norfolk Contemporary Arts Society; Past Chairman, Isle of Wight Council for the Arts, Vice-Pres., Isle of Wight Art Society; *b* Edinburgh, 17 Feb., 1911. *m* Rosemary Britten. one *s.* two *d. Exhib:* R.A., R.B.A., U.S.A., Canada, Australia, Bermuda; one-man shows: London, York University, Norwich, King's Lynn, Sudbury, Ipswich, Aldeburgh, Henley, Portsmouth. *Work in collections:* B.M., Norwich Castle Museum, Wolverhampton A.G., Contemporary Arts Society, Eastern Arts Assoc., I.O.W. Cultural Services, Glasgow City A.G., Royal Naval Museum, Gustav Holst Museum, National Trust. *Commissions:* Review of The Cumberland Fleet, Royal Thames Yacht Club. *Publications:* illustrations for Dorothy Hammond Innes' Occasions (Michael Joseph, 1972), What Lands are These (Collins, 1981), and The Bembridge Redwings, David Swinstead (1997). *Signs work:* "CAVENDISH MORTON." *Address:* 6 Fairhaven Cl., Bembridge, I.O.W. PO35 5SX.

MOSELEY, Austin Frank, R.B.S.A. (1988), C.A.S. (1987), C.Eng.M.I.Mech.E. (1958); painter in oil, ink, pastel, charcoal; *b* Tividale, Staffs., 25 Apr., 1930. *m* Sylvia. two *s. Educ:* Dudley Technical College. *Studied:* Dudley School of Art. *Exhib:* R.B.S.A., Chelsea Arts Soc., Dudley Mid. Art, Llewellyn Alexander (London), John Noott (Broadway), R.O.I. *Work in collections:* Dudley Metropolitan County Borough, R.B.S.A, and many private and commercial collections. *Signs work:* "Austin Moseley." *Address:* 24 Raglan Cl., Sedgley, Dudley, W. Midlands DY3 3NH.

MOSELEY, Malcolm, B.A. (1969), M.A. (1973); painter; *b* Birmingham, 1947. *m* Christine. one *s.* one *d. Studied:* Birmingham College of Art (1965), Winchester School of Art (1966-69), Central School of Art (1969-70), R.C.A. (1970-73). *Exhib:* R.A., R.S.W., London Group, Mall Galleries, Barbican, Eastern Open, New English, Laing Landscape, Suffolk Group. *Work in collections:* Ipswich Museums, P. & O., McDonalds, Hammersmith and Fulham Council. *Clubs:* Ipswich Art Soc., Suffolk Group. *Signs work:* "M.M." *Address:* 133 Norwich Rd., Ipswich, Suffolk IP1 2PP.

MOUNT, Paul Morrow, A.R.C.A. (1948); sculptor; *b* Newton Abbot, 8 Jun., 1922. *m* June Miles. one *s.* one *d. Educ:* Newton Abbot Grammar School. *Studied:* R.C.A. (1940-1941 & 1946-1948) under Gilbert Spencer, Percy Horton. *Exhib:* Architectural Assoc., Drian Gallery, Whibley Gallery, South West Arts, Marlborough, New Art Centre, Beaux Arts Gallery, Penwith Gallery, Falmouth Art Gallery. *Work in collections:* Hyde and Fermi, U.S.A., Dept. of Environment, Stanley Picker Trust, Cornwall County, Exeter University. *Commissions:* Swiss Embassy; Chase Manhattan Bank; Tafawa Balewa Sq., Lagos, Nigeria; Ibadan University, Cocoa House, Ibadan; Cabinet Offices, Accra; British Steel, York House, Bristol; C.W.S., Falmouth. *Publications:* Agnes Holbrook, under pseudonym, Andrew Morrow, Minerva Press (2001). *Signs work:* "Paul Mount." *Address:* Nancherrow Studio, St. Just, Penzance, Cornwall TR19 7LA.

MOUNTFORD, Derylie Anne, S.W.A. (1988); artist in pencil, etching, oil and water-colour; *b* London, 17 June, 1943. *m* Malcolm Mountford, B.A.(Oxon.). two *s.*

Educ: Montessori, Wimbledon. *Studied:* Byam Shaw School of Art (1960-62, Peter Greenham, Bernard Dunstan), St. Martin's School of Art (1963), University of Brighton (B.A. Hons. History of Design, 1998). *Exhib:* R.A., R.B.A., R.M.S., S.W.A., N.S.P.S., C.D.S.; one-man shows: Japan (1986, 1988), Lyric Theatre, Hammersmith (1990), Cambridge (1988); group shows: Cambridge, Ely, Saffron Walden, Salisbury, London, Sussex, etc. *Work in collections:* Addenbrookes Hospital Trust. *Signs work:* "Derylie Mountford" (etchings), "D. Mountford" (paintings). *Address:* 3 Belle Vue Gdns., Brighton, Sussex BN2 2AA.

MOWAT, Jane Catherine, B.A. (Hons.) History of Art, P.G.C.E. (Art); artist/printmaker in woodcuts; *b* Stamford, Lincs., 5 Apr., 1956. one *s.* one *d.* *Studied:* Courtauld Inst. of Art - Art History (1975-78, Anita Brookner, George Zarnecki). *Exhib:* many Open Exhbns. in South West, including R.W.A., and London, Royal Academy, Curwen Gallery, Air Gallery, National Print at Mall Galleries. *Commissions:* Screen for Russell-Cotes Museum, Bournemouth. *Publications:* illustrated: You and Your Child's Behaviour (Birmingham and Redditch Health Authority, 1984). *Clubs:* Printmakers Council, Somerset Printmakers. *Signs work:* "Jane Mowat." *Address:* 5 Palmerston Rd., Taunton, Som. TA1 1ES.

MOXLEY, Ray, F.R.I.B.A., R.W.A., Hon. F.(W.Eng.); *b* 28 June, 1923. *m* Ann. one *s.* two *d. Educ:* Caterham. *Studied:* architecture: Oxford (1940-42 and 1946-49). *Exhib:* R.W.A. annual 1960 onwards, A.C.A. Salons at the Royal Academy (1982, 1984, 1986). *Commissions:* architect of Chelsea Harbour and Exhibition Centres; Vice-president R.I.B.A. (1971-74), Chairman A.C.A. (1974-76). *Publications:* Building Construction (Batsford), Fee Negotiations (A.P.), Architects Eye (G.P.C.), Building Management by Professionals (Butterworth). *Signs work:* "Ray Moxley." *Address:* 10 The Belvedere, Chelsea Harbour, London SW10 0XA.

MOYSE, Arthur, artist in collage, water-colour, pen and ink; art critic for Freedom Press, London Correspondent for Chicago Industrial Worker; *b* London, 21 June, 1914. *Educ:* Addison Gardens L.C.C. Primary School. *Exhib:* Angela Flowers Gallery, Woodstock and others. *Work in collections:* Transport Museum. *Publications:* More in Sorrow, Zero One, Revolutionary Manifesto, Peterloo. *Clubs:* Hon. Mem. Chelsea Arts. *Signs work:* "Arthur Moyse." *Address:* 39 Minford Gdns., W. Kensington, London W14 0AP.

MUIR, Jane, artist, in mosaic, etching and water-colour; *b* 1929. *m* A. W. E. Muir. two *s. Educ:* Rye St. Antony School. *Studied:* Oxford University, Teesside College of Art. M.A. Oxon (1950), Dip. Architectural Decoration (1969), F.C.S.D. (1974). *Exhib:* numerous. Founder Mem. International Assoc. of Contemporary Mosaic Artists, U.K. exhibitor Ravenna (1980), Trier (1984), Louvain (1986), Tokyo (1994), Alexandria (1996), Exeter (1999), Touring Anglo-Italian Mosaic Exhbn. (2000). Patron, British Assoc. for Modern Mosaic. *Work in collections:* Public: Oxon County Museum, Buckinghamshire County Museum, Glynn Vivian A.G., Open University, St. Anne's College, Oxford; Ruskin Gallery, Sheffield; Corning Museum, U.S.A. Major Commissions: St. Anne's College Oxford; Open University; Princes Sq., Glasgow; Longmarket, Canterbury; Becket's Well, Northampton; Doha, Arabian Gulf. *Publications:* videos: 'Mosaic as Art', 'New Directions in Mosaic'. *Clubs:* Art

Workers' Guild Soc. of Designer Craftsmen. *Signs work:* "Muir." *Address:* Butcher's Orchard, Weston Turville, Aylesbury, Bucks. HP22 5RL.

MUIRDEN, Philip, R.A. David Murray Student, N.D.D., A.T.D.; Lecturer, Mansfield College of Art (1965-72), Senior lecturer, Newport College of Art (1975-); *b* Oct., 1932. *Educ:* Haverfordwest Grammar School. *Studied:* Cardiff College of Art, Cardiff University. *Exhib:* R.A. (5 yrs.), Sunday Times Water-colour of the Year (2 yrs.), Hunting Group - Britain in Water-colour; one-man shows include Newport Gallery (2). *Work in collections:* Arts Council of Wales, Contemporary Art Soc., Mold Council, Newport Museum, Newport Council S.Glam. *Publications:* Poems TV B.B.C. Wales, and Swap Shop National B.B.C.; articles for Art News and Review. *Clubs:* The Welsh Group, W.S.W. *Signs work:* "PHILIP MUIRDEN" or "MUIRDEN." *Address:* 6 Hill St., Hakin, Milford Haven SA73 3LP.

MULES, Joanna Mary, B.Ed. (1977), A.R.U.A. (1990); artist in pastel, print-making, water-colour; art teacher, Rockport School, part-time lecturer, School of Architecture, Queen's University, Belfast; *b* Hants., 4 Sept., 1949. *m* Marcus Patton. three *s. Educ:* Elmhurst Ballet School, Camberley, Surrey (1957-63), Londonderry High School (1963-66). *Studied:* Belfast College of Art and Design (1966-68). *Exhib:* Bell Gallery, Arts Club, Belfast. *Work in collections:* D.O.E., but mainly private collections. *Commissions:* National Self-portrait Collection, Limerick. *Publications:* Gape Row, Night of the Big Wind. *Clubs:* R.U.A. *Address:* Ingledene, Sans Souci Park, Belfast BT9 5BZ. *Email:* jpatton@rockportschool.com

MULLEN, Kay, S.W.A. (1993), S.B.A. (1995), A.R.M.S. (1998); self taught painter in water-colour gouache, pastel and mixed media; Winner of Alexander Gallery Award, S.W.A. (1999); *b* Mottingham, Kent, 3 Sept., 1959. one *d. Educ:* Nonsuch High School for Girls, Cheam, Surrey. *Studied:* City and Guilds, - teaching of adults in further education. *Exhib:* S.W.A., S.B.A. and R.M.S. at Westminster Central Halls, many mixed exhbns. *Commissions:* numerous for private collections. *Publications:* work repro.: Medici, The Paper House Group and Quatro Publishing. *Address:* 1b Parkhurst, Epsom, Surrey KT19 8QZ.

MULLETT, Vivien, A.R.M.S. (1992), H.S. (1990), B.A. Fine Art (1974); artist in water-colour, graphic designer; *b* Oxford, 1952. *Educ:* Milham Ford School, Oxford. *Studied:* Reading University (1970-74). *Exhib:* R.A. Summer Show, R.M.S., H.S., M.A.S.-F. *Publications:* illustrated The Night Watchman - collection of stories. *Signs work:* "VM." *Address:* 111 Penwith Rd., Earlsfield, London SW18 4PY.

MULLINGS, Pam, freelance artist of British wildlife in gouache; *b* Littlehampton, 18 Jan., 1940. *m* Maurice. one *s.* one *d. Exhib:* London and West Country. *Clubs:* H.S., A.R.M.S. *Signs work:* "Pam Mullings." *Address:* 'Rough Close', 13 Park Lane, Seend Cleeve, Melksham SN12 6PT.

MULLINS, Edwin Brandt, B.A., M.A. (Hons.) Oxford University (1957); writer and film-maker, mainly on art subjects; *b* London, 1933. *m* Gillian Brydone (d. 1982). one *s.* two *d.*; Anne Kelleher (1984). *Educ:* Midhurst Grammar School and Oxford University. *Publications:* numerous books and over 200 television films. *Address:* 25 The Crescent, Barnes, London SW13 0NN.

MUMBERSON, Stephen Leonard, R.E. (1995), M.A. (1981), B.A. (Hons.)

(1977); Reader in Fine Art Printmaking; *b* Beaconsfield, 16 Feb., 1955. *Educ:* Secondary Modern School, Bucks. *Studied:* Brighton Polytechnic (1977-78), R.C.A. (1978-81, Prof. Grant, Prof.Chris. Orr), Cité des Arts, Paris (1980). *Exhib:* R.E., Bankside London, Art Now London, P.M.C. *Work in collections:* V. & A., U.S.A., Japan, S.America, Europe, Canada, Zambia, Zimbabwe. *Signs work:* "Stephen Mumberson" or "S. Mumberson." *Address:* c/o Fine Art Dept., School of Art, Design and Performance, Middlesex University, Quicksilver Pl., Western Rd., London N22 6XH.

MUNDY, William Percy, R.M.S., M.A.A., M.A.S.F., H.S.; self taught artist in water-colour and oil, miniaturist, portrait and Trompe l'oeil painter; *b* Wokingham, 30 Oct., 1936. *Educ:* Forest School, Berks. *Exhib:* R.A., R.M.S., R.P. Awarded "Exhibit of the Year" at 1980 and 1982 R.A. Summer Exhbns; Silver medal, Paris Salon (1982); Gold Memorial Bowl, R.M.S. (1986); Bell Award (1987); Best of Show M.A.S.F. (U.S.A.) (1997); Bell Award (1996, 2000); Best of Show H.S. (2001). *Work in collections:* H.M. The Queen; H.R.H. The Duke of Edinburgh; H.M. King Bhumipol Aduladej of Thailand; The Yang di Pertuan Agong of Malaysia; H.R.H. The Sultan of Johor; H.R.H. The Sultan of Oman; V. & A., London; Cincinatti Museum of Art, U.S.A. *Clubs:* Tanglin, Singapore; Phyllis Court, Henley. *Signs work:* "W. P. Mundy." *Address:* 2 Marsh Mills, Wargrave Rd., Henley-on-Thames, Oxon. RG9 3JD.

MUNSLOW, Angela E., H.N.C., Grad.R.I.C., B.Ed.Hons.; sculptor in bronze, resin, terracotta, ceramic, cement and plaster, glass; figurative painter in oil, water-colour and pastel; *b* Sandbach, Ches. *m* Peter. two *s. Educ:* Ravenscroft Hall School, Cheshire; N.Staffs. Polytechnic (now Staffs. University); Crewe and Alsager C.H.E. (now Manchester University). *Studied:* sculpture: Sir Henry Doulton School of Sculpture. *Exhib:* Expo '92 Seville; group shows: St. Martin in the Fields, Mall Galleries, Westminster Gallery, and galleries in the North-West and Midland regions. *Work in collections:* Royal Doulton Museum, Stoke-on-Trent, Stapeley Water Gdns., Nantwich Ches., The Gallery, Manchester Art House; private collections. *Commissions:* 'Harmony' (Stapeley Water Gdns.); 'Heredities'; Garden Sculpture - a series of fairies (Tile House Statuettes). *Clubs:* S.W.A., Soc. of Staffordshire Artists. *Signs work:* "A.E. Munslow" and see appendix. *Address:* Mayfield Studio, 65 Station Rd., Alsager, Stoke-on-Trent ST7 2PD.

MURISON, Neil, A.T.D. (1951), R.W.A. (1979); painter in oil and acrylic; Co-ordinator, Dept. of Foundation Studies, Bristol Polytechnic (1961-87); previously art master, Queen Elizabeth's Hospital, Bristol (1952-61); *b* Bath, 10 Oct., 1930. *m* (1) Valerie Elizabeth John. one *s.* one *d.*; (2) Sheila May Tilling (1985). *Educ:* Bristol Grammar School. *Studied:* West of England College of Art (1946-51). *Work in collections:* Nuffield, Wills Tobacco Co., Bank of America, Skopje Modern Art Museum, Yugoslavia, Trumans Breweries, Bridgwater Public Library, Bristol, Devon, Leeds, Herts., Hull, Leics., Liverpool, Surrey and West Riding of Yorks, Educ. Authorities. *Signs work:* "Murison." *Address:* 110 Redland Rd., Redland, Bristol BS6 6QU.

MURPHY, Richard, B.A. (Hons.), Dip.Arch., F.R.S.A., A.R.I.A.S., A.R.S.A., R.I.B.A.; architect; recipient of ten R.I.B.A. awards; *b* Cheshire, 24 Apr., 1955.

Educ: Newcastle and Edinburgh Universities. *Commissions:* Fruitmarket Gallery, Dundee Contemporary Arts, Stirling Tolbooth Arts Centre. *Publications:* The Works of Richard Murphy Architects (1977), two books on Carlo Scarpa. *Signs work:* "Richard Murphy." *Address:* 34 Blair St., Edinburgh EH1 1QR. *Email:* mail@richardmurphyarchitects.com

MURRAY, Dawson Robertson, D.A. (1965); Post-grad (1966); B.A. Hons. (1982); R.S.W. (1988); R.G.I. (1995); Head of Art and Design, Bolcair Academy (1976-94); President, Glasgow Group of Artists (1990-94); Vice President, R.S.W. (1993-96); painter in water-colour, acrylic, etching; atmospheric abstractions of garden themes; *b* Glasgow, 25 June, 1944. *m* Liz Murray. two *d. Educ:* Albert Senior Secondary, Glasgow. *Studied:* Glasgow School of Art (1961-66), L'Accademia delle Belle Arti, Venice (1966). *Exhib:* solo: Nancy Smillie Gallery, Glasgow (1997), Richard Demarco Gallery (1995, 1990); group shows: Encuentro Acuarela Santa Cruz (1994), Scottish Etching, G.P.S., (1994), 5th Drawing Triennale, Wroclaw (1992), Mini-print Cadaques (1988), Winter Festival Sarajevo (1988), Galleria del Cavallino, Venice (1983). *Work in collections:* S.A.C., B.B.C. Scotland. *Signs work:* "Dawson Murray." *Address:* The Old Post Office, Kilmany, Cupar, Fife KY15 4PT.

MURRAY, Donald, B.A., D.A.; artist and designer in calligraphy, water-colour and pastel; Head of Art, Robert Gordon's College, Aberdeen; *b* Edinburgh, 1940. *m* Mary F. Low. two *s. Educ:* George Heriot's School, Edinburgh. *Studied:* Edinburgh College of Art (1958-63). *Exhib:* R.S.W., S.S.A., Pitlochry Festival Theatre, Aberdeen Artists' Society. *Work in collections:* Edinburgh District Council, Heriot-Watt University, Moray House College of Education, Edinburgh Merchant Company. *Commissions:* Illuminated scrolls and miscellaneous formal calligraphy: Aberdeen City Council; Orkney Islands Council. *Publications:* illustrated Growing up in the Church, Christian Symbols, Ancient and Modern. *Signs work:* "Donald Murray." *Address:* Manorlea, Commerce St., Insch, Aberdeenshire AB52 6JB.

MURRAY, Liz, D.A. (1965), S.S.A. (1991), R.S.W. (1992); painter in mixed media - collage including stitched and moulded paper; *b* Aberdeen, 1943. *m* Dawson Murray. two *d. Educ:* Dundee High. *Studied:* Duncan of Jordanstone College of Art, Dundee (1961-65). *Exhib:* regularly at R.S.A., R.S.W., S.S.A., R.G.I., S.A.A.C.; work featured in many touring exhbns. in Scotland, and selected for group exhbns. in Italy, Poland, Germany, Bosnia and Canaries. *Work in collections:* Scottish Arts Council, Renfrewshire Educ. Authority, Lanarkshire Educ. Authority, Hamilton District Libraries, City Art Space, plc. *Signs work:* "Liz Murray." or "L.M." *Address:* The Old Post Office, Kilmany, Cupar, Fife, KY15 4PT.

MUSGRAVE, Barbara, N.D.D.; sculptress specialising in portraiture and animals; painter in oil; *b* London 1937. *m* Peter Musgrave. one *s.* two *d. Educ:* Maltman's Green, Gerrards Cross. *Studied:* Regent St. Polytechnic (1955-59) under Mr. Deeley. *Exhib:* Harrow Art Soc., Mall Galleries, Compass Theatre, Ickenham, Smiths Covent Garden, Cow Byre Ruislip. *Signs work:* "B. Musgrave" or "B.M." *Address:* 25 Bury St., Ruislip, Middx. HA4 7SX.

MUSKER, Alison Awdry Chalmers, R.W.S., Agnes Reeve Award (1989 & 1991); painter in water-colour and gouache; *b* Southampton, 9 Sep., 1938. *m* Roger. one *s.* two *d. Educ:* Sherborne. *Studied:* in Paris. *Exhib:* five solo exhibs., incl.,

Gallery in Cork Street, and Royal Geographical Soc., London; group exhibs. R.A., N.E.A.C., Singer And Friedlander (1989, 1999, 2000). *Work in collections:* H.M. The Queen Mother, H.R.H. The Prince of Wales, Peter Boizot, and others. *Publications:* Artist's Manual pub. Collins. *Clubs:* Chelsea Art Society. *Signs work:* "A.C.Musker." *Address:* Rose Cottage, Beech Hill, Reading RG7 2AZ.

MUSZYNSKI, Leszek Tadeusz, D.A. (Edin.); artist in oil, pastel, water-colour, drawing, lithograph; Retd. Head of Painting School, West Surrey College of Art and Design; *b* Poland, 19 Apr., 1923. *m* Patricia. one *s. Educ:* in Poland. *Studied:* Edinburgh College of Art (W. Gillies, J. Maxwell, W. MacTaggart); Travelling Scholarship to Paris, Florence, Arezzo, Assisi. *Exhib:* R.S.A. Edinburgh; one-man shows: London, Edinburgh, Copenhagen, Basle, Dallas, Texas, Warsaw, Cracow, Poznan. *Work in collections:* V. & A., N.P.G., L.C.C., National Museum, Poland, Museum of Art, Dallas, Texas, Museum, Durban, S. Africa. *Signs work:* see appendix. *Address:* West Wing, Bramshott Ct., Liphook GU30 7RG.

MYERS, Bernard, N.D.D. (1951), A.R.C.A. (1954), Hon. F.R.C.A., Hon. Prof. R.C.A.; painter in oil, water-colour, oil pastel, printmaker; taught at various London art schools and R.C.A.; Visiting Prof., Indian Inst. of Technology, New Delhi (1968-72), Prof., Brunel University (1980-85); *b* London, 22 Apr., 1925. *m* Pamela Blanche Fildes. *Studied:* St. Martin's (1947-49), Camberwell School of Art (1949-51), R.C.A. (1951-54). *Signs work:* "B. Myers" or "B.M." *Address:* 5 St. Peter's Wharf, Hammersmith Terr., London W6 9UD.

MYERS, Mark Richard, B.A.(Hons.), R.S.M.A. (1975), President R.S.M.A. (1993-1998), A.S.M.A. (1978), Fellow, A.S.M.A. (1979); marine artist in oils and acrylic on canvas and water-colour; *b* San Mateo, Calif., U.S.A., 19 Nov., 1945. *m* Peternella Bouquet. one *s.* two *d. Educ:* Pomona College, Calif. *Exhib:* R.S.M.A., A.S.M.A., New York, London, Seattle. *Work in collections:* National Maritime Museum, Greenwich, San Francisco Maritime Museum, N. Devon Maritime Museum. *Publications:* various maritime books illustrated. *Signs work:* "Mark Myers," "Mark Richard Myers" or "Myers." *Address:* The Old Forge, Woolley, Bude, Cornwall EX23 9PP.

MYERSCOUGH, Ishbel, B.A., Post Dip. & Distinction; painter in oil; *b* London, 5 Nov., 1968. *m* Cormac Alexander. *Educ:* Highbury Hill High School, City of London Girls School. *Studied:* Glasgow School of Art (1987-1991), Slade (1993-1995). *Exhib:* three solo exhibs., Anthony Mould Contemporary, London (1992, 1996, 2001), B.P. Portrait Award, National Portrait Gallery (1990, 1991, 1992, 1993, 1995); various group exhibs. including Flowers East and National Portrait Gallery. *Work in collections:* Natwest Bank, Christies, National Portrait Gallery, M.C.C. *Commissions:* Helen Mirren for National Portrait Gallery, Graham Gooch for M.C.C., private and public paintings and portraits. *Publications:* catalogues for solo exhibs., 'British Sporting Heroes', National Portrait Gallery, 'British Figurative Art Part 1', Flowers East, 'Die Kraft Der Builder', Berlin, 'Treasures from the National Portrait Gallery,' Japan. *Signs work:* "I M" or "I Myerscough" on verso. *Address:* 81B St. Peter's St., London N1 8JR.

MYERSON, Ingrid, B.A., M.B.A. (1986), U.A.; sculptor in bronze, stone, stainless steel, Perspex; *b* 30 June, 1960. *m* Brian Alan. two *s.* one *d. Studied:* University of Witwatersrand, Hampstead Institute. *Exhib:* Business Design Centre, Mall Galleries, Westminster Gallery, Expo Geneva, Les Hirondelles Geneva, McHardy Sculpture Gallery, London, Cato Gallery, London, Affordable Art Fair, Phillips Ltd, London. *Commissions:* private and business: England, Switzerland, S. Africa, U.S.A. *Clubs:* U.A. *Address:* Shawford Park, Shawford nr. Winchester, Hants. SO21 2BP.

MYNOTT, Gerald P., S.S.I.; topographical artist, printmaker and calligrapher; *b* London, 1957. *Studied:* Reigate College of Art; College of Arms, London; Vienna Kunstlerhaus, Austria. *Exhib:* Francis Kyle Gallery, London, continuously from 1980, New York (1984), Bath Festival (1983), Arts Club, London (1987). *Work in collections:* V. & A., Tate Gallery (Curwen Archive), The Savoy Group, Chevening Estate, U.S.A., Tokyo. Lloyds Printmakers Award (1981). *Publications:* work repro.: The Times, The Observer, Tatler, Radio Times, Weidenfeld and Nicolson, Penguin Books, V. & A. Publications, The Field, B.B.C. *Clubs:* Arts. *Address:* 3 Belgrave House, 157 Marine Parade, Brighton, Sussex.

MYNOTT, Katherine S., B.A.; illustrator/printmaker in gouache, line and lino; *b* London, 1962. one *s. Studied:* Heatherley School of Art, Central School of Art and St. Martin's School of Art. *Publications:* work repro.: Vogue, Radio Times, Daily Telegraph, Tatler, Harpers and Queen, B.B.C., Palace Pictures, Cosmopolitan, Time Out, Over 21, 19, The Observer, The Listener, I.P.C., New Society, Economist, etc. *Signs work:* "K. Mynott." *Address:* 23 Mount Park Rd., London W5.

MYNOTT, Lawrence, M.A. (R.C.A.), A.O.I.; portrait painter, illustrator in watercolour, oil, line and gouache; lecturer and art writer; *b* London, 1954. *Studied:* Chelsea School of Art (1972-76), Royal College of Art (1976-79). *Exhib:* R.A., European Illustrators, Folio Soc., Thames Television; two one-man shows of portraits at Cale Art, Chelsea. *Work in collections:* N.P.G., National Gallery of Wales, Hull A.G., Arts Council. Awarded D. & A.D. silver award (1985). Lecturer at V. & A., 'The Sitwells as Patrons', Neo-Romanticism, The Rococo Revival. *Publications:* work repro.: Radio Times, Vogue, Tatler, Harpers and Queen, The Observer, Penguin Books, Macmillans, Hamish Hamilton, etc. *Clubs:* Chelsea Arts. *Signs work:* "Lawrence Mynott," "Mynott" or monogram "L.M." *Address:* c/o "The Organisation", 69 Caledonian Rd., London N1. (Agent).

MYNOTT, Patricia, film designer, illustrator and natural history artist working in water-colour, line and gouache; *b* London, 1927. *m* Derek Mynott, N.E.A.C. (d. 1994). two *s.* one *d. Educ:* Dominican Convent, Chingford. *Studied:* S.W. Essex School of Art. Films: National Screen Service, National Savings, Film Producers Guild. *Publications:* illustrated, Marine Life of the Caribbean, Guide to the Seashore, Beaches and Beachcombing, Folklore of Fossils, The Curious Lore of Malta's Fossil Sharks Teeth, Edible Seaweeds; children's books: Encyclopedias, Educational Teaching Alphabet. Publishers: Blackies, Readers Digest, Paul Hamlyn, Michael Joseph, Macdonalds, Pitmans, Sacketts. *Signs work:* "Patricia Mynott" or "Barton." *Address:* The Arts Club, 40 Dover St., London W1X 3RB.

N

NAGL, Hazel Anna, R.S.W. (1988), R.G.I. (2000); painter in mixed media of still life and landscape, mainly Scottish gardens; *b* Glasgow, 2 Nov., 1953. *m* Geoff Keanie. one *d. Educ:* North Kelvinside Senior Secondary School. *Studied:* Glasgow School of Art under Donaldson, Robertson, Shanks. *Exhib:* R.S.W., R.G.I., R.S.A. Thomsons, London, Roger Billcliff; solo exhibs, Open Eye, Stenton, G.A.C. *Work in collections:* Royal Bank of Scotland, Glasgow University, Fleming Collection, Arthur Anderson, Scottish and Newcastle Breweries. *Clubs:* Glasgow Art Club. *Signs work:* "NAGL." *Address:* Lawmarnock House, 2 Troon Drive, Bridge of Weir, Renfrewshire PA11 3HF.

NALECZ, Halima, F.F.P.S.; Dip. U.S.B. (Wilno), Dame Chevalier d'Honneur (18 May, 1957); Bronze Medal, Europe prize for painting, Kursaal, Ostend,Belgium (1969, 1971); painter in oils and mixed media; Founder and Director of Drian Galleries, London; *b* Wilno, Poland, 2 Feb., 1917. *m* Zygmunt Nalecz, writer. *Educ:* Lycée, Wilno. *Studied:* under Professor Roube, Professor Szyszko-Bohusz, Professor Zahorska, and in Paris under H. J. Closon. *Exhib:* most municipal and public galleries in England, and W.I.A.C., A.I.A., Free Painters and Sculptors, London Group, Salon de Réalités Nouvelle, Galerie Collette Allendy, Salon des Divergences, Galerie Creuze (Paris); one-man exhbns. at Walker Galleries, London (1956), New Vision Centre, London (1957, 1959), Ewan Phillips, London (1967), County Town Gallery, Lewes (1967), Drian Galleries, London (1968-69), R.A. Summer Exhbn. (1967, 1968, 1969), S.S.W.A., Edinburgh. *Work in collections:* Britain, France, Spain, Italy, Germany, Australia, U.S.A., Sweden, Nuffield Foundation, London, National Gallery of Israel, Bezalel, Jerusalem, National Museum in Warsaw, Gdansk, Poznan. *Publications:* work repro.: Quadrum, Apollo, Arts Review, Art and Artists, Wiadomosci, Art International, etc.; prefaces to catalogues by Denis Bowen and Pierre Rouve. Paintings featured in film, The Millionairess. *Clubs:* A.I.A., W.I.A.C., Hampstead Artists Association, Free Painters and Sculptors, Polish Hearth. *Signs work:* see appendix. *Address:* 7 Porchester Pl., Marble Arch, London W2 2BT.

NAPP, David, Dip. C.S.D., Elizabeth Greenshields Foundation award (1986, 1990); artist in chalk, pastel, oil and water-colour; sessional lecturer, Kent Inst. of Art and Design; *b* London, 5 Mar., 1964. *Educ:* Queen Elizabeth's School, Faversham. *Studied:* Canterbury College of Art (1981-85). *Exhib:* Bourne Gallery, Reigate (1987-), Art London (1989, 1990, 1991), Walker Galleries, R.W.S., R.B.A., P.S., Napier Gallery Jersey. *Publications:* illustrations: Encyclopaedia of Pastel Techniques (Headline); Colour: How to see it, how to paint it; How to Paint Trees, Flowers and Foliage; Pastels Workshop. *Signs work:* "David Napp" and date. *Address:* Windmill Cottage, Mill La., Barham, Canterbury, Kent CT4 6HH.

NAPPER, Helen, B.A. (1980), M.F.A. (1983), P.G.C.E. (1985); painter in oil on board; *b* Wivenhoe, 29 Mar., 1958. *Educ:* Friends School, Saffron Walden; Colchester County High School for Girls. *Studied:* Colchester Art School, Wimbledon Art School (Maggi Hambling, Colin Cina), Reading University (Adrian Heath, Terry Frost), London University Central School of Art (Norman Ackroyd,

Bernard Cheese). *Exhib:* Sue Rankin Gallery (1989-91), L.A. Contemporary Art Fair (1989, 1990), Olympia Art, London (1990, 1991) with Sue Rankin Gallery, Tatistcheff and Co., N.Y. and L.A. (1992, 1993). *Work in collections:* Citicorp Bank, London. *Signs work:* "Helen Napper." *Address:* 5 Castle Hill, Orford, Suffolk.

NASH, David, R.A. (1999), B.A. (Hons.) Fine Art (1967); artist/sculptor in wood; Hon. Doc. Kingston University; Research Fellow, University of Northumbria; *b* Esher, Surrey, 14 Nov., 1945. *m* Claire Langdown. two *s*. *Studied:* Kingston College of Art Foundation Course (1963-64), Brighton College of Art (1964-65, painting), Kingston College of Art (1965-67, sculpture), Chelsea College of Art (1969-70, post-grad.). *Exhib:* Forest of Dean, Sculpture Trail, Walker Art Centre, Minneapolis, U.S.A., Nagoya City Museum, Japan, Guggenheim Museum, N.Y., Muhka Antwerp, Kröller Müller Museum, Holland. *Work in collections:* Tate Gallery, London, Guggenheim Museum N.Y., British Council. *Commissions:* 'Eighteen Thousand Tides' Eastbourne, public sculpture (1996), 'Divided Oaks' and 'Turning Pines' (planted sculptures) Ottorlo, Netherlands (1985). *Publications:* The Sculpture of David Nash by Julian Andrews; Forms into Time (with essay by Marina Warner); Black and Light (essay by Dr. Judith Collins). *Address:* Capel Rhiw, Blaenau Ffestiniog, Gwynedd LL41 3NT.

NASH, Tom, A.T.D., R.C.A.; artist in oil, P.V.A., gouache, collage, murals in retroreflective plastics, etc.; awarded Geoffrey Crawshay Memorial Travelling Scholarship; West Wales Association for the Arts, Research Award; *b* Ammanford, 1931. *m* Enid Williams. two *d*. *Educ:* Llandeilo. *Studied:* Swansea, Paris, Provence; associated with Paul Jenkins in Paris. *Exhib:* one-man and mixed exhibitions in London, provinces, Washington, D.C., Argentine, Toronto, Japan. *Work in collections:* National Museum of Wales, Nuffield Foundation, Arts Council, Clare, Churchill, Pembroke Colleges, Cambridge, various county collections, Caerleon College of Education, Glynn Vivian Art Gallery, Swansea, Steel Company of Wales, C.A.S., Caiman Museum, Argentina, Wadham College, Oxford, University of Wales, India Rubber Co., Macco Corp., California, Brasenose College, Oxford, Trinity College of Education, 3M United Kingdom Limited, University of Bradford, Church of Wales Collection, I.T.V., British Petroleum Co., B.B.C., National Library of Wales, Conservetoire Darius Milhaud, Aix en Provence; private collections in Britain, France, Germany, U.S.A., Canada, New Zealand. *Commissions:* 3M U.K. Ltd., B.B.C., University of Bradford, Brecon Jazz Festival, P.T.P. Ltd., S.W. Police Authority, Prestige Hotels, Cardiff Festival, Brasenose College Oxford. *Publications:* I.T.V. biographical films, B.B.C. biographical films, national and international publications, 3M/UK/France publications. *Clubs:* Brecon. *Signs work:* "Tom Nash." *Address:* Clydfan, Llandeilo, Wales SA19 6HY.

NASON, Kristine, painter in water-colour, draughtsman in graphite pencil; portrait painter, equestrian artist, illustrator, tutor; *b* Matlock, Derbyshire. *m* L.B.Giwa. one *s*. one *d*. *Educ:* Basingstoke High School. *Studied:* Portsmouth College of Art and Design. *Exhib:* London, Toronto, and various group exhibs. and galleries throughout U.K. *Work in collections:* private collections worldwide. *Commissions:* U.K. and international clients. *Publications:* 'Running for Real', Macmillan, illustrated. *Clubs:* S.A.A. Professional Associate. *Signs work:* "Kristine Nason." *Address:* 1 Savory Walk, Foxley Fields, Binfield, Berks. RG42 4LP. *Email:* kristinenason@talk21.com

NEAGU, Paul, sculptor, painter, Anglo-romanian; lecturer (1972-91); *b* Bucharest, 1938. *Educ:* Inst. 'N. Grigorescu' Bucharest (1959-65). *Exhib:* over forty five solo exhibs.; major works: 'Palpable and tactile objects' (1965-90), 'Anthropocosmos (1968-81), 'Performance' (1969-77), 'Hyphen' (1974-93), 'Nine Catalytic Stations' (1975-87), 'Unnamed' (1983-92), 'Newhyphen' (1991-93), 'Ten right angles' (1994), 'Unnamed (Eschaton)(1997), 'Endlessedge Hyphen' (1999). *Work in collections:* U.K., U.S.A., Japan, Germany, Romania, France, Ireland, Austria, China. Outdoor sculpture: Middlesbrough, Bucharest, Guilin (China), Ottawa, Timisoara (Rom.). *Publications:* 'Palpable Art' (1969), 'Generative Arts' (1977), 'Hyphen' (1985), 'Deep Space and Solid Time' (1988), 'Epagoge' (1993), 'Reorganisation of nothing' (1996), 'A Derridean Tornado' (2000). *Clubs:* Founder: Generative Art Trust. *Signs work:* "Paul Neagu" or "P. Neagu." *Address:* 31c Jackson Rd., London N7 6ES.

NEAL, Arthur Richard, Dip.A.D.; painter/printmaker in oil, water-colour and etching; *b* Chatham, 15 Mar., 1951. *m* Jane. one *s.* one *d. Educ:* Reeds School. *Studied:* Camberwell School of Art. *Exhib:* R.A. Summer Shows, Cadogan Contemporary. *Publications:* Illustrated Poems of Edward Thomas. *Clubs:* N.E.A.C. *Signs work:* "ARN" or "ARNEAL" or not at all. *Address:* 32 Duke St., Deal, Kent CT14 6DT.

NEAL, Charles William, B.Sc. Hons. (1980); landscape painter in oil; *b* Carshalton, 27 Nov., 1951. *m* Susan Ann. one *s. Educ:* Highview High School/City of London University. *Studied:* initially private tuition with Malcolm Domingo and Francis Lane-Mason; later self taught to perfect style and technique. *Exhib:* Omell Gallery (1982); R.B.A.: Omell Gallery (1983), Godalming Gallery (1984), Harrods Picture Gallery (1985); annual, national, international exhbns.: Campbell's of Walton Street and Astley House Fine Art, Glos. *Work in collections:* one royal and many private and commercial collections both national and international. Gallery affiliation: Campbell's of Walton Street, 164 Walton St., London SW3 2JL; Astley House Fine Art, Moreton-in-Marsh, Glos., GL56 0LL. *Signs work:* C. Neal." *Address:* Woodside Cottage, 4 Cotswold Park, Woodmancote, Cirencester, Glos. GL7 7EL.

NEAL, James, A.R.C.A. (1939); artist; *b* Islington, 18 Jan., 1918. *m* Doreen Barnes. two *s.* one *d. Educ:* St. John Evangelist. *Studied:* St. Martin's School of Art; R.C.A. *Exhib:* R.A., R.S.A., N.E.A.C., London Group, Redfern Galleries; one-man shows Trafford Gallery, Wildensteins, etc. *Work in collections:* Nottingham A.G., Wakefield A.G., Ferens A.G., Hull, Beverley A.G., Graves A.G., Sheffield, London County Council, Hull Educ. Com., W. Riding Educ. Com., East Riding Educ. Com., Derbyshire Educ. Com., Durham Educ. Com., etc. *Signs work:* "James Neal." *Address:* 205 Victoria Ave., Hull, N. Humberside HU5 3EF.

NEAL, Trevor, self taught artist in oil; *b* York, 1947. *m* Sharon. one *d. Exhib:* Graves A.G. (1972-75, 1977), White Rose Gallery Bradford (1974), R.A. (1975, 1980, 1981, 1992), Art Centre St. Petersburg, U.S.A. (1980, 1982), Anderson Marsh Galleries St. Petersburg (1983), Ginnel Gallery Manchester (1988), Evander Preston Gallery St. Petersburg (1988, 1989, 1991), S. Yorks. Open Cooper A.G. Barnsley (1989), Ferens A.G., Hull (1995, 1996, 1997), Roy Miles, London (1994, 1995), Art Miami, Florida (1998), Leighton House, London (2001). *Work in collections:* U.K., U.S.A., France, Germany, Israel. *Commissions:* U.K., U.S.A., Germany.

Publications: "Dreams" (The Bridgewater Book Co., 1996). *Clubs:* Soc. of Tempera Painters. *Signs work:* see appendix. *Address:* Fossdale Towers, 23 Fossdale Rd., Sheffield S7 2DA. *Email:* painter@trevorneal.co.uk

NEALE, John, self taught landscape and seascape painter in oil and water-colour; *b* 13 Sept., 1944. divorced. two *s.* two *d. Studied:* self taught, but privately helped by Edward Seago. *Exhib:* Omell Galleries, Quantas Galleries, Frost and Reed, Bristol, John Noott, Broadway, Chime Gallery, N.Y., etc. *Work in collections:* in Europe and U.S.A. *Signs work:* "John Neale." *Address:* Maple Leaf House, 59 Maidenhead Rd., Stratford-on-Avon CV37 6XU.

NEASOM, Norman, R.W.S. (1978), R.B.S.A. (1947), Hon.S.A.S. (1976); artist in water-colour and gouache; retd. art master; *b* Tardebigge, 7 Nov., 1915. *m* Jessie Mary. two *d. Educ:* Redditch County High. *Studied:* Birmingham College of Art (1931-35, Harold H. Holden, Michael Fletcher, Fleetwood Walker, R.A., W.F. Colley, H. Sands). *Exhib:* R.A. (1970, 1974, 1976), R.W.S., R.B.S.A., Stratford Art Soc., Mall Galleries. *Work in collections:* West Midland Arts Council and various private collections. *Publications:* work repro.: articles for Leisure Painter, covers for Reader's Digest. *Clubs:* Redditch Sailing (founder). *Signs work:* "N. NEASOM" and date. *Address:* 95 Bromfield Rd., Redditch, Worcs. B97 4PN.

NEILAND, Brendan, R.A. (1992), Dip.A.D. (1966), M.A. (1969), Silver Medal R.C.A. (1969); painter in acrylic on canvas, printmaker in silkscreen, lithography; Prof. of Painting, University of Brighton (1996); Visiting Prof., Loughborough University (1998); Keeper, Royal Academy of Arts (1998); *b* Lichfield, 23 Oct., 1941. *m* Hilary. two *d. Educ:* St. Philip's G.S., B'ham; St. Augustine's Seminary, Ireland. *Studied:* B'ham College of Art (1962-66, William Gear, John Walker, Ivor Abrahams), R.C.A. (1966-69, Carel Weight, Roger de Grey). *Exhib:* Angela Flowers Gallery, Fischer Fine Art, Redfern Gallery. *Work in collections:* Tate Gallery, V. & A., British Council, Arts Council. *Commissions:* National Bank of Dubai (1997). *Publications:* "Brendan Neiland on Reflection" (Motivate Publishing, Oct. 1997). *Clubs:* Chelsea Arts. *Signs work:* "Brendan Neiland" on all prints and paper work; "NEILAND" stencilled onto back of canvas on stretcher. *Address:* 2 Granard Rd., London SW12 8UL; and Crepe, La Greve sur Mignon, Courcon 17170, France.

NEILL, Errol James, LL.B. (Lond.), Paris Salon: Silver Medallist (1980), Gold Medallist (1981); solicitor; artist in oil and pastel; *b* Doune, Perthshire, 15 Aug., 1941. *m* Audrey Bradbury. one *s.* two *d. Educ:* Christ Church, Preston. *Exhib:* R.B.A., R.O.I., R.S.M.A., N.E.A.C., U.A., S.E.A., Lancashire Art, Société des Artistes Francais, Paris, Deauville, N.Y., Melbourne, Australia. *Work in collections:* Britain, France, Eire, U.S.A., S. America. *Publications:* Travelling the Turf 1987 to 1992. *Clubs:* Law Soc. Art Group. *Signs work:* "ERROL NEILL." *Address:* Bridge House, 217 Chapel La., New Longton, Preston, Lancs. PR4 4AD.

NEILL, William Andrew Knight, Dip.A.D. (Fine Art) Leeds (1966), A.T.C. Goldsmiths' (1967), S.WL.A. (1990); wildlife and landscape artist in water-colour; *b* Middlewich, Ches., 22 Aug., 1943. *Educ:* Sandbach School. *Studied:* Leeds College of Art, Goldsmiths' College. *Exhib:* annually with S.WL.A., Kranenburg & Fowler Fine Arts, Oban. *Work in collections:* Nature in Art, Wallsworth Hall. *Commissions:* Scottish Natural Heritage, and The Western Isles Health Board.

Publications: illustrations in: British Birds, Scottish Birds, etc.; illustrated, Scottish Wildlife Trust, Discovery Book of Western Isles. *Address:* Rannachan, Askernish, SouthUist., Western Isles HS8 5SY.

NELLENS, Roger, painter in oil on canvas; *b* Liege, Belgium, 11 May, 1937. one *s.* two *d. Educ:* College St. Michel et St. Louis, Brussels, and London Academy; autodidact. *Work in collections:* Collection de l'Etat Belge; Musée d'Ostende; Collection de la Flandre Occidentale, Bruges; Museum Boymans-van Beuningen, Rotterdam; Musée d'Art et d'Industrie, St. Etienne France; CNAC, Paris; McCrory Corp., N.Y.; Tate Gallery, London; Musée d'Art Moderne, Brussels; The Menil Foundation, Houston; Centre Pompidou, Paris. *Signs work:* on the back; see appendix. *Address:* Fort St. Pol, Zoutelaan, 280, 8300 Knokke-Heist, Belgium.

NELSON, Kathleen, R.M.S. (1984), H.S.F. (1982); Hon. Men. Gold Memorial Bowl award R.M.S. (1985, 1994), Drummond award R.M.S. (1984), Llewellyn Alexander subject miniature award R.M.S. (1996); Llewellyn Alexander Masters award (1997), Presidents award Hilliard Soc. (1998); wildlife, natural history artist in water-colour and oil; *b* Durham City, 12 Mar., 1956. *Educ:* Durham Wearside. *Exhib:* R.M.S., H.S., Medici Gallery, Llewellyn Alexander Gallery; solo shows: Darlington A.G., Durham A.G. *Work in collections:* Darlington A.G., Diploma Collection, R.M.S. *Publications:* chapter with illustrations, The Techniques of Painting Miniatures by S. Burton (B.T. Batsford Ltd., 1995). *Signs work:* "Kathleen Nelson." *Address:* 18 Beverley Gdns., Chester-le-Street, Co. Durham DH3 3NB.

NEUENSCHWANDER, James Brody, Ph.D., M.Phil., A.B.; calligrapher, lettering artist, graphic designer; *b* Houston, Texas, 8 Sept., 1958. *Educ:* Princeton University, Courtauld Inst. *Studied:* Roehampton Inst. under Ann Camp. *Exhib:* Princeton University Library, Museum of Fine Arts, Houston, Gallerie Comptoir des Ecritures Paris, Torre di Malta, Padua, Vizo Gallery, Brussels. *Work in collections:* Princeton University, Westminster Cathedral. *Publications:* Modern German Calligraphy - Special issue of Letter Exchange Magazine; Letterwork - Creative Letterforms for Graphic Design (Phaidon, London 1993). Collaborated with Director Peter Greenaway on several films, including Prospero's Books, The Baby of Mâcon and The Pillow Book. *Signs work:* "Brody Neuenschwander." *Address:* Spinolarei 2, 8000 Bruges, Belgium.

NEVE, Margaret, R.W.A. (1995); painter in oil on wood panels; *b* Wolverhampton, 29 Mar., 1929. *m* James Sutton. two *s. Educ:* privately. *Studied:* Birmingham College of Art (1946-49), R.A. Schools (1949-55, B. Fleetwood Walker). *Exhib:* Hamilton Gallery (1967), Marjorie Parr Gallery (1976), Gilbert Parr Gallery (1977, 1979), New Grafton Gallery (1981), Montpelier Studio (1987, 1990, 1994), Montpelier Sandelson Gallery (1998). *Work in collections:* Birmingham A.G. *Publications:* monograph: Margaret Neve (Montpelier Sandelson, 1998). *Signs work:* "M. Neve." *Address:* 18 Greville Pl., London NW6 5JH.

NEVETZ: see COX, Stephen B.

NEVIA: see ROGERS, Joseph Shepperd.

NEWBERRY, John Coverdale, R.W.S. (1995), B.A. Dunelm (1960), M.A.Oxon. (1989); Water-colour Foundation prize R.W.S. Open (1990); painter of landscapes in water-colour and figure compositions in oil; tutor, Ruskin School of Drawing, Oxford (1963-89); *b* Horsham, 8 May, 1934. *Educ:* Kingswood School, Bath; School of Architecture, Cambridge. *Studied:* King's College, Newcastle upon Tyne (1957-60, Lawrence Gowing, Victor Pasmore). *Exhib:* R.W.S., O.A.S., R.A., R.I., N.E.A.C., Singer & Friedlander, numerous one-man shows mostly in Oxford: Ashmolean (1978), Chris Beetles (1990, 1991), Duncan Campbell (1993, 1994, 1996, 1998, 2001). *Signs work:* "Newberry." *Address:* Moulin de Sourreau, 24230 Vélines, France.

NEWBURY, Brian James, F.R.S.A., Mem. B.A.D.A.; specialist in marine, military, sporting and topographical prints, paintings and water-colours, ship models, etc.; Chairman and Managing Director of the Parker Gallery; *b* London, 24 Dec., 1941. widower. one *s. Educ:* Bembridge School, I.O.W. *Clubs:* Naval. *Address:* 49 Peplins Way, Brookmans Park, Herts. AL9 7UR.

NEWCOMB, Tessa, B.A. (Hons.) Fine Art 1976; painter in oil; *b* Suffolk, 20 May, 1955. one *s.* one *d. Studied:* Bath Academy of Art (1973-76), Wimbledon School of Art (1977). *Exhib:* Crane Kalman, Cadogan Contemporaries, Lena Boyle, London, many other regional galleries. *Work in collections:* Bradford Metropolitan Museum, Whitworth A.G. *Publications:* jacket illustrations for Julia Blackburn's 'Daisy in the Desert' and the paper back edn. 'The Emperor's Last Island' (both Secker & Warburg, 1994); Canns Down cards - four images, What's Cooking, 50 booklets, hand printed styrofoam prints for Aldeburgh Foundation. *Signs work:* "TN" joined. *Address:* Driftwood, Back Rd., Wenhaston, Halesworth, Suffolk IP19 9EB.

NEWELL, Robert Alan, B.A.Hons. (1977). M.A. (1984), P.G.C.E. Art (1981); artist in water-colour, oil, drawing, lecturer; Senior lecturer, Head of Painting, Swansea Inst H.E.; *b* 4 Dec., 1952. *m* Eileen Valerie Newell. *Studied:* Wimbledon School of Art (1973-77), University of Reading, School of Educ. (1980-81), Goldsmiths' College (1982-84). *Exhib:* R.A. Summer Show, Glynn Vivian A.G., other galleries in Wales, London, Dusseldorf, etc. *Address:* 1 Pantyblodau Rd., Blaenau, Ammanford, Carmarthenshire SA18 3BX.

NEWLAND, Anne, Edwin Abbey Major Scholarship (1938); *b* Wilts., 11 Jan., 1913. *Educ:* Byam Shaw Art School (1934-38). *Address:* 4 Vaughan Rd., London SE5 9NZ.

NEWSOME, Victor George, artist in egg tempera; *b* Leeds, 16 June, 1935. one *s.* one *d. Studied:* Leeds School of Art, British School at Rome. *Exhib:* A. d'Offay, Anne Berthoud, Marlborough Fine Art, Grosvenor Gallery. *Work in collections:* Arts Council, Contemporary Arts Soc., British Council, Ferens Art Gallery, Whitworth Art Gallery. *Address:* 4 Elizabeth Mews, London NW3 4TL.

NEWTON, Joanna Dawson, Dip. in Art (1982); artist in oil on canvas, charcoal drawing; *b* Oxford, 24 Apr., 1958. *Educ:* Headington School, Oxford. *Studied:* Byam Shaw School of Art (1979-82, P. Gopal-Chowdhuny, N. Volley). *Exhib:* Whitechapel Open, N.P.G., John Player award, R.A. Summer Exhbn., Picture Brokers Exhbn. *Clubs:* Chelsea Arts. *Signs work:* "Joanna D. Newton." *Address:* 60 St. Dionis Rd., Fulham, London SW6.

NEWTON, William Alexander, sculptor, specialising in lost wax casting in bronze and silver, mainly animals; creator of The Derby Trophies, Epsom (1998, 1999, 2000, 2001, 2002); *b* Alford, Somerset. *m* Sharon. one *s.* one *d. Exhib:* solo exhibs. at Park Walk Gallery (1995, 1997, 2000), and other group exhibs. *Signs work:* "Newton" or "W. Newton." *Address:* The Rosary, West Hill, Wincanton, Somerset BA9 9BY. *Second Address:* c/o Jonathan Cooper, Park Walk Gallery, 20 Park Walk, London SW10 0AQ.

NEWTON-DAVIES, Diana Elizabeth: see WHITESIDE, Diana Elizabeth Hamilton.

NG, Kiow Ngor, Dip.F.A. (1989); artist in painting and printmaking; *b* Singapore, 6 Apr., 1963. *Studied:* Nan Yang Academy of Fine Arts (1986-89), Slade School of Fine Art (1991-93). *Exhib:* London Group (1992), R.A. Summer Show (1992, 1993). *Signs work:* see appendix. *Address:* 9a Kang Choo Bin Rd., Singapore 1954.

NGUYEN, Tân-Phuoc, Mem. Confédération Internationale des Associations des Experts et du Conseils auprès du Conseil Economique et Social de l'Onu; Président Asia-Africa Museum (fondé en 1961); Président de la Chambre Internationale de Commerce Vietnam-Suisse; art expert on Asiatic archaeology and Africa Art, specialised in the founding of Fine Art Collections and Muséums, historian, writer; *b* 11 Oct., 1932. *m* Hélène Gerber. two *s. Educ:* Saigon, S. Vietnam, and Paris. *Studied:* l'Institut Hautes, Etudes Indochinoises, and Ecole du Louvre. *Publications:* Archéologie asiatique, Netzuke, La Culture de Ban-Chiang (Siam) 7.000-5.000 ans, Fouilles archéologiques à Ban-Chiang. Conférencier invité à Davos Symposium (from 1985) by W.E.F. *Clubs:* Musée d'Ethnographie, Musée des Collections Baur-Duret, Union Internationale des Experts, Croix Rouge Suisse, Intérêt de Genève, Kiwanis International, Président, Asia-Africa Museum (GVA) (1993), Chevalier du Tastevin, Expert membre C.I.D.A.D.E.C., O.N.U., Tennis Club Geneva. *Address:* 30 Grand Rue, Genève 1204, Switzerland.

NICHOLAS, Peter, N.D.D. (1956), A.R.C.A. (1962), F.R.B.S. (1993); sculptor in stone, bronze, G.R.P.; *b* Tredegar, S. Wales, 1934. *m* Marjorie (decd.). one *s.* two *d.* ; *m* Annie. one *s.* two *d. Educ:* Ebbw Vale County Grammar School. *Studied:* Cardiff College of Art (1951-56, Frank Roper, Geof Milsom), R.C.A. (1958-61, John Skeaping). *Exhib:* Jonathan Poole Fine Art. *Work in collections:* U.K., Europe, U.S.A. *Commissions:* 1990-2000 include: The Celtic Manor Hotel, Cwmbran New Town, Rotheram Met. Bor. Council, Merthyr Tydfil, Royal Caribbean Cruise Line, Aberystwyth, Mountain Ash, Penarth Town. *Publications:* Art in Architecture an Architects Choice (Eugene Rosenberg), The Encyclopedia of Sculpture Techniques (John Mills), Teaching Art in Wales (Alan Torjussen), Debrett's People of Today. *Signs work:* "P.W. NICHOLAS." *Address:* Craig-y-Don, Horton, Gower, W. Glam. SA3 1LB.

NICHOLS, Patricia Mary, R.M.S., S.W.A.; portrait painter in miniature and full-size portrait drawings in sanguine, chalk; Mem. Royal Society of Miniature Painters; and Soc. of Women Artists; teaches miniature painting at the West Norfolk Art Centre; *m* the late John Trevor Nichols, M.C.I.T. one *s.* one *d. Educ:* innumerable private schools. *Studied:* Central School of Arts and Crafts London. *Exhib:* R.I., Mall Galleries, Westminster Gallery and many others. *Commissions:* has undertaken many important, including royal, commissions. *Publications:* work repro.: The Artist, Illustrated county magazines and newspapers. *Signs work:* "Patricia Nichols."

Address: Sealand, Wodehouse Rd., Old Hunstanton, Norfolk PE36 6JD.

NICKS: see KANG, K.S.

NINNES, Lesley Marian, H.N.C. Art And Design (Illustration); painter in alkyds - fast drying oils; partner in Art Space Gallery, St. Ives; *b* Redruth, Cornwall, 7 Dec., 1953. two *d. Educ:* St. Ives School. *Studied:* Cornwall College. *Exhib:* group exhibs. Cornwall, Devon and France. *Work in collections:* private collections in U.K. and abroad. *Publications:* colour illus. for 'The Endemic Plants of St. Helena' and pen and ink illus. for F.A.O. pub. on Inland Fisheries. *Clubs:* St. Ives Soc. of Artists, Penwith Soc. of Artists - assoc. member. *Signs work:* "L. Ninnes." *Address:* 8 St. Johns Walk, St. Ives, Cornwall TR26 2JJ. *Email:* lninnes@eurobell.co.uk

NOAD, Julie Ann, B.A. Hons. Fine Art (1978); painter in oil; figurative painter of interiors and views through windows preoccupied by light and colour; *b* Essex, 29 Oct., 1955. one *s. Educ:* William Edwards School, Essex. *Studied:* Camberwell School of Art (1975-1978), under Antony Eyton R.A. *Exhib:* N.E.A.C., Mall Galleries, John Russell Gallery, Chappel Galleries, South London Gallery. *Work in collections:* private collections, U.K., Europe, America. *Publications:* illustrations for Agenda, P.N. Review. *Signs work:* "J Noad." *Address:* Turkey Hall, Metfield, Suffolk IP20 0JX.

NOAKES, Michael, P.P.R.O.I., R.P., C.P.S., Hon. N.S., Hon. U.A., Cert. R.A.S., N.D.D.; landscape and portrait painter (subjects include H.M. the Queen, other members royal family, etc.); Chairman (1971) Contemporary Portrait Society; Pres. Royal Institute of Oil Painters (1972-78); art critic (1964-68), B.B.C. Television; *b* Brighton, 28 Oct., 1933. married. two *s.* one *d. Educ:* Downside. *Studied:* R.A. Schools. *Exhib:* R.A., R.O.I., R.P., R.B.A., N.S., etc. *Work in collections:* H.M. the Queen, H.R.H. the Prince of Wales, B.M., National Portrait Gallery, etc. *Publications:* A Professional Approach to Oil Painting (Pitmans, 1968); work repro.: widely. *Signs work:* "Michael Noakes," with date underneath. *Address:* 146 Hamilton Terr., London NW8 9UX.

NOELLE: see SIMPSON, Noelle.

NOOTT, Edward John, B.A., R.B.S.A. (2001); painter in oil; *b* W. Midlands, 4 Oct., 1965. *m* Denise Cardone. one *s.* one *d. Educ:* Cheltenham College. *Studied:* Gloucestershire College of Art, Cheltenham, Trent Polytechnic College, Nottingham, State University of N.Y. *Exhib:* John Noott Galleries, R.B.S.A., R.O.I. *Publications:* work reproduced by The Art Group, Robertson Collection. *Signs work:* "Edward Noott." *Address:* c/o 14 Cotswold Ct., Broadway, Worcs. WR12 7AA.

NORBURY, Ian, B.A. (1979); sculptor in wood, metal, semi precious stones; *b* Sheffield, 21 Aug., 1948. *m* Betty Ann. two *s.* one *d. Educ:* Andover Grammar; St. Paul's College, Cheltenham. *Studied:* St. Paul's College, Cheltenham (Harold Sayer, R.E., R.W.A., A.R.C.A.). *Exhib:* annual one-man. *Work in collections:* Tower of London, Fine Art Museum of the South of Mobile, U.S.A., many private collections. *Publications:* Techniques of Creative Woodcarving, Projects for Creative Woodcarving, Relief Woodcarving and Lettering, Fundamentals of Figure Carving, Carving Facial Expressions. *Signs work:* "IAN NORBURY," "I. NORBURY" or

"I.N." *Address:* Ballycommare, Tournafulla, Co. Limerick, Eire.

NORDEN, Gerald, A.R.C.A. (1937); still-life painter in oil; *b* Hampstead, London, 28 June, 1912. *m* Lilian Moorhead. one *s.* two *d. Educ:* Arnold House, NW8. *Studied:* Thanet School of Art (J. Moody, B. Willis), R.C.A. (Gilbert Spencer, Percy Horton). *Exhib:* Trafford Gallery (1969-75), King St. Gallery (1976-86), Catto Gallery (1991-93). *Publications:* A Practical Guide to Perspective (Longman). *Signs work:* "NORDEN." *Address:* 11 Julian Rd., Folkestone, Kent CT19 5HP.

NORLAND (NEUSCHUL), Khalil, M.A. Physics (Oxon.); artist-painter in mixed media; *b* Aussig (Usti), Czechoslovakia, 25 Mar., 1934. *m* Layla Shamash. three *s. Educ:* Merton College, Oxford. *Studied:* Ruskin College of Art, Oxford (1953-57), Slade School of Art London University (1959-60). *Exhib:* Artist House, Jerusalem (1959), Woodstock Gallery, London (1961), Gallerie Lambert, Paris (1964), Camden Arts Centre, London (1987), Queen Elizabeth House, Oxford (1987), Loggia Gallery, London (1988), Haus am Lützowplatz, Berlin (1991). *Signs work:* see appendix. *Address:* 25 Southmoor Rd., Oxford OX2 6RF.

NORMAN, Barbara, Paris Salon bronze medal (1975), silver medal (1976); glass engraver in diamond point, flexible drive drill; *b* London. *Studied:* Stanhope Institute and glass engraving at Morley College under Mary Stevens. *Exhib:* Bourne Hall, Ewell, New Ashgate Gallery, Farnham, Florida Gulf Coast Art Center, Clearwater, Florida, Tampa Bay Art Center, Florida. *Publications:* Engraving and Decorating Glass (David and Charles 1972, McGraw Hill, U.S.A. 1972); Glass Engraving (David and Charles 1981, ARCO, U.S.A. 1981, A. H. & A. W. Reed, Australia 1981). *Signs work:* "Barbara Norman." *Address:* 9 Downs Lodge Court, Church St., Epsom, Surrey KT17 4QG.

NORMAN, Michael Radford, R.S.M.A. (1975); artist/model maker, in pen and water-colour, often of river and coastal scenes; *b* Ipswich, 20 Aug., 1933. two *d. Educ:* Woodbridge School. *Studied:* Bournemouth School of Art, Regent St. Polytechnic. *Exhib:* R.I., R.S.M.A.; one-man shows, Colchester, Ipswich, Norwich, London. *Work in collections:* water-colour at D.O.E. *Commissions:* numerous. *Publications:* illustrated, The Suffolk Essex Border by John Salmon. *Signs work:* "Michael Norman" usually in black ink. *Address:* The Studio, Woolverstone, Ipswich, Suffolk IP9 1AX.

NORMAN, Richard, D.A. (1978), R.S.W. (1994); Cargill award R.G.I. (1991), Travelling Scholarship, Venice (1995); artist in water-colour and oil; teacher; *b* Glasgow, 15 June, 1956. *Studied:* Glasgow School of Art (1974-78, Dr. David Donaldson, James Robertson, Leon Morrocco). *Exhib:* regularly at R.G.I. and R.S.W.; one-man shows 1990-92: Kelly Gallery, Glasgow, Blythswood Gallery, Glasgow. *Clubs:* Glasgow Art. *Signs work:* "Richard Norman." *Address:* 185 Bath St., Glasgow G2 4HU.

NORRIS, David, Cert. R.A.S., F.R.B.S.: sculptor in bronze; Vice-Pres. Royal Soc. of British Sculptors; *b* São Paulo, Brazil, 26 Sept., 1940. *m* Carol. three *d. Educ:* Millfield. *Studied:* Guildford School of Art and R.A. Schools. *Exhib:* R.A., Mall Galleries, Royal Mint. *Work in collections:* 'Women and Doves' Stevenage Town Park; 'Britannia' for the Falklands Monument; 'Mother and Child' Portland Hospital;

Sir Barnes Wallis, R.A.F. Museum Hendon; 'Spindrift' 3.5m. high stainless steel spiral with bronze gulls for P. & O. liner Royal Princess; two life-size bronzes for Royal Caribbean Cruise Line; group of 'flying flamingos', Arndale Centre, Luton; bronze portrait of Maria Callas for the Royal Opera House, London; bronze relief portrait of General Sir David Fraser, Grenadier Guards; bronze 'Birds of Prey' for the Middle East. Awarded the Sir Otto Beit medal. *Signs work:* "David Norris." *Address:* The Orchard House, Cranleigh, Surrey GU6 8LR.

NORRIS, Katharine, B.A.(Hons.) graphic design and illustration; decorative mural artist and stenciller and fine artist of figurative work, landscape, life, decorative still life in acrylic, oil, pastel, coloured pencil, charcoal; *b* Worthing. *Educ:* Trinity School, Carlisle. *Studied:* Cumbria College of Art and Design (1977-78), Norwich School of Art (1978-81). *Clubs:* Life Drawing, Penrith. *Signs work:* "Kate Norris." *Address:* 30 Esk Bank, Longtown, Carlisle, Cumbria CA6 5PT.

NORRIS, Linda, B.A. (Hons.) Visual Art (1982); artist in mixed media; *b* Chichester, 22 June, 1960. *m* Denbeigh Vaughan. one *d.* *Studied:* U.C.W. Aberystwyth. *Exhib:* selected: 1998: New Academy Gallery, London, Martin Tinney Gallery, Cardiff; 1999: Attic Gallery, Swansea, Six Chapel Row Gallery, Bath; 2000: New Academy Gallery, London; 2000-2001: Adam Gallery, Bath; ongoing galleries in artist's home. *Work in collections:* Chevron U.K., General Medical Council. *Commissions:* Llandough Hospital, Penarth, Urdd Llangrannog. *Address:* The Manse, Trefgarn Owen, Haverfordwest SA62 6NE. *Website:* www.linda-norris.com *Email:* linda@linda-norris.com

NORTON, Maureen Joan, R.S.M. (1982), S.M. (1981); marine and landscape artist in oil on canvas and oil on ivorine; *b* Norwich, 1928. *m* Denis Norton. one *d.* *Exhib:* three one-man shows at Ancient House, Holkham, also soc. exhbns. at Mall Galleries, The Westminster Gallery; R.S.M. Golden Bowl Hon. mention (1996). *Work in collections:* America, Germany, Australia and Mexico. *Signs work:* "M.J. Norton." *Address:* 179 Wroxham Rd., Sprowston, Norwich NR7 8AG.

NOSWORTHY, Ann Louise, N.D.D. (1952), A.T.D. (1953); painter in oil, gouache, pastel and charcoal; *b* Stonehaven, Scotland, 24 Aug., 1929. *m* T. C. Nosworthy. one *s.* *Educ:* Beacon School, Bridge-of-Allan, Scotland. *Exhib:* one-man shows: Redcar, Yorks. (1968), Castle de Vide, Portugal (1966). *Work in collections:* Municipal Art Gallery, Port Allegre, Portugal. *Signs work:* "A. L. Nosworthy." *Address:* Brackengarth, Lealholm, Whitby, Yorks. YO21 2AE.

NOT, Philip James, self taught artist in oil; proprietor of Galerie Not; *b* 28 Feb., 1938. *m* Violet Vidot 'Une Belle Seychelleoise'. one *s.* two *d.* *Educ:* Holloway Grammar School. *Work in collections:* Etablisement de Reu (Arras, France), Lloyds Bank Plc. (Hampstead Village Branch). Noted for legal still life and local West Hampstead and Hampstead landscapes. *Signs work:* "P.J. Not" or "PJN" *Address:* 37 Narcissus Road, West Hampstead, London NW6 1TL.

NOYES, Margot, N.D.D. (1960); painter in oil; *b* London, 17 Aug., 1939; divorced. one *s.* one *d.* *Educ:* Fulham County Grammar School. *Studied:* Camberwell School of Arts and Crafts (1956-60, Robert Medley, Anthony Eyton, Richard Lee, Michael Salaman, Richard Eurich, Henry Inlander). *Exhib:* Many solo shows and mixed shows nationwide and overseas. *Publications:* 'Camberwell School of Arts & Crafts - Its Students & Teachers 1943-1960' by Geoff Hassel. A founder member of the Suffolk Group. *Signs work:* "M. Noyes," very small works initials only. *Address:* 51 London Rd., Halesworth, Suffolk IP19 8LS.

O

O'AIVAZIAN, Edman, painter in oil, water-colour and acrylic; designer; *b* Tehran, 10 Aug., 1932. *m* Thelma. two *s. Educ:* Tehran, Rome and London. *Exhib:* since 1948; Tehran, Venice (Biennale), New York, Boston, Jeddah, Yerevan, London - R.O.I., R.S.M.A., N.E.A.C.; prizes - 1st prize Iranian Contemp. Artists (1956), 1st prize Iranian Ministry of Culture Competition (1958), George Grimm prize R.O.I. (1998), Windsor and Newton Award R.O.I. (2000). *Work in collections:* Museums - San Lazaro, Venice; Aram Khachaturian, Yerevan; Aivazovski, Crimea; Armenian National Gallery, Yerevan; Modern Art, Yerevan. Private collections - Saudi Arabia, Oman, Tehran. *Commissions:* Boston, New York, Los Angeles, London; portraits for Saudi Royals, and Sultan Qaboos, Oman; Murals in Armenian churches; calligraphy and design of Grand Mosque, Riyadh; mural for Jeddah airport; designs for King Fahed Int. Airport Mosque; mosaic design for Sultan Qaboos Mosque, Muscat; mural for Nat. Museum, Riyadh. *Publications:* illus. Armenian Village (1984), Portraits of Poets (1970); Poems of Toumanian (1970); Komitas (1998). 2001 design of Armenian exhibition, British Library. *Clubs:* A.R.O.I.; Wapping Group of Artists. *Signs work:* "EDMAN." *Address:* 61a Fulham High St., London SW6 3JJ. *Email:* edman@lineone.net

OATES, Bennett, painter in oils, specialising in flowers and landscape; President, Guild of Norwich Painters; *b* London, 1 Jan., 1928. *m* Phyllis Mary, Art Historian and Designer A.R.C.A. two *d. Educ:* Raynes Park Grammar School. *Studied:* Wimbledon School of Art (1943-46, Gerald Cooper), R.C.A. (1948-51, Robin Darwin and Ruskin Spear). *Exhib:* three Continents. *Work in collections:* Stacy-Marks Gallery. *Clubs:* City Club, Norwich. *Signs work:* "Bennett Oates." *Address:* The Grange, Little Plumstead, Norwich NR13 5DJ.

O'BRIEN, Brigid: see GANLY, Rosaleen Brigid.

OCEAN, Humphrey, winner Imperial Tobacco Award (1982); artist-in-residence, Dulwich Picture Gallery (2002); *b* Pulborough, 22 June, 1951. *m* Miranda Argyle. two *d. Educ:* Ampleforth. *Studied:* Tunbridge Wells Art School (1967-69), Brighton College of Art (1969-70), Canterbury College of Art (1970-73). *Exhib:* R.A., Whitechapel Open, Haus der Kunst Munich, British Council; one-man shows: N.P.G. (1984), Ferens A.G. Hull (1987), Dulwich P.G., Whitworth A.G. and Tate Gallery, Liverpool (1991), Whitworth A.G., Manchester, Ormeau Baths Gallery, Belfast and Kapil Jariwala Gallery, London (1997-98), 'Painter's Eye' N.P.G. (1999). *Work in collections:* N.P.G., Imperial War Museum, Ferens A.G., Scottish N.P.G., R.A.F. Museum, Royal Collection, Hertford College, Oxford, Southwark

Collection, Wolverhampton A.G., U.E.A., National Maritime Museum, Port Authority, Zeebrugge. *Publications:* The Ocean View (Plexus 1982), Big Mouth (Fourth Estate 1990, and Brown Trout, San Francisco 1994). *Address:* 22 Marmora Rd., London SE22 0RX.

OCKENDEN, John Richard, B.Ed. (Hons.) (1978); artist in water-colour and acrylic; Vice Chairman, Deeside Art Group; *b* Cheltenham, 6 Aug., 1946. one *d.* *Educ:* Alsager C.H.E., Chester C.H.E. *Exhib:* one-man shows: Theatr Clwyd Gallery since 1988; many mixed shows in England and Wales, including International Spring Fair, N.E.C. B'ham. *Publications:* limited editions. *Signs work:* "John R. Ockenden." *Address:* 29 Marksway, Pensby, Wirral L61 9PB.

O'CONNELL, Richard Marcus, Dip. A.D. (Hons.) Norwich (1969), Cert. F.A. (Oxon. 1972); figurative painter in oil, acrylic, water-colour, poet; *b* Mumbles, Swansea, 19 July, 1947. two *d.* *Educ:* Swansea College of Art (1965-66), Ruskin School of Drawing, Norwich School of Art (1966-69), University of Oxford (1971-72). *Exhib:* one-man shows: Marlborough Fine Art, London (1974), St. David's Hall, Cardiff (1989, 1996), National Museum of Wales, Turner House, Penarth (1994), Washington Gallery, Penarth (2001). *Work in collections:* Balliol College, National Museum of Wales, Cardiff, Vale of Glamorgan Council, Barry. *Publications:* poetry book: 'Cardiff, my Cardiff' (Inika Press, Penarth, 1997); 'I Remember Swansea' (1999). *Signs work:* "R.M. O'Connell." *Address:* 26 Coronation Terrace, Penarth, Vale of Glamorgan, Wales CF64 1HN.

O'CONNOR, John, R.W.S., A.R.C.A.; painter, illustrator, wood engraver and author; *b* Leicester, 11 Aug., 1913. *m* Jenny Tennant. one *s.* *Educ:* Wyggeston School. *Studied:* Leicester College of Art; Royal College of Art. *Exhib:* one-man shows, Zwemmer Gallery (1955-68), Clare College (1965), New Grafton Gallery (1970-80), Broughton Gallery, Borders (1978 onwards); mixed shows, R.A., Bankside Gallery, London SE1 (R.W.S.), Rocket Gallery W1. *Work in collections:* N.Y. Public Library, Columbia University; public galleries, Oxford, Cambridge, and other Universities and Colleges. *Publications:* written and illustrated: Canals, Barges and People (Shenval Press), A Pattern of People (Hutchinson); Biography: Wood Engravings - John O'Connor (Whittington Press, British Art Library); books illustrated for Golden Cockerel Press, Dropmore Press, Boston Imprint, Limited Editions Club, N.Y., Florin Press, Whittington Press, Foulis Archives, Glasgow. Technical, several books on Graphic Arts. *Clubs:* Double Crown. *Signs work:* "John O'Connor." *Address:* Craigmore, Parton, Castle Douglas DG7 3NL, Scotland.

O'CONNOR, Marcel, B.A. (Hons.) Fine Art; artist/teacher in oil and wax encaustic painting; *b* Lurgan, Co. Armagh, 19 Nov., 1958. *Educ:* St. Michael's High School, Lurgan. *Studied:* Liverpool Polytechnic (1977-78), Brighton Polytechnic (1978-81), Cyprus College of Art (1983-84). *Exhib:* Scotland, Ireland, England, Cyprus, Hungary, Germany. *Work in collections:* City Arts Centre, Edinburgh. *Publications:* catalogues: 'Boundaries' in Edinburgh and Belfast; 4 Artists in Hungary; 'Europe 24' in Hungary; 'Europe 24 no.2' in Germany, bookcover artwork 'Scotland and Ulster'. *Signs work:* "Marcel O'Connor." *Address:* W.A.S.P.S. Studios (115), Patriothall, Stockbridge, Edinburgh.

ODDY, Mercy, S.W.A., H.S.; Seascape painter in water-colour, miniaturist;

Council Mem. Soc. of Women Artists, Mem. Hilliard Soc. of Miniaturists, Sec. Christchurch Arts Guild; *b* Southsea. *m* David Oddy. two *d. Exhib:* Solo show: Red House Museum and A.G., Christchurch, Dorset. Recent showings in London include Llewellyn Alexander, The Mall and Westminster Central Hall. *Work in collections:* internationally. *Clubs:* Christchurch Arts Guild, Romsey Art Group. *Signs work:* "Mercy Oddy" larger works; "M.O." miniatures. *Address:* 1 Lyme Cres., Highcliffe, Dorset BH23 5BJ.

O'DONOGHUE, Declan, M.C.S.D. (1986), F.S.C-D. (1991), M.Inst.P.I. (1991), M.S.D.I. (1991); designer and furniture maker in wood, metal, stone, glass; Director, Wilcogold Ltd. (1985), Adviser, Connemara West plc. (1992), Partner, S.F. Furniture (1980), Principal visiting tutor, Furn. Coll. Letterfrock (1988); *b* Cork, 18 Oct., 1960. *m* Fiona Mary Curry. two *d. Educ:* St. Vincent's College, Castleknock, Dublin. *Studied:* Parnham College (1978-80, R. Ingham). *Exhib:* National Theatre, Barbican, Camden Arts Centre, Mall Galleries, Bath Festival, Kilkenny Design Dublin, British Crafts Centre, British Crafts, Cheltenham. *Commissions:* National Gallery, Dublin, Guildhall, London. *Publications:* numerous exhbn. catalogues, articles, book features, B.B.C. (1981), H.T.V. (1992-93). Freeman City of London (1994), Liveryman Worshipful Co. of Furn. Makers (1994). *Clubs:* Royal Cork Yacht. *Address:* Street Farm, Acton Turville, Badminton, Glos. GL9 1HH.

O'FARRELL, Bartholomew Patrick, B.Ed.Hons. (Wales), Dip.A.D.; landscape painter in acrylic, pastel, water-colour; Lecturer in Illustration, Faculty of Art, W.G.I.H.E., Swansea (1981-85); *b* Ogilvie, Mid-Glamorgan, 11 Aug., 1941. *Educ:* Caerphilly Grammar School. *Studied:* Cardiff College of Art (1959-62), Polytechnic of Wales, Barry (1974-78). *Exhib:* Cornwall and S. Wales; annual one-man shows in Cornwall from 1986 onwards at Trelowarren, Helston Folk Museum, Camborne School of Mines Museum and Gallery, St. Austell Arts Centre, Falmouth A.G.; selected: National Museum of Wales, Albany Gallery, Cardiff; Celtic Art, Falmouth; Manor House Fine Arts; 3 Spires, Truro; Royal Cornwall Museum, Truro. *Work in collections:* National Library of Wales. *Publications:* The Encyclopedia of Acrylic Techniques; The Best of Acrylic Painting; Inspirational Portraits; Encyclopedia of Water-colour Landscape Painting; Water, How to paint it; Acrylic School. *Signs work:* "Bart O'Farrell." *Address:* Treleague Farm, St. Keverne, Helston, Cornwall TR12 6PQ. *Email:* bart@treleague.co.uk

OFFEN, John, B.A.(Hons.); designer and author; partner Ken Moore Design Associates; *b* 15 Mar., 1951. *Educ:* University of Exeter. Positions held: British Council, UNESCO, Attache, British Embassy, Tunis. *Publications:* A History of Irish Lace, Thoroughbred Style. *Address:* 33 Vicarage Ct., Kensington Church St., London W8 4HE.

OGDEN, Catherine, A.R.B.S.A. (1992), R.M.S. (1993), S.W.A. (1988); miniature seascape painter and flower pastelist; *b* London, 10 Apr., 1951. *Educ:* Plashet Secondary Modern, Kingsway College. *Exhib:* R.M.S., S.W.A., R.I., R.B.S.A., R.W.S., Mid 'Art' 86 Dudley, Laing Art collection competition, John Noott Gallery, Llewellyn Alexander Gallery. *Signs work:* "C. Ogden." *Address:* Forge House, Brimfield, Ludlow, Shropshire SY8 4NG.

OGILVY, Susan Pamela, R,H.S. Silver Gilt Medal (1995), R.H.S. Gold Medal

(1997); botanical illustrator in water-colour; *b* Bromley, Kent, 22 Mar., 1948. *m* A.R.W. Ogilvy. three *s*. *Educ:* Park School, Yeovil and St. Loyes School of Occupational Therapy, Exeter. *Studied:* Luton School of Art. *Exhib:* three solo exhibs. at Park Walk Gallery and group exhibs. at Tryon Gallery and R.H.S. *Work in collections:* Dr. Shirley Sherwood. *Commissions:* national. *Signs work:* "Susan Ogilvy" or a monogram of an S within an O. *Address:* c/o Jonathan Cooper, Park Walk Gallery, 20 Park Walk, London SW10 0AQ. *Email:* mail@jonathancooper.co.uk

O'GORMAN, Linda Helen, B.A. Hons. , graphics/illustration; artist and framer in monoprint and mixed media; *b* Woodend, Staffs., 8 July, 1948. *m* Tom O'Gorman. one *s*. four *d*. *Studied:* Gwent College of Art, Nuneaton School of Art and Bath Spa University. *Exhib:* Royal West of England Autumn open, Cheltenham open, Battersea Art Fair, Bath Society of Artists, Atrium Gallery Spring show, Society of Graphic Fine Artists, Bath Visual Arts Exhibition. *Clubs:* member Bath Area Network of Artists, Society of Graphic Fine Artists. *Signs work:* "L H O'Gorman." *Address:* 2 Beech View, Bath BA2 6DX. *Email:* lindaogorman@hotmail.com

O'HARA, D. Patrick, botanical sculptor (original works in porcelain, engraving and enamelling on crystal); *b* Windsor, 17 June, 1936. *m* Anna Greenwood, landscape painter. one *s*. one *d*. *Educ:* Haileybury and Reading University. *Studied:* Malvern Art School (1969-71). *Exhib:* Cartier, N.Y. (1972), Tryon and Moorland Gallery (1973), Chicago Flower Show (1975), Wexford Festival (1976), Victor Zelli (1978), R.H.S. (1979), Bank of Ireland (1980), Meister Gallery, Zurich (1980, 1981), Chester Beatty Library, Dublin (1984), United Nations (1984), EXPO, Osaka (1990), Royal Bot. Gdns. (1994), Huntington, California (1998), Ulster Museum, Belfast (2001). *Work in collections:* Lewis Ginter Botanical Gdn., Richmond, Va.; Flagler Museum, Florida; Jones Museum, Maine; International Museum of Wildlife Art, Gloucester; Chicago Horticultural Soc.; Gloucester City Museum; Adachi Inst., Tokyo; Smithkline Beecham Corp., Sumitomo Group; Jefferson Smurfit Foundation; Molecular Nature Ltd. *Signs work:* "Patrick O'Hara." *Address:* Manor House, Currabinny, Carrigaline, Co. Cork, Ireland.

OHL, Gabrielle, painter in oil, inks, stained glass; *b* Diego-Suarez, Malagsy. *Studied:* Paris Academie Julian (1949-50), Madrid Beaux Arts (1950-51), Melbourne Technical College of Arts (1951-53), Paris. *Exhib:* Paris salons: Independents, Marine, Automne, Femmes Peintres; Maison de l'Alsace Germany, U.S.A. One-man shows, Paris, Belgium, London, Italy, Malaya, Korea, Kuwait, Luxemburg, Sardinia, La Coupole, Paris, Stasburg, Rosheim, Barr, Alsace, MDIAC, Paris. Awards: Medaglia "Nuova Critica Europea" Italy (1969); Gold Medal, Paternoster Academy, London (1971), Palmes d'or, Paris-Critique (1977), Gold Medal, Baden Baden (1981), Bronze Medal, New York (1983), Gold Medal, Milan (1989), Prix Special, Nouvelle Figurtion, MDIAC. Paris (1995). *Signs work:* see appendix. *Address:* 10 Rue des Halles, Paris 75001.

OLDFIELD, Joy M., A.T.D. (1943); painter, sculptor and potter in oil, pastel, charcoal, clay and stone; *b* Hampstead, 1920. *m* John Oldfield. one *s*. two *d*. *Educ:* Camden School for Girls. *Studied:* Westminster and Central Schools of Art (1938-40, K. Jamieson, R. Millard), Regent St. Polytechnic Art School (1940-42, S.

Tresillian), Hornsey School of Art (1943). *Exhib:* R.P., S.W.A.; one-man show, Watatu Gallery, Nairobi (1980), Castle Park Frodsham (1994), and locally in Northwich. *Work in collections:* England, Scotland, Ireland and Kenya. *Signs work:* "Joy M. Oldfield." *Address:* White Lodge, West Rd., Weaverham, Ches. CW8 3HL.

OLIN, Leon, N.D.D. (1962), A.T.D. (1963); artist and illustrator in oil, water-colour, line drawing; Resident Artist and co-Proprietor, Gallery One, Fishguard, Pembrokeshire; *b* 28 May, 1939. *m* Sylvia Gainsford. *Studied:* Leicester and Brighton Colleges of Art (D.P. Carrington). *Exhib:* Numerous. *Work in collections:* Portsmouth Civic Gallery, Kallis Foundation, Beverly Hills. *Commissions:* Limited edition prints by Buckingham Fine Art. *Publications:* Pembrokeshire Architecture (Rosedale Pub.), Wildlife of St. James' Park (Brick by Brick L.H.A.G.), Food from the Countryside, Where have all the Cowslips gone, Out of This World (Bishopsgate Press), The Country Kitchen (Bell and Hyman). *Signs work:* "LEON OLIN." *Address:* Fron Haul, Rhos-y-Caerau, Goodwick, Pembrokeshire SA64 0LB. *Website:* www.abergwaun.com

OLIVER, Charles William, A.R.C.A. (1933), Liverpool Academy (1938); artist in oil; Vice-Principal, Laird School of Art, Birkenhead (retd.); *b* Youngstown, Ohio, U.S.A., 21 Apr., 1911. *m* Ena Landon Davies. two *s. Educ:* Wade Deacon Grammar School, Widnes, Cheshire. *Studied:* City School of Art, Liverpool, and R.C.A. under Sir W. Rothenstein (1930-34). *Exhib:* R.P.S., R.B.A., R.Scot.A., Liverpool Academy of Arts, Southport, R.Cam.A., Wirral Soc. of Arts. *Work in collections:* Liverpool, Birkenhead A.G.; Portraits: Liverpool University & John Moores Univ., Birkenhead School, Society of Anaesthetists, Chester Cathedral Library, etc. *Publications:* Anatomy and Perspective (Studio Vista, 1972). *Signs work:* "C. W. OLIVER" and date. *Address:* 1 South Bank, Oxton, Wirral CH43 5UP.

OLIVER, Dawn Nicola, H.S. (1999), M.A.S.-F. (1999); artist in water-colour, art tutor; gallery owner; *b* High Wycombe, 14 Apr., 1959. *Exhib:* R.M.S. Westminster, H.S. Wells, M.A.S.-F., Royal Soc. of Painters in Watercolour, Mall Galleries, etc. Work in collections internationally. *Clubs:* Chilterns Art Group. *Address:* 9 Hampden Rd., Stoke Mandeville, Bucks. HP22 5UF. *Email:* dawnoliver@hotmail.com

OLIVER, Kenneth Herbert, R.W.S., R.E., A.R.C.A., R.W.A.; etcher, lithographer, artist in water-colour; taught at Gloucestershire College of Arts and Technology, Cheltenham; *b* Norwich, 7 Feb., 1923. *m* Joyce Margaret Beaumont, A.R.C.A., R.W.A. three *d. Educ:* King Edward VI Grammar School, Norwich. *Studied:* Norwich School of Art and R.C.A. *Exhib:* R.W.S., R.W.A., R.A., R.E., provincial galleries and abroad. *Work in collections:* Royal West of England Academy, Bristol, Cheltenham A.G. *Signs work:* "KENNETH H. OLIVER." *Address:* Green Banks, Blakewell Mead, Painswick, Stroud, Glos. GL6 6UR.

OMAN, Julia Trevelyan, C.B.E. (1986), Hon. D.Litt. (1987), R.D.I., F.C.S.D., Des.R.C.A. Royal Scholar, R.C.A.; 1st Class; Silver Medal R.C.A.; Designer of the Year Award (1967); designer for films, theatre, television, books; Director, Oman Productions Ltd; *b* 11 July, 1930. *m* Sir Roy Strong, former Director, V. & A. *Educ:* R.C.A., London. *Exhib:* design of productions for: National Theatre, Royal Opera Covent Garden, Royal Ballet, Royal Shakespeare Co., Hamburg Opera, West End Theatres, Burg Theater Vienna, Boston Ballet, Stockholm Opera, Kassel Opera,

Glyndebourne, B.B.C. Television, films. *Work in collections:* V. & A. *Publications:* Street Children (photographs); Elizabeth R. (design); Mary Queen of Scots (design); Merchant of Venice (Folio Society), etc. *Signs work:* "Julia Trevelyan Oman." *Address:* The Laskett, Much Birch, Hereford HR2 8HZ.

ONIANS, Richard (Dick) Lathbury, M.A.(Cantab.), A.R.B.S. (1989); City and Guilds Art School Cert. of Merit (1968); sculptor in wood and stone, lecturer; Senior Carving Tutor, City and Guilds of London Art School; *b* Chalfont St. Giles, 19 May, 1940. *m* Frances Clare Critchley. *Educ:* Merchant Taylors' School, Northwood; Trinity College, Cambridge. *Studied:* City and Guilds of London Art School (1966-68). *Exhib:* Mall Galleries, Marjorie Parr Gallery, Century Galleries, Henley-on-Thames, Galleria Renata, Chicago, Clementi House Gallery, Edith Grove Gallery, Bow House Gallery, London. *Publications:* Essential Woodcarving Techniques: (G.M.C. Publications Ltd., 1997); Carving The Human Figure: (G.M.C. Publications Ltd., 2001). *Signs work:* "R.L.O." *Address:* Woodside, Commonwood, King's Langley, Herts. WD4 9BA.

OOZEERALLY, Barbara, B.A. Hons. Architecture; botanical artist in water-colour; *b* Poland, 18 Dec., 1953. *m* Shahood. one *s.* one *d. Educ:* Warsaw Politechnik. *Exhib:* S.B.A., S.G.F.A., S.F.P., R.H.S., Chelsea Flower Show. *Work in collections:* Dr Shirley Sherwood, U.K., and Mrs Barbara Macklowe, New York. *Publications:* book to be pub. 2003. *Signs work:* "B Oozeerally." *Address:* 45 Manor Close, London NW9 9HD. *Email:* barbara@barbaraoozeerally.co.uk

ORAM, Ann Alexandra, B.A.(Hons.) 1980, Post Grad. Dip. in Fine Art (1981), R.S.W. (1986); painter in water-colour, mixed media and oil; *b* London, 3 May, 1956. *m* David Cemery. one *s. Educ:* Grantown Grammar School, Inverness Royal Academy. *Studied:* Edinburgh College of Art/Heriot Watt University (1976-82). *Exhib:* one-man shows include: Thackeray Gallery, Scottish Gallery, Portland Gallery, Loomshop and Macauley Gallery; group shows: R.S.A., R.S.W., R.G.I., R.A., Stowell's Trophy, Royal Overseas League, Compass Gallery - New Generation, Corrymelia Scott, Duncan Miller Fine Art, Roger Billcliffe, S.T.V. Student Show. Air Fairs Bath, London, Manchester, New York. *Work in collections:* Britain and abroad. *Signs work:* "Ann Oram." *Address:* 10 West Court, Ravelston House Park, Edinburgh EH4 3NP.

O'REILLY, Faith, N.D.D., Dip. R.A., A.T.C.; oil and water-colourist; *b* Boston, Mass., U.S.A., 6 Aug., 1938. partner: Sandra Freeman, playwright. *Educ:* in U.S.A. and England. *Studied:* Berkshire College of Art, Royal Academy Schools, Hornsey and University of London. *Exhib:* group and solo shows: Midland Group Gallery; 273 Gallery, London; shows in Universities, Surrey, Sussex, Montpellier, Paris and Dieppe. *Work in collections:* U.S.A., France, Australia, Singapore, Britain. *Commissions:* 'Roman' Mosaic, Moorgate, London,. *Publications:* Snoopy's Guide to Computors, Btn. Poly, Mag. Helped to found Stanley Spencer Gallery, Cookham, Berkshire. *Clubs:* N.A.A. *Signs work:* "F.O.R." and "Faith O'Reilly." Returned to "O'Reilly" from adoptive name "Gibbon" in 1975. Studio in S. France; Le Vernet, 34240 Combes, and in Kemptown, Brighton BN2 2EB. *Address:* 13 Walpole Terr., Kemptown, Brighton, Sussex BN2 2EB.

O'REILLY, Richard, F.P.S.; artist in oil, water-colour, ink, wood; *b* London, 11

May, 1932. *m* P. Turner. two *s.* one *d. Educ:* Avondale School, Cheadle Heath, Ches. *Studied:* under William Redgrave, sculptor-draughtsman 'One to One'. *Exhib:* Guildhall London, Ragley Hall, Foyles's King's College, Vienna 9th International, P.S., Tattershall Castle, Cambridge Union, University of Essex, House of Commons, B.A.C., St. Martin-in-the-Fields, London. *Work in collections:* Loggia Gallery, The Investment Gallery, Paris, Berlin, Vienna, N.Y. *Publications:* work repro.: Arts Review. *Signs work:* "O'Reilly." *Address:* 12 Acanthus Rd., Battersea, London SW11 5TY.

ORGAN, Robert, D.F.A. (Lond.), R.W.A.; painter in oil, water-colour, sometimes tempera; *b* Hutton, Som., 27 Jan., 1933. *m* Valerie Barden. one *s.* three *d. Studied:* West of England College of Art, Slade School. *Exhib:* Beaux Arts, Bath (1983-95), Browse & Darby (1981-2001), R.W.A. (1995), Belloc Lowndes, Chicago (1995-97). *Work in collections:* Plymouth City A.G., Brighton and Hove A.G., Exeter Royal Albert Museum, Devon Educ. Com., Cornwall Educ. Com., R.W.A. Collection, Somerset C.C., S.W.A. Collection, Universities: Edinburgh, Exeter, Reading, Dorset County Hospital, Dorchester. *Publications:* various articles, art and architectural journals. *Signs work:* "Robert Organ" usually on back. *Address:* Lower Ridge, Wambrook, Chard, Som. TA20 3ES.

ORR, Chris, M.A. (1967), R.A. (1995); artist in painting, etching, lithography; Professor of Printmaking, Royal College of Art; *b* London, 1943. *m* Catherine Terris. one *s.* one *d. Educ:* Beckenham & Penge Grammar School. *Studied:* R.C.A. (1964-67). *Exhib:* R.A. Summer Exhbn.; one-man shows: London, America, Australia, France, Japan, Canada. *Work in collections:* V. & A., British Council, Arts Council, Science Museum, Royal Academy of Arts, Government Art Collection. *Publications:* John Ruskin (1976), Arthur (1977), Many Mansions (1990), The Small Titanic (1994), Happy Days (1999), Semi-Antics (2001). *Clubs:* Chelsea Arts Club. *Signs work:* "Chris Orr." *Address:* 7 Bristle Hill, Buckingham MK18 1EZ.

ORR, James, Royal College of Surgeons and Physicians award R.G. (1997); artist in acrylic; *b* Glasgow. *m* the late Elizabeth Inglis. one *d. Studied:* part time, Glasgow School of Art (1970-78). *Exhib:* R.S.A., R.G.I., R.W.A., P.A.I. *Work in collections:* Royal College of Surgeons and Physicians, London and Glasgow; H.R.H. The Duke of Edinburgh; Ayr Civic Collection. *Signs work:* "Orr." *Address:* 36 Gray St., Prestwick, Ayrshire KA9 1LX.

OSBORNE, Dennis Henry, N.D.D., A.R.U.A.; painter in oil, retd. teacher of art; *b* 23 Dec., 1919. *m* Maureen. one *d. Studied:* Heatherley School of Art (1946), Camberwell School of Art (1946-50, Pasmore, Coldstream, Minton, Monnington). *Exhib:* many including N.E.A.C., R.A., Hamilton A.G. Canada, O.S.A. Toronto Gallery, Queen's University Belfast, R.H.A. Dublin, Royal Academy, London (1952), Brooklyn Museum, New York – 20th Biennial International (1959); one-man shows: Ulster Arts Council (C.E.M.A.), Jorgensen Fine Art Dublin, Molesworthy Gallery, Dublin (2001); self portrait – Haverly Trust Award, etc. *Work in collections:* Hamilton A.G., Canada; National Self-portrait Collection, Limerick; UTV Belfast; Linen Centre and Museum, Lisburn, etc. *Publications:* Dictionary of Canadian Artist Vol.5, Dictionary of British Artists by Grant McWaters, 1900-1950, Dictionary of Royal Academy Exhibitors, 1905-1970, Camberwell School of Art - Teachers and

Students by Geoff Hassell, etc. *Signs work:* "D.H. OSBORNE." *Address:* 15 The Mews, South Street, Newtownards, Co. Down BT23 4JU.

OSBORNE, Stuart John, A.R.C.A., A.T.D., M.F.P.S.; sculptor, models portraits, figures and animals; stone and wood carver; *b* Weston-s-Mare, Som. *m* Margaret Cole, A.T.D., portrait and animal painter. one *d. Educ:* Kingsholme School, Weston-s-Mare. *Studied:* Bristol College of Art, and Royal College of Art, London. *Exhib:* societies: F.P.S., Galerie Salammbo, Paris, Vallombreuse, Biarritz, International, New York, Geneva, Loggia Gallery, Kulfurgeschichtliches Museum, Osnabruck. *Work in collections:* public and private, including portraits and animals. *Signs work:* "S.J. Osborne." *Address:* 64 Burton Manor Rd., Stafford ST17 9PR.

OSMOND, Edward, A.T.D., M.S.I.A., Carnegie Award; artist in oils, wash, line, illustrations, commercial drawing and book design; *m* C. M. ("Laurie") Osmond, sc. and painter. *Signs work:* in full, block caps. *Address:* Downland Cottage, Lullington Cl., Seaford, E. Sussex BN25 4JH.

OSTROWSKY, Oleh, B.A., M.Sc., Ph.D., F.I.E.D., Dip. Appreciation and Hon. plaque I.E.D.; artist in graphic art, lecturer in design, mechanical engineer; Prof. Emeritus, Lviv University, Ukraine; Lecturer in Engineering Design, Trent University and People's College, Nottingham; *b* Lviv, Ukraine, 16 Apr., 1925. two *d. Studied:* Madrid State Art Academy, Nottingham Trent University, London Polytechnic. *Exhib:* Italy, Spain, England and Ukraine. *Publications:* author and illustrator four text books in Engineering Design, album of artistic works, calendars, greetings cards, etc. *Clubs:* Nottingham Soc. of Artists. *Address:* 14 Clandon Drive, Sherwood, Nottingham NG5 2AN.

OTTEY, Piers Ronald Edward Campbell, B.A.(Hons.); painter in oil on canvas and panel, teacher/lecturer; *b* London, 27 Sept., 1955. *m* Annelise. two *s.* one *d. Educ:* King's College School, Wimbledon. *Studied:* Chelsea School of Art (1974-78, the late Patrick Symons, Myles Murphy). *Exhib:* R.A., Bath Contemporary Arts Fair, London, Sussex, Paris; one-man shows: Brighton (1988), Midhurst (1991), Stansted House (1994), Seaford College (1994), The Mill Studio, Sussex (1996), Bates Gallery, London (1996, 1998), Sheridan Russell Gallery, London (2000, 2001). *Work in collections:* England, France, Denmark, Canada. *Commissions:* Grant Thornton, Chichester Hospital. *Publications:* Exhibit 'A' Magazine, 4 page feature (2000). *Signs work:* "Ottey." *Address:* Bishop's Hill Cottage, Graffham, nr. Petworth, W. Sussex GU28 0QA.

OULTON, Therese, B.A. Hons. (Fine Art), M.A. (R.C.A.); painter in oil; *b* Shrewsbury, Salop., 20 Apr., 1953. *m* Peter Gidal. *Studied:* St. Martin's and Royal College of Art. *Exhib:* fifteen solo exhibs. since 1984 in London, New York, Los Angeles, Vienna, Berlin, Munich, Museum of Modern Art, Oxford etc., as well as group exhibs. Venice Biennale, Turner Prize at The Tate, Mellon Centre, Yale, Stockholm etc. *Work in collections:* Tate, Metropolitan, National Gallery of Australia, Harris Museum, Museum of Fine Art, Boston, British Museum, Leeds City Art Museum, V. & .A., St. Louis Art Museum, Missouri, Broadgate, Hoffman Collection, Berlin etc. *Publications:* monograph catalogues include Marlborough, London, Andrew Benjamin in 'Journal of Philosophy and the Visual Arts', Stuart Morgan's essay and interview in 'What the Butler Saw', Angela Moorjani's chapter in 'Loss and Lestness' etc. *Signs work:* "Therese Oulton." *Address:* 38 St. Stephen's Gardens, London W2 5NJ. *Email:* thereseoulton@btinternet.com

OVERTON, Alan, artist in acrylic; *b* Salisbury, Wilts., 27 Nov., 1946. *m* Petula. one *d. Exhib:* R.A. Summer Show, R.W.A., Royal Bath and West Show, N.A.P.A. (The Artist award Wales, 1999), S.W. Academy of Fine and Applied Arts, Exeter. *Work in collections:* Lord Bath, many private collections. *Clubs:* N.A.P.A., Frome Art Soc., Warminster Art Soc. *Signs work:* "A. Overton." *Address:* 26 Lynfield Rd., Frome, Som. BA11 4JB.

OWEN, Glynis, B.A. (Fine Art) (1966), A.T.C. (1967), F.R.B.S. (1990); sculptor in stone and bronze; *b* Gravesend, Kent, 22 May, 1945. married. two *s.* one *d. Educ:* Portsmouth High School, G.P.D.S.T. *Studied:* Portsmouth College of Art (1962-66), Goldsmiths' College (1966-67). *Exhib:* R.I.B.A. (1991), Glyndebourne Festival Opera (1996), Millennium Exhbn., Artmonsky Arts (1999), McHardy Sculpture Gallery (1999, 2001). *Work in collections:* Alton College, Hants. purchased by Hants. Architects Dept.; Stevenage Town Centre, life-size family group, commissioned by Stevenage Development Corp.; Portrait of Jacqueline du Pre for Music Bldg. St. Hilda's College, Oxford; Tate Modern, Resource. *Commissions:* private: Lake Como, Switzerland (1992), Nick Mason (Pink Floyd) (1997); national: Teaching Awards Trophy established by Lord Puttnam C.B.E. (2000). *Publications:* Carving Techniques by Glynis Beecroft (Batsford 1976), Casting Techniques by Glynis Beecroft (Batsford 1979). *Signs work:* "Glynis Owen." *Address:* The Studio, 52 Pilgrim's Lanc, Hampstead, London NW3 1SN.

OWEN, Muriel Sylvia, N.D.D., A.T.D., S.W.A., U.A., F.R.S.A.; painter in watercolour, lecturer; Head of Art and Deputy Principal, Dixon and Wolfe, Tutors, London SW1 (1969-82); Vice-Pres., Soc. of Women Artists; runs painting holidays worldwide – under the name "Muriel Owen Painting Holidays"; *b* Welwyn Garden City. *m* Edward Eardley Owen, M.A. three *s.* by previous marriage. *Educ:* Welwyn Garden City Grammar School. *Studied:* St. Albans School of Art (1946-50 under Gwen White and Christopher Sanders, R.P., R.A.), London University (1951). *Exhib:* R.I., S.W.A., U.A., Llewellyn Alexander Gallery, London; ten one-man shows, London, Fairfield Halls, Croydon, Yarmouth Castle, I.O.W. official galleries. *Work in collections:* 38 paintings English Heritage, I.O.W. Arts Council, Bank of England, Queen Elizabeth Military Hospital, Woolwich, Atomic Energy Commission, London. *Publications:* work repro.: St. Paul's, Westminster, floral, (Henry Ling), calendars and 32 cards (I.O.W. County Press), series of 4 art teaching videos. *Signs work:* "Muriel Owen." *Address:* Briarwood House, Church Hill, Totland, I.O.W. PO39 0EU.

OXENBURY, Helen Gillian, illustrator/writer in water-colour; Kate Greenaway medal (1969), Smarties award (1989), Boston Globe award, Kurt Maschler award (1985); *b* 2 June, 1938. *m* John M. Burningham. one *s.* two *d. Studied:* Ipswich School of Art and Central School of Arts and Crafts, London. *Publications:* illustrated: The Three Little Wolves and the Big Bad Pig (1993), Farmer Duck (1991), We're Going on a Bear Hunt (1989). *Signs work:* "Helen Oxenbury." *Address:* c/o Walker Books, 87 Vauxhall Walk, London SE11 5HJ.

OXLADE, Roy, M.A., R.C.A.; painter; *b* 1929. *Studied:* Bromley College of Art and with David Bomberg. *Exhib:* Young Contemporaries (1952-54), Borough Bottega Group (1954, 1955), Winnipeg Biennial (1st prize drawing, 1960), John Moores (1963, 1991), Hayward Annual (1982), Norwich Gallery 'Rocks and Flesh' (1985), Cleveland International (1989), Norwich Gallery, 'EAST' (1991, 1994), Velan, Turin (2000); one person shows: Vancouver A.G. (1963), New Metropole, Folkestone (1983), AIR Gallery (1983), Odette Gilbert Gallery (1985, 1987, 1988), Gardner Centre, University of Sussex (1990), Reed's Wharf Gallery, London (1993), Art Space Gallery, London (2001); two person show: Wrexham & Aberystwyth Arts Centres (1999). Korn/Ferry R.A. Picture of the Year (1997). *Work in collections:* South East Arts, Railtrack London, Deal Dallas, University College Oxford, J.C.R. *Publications:* David Bomberg (R.C.A. Papers 3 1981). *Address:* Forge Cottage, Newnham, Sittingbourne, ME9 0LQ.

OXLEY, Ursula Frances, Board of Educ. drawing exam. (1937); artist in black and white, crayon, conte, pastel and water-colour; specialist in child portraiture; *b* Ealing, 4 May, 1918. *m* Laurence Oxley. one *s.* one *d. Educ:* privately. *Studied:* Winchester School of Art under E. E. Anderson, A.R.C.A. (1935-39). *Exhib:* P.S., S.W.A., S.G.A., R.I., Guildford Art Soc., Woking Art Soc., N.S., Alresford Art Soc. *Publications:* illustrated 1971 and subsequent editions of History of Alresford, and Sketches of My Cat. *Clubs:* Alresford Art Soc. *Signs work:* "Ursula Oxley." *Address:* The Studio Bookshop, Alresford, Hants. SO24 9AW.

OXLEY, Valerie Mary, Cert.Ed. (1969), A.N.E.A. (1983), S.B.A. (1987); self taught botanical illustrator in pencil, water-colour, pen and ink; Tutor, botanical illustration, A.E.C.; *b* Manchester, 26 Sept., 1947. *m* Michael Oxley, M.Sc., C.Eng. one *d. Educ:* Abbeydale Girls' Grammar School, Sheffield; Hereford College of Educ. *Exhib:* S.B.A., R.H.S., Linnean Soc., Portico Gallery, Manchester, Durham A.G., Museum of Garden History, London. *Publications:* Art Editor 'Wild Flowers of the Peak District' published by the Hallamshire Press, Sheffield. *Clubs:* Vice President, Northern Soc. of Botanical Art, Chairman: Sheffield Botanical Gardens Florilegium Society. *Signs work:* "Valerie Oxley." *Address:* Brookside, Firbeck, Worksop, Notts. S81 8JZ.

P

PACE, Shirley, sculptor and artist in bronze, charcoal, pen and ink, conté, monochrome, the Ashling Collection representational, equestrian sculptor to Susse Fondeur, Paris; *b* Worthing, Sussex, 16 Feb., 1933. *m* Roy Pace. two *d. Educ:* Worthing Convent. *Studied:* Worthing School of Art (1948-51). *Exhib:* Mall Galleries, Alwin Gallery, many provincial and overseas galleries. *Work in collections:* Life and a quarter dray-horse, London; private collections: England, U.S.A., Bermuda, New Zealand, Australia, Hong Kong. *Clubs:* S.E.A., Chichester Art Soc. *Signs work:* "Shirley Pace." *Address:* Field House, Newells La., West Ashling, Chichester, W. Sussex PO18 8DD.

PACKARD, Gilian E., Des.R.C.A. (1962), F.S.D.C. (1963), F.R.S.A. (1975), F.C.S.D. (1977); first woman freeman of Goldsmiths' Company by special grant (1971); designer of jewellery in gold, platinum, silver and stones; Senior Lecturer, Sir John Cass Dept. of Arts, Design and Manufacture, London Guildhall University; *b* Newcastle upon Tyne, 16 Mar., 1938. *Educ:* Claremont School, Esher. *Studied:* Kingston-upon-Thames School of Art (1955-58), Central School of Arts and Crafts (1959), Royal College of Art (1959-62). *Work in collections:* Goldsmiths Hall, De Beers, V. & A. *Signs work:* "G.E.P." within oval, (Hallmark). *Address:* 8.2 Stirling Ct., 3 Marshall St., London W1V 1LQ.

PACKER, William John, N.D.D. (Painting), A.T.C., Hon. F.R.C.A., Hon. R.B.A.; painter in oil and water-colour; Art Critic, The Financial Times (since 1974); *b* Birmingham, 19 Aug., 1940. *m* Clare Winn. three *d. Educ:* Windsor Grammar School; Wimbledon School of Art (1959-63), Brighton College of Art (1963-64). *Exhib:* R.A.; group exhbns.: Angela Flowers, Cadogan, Contemporary and many other galleries. *Publications:* The Art of Vogue Covers (Octopus, 1980), Fashion Drawing in Vogue (Thames & Hudson, 1983), Henry Moore (with Gemma Levine) (Weidenfeld & Nicolson, 1985). *Clubs:* Chelsea Arts. *Signs work:* "W.P." or "W. PACKER." *Address:* 39 Elms Rd., Clapham, London SW4 9EP.

PAES, Rui, M.A., R.C.A. (1988), Dip. E.S.B.A.P. (1976-81); painter in oil and water-based media; *b* Pemba, Mozambique, 13 July, 1957. *m* Anabela Ribeiro da Cunha. one *s. Educ:* Escola de Belas Artes do Porto, Portugal (1976-81), Royal College of Art, London (1986-88); Calouste Gulbenkian Scholarship (1986-1988) and the Beal Foundation Grant. *Exhib:* England, Germany, Portugal and Spain. *Work in collections:* Museu de Arte Moderna, Oporto, Portugal, The Beal collection, U.S.A., and the Royal College of Art Permanent collection. *Commissions:* Mural painting in Egypt, England, France, Germany, Norway and Portugal. *Publications:* illustrations for ". do tempo inutil" by Gloria de Sant'anna (1975). *Clubs:* Chelsea Arts. *Signs work:* see appendix. *Address:* 2 Chelsea Farmhouse Studios, Milmans St., London SW10 0BY.

PAGE, Charles, R.I. (1988), M.S.I.A. (1955); painter, illustrator and graphic designer in water-colour, acrylic, mixed media, collage; *b* Leighton Buzzard, 17 Apr., 1910. *m* (1) Jessie Stevens (decd.). (2) Beryl Sheaves (decd.). one *s. Educ:* Luton Grammar School. *Studied:* Central School of Art and Crafts (1928-29). *Exhib:* R.I., R.W.S., R.S.A., R.B.S.A. and several provincial galleries. First recipient of Rowland Hilder Award at R.I. (1994). *Work in collections:* Luton A.G., Letchworth A.G. *Signs work:* "Charles Page." *Address:* 13 Carisbrooke Rd., Harpenden, Herts. AL5 5QS.

PAGE-ROBERTS, James, painter in oil, sculptor, artist in black and white, and writer; *b* Silchester, 5 Feb., 1925. *m* Margaretha Klees. two *s. Educ:* Wellington College, and Taft, U.S.A. *Studied:* Central School of Arts and Crafts and Old Vic School of Theatre Design. *Exhib:* one-man shows at Galerie de Seine, Reid Gallery, Kintetsu Gallery, Osaka, Qantas Gallery, Cambridge, Loft Gallery. *Publications:* Writer of over 700 articles on vines and wines, and author/illustrator of 14 books on vines, wines, cooking, docklands, household management and travel. *Signs work:* "P R" and "PAGE-ROBERTS." *Address:* 37 St. Peter's Grove, London W6 9AY.

PAINE, Ken, P.S., S.P.F.; portrait artist in pastel, oil, water-colour; Master

Pastellist of France; *b* 2 Nov., 1926. one *s.* two *d. Studied:* Worked with R.Q. Dunlop, R.A.; studied at Twickenham College of Art. *Exhib:* annually P.S., R.P., R.O.I., R.I. at Mall Galleries London, R.W.A., widely exhib. in and around London, U.S.A., France, Canada, Germany; solo exhbns. include Llewellyn Alexander Gallery, London; Edward Day Gallery, Ontario, Canada. *Commissions:* many which include Sir David Atkinson Air Marshal, Trevor McDonald broadcaster. *Publications:* (Biography) "Ken Paine - His Life and Work" by Michael Simonow. *Signs work:* "PAINE." *Address:* 8 Spring Gdns., E. Molesey, Surrey KT8 0JA.

PAINTER, Tom, F.R.B.S., R.B.A., A.R.C.A. (Sculpture, 1949) Travelling Scholar; sculptor in bronze, concrete, resin/fibre glass, wood, stone; *b* 29 Nov., 1918. *m* Muriel Jeffery, A.R.C.A. one *d. Educ:* Wolverhampton. *Studied:* Wolverhampton School of Art (R.J. Emerson). *Exhib:* R.B.S., R.B.A., R.A. *Work in collections:* U.K., U.S.A., Canada, Italy. *Signs work:* "Tom Painter." *Address:* 5 Garlies Rd., Forest Hill, London SE23 2RU.

PALMER, Prof. Herbert Ralph, awarded Scholarship of Art, Johannesburg, S. Africa (1932-36); F.R.B.S.; sculptor in all known media and painter in oil and water-colour; worked in the Art Dept., V. & A.; art teacher, Tower Bridge Institute, London (1950-51), Senior Professional Officer and Curator of Art, McGregor Museum, Kimberley, Cape Province (1974-76), Curator, Zululand Historical Museum, Eshowe, Natal (1980-); *b* Richmond Surrey, 13 Dec., 1915. *Studied:* Johannesburg Art School, and one-time pupil of Anton Van Wouw and P. H. Jowett. *Exhib:* in twenty leading galleries in London, New York, South Africa, Portugal. *Work in collections:* (1947) worked with Sir William Reid Dick, K.C.V.O., R.A., on the Roosevelt Monument. *Commissions:* numerous including two ecclesiastical figures, St. James Church, Fulham, London; bronze Mother and child, South Africa House, London; Dr. Basil Merriman Bronze, Carter Foundation, London, etc. *Publications:* There must be Sculpture (1989). Hobby: Violin-making. *Clubs:* Chelsea Arts. *Signs work:* "R. Palmer." *Address:* 91 Vausedale Rd., Queensburgh 4093, Natal, S. Africa.

PALMER, Jean C., B.A. (Hons.) Fine Art; painter in oil; part-time Tutor - Adult College, Lancaster; *b* Southport, 1961. *m* Peter Layzell. one *s.* one *d. Studied:* Southport College of Art (1977-79), University of Central Lancs. (1979-82). *Exhib:* R.A. Summer Shows (1992-99), various London exhbns. *Work in collections:* Manchester City A.G., NatWest Coll., Warrington Arts Council, Jerwood Foundation. *Signs work:* "J.Palmer" on reverse *Address:* 72 Vale Rd., Lancaster LA1 2JL.

PALMER, John Frederick, R.W.A. (1991); Cornelissen prize R.W.A. annual exhbn. (1985); graphic designer; artist in oil, water-colour, gouache; P.P., Bristol Savages; *b* Bristol, 11 Aug., 1939. *Educ:* Carlton Park, Bristol. *Studied:* West of England College of Art (1955-56, J. Arnold). *Exhib:* Bristol Artists, Arnolfini, R.W.A., Mall Gallery, First Sight. *Work in collections:* Bristol Savages, Leeds Bldg. Soc., NatWest Assurance, British Aerospace, Atomic Energy Authority, Wessex Collection, Block Busters, International Duty Free, private collectors. *Publications:* Drawing & Sketching (1993), Watercolour Landscape (1994). *Clubs:* Bristol Savages. *Signs work:* "J.F. Palmer." *Address:* 18 Haverstock Rd., Knowle, Bristol BS4 2BZ.

PALMER, Juliette, N.D.D. (1950), A.T.D. (1951); painter in water-colour, illustrator, author; *b* Romford, 18 May, 1930. *m* Dennis Palmer. one *d. Educ:* Brentwood County High School. *Studied:* S.E. Essex School of Art (1946-50, Alan Wellings, William Stobbs, Bernard Carolan). *Exhib:* R.A., R.I., N.E.A.C., R.O.I., R.W.A.; group gallery shows, Philadelphia, U.S.A., Sheffield, Windsor, Henley, Barnes, Bloomsbury; one-man shows, S. Australia, Tokyo, Cambridge, Chipping Norton, Cookham. Finalist in Hunting, Laing, Singer & Friedlander/Sunday Times National Art Competitions. *Work in collections:* Barking Library, Leicestershire Educ. Com. *Publications:* 60 children's books illustrated; author/illustrator, 6 children's picture/information books (Macmillan). *Signs work:* "Juliette Palmer." *Address:* Melmott Lodge, The Pound, Cookham, Maidenhead, Berks. SL6 9QD.

PALMER, Margaret, A.T.D., P.S., N.S.; portrait painter in oil and pastel, animal and genre painter, book illustrator; *b* London, 10 Sept., 1922. *m* R. G. W. Garrett. two *d. Studied:* Hornsey School of Art (1938-39), Salisbury School of Art (1939-41), Bournemouth College of Art (1941-42). *Exhib:* R.P., R.O.I., etc.; one-man shows in London, Guildford, Farnham, Leatherhead, works in worldwide collections. *Commissions:* Lord Howell, Lord Nugent, Sir David Rowe-Ham, Sir Richard Nichols, Sir Greville Spratt, Mother Teresa, Sandy Gall, Susan Hampshire, etc. *Publications:* written and illustrated, Honeypot and Buzz; also illustrated books published by Harrap, Heinemann, etc. *Signs work:* "Margaret Palmer." *Address:* Robins Oak, Wonersh, nr. Guildford, Surrey GU5 0PR.

PALMER, Robert Derrick, R.O.I. (1978), R.B.A. (1983); painter in oil; *b* Cambridge, 13 June, 1927. *m* Jean Parker. one *s.* one *d. Educ:* Central School, Cambridge. *Studied:* Cambridge School of Art (part-time 1951-58). *Exhib:* one-man shows, Richard Bradley Atelier, Norwich (1968), Hallam Gallery, E. Sheen, Fermoy Gallery, Kings Lynn (1980). Awarded De Laszlo Medal at R.B.A. exhbn. (1990), Alan Gourley Prize R.O.I. (1992). Mixed exhbns. include Royal Academy, Mall Galleries (R.B.A., R.O.I., N.E.A.C., Discerning Eye), Bourne Gallery, Reigate, Catto Gallery, London, St. James Gallery, Bath, Jerram Gallery, Salisbury, Century Gallery, Datchet. *Signs work:* "R. PALMER" or "R.P." *Address:* 8 St. Mary's Rd., Poole, Dorset BH15 2LH.

PALTENGHI, Julian Celeste, B.F.A.; Winner 1993 Hunting/Observer art prizes: Travel award - Australia; painter in oil, sculptor in plaster and bronze; *b* London, 28 Aug., 1955. *m* Katy. one *d. Educ:* Stowe, Bucks. *Studied:* Cambridge (1976-77), Loughborough College of Art (1978-81). *Exhib:* 'Critic's Choice' Clare Henry: Cooling Gallery, Beaux Arts Galleries, London and Bath, Swiss Artists in Britain: October Galleries, Stephen Bartley, Chelsea, Camden Annual, G.L.C. Spirit of London Festival Hall, Centre Georges Pompidou, Paris, Royal West of England Academy, (purchased by) Christie's Cooperate Collection. *Clubs:* Chelsea Arts. *Signs work:* "PALTENGHI." *Address:* 143 Old Church St., London SW3.

PANCHAL, Shanti, M.A. Bombay (1977), Byam Shaw, London (1980); painter in watercolour; resident artist, Hariss Museum, Preston (1994), Winsor and Newton Art Factory (2000); *b* Mesar, India. *Studied:* Byam Shaw, London. *Exhib:* over 25 solo exhibs. in U.K. and abroad. *Work in collections:* Arts Council, British Museum, Birmingham Museum, Walker Art Gallery, Liverpool, etc. *Commissions:* Imperial

War Museum (1998), De Beers (1996). *Publications:* exhib. catalogues, 'Earthen Shades', Cartwright Hall, Bradford; Castlefield Gallery, Manchester (1998); 'Windows of the Soul', Angel Row Gallery, Nottingham (1997); 'Private Myths', Pitshanger Manor Museum and Gallery, London (2000). *Signs work:* "Shanti Panchal" or in Gujarati. *Address:* 25 Locket Rd., Harrow, Middx. HA3 7ND.

PANCHERI, Robert, A.R.B.S., Dip. (1977); sculptor in wood and stone; *b* Bromsgrove, 22 June, 1916. *m* Bridget Milligan. two *s.* two *d. Educ:* Bromsgrove School. *Studied:* Birmingham School of Art (1934-39, William Bloye). *Work in collections:* statues: Winwick Lancs; Great Malvern Priory; Franciscan Friary, Chester; St. Peter's Church, Swinton, Manchester; sculpture panel, Sheldon Fire Station. *Signs work:* "R. Pancheri" lower case letters. *Address:* 12 Finstall Rd., Bromsgrove B60 2DZ.

PANNETT, Juliet, M.B.E. (1992), F.R.S.A.; portrait painter; Special artist to the Illustrated London News from 1958-64; *b* Hove, Sussex. *m* Major M. R. D. Pannett (died 1980). one *s.* one *d. Studied:* Brighton School of Art. *Exhib:* R.A., R.P., R.I. *Work in collections:* 22 portraits in National Portrait Gallery, Hove Art Gallery. Portraits include: H.M. The Queen; H.R.H. Prince Andrew and H.R.H. Prince Edward for H.M. The Queen; Lord Goodman; Lord Tonypandy; Lavinia Duchess of Norfolk for Arundel Castle; Oxford and Cambridge colleges. *Publications:* work repro.: Illustrated London News, The Times, Daily Telegraph, Radio Times, Birmingham Mail. Awarded freedom of Worshipful Company of Painter Stainers; Freeman of City of London (1960). *Signs work:* "Juliet Pannett." *Address:* Pound House, Poundstone Lane, Angmering Village, Sussex BN16 4AL.

PAOLOZZI, Sir Eduardo Luigi, Kt. (1989), C.B.E. (1968), R.A. (1979), Hon. Dr. (R.C.A.), D.Litt. (Glas.); sculptor; Visiting Professor, Royal College of Art; *b* Leith, Scotland, 7 Mar., 1924. *Studied:* Edinburgh College of Art, Slade School. *Exhib:* one-man shows, Mayor Gallery (1947), 30th Venice Biennale (1960), M.O.M.A. New York (1964), Rijksmuseum, Otterlo (1967), Stadtische Kunsthalle Dusseldorf, Tate Gallery (1971), V. & A. (1973, 1977), Nationalgalerie Berlin (1975), Kolnischer Kunstverein (1979), Royal Scottish Academy (1984), Museum Ludwig (1985). *Publications:* Eduardo Paolozzi by Winfried Konnertz (Dumont Verlag, 1984). *Signs work:* "Eduardo Paolozzi." *Address:* 107 Dovehouse St., London SW3 6JZ.

PARFITT, Margaret, C.B.E. (1980), S.R.N., S.W.A., C.A.S., S.E.L.A.S.; sculptor in wood and metal; *b* Romford, 23 Oct., 1920. *m* Ronald Parfitt. two *d. Educ:* Brentwood County High School. *Studied:* Evening Classes (Don Smith). *Exhib:* Sun Lounge, Fairfield (1991), Outwood Gallery (1988-90), Soc. of Women Artists. *Signs work:* "Margaret Parfitt' or "M.P." joined. *Address:* The White House, 165 Shirley Church Rd., Shirley, Croydon CR0 5AJ.

PARKER, Constance-Anne, A.T.D., F.R.B.S.; Lecturer, Archivist and Travelling Exhbns. Organiser, Royal Academy (1986-), Librarian, Royal Academy of Arts (1974-86), Assistant Librarian (1958-74); Landseer Scholar, Sir David Murray Scholarship, Leverhulme Scholarship; painter in oil, sculptor in wood and clay; *b* London, 19 Oct., 1921. *Educ:* privately. *Studied:* Polytechnic School of Art and Royal Academy Schools (four silver and three bronze medals). *Exhib:* R.A., London galleries and provinces. *Publications:* Mr. Stubbs the Horse Painter (1971), Royal Academy Cookbook (1981), Stubbs Art Animals, Anatomy (1984). *Clubs:* Reynolds. *Address:* 1 Melrose Rd., Barnes, London SW13 9LG.

PARKER, Gill, S.Eq.A. (1987); winner President's Medal S.Eq.A. (1992); sculptress in bronze, silver; *b* Amesbury. *Educ:* South Wilts. Grammar School. *Exhib:* solo shows: Sladmore Gallery, London (1984, 1987, 1989), S.Eq.A. (1984-96), National Horse Racing Museum, Newmarket (1991), Chute Standen (1992), Robert Bowman Ltd, London (Dec. 1999, June 2000), Kevin Anderson Gallery, Los Angeles (Nov. 2000). *Work in collections:* National Horse Racing Museum, Newmarket, World Wildlife Art Museum, Jackson Hole, Wyoming. *Commissions:* Habibti, Mrs.Moss, Precocious, Rainbow Quest, Sir Wattie, Dancing Brave, Middleroad. *Signs work:* "G. Parker" or "Gill Parker." *Address:* 18 Tibbs Meadow, Upper Chute, Andover, Hants. SP11 9HG.

PARKER, Walter F., A.R.C.A., M.S.I.A.D., A.T.D., F.R.S.A.; Principal, Hartlepool College of Art (1953-78); War Service in Middle East as F/Lieut. in R.A.F.; senior posts held at Preston and Hastings Schools of Art; since retirement in 1978 takes a number of regular painting schools in Britain specialising in watercolours and printmaking; *b* Carlisle, 11 May, 1914. *m* Joy E. Turk, contralto, Guildhall School of Music (decd.). *Educ:* Carlisle Grammar School (1922-30). *Studied:* Carlisle Art School (1930-35), Royal College of Art (1935-38), Courtauld Inst. (1938-39). *Clubs:* Pres., Lake Artists' Soc. and Life mem. (1996). *Signs work:* "Walter F. Parker." *Address:* 19 The Cliff, Seaton Carew, Hartlepool TS25 1AP.

PARKIN, Jane Maureen, S.Eq.A., S.W.A.; artist in oil and pastel; *b* Sheffield, 29 Aug., 1936. *m* Frank. one *d. Educ:* Wath Grammar School, S. Yorks. *Studied:* mainly self taught with five years tuition by P.K.C. Jackson, A.R.C.A. *Exhib:* S.Eq.A., Westminster Gallery, Christie's, Carisbrooke Gallery, every year since 1997 with the Society of Women Artists at Westminster Gallery. *Publications:* Limited edn. prints and Open prints by Rosensteils London/New York. *Signs work:* "Jane M. Parkin." *Address:* 103/109 Main St., Haworth, Keighley, W. Yorks. BD22 8DP. *Email:* frank.parkin@totalise.co.uk

PARKIN, Michael Robert, art dealer; chairman/managing director, Michael Parkin Fine Art Ltd.; *b* London, 1 Dec., 1931. *m* Diana Mary Frances. three *d. Educ:* Mill Hill and St. George's Schools; Magdalen College, Oxford. *Exhib:* at Michael Parkin Gallery, 11 Motcomb St., SW1. Cover British Art 1850-1950, have included The Cafe Royalists, Four for Whistler, The Fitzrovians, Claude Flight, A Salute to Marcel Boulestin and J. E. Láboureur, Jean Cocteau, Cecil Beaton Memorial Exhbn., Artists of the Yellow Book, Nina Hamnett, Walter Sickert, Walter Greaves, Rex Whistler and Stephen Tennant, Walter Bayes, Jaques Emile Blanche, Artists of Corsham - a Celebration, Sylvia Gosse, Therese Lessore, the 7 & 5 Society, Paul Stevenson and John Pawle, Hermione Hammond, Gwyneth Johnstone, Roland Collins, Philip Jones, Damian O'Brien. *Publications:* Old Chelsea (Newson, London 1975), Louis Wain's Cats (Thames & Hudson, London 1983), Louis Wain's Edwardian Cats (Thames & Hudson, New York 1983); in preparation: Modern British Art 1860-1960; Walter Greaves. *Clubs:* Beefsteak, Norfolk, B.A.F.T.A., Chelsea Arts. *Address:* Gunton Hall, Hanworth, Norfolk NR11 7HL.

PARKINSON, Gerald, painter in oil, gouache and water-colour; *b* Shipley, Yorks., 5 Nov., 1926. *m* Sylvia Mary. one *s*. *Educ:* Woodhouse Grove School, nr. Leeds. *Studied:* Bradford College of Art (1951-54). *Exhib:* R.A., West of England Academy, John Moores, Sussex Artists, Yorks. Artists, S.E.A.; one-man shows: London, Bologna, Stockholm, Brighton, York, Bristol, Monte Carlo, Lewes, Bradford, Hove, Tunbridge Wells. *Work in collections:* Glasgow, Brighton, Leicestershire C.C., L.C.C., Surrey C.C., West Riding C.C. *Commissions:* Mural for NatWest Bank. *Signs work:* "Gerald Parkinson." *Address:* The Gate House, Wootton Manor, Nr. Polegate, East Sussex BN26 5RY. *Email:* sales@conceptengland. freeserve.co.uk

PARKINSON, Richard Henry, Dip. A/D (1967); painter in oil on canvas/board, restorer, critic, designer, frame maker; Prop./M.D. The Studio, tutor for Pitman's Correspondence Courses since 1967, judge at Royal College for Parkinson/Henderson Prize since 1988, and Cheltenham Correspondence College; *b* Epsom, 23 Mar., 1947. *m* Susan Sanders. one *s*. one *d*. *Educ:* Ewell Castle, Epsom. *Studied:* Folkestone School of Art (1963-67), Heatherleys School of Art (1968-71). *Exhib:* R.A. since 1967, Wye, Henley, Wimbledon, R.W.A., Mall Galleries, R.B.A., Stockbridge, etc. *Work in collections:* Woolworth Holdings, various Boardrooms. *Commissions:* portraits various. *Publications:* Introductory Art (Pitman), Mounting Water-colours (The Artist). *Clubs:* Chelsea Arts. *Signs work:* "R.H.P." or "Richard Parkinson." *Address:* No. 3, Best Lane, Canterbury, Kent CT1 2JB.

PARR, Elizabeth, painter in water-colour and oil; paints the Lake District, Cornwall and teddy bears; *b* Horsham, W. Sussex. *m* Douglas Ashley (1999), (previously widowed in 1996). one *s*. two *d*. *Educ:* St Christophers, Horsham. *Studied:* Horsham School of Art and I.C.S. under Patrick Barclay. *Exhib:* eighteen solo exhibs. in Cornwall and The Cotswolds; group exhibs. at Mall Galleries and Westminster Galleries, London; work accepted by "Britain's Painters" for four consecutive years. *Work in collections:* various national and international collections incl. St Ives Gallery. *Publications:* greeting cards and prints. *Signs work:* "Elizabeth Parr." *Address:* The Beach House, Coverack, Nr. Helston, Cornwall TR12 6TE.

PARROTT, Denis William, N.D.D.(Painting) (1953), A.T.C. (1958), Ph.D. (1993), Fulbright Scholar, U.S.A. (1970-71), F.R.S.A. (1977), F.S.A.E. (1980); painter, printmaker; lecturer, University College, Northampton; *b* Dewsbury, Yorks., 22 Mar., 1931. *m* Kathleen Hendry. one *s*. *Educ:* Dewsbury Technical College. *Studied:* Dewsbury and Batley School of Art (1948-51), Camberwell School of Art (1951-53), Leeds College of Art (1957-58). *Exhib:* R.A., Mall Gallery, U.S.A., Centre International d'Art Contemporain de Paris and Galerie Salammbo, Paris. *Work in collections:* England, Europe and U.S.A. *Publications:* author for Schools Council. *Signs work:* "Denis W. Parrott." *Address:* 37 Bowling Green Rd., Kettering, Northants. NN15 7QN.

PARRY, David, S.WL.A.; wildlife artist in water-colour; *b* Liverpool, 23 June, 1942. *Educ:* in Tunbridge Wells. *Studied:* Tunbridge Wells School of Art, Central School of Art, London. *Exhib:* one-man shows, Brasted, Kent, Lanhydrock House, Cornwall PL22 0JN. *Signs work:* "David Parry." *Address:* Castle Cottage, Lostwithiel, Cornwall PL22 0JN.

PARRY, Leigh, M.A. (1946), P.S. (1966), P.P.S. (1983-88), R.B.A. (1988), P.S. (Canada) (1987), S.E.A. (1983); painter in pastel, oil and water-colour of equestrian subjects, landscapes, buildings, etc.; *b* London, 12 Apr., 1919. *Educ:* Uppingham; Pembroke College, Cambridge. *Studied:* St. Martin's School of Art (1945). *Exhib:* R.A., Paris Salon, New Grafton, Linda Blackstone, Pinner, R.B.A., N.E.A.C., P.S.; one-man shows, Canada and London. *Work in collections:* Kesteven C.C., Essex C.C., Lincolnshire museums, Midland Bank. *Publications:* illustrated Climbing and equestrian publications. *Signs work:* "Leigh Parry." *Address:* 6 Wharf Rd., Stamford, Lincs. PE9 2DU.

PARSONS, Denis Alva, M.B.E. (1993); sculptor in wood, stone and bronze; *b* Polesworth, Warwickshire, 14 Nov., 1934. partner Pamela Marshall. one *s*. one *d*. *Educ:* Tamworth Secondary Modern; apprenticeship to R. Bridgemen Ltd. (1950-55); Birmingham College of Art (1953-55, part-time). Work in various churches and public buildings. *Signs work:* see appendix. *Address:* Alderways, Fosseway La., Pipe Hill, Lichfield, Staffs. WS13 8JX.

PARSONS, Gwendolene Frances Joy, F.R.S.A. (1976), S.W.L.A. (1966); painter in watercolour, pastel, oil; tutor on Galleo sketching party holidays for 30 years; *b* Bollington, 9 Jul., 1913. *m* W.N.T. Parsons, A.R.I.B.A. (decd.). *Educ:* privately. *Studied:* Frome School of Art, Bridgwater Art School, Somerset. *Exhib:* solo exhibs., Red House Museum, Christchurch, Diss, Norfolk, recently, Madison, U.S.A. *Work in collections:* Russell Cotes Museum, Bournemouth, Ulster Museum, Belfast. *Commissions:* forty foot mural for Birdland, Bourton-on-the-Water (1969). *Publications:* 'Flower Painting' (F.Warne), 'Wildlife Painting' (Batsford), 'Days Out in Dorset', 'Days Out in Hampshire', (Thornhill Press), 'Holiday Painting and Wildlife Tales' (Natula Publications). *Clubs:* Bournemouth Arts, Lymington Palette Club, Southbourne Art Soc. (president for 14 years). *Signs work:* "Joy Parsons." *Address:* 3 Willow Pl., Bridge St., Christchurch, Dorset BH23 1ED.

PARTINGTON, Peter Norman, N.D.D., A.T.C., S.WL.A.; painter in water-colour, oil, drypoint etching, art lecturer; Com. mem. S.WL.A.; *b* Cambridge, 29 Sept., 1941. *m* Josephine. two *s*. one *d*. *Educ:* Poole Grammar School. *Studied:* Bournemouth College of Art and Design (1960-66), Middlesex Polytechnic (1967-68). *Exhib:* various galleries in London including Tryon Gallery, Glos., Wilts. *Work in collections:* Nature in Art Museum. *Publications:* illustrations, 'Down the River' H.E. Bates (Gollancz 1987), 'Painting Birds in Watercolour' (Collins 1989), 'A Floating World' own poetry and illustration, 'Learn to Draw' 'Birds', 'Wildlife', 'Farm Animals' (Harper Collins, 1998). *Signs work:* "Peter Partington." *Address:* The Hall, Kettlebaston, Suffolk IP7 7QA.

PARTRIDGE, John Arthur, antique dealer; Chairman, Partridge Fine Arts PLC; Com.; Hon. Treasurer, Society of London Art Dealers; *b* London, 6 July, 1929. married. two *s*. one *d*. *Educ:* Elstree and Harrow. *Address:* 144-146 New Bond St., London W1J 2PF.

PASCOE, Jane, B.A.(Hons.) Fine Art (1977), A.T.C. (1978), R.W.A. (1988); painter/sculptor/printmaker, teacher (Head of Art Dept.); *b* Bristol, 9 May, 1955. one *s*. *Educ:* The Redmaids School, Bristol (Bristol Foundation Scholarship 1966-73). *Studied:* Bristol Polytechnic Faculty of Art and Design, Dept. of Fine Art (1974-77),

Brighton Polytechnic School of Art Education (1977-78). *Exhib:* R.W.A., Eye Gallery, Bristol, Parkin Fine Art, Mall Galleries, London, Salisbury Arts Centre, Swindon Museum and A.G., Victoria Gallery, Beaux Arts Gallery Bath. *Work in collections:* R.W.A., Avon County Art Collection, Cheltenham and Gloucester Bldg. Soc. Art Collection. *Signs work:* "Jane Pascoe." *Address:* 14 Stoke Rd., Old Shirley, Southampton, Hants. SO16 6BD.

PASKETT, David, R.W.S. (2001), B.A. (1966), A.T.D. (1967), Queens Award (1965); painter in water-colour and oil; resident artist, Pitt Rivers Museum, Oxford (1993); *b* Potters Bar, 3 Jun., 1944. *m* Sally. two *d. Educ:* Mountgrace Comprehensive School, Potters Bar. *Studied:* Hornsey and Exeter Colleges of Art, teacher training at Liverpool College of Art. *Exhib:* Singer Friedlander Sunday Times Watercolour Competiition (1992-2001), prizewinner (1992); Hunting Observer Competition, R.W.A.; Pitt Rivers Museum; Oxford University (1993); Pastel Society (1994); R.W.S. open prizewinner (1994, 1999); Catto Gallery (1997). *Work in collections:* Philip Morris, Kerry International, Hutchison Whampoa, Honeywell, Shell, World Bank, Chase Manhattan, Jardines, Freshfields. *Commissions:* H.R.H. The Queen Mother's 100th Birthday Celebration, Hong Kong Jockey Club, Lord and Lady Wilson, Hong Kong Tourist Assoc., Time Life, Chinese University of Hong Kong. *Signs work:* "PASKETT." *Address:* 50 Bickerton Rd., Headington, Oxford OX3 7LS. *Website:* www.chineseimages.co.uk *Email:* paskettart@aol.com

PASMORE, Wendy, painter; teacher of painting at Sunderland College of Art, (1955-58), and at Leeds College of Art (1958-67); *b* Dublin, 1915. *m* Victor Pasmore (decd.). one *s.* one *d. Educ:* privately. *Studied:* art: privately. Mem. London Group. *Work in collections:* Tate Gallery, Arts Council, Leeds Education Committee. *Clubs:* Arts. *Address:* Dar Gamri, Gudja 2TN, Malta. *Second Address:* 12 St. Germans Pl., Blackheath, London SE3 0NN.

PASS, Derek Percy, artist in ceramic enamels, water-colour; ceramic artist, Royal Doulton (retd.); *b* Newcastle, Staffs., 19 Apr., 1929. *m* Doreen Odell. two *d. Educ:* Knutton Elementary School; Burslem School of Art. *Studied:* Stoke-on-Trent College of Art (1942) under Gordon Forsyth, R.I. and Reginald Haggar, R.I. *Exhib:* Trends, Britain in Water-colours, N.S. *Signs work:* "Derek Pass," "D. Pass" (ceramic). *Address:* 12 Thirlmere Pl., Clayton, Newcastle, Staffs. ST5 3QJ.

PASS, Donald James, N.D.D., R.A.S.; portrait and landscape painter in oil, pastel and water-colour; noted for works of a visionary nature; *b* Congleton, Ches., 9 Sept., 1930. *m* Anne Jacqueline Whitelegge. two *s.* three *d. Educ:* Macclesfield Kings School. *Studied:* Macclesfield School of Art, Stoke-on-Trent Regional College of Art, R.A. Schools (silver medal). *Exhib:* Drian Gallery - New Art Centre, Premio Lissone, Milan, Royal Soc. Portrait Painters, Royal Inst. Painters in Water-colours, Royal Water-colour Soc., Soc. of Art of the Imagination (1999) First Prize at Mall Galleries, also in 2000 adjudicator, 2001 Outsider Art Exhibition, New York, The Attic Gallery, Nashville, Tennessee. *Work in collections:* Gdansk National Museum, Poland, Stoke-on-Trent A.G., Yorkshire Educ. Com., Gallery of Contemporary Art Skopje, Yugoslavia, Gallery of Art Lissone, Milan, University of Keele, Church of St. Mary the Virgin, Elmley Castle, Worcs., Graves A.G., Sheffield, Sir John

Rothenstein, American Museum of Visionary Art, Baltimore, U.S.A., H.R.H. Duke of Edinburgh, Prince Edward (2001). *Commissions:* portraits: Sir Compton Mackenzie, Brigadier Sir Alex Stanier, Bt., D.S.O., M.C., Lt. Col. Sir John Miller, G.C.V.O., D.S.O., M.C. *Publications:* Apollo Magazine article by Sir John Rothenstein, Quarto Press, work included in Encyclopedia of Water-colour Techniques, Raw Vision Magazine and others. Mem. Art of the Imagination Soc., Vice Chairman; Dealer, Henry Boxer, Henry Boxer Gallery, 98 Stuart Court, Richmand, London; Dance Theatre Production 'Awakenings' based on Pass's visionary paintings, choreography by Katie Graham, music composed by Marcus Davidson, performances in Norwich Cathedral and Dorchester Abbey, Oxon. *Clubs:* Reynolds. *Signs work:* "D. Pass" or "DONALD PASS," and see appendix. *Address:* 2 Green Lane Lodge, Old Rd., Wheatley, Oxford OX33 1NY.

PATERSON, Donald M., D.A.; artist in water-colour, teacher; elected Mem. Royal Scottish Soc. of Painters in Water-colour; *b* Kyleakin, Isle of Skye, 28 Nov., 1950. *m* Alexandra. two *s. Educ:* Portree High School. *Studied:* Glasgow School of Art (1969-73). *Exhib:* one-man show: Fair Maids Gallery, Perth; mixed shows: 'Artists under 30' Third Eye Centre, Glasgow, Glasgow Herald Exhbn. Collins Gallery, Strathclyde University, R.S.A. Annual, G.I. Annual. *Signs work:* "D.M. Paterson." *Address:* Blaven, Torr Rd., Bridge of Weir, Renfrewshire PA11 3BE.

PATERSON, Michael Hugh Orr, B.A., F.R.S.A., F.M.A.; art restorer; freelance lecturer and archivist; trainee, City A.G., Birmingham (1953-54); asst., City A.G., Hereford (1954-55); asst.-in-charge, Municipal A.G., Oldham (1956); asst. keeper, City A.G., Leicester (1957-58); Curator, Russell-Cotes A.G. and Museums, Bournemouth (1958-66); Curator of Art, London Borough of Enfield (1966-81); Hon. Curator, Thomas Coram Foundation for Children to 1995; volunteer lecturer, National Trust; *b* London, 7 Dec., 1927. *m* Maureen Robinson. *Educ:* Kirkcudbright Academy; Cranleigh School; Manchester and Edinburgh Universities. *Address:* 24 Adamsrill Cl., Enfield, Middx. EN1 2BP.

PATTERSON, Janet, Slade Dip., Churchill Fellow (1987), M.A. (1993); painter/printmaker, art lecturer; Vice President, London Group (1991-92), Vice Chairman, Chelsea Arts Club (1996-97); major prizewinner Hunting Art Prizes (2000); *b* 13 Feb., 1941. one *s.* one *d. Studied:* Slade School of Fine Art (1960-64, Patrick George, Harold Cohen). *Exhib:* 'Natural Elements' University Sussex tour (1999), 'Dreamtime' Talbot Rice, Edinburgh (1988), London Group, R.A., etc. *Work in collections:* Scottish Arts Council, Unilever, Texaco, I.C.I., NatWest, Ciba-Geigy, Coopers & Lybrand, etc. Awards: French Government Scholarship (1964), R.W.S. award (1984), Winston Churchill Travel award (1987), Norwegian Travel Scholarship (1989), etc. *Commissions:* Dresdner Kleinwort Benson (2000). *Publications:* 'Dreamtime' catalogue (1988). *Clubs:* Chelsea Arts. *Signs work:* "J.P." *Address:* Studio 1, 71 Stepney Green, London E1 3LE. *Email:* janetpatterson_arts@hotmail.com

PATTERSON, Linda, B.A.Hons., S.B.A., S.F.P., Dip. Eur. Hum. (Open) 1999; painter in pastel, oil, acrylic, teacher, lecturer; Chairman, Christchurch and District Arts Council; *b* London, 3 Dec., 1942. *m* David. one *s.* one *d. Studied:* London and Bournemouth. *Exhib:* Westminster Central Hall, London, Bournemouth,

Christchurch, Salisbury, Romsey, Sofiero Castle, Sweden (1998), Société Jersiaise, Jersey (1999), St. Lo, France. Work in collections internationally. *Publications:* work repro: cards for Medici; published in 'Pastel Artist International' magazine. *Clubs:* Soc. of Botanical Artists, Soc. of Floral Painters, Christchurch Arts Guild, Romsey Art Group, Wessex Artists. *Signs work:* "L. PATTERSON." *Address:* 22 Heatherlea Rd., Southbourne, Dorset BH6 3HN.

PATTON, Eric Samuel, R.H.A. (1982); self taught painter in oil and water-colour; *b* Dundalk, Ireland, 29 Jan., 1925. *Educ:* Wellington National School, Dundalk Grammar School. *Exhib:* one-man shows: Dublin, Belfast, Galway, Longford, Wales, New York, Jeddah. *Work in collections:* Jeddah, Saudi Arabia. *Clubs:* United Arts, Dublin. *Signs work:* "Eric Patton." *Address:* 35 Kildare St., Dublin 2.

PATTON, Marcus, O.B.E., B.Sc., Dip.Arch., A.R.U.A.; architect/illustrator in ink, water-colour, screen printing; Trustee of 'In You We Trust' (artists' residency), and Belfast Print Workshop; *b* Enniskillen, Co. Fermanagh, 23 Aug., 1948. *m* Joanna Mules. three *s. Exhib:* various. *Work in collections:* B.B.C., Arts Council of N. Ireland, Ulster Television, Belfast City Council, Down Museum, etc. *Commissions:* B.B.C., U.T.V., etc. numerous posters. *Publications:* Ireland, Scotland, South West Ireland, 'Bugs, Bites and Bowels' (Cadogan Press), etc. *Clubs:* Tonk's. *Signs work:* signature usually hidden in a maze of lines. *Address:* Ingledene, Sans Souci Park, Belfast BT9 5BZ.

PAUL, Celia Magdalen, B.A. 1st. Hons. Fine Art (1981); painter in oil and etch-er; *b* Trivandrum, India, 11 Nov., 1959. one *s. Educ:* Edgehill College, Bideford, Devon. *Studied:* Slade School (1976-1981) under Prof. Lawrence Gowing. *Exhib:* Bernard Jacobson (1986), Marlborough Fine Art (1991, 1995 & 1999), Israel Museum (Bacon to Bevan) (1991), Musée Maillol, Paris (1998). *Work in collections:* Saatchi Collection, British Museum, Metropolitan Museum, New York, Fitzwilliam Museum, Cambridge, Galerie de Bellefeville, Montreal. *Publications:* School of London - Alistair Hicks, Women Painters by Lynn Bushell, Marlborough Fine Art catalogues. *Signs work:* "Celia Paul." *Address:* 50 Great Russell St., London WC1B 3BA.

PAVEY, Don, F.R.S.A., A.R.C.A.; director, Micro Academy producing art educa-tion videos and computer art software; author; lecturer in design and colour; a founder of the National Art Education Archive (Leeds Univ.). Freedom of the City of London (July, 1987); *Publications:* The Artist Colourmen's Story (about Winsor & Newton's Museum of Colour, 1985), Color (Architectural Digest of America, 1980), Art-based Games (Methuen, 1979), Methuen Handbook of Colour and Colour Dictionary (Methuen, 1961, 1967, 1978). Mem., Colour Group (Great Britain) - awarded the Isaac Newton Medal for researches into the psychology and history of colour (1997). *Address:* Studio House, 30 Wayside, Sheen, London SW14 7LN.

PAVITT, Diane, H.S., S.Lm.; self taught painter of miniatures specialising in por-traiture in water-colour on ivorine/polymin; *b* Brighton, 31 May, 1954. *m* John. one *s.* one *d. Exhib:* R.M.S., S.A.M.A.P., Hilliard & Limners Societies, several galleries etc. Work in collections internationally. *Clubs:* H.S., S.Lm. *Signs work:* see appen-dix. *Address:* 'Le Mas des Restanques', 521 Avenue des Sources, 06370 Mouans

Sartoux, France. *Email:* diane-pavitt@club-internet.fr

PAYNE, David, N.D.D., A.T.C. (1954); painter in oil and water-colour (triptychs); formerly senior lecturer in painting, Bedford College of Educ.; *b* Dover, 29 July, 1928. *m* Iris. one *s.* one *d. Studied:* Canterbury, Farnham and Brighton Colleges of Art until 1954, R.A. Schools (1980-81) (Guest student/Peter Greenham). *Exhib:* R.A. (1976, 1978-89, 1991-92, 1995-01), Singer & Friedlander/Sunday Times (1991-94), N.E.A.C. (1992-98), R.W.S. (1992-00), Portal Gallery (1984), Laing Gallery (1984), Ellingham Mill (1979, 1982), Ash Barn Gallery, Sotheby's (1981); one-man show, The Gallery, Wellingborough (1983-85), New Ashgate Gallery, Farnham (1987), Discerning Eye (1996, 2001). *Work in collections:* Beds. Educ. Loan Service and private collections. *Publications:* reviews, I.T.V. (1982), B.B.C.2 (1983), Academy Illustrated (1983, 1984, 1991). *Clubs:* Reynolds. *Signs work:* "David Payne." *Address:* 25 Willmers Cl., Bedford MK41 8DX.

PAYNE, Margaret A., N.D.D. (1959), A.T.C. (1960), B.A.(Hons.) History of Art (1981), M.A. (Art Educ.) (1983), R.E. (1975); graphic artist including computer graphics, painter in oil, etcher; Art Teacher at Ashton House School, Isleworth; Currently researching children's learning in N.C. Art at KS1 & 2; *b* Southampton, 14 Apr., 1937. *Educ:* St. Helen's School, Northwood, Middx. *Studied:* Harrow School of Art (1955-59), Goldsmiths' College (1959-60). *Exhib:* R.A., R.E., Paris Salon, Society of Women Artists, Young Contemporaries, R.I. *Work in collections:* Sheffield and Nottinghamshire C.C., Pictures for Schools circulation. *Publications:* in Journal of Art and Design Education (1993), Froebelian Principles and the Art National Curriculum. *Address:* 11a Wallorton Gdns., London SW14 8DX.

PAYNTER, Hilary, N.D.D. (1964), A.T.C. (1965), M.A. (Psych.Ed., 1982), A.R.E. (1984), F.R.S.A. (1986); wood engraver; educational psychologist; Hon. Sec. S.W.E., Council Mem. R.E.; *b* Dunfermline, 16 June, 1943. *m* Gerry Bradley. one *s.* one *d. Studied:* Portsmouth College of Art (Gerry Tucker). *Exhib:* S.W.E., R.E., Xylon, Switzerland; major engraving exhbns.: Durham (1982), Medici (1980), Hereford (1982), Sydney, Australia (1986-87), Ex Libris Internationals; one-man: Buckden (1976) and Kew (1985), R.A., etc. *Work in collections:* Hereford City A.G., Ashmolean Museum. *Publications:* contributions to: The Imprisoned Heart (Gryphon, 1979), Hilary Paynter's Picture Book (Carr, 1985). *Signs work:* "Hilary Paynter." *Address:* P.O. Box 355, Richmond, Surrey TW10 6LE.

PAYNTON, Colin Frank: see SEE-PAYNTON, Colin Frank.

PEACE, Dr. David, M.B.E., D.Sc.Tech., F.S.A., A.R.I.B.A., F.R.T.P.I.; glass engraver, lettering and heraldic designer; Master, A.W.G. (1973); first Chairman, Guild of Glass Engravers (1975), President (1980-86); Liveryman, Glaziers Co. (1977); *b* Sheffield, 13 Mar., 1915. *m* Jean Margaret Lawson, A.R.C.A. two *d. Educ:* Mill Hill; University of Sheffield, Hon.D.Sc.Tech. (1991). *Studied:* under Clarence Whaite. *Exhib:* 12 one-man shows; Retrospective (1990). *Work in collections:* V. & A., Fitzwilliam, Kettle's Yard, Brierley Hill Glass Museum, Corning Museum, N.Y., etc.; much presentation glass; windows in many churches; also engraved screens and doors - e.g. St. Nicholas, Liverpool, St. Albans Abbey, Westminster Abbey; memorial to G.M. Hopkins and John Betjeman, Poets Corner. Since 1986, much architectural glass in partnership with Sally Scott, e.g. St. John's College, Cambridge,

Norwich Cathedral, Lancaster and Sheffield Universities. *Clubs:* Arts. *Signs work:* see appendix. *Address:* Abbots End, Hemingford Abbots, Huntingdon, Cambs. PE28 9AA.

PEACOCK, Brian, A.R.C.A. Silver medal (1960), Prix de Rome, painting (1960); painter in oil on board; Head of Painting and Printmaking, Sheffield Polytechnic until 1988; *b* London, 1934. *Educ:* Sir Joseph Williamsons Mathematical School, Rochester. *Studied:* R.C.A. (1957-60, Carel Weight, Roger de Grey). *Exhib:* R.A., John Moores, Bristol Art Show; one-man shows include Piccadilly Gallery, John Davies Fine Art, Stow, Mistral Galleries, Dover St. *Work in collections:* Contemporary Arts Soc., Government Collection, D.O.E., M. of W., Nuffield Foundation, Free University Amsterdam, Pembroke College Oxford, many provincial and overseas galleries. *Signs work:* "B. Peacock." *Address:* 107 Meersbrook Pk. Rd., Sheffield S8 9FP.

PEACOCK, Carlos (Charles Hanbury), B.A.(Cantab.); writer and art critic; *b* 6 Oct., 1909. *m* Cynthia Howell . *Educ:* Uppingham and Cambridge. *Exhib:* Arranged: Constable Exhbn. at Aldeburgh Festival (1948), Pre-Raphaelite Exhbn. at Bournemouth (1951). *Publications:* Painters and Writers (Tate Gallery), co-author (with John Rothenstein) of essay on Tate Gallery in The Nations Pictures (Chatto and Windus, 1951), John Constable (John Baker Ltd.), Samuel Palmer (John Baker Ltd.), Richard Parkes Bonington (Barrie & Jenkins). *Address:* 26 Brompton Sq., London SW3 2AD.

PEARCE, Antony, B.A. (Exeter) (1963), F.R.S.A. (1990), A.N.S. (1991); teacher/full time artist in water-colour and acrylic since 1980; *b* Leigh, Essex, 21 July, 1933. *Educ:* Mayfield College, Sussex. *Studied:* self taught, but inspired principally by Rowland Hilder and Edward Seago. *Exhib:* Edwin Pollard Gallery, Wimbledon (annually), numerous one-man shows. *Publications:* by Sharpe's, Castlebar Graphics, Kingsmead Publications. *Clubs:* R.S.A. *Signs work:* "Antony Pearce." *Address:* 16 Sandra House, Hansler Gr., E. Molesey, Surrey KT8 9JL.

PEARCE, John Allan, Vice-Pres., Turner Society; painter in oils; retd. solicitor; *b* Sidcup, Kent, 1912. *m* Raffaella Baione. two *s. Educ:* Charterhouse and B.N.C. Oxon. *Studied:* with Giorgio de Chirico and privately. *Exhib:* R.A., N.E.A.C., R.B.A., R.O.I., Chelsea Art Soc., etc. *Clubs:* Travellers. *Signs work:* "A.P." *Address:* 32 Brompton Sq., London SW3 2AE.

PEARSON, Bruce Edward, B.A. Fine Art (1973), S.WL.A. (1978); painter in water-colour and oil; President, Soc. of Wildlife Artists (1994); *b* Newmarket, Suffolk, 20 Sept., 1950. *m* Sara Oldfield. two *d. Studied:* pre-Dip. Gt. Yarmouth College of Art and Design (1969-70), Leicester Polytechnic (1970-73). *Exhib:* many solo exhbns. in U.K., and group shows in U.S.A., Holland; Ministère de L'Environment, France; Natural History Museum, London. *Publications:* chapter with illustrations in 20th Century Wildlife Artists, Nick Hammond (Croom Helm, 1981); author and illustrator: An Artist on Migration (Harper Collins, 1991). *Signs work:* "B.P." (on some illustrative work), "BRUCE PEARSON" (on all other work). *Address:* The Old Plough, Caxton Rd., Great Gransden, Sandy, Beds. SG19 3BE.

PEARSON, James E., artist in oil, clay, bronze; William Boyd Andrews, Best of

Show, 1961; Gold Keys, 1951, 1954, 1956; Scholastic Art Awards, Carnegie Institute; art instructor, Woodstock, Comm. High School, Woodstock, Illinois, U.S.A.; Bachelor of Science in Education (1961), Master of Science in Education (1962), Master of Fine Art (1964); *b* Woodstock, Illinois, U.S.A., 12 Dec., 1939. *Educ:* McHenry Community High School, McHenry, Illinois; Northern Illinois University, Dekalb, Illinois. *Studied:* Northern Illinois University, Dekalb, Illinois. *Work in collections:* Northern Illinois University; over 100 private collections (company and individual). *Publications:* McHenry County, 1832-1968. *Signs work:* see appendix. *Address:* 5117 Barnard Mill Rd., Ringwood, Illinois, 60072, U.S.A.

PEARSON, Yvette L., B.A.Hons.; freelance graphic designer in oil and watercolour, fashion designer; visiting lecturer, South Devon College of Art and Design; *b* 16 May, 1962. *Studied:* South Devon College and Ravensbourne College of Art and Communication (1985). *Exhib:* South Devon. Work manufactured: Kirtle, Jester Dress. *Address:* 22 Central Ave., Paignton, S. Devon.

PEART, Tony, B.A. (Hons.) (1983), M.A. (1986); painter in oil; associate lecturer, Cumbria College of Art and Design; *b* Darlington, 23 June, 1961. *m* Sharyn Brown. one *d. Educ:* Eastbourne School. *Studied:* Cheltenham College of Art, Leeds Polytechnic, Newcastle Polytechnic. *Exhib:* Piccadilly Gallery (1988-). *Work in collections:* Carlisle A.G., Darlington A.G., Government Painting Coll., Rank Xerox, Newcastle University, Northern Arts. *Signs work:* "Tony Peart" always on reverse. *Address:* 4 Beanley Ave., Lemington, Newcastle upon Tyne NE15 8SP.

PECKHAM, Barry Arthur, S.E.A. (1984), R.O.I.; landscape, marine and equestrian artist in oil, water-colour, pastel, etching; *b* New Forest, Hants., 30 Dec., 1945. *m* Sarah Peckham. three *d. Educ:* Bartley School. *Studied:* Southampton College of Art. *Exhib:* R.A., R.I., R.O.I., P.S., R.S.M.A., S.E.A., N.E.A.C., R.W.A. *Work in collections:* Royal Marines, Poole. Awards: Royle prize (1984), Cuneo medal (1989), Crossgate Gallery award (1989), Pastel award (1990), Champagne Mumm Marine Artist (1990). *Signs work:* "B.A. PECKHAM." *Address:* Fletchwood Cottage, Busketts Way, Ashurst, Southampton, Hants. SO40 7AE.

PEDLEY, Nada Marija, R.M.S. (1994); sculptor in clay and terracotta; freelance sculptor, Royal Doulton; *b* 1 Aug., 1944. *m* John Pedley. two *s.* one *d. Studied:* Slovenija Ljubljana Commercial Art (1964-67), Horsham Art School (1974-78, ceramics: John Green). *Exhib:* R.M.S. (1987-), Doulton Gallery, Stoke-on-Trent. *Work in collections:* Doulton Gallery, Stoke-on-Trent. *Publications:* Royal Doulton Figures (Richard Dennis, 1994). *Signs work:* "Nada Pedley." *Address:* 9 Garrick Rd., Worthing, Sussex BN14 8BB.

PEGLITSIS, Nicholas, painter in oil, water-colour, pastel; awards: (1990, 1993) Beecroft Gallery Trustees Award for best painting in Essex open exhib., by public vote, (1993) short listed for the Bank of Cyprus (London) Ltd. art award, (2001) awarded prize for best landscape, Essex open exhib.; *b* Larnaka, Cyprus, 1938. *m* Jacqueline Taylor. two *d. Educ:* Southend High School. *Studied:* Goldsmith's College, London. *Exhib:* R.A.; R.W.S.; Minories, Colchester; Beecroft Gallery, Westcliff; Crome Gallery, Norwich; Furneaux Gallery, London; Chartwell Gallery, Southend; Melford Fine Arts, Suffolk. *Work in collections:* private collections in U.K., U.S.A., Canada, Australia, New Zealand, Germany, Denmark, Holland,

France, Spain, Cyprus; public collections, Municipal Gallery, Larnaka, Cyprus. *Commissions:* many private commissions, various subjects. *Publications:* Monograph: 'As John Constable Saw it'. *Signs work:* "Peglitsis" with date. *Address:* 25 Bridgwater Drive, Westcliff-on-Sea, Essex SS0 0DJ. *Email:* jacnnicat25 @aol.com

PELL, Robert Leslie, N.D.D. (Painting) (1948), F.R.S.A. (1968); painter in oil and gouache and lecturer; *b* Northampton, 24 Nov., 1928. *m* Pamela Crake. one *s.* one *d. Educ:* Technical High School, Northampton. *Studied:* Northampton School of Art and Camberwell School of Art and Crafts. *Exhib:* R.C.A. Galleries, R.B.A., Foyle's Gallery, Canaletto Gallery, Leicester Gallery (Artists of Fame and Promise), Piccadilly Gallery, Bear Lane Gallery, Oxford. *Work in collections:* University College and Balliol College, Oxford, Leicestershire, Reading, Surrey and Northumberland Education Committees, The John Lewis Organisation, Northampton Art Gallery, Coventry City Art Gallery, private collections in England, America and Finland. *Publications:* work repro.: La Revue Moderne, Art Review, The Artist, The Oxford Magazine, The Studio. *Clubs:* Royal Society of Arts. *Signs work:* "Pell" (written in italic script). *Address:* The Studio House, 141 High St., Brackley, Northants. NN13 7BN.

PELLING, John Arthur, A.R.C.A.; painter in oil on canvas; clergyman, Church of England; *b* Hove, 9 Aug., 1930. divorced. four *s. Educ:* Brighton, Hove and Sussex Grammar School. *Studied:* Brighton College of Art (1946-49) and Royal College of Art (1951-55), Chichester Theological College (1955-58). *Exhib:* nine one-man shows: London, Sussex University, Manchester, and including two latest exhbns., Air Gallery, Dover St., London. 'The Splitting Image' - Dilemma of Women as Priests (1998) and 'Double Exposure' (2001). *Work in collections:* National Gallery Poland, Nuffield Foundation, Vittorio 'de Sica private collection, Italy. At present full time painter in France and London. *Clubs:* Chelsea Arts . *Signs work:* "PELLING" (on paintings), "John Pelling" (on drawings). *Address:* 44 Redcliffe Rd., London SW10 9NJ.

PELLY, Frances, R.S.A., D.A.; sculptor in wood, stone, clay, paper; *b* Edinburgh, 1947. *Educ:* Morrisons Academy, Crieff. *Studied:* Duncan of Jordanstone, Dundee (1965-71, Scott Sutherland, Alistair Smart). *Exhib:* R.S.A., S.S.A., R.G.I.; solo shows, Collective Gallery, Edinburgh (1986), Crawford Art Centre, St.Andrews (1987), 'Nousts', travelling exhbn. in Highland Region and Norway (1992-93). *Work in collections:* Fine Art Soc., Scottish Arts Council, Dundee, BBC Glasgow, Perth, Dumfries, Orkney, Aberdeen, Royal Concerthall Glasgow, Banff, City Halls Glasgow and Fort William, Edinburgh, Kirkwall. *Commissions:* North Inch Perth, Orkney Art Soc., Parcelforce Glasgow, Mobil North Sea Banff, Strathclyde Regional Council Glasgow, Highland Regional Council Fort William, Orkney Arts Soc., Kirkwall, Museum of Scotland, Edinburgh. *Signs work:* Uses symbol of gibbous moon or red throated diver. Never signs work. *Address:* Quoyblackie, Rendall, Orkney KW17 2HA.

PELZ, Peter, M.A. (Cantab.) (1968); artist in oil, tempera, water-colour, drawing and etching; *b* Oxford, 18 Sept., 1945. *Educ:* King's College, Cambridge. *Studied:* Wigan, Lancs. (1957-63, Theodore Major). *Exhib:* Rebecca Hossack Gallery,

London. *Work in collections:* on commission (chief works): triptych at St. James's, Piccadilly; mural at St. Peter's, Morden. *Publications:* Prayer for the Day (Cairns). *Signs work:* "Peter Pelz" and date. *Address:* 28 Victoria Rd., Cirencester, Glos. GL7 1ES.

PEMBERTON, Christopher Henry, M.A. (1948); landscape, portrait and still life painter and draughtsman in oil, pencil, pen, water-colour and gouache; Head of Foundation Studies, Camberwell School of Art (1982-85; taught at Camberwell 1958-85); *b* London, 14 Mar., 1923. *m* Hester Riddell. four *s.* one *d. Educ:* Eton College, Christ Church Oxford. *Studied:* Camberwell School of Art (1948-50, Claude Rogers). *Exhib:* one-man shows: Woodlands, Blackheath (1977), Bury St. Edmunds A.G. (1977), Wells Centre, Norfolk (1987), Quay Theatre, Sudbury (1988), Gainsborough's House (1989), Cadogan Contemporary (1989, 1992), Swaffham Prior Festival (1998), Chappel Galleries, Essex (2001). *Work in collections:* Newnham College, Cambridge; Christ Church, Oxford. *Publications:* Gasquet's Cézanne (Thames & Hudson, 1991). *Signs work:* "C. Pemberton." *Address:* Place Farmhouse, Bardwell, Bury St. Edmunds, Suffolk IP31 1AQ.

PENDERED, Susan Marjorie Anne, M.C.S.P., R.I. (1983); painter in water based medium; Winner of the Winsor & Newton R.I. Award (1988); *b* London, 15 June, 1925. *m* John H. Pendered, G.P., M.B.E., M.B., B.S. one *s.* two *d. Educ:* Lillesden School for Girls, Hawkhurst, Kent. *Studied:* part-time at Brighton Polytechnic (1975-82, Norma Weller). *Exhib:* Mall Galleries, R.I., R.A. Summer Exhbn., R.W.A., Bristol, participated in travelling exhbn. to Vancouver, Canada and Seattle, U.S.A. (1986). *Work in collections:* work purchased by Hertford Education Authority. *Clubs:* Sussex Water-colour Soc., Attic Club Ditchling. *Signs work:* "S. Pendered." *Address:* Littleway, West Furlong La., Hurstpierpoint, W. Sussex BN6 9RH.

PENDERY, Carroll, S.W.A. (1997), S.F.P. (2000); artist in pastel, water-colour, oil, and gardener; *b* Leicester, 30 Dec., 1935. *m* Terence Pendery, B.Sc. two *s. Educ:* Gateway Girls School, Leicester. *Exhib:* by selection in Yorkshire, Birmingham, Peterborough and London. *Signs work:* "C. Pendery" or "Carroll Pendery." *Address:* 134 Station Rd., Cropston, Leicester LE7 7HE.

PENKETH-SIMPSON, Barbara, R.M.S., S.W.A.; Mundy Sovereign portrait award (1989), R.M.S. President's Special Commendation (1996), R.M.S. Gold Memorial Bowl (1997), R.M.S. Presidents special commendation (1998); self taught artist and miniaturist, larger oils and portraiture; *b* Crewe, Ches. *m* F.W. Simpson. one *s.* one *d. Exhib:* H.S., S.W.A., R.M.S., S.A.M.A.P. *Publications:* featured on Flier For, and included in Royal Society of Miniature Painters, Sculptors and Gravers 100 years of Miniatures. *Signs work:* see appendix. *Address:* 31 Meadowview Rd., Bexley, Kent DA5 1HP. *Email:* barbara@penketh7.fsnet.co.uk

PEPYS, Rhoda Gertrude, N.A.T.C. (South Africa); artist, portrait painter, tutor; *b* Port Elizabeth, 12 Mar., 1914 (née Kussel). *m* Prof. Jack Pepys (1938). two chil-dren. *Educ:* Collegiate, School of Arts and Crafts, Port Elizabeth; Silver Medal (1934). *Exhib:* one-man shows: S.A.; Italy; Paris (1962); London: Hampstead Art Cellar (1963), Barbican (1982), Studio 36 (1967-89); U.S.A.: Washington (1985); group shows in London: R.A. Summer Exhbn. (1966, 1989), Images of Italy (1987-

89), Israel Paintings (1988). *Commissions:* Univ. of London, Portrait of (1) Prof. G. Scadding (1974); (2) Prof. Jack Pepys (1979). Awards: Academie International de Lutèce, Paris, Silver Medal, (1978); Accademia Italia, Gold Medal (1980); Centauro D'Oro (1982). *Clubs:* Accademia Italia. *Signs work:* "Pepys" and "Rhoda Pepys." *Address:* 34 Ferncroft Ave., London NW3 7PE.

PEPYS, Sandra Lynn, B.A. (Hons.) London University; artist, art historian, lecturer; *b* Cape Town, 27 Jan., 1942. one *s.* one *d. Educ:* South Hampstead, S.O.A.S., University of London. *Studied:* Slade School of Art, also studied with Ruszkowski. *Exhib:* Solo shows include: London: Hampstead Art Cellar (1962, 1973-76), Studio 36 (annually from 1966-76), Duncan Campbell (1994, 1996, 1998, 2000); Paris: Galerie Tedesco (1962); Italy: Sperlonga (1962, 1965, 1999); Rome: Galleria Coppella (1965); Artists House Jerusalem (1979, 1982); group shows: London: Society of Landscape Painters, annually from 1989 at W.H. Patterson and Duncan Miller Fine Arts. "Venice in Peril", annually from 1992 at W.H. Patterson. "Images of Italy", Accademia Italiana, London. Arts Club Dover St. Florentine Artists Assoc. Soc. of Landscape Painters Rotunda Gallery Hong Kong (1995). R.A. Summer Exhbn. (frequently from 1973 to present). *Work in collections:* University of London, Municipality of Jerusalem. *Commissions:* mural paintings, London University (1966), British Railways (1967). Portraits include: Professor Sir Ernst Gombrich, O.M., Lady Alexander Fleming, Dr. Arnold Miles F.C.C.P., F.A.C.P. *Publications:* Contributor: Artists and Illustrators Magazine, The Art of Drawing and Painting, Jerusalem Post, Former Editor: Arts Club Journal, Arts Club, Dover St., London. Founder and Chairman, Society of Landscape Painters; Founder and Vice President, Small Painters Group; 1st Prize University of London Exhbn. (1966); Languages: fluent in Italian, French, Spanish, Hebrew. *Clubs:* Chelsea Arts Club. *Signs work:* "Sandra Pepys." *Address:* 36 Ferncroft Ave., London NW3 7PE.

PERKINS, Stuart M.G., R.M.S. (1991), M.A.A. (1990), A.T.D., N.D.D. 1st Class Hons.(1956), M.P.S.G., M.A.S.-F.; landscape miniaturist in water-colour and gouache with occasional still life; trained as a sculptor, and practised as a Studio Potter (1976-85); *b* Leicester, 4 July, 1935. *m* Joan Chatterley, A.T.D. three *d. Educ:* Alderman Newton Boys G.S., Leicester. *Studied:* Leicester College of Art (1952-56, Albert Pountney). *Exhib:* R.M.S., R.W.A., R.W.S. Summer Show, W.A.C.; many mixed exhbns. in England and Wales, miniature exhbns. in U.K., Canada, U.S.A., Australia and Japan. *Work in collections:* M.A.S.-F., G.M.A.S. Works mainly held in private collections in Canada, France, U.S.A. *Signs work:* "S. PERKINS, R.M.S, M.A.A.," (dated), "Stuart Perkins." *Address:* The Old School, Scowles, Coleford, Glos. GL16 8QT.

PERRIN, Brian, A.R.C.A., Rome Scholar (1954); painter/etcher; Head of Printmaking Dept., Wimbledon School of Art (1964-97); Mem. C.N.A.A. Fine Art Board (1978-90); *b* 19 Aug., 1932. *m* Jane Lisle. two *s. Educ:* Whitgift Middle School. *Studied:* Croydon School of Art (1948-51), R.C.A. (1951-54). *Exhib:* extensively in Europe and U.S.A., including international print Biennales. *Work in collections:* Library of Congress, Washington, V. & A., Arts Council, British Council; Museums of Art: Metropolitan N.Y., Perth, Jerusalem, Boston, Cincinatti, Glasgow. *Signs work:* "Brian Perrin." *Address:* 293 Kings Rd., Kingston-upon-Thames, Surrey KT2 5JJ.

PERRIN, Sally Jane, *b* Hoddesdon, 1964. *m* Graham Russell Perrin. one *d. Exhib:* Westminster Gallery with S.B.A. annually, Mall Galleries with R.S.M.A., Medici; solo show: Tudor House Gallery, Aldeburgh. *Publications:* work repro.: greetings cards for R.H.S. *Signs work:* see appendix. *Address:* 27 Hailey Lane, Hailey, Hertford, Herts. SG13 7NX. *Email:* sally-jane.perrin@virgin.net

PERRY, Jeffrey, N.D.D., A.T.D., N.A.P.A.; artist in acrylic; *b* West Bromwich, 10 Jan., 1935. *m* Sylvia. *Studied:* B'ham College of Art (Bernard Fleetwood-Walker). *Work in collections:* private: England, Wales, Ireland, U.S.A., Canada. *Clubs:* Chair, Blockley Art Soc., Fosseway Artists, R.B.S.A., Helios, N.A.P.A. *Signs work:* "PERRY." *Address:* 90 Badgers Lane, Broadway, Worcs. WR12 7QW.

PERRY, Roy, R.I. (1978); painter in oil, water-colour and acrylic; awarded R.I. Medal (1978), R.I. Council (1979); *b* Liverpool, 1935. *m* Sallie Charlton. one *s.* one *d. Educ:* John Lyon School, Harrow and Southampton University. *Exhib:* R.A., R.I., R.B.A., R.S.M.A., etc.; one-man shows, Oxford, Guildford, London, Henley and Cambridge. *Work in collections:* many large business corporations; The Fleet Air Arm Museum; H.R.H. The Duke of Edinburgh and other private collections throughout the world. *Publications:* work repro.: Lithographs, New York, Industrial Reviews and Laings Calendar. *Signs work:* "Roy Perry." *Address:* The Mill House, Donhead St. Mary, Shaftesbury, Dorset SP7 9DS.

PERRYMAN, Margot, M.A.; painter; tutor at Goldsmiths, Portsmouth, Ravensbourne, and Winchester Colleges of Art (1967-1974); By-Fellowship - Churchill College, Cambridge University (2002); *b* Plymouth, 1938. *m* Luc Delfanne. three *s. Studied:* Harrow School of Art (now Westminster University), The Slade. *Exhib:* ten solo exhibs., six two-man exhibs., plus numerous group exhibs. *Work in collections:* Tate Gallery, Arts Council of G.B., Govt. Art Collection U.K., B.B.C., Leicestershire County Education Authority. *Commissions:* various private commissions. *Signs work:* "Perryman." *Address:* 26 Leighville Dr., Herne Bay, Kent CT6 8UJ.

PESKETT, Tessa, B.A. (Hons.) Fine Art (1979), P.G.C.E. (1982), H.Postgrad.Dip.Painting (1992), R.O.I. (1994); Chadwick Healey prize for painting (1992), Anne LeClerc Fowle medal (1993); artist in oil, water-colour, charcoal; *b* Three Bridges, Sussex, 25 Apr., 1957. *Educ:* Beaumont School, St. Albans. *Studied:* Reading University (1975-79), City & Guilds of London Art School (1992). *Exhib:* R.A. Summer Shows, R.B.A., R.O.I., Linda Blackstone Gallery, Mall Galleries, Trinity A.G. Arundel, Parkview, Bristol, Laing Art Competition, London (1994-97), Atrium Gallery, Bournemouth University, solo show (1996), Albemarle Gallery, London (1996-97), Paris (1996), New York (NYAD 2000), Four Seasons Gallery, Wimborne (2001). *Publications:* Positive Health. Opened own gallery 'Aspects of Art' June 2001. *Clubs:* Friends of Studio 8. *Signs work:* "Tessa D. Peskett" and "T.P." *Address:* 63 Swanmore Rd., Boscombe, Bournemouth, Dorset BH7 6PD. *Website:* Internet: art.com/gallery *Email:* tessapeskett@hotmail.com

PETERSEN, David Thomas, N.D.D (1965), A.T.C. Lond. (1966), R.C.A.; sculptor; Head of Sculpture, Harrow School of Art (1967-1970), lecturer in Fine Art (1972-1974), senior lecturer in Fine Art (1974-1978), head of Sculpture and 3D, Dyfed College of Art (1978-1982); now full time sculptor; director of First Internat.

Festival of Iron, Cardiff (1989); visiting prof. at Makina Inst., St. Petersburg; visiting lecturer to World Congress in Aachen, Germany, ABANA conference, Birmingham, Alabama, and to Penland, North Carolina, U.S.A.; *b* Cardiff, 25 Feb., 1944. *m* Bronwen. three *s*. one *d*. *Educ:* Taunton School. *Studied:* Newport College of Art (1961-1965), London University, Inst. of Educ. (1965-1966). *Exhib:* numerous from 1963 onwards. *Work in collections:* Dyfed County Council, Cardiff City Council, London Borough of Harrow. *Commissions:* Cardiff City Council H.Q. building (1989), Mametz Wood Dragon, Somme, France (1987), Trinity College (1990), Millennium Beacon for Wales (2000). *Clubs:* past chairman of B.A.B.A. *Signs work:* "David Petersen." *Address:* Efail Y Tyddyn, San Clêr, Sir Gaerfyrddin SA33 4EJ. *Email:* petersen.myfyrfa@virgin.net

PETERSON, Peter Charles, N.D.D., V.P.R.B.A. (1988), R.B.A. (1978); mem. Landscape Soc. (1989), Vice Chairman, Soc. of Landscape Painters; Daler Rowney Prize (1983), First Prize (1988), De Laszlo medal (1994); artist in oil, water-colour and gouache; lecturer, Visual Research Dept. Chesterfield College of Art; senior lecturer, Fine Art Dept. Epsom College of Art; visiting lecturer, Falmouth College of Art (1986);two *d*. *Studied:* Hornsey College of Art. *Exhib:* R.A. Summer Exhbn. since 1968, R.B.A. since 1978, Falmouth A.G., Hallam Gallery, N.E.A.C., Crossgate Gallery, U.S.A.; one-man shows, Portal Gallery, Highgate, Southwell-Brown Gallery, Richmond, Gt.Yarmouth Museum; group shows, Odette Gilbert Gallery (1983-84), Southwell-Brown Gallery, Richmond, Alexander Gallery London. *Signs work:* "Peter Peterson." *Address:* Waratah House, 11 The Praze, Penryn, Cornwall TR10 8DH.

PETHERS, Ian Peter Andrew, S.B.A. (1989); artist in ink and wash, water-colour and acrylic of botanical, marine, architectural and mythical subjects including miniatures; *b* London, 23 Jan., 1956. *m* Marylou. *Educ:* Langley County School, Slough. *Studied:* at school under Thomas McCabe (1967-73), Marlow Community College under Jenny Riley (1983-1986). *Exhib:* S.B.A. Westminster Gallery since 1987, R.M.S. Westminster Gallery since 1999, various one-man shows. *Work in collections:* Permanent display of miniatures in Mayflower Gallery, Tavistock. *Commissions:* 2 murals in Callington, Cornwall. *Publications:* work repro.: greetings cards; illustrated Food and Travel Guides by Kingsley Media (1996-99), jacket cover designs for Kingsley, Plymouth and Alexander Associates, Fowey, wrote and illustrated 'Visions of Glastonbury', Bossiney Books (2001). *Clubs:* S.B.A. *Signs work:* "Ian Pethers." *Address:* Glenrock Studio, Drakewalls, Gunnislake, Cornwall PL18 9EE.

PETTERSON, Melvyn Lawrence, R.E. (1991), B.A. (1986); painter/printmaker in oil, etching, water-colour; partner, Artichoke Print Workshop; *b* Cleethorpes, 7 July, 1947. *m* Glynis. one *d*. *Educ:* Cleethorpes-Beacon Hill Sec. Modern. *Studied:* Grimsby Art School (Peter Todd, Alf Ludlam, Nev Tipper), Camberwell School of Art (Graham Giles, Francis Hoyland, Anthony Eyton, R.A., Ben Levene, R.A.). *Exhib:* R.A., N.E.A.C., R.O.I., Bankside Gallery, museums and galleries in U.S.A., France, Russia, China, Spain, Sweden, Finland, Mont Carlo. *Work in collections:* Oxford, Leicester, galleries in U.S.A. *Publications:* British Painters/Sculptors, Painting and Drawing, Art Review, Drawing and Painting the Landscape (Collins-Brown). *Clubs:* R.E. *Signs work:* "M.L. Petterson" or "M.L.P." *Address:* 92 Grove

Park, Camberwell, London SE5 8LE.

PETZSCH, Helmut Franz Günther, D.A. (Edin.) 1951; F.S.A. Scot.; painter in oil and water-colour; *b* Berlin, 13 Dec., 1920. *m* Catherine Oag Craigie. one *s.* two *d. Educ:* Hamburg and London. *Studied:* Edinburgh College of Art (1947-51). *Exhib:* R.S.A., S.S.A., '57 Gallery, Edinburgh. *Publications:* author of Architecture in Scotland (Longman). *Signs work:* "Helmut Petzsch." *Address:* 32 Canaan Lane, Edinburgh EH10 4SU.

PEVERALL, Adrienne, B.Ed., Dip. A.D.; printmaker of etchings and monoprint landscapes; ceramics tutor (1979-1982); *b* London, 15 Oct., 1939. *m* Ronald Peverall. two *s. Educ:* Southgate Grammar School. *Studied:* King Alfred's College, Winchester (1974-1978), Falmouth College of Art (1990-1992),. *Exhib:* annual group exhibs. with Penwith Printmakers, St. Ives Society, Falmouth Art Gallery; continuous exhib. at Small Print Gallery, Penzance. *Clubs:* Cornwall Crafts Assoc. *Signs work:* "A Peverall." *Address:* Kerrow Lodge, Bosullow, Penzance, Cornwall TR20 8NR.

PHILIPPS, Nicola Jane, artist in oil; *b* London, 27 Aug., 1964. *Studied:* City & Guilds; apprentice to Studio Cecil Graves, Florence (1986-88). *Exhib:* Malcolm Innes Gallery (3) including solo show (1977). *Commissions:* Scottish and Newcastle Breweries, The Irish Guards. *Signs work:* "Nicky Philipps." *Address:* c/o Fine Art Commission Ltd., 107 Walton St., London SW3 2HP.

PHILLIPS, Aubrey, R.W.A., P.S.; Gold Medal, Paris Salon (1966); artist in pastel, water-colour and oil, teacher; *b* Astley, Worcs., 18 June, 1920. *m* Doris Kirk. three *s. Studied:* Stourbridge School of Art (E. M. Dinkel), Kidderminster School of Art (W. E. Daly, C. J. Lavenstein). *Exhib:* F.B.A. Galleries, National Library of Wales, City A.G.'s of Worcester, Hereford and Gloucester. *Work in collections:* Worcester A.G., Worcester County Museum. *Publications:* Two works on pastel and one on water-colour publ. by Search Press; work repro.: Leisure Painter and Artist, Batsford. *Signs work:* "Aubrey R. Phillips." *Address:* 16 Carlton Rd., Malvern, Worcs. WR14 1HH.

PHILLIPS, Francis Douglas, painter and illustrator in water-colour, oil, acrylic, pastel, ink; *b* Dundee, 19 Dec., 1926. *m* Margaret Parkinson. one *d. Educ:* Dundee. *Studied:* Dundee College of Art (J. Milne Purvis). *Exhib:* R.S.A., R.S.W., R.G.I., R.I.; two 'Grampian' T.V. appearances (Feb. and July 1987) 'Tayside Artist'. *Work in collections:* National Trust for Scotland, English Speaking Union, Northern College of Educ., Aberdeenshire Health Board, Watson and Philip Plc., Glasgow Port Authority; private collections worldwide. *Publications:* work repro.: Limited Edn. Prints; illustrated over 100 books; covers on British and French Reader's Digest, The Artist Magazine, International Artist Magazine, Scots Magazine March 2001. *Signs work:* "Phillips." *Address:* 278 Strathmore Ave., Dundee DD3 6SJ.

PHILLIPS, John Edward, N.D.D. (Sculpture) 1958, A.T.C. (Lond.) 1961; fulltime sculptor and Artist in Residence; *b* Ealing, London, 28 June, 1937. *m* Valerie Maughan. one *s.* one *d. Educ:* Ealing College. *Studied:* Ealing School of Art (1953-58), Hornsey College of Art (1960-61). *Exhib:* various galleries, art centres, libraries, schools in London, Southern England and France. *Work in collections:* Hillingdon

Civic Centre, Uxbridge Library and various schools in the London area, Bucks., Herts. and Oxford. *Signs work:* "John Phillips." *Address:* Lanhael, Hedgerley Hill, Hedgerley, nr. Slough SL2 3RW.

PHILLIPS, Karen E, S.G.F.A.; artist in pencil - graphite and colour, pastel, photography and tattoo art; wildlife, portraits and fantasy; Karisma prize for drawing, Born Free Foundation Auctions; *b* Bromley, Kent, 7 Sep., 1966. *Studied:* self taught from life and nature. *Exhib:* S.W.L.A., S.G.F.A., Wildlife Art Soc., and various exhibs. throughout U.K. *Work in collections:* private collections in U.K., U.S.A., and Australia. *Commissions:* nationally and internationally. *Publications:* Absolute Press. *Clubs:* B.F.P. *Signs work:* 'K E Phillips." *Address:* 1 Brambleacres Cl., Sutton, Surrey SM2 6NJ.

PHILLIPS, Karen Erica, D.A.T.E.C. (1982), B.A.Hons. (1985), M.F.A. (1987); painter in oil, ink, charcoal, acrylic; *b* Kidderminster, 1 Nov., 1962. *Educ:* Franche Middle School, Kidderminster; Ilfracombe Comprehensive. *Studied:* North Devon College (1979-82, Robin Wiggins), Bristol Polytechnic (1982-85, Ernest Pascoe), Newcastle University (1985-87, Norman Adams). *Exhib:* New Theatre Gallery, Barnstaple (shared exhbn. with father), Zetland Studios, Bristol, Burton A.G., Bideford, Jigsaw, Barnstaple, Long Gallery, Newcastle, R.W.A., R.A., Vicarage Cottage Gallery, North Shields. *Signs work:* "K. Phillips." *Address:* 6 Laburnum Ct., Guidepost, Northumberland.

PHILLIPS, Rex, Cdr.R.N. (retd.); marine and landscape artist in oil and watercolour; *b* March, Cambs., 19 July, 1931. *m* Shirley Chadwick. one *s.* two *d. Educ:* Nautical College, Pangbourne. *Exhib:* R.S.M.A., A.F.A.S., and various one-man shows. *Work in collections:* Royal Naval, Royal Marines and Fleet Air Arm Museums, London and provincial galleries; private collections in U.K. and abroad, naval ships and establishments, R.N.L.I. and other institutions. *Signs work:* "Rex Phillips." *Address:* 15 Westbourne Ave., Emsworth, Hants. PO10 7QT. *Email:* fersa@cwctv.net

PHILLIPS, Tom, R.A. (1988), R.E., M.A. (Oxon.), N.D.D.; artist in oil, watercolour, book productions, television director (A TV Dante, etc.); *b* London, 25 May, 1937. *m* Fiona Maddocks, 1995. *Educ:* St. Catherine's, Oxford. *Studied:* Camberwell School of Art (Frank Auerbach). *Work in collections:* Tate Gallery, B.M., V. & A., Moma, N.Y., etc. Gallery (Graphics) Alan Cristea Gallery. *Publications:* A Humument (etc.). *Clubs:* S.C.C.C., Groucho. *Signs work:* "Tom Phillips." *Address:* 57 Talfourd Rd., London SE15 5NN; and Alan Cristea Gallery, 31 Cork St., London W1X 2NU. *Website:* www.tomphillips.co.uk

PHIPPS, Howard, B.A.(Hons.), R.W.A., S.W.E.; wood engraver, painter and illustrator; *b* Colwyn Bay, 1954. *Studied:* Fine Art, Cheltenham Art College (1971-75). *Exhib:* R.W.A., S.W.E., also at R.A. Summer Exhbns. where in 1985 awarded Christies Contemporary Print prize; one-man exhbns. include Dorset County Museum, Salisbury Museum (1993), Victoria Gallery, Bath (1994, 2001), Cassian de Vere Cole Fine Art, London (1996), Cheltenham Art Gallery (1997), Lymington Museum (2001). *Commissions:* commemoration print – Portsmouth Cathedral (1991), Thomas Hardy's Study, Dorchester (1993), Leeds Castle (2001). *Publications:* illustrated books for: Bloomsbury, Century, Perdix, Folio Soc.

(Shakespeare, Bronte, Tennyson) and Whittington Press who published the artist's own books Interiors (1985) and Further Interiors (1991). *Address:* Hilfield, Homington Rd., Coombe Bissett, Salisbury SP5 4ND.

PICARD, Bridget Margaret, painter in oil; tutor, Badminton School, Bristol (1942-1943), Penzance Art School (1960s); started Mousehole Pottery with husband; *b* Chesterfield, 26 June, 1922. *m* Bill Picard, potter. one *s.* two *d. Educ:* Chesterfield. *Studied:* Chesterfield Art School (1936-1939), Slade School, under Swarb and Rutherford (1939-1941). *Exhib:* galleries countrywide, mainly West Country. *Work in collections:* Tyne and Weir Civic Centre. *Clubs:* Newlyn Society of Artists. *Signs work:* "Biddy Picard." *Address:* Penaluna, Clodgy Moor, Paul, Penzance, Cornwall TR19 6UR.

PICHÉ, Roland, 1st Class N.D.D., A.R.C.A., F.R.B.S., Medal for Work of Distinction, R.C.A.; sculptor in resin, fibreglass, stainless steel, stone and bronze; lecturer in sculpture; Principal Lecturer, Canterbury College of Art; *b* London, 21 Nov., 1938. one *s.* two *d. Educ:* Romsey College, Embley Park, Hants. *Studied:* Hornsey College of Art (Mr. C. Anderson, A.R.C.A., 1956-60), Royal College of Art (Mr. B. Meadows, A.R.C.A., 1960-64). *Work in collections:* The Arts Council of Great Britain and Wales, São Paulo Museum, Gothenburg Museum, Sweden, National Gallery of Western Australia, M.O.M.A. New York, Aberdeen Scotland, Nene College, Northampton. *Publications:* Private View (B. Robertson and T. Armstrong-Jones), Dada, Surrealism (W. S. Rubin). *Signs work:* see appendix. *Address:* Victoria Studios, Tollesbury, Essex CM9 8RG.

PICKEN, Mollie, N.D.D. (1963), A.T.C. (1964); freelance artist in illustration, embroidery and fabric collage; *b* 13 Oct., 1940. *Studied:* Goldsmiths' College School of Art (1959-64) under Constance Howard and Betty Swanwick. *Work in collections:* Education Authorities. *Publications:* Illustrated books by Constance Howard; collaborated with Christine Bloxham to produce Love and Marriage (Pub. date: Feb. 1990). Art work for Oxfordshire Museum Services, Embroiderers Guild. *Clubs:* S.D.C.; Embroiderers' Guild, Assoc. of Illustrators. *Address:* The Old Post Office, Sibford Gower, Banbury, Oxon. OX15 5RT.

PICKING, John, N.D.D. (1960), D.A. Edin. (1962), A.T.D. (1966); painter and lecturer; Mem. Manchester Academy; ex Senior Lecturer in Fine Art, Manchester Polytechnic; *Studied:* Wigan School of Art, 1956-60 (Governors Medal); Edinburgh College of Art, 1960-63 (Postgrad. Scholarship); Scholarship to Spain 1963-64; Goldsmiths' College, London, 1965-66. *Exhib:* Scottish Gallery, Edinburgh, Colin Jellicoe Gallery, Manchester, Mercury Gallery, London, La Barcaccia galleries in Rome, Naples, Palermo etc.; since 1989 exclusive with Telemarket (Brescia) with galleries in Milan, Rome, Bologna etc.; many group exhibitions including Royal Academy, London and Galleria Borghese, Rome. *Work in collections:* Salford and Manchester Universities, Edinburgh Corp., Palermo Museo Regionale, private collections over the world. Work reflects interest in mixing painting languages, mythology, geology. Since 1979 painting full-time. Studios in Brescia and Sicily. *Address:* c/o Colin Jellicoe Gallery, 82 Portland St., Manchester M1 4QX.

PIDOUX, Janet Anne, S.W.A. (1992), S.O.F.A. (1997); painter in pastel; *b* High Wycombe, Bucks., 2 Sept., 1950. *m* Derek. one *s.* one *d. Educ:* Wellesbourne. *Exhib:*

S.W.A., S.WL.A., P.S. *Publications:* work repro.: greetings cards, limited edition prints. *Signs work:* "JANET PIDOUX." *Address:* c/o Penn Barn Gallery, By the Pond, Elm Rd., Penn, Bucks. HP10 8LB.

PIERCY, Rob, R.C.A.; painter in water-colour and mixed media; *b* Porthmadog, Wales, 22 Jan., 1946. *m* Enid. three *s. Studied:* Bangor under Selwyn Jones. *Exhib:* regularly in Singer and Friedlander/Sunday Times Watercolour; shortlisted in Garrick Milne Art Prize (2000). *Signs work:* "Rob Piercy." *Address:* Rob Piercy Gallery, Porthmadog, Gwynedd LL49 9BT. *Website:* www.robpiercy.com *Email:* gallery@robpiercy.com

PIERCY, Sioban, M.A., National Dip. Painting; printmaker in screen printing, art lecturer; Head of Dept. Galway and Mayo Inst. of Technology; *b* Rutland, 6 Jan., 1957. *m* Gerard O'Brien. *Studied:* Ravensbourne College of Art, Kent; Crawford College of Art, Cork; R.C.A. *Exhib:* International Print exhbns. Norway, Brazil, Germany, Poland, Slovina, Japan, Spain, Taiwan; numerous shows including one and two person in Dublin and London. *Work in collections:* private and public: U.K. and Ireland. *Publications:* 'Profile 4 - Sioban Piercy' (Gandon Edns., 1997). *Clubs:* Artists Assoc. of Ireland. *Signs work:* "SIOBAN PIERCY." *Address:* Rahard, Athenry, Co. Galway, Ireland.

PIERSON, Rosalind, landscape miniaturist in water-colour; *b* Tavistock, Devon, 14 Sept., 1954. *Educ:* St. Audries School, West Quantoxhead, Som. *Studied:* Ruskin School of Drawing and Fine Art (John Newberry). *Exhib:* R.A., Paris Salon, Silver Medal (1978), Gold Medal (1981); R.M.S. Drummond Award (1987), Twice Hon. Mention for Gold Bowl; Bilan de l'Art Contemporain, New York (1982), Silver Medal; Florida Miniature Art Society (1996), Best in Exhibition; Hilliard Soc. of Miniaturists, Co-founder (1981); M.A.A.; M.P.S.G. Washington D.C.; M.A.S.F. *Work in collections:* Miniature Art Soc., Florida, Hilliard Soc. of Miniaturists, Wells, Som. *Signs work:* "R. Pierson." *Address:* Brangwyn House, Kilworthy Hill, Tavistock, Devon PL19 0EP.

PIESOWOCKI, Leon, painter and printmaker in oil, water-colour and silkscreen; *b* Poznan, Poland, 9 Dec., 1925. two *d. Studied:* painting: Academy in Rome (1946-47), graphics: Sir John Cass College of Art, London (1949-52). *Exhib:* International Biennale of Graphis, Bradford, Krakow Poland, Frechen Germany, Biella Italy, Fredrikstad Norway. *Work in collections:* V. & A., Nuffield Foundation, National Museum Warsaw, Stedelijk Museum Netherlands, Boymans van Beunigen Netherlands, Arts Council, British Council, Dudley Museum and A.G., Northampton Central Museum, National Museum Poznan. *Clubs:* International Prizewinners Club, Krakow. *Address:* 26160 Manas, La Begude de Mazene, France.

PIKE, Celia, B.A.; artist in gouache and oil; *b* Surrey, 24 May, 1952. *m* Richard Morris. two *s. Studied:* Central College of Art and Design, St. Martin's School of Art, R.A. Schools post.grad. *Exhib:* R.A., Whitechapel, Mall Galleries. Work in collections internationally. *Publications:* work repro: prints, calendars, greetings cards. *Clubs:* S.W.A., H.S., S.F.A. *Signs work:* "CELIA PIKE." *Address:* 51 Estcourt Rd., Woodside, London SE25 4SE.

PIKE, Jonathan, B.A. (1971); painter in water-colour and oil; *b* Leatherhead, 17

Jan., 1949. two *d. Studied:* Central School of Art and Design, Falmouth School of Art. *Exhib:* one-man shows: London; mixed shows: throughout England and U.S.A. *Commissions:* Oxford University Press, The Clothworkers' Company. *Signs work:* "JONATHAN PIKE." *Address:* 26 Manor Lane Terr., London SE13 5QL. *Email:* jon@cminor.fsnet.co.uk

PIKE, Mark Walter, painter in oil, water-colour and acrylic; *b* Wilts., 22 Sept., 1938. *m* Lesley-Joan. *Exhib:* worldwide. *Work in collections:* private and corporate: worldwide. *Commissions:* best known for development of "Luminart" dual reality paintings. *Clubs:* N.A.A., Fine Art Guild, N.A.P.A. *Signs work:* "MARK PIKE," "PIKE" or "M.P." and see appendix. *Address:* Langley Studio, Rake, Liss, Hants. GU33 7JL.

PIKE, Septimus: see WATTS, Michael Gorse.

PIKESLEY, Richard Leslie, N.E.A.C., Dip. A.D. (1973), A.T.C. (1974); finalist, Hunting Group Prize (1981 and 1989), winner, E.F. Hutton Prize (1987), W.H. Patterson Prize (1988); painter in oil and water-colour; *b* London, 8 Jan., 1951. *m* Susan Margaret Stone. *Studied:* Harrow School of Art (1969-70), Canterbury College of Art (1970-73). *Exhib:* R.A., R.O.I., R.W.A., R.I.; one-man shows include New Grafton Gallery London (1990), Linfield Gallery, Bradford-on-Avon (1986), St. James's Gallery, Bath Festival (1986). *Clubs:* N.E.A.C. *Signs work:* "Richard Pikesley." *Address:* Middlehill Farm, Marrowbone Lane, Bothenhampton, Bridport, Dorset.

PILKINGTON, Richard Godfrey, M.A. (Cantab.); art dealer and publisher; Partner (Co-founder) Piccadilly Gallery, 16a Cork St., W1, since 1953; Chairman of Society of London Art Dealers (1974-77); editor The Art Bulletin (1951-60); Governor, Wimbledon School of Art (1991-2000); *b* Stafford, 8 Nov., 1918. *m* Evelyn (Eve) Vincent. two *s.* two *d. Educ:* Clifton and Trinity College, Cambridge. *Address:* 45 Barons Court Rd., London W14 9DZ.

PILKINGTON, Ruth Jane, R.O.I. (1976), S.W.A. (1985); painter in oil; *b* Manchester, 2 May, 1924. *m* Eric W. L. Pilkington (decd.). one *s* (decd.). one *d. Educ:* Ladybarn House School, Manchester and Maltman's Green, Gerrard's Cross. *Studied:* Johannesburg Technical College (1947-48), Macclesfield C.F.E. (1962-65). *Exhib:* R.B.A., R.O.I., Paris Salon, Manchester Academy, etc., other group exhbns., one-man show in Channel Islands (1976). *Work in collections:* Barreau A.G., Société Jersiaise, Jersey. *Signs work:* "Ruth J. Pilkington." *Address:* Sondela, La Rue à Don, Grouville, Jersey JE3 9DX, C.I.

PILLOW, Lorna Mary Carol, A.R.C.A.; Sir Frank Warner Memorial Medal; freelance textile, exhibition and graphic designer; taught, Croydon and Berkshire Colleges of Art; senior lecturer, West Surrey College of Art and Design (retd.); *b* Cork, Eire. widow of Peter John Palmer. one *s. Educ:* Wolverhampton and Leeds. *Studied:* Leeds, Hull and the Royal Colleges of Art. *Exhib:* Beverley Art Gallery, Ferens Art Gallery, Guildhall, R.W.S. Galleries, Mall Galleries, London, W.S.C.A.D. Gallery, Farnham, R.S.A. Travelling Exhibition, Design Centre, London. *Publications:* International Textiles; illustrated Geography of Flowering Plants. *Signs work:* "Lorna Pillow." *Address:* 33 Havelock Rd., Maidenhead, Berks. SL6 5BJ.

PINCUS, Helen Frances, B.A. Hons. (1982), M.F.P.S. (1984), M.S.D.C. (1993), Adult Educ. Dip. (1979); fibre and textile artist, designer, embroiderer in fibres, yarns, aluminium mesh, wood, piano wire and pure silk; freelance lecturer, writer and musician; *b* Acton, London, 22 Oct., 1938. *Educ:* Haberdashers' Aske's Acton Girls' School; Arts Educational Schools. *Studied:* Nottingham University; Loughborough College of Art and Design. *Exhib:* numerous one-man shows and mixed exhbns. both in the U.K. and abroad including Commonwealth Inst. A.G., Cork St. Fine Arts, Leighton House, Savaria Muzeum (Hungary), Galeria Bellas Artes (Spain), University of Surrey, Loggia Gallery, Contemporary Arts (Hong Kong), Hampton Court Palace, Guild Gallery, Bloomsbury Gallery, Vincent A.G. (Australia), Cecilia Colman Gallery, Metro Toronto Convention Centre (Canada), Del Bello A.G. (Canada), Strathclyde University, Barbican Centre, The Rotunda Gallery Hong Kong, Mall Galleries, London, dfn Gall., Manhattan N.Y.C., Tidedancers, Easton, Md. U.S.A. *Work in collections:* Savaria Muzeum, Hungary, Embroiderers' Guild Collection, Hampton Court Palace, The World Bank, U.S.A. *Clubs:* F.P.S., Soc. of Designer Craftsmen, The Colour Group (G.B.), Embroiderers' Guild, Cornwall Crafts Assoc., New Embroidery Group, Registered with the Crafts Council. *Signs work:* see appendix; or occasionally embroiders initials and year. *Address:* MoonGates, off Atlantic Rd., Tintagel, N. Cornwall PL34 0ED.

PINE, Diana, Assoc. Sussex Artists (1974, Hon. Sec. 1978-83); artist in watercolour, pastel and oil; documentary film director, Crown Film Unit, Wessex, etc. B.B.C.; part-time teacher, Mole Valley A.E.C. and Day Centre; *b* London. *Educ:* Jersey, France, London, P.N.E.U. *Studied:* Regent St. Polytechnic (1936-37) under Clifford Ellis, Chelsea Art School under H. S. Williamson, Central School; apprentice Edward Carrick for Art Direction, Films (-1940), Ernest Savage, Aubrey Sykes (1968-75). *Exhib:* R.I., P.S., S.W.A. (1976-86), Assoc. Sussex Artists, Horsham, Barns Green, Dorking Group. *Signs work:* "D. Pine." *Address:* 2 Lodge Close, North Holmwood, Dorking, Surrey RH5 4JU.

PINKNEY, Richard, N.D.D., A.T.D.; painter, sculptor and printmaker in oil, acrylic, gouache, intaglio, etc.; teacher, Ipswich, Colchester and St. Martin's Schools of Art, and Kingsway College; Director, Lady Lodge Arts Centre, Peterborough, Open College of the Arts; *b* 22 July, 1938. *m* Judith Foster, A.R.C.A. two *s. Educ:* Ipswich School. *Studied:* Ipswich Civic College, School of Art; West of England College of Art, Bristol. *Exhib:* solo shows: A.I.A. Gallery, London; Traverse Theatre, Edinburgh; Paperback Bookshop, Edinburgh; St. Martin's Schools of Art, London; Lady Lodge Arts Centre, Peterborough; Manor School of Ballet, Edinburgh; University College Suffolk; Christchurch Mansion, Ipswich; Sans Walk Gallery, London; group shows: graphics and mailart widely, U.K., Europe, U.S.A., Japan, S. America. *Work in collections:* Tate Gallery, V. & A., B.M.; public and private collections U.K. and worldwide. *Publications:* Circle, Tetrad, Trivia & Bad Presses. *Clubs:* Suffolk Group, Ipswich Arts Soc. *Signs work:* "R.P.," "R. Pinkney," "Richard Pinkney." *Address:* 10 The Street, Bramford, Ipswich, Suffolk IP8 4EA. *Email:* NoRedTram@LineOne.net

PINSKY, Michael, Doctorate in Fine Art, M.A.(R.C.A.), B.A. (Hons.) Fine Art (1991); artist in photography, sculpture, site-specific installation; *b* Scotland, 24 Nov., 1967. *Educ:* James Gillespies High School. *Studied:* Manchester Polytechnic

(1987-88), Brighton Polytechnic (1988-91, Bill Beach), R.C.A. (1993-95), University of East London (1998-2001). *Exhib:* one-man shows: Collective Gallery Edinburgh, The Warehouse Amsterdam, The Gantry Southampton, Open Eye Gallery Liverpool, Viewpoint Gallery Manchester, Stockport A.G., Crawford Arts Centre St. Andrews, Quay Arts Centre, I.O.W., Gatwick Airport, Metropole A.G. Folkestone, Gracefield Art Centre, Dumfries, McLellan A.G. Ayr, Dean Clough A.G. Halifax, Towner A.G. Eastbourne, Photofusion, London, Duncan of Jordanstone A.G. Dundee, Delfina London, Bonnington Gallery Nottingham, Leeds City A.G., Watershed, Cymar, Wiemar, Germany, Economist Gallery, London, East London Gallery; group shows worldwide. *Address:* 47 Earlsferry Way, London N1 0D2.

PIOTTI, Vittorio, Dip. of Artistic Maturity, Art-Liceum, Carrara (1967), Knighthood of Italian Republic (Cav.) (1978), R.W.A. (1983); Major Alpini Parachutists; sculptor in iron; *b* Brescia, Italy, 5 Mar., 1935. *m* Andreina. one *s.* one *d. Studied:* Art Liceum of Venezia; Art-Liceum of Carrara. *Exhib:* (1967-93): Brescia, Trento, Padova, Vicenza, Mantova, Cremona, Bari, Pavia, Biarritz and Parigi (France), Venezia, Pompeii, Cassino, Bolzano, Verona, Bergamo, Torino, Bristol (England), Genova, Monaco and Mainz (Germany). *Work in collections:* in Italy, Libya, France, England, Germany. Public monuments: in Italy and Germany, etc. *Signs work:* "V. PIOTTI" or "Vittopiotti." *Address:* via Columbaia 17, 25050 Rodengo, Saiano, Brescia, Italy.

PIPER, Raymond Francis Richard, F.L.S. (1974), M. Univ. (2000), H.R.H.A. (1999), R.U.A. (1975), U.W.S. (Hon. 1975); portrait painter, draughtsman, botanical illustrator; works in pencil, pastel, oil, water-colour; President, The Ulster Arts Club; *b* London, 6 Apr., 1923. *Educ:* Belfast High School. *Studied:* Belfast College of Art. *Exhib:* R.W.S. Galleries London, R.H.S. London, Ulster Museum, Dublin, etc. *Work in collections:* Arts Council of Northern Ireland, Ulster Museum, Royal College of Physicians, London, St. Columb's College, Derry, Irish National Portrait Collection, etc. *Commissions:* As professional portrait painter sitters have included Sir Adrian Boult, Lord Justice MacDermott, Lord Brookeborough and Sir Brian Faulkner (past Prime Ministers of Northern Ireland) several Lords Mayor of London and Belfast including Sir Frederick Hoare and Sir Bernard Waley-Cohen. *Publications:* at least 22, mainly on Ireland and botanical works, Shakespeare, etc. *Clubs:* Ulster Arts, United Arts (Dublin), The Irish Club (London). *Address:* 11c Notting Hill, Malone Rd., Belfast BT9 5NS.

PITFIELD, Thomas Baron, N.R.D., Hon. F.R.M.C.M.; artist in water-colour, reed-pen, lino-cut, lettering; composer; art master; *b* Bolton, Lancs., 5 Apr., 1903. *m* Alice Maud Astbury. *Educ:* Bolton and Manchester. *Studied:* Municipal School of Art, Bolton (apprenticed in Engineer's drawing-office). *Exhib:* R.A., Northern Academy of Fine Arts, and various one-man exhbns. *Publications:* Junior Course in Art Teaching, Senior Course in Art Teaching, The Poetry of Trees, Bowdon and "Limusicks" (40 limericks), (texts, script, illustrations), Recording a Region (drawings and hand-lettered script), and a large number of musical compositions; autobiographies: A Cotton Town Boyhood, No Song, No Supper, A Song after Supper; work repro.: Artist, Countryman, and other periodicals, calendars, etc. C.D. issued by R.N.C.M., of chamber music and songs. *Signs work:* see appendix. *Address:* Lesser Thorns, 21 East Downs Rd., Bowdon, Ches.WA14 2LG.

PITMAN, Primrose Vera, S.G.A. (1953), L.R.A.M., Gold Medal for Design; painter in water-colour, commercial artist in pencil; etcher; *Educ:* St. Hilda's School. *Studied:* Royal Albert Memorial School of Art under Burman Morrall and James Sparks. *Exhib:* R.W.A. and provincial galleries. *Work in collections:* Royal Albert Memorial Museum, City of Exeter. *Publications:* work repro.: of pencil drawing of Exeter Cathedral for Preservation Fund organized by Mayor of Exeter. Etchings and pencil drawings in This Jewel Remains (1942). *Clubs:* Exeter Art Soc., Kenn Group. *Signs work:* "Primrose V. Pitman." *Address:* Marlands, 4 Victoria Park Rd., Exeter.

PLATT, Eric Warhurst, A.R.C.A., Silver Medallist (1940); artist in line and wash, water-colour, etching, graphic design, and creative cut card relief; Vice Principal Doncaster College of Art; Head of Design, Doncaster M.Inst. of H.E. (retd. July 1980); *b* Cudworth, Yorks., 2 May, 1915. *m* Mary Elizabeth. one *s*. one *d*. *Educ:* Wakefield and Doncaster School of Art. *Studied:* R.C.A. under Malcolm Osborne, R.A., and Robert Austin, R.A. (1937-40). *Exhib:* R.A., Brighton, West Riding Artists exhbn., Yorkshire Artists exhbn., Doncaster A.G., Feren's Gallery, Hull, Graves Gallery, Sheffield, Liverpool, and Williamson A.G. Birkenhead. *Signs work:* "Eric Platt." *Address:* 18 Warren Hey, Spital, Wirral CH63 9LF.

PLINCKE, J. Richard, R.I., R.I.B.A., A.A.Dip.; water-colour and mixed media; work includes designs for tapestries, and stained glass windows at St. Mark's Church, Kempshot; *b* Woldingham, Surrey, 1928. *m* Rosemary D. Ball. two *d*. *Educ:* Stowe, Bucks. *Studied:* art: Southampton Inst. of Higher Educ., gaining Higher Cert. (Distinction); architecture: Architectural Assoc. School of Architecture, London. *Exhib:* R.A., R.W.A., R.I., R.S.M.A., Manor House Gallery, Chipping Norton, Linda Blackstone Gallery, Pinner, Shell House Gallery, Ledbury, also U.S.A., France and Jersey. *Work in collections:* Work included in a number of private collections. *Signs work:* "R.P." followed by the date. *Address:* The Studio, 2 St. Thomas Mews, Winchester, Hants. SO23 9HG.

PLOWMAN, Christopher Charles, B.A. Fine Art (1973), M.A. Printmaking (1976); artist in printmaking (etching) and sculpture (steel); *b* Fareham, 16 Sept., 1952. *m* Annie. one *s*. one *d*. *Studied:* Wolverhampton Polytechnic (1970-73), R.C.A. (1973-76). *Exhib:* Flowers East (1995), Jill George Gallery, London (1998). *Work in collections:* Tate Gallery, V. & A., British Museum. *Commissions:* Legal and General, Coca-Cola Schweppes, Maidstone Hospital, Derby City Council. *Signs work:* see appendix. *Address:* The Old Farmhouse, Cooks Lane, Lockerley, nr. Romsey, Hants. SO51 0JE.

PLUME, Anita Frances, B.A. Hons, Fine Art (1993-2000); painter in oil, water-colour, acrylic; hotelier; *b* 11 May, 1947. *m* David. one *d*. *Educ:* Glendale Grammar School, N. London. *Studied:* Falmouth College of Arts. *Exhib:* Mariners Gallery, St. Ives, Norway Gallery, St. Ives Soc. of Artists. *Signs work:* "Anita Plume" or "AP." *Address:* Polmark Hotel, Harlyn Bay, Padstow, Cornwall PL28 8SB.

PLUMLEY, Richard Harry, interior designer, painter in oil, water-colour and gouache, early sculpture, stage and theatre design, consultant; co-Director, Personal Choice Interiors; *b* Harrow, Middx., 5 Mar., 1944. *m* Snezana Nikolic. one *s*. one *d*. *Educ:* Orange Hill, Edgware. *Studied:* Harrow College of Art (1962). *Exhib:* one-man shows: George St. London (1969, 1972), Isle of Man (1994); mixed shows:

Windsor (1976), Douglas (1984), artfulhand (2000); retrospective exhbn. (1998). *Work in collections:* London, Chicago, Spain, Isle of Man, Gallery artfulhand I.o.Man, private and corporate collections. *Commissions:* Interiors Avon Castle, Ringwood, Creek Peel. *Publications:* Manx Life, Isle of Man Examiner and Courier. Recent return to stage design and painting on large scale. *Clubs:* Legion Players, Dramatic Personae. *Signs work:* "R.H. Plumley" or "R.P." *Address:* Seaforth House, 4 Crown St., Peel, I.O.M. IM5 1AJ. *Email:* plumleyr@hotmail.com

PLUMMER, Brian, painter in acrylic and water-colour relief; *b* London, 1934. *Studied:* Hornsey College of Art, R.A. Schools. *Exhib:* R.A., Expo Montreal, Barcelona Bienal (prizewinner), Toronto, Abbot Hall, Kendal, Lucy Milton, Galerie van Hulsen, Amsterdam, Rex Irwin Sydney, Sloane St. Gallery, Audun Gallery, Macquarie Galleries, Sydney, Gallerie St. Pierre, Bordeaux, Piano Nobile, London. *Work in collections:* D.O.E., St. Thomas' Hospital, Power Collection Sydney, Ministero Cultura Madrid, Mobil Oil Co., Lancaster University, Abbot Hall, Kendal. Armidale N.S.W. *Commissions:* mural: London Office, Western Asset, Pasadena, U.S.A. *Publications:* Brian Plummer - Landscape & Perception, text by Norbert Lynton & Susan King (University of Westminster). *Signs work:* "BRIAN PLUM-MER" on acrylics, hand written on water-colours. *Address:* 89 Palmerston Rd., London N22 8QS.

POLAINE, Peter David, N.D.D., F.C.S.D., F.R.S.A.; painter in oil, printmaker and stained glass artist; *b* London, 30 Apr., 1937. *m* Betty. two *s. Educ:* Harlow College. *Studied:* Walthamstow School of Art (1954-1959). *Exhib:* N.E.A.C., R.A., and other London and East Anglian galleries. *Signs work:* "PETER POLAINE" or monogram or both (see appendix). *Address:* Gardener's Cottage, Broke Hall Park, Nacton, Suffolk IP10 0ET. *Email:* peter@polaine.com

POLLARD, Malcolm, sculptor, draughtsman, teacher; *b* Raunds, Northants, 14 Mar., 1941. *m* Elke Kairies Addis. two *s. Signs work:* "MALCOLM POLLARD" christian name above surname. *Address:* 42 East Park Parade, Northampton NN1 4LA.

POLLARD, Michael Vincent, Dip. A.D. (1973), S.B.A. (1988); freelance artist, designer and model maker in oils, acrylics, water-colour, gouache and crayon; visiting tutor to junior and secondary schools; Council mem. S.B.A.; *b* Cambridge, 6 May, 1948. *Educ:* Harpur Secondary School, Bedford. *Studied:* Luton School of Art (1969-73). *Exhib:* Westminster Gallery, London, 'Flora', Sevenoaks, Rackhams, Birmingham and New York. Work in collections worldwide. *Commissions:* over 150 postage stamps designed for British Crown colonies and dependencies. *Publications:* books illustrated: Fairytales and romance: work repro.: greetings cards and calendars. Architectural models. *Clubs:* Hasselblad Forum. *Signs work:* see appendix. *Address:* Tara House, Dychurch Lane, Bozeat, Northants. NN29 7JP.

POLLOCK, (Sir) George F., Bt., M.A. (Cantab.), Hon. F.R.P.S., F.R.S.A., F.B.I.P.P., E.F.I.A.P., M.P.A.G.B.; artist-photographer, a-v producer; past President, Royal Photographic Society; *b* 13 Aug., 1928. *Educ:* Eton College and Trinity College, Cambridge. *Exhib:* numerous. *Work in collections:* British Council, R.P.S., National Gallery of Victoria, Musée de Photographie, Bièvres, Towner A.G., Eastbourne, Texas University, University of Surrey. *Commissions:* murals for Lloyds

Bank, British Petroleum. *Publications:* numerous articles on photography; "The Limits of Photography" - Prizewining essay. *Signs work:* "George F. Pollock." *Address:* 83 Minster Way, Bath BA2 6RL.

POOLE, David James, R.P. (1969), A.R.C.A.; artist; President, Royal Soc. of Portrait Painters (1983-91); Senior lecturer in Painting and Drawing, Wimbledon School of Art (1962-77); *b* 5 June, 1931. *m* Iris Mary Toomer. three *s. Educ:* Stoneleigh Secondary School. *Studied:* Wimbledon School of Art, R.C.A. *Exhib:* one-man shows: Zurich and London. Portraits include: H.M. The Queen, H.R.H. The Duke of Edinburgh, H.M. The Queen Mother, H.R.H. Prince Charles, H.R.H. Princess Anne, H.R.H. Princess Margaret, Earl Mountbatten of Burma and The Duke of Kent; also distinguished members of govt., industry, commerce, medicine, the academic and legal professions. *Work in collections:* H.M. The Queen and H.R.H. The Duke of Edinburgh; and in Australia, S. Africa, Bermuda, France, W. Germany, Switzerland, Saudi Arabia, U.S.A. *Address:* Trinity Flint Barn, Weston Lane, Weston, Petersfield, Hants. GU32 3NN.

POOLE, Greg, B.Sc. Zoology (1983); Mem. S.WL.A.; artist/illustrator in print-making and collage; *b* Bristol, 26 Oct, 1960. *Studied:* Foundation Course, Manchester Polytechnic (1989-90). *Exhib:* many mixed exhbns., annually with S.WL.A. *Work in collections:* Nature in Art Museums, Glos. Many private collections. *Publications:* At present working on a book for Editions Gallimard based on the Cote d'Azur; work repro.: Book covers for Blackwells, C.U.P. and Reed International, many magazine illustrations. Participant in Artists for Nature Foundation Projects on the Loire Estuary, France, and Bandavgarh, India. Recent Residences in France, Ireland and Barbados, *Address:* 1 Eagle Tap, Eagle Lane, Kingscliffe, nr. Peterborough PE8 6XD. *Website:* http://homepage.virgin. net/greg.poole *Email:* greg.poole@virgin.net

POOLE, Monica, A.R.E. (1967), R.E. (1975); Central School Diploma (1949); Member of the Art Workers' Guild; wood engraver; *b* Canterbury, 20 May, 1921. *m* Cmdr. A. G. M. Small, R.N., F.I.H.V.E. *Educ:* Abbotsford, Broadstairs. *Studied:* Central School of Arts and Crafts (1945-49). *Exhib:* R.A., R.E., etc. *Work in collections:* Fitzwilliam Museum, B.M., S.N.G.M.A., V. & A., Ashmolean Museum, Hunt Botanical Museum, Pittsburgh, U.S.A., National Museum of Wales, British Museum. *Publications:* The Wood Engravings of John Farleigh (1985). *Signs work:* "MONICA POOLE." *Address:* 67 Hadlow Rd., Tonbridge, Kent TN9 1QB.

POPE, Perpetua, D.A. (Edin.) 1947; painter in oil; lecturer in visual arts, Moray House College of Education (1968-73); *b* Solihull, Warwicks., 29 May, 1916. *Educ:* Albyn School, Aberdeen. *Studied:* Edinburgh College of Art under W. G. Gillies, John Maxwell, Leonard Rosoman. *Exhib:* one-man shows: Scottish Gallery, Stenton Gallery, Edinburgh; mixed shows: R.A., R.S.A., S.S.A., S.S.W.A., Aberdeen Artists, Stirling Gallery, Open Eye Gallery. *Work in collections:* H.R.H. The Duke of Edinburgh, Scottish Arts Council, Nuffield Trust, Argyll County Council, Robert Fleming Plc., Royal Bank of Scotland; works in private collections Britain, U.S.A. and France. *Signs work:* "Perpetua Pope." *Address:* 27 Dean St., Edinburgh EH4 1LN.

PORTELLI, Guy Anthony, A.R.B.S. (1998); sculptor; specialises in large corporate commissions; *b* Durban, S. Africa, 13 June, 1957. one *d. Educ:* Hugh Christie

School, Tonbridge. *Studied:* Medway College of Art (1974-1978). *Exhib:* various in U.K., London, Manchester, Edinburgh, Guernsey. *Work in collections:* Porsche Collection, Paris. *Commissions:* Sainsburys, Eagle Gates, Guernsey, Commomwealth Inst., London Pavillion, Piccadilly, Trafford Park, Manchester, Rowland Hill Monument. *Signs work:* "Guy Portelli" and date. *Address:* The Studio, 125 St. Mary's Rd., Tonbridge, Kent TN9 2NL. *Website:* www.portelli.sculptor.co.uk

PORTEOUS WOOD, James, R.S.W. (1945); landscape, mural and portrait artist in oils, water-colour, black and white; specialist in architectural subjects; art director and chief designer Asprey, Bond St. (1956-1980); designer of important gold and silver and objets d'art works in many of the premier world contemporary collections; murals and paintings in royal and presidential palaces in Near, Middle and Far East; *b* Edinburgh, 1919. married. one *s. Educ:* George Heriot's School. *Studied:* Edinburgh College of Art (1935-40) (Travelling Scholarship). *Exhib:* R.A., R.S.A., R.S.W., G.I., and several one-man shows. *Publications:* private editions with miniatures and calligraphy mainly on vellum, Midland Riches (Hancock), Yorkshire Sketchbook; work repro.: many editorial drawings mainly architectural, industrial, and portrait in national Press, top magazines and prestige books. *Signs work:* "PORTEOUS WOOD." *Address:* Caimbe Bridge, Arisaig, Inverness-shire PH39 4NT.

PORTSMOUTH, Delia, painter of landscapes, portraits, flowers, birds, wildlife in oils; *b* Mottram, Ches., 6 Aug., 1939. *m* A. C. Portsmouth. four *d. Educ:* Hyde and Bala Grammar Schools. *Studied:* self taught. *Exhib:* R.O.I., Hesketh Hubbard, Flower Painters' Summer Salon; one-man shows: Chester, Lampeter, Bala, Brantwood, St. Davids, Usher Gallery, Lincoln, Public Gallery, Oldham. *Work in collections:* National Library of Wales, National Museum of Wales, Liverpool Corp. and numerous private collections worldwide. *Clubs:* founder member, Modern Millais Association. *Signs work:* "Delia Portsmouth." *Address:* 14 Saffron Park, Kingsbridge, Devon TQ7 1RL.

PORWOL, Steven, painter in water-colour on paper; specializes in natural history painting, predominantly birds; *b* Ilford, London, 14 Feb., 1973. *Educ:* Ilford County High Grammar School. *Studied:* self taught. *Exhib:* Singer and Friedlander Watercolour Exhib., Art and Antiques Fair, Olympia (2001-2002), Park Walk Gallery (2001), Natural History Museum, Vienna (2001). *Commissions:* numerous in U.K. and Europe. *Signs work:* "Steven Porwol" or "S.Porwol." *Address:* c/o Jonathan Cooper, 20 Park Walk, London SW10 0AQ. *Email:* mail@jonathancooper.co.uk

POTTINGER, Frank, D.A. Sculpture (1963), R.S.A. (1991); sculptor in bronze, stone, wood, clay; *b* Edinburgh, 1 Oct., 1932. *m* Dr. Norah Smith, 1991. one *s-s.* two *s-d. Educ:* Boroughmuir School. *Studied:* Edinburgh College of Art (1958-63). *Exhib:* Richard Demarco Gallery, Yorkshire Sculpture Park, Landmark Scottish Sculpture Trust, Camden Arts Centre, Pier Arts Centre Orkney, Kildrummy Castle, S.S.W. Open, Royal Scottish Academy. *Work in collections:* Heriot Watt University, Hunterian Museum, I.B.M., Scottish Development Agency, Leeds Educ. Authority, Scottish Arts Council, Paisley Museum; private collections, U.K. and abroad. *Commissions:* L.A.S.M.O., The Woodland Trust, Motherwell District Council, Ellon Development, Aberdeenshire, Dundee University, Royal Mail, Western Isles Health Board. *Address:* 30/5 Elbe St., Edinburgh EH6 7HW.

POTTS, Ian N., N.D.D., R.A.S.Cert.; artist in water-colour; retd. Dept. Head, School of Art, University of Brighton; *b* 11 Apr., 1936. *m* Helen B. Bewick. one *s.* two *d. Studied:* Sunderland College of Art (1956-59), R.A. Schools (1959-63, H. Rushbury). *Exhib:* Barbican London, R.A. Summer Show, Brighton Museum, Amalgam Art London, Coombes Gallery London, S.C.R. Bath. *Work in collections:* V. & A., Arts Council, British Council, Towner A.G. Eastbourne. *Commissions:* Brighton Festival, Daystar, Contemporary Sundials. *Publications:* Water-colours and Landscapes (Bridgewater Press). *Address:* 12 Southdown Ave., Lewes, Sussex BN7 1EL.

POTTS, Kenneth Arthur, A.R.B.S. (1988), Dip.A.D., B.A. (1972), C.I.C. (1969); sculptor in bronze, stoneware, terracotta and fine porcelain; *b* Macclesfield, 16 Mar., 1949. *m* Anne. one *s.* one *d. Educ:* Stockport C.F.E. (1966). *Studied:* Stafford College of Art (1969), Stoke-on-Trent College of Art (1972). *Exhib:* R.A. Summer Show, Festival Hall, Sladmore Gallery, Art Expo N.Y., R.B.S. West of England Academy, Tokyo, etc. *Work in collections:* Dyson Perrins Museum, Raphael Djanogly Trust. *Commissions:* Bronze statue, Sir Edward Elgar, Worcester; bronze statue, A.E. Housman, Bromsgrove; mosaic panels, Holy Trinity, Sutton Coldfield; "Spitfire" mural, Longton, Stoke on Trent; Cassidy Memorial, Tamside Metropolitan Borough; Hogg Memorial, Edinburgh. *Signs work:* "Kenneth Potts." *Address:* Clater Pk., Bringsty, Worcester WR6 5TP.

POUNTNEY, Monica (née Brailey), cup for oils S.E.I.F.A.S. (1976); freelance artist in oil, water-colour, acrylic, pastel, etc.; *b* London. *m* D. H. Pountney. one *s. Studied:* Hammersmith School of Arts and Crafts (Carel Weight and Ruskin Spear), Central School (John Farleigh). *Exhib:* Federation of British Artists, U.A., S.W.A., R.I., N.S., and various mixed exhbns. *Work in collections:* landscapes in London, Moscow and U.S.A. *Commissions:* various. *Publications:* work repro.: books illustrated for Heinemann, Blackie and others. *Clubs:* U.A., L.A.G., Essex A.C. *Signs work:* "M.P." or full name. *Address:* 3 Thickwood House, Bedford Rd., S. Woodford, London E18 2AH.

POVER, Lesley, R.B.A.; sculptor (largely figurative and portraiture) in bronze, plaster, cement; *b* Plymouth, 1 Apr., 1950. two *s. Educ:* Devonport High, St. John's, Singapore. *Studied:* New College of Speech and Drama. *Exhib:* numerous provincial galleries, Woodlands, R.A., Mall Galleries, Islington Art Fair. *Work in collections:* life-sized bronze Lambeth Palace; various private collections. *Commissions:* Eric Liddell Sports Centre, Edinburgh University. *Signs work:* "L. Pover" or "Pover." *Address:* 78 Inverine Rd., Charlton, London SE7 7NL.

POVEY, Edward, B.Ed. (1978), R.C.A.; artist in oil, pencil and conté; *b* London, 1 May, 1951. *m* Alison Bone. two *s. Educ:* Crown Woods Comprehensive School, Eltham. *Studied:* Eastbourne College of Art and Design (1972-73), University of Wales (1974-78, Selwyn Jones). *Exhib:* Martin Tinney Gallery, Cardiff; Meridian Contemporary Arts, Hay-on-Wye; Mostyn Gallery, Llandudno; Jan de Maere Galleries, Brussels; Gallery Gerard, The Hague; Midtown Payson Galleries, N.Y.; Horwitch Newman Gallery, Scottsdale, U.S.A. *Work in collections:* University of Wales at Bangor, Laguna Gloria Museum in Austin, Texas. *Publications:* chapters and photographs in: Painting The Town by Cooper and Sargent (Phaidon Press

1979), Wales on Canvas by Hywel Harries (Lolfa Press 1983), Gwynedd by Ian Skidmore (Robert Hale 1987). *Signs work:* "Edward Povey" or "Povey." *Address:* The Studio, Meirion Rd., Bangor, Gwynedd LL5 2BY.

POWELL, Christopher Alan, LL.B. (1957), B.A. (2000); former journalist; painter mainly in oil with occasional water-colour and tempera of landscapes, seascapes, city scenes, still life and flower studies; former sub-editor on The Times (1968-92); *b* Newcastle upon Tyne, 11 July, 1935. *Educ:* Queen Elizabeth Grammar, Hexham. *Studied:* part time at City Literary Inst., London (Cecil Collins). Studied law at King's College, Newcastle upon Tyne, Arts with Open University. *Exhib:* Mall Galleries, Leighton House, various art societies in London. *Work in collections:* U.K., U.S.A., Japan. *Signs work:* "C.A. POWELL." *Address:* Flat A7, Sloane Ave. Mans., Chelsea, London SW3 3JF.

POWELL, John, A.R.C.A.; painter; *b* Nottingham, 27 Aug., 1911. *m* Freda Heathcote. one *d. Studied:* R.C.A. under Gilbert Spencer (1935-39) and Nottingham Art College (1932-35). *Exhib:* R.A., R.B.A., R.O.I., N.E.A.C., London Group, S.M.A., N.S., United Artists, Pastel Society, also mixed and travelling exhbns. in London and provincial galleries. Main exhbns.: New Ashgate Gallery, Farnham (1981), Bosham Walk Gallery, W. Sussex (1990), Eastgate Gallery, Chichester (1994). *Work in collections:* Bristol Educ. Com. (Harbour, Tenby), Manchester Educ. Com., (Child at Breakfast, Fair at Twilight); and private collections. *Signs work:* "John Powell" on back or under mat. *Address:* Fishbourne Farmhouse, Fishbourne, Chichester, W. Sussex PO18 8AW.

POWELL, Sir Philip, C.H., O.B.E., R.A., F.R.I.B.A., A.A. Dip. (Hons.), R.I.B.A. Gold Medallist (1974); Treasurer R.A. (1985-95), Member, Royal Fine Art Commission (1969-94); architect (Powell and Moya, 1946-91); *b* Bedford, 15 Mar., 1921. *m* Philippa (née Eccles). *Educ:* Epsom College. *Studied:* Architectural Assoc. Works include Churchill Gdns., Pimlico; South Bank Skylon; British Pavilion, Expo. '70, Osaka; Hospitals at Swindon, Slough, High Wycombe, Maidstone, Hastings, Ashington, Great Ormond Street; Wolfson College, Oxford; new buildings at Brasenose, Christ Church and Corpus Christi, Oxford, and St. John's and Queens' Colleges, Cambridge; Chichester Festival Theatre; Museum of London; Queen Elizabeth II Conference Centre, Westminster. *Clubs:* Chelsea Arts. *Address:* 16 The Little Boltons, London SW10 9LP.

POWELL, Roy Owen, N.D.D. (1956), A.T.D. (1959); landscape figure and still life artist in oil on canvas, charcoal and pencil drawings; retd. art teacher; *b* Chepstow, 3 Dec., 1934. *Educ:* Monmouth School and West Mon School, Pontypool. *Studied:* Cardiff College of Art (1952-56, Eric Malthouse, J.C. Tarr). *Exhib:* National Gallery of Wales, 1996 (with the work of my father - 1906-85 - a primitive painter); one-man shows: Brecknock Museum (1994), International Pavilion, Llangollen, Washington Gallery, Theatre Brecheiniog; various group shows in England, Wales and Scotland including Celtic Vision. *Publications:* articles for Planet' magazine. *Clubs:* The Welsh Group. *Signs work:* "R.O. Powell." *Address:* 10 Mill St., Brecon, Powys LD3 9BD.

PRENDERGAST, Peter, R.W.A., R.C.A., D.F.A. (1967), M.A. (1970), Hon. Doc. Letters, University of Glamorgan; painter draughtsman/landscape painter in water-colour, oil, charcoal, pencil and ink on paper, canvas, board; prizewinner, Singer Friedlander/Sunday Times Water-colour competition (1996); *b* 27 Oct., 1946. *m* Lesley. two *s*. two *d*. *Educ:* Cardiff. *Studied:* Slade School of Fine Art (William Coldstream, Frank Auerbach, Jeffery Camp), Reading University. *Exhib:* Mostyn Gallery touring to Swansea, Durham, London, Tate Gallery, Norwich A.G., A.C.G.B. touring show, National Parks Exhbn., V. & A., also toured U.S.A., Land and Sea exhbn. with Len Tabner, Scarborough (1992), National Museum of Wales (1993-94), Agnews, London, Boundary Gallery, London, Royal Academy and Barcelona tour, Angela Flowers British Landscape (1999), Martin Tinney, Cardiff. *Work in collections:* Tate Gallery, B.M., A.C.G.B., W.A.C., Contemporary Art Soc., National Museum of Wales, etc. Paintings from Wales - Agnews London (1994), Barings Bank. *Commissions:* National Trust, National Museum of Wales. Agents: Boundary Gallery, London NW8 0RH. *Clubs:* 56-Group, Wales. *Signs work:* "Peter Prendergast." *Address:* Tan-y-Craig, Deiniolen, Caernarfon LL55 3EE.

PRENTICE, David, landscape painter; co-founder/director, Ikon Gallery, B'ham. (1964-71); taught at School of Fine Art, B'ham (1968-86), Ruskin, Oxford (1986-87), U.C.E., Birmingham and Fine Art B.A., Trent Polytechnic (1986-93); *b* 4 July, 1936. *m* Dinah Prentice, artist. four *d*. *Educ:* Moseley School of Art, B'ham. *Studied:* B'ham College of Art and Crafts. *Exhib:* Serpentine, Betty Parsons, N.Y., Gainsborough's House, Suffolk, Art First, London. Winner of the Singer & Friedlander/Sunday Times water-colour prize (1990, 1996, 1999). *Work in collections:* M.O.M.A., N.Y., Albright Knox, Buffalo, House of Commons, Arts Council, Art Institute of Chicago. Patron: Autumn in Malvern Festival. Trustee: George Jackson Educational Foundation. Represented by Cowleigh Gallery, Malvern and John Davies Gallery, Stow-on-the-Wold. *Signs work:* "David Prentice." *Address:* Ashdown Villa, 9 Hanley Terr., Malvern, Wells, Worcs. WR14 4PF. *Email:* dinah.prentice@virgin.net

PREST, Harry, Albert, Le Bealle, A.R.I.B.A. (1948-1966 - resigned); painter in oil and watercolour; specialises in paintings of coastal scenery of Cornwall; *b* Nr Shrewsbury, 25 Oct., 1914. *m* Lily Hillage (decd.). two *s*. *Educ:* Shrewsbury Priory County School for boys. *Studied:* mainly self taught. *Exhib:* St Ives Society of Artists and various other galleries in England. *Work in collections:* numerous private collections in Britain, Europe and U.S.A. *Clubs:* St Ives Society of Artists. *Signs work:* "HARRY PREST." *Address:* 6, Northfield Drive, Truro, Cornwall TR1 2BS.

PRESTON-GODDARD, John, Professional painter, oil, water-colour, gouache; *b* Liverpool. *m* Kathleen Preston-Goddard, art gallery owner (Who's Who World of Women). *Exhib:* foremost London galleries, Moscow and Croydon. *Work in collections:* Britain, U.S.A., Europe, Australia, Japan and S.Africa. *Signs work:* "PRESTON GODDARD." *Address:* Studio House, Selborne Rd., Croydon CR0 5JQ.

PRETSELL, Peter, D.A. (Edin.); artist in printmaking, painting; lecturer in printmaking, Nene College, Northampton; lecturer, Edinburgh College of Art (1985); Head of Printmaking, E.C.A.(1999); *b* Edinburgh, 1942. *m* Philomena Pretsell. three *s*. *Educ:* George Heriots School, Edinburgh. *Studied:* Edinburgh College of Art (1960-65). *Exhib:* New 57 Gallery, Printmakers Workshop, S.S.A. and Fruitmarket Gallery (Edinburgh), Northampton, Birmingham, Newcastle, Kettering, Bedford,

Thumb Gallery, London, Bradford Print Biennale prizewinner, Humberside Print Competition prizewinner. *Work in collections:* V. & A., Scottish Arts Council, Edinburgh Corp., Hull, Northampton A.G. *Signs work:* "Pretsell." *Address:* c/o Edinburgh College of Art, Edinburgh EH3 5QD.

PRICE, E. Jessop, H.R.S.W.A. (1987), S.W.A. (1951), Mem. of Council (1956); painter in oils; *b* Ashby-de-la-Zouch. *m* Rev. A. Jessop Price. four *s. Educ:* Ashby and Versailles. *Studied:* St. Ives School of Art (Leonard Fuller), St. Martin's School of Art (Archibald Zeigler), Heatherley's (Iain Macnab). *Exhib:* one-man show at R.W.S. Gallery (1949), S.W.A., R.O.I., Bradford Art Gallery, City of London Guildhall, etc.; awarded Freedom of the Worshipful Company of Painter Stainers in 1957. *Work in collections:* St. Paul's Cathedral, Chase National Bank, N.Y., Newton Chambers, etc. *Publications:* work repro.: The Soho Gallery, Daily Telegraph, etc. *Signs work:* "E. Jessop Price." *Address:* Sefton, Stade St., Hythe, Kent CT21 6DY.

PRICE, Stephen Jon, M.A., F.M.A.; Head of Museums and Art Gallery, Bristol; *Address:* City of Bristol Museum and Art Gallery, Queen's Rd., Bristol BS8 1RL.

PRICE, Trevor, R.E., B.A.Hons.; artist/printmaker; *b* Cornwall, 18 July, 1966. *Studied:* Falmouth School of Art (1984-85), Winchester School of Art (1985-88). *Exhib:* solo shows: Original Print Gallery (2002), Rostra Gallery, Bath (2001), Printspace, London (2001), Zella Gallery, London (1996, 1998), Montpellier Gallery, Cheltenham (1999), Pyramid Gallery, York (1997), C.C.A., Bath (1997); group shows: National Print Exhbn., London (1995-2001), Royal Soc. of Painter Printmakers, London (1996-2001). *Work in collections:* Bank of England, Yale University, U.S.A. *Commissions:* Etching for P. & O. (1994 & 2000). Printmaking Today Award (1997). *Signs work:* "Trevor Price." *Address:* Studio 30, Clink Street Studios, London SE1 9DG.

PRIESTNER, Stephen Miles, artist in oil, pastel, water-colour, collages; sign-writer, life-guard, film projectionist; *b* Altrincham, Ches., 1 May, 1954. *m* Ann, nee Warburton. *Educ:* Dodoma School, Tanzania (1959-61), Ellesmere College, Salop. (1967-70), Blackpool College of Art (1971-72), Manchester Polytechnic (1972-74). *Studied:* École des Beaux Arts, Paris (1978, B. Neiland). *Exhib:* Olympian Arts, London (1993), Salford Museum (1988), New York City, Art Competition Winner (1994), Nice, Milan, Stockholm, Venice, Barcelona (1998). *Work in collections:* Ghent Museum, Belgium; M.O.M.A., New York (prints); Musée d'Art Moderne, Paris; Bradford Art Gallery, Tate Gallery. *Publications:* work repro.: The Artist, Apollo Magazine, New York Post (review), Contemporary Art, N.Y., etc.; book: New Art International, N.Y., Art News, Art Monthly, Modern Painters. *Signs work:* "Stephen M. Priestner." *Address:* 23 Booth St., Stockport, Cheshire SK3 9DG.

PRITCHARD, Marion Ruth, S.W.A. (1987), S.O.F.A. (1994); painter and illus-trator in oil and water-colour; *b* London, 10 Nov., 1934. *m* Ronald Pritchard. two *s.* one *d. Educ:* Minchenden Grammar School. *Studied:* Hornsey College of Art and Crafts (1951-56, graphic design). *Exhib:* R.A., R.B.A., R.I., R.O.I., S.W.A., S.WL.A., S.G.A., S.B.A., R.M.S., S.O.F.A.; mixed exhbns. at several London gal-leries. *Publications:* work repro.: greetings cards for Medici, Royle, Bucentaur, Camden Graphics, Hallmark. *Signs work:* "Marion Pritchard." *Address:* 50 Arnos Grove, Southgate, Londn N14 7AR.

PROCKTOR, Patrick, R.A., R.W.S., R.E.; painter and etcher; *b* Dublin, 12 Mar., 1936. *m* Kirsten Benson, née Bo-Andersen (decd.). one *s.* one *d. Studied:* Slade School (1958-62). *Exhib:* since 1963 seventeen one-man shows at Redfern Gallery, London, and other one-man shows abroad. Works represented in numerous public collections. *Publications:* author of One Window in Venice, publ. 1974 (16 water-colour views, published by Galleria Cavallino, Venice); new edition of The Rime of the Ancient Mariner by S. T. Coleridge with twelve etching illustrations, publ. 1976 by Editions Alecto, London; A Chinese Journey, suite of acquatint landscapes of China, publ. 1980 by Editions Alecto; Patrick Procktor, monographs by Patrick Kinmonth publ. by Cavallino 1986, Self portrait, memoir publ. 1993 by Weidenfeld & Nicholson; P. Procktor, monograph by John McEwen, publ. 1997 by Scolar Press. *Clubs:* Garrick. *Address:* c/o Royal Academy of Arts, Piccadilly, London W1V 0DS.

PROCTER, (née PALMER), Marjorie, A.T.D. (1940); artist in water-colour, pencil and wash; art teacher, Ealing School of Art (1943-74); art teacher, Liverpool Inst. for Boys (1941-43); *b* Birmingham, 17 Feb., 1918. *m* Kenneth Procter, painter (decd.). *Educ:* Wade Deacon Grammar School, Widnes. *Studied:* Liverpool City School of Art (1935-40). *Exhib:* R.A., R.I., R.B.A., Nat. Soc., United Soc. of Artists, S.M.A., S.W.A., R.I. Summer Salon, Britain in Water-colour. *Signs work:* "Marjorie Procter," either written or in block capitals. *Address:* Spring Cottage, Woonton, Almeley, Herefordshire HR3 6QL.

PROUD, Alastair Colm, artist in oil and water-colour, specialising in wildlife and landscape; *b* Dublin, Rep. of Ireland, 2 Oct., 1954. *m* Jill Paula. one *s.* one *d. Exhib:* 'Birds in Art' Leigh Yawkey Museum of Art, U.S.A., Mall Galleries, London. *Work in collections:* Sultan of Oman. *Publications:* illustrator: Birds of Prey of British Isles; Wildfowl of British Isles and North West Europe. *Clubs:* S.WL.A. *Address:* Plas Bach, Newchurch, Carmarthen, Carms. SA33 6EJ, S. Wales.

PROWSE, Alexander Reginald, P.S.; painter in pastel, oil and water-colour; *b* London, 23 June, 1949. *m* Janet Prowse. *Studied:* Harrow School of Art (Christopher Saunders, R.A., Ken Howard, R.A.). *Exhib:* one-man shows: London, Mexico, Venezuela; N.E.A.C., P.S., R.S.M.A., R.P., R.I., R.M.S. *Work in collections:* Lord & Lady Sainsbury, Hotel de Ville, Paris, Sadlers Wells Theatre. *Signs work:* "Alex Prowse." *Address:* Cascade Art Gallery, Pool of Little Venice, Blomfield Rd., London W9 2PA. *Website:* www.littlevenicelondon.co.uk *Email:* a@littlevenicelondon.co.uk

PRYSE: see SPENCER PRYSE, Tessa.

PULLAN, Margaret Ida Elizabeth, Paris Salon: Gold Medal (1972), Silver Medal (1967); artist in oil; *b* Saharanpur, U.P., India, 6 Nov., 1907. *Educ:* Highfield, Oxhey Lane, Watford, Herts. *Studied:* privately. *Exhib:* Paris Salon (1957-58, 1963 (hon. mention), 1965-71), R.P., R.B.A., Leicester Galleries, Bournemouth, Bradford, Cartwright Memorial Hall, United Soc. of Artists. *Work in collections:* Rugby A.G. *Signs work:* see appendix. *Address:* Cedars Rest Home, 90 Warwick Park, Tunbridge Wells, Kent TN2 5EN.

PULLAN, Tessa, S.Eq.A. (1988), F.R.B.S. (2001); sculptor in wood, clay, stone, bronze; *b* London, 20 Dec., 1953. married. one *s.* one *d. Educ:* Tudor Hall. *Studied:*

apprenticeship with John Skeaping, R.A. (1971-74), City & Guilds of London Art School (1974-77, James Butler), R.A. Schools (1977-80, Willi Soukop, R.A.). *Exhib:* R.A. Summer Shows, Cork St. Fine Arts, Ackermann (London and N.Y.), S.Eq.A., Christies, London Contemporary Art Fair, Bruton St. Gallery, etc.; solo shows: Quinton Green Fine Arts, London, John Hunt Gallery, Frank T. Sabin, London. *Work in collections:* N.P.G., National Horse Racing Museum, Newmarket, Yale Center for British Art, Clare College, Cambridge, Virginia Museum of Fine Art, Paul Mellon Center for Studies in British Art, Virginia Historical Soc., Fitzwilliam Museum. *Signs work:* "Tessa Pullan" and see appendix. *Address:* Granby House, Kings Lane, Barrowden, Rutland LE15 8EF.

PULLÉE, Edward, C.B.E. (1967), A.R.C.A. (1929), F.S.A.E. (1945), N.E.A.C. (life mem.); artist in oil and water-colour; retd. Chief Officer, N.C.D.A.D. (1967-74); *b* London, 19 Feb., 1907. *m* Margaret, A.R.C.A., N.E.A.C. one *s. Educ:* St. Martin's School, Dover. *Studied:* Dover School of Art (1922-26), R.C.A. (1926-30, Profs. William Rothenstein, Randolph Schwabe, Malcolm Osbourne). *Exhib:* R.A., N.E.A.C., London and provincial galleries. *Work in collections:* Leeds City A.G., Leicester City A.G. *Signs work:* "Pullee." *Address:* c/o Michael E. Pullée, 48 Wray Common Rd., Reigate, Surrey RH2 0NB.

PULLÉE, Michael Edward, Des.R.C.A., F.C.S.D., N.E.A.C., F.R.S.A.; artist in oil, designer and educational consultant; former H.M. Inspector of Schools; *b* London, 8 Sept., 1936. *m* Sheila Mary Threadgill. two *d. Educ:* Bootham School, York. *Studied:* Leeds College of Art, R.C.A. *Exhib:* New English Annual, Pattersons, R.A. Summer Exhbn., Bankside. *Clubs:* N.E.A.C. *Signs work:* "Michael E. Pullée." *Address:* White Gables, 48 Wray Common Rd., Reigate, Surrey RH2 0NB.

PURNELL, John, Ph.D., M.A., B.A.Hons., F.R.G.S., F.R.S.A., F.B.P.A., A.R.P.S., A.B.I.P.P., L.C.G.I., M.Ph.E.; art and photography tutor, University researcher; *b* Birmingham, 8 Jan., 1954. *Studied:* Bournville College of Art and Design; Cardiff Inst. of Higher Education; University of Wales Institute, Cardiff. *Clubs:* Mensa. *Signs work:* "John Purnell" and see appendix. *Address:* Flat 3, 4 West Luton Place, Adamsdown, Cardiff CF24 0EW.

PUTMAN, Salliann, B.A. (Hons.) Fine Art, R.W.S., N.E.A.C.; painter in oil and water-colour; *b* London, 20 Apr., 1937. *m* Michael. one *s.* one *d. Studied:* West Surrey College of Art and Design, Farnham (1988-93). *Exhib:* one and two-man shows: London, Windsor, Stockbridge; R.A., Mall Galleries, N.E.A.C., R.B.A., R.O.I., R.I., P.S., Bankside Gallery, W. H. Pattersons Gallery, New Grafton Gallery. *Signs work:* water-colours: "Salliann Putman," oils: "S.P." *Address:* 3 Pinecote Drive, Sunningdale, Berks. SL5 9PS.

PYE, Patrick, Mem. of Aosdána and R.H.A.; painter in tempera and oil, stained glass artist, etcher - an artist of the sacred theme; *b* Winchester, 1929. *m* Noirin Kennedy. two *d. Educ:* St. Columba's College, Dublin 16. *Studied:* National College of Art, Dublin (1951-54), Jan van Eyck Akad., Maastricht (1957-58). *Exhib:* many one-man shows, (Jorgensen Fine Art); Dublin, R.H.A. Annual, etc. *Work in collections:* Municipal Gallery Dublin, Crawford Gallery, Cork. *Commissions:* Stations of the Cross, Killerney; Wall Hanging, The Transfiguration, Maynooth University and many others. *Publications:* author: Apples and Angels; The Time Gatherer (on El

Greco) publ. by Veritas (1981) & Four Courts Press (1991) respectively. *Signs work:* "Patrick Pye." *Address:* Pyerstown, Tallaght, Dublin 24, Ireland.

PYE, William, A.R.C.A., F.R.B.S., Hon.F.R.I.B.A.; sculptor; *b* 16 July, 1938. *m* Susan. one *s.* two *d. Educ:* Charterhouse. *Studied:* Wimbledon School of Art (1958-61) under Freda Skinner, R.C.A. Sculpture School (1961) under Prof. B. Meadows. *Work in collections:* Arts Council, Museum of Modern Art, N.Y., Contemporary Art Soc., G.L.C., Royal Albert Memorial Museum, Exeter, Graves City A.G., Sheffield, Middlesbrough City A.G., Birmingham City A.G., Szépmúvészeti Muzeum, Budapest, National Museum of Wales, Wakefield A.G., National Portrait Gallery, London. *Commissions:* Water Wall, British Pavilion Expo '92, Seville; Slipstream and Jetstream, Gatwick Airport; Chalice, Fountain Square, London WC1; Cristos, St. Christopher's Place, London; Derby Cascade; British Embassy Oman; Antony House, Cornwall; Cader Idris, Central Sq., Cardiff; Prism, Hong Kong Airport. *Signs work:* see appendix. *Address:* 43 Hambalt Rd., Clapham, London SW4 9EQ.

PYNE, Doris Grace, A.T.D. (1934), oil painting cert., Slade School; freelance artist in water-colour, art teacher; *b* Wealdstone, 8 Oct., 1910. *Studied:* Hornsey School of Art (1930-34, Norman Janes, A.R.C.A., R.E., Douglas Percy Bliss, M.A.), Slade School (Randolph Schwabe). *Exhib:* one-man show, Salon des Nations, Paris (1984), Mall Galleries, London (1982); Norwich (1967, 1969, 1972, 1978), Park Gallery, Chislehurst (1973), Aldeburgh (1974), International Art Centre, London (1975), frequent exhib. R.I., Graphic Artists, Mall Galleries. *Clubs:* F.B.A., Bromley Art Soc. *Signs work:* "PYNE." *Address:* 32 Clarendon Way, Marlings Pk., Chislehurst, Kent BR7 6RF.

PYTEL, Walenty, N.D.D. (1961), A.R.B.S.; sculptor in bronze and mild steel; *b* Poland, 10 Feb., 1941. *m* Janet Mary. one *s.* one *d. Studied:* Hereford College of Art (1956-61). *Exhib:* Tokyo (1988), Marbella (1985), U.S.A., Germany, France, Jersey, S.WL.A. Mall Galleries (award winner 1988). *Work in collections:* Hereford, Worcester and Stockport; permanent: New Palace Yard Westminster, B'ham International Airport, Beaulieu, Berkeley Hotel London, J.C.B. Uttoxeter, County Hall, Llandrindod Wells. *Commissions:* South Herefordshire District Council 1997 'Landing Ducks'; 'Swans'; 'Leaping Salmon'. Gracemount Developments Ltd. Royal Caribbean Cruiseline; Lloyds Bank Trophy; Lloyds of London; Yamazaki Machinery Ltd. *Publications:* London Art and Antiques Guide (1991), Debrett's Distinguished People of Today (1988-95), Into the New Iron Age (Amina Chatwin 1995). *Signs work:* "WALENTY PYTEL," "W. Pytel" or "W.P." *Address:* Hartleton, Bromsash, Ross-on-Wye HR9 7SB.

Q

QUANTRILL, David James, artist in most media; *b* Lowestoft, 11 July, 1938. *m* Angela. one *s.* one *d. Studied:* Lowestoft College (part-time). *Exhib:* P.S. since 1985, First Britains Painters (1988), Eastern Open since 1985, Work on tour (1988), Laing

Exhbn. Gainsborough's House. *Work in collections:* Norwich Castle; private collections U.K., U.S.A., Europe. *Signs work:* "Quantrill." *Address:* 18 Carlton Sq., Lowestoft, Suffolk NR33 8JL.

QUIGLEY, Vlad, artist and portraitist in monochrome, linear, Art Nouveau; works in collaboration with Viola D'Amour; *Studied:* Southampton Inst. of Art and Design, Northbrook College under Joe Orlando (E.C. Comics). *Exhib:* Pop Art Nouveau portraits of Viola D'Amour, Fairfield Halls, Vampyria, Hippodrome, Damned U.S. Tour, Big Draw, Alfresco, Vampire Viola, Frogpond, The 100 (100 years of comic art), A.D. 2000, Shock, Anglo-French Aubrey Beardsley Centenary. *Commissions:* private portraits for clients, models, actresses, model agencies. *Publications:* Viola D'Amour, Viola D'Amour's Phantom Sword, Dracula's Guest, Bride of Dracula, Varney the Vampyre, Taloola, Eulalie, Vampire Viola, O.M.L.R.P., Time Machine, Space Vampires, 21st. Century Ghouls, Comics Forum, Queen of the Chickens, Viola and the Vampires, Crimson, Demeter, Velvet Vampyre, Fantagraphics, Rockin' Times, The Pier, Puppy Shrine, Witchfinder General, Betty and the Boobies, various C.D. covers, advertising art and graphics. *Clubs:* C.C.G. *Signs work:* see appendix. *Address:* c/o 276a Lower Addiscombe Rd., Croydon, Surrey CR0 7AE.

QUINN, Máire Catherine, B.A. Hons Fine Art (1984); National Portrait Gallery award finalist (1988), R.W.S. Elizabeth Scott Moore prize winner (2001); artist in oil, water-colour, printmaking, sculpture, textile; *b* Armagh City, N. Ireland, 4 Aug., 1961. *Studied:* University of Ulster. *Exhib:* N.P.G., Whitechapel Gallery, South London Gallery, Bankside Gallery, Museum of London, plus solo and group exhibs. in U.K. and abroad. *Commissions:* private, national and international. *Signs work:* "Máire Quinn." *Address:* Eliot Lodge, 295 Hither Green Lane, London SE13 6TH.

QUINN, Mary P. (née McLAUGHGLIN), Hons. sculpture (1986); sculptor in bronze portrait busts and statues; *b* Co. Down, N.I., 26 May, 1943. three *d. Educ:* St. Dominic's High School, Belfast. *Studied:* Richmond Adult College (1982-89). *Exhib:* many group shows since 1985. *Work in collections:* many bronze busts and statues in Ireland, England and U.S.A. including life-size statue of John Wesley in Virginia Wesleyan College, Virginia, U.S.A. *Commissions:* Frank Sinatra, Frankie Dettori (bronze busts). *Clubs:* F.P.S., S.C.A. *Signs work:* "Mary Quinn." *Address:* 1 Exeter Rd., Hanworth, Feltham, Middx. TW13 5PE. *Email:* maryquinnsculptures@hotmail.com

R

RACZKO, Julian Henryk, Dip. Eng. (Warsaw, 1963); artist; Prof. of Art, Warsaw Academy of Fine Arts; *b* Warsaw, 2 Jan., 1936. *m* Malena Raczko, architect. two *d. Educ:* Warsaw Technical University. *Studied:* voluntary basis at Warsaw Academy of Fine Art (1963-65, Prof. Alexander Kobzdej). *Exhib:* one-man shows: Poland, Denmark, Norway, Sweden, France, Germany, C.K. Norwid art critics award

1980. *Work in collections:* National Museums of Warsaw, Wroclaw, Poznan, Cracow, Arts Museum Lodz, galleries of Chelm, Bydogoszcz, National Gallery of Arts, Washington, Museum of Modern Art, Hünfeld, Van Reekum Museum of Apeldoorn, Fyns Kunstmuseum, Odense. *Signs work:* "Julian H. Raczko." *Address:* J. Bruna 34 m 35, 02-594 Warsaw, Poland.

RAE, Barbara, C.B.E., R.A., R.S.A., R.S.W., R.G.I.; painter and printmaker; *b* Falkirk, Scotland, 10 Dec., 1943. one *s. Educ:* Morrisons Academy, Crieff. *Studied:* Edinburgh College of Art under William Gillies, Robin Phillipson. *Exhib:* recent solo exhibs., Art First, London (1994, 1996, 1997), Waxlander Gallery, Santa Fe, U.S.A. (1996), Bohun Gallery, Henley-on-Thames (1996), Galleri Galtung, Oslo (1998), Painted Desert, Art First, London (1999); recent group exhibs., Eigse '94, Carlow Arts Festival, Ireland (1994), Hunting Group Awards, London and Wales (1994-1996), A Scottish Renaissance, Rotunda Gallery, Hong Kong (1996), R.A. Summer Exhibs. (1997-1999). *Work in collections:* public collections include, Aberdeen Art Gallery, Birmingham City Art Gallery, British Museum, City Arts Centre, Edinburgh, Contemporary Arts Soc., London, Derby Museum and Art Gallery, Dundee Art Gallery, Glasgow Museum and Art Gallery, Hunterian Art Gallery, Glasgow, Museum of Art for Woman, Washington, U.S.A., Perth Art Gallery and Museum, Scottish National Gallery of Modern Art, Edinburgh, Scottish Office, Edinburgh, University of Edinburgh, Whitworth Art Gallery, Manchester. *Clubs:* Glasgow Art Club. *Signs work:* "Barbara Rae." *Address:* c/o Art First, 9 Cork St., London W1X 1PD. *Email:* barbararaera@aol.com

RAE, Fiona, painting; *b* Hong Kong, 10 Oct., 1963. *Studied:* Croydon College of Art (1983-84), Goldsmiths' College, London (1984-87). *Exhib:* selected solo shows 1999: Luhring Augustine Gallery, N.Y., Komji Ogura Gallery, Nagoya; 1997: Saatchi Gallery, London (with Gary Hume), British School at Rome; 1996: Contemporary Fine Arts, Berlin; 1993-94: Inst. of Contemporary Arts, London; 1992: Kunsthalle Basel, Basel; 1991: Waddington Galleries, London; 1990: Third Eye Centre, Glasgow. *Work in collections:* includes Tate Gallery, London; Arts Council; Walker A.G., Liverpool; Muse Departemental de Rochechouart, Haute-Vienne; Hamburger Bahnhof, Berlin; Sintra Museum of Modern Art, Portugal. *Publications:* work repro.: numerous exhbn. catalogues, articles, reviews. *Address:* Luhring Augustine Gallery, 531 West 24th St., New York, N.Y. 10011, U.S.A.

RAE, John, works in mixed media, often in combination with PVA, and also makes screen and mono prints and etchings, and draws in conté and pencil. Subjects include landscape, plants and trees, buildings, people, and life paintings. Formerly a lecturer in Architecture at University College London, the Architectural Association, and at Hornsey College of Art. He has travelled and painted in Australasia, Africa, and the New World; *b* Exeter, 1931. *Exhib:* Australian and British galleries, see www.thomasplunkett.com. *Publications:* Sketch Book of the World. *Signs work:* "John Rae." *Address:* 14 Orchard St., St. Albans, Herts. AL3 4HL.

RAEBURN, Kenneth Alexander, D.A.(Edin.) (1966); Post Grad. Scholarship (1966-67); sculptor in bronze, resins and wood, of free-standing figures, portraits and relief murals; principal teacher of art, Comprehensive School; *b* Haddington, E. Lothian, 9 June, 1942. *m* Helen Raeburn. one *s.* one *d. Educ:* Trinity Academy,

Edinburgh. *Studied:* School of Sculpture, Edinburgh College of Art under Eric Schilsky. *Exhib:* R.S.A., S.S.A., various group exhbns. in Scotland, Salon des Nations Exhbn., Paris (1983); one-man show, Metropolis Galerie d'Art, Geneva (1985). *Work in collections:* commissioned panel depicting Baptism of Christ by St. John, in St. John the Baptist Primary School, W. Lothian (awarded Saltire Society Commendation, 1972); commissioned woodcarving of St. Columba in St. Columba's Church, Boghall, West Lothian; commissioned life-sized seal, with her pup, (concrete), South Queensferry; work in numerous private collections in U.K. *Signs work:* "Raeburn." *Address:* 46 Belsyde Ct., Linlithgow, W. Lothian EH49 7RW.

RAMSAY, Alexander, Dip. A.D. (Hons.), 1968, H.D.A. (1969); artist in oil paint and drawing media; Senior lecturer in Fine Art, Central/St. Martin's School of Art; *b* London, 23 Mar., 1947. *m* Tricia Gillman. two *s.* one *d. Studied:* Chelsea School of Art (1964-69). *Exhib:* one-man shows: Hatton Gallery Newcastle, Newcastle Polytechnic Gallery, Creaser Gallery London, Castlefield Gallery Manchester, South Square Gallery Bradford. *Clubs:* London Group. *Signs work:* "Alex Ramsay." *Address:* 149 Algernon Rd., London SE13 7AP.

RAND, Keith John, B.A, Hons. (1981), A.R.S.A. (1996); sculptor in wood including various landscape structures, stiles, footbridges, and seating, all site-specific; *b* Germany (British nationality), 25 Oct., 1956. *Educ:* Woodroffe School, Lyme Regis, Dorset. *Studied:* Winchester School of Art (1979-1981). *Exhib:* ten solo exhibs. in U.K. since 1982. *Work in collections:* Aberdeen Art Gallery, Obihiro Internat. Building, Japan, private collections Europe, U.S.A. and Japan. *Publications:* exhib. catalogues, works 1987-1992. *Signs work:* "KR" or "RAND." *Address:* 10 St. Margaret's Cl., Salisbury, Wilts SP1 2RY.

RANDALL, Carl, B.A, Hons. in Fine Art, R.B.A; painter in oil, and water-colour, sculptor in wood and mixed media, draughtsman in pencil and charcoal; *b* South Shields. *Studied:* Slade School of Fine Art, University College, London. *Work in collections:* Singer and Friedlander Bank, Railtrack Plc. *Signs work:* "CARL RANDALL." *Address:* 22 Ryton Court, South Shields, Tyne and Wear NE33 4HS. *Website:* www.carlrandall.net *Email:* carl@carlrandall.net

RANDALL, Edward Mark, graphic designer, painter in oil, pastel, water-colour; *b* Coventry, 24 Feb., 1921. *m* Marjory. two *s.* one *d. Educ:* Coventry Technical College. *Studied:* Coventry Art School, Hornsey and Central Schools. *Work in collections:* Marks and Spencer, Plessey Co. private collection, R.C.M. Printing Group. *Signs work:* "Mark Randall." *Address:* B7 Argyll House, Seaforth Rd., Westcliff-on-Sea, Essex SS0 7SH.

RANDALL-PAGE, Peter, B.A. (Hons.) 1977, Hon. Doctorate of Arts, University of Plymouth (1999); sculptor in stone; *b* Rochford, Essex, 2 July, 1954. *m* Charlotte Eve Randall-Page. one *s.* one *d. Studied:* Bath Academy of Arts (1973-77). *Exhib:* 'Sculpture and Drawings 1980-1992' Leeds City A.G. (1992), 'In Mind of Botany' R.B.G. Kew (1996), 'Nature of the Beast', Nottingham, Sheffield and Eastbourne (2001). *Work in collections:* Tate Gallery, British Museum, etc. *Commissions:* National Trust (1995), L.D.D.C. London (1996), Manchester City Council (1996), Hunters Sq. Edinburgh (1996), sculpture at Goodwood (2000). *Publications:* Peter Randall-Page: Sculpture and Drawings 1977-1992; Granite Song (1999), Nature of the Beast (2001). *Address:* P.O. Box 5, Drewsteignton, Exeter, Devon EX6 6YG. *Website:* www.peterrandall-page.com *Email:* randalpage@aol.com

RANDLE, Susan Ann, Dip.H.E.; painter, muralist and graphic artist in oil, water-colour, gouache, pen and ink; *b* Portsmouth, 16 June, 1936. *m* Dave Randle, writer. one *s.* one *d. Educ:* Dominican Convent, Harare, Zimbabwe. *Studied:* Dartington College of Art, Totnes (1978-80, Chris Crickmay, John Gridley). *Exhib:* Carlos Gallery, London, Arnolfini, Bristol; one-man show: Bruyas Gallery, Torquay. *Signs work:* "Sue Randle." *Address:* 2a Granville Rd., Sidcup, Kent DA14 4BN.

RANK-BROADLEY, Ian, H.D.F.A. (Lond.) (1976), Boise scholar (1976), F.S.N.A.D. (1990), F.R.B.S. (1994), A.W.G. (1995); sculptor and medallist in bronze; *b* Walton-on-Thames, 4 Sept., 1952. *m* Hazel Rank. one *s.* one *d. Studied:* Epsom School of Art (1970-74, Bruce McLean), Slade School of Fine Art (1974-76, Reg Butler). *Exhib:* Adonis Art, Simmons & Simmons. *Work in collections:* British Museum, Fitzwilliam Museum, Cambridge, Staatliche Museen, Berlin, Rijksmuseum, Leiden, N.P.G. London, Royal Swedish Coin Cabinet, Royal Mint, Goldsmiths' Hall, London, H.M. The Queen Mother. *Commissions:* effigy of H.M. The Queen on U.K coinage from 1998, Golden Jubilee Hallmark, new effigy of H.M. Queen for Golden Jubilee crown & medal. Freeman of the Goldsmiths' Company; Granted Freedom of City of London (1996). *Signs work:* see appendix. *Address:* Stanfields, Kingscourt La., Rodborough, Stroud, Glos. GL5 3QR.

RANKIN, Stella, painter in oil; *b* London, 1915. *Studied:* St. Martin's, London (1956-58), Goldsmiths' College of Art (1958-61, Kenneth Martin). *Exhib:* Royal Festival Hall, Barbican, (F.P.S.) Guildhall, London, (Art for Sale) Whiteley's, Christie's (Imperial Cancer Research) London, The London Group, Artists International, Studio Club, W1, Market Cross Gallery, Bury St. Edmunds, Galerie Internationale, New York, U.S.A.A.F., Lakenheath, Inst. of Education, Corn Exchange, Saffron Walden White Hart, Braintree, Beecroft Gallery, Westcliff-on-Sea, The Crypt, St. Martin-in-the-Fields, R.A.; solo shows: Oriel Gallery, Aberystwyth, Halesworth Gallery, Suffolk, Mercury Gallery, Colchester, Loggia Gallery, SW1, Chappel Gallery, Essex, Cinema Gallery, Aldeburgh, Oakwood Gallery, Maldon, Prettygate Library, Colchester. *Work in collections:* Chelmsford Museum; and private collections. *Signs work:* "Stella Rankin" or "S.R." *Address:* 7 Constitution Hill, Sudbury, Suffolk CO10 2PT.

RASMUSSEN, Roy, F.F.P.S. (1961); sculptor in hand beaten and welded alu-minium; Co-Director, Woodstock Gallery, London (1958-67); Director, Loggia Gallery, London (1984 to present); *b* London, 29 Apr., 1919 . *Exhib:* British Council, Berlin (1961); Réalités Nouvelles, Paris (1966); John Whibley Gallery, Cork St., London (1968-77); New Directions 1999, Loggia Gallery, London; F.P.S. exhbns. (1957-99); and many London galleries, including one-man shows. *Work in collections:* Towner Gallery and Museum, Eastbourne, Paris, Berlin and U.S.A. *Publications:* The Free Painters and Sculptors 1952-1992 (author). *Signs work:* "RASMUSSEN." *Address:* 123 Canterbury Rd., N. Harrow, Middx. HA1 4PA.

RAVERA, John, P.P.R.B.S., F.R.S.A.; President, R.B.S. (1988-90); sculptor in clay; *b* Surrey, 27 Feb., 1941. *m* Daphne. one *s. Studied:* Camberwell School of Art (1954-62). *Exhib:* R.A. (1975, 1976), Alwin Gallery (1977), Woodlands (1977),

Bexleyheath (1985), Haywards Heath (1985), Johannesburg S.A. (1995), Chris Beatles Gallery (1996). *Commissions:* Major commissions: Academy of Arts Hong Kong (1982), Morgan's Walk London (1983), London Dockland Development, bronze bust (1986), Bayswater London, bronze group of children (1987), Barbican London, bronze group dolphins (1989), Elstree London, stainless steel abstract (1989), Tokyo (1994), Maidenhead (1996), Reading (1996). *Signs work:* "John E. Ravera." *Address:* Studio, 82 Latham Rd., Bexleyheath, Kent DAG 7NQ.

RAWLINGS, Raymond, commercial artist in water-colour (retd.); *b* Windsor, 26 Apr., 1934. *m* Frances. three *d. Studied:* apprenticed to major art studio (London) producing artwork for major multi national companies (1951). *Exhib:* Oxford, R.W.A. Work in collections worldwide. *Clubs:* Oxford Art Soc. *Address:* 1 Chestnut Close, Fawley, nr. Wantage, Oxon. OX12 9YW.

RAWLINS, Janet, N.D.D. (Illustration), A.T.D., book illustration, fabric collage, gouache, water-colour; *b* Horsforth, Leeds, 3 May, 1931. *m* John G. Leyland, F.C.A. one *s. Educ:* Gt. Moreton Hall, Ches. *Studied:* Leeds College of Art. *Exhib:* R.A., northern galleries. *Work in collections:* Bradford, Harrogate and Batley Art Galleries, Leeds, Huddersfield, West Riding, Leicester and Essex Education Committees, Leeds Permanent Building Society, I.W.S., N.C.B., I.C.I. *Publications:* children's books by William Mayne and Jane Gardam; compiled and illustrated A Dales Countryside Cookbook (1993). *Signs work:* "Janet Rawlins." *Address:* West End House, Askrigg, Wensleydale, N. Yorks. DL8 3HN.

RAY: see HOWARD-JONES, Ray.

RAY, Karen, painter in oil, water-colour, pencil, coloured pencil, lecturer; *b* Queensland, Australia, 8 Dec., 1931. *m* Stuart Ray (decd.). three *s. Studied:* Walthamstow School of Art (Stuart Ray, John Tichell, Fred Cuming); R.A. Schools (Peter Greenham). *Exhib:* many times in the R.A. Summer Exhbn. *Signs work:* "K. Ray." *Address:* 91 Mountview Rd., London N4 4JA.

RAYMENT, Brenda, A.R.M.S. (1991); artist in oil on ivorine; *b* Paddock Wood, Kent, 5 May, 1951. *m* Laurence Rayment. one *s.* one *d. Educ:* Kidbrooke School. *Studied:* Bexley A.E.C. (1980-90, Barry Shiraishi, R.M.S.). *Exhib:* S.W.A., R.M.S. *Address:* Heather Cottage, 5 Gwel-an-Garrek, Mullion. Cornwall TR12 7RW.

RAYNER, Desmond, L.G.S.M.; self taught artist in gouache, charcoal, pencil, oil; literary agent, writer, actor; *b* London, 31 Oct., 1928. *m* Claire Rayner. two *s.* one *d. Educ:* theatre: Guildhall School of Music and Drama. *Exhib:* Heals, London; Embankment Gallery, Tattershall Castle, London; Grays, Mayfair; Talent Store, Belgravia; October Gallery, U.S.A.; Mall Galleries, London; Seven Dials Gallery, London; Barbican Centre, London; Wylma Wayne Fine Art, London; Building Centre, London; Charisma Gallery, Harrow, etc. *Work in collections:* U.S.A., Canada, Australia, U.K. *Publications:* The Dawlish Season, The Husband (novels). Work can be viewed by appointment at own address below. *Signs work:* "RAYNER." *Address:* Holly Wood House, Roxborough Ave., Harrow-on-the-Hill, Middx. HA1 3BU.

RAYNER, Martin, Dip. Art (Drawing and Painting), Post Dip. Art, A.R.S.A.; sculptor in painted carved wood; full time artist and part time lecturer in visual studies; now studying social work at Dundee University; *b* Haddington, East Lothian, 21 Nov., 1946. one *s.* three *d. Educ:* Dunbar Grammar School, East Lothian. *Studied:* Duncan of Jordanstone College of Art (1976-1981), Dundee University under Alberto Morrocco. *Exhib:* R.S.A., and numerous both national and international. *Work in collections:* private collections in Switzerland, France, Canada, U.S.A., Sweden, Belgium, Holland, England, Scotland; public collections in Aberdeen Art Gallery, Dundee Art Gallery, Kirkcaldy Art Gallery, Fife. *Commissions:* Duke of Atholl, Atholl Estates, Kirkcaldy Art Gallery, Burntisland Leisure Center, Fife, Wurzburg City Council, Bavaria, Germany, Scottish Nuclear H.Q., East Kilbride, Dairsie Medieval Castle, Fife, Dundee City Council, Fife Council Health Centre, Rosyth, Fife. *Publications:* Encyclopaedia of Sculpting Techniques (1995), London, Quarto; Craft Magazine (Issue no. 108, Jan/Feb. 1991). *Signs work:* "Martin Rayner." *Address:* 18 Grove Rd., Broughty Ferry, Dundee DD1 5JL.

RAYNOR, Trevor Samuel, Mem. Associé, Société des Artistes Français (1977); textile designer, artist in oil and water-colour and floral subjects in gouache; *b* Oldham, 13 May, 1929. *m* Margaret Joyce Marwood. one *s. Educ:* Werneth Council School. *Studied:* Oldham School of Art (1942-45), Manchester School of Art (1945-49). *Exhib:* Paris Salon (1975, 1976, 1977); one-man shows, Salford City A.G., Swinton Memorial A.G. Work in private collections. *Publications:* work repro.: prints of floral work. *Signs work:* "RAYNOR" or "T.S. RAYNOR." *Address:* 1 Hollin Cres., Greenfield, Oldham OL3 7LW.

READ, Sue, R.I. (1985), N.D.D. (1963), A.T.D. (1964); artist in water-colour; *b* Slough, 1941. *m* Robert Read (divorced). three *s. Educ:* Aylesbury Grammar School. *Studied:* High Wycombe School of Art (1959-63), Royal West of England College of Art (1963-64). *Exhib:* Mall Galleries, R.A. Summer Exhbn., Shell House Gallery, Ledbury. *Signs work:* "S.R." *Address:* Primrose Cottage, Water Stratford, Buckingham MK18 5DS.

READING, Peter William, M.S.I.A. (1957); painter in oil, acrylic, pastel, water-colour and etcher; design consultant, (retired 1990); *b* London, 3 Aug., 1933. *m* Doreen Rita. two *d. Educ:* Edmonton County Grammar School. *Studied:* Hornsey and London School of Printing (part time). *Exhib:* London, Henley-on-Thames, Bournemouth, Gloucester, Plymouth, Penzance, St. Ives, Brest, France, Minneapolis, U.S.A.; two solo exhibs. annually, Mariners Gallery, St. Ives. *Work in collections:* various private collections in U.K. and U.S.A., and St. Ives Gallery. *Clubs:* St. Ives Soc. of Artists. *Signs work:* "Peter Reading" and date. *Address:* 5 Higher Tamar Terr., Gunnislake, Cornwall PL18 9LP. *Website:* www.peter-reading.com *Email:* enq@peter-reading.co.uk

REAL, Jacqueline, F.F.P.S. (1992); contemporary painter in acrylic, collage and mixed media; *b* Zürich, 5 Oct., 1931. *m* Christopher Butler. one *s.* one *d. Studied:* in Zürich (1975-78), Academy of Modern Art, Masterclass, Salzburg (1979), Painting Course in Meran (1980). *Exhib:* solo and group shows: Switzerland, England, U.S.A. and Germany. *Work in collections:* Switzerland, England, U.S.A., Germany, including Oeblikon Contraves, Zürich, Mark Rich Switzerland, Union Bank of Switzerland Zürich and London, Zürich Insurance, Credit Swiss Bank Zürich, British Government, Johnson & Johnson, Tokai Bank, Bank of Austria, Crown Court Truro.

Publications: New Visions, St. Ives Painters. Represented by: International Art Consultants, London, White Gallery, Hove, Wills Lane Gallery, St. Ives, New Millennium Gallery, St. Ives, Galerie Ruth Schwarzer, Pfäffikon (Zürich), Contemporary Art Gallery, Bonstetten (Zürich), Lelipis Art Place, Ascona. *Clubs:* F.P.S., Soc. of Swiss Painters, Sculptors and Architects, Eastbourne Group of Artists. *Signs work:* "J. Real." *Address:* 7 Bath Court, Kings Esplanade, Hove BN3 2WP.

REDDICK, Peter, D.F.A. (Slade, 1951), R.E. Hon. Retd., R.W.A.; printmaker and wood-engraver, freelance illustrator; *b* Essex, 1924. *Studied:* Slade School of Fine Art (1948-51); Gregynog Arts Fellow (1970-80). Chairman, Bristol Printmakers Workshop. *Signs work:* "Peter Reddick." *Address:* 18 Hartington Park, Bristol BS6 7ES.

REDFERN, June, D.A. (1972); prizewinner, Scottish Young Contemporaries; Artist in Residence, National Gallery (1985); painter in oil and water-colour; *b* St. Andrews, Fife, 16 June, 1951. one *d. Educ:* Dunfermline High School, Fife. *Studied:* Edinburgh College of Art (1968-73, Robin Philipson, David Michie, Elizabeth Blackadder, John Houston). *Exhib:* many throughout Britain and U.S.A. including National Gallery, London (1985). *Work in collections:* S.N.G.M.A., National Gallery London, B.B.C. Television, Robert Fleming plc, Arthur Andersen, Texaco, Hiscox Holdings. *Signs work:* "June Redfern" on reverse of oils only. *Address:* 12 Lawley St., London E5 0RJ.

REDINGTON, Simon, B.A. (Fine Art), Postgrad.Dip. in Art Therapy, Cert. of Advanced Printmaking; artist/printmaker in etching, woodcuts, letterpress, painting, mixed media; *b* London, 28 Sept., 1958. *Educ:* Pimlico School. *Studied:* Goldsmiths' College, Hertfordshire College of Art, Central St. Martin's College of Art. *Exhib:* N.P.G., R.A. Summer Show, Slaughterhouse Gallery, Southbank Picture Show, Royal Festival Hall, Bankside Gallery. *Work in collections:* V. & A., Theatre Museum, Ashmolean Museum, N.Y. Public Library, Harvard University, Yale Center for British Art, Museum of London, Newberry Library, Chicago. *Commissions:* Peter O'Toole as Jeffery Bernard, Shaftesbury Theatre, London. *Publications:* see website. *Clubs:* R.E. *Signs work:* "S. Redington." *Address:* 149 Archway Rd., London N6 5BL. *Website:* www.kamikazepress.com

REDVERS, John Stephen, (formerly PIGGINS, John Redvers Stephen, changed 1979), Slade Dip. (1948), P.S. (1984); portrait painter in pastel, oil; *b* Birmingham, 18 July, 1928. *m* Mary Pennel. one *s.* two *d. Educ:* Solihull School, Warwickshire. *Studied:* Slade School of Art (1945-48, Prof. Randolph Schwabe), Ruskin School of Art, Oxford (1950, Prof. Albert Rutherston). *Exhib:* R.P., P.S., Hopetoun House, W. Lothian (1977); one-man show, Chakrabongse Palace, Bangkok (1962). *Signs work:* "JOHN REDVERS" or "REDVERS" ("J.R.S. Piggins" or "John Piggins" pre 1979). *Address:* Tweenhills, Hartpury, Gloucester GL19 3BG.

REES, Darren, B.Sc. (Hons.) (1983), S.WL.A. (1985); self taught artist in water-colour of natural history particularly birds; *b* Andover, Hants., 15 Mar., 1961. *m* Gwynneth Jane Rees (Kenny). one *s.* one *d. Educ:* Southampton University. *Exhib:* S.W.L.A., Artists for Nature Foundation, Holland, Sweden, Poland, U.S.A. *Work in collections:* Lloyds, Les Ecrins National Park, Leigh Yawkey Museum Wisconsin, Stirling Council. *Commissions:* Awards: B.B.C., R.S.P.B., Lloyds. *Publications:*

Bird Impressions, Portrait of Wildlife on a Hill Farm, Birds by Character. *Awards:* R.S.P.B. Fine Art Award, Natural World Award, Young European Bird Artist Award. *Signs work:* "Darren Rees" or "DR" *Address:* New East Frew, Thornhill, Stirling FK8 3QX.

REES-DAVIES, Kay, A.L.C.M. (1976), S.B.A. (1994), R.H.S. Silver-Gilt Medal (1993); Cert. Botanical Merit, S.B.A. (1994); R.H.S. Gold Medals (1996, 1998); freelance botanical artist; *b* Brighton, 17 June, 1936. *m* John Rees-Davies. one *s.* one *d. Educ:* Bretton Hall College (1954-56), courses in Botanical Art, Adult Study Centre, Gwynedd (1988-89). *Exhib:* several solo and joint exhbns. in Wales; S.B.A., London; R.H.S.; Waterman Fine Art, London; Gordon-Craig Gallery. *Work in collections:* R.H.S. Lindley Library; Hunt Inst. for Botanical Documentation, Carnegie Mellon University, Pittsburgh U.S.A.; Library, R.B.G., Kew; Shirley Sherwood Collection. *Publications:* illustrated 'Plantas Endemicas e Avores Indigenas de Cabo Verde (1995); 'Contemporary Botanical Artists' Shirley Sherwood Collection (1996); 'Fine Botanical Paintings' – Gordon Craig Gallery (2000). *Address:* 6 Balmoral, The Promenade, Llanfairfechan, N.Wales LL33 0BU.

REEVE, Marion José, N.D.D. (1953), M.F.P.S. (1968); landscape painter in oil, acrylic and gouache; retd. civil servant, Building Research Establishment; *b* Watford, 26 Sept., 1926. *m* Albert Edward Butcher (decd.). *Educ:* St. Joan of Arc Convent, Rickmansworth. *Studied:* Watford College of Technology, School of Art (1947-53) under Alexander Sutherland, M.A. *Exhib:* one-man show: Loggia Gallery (1974), Young Contemporaries (1954), F.P.S. Annual and Travelling exhbns. at Kings Lynn Festival, South of France, etc. *Work in collections:* St. Michael and All Angels Church, Watford (Stations of the Cross), also design for Christ in Majesty. *Clubs:* Watford and Bushey Art Soc. *Signs work:* "M. Reeve" and date. *Address:* 10 Kelmscott Cres., Watford, Herts. WD18 0NG.

REEVES, Philip Thomas Langford, A.R.C.A. (1954), R.E. (1963), R.S.W. (1959), A.R.S.A. (1971), R.S.A. (1976), R.G.I. (1981); painter-etcher; *b* Cheltenham, 7 July, 1931. *m* Christine MacLaren (decd.). one *d. Educ:* Naunton Park Senior Secondary School, Cheltenham. *Studied:* Cheltenham School of Art (1945-49), Royal College of Art (1951-54). *Work in collections:* Arts Council of Gt. Britain, V. & A., Contemporary Art Soc., Gallery of Modern Art, Edinburgh, Glasgow A.G., Glasgow University Print Collection, Aberdeen A.G., Paisley A.G., Milngavie A.G., Dundee A.G., Edinburgh University, Stirling University, Dept. of the Environment, British Government Art Collection. *Signs work:* "Philip Reeves." *Address:* 13 Hamilton Drive, Glasgow G12 8DN.

REGO, Paula, F.R.C.A.; painter in various mediums; D. Litt. (Honoris Causa) University of St. Andrews, Scotland, and University of East Anglia; *b* Lisbon, Portugal, 26 Jan., 1935. *m* Victor Willing (decd.). one *s.* two *d. Educ:* St. Julian's, Portugal. *Studied:* Slade School of Fine Art. *Work in collections:* Gulbenkian Foundation, Lisbon; National Gallery, London; Tate Gallery, London; Saatchi Collection, London. *Commissions:* National Gallery, Sainsbury Wing Brasserie, mural. *Publications:* Paula Rego by John McEwen (Phaidon Press), Peter Pan (Folio Soc.), Nursery Rhymes (Thames & Hudson), Pendle Witches (Enitharmon Press). *Address:* c/o Marlborough Fine Art, 6 Albemarle St., London W1X 4BY.

REID, Paul John, M.A. (Hons.) Fine Art: painter in oil; *b* Perth, 21 Apr., 1975. *Studied:* Duncan of Jordanstone College of Art, Dundee (1994-98). *Exhib:* Rendezvous Gallery, Aberdeen, Scottish Gallery, Edinburgh. *Work in collections:* Flemings of London. *Signs work:* "REID." *Address:* 21 Perth Rd., Scone, Perth PH2 6JJ.

REID, Sir Norman Robert, Kt. (1970), D.A. (Edin., 1937), D.Litt., F.M.A., F.I.I.C., joined Tate Gallery, 1946; appointed Director, 1964; Chairman, British Council Fine Arts Committee; Fellow and Vice-Chairman, International Institute for Conservation of Historic and Artistic Works; Member, British National Cttee. of I.C.O.M.; Mem. Culture Adv. Cttee.; President, Council of the Rome Centre; *b* London, 27 Dec., 1915. *m* Jean Bertram. one *s.* one *d. Educ:* Wilson's Grammar School. *Studied:* Goldsmiths' College, Edinburgh College of Art (1933-38) and Edinburgh University. *Work in collections:* paintings in Tate Gallery, S.N.G.M.A. and the Government Art Collection. *Clubs:* Arts. *Signs work:* "Reid." *Address:* 50 Brabourne Rise, Beckenham BR3 6SH.

REILLY, Kevin Patrick, F.I.G.A. (1994); painter in oil, water-colour and pastel; tutor, lecturer, founder of Hermes Galleries; studied humanities, Open University (1979-1984); *b* Lancs., 1949. *m* Diane. one *s.* one *d. Educ:* Sts. John Fisher and Thomas More, Lancs. *Studied:* Wirral Art College (1978) under Philip Smith. *Exhib:* I.G.A., British Soc. Oil Painters, Watercolour, Pastels, Liverpool Academy; solo exhibs. Laing, Manchester, and in Cumbria, Liverpool, Wirral, Ireland. *Work in collections:* various private collections in U.K., Eire, U.S.A., Australia, Spain, Italy. *Commissions:* National and international, Artist and Illustrator Magazine, Wet Day in Dublin, (Feb. 1996). *Publications:* magazine articles, national and international, Hermes publications, prints, gift cards, postcards, limited editions. *Signs work:* "Kevin Reilly." *Address:* 6 Cromarty Rd., Wallasey, Wirral, Merseyside CH44 2BH.

REILLY-DEAS, Anne, business studies, qualified for "Mensa" genius score; self taught artist in oil, water-colour, pastel, mixed media; writer, accounting executive; *b* Mullingar, 28 Nov., 1950. *m* Arthur Deas, scientist (divorced). *Educ:* Loreto, Bloomfield, Rosse, Christie Colleges. *Exhib:* Tullynally Castle, R.H.A., Westmeath County Library, Alliance Francaise, Longford Library, Granard Library, Caley House, Orchard House, Allen Manor, Cheltenham Show, selected for New York Prestige Artists Debut 2000, National Irish Bank, dfn Gallery N.Y., Christie Wild Int., Texas, etc. *Publications:* work repro: catalogues, articles, exhbns. Work in private collections at home and abroad. *Signs work:* "Anne Deas", "Reilly-Deas." *Address:* "Greenville", Dublin Rd., Castlepollard, Co. Westmeath, Ireland.

REITER, Laura, B.A. (Hons.) (1986), M.A. (1989), R.E. (1989); painter in oil, acrylic and water-colour, printmaker mainly in silkscreen/linocut; teacher/lecturer; *b* London, 25 Aug., 1950. three *d. Educ:* Brondesbury and Kilburn High School. *Studied:* Kingston School of Art (1983-86), Wimbledon School of Art (1986-89), Middlesex University. *Exhib:* Bankside Gallery, Barbican, London, Manchester Royal Exchange Theatre Gallery, Brunel University Gallery. *Publications:* article, 'The Artist Magazine' (Oct. 1995). *Signs work:* "Laura Reiter." *Address:* 5 Norman Crescent, Pinner, Middx. HA5 3QQ. *Email:* laura.reiter@virgin.net

RELFE, Elizabeth Anne Harvey (Liz), S.F.P. (2000), S.W.A. (1993), F.E.T.C.

(1980); painter in water-colour and pastel, teacher; lecturer in drawing, water-colour and mixed media: Surrey Adult and Continuing Educ. Service; *b* Harrow, Middx., 21 Dec., 1943. *m* John Relfe (divorced). two *d. Educ:* Paddington and Maida Vale High School for Girls. *Studied:* with John Kingsley Sutton (1972-75), Edward Wesson (1977-82). *Exhib:* S.W.A., Britain's Painters, numerous mixed and solo shows in London and South East. *Work in collections:* Surrey Heath Museum. *Publications:* five teaching videos. *Signs work:* "Liz Relfe" or "L.R." *Address:* 12 Riverside Ave., Lightwater, Surrey GU18 5RU.

REMFRY, David, R.W.S.; painter in oil and water-colour; *b* Sussex, 30 July, 1942. *Studied:* Hull College of Art (1959-64). *Exhib:* solo shows: Mercury, London (1978/80/82/84/86/88/90/92/94/97), Edinburgh (1983), New Grafton Gallery (1973), Editions Graphiques (1974), Old Fire Engine House, Ely (1975/77/79/81/83/86/90/92/94), Ferens A.G., Hull (1975), New Art Centre, Folkestone (1976), Ankrum Gallery, Los Angeles (1980/81/83/85/87), Bohun Gallery, Henley (1978/81/83/85/87/89/91/93/96), Galerie de Beerenburght, Holland (1979/80/83/86), Middlesbrough A.G. (1981), Zack Shuster Gallery, Florida (1986/88/90), Margaret Lipworth Fine Art, Florida (1992/93/97), N.P.G. (1992), Portal Gallery, Bremen, Germany (1993/95), Tatistcheff Gallery, N.Y. (1996), Elaine Baker Gallery, Florida (1999, 2002), Boca Raton Museum of Art (1999, 2002), Neuhoff Gallery, N.Y. (1999, 2001), Bohun Gallery, Henley on Thames, Neuhoff Gallery, New York. *Work in collections:* N.P.G., V. & A., Middlesbrough A.G., Minneapolis Museum of Art, U.S.A., Swarthmore College, Pennsylvania, U.S.A., Museo Rayo, Colombia, South America, Boca Raton Museum of Art, Florida, U.S.A., Royal Collection, England, Whitworth Art Gallery, Manchester. *Clubs:* Chelsea Arts, Groucho, Colony. *Signs work:* "David Remfry." *Address:* 19 Palace Gate, London W8 5LS.

REMINGTON, Mary, A.R.C.A. (Lond., 1933), N.E.A.C. (1954), R.O.I. (1962); painter in oil; *b* Reigate, Surrey, 1910. *Educ:* privately. *Studied:* Redhill School of Art; awarded scholarship to Royal College of Art (1930) under Sir William Rothenstein; later at Académie de la Grande Chaumière, Paris. *Exhib:* R.A., N.E.A.C., R.O.I., R.B.A., Arts Council and principal provincial galleries. *Work in collections:* Grundy Gallery, Blackpool; Brighton Municipal Gallery; Kensington Public Library; Tower Hamlets Public Library; private collections: Italy, Germany, Belgium, Persia, Switzerland, Canada and Gt. Britain. *Signs work:* "Mary Remington." *Address:* White Post Studio, 13 Stanley Rd., Sutton, Surrey SM2 6TB.

RENTON, Joan Forrest, D.A., R.S.W.; painter and teacher in oil, water-colour and mixed media; *b* 1935. *m* Professor R. S. Renton. two *s.* one *d. Educ:* Dumfries Academy and Hawick High School. *Studied:* Edinburgh College of Art, Post.Dip. Travelling Scholarship. *Work in collections:* H.R.H. the Duke of Edinburgh, Yorkshire Educ. Dept., Scottish Hospitals, Lothian Region Collection, Royal College of Physicians, Paintings in Hospitals and Jean Watson Trust; private collections in Europe, U.K., U.S.A. and N.Z. *Signs work:* "Joan Renton." *Address:* Holmcroft, 4 Tweeddale Ave., Gifford, E. Lothian EH41 4QN.

RETTER, Janet Elizabeth, B.A. (Hons.) Fine Art (1977), A.R.M.S. (1998), H.S.; Suzanne Lucas award H.S. (1997), Hon. Mention R.M.S. (1998); miniature painter in water-colour; *b* Bristol, 5 Jan., 1955. *m* Wilfred Retter. one *s.* one *d. Educ:* Helsby Grammar School. *Studied:* University of Leeds (1973-77). *Exhib:* R.M.S., H.S. *Clubs:* R.M.S.,H.S., Northamptonshire Town and County Art Soc. *Signs work:* "J.R." or "J. RETTER." *Address:* The Old Bakehouse, Woodend, Towcester, Northants. NN12 8RX.

REYNOLDS, Daphne, Chairman, Women's International Art Club (1964-67); Fellow, Printmaker's Council (1973); Founder, Gainsborough's House Printworkshop (Chairman 1978-79); painter in oil, gouache, and engraver in mezzo-tint; *b* Huddersfield, 12 Jan., 1918. *m* Graham Reynolds (q.v.). *Educ:* Wentworth School, Huddersfield. *Studied:* Huddersfield School of Art (1934-36). *Exhib:* solo shows: Galerie Creuze, Paris (1959), Drian Galleries (1961, 1964), City of Oldham A.G. (1969, 1975), Angela Flowers (1975), Gainsborough's House, Sudbury, Suffolk (1976, 1989), Ipswich City A.G. (1977), Albany Gallery, London (1991, 1993), Haylett Gallery, Colchester (1995), Chappel Gallery, Essex (1996, 1998), Flowers East (1998), Christchurch Mansion, Ipswich (1999), etc. *Work in collections:* Arts Council, V. & A., B.M., Bibliotheque Nationale, Paris, I.C.I., National Galleries in Australia and N.Z., Minneapolis Inst. of Fine Art, New Orleans Museum, Library of Congress, Washington D.C., Government Art Collection, etc. *Signs work:* "Daphne Reynolds." *Address:* The Old Manse, Bradfield St. George, Bury St. Edmunds, Suffolk IP30 0AZ.

REYNOLDS, Graham, C.V.O. (2000), O.B.E. (1984), B.A. (1935), F.B.A. (1993); keeper, Dept. of Prints and Drawings, and Paintings, V. & A. (1959-74); hon. keeper of Portrait Miniatures, Fitzwilliam Museum (1994-); *b* 10 Jan., 1914. *m* Daphne Reynolds (q.v.) née Dent. *Educ:* Highgate School and Queens' College, Cambridge. *Publications:* Twentieth-century Drawings (1946), Nicholas Hilliard and Isaac Oliver (1947) 2nd edition (1971), English Portrait Miniatures (1952) 2nd edition (1988), Painters of the Victorian Scene (1953), The Constable Collection, Victoria and Albert Museum (1960) 2nd edition (1973), Constable, the Natural Painter (1965), Victorian Painting (1966) 2nd edition (1987), Turner (1969), A Concise History of Water-colours (1971), Portrait Miniatures, Wallace Collection (1980), Constable's England (1983), The Later Paintings and Drawings of John Constable (1984), awarded Mitchell Prize (1984), English Watercolours (1988), The Early Paintings and Drawings of John Constable (1996), European Miniatures in the Metropolitan Museum of Art (1996), (with K. Baetser), Sixteenth and Seventeenth Century Miniatures in Collection of H.M. The Queen (1999). *Address:* The Old Manse, Bradfield St. George, Bury St. Edmunds Suffolk IP30 0AZ.

REYNOLDS, Vicki, B.A.(Hons.) (1976), Dip.R.A.S. (1979); British Inst. award (1978), Richard Ford scholarship (1980), S.J. Solomon silver medal for painting (1979); prizewinner, The Spirit of London; painter in oil, water-colour, charcoal, sculptress in clay; part-time assistant, Royal Academy; *b* Portsmouth, 8 June, 1946. divorced. *Educ:* Paulsgrove and Southsea Schools, Portsmouth. *Studied:* Goldsmiths' College (1972-76, John Thompson), R.A. Schools (1976-79, Peter Greenham). *Exhib:* Stowells Trophy, New Contemporaries, Three College Show, R.A. Summer Exhbn., Vortex Gallery; group shows, R.A., The London Group, Gallery 10. *Signs work:* "V.R." *Address:* 4 Whidborne Cl., St. John's Vale, London SE8.

RHOADES, Peter G., C.F.A.Oxon. (1958), N.D.D. Painting (1959), M.A. Cardiff (1992), R.E. (1989); artist/lecturer in printmaking, drawing, photography; Tutor in Art, Christ Church College, Oxford, Visiting Tutor in Drawing, Ruskin School of Drawing, University of Oxford, Lecturer, Abingdon College; *b* Watford, 6 May, 1938. partner: Jane Harrison. one *s.* three *d. Educ:* Bryanston School. *Studied:* Ruskin School of Drawing (1955-59, Percy Horton), Central School of Art and Crafts (1960-61, William Turnbull, Alan Davie), Cardiff Inst. of Higher Educ. (1990-92, John Gingell). *Exhib:* periodic one-man shows, numerous selected exhbns. in Britain, Europe and U.S.A. *Work in collections:* Ashmolean Museum Oxford, John Radcliffe Hospital Oxford, Art in Hospitals, The Museum, Trondheim, Norway. *Signs work:* "PETER RHOADES" or "P.G.R." *Address:* Seven Stars, Spurt St., Cuddington, Aylesbury, Bucks. HP18 0BB.

RHYS-JAMES, Shani, B.A.Hons.; Hunting/Observer first prize (1993), Gold medal, Eisteddfod (1992), B.P. Portrait prize (1994), B.B.C. Wales Visual Artist of the Year (1994); artist in oil on canvas, gesso and linen; *b* Melbourne, Australia, 2 May, 1953. *m* Stephen West, artist. two *s. Educ:* Parliament Hill Girls' School. *Studied:* Loughborough (1972-73), St. Martin's (1973-76, Freddie Gore, Jennifer Durrant, Gillian Ayres, Albert Herbert). *Exhib:* mixed shows: Disclosures, Touring to Barcelona, Reclaiming the Madonna, Intimate Portraits Glyn Vivian, In the Looking Glass, Usher; solo shows: Blood Ties Touring, Beaux Arts Bath, Martin Tinney, Cardiff, Facing the Self, Mostyn Llandudno, touring, Stephen Lacey London (2000), Aberystwyth Art Centre (2003). *Work in collections:* National Museum of Wales, Newport Museum, Contemporary Art Soc., Glyn Vivian, Swansea, B.B.C., Lincoln Museum, Birmingham Museum and Art Gallery, Wolverhampton Museum & Art Gallery, National Library of Wales. *Publications:* Art Today (Phaidon), Edward Lucie-Smith: Facing the Self, Welsh Artists Talking, Prof. Tony Curtis. *Clubs:* R.Cam.A. *Signs work:* "Shani Rhys-James." *Address:* Dolpebyll, Llangadfan, Powys SY21 0PU, Wales.

RICE, Cecil, B.A. (Hons.) Fine Art (1983), P.G.C.E. (1989); artist in water-colour and oil; *b* Nottingham, 3 Mar., 1961. *m* Linda. one *s. Studied:* Brighton College of Art (1979-83). *Exhib:* Brighton, London, Suffolk, Norfolk; one-man shows: Red Pot Gallery London, Clairmonte Galleries Brighton, Ropner Gallery, London. Work in collections internationally. *Publications:* work repro.: fine art screen prints (Chapel Green Prints). *Address:* 14 Granville Rd., Hove, E. Sussex BN3 1TG.

RICE, Elizabeth Helen, S.B.A., R.H.S. Gold Medal; botanical painter in water-colour; illustrator; *b* Canterbury, 4 Apr., 1947. *Educ:* Ashford School, Kent. *Studied:* Exeter College of Art (1963-65), bursary to study wallpaper design with Arthur Sanderson & Sons (1965-70). *Exhib:* Mall Galleries, Medici Gallery, Pawsey & Payne, St. James's, Jersey Wildlife Preservation Trust, C.I., McEwan Gallery, Scotland, etc. *Work in collections:* H.R.H. The Princess of Wales, Sultan of Oman, Sissinghurst Castle, Kent. *Publications:* contributor to Collins Fieldguide to Crops of Britain and Europe, Reader's Digest Fieldguide to Butterflies, Collins Gem Guide to Herbs, etc. *Signs work:* "Elizabeth H. Rice." *Address:* 33 Peel St., London W8 7PA.

RICE, Seán, Prix de Rome (1953-55); sculptor/painter in bronze, mixed media, oil and water-colour; *b* London, 5 Nov., 1931. *m* Janet Teniers. two *s.* one *d. Educ:*

Brighton and Hove County Grammar School. *Studied:* Brighton College of Art (1947-51, James Woodford, R.A.), R.A. Schools (1951-53, Maurice Lambert, R.A.), British School at Rome (1953-55). Winner of Constance Fund Sculpture competition (1970). *Exhib:* R.A.; one-man shows: 15 in G.B. and Italy, eight at Alwin Gallery London; Art Scene London. *Commissions:* Noah Fountain, Chester Zoo; Poseidon Fountain, Gravesend; Atlantic Tower Sculptures, Liverpool; Stations of the Cross, Metropolitan Cathedral, Liverpool. *Signs work:* "Rice" or not at all. *Address:* 72 Mandeville St., Liverpool L4 5TL.

RICHARDS, E. Margaret (née Turner), exhbn. scholarship R.C.A. (1940), Drawing prize (1943), A.R.C.A. (Painting) (1943), M.F.P.S. (1976); artist in oil and water-colour; *b* Kingston, Surrey, 29 Dec., 1918. *m* E. M. Richards, LL.B. three *s.* one *d. Educ:* St. Paul's Convent, Teddington. *Studied:* Kingston School of Art (1935) under Reginald Brill, R.C.A. (1939-40) under Gilbert Spencer. *Exhib:* R.A., R.O.I., London Group, R.B.A., N.E.A.C., Trends. *Clubs:* F.P.S. *Signs work:* "E. Margaret Richards" on back, sometimes "Peggy E. M. Turner." *Address:* 3 Cheapside, Horsell, Woking GU21 4JG.

RICHARDS, Patricia, N.D.D.; freelance display artist, art tutor with Adult Educ. including art for the handicapped, pre-school toddlers and paper sculpture for primary school children; diversional therapist for the elderly (retired), Clare House Nursing Home, Walton, Surrey; artist in oil, water-colour, pencil and pen work; demonstrator of varied crafts; private art tutor for the over 60's; *b* New Malden, Surrey, 9 Nov., 1935. divorced. one *s.* one *d. Educ:* Wimbledon County Grammar School. *Studied:* Kingston Art School (1950-55, Reginald Brill). *Exhib:* Graphic Artists (1984), Heritage '84 (National Trust), R.A. (1984), Mall Galleries, Festival Hall, London, Guildford House, Blaydon Gallery, Parkshot Gallery, Richmond, Garden Gallery, Kew, Boathouse Gallery, Walton; one-man show, Trends (F.P.S.) and Esher. Work in private collections. *Signs work:* "P. Richards" or "P.RICHARDS." *Address:* 39 Woodlands, Meadowlands Pk., Weybridge Rd., Addlestone, Surrey KT15 2RQ.

RICHARDSON, Barbara E., B.A. (Hons.), R.B.A. (1996); painter in oil and water-colour; *b* 29 June, 1944. two *s. Studied:* Chelsea School of Art (1975-79). *Exhib:* N.P.G. Portrait Award, R.A., N.E.A.C., London Group Open, Discerning Eye, R.O.I., R.P., R.B.A., R.W.S., Singer & Friedlander/Sunday Times. *Signs work:* "B.R." (oils), "Barbara Richardson" (water-colours). *Address:* 27 Potterne Cl., London SW19 6RX.

RICHARDSON, Geoffrey Philip, landscape artist in oil, water-colour, etching, drypoint; *b* Woodbridge, 15 Apr., 1928. *Educ:* Woodbridge Elementary School. *Studied:* Ipswich School of Art (1940-44) under A. Ward, A.R.C.A., A. W. Bellis, A.R.C.A., Miss E. Wood, A.R.C.A. *Exhib:* R.I., N.S. Summer Salon; one-man shows, Haste Gallery, Ipswich, Deben Gallery, Woodbridge; and various group shows. *Work in collections:* England, America, Germany, Turkey, New Zealand. *Clubs:* Ipswich Art. *Signs work:* "G. Richardson", followed by date and monogram, paintings, and "G" engraved in etchings and drypoint. *Address:* 21 Old Barrack Rd., Woodbridge, Suffolk IP12 4ET.

RICHARDSON, Ilana, Dip. A.D. (1968); painter in water-colour and oils, screen printer; *b* Haifa, Israel, 1946. *m* Crispin Ellison. two *d. Studied:* Betzalel Academy of Art, Jerusalem (1963-67), Hornsey College of Art (1967-68). *Exhib:* C.C.A. Galleries London, Oxford, Bath, Window Gallery Brighton, R.A., Catto Gallery, Tidal Wave Gallery, Hereford, and many exhbns. abroad. *Publications:* participated as artist in The New Guide to Screen Printing by Brad Faine. Prints published by C.C.A. since 1982 printed at Coriander Studio London. Posters published by the art group and Ikea. Gicleé prints published by the Artist. *Signs work:* "Ilana Richardson." *Address:* 175 Ramsden Rd., London SW12 8RF.

RICHARDSON, Philip David, B.A. (Hons.) 1974; painter in oil and water-colour; *b* Harpenden, 11 Oct., 1951. *Studied:* St. Albans School of Art (1970-71), Liverpool College of Art (1971-74). *Exhib:* recent solo shows include: Highgate Fine Art, London (2001, 1999), Enid Lawson Gallery, London (2001, 1999), The Cottage Gallery, Huntingdon (2001, 1998); has particpated in group shows at all the above galleries plus: Francis Iles Gallery Rochester, Patisserie Valerie London, Star Gallery Lewes, New Grafton Gallery London, Rowley Gallery London, Whittlesford Gallery Cambridge, etc. *Address:* Amery, Theobalds, Hawkhurst, Kent TN18 4AJ.

RICHARDSON, Ray, B.A. (Hons.) 1987; artist in oil and printmaking; *b* London, 3 Nov., 1964. *m* Gila. two *s. Studied:* St. Martin's School of Art (1983-84), Goldsmiths' College (1984-87). *Exhib:* Boycott Gallery, Brussels (1989, 1992, 1995, 1998, 2000, 2001), Galerie 31, Lille (1990), Gallery Aoyama, Tokyo (1999), Galerie Alain Blondel, Paris (1994, 1996, 1998, 2000), Beaux Arts, London (1994, 1996, 1999), Mendenhall Gallery, L.A. (1998), Gallery Fabien Fryns, Marbella (2002). *Work in collections:* de Beers, J.P Morgan, N.P.G. London, Kasen-Summer, N.Y., Tama University, Tokyo, R.C.A. London, V. & A. Museum, London. *Commissions:* Sir Matt Busby (commemoration sculpture), Lennox Lewis (portrait), paintings for the R.S.C. *Publications:* Ray Richardson: 'One Man on a Trip', 'Oil on Canvas', 'British Figurative Painting', 'British Sporting Heroes'. *Clubs:* Royal Brussels British F.C., Old Roan F.C., King Vic F.C. *Signs work:* "RAY RICHARDSON." *Address:* Delfina Studios, 50 Bermondsey St., London SE1 3UD.

RICHMOND, Donald Edward, N.D.D., painting (1952), A.T.C., London (1953); painter and theatrical designer; hon. treas. (1952), hon. adviser (1953), Young Contemporaries; senior lecturer in stage design, West Midlands College (since 1966); *b* Ilford, Essex, 13 Aug., 1929. *Educ:* Ilford County High School. *Studied:* S.W. Essex Technical College and School of Art (1946-48 and 1950-52), Brighton College of Art (1952-53). *Exhib:* Young Contemporaries, R.B.A. galleries (1952-53). Designer: Tower Theatre, N.1 (1956-61); English première Goyescas (Granados), Morley College (1965-66). *Signs work:* "DON RICHMOND." *Address:* Portsea House, 3 Sea Lane Cl., E. Preston, W. Sussex BN16 1NQ.

RICHMOND, Robin, B.A., M.A.; artist in water-colour, pastel, mixed media, oil; writer and broadcaster; *b* Philadelphia, U.S.A., 7 Nov., 1951. *m* Dr. James Hampton. one *s.* one *d. Educ:* St. George's English School, Rome. *Studied:* Chelsea School of Art (1969-74). *Exhib:* (selected) Mercury Gallery (1989, 1990, 1992), Barbican Centre (1992); group shows: (selected) Cleveland Biennale (1990), Southwestern Arts, Dallas (1993), etc. *Work in collections:* San Francisco Fine Art Museum, Middlesbrough A.G., M.O.M.A. (N.Y.). *Publications:* (selected) illustrated: The

Magic Flute (Faber); author: Michelangelo and the Creation of the Sistine Chapel (Barrie and Jenkins, 1992), Introducing Michelangelo (Little Brown, 1992), Story in a Picture, Vols. I, II (Ideals, 1992, 1993), Frida Kahlo in Mexico (Pomegranate, 1993). *Signs work:* "Robin Richmond." *Address:* c/o Rebecca Hossack Gallery, 35 Windmill St., London W1.

RIDLEY, Martin Friedrich, H.N.D.; artist and wildlife illustrator; *b* Liverpool, 9 Aug., 1967. *Educ:* Calday Grange Grammar School, Wirral. *Studied:* Carmarthenshire College of Technology and Art (1985-88). *Exhib:* 'Birds in Art' Leigh Yawkey Woodson Art Museum, Wausau, Wisconsin, U.S.A., Nigel Stacy-Marks Gallery, Perth, Scotland, The Wildlife A.G, Lavenham, Suffolk, S.WL.A., 'Wild in de Natur' Enschede, Holland, Theatre in the Forest, The Grizedale Soc. Cumbria, St. Helier Gallery, Jersey, John Noott Galleries, Carousel Gallery, 'Nature in Art' Wallsworth Hall, Glos. *Publications:* The Best of Wildlife Art (North-light Books, 1997). *Signs work:* "Martin Ridley." *Address:* c/o John Noott Galleries, 14 Cotswold Ct., Broadway, Worcs. WR12 7AA.

RIDLEY, Philip, B.A.(Hons.); artist in oil and charcoal; *b* London, 29 Dec., 1962. *Educ:* St. Martin's School of Art. *Exhib:* The Vinegar Blossoms. *Signs work:* "Philip Ridley." *Address:* c/o Lamont Gallery, 65 Roman Rd., Bethnal Green, London E2 0GN.

RIGDEN, Geoffrey, N.D.D. (1963), A.R.C.A. (1966); painter/sculptor in acrylic, oil, canvas, wood; visiting artist, Cyprus College of Art; *b* Cheltenham, 22 July, 1943. *Educ:* King's School, Gloucester, Grammar School, Weston-super-Mare. *Studied:* Somerset College of Art, Taunton (1960-63, Terence Murphy), R.C.A. (1963-66). *Exhib:* John Moores Liverpool (prize, 1965), Tolly Cobbold (prize, 1977), Hayward Annual (1980-82); one-man shows: Francis Graham-Dixon Gallery (1988, 1990, 1993, 1995). *Work in collections:* Arts Council, Contemporary Art Soc., Eastern Arts Assoc. *Signs work:* "Rigden." *Address:* c/o Francis Graham-Dixon Gallery, 17 Gt. Sutton St., London EC1V 0DN.

RILEY, Bridget, C.B.E. (1972), A.R.C.A.; 1st English painter to win the major Painting Prize at Venice Biennale (1968); painter; *b* London, 1931. *Studied:* Goldsmiths' College of Art; Royal College of Art. *Work in collections:* Arts Council, Tate Gallery, V. & A., British Council, Museum of Modern Art, New York, Albright Knox Gallery, Buffalo, Gulbenkian Foundation, Art Gallery of Victoria, Melbourne, Stuyvesant Foundation, Chicago Institute, Whitworth A.G., Manchester, Power Gallery of Contemporary Art, Sydney, Walker A.G., Liverpool, Dept. of the Environment, Fitzwilliam Museum, Cambridge, Scottish National Gallery of Modern Art, Edinburgh, Ulster Museum, Belfast, Museum Boymans van Beuningen, Rotterdam, Stedilijk Museum, Amsterdam, Ohara Museum, Okayama-Ken, National Gallery of Australia, Canberra. *Address:* Karsten Schubert Ltd., 41-42 Foley St., London W1P 7LD.

RIMMINGTON, Eric, artist in oil and charcoal; *b* Portsmouth, 14 June, 1926. *m* Sonia Michaels. one *d. Studied:* Slade School of Fine Art. *Exhib:* many mixed exhbns. in public and private galleries since 1963, R.A., Mercury Gallery (1983-99). *Work in collections:* Bradford City A.G., Gulbenkian Foundation, Scarborough A.G., Museum of London. *Signs work:* "E.R." "Eric Rimmington" or not at all. *Address:*

c/o Mercury Gallery, 26 Cork St., London W1X 1HB.

RISOE, Paul Schjelderup, Dip. A.D. (Painting) (1968), A.T.C. (1972); painter in acrylic on board, work based on landscape; Head of Art History Dept., Downe House, Newbury, Berks.; *b* Calcutta, 19 Mar., 1945. *m* Clare Perry. two *s.* one *d. Educ:* Christ College, Brecon. *Studied:* Epsom (1963-65, Leslie Worth), Chelsea (1965-68, Brian Young, Jeremy Moon). *Exhib:* Young Contemporaries, R.A.; one-man shows, London, Middlesbrough, Newbury; various mixed exhbns. *Work in collections:* B.P. International, Leicester Educ. Authority etc. *Signs work:* "Paul Risoe." *Address:* Nuttage House, Bucklebury, Reading, Berks. RG7 6RP.

RITCHIE, Paul Stephen, Dip.A.D. (1972); etcher and intaglio printmaker; established and runs, Manchester Etching Workshop; formerly ran, Two Rivers Paper Co. (1984-88); *b* Chatham, 29 Oct., 1948. *Educ:* Taunton School. *Studied:* Somerset College of Art, Manchester College of Art and Design (Norman Adams, Brendan Neiland), Croydon College of Art. *Exhib:* R.A., R.S.A., S.A.C., M.A.F.A., Whitworth A.G. *Work in collections:* Arts Council, S.A.C., Johnsonian, S.N.G.M.A., Hunterian, Aberdeen A.G., Salford A.G., Bradford A.G., Oldham A.G., Rochdale A.G. *Publications:* in conjunction with V. & A. and B.M.: facsimile edition of William Blake's Songs of Innocence and of Experience (1983). *Signs work:* "Paul Ritchie." *Address:* 14A Edinburgh Rd., South Queensferry, West Lothian EH30 9HR.

RIZVI, Jacqueline Lesley, R.B.A. (1992), R.W.S. (1986), A.R.W.S. (1983), N.E.A.C. (1982), Dip.A.D. (1966); painter; *b* Dewsbury, Yorks., 25 June, 1944. *m* Syed Muzaffar Rizvi. one *d. Educ:* Whitley Bay Grammar School. *Studied:* The Polytechnic, Regent St. (1962-63), Chelsea School of Art (1963-66, Patrick Symons, R.A., Norman Blamey, R.A.). *Exhib:* R.A., R.I., R.S.M.A., N.E.A.C., R.W.S., R.B.A., I.C.A.F.; Bath Festival; London Chamber of Commerce; Sothebys; World of Watercolours, Park Lane; Lineart, Ghent; 20th Century British Art Fair; Minton Fine Art Toronto; Ruthven Gallery, Ohio; Glyndebourne; The Upstairs Gallery, R.A.; New Grafton Gallery; The New Academy Gallery; Agnews, National Trust Foundation for Art; Fosse Gallery; Patterson Gallery; Milne and Moller; Tokyo; St. James' Art Group; The Arts Club; The Hague; Castle Museum, Norwich; Catto Gallery; Waterman Fine Art; Exchange Quay, Manchester; Visions of Venice; S.A.V.E., The Heart of the City; Duncan Miller; Albany Gallery, Cardiff; Malcolm Innes, Edinburgh; Bilbao; Seville; Barcelona; Gorstella Gallery, Chester; City Gallery; Duncan Cambell; Thompsons Gallery; Whittington Gallery, Amersham; Discerning Eye; County Gallery, Maidstone; Piers Feetham; Mexico City; Crown Estates Millenium, New Academy/Curwen; Vaila Fine Art, Shetland; Royal Cornwall Museum; six one-man shows: The Sallyport Tower, Newcastle-upon-Tyne, Cale Art, Chelsea, New Grafton Gallery, The Upstairs Gallery, R.A., The New Academy Gallery. *Work in collections:* murals for The Medical School, St. Mary's Hospital, Paddington; London Underground Ltd., London Clubs Ltd., Shell, Amoco, Davy Corporation. *Commissions:* three murals for The Medical School, St. Mary's Hospital, Paddington; London Underground Ltd.; London Clubs Ltd. *Clubs:* The Arts, Dover Street. *Signs work:* "J.L.R." and year. *Address:* 24 Sunny Gardens Rd., Hendon, London NW4 1RX.

RIZZELLO, Michael Gaspard, O.B.E. (1977), Prix de Rome (1951), P.P.S.P.S. (1968-73), P.P.R.B.S. (1976-86), F.C.S.D. (1977); sculptor and chartered designer; *b* London, 2 Apr., 1926. *m* Sheila Semple Maguire. one *d. Educ:* Oratory Boys School. *Studied:* R.C.A. (1947-50), British School in Rome (1951-53). *Work in collections:* London, Cardiff, Dublin and Saudi Arabia, etc.; Welsh National Memorial: David Lloyd George; busts: Sir Thomas Beecham: Royal Opera House, Royal Festival Hall and St. Helens, Lancs.; Nelson Mandela: Dublin, Tanzania and London. *Clubs:* Reform. *Signs work:* "Rizzello." *Address:* Melrose Studio, 7 Melrose Rd., London SW18 1ND.

ROBARDS, Audrey, R.D.S.Hons.; freelance artist in water-colour, oil, collage; *b* B'ham, 1924. *m* Jack Robards. two *s.* one *d. Educ:* Park House School, Malvern. *Studied:* B'ham College of Art (Alex Jackson), Sutton Coldfield College of Art (Dennis Greenwood), Bournville College of Art (Alex Jackson). *Exhib:* numerous one-man shows in the Midlands. *Work in collections:* hotels, boardrooms, theatres in G.B. and various European venues. *Clubs:* Stratford on Avon Art Soc., Sutton Coldfield Soc. of Arts, Worcs. Soc. of Arts. *Signs work:* "Audrey Robards." *Address:* Ivy Cottage, Main St., Wick Pershore, Worcs. WR10 3NU.

ROBERT, Mary, M.A. R.C.A. (1985), B.A. (1973); photographer and graphic artist in photographic and mixed media; Senior lecturer and Lens Media Programme Co-ordinator at Richmond International University, London; Tutor in Photography, Royal College of Art; *b* Atlanta, Georgia, 11 Dec., 1951. *Educ:* Miami University, Oxford, Ohio; University of Akron, Akron, Ohio; R.C.A., London. *Exhib:* U.S.A., U.K., France, Japan, Mexico. *Work in collections:* Bibliothéque Nationale, Paris, N.P.G. London, Indianapolis Museum, U.S.A., and private collections in U.S.A., Britain, Europe, Asia. *Signs work:* "Mary Robert." *Address:* 47 Creffield Rd., London W5 3RR.

ROBERTS, Gladys Gregory, R.C.A.; artist in oil and acrylic; *b* Rhyl. *m* Prof. E. J. Roberts, M.A., M.Sc. (decd.). one *d. Educ:* Pendre Private School, Prestatyn. *Studied:* Bangor Technical College (1959-63). *Exhib:* Royal Cambrian Academy of Art, Tegfryn Gall., Menai Bridge, Anglesey. *Signs work:* "G. Roberts." *Address:* "Bryn Llinos", Victoria Drive, Bangor LL57 2EY.

ROBERTS, John Vivian, R.W.S., R.E., A.R.C.A., R.C.A.; artist in acrylic, mixed intaglio media, water-colour; *b* Tredegar, Mon., 26 Jan., 1923. *m* Gwendoline Thomas. one *s.* one *d. Educ:* Cathays High School, Cardiff. *Studied:* Cardiff School of Art (1939-42), Royal College of Art (1947-51), Engraving School under Prof. Robert Austin. *Work in collections:* Arts Council, Nat. Mus. of Wales, National Library Wales. *Commissions:* many portraits. *Publications:* books illustrated for a variety of publishers. *Signs work:* "John Roberts." *Address:* Ty Meini 16 Cross Sq., St. Davids, Dyfed SA62 6SE.

ROBERTS, Marguerite Hazel: see HARRISON, Marguerite Hazel.

ROBERTS, Phyllis Kathleen, R.O.I. (1961); Paris Salon Silver Medal (1959) and Gold Medal (1964); portrait and landscape painter in oil, and sculptor; *b* London, 11 June, 1916. *m* A. Gwynne Roberts, F.C.I.I. (decd.). *Educ:* Clifton College, London. *Studied:* Hornsey College of Art. *Exhib:* R.A., Paris Salon, R.O.I.,

N.E.A.C., R.B.A., R.P., Contemporary Portrait Society, and principal provincial municipal art galleries, etc. *Work in collections:* British Isles, France, Portugal, Spain, etc. *Publications:* articles in Leisure Painter, etc. *Signs work:* see appendix. *Address:* 34 Rock Gardens, Bognor Regis, PO21 2LE.

ROBERTSON, Anderson Bain, D.A. (1955), A.T.C. (1956), B.A.Hons. (1982); painter in oil and water-colour; formerly Principal Art Master, Prestwick Academy; *b* Bristol, 22 Oct., 1929. *m* Mary M.M. Christie. two *s. Educ:* Ardrossan Academy, Ayrshire. *Studied:* Gray's School of Art, Aberdeen (1951-52, Robert Sivell), Glasgow School of Art (1952-55, 1981-82, David A. Donaldson, William Armour, Jack Knox). *Exhib:* R.S.A., R.S.W., R.G.I., S.S.A., R.P., V.A.S. *Work in collections:* Many private collections. Elected professional member of Visual Arts Scotland (1996). *Clubs:* Glasgow Art. *Signs work:* "Anderson B. Robertson." *Address:* "Window Rock", Sandy Beach, Innellan, Argyll PA23 7TR.

ROBERTSON, Barbara Janette, D.A. (1970), S.S.A. (1974), Lily MacDougall, S.S.W.A. (1975); printmaker in linoprint, part-time lecturer; *b* Broughty Ferry, Dundee, 16 Aug., 1945. *Educ:* Blairgowrie High School. *Studied:* Duncan of Jordanstone College of Art, Dundee (1965-71) under Ron Stenberg, Josef Sekalski. *Exhib:* Aberdeen Art Centre, Print Exchange, Galerie Tendenz; Contributor R.S.A. (1973-75), Prints in Folios of Compass Gallery, Glasgow, Glasgow Print Workshop, Molesey Gallery, Kingston on Thames. *Work in collections:* Leeds, Aberdeen, Glasgow, Stirling, Angus. *Publications:* illustrated The Cuckoo's Nest by Carl McDougall; The Oath Takers, Sea Green Ribbons, by Naomi Mitchison. *Signs work:* "Barbara Robertson." *Address:* 10 The Row, Douglastown, Forfar DD8 1TL, Scotland.

ROBERTSON, Richard Ross, F.R.B.S. (1963), R.S.A. (1977); sculptor in clay, wood, stone; retd. lecturer, Aberdeen Art College; *b* Aberdeen, 1914. *m* Kathleen Matts. two *d. Studied:* Glasgow and Aberdeen Schools of Art (1934-38, Benno Schotz, T.B. Huxley Jones). *Exhib:* R.S.A. Edinburgh, Glasgow Inst., Open Eye Gallery, Kingfisher Gallery Edinburgh. *Work in collections:* Aberdeen A.G., Peterhead A.G., Metropolitan Gallery, N.Y., Boston University. *Signs work:* "R.R. Robertson." *Address:* Creaguir, Rosemount, Woodlands Rd., Blairgowrie.

ROBERTSON, Seonaid Mairi, Dip. in Design and Crafts, Edinburgh (1935), A.T.D., Postgrad. Dip. in Psychology, London University (1947); educator, lecturer, craftswoman; fellow of Edinburgh College of Art (1944-47), Founder/Mem. and senior lecturer, Bretton Hall (1948-54), Senior Research Fellow in Educ., Leeds University (1954-57), Deputy Head A.T.C. Goldsmiths' College, London (retd.); *b* Perth, Scotland, 1912. *Educ:* Edinburgh University and College of Art. Visiting Prof. or Lecturer in seven U.S.A. Universities, and in Brazil, Canada and Germany. Founder/Mem. W.C.C., I.N.S.E.A., British Soc. of Aesthetics. *Exhib:* London, Manchester, Edinburgh, U.S.A. and Brazil. *Publications:* Creative Crafts in Education, Rosegarden and Labyrinth, Dyes from Plants, Using Natural Materials, articles in Craftsman Potter, Studio Potter, Parabola, etc. *Signs work:* "S.M.R." *Address:* Alterra, 1935 South Federal Highway, Boynton Beach, Florida 33435.

ROBERTSON, Sheila Macleod, R.S.M.A., Mem. St. Ives Society of Artists; artist in oil, water-colour; *b* London, 1927. *Educ:* St. Michael's School, Leigh-on-

Sea. *Studied:* Watford Art School, Central School of Arts and Crafts. *Exhib:* R.O.I., R.S.M.A., S.W.A. and St. Ives. *Work in collections:* R.S.M.A. Diploma Collection. *Signs work:* "S. M. ROBERTSON" and see appendix. *Address:* Flat 7, 1 Pentland Drive, Edinburgh EH10 6PU.

ROBINSON, Barbara, Prize for Portrait, Marlborough Fine Art, Prize and Medal, City of Monaco/Medal, City of Rodez; painter in oil, gouache, pencil; *b* London, 7 Mar., 1928. *m* Walter Robinson (decd.). two *s. Educ:* Lycée Français du Royaume Uni, Kensington High School. *Studied:* Slade and Ruskin Schools (1943-45, Prof. Randolph Schwabe), Ruskin School of Drawing (1945-47, Albert Rutherston). *Exhib:* New Art Centre, London (1959-74), French, Swiss and American Galleries (1975-94), Nîmes (1987), Sommières (1994), Bruton St. Gallery, London (1999, 2000). *Work in collections:* Contemporary Art Soc. London; City Halls Monaco, Sommières, Rodez and Pamiers; Museums of La Rochelle, Frontignan, Nimes. *Publications:* Lumières du Barbara Robinson by Geneviève Conte (1985), D'Autres Lumières du Barbara Robinson by Marc Moulin (1997). *Signs work:* see appendix. *Address:* 30260 Vic-le-Fesq (Gard), France.

ROBINSON, Basil William, F.B.A., F.S.A., M.A., B.Litt. (1938); museum curator (retd. 1976); deputy keeper, Victoria and Albert Museum (1954), keeper (1966), Keeper Emeritus (1972); President, Royal Asiatic Society (1970-73); *b* London, 20 June, 1912. *m* 1st., Ailsa Mary Stewart (decd. 1954). 2nd, 1958, Oriel Hermione Steel. one *s.* one *d. Educ:* Winchester, Corpus Christi (Oxford). *Publications:* A Primer of Japanese Sword Blades (1955), Descriptive Catalogue of the Persian Paintings in the Bodleian Library (1958) and other books, booklets, articles and reviews on Persian and Japanese Art. *Address:* 41 Redcliffe Gdns., London SW10 9JH.

ROBINSON, Gillian, M.A. (1984), Ph.D. (1989); Isis Gallery award best contemporary work, Artists in Essex award winner; painter in mixed media; senior lecturer in art; *b* 30 June, 1944. *m* John Robinson. three *s.* one *d. Studied:* University of London. *Exhib:* Bloomsbury Gallery London, Elizabeth Soderberg Gallery Israel, Sabae Contemporary Art Centre, Japan. *Work in collections:* Epping Forest Museum, Archive of the Karelian Republic Art Museum, Petravodska, Russia; and private collections. *Publications:* Sketchbooks: Explore and Store (Hodder & Stoughton, 1995). *Signs work:* "Gillian Robinson." *Address:* Coolmore Lodge, High St., Thorpe-le-Soken, Essex CO16 0EG.

ROBINSON, Hilary, B.A.(Hons.) (1979), M.A. (1987); lecturer, writer, artist; senior lecturer, research co-ordinator, University of Ulster; *b* U.K., 25 June, 1956. *m* Alastair MacLennan. *Educ:* John Mason School, Abingdon. *Studied:* University of Newcastle upon Tyne (1975-79, Prof. Kenneth Rowntree), R.C.A. (1985-87, Prof. Christopher Frayling). *Exhib:* U.K., Italy, Hungary. *Publications:* author: Feminism-Art-Theory 1968-2000 (Blackwells, 2001), Visibly Female: Feminism and Art Today (Camden Press 1987, Universe (N.Y.) 1988), The Rough Guide to Venice (1989, 1993); many catalogue essays including: Mothers, Ikon Gallery, Birmingham (1990), Sounding the Depths, I.M.M.A., Dublin (1992), Louise Bourgeois, M.O.M.A. Oxford (1996); Editor, Alba (1990-92). *Address:* School of Art and Design, University of Ulster, Belfast BT15 1ED.

ROBINSON, Ivor, M.B.E., artist-bookbinder; Hon. Fellow of Oxford Brookes University, Fellow of Designer Bookbinders (President 1968-73); *b* 28 Oct., 1924. *m* Olive Trask one *d.* one *s. Studied:* Bournemouth School of Art (1939-42). Royal Navy (1942-45). Lectureships: Salisbury School of Art (1946-52), London School of Printing and Graphic Arts (1953-58), Oxford Polytechnic (1959-89). *Exhib:* major one-person shows: Hantverket, Stockholm (1963); Galleria del bel Libro, Ascona (1969); two person show: Prescote Gallery, Cropredy with Hilary Robinson showing Works on Paper (1981); ninety group exhbns. (1951-2001). *Work in collections:* British Library, V. & A., Bodleian Library, Crafts Council, Keatley Trust, Danish Royal Library; Royal Library, The Hague; Swedish Royal Library; Röhsska Museum, Gothenburg. Awards: Triple Medallist, Prix Paul Bonet, Switzerland (1971). *Signs work:* "IR" and date. *Address:* Trindles, Holton, Oxford OX33 1PZ.

ROBINSON, Jim, F.B.S.P. (1988); line artist (printing industry) in acrylic, pencil, scaperboard; *b* Leeds, 12 Apr., 1928. *m* Anne. one *s.* one *d. Studied:* Leeds College of Art (1941-43). *Exhib:* Yorkshire Artists Ilkley, Yorkshire Itinerants, numerous venues throughout Yorkshire. *Commissions:* various. *Clubs:* Horsforth Arts Soc. *Address:* 33 Grove Farm Cl., Cookridge, Leeds LS16 6DA.

ROBINSON, Leslie Ernest, B.A. (Hons.) 1968, Post Grad. (1969); painter in water-colour, acrylic, pen and ink; Artists' Manager, Art Exhbn. Promoter; *b* Consett, Co. Durham, 1947. *m* Jill Robinson. *Studied:* Sunderland College of Art and Design, Manchester University. *Exhib:* numerous worldwide. *Work in collections:* U.K., Europe, Australia and Gulf States. *Publications:* wrote, photographed and published 'The Materials of the Artist' - a visual 15 series course. *Clubs:* Falmouth Arts Soc., Royal Cornwall Polytechnic Soc. *Address:* Lemon Court, Carclew, Perranarworthal, Truro, Cornwall TR3 7PB. *Email:* lescornwallart@aol.com

ROBINSON, Peter Lyell, B.A.(Hons.) (Geog. Geol.); sculptor in clay, plaster, bronze, stone; *b* Melbourne, Australia, 12 Apr., 1962. *m* Kate MacNab. one *s.* one *d. Educ:* King's School, Bruton. *Studied:* Durham University. Apprenticed to sculptor John Robinson (1987-90). *Exhib:* London: Alwin Gallery, Harrods F.A. Gallery, McHardy Sculpture Co., Art Scene; Arlesford Gallery Hants., Beaver Galleries, Australia, McHardy Sculpture Company at Butler's Wharf, The Garden Door at Ladbroke Sq., Alwin Gallery at Tunbridge Wells. *Signs work:* "LYELL." *Address:* Bralorne, Charlton Horethorne, Sherborne, Dorset DT9 4PQ.

ROBINSON, Sonia, N.S.A. (1977), R.S.M.A. (1979), S.W.A. (1990), Past Chairman of St. Ives Soc. of Artists; paints in oil, water-colour and gouache; *b* Stockport, 24 May, 1927. *Educ:* Glasgow High School; Manchester High School; Copthall School, Mill Hill, London. *Studied:* Manchester School of Art (1943-45), Hornsey Art School (1945-47). *Exhib:* London: R.S.M.A., R.I., Singer and Friedlander (Mall Galleries), S.W.A. (Westminster Galleries), Orangery, Holland Park, St. Katharine's Dock, Thackeray Gallery, R.A. Summer Exhbn. and Heals, shared R.S.M.A. exhbns. at Century Gallery, Datchet, Bruton St. Gallery London, Guildford House Gallery, Guildford. Solo show at Coach House Gallery, Guernsey and the Mariners' Gallery, St. Ives (1990-94 and 1996). Exhibits regularly at the St. Ives Soc. of Artists Norway Gallery, Lyonesse Gallery, Lands End, and the Passmore Edwards Gallery, Newlyn Cornwall. Exhbns. abroad: Mystic Maritime Gallery,

Connecticut, U.S.A., Prouds, Sydney, Australia, Vancouver, Canada and Pont Aven, France. *Publications:* A Celebration of Marine Art (Fifty Years of the Royal Society of Marine Artists), and Marine Painting by James Taylor. *Signs work:* "SR" on oils; "Sonia Robinson" on gouaches and water-colours. *Address:* 3 Paul La., Mousehole, Penzance, Cornwall TR19 6TR.

ROBINSON, Virginia Susanne Douglas, artist in pastel, oil, acrylic; *b* London, 27 July, 1933. *m* Lowther. *Educ:* privately. *Studied:* Brighton College of Art, R.A.S. *Exhib:* R.A., Bradford, York, Cheltenham, Gottingen, Annecy. *Clubs:* Cheltenham Group of Artists. *Signs work:* "Virginia S.D. Robinson." *Address:* 49 The Green, Southwick, Brighton BN42 4FY.

ROBINSON, Wayne, B.A.Hons, Fine Art (1981), M.A., Fine Print (1991); painter, printmaker-woodcut; lecturer, St. Helens College of Art; *b* Peterborough, 19 May, 1959. *m* Amy. one *d. Studied:* Cambridge College of Art, Loughborough College of Art and Design, Manchester Metropolitan University. *Exhib:* widely throughout Britain and Europe. *Work in collections:* Malta, U.S.A., Germany. *Signs work:* "W Robinson." *Address:* 254 Dentons Green Lane, St. Helens, Merseyside WA10 6RY. *Email:* wjrobinson@talk21

ROBOZ, Zsuzsi, painter in oils, acrylics, pencil, charcoal and pastel; *b* Budapest. married. *Studied:* Regent St. Polytechnic, R.A. under Peter Greenham, and in Florence under Annigoni. *Exhib:* solo shows include 'Revudeville' at Theatre Museum (1978) at V. & A., London, Lincoln Centre N.Y. (1989), David Messum, Cork St. (1995, 1997, 1999, 2000). *Work in collections:* Museum of Fine Arts, Budapest, National Portrait Gallery, Tate Gallery, V. & A., Royal Festival Hall, London, Bradford Museum, Graves A.G., Sheffield, Cambridge University. *Publications:* Women and Men's Daughters, Chichester 10 - Portrait of a Decade, British Ballet To-day, British Art Now with E. Lucie-Smith (1993). *Clubs:* Chelsea Arts, Arts Club, Dover St. *Signs work:* "Roboz." *Address:* The Studio, 76 Eccleston Sq. Mews, London SW1V 19N.

ROBSON, Hugh Mather, artist in oil, gouache, pen and ink; *b* Hinckley, Leics., 28 June, 1929. *m* Barbara Ann Mills. four *d. Educ:* Hinckley Grammar School. *Studied:* Fine art: St. Martin's School of Art (1945-49, William Craig, Russell Hall); Slade School of Art (1949-53, Lucien Freud, Sam Carter, tutor). *Exhib:* Arthur Jeffress, Trafford Gallery, Windsor Fine Arts, King St. Gallery, Mallets at Bourdon House, Colefax and Fowler, Nina Campbell's and Stephanie Hoppens Gallery. Murals include Crockfords, Park Lane Hotel, Belfry Club, Capital Hotel, 45 Park Lane, Croix des Gardes and many private houses. Visuals of gardens for Peter Coats; visuals of interiors for Interior decorators including John Siddley, Nina Campbell and Colefax and Fowler. Fabric designs for Nina Campbell. Bookplates, letterheads and tile designs. A series of Genre Singerie water-colours (96 to date), also a series of 20 military pansy figures (signed EWL). *Publications:* articles in House and Garden, Country Life, Connaissance des Arts, World of Interiors, Harpers, Southern Accents, etc. *Signs work:* "Hugh Robson." or "H. M. Robson." *Address:* 47 Loraine Rd., London N7 6HB.

ROCHE, Helen, D.A. (Edin.); painter in acrylic and mixed media; theme of work includes abstract and semi abstractions based on natural and man made objects; *b*

Limavady, Co. Derry, 23 Mar., 1945. *m* Laurence Roche, D.A. (Edin.). *Studied:* Edinburgh College of Art (1963-67). *Exhib:* R.S.A., R.W.A., S.S.A., R.S.W., S.S.W.A., and numerous other exhbns. *Work in collections:* private collections in Britain and abroad. *Signs work:* "Helen R." *Address:* 67 Valley View Rd., Stroud, Glos. GL5 1HW.

ROCHE, Laurence, N.D.D., D.A.(Edin.), G.R.A.; marine, landscape and industrial painter in oil and acrylic; *b* Goodwick, Pembs., 1 May, 1944. *m* Helen Roche, D.A.(Edin.). *Educ:* Fishguard County Secondary School. *Studied:* Swansea College of Art (1961-65), Edinburgh College of Art (1965-68); Postgrad. scholarship; Moray House College of Educ., Edinburgh (1969-70). *Exhib:* Many group and one-man exhbns. *Work in collections:* in U.K. and abroad, corporate and private. *Commissions:* 1999: Millennium Dome, (3 paintings, 2 works), all done for Sir Robert McAlpine, 2000/2001 West Quay Development, Southampton. President, Guild of Railway Artists, (1998-) *Signs work:* "Laurence Roche." *Address:* 67 Valley View Rd., Stroud, Glos. GL5 1HW.

RÖDER, Endre Zoltán Eugene, painter in oil on canvas and acrylic on paper; formerly art gallery educ. officer, senior lecturer (Art History); *b* Budapest, 17 Aug., 1933. *m* Carole. one *s*. *Educ:* St. John's College, Southsea. *Studied:* School of Art, Malta; College of Art, Portsmouth; Sheffield College of Art (1956-60, W.S. Taylor, Eric Jones). *Exhib:* R.O.I., various Open Shows (provinces), but generally in private galleries in England, Scotland, U.S.A. and France. *Work in collections:* Sheffield City A.Gs., Sheffield University, etc. *Signs work:* "RÖDER." *Address:* 50 Clifford Rd., Sheffield S11 9AQ.

RODGER, Willie, A.R.S.A. (1989), R.G.I. (1994); artist in lino and woodcuts; Hon. Degree of Doctor of the University of Stirling (1999); *b* Kirkintilloch, 3 Mar., 1930. *m* Anne Henry, illustrator. two *s*. two *d*. *Educ:* Lenzie Academy. *Studied:* Glasgow School of Art (1948-53, Lennox Paterson). *Exhib:* many one-man since 1964, also group in U.K. and abroad, including R.S.A., R.A., S.S.A., R.G.I.F.A., Glasgow Group, 'In Between the Lines' retrospective, Collins Gallery, Glasgow (1986); now exhibits mainly 'The Open Eye Gallery' Edinburgh, transparencies of paintings, Bridgeman Art Library, London. *Work in collections:* V. & A., S.A.C., numerous public collections in U.K. *Commissions:* Enamel mural, Exhibition Station, Glasgow, (Scot Rail, 1987); illustrations and mural, Dallas D.H.U. Distillery, Forres (Historic Scotland, 1987-88); designs, stained glass windows, St. Mary's Parish Church, Kirkintilloch (1987-93); street banners, 200th Anniversary, Union St., Aberdeen (1994), edition of linocut prints P & O Ferries (2000), linocut illustrations "Finding Alba', Scottish Television (2000). *Publications:* Scottish Historical Playing Cards (1975); illustrated, The Field of Thistles (1983); Willie Rodger, Open Eye Gallery, Edinburgh (1996); Willie Winkie, Strathpride Universality Ltd., Glasgow (1997). Artist in Residence, University of Sussex (1971); Saltire Awards for Art in Architecture (1984-87). *Signs work:* "Willie Rodger." *Address:* Stenton, Bellevue Rd., Kirkintilloch G66 1AP.

RODGERS, Harry Stewart, painter in acrylic, pastel; *b* Stamford, 18 July, 1920. *m* Pamela Codd (decd.). *Educ:* Stamford School. *Studied:* with Ian Macnab (1951-52). *Exhib:* Boston, Stamford, London, Dublin. *Work in collections:* Lincolnshire

Arts. *Clubs:* R.A.F.A. *Signs work:* "H.S. Rodgers" or "Roger." *Address:* 1 Tinwell Rd., Stamford, Lincs. PE9 2QQ.

ROGERS, Carol Ann, A.U.A. (1997); artist and tutor, water-colourist and print-maker; *b* Enfield, 12 Dec., 1944. *m* Dennis. one *s. Studied:* West Herts. College, Harrow Arts Centre. *Exhib:* U.A. regularly, London and Herts. *Clubs:* U.A., Herts. Visual Arts Forum, Watford Area Arts Forum, Watford and Bushey Art Soc. *Address:* Oxhey Hall Cottage, Hampermill Lane, Oxhey, Watford, Herts. WD19 4NU.

ROGERS, John Boydell, M.A.; Welsh National Eisteddfod First prize (1980), Hunting Art prizes (1995), Arts Council of Wales Travel grant (1995); painter acrylic and oil; retd. teacher Goldsmiths' College (1987); *b* Leigh, Lancs., 1934. *m* Johanna Willson. three *s.* one *d. Educ:* Hyde County Grammar School. *Studied:* Bretton Hall, University of Birmingham, University of London, Goldsmiths' College. *Exhib:* Arnolfini (1962-63), Camden Arts Centre (1980), Sheffield City Gallery Mappin (1977), Glyn Vivian Gallery, Swansea (1997), Barbican Arts Centre (1996), Islington International Arts Fair '95. *Work in collections:* Museum of Modern Art, Wales, private collections in U.S.A., Europe, S.E. Asia. Glider and power pilot. *Signs work:* "J.B. Rogers" back of painting, "J.B.R." and date on front of drawings. *Address:* Le Bourg, 24320 Chapdeuil, France.

ROGERS, John Rowland, painter, mainly landscapes, in water-colour and oil; Art Com., W.A.C., Mem. W.C.S.W.; *b* Cardiff, 28 May, 1939. married. three *s. Studied:* Cardiff (John Roberts, Phil Jennings, David Tinker). *Exhib:* R.S.M.A., I.C.A., W.A.C. (touring); Pascoe Gallery, Winnipeg; Mostyn Gallery, Wales; 'Journey in Morocco' (1983), Cardiff; Edwin Pollard Gallery, London; John Rogers' retrospective (touring) (1991); Royal Society of Arts, London (1999). *Work in collections:* Haverfordwest County Museum, West Wales Arts, W.A.C., Museum and A.G., Newport, Gwent, National Library of Wales, Aberystwyth, Contemporary Art Soc. for Wales, The Museum of Modern Art, Wales. *Signs work:* "John Rogers." *Address:* Peter's La., St. Davids SA62 6NT, Wales.

ROGERS, Joseph Shepperd (Nevia), B.A. (1967), M.F.A. (1969), Instructor, Corcoran School of Art, Columbia Inst. of Art (1970-72), M.P.S.G.S (Jamieson Award, 1982); artist in oil and collage; V.P., American Art League Admission Com., Arts Club of Washington; *b* Washington, D.C., 10 Mar., 1943. *Educ:* Longfellow School for Boys, Bethesda, Md. *Studied:* Corcoran School of Art, D.C., Greensboro College, N.C., (Irene Cullis, U.N.C.G., M.F.A., Gilbert Carpenter, Peter Agostini, Stephen Antonakos), American University (Dr. Turak). *Exhib:* "Five American Artists" Galerie Geilsdorfer, Köln, W. Germany (1982), "Art on Paper" Weatherspoon Gallery, U.N.C.G. (1970-80), "New Members" Spectrum Gallery, Georgetown, D.C.: seven one-man shows, etc. *Work in collections:* University of Maryland, "Maryland Collection", main altar collage, Chapel, Bishop Dennis J. O'Connell School, Arlington, Va. *Clubs:* Soc. of Architectural Historians, Arts Club of Washington, N. Va. Fine Arts Assoc., American Assoc. of Museums. *Signs work:* see appendix. *Address:* Bealls Pleasure, P.O. Box 1268, Landover, Md., U.S.A.

ROGERS, Lord Richard George (Rogers of Riverside) , Baron 1996 (Life Peer), Kt.1991; M.Arch., R.I.B.A.; Richard Rogers Partnership, Rogers P.A. Technical and Science Centre; Piano and Rogers, France; *b* 23 July, 1933. *m* Ruth

Elias (1973) . three *s. Educ:* Architectural Assoc. (graduate, Dip.); Yale Univ. (Fulbright, Edward D. Stone, and Yale Scholar, M.Arch), R.I.B.A. Chairman, Tate Gallery (1984); Royal Gold Medal for Architecture (1985); Royal Academician; Hon. Fellow Royal Academy of the Hague; Hon. Fellow American Institute of Architects; Saarinen Professor Yale University (1985); Mem. United Nations Architects Committee; IBM Fellow; Mem. R.I.B.A. Council; Visiting Lecturer/Professor: U.C.L.A., Princeton, Harvard, Berkeley, Cornell U.S.A., McGill Canada, Hong Kong University, Aachen Germany, Cambridge University England. Winner of internat. competition from 680 entries for Centre Pompidou (1 million sq. ft. in Paris for Min. of Culture) (1977); winner of Lloyd's internat. competition for 600,000 sq. ft. Headquarters in City of London (1978). Projects include: Music res. centre for Pierre Boulez and Min. of Cultural Affairs, Paris (1977); B. & B. Factory, Como, Italy (1972); P.A. Science Lab. Princeton, U.S.A. (1984); Urban Conservation, Florence Italy (1984); HQ Wellcome Pharmaceuticals Esher U.K. (1984); Cummins/Fleetguard factory, Quimper, France (1980); Electronics Factory for Reliance Controls Ltd., Swindon U.K. (1967); P.A. Technology Centre, Phases 1, 2 and 3, near Cambridge U.K. (1975); Inmos semi-conductor manufg. facilit, Newport, S. Wales (1982). Prizes: include: Fin. Times Indust. Arch. Award for Most Outstanding Indust. Bldg. 1967, (Reliance Controls, Swindon), and 1976 (Patscentre) and 1983 (Inmos); Auguste Perret Prize, Internat. Union of Architects (1978), Premier Europeo Umberto Biancamano (1979), Royal Institute of British Architects Research Award (1970), Royal Institute of British Architects Commendations (1976), British Steel Structural Design Award (1975, 1982), Eurostructpress Award (1983), Architectural Design Awards (1964, 1965, 1968). Subject of BBC documentary, Building for Change (1980). *Publications:* incl. contribs. to Architectural Design, Global Arch. and Arch. and Urbanism. Monograph. G.A. Beaubourg. *Address:* (offices and studios) Thames Wharf, Rainville Rd., London W6 9HA.

ROGERSON, Joyce, F.R.S.A. (1998); R.M.S. (1986); S.W.A. (1986), wildlife artist and miniaturist in water-colour, for miniatures vellum; Vice Pres. S.W.A. (1997-); *b* Yorkshire. *m* Ronald Rogerson, A.M.R.Ae.S., I.Eng.Cei., retd. aeronautical engineer. one *s.* one *d. Educ:* Mayfield Girls School, Walton-on-Thames. *Studied:* art: Chertsey Trust. *Exhib:* R.M.S., S.W.A., H.S., M.A.S.-F. (U.S.A.), G.M.A.S. (U.S.A.), U.S.M. (Ulster), Mall Galleries, Westminster Gallery, Medici Gallery, Llewellyn Alexander Gallery, Soc. of Wildlife Art of the Nations. *Commissions:* worldwide, and designs for greetings cards. *Publications:* Included in: Technique of Painting Miniatures, Royal Miniature Society 100 Years, Magic of Miniatures. *Signs work:* "Joyce Rogerson." *Address:* 84 Cobham Rd., Fetcham, Surrey KT22 9JS.

ROMER, Caroline Eve, Byam Shaw Dip. (Painting); painter in oil, water-colour, etching; *b* Braughing, Herts., 25 Sept., 1955. *m* David Marzo. three *d. Educ:* Ware Grammar School for Girls. *Studied:* Cambridge Polytechnic (1972-73), Byam Shaw School of Art (1974-76). *Exhib:* R.A., R.B.A., N.E.A.C.; one-man shows, Brotherton Gallery (2), Prades Festival, Thackeray Gallery (1989, 1991, 1993), Lineart, Belgium, 20th Century British Art Fair, France, Spain. *Signs work:* "C.E. Romer." *Address:* Casa Moline, Escalarre, Esterri de Aneu, Prov. de Lerida, Spain.

ROMER, Philippa Maynard, portrait painter in oil; *b* Hitchin, Herts. *Studied:*

Cambridge School of Art and R.A. Schools. *Exhib:* R.A., R.P., R.B.A., N.E.A.C., S.W.A. *Signs work:* "Philippa Romer." *Address:* North End Farm, Littlebury, Saffron Walden, Essex CB11 4TW.

RONALDSON, David Bruce, B.A. (Hons.), P.G.C.E.; artist in oil, water-colour and egg tempera, freelance art historian; *b* Felsted, 20 Jan., 1950. *Studied:* Newcastle University. *Work in collections:* U.K., Europe, U.S.A. *Address:* 2 The Terrace, Felsted, Dunmow, Essex CM6 3ER.

RONN: see HILL, Ronald James.

ROONEY, Michael John, R.A. (1991), R.E. (2001), N.D.D. (1964), A.R.C.A., M.A. (1967); painter in gouache, water-colour, tempera, oil; printmaking in etching, collographs, drypoint, monoprint; *b* Epsom, 1944. *m* (1) Patricia Anne (decd.); one *s.* one *d.* (2) Alexandra. one *s. Educ:* Sutton School of Art (1959-62), Wimbledon School of Art (1962-64), R.C.A. (1964-67), British School at Rome (1967-68; Rome Scholar). *Exhib:* Royal Academy, Mercury Gallery (London), Portal Gallery (London), Arts Council Touring 'Fragments against Ruins' (1981), 'Headhunters' (1984), 'After Ausschwitz' (London, Manchester, Sunderland, Dresden, 1995), De Vreeze Gallery (Amsterdam), Seasons Gallery (The Hague). Ten years retrospective 1980-1990 (Folkestone, Eastbourne, Hastings). Art Fairs: Chicago, New York, Basle, London, Bath, Galerie Franziskanergasse (Salzburg, 1999), Broderick Gallery, Portland (Oregon, U.S.) (1999/2001). *Work in collections:* Hove Museum, Towner (Eastbourne), Rye A.G., University of Aston, Museo Ralli (Uruguay), De Beers (London), Bolton Museum, Ambro Bank (Amsterdam), Tullie House (Carlisle). *Commissions:* 'Annunciation' (mosaic, Franciscan Basilica, Nazareth, 1968), Gulbenkian Foundation Printmakers' Award (1984), Financial Times centenary (1988), 'Brick Lane' (London Underground Poster, 1991), 'Aesop's Fables' (tapestry for T.S.B. HQ in Birmingham, 1991). *Publications:* Country Life - P. Kitchen 'A Vision for Europe' (1991). Artist in Residence, Towner Art Gallery, Eastbourne (1984), Korn Ferry Premium Award (R.A., 1990). *Clubs:* Chelsea Arts. *Signs work:* "M.R." joined, from 1996. *Address:* The Old Sorting House, 19 Alder Rd., Mortlake, London SW14 8ER. *Email:* mick.rooney@ukgateway.net

ROPER, Geoffrey John, painter in oils and water-colours, illustrator; *b* Nottingham, 30 July, 1942. *Educ:* Nottingham Sec. Art School. *Studied:* Nottingham College of Art (1958-60); Edinburgh College of Art (1960-65) under Sir Robin Philipson, P.R.S.A. *Exhib:* Figurehead Gallery, Edinburgh (1992), Murray Motor Co., Edinburgh (1994), Open Eye Gallery, Edinburgh (1995, 1997-99), Fine Art Society (1972, 1974, 1975, 1977, 1980, 1988), Teesside A.G. (1972), Great King St. Gallery, Edinburgh (1970, 1971, 1972), Middlesbrough Civic A.G. (1968), King St. Gallery, Dublin (1968), David Letham, Edinburgh (1967, 1968, 1969), Douglas Foulis Gallery, Edinburgh (1967), William St. Gallery, Edinburgh (1964, 1965, 1966), Silver Coin Gallery, Harrogate (1965, 1966), Loomshop Gallery (1997). *Work in collections:* Middlesbrough Civic Art Galleries, Edinburgh New Town Conservation Com., New University of N. Ireland. *Publications:* illustrated books, poems - Sydney Goodsir-Smith; Stanley. R. Green; Suburb of Belsen; mainstream pub. 'Destiny's Daughter; Newhall House, illustrations; McDonald Press, 100 life paintings. *Signs work:* see appendix. *Address:* Whinstane Cottage, Pumpherstone

Farm, Mid Calder, Scotland EH53 0HR.

ROPER, June Morgan, mural painter in oil and acrylic; *b* Kirkaldy, Fife, 7 June, 1940. *m* Geoffrey John Roper. *Studied:* Edinburgh College of Art (1958-62, Sir Robin Philipson, Sir William Gillies, John Maxwell). *Exhib:* Douglas & Foulis, Torrance Gallery, Loomshop Gallery, Kilbarchan Gallery. *Commissions:* A. Fletcher of Saltoun, Travel Scotland Ltd., H. Cathie, Sangster Distillers Jamaica, Dr. Melvin of Edinburgh, Mr. & Mrs. D. Workman of Edinburgh, Hunter Carson Co. Ltd., Torphichen. *Address:* Whinstane Cottage, Pumpherston Farm, Mid Calder, Scotland EH 53 0HR.

ROSCINI, Count M., F.R.S.A. (1967), M.F.P.S. (1985), B.A. (1960); sculptor in bronze; *b* Rome, 22 Dec., 1933. *m* divorced. one *d. Educ:* Rome and Cambridge University. *Studied:* Accademia dell'Art Rome. *Exhib:* Hamilton Gallery, Drian Gallery, Loggia Gallery, Salon de Provence, Grenoble, Tevere Expo Rome. *Work in collections:* Morristown N.J., Manilla, Lambeth Palace. *Publications:* Sounds of the Cross by David Owen. *Signs work:* "Roscini." *Address:* 19a Annandale Rd., Greenwich, London SE10 0DD.

ROSE, Christopher Andrew, Biology B.Sc. Hons. (1981); artist in acrylic and oils; *b* Uganda, 27 Aug., 1959. *m* Elaine Smith. *Educ:* Rydens County Secondary School, Hersham, Surrey; Nottingham University. *Exhib:* S.WL.A.; Wildlife A.G., Lavenham; many mixed exhbns. in U.K., France, Holland, Spain, U.S.A., Japan, Singapore. *Publications:* Swallows and Martins of the World (Christopher Helm, 1989), Complete Book of British Birds (R.S.P.B. and A.A., 1988), and many other publications. *Signs work:* "Chris Rose." *Address:* Maple Cottage, Holydean, Bowden, Melrose, Scotland TD6 9HT.

ROSE, Diana Cecilia, M.F.P.S. (1976); artist in oil; *b* Chiswick, 12 June, 1921. *m* Donald Rose. *Educ:* Lourdes Mount Convent, Ealing and Westcliff High School for Girls, Westcliff-on-Sea. *Studied:* Southend-on-Sea Art School (1948-60 part-time) under Leo Hardy; St. Martin's Art School (1946-47) under A. Ziegler. *Exhib:* Whitechapel A.G., Mall Galleries, Trends, Barbican A.G., Beecroft A.G., Southend-on-Sea. *Work in collections:* Britain, U.S.A. and Sweden. *Address:* 19b Cliff Parade, Leigh-on-Sea, Essex SS9 1AS.

ROSE, Jean Melville, artist/painter in water-colour and powdered colour; retired art teacher; *b* 29 Apr., 1929. married. two *s. Studied:* Bath Academy of Art, Corsham (Kenneth Garlick, William Scott, Peter Potworowski, Clifford Ellis, Kenneth Armitage). *Exhib:* Portal Gallery, London, Woodstock Gallery, London, Ancrum Gallery, Los Angeles, (three shows) and may others. *Work in collections:* H.S. Ede Kettles Yard permanent collection, Cambridge. *Commissions:* Fresco through Country Works Gallery, Montgomery, Wales. *Clubs:* Cambridge Soc. of Painters and Sculptors. *Signs work:* "JEAN ROSE." *Address:* 1 Wingfield House, Wingfield, Trowbridge, Wilts. BA14 9LF.

ROSE, Muriel (Miss), R.O.I. (1966), R.B.A. (1968), W.I.A.C. (1967), F.F.P.S., N.S.; painter in oils, designer, printmaker, ceramic sculptor, potter; Lecturer in ceramics and painting in Adult Education; *b* London, 1923. *Educ:* Richmond Grammar School. *Studied:* Richmond School of Art, pottery at Hammersmith

College of Art. *Exhib:* R.A., R.B.A., R.O.I., Royal Scottish Academy, R.W.A., Paris Salon, Gallery Creuze, Paris, U.S.A., South Africa, National Museum of Wales, Glasgow Institute of the Fine Arts. *Work in collections:* Oxford, Nottingham E.C., Herts E.C., Welsh E.C., Univ. of Texas A.G., Danish Court of Justice, Lady Docker, Mrs. Michael Foot, etc. *Signs work:* "Muriel Rose." *Address:* 9 Temple Sheen, London SW14 7RP.

ROSEMAN, Stanley, B.F.A. (1967), M.F.A. (1972); painter, engraver, draughtsman and sculptor in oil, drypoint, engraving, chalk, pen and ink, bronze; *b* Brookline, Mass., 4 Sept., 1945. *Studied:* The Cooper Union for the Advancement of Science and Art, N.Y.C. (1965-67), Pratt Inst., N.Y.C. (1970-72). *Exhib:* (among others) N.Y.C., Zurich, Vienna, Oxford, Dublin, London, Bordeaux, Philadelphia, New Hall, Brussels, Washington, Paris. *Work in collections:* (among others) British Museum; V. & A.; Ashmolean; National Gallery of Art, Washington D.C.; Los Angeles County Museum of Art; California Palace of the Legion of Honor, San Francisco; Bibliothèque Nationale, Paris; Musée des Beaux-Arts, Lille; Musée des Beaux-Arts, Rouen; Musée d'Art Moderne, Strasbourg; Musée des Beaux-Arts, Bordeaux; Musée Ingres, Montauban; Musée d'Art Moderne, Brussels; Teylers Museum, Haarlem; Prentenkabinet der Rijksuniversiteit, Leyden; Museum of Modern Art, Rio de Janeiro; National Museum of Wales, Cardiff; National Gallery of Ireland, Dublin; Vatican Museum, Vatican City; Staatliche Graphische Sammlung, Munich; Museum of Fine Art, Budapest; Israel Museum, Jerusalem; Albertina, Vienna; China Museum of Fine Arts, Beijing; H.M. The Queen. *Publications:* Stanley Roseman and the Dance-Drawings from the Paris Opera (Ronald Davis, Paris, 1996); Stanley Roseman - Dessins sur la Dance à la Opéra de Paris (Bibliothèque Nationale de France, Paris, 1996). *Signs work:* see appendix. *Address:* B.P. 219, 75765 Paris Cedex 16, France.

ROSEN, Hilary, B.A. (1976), M.A. (1980); painter in water-colour; part-time art lecturer; *b* London, 3 Sept., 1953. married. one *s.* one *d. Educ:* J.F.S. Comprehensive School, London. *Studied:* Trent Polytechnic (1973-76, Derek Carruthers), R.C.A. (1978-80, Peter de Francia). *Exhib:* solo shows: Royal National Theatre, Galerie Rose Hamburg, Strausberg Galerie Berlin, Galerie Fischinger Stuttgart; mixed shows: R.A., Singer and Friedlander, Arthur Andersen, Boundary Gallery, London. *Work in collections:* Neville Burston Coll., Zeiss, Hamburg, Imperial College; private and public collections in Munich, Hamburg, New York, Paris, Arthur Andersen, B.T., British Gas, Liberty, Brown Part Works Publisher, Brompton Hospital. *Publications:* Dorling Kindersely: Water-colour Still Lives. *Clubs:* Chelsea Arts. *Signs work:* "H. Rosen." *Address:* Chisenhale Studios, 64-84 Chisenhale Rd., London E3.

ROSMAR: see BOOTH, Rosa-Maria.

ROSOMAN, Leonard, O.B.E. (1981), A.R.A. (1960), R.A. (1970); artist and teacher; teacher of illustration, Camberwell School of Art; teacher of mural decoration, Edinburgh College of Art; tutor at the Royal College of Art, London; *b* Hampstead, London, 27 Oct., 1913. *Educ:* Deacons School, Peterborough. *Studied:* King Edward VII School of Art, Durham University; Central School of Arts and Crafts; R.A. Schools. *Exhib:* Fine Art Society, Roland, Browse & Delbanco, Leicester

Galleries, Leger Gallery, St. George's Gallery, Sheffield, Bradford, Edinburgh, Dublin, and provincial galleries, and Lincoln Center, N.Y., State University of New York at Albany. *Work in collections:* Tate Gallery, London, Nat. Portrait Gallery, London , Royal Academy, London, Aberdeen A.G., Royal College of Art, London, Bradford City A.G. *Commissions:* murals: vaulted ceiling, Lambeth Palace Chapel, Royal Academy Restaurant, London. *Publications:* Mad Meg, Pieter Breughel; illustrated: Old Testament, Exodus (O.U.P); Aldous Huxley's Brave New World, and Point Counterpoint; Thomas Mann's Buddenbrooks; Evelyn Waugh's Brideshead Revisited (all Folio Soc.). *Clubs:* Arts, Dover St., Chelsea Arts. *Signs work:* "Leonard Rosoman." *Address:* 7 Pembroke Studios, Pembroke Gdns., London W8 6HX.

ROSS, Alastair Robertson, C.St.J., F.R.B.S., A.R.S.A.; sculptor; Lecturer in Fine Art, Duncan of Jordanstone College of Art, Dundee; D.A. (1965), Post-grad. (1966), F.R.S.A. (1966), F.S.A.Scot. (1971), A.R.B.S. (1968), F.R.B.S. (1975), A.R.S.A. (1980), Mem. of Council, S.S.A. (1972-75), Scottish Mem. of Council, R.B.S. (1972-92), Vice Pres., R.B.S. (1988-90), Hon. F.R.I.A.S. (1992), Mem. of Council, Royal Scottish Academy (1998-2000); *b* Perth, Scotland, 1941. *m* Kathryn Wilson. one *d. Educ:* St. Mary's Episcopal School, Dunblane, McLaren High School, Callander. *Studied:* Duncan of Jordanstone College of Art, Dundee. Work in numerous collections in this country and abroad. Awards: Dickson Prize (1962), Holokrome Award (1962), S.E.D. Travelling Scholarship (1963), R.S.A. Chalmers Bursary (1964), R.S.A. Carnegie Travelling Scholarship (1965), Duncan of Drumfork Scholarship (1965), S.E.D. Post-grad. Scholarship (1965-66), bronze and silver medallist Paris Salon, Sir William Gillies award of R.S.A. (1989), Sir Otto Beit Medal of R.B.S. (1989), Freeman of the City of London (1989). *Signs work:* see appendix. *Address:* Ravenscourt, 28 Albany Terr., Dundee DD3 6HS.

ROSS, Michèlle, B.A.(1985) Illustration and Applied Drawing; freelance illustrator/artist in water-colour; *b* Morpeth, Northumberland, 9 Mar., 1964. *Educ:* Hustler Comprehensive, Middlesbrough. *Studied:* Cleveland College of Art (1980-82), Harrow School of Art (1982-85). *Exhib:* solo show: Talent Store Gallery, Belgravia, London (1988), S.B.A. Open Exhibitions, The Mall Galleries, London, Westminster Halls, London. *Publications:* work repro.: illustrated numerous books for adults and children, including Dorling Kindersley Eye-Witness Guides, greetings cards, calendars, posters and packaging. *Clubs:* S.B.A. (1987). *Signs work:* "Michèlle Ross." *Address:* c/o The Conifers, Moorsholm, Saltburn-by-the-Sea, Cleveland TS12 3JH.

ROSS-CRAIG, Stella, F.L.S.; artist in water-colour, pencil, and pen and ink; *b* Aldershot, Hants, 19 Mar., 1906. *m* J. Robert Sealy, B.Sc., F.L.S. *Educ:* privately. *Studied:* Thanet Schools of Art, and botany at Chelsea Polytechnic. *Work in collections:* Reference Collection, Herbarium of Royal Botanic Gdns., Kew (approx. 500 water-colours, several hundred pen-and-ink and pencil drawings); Hunt Botanical Library, Pittsburgh, Penn., U.S.A. *Publications:* work repro.: Drawings of British Plants; Hooker's Icones Plantarum, Botanical Magazine, and many other scientific publications. *Signs work:* "SR-C" or "Stella Ross-Craig." *Address:* 15 Grosvenor Rd., Richmond, Surrey TW10 6PE.

ROSSER, John, N.D.D. (1952); painter; *b* London, 8 June, 1931. *m* Margaret Rosser. *Studied:* Regent St. Polytechnic and Watford School of Art (1947-52) under

A. J. B. Sutherland. *Exhib:* R.A., R.B.A., N.E.A.C., R.I., Young Contemporaries, Medici Gallery, Compton Gallery, Windsor, Neville Gallery, Sandford Gallery, Paris Salon; one-man shows: Brian Sinfield Gallery, Burford (1987), Hallam Gallery, SW14 (1989); finalist in the Hunting Group art prizes (1981); Chelsea Library (1992), Radisson Hotel, Brussels (1997). *Work in collections:* Watford Museum, Goodwood House. *Publications:* work repro.: Elgin Court, Simon and Schuster, Australia, Foyles Books, Rosenstiels, Medici, Reader's Digest Publications. *Signs work:* capital R. *Address:* 4 Beachview, 91 Banks Rd., Sandbanks, Poole, Dorset BH13 7QQ.

ROSSIE, Kay, Dip.F.A., A.Dip., F.F.P.S.; abstract painter/sculptor in acrylic, water-colour, oil, wood, metal constructions; *b* Porthcawl, 1940. one *s. Studied:* Croydon College of Art (1983-86), one year advanced sculpture (1986-87). *Exhib:* one-man show, Loggia Gallery, London; many mixed exhbns. of painting and sculpture, including Trends, Phillips, G.E.C. Management College, Business Design Centre, Royal Society of Birmingham Artists, N.Y.A.D. 2000 Manhattan, New York. *Work in collections:* Croydon College, Price Waterhouse. *Commissions:* Kenetic Sculpture for First Light Ltd. *Publications:* included in international biographies. *Clubs:* F.P.S., London, Reigate Soc. of Artists. *Signs work:* "Kay Rossie." *Address:* 12 Brokes Cres., Reigate, Surrey RH2 9PS.

ROWAN, David Paul, R.B.A. (1979), R.A. Schools Post. Grad. Cert. (1972-75), Dip.A.D. (Painting, 1969-72); artist in acrylic; *b* Colne, Lancs., 28 Apr., 1950. *Studied:* Maidstone College of Art (1969-72, D. Winfield, R.B.A., W. Bowyer, R.A.), R.A. Schools (1972-75, P. Greenham, C.B.E., R.A., Margaret Green, John Holden). *Exhib:* R.B.A., Mid-Pennine Arts, Colne. *Work in collections:* F. Kobler, London; A. Whalley, Windsor. *Signs work:* "DAVID ROWAN" or "D.P. Rowan." *Address:* 1 Sandown Rd., London SE25 4XD.

ROWAN, Evadné Harris, M.C.S.D. (1952), A.I.A. (1949); freelance artist in pen and ink, water-colour, oil, lithography; *b* Warsash, Hants. *m* F. H. Paul. *Studied:* Gloucester School of Arts and Crafts and Central School of Arts and Crafts, Southampton Row. *Exhib:* Senefelder Club and Artists International Assoc. *Publications:* work repro.: Radio Times, Sunday Times, Heinemann, Macmillan, Penguin Books, Methuen, Harvill Press, Rupert Hart-Davis, Odhams, Collins, Putnams, G.P.O., Dents, O.U.P., Michael Joseph, Ward Lock, Longmans, B.B.C. *Signs work:* "Evadné Rowan." *Address:* Flat 7, 35 Elm Pk. Gdns., London SW10 9QF.

ROWBOTHAM, Mark A., Dip.A.D., P.S. (1992); painter in oil and pastels; Mem. Pastel Soc., winner Patterson Award; *b* Sarawak, Borneo, 1959. *m* Sherree E. Valentine-Daines. one *s.* two *d. Studied:* Epsom School of Art (1977-81). *Exhib:* R.B.A., R.O.I., R.W.S., R.P., N.E.A.C., P.S. *Signs work:* "M.A.R." *Address:* Misty Ridge, 126 The Street, Ashtead, Surrey KT21 1AB.

ROWE-EVANS, Prue, B.A. (Lond.), Dips. in Painting and Printmaking (mid-Warwickshire C.F.E.), F.F.P.S.; painter; *b* London, 30 July, 1921. *m* Adrian. one *s. Educ:* Frognal School, Hampstead; University College, London. *Studied:* Slade; Mid-Warwickshire C.F.E. *Exhib:* numerous mixed and one-man exhbns. in the Midlands, and in London at the Mall Gallery, the Loggia Gallery and Llewellyn

Alexander. *Work in collections:* private collections in U.K., Europe, U.S.A., and Hong Kong. *Clubs:* Fellow, Free Painters and Sculptors, Coventry and Warwickshire Soc. of Artists; Assoc. of Midland Artists. *Signs work:* "P. ROWE-EVANS" or "Prue Rowe-Evans." *Address:* 48 New St., Kenilworth CV8 2EZ.

ROWLAND, Dawn, F.R.B.S.; sculptor in stone and bronze; member R.B.S. and M.A.F.A.; *b* London, 24 Sept., 1944. *m* Prof. Malcolm Rowland. two *d. Educ:* Orange Hill Girls' Grammar School. *Exhib:* Chelsea Harbour Sculpture (1993), Chichester Festival (1994), Konishi Gallery Kyoto, R.A. Summer Show, Salford A.G., Hannah Peschar Sculpture Garden, Air Gallery, London (2000), Newby Hall Sculpture Park. *Signs work:* "DAWN" in semicircle with date under. *Address:* The Pines, 39 Bramhall Park Rd., Bramhall, Stockport, Ches. SK7 3NN.

ROWLETT, George Goldie, painter of land and seascapes, portrait and figure in oil; *b* Troon, Ayrshire, 29 June, 1941. *m* Marion Sneller. two *s. Educ:* De Aston Grammar, Market Rasen. *Studied:* Grimsby School of Art (1960-62), Camberwell School of Art (1962-65), R.A. Schools (1965-68). *Exhib:* one-man shows: Grimsby Museum (1962), Greenwich Theatre Gallery (1975), Woodlands Gallery (1982), Zur Torkel Zehn, Konstanz (1985, 1986, 1987, 1991), D.M. Gallery (1987), Everard Read Gallery, Johannesburg (1987, 1988, 1990), Smith-Jariwala Gallery (1989), Cleveland Bridge Gallery, Bath (1989), Albemarle Gallery (1990, 1992, 1995), Art Space Gallery (1993, 1995, 1997), Belloc Lowndes, Chicago (1995), Grant Fine Art, Newcastle, N. Ireland (1996); mixed shows: R.A., Whitechapel Open, Cleveland Drawing Biennale, N.P.G., Hayward Annual 'A Singular Vision', Hunting Group, Spirit of London, South Bank Picture Show, London Group, Druce-Constable, Zur Torkel Zehn, Read Stremmel San Antonio, Everard Read, Architectural Arts Co. Dallas, Elizabeth Gordon Durban, Cleveland Bridge, Albemarle, Henry Wyndam, National Trust Centenary - Christies, Grant Fine Art, Belloc Lowndes, Art Space Gallery, Chicago Art Fair, Glasgow Art Fair. *Work in collections:* Grimsby Museum, Northern Arts, Cleveland Museum Service, Nuffield Foundation, Baring Bros., Manny Davidson Discretionary Trust, Equitable Real Estate Investment, Atlanta, Ga., Kelmac Group, Price Forbes Ltd., Auto & General Ltd., Innovative Marketing Ltd., Ken Solomon Ltd., African Salt Works Ltd., Weedon Minerals, Anglo American Ltd., A.G. Diamond Cutters, Mesquite Investments, Philip Loot's Assoc., Sumrie of London, Stephen Fauke Interiors, Altron Ltd., Charles Glass Soc., Rose Gardens Ltd., Nedfin Bank Ltd., Head Interiors, Momentum Components, Grinrod Unicorn Group Ltd., Voicevale Ltd. Gallery: Art Space Gallery, 84 St. Peter's St, London N1 8JS. *Signs work:* "George Rowlett." *Address:* 23 Farrins Rents, London SE16 1NF.

ROWSELL, Joyce (née Gwyther), B.A., H.S.F., M.A.S.-F.; oil painter, minia-turist, illustrator; *b* S. Wales, 20 Nov., 1928. *m* Geoffrey N. Rowsell. two *s. Educ:* Coborn School, Bow, and Bishop Fox's School, Taunton. *Studied:* History of Art degree from Courtauld Inst. *Exhib:* regularly with the Hilliard Society from 1982, the Llewellyn Alexander Gallery from 1993, Florida from 1995, the World Federation of Miniature Artists from 1995; from 1997 with many American Societies and Galleries in N. Jersey, New York, N. Carolina, New Mexico etc.; at times with the Royal Miniature Society, Royal Birmingham Society, Bath Society, and Cider Painters of America and France; recently with the Medici Gallery, London and the Cornelius Gallery, Ross on Wye. *Work in collections:* Dutch Foundation of Miniature Art.

Commissions: portraits of people, houses, horses, events (e.g. celebrations, meets, fairs, shows). *Publications:* illustrations, book jackets. Since 1996, gained 18 commendations, prizes or awards. *Clubs:* Hilliard Society of Artists, New Mexico Art Society, Miniature Art Society of Florida, World Federation of Miniature Artists. *Signs work:* "Joyce Rowsell" or "JR" on very small paintings. *Address:* Spring Grove Farm, Milverton, Som. TA4 1NW. *Website:* www.spring-grove-gallery.com *Email:* joyce@rowsell.net

ROWSON, Hugh Thomas, B.A., D.A., R.S.W.; artist in water-colour, acrylic, printmaking; former Educ. Officer, Aberdeen A.G.; former V.P., Aberdeen Artists Soc., mem. Peacock Visual Arts, Aberdeen, mem. Royal Scottish Soc. of Painters in Water-colour, Edinburgh (since 1980); *b* Aberdeen, 4 Aug., 1946. *m* Lesley (divorced). two *s. Studied:* Grays School of Art, The Robert Gordon University (1965-70, Alexander Fraser, Ian Fleming), Aberdeen College of Education (1970-71), Open University (1972-76). *Exhib:* Aberdeen University, Aberdeen Arts Centre, Peacock Printmakers (1997), Riverside Gallery, Stonehaven (1999), Queens Road Gallery, Aberdeen (2000). *Work in collections:* Grampian Hospitals Art Trust, Gray's School of Art, Aberdeen, private collections. *Publications:* Children's Guide to Aberdeen Art Gallery. *Signs work:* "Hugh T. Rowson" or "H.T.R." *Address:* 276 Union Grove, (Ground Floor Flat East), Aberdeen AB10 6TQ, Scotland.

ROXBY, Brian, R.O.I. (1993); painter in oil, acrylic and water-colour; *b* 25 Oct., 1934. *m* Christina Mary (decd.). one *s.* two *d. Educ:* St. Cuthbert's Grammar School, Newcastle upon Tyne. *Studied:* Sunderland College of Art (1951-55, Harry Thubron), R.C.A. (1955-58, Leonard Rosoman, Robert Buhler). *Exhib:* R.B.A., N.E.A.C., R.I., R.O.I., Contemporary British Painters, Wildenstein (1958); one-man shows: Queen's Hall Gallery, Hexham (1988), Trevelyan College, Durham (1989). *Work in collections:* National Gallery of Wales and Government Art Collection. *Signs work:* "B. Roxby." *Address:* The Chestnuts, 21 High St., Walcott, Lincoln LN4 3SN.

ROY, Michael (Michael Roy Presley-Roy), A.T.C. (1970) Reading University, D.A.E. (1976) London University; artist (drawing, painting, multi media) landscapes, religious themes, figurative flower-pieces, abstract motifs; *b* London, 20 Apr., 1928. *Educ:* Upton Grammar, Berks. *Studied:* Newland Park College (1967-70, David Bowers), Post Grad Centre, Hornsey College of Art (1973-76, Eric Sonntag). *Exhib:* Reading A.G., Windsor Parish Church, Southampton Civic A.G., Southern Arts Database, Winchester, Leeds Metropolitan University. *Work in collections:* numerous private and public, U.K. and abroad. *Publications:* Author: "The rôle of the Art Teacher" (1976); "The Art Lark" (1992). Profile/feature p.182 "International Panorama of Contemporary Art" (r & p/d'arte Verona, Italy 1998), p.61 "British Contemporary Art" (Gagliardi, London 1993), p.335 "Dictionary of International Biography" (Cambridge, I.B.C.,1999), pps 214/215 '2000 Outstanding Artists & Designers of the 20th Century' (Cambridge, I.B.C., 2001). *Signs work:* "Michael Roy" with symbol of small spider and date, see appendix. *Address:* "La Palette",13 Lapthorn Close, Bridgemary, Hants. PO13 0SR. *Website:* www.axisartists.org.uk/all/ref5238.htm

RUDD, Bob, B.A. (1973), R.I. (1995); painter in water-colour and oil; *b* Ipswich, Suffolk, 18 Jan., 1944. *m* Jennifer Cuff. two *s. Studied:* Ipswich Art School (1960-

63), Bath Academy of Art (1969-73, Adrian Heath). *Exhib:* R.A., R.I., R.W.A. and many mixed exhbns. and one-man shows in London and Edinburgh. *Work in collections:* 15 works in the permanent collection of the Houses of Parliament. *Address:* 38 The Causeway, Chippenham, Wilts. SN15 3DB.

RUDDUCK, Ron, F.F.P.S. (1990), Mem. S.S.S. (1997), L.R.B.S. (1999), A.R.B.S.; sculptor in steel, copper and bronze; *b* 1 Apr., 1932. *m* Annette. two *d. Educ:* Chiswick School. *Studied:* Richmond and Kingston Colleges, Middlesex Polytechnic. *Exhib:* 'Age of Shakespeare' British Council, Athawes Gallery W. London, Loggia Gallery W1, R.S.B.A., Boxfield Gallery, Stevenage, Bettina Fine Art, London. *Work in collections:* F.P.S., London, Belfast U.S.A. *Address:* 53 Axbridge, Forest Park, Bracknell, Berks. RG12 0XB. *Website:* www.rbs.org.uk *Email:* ronald.ruddock@ntlworld.com

RUDLING, Laurence John, B.Ed. (Cantab.) 1972, M.A. (Sussex) 1981; artist-printmaker in etching, pastel, drawing; lecturer; adult educ. tutor; *b* 3 June, 1950. *m* Larry (Larraine). *Studied:* Keswick Hall College of Educ., Queen's College, Cambridge (art history). *Exhib:* R.A. Summer Show, P.S., R.W.A. Bristol, R.E. National Print Exhbn., South West Academy of Fine & Applied Arts. *Work in collections:* Devon C.C. *Clubs:* Devon Guild of Craftsmen. *Signs work:* "LAURIE RUDLING." *Address:* 6 South St., Totnes, Devon TQ9 5DZ. *Email:* laurie@therudlings.fsnet.co.uk

RUFFING, A. E., professional artist in water-colour; *b* Brooklyn, N.Y. *m* George Ruffing. one *d. Educ:* Cornell University, Drexel Institute of Technology. *Studied:* under John Pike (1964). *Work in collections:* Metropolitan Museum of Art, Smithsonian Institute, Library of Congress, Brooklyn Museum, Harvard University, Institute of Early American History and Culture, Albany Institute of History and Art, Atwater Kent Museum, Johnston Historical Museum, N.Y. Historical Society. *Signs work:* "A. E. Ruffing." *Address:* 1200-206 New World Circle, Raleigh, N.C. 27615, U.S.A.

RUNAGALL, Alan Trevor, R.S.M.A., marine artist in water-colour; worked for thirty five years with Port of London Authority in India and Tilbury Docks; *b* Rochford, Essex, 26 May, 1941. *m* Carol. two *d. Educ:* Southend High School. *Studied:* self taught. *Exhib:* various solo and group exhibs. throughout U.K. *Work in collections:* Southend Museums Service, various shipping companies. *Commissions:* P.L.A., Port of Tilbury London Ltd. *Clubs:* Wapping Group of Artists., East Anglian Group of Marine Artists. *Signs work:* "Alan Runagall." *Address:* 7 Albany Rd., Rayleigh, Essex SS6 8TE. *Email:* alan.runagall@tesco.net

RUNAYKER, Irene, N.D.D. (1958); painter in acrylic; *b* London, 11 May, 1937. two *s. Educ:* Sarah Bonnell Grammar School, London. *Studied:* Camberwell School of Art (1954-58), 2 yrs. drawing Merlyn Evans Central School (1960-61). *Exhib:* NYAD2K Show, New York, U.S.A. (2000), Green Man Gallery, Eastborne; 1998: Sussex Open, Brighton A.G., ARTWAVE, Crypt, Seaford; Star A.G., Lewes; 1996-97: Cable and Wireless, London; 1995: Jeu de Paume, Albert, France; 1993-96; XO Gallery, London and Windsor; 1992-93: Städisches Museum, Gelsenkirchen, Germany, 'Art and Sport', Kensington and Chelsea Borough; 1993: 'Women in Conflict', Liverpool Albert Dock; 1990: New Myths, Submarine Gallery, NI. *Work in* *collections:* London Borough of Camden, University of Technology, Sydney, Australia, Our Lady of Dolours, London, Hallfield School, London. *Publications:* ref. in: Camberwell Students and Teachers 1943-1960 (Antique Collectors, Woodbridge, 1995), Edgell Rickword by Charles Hobday (Carcarnet Press). *Clubs:* I.A.A; I.N.I.V.A.; Landscape and Art; F.W.A.; N.A.A.; Sussex Art. *Signs work:* "Runayker"; before 1982 "Runacre." *Address:* 1 Matlock Rd., Eastbourne BN20 7RA.

RUNSWICK, Eddie, Director of Community and Leisure Services, Borough of Blackburn; *Address:* Town Hall, Blackburn BB1 7DY.

RUSH, Maureen Elizabeth, freelance artist in water-colour and pastel; Adult Educ. teacher; mem. Yorkshire Water-colour Soc.; *b* Surrey, 1938. *m* Christopher John Rush. three *s. Educ:* Roseberry County Grammar School, Epsom. *Studied:* primarily self taught, influenced by Edward Wesson and the English Water-colour Impressionist School. *Exhib:* many joint and solo shows. *Work in collections:* Royal Tunbridge Wells A.G. *Signs work:* "Maureen Rush." *Address:* Weaver's Cottage, 3 New Row, Birstwith, Harrogate, N.Yorks. HG3 2NH.

RUSHMER, Gordon, landscape and war artist in oils and water-colour; *b* Petersfield, 12 July, 1946. *m* Shirley Ann Holland. one *s.* one *d. Educ:* Petersfield School. *Studied:* Farnham School of Art (1962-67). *Exhib:* Furneaux Gallery, Edwin Pollard Gallery, Ceri Richards Gallery, R.I., Ashbarn Gallery, New Ashgate Gallery, Peter Hedley Gallery, Kingsmead Gallery, Dragon St. Gallery, Petersfield, Gallery East, N.Y., David Curzon Gallery, Gallery 238, Francis Iles Gallery, Weald & Downland Museum, Royal Marines Museum. *Work in collections:* National Library of Wales, I.C.I., Nelson Mandela, Royal Marines, Royal Netherlands Marine Corps., H.M. Foreign and Commonwealth Office, Princess of Wales' Royal Regiment. *Commissions:* British Embassy Warsaw, Series on Conflicts in Bosnia, Cambodia, Kosovo and Eritrea. *Publications:* Art Business News U.S.A., Artists and Illustrators Magazine. *Signs work:* "Gordon Rushmer." *Address:* 2 Sherwood Cl., Liss, Hants. GU33 7BT. *Email:* GordonRushmer@btinternet.com

RUSHTON, James, A.R.C.A., R.W.S., N.E.A.C.; artist in oil and water-colours; principal lecturer (retd.); *b* Newcastle-u-Lyme, 15 Jan., 1928. widower. one *s.* one *d. Studied:* Burlem School of Art; Royal College of Art. *Exhib:* R.A. R.W.S. and N.E.A.C. annual exhbns. Work in private collections. *Commissions:* portrait, Dr. Derek Ferrington. *Publications:* illustrations for, Maxwells Ghost, On a Shoe String to Coorg, Archaeology Publications (Quality Book Club, London). *Signs work:* "J Rushton." *Address:* 17 Gower St., Newcastle-u-Lyme, Staffs. ST5 1JQ.

RUSPOLI, Francesco Mario Robert, Silver Medal, Rome & Villeneuve (1985), Silver Medal, French Institute (1986), Eugene Fromentin Award (1987), Gold Medal, French Institute (1988), Knight of the Art, Italy (1998), Bronze Medal, Paris (1991); theatre designer of set and costumes; *b* Paris, 11 Dec., 1958. *Studied:* Central St. Martin, London under Pamela Howard. *Exhib:* America and Europe. *Commissions:* Rating and Evaluation Assoc., M.G.A., Temple. *Signs work:* "F Ruspoli." *Address:* 54 Chestnut Gr., London SW12 8JJ. *Website:* www.multimania.com/ruspoli *Email:* f.ruspoli@virgin.net

RUSSELL, Caroline, B.A. (Hons.) 1989, L.R.B.S.; sculptor, work cast in foundry bronze and bronze resin; *b* London,12 June, 1968. *Studied:* privately under Patricia Finch, F.R.B.S. *Exhib:* Air Gallery, Gallery 27 London. *Work in collections:* various private collections. *Commissions:* large sculpture - Lehmann Communications plc. Entrance Hall. *Signs work:* "C. RUSSELL." *Address:* Russell Sculptures, 50 The Drive , Edgware, Middx. HA8 8PT. *Email:* russellsculpture@aol.com

RUSSELL, Christine Gillian, S.W.A.; self taught professional artist specialising in pastel still life and other subject matter; *b* London, 4 Apr., 1952. *m* Sidney Stephen Russell. one *s.* one *d. Educ:* Tollington Park School, London. *Exhib:* S.W.A., U.A., P.S., R.B.S.A.; Bourne Gallery, Reigate (solo show), Alexander Gallery, Bristol, John Noott Gallery, Broadway, Century Gallery, Datchet, Royal Gallery, Tunbridge Wells, Thornbury Castle, South Glos. (solo show); many mixed exhbns. Many works in private collections. *Publications:* entry in S.W.A. Exhibitors 1855-1996, work illustrated in 'Masterstrokes: Pastel' and 'Painting Great Pictures from Photographs' (Quarto), 'International Artist' Magazine, 'Pastel Artist International' magazine and 'The Artist's Sketchbook' (Quarto). *Signs work:* "C.G. Russell" (originals) "Christine Russell" (prints). *Address:* 58 St. Davids Rd., Thornbury, South Glos. BS35 2JJ. *Website:* www.christinerussell@ukonline.co.uk

RUSSELL, Edwin John Cumming, F.R.B.S., Cert. R.A.S., R.A. Gold Medal for sculpture; Sir Otto Beit Medal for sculpture (1991); sculptor in bronze, stone, wood; *b* Heathfield, 4 May, 1939. *m* Lorne McKean, sculptor. two *d. Studied:* Brighton College of Art and Crafts (1955-59), Royal Academy Schools (1959-63). *Work in collections:* Crucifix, and St. Michael, St. Paul's Cathedral; Bishop, Wells Cathedral; Dolphin Sundial, Greenwich; Sundials for Oman University and Dubai Parliament Sq.; Mad Hatters Tea Party, Warrington; Lion and Lamb, best shopping centre (1987); Alice and White Rabbit, Guildford; Panda, W.W.F., H.Q.; Forecourt Sculpture, Rank Xerox U.K., H.Q. *Signs work:* "E.R." *Address:* Lethendry, Hindhead, Surrey GU26 6BE.

RUSSELL, Jim, R.B.A.; painter and illustrator in oil and water-colour; *b* Walsall, Staffs., 30 June, 1933. *m* Becky. one *s.* one *d. Educ:* Royal School, Wolverhampton. *Studied:* Birmingham College of Art. *Exhib:* R.A., John Moores, R.B.A., F.B.A., Bankside, Laing, Singer & Friedlander, Hunting, etc.; one-man shows: Amalgam, Drian London, Alpha House Sherborne, Boxfield Stevenage. *Work in collections:* Liverpool University, various L.E.A.'s. *Commissions:* various theatre rehearsal drawings, Wine Soc. *Publications:* work repro.: Radio Times, Punch, newspapers, theatres, etc. *Address:* 10 Milton Rd., London SE24 0NP.

RUSSELL, Kathleen Barbara, D.A.Edin. (1962); Membre Associé Société des Artistes Français; artist in oil, pastel, gouache and water-colour; *b* Edinburgh, 1940. *m* John Caskey. *Educ:* The Mary Erskine School for Girls. *Studied:* Edinburgh College of Art (1958-63) under Sir Wm. Gillies, R.A., R.S.A. and Sir Robin Philipson, P.R.S.A. *Exhib:* one-man shows since 1965. *Work in collections:* Watson Coll., Edinburgh Corp. Schools Coll., Nuffield Collection, Durham University, Kings College, London, Royal Botanic Gardens, Kew. *Publications:* illustrated Magnus the Orkney Cat. *Signs work:* "Kathleen Russell" or "K. Russell" or "K." *Address:* 113 Laleham Rd., Catford, London SE6 2JD.

RUSSELL, Pat, F.S.S.I., F.C.L.A.S.; textile artist in fabric collage, lettering artist, calligrapher; *b* Wembley, 17 Aug., 1919. *m* Birrell Russell. one *s*. one *d*. *Educ:* Farnborough Hill. *Studied:* Chelsea College of Art under M. C. Oliver. *Exhib:* Oxford Gallery and various group exhbns. *Work in collections:* V. & A., Oxford City and County Museum, Reading Museum. *Publications:* Lettering for Embroidery (Batsford); Decorative Alphabets Throughout the Ages (Bestseller Publications). *Signs work:* "Pat Russell." *Address:* 48 East Saint Helen's St., Abingdon OX14 5EB.

RUST, Graham Redgrave, artist (muralist, illustrator and botanical painter) in water-colour and water-based paints; *b* Hatfield, 17 Feb., 1942. *Educ:* St. Dominics School. *Studied:* Polytechnic School of Art, Regent St. (1958-60), Central School of Arts and Crafts (1960-61), under Sir Lawrence Gowing, and Norman Blamey, R.A., National Academy of Art, N.Y. (1962). *Exhib:* First exhib. R.A. (1965), over 20 one-man exhbns. since 1964. *Commissions:* Private mural commissions in various country houses in England. Largest work, the South staircase, Ragley Hall, Warwickshire for the Marquess of Hertford (1969-83). Public mural commission, The Theatre, Chipping Norton, Oxon. (1996). *Publications:* The Painted House (1988), Decorative Designs (1996), Needlepoint Designs (1998), The Painted Ceiling (2001). *Clubs:* Brooks'. *Signs work:* "GRAHAM RUST" or "G.R. Rust." *Address:* The Old Rectory, Somerton, Suffolk, IP29 4ND.

RYAN, John Gerald Christopher, freelance artist, illustrator, writer and cartoon film-maker; *b* Edinburgh, 4 Mar., 1921. married. one *s*. two *d*. *Educ:* Ampleforth College. *Studied:* Regent St. Polytechnic. *Exhib:* R.A. Creator "Captain Pugwash" "Sir Prancelot" and various other children's cartoon characters. *Publications:* work repro.: internationally in various magazines and picture-books. Cartoonist 'Catholic Herald' since 1967. *Signs work:* "JOHN RYAN." *Address:* Gungarden Lodge, The Gungardens, Rye, E. Sussex TN31 7HH.

RYAN, Thomas, P.P.R.H.A., D.Litt., A.N.C.A.D., Hon.R.A., Hon.R.S.A.; painter in oil, water-colour, pastel, red chalk, coin and medal designer; President, United Arts Club, Dublin, and Limerick Art Soc.; Council mem. Stamp Design Com. An Posz; *b* Limerick, Ireland, 16 Sept., 1929. *m* Mary Joyce. four *s*. two *d*. *Educ:* Christian Brothers School, Limerick. *Studied:* Limerick School of Art (Richard Butcher, A.R.C.A.), National College of Art, Dublin (Seän Keating, Maurice McGonigle). *Exhib:* many one-man and mixed shows in Ireland, G.B., Ukraine, U.S.A., Latvia. *Work in collections:* National Gallery of Ireland, President of Ireland official residence, Cardinal's residence Armagh, European Court, E.E.C. Brussels, St. Patrick's College, Maynooth, Kings Inns, Dublin, Royal College of Surgeons, Trinity College Dublin, University College, Dublin, University College, Galway, Limerick University, Dublin Castle, Leinster House (Dáil Eireann), National University of Ireland, Royal Hibernian Academy, Archbishop of Cashel, McKee Barracks (Chief of Staff), Government Buildings (Taoiseachs Office), Pro-Cathedral, Christ Church Cathedral, N.C.E.A.; Office Public Works. *Clubs:* Arts Dublin, Friendly Brothers of St. Patrick, Dublin. *Signs work:* "Thomas Ryan." *Address:* Robertstown Lodge, Robertstown, Ashbourne, Co. Meath, Ireland.

RYDER, Betty Pamela Dorothy, landscape painter in oil on canvas and board; *b* London, 5 Jan., 1924. *m* P.B.H. Furlong, D.F.C., F.R.I.C.S. two *s*. one *d*. *Educ:* L.M.S., Parsons Green. *Studied:* Epsom School of Art - mature student (1969-75,

John Morley). *Exhib:* N.E.A.C., R.B.A., R.A., Lincoln Joyce, Bookham, David Curzon Gallery, Church Rd., Wimbledon. *Signs work:* "B. Ryder." *Address:* 22 Lansdowne Rd., Wimbledon, London SW20 8AW.

RYDER, Susan, R.P. (1992), N.E.A.C. (1980), N.D.D. (1964), David Murray Travel scholarship (1964); N.E.A.C. Critics prize (1990, 1993), Barney Wilkinson prize (1990), Alexon Portrait Competition (1991); painter in oil and water-colour; *b* Windsor, 1944. *m* Martin Bates. one *s*. one *d*. *Studied:* Byam Shaw School of Painting (1960-64, Maurice de Sausmarez, A.R.A., Bernard Dunstan, R.A.). *Exhib:* R.A., Portrait Painters, N.E.A.C.; one-man shows, Haste Gallery, Ipswich (2), W.H. Patterson, Albemarle St., W1. (1989, 1995, 1999). *Work in collections:* "Miss Pears 1984" Pears Collection, several at Allen and Overy, and James Capel Co. Ltd., Royal Automobile Club. *Commissions:* H.R.H. The Princess of Wales (1982); H.M. The Queen (1997). *Signs work:* "Ryder." *Address:* 17 Queen's Gate Place, London SW7 5NY. *Email:* paintings@susanryder.co.uk

RYLAND, Christopher, B.A. Fine Art (1972), A.T.C. (1975), S.B.A. (1995); artist specialising in flower painting in water-colour, also runs art courses from his studio; *b* Eastbourne, Sussex, 2 Feb., 1951. *m* Pamela Ryland. *Studied:* Goldsmiths' College School of Art, University of London. *Exhib:* The Barbican, London, Antony Dawson Fine Art, London, Medici Galleries, London, R.B.A., Mall Galleries, London, recently two solo exhbns. at John Russell Gallery, Ipswich. *Commissions:* Wedgewood, Royal Doulton. Winner of S.B.A. President's Award 2001. *Signs work:* "Ryland" or "RYLAND." *Address:* 35 Gainsborough St., Sudbury, Suffolk CO10 2EU.

S

SADDINGTON, Donald William, N.A.P.A.; painter in oil, pastel, water-colour, acrylic, specialising in landscape and marine; Tutor in Art Workshops; *b* Dartford, 31 Aug., 1935. *m* Vivienne Crouch (decd.). one *s*. one *d*. *Educ:* Wordsworth Secondary. *Studied:* London College of Printing and Graphic Arts (1950-55), Cricklade College, Andover. *Exhib:* R.I., P.S., R.W.S., R.W.A., R.B.S.A., City A.G., Southampton, Wykeham Galleries, Stockbridge, Westminster Gallery, International Water-colour Exhbn., France and one-man shows in England and France. *Work in collections:* G.P.M.U., Salisbury. *Clubs:* S.G.A. *Signs work:* "D. Saddington." *Address:* 85 Highlands Rd., Andover, Hants. SP10 2PZ.

SAHAI, Virendra, O.B.E., Dip.T.P., A.R.I.B.A., F.R.S.A.; painter in oil and water-colour; *b* Shahjehanpur, India, 25 June, 1933. *m* Ingrid Clara Marie. one *s*. *Educ:* trained as an architect and townplanner. *Studied:* painting: Central School of Art. *Exhib:* one-man shows: New Vision Centre and Biggins Gallery, London (1961), Commonwealth Institute, London (1966), Galerie Suzanne de Coninck, Paris (1967), Bear Lane Gallery, Oxford (1967), Horizon Gallery, London (1991); group and mixed exhbns.: Redfern Gallery, London, Commonwealth Biennale of Abstract Art (1961-67), Kettle's Yard, Cambridge (1996), Reading Museum, Bradford Museum,

Brighton Museum, Beaune Gallery, Paris, and several others. *Work in collections:* Bradford Museum, Councils for Art Education, Leicester and Oxford; private collections in England, Nigeria, U.S.A., Canada, Germany, Hong Kong and Spain. *Publications:* Guardian, Art International, Discovering an Historic City - Cambridge. *Signs work:* see appendix. *Address:* 39 New Rd., Barton, Cambs. CB3 7AY. *Email:* icm@newroad0.freeserve.co.uk

ST. JOHN ROSSE, Nicholas David, figurative artist in oil, pencil, pastel, gouache, tempera; twice Elizabeth Greenshields Foundation; *b* London, 18 Sept., 1945. *m* Chantale. two *s. Educ:* University College School. *Studied:* under Pietro Annigoni, Florence, and at the Scuolo del Nudo of the Florence Academy, early 60's. *Exhib:* regular one-man shows and group shows London, nationwide and the Continent. *Work in collections:* E. Greenshields Foundation, Montreal, Britannia Royal Navy College, Dartmouth. *Commissions:* portrait/figure, religious, houses. *Publications:* series of illustrated articles on egg tempera painting 'Artist' magazine (1980). *Clubs:* St. Ives Soc. of Artists. *Signs work:* "N. St. John Rosse." *Address:* St. Adwen, Trethevy, Tintagel, Cornwall PL34 0BE.

SALAMAN, Christopher, artist in oil, bronze and resin bronze; *b* Dorking, 4 Nov., 1939. married. one *s. Educ:* Bedales School. *Studied:* Camberwell School of Art and Crafts under Karel Vogel. *Exhib:* Woodstock Gallery, Upper Street Gallery, Mall Galleries, Margaret Fisher Gallery. *Signs work:* "Christopher Salaman." *Address:* West Park Lodge, High Ongar, Essex.

SALMON, Martin, illustrator in water-colour and gouache; designer (Advertising); *b* Barnehurst, Kent, 19 Apr., 1950. *m* Janice. *Educ:* Dartford Technical School. *Exhib:* Edwin Pollard Gallery, Limpsfield Water-colours. *Work in collections:* Hong Kong, N.Z., Italy, N. America, etc. *Signs work:* "Martin Salmon." *Address:* 17 Dome Hill, Caterham, Surrey CR3 6EE.

SALMOND, Ronald, A.T.D. (1938), S.G.A. (1967); wood engraver, etcher, painter, etc.; Head of Art Dept., Preston Manor High School, Wembley (retd.); *b* Hornsey, 30 Dec., 1912. *m* Mary. one *s. Educ:* Tollington Grammar School. *Studied:* Hornsey College of Art (printmaking under Norman Janes). *Exhib:* R.A., R.E., R.B.A. *Work in collections:* South London A.G., Ashmolean Museum. *Signs work:* "Ronald Salmond." *Address:* 13 Treve Ave., Harrow, Middx. HA1 4AL.

SALTER, Anthony, graphic designer and printmaker in etching; *b* London, 2 Mar., 1949. *Studied:* Goldsmiths' College of Art (1966-69). *Exhib:* R.A., R.S.P.E.E., P.M.C. *Work in collections:* Rank Zerox, London Borough of Greenwich. *Signs work:* "ANTHONY SALTER." *Address:* 34 Lizban St., London SE3 8SS.

SALTER, Rebecca, B.A. Art and Design; artist in acrylic on canvas, works on paper, woodcut prints; *b* Sussex, 24 Feb., 1955. *m* Geoffrey Winston. *Educ:* Bristol Polytechnic (1974-77). *Exhib:* extensively in Britain and Japan; solo shows: Jill George Gallery (1994, 1996), New York (1997). *Work in collections:* Tate Gallery, British Museum, Portland Museum and San Francisco Museums of Modern Art, Library of Congress, Washington, British Council. *Publications:* Exhibition catalogue (1996, 1998, 1999). *Signs work:* "REBECCA SALTER." *Address:* c/o Jill George Gallery, 38 Lexington St., London W1R 3HR.

SALTZMAN, William, B.S. Education, University of Minnesota (1940); easel and mural painter, designer, teacher; Prof. Emeritus, Macalester College (since 1984); Director-resident artist, Rochester Art Centre, Rochester, Minn. (1948-63), Freelance Studio, Minneapolis, Minn. (since 1963); Prof. of Art, Macalester College, St. Paul, Minn. (since 1966); currently painting and designing stained glass and sheet copper sculpture reliefs for many architectural commissions; exhibiting paintings widely coast to coast; (3) I.F.R.A.A. National awards; Regional/National awards; *b* Mpls., Minn., 9 July, 1916. *m* Muriel. one *s.* two *d. Educ:* University of Minnesota; Art Students League, N.Y.C. *Studied:* as above. *Signs work:* see appendix. *Address:* Studio: 5916 Walnut Drive, Edina, Minn. 55436-1750.

SAMUELSON, Becky, H.S., U.A.; marine and landscape artist in pastel and gouache; teacher, Adult Educ. I.O.W.; *b* Oxon, 13 July, 1959. *m* Colin. one *s.* one *d. Educ:* self taught. *Exhib:* London (various), Kendall's Fine Art Cowes, Turnpike Gallery Petersfield, Bembridge Gallery I.O.W., H.S., Century Gallery, Datchet. *Work in collections:* private. *Publications:* work repro.: greetings cards, prints for Shanklin Chine, Sailing Clubs, Appuldurcombe House, Priory Hotel, calendar and local cards. *Signs work:* "B. SAMUELSON." *Address:* Kempsford, Hilbre Rd., St. Helens, Ryde, I.O.W. PO33 1TJ. *Website:* www.samuelsonc.freeserve.co.uk *Email:* colin@samuel-sonc.freeserve.co.uk

SANDERS, Rosanne Diana, S.B.A.; botanical painter in water-colour and print-maker; four R.H.S. gold medals, R.A. miniature award; *b* Stoke Poges, Bucks., 21 June, 1944. one *s. Educ:* Roedean. *Studied:* High Wycombe College of Art. *Exhib:* Hunt Institute, U.S.A., S.B.A., Westminster, Tryon & Swann Gallery, London, R.H.S., Devon Guild, and various galleries in Britain; solo exhib., Hortus, London. *Work in collections:* Dr. Shirley Sherwood, V. & A. Museum, First National Bank, Johannesburg, S. Africa. *Commissions:* stamps - commemorative plates for H.M. Queen Elizabeth and the Queen Mother. *Publications:* The English Apple, Phaidon Press; Portrait of a Country Garden, Aurum Press; Painting The Secret Life of Nature, Search Press; A Little Book of Old Roses, Appletree Press; The Art of Making Wine, Aurum Press. *Signs work:* "RDS" and on prints "Rosie Sanders." *Address:* c/o Jonathan Cooper, Park Walk Gallery, 20 Park Walk, London SW10 0AQ. *Website:* rosiesanders@onetel.co.uk *Email:* rosiesanders@btinternet.com

SANDERS, Susan Mary, D.F.A. (1968), R.A. Schools Post Grad. Cert. (1971); painter in oil, water-colour, pencil, chalk and gouache; Partner, The Studio, Wye Art Gallery; *b* Haslemere, 11 Aug., 1946. *m* Richard Henry Parkinson. one *s.* one *d. Educ:* St. Mary's School, Baldslow Hastings. *Studied:* Byam Shaw School (1964-68), R.A. Schools (1968-71). *Exhib:* R.A. Summer Exhbn. (1971-98), R.W.A., (1983-88), Mall Galleries (1986-89), Bath, Bristol, Stockbridge, etc. *Work in collections:* Merchant Navy Pensions London, B.& Q. Southampton, and various board-rooms and offices. *Publications:* work repro.: Whatmans Ltd. Calendar (1989), advertising of B.& Q. Southampton. *Clubs:* Reynolds, R.A. Schools. *Signs work:* "S. Sanders," "Susan Sanders," or "S.S." *Address:* 3 Best Lane, Canterbury, Kent CT1 2JB.

SANDERSON, C. J., 1st prize Corfu Landscapes (1967); Dip. d'Honneur Salon International Biarritz (1974); artist in oil, acrylic, water-colour, pastel, gouache, pencil, etching, Indian ink, stone, clay and wood; *b* London, 18 Aug., 1949. *Educ:* Millfield. *Studied:* Byam Shaw School of Art (1967-71) under Maurice de Sausmarez and Ruskin Spear, R.A. *Exhib:* one-man shows: Woodstock Gallery (1974), Gallery Vallombreuse (1974), Gallery Mouffe (1974), Drian Gallery (1979); mixed shows: John Neville (1974), Ashgate Gallery (1973, 1974), Paris Salon (1974), R.A. (1970, 1972, 1973, 1983, 1984, 1985), Wylma Wayne Gallery (1983), Roy Miles Gallery (1995), Grosvenor Gallery (1995), Bruton St. Gallery (1995), Highgate Fine Art (1999), Cornelius Gallery (1999-2001), Finalot Fine Art (2001), Galerie Tamenega, Paris, and 2 websites: artdirectukltd and finalotgal and other mixed shows London and abroad. *Work in collections:* D. J. Redwood White, London, and Paris. *Publications:* Noo 1995 Critics Choice Sunday Telegraph. *Clubs:* The Organ. *Signs work:* "C.J. Sanderson." *Address:* 7 Gordon Pl., London W8 4JD.

SANDERSON, Roger, N.D.D. (1951), S.G.F.A. (1985-96), A.O.I. (1980), S.C.A. (1986); painter in water-colour, illustrator, designer (landscapes, figurative, humorous); Senior tutor, Linguaphone Institute's Paris School of Art (1982-94); *b* London, 23 Nov., 1923. *m* Hilde Kokorz. one *s.* three *d. Educ:* Dulwich College. *Studied:* Croydon and Epsom Art Schools (Barbara Jones, Michael Cadman, Leslie Worth, Ray Evans). *Exhib:* R.I., R.W.S. Open, R.B.A., P.S., U.A., etc. H.W. Peel prizewinner - drawing S.G.F.A. (1992). Private and corporate collections. *Publications:* illustrations for leading publishers. *Signs work:* "ROGER SANDERSON," see appendix. *Address:* Bucklers Lodge, St. Ives, Ringwood, Hants. BH24 2NY.

SANDLE, Michael Leonard, R.A., F.R.B.S., D.F.A. (Lond.); artist in watercolour and ink, sculptor in bronze; Prof. at The Academy for Visual Arts, Karlsruhe, W. Germany; *b* Weymouth, 18 May, 1936. divorced . *m* Demelza Spargo, 1988. one *s. Educ:* Douglas High School. *Studied:* Douglas School of Art, I.O.M. (1951-54), Slade School of Fine Art (1956-59). *Exhib:* group: Young Contemporaries (1957-59), Grabowski Gallery, London (1964, 1966), British Sculptors '72, R.A. (1972), Hayward Annual (1978), Träume vom Frieden, Recklinghausen (1982), etc.; one-man: Drian Gallery (1963), Haus am Lützowplatz, Berlin (1975), Allen Gallery, Vancouver (1975), Fischer Fine Art (1981, 1985), Wilhelm Lehmbruck Museum (1984), Whitechapel (1988), Württembergischer Kunstverein, Stuttgart (1989), Ernst Museum, Budapest (1990), etc. *Work in collections:* Arts Council, British Council, B.M., Imperial War Museum, Leics. A.G., Leics. Educ. Authority, Metropolitan Museum, N.Y., Museum des 20. Jahrhunderts, Vienna, Neuberger Museum of Modern Art, U.S.A., Neue Sammlung, Munich, National-Galerie, Warsaw, Preston Art Museum, Tate Gallery, V. & A., W. German Government, etc. *Signs work:* "Michael Sandle." *Address:* Schloss Scheibenhardt, D 71635 Karlsruhe, W. Germany.

SANDWITH, Noelle, artist in line (particularly people), water-colour, oil, egg tempera, acrylic, pastel, etching; *b* 1927. *Educ:* Carshalton House, Surrey. *Studied:* Kingston-on-Thames, Croydon and Heatherley's. *Exhib:* R.A., R.B.A., S.W.A., Brighton A.G., Waldorf Astoria, New York; one-man show: Foyle's Art Gallery. *Work in collections:* Royal Naval College, Greenwich, Starr Commonwealth, Albion, Michigan, U.S.A., Royal Free Hospital, London, Auckland Inst. and Museum, N.Z., National Museum of Australia, British Museum, London. *Commissions:* Edith Wertheimer Memorial, Royal Free Hospital. *Publications:* work repro.: The Times,

Sydney Morning Herald, R.A. Illustrated, Revue Moderne, Frost & Reed, etc. *Signs work:* "Noelle Sandwith." *Address:* Cottage No. 1, John Howard Cottages, Roedean Rd., Brighton, E. Sussex BN2 5RY.

SANFORD, Sheila, R.I., R.M.S., M.A.A., H.S.; water-colour artist, miniaturist; *b* Singapore, 1922. *m* Roy Sanford. three *s*. *Educ:* Brentwood School, Southport. *Studied:* St. Martin's School of Art. *Exhib:* Llewellyn Alexander (Fine Paintings) Ltd.; David Curzon Gallery; M.A.S.-F.; R.I.; R.M.S.; H.S.; R.A. Summer Exhbn. *Work in collections:* M.A.S.-F., Llewellyn Alexander (Fine Paintings) Ltd., M.A.A., R.M.S. *Signs work:* "Sheila Sanford." *Address:* Sheepwash Cottage, Uploders, Bridport, Dorset DT6 4PH.

SANZ-PASTOR Fz. de PIÉROLA, Consuelo, Doctor of History; Chairman of I.C.O.M. National Committee (1981-84); Mem. Hispanic Society of America (since1959); Directora Museo Cerralbo (1942-86); Inspectora Museos Bellas Artes (1963-69); Chairman of Sup. Council of Museums (1980-82); Mem., Trustees the Prado Museum (1980-85); Directora Honoraria Museo Cerralbo (since 1986); *b* Madrid. *Publications:* Guia Museo Cerralbo (4th ed. 1981), Catálogos Exposiciones A. Berruguete (1960), San Pablo en el Arte (1963), Francisco de Zurbarán (1964), Museos y Colecciones de España (5th ed. 1990), Guia Museo Casas Reales (Rep. Dominicana 1976), Museo Cerralbo: Catálogo de Dibujos (1976). *Address:* Juan Hurtado de Mendoza 9-28036 Madrid.

SAPIEHA, Christine, S.W.A., A.P.A.; painter in acrylic, portraits, sculpture; therapist; *b* Vienna, 5 May, 1934. *m* Adam Fremantle. two *s*. *Educ:* The Brearley, N.Y.C., Georgetown University, Washington D.C. *Studied:* Abbott School of Art, Washington D.C. (1951-52), Parsons School of Design, N.Y.C. (1952-56). *Exhib:* Mall Galleries, Spirit of London, R.A. Summer Show, Francis Kyle, Stable Gallery, Ice House, Bush House, Beach Thomas Gallery, Burford, Gallery East, N.Y., Westminster Gallery. *Work in collections:* Sheldon Weisfeld, Brownsville, Tex., W.A.S.L. *Publications:* illustrated science and fiction for children. *Signs work:* see appendix. *Address:* 20 Macduff Rd., Battersea, London SW11 4DA.

SAPP, Prudence Eugenie (née Williams), School Cert. with Hons. in Art and English (1945); painter in oil; *b* London, 11 Mar., 1928. *m* Reginald Walter. *Educ:* Wycombe Abbey; Benenden School, Kent; English School of Languages, Chateau d'Oex, Switzerland. *Studied:* C.F.E. Bognor Regis (1964), portraiture at Epsom A.E.C. (1974, Reg Sapp). *Exhib:* one-man shows: Hyde Park Gallery (1992, 1993); two-man shows: Barnes Gallery, SW13 (1994, 1995); Mall Galleries since 1974; R.A. Summer Exhbn. (1987, 1992-95). *Work in collections:* America, Sweden, Japan. *Clubs:* Chelsea Art Soc. *Signs work:* "Prue Sapp." *Address:* 19 Waterer Gdns., Tadworth, Surrey KT20 5PB.

SAUMAREZ SMITH, Romilly, Fellow of Designer Bookbinders; bookbinder; *b* London, 10 Feb., 1954. *m* Charles Saumarez Smith. two *s*. *Studied:* Camberwell School of Art and Crafts (1975-78). *Exhib:* many bookbinding exhbns. since 1982. *Work in collections:* Crafts Council, V. & A., N.Y. Public Library, H.R.C., Austin Texas, British Museum. *Publications:* reviews and articles for Crafts Magazine. *Address:* 13 Newell St., Limehouse, London E14 7HP.

SAUNDERS, Jutta Gabrielle, Slade Dip.; painter in oil and water-colour, portrait sculptor; tutor; *b* 10 July, 1929. *m* Vernon Saunders. one *s.* one *d. Educ:* The Hall School, Somerset, St. Maurs, Weybridge. *Studied:* Kingston School of Art (1945-48), Slade School of Fine Art (1948-51) under William Coldstream, John Piper; sculpture under F.E. McWilliam. *Exhib:* R.A., R.W.A., Leicester, London and provincial galleries. *Work in collections:* in England, U.S.A., Brazil, Germany, France, Sweden and Canada. *Signs work:* "J.S." or "J.G.S." or "J. Saunders." *Address:* Flint House, Oatlands Mere, Weybridge, Surrey KT13 9PD.

SAVAGE, Judith, L.D.A.D.; artist in oil on canvas; *b* Sydney, Australia. one *s. Educ:* Australia. *Studied:* Interior Design and Decoration and Mural Design, Chelsea College of Art (1977-80). *Exhib:* London: Loggia Gallery, Leighton House, C.W.A.C., etc. Specialises in colour: therapeutic, psychological, symbolic aspects. Studies in art therapy, psychology, sociology (1991-92). Guest Lecturer Chelsea College of Art. Currently working St. Bernards Psychiatric Hospital, Ealing. *Signs work:* "J. Savage." *Address:* 32 Mansell Rd., The Vale, London W3 7QH.

SAVEGE, Roma, painter in oil, gouache, tempera, sculptor in welded steel and glass: sand, blasting, gilding, colouring and engraving; Hon. mem. N.S.; *b* Christchurch, N.Z., 17 July, 1907. *m* R.M. Savege, O.B.E., M.C., F.R.C.S. six *s. Educ:* Queenwood, Eastbourne. *Studied:* Canterbury College of Art, N.Z., and Richmond and Hounslow Colleges, England. *Exhib:* one-man shows, Richmond Hill Gallery, R.A.G., Contemporary Portrait Soc., Circuit Painters, N.E.A.C., Guildhall, etc. Now working in computer graphics with Don Pavey. *Clubs:* N.S., F.P.S., I.P.I., R.A.S. *Signs work:* "Roma Savege." *Address:* Pembroke House, The Green, Richmond, Surrey TW9 1QF.

SAWYERS, David Robert, A.T.C. (1964), A.R.E. (1964), M.A. (1983); topographical draughtsman in pen and ink with water-colour washes; *b* Brighton, 29 Apr., 1941. *m* yes. *Educ:* Varndean Grammar School, Brighton. *Studied:* Brighton College of Arts and Crafts (1959-64), University of Sussex (1982-83). *Exhib:* Gardner Centre, Bankside Gallery, Corn Exchange and Gallery, Brighton Museum and Library. *Work in collections:* held by Leoframes, 70 North Rd., Brighton. *Signs work:* "D.R. Sawyers." *Address:* 19 Foundry St., Brighton BN1 4AT.

SAYERS, Brian, B.A. (1978); painter in oil on canvas; *b* Bromley, Kent, 3 Oct., 1954. one *d. Educ:* St Olave's Grammar School, Kent. *Studied:* Slade School of Fine Art (1974-78, Jeffery Camp, Patrick George). *Exhib:* R.A., N.P.G., Long & Ryle, Hohental & Littler, Munich, Discerning Eye, Mall Galleries (1st Prize). *Signs work:* "Brian Sayers" on reverse. *Address:* 27a Walterton Rd., London W9 3PE.

SCAMPTON, Ann Barbara, F.R.I.B.A., R.W.A.; chartered architect, painter in water-colour; *b* Shanghai, 2 Feb., 1933. three *d. Studied:* Royal West of England Academy School of Architecture. *Exhib:* R.W.A. Bristol. *Signs work:* "A.S." or "A. Scampton." *Address:* 10 Belvedere, Chelsea Harbour, London SW10 0XA.

SCHAVERIEN, Pat, B.A, Hons. in Fine Art (1974), Slade Higher Dip. in F.A. (1976); printmaker in etchings-collographs and linocuts; *b* London, 12 Oct., 1951. *m* Charles Frydman. *Educ:* Middlesex Polytechnic (1970-74). *Studied:* Slade School of Fine Art (1974-76). *Exhib:* R.A. Summer Exhbns. and mixed shows. *Work in* *collections:* V. & A., Museum of London, British Council, Guildhall Library, City of London. *Commissions:* The site of Bracken House, London, by the Museum of London, Henderson Assoc. Bldg., Broadgate, London. *Address:* 12 Frognal Lane, London NW3 7DU.

SCHLEE, Anne H., P.P.N.S.; artist in water-colour, acrylic, ink; Cert. Fine Art (1972); Hon. Officer, National Soc. Painters, Sculptors and Printmakers (1989); *b* Shanghai, China, 1931. *m* Charles A. Schlee. three *d. Educ:* Katharine Branson School, California. *Studied:* International School (1962-65, Chinese art: Chow Chian-Chui), Famous Artists' School (1970-72, Charles Reid, John Pellew, Joseph Laskar, Ray Peese). *Exhib:* Hong Kong, N.S., Chelsea Art Soc., Ridley Art Soc., Women Painters of Washington, Rogue Gallery and Art Center. *Work in collections:* Guildford House Museum and Gallery, University of W.A. Medical Centre – permanent art collection; private collections in U.S.A., Canada, Australia, U.K., etc. *Publications:* work repro.: Best of Water-colour Series - Textures (Rockport). *Clubs:* N.S., W.P.W. *Signs work:* "Anschlee." *Address:* 6554 Monte Vista Drive N.E., Bainbridge Island, W.A. 98110, U.S.A.

SCHLEE, Nick, M.A. (Oxon.); painter in oils; *b* 17 July, 1931. *m* Ann Acheson Schlee. one *s.* three *d. Educ:* Rugby School (1942-47), Oxford (1952-55). *Studied:* Evening Classes, Art Students League New York, Central School London, Morley College, Putney Art School, Slade. *Exhib:* one-man, Flying Colours Gallery, Edinburgh (1992), Barbican Centre, University of Liverpool (1994), Christchurch Picture Gallery, Oxford (1996), Gallery 27, London (1998, 2000). *Address:* Galvey, Upper Basildon, nr. Reading RG8 8LU.

SCHMOOK, Bernhard, structural engineer, sculptor in wood, metal, ceramics; Assistant to Prof. P. K. King; *b* Austria, 13 Sept., 1965. *m* H.A. Alele. *Studied:* HTLB Saalfelden (Prof. J. Kahapka). *Exhib:* Hall Place, Bexley. *Commissions:* Ironbridge Steel Sculpture Museum, Kirishima Sculpture Park, Kagoshima, Japan. *Clubs:* Public Monuments and Sculpture Assoc. *Signs work:* "B. SCHMOOK" and see appendix. *Address:* 15 Banyan House Studio, Lithos Rd., London NW3 6ES.

SCHOFIELD, Roy Malcolm, N.D.D. (1953), M.S.I.A. (1973), G.R.A. (1986); illustrator in pen, ink and wash, painter in watercolour and mixed media; art director, Field Enterprises Educational Corp. (1962-1967), tutor, Sutton College of Liberal Arts (1979-1983); *b* Huddersfield, 8 Jul., 1933. *m* Dorothy. one *s. Educ:* Hillhouse School. *Studied:* Huddersfield School of Art (1948-1953). *Publications:* illustrator and designer of many books for Brockhampton Press, Holmes McDougal, Edward Arnold, Macdonald, Ginn & Co., Cornelsen, Berlin, and own imprint, 'Travel About Books' for children. *Signs work:* "Roy Schofield." *Address:* 39 Northey Ave., Cheam, Surrey SM2 7HS.

SCHOFIELD, Sara Anne, F.S.B.A. (1986); R.H.S. Gold medal (1987, 1991); artist, primarily botanical, in water-colour, chromacolour, pastel; *b* London, 21 May, 1937. *m* John Schofield. one *s.* one *d. Educ:* Ashford County Grammar School. *Studied:* Twickenham College of Art. *Exhib:* solo shows: London (3); solo and group shows: R.W.S., R.B.A., R.I., and S.B.A. regularly. *Work in collections:* Hunt Inst. of Botanical Documentation, Shirley Sherwood Collection of Contemporary Botanical Artists. *Commissions:* numerous series of collectors plates, several of them Royal commemoratives. *Clubs:* Founder mem. S.B.A. *Signs work:* "SARA ANNE SCHOFIELD" or "S.A.S." *Address:* 40 Grove Wood Hill, Coulsdon, Surrey CR5 2EL.

SCHWARZ, Hans, R.B.A. (1981), R.W.S. (1982), N.E.A.C (1982), R.P. (1990), Hunting Group Prize (1981); painter in water-colour and oil; *b* Vienna, 29 Dec., 1922. *m* Lena. two *s. Educ:* Vienna. *Studied:* Vienna Kunstgewerbeschule (1937-38), Birmingham College of Art (1941-43). *Exhib:* R.W.S., R.A., R.B.A., N.E.A.C., R.P.; eighteen one-man shows since 1960: A.I.A., Camden Arts Centre, Cambridge, Thackeray Gallery. *Work in collections:* Glasgow A.G., National Maritime Museum, Newport A.G., Halifax N.Z. A.G., Oxford University, N.P.G. *Publications:* Studio Vista: Figure Painting; Colour for the Artist; Painting in towns; four for Pitmans, etc. *Signs work:* see appendix. *Address:* c/o R.W.S., Bankside Gallery, 48 Hopton St., London SE1 9JH.

SCOTT, Dafila Kathleen, S.WL.A. (1991), M.A. (1975), Ph.D. (1978); painter in oil, water-colour; *b* London, 9 June, 1952. *m* Tim Clutton-Brock. one *s.* one *d. Educ:* Badminton School, Millfield School, Oxford University. *Studied:* in the studios of Peter Scott (during childhood), Thomas Newbolt and Robin Child. *Publications:* illustrated Antarctica: A Guide to the Wildlife by Tony Soper (Bradt Publications, 1994). *Signs work:* "Dafila Scott" or "DKS." *Address:* White Roses, The Hythe, Reach, Cambs. CB5 0JQ.

SCOTT, David Henry George Montagu Douglas, landscape painter and illustrator in oil and water-colour; *b* Edinburgh, 29 Jan., 1945. *m* Laura Harmsworth. two *d. Educ:* Eton. *Studied:* Byam Shaw School of Art (1963-66, Maurice de Sausmarez), R.A. Schools (1966-67, Peter Greenham). *Exhib:* R.A., R.B.A., R.P., Rutland Gallery, Thomas Gibson Fine Art, Maclean Gallery, The Scottish Gallery, French Embassy, Wildenstein 'Venice Observed', etc. *Work in collections:* Dublin Art Museum, Thameside Council. *Commissions:* Jaguar Showrooms Belfast; Wembley Stadium 1990 Cup Final. *Publications:* illustrated five children's books for Walker Books and Methuen; contributed to 'The Children's Book' (Walker Books), 'Open Door' Series (Thomas Nelson). *Signs work:* "D.S." dated. *Address:* 19 Petworth St., London SW11 4QW.

SCOTT, I. Borg, Associate, Société des Artistes Français, F.R.S.A.; artist in oil and sanguine chalk; *b* 4 Feb., 1940. *Studied:* under Leonard Boden, R.P., and F. Wyatt, V.P.S.W.A., R.M.S. *Exhib:* Salon des Artistes, France; Salon Sony, Osaka, Japan; European Art, Auckland, N.Z.; Roy Miles, London; group shows: Westminster Gallery; Gagliardi Gallery, etc. *Signs work:* "I. Borg Scott." *Address:* 8 Colinwood, Colinwood Rd., Farnham Common, Berks. SL2 3LN.

SCOTT, Irene Mary, D.A. (Edin.) (1965), B.A.(Hons.) (1990), M.A. (1994), R.S.W. (1989); artist in water-colour, oil, printmaking; elected professional mem. S.S.A. (1987); *b* Penicuik, Midlothian, 31 Dec., 1942. *m* Brian S. Duffield. four *s.* one *d. Educ:* Lasswade High School. *Studied:* Edinburgh College of Art (1961-65). *Exhib:* R.S.A., R.S.W., S.S.A., various solo and group exhbns., etc. *Work in collections:* Britain, Canada, N. Ireland, Norway, Poland and U.S.A. *Commissions:* Iona Abbey Ltd. (1997). Member of Board of Directors AXIS (Visual Arts Information Service, 1997). *Signs work:* "Irene M. Scott." *Address:* 55 Fairfield Rd., Inverness IV3 5QP.

SCOTT, Judy, N.D.D. (1961), C.S.D. (1962); figurative painter in gouache and oils, printmaker; *b* Herts., 7 Nov., 1939. *Studied:* Maidstone College of Art (1956-58, Dick Lee), Central School of Arts and Crafts (1958-62), mid 80's, Dick Lee. *Exhib:* solo shows: Abbott & Holder, and Cadogan Gallery, London, Bircham Gallery, Norfolk; selected mixed shows: New Grafton, N.E.A.C., R.P., R.I., R.W.S., Garrick-Milne and John Boulton Fine Art, Shropshire; winner of R.W.S. Abbott & Holder Travel prize (1993) and National Print Exhibition, St. Cuthbert's Mill prize (2001). *Commissions:* portraits and theatre prints. *Signs work:* "J. Scott." *Address:* 4 Church Cottage, Bale, Fakenham, Norfolk NR21 0QZ.

SCOTT, Sally, painter in oil, pastel, drawing, glass engraver in sandblasting and engraving on flat architectural glass; Partnership with David Peace, Peace and Scott (1986); *b* London, 28 Jan., 1939. *m* Tony Guy, graphic designer (decd.). one *s.* one *d. Educ:* Benenden School, Kent. *Studied:* Croydon College of Art (1957-59), R.A. Schools (1959-62). *Work in collections:* glass work in Norwich, Leicester, Llandaff, St. Albans Cathedrals, Westminster Abbey, Lancaster, Sheffield, Oxford and Cambridge Universities; private collections in France and England. *Publications:* contributed to Drawing, Seeing and Observing by Ian Simpson (1992), co-author, Engraved Glass in Architecture (Peace and Scott, 1995). *Clubs:* A.W.G., Fellow, Guild of Glass Engravers, Art and Architecture. *Signs work:* "Sally Scott." *Address:* The Cottage, Cambalt Rd., London SW15 6EW.

SCOTT-KESTIN, Colin, R.M.S. (1995), H.S. (1989), A.S.Eq.A. (1994); painter in oil, water-colour and gouache of landscapes, equestrian and other animal subjects, especially miniatures; *b* 14 Jan., 1921. *m* Mary Widdows. *Educ:* St. Giles School, St. Leonards-on-Sea. *Studied:* Beckenham School of Art (1938-39, Henry Carr, R.P.). *Exhib:* R.M.S., H.S., S.Eq.A., M.A.S.-F., Llewellyn Alexander (Fine Art), where awarded a Commendation of Excellence (1995, 2001). *Work in collections:* war sketches, Royal Signals Museum, Blandford. *Signs work:* "C. SCOTT-KESTIN." *Address:* Strapp Cottage, Skillgate La., Chiselborough, Som. TA14 6TP.

SCOTT-MILLER, Melissa Emma, B.A. Hons., R.P.; painter in oil; *b* London, 17 Jul., 1959. *m* Frank Walsh (partner). one *s.* one *d. Educ:* Queens College, London. *Studied:* Slade School of Fine Art (1977-1981). *Exhib:* Albemarle Gallery (1989), Grosvenor Gallery (1995). *Signs work:* "Melissa Scott-Miller." *Address:* Flat G, 5 Lonsdale Sq., London N1 1EN.

SCOTT-TAGGART, Elizabeth Mary Josephine, N.D.D.; sculptor working mainly as wood-carver; *b* nr. Croydon, 10 Oct., 1927. *Educ:* Old Palace School, Croydon. *Studied:* Central School of Arts and Crafts, and St. Martin's, London (1945-49). *Exhib:* R.A.; group shows: R.B.A., Trends at Mall Galleries, Loggia Gallery, Wooburn and Cookham Festivals; one-man shows at Century Galleries, Henley-on-Thames. Full mem. F.P.S. Has recently started studying and practising Chinese Brush Painting. *Signs work:* "est." *Address:* 96 Gregories Rd., Beaconsfield, Bucks. HP9 1HL.

SCOULLER, Glen, D.A. (1972), R.G.I. (1989), R.S.W. (1997); artist in oil and water-colour; *b* Glasgow, 24 Apr., 1950. *m* Carol Alison Marsh. two *d. Studied:* Glasgow School of Art (1968-73, David Donaldson). *Exhib:* solo shows: John D. Kelly Gallery, Glasgow (1977), The Scottish Gallery, Edinburgh (1980), Fine Art

Soc., Glasgow (1985, 1988), Harbour Arts Centre, Irvine (1986), Fine Art Soc., Edinburgh (1989), Portland Gallery, London (1989, 1992, 1994, 1998), Macauley Gallery, Stenton (1990, 1993, 1996), French Inst., Edinburgh (1990), Open Eye Gallery, Edinburgh (1992, 1994, 1997, 2000), Roger Billcliffe Fine Art, Glasgow (1992, 1995, 1998), Everard Read Gallery, Johannesburg (1997), Corrymella Scott Gallery, Newcastle upon Tyne (1999), Everard Read Gallery, Capetown (2000). Regular exhibitor: Royal Scottish Academy, Edinburgh, R.G.I., R.S.W. *Work in collections:* Argyll C.C., S.A.C., Argyll Group, Leeds Educ. Authority, Lillie A.G., United Distillers PLC, Edinburgh Tapestry Co., Arthur Anderson & Co., Ford Collection U.S.A., Ross Harper & Murphy, Scotts Restaurant PLC, Dunedin Fund Managers, Scottish Amicable Assurance Co. Ltd., Craig Capital Corp. U.S.A., October Restaurant, Enterprise Oil London, MISYS PLC, Cargill Inc., Royal Bank of Scotland PLC, Clydesdale Bank PLC, Drambuie PLC, Edinburgh Fund Managers, Touche Ross, Scottish Office, Edinburgh, First National Bank of South Africa, Paintings in Hospitals, Scotland, Flemings Clyde Property, Tuscan Square Restaurant, Edinburgh; private: Japan, U.S.A., Singapore, Australia, France, Holland, Switzerland, Greece, Norway, S. Africa, and the U.K. *Publications:* Italian Sketchbook/W. Gordon Smith; Who's Who in Scotland (1999). *Clubs:* Glasgow Art. *Signs work:* "SCOULLER." *Address:* East London Hill Farm, Darvel, Ayrshire KA17 0LU.

SCROPE-HOWE, Pat, F.R.G.S., Sociétaire of Société des Artistes Indépendants Paris (1973); Sociétaire of Artistes Français Le Salon Paris (1975); painter in oil, pastel, acrylic, water-colour; sculptor in cire perdue and GRP/bronze; *b* London, 27 Jan., 1926. married. two *s. Studied:* Torbay Art School (1958-59), Saskatchewan Art Council (1959-60), Bourneville Art School (1961-62), Manchester Fine Arts (1963-69), Florence, Rome and Venice. Also travelled and painted in France, U.S.A., Spain, Egypt, Far East, South America and the Caribbean. Studied under Harry Rutherford (pupil of Sickert) for portraiture and studies in pastel and oils, Terry McGlynn for abstract and experimental art, Ian McDonald Grant for History of Art, life and composition. *Exhib:* Paris: Salon des Nations (1984), Grand Palais (Indépendants and Artistes Français) since 1973; provinces: Salford Open (1964), Withington, Liverpool Open (bi-annual), Colin Jellicoe Gallery, Manchester College; London: R.S.M.A. Boat Show and National Tour (1969-73). Painting rented via R.S.M.A. for a Polaris Submarine which went under North and South Poles (1973); London International Open, S.W.A. and their National Tour (1972), Laing Competition (1975), Hesketh Hubbard Soc., U.A., Long Gallery, Isleworth (solo show), Royal Horticultural Art Exhbn., Festival of Paintings and Graphic Art (1972); Ireland: Kilkenny (solo show), Dunmore East, Waterford (Studio, permanent solo show). *Work in collections:* Canada, Australia, Gt. Britain, Ireland and the continent. Has appeared on CKBI TV (Canada) to talk on art. *Signs work:* "Pat Scrope-Howe." *Address:* Maudwill, Flat 3, 9 Barton Terr., Dawlish, Devon EX7 9QH.

SCRYMGEOUR WEDDERBURN, Janet, F.R.B.S. (1980), R.S.A. Ottillie Helen Wallace Scholarship (1972), R.S.A. Benno Schotz Prize (1973), Paris Salon bronze medal, silver medal; sculptor in clay and bronze, stained glass window designer; *b* Winchester, 14 Aug., 1941. *m* Mervyn Fox-Pitt. one *s.* two *d. Educ:* Kilgraston, Convent of the Sacred Heart, Bridge of Earn, Perthshire. *Studied:* with

Alastair Ross, F.R.B.S. (1970-71). *Exhib:* R.S.A. (1971-76, sculpture); Paris Salon (1972, 1973, sculpture). *Work in collections:* East Window of the Episcopal Church of St. James the Great, Cupar, Fife; West Window the Chapel Royal, Falkland Palace; Meditation Window Bedale Church, Yorks.; Victory and Freedom Windows, R.A.F. Leuchars, St. Paul's Church (1993), Sir Nicholas Fairbairn, M.P. (Scottish National Portrait Gallery), (posthumous) The Marquis of Bute, National Museum of Scotland. *Commissions:* St. Columba 1997 (Diocese of Dunkeld), Admiral Lord Duncan, 1997 (Camperdown Trust), Dundee Sea Gate (seven foot high), The Cosmic Christ (crucifix 8ft.) Carnoustie (1998), The Stobhall Madonna (6ft. bronze) Stobhall, Perthshire (1998), The Annunciation (3ft. bronze figures) (1999). *Signs work:* "J.S.W." *Address:* Grange Scrymgeour, Cupar, Fife. KY15 4QH.

SCULL, Paul Harvey, B.A.Hons. (1975), H.D.F.A. (1978), R.E. (1986), M.Ed. (1988); artist; Senior Lecturer in fine art, University of Wolverhampton; *b* London, 1953. *m* Dawn. *Educ:* Kimbolton School, Cambs. *Studied:* Northampton School of Art (1971-72), Maidstone College of Art (1972-75), Slade School of Fine Art (1976-78), University of Wales, Cardiff (1984-88). *Exhib:* Whitworth A.G., Manchester; Museum of Modern Art, Wales; Manchester City A.G.; University of Keele Gallery; Taipei Museum of Fine Art, Taiwan. *Work in collections:* Rank Xerox; Oxigen Foundation, Hungary; Xantos Janos Museum, Gyor; Mappin A.G., Sheffield; H.M.K. (Fine Arts) New York; West Midlands Arts. *Signs work:* "Paul Scull." *Address:* Fair View, Brockhampton, Hereford HR1 4SQ.

SCULLARD, Susan Diane, B.A. (Hons.), M.A.; freelance illustrator in wood engraving, pen and ink, water-colour; *b* Chatham, 20 Apr., 1958. *m* Jeremy Duncombe. one *s. Educ:* Chatham Grammar School. *Studied:* Camberwell School of Art (John Lawrence), R.C.A. (Yvonne Skargon). *Exhib:* regularly with S.W.E., R.A. Summer Show (1999), New Ashgate Gallery Farnham, Open Eye Gallery Edinburgh, Crooked House Gallery Lavenham, Craft Gallery Cranbrook, Watergate St. Gallery Chester, Line Gallery Linlithgow, Tidal Wave Gallery Hereford, Art in Action Gallery Waterperry nr. Oxford. *Publications:* illustrations for Folio Soc. books, Canterbury Tales, Shakespeare; children's books: The Great Round the World Balloon Race, and Miss Fanshawe and the Great Dragon Adventure. *Clubs:* S.W.E. *Signs work:* "Sue Scullard." *Address:* Beech Hill Cottage, Glassenbury Rd., Cranbrook, Kent TN17 2QJ.

SCULLION, Anthony Kevin, B.A. Hons., Painting; painter in oil; *b* East Kilbride, 3 June, 1967. *Educ:* St. Bride's High School, East Kilbride. *Studied:* Glasgow School of Art (1988-1992). *Exhib:* solo and group exhibs. in S. Africa (1995-1998), solo exhib., Flying Colours Gallery, London (2000). *Signs work:* "A S" on verso. *Address:* c/o Flying Colours Gallery, P.O. Box 9361, London SW3 3ZJ. *Email:* art@flyingcoloursgallery.com

SEAGER, Harry Abram, A.T.D. (Birm., 1955); sculptor in glass and mixed media, cast and constructed metals; Senior Lecturer, College of Art, Stourbridge, W. Midlands; *b* Birmingham, 9 May, 1931. *m* Marie. one *s.* one *d. Educ:* Holly Lodge Grammar School, Smethwick, Warley, W. Midlands. *Studied:* College of Art, Birmingham. *Exhib:* Gimpel Fils London, Rotterdamse Kunstkring, Camden Art Centre, Fondation Maeght, S. France, Middleheim Park Antwerp, Perth, Economist

Bldg London. *Work in collections:* City Art Gallery, Leeds, C.A.S., London, Joseph H. Hirshorne Coll., U.S.A., D.O.E. London, V. & A., W. Midlands Arts; private collections in Canada, U.K., U.S.A., Holland, Italy. *Commissions:* London Hilton Park Lane, Hilton, Mauritius. *Publications:* Open Air Sculpture in Britain, W. Strachan Tate Gallery (A. Zwemmer Ltd); International Modern Glass, Geoffrey Beard Barrie & Jenkins, London; Public Sculpture of Birmingham, George Yoszopy, Liverpool University Press. *Address:* 1 Baylie St., Stourbridge, W.Midlands DY8 1AZ.

SEAL, Norman, painter in oil, ink, water-colour, calligrapher; *b* Warsop, Notts., 26 Feb., 1921. one *s.* one *d. Educ:* Mansfield Technical College. *Studied:* Mansfield College of Art (1963). *Exhib:* Nottingham Castle (1965), Fermoy, Kings Lynn (1978), Hudson Gallery, Wisbech (1978), Assembly House, Norwich (1978, 1990), Municipal Gallery, Mansfield (1981), Angles Theatre, Wisbech (1988), Central Library, Cambridge (1988). *Clubs:* Cambridge Arts Forum. *Signs work:* "N. Seal" and see appendix. *Address:* 15 Westfield Rd., Wisbech, Cambs. PE13 3EU.

SEARLE, Ronald, *b* Cambridge, 3 Mar., 1920. *Studied:* Cambridge School of Art (1936-39). *Exhib:* Leicester Galleries (1948, 1950, 1954 and 1957); Kraushaar Galleries, New York (1959); Bianchini Gallery, New York (1963); Kunsthalle, Bremen (1965); Wilhelm-Busch Museum, Hanover (1965, 1976); Wolfgang Gurlitt Museum, Linz, Austria (1966); Galerie La Pochade, Paris (1966, 1967, 1968, 1969, 1971, 1976); Galerie Carmen Cassé, Paris (1975, 1977), Galerie Gurlitt, Munich (1967, 1969, 1970, 1971 and 1973); retrospectives: Bibliothèque Nationale, Paris (1973), Prussian National Gallery (1976), etc. *Clubs:* Garrick. *Signs work:* see appendix. *Address:* c/o Tessa Sayle, 11 Jubilee Pl., London SW3 3TE.

SEDDON, Richard Harding, P.R.W.S., A.R.C.A., Ph.D.; painter in oil and water-colour, and writer on art; *Educ:* King Edward VII School and Reading University. *Studied:* Sheffield College of Art (1932-36); Royal College of Art (1936-39). *Exhib:* R.A., R.W.S. *Work in collections:* H.M. The Queen, V. & A., Imperial War Museum, Sheffield, Leeds, Derby, Southport, Reading, Philadelphia (U.S.A), Neufchatel (France). *Publications:* The Academic Technique of Oil Painting (1960), A Hand Uplifted (War Artist Memoirs) (1963), Art Collecting for Amateurs (1965), A Dictionary of Art Terms (1982) (with K. Reynolds), The Artist's Studio Book (1983); art criticism in The Guardian and most art journals; London art critic of Birmingham Post (1961-70); of Yorkshire Post since 1974. *Address:* 6 Arlesey Cl., London SW15 2EX.

SEE-PAYNTON, Colin Frank, R.C.A. (1993), R.E. (1986), S.WL.A. (1986), S.W.E. (1984), A.R.E. (1983); painter, etcher and engraver in water-colour, etching and wood engraving; *b* 1946. *m* Susie See. *Educ:* Bedford. *Studied:* Northampton School of Art (1963-65, Henry Bird). *Exhib:* R.A., R.E., R.W.S., S.W.E., S.WL.A. *Work in collections:* Ashmolean Museum Oxford, Beecroft A.G., Southend, Bedford C.C., Fremantle Museum, Australia, National Museum of Wales, National Library of Wales, S.W.A.N., and others. *Publications:* illustrations in many private press and commercial publications, The Incisive Eye - Colin See-Paynton Wood Engravings 1980-1996 (Scolar Press, 1996). *Signs work:* see appendix. *Address:* Oerle Hall, Berriew, Powys, Wales SY21 8QX.

SEELEY, Eric Charles, B.A. Hons. (1973), Cert R.A.S. (1976), A.T.C. (1977); painter, printmaker; British Inst. Fund Award in Fine Art, Armitage Prize (silver medal) for painting, Landseer Prize (bronze medal) for painting, Arthur Hacker Prize (silver medal) for portrait painting, Laing Art Show winner (1977, 1993); *b* Luton, 2 Dec., 1951. one *d*. *Studied:* Luton School of Art (1968-1970), Kingston Polytechnic (1970-1973), R.A. Schools (1973-1976), under Ruskin Spear, David Tindle, Gertrude Hermes, Peter Greenham, London University, Goldsmiths (1976-1977). *Exhib:* R.A., John Player Awards, National Gallery, Marryat Gallery, Leighton House, Famagusta, Cyprus. *Work in collections:* U.K. and abroad. *Clubs:* Reynolds Club, R.A. *Signs work:* "Eric Seeley." *Address:* 4 Irwin Rd., Bedford, Beds. MK40 3UL. *Email:* seeley@studio44.fsnet.co.uk

SEGAL, Hyman, R.B.A.; artist in charcoal and all mediums; founder mem. Penwith Soc.; *b* London, 26 May, 1914. *m* Diane Christie. *Educ:* Elementary and J.F.S., London. *Studied:* St. Martin's (Leon Underwood, Vivian Pitchforth). *Exhib:* one-man shows: Bankfield Museum, Halifax, Batley, Nairobi, E. Africa, International Club, Manchester, Downings Bookshop, Heffer Gallery, Castle Gallery, St. Ives, The Crypt, St. Ives, Penwith Soc., St. Ives Soc. of Artists. *Work in collections:* 'Bernard Leach' National Museum of Wales, 'Study of a Footballer' Manchester City A.G., The Sloop Inn, St. Ives permanent exhbn. since 1948. *Publications:* "Familiar Faces of St. Ives"; "Art Colony"; "As I was Going to St. Ives.". *Clubs:* Chelsea Arts. *Signs work:* "Segal." *Address:* 10 Porthmeor Studios, St. Ives, Cornwall TR26 1NG.

SELBIE, Rosy, artist in oil, water-colour, pastel; *b* Wales. *m* Robert, civil engineer. one *s*. one *d*. *Educ:* Birtwhistles, London SW1. *Studied:* Sir John Cass Foundation, Whitechapel. *Exhib:* solo shows: Knapp Gallery, Burghclere Manor; numerous mixed shows including Mall Galleries, dfn Gallery, Broadway, Manhattan, New York, U.S.A. *Work in collections:* Regents College, London, Test Valley Hampshire and in many private collections. *Publications:* Southern Arts Visual Art Index. *Clubs:* Sloane. *Signs work:* "Selbie." *Address:* Fellowes Cottage, Hurstbourne Priors, Whitchurch, Hants. RG28 7SE. *Website:* www.livingwithpaintings.com *Email:* selbie@livingwithpaintings.com

SELBY, William, R.B.A. (1989), R.W.S. (1992), R.O.I. (1982), N.E.A.C. (1994), R.S.W. (1998); painter; *b* Fitzwilliam, nr. Pontefract, Yorks., 26 Dec., 1933. *m* Mary. *Educ:* Fitzwilliam Secondary Modern. *Exhib:* R.A. Summer Exhbns. from 1972; solo shows: Adam Gallery, Bath (1995, 1997, 1999, 2001), Thomsons Gallery, Dover St., London (1997, 1999), City Gallery (1998, 2000). *Work in collections:* Mapin Gallery, Sheffield. Prizes: Christina Leger award R.O.I. (1985, 1987), Chris Beetle award (1986), L. Cornelissen & Son award R.O.I. (1988), Le Clerc Fowle medal R.O.I. (1994), Granada award, Mancaster Academy N.S. (1995), Macfarlane award R.G.I. (1995), Llewellyn Alexander award N.E.A.C. (1995). *Clubs:* Leeds Fine Art. *Signs work:* "SELBY" or "WILLIAM SELBY." *Address:* 'Stonehaven', 11 Greenbank Rd., Brixham, S. Devon TQ5 9ND.

SELL, Richard, A.T.D. (1949); artist in lithography, water-colour, drawing; Vice Pres. Cambridge Drawing Soc.; *b* Berkhamsted, 26 Jan., 1922. *m* Jean Bryant. one *s*. one *d*. *Educ:* Berkhamsted School. *Studied:* Chelsea School of Art (Brian Robb, Morland Lewis, Harold Jones, Ceri Richards, Ella Griffin). *Exhib:* one-man shows: Old Fire Engine House Ely, Heffer Gallery Cambridge, Trumpington Gallery

Cambridge; R.A. Summer Shows, National Exhbn. Prints and Drawings R.I. Gallery (1964), E. Anglian Art Today R.I. Gallery (1969), Mall Prints (1971, 1972, 1973), Art in Business, Arthur Young, Cambridge (1987, 1988), Anglesey Abbey, Cambridge (July 2001). *Commissions:* portrait drawings for several Cambridge colleges; lithographs for Lloyd's Register of Shipping, Emmanuel College Cambridge, Pembroke College Cambridge, St. Catharine's College, Cambridge. *Signs work:* "Richard Sell 1998." *Address:* 22 Station Rd., Fulbourn, Cambridge CB1 5ES.

SELWAY, John Henry, artist in mixed media; lecturer; *b* Askern, Yorks., 11 July, 1938. *m* Margaret. one *s.* one *d. Studied:* Abertyleri Technical School, Newport School of Art, R.C.A. *Exhib:* one-man shows: Roland, Browse & Delbanco, Browse Darby, Christopher Hull, Jeffrie Museum. *Work in collections:* A.C.G.B., Welsh Arts Council, National Museum Wales, Leeds City A.G., Ferens Gallery Hull, Glynn Vivian, Johannesburg A.G., Nuffield Foundation, de Beers; private: U.S.A., G.B., U.S.S.R., Europe. *Address:* Park View, Roseheyworth Rd., Abertyleri, Blaenua, Gwent NP3 1SB.

SELWYN, William, R.C.A.; artist in water-colour, mixed media; *b* 4 Dec., 1933. *m* Mary Ann Jones. one *s.* one *d. Educ:* Bangor Normal College. *Work in collections:* National Library of Wales, Gwynedd C.C., Anglesey C.C., University of N. Wales, Bangor. Award: Welsh Artist of the Year (2001). *Address:* Bron Eryri, Aelygarth, Caernarfon, Gwynedd LL55 1HA.

SEMMENS, Jennifer Anne, B.A.(Hons.) (1986); painter in mixed media on paper and etcher; *b* Penzance, 12 Jan., 1964. *m* Roger Asbury. two *d. Educ:* in Penzance, Cornwall. *Studied:* Falmouth School of Art (1982-83), Gloucestershire College of Arts and Technology, Cheltenham (1983-86). *Exhib:* New Ashgate Gallery, Farnham; Coram Gallery, London; Marsden Contemporary Art, London; Gibbs Gallery, Canterbury; On Line Gallery, Southampton, 3D Gallery, Bristol, Candover Gallery, Alresford. *Publications:* 'Twenty-Two Painters (who happen to be women) St. Ives' by Marion Whybrow; 'Drawing Towards the End of the Century' by Newlyn Society of Artists. *Clubs:* Penwith Soc. of Artists. *Signs work:* "J. Semmens." *Address:* Higher Barn, Bone Farm, Bone Valley, Heamoor, Penzance, Cornwall TR20 8UJ.

SEMPLE, Patricia Frances, S.S.A. (1980), R.S.W. (1987); painter of expressionist landscape in water-colour, ink, oil, charcoal; tutor, Open College of the Arts; *b* Kintyre, Argyll, 3 July, 1939. *Educ:* Lasswade Grammar. *Studied:* Edinburgh College of Art (1958-63), post. grad. (1963-64). *Exhib:* Stirling Gallery, Art Space Aberdeen, Edinburgh University, Aberdeen University, Dundee College of Art, Open Eye Gallery Edinburgh, regularly with R.S.A., S.S.A., R.S.W.; group shows: Glasgow Group, Scottish Gallery, Compass Gallery, Arts Council Travelling Exhbn. Scotland and Yugoslavia. *Work in collections:* S.A.C., Aberdeen A.G., B.B.C., Globus, Gateway Inc. N.Y., Educ. Inst. of Scotland, Grampian TV, Aberdeen Hospitals, Shell U.K. *Signs work:* "Pat Semple." *Address:* Tigh-Nan-Uiseagan, By Drumnadrochit, Inverness-shire.

SENFT, Nadin, A.R.B.S. (1980), City and Guilds D.F.A. (1968); sculptor in bronze, stone, wood, perspex; *b* London, 8 Mar., 1932. *m* Dr. Paul Senft (decd.). *Educ:* St. Mary's Abbey, London; Eversley, Lymington, Hants. *Studied:* Leicester

College of Art; City and Guilds of London College of Art, Kennington. *Exhib:* R.A., Alwin Gallery, Royal Exchange, Jordan Gallery, Annely Juda Fine A.G., Hertford Museum, Sutton College of Art, Natalie Stern Gallery, Richard Demarco Gallery, Edinburgh, Scone Palace, Perth, Herbert Museum and A.G. Coventry, Aim Gallery, Milton Keynes. *Commissions:* 'St. George and the Dragon', St. George's Centre, Preston; 'Seated Bronze Figures' Guildhall Sq., Portsmouth; Royal Inst. of Chartered Surveyors Trophy (sculpture of Logo in perspex for annual presentation); The Fasson Trophy (6 aluminium sculptures); Bronze Crucifixion, St. Gregory's, Tredington; Madonna and Child, painted wood carving, St. George's, Brailes. *Publications:* Sixteen Stories as they Happend by Michael Bullock. Award: First Prize Winner W. Mid. Arts Open Exhibition (1999). *Signs work:* "Nadin Senft" and see appendix. *Address:* Willowbrook, Cotswold Cl., Tredington, Warwicks. CV36 4NR.

SENIOR, Bryan, painter of figures, landscape, still-life; *b* Bolton, 1935. *Exhib:* one-man shows include: Crane Kalman Gallery, London (1965, 1968, 1971), Demarco, Edinburgh (1970, 1973), Vaccarino, Florence (1968, 1970, 1975), Pucker-Safrai, Boston, U.S.A. (1968), Bolton A.G. (1961), Fieldborne Galleries, London (1972), Ashgate Gallery, Farnham (1973), Exeter Museum (1974), Exeter University (1975), Galleria Acropoli, Milan (1976), Lad Lane Gallery, Dublin (1977), Architectural Assoc., London (1982), Hampstead Museum (1983), Manor House, Finchley (1989), Tricycle Gallery (1990), Hooper Gallery, London (1991), Tunbridge Wells Museum (1998, 2000). Prizes include: G.L.C. 'Spirit of London'; Druce Competition. *Address:* 134 Upper Grosvenor Rd., Tunbridge Wells, Kent TN1 2EX.

SEROTA, Nicholas Andrew, Director, Tate (since 1988); *b* 27 Apr., 1946. *m* Angela Mary Beveridge (marr. diss. 1995); two *d. m* Teresa Gleadowe (1997). *Educ:* Haberdashers' Askes School, Hampstead and Elstree; Christ's College, Cambridge (B.A.). *Studied:* Courtauld Inst. of Art, London (M.A.). *Publications:* Experience or Interpretation: The Dilemma of Museums of Modern Art 1996 (Neurath Lecture, National Gallery, 1996). Hon. Fellow, Queen Mary and Westfield College; Univ. of London (1988), Hon. D. Arts, London Guildhall (1990), Hon. D. Litt. City University (1990), Hon. F.R.I.B.A. (1992), Hon. D.Litt. Plymouth University (1993), Hon. D.Litt. Keele University (1994), Hon. Fel. Goldsmiths (1994), Hon. D.Litt. South Bank University (1996), Sen. Fel. R.C.A. (1996), Hon. D.Univ., University of Surrey (Wimbledon School of Art, 1997), Hon. D. Litt. Exeter (2000), Hon. D. Litt. London Institute (2001). Regional Art Officer and Exhbn. Organiser, Arts Council of G.B. (1970-73); Director, Museum of Modern Art, Oxford (1973-76); Director, Whitechapel A.G. (1976-88). Mem., Fine Art Advisory Com., British Council (1976), Chairman 1992; Trustee, Public Art Development Trust (1983-87); Trustee, Architecture Foundation (1992-). Selector 'A New Spirit in Painting', R.A. (1981), Carnegie International, Carnegie Museum of Art, Pittsburgh (1985, 1988). *Address:* Tate, Millbank, London SW1P 4RG.

SETCH, Terry, D.F.A. (Lond., 1959); painter; *b* London, 11 Mar., 1936. *m* Dianne Shaw. one *d. Educ:* Sutton and Cheam School. *Studied:* Sutton School of Art (1950-54), Slade School of Fine Art (1956-60). *Work in collections:* Tate Gallery, Arts Council of G.B., Welsh Arts Council, Aberystwyth University, Contemporary Arts Soc. of Wales, V. & A., University College, London, Gallery of Modern Art,

Lodz, Poland, Swansea University, British Council, National Museum of Wales, Contemporary Arts Soc., Coleg Harlech, Wakefield City A.G., Glynn Vivian Museum and A.G., Northampton A.G., Rugby Borough Council, Leicestershire Educ. Authority, Cardiff C.C., Glamorgan Educ. Authority, Normal College Bangor. *Commissions:* National Museum and Galleries of Wales, painting for the restaurant, Cardiff. *Publications:* New Work by Terry Setch, pub. Welsh Arts Council, National Museum of Wales, Camden Arts Centre (1992); Terry Setch a Retrospective, pub. University of Wales Institute, Cardiff (2001). *Clubs:* Chelsea Arts, London; Cardiff Arts Club. *Signs work:* "Terry Setch." *Address:* 111 Plymouth Rd., Penarth, Vale of Glamorgan CF64 5DF, S. Wales.

SEWARD, P., A.R.C.A., Hon. Retd. A.R.E., R.W.S., Rome Scholar, Dip. in Paper Conservation; artist in pen and ink, water-colour, etching and lithography; *b* London, 1926. *Studied:* Royal College of Art, Camberwell School of Art and Crafts (Conservation of Prints and Drawings). *Exhib:* R.A., Bankside Gallery, Curwen Gallery, Barbican, London, Flitcroft Gallery, London. *Work in collections:* Mr. & Mrs. A. Walsh, Mrs. Finch-Knightley, Mrs. Ivan Fox and Bankside Gallery. *Publications:* children's books, cookery books. *Signs work:* "P. Seward" or "Prue Seward." *Address:* 30 Sekforde St., London EC1R 0HH.

SEWELL, Peggy Joan Kearton, M.F.P.S. (1986); painter of landscapes and flowers in oil on canvas; Freeman of the Worshipful Company of Painter-Stainers, London; *b* London, 18 Dec., 1920. *m* Robert H. Sewell, Ch.M., F.R.C.S. two *d. Educ:* Manchester High School, and Merchant Venturers College, Bristol. *Studied:* Croydon Art College and privately with Richard Walker, N.D.D., A.T.D. *Exhib:* Guildhall London, Royal Exchange, Fairfield Halls Croydon, Loggia Gallery, London and Painters Hall, London. *Work in collections:* in the U.K., Ireland, Spain and France. *Clubs:* Croydon Art Soc., Purley Art Group, F.P.S., Tandridge Art Soc. *Signs work:* "Joan Sewell." *Address:* 4 Bayards, Warlingham, Surrey CR6 9BP.

SEYMOUR, Jack, N.D.D. (1954), Ad.Cert.Ed. (1962); painter of landscapes, interiors and portraits in oil, pencil and water-colour; *b* London, 23 Apr., 1928. one *s.* two *d. Educ:* Southall Technical School. *Studied:* Harrow School of Art (1948-52, C. Sanders, T. Ward), Gloucester College of Art (1952-54, R.S.G. Dent), St. Paul's College, Cheltenham (1960-62, H.W. Sayer). *Exhib:* R.B.A., R.P., R.A., R.W.A.; one-man show, Stroud, Gloucs.; provincial galleries, travelling exhbns. and abroad. *Work in collections:* Britain and abroad. *Signs work:* "SEYMOUR" and year. *Address:* 3 Holeground, School Hill, Wookey Hole, Som. BA5 1BU.

SHACKLETON, Keith Hope, R.S.M.A., S.WL.A., Hon.Doctor of Laws; oil painter, writer, naturalist, T.V.; *b* Weybridge, 16 Jan., 1923. *m* Jacqueline. two *s.* one *d. Educ:* Melbourne, Australia, Oundle. *Work in collections:* R.S.M.A. Maritime Museum, Greenwich, Birkenhead, Belfast A.G., LYW Art Museum Wisconsin, U.S.A. *Publications:* Wake, Tidelines, Wild Animals in Britain, Ship in the Wilderness, Wildlife and Wilderness, Keith Shackleton: An Autobiography in Paintings. *Clubs:* Itchenor Sailing. *Signs work:* see appendix. *Address:* Woodley Wood Farm, Woodleigh, Kingsbridge, Devon TQ7 4DR.

SHANKS, Duncan Faichney, D.A., A.R.S.A. (1972), R.G.I. (1983), R.S.W. (1987), R.S.A. (1990); artist in oil; *b* Airdrie, 30 Aug., 1937. *m* Una Brown Gordon.

Studied: Glasgow School of Art. *Exhib:* Art Spectrum, Contemporary Art from Scotland (1981-82), Five Glasgow Painters, Scottish Painting - Toulouse, About Landscape - Edinburgh Festival, Scottish Painting - Rio de Janeiro, Ten Scottish Painters - London, Scottish Painting - Wales, Bath, Basle, London Art Fairs; one-man shows: Stirling University, Scottish Gallery, Fine Art Soc. - Glasgow and Edinburgh, Talbot Rice Gallery, Edinburgh (cat.), Crawford Centre, St. Andrews, Maclaurin Gallery, Ayr, Glasgow A.G. (1990), Touring Exhbn. Wales (1991-92) (Cat.), Billcliffe Fine Art (1992). *Work in collections:* A.C.G.B., Scottish Art Council, Glasgow, Dundee and Swansea A.Gs., Hunterian Museum, Edinburgh University, City Art Centre, Edinburgh, Lillie A.G., Government Art Collection, Scottish TV., 'Talking Pictures', STV film. Provost's prize for contemporary art (G.O.M.A.) 1996. *Signs work:* "SHANKS." *Address:* Davingill House, Crossford By Carluke, Clyde Valley ML8 5RA.

SHANKS, Una Brown, D.A. (Textiles) (1962), R.S.W. (1988); artist in water-colour, pen and ink; *b* Hartwood, 9 June, 1940. *m* D.F. Shanks. *Educ:* Wishaw High School. *Studied:* Glasgow School of Art (1958-62). *Exhib:* Scottish Artists Shop (1987), Fine Art Soc. (1988, 1989, 1993). Awards: Alexander Stone R.G.I. (1990, 1991), Betty Davies R.S.W. (1993). *Signs work:* "Una B. Shanks." *Address:* Davingill House, Crossford By Carluke, Clyde Valley ML8 5RA.

SHARP, Elizabeth, S.Eq.A. (1988), A.S.E.A. (1984), S.W.A. (1986), B.H.S.A.I. (1969); artist in oil and acrylic, China and silk painting, also sculptor specializing in golfing, animal and equestrian subjects, presentation items and trophies, in hand painted porcelain; *b* 7 Jan., 1947. *Educ:* Kesteven and Grantham Girls' High School. *Studied:* Leicester College of Art and Design (1965-66), Stoke Rochford College (1966-70). *Exhib:* regularly with S.E.A. and S.W.A. in London; occasionally one-man shows, Napier Gallery, St. Helier, Jersey. *Work in collections:* sculpture in Victoria Centre, Sydney, Australia; Flying Horse Centre, Nottingham; Reindeer Court, Worcester. *Commissions:* Lords Cricket Club, Hunt committees, societies, corporations. *Publications:* work repro.: numerous prints and cards. Breeds American Morgan horses, avid golfer. *Clubs:* B.C.P.A.A., British Horse Soc. *Signs work:* "Elizabeth Sharp." *Address:* Stanton Court, Denton, Grantham, Lincs. NG32 1JT.

SHAVE, Terry, B.A.(Hons.), H.D.F.A. (Slade); artist in oil, acrylic on canvas, etching; lecturer; Head of Painting, Staffordshire Polytechnic; Professor of Fine Art (1998); *b* 8 June, 1952. *m* Helena. three *s.* one *d. Studied:* Loughborough College of Art (1972-75), Slade School of Fine Art (1975-77). *Exhib:* Anderson O'Day Gallery, John Moores Liverpool Exhbn. (Prizewinner), Ikon Gallery Birmingham, City Gallery Stoke. *Work in collections:* A.C.G.B., Unilever, B'ham City Museum and A.G., Stoke Museum and A.G. *Signs work:* "Terry Shave." *Address:* 19 Park Ave., Wolstanton, Staffs. ST5 8AY.

SHAW, Barbara Nancy, R.H.S. Gold medallist (1980), Grenfell medals (1976, 1977); botanical artist in water-colour; *b* Dartmouth, Devon, 28 Sept., 1922. *m* Denis Latimer, surgeon. three *s.* one *d. Educ:* Fairview College and Hampton Court School. *Studied:* Dartington (for a time). *Exhib:* Chagford Galleries (1977), Thompson Gallery, Aldborough and London, etc. *Work in collections:* U.K., U.S.A., Germany, Japan. *Commissions:* several national collections and others. *Publications:* author and illustrator: The Book of Primroses (David & Charles 1991), illustrations in The Plantsman, illustrator: Foliage and Form by Phillipa Rakusen, and others. *Clubs:* S.B.A., S.M. *Signs work:* see appendix. *Address:* Tan Cottage, West Lane, Cononley, nr. Skipton, N. Yorks. BD20 8NL.

SHAW, Sax Roland, D.A. (Edin.), F.M.G.P.; former Head of Stained Glass Dept., Edinburgh College of Art (retd. 1984); works in tapestry, stained glass, mural decoration, water-colour paintings; *b* Huddersfield, 5 Dec., 1916. *m* Mary. two *s. Educ:* Almondbury Grammar School. *Studied:* Huddersfield, Edinburgh, Paris. *Work in collections:* private and public buildings in Edinburgh, London, New York, San Francisco, Iceland. At present working on windows and tapestries for the Marquis of Bute. *Signs work:* "Shaw." *Address:* 25 Howe St., Edinburgh EH3 6TF.

SHEARD (née MOIR), Rosalind Elizabeth Allaway, H.S., S.Lm., A.U.A.; artist in oil and water-colour; *b* Penzance, 9 Sept., 1940. *m* Michael. two *s.* one *d. Educ:* Chiswick County Grammar School. *Studied:* Webber Douglas Academy of Dramatic Art. *Exhib:* R.A., Medici Gallery, Llewellyn Alexander Gallery; 'Discerning Eye' Mall Galleries; R.M.S., H.S., S.W.A., U.A., S.Lm., Chichester, Tunbridge Wells, Leeds, Aberdeen, London, Inside Art Gallery, Ryde, Kendalls Fine Arts, Cowes, Alchemist Gallery, Yarmouth. *Clubs:* I.O.W. Art, A.P.K. Group. *Signs work:* Work numbered on the back commencing "R.S.", miniatures: "ROS SHEARD." *Address:* c/o 9 Westfield Park, Ryde, I.O.W. PO33 3AB. *Website:* www.londonart.co.uk *Email:* ros@seachest.freeserve.co.uk

SHEATH, Janet, R.M.S. (1998), S.W.A. (1995), H.S. (1992); self taught artist in miniatures, water-colour, dry mediums and egg tempera; *b* Portsmouth, 1952. *m* Robert J.C. Sheath. two *d. Educ:* Cowplain Secondary Modern School for Girls. *Exhib:* R.A., R.M.S., S.W.A., S.B.A., H.S., Llewellyn Alexander, Medici. *Signs work:* "Janet Sheath" or "J. SHEATH." *Address:* 4 Cupressus Ave., Winford, Sandown, I.O.W. PO36 0LA.

SHELBOURNE, Anita, painter in oil, water-colour, acrylic, mixed media; Art Flight, Irish Arts Council Aer Lingus Travel Award, De Veres Award for a Work of Distinction, R.H.A., Oireachtas, Landscape Award; *b* 17 Jul., 1948. *Educ:* Holy Faith Convent, Dublin. *Studied:* Trinity College, Dublin. *Exhib:* 12 solo exhibs. and group exhibs. at R.H.A., Oireachtas, Taylor Galleries, Boyle Festival, Wexford Festival. *Work in collections:* Irish Arts Council, Irish Embassies, Greece and Japan, Bank of Ireland, Ulster Bank, Trinity College, Dublin, Jefferson Smurfit Group, University College, Dublin, Embassy of The Republic of Korea, Haverty Trust, and collections in Milan, Rome, Sardinia. *Publications:* Irish Woman Artists, Dorothy Walker (1987), The Female Vision, Brian Fallon (1990), Irish Arts Review Year Book (1998). *Clubs:* United Arts Club. *Signs work:* "ANITA SHELBOURNE." *Address:* 76 Willowfield, Park Ave., Sandymount, Dublin 4, Ireland.

SHEPHARD, Rupert, Hon. A. L'Accademia Fiorentina; R.P., N.E.A.C.; painter, graphic artist; Slade Dipl.; lecturer, Central School, St. Martin's School of Art (1945-48); Professor of Art, University of Cape Town (1948-63); *b* 12 Feb., 1909. *m* 1st, Lorna Wilmott (decd., 1962). one *s.* two *d.* 2nd, Nicolette Devas (1965). *Exhib:* one-man: Calmann Gall. (1939), Agnews (1962, 1980), Upper Grosvenor Gall. (1966, 1970), Kunsthalle, Bielefeld, Germany (1973), Collectors Gall., Johannesburg

(1975), Patrick Seale Gall. (1975, 1979), Sally Hunter Gall. (1985, 1987, 1989, 1991), National Museum of Wales, Parkin Gallery (1977), Cape Town (seven) and Johannesburg (three) (1949-63); general: London: R.A., R.P., etc.; Venice Biennale (1958), São Paulo Bienal (1957), Ljubljana Biennale (1955, 1957, 1959, 1961). *Work in collections:* C.E.M.A. British Museum, War Artists, National Portrait Gall., National Museum of Wales, South African National Gall., Johannesburg Municipal Gall. *Publications:* illustrated: Capescapes (1954), Passing Scene (1966). *Address:* 68 Limerston St., London SW10 0HJ.

SHEPHEARD, Sir Peter (Faulkner), Kt. (1980), C.B.E. (1972), B.Arch., Liverpool (1936), P.P.R.I.B.A., M.R.T.P.I., P.P.I.L.A.; architect, town planner, landscape architect, draughtsman and illustrator. In private practice (Shepheard, Epstein & Hunter) (1948-1989); Prof. of Environmental Design (and Dean 1971-76) of the Graduate School of Fine Arts, University of Pennsylvania, Philadelphia (1959); mem. National Parks Commission (1966-68), Countryside Commission (1968-71), Royal Fine Art Commission (1968-71), Artistic advisor, Commonwealth War Graves Commision (1977-), Master, Artworkers Guild (1984); *b* Birkenhead, 1913. *m* Mary Bailey. one *s.* one *d. Educ:* Birkenhead School. *Studied:* Liverpool School of Architecture and Dept. of Civic Design. *Exhib:* R.A., etc. *Publications:* Modern Gardens (Arch. Press, 1953), Gardens (C.O.I.D., 1969); illustr.: A Book of Ducks and Woodland Birds. *Signs work:* "Peter Shepheard." *Address:* 21 Well Rd., London NW3 1LH.

SHEPHERD, David, O.B.E. (1979), F.R.S.A. (1986), F.R.G.S. (1988); artist; *b* 25 Apr., 1931. *m* Avril Gaywood. four *d. Educ:* Stowe. *Studied:* under Robin Goodwin (1950-1953); started career as aviation artist, founder member of Guild of Aviation Artists; many worldwide trips for aviation and military paintings for Services; began specializing in African wildlife subjects (1960). *Exhib:* R.A., R.P.; one man exhbns. London (1962, 1965, 1971, 1978, 1999), Johannesburg (1966, 1969), New York (1967). *Work in collections:* 15ft reredos of Christ for Army Garrison Church, Bordon, Hants (1964). Portraits: H.E. Dr Kenneth Kaunda, President of Zambia (1967), H.M. The Queen Mother (1969), H.E. Sheikh Zaid of Abu Dhabi (1970). *Publications:* Artist in Africa (1967), The Man who Loves Giants (1975), Paintings of Africa and India (1978), A Brush with Steam (1983), David Shepherd: The Man and his Paintings (1985), An Artist in Conservation (1992), David Shepherd, My Painting Life (1995). In 1984 David founded The David Shepherd Conservation Foundation, a registered charity, to raise funds and awareness for endangered animals. Awards: Order of Golden Ark by H.R.H. Prince Bernhard of The Netherlands (1973), Hon.D.F.A.Pratt Inst. N.Y. (1971), Hon. Doctor of Science, Hatfield Polytechnic (1990), Member of Honour, World Wildlife Fund (1979), Order of British Empire (1979), Officer (Brother) of the Order of St. John (1996). Life story subject of BBC TV documentary "The Man Who Loves Giants" (1971), Harlech TV documentary, "Elephants and Engines", etc. Auctioned five wildlife paintings in U.S.A. in 1971 and raised funds for Bell Jet Ranger Helicopter for anti-poaching work in Zambia, in return President Kaunda presented an 1896 steam locomotive, its return to Britain subject of BBC TV documentary "Last Train to Mulobezi" (1974); painted "Tiger Fire" 1973, raised £127,500 for Operation Tiger (1973). Purchased two mainline steam locomotives 92203 Black Prince, and 75029

The Green Knight (1967) and founded The East Somerset Steam Railway, Cranmore, Somerset, a registered charity and fully operational steam railway. Videos: The Man who Loves Giants: The Most Dangerous Animal; Behind the Scenes, In Search of Wildlife I and II. Ambition: to drive Black Prince into Waterloo Station. Recreations: driving steam locomotives and raising money for wildlife. *Address:* Brooklands Farm, Hammerwood, East Grinstead, West Sussex RH19 3QA.

SHEPHERD, Gerald, F.F.P.S. (1990); painter and graphic artist in oil, acrylic, ink and pencils; currently co-ordinating the 'Artists for Animals' project; Director, Ionist Art Group; *b* 1955. *m* June Taylor. one s-d. *Exhib:* solo and group exhbns. in London and south of England, including Loggia Gallery, London. *Work in collections:* Surrey University, Stevenage Art and Leisure Centre; private collections. *Publications:* edited, Ion Exchange Magazine. *Clubs:* Founded: Ionist Art Group, Process Art, Artists for Animals; F.P.S., Marlborough Artists, Andover Art Soc., Wallop Artists. Organizes "Modern Wiltshire Artists" Exhbns. *Signs work:* usually "G.S." occasionally "GERALD SHEPHERD"; signature often incorporated into composition. *Address:* 56 Mylen Rd., Andover, Hants. SP10 3HG. *Website:* www.ionistart.com *Email:* geraldshepherd@ionistart.com

SHEPHERD, Philip, R.W.S. (1977); Gold medal Paris Salon (1976); artist in water-colour, oil, wood engraving; *b* London, 4 May, 1927. two *d*. *Studied:* Harrow College of Arts and Crafts (1941-45), Birmingham College of Arts and Crafts (1948-50). *Exhib:* R.W.S. *Work in collections:* Fitzwilliam Museum Cambridge, Whitworth A.G. Manchester (wood engravings). *Signs work:* "Philip Shepherd, R.W.S." *Address:* 52 Aston Cantlow Rd., Wilmcote, Stratford-upon-Avon, Warwickshire CV37 9XZ.

SHEPHERD, Valerie Mary, S.W.A. (1987), Cert.A.D.; graphic artist, sculptor and printmaker, paints in water-colour, oil and mixed media; *b* Orpington, Kent, 5 Feb., 1941. *m* Norman Shepherd, dental surgeon. one *s*. two *d*. *Educ:* St. Philomena's Convent. *Studied:* Gyula Sajo Atelier; Brighton Polytechnic. *Clubs:* S.W.A., W. Sussex Art, Arun Art Soc., Assoc. of Sussex Artists. *Signs work:* "Valerie Shepherd." *Address:* Bacon Hall, Poling, nr. Arundel, Sussex BN18 9PU.

SHEPPARD, Liz, Intermediate in Arts Crafts (1953), N.D.D. Painting (1955), A.T.D. (Lond. 1956), Scholarship Pratt bequest (1956, to Italy); painter, printmaker in etching; *b* Tonbridge, 20 Dec., 1933. *m* Clive Sheppard, sculptor (decd.). two *s*. one *d*. *Educ:* St. Albans Girls Grammar School. *Studied:* St. Albans School of Art (1950-52), St. Martin's College of Art (1952-55), London University Institute (1955-56). *Exhib:* Digswell House, Bear Lane Gallery, Oxford, City Gallery, Milton Keynes, R.A. Summer Exhbn. (1977, 1978), Cartoon (1978), Wavendon Festival (1979), Margaret Fischer (1980), Bedford School (1990), Leighton Buzzard Arts Centre (1990), Milton Keynes Exhbn. Gallery (1991), Bromham Mill Gallery, Bedford (1992), Art in Milton Keynes (1993), New Studio Gallery Olney (2001). *Work in collections:* H.R.H. The Princess Margaret; John Dankworth and Cleo Laine; The Open University; Milton Keynes Development Corp.; M.K. Hospital; Anglian Water, Huntingdon; Bedford Art Loan Collection; Bedfordshire Library; Leicester Royal Infirmary; Ernst and Young, etc. *Publications:* writes for Printmaking Today since 1994. Millenium Artist in Residence, Woburn Schools Cluster (2001). *Clubs:* Friends of Royal Academy. *Signs work:* "Liz Sheppard."

Address: 6 Leighton St., Woburn, Milton Keynes MK17 9PJ.

SHEPPARD, Maurice, P.P.R.W.S., M.A. (R.C.A.), Dip.A.D.; professional painter in oil and water-colour; *b* Llangwm, Pembrokeshire, 25 Feb., 1947. *Educ:* Haverfordwest Grammar School. *Studied:* Loughborough College of Art; Kingston College of Art under Alfred Heyworth; R.C.A. under Hamilton-Fraser, Buhler, Spear, Weight. *Exhib:* London and abroad. *Work in collections:* V. & A., National Museum of Wales, Cardiff, B'ham Museum and A.G., B.M. *Publications:* Old Water-colour Soc. Club Annual Vol. 59. *Signs work:* "Maurice Sheppard." *Address:* 33 St. Martin's Pk., Crow Hill, Haverfordwest, Pembrokeshire SA61 2HP, Wales. *Second Address:* 14 Apsley St., Rusthall Common, Tunbridge Wells, Kent TN4 8NU.

SHEPPERSON, Patricia Ann, artist in pastel and oils, wildlife, still life and landscape; *b* London, 1929. *m* Desmond Vereker. one *s.* one *d. Educ:* Holy Trinity Convent, Bromley. *Studied:* Heatherley School of Art (1959-62, Patrick Larking, R.O.I.), Sir John Cass School of Art (1963-67), studied drama at Guildhall School of Music and Drama (1946-49). *Exhib:* one-man shows, London and The Hague, mixed exhbns., R.A., Mall Galleries. *Work in collections:* U.K. and abroad. *Signs work:* "Patricia Shepperson." *Address:* 2 Grange Rd., Norwich, Norfolk NR2 3NH.

SHERLOCK, Siriol Ann, B.A.Hons. (1977), S.B.A. (1988); R.H.S. Gold Medal (1993, 1994, 1995, 1999); textile designer, water-colour painter, botanical artist; *b* Nantwich, 28 Aug., 1954. *m* Stephen Paul Sherlock. two *d. Educ:* Fernhill Manor School; Brockenhurst College. *Studied:* Winchester School of Art (1973-77). *Exhib:* many galleries in south of England, The Hillier Gdns. and Arboretum (1990, 1993, 1996), Kew Gdns. Gallery (1992), Sweden (1998), Jersey (1999). *Work in collections:* The Hunt Inst., Pittsburgh, U.S.A., The Hillier Gdns. and Arboretum, Romsey, The Royal Horticultural Soc, The Shirley Sherwood Collection. *Commissions:* R.H.S. 'Chelsea Flower Show Plate' (1999). *Publications:* work repro.: in The Kew Magazine, The New Plantsman, Contemporary Botanical Artists; Exploring Flowers in Water-colour by Siriol Sherlock (B.T. Batsford, 1998). *Clubs:* S.B.A., President, Society of Floral Painters. *Signs work:* "Siriol Sherlock." *Address:* Elizabethan Cottage, Michelmersh, nr. Romsey, Hants. SO51 0NW.

SHETLAND, Ilric, Hornsey Dip.; painter; *b* London, 24 Oct., 1946. *Educ:* Forest Hill Comprehensive School. *Studied:* Hornsey College of Art (1966-69), Goldsmiths' College of Art. *Exhib:* International Cultural Centre, Antwerp, Gamstyl, Brussels, Basle, Serpentine Gallery, London, Treadwell Gallery, London, Patrick Seale Gallery, London, Angela Flowers. *Publications:* The Male Nude. *Clubs:* Space Studios. *Signs work:* "Ilric Shetland." *Address:* 76a Lauriston Rd., London E9 7HA.

SHIELDS, Christopher Ronald, Dip.A.D. (1973); artist in water-colour, gouache and acrylic; *b* Sale, Ches., 7 June, 1954. divorced. one *d. Educ:* Sale Moor Secondary School. *Studied:* Northwich College of Art and Design (1970-73). *Exhib:* Warrington Museum and A.G. (1983, 1986, 1989, 1992), Wildfowl Trust Martin Mere (1985), Towneley Hall A.G. and Museum, Burnley (1988), Stockport A.G. (1991), plus several other one-man shows in private art galleries throughout Gt. Britain. *Work in collections:* Trafford Borough Council's Art Archives, City of Wakefield Educ. Resource Service Collection. *Publications:* published in Gt. Britain, Europe, N. America and Japan. Illustrated over 100 books including Collins Guide -

Seashore of Britain and Europe, Collins New Generation Guide - Wild Flowers, Collins Gem Guide - Pond Life, Tracks and Signs of the Birds of Britain and Europe (A & C Black Publishing); plus commissions for B.B.C. publications, the R.S.P.B. and the Worldwide Fund for Nature. *Signs work:* "Chris Shields" - always includes moth or butterfly in every work. *Address:* 2 Bramble Walk, Sale, Ches. M33 5LL.

SHIELDS, Mark, B.A. (1985), P.G.C.E. (1989), A.R.U.A.; painter, mostly in acrylic; *b* Co. Down, N. Ireland, 22 Feb., 1963. *Educ:* Regent House School, Newtownards, Co. Down. *Studied:* University of Ulster (1981-1985 & 1988-1989). *Exhib:* R.A., R.I., R.O.I., N.P.G., Florence Biennale, 3 solo exhibs., Grosvenor Gallery, London. *Work in collections:* National Gallery of Ireland, Ulster Museum. *Publications:* 'Inhabitants of the Dream Courtyard' and exhib. catalogues, Grosvenor Gallery. *Signs work:* "MS" monogram. *Address:* c/o Grosvenor Gallery 18 Albemarle St., London W1.

SHIPSIDES, Frank, M.A.; painter in oil and water-colour, specialising in marine painting; President, Bristol Savages (1974-75); *b* Mansfield, Notts., 1908. *m* Phyllis. one *s.* one *d. Educ:* King Edward School, Mansfield. *Studied:* Mansfield College of Art (1923) under Buxton; Nottingham College of Art (1925) under Else. *Exhib:* Alexander Gallery, Bristol 8. *Work in collections:* Bristol Maritime Heritage Centre "Visit of H.M. The Queen", Bristol Council House, H.M.S. Bristol paintings 1653-1983. *Publications:* Frank Shipsides Bristol; Somerset Harbours; Bristol Impressions; Original Graphic - Days of Steam & Sail; Bristol: Portrait of a City; Bristol: Maritime City. *Clubs:* Bristol Savages (Pres. 1983-84). *Signs work:* see appendix. *Address:* 5 Florence Pk., Bristol BS6 7LS.

SHIRAISHI, Barry Toshio, teacher (painting and sculpture);Vice Pres. Royal Soc. of Miniature Painters, Sculptors and Gravers; *b* Woolwich, London, 5 May, 1938. *m* Colleen Powell. two *s.* three *d. Studied:* Woolwich Polytechnic School of Arts (1950-54, Heber Matthews). *Exhib:* Geneva, Frankfurt, Paris and London. *Work in collections:* Franklin Mint Museum, Philadelphia. *Commissions:* Channel Tunnel Products and Franklin Mint. *Address:* 34 Paget Rise, Plumstead, London SE18 3QQ.

SHIRLEY, Rachel, B.A.Hons. (1986); animal, landscape and figures in oil; Daler Rowney art prizewinner (Spring 1995 and Autumn 1998), winner of Best Professional Abstract Painting in the S.A.A. Competition (2001); *b* Nuneaton, 26 May, 1965. *Studied:* N. Warwickshire College of Art, Nuneaton (1981-83), Kingston Polytechnic School of Fine Art (1983-86). *Exhib:* one-man shows: Museum and A.G., Nuneaton (1987), Hinckley Municipal A.G., Leics. (1988), Whitmoors Fine A.G., Leics. (1989); group shows: Hurlingham Gallery, London, Warwick University, Twycross Zoo Gallery, Leics. *Work in collections:* Midland private collections. *Publications:* work repro.: Rosenstiels Fine Art Ltd., The Guild of Master Craftsmen Publications Ltd. *Signs work:* "Rachel Shirley." *Address:* 65 Gipsy Lane, Whitestone, Nuneaton, Warwickshire CV11 4SH.

SHIRLEY, Sidney Raymond, Médaille d'Argent (Paris Salon, 1981); still life artist in oil; *b* Coventry, 27 Nov., 1930. *m* Sylvia Denise Elizabeth. six *d. Studied:* privately. *Exhib:* one-man shows, Museum and A.G., Nuneaton (1968, 1974, 1982, 1993); group shows, R.A., N.E.A.C., R.B.A., R.O.I., R.B.S.A., New King's Rd., and 20th Century Galleries, London. *Work in collections:* Australia, N.Z., France,

Austria, U.K. *Publications:* work repro.: R.A. Illustrated, La Revue Moderne, Le Monde, etc. Work reviewed BBC-CWR (1993). *Clubs:* Membre Associé, Société des Artistes Français, Founder mem, Bedworth Civic and Arts Soc. (1969). *Signs work:* "R. SHIRLEY" or "R.S". *Address:* 65 Gipsy Lane, Whitestone, Nuneaton, Warwickshire CV11 4SH.

SHIRREFF, Jack Robert, N.D.D., A.T.D., A.R.E.; artist in intaglio; Director of 107 Workshop; *b* Sri Lanka, 11 July, 1943. *m* Patricia. *Educ:* Sutton Valence. *Studied:* Brighton Polytechnic. Lecturer, Bath Academy of Art (1965-85). Currently engaged in producing and publishing work by Howard Hodgkin, Joe Tilson, Jim Dine, Oleg Kudryashov, David Inshaw, Gillian Ayres. *Publications:* S.W. Hayter: Eluard; S.W. Hayter: Death of Hektor; produced The Way We Live Now: Hodgkin/Sonntag. *Signs work:* "J. Shirreff." *Address:* 107 Workshop, The Courtyard, Bath Rd., Shaw, nr. Melksham, Wilts. SN12 8EF.

SHOA, Nahem, B.A.(Hons); artist in oil; *b* 4 Oct., 1968. *Educ:* Holland Park Comprehensive. *Studied:* London College of Printing (1987-88), Manchester School of Art (1988-91). *Exhib:* R.A. Summer Show (1992, 1993), Discerning Eye Mall Galleries (1992), winner Carol Foundation award R.P., Mall Galleries (1992), B.P. National Portrait award N.P.G. (1993), Elizabeth Greenshield award (1994), The Sacred Body, James Colman Fine Art (1996), Modern British Art Show, R.C.A. (1996, 1997), Art 98-99 Business Design Centre (1997-98). *Commissions:* Peter Mandelson, M.P., Dr. Mary Cowling, Lady Kate Douglas, Lord Queensbury. *Publications:* The Amazing Aventures of Nahem Shoa, Montpelier Sandleson (1999). *Signs work:* "N. Shoa." *Address:* 69 Princes Sq., London W2 4NY.

SHORE, Jack, A.T.D. (1943); artist in collage, acrylics and drawing in various media; President, Royal Cambrian Academy of Art (1976-82); *b* Ramsbottom, Lancs., 17 July, 1922. *m* Olive Brenda Shore. one *s.* one *d. Educ:* Haslingden Grammar School. *Studied:* Accrington and Manchester Schools of Art (1938-43, S. V. Lindoe, John M. Holmes). *Exhib:* R.Cam.A.; one-man shows, Theatre Clwyd, N. Wales (1979), R.Cam.A., Conwy (1980), Oriel Gallery, Bangor (1984). *Work in collections:* Bury A.G., and University College, N. Wales; private collections U.S.A., G.B. *Signs work:* "J. Shore." or "J.S." *Address:* 11 St. George's Cres., Queen's Pk., Chester CH4 7AR.

SHORES, Margot, painter in oil and acrylic; lecturer in painting, University of Newcastle upon Tyne (1985-90); visiting lecturer, R.A. Schools (1987-88); *b* 1961. *Exhib:* 'Young Masters' Solomon Gallery (1985), R.A. Summer Show (1986-87), Cleveland Drawing Biennale (1989). *Signs work:* "Margot Shores." *Address:* 70 On the Hill, Old Whittington, Chesterfield, Derbyshire S41 9HA.

SHORTHOUSE, G. Sydney, R.M.S., M.A.A., M.A.S.-F., H.S., F.I.D. (1969-83); retd. Company Director; artist in water-colour, mainly miniature portraiture; Display and Advertising Manager, Leicester Corp., Area Design Manager, E. Midlands Gas Board, Design Director, City Design and City Leather Companies; *b* Whitwick, Leics., 1925. married. one *s.* one *d. Educ:* Hugglescote School. *Exhib:* R.M.S., Hilliard Soc., Florida and Washington D.C. *Commissions:* The Garter Principal King of Arms, Lady Hilda Swan, The Governor of Anguilla, The Lord Provost of Perth, Scotland, The Pro-Chancellor of Edith Cowan University, W. Australia, Anastasia,

Baroness Peter Hatvany. *Publications:* R.M.S. - One Hundred Years; The Techniques of Painting Miniatures; The Magic of Miniatures. Awards: Hon. men. (1988, 1989, 1991, 1994, 1995, 1996) R.M.S. Gold Bowl award; 1st International Portrait award Washington D.C. (1989); 2nd International Portrait award Florida (1990); Best In Exhbn. (1987), Bell award (1989) Hilliard Soc.; Suzanne Lucas award (1985); Mundy Sovereign Awards R.M.S. (1991); Excellence in all Entries award and 1st International Portrait award Florida (1995). *Signs work:* see appendix. *Address:* The Barn, Main St., Wilson, Derbyshire DE73 1AD.

SHRAGER, Ann Jessica, N.E.A.C. (1975); artist in oil and water-colour; *b* London, 9 Jan., 1948. *m* Martin Anderson. two *s. Studied:* Byam Shaw (1967-70, Maurice De Saumarez), R.A. (1970-73, Peter Greenham). *Exhib:* mixed: R.A., N.E.A.C., New Grafton, Erica Bourne, British Art at Auction, Bilan de L'Art Contemporian, Paris; one-man: Michael Parkin (1976, 1978, 1979, 1996), Olympia, James Huntington-Whiteley; two-man show: New Grafton Gallery (April 2002). *Publications:* book cover design for Remember Your Gramer! (Winged Lion Publishers). *Signs work:* "A.J.S." *Address:* 3 Maids of Honour Row, The Green, Richmond, Surrey TW9 1NY.

SHUKMAN, Barbara Benita, Jacox Students Painting Prize, Edmonton, Canada (1968), John Radcliffe Purchase Prize, Oxford (1983); painter in acrylic on paper and canvas, and inks on silk, and printmaker, etchings, etc.; *b* London, 25 Nov., 1934. *m* (1) Harold Jacobs. one *s.* two *d.* (2) Harold Shukman. *Educ:* U.S.A. primary schools; Queen's College, London. *Studied:* University Saskatchewan, Regina, Canada (1963-65), University Alberta, Edmonton, Canada (1966-70). *Exhib:* group shows: Canada, U.K., Spain; solo shows: U.K., U.S.A. *Work in collections:* U.S.A.: Solomon Guggenheim Museum, N.Y.; Georgia Museum of Art; New Orleans Museum. Turkey: Sheraton Voyager, Antalya. Barbados: Sandy Lane Hotel. U.K.: Sedgwick Group; British and Commonwealth; Sarm Film Studios; Bain and Co.; Jardine and Co.; Strutt and Parker; Chartwell Land: Christiana Bank; Booz Allen, (all London). John Radcliffe Hospital Oxford. *Signs work:* "Barbara Shukman." *Address:* 11 Cunliffe Cl., Oxford OX2 7BJ.

SHURROCK, Christopher, A.T.D.; painting, sculpture, print; *b* Bristol, 1939. *Studied:* painting: West of England College of Art, Postgraduate Cardiff, A.T.D.(Dist.). Art Advisor, University Settlement, Bristol, Cardiff College of Art, Foundation Dept. 1962-91 (Senior Lecturer/Director). Consultant Art and Design. *Work in collections:* National Gallery of Slovakia, Bratislava, National Museum/Gallery of Wales, University of Wales, A.C.W., C.A.S.W., John Caroll University, Ohio, etc. *Publications:* Studio International (June, 1966) D'Ars Agency N36-37 (1967), Art and Artists (Jan. 1969), Art in Britain, 1969-70 (Dent), Studio International 991/2 (1981), Art in Wales 1850-1980. *Address:* 9 Min-y-Nant, Rhiwbina, Cardiff CF14 6JR.

SIDERY, Vera Ethel, painter in pastel and oil; *b* 3 Aug., 1916. *m* Albert Sidery (decd.). two *s.* two *d. Educ:* Tottenham High School. *Studied:* with Leonard and Margaret Boden. *Exhib:* P.S., Mall Galleries, London; one-man show, Broomfield Museum, Southgate. *Clubs:* P.S., Enfield Art Soc. *Signs work:* "V.E. Sidery." *Address:* 8 Roedean Cl., Enfield EN3 5QR.

SIDOLI, Dawn Frances, R.W.A. (1987), N.E.A.C. (1990), Teacher's Cert. (1956); painter, printer; *b* Gosport, Hants., 24 Nov., 1933. *m* Frank Sidoli. two *s.* one *d. Educ:* Wigton High School, Cumbria; Notre Dame Convent, Northampton. *Studied:* Northampton Art School (1949-52). *Exhib:* R.A. from 1977, R.W.A., N.E.A.C., Cardiff, etc. Finalist, Laing '85, '86, Hunting Group '86, '87, '89, Inveresk, Singer and Friedlander w/col. Comp., Laing National First Prize '88, Discerning Eye Comp. (1997). *Work in collections:* R.W.A., Mid-Glamorgan C.C., Cardiff School of Economics (Schools Art, Avon, Cardiff, Salisbury), Hewlett Packard. *Clubs:* Bath Soc. of Artists, Clifton Arts. *Signs work:* "Dawn Sidoli" or "SIDOLI." *Address:* 10 Elgin Pk., Redland, Bristol BS6 6RU.

SILBER, Evelyn Ann, Ph.D.(Cantab.), M.A.(Cantab.), M.A. (University of Pennsylvania), F.M.A.; art historian and museum curator; Director, Leeds Museums and Galleries; *b* Welwyn Garden City, 22 May, 1949. *Educ:* Hatfield Girls' Grammar School. *Studied:* history of art: New Hall, Cambridge (1968-72), University of Pennsylvania (Thouron Fellowship, 1972-73), Clare Hall, Cambridge (Leverhulme Fellowship, 1975-78). *Exhib:* organised: Jacob Epstein, Sculpture and Drawings, Leeds City A.G., and Whitechapel A.G. (1987). *Publications:* The Sculpture of Jacob Epstein (Phaidon, 1986), Gaudier - Brzeska: Life and Art (Thames and Hudson, 1996); catalogues, articles, lectures. *Clubs:* Royal Overseas League. *Address:* Director, Hunterian Museum and Art Gallery, University of Glasgow, Glasgow G12 8QQ.

SILLMAN, Norman H., A.R.C.A., F.R.B.S.; sculptor, coin and medal designer, Royal Mint; Fine Art Dept. (retd.), Nottingham Polytechnic; *b* May, 1921. *m* Gillian M. one *d. Educ:* Pyramid Hill, Australia. *Studied:* Blackheath Art School, Royal College of Art. *Exhib:* R.A., R.B.A., London Group, Midland Group, Arts Council "Sculpture in the Home" Exhbn., R.C.A. Open Air Exhbn.; medals exhib. in Europe and U.S.A. *Work in collections:* B.M., Derby Educ. Coll., Kelham Hall, Notts. Designed R.I.B.A. Awards (1990), British coins: £2 (1986), four £1 (1994), various overseas. *Commissions:* sculpture 16ft. Staythorpe Power Station, Notts. and various. *Publications:* articles, Saeculum (1981), Tubingen; Jour. Indian Anthrop. Soc. (1983). *Signs work:* "N. Sillman." *Address:* 33 Church St., Eye, Suffolk IP23 7BD.

SILVERMAN, Lisa Nicole, B.A. (Hons.) 1991, P.G.C.E. (1997); painter in oil, printmaker, art teacher; *b* London, 26 June, 1968. *Studied:* Exeter College of Art (1987-91), Ecole des Beaux Arts, Toulouse (1989-90). *Exhib:* London: Mall Galleries, Barbican Centre, Battersea Arts Centre, Suburb Gallery, Railings Gallery, International A.G., Smith's Galleries, Ben Uri A.G., Business Design Centre. *Work in collections:* Apthorp Fund for Young Artists. *Address:* 2 Danescroft, 21 Torrington Park, London N12 9AG.

SILVERTON, Norma, M.A., N.S., H.N.D., F.E.T.C.; artist/printmaker in etching, lithograph, silkscreen, 2D and 3D; *b* Birmingham, 1941. married. one *s.* two *d. Educ:* in Birmingham. *Studied:* Byam Shaw School of Art, Camberwell College of Art. *Exhib:* solo shows: Tel Aviv, Israel and London; and continually in group shows in U.K. and abroad. Curated print exhbns. between U.K., Israel and Germany. *Work in collections:* Scarborough Municipal A.G., Ben Uri Museum Collection. *Publications:* Eye Music - a collection of nine lithographs, Unspoken Poems - a collection of ten etchings. *Clubs:* Printmakers Council, N.S.P.S. *Signs work:* "Norma Silverton." *Address:* 13 Linden Lea, London N2 0RF.

SIMCOCK, Jack, painter; *b* Biddulph, Staffs., 6 June, 1929. *m* Suzanne, partner (1998). *Exhib:* over 50 one-man shows, England and abroad. Work in many public art galleries and private collections at home and abroad. Major retrospective, Potteries Museum and Art Gallery (2001). *Publications:* Simcock, Mow Cop, autobiography (1975), Midnight Till Three, volume of poems (1975). *Signs work:* "SIMCOCK." *Address:* 13 Primitive St., Mow Cop, Stoke-on-Trent ST7 3NH.

SIMMONDS, Jackie, H.N.D.; artist in pastel and water-colour; *b* Oxford, 27 Dec., 1944. *m* Geoffrey Simmonds. two *d. Educ:* Preston Manor Grammar. *Studied:* Harrow School of Art (1978-82). *Exhib:* Linda Blackstone Gallery, Pinner, P.S., R.I., R.W.A., R.S.B.A., Britain's Painters (1992). *Publications:* Pastels Workshop (Harper Collins, 1994). *Signs work:* "Jackie Simmonds." *Address:* 23 Linksway, Northwood, Middx. HA6 2XA.

SIMMONS, Fay, N.D.D. (1959), Cert.R.A. (1963), Leverhulme Scholarship (1963), A.R.B.S. (1976); sculptor in bronze or gesso composition with mixed media; V.S.O. Business/Social Development, Uganda; *b* New Zealand, 1938. *m* Sean Mullaney (decd.). *Educ:* Stella Maris Convent, Bideford. *Studied:* Bideford School of Art; Hammersmith College of Art; R.A. Schools. *Exhib:* R.A., Nicholas Treadwell Gallery, A.I.A., Alec Mann Birmingham, XVIII Gallery Knightsbridge, Jersey, Guernsey, Gallery Oste Hamburg, New York, Washington. First woman awarded the President's Prize for Sculpture, R.A. Schools (1963). *Clubs:* R.B.S. *Signs work:* "F.S." *Address:* 54 Coburg Cl., Greencoat Pl., London SW1P 1DP.

SIMMONS, Rosemary, N.D.D. (1953), Hon. R.E. (1990); artist in relief printmaking, water-colour; writer; Founder Editor, Printmaking Today, now retired as editor; *b* Brighton, 19 Oct., 1932. *m* Anthony Christie, M.A., F.S.A. *Studied:* Chelsea School of Art (1949-53). *Exhib:* International Gdn. Festival (1984), Museum of Gdn. History (1985), St. John's, Smith Sq. (1987). *Work in collections:* Tate Gallery print collection. *Publications:* Collecting Original Prints (1980), Complete Manual of Relief Printmaking with Katie Clemson (1988). *Signs work:* "Simmons." *Address:* Greendown Bungalow, Greendown Place, Combe Down, Bath BA2 5DD.

SIMONDS, Gillian Betty, N.D.D. (1956); artist in acrylic; *b* London, 8 June, 1935. *m* Brian Simonds. one *d. Educ:* Henley Grammar School. *Studied:* Folkestone and Dover Art Schools (1952-54), Canterbury College of Art (1954-56), Folkestone Arts Centre (1979-85, Beryl Bell). *Exhib:* Shepway Show, Folkestone; with N.A.P.A.: Newcastle-under-Lyme, Ludlow, R.B.S.A. Gallery B'ham, Westminster Gallery, London, Durham Art Gallery. *Commissions:* Mr. A. Hobbs, Mrs. M. Eason. *Publications:* illustrated: From My Reading to Yours (Prometheus Trust), pencil drawings; 'One Pair of Boots' by Tony Hobbs (Logaston Press 2000), pen & ink drawings. *Clubs:* N.A.P.A. *Signs work:* "Simonds." *Address:* Stonehurst, Quarry Rd., Hythe, Kent CT21 5HA.

SIMPSON, Alan John, R.S.M.A., I.S.M.P.; marine and landscape artist in oil, water-colour, pastel; *b* Basingstoke, 22 July, 1941. *m* Denise. two *s. Studied:* informal training at College of Art, Bournemouth. *Exhib:* R.S.M.A., R.O.I., R.I., Britain in Water-colour, Mystic, Seaport, U.S.A., Richard Beard Gallery, Vancouver, Harrison Galleries, Vancouver. *Signs work:* "Alan Simpson." *Address:* 24 Waltham Rd., Bournemouth BH7 6PE.

SIMPSON, Cathy, B.A.(Hons.), A.R.B.S.A., R.M.S., H.S.; freelance illustrator in water-colour and gouache; Head of Art, Bromsgrove School; *b* Kingston on Hull, 15 Nov., 1959. *Educ:* Christ's Hospital Girls' School, Hertford; Leicester University. *Studied:* Central St. Martin's School of Art. *Exhib:* R.I., S.WL.A., S.W.A., S.B.A., R.M.S., H.S., R.B.S.A., M.A.S.-F. *Signs work:* see appendix. *Address:* 23 The Dock, Catshill, Bromsgrove, Worcs. B61 0NJ.

SIMPSON, Helen Elizabeth, B.A. (1990), M.A. (1992), A.M.A. (1998), F.R.S.A; Curator; *b* Weston-super-Mare, 12 Nov., 1968. *Studied:* University College, London (Ancient History and Egyptology, 1987-90), University of Leicester (Museum studies, 1991-92). *Clubs:* Fellow of R.S.A. *Address:* The New Art Centre, Sculpture Park and Gallery, Roche Ct., East Winterslow, Wilts. SP5 1BG.

SIMPSON, Ian, A.R.C.A. (1958); Abbey Travelling Scholar (1958); freelance artist-writer in oil, acrylic and drawing media; Principal, St. Martin's School of Art (1972); Assistant Rector, The London Institute, Head of School, St. Martin's School of Art (1986-88); Course Director, Open College of the Arts (1997-99), Consultant (1999-); *b* Loughborough, Leics., 12 Nov., 1933. *Educ:* Bede Grammar School, Sunderland. *Studied:* Sunderland College of Art (1950-53); Royal College of Art (1955-58). *Exhib:* R.A. since 1956; solo exhbn.: Durham, Cambridge, Blandford, Dorset, Chappel, Essex. *Work in collections:* Glasgow City A.G., Nuffield Foundation, Hull Education Authority, Northumberland Education Authority, London Borough of Camden. *Publications:* Eyeline (B.B.C.), Picture Making (B.B.C.) Drawing: Seeing and Observation (Van Nostrand Reinhold) 3rd Revised Edn. (A. & C. Black 1992), Ian Simpson's Guide to Painting and Composition (Warnes), Painters Progress (Allen Lane) re-published as "Practical Art School" (Tiger Books 1995), The Encyclopedia of Drawing Techniques (Headline), The Challenge of Landscape Painting (Collins 1990), The New Guide to Illustration (Chartwell Books 1990), Anatomy of Humans (Studio Editions 1991), Collins Complete Painting Course (Harper Collins 1993), Collins Complete Drawing Course (Harper Collins 1994). T.V. Programmes written and presented: Eyeline (B.B.C. 1968), Picture Making (B.B.C. 1972), Reading the Signs (B.B.C. 1976). *Clubs:* Suffolk Group. *Signs work:* "Simpson." *Address:* Motts Farm House, Chilton St., Clare, Sudbury, Suffolk CO10 8QS.

SIMPSON, Leslie, F.R.S.A. (1985); portrait artist in oil and water-colour working to commission on all subjects; Director, Soc. of Miniaturists, British Water-colour Soc., British Soc. of Painters; Founder, Yorkshire Artists Exhbn. (1981); Principal, International Guild of Artists; *b* Horsforth, 28 May, 1930. *m* Margaret. one *s. Educ:* Bridlington School. *Studied:* Hull College of Art. *Work in collections:* portrait of the full Wakefield City Council (1974); portraits of the Lady Lord Mayors of Leeds, Bradford, Sheffield and London; 'The Winning Throw' portrait of Tessa Sanderson, Los Angeles Olympics (1984). Descendant of James Simpson (1791-1864) leading non-conformist architect in the North, and John Simpson official portrait artist to Queen Donna Marie II of Portugal (1837). *Signs work:* "Leslie Simpson." *Address:* Briargate, 2 The Brambles, Victoria Drive, Ilkley, W.Yorks. LS29 9DH.

SIMPSON, Noelle, painter, colourist of joyous landscapes, nudes, interiors and portraits in oil on canvas, original limited edition prints; *b* Auckland, N.Z., 10 Aug., 1950. one *d. Educ:* Chatelard, Switzerland; Moreton Hall, Shropshire. *Studied:* under Philip Sutton, R.A., and Frederick Deane, R.P. (1985), Van Wieringen, Bali (1986-90). *Exhib:* J. Weston Gallery, London (1985), Symon Gallery, Bali (1987), Bowmoore Gallery, London (1991), Hilton International, Bali (1992), Gagliardi Gallery, London (1992, 1994), Pacific Rim Gallery, San Diego (1993), Los Angeles (1995-97), Auckland, N.Z. (1998-99). *Work in collections:* Agung Rai Museum, Bali. *Publications:* Then Till Now - Noelle Simpson. *Signs work:* see appendix. *Address:* 18 Cottesmore Gdns., London W8 5PR.

SIMS-WILLIAMS, Dorothy Audrey Constance, F.R.S.A., Hon. Mention, Paris Salon, R.A.S. Cert., Leverhulme Leaving Scholar Silver and Bronze medal; artist in oil and pastel, teacher, lecturer; *b* Disley, Ches., 26 May, 1909. *m* Rev. L. T. Sims-Williams. three *s.* one *d. Educ:* privately. *Studied:* Stockport Art School (1926-28), R.A. Schools (1928-33) under W. W. Russell, R.A. and F. E. Jackson, A.R.A. *Exhib:* R.P and various London exhbns., R.W.A. Bristol, Dorset Art Weeks. *Work in collections:* St. Matthew's Church, Stockport; St. John's Church, Hopwood, Lancs.; St. Andrew's Church, Dearnley, Lancs.; Bridport Museum. *Commissions:* portraits. *Clubs:* Reynolds. *Signs work:* "D. Sims-Williams." *Address:* Stonehayes, Westcliff Rd., Charmouth, Dorset DT6 6BG.

SINCLAIR, Elizabeth, N.D.D. (1950), A.T.D. (1958), M.F.P.S. (1986), Visual Arts Dip. (1969), Dip. in History of Art (1972); painter in oil, pastel, acrylic and water-colour; *b* Glasgow, 18 Jan., 1933. *Educ:* 'Wings', Charlton Pk., Wilts. *Studied:* Plymouth School of Art, Bath Academy of Art, London University. *Exhib:* one-man shows: Hong Kong, Italy; group shows: Hong Kong, Germany, Plymouth, London, Reigate, etc., Surre Open Studios. *Work in collections:* Plymouth A.G. *Clubs:* Reigate Soc. of Artists, North Weald Group, F.P.S. *Signs work:* "E. Sinclair." *Address:* 10 Cockshot Hill, Reigate, Surrey RH2 8AE.

SINCLAIR, Helen, B.F.A.(Hons.) (1976); sculptor in cast stone and metal; *b* S.Wales, 27 Feb., 1954. *m* Terry Ryall, sculptor. *Educ:* Llanelli Girls' Grammar School. *Studied:* Dyfed School of Art, Wimbledon School of Art (1973-76, Peter Startup, Jim Turner). *Exhib:* Heifer Gallery, Highbury, Montpellier Gallery, Cheltenham and Stratford-upon-Avon, Online Gallery, Southampton, Gordon Hepworth Gallery, Exeter, Edith Grove Gallery, Fulham, Flying Colours Gallery, Chelsea, Fairfax Gallery, Tunbridge Wells. *Work in collections:* Bultarbo Estate, Sweden, Grand Theatre, Swansea. *Commissions:* Trophy for W. Wales Tec Management Awards; Wall Reliefs, Castle Square, Swansea. *Signs work:* "Helen Sinclair" or "H.S." *Address:* Rhossili Farmhouse, Rhossili, Gower, Swansea SA3 1PL.

SINCLAIR, N. T., M.A., F.M.A.; Senior Curator; *Address:* Museum and Art Gallery, Borough Rd., Sunderland SR1 1PP.

SINNOTT, Kevin, artist in oil on canvas; *b* Wales, 1947. *m* Susan. three *s.* one *d.* *Studied:* Cardiff College of Art (1967-68), Gloucester College of Art (1968-71), R.C.A. (1971-74). *Exhib:* one-man shows: Ikon Gallery (1980), Blond Fine Art (1982, 1984), Chapter Arts Centre, Cardiff (1984), Bernard Jacobson Gallery (1986, 1987, 1988, 1990), Flowers East (1992, 1994, 1996), Caldwell/Snyder N.Y. (2000), Martin Tinney, (2001). *Work in collections:* British Council, B.M., A.C.G.B., R.C.A., Whitworth Manchester, Wolverhampton City Gallery, Unilever, Deutsche Bank A.G. London, Metropolitan Museum of Art, N.Y., National Museum of Wales. *Clubs:* Chelsea Arts. *Signs work:* initials right hand corner. *Address:* Ty'r Santes Fair, Pont-y-Rhyl, Bridgend CF32 8LJ.

SITWELL, Pauline, S.W.E., R.A. Dip. (1937), L.I.S.T.D., F.R.G.S.; painter, printer, poet and lecturer; oil, water-colour, wood engraving, lithography, etc.; *b* Malta, 5 Oct., 1916. *Educ:* full stage training and young career. *Studied:* St. John's Wood School of Art (1930), Royal Academy Schools of Art (1933-37). *Exhib:* S.W.E., R.S.M.A., and Mall Prints tour of G.B., etc.; Laureat Paris Salon de Printemps, Auribeau s/Siagne, France (1988); one-man show sponsored by Westminster City Council, many others. *Work in collections:* works in seven countries. *Commissions:* many and various. *Publications:* Green Song; Train Journey to Deal and other Poems (Outposts, 1981). *Clubs:* Royal Academy, Reynolds (Hon. Treasurer, retd. after 20 years), S.I.A.C., B.S.C.G., S.W.E., etc. *Signs work:* "Pauline Sitwell" and see appendix. *Address:* 46 Porchester Rd., London W2 6ET.

SKEA, Janet, B.F.A. (1968); painter in water-colour, tempera and oils; *b* Johannesburg, S.Africa, 15 Sept., 1947. *Educ:* Parktown Girls' High, Johannesburg. *Studied:* Stellenbosch University (1965-68, Prof. Otto Schröder). *Exhib:* widely in the U.K., including St. Ives Soc. and Mariners; Look, Helmsley; Bourne, Reigate; R.W.A., Bristol; London: Bankside, Churzee Galleries, Llewellyn Alexander, Mall with the R.I., Singer and Friedlander, Sunday Times Competition, and others, Medici, and with Manya Igel; solos: Museum of Garden History (1985), Heifer (1994), Financial Times (1995). *Signs work:* "Janet Skea" dated on reverse. *Address:* 30 Queen St., Penzance, Cornwall TR18 4BH.

SKILLINGTON, Nancy: see TALBOT, Nancy Wilfreda Hewitt.

SKINNER, John, B.A. (Hons.) Fine Art (Painting); artist in oil painting; *b* Kent, 19 Aug., 1953. *m* Mary Skinner. one *s. Educ:* Brighton Polytechnic (1973-76). *Address:* The Abbotsbury Studio, 11a Rodden Row, Abbotsbury, Dorset DT3 4JL.

SLADE, Jacqueline, U.A. (1999); artist in acrylic, water-colour, mixed media; *b* Nottingham, 14 Sept., 1940. one *s. Studied:* Bournemouth College of Art and Design. *Exhib:* Gagliardi, Mall Galleries, British Natural History Museum travelling exhbn., Southampton, Westminster Gallery. *Commissions:* work commissioned and in private collections. *Publications:* Portman Bldg. Soc. calendar (1998), Christchurch Leisure and Tourism promotional literature (1995), greetings cards for Greyhound Racing Trust (1998). *Clubs:* U.A. *Signs work:* "Jacqui Slade." *Address:* 2 Beech Cres., Surrey Hills Pk., Bexhill Rd., Tadworth, Surrey KT20 7LY.

SLANEY, Noël, R.S.W.; artist in Batik oils and water-colour; *b* Glasgow, 26 Dec., 1915. *m* George Frederick Moules, painter. four *d. Educ:* Girls' High School,

Glasgow. *Studied:* Glasgow School of Art under the late Hugh Adam Crawford, R.S.A., D.A. (1937), Post Dip. with distinction (1939). *Work in collections:* water-colours in Aberdeen and Dundee; oils in Arts Council, Glasgow A.G., Lillie A.G. Milngavie, Hunterian Museum Glasgow. *Signs work:* "Slaney." *Address:* c/o MacKinnon, 12 Woodvale Ave., Giffnock, Glasgow G46 6RQ.

SLATER, Richard, N.D.D. Illustration (1950), A.T.D. (1951), N.D.D. Painting/Lithography (1954), R.I. (1999); printmaker and painter in oils and water-colour; formerly principal lecturer, College of S.M. & S.J., Chelsea and Plymouth (1960-1980); 1st prize S.W. Open Figurative Art Comp. (1991), R.I. medal (1992); *b* Tottenham, London, 1927. *m* Mavis. three *d. Educ:* Tottenham Grammar School. *Studied:* Hornsey School of Art (1943-1945, 1948-1954). *Exhib:* R.A., R.S.M.A., R.I., first solo exhib. at Whibley Gallery (1974), art centres in Plymouth and Cornwall, various galleries in S.W. and S. England. *Publications:* illustrations for Cambridge Univ. Press, lithographic editions for Consolidated Fine Arts, New York. *Clubs:* assoc. member St Ives Soc. of Artists. *Signs work:* "R E Slater R.I." *Address:* The Barn, Ducky Lane, Landrake, Saltash, Cornwall PL12 5DL.

SLICER, Sheila Mary, A.R.M.S. (1978); first prize M.A.S.-F. (1983, 1986, 1992); President, A.S.M.A. (Vic.); freelance miniature portraitist in water-colour; miniature restorer, lecturer; *b* Yorks., 26 Sept., 1930. *m* Robert Slicer. two *d. Educ:* Bradford Girls Grammar School. *Studied:* Bradford Regional College of Art (1946-49). *Exhib:* R.M.S., M.A.S.-F., Andorra, Yorks. Water-colour Soc., Brighouse and Bradford Art Clubs, Victoria, New South Wales, Queensland and Tasmania, Australia, Hilliard Soc., Royal Pastel Soc. and Sweden. *Work in collections:* England, Bermuda, Florida, Australia, Hong Kong, Andorra, America, Japan. *Clubs:* R.M.S., M.A.S.-F., H.S., M.A.A., Victoria, N.S. W. and Queensland Miniature Socs., Australia, Tasmania. *Signs work:* "Sheila M. Slicer." *Address:* Faraway, 1655 Don Rd., Launching Pl., Victoria 3139, Australia.

SLOAN, Bob, R.U.A., D.A., A.T.D.; Mont Kavanagh award (1983), R.U.A. medals: Silver (1983), gold (1988, 1999); sculptor in mixed media; Lecturer in Fine Art, University of Ulster; *b* Belfast, 10 Apr., 1940. *m* Veronica. one *s.* one *d. Studied:* Belfast College of Art (1959-63), Central Schools, London (1963-64). *Exhib:* Belfast, London, Liverpool, Dublin, N.Y., Kassel Germany. *Work in collections:* Ulster Museum, N.I. Arts Council, Arts Council of Ireland, National Self-Portrait Collection; private collections in Ireland, England, America. *Commissions:* Northern Bank, Strabane District Council, N.I. Tourist Board, Belfast Newsletter, Diocese of Derry, N.I. Housing Executive. *Signs work:* "R.W. Sloan" and see appendix. *Address:* 58 Upper Mealough Rd., Belfast BT8 8LR.

SLOAN, Victor, visual artist/lecturer - photography, video, printmaking, painting and drawing; Awards: British Council, Arts Council of N.Ireland, Dept. of Foreign Affairs (Ireland), An Chomhairle Ealaion, Arts Council of Ireland, Gold Medal and Connor Prize (R.U.A.); *b* Dungannon, Co. Tyrone, 16 July, 1945. *m* Katherine Joyce Sloan. two *s. Studied:* Belfast and Leeds Colleges of Art - Fine Art Painting (1963-69). *Exhib:* Orchard Gallery, Derry; Ormeau Baths Gallery, Belfast; Douglas Hyde Gallery, Dublin; Gallery of Photography, Dublin; Ulster Museum, Belfast; Barbican Centre, London; Cartwright Hall, Bradford; Cornerhouse, Manchester; Royal

Festival Hall, London; Arnolfini, Bristol; also exhbns. worldwide. Represented both Ireland and Britain in many major exhbns. *Work in collections:* Imperial War Museum; National Photographic Archives; Dublin City University; Arts Council; National Self-Portrait Collection of Ireland; North West Arts Trust; British Telecommunications; National Museum of Photography, Film and Television; Ulster Museum; also public and private collections in U.S.A., Canada, Europe, Australia, Asia. *Publications:* 'Marking the North - The Work of Victor Sloan' (England); 'Walls' (Northern Ireland); 'Borne Sulinowo' (Poland); 'Stadium' (Germany); 'Acts of Faith' (Ireland); 'Victor Sloan: Selected Works 1980-2000' (Northern Ireland). *Signs work:* "VICTOR SLOAN." (see appendix) *Address:* Rosedale House, 10 Church Rd., Portadown, Co. Armagh BT63 5HT. *Website:* www.bigfoot.com/~victorsloan *Email:* victorsloan@bigfoot.com

SLOWE, Vikki, R.E.; printmaker; *b* London, 24 May, 1947. *m* Martin Slowe. two *d. Educ:* Camden School for Girls. *Studied:* London College of Fashion; Camden Arts Centre. *Exhib:* R.A., R.E., Japan & U.S.A. *Work in collections:* Smithsonian Inst., Washington, Tel Aviv Museum, Israel, Ashmolean Museum, Oxford. *Signs work:* "Vikki Slowe." *Address:* 35 Ornan Rd., London NW3 4QD.

SMAIL, Elizabeth Ann, F.L.S. (1991), F.S.B.A. (1985); Cert. of Botanical Merit (S.B.A. Exhbn. 1993 & 2000); botanical artist in water-colour, gouache; Personnel Officer, Council Mem. (Ex-officio), Soc. of Botanical Artists (1988-95); *b* Ross-on-Wye, 5 Mar., 1942. *m* Norman Smail. *Educ:* Ross-on-Wye. *Studied:* Hereford College of Art (1958-62). *Exhib:* Mall Galleries (1986, 1987), Westminster Gallery (annually since 1988), Hereford Museum and A.G. (1991), Sevenoaks Wildfowl Trust annually since 1994; 21 other centres worldwide since 1984. *Work in collections:* Hunt Inst. of Botanical Documentation, Pittsburg; Marine Soc., London; private collections throughout the world. *Publications:* work repro.: illustrations for articles in various publications; designs for reproduction on greetings cards and ceramics. *Clubs:* S.B.A. *Signs work:* "Elizabeth Smail." *Address:* 25 Walton Rd., Tonbridge, Kent TN10 4EF.

SMAIL, Janice Ann, U.A.; Council mem. U.A. (1995-98), Teacher's Cert. (1962), C. & G. Fashion (1980); painter in oil, pastel, and water-colour; *b* Bury St. Edmunds, Suffolk. *m* Peter. one *s.* one *d. Educ:* Whitelands College, Putney. *Studied:* University of London Inst. of Educ., Reigate College of Art. *Exhib:* Westminster Gallery, London with U.A.; solo shows: Surrey and Cambs. Work in collections internationally. *Clubs:* U.A., Cambridge Drawing Society. *Signs work:* "Jan Smail." *Address:* Woodlands, 24 North Rd., Whittlesford, Cambs CB2 4NZ.

SMART, Jeffrey, painter in oil, pen and ink; *b* Adelaide, S. Aus., 26 July, 1921. *Educ:* Pulteney Grammar School, Adelaide. *Studied:* S.A. School of Arts, Adelaide (1940), Grand Chaumiere (1948) under McEvoy, Academie Montmartre (1949) under Fernand Leger. *Exhib:* Whitechapel (1962), Tate Gallery (1963); one-man shows: Redfern Gallery (1967, 1979, 1982), Galleria 88 Rome (1968), Leicester Galleries (1970). *Work in collections:* National Galleries of Sydney, Melbourne, Adelaide and Perth, Mertz Coll., Corcoran Gallery, Washington, Yale University, Von Thyssen Coll., Lugano, De Beers Coll., 20th Century Art, London. *Publications:* work repro.: Art International (May, 1968), Present Day Australian Art (Ure Smith),

Masterpieces of Australian Art (1970), 200 Years of Australian Art (1971), The Moderns (Phaidon Press, 1976), Jeffrey Smart (S. McGrath, Art International Vol. XXI/I, 1977), Jeffrey Smart (David Malouf, Art International, Nov. 1982); Jeffrey Smart by Peter Quartermaine (Gryphon Press, 1983). Documentary film BBC "Omnibus" (1984). *Signs work:* "Jeffrey Smart." *Address:* c/o Redfern Gallery, Cork St., London.

SMITH, Barry Edward Jervis, B.A.; artist/illustrator in water-colour; *b* Sydney, Australia, 27 Apr., 1943. *Educ:* Coburg High School; University of Melbourne (1961-66). *Exhib:* group shows in London; one-man shows: Nantes, Edinburgh, Sweden and Australia. *Publications:* written and illustrated several children's books. *Signs work:* "B. Smith" or "Barry Smith." *Address:* P.O. Box 846, London E8 1ER. *Email:* bookart@gpo.sonnet.co.uk

SMITH, Basil, M.C.S.D. (1958), M.S.T.D. (1965), F.S.B.A. (1985), M.G.M.A. (1992); freelance artist in water-colour and acrylic; *b* Hove, 1925. *m* Mavis Grant. three *s.* one *d. Educ:* Xaverian College, Brighton. *Studied:* Brighton College of Art and Crafts (1940-42, 1946-48, Charles Knight). *Exhib:* R.I., Mall Galleries, Sussex Artists, Wildlife Artists, Westminster Gallery, Donnington, Limerock U.S.A. *Publications:* illustrated: The Principles of Gardening, The Good Cook, Vegetables, Graham Hill's Motoring Racing Book, Food from your Garden. Over 400 paintings of flora and fauna, all types of transport through the ages for American First Day Covers. *Signs work:* "BASIL" and see appendix. *Address:* 53 Davidgor Rd., Hove, E. Sussex BN3 1RA.

SMITH, C. Philip, A.R.C.A. (1st Class) (1954), M.D.E. (1970), Fellow and Past President (1977-79) Designer Bookbinders; Presidium of Honour (Czech) (1989); several international Gold, Silver Medals; book artist, bookbinder, painter, author, inventor (Patents: maril, lap-back book-structure); Editor, The New Bookbinder (1980-95); British Museum team Florence flood 1966-67; awarded M.B.E. for services to art (2000); *b* Southport, Merseyside, 10 June, 1928. *m* Dorothy M. Weighill, artist. three *s. Educ:* Ackworth School, Yorks. *Studied:* Southport School of Art (1949-51), R.C.A. (1951-54, Roger Powell); Sydney Cockerell bindery (1957-61). *Exhib:* several solo U.K. and abroad, over 150 book-art, binding exhbns. U.K., U.S.A., France, Germany, Holland, Belgium, Luxembourg, Spain, Norway, Czechoslovakia, S. America, Canada, Japan, S. Africa, etc.; painting exhbns. include John Moores, R.B.A., etc. *Work in collections:* V. & A., B.M. (B.L.), Royal Collection, Bibliothèque Historique, Paris, Royal Library Holland, and other major public collections U.K., U.S.A., Spain and around the world. *Publications:* The Lord of the Rings and Other Bookbindings, (1970); New Directions in Bookbinding (London and N.Y. 1975); The Book: Art & Object (1982); Book Art: Concept and Making, in prep.; numerous exhbn. catalogues, articles and reviews internationally. *Clubs:* Designer Bookbinders, Meister der Einbandkunst, Canadian G. of B.B.A., Soc. of Bookbinders, Center for Book Arts, N.Y., Hon. Fellow Soc. of Czech Bookbinders. *Signs work:* "Philip Smith." *Address:* The Book House, Yatton Keynell, Wilts. SN14 7BH. *Email:* PDSBookarts@aol.com

SMITH, Caryl, S.B.A. (1997); mainly self taught artist in pastel and water-colour, mostly flowers and gardens; *b* Wiltshire, 21 Oct., 1943. *m* V. J. Smith. two *s.*

Exhib: galleries in the Cotswolds, Wiltshire and Sussex. *Publications:* greetings cards. *Clubs:* S.B.A., S.F.P. *Signs work:* paintings "CARYL." *Address:* 2 Willowhayne Close, Angmering on Sea, W. Sussex BN16 1PF.

SMITH, Colin Hilton, B.A.(Hons.), M.A.(R.C.A.); Harkness Fellow (Yale University), Royal Overseas League joint first prizewinner; painter in oil on canvas, acrylic etc. on paper; associate lecturer, Loughborough University; *b* Harpenden, Herts., 21 Feb., 1953. divorced. one *s. Educ:* Hitchin Boys Grammar School. *Studied:* St. Albans School of Art (1971-72), Falmouth School of Art (1972-75), R.C.A. (1975-79), Yale (1983-85). *Exhib:* solo shows: Adair Margo Gallery, El Paso, Texas U.S.A. (1999), Musikpaviljongen, Grenadjarstaden, Örebro, Sweden (1999), British Council Art Centre, Buenos Aires (1998), 6 Chapel Row Contemporary Arts, Bath (1998), VIP Lounge, Virgin Airways, Heathrow Airport (1997), Galleri M, Stockholm (1997), Arte.X.Arte, Buenos Aires (1996), Wilmer, Cutler and Pickering, Berlin (1995), University of Northumbria Gallery, Newcastle-upon-Tyne (1995), Chelsea Arts Club, London (1995), Galleri M, Stockholm (1995), Big Paintings for the Barbican, London (1993), Gallery Three Zero. N.Y. (1993), Kunst Europa, Kunstverein Freiburg, Germany (1991), Anderson O'Day Gallery (1991), Ruth Siegal, N.Y. (1986), Art Iteinera '83, Volterra, Italy (1983), Nicola Jacobs Gallery, London (1982, 1984, 1987, 1989). *Work in collections:* Tate Gallery, London, British Council, Buenos Aires, NatWest Group, London, Royal Palm Hotel, Phoenix, Arizona, Scottish Equitable, Edinburgh, Museum of Modern Art, Tel Aviv (Herrmann's Bequest), Virgin Communications, London, Wilmer, Cutler and Pickering, Berlin, BML Corporate Management, Frankfurt, Arthur Anderson, Newcastle, Amerivox Scandinavia, Stockholm, Duke and Duchess of Westminster, Coopers Lybrand, London, Hunting Group Plc., British Airways, Kettering A.G. and Museum, Kettering, Arthur Andersen, London, EMI Worldwide, London, British Standards Inst., London, Pearl Development, London, Contemporary Art Soc., London, Pepsi Cola, London, Prudential Holborn, London, A.C.G.B., Unilever, London, Royal College of Art, London. *Clubs:* Chelsea Arts. *Signs work:* "Colin Smith." *Address:* 27 Orsman Rd., London N1 5RA.

SMITH, David Henry, M.Art, R.C.A. (1971), Hugh Dunn Plaque (1971); artist in oil and water-colour; *b* Cleethorpes, 29 Oct., 1947. *m* Irena Ewa Flynn. *Educ:* Elliston Secondary Modern School, Cleethorpes. *Studied:* Grimsby School of Art (1965-68); R.C.A. (1968-71). *Exhib:* one-man shows, New Art Centre, London (1970-72), Fischer Fine Art, London (1974, 1976, 1978, 1981), Vienna (1976), W. Germany (1976), Sweden (1979). *Work in collections:* Arts Council, Contemporary Art Soc. *Signs work:* "D. H. Smith." *Address:* Hall Lodge, Holton-cum-Beckering, Wragby, Lincoln.

SMITH, Edward John Milton, A.T.D. (1952), N.D.D. 2nd Cl. Hons. (1951), F.S.A.E.; artist in lettering, writing and illumination; Principal Lecturer, Subject Leader (Art) P.G.C.E. Course, Leeds Polytechnic 1963-85 (now retd.); art teacher, West Monmouth School, Pontypool (1952-62); visiting lecturer, Newport College of Art (1954-62); President N.S.A.E. (1972); *b* Stonehouse, Glos., 3 May, 1922. *m* Doreen. one *s.* two *d. Educ:* Central School, Stroud, Glos. *Studied:* Stroud School of Art (1936-38), Gloucester College of Art (1939-40), Leeds College of Art (1946-52). *Signs work:* see appendix. *Address:* Glevum, 30 Burnham Rd., Garforth, Leeds, Yorks. LS25 1LA.

SMITH, Gregor, R.S.W., D.A. (1966), Post-grad. scholarship (1967); artist in oil and water-colour, teacher; *b* Renton, Dunbartonshire, 15 July, 1944. *m* Elizabeth. *Educ:* Wishaw High School. *Studied:* Edinburgh College of Art (1962-67). *Exhib:* R.S.A., R.S.W., Compass Gallery, Glasgow, numerous group and one-man shows. *Work in collections:* H.R.H. The Duke of Edinburgh, S.A.C., numerous educ. authorities and district councils. *Signs work:* "Gregor Smith." *Address:* Auchendarroch House, Shore Rd., Kilcreggan, Helensburgh, Dunbartonshire G84 0HQ.

SMITH, Ivor Stanley, M.A., LL.D., R.I.B.A., A.A. Dip.; consultant architect; educational consultant, Professor Emeritus; *b* Leigh-on-Sea, Essex. *m* Audrey. one *s*. three *d*. *Educ:* Southend School of Art; Bartlett, Cambridge; A.A. Schools of Architecture. *Signs work:* "Ivor Smith." *Address:* The Station Officer's House, Prawle Point, Kingsbridge, Devon TQ7 2BX.

SMITH, Jack, artist in oil; *b* Sheffield, 18 June, 1928. *m* Susan. *Educ:* Nether Edge Grammar School. *Studied:* R.C.A. (1949-52). *Exhib:* twenty-seven one-man shows in England. *Work in collections:* Tate Gallery, Arts Council, Berlin Internatioal Gallery, Guggenheim Museum, Gottenburg Museum. *Publications:* Jack Smith, A Painter in Pursuit of Marvels, text Prof: Norbert Lynton. *Signs work:* "Jack Smith" or "Jacksmith." *Address:* 29 Seafield Rd., Hove, Sussex BN3 2TP.

SMITH, Jesse, B.A. (Hons.) 1988, Postgrad. Dip. (1992); artist in mixed media, visiting lecturer; *b* London, 5 Aug., 1966. *m* Sharon Purves. one *d*. *Studied:* Norwich School of Art (1985-88), R.A. Schools (1989-92). *Exhib:* solo shows: One Gallery, Brick Lane, London (1999), Ozten Zeki Gallery, Walton St. London (1997-98); group shows: Bow Wow, Holland Pk. (1999), Clink St. Gallery, London Bridge (1999), R.A. Summer Show (1999), Studio 3 Gallery, Old St. London (1995-98). *Address:* 67 Whipps Cross Rd., Leytonstone, London E11 1NJ.

SMITH, Joan, M.A. (Hons.) (1987), Postgrad. Dip. in Painting (1988), M.F.A. (1989); artist in acrylic, oil and mixed media on canvas and paper, lithography; Lecturer in Drawing and Painting, Edinburgh College of Art; *b* Dundee, 28 June, 1964. *Educ:* Monifieth High School, Dundee. *Studied:* Edinburgh University (1982-87, Prof. Fernie), Edinburgh College of Art (1982-89, Prof. David Michie). *Exhib:* solo shows: Collective Gallery, Edinburgh (1992), Crawford Art Centre, St. Andrews (1993); many group shows, Pier Art Centre, Orkney (1994), Christopher Boyd Gallery, Galasheils (1995). *Work in collections:* R.S.A., Edinburgh College of Art, Edinburgh City Art Centre, Heriot Watt University, Glasgow Museums and Art Galleries. *Publications:* Drawing Comparisons (1997). *Signs work:* "Joan Smith." *Address:* 14 Coillesdene Gdns., Edinburgh EH15 2JS.

SMITH, Keir, B.A. Fine Art (1973); artist and teacher in cast bronze; *b* Gravesend, Kent, 1950. *m* Clare. *Studied:* University of Newcastle upon Tyne (1969-73), postgraduate study, Chelsea School of Art (1973-75). *Exhib:* selected solo shows: 'Mark/Meaning' A.I.R. Gallery, London (1977); 'Like Nimrod's Tower' Acme Gallery, London (1980); 'Sailing Ancient Seas' Ceolfrith Gallery and Ikon Gallery (1982); 'Navigator' Rochdale A.G. and nautical tour (1984); 'The Dreaming Track' Laing Gallery, Newcastle upon Tyne and Wolverhampton A.G. (1989); 'Flint Sepulchre' Mead Gallery and Bury St. Edmunds A.G. (1994); 'Ognissanti' Concourse Gallery, Barbican Centre (1998). *Commissions:* 'The Iron Road' Forest of

Dean (1986); 'The Way of Clouds' Usher Gallery, Lincoln (1990); 'From the Dark Cave' Henrietta House, London (1992); 'Stefano' - Enabled by Sculpture at Goodwood (1997). *Address:* 19 Florence Rd., New Cross, London SE14 6TW.

SMITH, Leo Illesley Gibbons, P.U.A.; Pres. United Society of Artists, past mem. of Executive Council, Federation of British Artists, past Vice-Pres. Soc. of Graphic Fine Arts, past Pres. Herts. Visual Arts Forum; painter in water-colour, pastel, acrylic, landscape, portrait, works of the imagination; Art Director in publishing and advertising, illustrator, typographer; latterly art editorial, Radio Times; *b* Cobham, Surrey. *m* Constance Hilda (decd.). one *d. Educ:* Queen Elizabeth's Grammar School Kingston. *Studied:* Hornsey College of Art (1945-49). *Exhib:* Mall Galleries, R.B.A., R.I., R.P., P.S., N.E.A.C., R.W.S.; several one-man shows. *Work in collections:* Ealing Educ. Com. *Publications:* U.A. News and Views. *Signs work:* "Leo Gibbons Smith" or "L.I.G.S." *Address:* 207 Sunnybank Rd., Potters Bar, Herts. EN6 2NH.

SMITH, Liz, S.F.P. (1996), H.S. (1998); artist in water-colour, oil, acrylic; *b* Romsey, Hants., 13 Sept., 1927. *m* Colin Smith. two *s. Studied:* Adult Education (Robert Palmer, R.O.I., R.B.A.). *Exhib:* S.F.P. at Castle Sofiero, Sweden; Societé Jersaise, St. Helier, Jersey; and Mottisfont Abbey, Hampshire; H.S.: Mall Galleries and Wells, Somerset; also exhibited at Castle Bosjokloster, Sweden, and Geras, Austria; "Spirit of the Garden" open exhibition at Salisbury Museum, Wilts. *Clubs:* Boscombe Art Circle. *Address:* 26 Herbert Ave., Parkstone, Dorset BH12 4EE.

SMITH, Marion, B.A. Hons, (1987-1991), A.R.S.A. (1998); visual artist, mainly sculpture in wood, stone, plaster, mixed media; technician, fine art, Glasgow School of Art; *b* St. Andrews, 14 Feb., 1969. *Studied:* Grays School of Art, Aberdeen. *Exhib:* solo exhib., Crawford Arts Centre, St. Andrews (1997); Iwate Art Festival, Japan (1998); Scandex, Stavanger, Norway (1995); Lulea, Sweden; Kemi, Finland; Haddo Arts Trust, Tarves, Aberdeenshire (1994); Tyrebagger Forest, Aberdeen; Gyle Shopping Centre, Edinburgh. *Commissions:* House for an Art Lover, Bellahouston Park, Glasgow (1999); Hamilton Town Centre, South Lanarkshire (2000). *Signs work:* "Marion W Smith." *Address:* 66 Fergus Drive, Glasgow G20 6AW.

SMITH, Peter William, D.F.C.; artist in oils and water-colour; *b* New Malden, Surrey, 3 July, 1920. *Educ:* Whitgift, Croydon. *Studied:* Reigate Art School. *Exhib:* East Sussex Art Club, Hastings (1947 and 1948), International Amateur Art (1969). *Signs work:* "Peter Smith." *Address:* Dean Cottage, Blanks Lane, Newdigate, Surrey RH5 5ED.

SMITH, Richard Michael, B.A. (Hons.) (1993); winner, Carroll Foundation award (R.P.); painter in oil on canvas, pastel, pencil; *b* Warlingham, Surrey, 15 June, 1957. three *s.* one *d. Educ:* Caterham School. *Studied:* Coventry Art School (1977-80, Colin Saxton, Harry Weinberger), and in studio of John Ward, R.A. *Exhib:* R.A. Summer Exhbns., R.P., Brian Sinfield Gallery, Burford, Portland Gallery, London, David Messum Gallery, London. *Work in collections:* G.L.C. *Commissions:* Dr. Robert Runcie, Past Archbishop of Canterbury; Lord Plumb, Past President of European Parliament; Mr. Justice Owen; Mr. John Fenwick. *Signs work:* "Richard Smith," "R.S." or "R.M.S." *Address:* Flat 5, Stangrave Hall, Godstone, Surrey RH9 8NB.

SMITH, Rita, B.A. (Hons.) (1978), H.D.F.A. (Lond.) (1980), Boise Travelling Scholarship (1980); artist in water-colour; *b* London, 9 Mar., 1946. two *s. Educ:* Collingwood School for Girls. *Studied:* Camberwell School of Art (1974-78), Slade School of Fine Art (1978-80). *Exhib:* solo: University of Surrey, Plymouth Arts Centre; selected mixed shows include, The Whitechapel, R.A., South London A.G., Grundy Gallery, Blackpool, Plymouth and Truro Museums, Singer and Friedlander/Sunday Times Water-colour Competition, Gallery 27, Cork Street, Gillian Jason Gallery. Winner, The Guinness award at R.A. (1993). *Signs work:* "RITA SMITH." *Address:* 1 Gnaton Terr., Albaston, nr. Gunnislake, Cornwall PL18 9AG.

SMITH, Stan, R.W.S.; painter/draughtsman; Hon. Life President, London Group; former Head of Fine Art, Ruskin School, University of Oxford; Fellow, Linacre College, Oxford (1981); Chairman, Chelsea Arts Club (1994); *b* Hull, 1929. *Exhib:* widely in U.K. and abroad. Work in national, corporate and private collections worldwide. Prizewinner: R.A. and Hunting Group. *Publications:* include books, articles and videos on art and art theory. Consultant on magazines, TV and radio programmes. *Clubs:* The Arts Club, Chelsea Arts, Grouchos. *Address:* 1 Brunswick Cl., Twickenham, Middx. TW2 5ND.

SNELLING, John, F.R.S.A. (1966); landscape and marine artist in water-colour and oils; *b* Greenwich, 15 Nov., 1914. *m* Margaret Snelling. three *s.* one *d. Educ:* Camberwell School of Art. *Studied:* under Horace Brodzky. *Exhib:* Mall Galleries, Guildhall Gallery and numerous one-man shows. *Work in collections:* Great Britain, U.S.A., S.A., Finland, Norway, Germany, Italy, etc. *Publications:* written and illustrated: Painting Defects (Spon), Painters Book of Facts (Technical Press). *Signs work:* see appendix. *Address:* 306 Wennington Rd., Rainham, Essex.

SNOW, Graham, Dip.A.D. (1968), H.Dip. (1972); Mombusho scholar, Japan (1974-77), Artist in Residence, Cambridge University (1977-81); artist in oil and water-colour; *b* Exeter, 28 Oct., 1948. *Educ:* Colfox School, Dorset. *Studied:* Bournemouth College of Art (1966-68), Hornsey College of Art (1968-70), Slade School of Fine Art (1970-72). *Exhib:* one-man shows in London, New York and Tokyo. *Work in collections:* Arts Council, Chase Manhattan Bank, Texaco, etc. *Signs work:* "G. SNOW." *Address:* c/o Grob Gallery, 20 Dering St., London W1R 9AA.

SNOWDEN, Hilda Mary, B.A. (Hons.) Open University, F.I.A.L.; artist in pastels, oils, water-colour, embroidery, sculpture; *b* Bradford, 13 Apr., 1910. *Educ:* Grange Upper School, Hillcroft College, Surbiton. *Studied:* Regional College of Art, Bradford, Positano Art Workshop, Italy. *Exhib:* London, Bradford, Harrogate, Ilkley. *Publications:* author and illustrator, Dalesman (Nov. 1985); Under Stag's Fell - A History of Simonstone-Wensleydale (1989); author, Bradford Antiquary (1987). *Signs work:* see appendix. *Address:* Flat I, Victoria Mans., Dawson St., Thackley, Bradford BD10 8LH.

SOAR, John Richardson, M.A. (1966), B.Sc. (1952), A.R.M.S. (1996), H.S. (1989); landscape painter in pastel (from miniature to large size pastel paintings); Principal, Swindon Technical College and School of Art (retd. 1984); Inspector of Further Education for Essex C.C. (1965-70); *b* London, 30 May, 1927. *m* Miriam Theresa. one *s.* one *d. Educ:* West Ham Municipal College; King's College, London.

Exhib: U.A. (annually), Westminster Gallery; Hilliard Soc. of Miniaturists (annually), Wells; R.M.S. Westminster Gallery (annually); World Exhbn. of Miniatures (1995); regular contributor to Medici Gallery and Llewellyn Alexander Gallery, London. *Work in collections:* mostly in West of England, U.S.A., Canada and various European countries. *Clubs:* Guild of Wiltshire Artists. *Signs work:* "JOHN SOAR." *Address:* 81 Chestnut Springs, Lydiard Millicent, Swindon, Wilts. SN5 9NB.

SOBIEN, Inka, Grand Prix Humanitaire de France avec Medaille d'Argent (1977), La Palme D'or, Belgo-Hispanique (1977); artist; lecturer, Hornsey College of Art and Central Academy of Film, Art and Drama, London (1963-66), St. Martin's School of Art (1963-67); *b* 25 Feb., 1939. *m* Stewart Steven. one *s. Studied:* St. Martin's School of Art (1959-63). *Exhib:* one-man shows: Upper St. Gallery, London (1974), Gallerie Raymond Duncan, Paris (1975), New Jersey (1975), Ligoa Duncan, N.Y. (1975), Philadelphia (1975), Florida (1976), Festival International de Peinture et d'Art Graphico-Plastique de St. Germain-des-Pres, Paris (1976), Scribes Writers' Club, London (1978), Little Palace, Warsaw (1979), B.W.A. Gallery, Cracow (1979), Avant Garde Gallery, Wroclaw (1979), Barbican Centre (1985), Budapest (1985), Camden Arts Centre (1989); mixed shows: Grande Palais Paris; London: Marjorie Parr Gallery, Gallery XVIII, Annely Juda Fine Art, Leinster Fine Art, Salomon Gallery, Inka's Extravaganza ('97, '98, 2001). *Work in collections:* National Museum, Warsaw and Cracow, Museum of Modern Art, Budapest. *Signs work:* "Inka Sobien." *Address:* 20 Woodstock Rd., London W4 1UE.

SOKOLOV, Kirill Konstantinovich, painter, printmaker, illustrator, sculptor, engraver; Hon. editor, "Leonardo"; *b* Moscow, 27 Sept., 1930. *m* Avril Pyman. one *d. Educ:* Special Art School, Moscow (1942-49). *Studied:* Surikov Institute, Moscow (1949-56). *Exhib:* Gulbenkian Gallery, Newcastle, Durham University, St. Helier, C.I., London University, Bishopsgate Foundation, Academy of Art, Riga, House of Artists, Krymskaia Naberezhnaia, Moscow, Art Gallery, Perm, Hatton Gallery and Laing Gallery, Newcastle, and various venues in U.S.S.R., China, U.S.A., Norway, Germany. *Work in collections:* Pushkin Museum, Trediakov Gallery, Latvian State Museum of Arts, Graphic Archive, Munich, Perm Gallery, Optyno-Pustyn, Taras Shevchenko, Dostoevsky and Aleksandr Blok Memorial Museums, Shakespeare Memorial Museum, Stratford-on-Avon, V. & A., Faust Soc., Knittlingen, Lyric Theatre, Hammersmith, Theatre Royal, Newcastle, Hatton Gallery, Newcastle. *Publications:* over 60 titles in Russian and English. *Signs work:* "Kirill Sokolov," also "K.S." and "K.C." (until 1974 in cyrillic). *Address:* 213 Gilesgate, Durham DH1 1QN.

SOREL, Agathe, R.W.S., R.E., Churchill Fellow (1967), Fellow, Printmakers Council; printmaker, sculptor, lecturer; *b* Budapest, 1935. *m* G. Sitkey. one *s. Studied:* Academy of Fine Art, and Academy of Applied Art, Budapest; Camberwell School of Art and Crafts (Michael Rothenstein, S.W. Hayter); Atelier 17, Paris. *Exhib:* one-man shows: Curwen Gallery, London, Arleigh Gallery, San Francisco, Philadelphia Print Club, Camden Arts Centre, O.U.P., Robertson Gallery, Ottawa, Mälargalleriet, Stockholm, Sculpture at Paul Kövesdy Gallery, N.Y., Galerie Geiger Kornwestheim, Germany, Städtische Galerie Filderstadt, Germany; retrospective exhbn. Herbert Read Gallery, Canterbury, Highgate Fine Art, Galerie La Hune, Paris.

Work in collections: in 33 major museums including B.M., Tate Gallery, Los Angeles Museum of Art, Philadelphia Museum of Art, Chicago Art Inst., National Gallery, Washington. *Publications:* illustrated: Jean Genet, Le Balcon, 'Catalana Blanca' in collaboration with Lorand Gasper; 'The Book of Sand' in collaboration with David Gascoyne. *Clubs:* R.W.S., R.E., Printmakers Council. *Signs work:* "Agathe Sorel." *Address:* Dorrell Hall, 43 London Rd., London SE23 3TY.

SORRELL, Adrian, sculptor in wax and clay cast in bronze, painter; lecturer, Bolton College of Art (1961-75); *b* Salford, 1932. *Studied:* Salford School of Art (1949-54). *Exhib:* Sladmore Gallery, London (1972-78), Les Animaliers, 150 Years of Animal Sculpture, Sladmore Gallery (1976), Morris Singer Exhbn., Dubai (1977), Sportsmans Edge Gallery, N.Y. (1978), Moorland Gallery, London (1979), Dominion Gallery, Montreal (1980), R.A. Summer Exhbn. (1980-89), Tryon Moorland Gallery, London (1983, 1987), Liverpool Museum (1985), Church St. Gallery, Stow (1987), Reid Stremmel Gallery, Texas (1986-87). *Signs work:* "SORRELL." *Address:* 74 Ringley Rd., Whitefield, Lancs. M25 7LN.

SORRELL, Richard, Dip.A.D. (1969), R.A. Schools Post. Grad. Cert. (1972), R.W.S. (1978), R.B.A. (1989), N.E.A.C. (1995); artist in oil, water-colour and acrylic; *b* Thundersley, Essex, 24 Sept., 1948. *m* Doreen Burke (divorced). two *s.* *Educ:* Eton House School, Thorpe Bay, Essex. *Studied:* Walthamstow Art School (1965-66), Kingston College of Art (1966-69), R.A. Schools (1969-72). *Exhib:* R.A., R.W.S., N.E.A.C., Bourne Gallery, Reigate, Agnews, Cadogan Gallery, Leamington A.G. *Work in collections:* V. & A., Museum of London, National Trust. *Publications:* The Artist, Country Life. *Clubs:* Art Workers Guild. *Signs work:* "Richard Sorrell." *Address:* The White House, Chapel Lane, Mickleton, Glos. GL55 6SD.

SOULAGES, Pierre, painter; *b* Rodez, France, 24 Dec., 1919. *m* Colette Llaurens. *Exhib:* one-man shows in Museums of Hannover, Zurich, Essen, De Hagen (1960-61), Copenhagen (1963), Houston (1966), Paris (1967, 1979), Buffalo, Pittsburgh, Montréal (1968), Mexico, Caracas, Rio de Janeiro, Sao Paulo (1975-76), Liège et Salzburg (1980), Tokyo (1984), Kassel, Valencia, Nantes (1989), Séoul, Pekin, Taipei (1994), Paris, Montréal, Sao Paulo (1996), Hamburg, Zaragoza (1997). *Work in collections:* Centre G. Pompidou, Paris, Museum of Modern Art, Guggenheim Museum, N.Y., National Gallery, Washington, National Gallery of Australia, Canberra, Museo de Arte Moderna, Sao-Paulo, Tate Gallery, London, etc. *Signs work:* see appendix. *Address:* 18 rue des Trois-Portes, 75005 Paris, 5.

SOUZA, F. N., painter; founder of Progressive Artists Group, Bombay (1948); *b* Goa, 12 Apr., 1924. *m* 1st. Maria Figuereido (divorced). one *d.* 2nd. Liselotte Kristian (in common law). three *d.* 3rd. Barbara Zinkant (divorced). one *s. Educ:* St. Xavier's College. *Studied:* Sir J. J. School of Art; Central School of Art; Ecole des Beaux Arts; Italian Govt. Scholarship. *Exhib:* one-man shows, London, Paris, Stockholm, Copenhagen, Johannesburg, Germany, U.A.E., U.S.A., etc.; retrospective exhbns., London, New Delhi, Leicester, Detroit; Minneapolis Int. Art (1972); Expo '67, Montreal; Commonwealth Inst., London (1977); Contemporary Indian Artists (N.Y., 1978); Festival of India, R.A. and Oxford (1982), etc. *Work in collections:* New Delhi, Tate, Haifa, Melbourne, etc. *Publications:* Words and Lines (autobiography); The White Flag Revolution (1982); New Poems (1985). *Signs work:* see appendix. *Address:* 148 West 67 St., New York, N.Y. 10023, U.S.A.

SPACKMAN, Sarah, B.A. (1981); painter in oil, water-colour, gouache, charcoal; *b* Reading, Berks., 19 Feb., 1958. *Educ:* Abbey School, Reading. *Studied:* Byam Shaw School of Art (1977-78), Camberwell School of Art (1979-81). *Exhib:* Austin Desmond Fine Art, Cadogan Contemporary, New Ashgate Gallery, Farnham, Solomon Gallery, Dublin, Mitchell Gallery, Toronto, Canada. *Work in collections:* Contemporary Art Collection, Allied Irish Bank, many private collections worldwide. *Publications:* several paintings as posters and cards by The Art Group. *Signs work:* "S.S." *Address:* 12 Henley St., Oxford OX4 1ER.

SPAFFORD, George, M.A., B.C.L., R.C.A. (1990); artist in acrylic; *b* Manchester, 1 Sept., 1921. *m* Iola. one *s.* one *d. Educ:* Rugby, Oxford. *Signs work:* "G.S." *Address:* 57 Hawthorn La., Wilmslow, Ches. SK9 5DQ.

SPAFFORD, Iola Margaret, D.F.A. (1953), R.C.A. (1984), mem. M.A.F.A.; artist in oil, pen and ink, water-colour, etching; *b* Cambridge, 24 Aug., 1930. *m* George Spafford. one *s.* one *d. Educ:* Queen Anne's, Caversham. *Studied:* Bristol Art School (1947), Nottingham Art School (1948-50), Slade School of Fine Art (1950-54). *Exhib:* 7 one-man shows, Tib Lane Gallery, Manchester. *Work in collections:* Manchester A.G. (Rutherston Collection), Salford A.G., and many private collections here and abroad. *Signs work:* "Iola Spafford." *Address:* 57 Hawthorn La., Wilmslow, Ches. SK9 5DQ.

SPENCE, Leslie James Arthur, painter in oil; gallery owner; *b* Wallasea, 30 Sep., 1934. *m* Mary. two *s.* one *d. Educ:* Leeds. *Studied:* under Prof. George McTaque. *Exhib:* R.S.M.A., R.B.A., Royal Society, Birmingham Artists; solo exhibs. throughout U.K. *Work in collections:* Westward T.V., Rowntrees of York. *Commissions:* R.N. Devonport, Norwegian Royal Navy, Rowntrees of York, Arndale Developments, Royal Marines, Plymouth Sound Radio, Leeds Regional Hospital Board, Chandos Records. *Publications:* reproductions published by Northern Editions, Solomon and Whitehead and others. *Clubs:* St. Ives Soc. of Artists. *Signs work:* "L J A Spence." *Address:* Clifton Farmhouse, Landulph, Saltash, E. Cornwall PL12 6QG.

SPENCER, Charles Samuel, lecturer and art critic; Former editor: Art and Artists, and Editions Alecto Collectors Club; former art critic London Daily Mail, New York Times European Edition; *b* London, 26 Aug., 1920. *Publications:* author: Erté (1970); A Decade of Print Making (1973); Leon Bakst (1973), enlarged and revised (1995); Cecil Beaton (1975), enlarged and revised (1995); The World of Serge Diaghilev (1974); editor: The Aesthetic Movement (1973); The World of Flo Ziegfeld (1974); Alecto Monographs on Kenneth Armitage, Colin Lanceley, Tom Phillips, Achilles Droungas, Ed Meneely, Harald Becker, Paulo Legnaghi, Igino Legnaghi. *Address:* 24a Ashworth Rd., London W9 1JY.

SPENCER, Claire, N.D.D. (1958), A.R.C.A. (1963), A.T.D. (1973), R.B.S.A. (1980), P.S. (1985); painter in oil, water-colour and pastel; *b* Kingsbury, Middx., 17 May, 1937. one *s. Educ:* Harrow County School for Girls. *Studied:* Hornsey College of Art (1954-58), R.C.A. (1960-63), Accademia di Belle Arti, Perugia (1966). Numerous individual and group exhbns. *Work in collections:* Nuffield Collection,

West Midlands Arts Collection. *Publications:* contributor to The Artist Magazine. *Signs work:* "Claire Spencer" and see appendix. *Address:* 10 Sandbourne Drive, Bewdley, Worcs. DY12 1BN.

SPENCER, Gwen, N.S.; painter in oil, pastel and water-colour; Hon. sec., National Soc. of Painters, Sculptors and Printmakers (Full mem. since 1980); *b* Argentine, 2 Oct., 1927. *m* Christopher Spencer, F.C.A. two *s.* one *d. Educ:* St. Hilda's College, Buenos Aires. *Studied:* Atelier Josse, Buenos Aires, and Putney School of Art. *Exhib:* N.S., R.O.I., P.S., Ridley Soc. *Work in collections:* U.K., N. and S. America, Italy, Holland, Denmark, India and Australia. *Publications:* work repro.: Medici Soc. *Signs work:* "Gwen Spencer" or "G. Spencer." *Address:* 122 Copse Hill, Wimbledon, London SW20 0NL.

SPENCER, Liam David, B.A.; artist in oil paint; *b* Burnley, 1964. *m* Heather Walker. two *s. Educ:* Manchester Polytechnic (1983-86). *Exhib:* touring exhbns."Windows on the City" (1996-97), "The Mancunian Way" (1997-98), "Urban Panoramas" (2000) – The Lowry, Salford. *Work in collections:* Towneley Hall A.G. and Museum, Burnley, Manchester City A.G., Readers Digest, N.Y. *Commissions:* Price Waterhouse, Manchester, Arthur Andersen, Addleshaw, Booth & Co. *Publications:* 'Article of Faith' Richard Kendal Art Review (Oct. 1996), 'Landscape Next Door' Laura Gascoigne Artists and Illustrators (Sept. 1997). *Signs work:* "L.S." or not at all. *Address:* 67 Albert Terr., Cloughfold, Rossendale BB4 7PY. *Email:* liam.spencer@lineone.net

SPENCER, Pamela Mary, artist in oil, water-colour, pencil; *b* Manchester, 11 Jan., 1924. *Educ:* P.N.E.U. Schools, Queen's College, Radbrook College of Domestic Science (Shrewsbury). *Studied:* St. Martin's School of Art under J. Bateman, Barry Craig, J. L. Wheatley, H. A. Freeth, K. Martin (1945-51). *Exhib:* R.A., N.E.A.C., S.W.A., N.S., R.B.A., R.O.I., P.S., Russell-Cotes Museum, and other provincial galleries. *Signs work:* "Pamela M. Spencer" or "P. M. Spencer." *Address:* 33 Damer Gdns., Henley-on-Thames, Oxon. RG9 1HX.

SPENCER, Sarah, B.A. (Hons.) (1988), Post. Dip. R.A. Schools (1991); painter in oil, charcoal, pastel; part-time lecturer, Canterbury College; *b* Sevenoaks, 26 Sept., 1965. *Educ:* Tonbridge Grammar School, West Kent College of F.E. *Studied:* Camberwell School of Art and Crafts (1985-88), R.A. Schools (1988-91). *Exhib:* solo shows: New Grafton Gallery, Waterman's Fine Art; many mixed shows. *Work in collections:* West Wales Arts Council. *Signs work:* full signature on reverse of works, sometimes "S.S." on front. *Address:* 7 Marine Terr., Whitstable, Kent CT5 1EJ.

SPENCER PRYSE, Tessa, R.B.A. (1986); painter of portraits, landscapes and interiors in oil, water-colour, lithography; *b* Highcliff on Sea, 28 Sept., 1939. *m* E.D.A. Cameron. one *s.* one *d. Educ:* France and Switzerland. *Studied:* Byam Shaw School of Art (1960-64, Peter Greenham, Bernard Dunstan). *Exhib:* R.A., R.P., R.B.A., N.E.A.C., R.S.A., R.W.S.; one-man shows: Phoenix Gallery, Lavenham, Hayletts Gallery, Colchester, Alpine Gallery, London, John Russell, Ipswich, Arthur Andersen, London, Llewellyn Alexander, London, Davies and Tooth, London. *Work in collections:* Essex Museum. *Signs work:* "PRYSE." *Address:* 12 Alma St., Wivenhoe, Colchester, Essex CO7 9DL.

SPENDER, Humphrey, Hon. Des. R.C.A., D. Litt. Sussex; painter, photographer; designer, textiles, wallpapers, carpets; four C.O.I.D. Awards; *b* London, 19 Apr., 1910. *m* Pauline Wynn. two *s*. *Studied:* Architectural Assoc. *Exhib:* one-man: Redfern, Leicester Galleries, New Art Centre, Windsor, Farnham, Colchester, Bristol; group: C.A.S., Arts Council, John Moores, Bradford, Aldeburgh, R.A. *Work in collections:* V. & A., N.P.G., M. of W., Southampton, Wolverhampton, Brighton, Manchester, Johannesburg. Murals: Festival of Britain, P. & O. Liners Orcades, Orsova, Oriana, Canberra, Shell Centre, Pilkingtons. *Publications:* Worktown People (Falling Wall Press, 1982), Lensman (Chatto & Windus, 1987), Humphrey Spender's Humanist Landscapes (Yale Univ. Press). *Address:* The Studio, Ulting, Maldon, Essex CM9 6QX.

SPENDLOVE, Gerald Hugh, A.T.D. (Dist.) (1954), F.S.D.C. (1972); designer-craftsman in calligraphy, lettering and ceramics; formerly Head of Ceramics, Herts. College of Art, St. Albans; Chairman, Soc. of Designer-Craftsmen (1979-81); *b* Derby, 1929. *m* Valerie Spendlove. one *s*. three *d*. *Educ:* Salisbury School of Art (1949-51), L.C.C. Central School of Art (1951-53), N.D.D. Pottery and Calligraphy: Inst. of Education, London University (1953-54). *Exhib:* Nottingham, Southampton, Bath, York, St. Albans, London, Winchester. *Work in collections:* H.M. the Queen, Herts. C.C., Australia, France; private collections in U.S.A., France, Norway, Germany, Nigeria, U.K. *Commissions:* numerous commissions, hand produced, all forms of lettering; stoneware and porcelain. *Signs work:* "G. H. Spendlove", stamp GHS in square. *Address:* The Sycamores, New Rd., Swanmore, Hants. SO32 2PE.

SPIBEY, Kenneth Richard, A.S.G.F.A., A.U.A.; painter in water-colour, pen and ink, calligrapher; retired school teacher; *b* Market Drayton, Salop., 9 Nov., 1934. *m* Janet. one *s*. one *d*. *Educ:* Oswestry School, Salop. *Studied:* Mid Cheshire College of Art, Padgate College of Education. *Exhib:* R.I., N.E.A.C., Laing Exhibs. *Publications:* illustrated guidebook to Englesea Brook Museum of Primitive Methodism. *Signs work:* "Kenneth R. Spibey." *Address:* Waneshill, Church Rd., Aston Juxta Mondrum, Nantwich, Cheshire CW5 6DR.

SPRAKES, John, R.O.I., R.B.A., F.R.S.A.; Andrew Grant scholarship, D.A. (Edin.) post grad.; prizewinner Singer Friedlander/Sunday Times water-colour (1992); artist in tempera, oil, acrylic; *b* 17 Oct., 1936. *m* Barbara Ann. three *s*. *Studied:* Doncaster College of Art, Edinburgh College of Art (1954-57). *Exhib:* R.A., Mem. of The Manchester Academy; Manchester Academy (prize 85), Barclays Bank award (1986, 1991), P/P award (1989), group and one-man shows. Work in public and private collections. Agent in London, J. Corless, Blackheath Gallery. *Signs work:* "John Sprakes" or "J. Sprakes." *Address:* 39 Douglas Rd., Long Eaton, Nottingham NG10 4BH.

SPURRIER, Raymond, R.I., R.W.A.; writer, illustrator, painter, printmaker; Hon. Secretary R.I.; *b* Wellingborough, 1920. *Educ:* Wellingborough Grammar School. *Studied:* part-time at St. Martin's and Central School. Practising town planner until 1980 and part-time freelance illustrator and writer. *Exhib:* R.A., R.W.A., R.I., etc.; finalist Hunting Group prize competition (1980, 1982); Winsor & Newton R.I. Award (1984). *Work in collections:* Dept. of the Environment and private. *Publications:* work repro.: R.A. Illustrated and calendar; contributor: The Artist

Magazine and instructional art books; author: Sketching with Raymond Spurrier; part author: Mastering Water-colour. *Signs work:* "Raymond Spurrier." *Address:* Halstead Cottage, Halstead, Sevenoaks, Kent.

SQUIRE, Geoffrey, D.F.A. (Lond.) 1948, A.R.S.A. (1977), R.G.I. (1980), R.S.W. (1983); painter in oil, acrylic, water-colour, pastel; retd. senior lecturer, Glasgow School of Art (1988), Governor (1988-91); *b* Yorks., 21 Feb., 1923. *m* Jeanmarie. one *s.* one *d.* *Studied:* Leeds College of Art (1939-41); Slade School of Art, Oxford (1941-42), London (1946-48, Randolph Schwabe). *Exhib:* Yorks., Glasgow, Fife, Edinburgh. *Work in collections:* Glasgow A.G., Greenock A.G., Paisley A.G., Dunkeld A.G., Jordanhill College of Educ., Royal Scottish Academy, Royal and Ancient Golf Club, New College, Edinburgh, Royal Hospital, Edinburgh, Court of the Lord Lyon, King of Arms, H.R.H. The Princess D. Maria Cristina, Duchess of Bragança. *Signs work:* "SQUIRE." *Address:* The Studio, Links Pl., Elie, Fife KY9 1AX.

STABELL, Waldemar Christian, painter in oil, wax drawings; *b* Hillsborough, N.B., Canada, 1913. *m* Margit Baugstö. one *s.* one *d.* *Educ:* Canada, Norway. *Studied:* Scandinavia, Anglo-French Art Centre, London, Brighton College of Art (etching). *Exhib:* first one-man show in London (1947), St. George's Gallery; several one-man shows and mixed exhibitions. *Publications:* Edvard Munch and Eva Mudocci; Bernt Tunold 1877-1977; Phillip King - En Engelsk Billedhugger (1969); British Artists at the Voss Summer School of Fine Arts; work repro.: Studio, Canada's Weekly, Contact Book, Arts Review, London. Founder of the Voss School of Fine Arts (1964) Voss, Norway. *Signs work:* "Stabell." *Address:* Sydneskleven 31, 5010 Bergen, Norway.

STAFFORD, C. Carolyn, C.P.S., S.G.F.A., P.M.C., N.S., A.U.A., N.D.D., D.A. (Manc.) (1955), Dip. Fine Art (1957); painter in oil and water-colour, printmaker in etching, woodcut, lino; tutor; *b* Bolton, 1935. *m* Gordon Clough, broadcaster (decd.). one *s.* three *d.* *Educ:* Bolton School. *Studied:* Bolton School of Art, Manchester College of Art (Ralph Downing, Ian Grant), Slade School of Fine Art (William Coldstream, Claude Rogers, Anthony Gross), Esmond Scholar British Inst. in Paris, etching with S.W. Hayter (1957-58). *Exhib:* John Moores, Liverpool, R.A., Bankside Open Prints, London Group, Arts Council tours, R.I., R.B.A., Printmakers Council, Malta, U.S./U.K., Art Olympia (1990-93), Pump House (1993), Contemporary Portrait Soc., Northern School (Pelter-Sands and touring exhbn.), Lvov (1991), New Academy Gallery (1991), Paris (1994, 1996), Universities of Bristol, Cambridge, London, Oxford and Surrey (1980-90), Tel Aviv, Ben Uri, Curwen, F.P.S., Munich (1997), North-South Printmakers Barbican (1999). *Work in collections:* Slade School, D.O.E., Bolton School (Girls Div.), Bolton A.G., Lvov A.G., Landau A.G. *Publications:* Arts Review. *Signs work:* "Carolyn Stafford," "Carolyn Stafford Clough" or "C. STAFFORD." *Address:* 52 Ellerton Rd., London SW18 3NN.

STAGE, Ruth, B.A. Hons., P.G. Dip. N.E.A.C.; painter in egg tempera; *b* 8 Nov., 1969. *Educ:* Blakeston Comprehensive. *Studied:* Newcastle University, R.A. Schools. *Exhib:* 4 solo exhibs., New Grafton Gallery. *Work in collections:* A T Kearney, Charing Cross Hospital, Durham University, Hiscox Plc. *Commissions:* Chevron U.K. Calendar. *Clubs:* Egg Tempera Soc. *Signs work:* "R Stage." *Address:* 13a Wyneham Rd., London SE24 9NT.

STAHL, Andrew, Slade D.F.A., Slade H.D.F.A.; painter in oil, water-colour, acrylic; senior lecturer, Slade School of Fine Art; *b* London, 4 July, 1954. *m* Kumiko Tsuna. one *s*. two *d*. *Studied:* Slade School of Fine Art. *Exhib:* many one-man and group shows in U.K. and abroad. *Work in collections:* Arts Council, British Council, British Museum, Contemporary Arts Soc., City Museum Peterborough, Leics. Educ. Authority, Metropolitan Museum of Art, New York. Ex Rome Scholar and Wingate Scholar. Represented by Angela Flowers Gallery. *Signs work:* back of work usually "ANDREW STAHL" or "A. STAHL." *Address:* 1 Old Oak Rd., London W3 7HN.

STAINTON, Frances: see EASTON, Frances.

STANDEN, Peter, D.A. (Edin.); works in oil, acrylic, etching: subjects allegorical, imaginary future ruins, and cats; Mem. Edinburgh Printmakers Workshop; Scottish Art Council Awards incl. 'Artist in Industry' Ferranti plc (1987); *b* Carshalton, 3 Apr., 1936. *m* Helen. one *s*. one *d*. *Educ:* Epping Secondary. *Studied:* Nottingham College of Art (1954-56), Edinburgh College of Art (1956-59). *Exhib:* one-man shows: 'Up the Nile' Commonwealth Inst., Edinburgh (1965), 'Paintings' New 57 Gallery, Edinburgh (1977), 'Mr. Cat' Traverse Theatre Club, Edinburgh (1985), 'Looking Back to the Future' P.M.W. Edinburgh (1988); group shows: 'Art into Landscape' I and III Serpentine Gallery, London (1974, 1979), '5 Scottish Printmakers' selected by Peter Fuller, P.M.W. Edinburgh Festival (1983), 'Ljubljana Biennial' Yugoslavia (1987). *Work in collections:* H.M. The Queen, Windsor Castle, Hamilton A.G., Ontario, City of Edinburgh, Moray House College Edinburgh, Eastern General Hospital Edinburgh, The University of Edinburgh, Royal Bank of Scotland. *Publications:* etchings included in "Edinburgh Suite" (1992) and "The Sea, the Sea" portfolios (Pub. by E.P.M.W., Edinburgh). *Signs work:* prints: "P. Standen" (pencil signature); paintings: "P. STANDEN." *Address:* 5 Lee Cres., Portobello, Edinburgh EH15 1LW. *Email:* peterstanden@edinburghetchings.com

STARR, Marion, artist in oil; *b* Hitchin, Herts., 19 Apr., 1937. *m* Christopher Fielder. two *d*. *Educ:* various Grammar Schools in U.K. and abroad. *Studied:* Chinese brush painting and the Sogetsu School discipline of flower arrangement while in the Far East. *Exhib:* R.A. Summer Exhbn. (since 1979), R.W.A., R.O.I., R.B.A., N.E.A.C., Laing, Spirit of London, Rye Soc. of Artists, Chichester City of Culture Open Art Exhbn., 'A Celebration of the Romney Marsh' at Sassoon Gallery, Folkestone and Marsh Gallery, New Romney; New Grafton Gallery, Easton Rooms and Stormont Studio, Rye, Neville Gallery, Canterbury, Attendi Gallery, Chiswick, Anna-Mei Chadwick Gallery, Fulham, Talents Fine Arts, Malton. Major winner, Laing Landscape Painting competition (1994). *Signs work:* "M.S." or "Marion Starr." *Address:* 23 Military Rd., Rye, E. Sussex TN31 7NX.

STAUVERS, Feliks, R.V.D.S. Arts Academy School (Riga, Latvia); Diploma of Merit, University of Art, Italy; artist in oil, water-colour, dry pigments, restorer, art historian, lecturer in Art and Old Master Paintings; *b* Riga, Latvia, 22 Apr., 1926. *m* M. E. Stauvers. two *s*. *Educ:* Latvia. *Studied:* Riga Government Arts Academy School (1939-44) under, Prof. Brumel, Dr. V. Luans, Daluns Paks, R.V.D.S. *Exhib:* Nuneaton, Coventry, London, Paris. *Work in collections:* Nuneaton Museum A.G., Riga Government A.G., Latvia, Coventry Museum/A.G. *Clubs:* Former Associate of

I.I.C. London. *Signs work:* "Feliks Stauvers." *Address:* 83 Windmill Rd., Exhall, Coventry CV7 9GP.

STEAD, David Thomas Kirby, B.A. (Hons.); artist in oil on canvas, and water-colour; *b* Ripon, Yorks., 14 Apr., 1959. *m* Rebecca Susan. one *s.* three *d. Studied:* Harrogate and Wimbledon. *Exhib:* Ariel Centre, Devon, Henry Brett Gallery, Stow, Coves Quay Gallery Salcombe, Thompson Gal. Stow., Art Co. Leeds, etc. Work in collections internationally. *Work in collections:* U.K., America, Europe, Far East. *Commissions:* album covers for 'Just Music' records. *Address:* 3 Seymour Villas, Totnes, Devon TQ9 5QR.

STEEL, Hilary, B.A. Hons. (1985), Dip. Arch. (1988); draughtsman in pen and pencil; freelance architectural illustrator; specialises in architectural elevational drawings; *b* Carshalton, 17 Mar., 1964. *m* Adrian Odey. one *s. Studied:* Brighton University School of Architecture. *Exhib:* R.A. Summer Exhib. (2000-2001). *Commissions:* Medici Gallery Cards (2001). *Signs work:* "Hilary Steel." *Address:* 132 Lower Church Rd., Burgess Hill, W. Sussex RH15 9AB. *Email:* h.steel@btclick.com

STEPHENS, Ian, N.D.D. (1961), R.E. (1984), S.W.E. (1984) (Chairman 1992-95); artist in wood engraving, water-colours; *b* Gt. Linford, Bucks., 19 May, 1940. *m* Valerie. two *s. Educ:* Wolverton Technical School. *Studied:* Northampton School of Art (1956-61). *Exhib:* R.E. (1975 onwards), Fremantle, Jeune Gravure Contemporaine, Paris, Humberside (1985); one-man show Daventry (1989, 1993), British Miniature Print International, Bristol (1989, 1997), Cadaqués (1991, onwards). *Work in collections:* Northants C.C., Notts. C.C., Surrey C.C., Warwicks. Museums, Kettering B.C., Daventry D.C., Fremantle Arts Centre, Ashmolean Museum Oxford, Northampton Central Museum and A.G. *Signs work:* "I. Stephens" or "Ian Stephens." *Address:* 46 Yardley Drive, Northampton NN2 8PE.

STEPHENS, Nicholas Anthony, N.D.D. (1960), A.R.C.A. (1963), Harkness Fellowship, U.S.A. (1963-65), Arts Council Major award (1977), A.R.B.S. (1981); sculptor in bronze; Principal Lecturer in Fine Art, Glos. College of Art and Technology; visiting teaching: U.C. Davis, California (1971), Victoria College, Prahran, Australia (1983); *b* Nottingham, 6 June, 1939. *m* Jenifer Beesley (divorced 1984). two *s. Educ:* Nottingham High School. *Studied:* Central School (Wm. Turnbull), R.C.A. (1960-63, Lord Queensbury), Pratt Inst., N.Y. (1964), San Francisco Art Inst. (1965, James Melchert). *Exhib:* Davis Cal. (1971), S.W. Arts (1978), The State of Clay (1978-80), R.A. (1980, 1981, 1983, 1984), R.B.S. Scone Palace (1983), Park Gallery Cheltenham (1982, 1985), St. Donat's Castle, Wales (1983), Nicholas Tredwell Gallery (1985), Air Gallery, Harkness Arts (1985), St. David's Hall, Cardiff (1988). *Signs work:* "N.A. STEPHENS." *Address:* The Red House, Bredon, Tewkesbury, Glos. GL20 7LM.

STEPHENSON, Christine Frances, N.D.D. (1957), A.T.D. (1958), S.B.A. (1997), R.H.S. Silver Medal (1996), Gold Medal (1997), Cert. of Botanical Merit S.B.A. (1999); botanical artist in water-colour; *b* Winchester, 3 Apr., 1937. *m* Jack Stephenson, artist. two *s. Educ:* St. Swithun's School, Winchester. *Studied:* Bournemouth College of Art (1953-58). *Exhib:* R.H.S., S.B.A., Lucy B. Campbell Gallery, London, Gordon-Craig Gallery, London. *Work in collections:* Hunt Institute for Botanical Documentaion, Pittsburgh, U.S.A. *Commissions:* many. *Publications:* "Woottens" catalogue, Gordon-Craig catalogue. *Signs work:* "C.F.S." *Address:* 3 Causeway Cottages, Middleton, nr. Saxmundham, Suffolk IP17 3NH.

STETTLER, Michael, D.Sc.; art historian; architect; Director of Bernese Historical Museum from 1948 to 1961; Director Abegg Foundation (1961-77); P. Helvetia Foundation (1965-71); *b* Berne, 1 Jan., 1913. *m* Barbara von Albertini. four *d. Educ:* Berne. *Studied:* Zürich Inst. of Technology and University under J. Zemp and H. Wölfflin, and at Rome. *Publications:* Das Rathaus zu Bern (1942), Inventory of Historical Monuments of Canton Aargau (Vol. I, 1948, Vol. II, 1953); Swiss Stained Glass of the 14th Century (English Edition, 1949); Of Old Berne (1957); Rat der Alten (1962); Bernerlob (1964), Neues Bernerlob (1967); Aare, Bär und Sterne (1972); Machs na (1981); Ortbühler Skizzenbuch (1982); A la Rencontre de Berne (1984); Sulgenbach (1992), Lehrer und Freunde (1997). *Address:* Ortbühl, CH-3612 Steffisburg, Switzerland.

STEVENS, Chris, B.F.A. (Hons.); artist in oil; *b* Basingstoke, 1956. *Studied:* University of Reading (1974-78). *Exhib:* one-man shows: U.K., London and Holland; group shows: London, Germany and U.S.A; shows with Sue Williams, London. *Work in collections:* National Gallery of Wales. *Address:* Space Studios, Deborah House, Retreat Pl., London E9.

STEVENS, Helen M., S.W.A. (1989); artist in pure silk hand embroidery, writer; *b* Belmont, Surrey, 2 Oct., 1959. *m* Brian Rayner. *Educ:* Bury St. Edmunds County Grammar School. *Exhib:* S.W.A., Soc. of Wildlife Art in Nature; numerous solo shows every two years. *Work in collections:* Palace of Westminster. *Publications:* author and illustrator: 'The Embroiderers Countryside', 'The Embroiderers Country Album'; 'The Timeless Art of Embroidery' and 'The Myth and Magic of Embroidery' (David & Charles). *Signs work:* "Helen M. Stevens." *Address:* 3 The Green, Flempton, Bury St. Edmunds, Suffolk IP28 6EL.

STEVENS, Margaret Cecilie, V.P.S.B.A. (1997-), S.G.F.A.; R.H.S. Silver Gilt Lindley medal (1989), Gold (1990), Cert. Botanical Merit, S.B.A. (1998); freelance botanical and miniature artist in water-colour; Adult Class Tutor at two Arca Colleges; Exec. Vice President, Soc. of Botanical Artists since 1997; *b* Brixham, Devon, 14 Oct., 1937. *m* Derek Stevens (decd.). *Educ:* Dartmouth Grammar School. *Exhib:* solo shows; Penrhyn Castle, National Trust; mixed exhibitions: S.B.A., Westminster, Llewellyn Alexander Gallery, R.M.S., Hilliard, Linnean, S.G.F.A. - all regularly. *Work in collections:* Hunt Inst. for Botanical Documentation, Pittsburgh; numerous private collections worldwide. *Commissions:* large collection of old roses for private buyer, Fine Art prints, greetings cards, etc., Chelsea plate (1993, Franklin Mint), Royal British Legion plates (Bradford Exchange). *Publications:* 'An Introduction to Drawing Flowers' (1994), 'The Gourmet Garden' (2001). *Clubs:* Founder mem. S.B.A., S.G.F.A. *Signs work:* "Margaret Stevens" and see appendix. *Address:* 1 Hen Gapel, Gerlan, Bethesda, Gwynedd LL57 3ST.

STEVENS, Meg, B.A. (Hons.) Fine Art, M.A. Art History, R.C.A.; landscape painter in oil, gouache, pen and ink wash; *b* Leeds, 8 Feb., 1931. *m* Roger Stevens. two *d. Studied:* Reading University. *Exhib:* Royal Cambrian Academy (members annual show), St. David's Hall, Cardiff, Oriels Ynys Mon, R.S.P.B., Nature in Art.

Tours four N.F.S. travelling shows annually in support of habitat conservation 'Grass' (old common) 'Flowerscapes, 'Trees' and 'Towpath'. *Work in collections:* S.W.A.N., and several private owners. *Publications:* own booklets (two) with pictures of my work on each page. *Signs work:* "Meg Stevens." *Address:* Bridge House, Llanfrynach, Brecon, Powys LD3 7BQ.

STEVENSON, David John, painter in egg tempera and oil; *b* Leicester, 26 Nov., 1956. *m* Alison Wilkins. two *s. Educ:* Guthlaxton College, Leicester. *Exhib:* Leicester Museum, Loseby Gallery, Leicester, Tettenhall Gallery, R.A. *Clubs:* Leicester Soc. of Artists. *Signs work:* "D. Stevenson." *Address:* 15 Wartnaby St., Market Harborough, Leics.

STEVENSON, Richard Lee, printmaker, etching, intaglio, relief printing, oils; *b* Penzance, 9 Apr., 1955. *Studied:* Falmouth School of Art, North Staffs. Polytechnic, Penzance School of Art (Sue Lewington). *Exhib:* R.W.A. Mall Galleries, London, Victoria Galleries, Bath, Small Print Gallery, Penzance, The Contemporary Print Show, The Barbican. *Commissions:* Linocut cover design for the 18th International Celtic Film And Television Festival catalogue. *Publications:* Ten Penwith Printmakers (1998). *Clubs:* St. Ives Soc. of Artists, Cornwall Crafts Assoc., Penwith Printmakers. *Signs work:* "Lee Stevenson." *Address:* Little Trevarrack, Brandy Lane, Rosudgeon, Penzance, Cornwall TR20 9QB.

STEWART, Barbara Jean, painter in oil, mixed media and pastel; archivist Pastel Soc.; *b* York, 18 Nov., 1929. *m* Rae Stewart (decd.). three *d. Studied:* Leeds College of Education, but mainly self taught. *Exhib:* mixed shows countrywide. *Work in collections:* R.W.A. *Clubs:* R.W.A., P.S., R.B.S.A. *Address:* 29 Meadowcourt Rd., Oadby, Leics. LE2 2PD.

STEWART, Charles William, taught at Byam Shaw School (1950-58); artist and illustrator in water-colour, pen and ink; *b* Ilo-Ilo, Panay, Philippine Islands, 18 Nov., 1915. *Educ:* Radley College. *Studied:* The Byam Shaw School of Drawing and Painting (1932-38) under Ernest Jackson. *Publications:* illustrated: Pendennis (Thackeray), Limited Editions Club, N.Y.; Vathek (Beckford), Bodley Head; The Lady of the Linden Tree (Barbara Leonie Picard), O.U.P.; Grimbold's Other World (Nicholas Stuart Gray), Faber; The Visiting Moon (Celia Furse), Faber; Uncle Silas (Sheridan LeFanu) Folio Soc.; Mistress Masham's Repose (T.H. White) Folio Soc., Ghost Stories, Folio Society: selected and illustrated by C.W.S., etc. *Signs work:* "Charles W. Stewart." *Address:* Flat 1, Ritchie Court, 380 Banbury Rd., Oxford OX2 7PW.

STEWART, John Dunlop, M.S.I.A. (1947-70), N.R.D. (1945), probationer, R.I.B.A. (1944); industrial designer and product design consultant; founder and hon. sec., Paisley Rocketeers' Society (1936-39 and from 1968); designer and producer of multiple originals - numbered and initialled rocket mail flown in experimental models; draughtsman-designer, Universal Pulp Containers Ltd. (1941-48); designer-photographer, H. Morris & Co. Ltd., Glasgow (1948); designer, Design Industries, Beckenham (1949-52); Burndept-Vidor Ltd., Erith (1952-56); Scottish Aviation Ltd (1956-59); *b* Paisley, 3 Sept., 1921. *Educ:* John Neilson Inst., Paisley. *Studied:* Glasgow School of Art, Glasgow School of Architecture and Royal Technical College, and Govt. Training Centre, Thornliebank. *Exhib:* Paisley Museum and A.G.; 'Britain Can Make It', London; Transport Museum Glasgow; Museum of Flight, nr. Edinburgh.

Publications: 'The Paisley Rocketeers' by Donald Malcolm; countless press articles; T.V. demonstrations. *Address:* Greystone, 15 Bushes Ave., Paisley PA2 6JR.

STEWART-JONES, Elizabeth, painter, mainly of portraits, in oil and gouache; *b* Lewes, 10 Nov., 1910. *m* Major F.H.D. Pulford. two *d.* *Studied:* Chelsea School of Art. *Exhib:* pre-war open: S.W.A. (1932, 1934, 1936, 1938), R.A. (1935), R.O.I. (1937, 1938), N.E.A.C., London Group, Artists International (1938), Paris (1939); post-war open: R.B.A., R.A., R.W.A., N.S., F.P.S., etc. Current paintings mostly abstract portraits based on the colour of sound. *Commissions:* various. *Signs work:* "E.S-J." or "E. Stewart-Jones." *Address:* Penlanole, nr. Llandrindod-Wells, Powys LD1 6NN.

STEYN, Carole, sculptor, painter, pastellist and engraver - abstract, pop art and figurative; *b* Manchester. two *s.* *Educ:* Wycombe Abbey. *Studied:* Académie Julian, Paris (1954), St. Martin's School of Art (1955-57). *Exhib:* eight solo shows: Drian Galleries (1971, 1975, 1981 (First Retrospective Exhbn.), 1985), Jablonsky Galleries, London (1987), Galerie Harounoff, London (1991); twenty group shows: all in London (1968-97); Lauderdale House (1997). *Work in collections:* National Museum, Warsaw, Poland (Nalecz Collection), Sheffield City Museum, National Museum, Gdansk, Poland, Ben Uri Collection. *Commissions:* British Telecom (1985). *Publications:* work repro.: in Apollo "The Select Few" (1975), Arts Review (1975, 1981), listed in Le Benizet (1999); Radio broadcast B.B.C. (1971), Open House (1975) and B.B.C. Manchester (1985). Television B.B.C. 1 (1971) and B.B.C. 2 (1989). *Signs work:* "C. Steyn." *Address:* 12 Rosecroft Ave., London NW3 7QB.

STIEGER, Jacqueline, sculptor/jewellery/medals - lost wax technique, casting, bronze and precious metals; *b* London, 26 Jan., 1936. two *s-s.* *Educ:* Bedales, Hants; The Mount School, York. *Studied:* Edinburgh College of Art (1952-58) under W. Gillies. *Exhib:* Goldsmiths' Hall, Galerie Riehentor, Basel. *Work in collections:* Eidgenosische Kunstkommission, Bern Ch; Museum of Medallic Art, Cracow, Poland; Goldsmiths' Hall Collection; B.M. *Commissions:* Plaque to commemorate Second World War, The Reform Club, London (1995), Bronze Sculpture, St. Clare's Oxford (1997). *Signs work:* "J. Stieger." *Address:* Welton Garth, Welton, N. Humberside HU15 1NB.

STOBART, Jane, R.E. (1986); artist printmaker specialising in etching; lecturer at Goldsmiths' College; Fellow, Royal Society of Printmakers; Mem., Wynkyn de Worde Soc.; *b* S. Shields, Tyne and Wear, 10 Nov., 1949. *m* Mustafa Sidki. *Educ:* S.E. Essex Technical School, Dagenham. *Studied:* Hornsey College and Central School. *Exhib:* Bankside Gallery, Royal Academy, Gainsborough's House, Bradford Print Biennale, Manhatten Graphics Center, N.Y., Barbican. *Work in collections:* Ashmolean Museum, Museum of London, Smithsonian Inst., U.S.A. *Commissions:* National Grid (1995), Smithsonian Inst., U.S.A. (1996), Florence Nightingale Health Centre, Harlow (1997). *Publications:* 'Printmaking for Beginners' (A. & C. Black). *Address:* 47 Potter St., Harlow, Essex CM17 9AE. *Email:* jstobart.printmaker@virgin.net

STOCK, Andrew Nicholas, A.R.E., S.WL.A.; Richard Richardson award for bird illustration (1980); P.J.C. award for individual merit (1990), prizewinner in Natural World fine art awards (1989, 1990), runner-up in BBC World Magazine's Wildlife

Artist of the Year (1991); Bird Illustrator of the Year (1995); Council mem. S.WL.A. (1992-94), secretary (1995-) Governor F.B.A. (1997-); self taught painter in water-colour, etching, oil, pen and ink; *b* Rinteln, W. Germany, 25 Mar., 1960. *m* Melanie Vass (divorced 1995). one *d. Educ:* Sherborne School, Dorset. *Exhib:* S.WL.A., Tyron Gallery, Royal Academy, etc.; one-man shows: Malcolm Innes Gallery, London (4), Alpine Club Gallery, London (2), Gallery in Cork St., London (1), The Mall Galleries (3), Edinburgh and Cerne Abbas, Dorset (2). *Commissions:* M.A.F.F., 29 Commando R.A., The Sultan of Oman. *Publications:* illustrated Driven Game Shooting by D. Bingham (Unwin Hyman, 1989). *Signs work:* "Andrew Stock." *Address:* The Old School House, Ryme Intrinseca, Sherborne, Dorset DT9 6JX. *Email:* Andrewstock1@compuserve.com

STOCKHAM, Alfred Francis, A.R.C.A. (1966), Rome Scholar (1967), Granada Arts Fellow (1968), R.W.A. (1992); painter in oil; *b* London, 1 Jan., 1933. *m* Catherine Bellohoubek. *Studied:* Camberwell School of Art (1960-63, Robert Medley), R.C.A. (1963-66, C. Weight), Rome Scholar (1966-67). *Exhib:* Il Capittello, Rome, Munster, Germany, Arts Fair, New York, R.A., R.W.A. *Work in collections:* Bradford City Museum, Bristol City Museum, G.L.C., M. of W., Arts Council (N.I.), York City A.G. *Signs work:* "A.S." front; "Alfred Stockham" back. *Address:* 75 Woodhill Rd., Portishead, Bristol BS20 9HA.

STOCKHAUS, Eva H. M., R.E.; artist in wood-engraving; Mem. Swedish Printmakers' Assoc.; Mem. British Soc. of Wood Engravers; Hon. Retd. Mem. Royal Soc. of Painter-Printmakers; *b* Gothenburg, Sweden, 4 Apr., 1919. *m* Bengt Stockhaus. one *s.* one *d. Educ:* Stockholm University; art studies Stockholm and London. *Work in collections:* V. & A., London; National Museum, Stockholm; Nasjonalgalleriet, Oslo; New York Public Library; Graphische Sammlung Albertina, Vienna; various museums Scandinavia etc. Recipient artist's grant of the Swedish State (1975, 1976). *Signs work:* "Eva Stockhaus." *Address:* Pontonjärgatan 16, 11237 Stockholm, Sweden.

STOKER, Richard, J.P. (1995), F.R.A.M. (1973); self employed artist in oils, poster paint, pen, pencil; composer, author; Com. mem. and treasurer, R.A.M. Guild; concert com. B.A.C.S.; *b* Castleford, Yorks., 8 Nov., 1938. *m* Dr. Gillian Stoker, Ph.D., M.A., B.A. (Hons.). *Studied:* Huddersfield School of Art (now University) under Sugden and Napier (1954-58) and privately under H.R.M. Irving, Huddersfield (1958-59); in Paris with Nadia Boulanger (1962-63). *Exhib:* Lawrence House (two one-man shows), Lewisham Soc. of Arts Summer Exhbn. (1992), Tudor Barn, Eltham (1990), Blackheath Art Soc. Exhbn. (1989, 1990, 1991), Lewisham Arts Festival (1990, 1992). Work in private collections and on CD's. *Commissions:* Arts Council, London. *Publications:* Open Window - Open Door (Regency); Words Without Music (Outposts, 1971); Tanglewood (novel) (Merlin); Diva (novel) (Minerva); Collected Short Stories (Minerva, 1997). Portrait painted by John Bratby, R.A. (1983). Steering Group mem. and treasurer, Lewisham Visual Arts Festival (1990, 1992). Nominated: 'Man of the Year 1997' by the American Biographical Soc. (1997), three Editors Awards: National Library U.S.A. *Clubs:* Blackheath Art Soc. (1988), Lewisham Arts Soc. (1990), elected to International and London P.E.N. (1996), R.A.M. Guild (1986), Founder mem. Atlantic Council (1993), Euro - Atlantic Group (1993), R.S.L. (1994). *Signs work:* "Stoker" or "R.S." or not at all. *Address:*

38 Lee Rd., Blackheath, London SE3 9RU.

STOKES, Vincent, B.A. (Hons.) Photography and Semiotics; designer/photographer; art director; *b* 9 Jan., 1964. *Studied:* London College of Printing (1986-89, Ann Williams, Peter Osborn). *Exhib:* Camera Work U.K., Camera Work San Francisco, Photographers Gallery, Arnolfini Bristol, New Orleans, Buffalo, Vancouver, N.Y. *Signs work:* see appendix. *Address:* 14 Beckley House, Hamlets Way, London E3 4SZ.

STOKOE, Michael Arthur, N.D.D. (1957); painter; ex-senior lecturer, Ravensbourne College of Design; *b* London, 1933. *m* Gillian Stacey. one *s.* one *d. Educ:* King's School, Bruton. *Studied:* St. Martin's School of Art (1953-57). *Exhib:* R.A., R.B.A., R.O.I., R.S.O.P.P., Young Contemporaries, Arts Council, Belfast, Piccadilly Gallery, Arnolfini Gallery, Hamilton Gallery, John Moores, New Gallery, Belfast etc.; one-man shows: Temple Gallery, Drian Galleries, Bear Lane Gallery, Nottingham City A.G., Oxford Gallery, Anna Mei Chadwick Gallery, Zella Gallery. *Work in collections:* Arts Council of N. Ireland, V. & A., W.A.G., Ferens A.G., Hull, Leeds City A.G., I.C.I., etc., and 20 educational authorities. *Publications:* prints with editions Alecto, Collectors Guild. *Signs work:* "STOKOE." *Address:* 44 Stockwell Park Cres., London SW9 0DG.

STONES, Anthony, F.R.B.S. (1992), V.P.S.P.S.; sculptor in clay for bronze; *b* Glossop, Derby., 8 Feb., 1934. *Educ:* St. Bede's College, Manchester. *Studied:* Manchester Regional College of Art (1950-51). *Work in collections:* bronze portrait heads: John Piper in Reading Civic Centre; Prof. Dorothy Hodgkin, O.M., Somerville College, Oxford; Sir Ronald Syme, O.M. and Sir Isaiah Berlin, O.M., Wolfson College, Oxford; Liam Ó Flaherty, National Gallery of Ireland; Sean Ó Faolin, Irish Writers Museum, Dublin. *Commissions:* commemorative bronze figures: The Hon. Peter Fraser, Wellington, N.Z.; Lord Freyberg, V.C., Auckland, N.Z.; Jean Batten, Auckland International Airport; Victorian Navvy (1992), Gerrards Cross Railway Station; Seven Pacific Explorers for New Zealand Pavilion Expo 92 Seville; Captain James Cook, Gisborne, New Zealand (1994); The Pioneer Wine Maker, Waitakere City, New Zealand (1995); equestrian statue of "Bonnie Prince Charlie", Derby (1995); Captain James Cook, National Maritime Museum, Greenwich (1997); Blair 'Paddy' Mayne, Newtownards, Northern Ireland (1997); 'King' and 'Queen', 'Orpheus and Eurydice', four bronze statuettes for Royal Caribbean Cruise Line A/S (1997). *Publications:* edited: Celebration (Penguin Books, 1984); wrote and illustrated: Bill and the Ghost of Grimley Grange (Wolfhound Press, 1988; Puffin Books, 1994), Bill and the Maze at Grimley Grange (Wolfhound Press, 1990); 'Venus and Cupid': a relief carving by Michelangelo? papers of The British School at Rome Vol. LXI (1993). *Signs work:* "Anthony Stones." *Address:* 42 Beauchamp Pl., Oxford OX4 3NE.

STONES, Thomas Fiendley, O.B.E. (1981), B.A. (Admin.), F.M.A.; *b* Astley, Lancs., 25 July, 1920. *m* Elizabeth Mackie (decd.). one *d. Educ:* Leigh Grammar School and Manchester University. *Studied:* Served R.A.F. (1941-46); Keeper of the Rutherston Collection, Manchester City Art Galleries (1946-52); Keeper of Modern European Dept. and Print Dept., Royal Ontario Museum of Archæology, Toronto; special lecturer in art and archæology, University of Toronto (1953-54); British

Council, Fine Arts Dept., Fine Arts Officer, Paris; Cultural Attaché, British Embassy, Budapest; etc. *Address:* c/o National Westminster Bank, P.O. Box 2162, 20 Dean St., London W1A 1SX.

STONYER, Andrew Allan, B.A. (1966), A.A. Dip. Arch. (1974), Ph.D. (1978); sculptor; Prof. in Fine Art, Cheltenham and Gloucester C.H.E.; *b* Sibbertoft, Leics., 11 Oct., 1944. *m* Linda. one *s*. one *d*. *Studied:* Northampton School of Art (1960-63), Loughborough College of Art and Design (1963-67), Architectural Assoc. (1970-72), Leicester Polytechnic/Slade School of Fine Art (1975-78). *Exhib:* R.A., Ikon Gallery, Cairn Gallery, Barbican Centre, Art 45 and Terre des Hommes, Montreal. *Work in collections:* Ottawa, Hague, Leicester, etc. *Commissions:* Leicester City Council, Cheltenham Racecourse, Ottawa City Council, Laval - Montreal, Newcastle Metro, etc. *Publications:* Leonardo Vol.18.No.3, The Structurist No.27/28. *Clubs:* Chelsea Arts, R.W.A. *Address:* Eastmead, Watery Lane, Newent, Glos. GL18 1QA.

STOPS, John, N.D.D., A.T.D., R.W.A.; retd. lecturer, landscape painter in oil, water-colour, lino, gallery organiser; Gallery Organiser, Guild Gallery, Bristol; *b* Radlett, 24 Mar., 1925. *m* Susan. one *s*. one *d*. (decd.). *Educ:* Repton School. *Studied:* Northampton, Leeds (1947-52, Alicia Boyle, Henry Bird). *Exhib:* numerous, mainly Bristol, own gallery St. Davids (1969-89). *Work in collections:* Northampton A.G., Royal West of England Academy. *Clubs:* R.W.A., Bath Soc. of Artists. *Signs work:* "John Stops" and year. *Address:* 9 Freeland Pl., Hotwells, Bristol BS8 4NP.

STOREY, Terence, P.P.R.S.M.A., F.R.S.A.; marine and landscape artist in oils and water-colour; *b* Sunderland, 17 Apr., 1923. *Educ:* Sunderland Art School and Derby College of Art. *Exhib:* N.S., R.B.A., R.S.M.A., R.O.I., N.E.A.C. and S.WL.A. *Work in collections:* H.R.H. the Prince of Wales, R.S.M.A. Diploma Collection, Derby A.G., The Picture collection of the Port of London Authority, and private collections in U.S.A., Canada, Australia, New Zealand, Germany and the U.K. *Commissions:* Sultan of Oman, The Royal Eagles Club, The Royal Burnham Yacht Club, The Forth Ports - Tall Ships Gathering - Leith. *Publications:* work repro.: Rolls-Royce Ltd., Medici Soc., Royles, Winsor and Newtons, 20th Century British Marine Art, Square Rigged Sailing Ships, Marine Painting, A Celebration of Marine Art and numerous shipping lines. *Signs work:* see appendix. *Address:* Merlewood, 6 Queensway, Derby DE22 3BE.

STOREY, Warren, R.W.A. (1957), V.P.R.W.A. (1988-Mar.93), A.T.D. (1950), Brit. Inst. Scholarship (1948); painter, general and ecclesiastical designer, mural artist; Head of Weston-super-Mare School of Art (1958-84); extra mural art history lecturer, Bristol University; *b* S. Shields, 19 Aug., 1924. *m* Lilian Evans. five *d*. *Educ:* S. Shields High School. *Studied:* S. Shields School of Art under Ernest Gill, A.R.C.A. (1941-44), and Regent St. Polytechnic School under Wm. Matthews and Norman Blamey (1947-50). *Exhib:* R.A., R.B.A., R.W.A., etc. *Work in collections:* R.W.A., St. Monica Home, Bristol, Somerset C.C., Walsall, Casa Piccolo Valletta, Weston-super-Mare Museum. *Commissions:* Harvey's Sherry Bristol, various churches, Windwhistle Junior School mural, private portraits. *Publications:* contributor to Leisure Painter since 1987. *Signs work:* "Storey" and date. *Address:* 14 Leighton Cres., Weston-super-Mare BS24 9JL.

WHO'S WHO IN ART

STORK, Mary, B.A., Slade Dip.; painter in pastels; figure painter; *b* Portsmouth, 5 Sep., 1938. one *s.* two *d. Educ:* Beadales, The Hall School. *Studied:* West of England College of Art, under Paul Feiler (1955), The Slade, London University, under Frank Auerbach, Keith Vaughan (1958). *Exhib:* David Messum, Cork St., Thompsons, Dover St., and many others. *Signs work:* "Stork." *Address:* 19 St. Mary's Terr., Penzance, Cornwall TR18 4DZ. *Email:* marystork@storkfsbusiness.co.uk

STRAFFORD, Judy, artist in oil and water-colour; *b* 6 Mar., 1932. *m* Thomas Strafford. one *s.* two *d. Studied:* Brighton College of Art. *Exhib:* solo and group shows: London, New Dehli, Alresford, Bristol, etc. Work in collections internationally. *Publications:* illustrated: The Green Home by Karen Christensen; work repro.: 1993 Good Hotel Guide, greetings cards, Limited Edn. prints. Workshops in water-colour, oil and mixed media in England, Italy, Turkey & Canada. *Clubs:* Chelsea Arts. *Address:* Apple Tree Cottage, Easton, Winchester, Hants. SO21 1EF.

STREVENS, Bridget Julia, M.A. (Cantab., 1979); artist and illustrator in oil, water-colour, line, and multimedia designer; *b* Ongar, Essex, 24 Sept., 1956. *m* (1) Stephen Romer. one *s.* (2) Michael Finch. one *d. Educ:* King's College, Cambridge University. *Studied:* Ecole Nationale Superieure des Beaux Arts, Paris. *Work in collections:* Epping Forest District Museum. *Publications:* CD-Rom 'Star Act' (Herisson Fox/Hachette), 'Toto's Travels' (Little, Brown & Co.), 'En Route' (Albin Michel, Fr.), Bayard Presse, France, Milan Presse, France. *Signs work:* "B. Strevens" or "Biddy Strevens." *Address:* 59 Rue de Meaux, 60300 Senlis, France. *Email:* b@bridgetstrevens.com

STRONG, Sir Roy, Ph.D. Fellow Ferens (1976), Prof. of Fine Art (1972), Hon.D.Litt. (Leeds) (1983), Hon.D.Litt. (Keele) (1984); writer and historian; Director, Victoria and Albert Museum (till Dec. 1987); *b* London, 23 Aug., 1935. *m* Dr. Julia Trevelyan Oman. *Educ:* Edmonton County Grammar School; Queen Mary College, London; Warburg Inst., London. *Publications:* author: Portraits of Queen Elizabeth I (1963), Holbein - Henry VIII (1967), Tudor - Jacobean Portraits (1969), The English Icon: English - Jacobean Portraiture (1969), Van Dyck: Charles on Horseback (1972), Splendour at Court: Renaissance Spectacle - the Theatre of Power (1973), Nicholas Hilliard (1975), The Cult of Elizabeth: Elizabethan Portraiture - Pageantry (1977), And When Did You Last See Your Father? (1978), The Renaissance Garden in England (1979), Britannia Triumphans: Inigo Jones, Rubens and Whitehall Palace (1980), The English Renaissance Miniature (1983), Art - Power (1984), Strong Points (1985), Henry, Prince of Wales - England's Lost Renaissance (1986), Creating Small Gardens (1986), Gloriana, Portraits of Queen Elizabeth I (1987), A Small Garden Designer's Handbook (1987), Cecil Beaton, The Royal Portraits (1988), Creating Small Formal Gardens (1989), Small Period Gardens (1992), A Celebration of Gardens (1992), Successful Small Gardens (1994), A Country Life (1994), William Larkin (1994), The Tudor and Stuart Monarchy, I, Tudor, II, Elizabethan (1995), III, Stuart (1996), The Story of Britain (1996), The Roy Strong Diaries 1967-1987 (1997), The Spirit of Britain (1999); other books jointly with Julia Trevelyan Oman, J.A. van Dorsten, Stephen Orgel, Colin Ford and J. Murrell; contributor to numerous books and learned journals. *Clubs:* Garrick. *Address:* The Laskett, Much Birch, Herefordshire HR2 8HZ.

STUART, Gordon, R.C.A. (2000), W.S.W. (1995); painter in oil, water-colour and draughtsman; lecturer, Heatherleys School of Art, Dyfed College of Art (1975-1982); artist in residence, U.K. Year of Literature (1995), artist in residence, Dylan Thomas Centre (since 1996); *b* Toronto, Canada, 30 May, 1924. *m* Mair Jenkins. *Educ:* Toronto Schools (1931-1946). *Studied:* Central Technical College, Toronto, Ontario College of Art, St. Martin's, London, University of London. *Exhib:* numerous, Toronto, Vancouver, England, Wales. *Work in collections:* H.R.H. Prince of Wales, Contemporary Art Soc., Wales, Canadian High Commission, London, National Portrait Gallery, Ontario College of Art, Buffalo University, New York, National Library of Wales, Glynn Vivian Art Gallery, Swansea. *Publications:* Dylan Thomas Trail, illustration, Dylan the Bard, Sinclair, illustration. *Signs work:* "Gordon Stuart." *Address:* 15 Richmond Rd., Uplands, Swansea, W. Glamorgan SA2 0RB. *Email:* mairgordon@ntlworld.com

STUART, Kiel, A.P.S.; artist in papier mache, mixed media and fibre, writer; Editor, Poetry Bone; *b* N.Y.C., 1951. *m* Howard Austerlitz. *Studied:* Suny New Paltz, Suny Stony Brook. *Exhib:* Lynn Kottler Galleries, N.Y.C.; Gallery II RSVP, Virginia; Artforum, Mills Pond House, N.Y.; Myths, Music and Magic, East End Arts Council, N.Y.; Gallery North, Setauket, N.Y. *Work in collections:* National Museum of Women's Art, Washington DC. *Publications:* cover, Island Women Anthology (N.S.W.W.A. Press). *Signs work:* see appendix. *Address:* 12 Skylark Ln., Stony Brook, N.Y. 11790, U.S.A.

STUART-SMITH, Susanna J., B.Mus., Dip.Ecol., Gold medal (R.H.S.); botanical artist in water-colour, pencil, ink; freelance botanical illustrator working at R.B.G. Kew; experienced in fieldwork abroad (Oman), orchid illustration; botanical illustration tutor; *b* B'ham, 26 May, 1943. *m* Richard Clymo, ecologist. *Educ:* Universities of London, Cambridge, Kent. *Studied:* trained: R.B.G. Edinburgh (1984), R.B.G. Kew (1993). *Exhib:* R.H.S. London; R.B.G. Edinburgh; R.B.G. Kew; Linnean Soc. London; Hunt Inst., U.S.A.; World Orchid Conference, Glasgow. *Work in collections:* R.B.G. Edinburgh, R.B.G. Kew. *Publications:* illustrated: 'Plants of Dhofar, Southern Region of Oman', Miller and Morris (Sultanate of Oman 1988); 'The New R.H.S. Dictionary of Gardening' (Macmillan Press Ref. Books 1992); 'The Orchids of Belize' (1996), 'Orchids of Bhutan', 'Orchids of Borneo'; reference books and scientific publications. *Signs work:* "Susanna Stuart-Smith" or "S.S.S." *Address:* 49 High St., Robertsbridge, E. Sussex TN32 5AL.

STUBBS, Constance, A.R.C.A.; painter and etcher in collage and acrylic; *b* Cheltenham, 6 Aug., 1927. *m* Harold Yates. two *s.* one *d. Studied:* Cheltenham School of Art, Royal College of Art (1949-51, Carel Weight, Ruskin Spear, John Minton, Barnett Freedman). *Exhib:* mixed shows: R.A., Hayward, Mall Galleries, C.P.S., S.C.A., Print Biennale-Berlin, Cracow and Rijeka; solo shows: Anglo Hellenic League Athens, John Russell Ipswich, Chappel Essex, Market Cross and St. Johns St., Bury St. Edmunds, Oxford Gallery, Chelmsford Festival. *Work in collections:* the late Princess Marina, Christchurch Mansions Ipswich, Unilever, Prudential, Sir Hugh Casson, Courtauld Private Collection, etc. *Signs work:* "C. STUBBS." *Address:* The Willows, Bell Corner, Pakenham, Suffolk IP31 2JT.

STUBLEY, Trevor Hugh, D.A. (Edin.) (1951), R.P. (1974) Vice-President (1994-

99), R.S.W. (1990), R.B.A. (1991), R.W.S. (1995); painter; *b* Leeds, 27 Mar., 1932. *m* Valerie Churm. four *s*. *Studied:* Leeds College of Art (1947-49); Edinburgh College of Art (1949-53). *Exhib:* Edinburgh, London. *Work in collections:* N.P.G., M.of.D., I.E.E., Palace of Westminster, British Library, B.M., Windsor Castle, five Oxford Colleges, Art Galleries: Doncaster, Harrogate, Huddersfield, Hull, Leeds, Lincoln, Manchester, Sheffield, Wakefield, nine University collections. *Commissions:* H.M. The Queen (1986), Lord Hailsham of Marylebone (1992). *Publications:* work repro.: illustrated over 400 children's books. Prizes: Hunting Group (1986), Singer & Friedlander (1990). *Clubs:* Arts. *Signs work:* "Stubley." *Address:* Trevor Stubley Gallery, Greenfield Rd., Holmfirth, nr. Huddersfield HD7 2XQ.

STULTIENS, Jeff, Dip.A.D. (1966), R.P. (1990); First Prize - The Portrait Award, National Portrait Gallery (1985); Hon. Sec. R.S.P.P.; Senior Lecturer at Hertfordshire College of Art and Design (1974-1987); painter in oil; *b* Blackpool, 12 Sept., 1944. *m* Catherine Knowelden. *Educ:* Hutton and Tiffin Schools. *Studied:* Kingston School of Art under Alfred Heyworth and Camberwell School of Art under Robert Medley R.A. (1961-1966). *Exhib:* John Player Portrait Award - N.P.G., British Portraiture 1980-85, Drawings for All, R.S.P.P., Hunting/Observer, Nikkei Exhbn. - Tokyo, The Portrait Award 1980-89. *Work in collections:* N.P.G., Merton and Oriel Colleges - Oxford, National Heart and Lung Inst., R.N.L.I., Royal Medical Foundation, R.A.M. Many other public and private commissions. *Signs work:* "Stultiens." *Address:* 26 St. George's Cl., Toddington, Beds. LU5 6AT.

SULLIVAN, Jason, B.A. (1979); painter in oil; *b* Poole, Dorset, 31 Mar., 1958. *m* Una. one *s*. *Educ:* Queen Elizabeth Grammar School, Horncastle, Lincolnshire. *Studied:* Grimsby College of Art (1974-76, Mr. Todd), Sheffield College of Art (1976-79, Mr. Peacock). Numerous exhbns. *Signs work:* see appendix. *Address:* 19 Meersbrook Pk. Rd., Sheffield, S. Yorks.

SULLIVAN, Wendy, poet, painter; *b* London, 18 May, 1938. *Educ:* Notre Dame High School, Battersea; attended Sir John Cass and Goldsmiths' Colleges; life drawing Leonard McComb, R.A.; anatomy Prof. Pegington, F.R.S. (U.C.H.). *Exhib:* R.A. Summer Shows, Galerie Dagmar, Portobello Opens, South Bank Show, Tamsins, Satay, Cooltans, Paperworks IV, Brixton Gallery, Le Creole, The Carrot Cafe, W. Norwood Library, First Sight Gallery, Bristol, The Ritzy, Brixton Library, Z Bar. *Work in collections:* on loan/and collections: Galerie Dagmar, Breast Screening Clinic Camberwell, St, John's Church, Brixton, Lambeth Archives, Movement for Justice. Artist-in-Residence, A.S.C. Studios, Brixton (2000/2001). *Signs work:* "Wendy Sullivan" and see appendix. *Address:* 127 Crescent La., London SW4 8EA. *Email:* panic.brixtonpoetry@which.net

SUMMERS, Leslie John, F.F.P.S. (1968); sculptor in bronze, perspex (acrylic); *b* London, 2 Nov., 1919. *m* Prof. Janet Margaret Bately C.B.E., F.B.A. two *s*. *Educ:* Dulwich College and London University. *Studied:* Chelsea School of Art. *Exhib:* R.A., R.B.A., Walker A.G., Cork St. Gallery, Alwin Gallery, Richmond Gallery London, Brussels Exhbn., Vth International Bienal Barcelona (Prizewinner). *Work in collections:* National Museum of Wales (purchased by Contemporary Art Soc. of Wales); Hull University, U.S. Atomic Energy Commission, Nat. Exhbn. Centre, Birmingham, Brighton Centre, Rochester Museum of Western Art, N.Y., G.L.C.,

British Tourist Authority, Art Scene, Beaux Art Gallery, Bath, Johnathan Poole Gallery, London, etc. *Publications:* work repro.: Studio International, Exploring Sculpture, Creative Plastics. *Signs work:* see appendix. *Address:* 86 Cawdor Cres., London W7 2DD.

SUMSION, Peter Whitton, A.R.C.A. (1955); painter in oil and printmaker in relief and mono prints, drawing, lecturer; Lecturer, Glasgow School of Art (retd. 1995); *b* Gloucester, 23 Aug., 1930. *m* Sarah Noble. two *s.* two *d. Educ:* St. George's Choir School, Windsor, St. Thomas' Choir School, New York City, Rendcomb College, Glos. *Studied:* Cheltenham School of Art (1949), Chelsea School of Art (1950-52), R.C.A. (1952-55, Carel Weight, John Minton, Robert Buhler). *Exhib:* one-man, Drawing Schools Gallery, Eton College (1960, 1978), Bury St. Edmunds Gallery; group shows, R.P., R.G.I. *Work in collections:* Brewhouse Gallery, Eton College. *Signs work:* "Peter Sumsion." *Address:* Bachie Bhan House, Cairndow, Argyll PA26 8BE.

SUNLIGHT, Benjamin Clement, professional artist; painter in oils and printmaker; *b* Brighton, 7 Apr., 1935. *m* Vivien Baskin. *Educ:* Clifton and Magdalene College, Cambridge. *Studied:* London Central School of Art and Design (Mural Diploma, 1962) under Alan Davie, Hans Tisdall, Harold Cohen and Tony Harrison. Part-time teacher, Hornsey College of Art (1964-65), Cranfield Institute of Technology (1973-74); Fellow and Vice-Chairman, Free Painters and Sculptors (1965-68); Mem., International Arts Guild; Gold Medallist, International Academy, Rome and Italian Academy, Palma. *Signs work:* "Ben Sunlight." *Address:* 16 Sydney Rd., Richmond, Surrey TW9 1UB.

SURREY, Kit, Dip.A.D. Theatre design (1968); theatre designer and artist in several media, mainly pastel and charcoal drawing; *b* B'ham, 23 June, 1946. *m* Meg Surrey (née Grealey). one *s.* one *d. Educ:* Tauntons Grammar School, Southampton. *Studied:* Southampton College of Art (1963-65), Wimbledon School of Art (1965-68). *Exhib:* R.A., International Drawing Biennale Cleveland (1991), Cheltenham International Open (1994), S. W. Academy of Fine Art (2000, 2001), Soc. of British Theatre Designers (1976, 1978, 1983, 1999), International Organisation of Scenographers, Berlin (1981), Moscow (1982). *Work in collections:* R.S.C. Coll., Stratford, many private collections. *Publications:* included in British Theatre Design - The Modern Age, 'Time & Space', Design for Performance 1995-1999. *Signs work:* "KIT SURREY" or not at all. *Address:* Rock Cottage, Balls Farm Rd., Alphington, Exeter, Devon EX2 9HZ. *Email:* kit@surreyk.freeserve.co.uk

SURRIDGE, Mark, B.A. Hons. (1984); painter in oil; part-time lecturer at Falmouth College of Art; *b* London, 6 Aug., 1963. *m* Lisa Wright. two *s. Studied:* Maidstone College of Art (1981-1984). *Exhib:* Beardsmore Gallery, solo exhib. (2000), New Millennium Gallery, St. Ives, solo exhib. (2001), many open exhibs.; Hunting Art Prizes, prizewinner (2001), Royal Overseas League (1995 & 1998), Newlyn Art Gallery, Merriscourt Gallery, Oxon. *Commissions:* three editions of lithographic prints for Club Quarter, London. *Clubs:* Newlyn Soc. of Artists. *Signs work:* "Mark Surridge." *Address:* Chapel House, Crelly, Helston, Cornwall TR13 0EY.

SUTHERLAND, Carol Ann, B.A.Hons. (1973); artist in water based mixed media oil; *b* Greenock, Scotland, 16 Mar., 1952. three *s*. *Educ:* St. Columba School for Girls, Kilmacolm, Renfrewshire. *Studied:* Glasgow School of Art (1969-73, Donaldson, Goudie, Grant, Robertson). *Exhib:* Mercury Gallery. *Work in collections:* McNay Museum, San Antonio, Tex., Middlesbrough A.G., Paintings in Hospitals. *Publications:* Leafy and Adam at the Seaside (handmade artist's book). *Signs work:* "Carol Ann Sutherland" or "C.A.S." *Address:* c/o Mercury Gallery, 26 Cork St., London W1X 1HB.

SUTTON, Linda Olive, M.A. (R.C.A.) (1974); painter in oil on canvas, etching, water-colour, books; *b* Southend-on-Sea, 14 Dec., 1947. *Educ:* Southend College of Technology. *Studied:* Winchester School of Art (1967-70), R.C.A. (1971-74). *Exhib:* one-man shows, Galerij de Zwarte Panter, Antwerp; Bedford House Gallery, London; L'Agrifoglio, Milan; World's End Gallery, London; Ikon Gallery, Birmingham; Chenil Gallery, London; Royal Festival Hall, London; Stephen Bartley Gallery, London (1986); Beecroft Gallery, Westcliff-on-Sea (1987); Christopher Hull Gallery (1988); Jersey Arts Centre (1988); Beaux Arts, Bath (1988); Austin/Desmond, Bloomsbury (1989); Isis Gallery, Essex (1993); Lamont Gallery, London (1993); Pump House Gallery, Battersea Park (1994); Sutton House (National Trust) (1994); Chappel Galleries, Essex (1995); Bromham Mill, Beds. (1995); Piers Feetham Gallery, London (1995); Lamont Gallery, London (1996); John Bloxham, Fine Art (1996); Emscote Lawn, Warwick (1996); Six Chapel Row, Bath (1997); Fosse Gallery, Stow-on-the Wold (1998); Workhouse Gallery, Chelsea (2000, 2001). *Work in collections:* Royal Academy of Arts, Chantrey Bequest for Tate, Sainsbury's Collection. *Publications:* Limited Edition of etchings and poems in collaboration with Brian Patten (1996), Limited Edition Books of paintings and text of Shakespeare's "The Tempest" (1999), Ovid's Metamorphoses I and II (2000, 2001). *Clubs:* Chelsea Arts, Colony Rooms. *Signs work:* "Linda Sutton." *Address:* 192 Battersea Bridge Rd., London SW11 3AE.

SUTTON, Philip, R.A. (1989); artist in oil and water-colour; *b* Poole, Dorset, 20 Oct., 1928. *m* Heather. one *s*. three *d*. *Studied:* The Slade School of Fine Art. *Exhib:* Roland, Browse & Delbanco (1954-79), Australia, S. Africa and U.S.A., Berkeley Square Gallery, London, Piano Nobile, London. *Work in collections:* Tate Gallery, etc. *Commissions:* Post Office, stamps design. *Signs work:* "Philip Sutton." *Address:* 3 Morfa Terr., Manorbier, Tenby, Pembrokeshire SA70 7TH, Wales.

SWAIN, Dorothy Louisa, artist in oil; private art teacher; *b* Wimbledon, 21 July, 1922. *m* A.C. Swain. two *s*. two *d*. *Educ:* Wimbledon College of Art. *Studied:* Royal College of Art (Charles Mahony, Gilbert and Stanley Spencer, Paul and John Nash). *Exhib:* R.A., R.C.A., Russell Cotes Gallery. *Work in collections:* Premier Gallery, Eastbourne. *Signs work:* "D.L. Swain." *Address:* Hawthorn, West St., Mayfield, E. Sussex TN20 6DR.

SWALE, Suzan Georgina, Dip. A.D. (Hons.) 1969, M.A. (R.C.A.) Painting (1972); artist/lecturer in paint, photo media, text, print, performance; Lecturer, Central/St. Martin's School of Art, Tutor, Morley College; *b* Nottingham, 30 Apr., 1946. *m* Robert Coward. one *s*. one *d*. *Studied:* Pre-Dip. Derby (1965-66), Bristol Polytechnic (1966-69, Hassel Smith), R.C.A. (1969-72). *Exhib:* 'A Catalogue of Fear' retrospective Gardner Arts Centre, Brighton (1998); exhibits widely solo and group shows. Work in public and private collections. *Publications:* 'A Catalogue of Fear' Collective Works - Suzan Swale. Professional membership: Artists Union (1983), I.A.A. (U.K.) (1979-86), London Group - mem. Working Party and Selection Com. (1987), R.C.A. Soc. (1993). *Signs work:* "Suzan Swale." *Address:* 217 Brecknock Rd., Tufnell Park, London N19 5AA.

SWAN, Ann, S.B.A., S.G.F.A.; R.H.S. Silver-gilt medal (1990), Gold medal (1991, 1993, 1997), Joint Gold (1999); botanical artist in pencil, coloured pencil, oil pastel, water-colour, drypoint engraving; *b* England, 7 Apr., 1949. *Educ:* Gravesend Grammar School for Girls. *Studied:* Manchester College of Art and Design. *Exhib:* R.H.S. Hampton Ct. International Flower Show (1990, 1991, 1994-97), S.B.A. (1991, 1992, 1994-97), R.H.S. (1990, 1991, 1993, 1997), Century Gallery Henley (1991), Lyric Theatre Hammersmith (1992), R.B.G., Kew (1994), Hunt Inst. of Botanical Documentation, Pittsburgh, U.S.A. (1996), R.H.S. Chelsea Flower Show (1998-99). *Work in collections:* The Shirley Sherwood Collection, National Collection of Lycastes, Beckenham, Kent. *Publications:* work repro.: limited edns. prints, and greetings cards. *Signs work:* "Ann Swan." *Address:* 55 Railway Rd., Teddington, Middx. TW11 8SD. *Website:* annswan.co.uk *Email:* ann@annswan.co.uk

SWANN, Marilyn, F.F.P.S.; painter; Women's Art Library, Fulham; *b* Kent, 1932. *Studied:* Woolwich Poly. (1945-50), Central, Chelsea and Sidcup (evenings). *Exhib:* Trends (Mall, Wieghouse, Barbican, Bloomsbury Galleries, etc.), F.P.S. shows since 1973, St. Martin's Crypt, Trafalgar Sq.; solo shows, Brangwyn Studio (1976/7), Univ. of Surrey, Old Bull, Barnet (1978), Loggia Gallery (1984), Holland Park Orangery (1987), Hall Place and various other venues in Bexley. *Work in collections:* Univ. of Surrey, Wilfred Sirrel Collection, Westminster Arts Council, Queen Mary's Hospital, Sidcup. *Clubs:* A.C.S.A.C. *Signs work:* "SWANN." *Address:* Cheltenham GL52 2JJ.

SWETCHARNIK, Sara Morris, Fulbright Fellow, Spain (1987-88, 1988-89); painter, sculptor; *b* Shelby, N. Carolina, 1955. *m* William Swetcharnik. *Studied:* Art Students League, N.Y.; Schuler School of Fine Art, Baltimore, Maryland. *Exhib:* Arts in Embassies, Honduras (1997-98). Residency Fellowship, Virginia Center for Creative Arts, Sweet Briar, Virginia (1990); Workshop instructor, Landon School, Washington D.C. (1991-96); Artist's Residency Fellowship, American Numismatic Assoc. Conference, The American Numismatic Museum, Colorado Springs, (1994). *Clubs:* Fulbright Assoc., Delaplaine Visual Art. *Signs work:* "Sara Morris Swetcharnik." *Address:* 7044 Woodville Rd., Mt. Airy, Maryland 21771-7934, U.S.A.

SWETCHARNIK, William Norton, P.S.A., Fulbright Fellow: Spain (1987-89), Honduras (1994-95), Yaddo Foundation (1987), Cintas Foundation (1985), Millay Colony for the Arts Fellowship (1983), Stacey Foundation (1983); painter in oil, pastel, tempera, encaustic; *b* Philadelphia, Pennsylvania, 1951. *m* Sara Morris. *Educ:* Sandy Spring Friends School, Maryland. *Studied:* Rhode Island School of Design, University of California, New York Art Students League. *Exhib:* Springville (Utah) Museum of Art, Butler Inst. of American Art, Youngstown, Ohio, Washington County (Maryland) Museum of Art, National Arts Club, N.Y.C., Hermitage Museum,

Norfolk, Virginia. *Signs work:* "Wm. Swetcharnik." *Address:* 7044 Woodville Rd., Mt. Airy, Maryland 21771-7934, U.S.A.

SWINGLER, Brian Victor, N.D.D., A.T.D., R.B.S.A. (1986); artist in water-colour and acrylics; part time teacher at Birmingham, Hereford and Worcester; *b* Birmingham, 8 July, 1939. divorced. two *s. Educ:* Yardley Grammar School. *Studied:* Birmingham Art School (1962-65, Gilbert Mason, Roy Abell). *Exhib:* main-ly at Potter Clarke Gallery, St. Ives, also at Compendium Gallery, Ombersley Gallery, R.B.S.A., Timaeus Gallery, Helios Gallery, Cedric Chivers Gallery, Pictures, Henry-Brett Gallery, Richard Hagen Gallery, New Gallery, Moseley Gallery, Bankside, Frames, Noott Gallery. *Work in collections:* R.B.S.A. Gallery. *Commissions:* many public and private portrait commissions. *Publications:* work repro.: Artist Magazine and Leisure Painter. *Clubs:* V.P.R.B.S.A. *Signs work:* "B.V. Swingler." *Address:* 17 Beverley Rd., Rubery, Birmingham B45 9JG.

SYKES, Barbara, B.A. (Hons.) Fine Art (1993); painter in water based paint on paper, and charcoal; textile designer (1962-75); *b* Doncaster, 4 Mar., 1944. *m* Jeffrey. two *s.* one *d. Studied:* Bretton Hall, University of Leeds (1990-93, Tom Wood). *Exhib:* Mall Galleries, R.A. Summer Show, Djanogley Gallery (Nottingham University), Logos London, Dean Clough, Halifax, Huddersfield Art Gallery, Peterborough Museum and Gallery, N.Y., Bury Art Gallery, etc. Both solo and group. *Work in collections:* Studio: Dean Clough, Halifax, and internationally. Both public and private collections locally, nationally, internationally *Publications:* work repro.: magazines, cards, etc. *Clubs:* M.A.F.A. *Signs work:* "Barbara Sykes" on request. *Address:* The Hollows, Shore Edge, Shaw, Oldham, Lancs. OL2 8LJ. *Email:* barbarasykes@supanet.com

SYKES, Sandy, B.A.Hons. (1966), M.A. (1987); printmaker, painter and maker of artists books; *b* Yorkshire, 13 Mar., 1944. *Studied:* Leeds Metropolitan University (1962-66), Middlesex University (1966-67), Wimbledon College of Art (1984-87). *Exhib:* recent solo shows: Manhattan Graphic Centre, N.Y. (2002), 'Manhattan Transfer' London Print Studio (1998), Crossley Gallery Dean Clough (1995), Brahm Gallery, Leeds (1995), Pentonville Gallery (1988), Creaser Gallery (1988), Hardware Gallery (1988, 1991, 1995, 1997), Wakefield A.G. (1988-89); many group shows in Britain, America, Russia and Europe. *Work in collections:* Tate Britain, M.O.M.A. N.Y., Metropolitan Museum of Art N.Y., British Arts Council, V. & A., Merrill Lynch, Yale University, U.S.A, etc. *Commissions:* Oxfam (1992), B.B.C. (1990), etc.,; residencies include: Senigallia, Italy (1991); Manhattan Graphic Centre, N.Y. (1998); Nagasawa, Japan (2001). *Publications:* Lament for Ignacio Sanchez Mejias by Federico Garcia Lorca; 'Paradise is Always Where You've Been' (1999) ISBN 1902111002; 'The Dante Series' catalogue (1997) ISBN 190211001. Represented in video 'Etching' Brighton University; 'The Wood Engraving and Woodcut in Britain 1890 to 1990,' by James Hamilton; Digital Data Bases 'Art View', New York and 'Axis', 'The Best of Printmaking: An International Collection.' *Clubs:* Chelsea Arts. *Signs work:* "Sandy Sykes." *Address:* 12 Kirkley Rd., London SW19 3AY.

SYKES, Thelma Kathryn, B.A. Hons. (1962), A.S.W.L.A. (1999), S.W.L.A. (2001); relief printmaker, linocut, woodcut; artist and writer; artist in residence, Nature in Art, Gloucester (2000-2001); *b* Heckmondwike, Yorks., 29 Apr., 1940.

Educ: Durham University. *Studied:* self taught and short courses under John Busby, Richard Bawden. *Exhib:* S.W.L.A., Mall Galleries, London (1996-2001), Printmakers Council, Royal National Theatre (2001), Soc. of Wood Engravers (1999-2001), Internat. Festival of Printmaking, Chong Qing, China (2000). *Work in collections:* Nature in Art, Wallsworth Hall, Gloucester, Powergen. *Publications:* European Atlas of Breeding Birds, Academic Press (1997), Birdwatchers Yearbook (1985-1996). *Signs work:* "Thelma K Sykes' or book illustrations, "TKS." *Address:* Blue Neb Studios, 18 Newcroft, Saughall, Chester CH1 6EL.

SYLVESTER, Diana, R.W.A. (1986), R.O.I.; artist in oil; Ex. Wilts. County Council part-time lecturer; ex. Sec. Bath Soc. of Artists; *b* Bath, Som., 16 Mar., 1924. *m* Robin Sylvester. three *s.* one *d. Educ:* Bath High School. *Studied:* Chippenham Technical College, Corsham and Bristol Polytechnic. *Exhib:* R.A., R.W.A., R.O.I., etc. *Work in collections:* R.W.A., Bristol Schools Art Service. *Clubs:* Bath Soc. of Artists. *Signs work:* "DIANA SYLVESTER." *Address:* Upper Farm, South Wraxall, nr. Bradford-on-Avon, Wilts. BA15 2RJ.

SYMONDS, Ken, N.D.D., P.S.; artist in pastel, oil, water-colour; *b* 18 Jan., 1927. *m* Jane. one *s.* one *d. Educ:* Euclid St. Grammar School, Swindon. *Studied:* Regent St. Polytechnic, London (1948-52, Norman Blamey, R.A.). *Exhib:* regularly in Cornwall, Mall Galleries, Europe, U.S.A. *Work in collections:* Government Collection, Plymouth C.C., Guernsey, etc. *Publications:* Around the Penwith. *Signs work:* "Symonds." *Address:* St. Andrew's Studio, Fore St., Newlyn, Cornwall TR18 5LD.

SYMONDS, Peter John, B.A.; landscape painter in oil of architectural and marine subjects; *b* Woking, 15 Jan., 1964. *m* Vanessa. one *s. Studied:* Leicester University. *Exhib:* four solo shows S.E. England, mixed shows nationwide. *Commissions:* Lloyds Bldg. London, numerous private commissions home and abroad. *Publications:* work repro.: Limited Edn. prints (Solomon & Whitehead). *Signs work:* "Peter Symonds." *Address:* Magpies, Vicarage Lane, Send, Woking, Surrey GU23 7JN.

SYNGE, Pamela: see de MEO, P.

T

TABB, Barrington Moore, R.W.A. (1999); self taught painter in oil; *b* Almondsbury, Glos., 25 Apr., 1934. *m* Grace Pearn. two *d. Exhib:* Olympia Fair, London (4 yrs.), Wimbledon Gallery (1980), Christopher Hull Gallery (1982), Neville Gallery, Bath (1986), Cleveland Bridge Gallery (1990), Black Swan Gallery, Frome (1997), R.W.A. (1998), etc. *Work in collections:* 14 paintings Wessex Collection Longleat House. *Signs work:* "B.M.T." or "BT." *Address:* 10 Frys Hill, Brislington, Bristol BS4 4JW.

TABER, A. Lincoln, artist; *b* Colchester, 1970. *Studied:* City and Guilds School of Art (1989-92). *Exhib:* R.A. Summer Show, New Grafton Gallery. *Commissions:*

murals, portraits. *Clubs:* Chelsea Arts. *Address:* 6 Hermes House, Arodene Rd., London SW2.

TABER, Jacqueline, artist and picture restorer; *b* London, 1946. *m* the late A. Lincoln Taber, painter. one *s. Educ:* Paris (one year). *Studied:* Florence (Signorina Simi), Gabinetto del Restauro, Uffizi Museum. *Exhib:* R.A. Summer Exhbn., New Grafton Gallery, Hayletts Gallery, Colchester, Mall Galleries. *Publications:* A Bit of Trompe - The Art of Lincoln Taber. *Clubs:* Chelsea Arts. *Address:* 33 Cleveland Gdns., London SW13 0AE.

TAIT, Renny, painter; *b* Perth, Scotland, 27 June, 1965. *m* Valerie Anderson. one *d. Studied:* Edinburgh College of Art, Royal College of Art. *Exhib:* regularly with Flowers East, London. *Signs work:* "Renny J. Tait" on back of painting. *Address:* 26a Lygon Rd., Edinburgh EH16 5QA.

TAIT, Wendy Ann, water-colour artist and demonstrator; *b* Derby, 19 Apr., 1939. *m* H.D.L. Tait. two *s.* two *d. Studied:* Joseph Wright School of Art, Derby (1952-55), Adult Educ. (1974-78, Roy Berry). *Exhib:* numerous Derbyshire galleries; demonstrations regularly given to local clubs and societies and for 'Maimeri' artists materials at N.E.C. and Business Design Centre, London; Residential courses and dayschools, Midlands and Yorkshire area. *Commissions:* 1999 'Autumn Flowers' nine designs for Government of Jersey Philatelic Bureau. *Publications:* work repro.: greetings cards by Robertson Collection; book 'Watercolour Flowers' (Search Press). . *Clubs:* B.W.S., S.F.P. *Signs work:* "W.A. Tait." *Address:* Harwen, 1 Chevin Rd., Duffield, Derbys. DE56 4DS.

TAJIRI, Shinkichi, William and Noma Copley Award for sculpture (1959); John Hay Whithey Found. Opp. Fellowship (1960); Mainichi Shibum Prize, Tokyo Biennale (1963); sculptor in bronze and brass; Prof. of Sculpture, Hochschule für Bildende Kunste, W. Berlin (retd. 1989); *b* Los Angeles, 7 Dec., 1923. *m* Ferdi (decd.). two *d. m* Suzanne Van Der Kapellen (1976). *Educ:* Los Angeles. *Studied:* under Donald Hord, San Diego (1948-51); O. Zadkine and F. Leger, Paris. *Work in collections:* Stedelijk Museum, Amsterdam, Gemeente Museum, Den Haag, Modern Museum, Stockholm, Town of Arnhem, Holland, Museum of Modern Art, N.Y., etc. *Signs work:* see appendix. *Address:* Kasteel Scheres, 5991 NC Baarlo, Limburg, Holland.

TAKEDA, Fumiko, B.A. (1989), M.A. Hons. (1991); artist in etching; lecturer since 1992, Tokyo Y.M.C.A. Inst. of Design; lecturer since 1999, Tokyo University of Fine Art and Music; *b* 26 July, 1963. *Studied:* Tokyo University of Fine Art and Music (1985-89), The Graduate School of Tokyo University of Fine Art and Music (1989-91). *Exhib:* over seventeen solo exhbns. since 1990, R.A. (1997), The 2nd and 3rd Sappro International Print Biennial Exhbn. (1993, 1995), The 23rd International Biennial of Graphic Arts in Ljubljana, Slovenija (1999). *Work in collections:* Tokyo University of Fine Art and Music. *Signs work:* "Takeda, F." *Address:* 2-10-21, Takagi-cho, Kokubunji-shi, Tokyo 185, Japan. *Email:* pajaco@dream.com

TALBOT, Nancy Wilfreda Hewitt, D.A. (Lond.) (1948); painter in oil and stage designer; consultant, Talbot Film Productions; teacher of painting for Hampshire (1950-66); *b* Coventry, 31 Aug., 1925. *m* Major Leon Talbot. *Educ:* Leamington

High School, Leamington Spa. *Studied:* Ruskin Drawing School, Oxford (1945) (Albert Rutherston), Slade School, London (1945-48) (Randolph Schwabe, Vladimir Polunin). *Exhib:* first one-man show, Alfred Herbert Gallery, Coventry (1965). *Work in collections:* mural and portrait commissions, privately owned. *Signs work:* "Nancy Talbot" or "Nancy Skillington." *Address:* Greensleeves, Avon Castle, Ringwood, Hants. BH24 2BE.

TALBOT KELLY, Chloë Elizabeth, M.C.S.D. (1968), S.WL.A. (1964), M.B.O.U. (1960); freelance bird artist/illustrator in water-colour, gouache and black and white; *b* Hampstead, 15 July, 1927. *m* Jeffrey Smith. one *s. Educ:* St. George's School for Girls, Convent of the Sacred Heart; adviser, father and Bird Room, B.M.N.H. *Exhib:* S.WL.A. and provincial galleries in U.K., Australia and Canada. *Commissions:* various. *Publications:* work repro.: Field Guides to Birds N.Z, Seychelles, Fiji, Tonga and Samoa; contributor to New Dictionary of Birds, African Handbook of Birds etc. *Clubs:* British Ornithologists. *Signs work:* "C.E. Talbot Kelly" semi printed in paint or written, or initials only. *Address:* 22 St. Philip's Rd., Leicester LE5 5TQ.

TAMBURRINI, Mosé, sculptor, direct carver in marble, stone and wood - bronze casts from these; International Affiliate Royal Soc. of British Sculptors; *b* Buenos Aires, 29 Nov., 1905. *Educ:* St. Martin's School of Art. *Exhib:* recent one-man shows: Bexhill Museum, Redchurch Gallery, London. *Work in collections:* John Hunt Galleries; Nicholas Bowlby Gallery; private collections in U.K., Europe and U.S.A. *Signs work:* "M. TAMBURRINI" carved on marble, stone pieces; engraved on bronzes. *Address:* 21 Glenleigh Pk. Rd., Bexhill, E. Sussex TN39 4EE.

TAMPLIN, Heather, M.F.P.S. (1984); artist in oil, water-colour and computer generated images; *b* Caterham, 4 Aug., 1950. one *s.* one *d. Studied:* Wimbledon College of Art (1967). *Exhib:* Loggia Gallery and Barbican with F.P.S., Mall Galleries, Fermoy Centre, King's Lynn; one-man shows locally, dfn Gallery, Broadway, N.Y. *Commissions:* A series of 34, computer generated/manipulated images, to project during performances of Alison Burns choral work "The Raven" with words by Tony Bonning. Member of North Norfolk exhibition project. *Signs work:* "H. TAMPLIN." *Address:* Orchard House, The Green, Aldborough, Norfolk NR11 7AA.

TARRANT, Olwen, P.R.O.I.; oil painter, sculptor, lecturer, art teacher; *b* Newport, Gwent, 1927. *m* John Tarrant, BBC and Fleet St. journalist and author. *Educ:* Newport High School, Gwent. *Studied:* Sir John Cass School of Art. *Exhib:* R.O.I. (Llewellyn Alexander Gallery award, 1997, Alan Gourlay Memorial award, 1998, Cornelissen Prize, 1987), R.B.A., N.S., Albemarle, Medici, City, Fosse, Century and others. *Work in collections:* London Polytechnic, Warburg, the late Sir Charles Wheeler, P.P.R.A. *Publications:* work repro.: Art text books, cards, calendars, Artists and Illustrators, Leisure Painter, The Artist. *Signs work:* "Olwen Tarrant." *Address:* High Ridge, 4 Yew Tree Lane, Upper Welland, Malvern, Worcs. WR14 4LJ. *Second Address:* Las Encinas de Siller, 3, Calle Urxella, 33, Puerto Pollensa, Mallorca.

TARRANT, Peter Rex, F.N.D.D.; artist in oil; *b* Shropshire, 1943. *Educ:* Morville School. *Studied:* Shrewsbury Art School. *Work in collections:* Birmingham

City Museum and A.G. *Address:* 10 Lower Bromdon, Wheathill, Burwarton, nr. Bridgnorth, Salop. WV16 6QT.

TARRANT, Terence Richard, F.M.A.A.; medical artist; ophthalmic artist at Theodore Hamblin Ltd. (1945-48); ophthalmic artist at Queen Alexandra's Military Hospital, Millbank (1948-50); medical artist at Inst. of Ophthalmology, London (1950-84); *b* London, 7 Jan., 1930. married. one *s.* two *d. Educ:* London. *Studied:* Camberwell School of Arts and Crafts. *Work in collections:* Moorfields Eye Hospital. *Publications:* Stallard's Eye Surgery, Roper-Hall; Clinical Ophthalmology, J.J. Kanski; System of Ophthalmology, Duke-Elder; Management of Vitreoretinal Disease, Chignell and Wong; Contact Lens Complications, N. Efron. *Signs work:* "TARRANT" with tops of the Ts joined. *Address:* 'Woodlands', Rectory Lane, Child Okeford, Blandford Forum, Dorset DT11 8DT.

TARRAWAY, Mary, B.Sc. Special Botany, P.G.C.E., S.B.A., S.F.P.; R.H.S. Silver-gilt medallist Grenfell range; self taught artist in water-colour, ink, etching with aquatint; retd. Deputy Head, Parkstone Grammar School, Poole, and teacher of 'A' level biology; Council mem. Dorset Natural History and Archaeological Soc., Life mem. Dorset Wildlife Trust; *b* Wimborne, Dorset, 29 Mar., 1928. *m* Harold George Tarraway. *Exhib:* S.B.A. Westminster Gallery (1991-99), R.H.S. London (1991-99), Britain's Painters, '91 winner of Osborne & Butler award Best Flower Painting; solo shows: Hillier's Gdns. Romsey, Dorset County Museum (4), 8th International Exhbn. Hunt Inst. U.S.A. (1995). *Work in collections:* Hunt Inst. for Botanical Documentation, Pittsburgh, Shirley Sherwood Collection of Contemporary Botanical Art. *Publications:* work repro.: Wild Flower greetings cards. *Clubs:* S.B.A., Dorset Wildlife Trust, Dorset Natural History and Archaeological Soc., S.F.P., Poole Printmakers, Christchurch Arts Guild. *Signs work:* "Mary Tarraway." *Address:* 6 Pearce Ave., Parkstone, Poole, Dorset BH14 8EQ.

TATE, Barbara, P.S.W.A., R.M.S., F.S.A.B.A., F.R.S.A., I.A.A., Ass. Société des Artistes Français; Silver Medal, Paris Salon (1968); Gold Medal, Paris Salon (1969); Prix Marie Puisoye (1971); Special Mention Palme d'or des Beaux-Arts, Monte Carlo (1972); Laureat Grand Prix de la Côte d'Azur (1972); painter in oil; Hon. President, Society of Women Artists; Hon. Prof. Thames Valley University; *b* Uxbridge, Middlesex. *m* James Tate, also a painter. one *d. Educ:* Dormers Wells School, Southall. *Studied:* Ealing School of Art (1940-45, under T. E. Lightfoot, A.R.C.A., T. Bayley, A.R.C.A., J. E. Nicholls, A.R.C.A.) and Wigan Art School (1945-46). 1957-58, under Peter Coker, R.A., A.R.C.A. *Exhib:* BBC2 Television, Royal Academy, Royal Society of Portrait Painters, Royal Institute of Oil Painters, Royal Society of British Artists, New English Art Club, National Society, Royal Society of Miniature Painters, Sculptors and Gravers, United Society of Artists, Society of Women Artists, Hesketh Hubbard Art Society, Royal Institute, Free Painters and Sculptors, R.W.S. Galleries' Flower Painting Exhbn., Chenil Galleries, Chelsea, Paris Salon, Salon Terres Latines, Salon du Comparaisons, Ville Eternal, Rome, Nice, Monte Carlo, Royal Festival Hall. *Publications:* work repro.: The Green Shawl, Clematis, Nasturtiums, Golden Girl, Marigolds, King's Pawn, Moon Goddess, Josephine, Marigold, Daisy, Scabious, Poppy, as prints for hanging, published by Solomon & Whitehead, London, and Marigold published by Felix Rosenstiel's Widow and Son. *Signs work:* see appendix. Some work done in collaboration with husband (see appendix). *Address:* Willow House, Ealing Green, London W5 5EN.

TAULBUT, John Maurice, R.W.A.; Jack Goldhill award for sculpture R.A. (1987); sculptor in stone, wood and bronze, teacher; *b* Gosport, 19 Jan., 1934. *m* Janet Marian Rickards. three *s. Educ:* Portsmouth College of Art, Highbury Technical College. *Studied:* Eaton Hall College of Educ., Retford. *Exhib:* R.A., R.B.A., R.W.A., S.WL.A., R.S.M.A., Sotheby's, Southampton A.G., Swindon A.G., Oxford Soc., Cheltenham Soc., 3D Gallery, Bristol, Rooksmoor Gallery, Bath, Ceri Richards Gallery, Swansea, Ash Barn, Petersfield, Swansea Arts Workshop, Barry Keene Gallery, Henley on Thames, The McHardy Sculpture Co. *Work in collections:* Royal West of England Academy, Grand Pavilion, Porthcawl, and private collections. *Commissions:* Madonna and Child, Parish Church, Llansteffan. *Signs work:* "John Taulbut." *Address:* 40 Crawte Ave., Holbury, Southampton SO45 2GQ.

TAVENER, Robert, R.E., A.T.D., N.D.D.; illustrator and printmaker; formerly Deputy Principal, Eastbourne College of Art and Design; *b* London, 1920. one *d. Studied:* Hornsey College of Art (1946-50). *Exhib:* 30 one-man exhibitions; work selected for eight Arts Council exhibitions. *Work in collections:* over 2000 prints purchased for national collections in U.K. and abroad by galleries, museums, local educational authorities. *Publications:* illustrated series of children's books for Longmans Green and Oxford University Press; and commissioned work for B.B.C., London Transport, G.P.O., Shell, I.C.I., Nuffield Foundation, etc. *Clubs:* Senior Fellow, Royal Soc. of Painter Printmakers (retd.). *Signs work:* see appendix. *Address:* Tussocks, Link Rd., Meads, Eastbourne BN20 7TA.

TAYLOR, Alan, N.D.D. (1954), A.R.C.A. (1957); artist in water-colour, gouache, ink, chalks; T.V. Designer/Art Director; retd. from T.V., painting full time, now producing computer art and writing novels; *b* India, 5 June, 1930. *m* Rachel Taylor. *Studied:* R.C.A. (Prof. John Skeaping, Leon Underwood). *Exhib:* one-man shows: three in Wales, one in Holland; mixed shows: Wales, England, France, Holland and U.S.A.; one-man show in computer art: Newport (Nov., 1997). *Work in collections:* University of Wales, Bangor, University of Wales, Cardiff, B.B.C., Welsh Tourist Board. *Commissions:* Computer landscape and portrait commissions (private), computer images for T.V. Channel S4C. *Publications:* illustrated Song of the Harp (Christopher Davies); illustrations for B.B.C. T.V. and H.T.V. Listed in Welsh Arts Council and Axis slide libraries, published novel 2001 'One Day as a Tiger' set in India – published by Authors on Line. *Signs work:* see appendix. *Address:* 75 Preston Ave., Newport, S. Wales NP20 4JD. *Email:* a.taylor6@ntlworld.com

TAYLOR, Alan, B.A.(Hons.) (1973), A.T.C. (1974); painter in acrylic; *b* Wembley, Middx., 1942. *m* Josephine. one *d. Educ:* Hornchurch Grammar School. *Studied:* Colchester School of Art (1963-65, drawing: John Nash), Stourbridge College of Art (1965-68 and 1972-73), University of Sussex Art Teachers' Certificate (1973-74). *Exhib:* Midland Young Contemporaries (1966-67), London, Trends in Modern Art (1966), Corning Museum, N.Y. (1968), numerous mixed and one-man shows Birmingham, London, Colchester, Wivenhoe, Exeter, Chudleigh, Sidmouth, Normandy. *Work in collections:* U.K., Europe, Middle East, Australia, U.S.A. Works mainly to commission. *Signs work:* "ALAN TAYLOR." *Address:* La Chapelle,

Foulognes, 14240 Caumont L'Evente, Calvados, Normandie, France.

TAYLOR, James Spencer, A.R.C.A. (1948), B.Sc.(Econ.) (Hons.) (1952), F.R.S.A., M.M.A.F.A.; painter; lecturer, Bolton College of Art (1948-79); *b* Burnley, 7 May, 1921. *m* Joyce B. Haffner. one *s.* one *d. Studied:* Burnley School of Art, Slade School of Fine Art, Royal College of Art (1945-48). *Exhib:* Red Rose Guild of Craftsmen, Crafts Centre of Gt. Britain, Society of Designer Craftsmen, Arts Council Touring, R.A., R.W.S., R.B.A., R.I., V. & A., C. of I.D., and many provincial galleries. *Work in collections:* Towneley Hall A.G., Burnley; Bolton A.G. Executed many commissions in Great Britain and abroad. *Publications:* 'Noel H. Leaver, A.R.C.A.' biography, published 1983. *Signs work:* "JT" (books, 1948-70), "J. S. Taylor" or "JST" (paintings). *Address:* 7 Leaverholme Cl., Cliviger, Burnley, Lancs. BB10 4TT.

TAYLOR, Jane Winifred, A.R.C.A. (1946), R.W.S. (1988), R.B.A. (1988); artist in gouache, private tutor; *b* Sheffield, 20 June, 1925. *m* Leslie Worth. one *s.* three *d. Educ:* Sheffield High School G.P.D.S.T. *Studied:* Sheffield College of Art (1941-43, Eric Jones), R.C.A. (1943-46, Gilbert Spencer). *Exhib:* R.B.A., R.W.S., R.A., Linfield Gallery, Jon Leigh Gallery, and others. *Work in collections:* Graves A.G. Sheffield, and various Educ. authorities, several private collections. *Publications:* magazine articles on drawing and painting. *Signs work:* "Jane Taylor." *Address:* 11 Burgh Heath Rd., Epsom, Surrey KT17 4LW.

TAYLOR, Joan D., A.T.D. (1946); textile designer and printer and painter; instructor in printed textiles, Laird School of Art, Birkenhead (1946-67); *Educ:* St. Edmund's College, Liverpool. *Studied:* Liverpool College of Art. *Exhib:* R.A., N.E.A.C., Liverpool Academy of Arts, Bluecoat Display Centre, Liverpool. *Signs work:* paintings: "J. D. Taylor." *Address:* 79 Grosvenor Rd., Birkenhead L43 1UD.

TAYLOR, John Russell, B.A.(Cantab.1956), M.A.(Cantab.1959); writer; Art Critic, The Times since 1978; *b* Dover, 19 June, 1935. *Educ:* Jesus College, Cambridge; Courtauld Inst., London. *Publications:* The Art Nouveau Book in Britain; The Art Dealers; Impressionism; Edward Wolfe; Bernard Meninsky; Impressionist Dreams; Ricardo Cinalli; Muriel Pemberton; Claude Monet: Impressions of France; Bill Jacklin; The Sun is God: The Life and Work of Cyril Mann; etc. *Address:* The Times, 1 Pennington St., London E1 9XN.

TAYLOR, Joyce Barbara, Oxford Delegacy, A.T.D., C.G.L.I. (Embroidery); lecturer, Bolton College of Adult Education; artist in embroidery and water-colour; *b* Burnley, 6 Aug., 1921. *m* James S. Taylor. one *s.* one *d. Educ:* Burnley High School. *Studied:* Burnley School of Art, Manchester College of Art. *Exhib:* Red Rose Guild of Craftsmen, Embroiderers Guild, Whitworth A.G., R.W.S. Galleries, London, Manchester and Hereford Cathedrals, Haworth A.G., Accrington. *Commissions:* Altar Frontals etc. for Bolton and Walmsley Parish Churches, and other churches; Banners and other work in private collections in England and U.S.A. *Signs work:* "J.B.T." and "Joyce B. Taylor." *Address:* 7 Leaverholme Cl., Cliviger, Burnley, Lancs. BB10 4TT.

TAYLOR, Kate Dornberger, B.A. (1948); water-colour, acrylic and oils; *b* Pittsburgh, Pa., U.S.A., 26 July, 1926. *m* Kenneth T. Taylor, retd. Antique Dealer.

Educ: Peabody High School; Chatham College. *Studied:* Chatham College (1944-48, Charles Le Clair): later under Murray Hantman in Maine and N.Y.C. (1955-60) and Walter Houmère. *Exhib:* R.M.S., M.P.S.G.S., M.A.S.-F., G.M.A.S., C.P.A. and several galleries and art shows. Work in many private collections. *Signs work:* "DORN-BERGER" or monogram "K.D.T." *Address:* Jokers, High St., Curry Rivel, Som. TA10 0ET.

TAYLOR, Martin, B.A.(Hons.) (1975), A.T.D. (1976); artist in water-colour and acrylic, etcher; *b* Hayes, Middx., 10 May, 1954. *m* Marianne Read. one *s.* one *d.* *Studied:* Ealing School of Art, Wimbledon School of Art, Goldsmiths' College. *Exhib:* Bankside Gallery (1986-94), Contemporary British Water-colours (1983-93), Mercury Gallery, Cork St., Catto Gallery, Hampstead, London, Edwin Pollard Gallery, Wimbledon, Linda Blackstone Gallery Pinner, Savage Fine Art, Northampton, R.A. Exhbns. (1982, 1985), Singer & Friedlander/Sunday Times water-colour exhbns. (1987-97). *Work in collections:* The Prudential. *Publications:* contributor to: Encyclopaedia of Water-colour Techniques (Quarto), Buildings (Quarto), Acrylics Masterclass (Quarto), Encyclopaedia of Drawing Techniques (Quarto); articles in The Artist magazine. *Signs work:* "Martin Taylor." *Address:* 13 St. Georges Ave., Northampton NN2 6JA.

TAYLOR, Michael John, Dip.Arch. (1953), A.R.I.B.A. (1955), V.P.S.G.F.A., F.S.A.I., U.A.; architectural illustrator in water-colour, gouache, linocuts; *b* Scarborough, 22 Sept., 1930. *m* Molly Crowther. one *s.* one *d.* *Educ:* Scarborough Boys High School. *Studied:* Leeds College of Art, School of Architecture (1948-53). *Exhib:* R.A., R.I., R.S.M.A., S.G.F.A., U.A., "Not the RA" Llewellyn Alexander Gallery, Laing, Singer and Friedlander and Hunting competitions; one-man shows: Bath, Canterbury, Harrogate. *Work in collections:* R.A.C. Pall Mall, Hertfordshire C.C. Museums Service. *Publications:* book jackets for Foyle, Hodder and Stoughton. *Signs work:* "Michael J. Taylor" and see appendix. *Address:* 4 Sewell Ave., Wokingham, Berks. RG41 1NS.

TAYLOR, Michael Ryan, R.P. (2001), B.A.Hons.(Lond.); artist in oil; *b* Worthing, 17 Feb., 1952. *m* Caroline. one *s.* one *d. Educ:* Worthing High School for Boys. *Studied:* Goldsmiths' School of Art (1970-73). *Exhib:* Morley Gallery, N.P.G. John Player Award (winner 1983), Millfield Open (winner 1989), Hunting Group Art Prize (3rd prize 1989), R.A., Worthing A.G., Quay Arts Centre, I.O.W., Beaux Arts, Bath, and Beaux Arts, London (1993, 1997), Royal Society of Portrait Painters. *Work in collections:* N.P.G., Christchurch Hall, Oxford, Robinson College, Cambridge. *Commissions:* Julian Bream (1984) N.P.G.; P. D. James (1996) N.P.G. *Address:* 1 Upper St., Child Okeford, Blandford Forum, Dorset DT11 8EF. *Website:* www.mrtaylor.co.uk *Email:* michael@www.mrtaylor.co.uk

TAYLOR, Mrs. M.: see BRIDGE, Muriel Elisabeth.

TAYLOR, Newton: see TAYLOR, William Henry.

TAYLOR, Pam, A.R.B.S. (1980), S.P.S. (1975); sculptor in bronze, resin bronze; *b* Pontypridd, 13 May, 1929. *m* Peter William Taylor. two *s. Educ:* South Shields and Wick High Schools. *Studied:* Sir John Cass College School of Art (1947-50). *Exhib:* Mall Galleries, Guildhall, Royal Exchange. *Work in collections:* Principal works:

R.A.F. and Allied Air Forces WW2 Monument, Plymouth Hoe; R.A.F. and Battle of Britain Museums, Hendon; Shakespeareplatz, Berlin; Colgate-Palmolive Head Office; Bancrofts School; Tobacco Dock London; Georgetown Guyana; bronze bust of Shakespeare in Shakespeare's Globe Theatre, London; R.A.F. North Coates Strike Wing Memorial; Hordle Walhampton School – child figures. *Commissions:* All the above were commissions as well as numerous portrait commissions. *Clubs:* Royal Soc. of British Sculptors. *Signs work:* see appendix. *Address:* Merrydown, 88 Haltwhistle Rd., S. Woodham Ferrers, Chelmsford, Essex CM3 5ZF.

TAYLOR, Sean, Hons.D.F.A. (1982), M.A.F.A. (1983), F.F.A. (1989); sculptor in mixed media; Senior Lecturer in Sculpture, Limerick School of Art and Design, Ireland; Chairman, Artists Assoc. of Ireland; Com. mem. Infusion, The National Review of Live Art, Limerick, Ireland; *b* Cork, 16 Aug., 1959. partner. one *d. Educ:* Presentation Brothers College, Cork. *Studied:* Crawford College of Art and Design, Cork (1979-82), University of Ulster, Belfast, N.I. (1982-83), Kunstenacademie, Rotterdam (1988-89). *Exhib:* 24 one-man shows since 1983 worldwide. *Work in collections:* museums in Poland, Mexico; commissions in Glasgow. *Publications:* 16 catalogues. Work on axis website (UK) http://www. Imu.ac.uk/ces/axis *Signs work:* "Sean Taylor." *Address:* Lismullane, Ballysimon, Co. Limerick, Rep. of Ireland.

TAYLOR, W. S., A.R.C.A., M.Phil.; painter; editor of Manuals Series for Thames and Hudson Ltd.; Dean of Faculty, Sheffield Polytechnic (1972-75)(now Sheffield Hallam University); *b* 26 Sept., 1920. *m* Audrey Wallis. one *d. Educ:* City Grammar School, Sheffield. *Studied:* Sheffield College of Art and R.C.A. (1939-43). *Exhib:* R.A., etc. *Work in collections:* various. *Publications:* Catalogue of Burne-Jones Exhbn., Sheffield City Art Galleries (1971). *Address:* Lower Manaton, South Hill, Callington, Cornwall PL17 7LW.

TAYLOR, Wendy Ann, C.B.E. (1988); sculptor; Mem. Royal Fine Art Commission (1981-99); Specialist Adviser, Com. for Arts Design (1988-91); Mem. Advisory Group P.C.F.C. (1989-90); F.Z.S. (1989-); Mem. Design Advisory Panel, London Docklands Development Corp. (1989-'98); Trustee, L.A.M.A. (1993-), F.Q.M.W. (1993-), F.R.B.S. (1994-) Council Mem. (1999-2000); F.S.S.M. *m* 1982, Bruce Robertson. one *s. Educ:* St. Martin's School of Art, L.D.A.D. (1st Dist.). *Exhib:* ten one-man shows: (1970-92); over 100 group exhbns. (1964-82). *Work in collections:* G.B., U.S.A., Eire, N.Z., Germany, Sweden, Qatar, Switzerland, Seychelles. *Commissions:* Major commissions: over fifty throughout the U.K. *Publications:* 'Wendy Taylor' monograph by Edward Lucie-Smith (1992). *Signs work:* see appendix. *Address:* 73 Bow Rd., London E3 2AN.

TAYLOR, William Henry (Newton Taylor), A.R.C.A. (1934), A.R.E. (1957), Free Studentship (1932), Prix-de-Rome Finalist in Engraving (1935); artist in oil (portrait and landscape), water-colours, etching and engraving on metal and wood; Head (retd.) School of Art, Amersham; lecturer, demonstrator, critic; *b* Normanton, Yorks., 31 Aug., 1911. *m* Elsie May Newton (decd.). three *s. m.* Monica Newton Taylor. *Educ:* Normanton Boys' Grammar School, Yorks. *Studied:* Wakefield School of Art; Leeds School of Art; R.C.A. *Exhib:* Yorks. Artists Soc., Bucks. Art Soc., R.P.E., R.B.A., R.A. *Signs work:* "NEWTON TAYLOR" in two lines. *Address:* Newstone Bungalow, Bovingdon Green, Marlow, Bucks. SL7 2JL.

TAYLOR WILSON, Joanne, M.A. Fine Art (Edin. 1977), A.T.C. Goldsmiths' College (1978), R.A. Schools Post. Grad. Cert. (1981), Elizabeth Greenshields Scholarship (1981-82); still life, landscape and portrait painter in oil and water-colour; Mem. of Manchester Academy of Arts (1985); *b* Bolton, Lancs., 12 Sept., 1953. *m* Ivan Wilson, R.I.B.A. one *s.* one *d. Educ:* Canon Slade Grammar School, Bolton. *Studied:* Edinburgh College of Art (1972-77), R.A. Schools (1978-81, Peter Greenham, R.A.). *Exhib:* Royal Scottish Academy (1975, 1987), R.A. (1979, 1980, 1982, 1983, 1986, 1987), R.B.A. (1980), Manchester Academy (1979-83, 1985-97), Manchester; one-man show, Bolton A.G. (1979), Howarth A.G., Accrington (1991), Towneley Hall, Burnley (1999). *Work in collections:* Bolton A.G., West Midlands College of Education. *Signs work:* "J. TAYLOR WILSON" or "J.T.W." *Address:* 4 Beechwood Ave., Clitheroe, Lancs. BB7 1EZ.

TEASDILL, Graham, F.R.S.A., F.R.N.S., F.Z.S., F.M.A.; Museum and Art Gallery Curator (retd.); *b* Horsforth, 5 Oct., 1935. *m* Nova Ann Pickersgill of Horsforth, 22 July, 1960. one *s.* two *d.* (see Morris, Caroline Nova; Andrews, Pauline Ann). *Educ:* Ilkley Grammar School. Assistant at Ilkley (1950-55), Leeds (1955-56) and Huddersfield (1956-60); Assistant Curator, Cheltenham (1960-62); Curator, Batley (1962-66), Russell-Cotes A.G. and Museum, Bournemouth (1966-88). President, Yorkshire Federation of Museums (1966-67); South-Eastern Federation (1969-70). *Address:* 99 Carbery Ave., Southbourne, Bournemouth BH6 3LP.

TEBBS, Margaret, Freelance botanical illustrator in ink and water-colour; free-lance artist: R.B.G. Kew, Natural History Museum, New Plantsman, etc.; *b* 5 Sept., 1948. *Educ:* Manor School, Ruislip. *Studied:* Ealing College of Art. *Exhib:* Westminster Gallery, London, Everard Read Gallery, South Africa. *Publications:* numerous illustrations for Kew Bulletin, Flora of Arabia, B.S.B.I. Publications, Wild Flowers of Europe (New Holland), Flora Zambesiaca, Flora of Bhutan, Flora of Egypt. *Signs work:* "M. Tebbs." *Address:* c/o Royal Botanic Gdns, Kew, Richmond, Surrey TW9 3AB.

TEMPEST, Victor, A.R.C.A. (1935); artist in oil and tempera; *b* Swaffham, Norfolk, 23 Mar., 1913. *Studied:* Woolwich Polytechnic School of Art (1927-32), R.C.A. (1932-36, Sir William Rothenstein). *Exhib:* R.A., R.B.A., N.E.A.C., and provincial galleries. *Work in collections:* City of Leicester A.G., Wolverhampton Municipal A.G., R.A., New York, Tokyo. *Signs work:* "Tempest." *Address:* 12 Forest Ridge, Keston Pk., Keston, Kent BR2 6EQ.

TEMPLE, Nigel Hal Longdale, Ph.D., M.Litt. in Architecture, N.D.D., A.T.D., F.S.A.E., R.W.A.; painter; architectural and garden historian; Hon. Registrar of Research, Garden History Soc., Companion of the Guild of St. George; *b* Lowestoft, 1926. *m* Judith Tattersill. one *s.* one *d. Studied:* Farnham, Sheffield, Bristol, Keele. *Exhib:* R.W.A.; Städtisches Museum, Göttingen; Musée du Château d'Annecy; Cheltenham Festivals; University of Reading; University of Bristol; New Ashgate; Cheltenham A.G.; Bruton St. Gallery; Thelma Hulbert Gallery. *Publications:* author: Farnham Inheritance (1956, 1965), Farnham Buildings and People (1963, 1973), Looking at Things (1968), Seen and Not Heard (1970), John Nash and the Village Picturesque (1979), George Repton's Pavilion Notebook: a catalogue raisonné (1993); contributor: Porzellan aus China und Japan (1990). *Signs work:* "Nigel

Temple" and date. *Address:* 4 Wendover Gdns., Cheltenham GL50 2PA.

TENGBERG, Violet, City of Gothenburg award for cultural achievement (1966), Bronze Medal, Europe Prize for painting (1971), Ostende, Belgium; Accademico Tiberino, Rome, Il Premio Adelaide Ristori, Rome (1984); City of Gothenburg Hon. Award (1987); Swedish Artists Foundation (1995); artist in oil and graphic work, and enamels on iron; poet, has published poetry books, 'Vision of the World Egg' (1996, 1997), 'Poetish Inspiration' (1999); *b* Munktorp, Sweden, 21 Feb., 1920. *m* J. G. A. Tengberg, D.H.S. one *s.* one *d. Educ:* Dipl. Academy of Fine Arts, "Valand" (1958-63), B.A. in Art History, Gothenburg University (1997). *Exhib:* 19 one-man shows, Stockholm, Helsinki, London, Brussels, Paris, Rome, Viterbo, etc.; nearly 200 group shows all over Europe; Riksutställningar travelling exhbn.; 2nd Enamel Triennial, Trondheim, Norway (1993); group exhbn.: Enamel Artists from the Northern Countries, Kecskemet (1993); Szegred, Budapest, Hungary; Vienna, Austria; Germany (1994); 3rd International and enamel ausstellung, Coburg, Germany (1995). Official invite to exhibit in India, New Delhi and The Government Museum of Chandigarh (1997). *Work in collections:* Museums and official collections in Sweden including: Museet i Halmstad, Kalmar Art Museum; Institut Tessin, Paris; Musée de Pau and Musée de Caen, France; Bibliothèque Nationale, Paris; Musée Vatican, Italy; Tate Gallery, London; Museo Nationale, Gdansk, Poland; Galleria Nationale, Varsavia, Poland; Museo di Viterbo, Italy; National Gallery of Modern Art, New Delhi, The Government Museum of Chandigarh, India. *Publications:* Swedish Art Lexicon, part V, Allhem; Enciclopedia Universale "SEDA" della Pittura Moderna, Milano, etc. (colour ill.); "Violet Tengberg - Paintings, drawings, graphics and poems" (1982) in three languages and with 45 colour reproductions; Creative Mysticism - a Psychological Study of Violet Tengberg's religious visions and artistic creations by Prof. Antoon Geels (University of Lund, 1989). Essays by (Prof.) J.P. Hodin, Teddy Brunius (Prof. art History, University of Copenhagen) and Benkt-Erik Benktson (Prof. University of Gothenburg); Violet Tengberg: paper on William Blake's poem "The Tygor" of "Songs of Innocence and of Experience" (Gothenburg University of Art Dept. 1994), M.A. paper on William Blake's "World of Ideas" (1997). *Clubs:* A.I.A., W.I.A.C., F.P.S., K.R.O. *Signs work:* "VT," "Violet Tengberg." *Address:* Götabergsgatan 22, 41134 Gothenburg, Sweden.

TERRY, John Quinlan, F.R.I.B.A. (1962); architect, artist in pen and ink, water-colour, linocut; *b* London, 24 July, 1937. *m* Christine. one *s.* four *d. Educ:* Bryanston School. *Studied:* architecture: Architectural Assoc., London. *Exhib:* R.A. Summer Show since 1962, Biennale in Venice (1980), San Francisco (1982), Paris (1981), Real Architecture Building Centre (1987); one-man shows: Rye A.G. (1980), Architectural Design (1981), Anthony Mould Gallery (1986), Judd St. Gallery (1987), Vision of Europe, Bologna (1992). *Address:* Old Exchange, Dedham, Colchester, Essex CO7 6HA.

THELWELL, Norman, A.T.D. (1950); landscape painter, cartoonist and free-lance illustrator in pen, line and wash, water-colour, oils and gouache; teacher of design and illustration, College of Art, Wolverhampton (1950-56); now freelance; *b* Birkenhead, Ches., 3 May, 1923. *m* Rhona E. Ladbury. one *s.* one *d. Educ:* Rock Ferry High School, Birkenhead. *Studied:* Liverpool College of Art under H. P. Huggill, A.R.C.A., M.A., A.R.E., principal, and G. H. Wedgwood, A.R.C.A., teacher of graphic design (1947-50). *Signs work:* see appendix. *Address:* Herons Mead, Timsbury, Romsey, Hants. SO51 0NE.

THEXTON, Ronald, painter in oil; retd. oral surgeon; *b* Burton, Westmoreland, 21 Feb., 1916. *m* Barbara J. Stevens. one *s*. one *d*. *Educ:* Solihull School, Birmingham and Edinburgh Universities. *Studied:* Edinburgh (evenings); private assistance from James Cowie, R.S.A., Hayward Veal, Allen Gwynne-Jones, R.A. *Exhib:* R.A., R.B.A., R.W.A., S.S.A. *Work in collections:* Newport (Gwent) Corp., Thamesdown Corp., Frank Slide Interpretive Centre, Alberta, Canada. *Signs work:* "Thexton." *Address:* Tallett Steps, Barnsley, Cirencester, Glos. GL7 5EF.

THICKE, Thelma Gwendoline, N.D.D., A.T.D., Dip. H.E., M.F.P.S.; dealer in fine art, restorer and painter in oil and water-colour; principal: Thicke Gallery, and Swansea Antique Club; retd. lecturer, Faculty of Art and Design, W. Glamorgan Inst. of Higher Educ., Swansea, also Swansea University, Faculty of Educ.; *b* 20 Aug., 1921. *Educ:* St. Leonards-on-Sea. *Studied:* Hastings School of Art (Vincent Lines), West of England College of Art, Bristol University, B'ham University (1966-67). *Exhib:* R.A., R.B.A., N.E.A.C., F.P.S., R.W.S. Valuations and restoration of oils and water-colours. *Clubs:* Royal Overseas League, L.A.P.A.D.A. *Signs work:* "T.G. Thicke." *Address:* 14 Valley View, Sketty, Swansea SA2 8BG, S. Wales.

THISTLETHWAITE, Ann, N.D.D. painting; artist, landscape painter in oil, pastel and charcoal; *b* Birmingham, 22 Oct., 1944. *Educ:* Edgbaston Church of England College. *Studied:* Birmingham College of Art and Design (1961-66) under Gilbert Mason and Mr. Francis. *Exhib:* one-man shows: London, Birmingham, Worcester, Tunbridge Wells, Malvern, R.B.A., R.O.I., R.S.M.A., P.S., Contemporary Art. (Royal Overseas Commonwealth Art 1st Prize (1969) presented to H.M. the Queen). *Work in collections:* J. M. Beaul, Michigan. *Signs work:* "Ann Thistlethwaite." *Address:* 4 King George Ave., Droitwich, Worcs. WR9 7BP.

THOMAS, David Arthur, B.A. (1972), P.G.C.E. (1982); artist in oil and acrylic; retd. teacher; *b* Croydon, 30 Apr., 1928. *Educ:* Wallington County Grammar School. *Studied:* Croydon Polytechnic (1949-53), Farnborough Technical College (1962), Roehampton Adult Inst. (1982). *Exhib:* Compass Theatre Co., Sheffield; several one-man shows. *Clubs:* F.P.S. *Signs work:* "D. THOMAS." *Address:* 21 Baileys Rd., Southsea, Hants. PO5 1EA.

THOMAS, Glynn David Laurie, L.S.I.A. (1967), R.E. (1975); freelance artist in etching; taught printmaking, Ipswich Art School (1967-79); *b* Cambridge, 7 Apr., 1946. *m* Pearl. two *s*. *Studied:* Cambridge College of Art (1962-67). *Exhib:* mixed and one-man shows incl. R.A., National Print Exhbn. Pall Mall Gal., Barbican, Cambridge Contemporary Art, John Russell, Ipswich, Printworks, Colchester, Royal Exchange, Manchester, Lyric, Hammersmith, Aldephi, New York, Toronto, Hong Kong. *Work in collections:* Museum of London, Ashmolean and Ipswich Museum. *Commissions:* Christies Contemporary Art. *Publications:* Victorian Cambridge, Illustrated Journal of Nepal. *Address:* Lodge Cottage, Bluegate Lane, Capel St. Mary, Ipswich IP9 2JX. *Website:* www.glynnthomas.com *Email:* studio@glynnthomas.com

THOMAS, Jean, Dip.A.D. Fine Art (Bristol, 1974); painter/printmaker in oil on canvas; *b* Haverfordwest, 1950. *m* Paul Preston, goldsmith. one *s.* one *d. Educ:* Taskers, Haverfordwest. *Studied:* Newport College of Art (1969-71), Bristol Polytechnic (1971-74). *Exhib:* Welsh National Eisteddfod, R.S.P.P., R.S.B.A., R.S.P.M., Galerie d'Or Hamburg, Fountain Fine Art Llandeilo, Manor House Cardiff; and numerous exhbns. G.B.H., Germany, Austria. *Commissions:* portraits for: Earl of Halifax, Lady Brooksbank, Judge Haworth, plus commissions for Christie's, and Northallerton Council for Duke and Duchess of York. Recently worked on large mural and now flag/banner sculpture. *Address:* The Old Smithy, Llandeilo, Haverfordwest, Pembrokeshire SA62 6LD.

THOMAS, Margaret, R.W.A., R.B.A., N.E.A.C.; painter; *b* 26 Sept., 1916. *Studied:* Slade School (1936-38), R.A. Schools (1938-39). *Exhib:* R.A., R.W.A., and R.S.A.; one-man exhbns. include Leicester Galleries (1949 and 1950); Aitkin Dott's Edinburgh (1952, 1955 and 1966); Canaletto Gallery (1961); Howard Roberts, Cardiff (1963); Minories, Colchester (1964); Queen's University, Belfast (1967); Mall Galleries (1972); Octagon, Belfast (1973); Scottish Gallery, Edinburgh (1982); Sally Hunter Gallery, London (1988, 1991, 1995, 1998); Royal West of England Academy (1992); Messum's Gallery, London (Sept. 2001). *Work in collections:* H.R.H. Duke of Edinburgh; Chantrey Bequest; Arts Council; Exeter College, Oxford; Min. of Educ.; Min. of Works; Paisley, Hull and Carlisle Art Galleries; G.L.C.; Edinburgh City Corporation; Steel Company of Wales; Financial Times; Nuffield Foundation Trust; Scottish National Orchestra; Robert Fleming; Lloyds of London, and the Warburg Group. *Commissions:* National Library of Wales (portrait of Sir Kyffin Williams R.A.). *Signs work:* see appendix. *Address:* Ellingham Mill, Bungay, Suffolk NR35 2EP.

THOMAS, Norma Marion, B.A. (1980), N.S.A.M., Cert. in Art; artist in oil, water-colours, restoration; *b* Hawarden, Ches., 9 Jan., 1922. *m* Leslie Gurwin Thomas, A.T.D. (decd.). three *s. Educ:* Hawarden Grammar School; Normal College, Bangor. *Studied:* Liverpool School of Art, Goldsmiths' and Hornsey College of Art. Art mistress in Liverpool, Wisbech and Wirral Grammar School. Own studio and exhbn. gallery. Paintings in Gt. Britain and abroad. *Signs work:* "Norma M. Thomas." *Address:* Old School Studio, Blaenporth, Cardigan SA43 2AP.

THOMAS, Robert John Roydon, A.R.C.A. (1952), Otto Beit Medal R.B.S. (1963), R.B.S. Silver Medal (1966); sculptor in bronze, stone; Past-President, Society Portrait Sculptors; Past V.P.R.B.S.; *b* Cwmparc, Treorchy, Rhondda, Glam., 1 Aug., 1926. *m* Mary Gardiner, Des. R.C.A. two *s.* one *d. Educ:* Pentre Grammar School, Rhondda. *Studied:* Cardiff College of Art (1947-49), R.C.A. (1949-52). *Exhib:* R.A. and various London galleries. *Work in collections:* Sculptures at Coalville, Leics., Birmingham City Centre, Blackburn Town Centre, Ealing Broadway Centre, London, Cardiff, Swansea, Rhondda; portraits include, H.R.H. Princess Diana, Viscount Tonypandy, Lord Parry, Lord Chalfont, Aneurin Bevan, Cliff Morgan, Sir Geraint Evans, Sir Julian Hodge, Dame Gwyneth Jones, Gwyn Thomas, Ryan, Carwyn James. *Signs work:* "Robert Thomas sculptor." *Address:* Villa Seren, 23 Park Rd., Barry, Vale of Glam. CF62 6NW.

THOMAS, Shanti, artist in oil, pastel and charcoal, teacher; Artist in Residence, Gatwick Airport (1993); *b* London, 3 Dec., 1949. *Studied:* School of Signa Simi

(1965), Academy of Fine Arts, Florence (1965-67), Camberwell School of Art and Crafts (1971-73, Sargy Mann). *Exhib:* Commonwealth Inst. (1987), Ikon touring (1984, 1989), Whitechapel Open (1987, 1989), Athena Arts Award Open, Barbican (1987), 'Critical Realism' Nottingham, Camden Arts Centre (1988), 'Black Art, Plotting the Course' Oldham (1988), 'The Artist Abroad' Usher Gallery, Lincoln (1989). *Work in collections:* A.C.G.B., Leicester Schools, and private collections. *Publications:* Birthday Book, Women's Artist Diary (1988), catalogues, Critical Realism, Black Art, The Artist Abroad, etc. *Signs work:* "Shanti Thomas." *Address:* 18 Cornwall Rd., London N4 4PH.

THOMPSON, Hilli, B.A.Hons. (1967), M.Phil. (1971), P.G.C.E. (1977); artist/botanical illustrator in linocut, etching, pen, pastel, acrylic; *b* London, 3 Apr., 1946. *Educ:* Brondesbury and Kilburn Grammar School; Universities of Newcastle (1964-67), Ulster (1968-71), Leeds (1971-77). *Exhib:* frequently at botanical socs. of British Isles, S.B.A.; solo shows: Ipswich/E. Anglia. *Work in collections:* Norwich City Museum. *Publications:* The New Flora of British Isles by C.A. Stale (C.U.P.). *Signs work:* "Hilli." *Address:* 42 Dover Rd., Ipswich, Suffolk IP3 8JQ.

THOMPSON, Kevin Barry, self taught artist in oil, acrylic, water-colour; *b* Dorking, Surrey, 11 Mar., 1950. *m* Vanessa Jane. one *s.* one *d. Educ:* Roman Hill School, Lowestoft; studied general design at Lowestoft College (1985-87). *Exhib:* R.O.I., R.S.M.A.; one-man shows: Norwich (1982), Aldeburgh (1986), Southwold (1989), Gt. Yarmouth (1991). *Work in collections:* Many works are held in private collections, both in Gt. Britain and abroad. *Clubs:* Norfolk and Norwich Art Circle, Oulton Broad Art Circle. *Signs work:* "KEVIN.B. THOMPSON." *Address:* 24 Pound Farm Drive, Lowestoft, Suffolk NR32 4RQ.

THOMPSON, Liam, B.A. Hons. (1978); self employed artist in water-colour and oil; Adult Educ. tutor, creative studies curriculum leader; *b* Larne, Co. Antrim, 20 Nov., 1956. *Educ:* Campbell College, Belfast. *Studied:* Newcastle College of Art and Design (1974-75), Chelsea School of Art (1975-78), City and Guilds of London Art School (1978-79, Peter Coker, R.A.). *Exhib:* R.A. Summer Shows (1983-97). *Work in collections:* National Trust, U.T.V. Collection. *Commissions:* National Trust, Storm Damage at Nymans, Sussex, Mount Stewart House, Co. Down. *Publications:* work repro.: Leisure Painter Magazine (1990-97). *Signs work:* water-colours and oils: signed on back. *Address:* Stone Cottage, Hogbens Hill, Selling, Faversham, Kent ME13 9QU.

THOMSON, Diana (née Golding), B.A., F.R.B.S.; sculptor in bronze, terracotta, wood, resin; *b* Manchester, 1939. *m* Alexander Thomson, B.S.C., Cinematographer;. one *d. Educ:* Cheltenham Ladies' College. *Studied:* Kingston Polytechnic Sculpture Dept. (1976-79). *Exhib:* R.A., R.W.A., New College, Oxford, Margam Park, S. Wales, and various group shows including "Free Range" Simmons Gallery, London W.C.1 (2000). *Commissions:* 'Woking Market' bronze plaque 7'3" x 4'6" at Network House, Bradfield Cl., Woking; 'Father and Child' bronze over life-size at Central House, off New St., Basingstoke; 'The Swanmaster' 7' bronze at Fairfield Ave., Staines; 'The Hurdler' bronze life-size, at APC International, The Lodge, Harmondsworth, Middx.; 'The Inheritors' bronze life-size group; 'Portrait of Yvonne de Galais and her daughter' life-size group; 'The Bargemaster' 7' bronze at Data-

General Tower, Brentford, Middx.; 'Portrait of D.H. Lawrence' bronze life-size, at Nottingham University; 'The First Cinematographer' bronze life-size homage to William Friese-Greene, sited at Shepperton Studios, Middx.; Pinewood Studios, Bucks; Panavision U.K. Ltd., Greenford, Middx.; and Panavision, L.A., Calif., U.S.A. (1999). *Signs work:* "D.C. Thomson" or "D.C.T." and the year. *Address:* The Summerhouse, 64 Mincing La., Chobham, Surrey GU24 8RT.

THOMSON, George L., D.A. (Edin.), S.S.A., F.S.S.I.; calligrapher; principal art teacher (retd.); *b* Edinburgh, 15 Dec., 1916. *Studied:* Edinburgh College of Art (1932-37). *Publications:* Better Handwriting (Puffin, 1954), Traditional Scottish Recipes (1976), New Better Handwriting (1977), Scribe (1978), Christmas Recipes (1980), Rubber Stamps (1982), Traditional Irish Recipes (1983), (Canongate), Dear Sir, (1984), The Calligraphy Work Book (1985), The Calligrapher's Book of Letters (1990) (Thorsons), The Art of Calligraphy (1987, Treasure Press), My Life as a Scribe (Canongate, 1988), others in preparation. *Signs work:* "George L. Thomson." *Address:* The White Cottage, Balgrie Bank, Bonnybank, by Leven KY8 5SL.

THORNBERY, Mary, painter in oil; *b* Bredhurst, Kent, 23 May, 1921. *m* Michael Dobson, F.R.A.M. one *s*. *Studied:* painting: London, Florence, Rome. *Exhib:* R.A., London Group, W.I.A.C., New English Art Club, Royal West of England Academy, Bristol (permanent collection). *Signs work:* "MARY THORNBERY." *Address:* Rose Hill, Brechfa, Carmarthen, W. Wales SA32 7RA.

THORNTON, Leslie, A.R.C.A. (1951); *b* Skipton, 1925. *Studied:* Leeds College of Art (1945-48), R.C.A. (1948-51). *Exhib:* One-man shows, Gimpels Fils (1957, 1960, 1969); Retrospective, Manchester (1981); I.C.A. (1955); Berne (1955); British Council Young Sculptors Exhbn. (Germany, 1955-56), Sweden (1956-57); São Paolo Biennal (1957); Holland Park (1957); C.A.S. Religious Theme Exhbn., Tate Gallery; British Embassy, Brussels (1958); Middelheim Biennial, Antwerp (1959). *Work in collections:* Museum of Modern Art, New York; Arts Council of Gt. Britain; Leeds Art Gallery; Felton Bequest, Australia; Albright Museum; Fogg Art Gallery; National Gallery of Scotland; private: U.K., Europe, U.S.A. and S. America. *Address:* Stable Cottage, Chatsworth Pl., Harrogate HG1 5HR.

THORPE, Hilary, B.A. (Hons.) Woven Textiles; painter in acrylic, fine art weaver in wool and silk; *b* Elsecar, Yorks., 9 Apr., 1959. *m* Ian Clayton. *Studied:* West Surrey College of Art and Design. *Exhib:* solo shows: Cowes and London. *Work in collections:* Cowes Maritime Museum. *Commissions:* two woven hangings, private client, Tollesbury Essex (1998). *Address:* 7 Solent View Rd., Cowes, I.O.W. PO31 8JY.

THURGOOD, Gwyneth, N.D.D. (1958), A.T.D. (1959), F.N.S.E.A.D. (1970); artist/teacher in painting, etching, stained glass; *b* Swansea, 2 Apr., 1938. *m* Anthony Thurgood. one *s*. *Educ:* Neath Girls' Grammar School. *Studied:* Swansea College of Art, B'ham College of Art. *Exhib:* eight solo shows: art/science (1987-97) including B.A. Meeting (1993), Science Museum, London (1995). *Work in collections:* Universities of Surrey, Manchester, Kent and Warwick. *Commissions:* University of Warwick. *Publications:* illustrated: papers - three international journals, catalogues; Meridian Television The Gallery (1994, 1995), Meridian Tonight, interview (1997). *Signs work:* "Gwyneth Thurgood" or "Thurgood." *Address:* Serengeti, Pilgrims Way, Harrietsham, Maidstone, Kent ME17 1BT.

THURSBY, Peter, P.P.R.W.A., F.R.B.S., Hon. D.Art; sculptor in bronze, stainless steel & sterling silver; *b* Salisbury, 1930. *m* Maureen Suzanne Aspden. *Educ:* Bishop Wordsworth's School, Salisbury. *Studied:* West of England College of Art, Bristol and Exeter College of Art. *Exhib:* solo shows: Arnolfini Gallery; A.I.A. Gallery; Plymouth City A.G. (2); Marjorie Parr Gallery (3); Westward TV Studios, Plymouth; Northampton Museum and A.G.; Royal Albert Museum and A.G., Exeter (2); University of Sheffield; Haymarket Theatre, Leicester; Nottingham Playhouse; University of Exeter; Alwin Gallery; R.W.A. Bristol, Bruton St. Gallery London (2). 1987 awarded R.B.S. Silver Medal. *Work in collections:* Arnolfini Gallery; A.T.E.I. London; Gloucester Regt.; Plymouth City A.G.; R.W.A. Bristol; University of Exeter; Westminster College Oxford; National Guard of Saudi Arabia; Newcastle College of Arts and Technology; Wates Built Homes Ltd.; Exeter Museum & Art Gallery; Temple – Japan; President, Royal West of England Academy, Bristol (1995-2000). *Commissions:* Croydon, Exeter, Dallas and New York State, U.S.A., Harrow, London (2), Plymstock, Tunbridge Wells, Uxbridge, Berlin. *Clubs:* Chelsea Arts. *Signs work:* "P.T." *Address:* Oakley House, Pinhoe, Exeter EX1 3SB.

THYNN, Alexander (7th Marquess of Bath), B.A., M.A.(Oxon.); painter in oil, novelist; *b* London, 6 May, 1932. *m* Anna Gael. one *s.* one *d. Educ:* Eton and Christchurch, Oxford. *Studied:* Paris: Grande Chaumiere (Henri Goetz), Academie Julian (Andre Planson), Academie Ranson (Roger Chastel). *Work in collections:* murals at Longleat House. *Publications:* Lord Weymouth's Murals by Alexander Thynn; novels, The Carry-Cot (W. H. Allen 1972), The King is Dead (Longleat Press 1976), Pillars of the Establishment (Hutchinson 1981), Strictly Private (an autobiography). *Address:* Longleat House, Warminster, Wilts. BA12 7NN. *Website:* www.lordbath.co.uk *Email:* lordbath@btinternet.com

TIDNAM, Nicholas Rye, N.D.D. (1961); painter in oil and water-colour, illustrator, lecturer; visiting lecturer, Kent Institute of Art & Design; *b* Oadby, Leics., 13 May, 1941. *m* Ruth Murray. one *s.* one *d. Educ:* Kings Park, Eltham. *Studied:* Camberwell School of Art (1957-61), Michael Rothenstein R.A., Frank Martin, Henry Inlander, Richard Lee, Bernard Dunstan R.A., Peter Weaver R.I. *Exhib:* Mercury Gallery, London, R.A., N.E.A.C., R.B.A., Drew Gallery, Canterbury, The Peter Hedley Gallery, Wareham, The Fly Gallery, Saffron Walden. *Work in collections:* Unilever, Leics., Notts. and W. Riding Educ. authorities and numerous private collections in U.K., U.S.A., France, Germany. *Publications:* work repro.: magazine illustrations. *Clubs:* Savage, The London Sketch Club. *Signs work:* "Nicholas Tidnam" or "N.T." *Address:* 16 Roebuck Rd., Rochester, Kent ME1 1UD.

TIERNEY, James Richard Patrick, Dip.A.D.(1966), Postgrad. Dip. in Printmaking (1967); artist in all painting and printmaking media; principal lecturer; *b* Newcastle upon Tyne, 23 May, 1945. *m* Janet Rosemary. one *d. Educ:* The Royal Grammar School, Newcastle. *Studied:* Sunderland Polytechnic (1961-66, David Gormley), Brighton Polytechnic (1966-67, Jennifer Dickson). *Address:* Maple Cottage, Holt End La., Bentworth, Nr. Alton, Hampshire GU34 5LF.

TIERNEY, Robert, D.A.Dip. (1956); International artist, Cos.; textile designer/graphics, etc.; artist in water-colour, oil, design colours; début U.K. and Paris (1958); since 1958 annually engaged by numerous companies throughout three continents; *b* Plymouth, 9 Aug., 1936. *Studied:* Plymouth College of Art (Joan Lee, A.T.D.), Central School, London (1956-58, Alan Reynolds). *Exhib:* from 1959, London Design Centre, Paris, Vienna, Italy, Australia, Sweden, Denmark, U.S.A., Canada, Munchen, Switzerland; five tours of Japan (1977-81), U.S.A. tour (1981), exhbns. in European, U.S.A., Far East cities (1982, 1983, 1984, 1985). *Work in collections:* Boston Museum of Fine Arts (1981), honoured by five works accepted by V. & A. Museum (1986), etc., and private collections. *Signs work:* "Tierney" or "Robert Tierney." *Address:* Chub Cottage, 31 Church St., Modbury PL21 0QR.

TILL, Michael John, S.G.F.A.; artist in graphic, engraving, etching, pastel; Insurance Broker; *b* Sri Lanka, 23 Mar., 1939. *m* Kathleen Margaret. one *s.* (decd.). two *d.* *Educ:* St. George's College, Weybridge. *Studied:* City and Guilds (1970-72 part-time). *Exhib:* S.G.F.A. *Clubs:* Bosham S.C., R.C.Y.C., Royal London Y.C. *Signs work:* see appendix. *Address:* 57 Southway, Carshalton Beeches, Surrey SM5 4HP.

TILLEY (née Fisher), Nicola Jane, painter in watercolour; tutor and demonstrator; *b* Ismailia, Egypt, 31 Jan., 1956. *m* Peter George. two *s.* one *d.* *Educ:* Maidstone Grammar School for Girls. *Studied:* Penzance Art School, under Colin Scott. *Exhib:* various in Cornwall, Exeter, Mall Galleries, London, St. Ives Soc. of Artists. *Work in collections:* many private collections at home and abroad. *Publications:* article in Artists and Illustrators magazine (Sept. 2001). *Clubs:* St. Ives Soc. of Artists. *Signs work:* "Nicola Tilley." *Address:* Evergreen Cott., Townshend, Hayle, Cornwall TR27 6AQ.

TILLING, Robert, R.I. (1985); painter in water-colours and acrylic; lectures include Tate Gallery and Exeter University; awarded R.I. Medal (1985); prizewinner, International Drawing Biennale (1989); R.I. Members Award (1995); *b* Bristol, 1944. *m* Thelma, N.D.D. two *d.* *Educ:* Bristol; studied art, architecture and education Bristol and Exeter. *Exhib:* one-man exhbns. include London, Bristol, Exeter, Southampton, Guernsey, and Jersey; various mixed exhbns. include the R.A., R.W.S., Barbican Centre (1988). *Work in collections:* include Lodz Museum, Poland and the States of Jersey, Cleveland Museum. *Publications:* illustrations to 'Twenty One Poems', by Charles Causley C.B.E., (Cellandine Press); various reviews/criticism on jazz and blues in many magazines. *Signs work:* "Robert Tilling." *Address:* Paul Mill, La Rosiere, St. Saviour, Jersey JE2 7HF.

TILLYER, William, artist in acrylic on canvas and panel, water-colour, print; French Government Scholarship (1962); Artist in Residence, Melbourne University (1981-82); *b* Middlesbrough, 1938. *m* Judith. one *s.* one *d.* *Studied:* Slade School of Fine Art (1960-62, William Coldstream, Anthony Gross), Atelier 17, Paris (1962, gravure under William Hayter). *Exhib:* one-man shows: Bernard Jacobson Gallery (1978-80, 1983, 1984, 1987, 1989, 1991), Wildenstein & Co. (1991, 1994), Andre Emmerich, N.Y. (1994), Whitworth A.G., Manchester (1996). *Work in collections:* V. & A., A.C.G.B., Tate Gallery, M.O.M.A. (N.Y.). *Publications:* illustrations for A Rebours by J.K. Huysmans, 'William Tillyer: Against the Grain' monograph by Prof. Norbert Lynton, published October 2000 by 21 Publishing. *Signs work:* surname on back. *Address:* c/o Bernard Jacobson Gallery, 14a Clifford St., London W1X 1RF. *Website:* www.jacobsongallery.com *Email:* William@Tillyer.com

TILMOUTH, Sheila, Dip.A.D. (Hons.), A.T.C.; artist in oil on gesso panel; *b*

London, 25 Sept., 1949. two *s.* one *d. Educ:* Latymer Grammar School, London. *Studied:* Hornsey College of Art (1969-72, Jack Smith, Nigel Hall, Norman Stevens), Byam Shaw School (1974-75, Bill Jacklin), Finnish Academy, Helsinki (1973). *Exhib:* R.A. Summer Exhbn., Alresford Gallery, Hants., Albemarle Gallery, London, Llewelyn Alexander Gallery, London, Old School House, Norfolk. *Work in collections:* Calder Museums. *Publications:* Limited Edn. prints (Buckingham Fine Arts, and Contemporary Arts Group). *Signs work:* "ST 2002" *Address:* 29 Royd Terrace, Hebden Bridge, W. Yorks. HX7 7BT. *Email:* sheila@sheilatilmouth.co.uk

TILSON, Joe, painter, sculptor; *b* London, 24 Aug., 1928. *m* Joslyn. one *s.* two *d. Studied:* St. Martin's School of Art (1949-52), R.C.A. (1952-55). *Exhib:* Venice Biennale (1964), Marlborough Gallery (1960-77), since 1977 Waddington Galleries, internationally since 1961. *Work in collections:* major museums in Gt. Britain, U.S.A., Italy, S. America, Australia, Germany, Holland, Denmark, Belgium, N.Z., etc. *Signs work:* "Joe Tilson." *Address:* 93 Bourne St., London SW1W 8HF.

TINDLE, David, R.A. (1979), Hon. F.R.C.A. (1984), M.A. (Oxon.) (1985); painter in egg tempera; Ruskin Master of Drawing, University of Oxford (1985-87), Hon. Fellow at St. Edmund Hall, Oxford; Hon. mem. R.B.S.A.; *b* Huddersfield, 29 Apr., 1932. *Studied:* Coventry School of Art (1945-47). *Exhib:* Fischer Fine Art since 1985, Piccadilly Gallery (1954-83), Galerie XX, Hamburg (1974, 1977, 1980), Redfern Gallery (1994). *Work in collections:* Tate Gallery, Manchester City A.G., Wakefield, Coventry, Whitworth, A.G.'s., Bradford, Huddersfield, R.A., N.P.G. Agents: Redfern Gallery, Cork St., London. *Signs work:* "David Tindle" or "D.T." *Address:* 16 Place de la Mairie, 56580 Rohan, Morbihan, France.

TINSLEY, Francis, M.A. (1971); lecturer, painter in oil, etching, woodcut; Sen. lecturer, Camberwell College of Arts; *b* Liverpool, 30 Mar., 1947. *m* Jennifer. *Studied:* Camberwell College of Arts (1967-70), Chelsea College of Art (1970-71). *Exhib:* one-man and mixed shows in London *Work in collections:* Flyde Museum, Blackpool, Hereford Museum, and Liverpool. *Publications:* Practical Printmaking. *Clubs:* Chelsea Arts. *Signs work:* "FRANCIS TINSLEY." *Address:* 28 Ewell Court Ave, Epsom Surrey KT19 0DZ.

TIPPETT, Jane, freelance artist in water-colour, tempera, also lithography, and teacher; *b* London, 25 Feb., 1949. *Studied:* Gloucestershire College of Art and Design, R.A. Schools (1977-80). Artist in Residence, Oundle School (1980-82). *Exhib:* R.A. Summer Exhbn. (1978-90), Agnew's Albermarle St. Gallery (1982), Church St. Gallery, Saffron Walden (1983, 1984, 1986); 14 lithographs made at the Curwen Studio. *Signs work:* "Jt." *Address:* 11 Cantelupe Rd., Haslingfield, Cambridge CB3 7LU

TISDALL, Hans, painter and designer; *b* 1910. *Exhib:* London, Paris, Rome, Brussels, Germany, Spain, Switzerland. *Commissions:* murals, tapestries. *Signs work:* see appendix. *Address:* 7 Brunel House, 105 Cheyne Walk, London SW10 0DF.

TITCOMBE, Cedric Anthony, N.D.D. (1962); painter and screen-printer in charcoal, oil, screen prints; *b* Gloucester, 11 Dec., 1940. divorced. two *s.* two *d. Educ:* Crypt Grammar School, Gloucester. *Studied:* Gloucester College of Art (1959-

63, James Tucker, John Whiskerd, Gordon Ward). *Exhib:* R.A., R.W.A., and numerous mixed shows. *Work in collections:* Trevor Barnes, etc. *Signs work:* "TITCOMBE." *Address:* 72 Priory Rd., Gloucester GL1 2RF.

TITHERLEY, Hazel M., R.C.A. (1985), A.T.C., A.T.D.(Manc.); painter in oil, acrylic and water-colour; *b* Little Singleton, Lancs., 4 Mar., 1935. *m* Philip Titherley, F.R.I.B.A., M.R.T.P.I. (decd.). one *s. Educ:* Queen Mary School, Lytham. *Studied:* Blackpool School of Art (1953-58), Manchester Regional College of Art (1958-59). *Exhib:* over 30 solo, many open and groups shows. Exhibits with Royal Cambrian Academy, English 7, North West Design Collective. *Work in collections:* Salford A.G. and private collections in Europe, U.S.A., and Far East. Studio-gallery open by appointment. *Clubs:* Founded New Longton Artists (1969). *Signs work:* "Hazel Titherley." *Address:* Woodside, Woodside Ave., New Longton, Preston, Lancs. PR4 4YD.

TODD, Daphne Jane, R.P. (1985), N.E.A.C. (1984), F.R.S.A. (1997), Hon. S.W.A. (1996), H.D.F.A.(Lond.) (1971); awards: 2nd prize John Player award (1983), G.L.C. prize (1984), 1st prize Hunting Group (1984), Ondaatje prize for Portraiture & Gold Medal of Royal Soc. of Portrait Painters (2001); painter in oil on panel; Hon. Sec. R.P. (1990-91); Director of Studies, Heatherley School of Art, Chelsea (1980-86); President R.P. (1994-2000); Governor, Heatherley School of Art (1986-); Governor, Federation of British Art (1995-2000), Worshipful Co. of Painter Stainers; Freedom, City of London (1997), Hon. Doctorate of Arts, D.M.U. (1998); *b* York, 27 Mar., 1947. *m* Lt.Col. P.R.T. Driscoll. one *d. Educ:* Simon Langton Grammar School, Canterbury. *Studied:* Slade School (1965-71). *Exhib:* R.A., R.P., N.E.A.C., Patterson Gallery, retrospective Morley Gallery (1989). *Work in collections:* Chantrey Bequest; University College, London; Royal Holloway A.G. and Museum; H.Q. Irish Guards; Pembroke College, Cambridge; Lady Margaret Hall, Oxford; St. David's University; N.P.G.; St. Catharine's College, Cambridge; Science Museum; De Montfort University; N.U.M.A.S.T.; Institution of Civil Engineers; Bishop's Palace, Hereford; University College, Oxford. *Commissions:* incl.: H.R.H. The Grand Duke of Luxembourg, K.G.; Dame Janet Baker, D.B.E.; Spike Milligan, Hon. C.B.E., Lord Sainsbury, Lord Sharman. *Publications:* occasional articles in The Artist. *Clubs:* Chelsea Arts, The Arts. *Signs work:* "D. Todd." *Address:* Salters Green Farm, Mayfield, E. Sussex TN20 6NP.

TODD, James Gilbert, M.A. (1965), M.F.A. (1970), R.E. (1997); artist in painting and wood relief printmaking; Prof. of Art and Humanities, University of Montana; *b* Minneapolis, Minn., 12 Oct., 1937. *m* Julia. three *s. Educ:* Chicago Art Inst., College of Great Falls, University of Montana (1965-70, Rudy Antio, Donald Bunse, James Dew). *Exhib:* North and South America, England, Europe, Russia, Asia. *Work in collections:* U.S.A., England, Europe, Asia, Canada. *Publications:* numerous articles on artists and art theory, and four books illustrated. *Clubs:* Northwest Print Council, S.W.E., R.E., American Assoc. of University Professors. *Signs work:* "James G. Todd" or "TODD." *Address:* 6917 Siesta Drive, Missoula, Montana 59802, U.S.A.

TODD, Peter William, A.R.C.A. (1949); artist in oil; Head of Grimsby School of Art (1956-86); *b* Sheffield, 13 May, 1921. *Studied:* Sheffield College of Art, Royal

College of Art (1946-49). *Exhib:* R.A., London Group, R.B.A., N.E.A.C., New Grafton Gallery. *Clubs:* Caterpillar. *Signs work:* "Peter Todd." *Address:* School House, Walesby, nr. Market Rasen, Lincs. LN8 3UW.

TODD WARMOTH, Pip, B.A.(Hons.), M.A.; artist in oil; *b* 5 Oct., 1962. *Educ:* Caistor Grammar School. *Studied:* Grimsby, Camberwell, R.A. Schools. *Exhib:* Catto Gallery, New Grafton, Bellock-Lowndes, Chicago, Albemarle, L.K.F. Gallery, Hong Kong, China Club, Hong Kong, C.A.C.; group shows: R.A., Bonhams, Ice Gallery, N.Y. *Work in collections:* Franklin Trust, Kingston Lacey, Montecute - National Trust, London Transport, Standard Chartered Bank, Abn Ambro, H.R.H. Prince of Wales. *Commissions:* poster for London Underground, Crown Trust. *Publications:* work repro.: Country Life, House and Garden, Evening Standard, South China Morning Post, Hong Kong Standard, Artist Illustrators, Art Review. B.B.C. Breakfast Show, H.K. Radio 4 and 5, C.B.S., News International. *Clubs:* Dover St. Arts, Chelsea Arts. *Signs work:* "Pip T.W." *Address:* 396 Brixton Rd., London SW9 7AW.

TOLLEY, Sheila, R.W.A.; artist in all media; *b* Birmingham, 28 June, 1939. *Educ:* Richard C. Thomas School for Girls, Staffs. *Studied:* Bournemouth and Poole College of Art (1972-74, Edward Darcy Lister, R.C.A.). *Exhib:* R.A. Summer Exhbns. (1978-95), R.W.A. (1976-77, 1980-87). Twice winner of the Cornelissen Prize for Painting. *Work in collections:* U.K. and abroad. *Signs work:* "sheila tolley" and see appendix. *Address:* Flat 16 Hollybush House, 3 Wollstonecraft Rd., Boscombe Manor, Bournemouth, Dorset BH5 1JQ.

TOLSON, Roger Nicholas, B.A., M.A.; painter in oil; Collection Manager, Dept. of Art, Imperial War Museum; *b* Sheffield, 2 Dec., 1958. *Educ:* King Edward VII School, Sheffield; Oriel College, Oxford; Birkbeck College, London. *Studied:* Sir John Cass College of Art (1986-90). *Exhib:* R.A. Summer Show (1986-87), Hunting Group (1987), Whitechapel Open (1988, 1989, 1992), N.E.A.C. (1988); one-man show: Cadogan Contemporary (1990). *Address:* 51 Albion Rd., London N16 9PP.

TOMALIN, Peter John, R.I.B.A. Dip.Arch. (Leics. 1964), F.S.A.I. (1978), U.A. (1978); first prize in B.B.C. Christmas painting competition (1977); self employed architectural illustrator and water-colour artist; *b* Kettering, 18 Oct., 1937. *m* Marjorie Elizabeth. two *s. Educ:* Kettering Technical College, Leicester School of Architecture. *Studied:* Northampton School of Art (1976-79, Peter Atkin, Frank Cryer). *Exhib:* Mall Galleries, U.A., R.I., Grosvenor Gallery, Hitchin, Northampton A.G. *Clubs:* Northampton Town and County Art Soc., S.A.I. *Signs work:* "Peter Tomalin." *Address:* 170 Sywell Rd., Overstone, Northampton NN6 0AG.

TOMBS, Sarah Jane, B.A. (Hons.) 1983, M.A. (R.C.A.) 1987; sculptor in welded steel, stone; Sculpture Fellow, Keele University; *b* Herts., 17 Nov., 1961. *Studied:* Wimbledon School of Art (1981-83, Glynn Williams), Chelsea School of Art (1983-84), R.C.A. (1984-87). *Exhib:* Cannizaro Pk. Wimbledon (1981-84), Christopher Hull Gallery, Berkeley Sq. Gallery, Mall Galleries, Margam Pk. Glamorgan, R.C.A., Keele University, etc. *Work in collections:* Government Art Collection, Christie's Contemporary Collection, Linklater & Paines. *Commissions:* 'The Man at the Fire' National Gdn. Festival, Stoke on Trent and British Steel (1986); 'Sailing by Stars' Basingstoke Railway Station (1990); 'Breath of Life'

Hammersmith Hospital (1993); 'Beths Arch' Black Country Route, Wolverhampton (1996), etc. *Address:* 80a Nightingale Lane, Balham, London SW12 8NR.

TOMLINSON, Greta, Dip. F.A., N.A.P.A.; painter in water-colour, acrylic, oil, mixed media; *b* Burnley, 30 Jan., 1927. *m* Richard Edwards (decd.). one *d. Studied:* Burnley School of Art (Harold Thornton), Slade School, Oxford and London (Prof. Schwabe). *Exhib:* regularly with R.I., R.W.S., R.W.E. *Work in collections:* Southport A.G. *Publications:* Eagle Magazine for Boys, 'Dan Dare' (1950-54); fine art prints, cards. *Clubs:* Farnham Art Soc. *Signs work:* "G. TOMLINSON." *Address:* South Dunrozel, Farnham Lane, Haslemere, Surrey GU27 1HD.

TOMS, Peter Edward, A.R.S.M.A. (1997), R.M.S. (1995), A.R.M.S. (1991), H.S. (1991); marine and landscape painter, principal designer, British Aerospace, to 1982; full time painter since then; *b* Hayes, Middx., 28 May, 1940. *m* Patricia Mary Toms. five *s.* two *d. Educ:* Mellow Lane School, Hayes. *Studied:* engineering and design: Southall Technical College (1956-63). *Exhib:* R.S.M.A., R.I., R.M.S., R.B.A., N.S., U.A., numerous London and provincial one-man and other exhbns. including Alpine Club, Century, Edwin Pollard, Oliver Swann, Omell, Skipwith, Solent and Wykeham Galleries. *Work in collections:* P. & O. "SS Canberra", Royal Hampshire Regt., Royal Navy (H.M.S. "Osprey"), NV Amev Group (Utrecht), H.M. Land Registry, Astrid Trust and many other corporate and private collections. *Publications:* biographical note, R.M.S. Centenary Book '100 Years'. *Clubs:* Dorchester (past President 1991-98). *Signs work:* "Peter Toms." *Address:* 20 Egdon Glen, Crossways, Dorchester, Dorset DT2 8BQ.

TONG, Belinda Josephine, S.W.A., U.A.; painter in oil, pastel, water-colour and acrylic; *b* Woodford, Essex, 8 Sept., 1937. *m* Bernard Tong. two *s.* one *d. Educ:* Loughton County High School for Girls, Havering College. *Studied:* Open College of the Arts. *Exhib:* R.O.I., S.B.A., S.W.A., U.A., Essex Art Club, local galleries and societies. *Work in collections:* private collections in U.K. and abroad. *Signs work:* "B. Tong" (oil, acrylic and pastel), "Belinda Tong" (water-colour). *Address:* Grazebrook, Theydon Mount, nr. Epping, Essex CM16 7PW.

TONKS, John, A.T.D., F.R.B.S., V.P.R.B.S.; freelance sculptor in stone, wood, terracotta, bronze; part-time lecturer, Birmingham University; V.P., Royal Soc. of British Sculptors (1990-91); *b* Dudley, Worcs., 14 Aug., 1927. *m* Sylvia Irene. one *s.* one *d. Educ:* Dudley Grammar School. *Studied:* Wolverhampton and B'ham Colleges of Art specialising in sculpture (William Bloy, Albert Willetts, Tom Wright). *Exhib:* one-man shows: University of B'ham (1974, 1984), Ombersley Gallery, Worcs. (1983), Helios Gallery, B'ham (1984); V.B. Gallery, St. Louis, U.S.A. (1981), Poole Willis Gallery, N.Y. (1983), Liverpool International Gdn. Festival (1984), Gardens of New College, Oxford (1988), Garden Festival, Wales (1992). *Commissions:* Alexandre Hospital, Redditch; Pendrell Hall, Stafford; Gretna Green; B'ham Botanical Gdns. *Signs work:* "J.T." joined. *Address:* Downshill Cottage, Comhampton, Stourport-on-Severn, Worcs. DY13 9ST.

TOOP, Bill, R.I. (1979), M.C.S.D. (1971); artist and illustrator in water-colour, line and wash, line, with own gallery in Salisbury; *b* Bere Regis, Dorset, 27 May, 1943. *m* Elizabeth Thurstans. one *s.* one *d. Educ:* Weymouth Grammar School, Blandford Grammar School. *Studied:* Bath Academy of Art (1961-63, Robyn Denny,

Howard Hodgkin), Southampton College of Art (1964-66, Peter Folkes), Bristol Polytechnic Art Faculty (1967-68, Derek Crowe). *Exhib:* R.I., R.W.A., numerous one-man shows. *Work in collections:* The Sultan of Oman, Northern Telecom, British Gas, Whitbread Inns, Coutts & Co., The Sedgwick Group, N.F.U. Mutual and Avon Insurance, Royal School of Signals, Atomic Energy Authority, Inst. of Directors, etc. *Publications:* illustrated Portrait of Wiltshire (Pamela Street), National Gardens Scheme Handbook, etc. *Signs work:* "Bill Toop." *Address:* Bill Toop Gallery, 5 St. John's St., Salisbury, Wilts. SP1 2SB.

TOPHAM, John, F.P.S., I.A.A., Assoc. Internationale des Arts Plastiques; painter; *b* Hampstead, London. *m* Hazel Grimsey, painter. two *s. Studied:* Melbourne, Australia; Harrow and Ealing Schools of Art. *Exhib:* R.W.A., R.B.A., F.P.S., R.S.B.A., U.A., H.A.C., Camden Art Centre, Allsop Gallery, Anglo-French Exhbn., Poole Art Centre, Seldown Gallery, Hambledon Gallery, Archer Gallery, Minstrel Gallery, Colne Group, Parkway Gallery, Questers Gallery, Swiss Cottage Library, Olympus Gallery, Upton House Gallery, Poole Art Centre Open Exhbn. *Work in collections:* Nuffield Foundation, Camden Council; private collections in U.K. and U.S.A. *Clubs:* F.P.S., life mem. I.A.A., Assoc. Internationale des Arts Plastiques. *Signs work:* "Topham." *Address:* Holmstoke, West Milton, Bridport, Dorset DT6 3SJ.

TOVEY, Robert Lawton, A.T.D. (1947); painter in oil; *b* Birmingham, 3 Apr., 1924. *m* Annette Suzanne Hubler. *Educ:* The George Dixon Grammar School, Birmingham. *Studied:* Birmingham College of Art under B. Fleetwood-Walker (1939-43, 1946-47). *Exhib:* R.B.S.A., R.B.A., A.I.A., N.E.A.C., R.O.I., R.W.A., one-man shows, Geneva (1957, 1962, 1964, 1980, 1981, 1982, 1983, 1984, 1985, 1995), Baden (1973, 1976), Nyon (1978, 1985). *Work in collections:* Musée d'Art et d'Histoire, Geneva; Dudley A.G.; oil painting, The Red Scarf, for above (1953). *Signs work:* "R. L. TOVEY." *Address:* 2 Place de L'Octroi, 1227 Carouge, Geneva, Switzerland.

TOWNSEND, Storm Diana, N.D.D. (Sculpture) (1960), A.T.C. (1962), Siswa Lokantara Foundation Resident Fellowship Award, Indonesia (1960-61), Huntington Hartford Foundation Resident Fellowship Award, Calif. (1963); sculptor in bronze, cements; sculpture instructor, Albuquerque University, N.M., University of New Mexico in Albuquerque and The College of Santa Fe, N.M.; Associate sculptor, Alcazar Corp., Albuquerque (1987-99); New Mexico Museum of Natural History contracts (1987, 1988, 1991); *b* London, 31 Aug., 1937. *Studied:* London University, Goldsmiths' College (1955-60, Harold S. Parker, Ivor Roberts-Jones). *Exhib:* throughout U.S.A. *Work in collections:* Museum of New Mexico and the City of Albuquerque, public works, many private collections. *Commissions:* over life-size bronze "To Serve and Protect" commissioned by City of Albuquerque and others, N.M. (1984); "Bronze Trophy" for P.G.A. 'Charlie Pride International Senior Golf Classic' Albuquerque (1987); Three figure bronze 'Tres Culturas del Rio Grande' commissioned by Sunwest Bank, N.M. (1988). *Publications:* many and various articles and interviews in local and national publications. 1964 Resident Fellowship Award, Helene Wurlitzer Foundation, Taos, N.M. *Signs work:* "STORM." *Address:* P.O. Box 1165, Corrales, New Mexico, 87048, U.S.A.

TOWSEY, Mary, T.D.; landscape artist, oils; *b* Epsom, 24 July, 1936. three *d.* *Studied:* Goldsmiths' College University of London (1955-57), Epsom College of Art (1960-67). *Exhib:* Wintershall Gallery Bramley, Hallam Gallery London, Edwin Pollard Gallery, Ebury Gallery London, Wykeham Gallery London, Jonleigh Gallery Wonersh, Llewellyn Alexander Gallery, London, Galerie de Vétheuil, France, R.B.A., R.O.I., N.E.A.C., R.W.S., S.W.A., S.B.A. B.B.C.2 television series 'Painters', winner - Best Collection Paintings "Au Bout du Monde" Épone, France. *Work in collections:* Marie de Vétheuil - France, Government Art Collection. *Commissions:* The Great Hall, King's College, Wimbledon. *Signs work:* "Mary Towsey." *Address:* Ambelor, Lands End La., Lindford, Hants. GU35 0SS.

TRANT, Carolyn, D.F.A.(Lond.) (1973); artist in egg tempera, drawings, etchings and lithographs, artists books under imprint 'Parvenu Press'; *b* Middx., 29 Oct., 1950. two *s.* one *d. Educ:* North London Collegiate School. *Studied:* Slade School of Fine Art (1969-73). *Exhib:* New Grafton Gallery, Business Arts Gallery, Brighton Festival, London Artists Bookfair - Barbican, R.A. Summer Shows, etc. *Work in collections:* R.A., National Art Library (V. & A.), Library Collections across U.S.A. *Commissions:* E.S.C.C./S.E. Arts commission: 'Rituals and Relics' - Earthworks on the Downs, National Theatre - poster 'Blood Wedding' (Lorca). First Prize for 'Gawain', Soc. of Bookbinders competition for the complete book. *Signs work:* "Carolyn Trant" on back of work. *Address:* 17 St. Anne's Cres., Lewes, E. Sussex BN7 1SB.

TRATT, Richard, S.WL.A. (1981), S.B.A. (1987); painter in oil; *b* Enfield, 19 Oct., 1953. *m* Hilary Wastnage. two *d. Educ:* Crewe Grammar School. *Studied:* Northwich College of Art (1970-72), Dartington College of Arts (1972-74). *Exhib:* R.A., Mall Galleries, Robert Perera Fine Arts, Alresford Gallery, Peter Hedley Gallery, Isetan Gallery, Tokyo; twenty four one-man shows. *Work in collections:* S.W.A.N., Royal Palace of Oman. *Publications:* work repro.: Reynard Fine Art, Royles, McDonald, Rosenstiel's. First prize winner of national competition - 'Nature in Art'. *Signs work:* "Richard Tratt." *Address:* 10 Sharpley Cl., Fordingbridge, Hants. SP6 1LG.

TRAYHORNE, Rex, R.M.S. (1988); artist in water-colour and gouache; art teacher, demonstrator and writer; exhbns. organiser, Wessex Artists Exhbns.; *b* 13 Oct., 1931. *m* Geraldine. two *s.* (one s-*s*), two *d.* (one s-*d*). *Educ:* Newbury Grammar School. *Studied:* Reading College (1958). *Exhib:* R.I., R.M.S., R.W.S., local art societies, Wessex Artists Exhbns., etc. *Publications:* 'Adventure into Watercolour' (an instructional video). *Clubs:* Romsey Art Group, Ringwood Art Soc. *Signs work:* "Rex Trayhorne" R.M.S. *Address:* Stable House Studio, Newton Lane, Romsey, Hants. SO51 8GZ.

TRAYNOR, Mary, J.P.; artist in pen and ink, water-colour and mixed media; *b* 23 Mar., 1934. *m* Brian Traynor (decd.). one *s.* two *d. Educ:* Walthamstow Hall, Sevenoaks. *Studied:* Birmingham College of Art and Crafts, Theatre Design: Findlay James, Roy Mason. *Exhib:* National Museum of Wales, Welsh National Eisteddfod; one-man: Welsh Industrial and Maritime Museum (1988), St. David's Hall, Cardiff (1990), Manor House Fine Arts, Cardiff (1997), Washington Gallery, Penarth (2001). *Work in collections:* National Museum of Wales, Cardiff Magistrates, Professional

Offices, County of Cardiff, Gwent Health Authority, University of Wales, St. James's Palace, private. *Commissions:* public and private inc. C.A.D.W., University of Wales, Cardiff, Welsh Development Agency, and private companies. *Publications:* illustrated: Wales Tourist Board, Western Mail, National Museum of Wales, Cardiff City Council, C.A.D.W.; book: "Temples of Faith: Cardiff's Places of Worship" (2001). *Clubs:* The Victorian Soc., Cardiff Architectural Heritage Soc., Cardiff Civic Soc. *Signs work:* "Mary Traynor." *Address:* 72a Kimberly Rd., Penylan, Cardiff CF23 5DN.

TREANOR, Frances, P.S. (1978), A.T.C. (1967), N.D.D. (1966); L'Artiste Assoifee awards winner (1975), Diplome d'Honneur, Salon d'Antony, France (1975), George Rowney award (1982), Frank Herring award (merit) (1984), Conté (U.K.) award (1986), Government Print Purchase (1987); *b* Penzance, Cornwall, 1944. *m* (1) Frank Elliott, (2) Anthony Taylor (divorced). one *d. Educ:* Assumption Convent, Kensington; Sacred Heart Convent, Hammersmith. *Studied:* Goldsmiths' College (1962-66), Hornsey College of Art (1966-67). *Exhib:* London, Paris, Yugoslavia, Berlin. Stage set design commission 'As You Like It' O.U.D.S. Summer Tour (Japan, U.S.A., U.K.) 1988. *Publications:* Vibrant Flower Painting (David & Charles). *Signs work:* "Treanor" or "F.T." *Address:* 121 Royal Hill, London SE10 8SS. *Website:* www.axisartists.org.uk/all/ref5493.htm

TREE, Michael Lambert, portrait painter, etcher, draughtsman and illustrator; *b* New York, 5 Dec., 1921. *m* Lady Anne Tree. two *d. Educ:* Eton. *Studied:* Slade School of Fine Art. *Exhib:* Hochmann Gallery, N.Y. (1982), Fine Arts, London (1984), St. Jame's Gallery (1989), Lumley Cazalet (1995). *Publications:* illustrations to Summoned by Bells by John Betjeman (1960). *Clubs:* White's. *Signs work:* "M. Tree." *Address:* 29 Radnor Walk, London SW3.

TRELEAVEN, Richard Barrie, S.WL.A. (founder member), M.B.O.U.; artist in oil on canvas and board, alkyd, gouache, and graphite drawings, specialises in paint-ing birds of prey; company director of family business; *b* London, 16 July, 1920. *m* Margery (decd.). *Educ:* Dulwich College (1932-36). *Studied:* under G. E. Lodge. *Exhib:* S.WL.A. Art Exhbns. Bureau, Moorland Gallery, etc.; one-man show, Bude (1953), Launceston (1973, 1980). *Work in collections:* Batley and many private col-lections. *Commissions:* Hawk portraits and falconry scenes including book covers. *Publications:* Peregrine (1977); author and illustrator 'In Pursuit of the Peregrine' (Tiercel Press, 1998); and ornithological journals. *Clubs:* British Falconers. *Signs work:* "R. B. Treleaven." *Address:* Blue Wings, South Petherwin, Launceston, Cornwall PL15 7JD.

TREMLETT, Phillippa Mary, H.S.(1994), A.R.M.S. (1998), Llewellyn Alexander award H.S. (1998); self taught miniaturist in water-colour; *b* London, 1947. *m* Peter Ian. *Exhib:* annually R.M.S. and H.S., Llewellyn Alexander Gallery, London. *Work in collections:* private: London, Home Counties, Jersey, U.S.A. *Clubs:* R.M.S., H.S. *Signs work:* "PIPT." or "PIP TREMLETT." *Address:* 4 Paddock Cl., Ropsley, Grantham, Lincs. NG33 4BJ.

TRESS, David, painter in water-colour based mixed media, including gouache, ink and oil crayon, graphite, oil; *b* London, 11 Apr., 1955. *Educ:* Latymer Upper School, Hammersmith. *Studied:* Harrow College of Art (1972-73), Trent

Polytechnic, Nottingham (1973-76). *Exhib:* regularly in Wales, England, Ireland, recently Glynn Vivian Art Gallery, Swansea; Boundary Gallery, London; W. Wales Arts Centre; 'Landmarks', National Museum of Wales. *Work in collections:* National Museum of Wales, National Library of Wales, C.A.S.W., Glynn Vivian Art Gallery. *Commissions:* Royal Mail, one of their millennium stamps (1999). *Publications:* Exhbn. catalogues: Boundary Gallery, London (1995), West Wales Arts Centre (1997). *Signs work:* "David Tress." *Address:* 17 Castle St., Haverfordwest, Pembrokeshire SA61 2ED.

TREVENA, Shirley, R.I. (1994); self taught artist in water-colour; *b* London, 11 Sept., 1934. *m* Michael Pickerill. *Educ:* Drayton Manor Grammar School, Middx. *Exhib:* R.I. Mall Galleries, R.W.S. Bank St. Gallery, Nicholas Bowlby Gallery, Tunbridge Wells. *Publications:* numerous articles and reviews; examples of work in several books on water-colour painting and drawing. *Signs work:* "S. Trevena." *Address:* 27 Montpelier Cres., Brighton, E. Sussex BN1 3JJ.

TROITZKY, Nina, M.A. Fine Art, B.A. Hons; painter, installations & mixed media; *m* Philip Richardson. *Studied:* The City Lit London, London Guildhall University, University College Chichester, and Brighton University. *Exhib:* R.O.I., Mall Galleries, London Contemporary Art Fair, British Painters, Discerning Eye, Llewellyn Alexander, London, Chelsea Arts Club, S.W.A.N. Sydney, Australia, Mountbatten Gallery, Portsmouth, University College Chichester, Brighton University Gallery, Hotbath Gallery Bath, Stroud Gallery, Phoenix Gallery Brighton, Cheltenham & Gloucester Open and many provincial and European galleries, selected Exhbn. 1999 in Dostoyevsky Museum, St. Petersburg, Russia. *Work in collections:* V. & A. Museum, London, St. Richard's Hospital, Chichester, California State University of Long Beach, U.S.A., University College, Chichester. *Publications:* work repro.: Medici card. Mem. of 'Catalyst' Women, Arts and Science Group, Artel Studio Trust, East & West Cultural Artists Club. *Clubs:* Chelsea Arts. *Signs work:* "N.T." *Address:* 31 Westgate, Chichester, W. Sussex PO19 3EZ.

TROTH, Miriam Deborah, B.A. Hons. (1983); multi-media environmental artist and sculptor; Mem. Eco-design Assoc., and N.A.A.; *b* Edgbaston, 1 Oct., 1951. *Studied:* W. Surrey College of Art and Design (1980-83). *Exhib:* Barbican, British Commonwealth Inst., Swansea A.G., Coleridge Gallery, Bristol A.G., R.A., Bankside Gallery, Smiths Gallery, Royal Soc. of Artists Gallery, Salisbury Museum, Windsor Arts Centre, Christchurch Museum, Bournemouth University. *Work in collections:* London, Sydney, Detroit, Frankfurt, Wiltshire C.C. *Commissions:* Russell Cotes Museum, Bournemouth. *Signs work:* "Miriam Troth." *Address:* 125 Seafield Rd., Bournemouth, Dorset BH6 3JL.

TROWELL, Jonathan Ernest Laverick, N.D.D. (1959), R.A.S.Dip. (1962), F.R.S.A. (1983), N.E.A.C. (1986); painter in oil, pastel and water-colour; *b* Easington Village, Co. Durham, 1938. *m* Dorothea May Howard. *Educ:* Robert Richardson School. *Studied:* Sunderland College of Art, R.A. Schools. *Exhib:* New Bauhaus Cologne, Young Contemporaries, John Moores, R.A., Lee Nordnes N.Y., Bilan de Contemporain Paris, R.B.A., N.E.A.C.; one-man shows, Brod Gallery London, Century Gallery, Culham College Oxford, Richard Stone-Reeves New York, Osborne Gallery London, Stern Galleries Australia. *Work in collections:* Bank of Japan; Culham College, Oxford; de Beers (Diamond Co.); Oriental Diamond Co.; Ciba-Geigy; Imperial College of Science; R.C.A.; B.P. *Clubs:* Chelsea Arts. *Signs work:* "TROWELL." *Address:* Carr Farm, Old Buckenham, Attleborough, Norfolk NR17 1NN.

TRUZZI-FRANCONI, Jane, B.A. (1977); Angeloni prize (1979), Discerning Eye prize (1990); sculptor in bronze; Supervisor, Fiorini Fine Art Foundry; *b* London, 26 July, 1955. one *d. Educ:* Sydenham School. *Studied:* Goldsmiths' College of Art (1973-74), Ravensbourne College of Art (1974-77), R.C.A. (1978-79). *Exhib:* R.A., Mall Galleries, many mixed shows in London, E. Anglia, Kent and Surrey. *Signs work:* "J.E.T.F." *Address:* 4 Wolsey Cottages, Strickland Manor Hill, Yoxford, Suffolk IP17 3JE.

TUCKER, Patricia Rosa, (née Madden), N.D.D. (1950), A.T.D. (1951); oil and water-colour painter, art teacher; Past Chairman, Bromley Art Soc.; Visual Arts Officer, Bromley Arts Council (1970-87); Sec. Chelsea Open Air Art Exhbn. (1967-87); *b* London, 2 Jan., 1927. *m* L. Tucker. two *s.* one *d. Educ:* Mayfield, Putney, St. Catherines, Swindon. *Studied:* Swindon School of Art, West of England College of Art. *Exhib:* R.A., Bankside, Mall, etc.; one-man shows, London, Blackheath, Greenwich, Bromley, Chelsea, Gloucester and Denmark. *Work in collections:* Bromley, Gloucestershire, Kensington and Chelsea, Swindon. *Commissions:* portraiture, architectural landscapes. *Publications:* illustrations, Parenting Plus. *Clubs:* Croydon, Blackheath, Bromley, S.E.F.A.S. *Signs work:* "Patricia Tucker." *Address:* 5 Bromley Ave., Bromley, Kent BR1 4BG.

TUDGAY, Norman, A.T.D. (1949); painter in oil; formerly head of dept., Medway College of Art, principal, Bournemouth and Poole College of Art and Design; *b* Nantyglo, Wales, 21 Apr., 1925. one *s.* two *d. Educ:* Bishop Gore Grammar School, Swansea. *Studied:* Swansea College of Art (1940-1943 and 1947-1952), Guildford College of Art (1953-1956). *Exhib:* recently at Collyer-Bristow Gallery, London, Heseltine-Masco Gallery, Petworth. *Work in collections:* emulsion drawings, Kansas University, Lord Holme private collection. *Signs work:* "TUDGAY." *Address:* The Lodge, 11 Chaddesley Wood Rd., Poole, Dorset BH13 7PN. *Email:* n.tudgay@virgin.net

TULLY, Joyce Mary, U.A. (1978); artist in oil and water-colour, teacher; speaker at local societies; teaches calligraphy and exhibits examples of work; *b* Wooler, Northumberland. *Educ:* Duchess Grammar School, Alnwick. *Studied:* Hammersmith Art College (part-time) and private tuition with Mr. Harold Workman, R.O.I., R.B.A., R.S.M.A. *Exhib:* Paris Salon, R.O.I., R.B.A., Chelsea Artists, N.S., U.A., Ridley Soc. and in Australia, British Painting in 1979, Paxton House, Berwickshire, member of North Northumberland Art Connextions. *Work in collections:* Copeland Castle, and private collections in England, Europe and America. *Signs work:* "J. M. Tully." *Address:* Kia-ora, 26 Tenter Hill, Wooler, Northumberland NE71 6DG.

TURNBULL, Alan, B.A. (Hons.) Fine Art (1977), M.A. (1978); painter in oil, etching, lecturer; *b* Co. Durham, 3 Oct., 1954. *Studied:* Newcastle University, Chelsea School of Art. *Exhib:* one-man shows: Dresden State Theatre, Norwich 'King of Hearts', Cathedrals of Durham, Ripon, Newcastle and Norwich, Bradford University, Sandford Gallery London; group shows: R.A., R.S.A. Edinburgh, 7th

Mostyn Open, Compass Gallery Glasgow, Mappin A.G. Sheffield, 'Ketterer Kunst' Hamburg, Canterbury Museum, University of Seattle, Museum of Fine Art Ekaterinberg, Galeria de Arte Brasil, Communications Centre Munich. *Work in collections:* City of Dresden, London University, Northern Arts; private collections worldwide. *Signs work:* "Alan Turnbull." *Address:* The Cottage, Moor Rd., Bellerby, Leyburn, N.Yorks. DL8 5QX.

TURNBULL, William, sculptor and painter; *b* Dundee, 11 Jan., 1922. *m* Kim Lim. two *s. Studied:* Slade School of Fine Art (1946-48). *Exhib:* I.C.A. (1957), Waddington Galleries (1967, 1969, 1970, 1976, 1978, 1981, 1985, 1987, 1991, 1998), Tate Gallery (1973); one-man and major group shows worldwide. *Work in collections:* Arts Council, Tate Gallery, Scottish National Gallery of Modern Art; numerous provincial and overseas collections. *Signs work:* see appendix. *Address:* c/o Waddington Galleries, 11 Cork St., London W1X 1PD.

TURNER, Cyril B., M.P.S.G. (1985), M.A.A. (1988), I.G.M.A. (Fellow Fine Art 1994); Fine Art master miniaturist in most categories including illuminated miniatures; inventor of Lumitex, an acid free, ultra-violet proof substitute for ivory as a miniature base; introduced cold enamel as a medium for miniature paintings; miniaturist in oils, cold enamel, soft pastel, gouache, acrylic, egg tempera, water-colour, pigmented inks, silverpoint; *b* Aldeby, Norfolk, 10 Sept., 1929. *Educ:* Beccles Area School. *Exhib:* one-man exhibs.: Museum Galleries Gt. Yarmouth. Many other U.K. one-man miniature shows, R.A., Salon des Nations Paris, many U.S.A. International Miniature Shows, others Jersey, Canada, France, Bermuda, Ulster, Sweden, Bangladesh, Japan, S. Africa. *Work in collections:* Private, corporate and representative miniature permanent collections throughout the world. Awards: 116 miniatures have won awards, including Best of Show, Highest Merit, 1st Place. 41 painted on Lumitex/Lumitex Fino. *Publications:* author: Painting Miniatures in Acrylics (1990), miniature section of Painting in Acrylics (English, Danish and French edns. 1991). Currently engaged in writing and publishing a 21 pocket book Informative Series 'Painting Original Fine Art Miniatures' 1 Bases (Lumitex), 2 Bases Various (1993): 3 Landscapes in Water-colours, 4 Landscapes in Oils, 7 Selecting Subjects and Categories (1994): 5 Landscapes in Cold Enamel on Lumitex, 6 One Twelfth Scale Miniatures in Water-colour on Lumitex Fino, 8 Miniatures in Water-colour on Lumitex Fino (1995), 9 Miniatures in Oils on Lumitex Fino, 10 One Twelfth Scale Miniatures in Oils on Lumitex Fino (1997): 11 Miniatures in Water-colour (1998); 12 Miniatures in Oils, 13 Bases Supplement Celluloid (Ivorine) (1999), 14 Miniatures in Soft Pastel, 15 Miniatures in Gouache (2001-'02); Miniature books 2 Limited Edns. of Miniature Paintings (1997); Collecting Contemporary Original Fine Art Miniture Paintings (Limited Edn., 1998); Tasmania 2000 Turner Miniature Collections (Limited Edn. 2000); Miniature Artists of America Turner 2000 (Limited Edn., 2000); Clearwater Florida Turner Miniature Collections (Limited Edn., 2001). Founder of the Turner School of Miniature Paintings promoted by the Turner Travelling Exhibition of Contemporary Original Fine Art Miniature Paintings. *Signs work:* "C.B. Turner." *Address:* 6 Gablehurst Ct., Long Lane, Bradwell, Gt. Yarmouth, Norfolk NR31 7DS.

TURNER, Jacquie, B.A.; painting in mixed media on paper; *b* 27 Mar., 1959. *m* Nigel Wheeler. three *s.* one *d. Educ:* Rickmansworth School, Herts. *Studied:*

Winchester School of Art (1979-81). *Exhib:* Linda Blackstone Gallery, Pinner, Middlesex. *Work in collections:* Leics. Coll. for schools and colleges, Norsk Hydro Oslo, Adam Bank London, Shangri La Hong Kong. *Publications:* The Encyclopaedia of Acrylic Techniques by Hazel Harrison (Headline), How to Capture Movement in Your Paintings by Julia Cassels (Northlight Books), Artists Manual (Collins), Mixed Media Pocket Palette by Ian Sidaway (Northlight Books), Israel at 50 (Linda Blackstone Gallery). *Signs work:* "Jacquie Turner." *Address:* Fairview House, Chinnor Rd., Bledlow Ridge, Bucks. HP14 4AJ. *Website:* www.jacquieturner.com *Email:* jacquieturner@talk21.com

TURNER, Lynette, Hons.B.Sc. (Zoology, 1968), H.N.D.D. (Graphic design, 1970); printmaker in coloured etchings using zinc; *b* London, 28 May, 1945. *Educ:* Hall School, Wincanton, Som., Manchester University. *Studied:* Brighton Art School (1963), City and Guilds Art School (1969, etching), Manchester Art School. *Exhib:* Century Gallery, Henley (1976), Margaret Fisher Gallery (1976), R.A. (1977), S.E. London Art Group, Y.M.C.A., Gt. Russell St., WC1. (1983), R.A. Summer Show (1987), December 1989 exhbn. in Crypt of St. Martin-in-the-Fields, (etchings and water-colours), writing and illustrating comic strip adventures. *Clubs:* Falmouth's Royal Cornwall Polytechnic Soc. *Signs work:* "Lynette Turner." *Address:* Pendynas, Minnie Pl., Falmouth, Cornwall TR11 3NN.

TURNER, Martin William, N.D.D. (1961), R.O.I. (1974), N.S. (1975); painter in oil, acrylic and water-colour, printmaker; *b* Reading, 3 Oct., 1940. *Educ:* Gravesend Technical School. *Studied:* Medway College of Art under David Graham, C. Stanley Hayes. *Exhib:* R.A., R.O.I., R.B.A., N.S., R.S.M.A., R.E. *Work in collections:* Abbot Hall Gallery, Swansea University, Cardiff Museum, Glamorgan Educ. Com., Liverpool A.G. *Publications:* work repro.: articles for Leisure Painter. *Clubs:* R.I., N.S.P.S., Hampstead Artists' Council. *Signs work:* "Martin Turner." *Address:* 24 Marshall Rd., Rainham, Kent ME8 0AP.

TURNER, Peggy E. M.: see RICHARDS, E. Margaret.

TURNER, Prudence, freelance artist in oil on canvas; Scottish landscape painter specifically since 1966; plus portraiture, seascapes and dream-fantasies; *b* 15 Mar., 1930. *Studied:* in India, Egypt, France and England, learning from artists already famous. Nationally recognized in England in 1934. Fine Art Publication copyrights purchased from 1967 onwards and given international circulation, including limited editions of signed prints. *Work in collections:* U.K., and Overseas. *Commissions:* Professional: Constant, including royalty. *Signs work:* "Prudence Turner." *Address:* 49 Romulus Ct., Justin Cl., Brentford Dock Marina, Brentford, Middx. TW8 8QW.

TURNER, Silvie, publisher, writer, artist, curator, book/internet based projects; *b* 19 Oct., 1946. two *d. Studied:* Corsham (1965-68), University of Brighton (Post grad., 1968-70). Work in permanent collections worldwide. *Publications:* about 25 on various print, paper, book subjects. *Clubs:* Chelsea Arts. *Signs work:* "Silvie Turner." *Address:* 204 St. Albans Ave., London W4 5JU.

TURNER, William Ralph, R.C.A., F.R.S.A.; artist in oil and water-colour; *b* Chorlton-on-Medlock, 30 Apr., 1920. *m* Anne Grant (decd.). one *d. Studied:* Derby College of Art (1945). *Exhib:* R.B.A., R.I., R.C.A., O'Mell Galleries London,

Christopher Cole Galleries, Henley-on-Thames, Pitcairn Galleries, Knutsford, Boundary Gallery, London. *Work in collections:* Manchester Educ. Com., Stockport A.G., Saab (Manchester) Ltd.; private collections in New York, Los Angeles, Kenya, Portugal, Switzerland, Zaire. *Publications:* Cheshire Life Magazine. *Signs work:* "William Turner" and see appendix. *Address:* (studio) Renrut, 23 Gill Bent Rd., Cheadle Hulme, Cheadle, Ches.

TURPIN, Louis, Dip.Ad.(Hons.) Fine Art (1971); painter in oil on canvas; *b* 25 Apr., 1947. *m* Davida Smith. two *s*. *Educ:* Alleyns, Dulwich; Sunbury Grammar School, Sunbury-on-Thames. *Studied:* Guildford School of Art (1967-68), Falmouth Art School (1968-71). *Exhib:* Beaux Arts, Bath, N.P.G., Bohun Gallery, Henley-on-Thames, Rye A.G., R.A., R.S.P.P. *Work in collections:* Rye A.G., South East Arts, Towner A.G., Bath University, John Radcliffe Hospital, Oxford, Nat.West Bank. *Commissions:* Miss Pears, Bedruthan Steps Hotel. *Publications:* The Painted Garden by Huxley. *Clubs:* Rye Soc. of Artists. *Signs work:* "Louis Turpin." *Address:* 19 Udimore Rd., Rye, E. Sussex TN31 7DS.

TUTE, George William, N.D.D. Illustration, N.D.D. Painting, R.A.Cert., M.A. (R.C.A.), R.E., R.W.A.; artist in oil, water-colour, printmaking; freelance graphic designer, wood engraving; *b* Hull, 23 Mar., 1933. *m* Iris Tute. two *s*. *Educ:* Bainse Grammar School, Lancs. *Studied:* Blackpool School of Art (1951-54); Royal Academy Schools (1954-59); Royal College of Art (1981-82). *Exhib:* R.A., R.W.A., R.E.; private and public galleries. Exhibits prints and paintings, book illustration and general illustration for commissions, wood engraved illustrations and autographic prints. *Signs work:* "G. W. Tute." *Address:* 46 Eastfield, Westbury-on-Trym, Bristol BS9 4BE.

TWEED, Jill, F.R.B.S., F.R.S.A., Slade B.A.; sculptor in bronze; *b* U.K., 7 Dec., 1931. *m* Philip Hicks. one *s*. one *d*. *Studied:* Slade School of Art (F. E. McWilliam). *Exhib:* Bruton St. Gallery, London, Flowers East Gallery, London, Poole-Wills Gallery, N.Y., Dublin, Brussels. *Work in collections:* H.M. The Queen; Corps of the Royal Military Police, Chichester; Royal Engineers, Mill Hill, London; Austin Reed Ltd., London; Picker Collection, Kingston-upon-Thames. *Commissions:* Hampshire C.C.; Amec U.K. Ltd., London; Conseil Regionale de Normandie, Caen, France; K.C.C.; Oxon. C.C.; Gosport D.C.; Herts. C.C.; Kent C.C. *Signs work:* "Jill Tweed." *Address:* Royal Society of British Sculptors, 108 Old Brompton Rd., London SW7 3RA.

TYDEMAN, Naomi, B.Ed. (Hons.); self taught water-colourist, gallery owner; *b* Taiping, Malaysia, 5 June, 1957. *Studied:* Trinity College, Carmarthen. *Exhib:* R.I., W.S.W. *Work in collections:* Tenby Museum. *Clubs:* W.S.W. *Signs work:* "Naomi Tydeman." *Address:* 60 Bevelin Hall, Saundersfoot, Pembrokeshire SA69 9PQ.

TYSON, Rowell Edward Daniel, A.R.C.A., R.B.A.; painter in oil, water-colour and pastel; *b* London, 5 Jan., 1926. *m* (1) Kathleen. one *s*. (2) Monica. *Studied:* Tunbridge Wells School of Art, Beckenham School of Art, Royal College of Art (1946-1950), fourth year scholarship (1949-1950). Senior Mem of Royal Soc. of British Artists. *Exhib:* R.A., R.S.A., R.B.A., R.O.I., R.S.M.A., London and provincial galleries, touring exhbns., and Nevill Galleries, Canterbury. *Work in collections:* include Leo-Burnett, Miles Laboratories, Shell, Lopex, Leicester Educ. Com., Carlisle City A.G., K.C.C., Paxus, Sumicorp Finance Ltd., Merrill Lynch, Arthur

Andersen & Co., Qatar National Bank, Inst. of Directors. *Publications:* included in '20th Century British Marine Painting' by Denys Brook-Hart. *Signs work:* "ROW-ELL TYSON." *Address:* 29 Fisher St., Sandwich, Kent CT13 9EJ.

TYSON EDWARDS, Marian, D.F.A.; sculptor in bronze, cement fondu, terra-cotta; *b* Manchester, 2 Oct., 1937. *m* John T. Sharples. one *s.* one *d.* *Studied:* Liverpool College of Art and High Wycombe College of Art. *Exhib:* Mall Galleries, galleries in Henley, Birmingham, Chalfont, etc. *Work in collections:* Windsor and Eton Fine Art. *Signs work:* "M. Tyson Edwards." *Address:* Wispington House, Worster Rd., Cookham, Berks. SL6 9JG.

U

UGLOW, Euan, painter in oil; First Prize John Moores (1972); awarded Austin Abbey Premiere Scholarship; artist Trustee, National Gallery, London; teacher at Slade School of Art; Fellow, London Institute; *b* London, 10 Mar., 1932. *Educ:* Strand Grammar School for Boys. *Studied:* Camberwell School of Art and Slade School. *Exhib:* Beaux Arts Gallery, London (1961), Gardner Centre, Sussex University, Brighton (1969), Whitechapel A.G. (1974), Browse & Darby, London (1977, 1983, 1989, 1991, 1997, 1999), Salander O'Reilly, N.Y. (1993). *Work in collections:* Tate Gallery, Arts Council, Glasgow Art Gallery, Southampton Art Gallery, South Australia National Gallery, Liverpool University, Ferens A.G., Hull, Government Art Collection, Metropolitan Museum of Art, N.Y., British Council, London, British Museum, London. *Publications:* 'Euan Uglow' (Browse & Darby, 1998). Gallery & Agent: Browse & Darby, Cork St., W1. *Clubs:* Garrick. *Signs work:* "Euan Uglow." *Address:* 11 Turnchapel Mews, Cedars Rd., London SW4 0PX.

UHT, John, R.I. (1976); painter in oil and water-colour, sculptor in bronze, marble, wood, lead sheet; *b* Dayton, Ohio, 30 Aug., 1924. *m* Jill Gould. two *s.* one *d.* *Educ:* Danville High School, Illinois. *Studied:* University of Illinois Fine and Applied Arts College (1943-47, Marvin Martin, John Kennedy) and Ishmu Naguchi (1948). *Exhib:* Art, U.S.A. (1958), Reading Museum (1970), Edwin Pollard Gallery, Barry M. Keene Gallery, R.A., R.I. *Work in collections:* R.A. (bronze), Nelson Rockefeller (bronze). *Clubs:* R.I. *Signs work:* painting, "JOHN UHT," sculpture, "UHT." *Address:* 44 Dorchester Rd., Weymouth, Dorset DT4 7JZ.

UNDERWOOD, George, painter in oil, water-colour, acrylic; *b* Bromley, Kent, 5 Feb., 1947. *m* Birgit. one *s.* one *d.* *Educ:* Bromley Technical High School. *Studied:* Beckenham Art School (1963), Ravensbourne College of Art (1964-1965). *Exhib:* solo exhib., About Face, London (1997), group exhibs. in Japan, Copenhagen, Spain, U.K., R.A. Summer Exhibs. (1998 & 2001). *Work in collections:* David Bowie Collection (15 works). *Commissions:* Helena Bonham Carter, David Bowie, Mike Leigh (Topsy-Turvy film poster 1999). *Publications:* illustrated many book covers, authors include, Julian Barnes, John Fowles, William Styron, Russell Hoban. *Signs* *work:* "george underwood." *Address:* 90 Priory Rd., Hornsey, London N8 7EY. *Website:* www.georgeunderwood.com *Email:* underwoodgeorge@hotmail.com

UNDERWOOD, Keith Alfred, Leverhulme Research Award in Fine Art (France, 1957-58); realist painter in oil and water-colour; sculptor, restorer, designer; *b* Portsmouth, 21 June, 1934. *Educ:* Monmouth School (1946-53). *Studied:* Newport College of Art (1953-57) under the late Tom Rathmell, A.R.C.A, and the late Hubert Dalwood; West of England College of Art (1960-61), Diploma in Education. *Exhib:* Welsh Arts Council, Pictures for Schools, British Art for Moscow, Young Contemporaries, Mall Galleries, Chepstow locale. *Work in collections:* Margaret Cleyton Memorial restoration (St. Mary's, Chepstow 1984), Onitsha Cathedral, Nigeria (portrait bronze 1985), Earl of Worcester armorial sculpture (Chepstow Town Gate 1988); large historical mural, Drill Hall, Chepstow, and town map (1991); Caldicot town map (1994); twelve stained glass cartoons for windows in SS. Richard and Alexander, Bootle (1994); paintings in private collections: U.K., U.S.A., Australia, S. Africa and Netherlands. *Signs work:* "KAU" until c1974, "K. Underwood" and "Keith Underwood" thereafter, see appendix. *Address:* 1 Madocke Rd., Sedbury, nr. Chepstow, Monmouthshire NP16 7AY.

UPTON, Michael, Cert. R.A.S. (1962), Abbey Scholar (Rome Scholarships); artist in mixed media, lecturer; lecturer, Royal Academy Schools (1980); visiting lecturer various art colleges; *b* 5 Feb., 1938. *m* Susan E. Young. one *s.* one *d. Educ:* King Edward VI School, Birmingham. *Studied:* Birmingham College of Art (1954-58) under Gilbert Mason; R.A. Schools (1958-62) under Peter Greenham. *Exhib:* Various London and touring exhbns. *Work in collections:* include Arts Council, British Council and private collections. *Publications:* work repro.: Studio International, Artscribe, Flash Art, etc. *Clubs:* Chelsea Arts. *Signs work:* "Michael Upton." *Address:* c/o Anne Berthoud Gallery, 10 Clifford St., Bond St., London W1.

UTERMOHLEN, William C., painter; *b* Philadelphia, Pa., 1933. *Studied:* Pennsylvania Academy of Fine Art, Philadelphia; Ruskin School of Drawing, Oxford. *Exhib:* one-man shows: Traverse Theatre Gallery, Edinburgh Festival (1963), Bonfiglioli Gallery, Oxford (1965, 1967), Nordness Gallery, N.Y. (1967), Marlborough New London Gallery (1969), Galerie d'Eendt, Amsterdam (1970, 1971), Mead Art Museum, Amherst College, Amherst, Massachusetts (1974). Visiting artist, Amherst College (1972-74). Mural, Liberal Jewish Synagogue, St. Johns Wood, London (1981); mural, Royal Free Hospital, Hampstead (1985). *Publications:* illustrated, Ten war poems by Wilfred Owen (1995). *Signs work:* "Utermohlen." *Address:* 35 Blomfield Rd., London W9 2PF.

V

VAHEY, Lorna, B.A. Fine Art (1967); painter in oil, water-colour; narrative and autobiographical painter; *b* Pett, Sussex, 22 Apr., 1946. two *d. Educ:* Rye Grammar School. *Studied:* Brighton (1962-1967). *Exhib:* R.A., R.S.A., Alex

Gerrard, Chichester Open, Brighton Museum, Hastings Museum, Rye Art Gallery. *Signs work:* "L. VAHEY." *Address:* 145 Emmanuel Rd., Hastings, E. Sussex TN34 3LE.

VAIZEY, Marina (Lady Vaizey), B.A. Radcliffe, M.A. (Cantab.); Art Critic, Sunday Times (1974-91); Editor, N.A.C.F. (1991-94), Editorial Consultant, N.A.C.F. (1994-98); Art Critic, Financial Times (1970-74); Trustee, National Museums and Galleries on Merseyside, Imperial War Museum, South Bank Centre, Geffrye Museum, London Open House; *b* New York City, 16 Jan., 1938. *m* Lord Vaizey (decd. 1984). two *s.* one *d. Publications:* 100 Masterpieces of Art (1979); Andrew Wyeth (1980); Artist as Photographer (1982); Peter Blake (1985); Christo (1990); Christiane Kubrick (1990); organised Critic's Choice, Tooth's (1974); Painter as Photographer, Arts Council (1982-85); Shining Through (Crafts Council, 1995), Sutton Taylor (1999). *Address:* 24 Heathfield Terr., Chiswick, London W4 4JE.

VALENTINE, Barbara, N.D.D. (Illustration), R.M.S., H.S., M.A.S.-F.; miniaturist in oil and water-colour, art tutor; *b* London, 1943. *m* Louis Dodd. one *s.* one *d. Studied:* Goldsmiths' College (1960-64, Betty Swanwick). *Exhib:* R.A. Summer Exhibition, annual miniature shows at Medici and Llewellyn Alexander Galleries. Work in private collections internationally. *Publications:* work repro.: articles in art magazines, books on miniatures, fine art prints. *Clubs:* R.M.S., H.S., M.A.S.-F. *Signs work:* "B.V." *Address:* Mountfield Pk. Farmhouse, Mountfield, Robertsbridge, E.Sussex TN32 5LE.

VALENTINE, Dennis Robert, N.D.D.(1953), A.T.D. (1956); professional artist in oil, pen and ink, charcoal, water-colour; *b* Leicester, 12 Jan., 1935. *m* Anne Valentine. two *s.* two *d. Studied:* Leicester College of Art (D.W.P. Carrington). *Exhib:* Lincolnshire Artist Soc. regularly since 1966, Spectrum (Arts Council) 1971, Corby Glen Gallery, Lincs.: one-man show (1999): John Laing Art Competition Mall Galleries (1989). *Work in collections:* private collections. *Clubs:* Lincolnshire Artists Soc. *Address:* Wheelwright Barn, 6 East Rd., Navenby, Lincoln LN5 0EP.

VALENTINE-DAINES, Sherree E., Dip. A.D., U.A. (1983), S.W.A.; painter in oil; *b* Effingham, 1956. *m* Mark Alun Rowbotham. one *s.* two *d. Studied:* Epsom School of Art and Design (1976-80, Leslie Worth, Peter Petersen). *Exhib:* R.B.A., R.A., Tate Gallery, R.O.I., R.W.S., R.P., Royal Overseas League, N.E.A.C., U.A., P.S., Olympic Games Exhbn., Royal Festival Hall, Barbican, Laing Landscape, N.S.P.S. *Commissions:* include Test Cricket, 5 Nations Rugby, Royal Ascot, Henley Royal Regatta. *Signs work:* "S.E.V.D." *Address:* Misty Ridge, 126 The Street, Ashtead, Surrey KT21 1AB.

VANGO, David, self taught artist in oil and mixed media; early work mostly perceptual reductionism. Since 1994 large metamorphic abstract constructions; *b* London, 18 Feb., 1950. one *s. Studied:* private studies Witt Library, and galleries and museums U.K. and abroad. *Exhib:* 4 one-man shows: Vidal Gallery, Barcelona; Picture Workshop; Gallery Three; Loggia Gallery; 23 group shows, including: F.P.S. Gagliardi Gallery, Kings Rd.; Paxhaven Studio; Foresters Court; Black Horse Chambers. *Work in collections:* Japan, France, Spain, Germany, Italy, Australia, America, etc. *Commissions:* Large abstract construction (Nicron 1) for number, 10. (Lincoln). *Publications:* contributor to British Contemporary Art (1993), The BritArt

Directory (2000). *Signs work:* see appendix. *Address:* 68 Alexander Terr., Lincoln LN1 1JE. *Email:* vango@btinternet.com or Google to David Vango Homepage

VAN NIEKERK, Sarah Compton, R.E. (1976), S.W.E. (1974), R.W.A. (1992); wood engraver; Tutor, City and Guilds of London Art School (1978-2000), R.A. Schools (1976-86), West Dean College; *b* London, 16 Jan., 1934. *m* Chris van Niekerk. one *s.* two *d. Educ:* Bedales. *Studied:* Central School of Art, Slade School of Fine Art. *Exhib:* R.A., Bankside Gallery, U.S.A., 28 one and two-man exhbns., Artmonsky Arts, Royal Cambrian Academy, Victoria Gallery, National Print, etc. *Work in collections:* V. & A., Fitzwilliam, Ashmolean, National Museum of Wales, National Library of Wales, U.C.L.A., U.S.S.R., Fremantle Arts Centre, Graves, Hereford Museum. *Publications:* Folio Soc., Gregynog, O.U.P., Readers Digest, Pavilion, Virago, Rider. *Signs work:* "Sarah van Niekerk" in pencil. *Address:* Priding House, Saul, Glos. GL2 7LG.

VAN ROSSEM, Ru, Hon. Mem., Academy of Fine Arts, Florence; Premio Milano (1988); Euro-medal in gold, Bonn; Gold Medal Biennale, Perugia; M.A.I. International Graphic Prize, Biennales Gorizia, Italy, Malbork, Poland; Head of Graphic Department, Tilburg Academy of Fine Art, Holland; *b* Amsterdam, 19 Mar., 1924. *m* 1st Miriam Pollock (decd.); two *s.* one *d.* 2nd Marianne van Dieren. one *s. Educ:* Rijksmuseumschool of Fine Art; Grammar School, Zaandam. *Exhib:* most European countries and U.S.A. *Work in collections:* Rijksmuseum and Municipal Museum, Amsterdam, Boymans Museum, Rotterdam, Bibliothèque Nationale, Paris, Museum of Modern Art, New York, National Museum, Cracow, Cincinnati Museum, etc. *Commissions:* sculpture for St. John's Cathedral, 's Hertogenbosch. *Publications:* biography written by Frans Duister (1977, 1994). *Signs work:* "Ru Van Rossem." *Address:* Burg, Vonk de Bothstr. 54, 5037NL Tilburg, Holland.

VAN STOCKUM, Hilda, H.R.H.A. (1989); painter in oil; *b* Rotterdam, Holland, 9 Feb., 1908. *m* Spike Marlin (decd.). two *s.* four *d. Educ:* Ryks-Academy, Amsterdam. *Studied:* Dublin School of Art, André L'Hote, Paris. *Exhib:* regularly at R.H.A., Dublin. *Work in collections:* National Gallery, Dublin. *Publications:* 24 childrens books written and illustrated, including A Day on Skates, and The Winged Watchman. *Signs work:* "HvS." *Address:* 8 Castle Hill, Berkhamstead, Herts. HP4 1HE.

VEALE, Anthony McKenzie, self taught painter in oil and acrylic, sculptor (surrealist and figurative work) in bronze, wood, marble and stone; also abstract painting and minimalist work; *b* Tonbridge, 20 Oct., 1941. *m* Susan. one *s.* two *d. Educ:* Sevenoaks School. *Exhib:* Tryon Gallery (1979), 20th Century Gallery (1985), Mall Galleries (1992). Permanent exhbn. of bronzes in sculpture garden at Buckstone House. *Publications:* cartoon illustrations: 'Hippo, Potta and Muss' (Chatto, Boyd & Oliver U.K., 1969), 'A Lemon Yellow Elephant called Trunk' (Harvey House Inc. U.S.A., 1970). *Signs work:* "Tony Veale," "Anthony Veale" or "A.V." *Address:* Buckstone House, Upton Hellions, nr. Crediton, Devon EX17 4AE. *Email:* aveale@ukgateway.net

VENNING, Virginia, Mem. S.W.A.; sculptor in stone, wood, clay for bronze, terracotta, including portraits; painter in water-colour; *b* London, 1913. *m* Capt. E. D. T. Churcher, C.B.E., R.N. (decd.). *Educ:* privately. *Studied:* Paris and Florence;

Regent St. Polytechnic (1931), R.A. Schools (1934-39). *Exhib:* R.A. Summer Exhbn. (from 1933), S.W.A. *Work in collections:* portraits: wood and stone carvings for churches, (mostly in Somerset) and other buildings and gardens. *Signs work:* "V.M. Venning." *Address:* 26 Bimport, Shaftesbury, Dorset SP7 8AZ.

VERDIJK, Gerald, Silver Medal, Prix Europe (1966), Maris Prize (1964, 1967); painter; *b* Boxmeer, Holland, 1934. *Exhib:* one-man shows: Galerie Gunar, Düsseldorf, Galerie Orez, The Hague (1961, 1962, 1964, 1965, 1967, 1971, 1979), Galerie Potsdammer, Berlin, Casino Ostende, Museum Municipal, The Hague (1967), Von der Heidt Museum, Wuppertal (1968), Galerie Palette, Zürich Galerie Lock St. Gallen (1984), Groninger Museum (1970), Gemeente Museum, The Hague (1972), Galerie Peccolo Livorno (1978), Galerie La Citta, Verona, Galerie La Polena, Geneva, Galerie Jeanneret, Geneva (1979), Galerie E. München (1981), Brenda Taylor Gallery, New York (1996); Abbemuseum Eindhoven (1985), Stedelijk Museum, Amsterdam 1993 (retrospective), Noord Brabants Museum, Den Bosch (retrospective) 1998; group shows: Amsterdam, Delft, The Hague, Berlin, Wuppertal, Brussels, Belfast, Dublin, Cork; Bienale de Paris (1961), World Fair, Montreal (1967), London, Liverpool, Paris, Stockholm, Los Angeles, Frankfurt, Tokyo, Copenhagen. *Work in collections:* Museums of The Hague, Schiedam, Brussels, Wuppertal, London, Ostend, Rotterdam, Amsterdam, Osaka, Munich. *Signs work:* see appendix. *Address:* "Les Places" Marcillac-St. Quentin, par 24200 Sarlat, Dordogne, France.

VERITY, Charlotte E., Dip.F.A. (1977); artist in oil on canvas, water-colour, monoprint; *b* Germany, 1 June, 1954. *m* Christopher Le Brun. two *s.* one *d.* *Studied:* Slade School of Fine Art U.C.L. (1973-77). *Exhib:* solo shows: Anne Berthoud Gallery (1984, 1988, 1990), Browse & Darby (1998); many mixed shows. *Work in collections:* Arts Council, C.A.S., Derby A.G., San Diego M.O.C.A., and many corporate collections. *Publications:* illustrated catalogues 1990 and 1998 to solo shows. *Signs work:* "Verity." *Address:* 8 Love Walk, London SE5 8AD.

VERITY, Colin, A.R.I.B.A. (1965), R.S.M.A. (1975); architect, artist in oil, water-colour and gouache; retd. principal architect, Humberside C.C., Pres., Hornsea Art Soc., Mem. Fylingdales Group of Artists (N. Yorks.), Yorkshire Water-colour Soc.; *b* Darwen, Lancs., 7 Mar., 1924. *m* Stella Elizabeth Smale. one *s.* three *d.* *Educ:* Malet Lambert High School, Hull and privately. *Studied:* Hull School of Architecture. *Exhib:* R.S.M.A., Mystic Maritime Gallery, Connecticut, U.S.A., Francis Iles Gallery, Rochester, Ferens Gallery, Hull. *Work in collections:* National Maritime Museum, Greenwich, Sultanate of Oman, Ben Line, Harrison Line, P. & O. Line, Town Docks Museum, Hull, Kassos Steam Nav. Co., - 17 countries. *Commissions:* Numerous shipping cos., Lloyds and private. *Signs work:* "Colin Verity." *Address:* Melsa, Meaux, Beverley, E. Yorks. HU17 9SS.

VERNON-CRYER, Joan, A.R.C.A., R.W.S. (1970); painter in water-colour; *b* Blackburn, 21 Mar., 1911. *m* W. Fairclough. one *s.* one *d.* *Educ:* Blackburn High School and Blackburn Technical College. *Studied:* Royal College of Art (Painting School). *Exhib:* Hunting Group Competition, Mall Galleries (1990), Sunday Times Water-colour Exhbn., Mall Galleries, Glasgow Cultural Year (1990), The Art of the Garden, Victoria A.G., Bath and North-East Somerset (1997). *Publications:* work repro.: in Old Water-colour Society's volumes, Visions of Venice (Michael Spender, 1990); Water-colour Drawings and Artists Magazine (1991); La Exposicion Internacional de Acuarela (1992, 1995). *Signs work:* "Joan Vernon-Cryer." *Address:* 12 Manorgate Rd., Kingston-upon-Thames, Surrey KT2 7AL.

VERRALL, Nicholas Andrew, N.D.D. (1965); artist in oil, pastel, water-colour, etching and litho; *b* Northampton, 4 Jan., 1945. one *s.* one *d. Studied:* Northampton College of Art (1960-65). Full-time artist since 1970. Prizes: R.W.S. Barcham Green Prize for Water-colour, Royal Horticultural Grenfell Medal, R.A. Committee Prize from B.A.T. *Exhib:* R.A., R.W.S., R.E., R.B.A., R.P., and N.E.A.C.; mixed shows: Tryon Gallery, R.A. Upstairs Gallery, Abbott & Holder, Gallery 10; one-man shows: Upper Grosvenor, Langton Gallery Chelsea, Catto Gallery, Hampstead, Art Obsession Inc., Tokyo, and Brian Sinfield, Oxfordshire. *Work in collections:* City of London, B.A.T. Coll., Crown Life, Painshill Park Trust, Coys of Kensington. Private collections in Britain, France, America and Japan. *Publications:* Entry in 'Forty Years at Curwen Studios'. *Signs work:* "Nicholas Verrall." *Address:* The Orchard, Ivy La., Woking, Surrey GU22 7BY.

VICARY, Richard Henry, R.E., R.W.A.; printmaker, (woodcuts etc.), painting, typography; late Head Printmaking Dept., Shrewsbury School of Art; *b* Sutton, Surrey, 1918. *m* (1) Jean Bickford (1946). two *s.* (2) Deirdre Vicary. one *s.* one *d. Educ:* Judd School, Tonbridge. *Studied:* Medway School of Art (1936-39); Brighton College of Art (1946); Camberwell School of Art and Crafts; Central School of Art. *Exhib:* A.I.A., Whitechapel, R.W.S., R.W.A. (Bristol) and many private galleries. *Work in collections:* various Universities and Education Authorities. *Publications:* Manual of Lithography and Manual of Advanced Lithography, (Thames & Hudson, 1976, 1977). *Signs work:* "Richard Vicary." *Address:* The Holding, Dunns Heath, Berwick, Shrewsbury SY4 3HY.

VINCENT, Michael John, Cert.Ed. (Dist.) 1973, B.Ed. (Hons.) 1974, M.A. (1979), Dip. Ed. (1983); landscape and seascape artist in gouache and oil, pencil and ink; *b* Bury St. Edmunds, Suffolk, 1949. *m* Kaisa (decd.). one *d. Studied:* Chelsea School of Art (1968-69), London University (1970-74), Inst. of Educ. (1977-79). *Exhib:* throughout U.K., Finland, N.Z. Work in collections worldwide. *Publications:* work repro.: The Guardian, T.E.S., Artist and Illustrators Magazine, Countryman, The Somerset Magazine. *Clubs:* U.A. *Signs work:* "M. VINCENT." *Address:* 76 Main St., Walton, nr. Street, Som. BA16 9QN.

VINE, Edward, landscape/still life artist in acrylic, water-colour, oil, pastel; *b* Weymouth, Dorset, 10 May, 1943. *Exhib:* regular one-man shows at Peter Hedley Gallery, Wareham, Dorset; also exhibits at Westover Gallery, Bournemouth, and The Gallery Dorchester in Dorchester. Artist-in-Residence at "Max Gate", Thomas Hardy's Dorchester home now owned by the National Trust. *Signs work:* "Edward Vine." *Address:* 90 Easton St., Portland, Dorset DT5 IBT.

VOGEL, Suzi, S.B.A., S.W.A.; self taught botanical and landscape artist in oil on panel; *b* Kent, 1950. one *s. Exhib:* regularly with S.B.A. and S.W.A. Suzi Vogel paints to celebrate the beauty of the natural world. She belongs to a long established Kentish family of passionate writers, gardeners and horticulturalists. Now living and working in Dorset and working only in oils, she uses the finest traditional methods and materials, following in the footsteps of the Dutch and French masters of the sixteenth and seventeenth centuries. Her paintings combine the classically decorative with the botanically accurate and are appreciated and collected by connoisseurs of fine representational oil painting. *Publications:* example of work, picture and caption on page nine of "Drawing Flowers" by Margaret Stevens. *Signs work:* see appendix. *Address:* Flat 1, 22 Victoria Grove, Bridport, Dorset DT6 3AA.

VOJDAEVA, Olga Alexseevna, artist in acrylic and oil; *b* Crimea, Kerch, U.S.S.R., May 1972. *m* Nathaniel James Giles. *Studied:* Art School, St, Petersburg (1983-88). *Exhib:* Beechfield House, Corsham, The Gallery Cirencester, Royal Inst. of Artists Birmingham, The Highgate Gallery, London (1999), Westminster Gallery, London (1999). *Work in collections:* Lord Bath, Longleat House. *Commissions:* Gleeson Homes, Pizza Hut (U.K.) Ltd. *Clubs:* N.AP.A. *Signs work:* "Olga Vojdaeva." *Address:* 29a Bath Rd., Wootton Bassett, Wilts. SN4 7DF.

VOLLER, Peter Robert, painter in oils, acrylic polymer, painted wood and paper collage; *b* Fleet, Hants., 26 Sept., 1943. *m* Tessa Philpot. two *s.* one *d.* *Studied:* Farnham School of Art. *Exhib:* mostly in London, including R.A. and Discerning Eye, and nationally. *Signs work:* "Voller" or "Peter Voller." *Address:* 53 The Street, Wrecclesham, Farnham, Surrey GU10 4QS.

von HARTMANN, Sylvia, D.A. (Edin.) (1965), Post. Dip. (1966), R.S.W. (1983); artist in wax; *b* Hamburg, Germany, 8 Dec., 1942. *m* Hamish Dewar. one *s.* one *d. Educ:* Walddoerfer Schule, Hamburg-Volksdorf. *Studied:* Werkkunstschule, Hamburg (1961-63), Edinburgh College of Art (1963-66), Royal College of Art, London. *Exhib:* R.A., R.S.A. Edinburgh, R.S.W., R.G.I.F.A., The Scottish Gallery, Edinburgh, National Trust of Scotland, Grosvenor Gallery, London, Open Eye Gallery, Edinburgh, etc. *Work in collections:* Scottish Arts Council, Scottish National Gallery of Modern Art, City of Edinburgh Art Collection, Dundee Museum and Art Galleries, National Westminster Bank, Edinburgh, The Royal Infirmary, Edinburgh, H.M. The Queen, St. John's Hospital, Livingstone. *Publications:* Living Light, Books II and III (Holmes McDougall), The Scots Magazine (June, 1984), The Green Book Press Ltd., Bath. *Signs work:* "Sylvia von Hartmann." *Address:* Rhododendron House, 5 Whitehorse Cl., Canongate, Edinburgh EH8 8BU.

W

WADDELL, Heather, M.A. St. Andrews (1972), D.F.A. (1976), Cert. Ed. London (1977); author, photographer, art critic; *b* Scotland, 1950. *Exhib:* N.S.W. House A.G., (1980), ACME Studio (1977-80), Battersea Arts Centre (1979). *Work in collections:* N.P.G. 20th c. Archives, National Portrait Gallery 20th Century Collection. *Publications:* Articles on art: Artnews, Art and Australia, The Artist, Art Monthly, Glasgow Herald (1978-94), London correspondent, Vie des Arts (1979-89),

The Independent, The European (arts events editor, 1990-'91), The Times; author/photographer: London Art and Artists Guide (8th edn. 2000); The London Art World 1979-99 (2000); co-author, The Artists Directory (3rd edn. 1988); photographer: Glasgow Arts Guide; N.P.G. 20th C. Collection; contributor: Encyclopaedia of London (Macmillan), Henri Goetz (1986), Time Out Publications (1987-92), L'Ecosse (1988), Londres (1997), Edns. Autrement, Paris. *Address:* 27 Holland Park Ave., London W11 3RW. *Website:* www.hwlondonartandartistsguide.com *Email:* hw.artlondon@virgin.net

WADE, Jonathan Armigel, M.A. St. Andrews (1983); painter in oil and water-colour; mentioned in despatches (1991) - British Army (R.H.F.); *b* Virginia, U.S.A., 12 May, 1960. *m* Marie-Louise Maze. one *s.* one *d. Educ:* Lancing. *Exhib:* Paris Salon (1991), Cognac (1991, 1992), Clarges Gallery, London (1993, 1994, 1996, 2000), Sutton, Sussex (1995), Haddo House, Aberdeenshire (1995), Grimsby (1996, 1997), Arundel (1997), Alchemy Gallery, London (1998), Glasgow (1998). *Work in collections:* National Army Museum (over 120 sketches and paintings of Gulf Campaign, Bosnia and Northern Ireland), R.M.A. Sandhurst (water-colours), Gen. Norman Schwarzkopf (Gulf Oil), H.R.H. Duke of York (gift), and many private. *Commissions:* 59 completed including a Bosnian triptych for A. & N. Club. *Clubs:* Army and Navy. *Signs work:* "JONATHAN WADE," "J. Wade," J.A. Wade" or "Armigel Wade." *Address:* 32 Dudley St., Grimsby, N.E. Lincs. DN31 2AB.

WADSWORTH, Freda Muriel, M.B.E. (1979), F.M.A.A. (1968), F.F.P.S. (1984); painter of geometrical abstracts, using unique technique in gouache; lecturer in medical art, University of London (1956-79); Hon. Newsletter Editor, F.P.S.; *b* London, 31 Jan., 1918. *Educ:* Vardean School, Brighton. *Studied:* Brighton School of Art (1935-39, Charles Knight, R.W.S.). *Exhib:* one-man shows: Loggia Gallery (1979, 1982, 1985, 1988); numerous London group shows including Mall Galleries and the Barbican. *Signs work:* "Freda Wadsworth." *Address:* 11 Burnham Ct., Moscow Rd., London W2 4SW.

WADSWORTH, Hilda Marjorie, F.F.P.S. (1988); painter in gouache of 17th and 18th c. architectural and sculptural features in historic parks and gardens; design and display executive, British Cellophane Ltd. (1949-71), freelance design (1972-80), Hon. sec. Free Painters and Sculptors (1981-87); *b* London, 5 July, 1911. *Educ:* Brighton Polytechnic (1927-29). *Studied:* Brighton School of Art (1929-34, Charles Knight, R.W.S.). *Exhib:* solo shows: Loggia Gallery (1988, 1992); group shows in London at Mall Galleries, Barbican, Loggia Gallery. *Commissions:* six paintings purchased by P. & O. Cruises for the Oriana (1994). *Signs work:* "M. Wadsworth." *Address:* 11 Burnham Ct., Moscow Rd., London W2 4SW.

WAKEFIELD, Nicole, B.A. (Hons.) Fine Art (1983), P.G.C.E. (1991); artist in pastel, acrylic, clay; teacher; Mem. Royal Cambrian Academy; *b* Manchester, 27 Oct., 1960. *Studied:* Wolverhampton (1980-83), Blackburn (1979-80). *Exhib:* R. Cam. A., and locally. *Clubs:* local mountain clubs. *Signs work:* "Nicole." *Address:* 2 Tan y Bonc, Valley Rd., Llanfairfechan, Conwy LL33 0ET.

WALCH, Kenneth Charles Crosby, N.D.D. (1955); artist in oil, garden design; former A.E. art tutor with I.L.E.A. Hounslow, Bognor; *b* Wimbledon, 16 Sept., 1927.

m Olive Winifred (decd.). *Educ:* Bradfield College. *Studied:* National Gallery Art School, Melbourne (1952-53, Murray Griffin), St. Martin's School of Art (1953-55, Bateson Mason, F. Gore). *Exhib:* Belgium (Hof de Bist), London, Germany (Unna), Hong Kong (Nishiki), Dublin. *Work in collections:* Hof de Bist, Antwerp, Chichester Centre of Arts; private collections in U.K., Europe, America, Australia. *Clubs:* Chichester Centre of Arts, Friends of Pallant Ho, Chichester Art Soc., Quaker Fellowship of Arts. *Signs work:* block letters with pencil into wet paint, or colour code. *Address:* 193 Oving Rd., Chichester, W. Sussex PO19 4ER.

WALDRON, Dylan Thomas, B.A.Hons.; artist in egg tempera, acrylic, pencil and water-colour; *b* Newcastle-under-Lyme, 21 Aug., 1953. *m* Susan Dorothy Ann Waldron. *Educ:* King Edward VI Grammar School, Stourbridge. *Studied:* Stourbridge College of Art (1971-72), Wolverhampton Polytechnic, Faculty of Art and Design (1972-76). *Exhib:* R.A. Summer Exhbn. (1983 to 2001), Piccadilly Gallery, Cork St., London (1981-96), Mall Galleries, London (1988-'98). *Work in collections:* West Midlands Arts. *Clubs:* Leicester Soc. of Artists, Society of Tempera Painters. *Signs work:* "Dylan Waldron" paintings initialled "D.W." *Address:* 2 Hallaton Rd., Slawston, nr. Market Harborough, Leics. LE16 7UA.

WALES, Patricia Ann, S.W.A. (1995), S.F.P. (1997); artist in water-colour - flower paintings; *b* Hamilton, Ontario, 27 Feb., 1933. *m* Graham Wales. two *s.* *Exhib:* London, Paris, Sweden and Wessex Region. *Work in collections:* paintings in private collections in Australia, Americas and Western Europe. *Publications:* work repro.: greetings cards. *Clubs:* Lymington Art Group, Lyndhurst Art Group, Lymington Palette. *Address:* Willowbank, Widden Close, Sway, Hants. SO41 6AX.

WALKER, Edward Donald, marine artist in oil, publisher; owner, Sumar Publications; *b* 2 Aug., 1937. *m* Susan. one *s.* one *d.* *Educ:* Warbreck School, Liverpool. *Studied:* Liverpool College of Art (1950-56). *Exhib:* R.S.M.A., Paris Salon, Talbot Gallery, Ethos Gallery, Lancs., Harrods London, Fulmar Gallery, N. Wales, and galleries throughout U.S.A. *Work in collections:* Liverpool Museum and private collections worldwide. *Clubs:* Liverpool Nautical Research Soc., Fine Art Trade Guild. *Signs work:* "E.D. Walker." *Address:* 1 Richmond Grove, Lydiate, Merseyside L31 0BL.

WALKER, Richard Ian Bentham, N.D.D. (1947), A.T.D. (1949); Mem. United Soc. of Artists, Armed Forces Art Soc., Soc. of Graphic Fine Arts; portrait and land-scape painter; teacher of oil painting, Croydon Art School (1948-53); *b* Croydon, 18 Mar., 1925. *Educ:* Canford School, Dorset; Queen's College, Oxford; Founder's Prize, Royal Drawing Soc. (1938). *Studied:* Croydon School of Art (1945-48), London University (1949), Slade School. *Exhib:* R.A., R.P., R.B.A., R.O.I., Paris Salon, Imperial Institute, etc.; one-man shows, Oxford, Croydon, Mall Galleries (1978), Alpine Galleries (1981). *Work in collections:* Portraits of: Dr. Herbert Howells for Royal College of Music (1972); A. K. Chesterton (1973); Sir Reginald Wilson for the Brompton Hospital; Sir Thomas Holmes Sellors for the Middlesex Hospital; C.B. Canning (1989), John Hardie (1990), Ian Wallace (1991), all for Canford School; Sir William Penney, Reading A.G. (1953); London panorama, Museum of London (1978); Croydon Landscape (1939), for the Croydon Collection; Museum of Ness, Lewis; Kjarval Museum, Reykjavik. *Publications:* drawings of

Stokowski, Havergal Brian, Edmund Rubgra, etc., published Triad Press, London (1971-73); illustrations to C. Palmer's biography of Herbert Howells (1993). *Signs work:* "RICHARD WALKER" and see appendix. *Address:* 72 Coombe Rd., Croydon CR0 5SH.

WALKER, Roy, A.R.E. (1975); painter/etcher; Director, Print Workshop, Penwith Society of Arts, St. Ives, Cornwall; *b* Welling, Kent, 25 Aug., 1936. *m* Margaret Anne Walker. two *s.* one *d. Studied:* Gravesend School of Art (1951-52), Regent St. Polytechnic (1952-54); Central School of Art (1957-60). *Exhib:* one-man shows: Camel Gallery, Wadebridge, Orion Gallery, Penzance, Plymouth Art Centre; three-man show: Marlborough Graphics; joint shows: Penwith Society of Arts, Wills Lane Gallery, St. Ives, Newlyn Gallery. *Work in collections:* Print Room, V. & A. *Signs work:* "Roy Walker." *Address:* Warwick House, Sea View Terr., St. Ives; Studio: 6 Porthmeor Studios, Back Rd. West, St. Ives.

WALKER, Sandra, artist in water-colour; *b* Washington D.C., U.S.A. two *s.* one *d. Exhib:* many mixed and one-man shows: Singer & Friendlander (1st Prize); R.I., R.W.S., R.B.A., Galerie Mensch, Hamburg; Bourne Gallery; Alresford Gallery; Mall Galleries; Watermans, London; Gallery Henoch, N.Y., U.S.A., Franz Bader Gallery, Wash.D.C., Corcoran Gallery, Wash.D.C., Smithsonian Inst., Wash.D.C., National Geographic, Wash.D.C., Tregastel Salon International de la Peinture a l'Eau, France. *Commissions:* Baroness Thatcher: print of Parliament. *Publications:* work illustrated in: "Water-colour Step by Step" (Harper Collins, 1993), "How to Draw and Paint Texture" (Harper Collins, 1993), "Collins Complete Painting Course" (Harper Collins, 1993), "Shapes and Edges" (Sandstone Books, 1996), "Houses and Buildings" (Cassells Press, 1991). Designer of President's Medal of Freedom honouring Simon Weisenthal (U.S. Mint). *Clubs:* member, Royal Institute of Painters in Watercolour (London). *Address:* 39 Stewkley Rd., Wing, Leighton Buzzard, Beds. LU7 0NJ.

WALKLIN, Carol, A.R.C.A. (1953), R.E. (1986); graphic artist and printmaker; *m* Colin, A.R.C.A., co-Director 'Mullet Press'; tutor-lecturer in printmaking. *Studied:* Beckenham School of Art and Royal College of Art. *Exhib:* widely in U.K. including Bankside Gallery and Mall Galleries, London. *Work in collections:* National Portrait Gallery, London; U.K., U.S.A. and Europe. *Commissions:* BBC T.V. 'Jackanory', Post Office U.K. (stamp designs and air letters). *Clubs:* Senior Fellow, Royal Soc. of Painter-Printmakers. *Signs work:* "Walklin." *Address:* 2 Thornton Dene, Beckenham, Kent BR3 3ND.

WALLACE, Donald Ian Mackenzie, B.A. (Economics, Law), Cantab.; artist in pencil, ink, gouache; *b* Gt. Yarmouth, Norfolk, 14 Dec., 1933. *m* Wendy. three *d. Educ:* Loretto School. *Exhib:* S.WL.A. (annually). *Commissions:* several annually. *Publications:* Birds of the Western Palearctic (Field Characters, plates); five other books; many papers. *Clubs:* Soc. of Wildlife Artists. *Signs work:* "dim wallace." *Address:* Mount Pleasant Farm, Main Rd., Anslow, Burton-on-Trent, E. Staffs. DE13 9QE.

WALLER, Jonathan Neil, B.A. (Hons.), M.A. (Painting); artist in oil and charcoal; *b* Stratford upon Avon, 16 Apr., 1956. *Studied:* Nene College, Northampton (1979-80), Coventry (Lanchester) Polytechnic (1980-83), Chelsea School of Art

(1984-85). *Exhib:* one-man shows: Paton Gallery, London (1986, 1988), Flowers East, London (1990, 1992, 1993, 1994), New End Gallery, London (1997), Axiom, Cheltenham (1998); group shows: 1984: New Contemporaries, I.C.A. London, Midland View 3 (major prizewinner), 1988: London, Glasgow, N.Y., Metropolitan Museum, N.Y., New British Painting, Cincinnati (touring), 1991: Kunst Europa, Karlsruhe, Germany. *Work in collections:* Tate Gallery, London; Metropolitan Museum, N.Y. *Publications:* Jonathan Waller (Flowers East, 1990). *Signs work:* "J.W.2001." *Address:* 42 Hervey Park Rd., Walthamstow, London E17 6LJ.

WALLER, Margaret Mary, F.I.A.L. (1958, mem. of Council), A.T.D., Mem. Liverpool Academy (1953); painter in oils, portrait, landscape, and decorative church work in gold leaf, also water-colour and egg tempera; *b* Yorks., 13 Nov., 1916. *m* Stephen Bryant, 1989. *Educ:* Friary Convent School (Venice), Belvedere School (Liverpool). *Studied:* Liverpool College of Art (1934-37) and R.A. Schools (1937-39). *Exhib:* R.A., S.W.A., R.P., Paris Salon, Funchal, Madeira (1992); executed Altar-piece for the Chapel of St. John, Guernsey (1960); also large decorative panels for St. Stephen's Church (1964). Invited to U.S.A. (1986) to give exhbn. of water-colours. Commissioned to paint in St. Malo, France (1993). *Clubs:* Sandon Studios Soc. (Liverpool), Reynolds (London). *Signs work:* "MARGARET WALLER." *Address:* Les Sauterelles, St. Jacques, Guernsey GY1 1SW; and Mayfield Studio, Sark.

WALLIS, Linda Joyce, S.W.A. (1994), S.B.A., (1999); artist in oil; *b* 20 Sept., 1940. *m* Howard. one *s.* two *d. Studied:* largely self taught, local evening class, and Verrochio Art Centre, Casole d'Elsa. *Exhib:* Guildhall, Royal Exchange, Wesminster Gallery, and many provincial galleries. *Work in collections:* America, Canada, Japan. *Publications:* work repro.: C.D. covers, Limited Edn. prints, Medici cards. *Clubs:* Epsom and Ewell Art Group, Croydon Art Soc., Carshalton and Wallington, Oxshott. *Signs work:* "WALLIS." *Address:* 25 Langton Ave., Ewell, Surrey KT17 1LD.

WALPOLE, Josephine Ailsa, artist specialising in flower painting and botanical illustration; *b* Cockfield, Suffolk, 27 Apr., 1927. *m* Derek Walpole. one *s. Educ:* East Anglian School for Girls, Bury St. Edmunds; Notre Dame High School, Norwich. *Studied:* privately under Stuart Somerville. *Exhib:* London and East Anglia. *Publications:* 'Anna' Memorial, Biography of Anna Zinkeisen; Biography of Leonard Squirrell, R.W.S., R.E.; Leonard Squirrell, Etchings and Engravings; Life and Work of Martin Kidner; Vernon Ward (Biography); 'Roses in a Suffolk Garden'. *Signs work:* "J. Walpole." *Address:* The Green House, 15 Cooper's Rd., Martlesham Heath, Ipswich, Suffolk IP5 3SJ.

WALTERS, Kate, B.A. (Hons.) Fine Art; artist in oil on canvas; *b* London, 23 May, 1958. one *s. Studied:* Brighton College of Art (1978-81), Falmouth College of Art (1966-2000). *Exhib:* I.C.A., Raw Art, Millfield, Laing, Beatrice Royal. *Work in collections:* private: U.K. and Europe. *Clubs:* Penzance Arts. *Address:* Trevellas, 3 Tolver Rd., Penzance TR18 2AG.

WALTON, Barbara Louise, M.F.A. (Hons.) (1981), Post.Grad. Dip. Painting and Drawing (1982); painter in oil and acrylic paint on canvas and paper; *b* Bishop Auckland, 30 Dec., 1955. *m* Dursun Cilingir, doctor. *Educ:* Queen Anne Grammar School. *Studied:* Edinburgh University/College of Art (Elizabeth Blackadder, David

Michie). *Exhib:* York University (1982), Gloucester College of Art (1983), Paisley Art Inst. drawing competition (1987), N.P.G. portrait competition (1987, 1989), Mall Galleries Open (1989); solo shows: Mercury Gallery (1988, 1993), Grape Lane Gallery, York (1989); regular exhib. with Mercury Gallery since 1986. *Signs work:* "B.L. Walton" *Address:* 31 St. John's Rd., Exeter EX1 2HR.

WALTON, John, D.F.A. (Lond. 1949), R.P. (1976); portrait painter in oil and tempera; Principal, Heatherley School of Fine Art, London; Governor, Federation of British Artists, Mem., Royal Soc of Portrait Painters; *b* Birkenhead, 5 Dec., 1925. *m* (1) Annette d'Exéa. two *s*. one *d*. (2) Alice Low. *Educ:* Birkenhead School, Edge Grove School, Aldenham School. *Studied:* Ruskin School of Fine Art (1944-45, Albert Rutherston), Slade School of Fine Art (1945-49, Randolph Schwabe). *Exhib:* R.A., R.P., Paris Salon (Hon. mention), Academie des Beaux Arts, Institut de France. *Clubs:* Chelsea Arts. *Signs work:* "John Walton." *Address:* 30 Park Rd., Radlett, Herts. WD7 8EQ.

WANG, Elizabeth, F.S.B.A. (1987); Founder mem. Soc. of Botanical Artists, Medalife Art award (1990); artist in water-colour, oil, pencil, writer; *b* Slough, 1942. *m* M.K. Wang. two *s*. one *d. Educ:* Dr. Challoner's Grammar School, Amersham. *Studied:* part-time at St. Albans College of Art. *Exhib:* F.B.A. Mall Galleries; mixed shows: still-life and botanical works: S.B.A., R.A., R.I., Fine Art (Solihull); solo shows: recent religious works: Harpenden, Westminster Cathedral, Bar Convent Museum, York, St. Paul's Conference Rooms, Westminster. *Work in collections:* numerous private collections. *Publications:* illustrated: The Way of the Cross (Collins Liturgical 1988); written and illustrated: Teachings in Prayer, Vols. 1-4 (Radiant Light, 1999), My Priests are Sacred (Radiant Light, 1999), How to Pray (Radiant Light, 1999), Falling in Love (Radiant Light, 1999). *Signs work:* "Wang" or "E.W." *Address:* 25 Rothamsted Ave., Harpenden, Herts. AL5 2DN.

WANLESS, Tom, N.D.D. (1957), D.A.E. (1970), M.Ed. (1974), R.O.I. (1996), R.B.A. (1997); artist/printmaker in oil, water-colour and etching; *b* Philadelphia, Co. Durham, 19 July, 1929. *m* Marjorie. one *d. Studied:* Bede College, Durham University (1946-48), Sunderland College of Art (1952-57), Bristol University (1970-74, post graduate). *Exhib:* regular exhibitor in London and regional galleries; one-man shows: Smith A.G., Brighouse; Mercer A.G., Harrogate; Durham A.G.; Scarborough A.G.; Chandler A.G., Hunton. *Work in collections:* U.K., Europe, N. America and Australia. *Publications:* illustrated educational books for Collins, Schofield & Sims, and Harraps (1958-89). Prizes: Cornelissen Award (R.O.I., 1964), Charles Pears Award (R.S.M.A., 1964), Roberson Award (R.O.I., 1996). *Clubs:* Leeds Fine Art. *Signs work:* "T. Wanless." *Address:* 41 Badgerwood Glade, Wetherby, W. Yorks. LS22 7XR. *Email:* t.b.wanless@btinternet.com

WARD, Gordon, D.F.A. Lond., R.W.A.; artist in all mediums; formerly Head of Painting, Gloucestershire College of Arts and Technology; *b* N. Walsham, Norfolk, 1932. *m* Maureen Liddell. one *s*. two *d. Educ:* Paston Grammar School, N. Walsham, Norfolk. *Studied:* Norwich School of Art (1949-53), Slade School of U.C.L. (1955-57). *Work in collections:* Royal West of England Academy, Robert Fleming Holdings, The Royal Bank of Scotland, Prudential Assurance and various private collections in Europe, America and Australia. *Signs work:* "GORDON WARD" and date. *Address:* Prospect House, Oakridge Lynch, Stroud, Glos. GL6 7NZ.

WARD, J. S., A.R.C.A., V.P.R.P., R.A.; painter in oil and water-colour; *b* Hereford, 1917. *m* Alison Ward. four *s.* two *d. Educ:* St. Owens School, Hereford. *Studied:* R.C.A. under Gilbert Spencer. *Work in collections:* H.M. the Queen, N.P.G., R.A., Preston A.G., Maas Gallery, Hereford. *Publications:* Alphonse by George Ward; Cider with Rosie by Laurie Lee; Little Kingdom by Richard Church; Autobiography of H. E. Bates. *Clubs:* Athenæum. *Signs work:* "John Ward." *Address:* Bilting Ct., Bilting, nr. Ashford, Kent.

WARD, Joan, A.R.C.A. (1949); sculptor in resins, wood, stone, etc.; *b* London, 10 Jan., 1925. *m* T. W. Ward. one *s.* one *d. Educ:* Croydon High School for Girls. *Studied:* Bromley Art School, Royal College of Art (1945-48, Willi Soukop, Frank Dobson). *Exhib:* R.B.A, N.E.A.C., N.S., Coach House Gallery, C.I. (1987); group exhbns. in London Parks and Questers, Ealing, Wherry Quay and Grove House, Ipswich, Digby Gallery, Colchester, Chappel Galleries, Essex. *Clubs:* Suffolk Group and Ipswich Art Soc. *Signs work:* "Joan Ward." *Address:* Hollydene, Ipswich Rd., Holbrook, nr. Ipswich, Suffolk IP9 2QT.

WARD, Nicholas, Dip.A.D. (1971), R.A. Schools (1974), R.E. (1992); artist and printmaker in etching and pencil; *b* Gt. Yarmouth, 10 Jan., 1950. *m* Elizabeth Somerville. one *s. Educ:* Lowestoft County Grammar School. *Studied:* Lowestoft School of Art (1967-68), St. Martin's School of Art (1968-71, Alan Cooper, James Stroudley), R.A. Schools (1971-74, Denis Lucas, Peter Greenham). *Exhib:* R.A. Summer Shows (1982, 1984-87, 1990, 1994), R.E. Annual (1988-99), British Miniature Print (1989, 1994, 1997), Bradford Print Biennale (1990), National Print Exhbn. (1995-2001); one-man shows 1974-97. *Work in collections:* Norfolk Museums, Ipswich Museum. *Signs work:* "N. Ward." *Address:* 38 Bulmer La., Winterton-on-Sea, Gt. Yarmouth, Norfolk NR29 4AF.

WARDEN, Peter Campbell, A.R.B.A. (1982), R.B.A. (1994), D.A. (1976), Post. Dip. (1977); award, Robert Colquhoun (1976); 1st prize Devon and Cornwall Figurative Art competition (1992); painter in oil, water-colour, pen, pencil; *b* Vancouver, Canada, 19 Mar., 1950. *m* Lorna Hawes. one *d. Educ:* Lancing College. *Studied:* Glasgow School of Art (1972-77). *Exhib:* R.A., R.B.A., R.S.A., R.G.I., R.S.W.; one-man shows: Malaga, Marbella, Dumfries, Sterts. *Work in collections:* Kilmarnock and Loudon D.C.; Sociedad Economica, Malaga. *Publications:* work repro.: various art magazines. *Signs work:* "Peter C. Warden" and date. *Address:* 57 Sunrising, East Looe, Cornwall PL13 1ND.

WARMAN, Oliver Byrne, R.B.A., R.O.I.; painter in oil of landscapes, houses, gardens, boats, cattle; Chief Executive, Federation of British Artists; Director, Arts News Agency (1983-92); *b* London, 10 June, 1932. Former regular officer Welsh Guards. *Educ:* Stowe, Exeter University, Royal Military College of Science, Staff College Camberley, Balliol College, Oxford. *Studied:* Exeter University. *Exhib:* R.A., R.B.A., R.W.A., N.E.A.C., R.S.M.A., R.O.I. *Work in collections:* Lancaster House, all major Banks, Sultan of Oman, Emir of Kuwait, American Embassy. *Publications:* Royal Society of Portrait Painters (joint, 1984), Arnhem, 1944 (1971). *Clubs:* Cavalry and Guards, Chelsea Arts, Royal Cornwall Yacht. *Signs work:* "O.B.W." or "Oliver Warman." *Address:* La Grange de l'Herbey, Merri, 61160 Trun,

Orne, France. *Email:* olivierwarman@aol.com

WARMAN, Sylvia (Mrs.), Ass. des A. Francais; portrait sculptor and painter; Wells Prize in Fine Art Reading University (1952); Owen Ridley Prize in Fine Art Reading University (1954); Bronze Medal (Sculpture) Paris Salon (1969); Silver Medal (Sculpture) Paris Salon (1973); Gold Medal Accademia Italia (1981); Hon. Sec. National Society Painters, Sculptors Printmakers (1978-83) Vice-President (1984/5); *b* St. Leonards on Sea, Sussex. *m* J. Royce Warman. three *d. Studied:* Reading University (1947-54). *Exhib:* various including R.A., London, and West of England R.A., five times Paris Salon. *Address:* 1 Chester St., Caversham, Reading RG4 8JH.

WARNER, Robert, artist in oil and water-colour; *b* Colchester, 14 Sept., 1947. *Studied:* Colchester Art School (1964-71, John Nash, Peter Coker). *Exhib:* R.O.I., N.E.A.C., R.I., R.A. (1974-84, 1986, 1988, 1991, 1992, 1993), R.A. Summer Exhibition (2000, 2001), Athena Art Awards (1987), Hunting Group (1988), Sunday Times Exhbns. (1988, 1990, 1992, 1996, 1997, 1998, 1999), Laing Art Competition (1990, 1991, 1992, 1994, 1996), Mall Galleries, prizewinner 32nd Essex Open 35th best water-colour; one-man shows: Minories, Colchester (1973), Mercury Theatre (1972, 1980, 1985), Chappel Gallery, Essex (2000). *Work in collections:* Epping Museum, private collections in Britain and America. *Publications:* work repro.: R.A. Illustrated (1980, 1988, 2000). *Clubs:* Colchester Art. Soc. *Signs work:* "R. Warner." *Address:* St. Elmer, Queens Rd., W. Bergholt, Colchester, Essex CO6 3HE.

WARNES, Robin, B.A.(Hons), R.A. Schools Cert. (Postgrad.); painter in oil, charcoal, pastel, acrylic, pencil; David Murray Studentship, Turner Gold medal for Landscape Painting (1980), regional prizewinner, Laing Landscape Exhbn. (1990); Artist in Residence, Ipswich Museums and Galleries (1989-90); *b* Ipswich, 13 Mar., 1952. *m* Vanessa. two *s.* one *d. Studied:* Ipswich School of Art (1972-74, Colin Moss), Canterbury College of Art (1974-77, Tom Watt), R.A. Schools (Peter Greenham, C.B.E., R.A.). *Exhib:* R.A., Federation of British Artists, Laing Landscape, John Russell Gallery Ipswich, Cadogan Gallery London, Chappel Gallery Colchester. *Work in collections:* Ipswich Borough Council, Suffolk C.C. *Signs work:* "R. Warnes" or "R.W." *Address:* 77 Rosehill Rd., Ipswich, Suffolk IP3 8ET.

WARREN, Michael John, N.D.D. (1958), S.WL.A. (1971); *b* Wolverhampton, 26 Oct., 1938. *m* Kathryne. one *s.* one *d. Educ:* Wolverhampton Grammar School. *Studied:* Wolverhampton College of Art (1954-58). *Exhib:* (recent): Wildlife Art Gallery, Lavenham, Suffolk, (1994/98); Hoste Gallery, Burnham Market, Norfolk (1996); In Focus Gallery, London (1996, '98, '99, 2000); Auditorium Sa Maniga, Cala Millor, Mallorca (2000), Conservatoire du Patrimoine Naturel de Savoie, Le Prieure, Le-Bourget-du Lac, France (2001), Focus Gallery, Nottingham (2001). *Work in collections:* Nature in Art. *Commissions:* 1985-87 Unicover Corporation U.S.A., paintings from 50 States; 1990-92 Unicover / Ducks Unlimited U.S.A., 50 paintings North American Wildfowl; Tarmac Calendar since 1995; work for R.S.P.B. *Publications:* 1984: 'Shorelines', Hodder & Stoughton, London & Times Books, N.Y.; 1998: 'Field Sketches', Arlequin Press, Chelmsford, England; 1999: 'Langford Lowfields 1989-99', Arlequin Press, Chelmsford, England; 2001: 'Le Lac du

Bourget' Gallimard, Conservatoire du Littoral, Paris, France. postage stamp designs: waterbirds – British Post Office; native & migratory birds, Republic of Marshall Islands (1990-92); conservation stamp designs: National Audubon Society, U.S.A. (1984-1997, 2001); U.K. Habitat Stamp (1996). *Clubs:* Nottinghamshire Birdwatchers (President). *Signs work:* "warren" (paintings), "Michael Warren" (prints). *Address:* The Laurels, The Green, Winthorpe, Notts. NG24 2NR. *Email:* mike.warren.birdart@care4free.net

WASIM, L., painter in oil and water-colours; nominated as an "Academic of Italy with Gold Medal" and Gold Plaque "Premio d'Italia 1986"; awarded Golden Centaur 1982 Prize with Gold Medal; and International Parliament U.S.A. Gold Medal of Merit; conferred Honoris Causa diploma "Master of Painting" from Salsomaggiore International Seminar of Modern and Contemporary Art, and Diploma of Merit from Italian University of Arts; Institute of Art Contemporer at Milano conferred the Great Gold Medal with the Institute's emblem in 24 carat gold on brass with box and relative certificate of merit for "Premio Milano 1988"; 20th Century Award Medal Achievement '96 from International Biographical Centre Cambridge, England; *b* Bandung, Java, 9 May, 1929. *m* Alisma Sudja. one *s.* one *d. Studied:* Graduated from The Central Academy of Arts, Beijing (1956). Instructor of Shanxi Provincial College of Fine Arts, Xian (1956-59). Court painter in Indonesian Presidential Palaces, Jakarta and Bogor (1961-67). Study tour in Asia and Europe (1975-80); participated several art exhbns. in Indonesia and Europe. *Work in collections:* Indonesian Palaces Museums, Jakarta and Bogor; The Asia and Pacific Museum, Warsaw, etc. *Signs work:* "L. Wasim" and see appendix. *Address:* J1 Tanah Sereal V no. 6, Jakarta Barat 11210, Indonesia.

WATERFIELD, Ken, S.WL.A. (1972); landscape and wildlife artist in oil and acrylics; *b* Watford, 7 Nov., 1927. *m* Enid. two *s.* two *d. Studied:* Watford School of Art (1940-43). *Exhib:* Mall Galleries, Medici, Guildhall London, Southern Regional Galleries; major one-man show, Winchester City Gallery (1979), 'Nature in Art' Gloucester (2000), Rome Biennale exhibitor (2001), Blacksheep Gallery, Hawarden (2001). *Work in collections:* Oxford C.C., King Alfred's College, Winchester. *Publications:* work repro.: illus. profiles, R.S.P.B. Magazine 'Birds' (Autumn, 1978); Oxford Mail (28 Oct., 1976). Winner, Natural World Art Award (1988, 1995). Entry Dictionary of International Biography (1999). *Signs work:* "Waterfield." Later work displays strong abstract characteristics. *Address:* Plaintiles, Uploders, Bridport, Dorset DT6 4NU.

WATERS, Linda Mercedes, B.A.Hons. (1977); painter, illustrator and designer in water-colour, pen and ink, oils, wood engraving; *b* Monmouthshire, 10 Nov., 1955. *Educ:* Chepstow School. *Studied:* Gwent C.H.E. Faculty of Art and Design, Newport (1974-77). *Exhib:* Royal West of England Academy, Medici Gallery, Oriel Cardiff, Llewellyn Alexander Gallery, etc. *Work in collections:* historic reconstructions of Chepstow in Chepstow Museum; many private collections. *Publications:* several books and magazines illustrated, particularly botanical, natural history and history. *Clubs:* 'Y Art ?' group. *Signs work:* "Linda Waters" or "L. Waters." *Address:* 41 Hardwick Ave., Chepstow, Monmouthshire NP16 5DS.

WATKINS, Frances Jane Grierson (Peggy), oil, water-colour, pencil artist;

jewellery; speciality, pencil portraiture; instructor silverwork and jewellery Hereford College of Art (1957-72); *b* 24 July, 1919. *m* Rev. Alfred Felix Maceroni Watkins. one *s* (decd). one *d*. *Educ:* Elms Private School, Herefordshire School of Art, Birmingham School of Jewellery. *Exhib:* R.A., R.S.A., R.B.A., R.W.A., R.B.S.A., National Eisteddfod, Herefordshire Arts and Crafts. *Work in collections:* Hereford A.G.; Lady Hawkins Grammar School; Agric. Exec. Com.; Hereford City Art Gallery; Hereford RDC (badge of office). *Commissions:* oil portrait of Mayor of Hereford, silver vase, Burghill, various jewellery, church. *Signs work:* "PEGGY WATKINS." *Address:* Leylines, 26 Southbank Rd., Hereford HR1 2TJ.

WATSON, Arthur James, D.A., A.R.S.A.; sculptor/printmaker; Course Director, Master of Fine Art, Duncan of Jordanstone College of Art and Design, Dundee; *b* Aberdeen, 6 June, 1951. *Educ:* Aberdeen Grammar School. *Studied:* Grays School of Art, Aberdeen (1969-74). *Exhib:* Venice Biennale (1990), New Directions, Sarajevo (1988), Common Ground, Utrecht (1995). *Work in collections:* Aberdeen A.G. and Museum, Scottish Arts Council. *Commissions:* North of Scotland Hydro Electric Board, University of Aberdeen, P. & O. Cruises, Monklands District Council, Forest Enterprise. *Signs work:* see appendix. *Address:* 16 Pilot Sq., Footdee, Aberdeen AB11 5DS.

WATSON, Heather, R.M.S. (1999), H.S. (1989); miniaturist painter in watercolour; *b* Coventry, 10 Mar., 1939. *m* William James Egerton Smith. *Educ:* Stoke Park School, Coventry. *Exhib:* R.A., R.M.S., Llewellyn Alexander (Fine Arts) Ltd., Medici Gallery, London, Linda Blackstone Gallery, Pinner, Hilliard Exhbns. Wells; solo shows: Dorset and N. Yorks, Nunnington Hall, National Trust Property, N. Yorks. *Signs work:* see appendix. *Address:* Dale Cottage, Dale End, Kirkbymoorside, N. Yorks. YO62 6EQ.

WATSON, Howard, painter in oil on canvas and soft pastel; *b* 13 Oct., 1930. *m* Patricia. one *s*. two *d*. *Studied:* Coventry School of Art. *Exhib:* Plumbline Gallery St. Ives, Herbert A.G. Coventry, Leamington Spa A.G., City A.G. Leicester, Warwick County Library. *Work in collections:* British Telecom H.Q. London, Reuters. *Commissions:* BMW Group Financial Services, Pizza Express Albangate, Charlotte St. London, Maidenhead, New Delhi, Walton-on-Thames, Gosforth, Newcastle on Tyne. *Clubs:* Birmingham Art Trust, Penwith Soc. of Arts (Associate). *Signs work:* "Howard Watson" and initials on verso. *Address:* Vincent Lodge, Percy St., Stratford on Avon CV37 6SL.

WATSON-GANDY, Basia, B.A.Hons., S.W.A., I.P.A., Grollo d'Ora Silver Medal (1980), Gold Medal (1981); painter on china, porcelain and ceramics using glazes, lustres, goldwork; lecturer and researcher in the Industry; lecturer. Founder Com. mem. and past president, B.C.P.A.A. Commissioned work in private collections throughout the world; *Publications:* many magazine articles; appearances on TV and radio. *Clubs:* S.W.A., Confraternity of Polish Artists, Virginia Water Art Soc. *Address:* Squirrel Court Studio, Hare La., Little Kingshill, Gt. Missenden, Bucks. HP16 0EF.

WATSON STEWART (née GIBB), (Lady) Avril Veronica, D.S.J. (1997), F.R.S.A. (1969), Hon.F.B.I.D. (1979), Hon.M.Aust.S.C. (1983); artist/calligrapher/lettering designer on vellum, glass, metals, stone; worldwide lecturer; *b* Glasgow. *m* Sir James Watson Stewart, Bt. (decd. 1988). *Educ:* Glasgow

High School for Girls, Glasgow and West of Scotland College of Commerce (now University of Strathclyde). *Studied:* Glasgow School of Art (1950, Prof. Colin Horsmann). *Exhib:* California, Norfolk, Va., St. Andrews, Dunfermline, Greenock A.G., National Library of Scotland, Australia. *Work in collections:* V. & A., and private collections. *Commissions:* glass doors in churches, all forms of architectural lettering or illuminated panels, calligraphy heraldry worldwide. *Clubs:* Royal Scottish Automobile. *Signs work:* owl followed by maiden name - see appendix. *Address:* Undercliff Court, Wemyss Bay. PA18 6AL Scotland.

WATT, Gilbert, D.A. (1946), A.R.B.S. (1982), Landseer bronze medal; Cert. of Merit (R.A. 1952), Prix de Rome (1952); sculptor in clay, stone, steel, wood; *b* Aberdeen, 19 Sept., 1918. *m* Irene Mae. *Studied:* Gray's School of Art, Aberdeen, under T.B. Huxley-Jones; R.A. Schools under Maurice Lambert; British School at Rome. *Exhib:* R.A.; R.S.A.; Rome; Leicester Galleries; Royal Festival Hall; Arts Council Travelling Exhbn.; G.I.; Aberdeen A.G.; Scone Palace; Shakespeare Birthplace Trust Exhbn.; Taliesin Art Centre, Swansea University; one-man show, Inverurie, Aberdeenshire. *Work in collections:* Britain, America, W. Germany. *Signs work:* "Gilbert Watt." *Address:* Riverside, 4 Ellon Rd., Bridge of Don, Aberdeen AB2 8EA.

WATTS, Brenda Mary, N.D.D. (1951), Cert. in Educ. (1973), S.B.A. (1998), C.B.M. (1997); Joyce Cummings Award (1999), G.M. (2001); botanical artist in water-colour, retd. teacher; *b* Ilford, Essex, 1932. *m* Michael Watts. two *s. Educ:* S.E. Essex (1948-51). *Exhib:* annually S.B.A. and R.H.S. *Work in collections:* Dr. Shirley Sherwood and Lindley Library. *Commissions:* private. *Signs work:* "B.W." in a lozenge. *Address:* Barrohill, Horsell Rise, Woking, Surrey GU21 4AY.

WATTS, Mrs. Dorothy, S.W.A. (1952), Mem. Federation of British Artists; artist in water-colour; early years, fashion designer for London and Northern papers; *b* London, 3 Apr., 1905. *m* A. Gordon Watts, LL.B., solicitor. *Studied:* Brighton College of Arts under J. Morgan Rendle, R.I., R.B.A. *Exhib:* R.A., R.I., R.B.A., S.W.A., Britain in Water-colours and provincial galleries. *Work in collections:* Hove Art Collection. *Publications:* work repro.: in Londoner's England, various Christmas cards and in newspapers, London and provincial. *Clubs:* S.W.A. *Signs work:* see appendix. *Address:* Southwoods, 65 Surrenden Rd., Brighton, Sussex BN1 6PQ.

WATTS, Joan Alwyn, A.R.M.S.; portrait miniatures and water-colour landscapes; *b* Birmingham, 19 Dec., 1921. *m* Ronald O. Watts. one *s.* one *d. Educ:* Birmingham College of Art. *Exhib:* Birmingham Soc. of Artists, Royal Miniature Soc., Paris Salon, various exhbns. in America and Australia; permanent exhbn. Art Bureau, London. *Publications:* The Royal Miniature Society 100 Years (a portrait min. requested for this publication). *Address:* Dial Cottage, Bannut Tree La., Bridstow, nr. Ross-on-Wye, Herefords. HR9 6AJ.

WATTS, Michael Gorse, (otherwise PIKE, Septimus - cartoonist), A.R.I.B.A. (1965), M.F.P.S. (1989); artist, cartoonist, illustrator, in ink, acrylic, water-colour; *b* Stepney, London, 3 Dec., 1934. *m* Meg Wattson Dean. three *s.* one *d.* by first marriage. *Educ:* St. Edward's School. *Studied:* Oxford School of Technology and Art (1951-54), S.W. Essex School of Art (1960-62). *Exhib:* Group, solo, etc., in Gt. Britain and the U.S.A. Work in private collections at home and abroad. *Publications:*

work repro.: numerous articles, cartoons and illustrations. *Clubs:* Free Painters and Sculptors, Chichester, Lewisham, Selsey. *Signs work:* see appendix. *Address:* 27 Sutherland St., London SW1V 4JU.

WATTS, Peter, F.R.B.S. (1970); sculptor in wood and stone; *b* Chilcompton, Bath, 12 Oct., 1916. *m* Anne Mary Coulson. two *s.* one *d. Educ:* Downside School. *Studied:* Bath School of Art (1937) under Clifford Ellis, apprenticed (1938) to Lindsey Clark, F.R.B.S., in London; also at City and Guilds School of Art, Kennington (1938-39). *Commissions:* Principal commissioned works in U.K.: Oban Cathedral (1951), St. Mary and St. Joseph's Church, Poplar, (1952), St. Mary's Church, Highfield St., Liverpool (1953), Bath Abbey, (West Front) (1959-60), Prinknash Abbey (1971), Downside Abbey (1974); in U.S.A.: Gethsemani Abbey, Kentucky (1955-64), St. John's Abbey, Collegeville, Minn. (1962), Sun of Justice Church, Benson, Vermont (1962-65), private collection of Mr. Chauncey Stillman, Amenia, N.Y. (1965-1970). *Signs work:* carved monogram, see appendix. *Address:* The Maltings, Wellow, Bath, Avon BA2 8QJ.

WATTSON DEAN, Meg, H.S., M.A.S.-F., M.P.S.G.; specialist in miniatures and glass engraving; artist/sculptor; *b* Luton, 11 Nov., 1929. *m* Michael Watts. one *s.* one *d. Educ:* Bedford High School. *Studied:* Rolle College, Exmouth (1968-70). *Exhib:* with R.M.S. (1989-99), Hilliard Soc., 'A Million Brushstrokes' at Llewellyn Alexander Gallery, Florida, Washington and Georgia Miniature Art Socs. (1991-99), Guild of Glass Engravers, Westminster Arts Council, 2nd World Miniature Art Exhibition (Australia 2000); two-person exhbns. with Michael Watts. *Work in collections:* Chelsea and Westminster Hospital, private collections U.K. and U.S.A. *Clubs:* Hilliard Soc., Guild of Glass Engravers, Miniature Art Socs. of Florida and Washington D.C. *Signs work:* "Meg Wattson Dean" and see appendix. *Address:* 27 Sutherland St., London SW1V 4JU.

WAUGH, Eric, A.R.C.A. (1953), R.I. (1990); artist in water-colour; *b* London, 15 Dec., 1929. two *s.* two *d. Studied:* Croydon School of Art (1946-50), R.C.A. (1950-53). *Exhib:* Ashgate Gallery, Farnham (1965-67), Geffrye Museum (1968), Roland, Browse & Delbanco (1971), Arte Benimarco, Spain (1980), Galeria de Arte Denia, Spain (1981), Galeria de Arte Javea, Spain (1982), R.A., R.I., R.B.A., London Group, Sport in the Fine Arts, Madrid. *Work in collections:* Mexico, U.S.A., Australia, Spain, U.K. *Publications:* articles written for various magazines; Painting in Acrylics - A Correspondence Course (Pitmans). *Signs work:* "Eric Waugh." *Address:* Pen-an-Vrea, St. Kew Highway, Bodmin, Cornwall PL30 3EG.

WAUTERS, Jef, artist (painter); *b* B9910 Mariakerke, 26 Feb., 1927. *m* Denise D'hooge. one *s.* one *d. Studied:* Sup. Inst. St. Lucas and Academy of Fine Arts, Ghent. *Exhib:* numerous one-man and group exhbns. *Work in collections:* New York, Chicago, San Francisco, Los Angeles, Paris, München, Brussels, Rome, Bern, The Haegue e.o. Diff. museums. *Publications:* Palet (300 numb. ex.), "Paris-Roma" sketch-book, (500 numbered ex.), Jef Wauters by J. Murez, Jef Wauters (Ed. Aro, Roma) by G. Selvaggi, Jef Wauters (ed. Arben Press Switzerland). *Signs work:* see appendix. *Address:* 7 Rode Beukendreef, 9831 St. Martens Latem, Belgium; and 3 rue Chérubini, Paris 2.

WEAVER, Felicity, N.D.D. City & Guilds; printmaker in etching and drawing; *b* Leeds, 11 Feb., 1930. *m* Peter Weaver. one *d. Exhib:* B'ham Museum and A.G., Greenwich Printmakers Gallery, LWT Terrace Gallery; group shows: R.E., R.W.A., R.B.S.A, R.P., Curwen Gallery, Barbican, C.P.S., P.S., etc., also Moscow, Paris, Landau, Belize, Belfast. *Work in collections:* B'ham Museum and A.G., Scarborough Archives, Lewisham Council, and private collections in England, Germany, America and Australia. *Clubs:* P.M.C., G.P.A. *Signs work:* "FELICITY WEAVER." *Address:* 36 Cator Rd., London SE26 5DS.

WEAVER, Peter Malcolm, R.I., Slade Dip.; painter in water-colour, sculptor in mixed media; Founder mem. Printmakers Council; teacher of drawing and lithography: Camberwell School of Art and Crafts (1957-87); *b* 10 June, 1927. *m* Felicity. one *d. Studied:* St. Martin's School of Art and Camberwell Schools of Art, Slade School of Fine Art, U.C.L. *Exhib:* galleries: Grosvenor, Nicholas Treadwell, Sloane St., Ikon, Primavera, Alresford, I.C.A., Whitechapel, Shell House Gallery, Manor House Gallery; Open exhbns.: R.A., R.W.S., R.B.A., R.W.A., N.E.A.C., R.I., London Group, Birmingham Museums and Art Gallery. *Work in collections:* V. & A., B'ham Museum and A.G., also Collections in U.K. and America. *Publications:* The Technique of Lithography and also Printmaking - A Medium for Basic Design. *Clubs:* The Arts Club, Dover St. *Signs work:* "P. WEAVER, R.I." *Address:* 36 Cator Rd., London SE26 5DS.

WEBB, Barbara, etcher; teacher for I.L.E.A.; *b* London, 18 Dec., 1933. *m* T.R. Webb. one *d. Educ:* South Hampstead High School. *Studied:* Cass School, Whitechapel, London, Corcoran School of Art, Washington, D.C., U.S.A. *Exhib:* R.A., St. John's Smith Sq. *Work in collections:* Government Art Collection, Camden Council. *Signs work:* "Barbara Webb." *Address:* 39b Rosslyn Hill, London NW3 5UJ.

WEBB, Elizabeth, A.R.C.M., (1953), G.R.S.M. (London) (1955); artist in oil on canvas or board; music teacher; *b* Fakenham, 7 Sept., 1931. *m* (1) Frank Rayer (decd.). (2) Graham Webb (decd.). two *s. Educ:* The Park School, Yeovil; Royal College of Music, London. *Studied:* Evening Classes with Mary Bairds (1989-93). *Exhib:* R.A., Paris Salon, Meridian International Center, Washington, Sui Loung Gallery, Hong Kong. *Signs work:* "Elizabeth Webb" and see appendix. *Address:* La Guelle, Guelles Rd., St. Peter Port, Guernsey, C.I. GY1 2DE.

WEBB, Kenneth, N.D.D., A.T.D.Hons., N.S., F.R.S.A., R.W.A.; artist in oil and acrylic; Head of Painting School, Ulster College of Art (1953-60); *b* London, 1927. *m* Joan Burch. two *s.* two *d. Educ:* Bristol Grammar School; Lydney Grammar School and School of Art. *Studied:* Gloucester College of Art and University College, Swansea. *Exhib:* one-man shows 1954 to 1994: Verhoff Washington D.C., Arts Council Belfast, Walker Galleries London, Toronto, San Francisco, Ritchie Hendricks Dublin, Kenny Galleries, Alexander Gallery Bristol, Geneva, Solomon, etc. *Publications:* Kenneth Webb (Shenval Press, London), Profile of an Artist by Thomas Kenny (Pub. 1990). *Signs work:* figurative work: "Kenneth Webb," non figurative work: "Webb." *Address:* Portland House, Chagford, Devon TQ13 8AR.

WEBB, Sarah Ann, B.A.(Hons.) (1978), S.W.A. (1994); Best of Show (1987) and Athena award (1992) Central South Art competition (U.S.A.); artist in oil; *b* Nashville, TN, 19 Feb., 1948. *m* Gary A. Webb, attorney. *Educ:* University of Tennessee. *Studied:* University of Tennessee and Vanderbilt University. *Exhib:* regular exhib. S.W.A. and Central South Art competition (U.S.A.), winner American Artists National Art competition, Grand Central Gallery (N.Y. 1985), Tennessee All State competition, numerous national and international group and solo shows; P.B.S. Television (U.S.A. 1994, 1995), Radio (U.S.A. 1985). Work in corporate and private collections worldwide. *Signs work:* "Sarah Webb." *Address:* P.O. Box 50134, Nashville, TN 37205, U.S.A.

WEBBER, Angela Mary, S.C.A.; painter and maker of religious images, writer on and tutor of animal painting; founder and secretary, S.S.S.A.; *b* London, 4 Jan., 1931. *m* Russell Arlen Bedingfield, art and antiques collector. *Studied:* Hull College of Art (1949-52). *Exhib:* O'Mell Gallery (1976), Solange de la Bruyere Gallery, Saratoga Springs, U.S.A. (1976-77), S.E.A. (1981), N.S. (1980), N.E.A.C. (1983). *Work in collections:* Martin S. Vickers, Stella A. Walker, Miss Wiesenthall, U.S.A. *Commissions:* various. *Publications:* work repro.: The Webber Prints, Quartilles International, etc. *Signs work:* "A. M. WEBBER." *Address:* 2 Marina Cottage, Willingdon Lane, Jevington, Polegate, Sussex BN26 5QH.

WEBBER, Michael H., A.T.D. (London); painter in oil and water-colour; *b* London, 30 June, 1926. *m* Miriam Broughton. two *d*. *Educ:* Kilburn Grammar School, London (1937-43). *Studied:* Northampton School of Art (1943-46), Chelsea School of Art (1946-48), Central School of Arts. *Exhib:* R.A., R.S.B.A., R.O.I., etc. *Work in collections:* Ben Uri Gallery, private etc. *Address:* 23a Alma Rd., Cheltenham, Glos. GL51 3LU.

WEBSTER, John Morrison, A.R.S.M.A. (1998); marine and landscape painter in oil, pastel, water-colour; former Naval officer; *b* Sri Lanka, 3 Nov., 1932. *Studied:* No formal art training. *Exhib:* one-man shows: Art Gallery of Nova Scotia (1976), London since 1980, Tryon and Swann, Cork St. (1996, 1999). *Work in collections:* H.M. The Queen, Naval establishments, and private collections in Canada, Australia, Holland, France, U.K. *Signs work:* "JOHN WEBSTER." *Address:* Old School House, Soberton, Southampton SO32 3PF.

WEBSTER, John Robert, A.T.C., D.A.E.; W.A.C. travel grant to Ireland (1991); artist in etching, printmaking, gouache; senior lecturer, St. Mary's College, Bangor, N. Wales (1968-75); Dip. in Art Educ., Leeds University Inst. (1975-76); Lecturer in Art Educ., U.C.N.W. Bangor (1977-89); part-time Curator, U.C.N.W. Art Gallery (1982-); *b* Bridlington, E. Yorks., 22 May, 1934. *m* Dorothy Lloyd Webster. one *s*. four *d*. *Educ:* Leeds G.S. *Studied:* Leeds College of Art (1951-55-57). *Exhib:* Mold, Conway (1969-), National Eisteddfod Llangefni (1983), Cardiff, Aberystwyth Open (from 1986), Birkenhead (1986), Anglesey Eisteddfod (1986), etc. *Work in collections:* Schools Museum, Cardiff, D.O.E., National Library, Aberystwyth. *Address:* Tyn' Cae, Paradwys, Bodorgan, Anglesey, Gwynedd LL62 5PF.

WEBSTER, Norman, R.W.S., R.E., A.R.C.A.; painter etcher; *b* Southend-on-Sea, 6 May, 1924. *m* Joan W. Simpson, A.R.C.A. three *s*. *Educ:* Dover Grammar School; Tunbridge Wells School of Art (1940-43, E. Owen Jennings, R.W.S.); Royal

Navy (1943-46); R.C.A. School of Engraving (1946-49, Malcolm Osborne, C.B.E., R.A., Robert Austin, R.A.). *Exhib:* Painter Etchers, R.W.S., R.A., Yorkshire Artists at Leeds, Bradford, Wakefield and Hull City A.G.'s., with Yorkshire Printmakers in Britain, U.S.A., Israel and Canada. *Work in collections:* Ashmolean Museum; Salford University; Leeds City A.G. and Arts Council of G.B. *Signs work:* "Norman Webster." *Address:* 48 The Drive, Cross Gates, Leeds LS15 8EP.

WEEKS, John Lawrence Macdonald, L.R.M.S. (1984), A.R.M.S. (1987), F.N.C.M. (1984); artist in oil and water-colour; private music teacher and organist; *b* Chelmsford, 28 Apr., 1954. *Educ:* Moulsham High School, Chelmsford. *Studied:* Colchester Inst. of H.E. (1973-74, John Buhler). *Exhib:* R.M.S. annual, Medici Gallery and one-man shows. *Signs work:* name followed by date and device (see appendix). *Address:* 47 Prescott, Hanworth, Bracknell, Berks. RG12 7RE.

WEERDMEESTER, Neil Jackson, B.A. (Hons.) Fine Art (1986), M.A. Fine Art (1994); artist in painting and photography; *b* London, 21 Feb., 1960. one *d. Studied:* Dartington College; Reading University; Winchester School of Art. *Exhib:* London, Barcelona, Antwerp. *Clubs:* London Group. *Address:* Lower Flat, 5 Gilmore Rd., London SE13 5AD. *Email:* neilweerdmeester@hotmail.com

WEGNER, Fritz James, M.C.S.D., Mem. Art Workers' Guild; freelance artist, retired lecturer, St. Martin's School of Art; *b* Vienna, 15 Sept., 1924. *m* Janet Wegner. two *s.* one *d. Studied:* St. Martin's School of Art. *Publications:* work repro.: book-jackets and illustrations for British, American and Continental publishers; cover designs and illustrations for magazines; educational publications; G.P.O. Christmas and Anniversaries sets of stamps. Examples of work reproduced in several manuals on illustration. *Clubs:* Chelsea Arts. *Signs work:* "Wegner." *Address:* 14 Swains Lane, London N6 6QS.

WEIL, Hanna, N.T.D. (1943); painter in oil, water-colour, gouache; tutor, Hammersmith School of Arts and Crafts (1945-48); St. Martin's School of Art (1945-87); *b* Munich, 19 May, 1921. one *d. Educ:* North London Collegiate School. *Studied:* St. Martin's School of Art (1940-43). *Exhib:* R.A., Leicester Galleries, Liverpool, Brighton, London Transport (posters), Pro Arte Kasper Gallery, Switzerland, Arthur Jeffress (Pictures) Ltd., 4 galleries Munich, Portal Gallery, Elaine Benson Gallery, U.S.A. *Commissions:* Still Life - Claus Hausmann, Munich. *Publications:* work repro.: Amalgamated Press, The Queen, Art News and Review, The Studio, The Artist; postcards, calendars, prints of paintings. *Signs work:* "H. Weil." *Address:* 34 Christchurch Hill, London NW3 1JL.

WEINBERGER, Harry, artist in oil and all kinds of drawing; *b* Berlin, 7 Apr., 1924. one *d. Educ:* Continent and England. *Studied:* Chelsea School of Art under Ceri Richards, and privately with Martin Bloch. *Exhib:* 34 one-man shows, including sixteen in London, one in Berlin and three in Stuttgart. Present gallery: Duncan Campbell Fine Art, 15 Thackeray St., Kensington Sq., London. *Signs work:* "HW." *Address:* 28 Church Hill, Leamington Spa, Warks. CV32 5AY.

WELCH, Robert Joseph, B.A. (1979), M.A. (1981); painter in oil and acrylic on canvas; *b* 22 Feb., 1956. *Educ:* Regis Comprehensive, Wolverhampton. *Studied:* Hull C.H.E. (1976-79, John Clarke), Manchester Polytechnic (1980-81, David

Sweet). *Exhib:* Castlefield Gallery, Manchester, Showroom Gallery, London, Winchester School of Art, Mall Galleries; one-man shows: Patricia Brown, Dulwich, Smith-Jariwala, London. *Signs work:* "Welch, R.J.W." *Address:* 4a Husbourne House, Chilton Grove, London SE8 5DZ.

WELCH, Rosemary Sarah, S.W.A., A.A.E.A.; artist in oil and pastel; *b* 24 May, 1943. *m* Anthony Crockford. *Educ:* private school Bournemouth, American High School, N.Y. *Studied:* St. Ives School of Painting (Leonard Fuller, R.A., R.O.I.). *Exhib:* Belfast, Mall Galleries, Omells, John Davies, St. Ives Soc. of Artists, American Academy Equine Art. *Work in collections:* Russell-Cotes Museum, Bournemouth. *Signs work:* "Rosemary Sarah Welch." *Address:* Forest Way, Valley Lane, Bransgore, Dorset BH23 8DX.

WELLINGS, Tricia, self taught artist in gouache, charcoal and ink and gouache; *b* Guildford, 20 Mar., 1959. *Educ:* Horsham High School. *Exhib:* Painters Hall, London EC2, Mall Galleries, London SW1, Edith Grove Gallery, London SW10, Wattis Fine Art, Hong Kong, Ramsay Galleries, Honolulu, Hawaii, Ropner Gallery, London SW6, Bartley Drey Gallery, London SW3. *Work in collections:* U.S.A., Australia, Mexico, U.K., Hong Kong, Ireland (Eire). *Clubs:* The Nine Elms Group of Artists. *Signs work:* "T. Wellings." *Address:* 5a Pentland Gdns., Wandsworth, London SW18 2AN.

WELLS, Peter, Dip.Soc. (Lond.) (1970), M.F.P.S. (1987); painter in oil, poet; *b* London, 12 Jan., 1919. *m* (1) Elisabeth Van der Meulen (decd.). (2) Gillian Anne Hayes-Newington. one *d. Educ:* privately, and Universities of London and Manchester. *Studied:* Hornsey School of Art - part-time (1952-54, J.D. Cast). *Exhib:* Hornsey Artists (1953), Ellingham Mill Art Soc. (1981), The Crest Gallery, London (1982), Minsky's Gallery, London (1982), Wells Arts Centre, Norfolk (1982), Loggia Gallery (1988), Fermoy Gallery, King's Lynn (Eastern Open Competition 1992), School House Gallery, Wighton, Norfolk (1991-). *Publications:* The One Time Press - illustrated edns. of the artist's work. *Clubs:* P.E.N. *Signs work:* see appendix. *Address:* Model Farm, Linstead Magna, Halesworth, Suffolk IP19 0DT.

WELTMAN, Boris, Nature micro miniaturist, draughtsman, cartographer, stylus; painter, water-colour; *b* London, 29 Nov., 1921. *m* Phyllis Joyce. *Educ:* Chatham House, Ramsgate; Folkestone College; art and light craft. Work in collections worldwide. *Exhib:* R.A., R.I., R.M.S., S.M. *Commissions:* Warburg Inst. London, and U.S.A. Universities, Rep. British Art, Tokyo Exhbn. (1977). *Publications:* educational books. *Signs work:* on back of micro miniature drawings and paintings, see appendix. *Address:* St. Luke's, The Drove, Monkton, Ramsgate CT12 4JP.

WELTON, Peter, B.A.; artist in water-colour; Emeritus Prof. of Fine Art, De Montfort University, Leicester; *b* Barnetby, Lincs., 15 Mar., 1933. *m* Liza. two *s. Studied:* King's College, Newcastle (Gowing, Pasmore and Hamilton). *Exhib:* Keele University (1997), Laing Gallery, Newcastle, Bar Convent Museum, York, Buxton Art Gallery, Jersey Arts Centre, Unicorn Gallery, London. *Work in collections:* Wimbledon 1997 "The New No. 1 Court", H.M. The Queen "Moored Boat" (1992), Peter Ogden: "The Jethou Suite" (1997), National Art Archive (London Transport), The Duke of Gloucester "Kimbolton School", Lady Conyngham "Udaipur 2001". *Publications:* "See What I Mean" with John Morgan (Edward Arnold, London,

1986), "Paint in Water-colour" (Patchings Farm, Nottingham); work repro.: Illustrated London News, The Artists Magazine; "Peter Welton's Sketch Diary 1999". Video "Peter Welton's Way with Water-colour" (1997). *Signs work:* "Peter Welton." *Address:* Orchard Cottage, Arnesby, Leics. LE8 5WG. *Email:* kbi39@dial.pipex.com

WERGE-HARTLEY, Alan, N.D.D. (Leeds) 1952, A.T.D.; painter in oil, pen and wash of marine landscapes, lecturer; senior lecturer Dept. of Education, Portsmouth Polytechnic (1962-90); *b* Leeds, 1931. *m* Jeanne Werge-Hartley. two *d. Studied:* Leeds College of Art (1947-53) under Maurice de Sausmarez and E. E. Pullée; Hornsey College of Art (1972-73) (sabbatical). *Exhib:* in group exhbns. and one-man shows in Hampshire from 1962. *Work in collections:* Portsmouth City Gallery and numerous private collections in England and abroad. *Signs work:* see appendix. *Address:* 5 Maisemore Gdns., Emsworth, Hants. PO10 7JU. *Email:* alanwerge@aol.com

WERGE-HARTLEY, Jeanne, N.D.D., F.S.D.C., F.R.S.A.; designer/jeweller/goldsmith; Founder Mem., Designer Jewellers Group; Vice-President and past Chairman, Soc. of Designer Craftsmen, member of the Association for Contemporary Jewellery; *b* Leeds, 1931. *m* Alan Werge-Hartley. two *d. Educ:* Leeds Girls' High School. *Studied:* Leeds College of Art (1948-52). *Exhib:* nationally and internationally. *Work in collections:* City of Portsmouth University, Portsmouth County Council, private collections in U.K. and abroad. *Commissions:* U.K., U.S.A., Europe, New Zealand, Japan. Freeman of the Worshipful Company of Goldsmiths and the City of London (1986). Included on Craft Council Index and BBC Domesday Project. *Signs work:* see appendix. *Address:* 5 Maisemore Gdns., Emsworth, Hants. PO10 7JU. *Email:* alanwerge@aol.com

WERNER, Max, B.A., M.A.; printmaker in etching, acrylic, pencil on paper; *b* Ghent, Belgium, 17 Oct., 1955. *m* Shireen. two *d. Educ:* College de la Berlière (Belgium). *Studied:* Byam Shaw School of Art (1979-82, Winn Jones, Chris Crabtree, John Lewis), Slade School of Fine Art (1983-85, B. dos Santos). *Exhib:* mixed and one-man shows in U.K., Belgium, France, Portugal, Switzerland, Germany, Ireland, Pakistan, Taiwan, Argentina. *Commissions:* collaborated with B. dos Santos to the decoration of the "Enter Campos" underground station, Lisbon, and to an etched limestone panel for the Nyombashi station, Tokyo. *Signs work:* "M. Werner." *Address:* Grenada 774, Acassuso 1641, Prov. de Buenos Aires, Argentina.

WESSELMAN, Frans, R.E. (1986); painter, etcher, stained glass artist; *b* The Hague, Holland, 1953. one *s. Studied:* printmaking and photography at Groningen College of Art (1976-78). Work concerned with the human figure, emotions and interactions. Sometimes literary sources (Shakespeare) are a starting point, from where my paintings develop into valid graphic, pictorial statements with strong colours and compositions. *Exhib:* R.E., R.A., R.W.S., R.W.A., and widely in the U.K., Holland, Ireland, Germany. *Work in collections:* Fitzwilliam, Ashmolean Museum; private collections in U.S.A., Japan, Australia. *Commissions:* limited edition print for Shropshire County Council, limited edition print for Galerie Inkt., Holland, commissions of paintings for private collectors. *Address:* 5 Green Mount, Cunnery Rd., Church Stretton SY6 6AQ.

WESSELOW, Eric, M.A., M.F.A., Prix de Rome, R.C.A., S.C.A., F.R.S.A.; past Pres. Independent Art Assoc. and Quebec Soc. for Educ. through Art; painter, artist in water-colour, acrylic, chalk and glass (patented system of coloured glass lamination), of portraits, landscapes, abstracts; teacher, linguist; *b* Marienburg, Germany, 12 Sept., 1911. *Educ:* Academy of Fine Arts, Koenigsberg. *Studied:* Philology, University Koenigsberg. *Exhib:* one-man shows: Montreal Museum of Fine Arts; Waddington Gallery, Montreal; N.Y. State University, Plattsburgh; Inaugural Exhbn. Eaton A.G., Montreal; Robertson Galleries, Ottawa; Toronto Dominion Centre; Ontario Assoc. of Architects, Toronto, etc. Represented in numerous national and international art exhbns. *Work in collections:* architectural laminated coloured glass relief windows and screens: Montreal Airport Dorval; Hospital Dortmund, W. Germany; Sanctuaries Congregation Beth-El, Montreal; Temple Emanu-El-Beth Sholom, Montreal; Temple Sinai, Toronto; Humbervalley United Church, Toronto; St. Dunstan of Canterbury Anglican Church, West Hill, Ontario; Baptistery Church of the Resurrection, Valois, Quebec. *Publications:* Sparks, illustrated own aphorisms (1980); New Sparks (1985 and 1992). *Signs work:* "Wesselow" or "W" followed by date or year. *Address:* 5032 Victoria Ave., Montreal, Quebec, Canada H3W 2N3.

WEST, Steve, Dip.A.D. (1969), R.A.S. Higher Cert. (1972), Prix de Rome (1972), A.R.B.S. (1992); sculptor in bronze, and a variety of media; *b* Warrington, 6 Apr., 1948. *m* Jenny. one *s.* one *d. Studied:* Liverpool College of Art and Design (1965-69), R.A. Schools (1969-72, Willi Soukop). *Exhib:* Crescent Gallery Scarborough, Oldknows Gallery Nottingham, Lanchester Gallery Coventry, Tabor Gallery Canterbury, Woodlands Gallery Blackheath, Prediger Schwabisch Gmund, Hart Gallery London, Derby Museum and Art Gallery, Doncaster Museum and Art Gallery, Buckenham Galleries Southwold, Wolverhampton Art Gallery. *Signs work:* "Steve West." *Address:* 17 Swift St., Barnsley, S. Yorks. S75 2SN.

WESTLEY, Ann, sculptor and printmaker; part-time lecturer, Braintree College; *b* Kettering, 5 Mar., 1948. *Studied:* Northampton School of Art (1965-67), Bristol Polytechnic (1967-70), Gulbenkian Rome Scholarship in Sculpture (1970-71). *Exhib:* Serpentine Gallery (1976), Out of Print, South Hill Arts Centre, Bracknell (1983), British Miniature Print Biennale (1990), A New Generation of British Printmakers, Xylon Museum, Germany (1992). *Work in collections:* Gulbenkian Foundation, Ashmolean Museum, Fredrikstaad Museum Norway. *Commissions:* Mural of four wood panels for Great Notley Community Centre commissioned by Countryside Properties and Braintree District Council (1997). *Publications:* Relief Printmaking (to be publ. by A. & C. Black, 2000). *Clubs:* R.E. *Signs work:* "Ann Westley." *Address:* Gore Cottage, 4 Gore La., Rayne, Braintree, Essex CM7 8TU.

WESTON, David J., B.A. (Hons.) Fine Art, R.M.S., B.W.S., H.S., B.S.M., U.A., M.A.S.F., C.M.S., F.R.S.A.; seascape and landscape painter in water-colour and other media; miniaturist; *b* 21 Sept., 1936. two *s.* one *d. Studied:* St. Albans School of Art and Design (University of Hertfordshire). *Exhib:* one-man shows: Clare Hall Cambridge, Grosvenor Gallery, Old Fire Engine House Ely and Conservatory Gallery. Has exhibited at New Academy, Llewellyn Alexander and Medici galleries; with U.A., R.M.S., R.S.M.A., R.B.A., R.I., N.E.A.C. and H.S. at Mall and Westminster Galleries, also with B.W.S. and B.S.M. at Ilkley. *Signs work:* "DAVID J. WESTON" or "D.J.W." (miniatures and small works). *Address:* Little Glebe, 11

Longcroft Ave., Harpenden, Herts. AL5 2RD.

WESTWOOD, John, A.R.C.A. (1948); graphic designer; Head of Typographic Design, later Director of Graphic Design, at Her Majesty's Stationery Office, London (1960-1978); *b* Bromley, 26 Sept., 1919. *m* Margaret Wadsworth. two *s. Educ:* Bromley County Grammar School. *Studied:* Bromley College of Art (1936-39) and R.C.A. (1940 and 1947-48). *Exhib:* South Bank (1951). *Commissions:* Binding designs for The Folio Society. *Publications:* articles on graphic design; International Meccanoman; printing trade press, etc. *Address:* The Malt House, Church La., Streatley, Reading RG8 9HT.

WHALLEY, Ann Penelope, N.D.D., A.T.D., A.T.C., S.W.A.; artist in water-colour and pastel; tutor and organiser for painting holidays abroad; *b* Yorks., 1 Apr., 1935. *m* Theo Whalley, N.D.D., A.T.D., A.T.C. four *s. Educ:* Pontefract Girls' High School. *Studied:* Leeds College of Art (1950-55, Mr. Pullé). *Exhib:* one-man shows: Albany Gallery, Cardiff, Fountain Gallery Llandeilo, Library Hall, Haverfordwest annually since 1981, Workshop, Wales (1983), Bloomfield Hall (1986), Coachhouse (1987), Henry Thomas Gallery, Carmarthen, Patricia Wells Gallery (1987); group shows: St. Ives Gallery (1984), Beacon Gallery, Painswick (1985), B.W.S. (1986), Laing Comp. (1987), S.W.A. (1987), R.I. (1986), Albany Gallery, Cardiff, Century Gallery, Henley-on-Thames, Bromley Gallery, Kent, Fountain Gallery, Llandeilo, Wold Gallery, Bourton on the Water. *Publications:* illustrated, About Pembrokeshire; author, Painting under a Blue Sky; author, Painting Water in Water-colour (Batsfords); articles for Artist and Illustrator, and Leisure Painter. *Signs work:* "Ann Whalley." *Address:* Haroldston House, Haverfordwest, Pembs. SA61 1UH.

WHEELER, Colin, S.G.F.A. (1986); graphic artist, illustrator and cartographer in ink, pencil and pastel; *b* Amersham, Bucks., 4 July, 1946. *Educ:* Alleyne's Grammar School, Stevenage. *Studied:* privately. *Exhib:* S.G.F.A., various one-man shows including Fermoy Gallery, King's Lynn, Lion Yard, Cambridge, Theatre Royal, Norwich, Denington Gallery, Stevenage. *Work in collections:* B.Ae., Stevenage and N. Herts. Museum. *Commissions:* 'Discover Hertford'; Stevenage Museum. *Publications:* travel and tourist brochures. *Signs work:* "Colin Wheeler." *Address:* 39 Plash Drive, Stevenage SG1 1LN.

WHEELER, Sir H. Anthony, Kt. (1988), O.B.E. (1973), P.P.R.S.A., P.P.R.I.A.S., F.R.I.B.A., M.R.T.P.I. (rtd.), B.Arch. (Strath.), Hon. R.A., Hon. R.G.I., Hon. R.B.S., Hon. Doc.Des., Robert Gordon's Inst. of Technology, P.R.I.A.S. (1973-75), P.R.S.A. (1983-90), Hon. Pres. Saltire Soc. (1995); architect and planner, Consultant, Wheeler & Sproson, Edinburgh and Kirkcaldy since 1986 when ceased to be senior partner; mem. of the Royal Fine Art Commission for Scotland (1967-85); trustee of the Scottish Civic Trust (1970-83); *b* Stranraer, Scotland, 7 Nov., 1919. *m* Dorothy Jean Wheeler. one *d. Studied:* architecture: Glasgow School of Architecture under Prof. W. J. Smith, and Glasgow School of Art; graduated 1948; John Keppie Scholar, Rowand Anderson Studentship R.I.A.S. (1948); R.I.B.A. Grissell Gold Medallist (1948); R.I.B.A. Neale Bursar (1949); 22 Saltire Awards and Commendations for Housing and Reconstruction; 12 Civic Trust Awards and Commendations. *Exhib:* R.S.A., R.A., R.G.I., S.S.A.A. *Clubs:* Scottish Arts, New Club. *Signs work:* "H. A. Wheeler." *Address:* South Inverleith Manor, 31/6 Kinnear Rd., Edinburgh EH3 5PG.

WHEELER-HOPKINSON, John Samuel, S.G.A. (1983); graphic artist in pen and ink, pencil and colour wash; *b* Prestatyn, N. Wales, 1 Mar., 1941. *m* Claire Follett. two *d. Educ:* Grammar School, Colne, and King's College, London. *Exhib:* Mall Galleries, London. *Signs work:* "J.W-H." and date as ideogram. *Address:* 4 Chemin de la Croix, 03500 Contigny, France.

WHIDBORNE, Timothy Charles Plunket, artist in oil, tempera, sanguine, lithography, sculptor; *b* Hughenden, Bucks., 25 July, 1927. *m* Wendy. *Educ:* Stowe School. *Studied:* St. Martin's Art School (1944), with Mervyn Peake, Chelsea (1945) and Pietro Annigoni, Florence (1949). *Exhib:* R.A., R.P., S.P.S., etc.; one-man show: Upper Grosvenor Galleries (1969). *Work in collections:* portrait of H.M. The Queen, H.Q. Irish Guards, London; St. Katherine of Alexandria, Worshipful Company of Haberdashers, London; H.M. The Queen Mother, the Inspection of the In-Pensioners Founder's Day at the Royal Hospital, Chelsea, 1991; The Duke of Devonshire, Proprietor of Pratt's Club, 1994; collection of Sir Paul Getty, K.B.E. and Lady Getty; St. Jude, 2000 Pheasantry Studios. *Clubs:* Chelsea Arts. *Signs work:* "T. Whidborne" or "T.W." *Address:* The Studio, 30 Albert Rd., Deal, Kent CT14 9RE.

WHISHAW, Anthony, R.A., R.W.A., A.R.C.A. (1955), Travelling Scholarship, R.C.A., Abbey Premier Scholarship (1982), Lorne Scholarship (1982-83), John Moores minor prize; *b* 22 May, 1930. *Exhib:* one-man shows: Madrid (1956), Roland, Browse and Delbanco (1960, 1961, 1963, 1965, 1968), I.C.A. (1971), New Art Centre (1972), Hoya (1974), Nicola Jacobs (1981, 1983, 1984), Mappin A.G. (1985), Barbican Centre (1994). *Work in collections:* National Gallery, Melbourne, Australia, Seattle Museum, Arts Council, Coventry Museum, Leicester Museum, Chantrey Bequest, Bolton A.G., Bayer Pharm., Western Australia A.G., Museo de Bahia, Brazil, Power A.G., European Parliament, Ferens A.G., Tate Gallery, Graves A.G. Sheffield. *Address:* 7a Albert Pl., Victoria Rd., London W8 5PD.

WHISKERD, Jennifer, B.A. Hons. Fine Art Painting; travel illustrator, Central Asia, Armenia, Syria, Eastern Europe, Islamic Africa; *b* Gloucester, 23 Mar., 1962. *Exhib:* international and national. Work in public and private collections. Fine Art tutor. *Commissions:* Gulfoil, Terrapin International. *Signs work:* "J.H. Whiskerd." *Address:* 2 Pittville Lawn, Cheltenham, Glos. GL52 2BD.

WHITAKER, David Malcolm, A.R.W.S. (2001), R.A.S. Cert. (Dist.) (1962, 1966), Mark Rothko Memorial award (1972), Lorne Scholarship (1999-2000); painter in water-colour, acrylic, oil; *b* Blackpool, 1938. *m* Frankie. three *s. Studied:* R.A. Schools (1962-66, Peter Greenham, Charles Mahoney, Derrick Greaves, William Scott, Derek Hirst). *Exhib:* 26 solo shows including West Berlin, Amiens in France, Oakland, California, Rebecca Hossack Gallery. *Work in collections:* A.C.G.B., Leicester Educ. Authority, Camden Library, Guildford C.C., National Gallery of Ireland, Salford University, York City A.G., L'Université de Picardy, Amiens. *Clubs:* Chelsea Arts, London Group. *Address:* 125 Elm Rd., New Malden, Surrey KT3 3HP.

WHITAKER, Rita Elizabeth, R.M.S., M.A.S.-F.; H.S. professional artist specialising in stoving enamel on copper; *b* 3 Sept., 1936. married. two *s. Educ:* Sion Convent, Worthing. *Studied:* Regent St. Polytechnic under Stuart Tresilian. *Exhib:* Royal Miniature Soc., R.A., Medici's, Hilliard Soc., Assoc. of Sussex Artists,

Miniature Art Soc. of Florida and various galleries throughout England and Wales. *Work in collections:* Royal Exchange and Baltic Exchange, London, and Carningli Centre, Newport, Pembrokeshire; private collections throughout the world. Top awards, Llewellyn Alexander Gallery, London, and Florida Miniature Art Soc. in America. *Signs work:* "R. E. Whitaker." *Address:* Foxley, Marlpit Lane, Seaton, Devon EX12 2HH.

WHITCOMBE, Susan Anne Clare, painter in oil and water-colour of equestrian portraits and landscapes; *b* London, 17 June, 1957. two *s. Educ:* N. Foreland Lodge, Hants. *Studied:* Heatherley School of Fine Art (John Walton, Bernard Hailstone). *Exhib:* S.E.A.; one-man shows: London (1981, 1988, 1993), Tokyo (1985, 1987), Melbourne (1982). *Signs work:* "Susie Whitcombe." *Address:* Redwood Cottage, West Meon, Hants. GU32 1JU.

WHITE, David, Des.R.C.A. (1959); potter, producing individual porcelain pots for sale in most of the leading galleries throughout the country; Joint Winner of the Duke of Edinburgh's Prize for Elegant Design (1960); *b* Margate, Kent, 27 June, 1934. *m* (1962) Diana Groves. one *s.* one *d. Studied:* Thanet School of Art (1950-54) and Royal College of Art (1956-59). Accepted as Full mem. Craftsmen Potters' Assoc. (Apr. 1991). *Address:* 4 Callis Court Rd., Broadstairs, Kent CT10 3AE.

WHITE, Helen Elizabeth, A.R.M.S. (1999), H.S.D.A.D. (1986), H.S. (1996); calligrapher, illuminator and miniaturist in gouache and gold; *b* Amersham, 26 July, 1965. *Educ:* Chesham High School. *Studied:* Reigate School of Art and Design (1984-86). *Exhib:* annually since 1996: Llewellyn Alexander Gallery - A Million Brushstrokes, R.M.S. and H.S.; R.A. Summer Show (1997). *Signs work:* "H.W." sometimes "H.E.W." *Address:* 115 Vale Rd., Chesham, Bucks. HP5 3HP.

WHITE, James, LL.D. (N.U.I.); Chairman, Irish Arts Council (1978-84); Director, National Gallery of Ireland (1964-80), Curator, Municipal Gallery of Modern Art, Dublin (1960-64); lecturer, Dublin and National Universities; *b* Dublin, 16 June, 1913. *m* Agnes Bowe. three *s.* two *d. Educ:* Belvedere College, Dublin. *Publications:* The National Gallery of Ireland (Thames & Hudson); Irish Stained Glass (Gill & Co.); Jack B. Yeats (Martin Secker & Warburg); John Butler Yeats and the Irish Renaissance (Dolmen Press); Masterpieces of the National Gallery of Ireland (Jarrolds, Norwich); Pauline Bewick, Painting a Life (Wolfhound Press); Gerard Dillon, A Biography (Wolfhound Press). *Address:* 15 Herbert Pk., Dublin 4.

WHITE, John Norman, N.D.D. (1951); painter, illustrator, oil, gouache, and water-colour; *b* Chipperfield, Herts., 27 Mar., 1932. *m* Irene White, potter. two *s. Educ:* Belmont Senior Modern School. *Studied:* Harrow School of Art (1945-51). *Exhib:* R.A., Young Contemporaries. *Work in collections:* Municipal collection Borken Germany. *Signs work:* "JOHN - WHITE." *Address:* Northwood Lodge, Bullockstone Rd., Herne, Herne Bay, Kent CT6 7NR.

WHITE, Laura, B.A.(Hons.); sculptor in stone, wood and bronze; *b* Worcester, 10 Mar., 1968. *Educ:* Alice Ottley School, Worcester. *Studied:* Worcester Art College, Loughborough College of Art and Design. *Exhib:* various mixed and solo shows in U.K. *Work in collections:* Art Scene London, Gallery Shurini London. *Signs work:* "LAURA WHITE" or not at all. *Address:* Flat B, 4 Corporation Oaks,

Woodborough Rd., Nottingham NG3 4JY.

WHITE, Lucy Annette, painter in egg tempera, oil, with prelim. sketches in conté crayon; modernist, landscapes, people, nature, usually combined, including design styles of 1950s; *b* Perth, Australia, 29 Oct., 1960. *Educ:* Perth Technical College. *Studied:* self taught. *Signs work:* "LAW." *Address:* Room 11, Everton Court, Milford Rd., Everton, Hants. SO41 0JG. *Website:* www.cornwallhumanists.org.uk

WHITE, Mary, A.T.D. ceramic artist and calligrapher; Rheinland-Pfalz Staatspreis (1982); *b* Croesyceiliog, Wales, 1926 née Rollinson. *m* Charles White, artist. *Studied:* St. Julian's High School; Newport Art College; Hammersmith Art College; London University Goldsmiths' College of Art. *Exhib:* Europe, U.S.A. *Work in collections:* British Museums: V.&.A., Fitzwilliam Cambridge, Newport, Cardiff, Winchester, Bristol, Norwich Castle, Swindon; Collections: Bath Study Centre, Leicester Educ. Authority, Aberystwyth Univ., Welsh Arts Council; U.S.A.: Pennsylvania State Museum; Museums in Germany: Kunstgewerbemuseum Köln, Veste Coburg, Westerwald, Berlin, Keramion, Deidesheim, Stuttgart, Mainz, Darmstadt. Many private collections. *Publications:* work repro.: Ceramic Review, Letter Arts Review, German Keramik Magazines; work in many books in G.B., Germany, France, Belgium and U.S.A. *Clubs:* Fellow C.P.A., Fellow S.S.I, Deutscher Handwerkskammer, Fellow C.L.A.S., Letter Exchange. *Signs work:* see appendix. *Address:* Zimmerplatzweg 6, 55599 Wonsheim, Germany.

WHITE, Michael B., painter in oil, water-colour; also etcher, serigrapher, lithographer; unique monoprints, trichoprints, bronze, charcoal; *b* 2 Jul., 1954. *Educ:* Sevenoaks School, Kent. *Studied:* Hastings College of Art and Design (1972-1974), Ravensbourne College of Art and Design (1974-1976), Brighton Polytechnic (1979-1981). *Exhib:* various including, R.A. Summer Exhib., B.P. National Portrait Gallery, Internat. Contemporary Arts Fair, Bath Arts Festival, N.E.A.C., Not the Royal Academy, London Group, Hildt Gallery, Chicago, Printmakers Council, national open prize winner. *Work in collections:* Foundation Wood, Fontenay, France; Stena, Oslo, Norway; Hildt Corpn., Chicago. *Commissions:* Eyre Estate, J.&J. Auen, Cochrane Co. *Clubs:* Chelsea Arts. *Signs work:* "M B White"or "M B W." *Address:* 143 Old Church St., London SW3 6EB. *Email:* white@lhd.dircon.co.uk

WHITEFORD, Joan, N.D.D. (1963), A.T.D. (1964); artist in etching and wood engraving; *b* St. John, Cornwall, 5 May, 1942. *m* David Whiteford. *Educ:* Grammar School, Tavistock, Devon. *Studied:* Plymouth College of Art (1958-63, William Mann, Jeff. Clements), Bournemouth College of Art (1963-64). *Exhib:* R.A., R.E., N.S., S.W.A., N.E.A.C., R.I., Mall Print. *Signs work:* "J. Whiteford." *Address:* Meadowside, Cockwells, Penzance, Cornwall TR20 8DB.

WHITEFORD, Kate, Dip.A.D. (1973), Dip.F.A. (1976) History of Art; Sargant Fellow, British School at Rome (1993-94); artist in oil on gesso, also land drawings; *b* Glasgow, 9 Mar., 1952. *m* Alex Graham. *Educ:* Glasgow High School. *Studied:* Glasgow School of Art (1969-73), Glasgow University (1974-76, History of Art, Prof. Martin Kemp). *Exhib:* Institute of Contemporary Art (1983), Riverside Studios (1986), Whitechapel A.G. (1988), Glasgow Museum and A.G. (1990). *Work in collections:* Tate Gallery, British Council, C.A.S., A.C.G.B., National Gallery of

Modern Art Edinburgh, S.A.C., Glasgow Museum and A.G. *Publications:* artists books published by Whitechapel A.G. (1988), Tetra Press and Advanced Graphics (1992), Cairn Gallery (1992), Sitelines (1992), Graeme Murray Gallery (1992). *Signs work:* "Whiteford" or "Kate Whiteford." *Address:* c/o Frith St. Gallery, 60 Frith St., London W1V 5TA.

WHITELEY, Alfred, A.R.C.A. (1952); Arts Council major award (1977); painter in oil, water-colour, lithography; *b* Chesterfield, 18 Nov., 1928. *m* Ottoline Reynolds. one *s.* one *d. Educ:* Tapton House, Chesterfield. *Studied:* Chesterfield School of Art (1945-47), R.C.A. (1949-52). *Exhib:* R.A., Odette Gilbert Gallery; one-man shows Odette Gilbert, Vorpal Gallery, N.Y. and Pride Gallery, The Pieter Breughal Gallery, Amsterdam. *Work in collections:* U.K., U.S.A., Germany, Switzerland, The Netherlands. *Publications:* work repro.: The Times, Sunday Times, Art Line, etc. *Signs work:* "Alfred Whiteley." *Address:* Fairfield, Mogador Rd., Tadworth, Surrey KT20 7EW.

WHITE-OAKES, Sue, M.C.S.D.; metal sculptor in copper and bronze; *b* 26 May, 1939. *m* Roger Oakes. two *s. Educ:* St. Martin's High School, London. *Studied:* Central School of Art. *Exhib:* Edinburgh, Glasgow, St. Andrews, London, Scottish Borders, Aberdeenshire and Ireland. *Publications:* articles: Craftsman Magazine and The Scotsman colour supplement. *Clubs:* C.S.D. *Signs work:* "Sue White-Oakes." *Address:* Tarfhaugh Farmhouse, West Linton, Peeblesshire EH46 7BS.

WHITESIDE, (formerly Newton-Davies), Diana Elizabeth Hamilton, miniature painter in water-colour; *b* London, 13 Jan., 1942. *m* John Newton Davies (1964-87). two *d. Educ:* Lycée Français de Londres, Glendower School, Sydenham House, Devon. *Studied:* Simi's and L'Accademia delle Belle Arti, Florence (1959-60), Camberwell School of Art (1961-62). *Exhib:* R.A., R.M.S., R.H.S., Tate Gallery, Mall Galleries, Anna-Mei Chadwick's, Westminster Gallery, Medici Gallery. *Commissions:* animal portraits. *Signs work:* "19 D.E.N.D. 85" (or relevant year pre 1987); "19 D.E.H.W. 99" (or relevant year from 1987). *Address:* Chapel Lands, Chailey, nr. Lewes, Sussex BN8 4DD.

WHITFORD, Christopher, artist in water-colour and acrylic; *b* Malvern, Worcs., 18 Feb., 1952. *m* Filippa. two *d. Studied:* Malvern. *Exhib:* R.M.S., John Noott, Broadway. *Signs work:* "C. Whitford" or "C.W." *Address:* c/o John Noott Twentieth Century, 14 Cotswold Ct., Broadway, Worcs. WR12 7DP.

WHITFORD, Filippa, artist in water-colour; *b* Italy, 22 Jan., 1951. *m* Christopher Whitford. two *d. Exhib:* R.M.S, R.W.S., John Noott, Broadway. *Signs work:* "Filippa Whitford." *Address:* c/o John Noott Twentieth Century, 14 Cotswold Ct., Broadway, Worcs. WR12 7DP.

WHITTEN, B. Janice E., Dip.Bact. (1960), F.R.S.H. (1990); bacteriologist and freelance artist in oil; *b* Middx., 15 July, 1937. *m* Don Whitten, designer (decd.). two *d. Educ:* Torquay Girls' Grammar School, Greenford Grammar School. *Studied:* Regent St., Chelsea, Harrow School of Art. *Exhib:* R.I. Gallery, mixed exhbns., Devon County Show, Royal Bath and West, Thelma Hulbert Gallery. *Publications:* illustrated: Modern Cereal Chemistry; Countryside Commission: The East Devon Way; Science of Bread; catalogues, articles. *Signs work:* capital W supporting initials

- see appendix. *Address:* Whitthayne, 26 Ryalls Court, Seaton, E. Devon EX12 2HJ.

WHITTEN, Jonathan Philip, B.A. Hons. (1977), P.G.C.E. (1978); teacher and potter in ceramic; Head of Art, Sir James Smith's School, Camelford; *b* Eastbourne, 23 Sept., 1954. *m* Sally Bowler. two *s. Educ:* Eastbourne Grammar School. *Studied:* Eastbourne College of Art and Design (1972-73, Geoffrey Flint, A.R.C.A.), University of E. Anglia (1974-77, Prof. Andrew Martindale), University of London (1977-78, William Newland); apprentice potter to Michael Leach (1978-79) and Roger Cockram (1980-81). *Exhib:* Brewhouse Gallery, Taunton (1979), Devon Guild of Craftsmen (1981), Leics. Guild of Craftsmen (1983-87), Cornwall (1990-01), etc. *Address:* Hale Farmhouse, St. Kew, Bodmin, Cornwall PL30 3HE.

WHITTEN, Miranda M.A., B.Sc.(Hons.) (1994), Ph.D. (2001), M.R.S.H. (1994), F.R.S.A. (1998); biologist, artist/illustrator in acrylic, pencil, ink; nature artist commissioned by E. Devon District Council; Post-Doctoral research assistant (immunology); *b* London, 25 Sept., 1972. *Educ:* Colyton Grammar School; Aston University; Swansea University. *Exhib:* mixed shows: Christie's, Devon County Show, Bath and West, Thelma Hulbert Gallery. *Publications:* illustrated: Countryside Commission: The East Devon Way; Nature in East Devon; Elefriends Recipe Book; catalogues, posterwork. *Signs work:* "M. Whitten." *Address:* Whitthayne, 26 Ryalls Court, Seaton, E. Devon EX12 2HJ. *Email:* mwhitten@care4free.net

WHITTEN, Philip John, A.R.C.A. (1949), F.R.S.A. (1952); armiger painter in oil; teacher, London University Inst. of Educ. (1968); senior lecturer; examiner, Cambridge and London University Insts. of Educ. (retd.); *b* Leyton, Essex, 19 June, 1922. four *s.* one *d. Educ:* Bishopshalt, Hillingdon. *Studied:* Hornsey College of Art (1937-40), R.C.A. (1946-49). *Exhib:* R.B.A., Dowmunt Gallery, Bond St., Towner Gallery, Cecil Higgins; Bedford, Shoreditch Colleges, private galleries in Weybridge, Walton and Eastbourne areas. *Work in collections:* Towner Gallery, Brunel University. Work sold by Christie's and Sotheby's. *Signs work:* "Philip Whitten." *Address:* 10 Beechwood Cres., Eastbourne BN20 8AE.

WHITTEN-LOCKE, Helena M.J., freelance artist in pen and ink, water-colour; scientific proof reader; *b* London, 9 Oct., 1970. *m* Tony Locke. *Educ:* Colyton Grammar School. *Exhib:* mixed shows: Devon County Show, Royal Bath and West; exhbn. designer: The Business Shop Agency. *Commissions:* sign writing, various house and pub exteriors in pen and ink. *Publications:* illustrated: Countryside Commission: The East Devon Way; catalogues, articles, posterwork. *Signs work:* "H.W.," "H.L." or "H. LOCKE." *Address:* 'The Rosary', Godford Cross, Awliscombe, E. Devon EX14 0PP.

WHITTINGHAM, Dr. Selby, B.A. (1964), M.A. (1968), Ph.D. (1975); art historian; founded Turner Soc. 1975 (Hon. Sec. 1975-76, 1980-84; Vice Chairman 1984-85); and Watteau Soc. 1984 (Sec. General and Editor); and J.M.W. Turner, R.A. (Co-Editor), 1988; and Donor Watch, 1995; *b* Batu Gajah, Malaya, 8 Aug., 1941. *m* Joanna Dodds. *Educ:* Shrewsbury School; Universities of Oxford and Manchester. *Publications:* An Historical Account of the Will of J.M.W. Turner, R.A. (1989, 1996); The Fallacy of Mediocrity: The Need for a Proper Turner Gallery (1992); World Directory of Artists' Museums (1995). *Address:* Turner House, 153 Cromwell Rd., London SW5 0TQ.

WHITTLESEA, Michael, R.W.S. (1985), N.E.A.C.; painter; *b* London, 6 June, 1938. *m* Jill. *Studied:* Harrow School of Art. *Exhib:* prizewinner, Singer Friedlander/Sunday Times Water-colour Competition. *Publications:* The Complete Watercolour Course (1987). *Clubs:* Chelsea Arts. *Signs work:* "Michael Whittlesea." *Address:* Richmond Cottage, High St., Hurley, Berks. SL6 5LT.

WHITTON, Judi, B.Sc. (Hons.) Physics (1966), M.Sc., Radiobiology (1967); painter in water-colour, teacher and demonstrator in water-colour; President, Palette Club; *b* St. Helens, 24 Nov., 1944. *m* Peter. three *d. Exhib:* solo shows: Painswick Town Hall (1995-00), St. George's Church, Upper Cam (1994, 1998). Work hung in Carousel Gallery, Chipping Sodbury, and The Artisan Gallery, Nailsworth. Work in collections internationally. *Commissions:* Series of paintings of Olleworth Park (1999). *Publications:* Book of Paintings (1999); Limited Edn. prints for Radio Times. *Clubs:* Fosseway Artists, Thornbury Art, Cotswold Collection, Tetbury Art, Palette Club, Raw Umber Club. *Address:* Street Farm, Upper Cam, Dursley, Glos. GL11 5PG. *Website:* www.watercolour.co.uk *Email:* judi@watercolour.co.uk

WILD, David Paul, D.F.A. Slade (1955), Abbey Major Scholarship to Rome (1955); artist in oil and water-colour; Founder Chairman, Friends of the Weavers Triangle; *b* Burnley, 14 Apr., 1931. *Educ:* Burnley Grammar School. *Studied:* Burnley School of Art, Slade School of Fine Art. *Exhib:* extensively in the north of England since 1957; Woodstock Gallery (1965), John Moores (1965, 1970), R.A. (1972-74), Arts Council 'Drawings of People' Serpentine Gallery. *Work in collections:* Manchester City A.G., Rutherston Coll., Granada TV, Arts Council of G.B., Walker A.G., Liverpool. *Signs work:* "D. Wild." *Address:* 66 Rosehill Rd., Burnley BB11 2QX.

WILDE, Louis, N.D.D. (1955), A.T.C. (1956), D.A.E. (1970), M.A. (1980); painter in oil and acrylic; ex-Principal, Halifax School of Art; *b* London, 14 Mar., 1921. *m* Janet Wilde. one *s.* one *d. Educ:* The Millbank School, Westminster. *Studied:* Leeds College of Art (1951-55, Tom Watt, Gavin Stuart), Leeds University (1955-56 and 1969-70), B'ham Polytechnic (1977-78), privately under George Dafters. *Exhib:* Chiltern Gallery, London; New Art Centre, Chelsea; Seven Dials Gallery, London; Edinburgh Festival; Manchester Academy; Piece Hall Gallery, Halifax; Contemporary British Art touring U.S.A./Canada; Lane Gallery, Bradford; City A.G. Bradford. *Work in collections:* Bradford City Art Galleries, International Shakespeare Globe Centre. *Publications:* contributor to: Systems Art Enquiry Two (B'ham Polytechnic), Index of British Studies in Art Education (Allison). *Clubs:* S.G.F.A. *Signs work:* "Louis Wilde," "L.W.W.," "L. Wilde" or "Louis." *Address:* 60 Park Lane, Baildon, Shipley, W. Yorks. BD17 7LQ.

WILES, Gillian, A.R.B.S., I.B.H.S.; sculptor/painter/illustrator; *m* Dr. Robin Catchpole. *Educ:* Royal Veterinary College, London. *Studied:* Cape Town University, and Heatherley, London. *Exhib:* one-man shows: Sladmore, London, John Pence, San Francisco, The Collector, Johannesburg; exhib. at Tryon, London, R.B.S., Denis Hotz, London, Sportsmen's Edge, N.Y., Collector's Covey, Dallas. *Work in collections:* bronze sculptures: Genesee Museum, N.Y.S., Toyota, Nikon, many international private collections. *Commissions:* many, international. *Publications:* work repro.: art gallery catalogues. *Signs work:* "Gill Wiles." *Address:*

c/o R.B.S., 108 Old Brompton Rd., London SW7 3RA.

WILKINS, William Powell, A.R.C.A.; artist in oil, lecturer and consultant; *b* Kersey, Suffolk, 4 Apr., 1938. *m* Lynne Brantly. two *d. Educ:* Malvern College. *Studied:* Swansea and Royal College of Art. *Exhib:* London, New York, San Francisco, Swansea. *Work in collections:* National Museum of Wales, Glynn Vivian Museum Swansea, Hirshorn Museum Washington D.C. *Address:* c/o Piccadilly Gallery, 16a Cork St., London W1X 1PF.

WILKINSON, John Charles, R.B.A.; artist in oil, water-colour, pen and ink, pencil; *b* Barnes, London, 20 July, 1929. *m* Sarah Goodwin, artist. one *s.* one *d. Educ:* Bradfield College; University College, London. *Studied:* R.A. Schools (1954-59). *Exhib:* two one-man shows, numerous mixed exhbns. *Signs work:* "J.C.W." and on back of work signs full name. *Address:* Orchard House, Alderholt Rd., Sandleheath, Fordingbridge, Hampshire SP6 1PT.

WILKINSON, Ronald Scotthorn, M.A., B.M., B.Ch. (Oxon.); physician, playwright, novelist, artist in oil, water-colour; *b* Melton Mowbray. two *d. Educ:* Shrewsbury School, Merton College, Oxford. *Studied:* under H. B. Hewlett. *Exhib:* Public Schools Exhbn., Leicester Soc. of Artists' Exhbn., R.A. Summer Exhbn. (1977); one-man show, Fine Art Trade Guild (1986). *Address:* 50 Hanover Steps, St. George's Fields, Albion St., London W2 2YG.

WILKINSON-CLEMENTSON, William Henry, R.E., A.R.C.A., F.I.A.L. (1946), Ph.D. (1980); line engraver and painter; Head of Dept. Engraving, City and Guilds of London Art School; *b* Bath, 1921. *m* Lady Margaret Ewer. one *d. Educ:* Winchester. *Studied:* Royal College of Art under Malcolm Osborne and Robert Austin, Heidelberg and Lindau, Germany, Fiorenza, Italy. *Exhib:* R.A., and 5 countries. *Work in collections:* Holland, Switzerland, Italy and America. *Clubs:* Chelsea Arts, Aviemore, Scotland, Swiss Alpine. *Signs work:* "HENRY WILKINSON." *Address:* Crane Cottage, Tatsfield, Westerham, Kent TN16 2JT.

WILLIAMS, Alex, N.D.D., A.T.D.; artist in oil on canvas; *b* Reading, 1942. *m* Celia. one *s.* two *d. Educ:* St. Peter's School, Cambs. *Studied:* St. Martin's School of Art (1962-66, Frdk. Gore, Peter Blake, Peter de Francia, David Tindle). *Exhib:* Helen Greenberg Gallery, Los Angeles (1977, 1982), Retrospective Hereford City Museum (1987), Fosse Gallery Stow on the Wold, The Kilvert Gallery, Clyro. *Work in collections:* National Library of Wales, National Trust, Hurst Newspapers, Hereford and Worcester City Museums; public and private collections in U.S.A. *Commissions:* has designed (restaurants) and painted many portraits of country houses. *Publications:* illustrated The Bird who Couldn't Fly (Hodder & Stoughton, 1988). Extensive collection of prints, greetings cards published and over 100 fine bone china designs distributed worldwide. *Signs work:* "Alex Williams '98." *Address:* Cliff House, Broadoak, Newnham on Severn, Glos. GL14 1JA. *Website:* www.alexwilliams.net *Email:* alexwilliams@beeb.net

WILLIAMS, Angela Elizabeth, S.G.F.A.; artist in drawing, water-colour, oil; college tutor; *b* Belfast, 15 Jul., 1948. *m* John Shelley (partner). *Studied:* Wimbledon School of Art. *Exhib:* London and U.K. including R.A. Summer Exhib., S.B.A., S.G.F.A., N.E.A.C. Drawing Scholar (2000). *Work in collections:* U.K. and abroad.

Publications: magazine articles, greetings cards, limited edition prints. *Signs work:* "A E Williams." *Address:* 16 Warren Park, Warlingham, Surrey CR6 9LD.

WILLIAMS, Charles, B.A. (Hons.) (1989), M.A. (R.A.S.) (1992); oil painter; *b* Evanston, Ill., U.S.A. *m* Alice Smith, artist. *Studied:* Maidstone College of Art (1986-89, Mike Upton, Peter Morrell, John Titchell), R.A. Schools (1989-92, Norman Adams, Mick Rooney, Roderic Barrett, David Parfitt). *Exhib:* Star Gallery Lewes, Coombs Contemporary, C.A.S., Mercury Gallery, N.E.A.C., R.A., R.O.S.L., N.P.G., Beaux Arts, Bath. *Work in collections:* T.V.S., Chevron (U.K.), K.I.A.D., British High Commission in Nairobi, Lily Savage, British Design Council, Alan Howarth M.P. *Publications:* Art Review (Sept., 1999). *Clubs:* Reynold's, N.E.A.C., Stuckists. *Signs work:* "C.W." or "VERSO." *Address:* 9 Swale View, Hernhill, Faversham, Kent ME13 9JS.

WILLIAMS, Emrys, B.A. Fine Art (1980); painter in acrylic and oil; Lecturer in art and design, Coleg Menai, Bangor; *b* Liverpool, 18 Jan., 1958. partner: Nathalie Camus. one *s. Studied:* Slade School of Fine Art (1976-80). *Exhib:* Benjamin Rhodes Gallery (1989, 1991, 1994), touring shows: 'Sunny Spells' Oriel Mostyn, Llandudno (1995), 'Various Fictions' Collins Gallery, Glasgow (1998). *Work in collections:* Metropolitan Museum of Art, N.Y., Arts Council of England, Government Art Collection. *Commissions:* National Museum of Wales. *Address:* 47 Cecil St., Cardiff CF2 1NW.

WILLIAMS, Glynn, sculptor in stone and bronze; Prof. of Sculpture, R.C.A., head of the School of Fine Art; *b* Shrewsbury, 1939. *m* Heather (divorced). two *d. Studied:* Wolverhampton College of Art (1955-60, 1960-61 Post Dip.); Rome Scholarship in Sculpture (1961-63). *Exhib:* one-man shows: including Blond Fine A.G. (1982), Bernard Jacobson Gallery (1985, 1986, 1988, 1991, 1994, 2000), Artsite Gallery, Bath (1987), Retrospective exhbn. at Margam Park, S. Wales (1992), Atkinson Gallery, Millfield (1997). *Work in collections:* A.C.G.B., Hakone Open Air Museum, Japan, V. & A., Tate Gallery, N.P.G. *Commissions:* Henry Purcell Memorial, City of Westminster (1996), "Gateways of Hands", Chelsea Harbour, memorial to Lloyd George to stand in Parliament Square commencing 2002. *Clubs:* Chelsea Arts. *Signs work:* "G.W." *Address:* c/o Bernard Jacobson Gallery, 14a Clifford St., London W1X 1RF.

WILLIAMS, Jacqueline E. E., B.A. (Hons.) (1985), Advanced Dip. (R.A.) (1988); artist in oil; *b* Lincoln, 2 Nov., 1962. *Educ:* Downlands School, Hassocks. *Studied:* Glos. College of Arts and Technology (1982-85), R.A. Schools (1985-88). *Exhib:* New Grafton Gallery, Barnes; solo show: Brian Sinfield Gallery; mixed shows: N.E.A.C., R.W.A., R.A. *Work in collections:* Cheltenham and Gloucester Bldg. Soc. H.Q., Contemporary Arts Soc. for Wales. *Clubs:* N.E.A.C., C.G.A. *Signs work:* "J.W." *Address:* Garden Flat, 73 Bath Rd., Cheltenham, Glos. GL53 7LH.

WILLIAMS, Joan Barbara Price, A.R.C.A., R.E., R.W.S.; printmaker and painter; *b* Pontypridd, S. Wales. *Educ:* High Wycombe High School. *Studied:* High Wycombe School of Art, Royal College of Art. *Exhib:* R.A., Bankside Gallery, International Biennales of Graphic Art, Ljubljana, Frechen, Germany, Biella, Italy. *Work in collections:* Arts Council, Welsh Arts Council, Sheffield, Oldham, Newcastle, Norwich, Glasgow and Hull Art Galleries and many private and public collections. *Clubs:* R.W.S., R.E. *Signs work:* "Joan Williams." *Address:* 1 Upper Mill, Wateringbury, Maidstone, Kent ME18 5PD.

WILLIAMS, Sir Kyffin, O.B.E. (1982), A.R.A. (1970), R.A. (1974), Hon.M.A. (Wales), D.L., Hon. D.Litt. Univ. of Wales (1993); artist in oil and water-colour, printing; Winston Churchill Fellow (1968); Hon. Fellow, Univ. College of Bangor, Swansea and Aberystwyth; Cymmrodorion Medal (1991); Knight Bachelor (1999); *b* Llangefni, Anglesey, 1918. *Educ:* Shrewsbury School. *Studied:* Slade School of Fine Art (1941-44). *Exhib:* Colnaghi (1947, 1949, 1970), Leicester Galleries (1951, 1954, 1957, 1967, 1970), Thackeray Gallery (1977, 1979, 1981, 1983, 1985, 1987, 1989, 1991, 1993) and in the provinces; retrospective exhbn. National Museum of Wales (1987). *Work in collections:* National Museum of Wales, Arts Council, Chantrey Bequest. *Publications:* autobiography, Across the Straits (Duckworth, 1973), A Wider Sky (Gwasg Gomer, 1991); illustrated, Gregynog, Kate Roberts (1981), Portraits (Gwasg Gomer, 1996), The Land and the Sea (Gomer, 1998), Drawings (Gomer, 1999). *Signs work:* "K.W." *Address:* Pwllfanogl. Llanfairpwll, Anglesey LL61 6PD.

WILLIAMS, Mary, R.W.A., S.W.A.; painter of landscape, marine and architectural subjects, also of flowers in water-colour and oil; *b* Ottery St. Mary, Devon. *Studied:* Exeter. *Exhib:* R.A., R.S.A., Paris Salon, R.I., R.B.A., etc., and in many municipal galleries; one-man show: R.A.M. Museum, Exeter (1974). *Work in collections:* Exeter Art Gallery, Sunderland Art Gallery, R.W.A. Bristol. *Signs work:* "Mary Williams." *Address:* Dormers, Orchard Close, Manor Rd., Sidmouth, Devon EX10 8RS.

WILLIAMS, Nicholas Charles, figurative painter in oil on canvas; *b* U.K., 1961. *Studied:* Richmond College (1977-79). *Exhib:* Brian Sewell's A Critic's Choice, Cooling Gallery, London; The Spectator Awards, Christie's, London; Hunting/Observer Awards, Mall Galleries, London; Bayer art prize, London; Garrick Milne Exhibition, London; winner of the Hunting art prize (2001). *Publications:* work repro.: cover of Steven Berkoff's Collected Plays, volume one. *Signs work:* "Nicholas Charles Williams." *Address:* Old Lifeboat Station, Towan Headland, Newquay, Cornwall TR7 1HS.

WILLIAMS, Susan, R.A. Schools Dip.; artist in oil and water-colour; *b* Lichfield, Staffs., 23 July, 1944. *m* Ben Levene. one *s. Educ:* Lichfield Central School. *Studied:* Stafford Art School, Byam Shaw School, R.A. Schools. *Exhib:* regularly at R.A. Summer Exhbn., Spirit of London (prizewinner), Ogle Gallery, Cheltenham, Hintlesham Hall Pictures, Ipswich, The Gallery Southwark Park, Bermondsey, Duncan Campbell Gallery, Waterman Gallery, London. Work in private collections. *Signs work:* "S.W." *Address:* 26 Netherby Rd., London SE23 3AN.

WILLIAMS-ELLIS, Bronwyn Mary, B.A. (1973), M.A. (1983), R.C.A. (2001); drawing and colour in 2D ceramics, including tiles; also on paper; ceramicist; *b* 20 Jan., 1953. *m* Louis Hodgkin (partner). *Studied:* Cardiff College of Art, under Frank Vining (1971-1973), S.G.I.H.E., Cardiff (1982-1983). *Exhib:* regularly, including, 1000 Years of Tiles (1991-1993), Ceramic Series, Aberwsytwyth Arts Centre (1991), Tremayne Applied Arts, St. Ives, Oriel Plas Gly-y-Weddw, Royal Cambrian

Academy (2001). *Work in collections:* Aberwsytwyth Arts Centre, private collections. *Publications:* work appears in Decorating With Tiles, Elizabeth Hilliard; Ceramics and Print, Paul Scott; Practical Solutions for Potters, Gill Bliss. *Signs work:* "B W Ellis", or "B W E." *Address:* Penclogwyn, Pentrefelin, Criccieth, Gwynedd LL52 0PU. *Second Address:* Old Orchard, 88a Walcot St., Bath, Avon BA1 5BD.

WILLIAMS-ELLIS, David Hugo Martyn, R.C.A. (1993), A.R.B.S. (1992); sculptor in clay for bronze and terracotta; *b* Ireland, 6 Apr., 1959. *m* Serena Stapleton. two *s*. two *d*. (one decd.). *Educ:* Headfort School, Ireland; Stowe School. *Studied:* in Florence (1977-78, Signorina Nerina Simi), Carrara (1979-80), Sir John Cass (1981-83). *Exhib:* London, Belfast, Paris, U.S.A., Japan, Argentina, South Africa. Many portrait busts and figures in private and public collections. *Clubs:* Arts, Lansdowne. *Signs work:* "D.W.E." dated with signet ring eagle on larger pieces. *Address:* 4 Walham Yard, London SW6 1JA.

WILLIES, Joan, R.M.S. (1976) (Eng.), M.A.A. (1995) (U.S.A.), H.S. (Eng.), Mem. Florida (Hon. mem.), Washington and Georgia Miniature Art Socs., U.S.A.; painter in oils, alkyds and water-colours, specialising in miniatures; *b* Bristol, England, 23 Dec., 1929. *m* Mark Willies. three *s*. *Educ:* Bristol Commercial College, art studies under private tutors. *Exhib:* R.M.S., R.I., S.W.A., U.A., H.S. (Eng.), U.S.A., Australia, Spain, Germany, Canada, Japan, Tiffanys, U.S.A.; permanent exhbn. Bilmar Hotel, Treasure Island, Florida. *Publications:* The Artist's Workbook 1 and 2; illustrated children's books, St. Francis of Assisi (worldwide prints) I.G.M.A. prints Ohio. Writer of articles, artist magazines; author, 'Miniature Painting techniques and applications' (pub. Watson & Guptil, N.Y. June 1995; English distributors Phaidon Press, London). Awards: numerous U.K. and U.S.A. Teacher: Workshops internationally and private groups at Joan Cornish Willies Studio, 1726 St. Croix Drive, Clearwater, Florida 34619. *Signs work:* "Joan Willies," or "Joan Cornish Willies, R.M.S., M.A.A., H.S." and see appendix. *Address:* P.O. Box 7659, Clearwater, Florida 34619, U.S.A.

WILLIS, Lucy, R.W.A. (1993); painter and printmaker in water-colour, oil, etching; *b* 15 Dec., 1954. *m* Anthony Anderson. one *s*. one *d*. *Educ:* Badminton School, Bristol. *Studied:* Ruskin School of Drawing and Fine Art, Oxford (1972-75). *Exhib:* eight solo shows at Chris Beetles, London since 1986; R.A., R.W.A., N.P.G., B.P. Portrait award (1st prize 1992), Mall Galleries, R.W.S., R.E., Curwen Gallery; London: solo shows (2000, 2001). *Work in collections:* N.P.G., R.W.A. *Commissions:* 'Year of the Artist' murals in Portland Prison (2000). *Publications:* 'Light, How to See it, How to Paint it'; 'Excursions in the Real World' by William Trevor (illustrations); Light in Water-colour (1997). *Signs work:* "Lucy Willis." *Address:* Moorland House, Burrowbridge, Bridgwater, Som. TA7 0RG.

WILLIS, Victor, M.A. Fine Art (1985); artist in oil; *b* London, 2 Aug., 1934. *m* Mary. two *d*. *Educ:* Dulwich College. *Studied:* Camberwell College of Art (1974), City & Guilds (1978), Goldsmiths' College (1985). *Work in collections:* London and abroad. *Commissions:* Swan Hellenic, British Rail, Anna Bornholt Assoc. *Publications:* articles illustrated: 'The Thames at Night', 'Light on Landscape'. *Clubs:* Chelsea Arts. *Signs work:* "Victor Willis." *Address:* Studio: Unit 8,

Shakespeare Business Centre, 245 Coldharbour Lane, London SW9 8RR.

WILLS, Joan, P.V.P.S.W.A., U.A., A.S.A.F., F.R.S.A.; mention hon. (Paris Salon); oil painter; past Vice-Pres., Soc. of Women Artists, Ass. Société des Artistes Français; Council Mem. United Soc. of Artists; *b* Shrewsbury. *m* Major-Gen. J. A. R. Robertson, C.B., C.B.E., D.S.O., D.L. one *d. Educ:* Albyn School, Aberdeen. *Studied:* Sir John Cass College, City and Guilds, London, and privately with the late Kenneth Green and the late Stanley Grimm. *Exhib:* R.O.I., R.B.A., S.W.A., U.A., R.M.S., N.S., Artists of Chelsea, Paris Salon. *Signs work:* "Wills." *Address:* 36 Marlborough Pl., London NW8 0PD.

WILLS, Richard Allin, N.D.D., A.U.A.; painter in oil and water-colour, etc.; art tutor; visiting lecturer; *b* Monmouth, 11 Sept., 1939. *m* Vera Elizabeth. one *s.* two *d. Educ:* King Henry VIII Grammar, Abergavenny. *Studied:* Newport College of Art (1956-61, Thomas Rathmell). *Exhib:* R.A., R.W.A., Welsh Young Contemporaries, R.S.P.P., U.A., W.C.S.W., P.S., R.W.S., R.I. *Work in collections:* British Steel Corp., Welsh Div. British Steel, Rank Xerox. *Commissions:* Welsh Office, Whitehall; Guildhall School of Music, London; Polytechnic of Wales; Yamazaki Mazak Europe; Royal Monmouthshire Royal Engineers; Royal Regiment of Wales Contemporary Art Society. *Publications:* Colllins: Complete Drawing Course, Watercolour Workshop; Headline: Encyclopedia of W/C Techniques. *Signs work:* "Richard A. Wills." *Address:* The Studio, Mansard House, Vine Acre, Monmouth, Gwent NP25 3HW.

WILSON, Arnold, M.A., F.S.A., F.M.A.; former Chairman of Trustees, Holburne of Menstrie Museum, Bath, and serves on numerous other Coms.; formerly Director, City Art Gallery, Bristol; *b* Dulwich, 1932. twice married. two *d.* by first marriage. *Educ:* Selwyn College, Cambridge, and Courtauld Inst. of Art. *Publications:* author: Dictionary of British Marine Painters (3 eds.); Dictionary of British Military Painters; Exploring Museums: South West England; numerous articles for Burlington Magazine, Apollo, Connoisseur, Country Life, etc. *Clubs:* Bristol Savages. *Address:* 4 George St., Bathwick Hill, Bath BA2 6BW.

WILSON, Arthur, artist in mixed media; ex-Vice President, London Group; *b* London, 31 Dec., 1927. *m* Ivy. three *s.* two *d. Studied:* Chelsea School of Art. *Exhib:* solo and mixed shows. Work in public and private collections. *Signs work:* "ARTHUR WILSON." *Address:* 22 Wingate Rd., Hammersmith, London W6 0UR.

WILSON, Chris, B.A.(Hons.) (1982), M.A. (1985); artist in oil and collage; *b* Belfast, 27 Dec., 1959. *m* Cindy Friers. one *s. Educ:* Belfast Royal Academy. *Studied:* Brighton College of Art (1979-82), University of Ulster (1984-85). *Exhib:* 'Shocks to the System' A.C.G.B. (1991), 'On the Balcony of the Nation' touring U.S.A. (1991-92), 'Shadows of Light' one-man touring Romania (1992), Bulgaria (1993). *Work in collections:* A.C.G.B., Arts Council of Ireland, Aer Rianta Dublin, Queens University Belfast; private collections in Ireland, England, Germany, U.S.A. *Signs work:* "CHRIS WILSON" or "C. WILSON" with date. *Address:* 44 Victoria Rd., Bangor, Co. Down BT20 5EX.

WILSON, David, M.F.P.S. (1976); painter in oil, acrylic, water-colour, gouache, etching, linocut; *b* Gillingham, Kent, 23 May, 1936. *m* Sheila. two *s.* two *d. Educ:*

Sir Joseph Williamson's Mathematical School, Rochester; Joint Services School of Linguists. *Studied:* Heatherley's (Evening classes 1976-77, Terry Shave). *Exhib:* R.A., R.B.A., Royal National Eisteddfod, N.E.A.C., S.G.A., R.Cam.A., F.P.S., and elsewhere in U.K., France and Ireland. *Work in collections:* National Library of Wales, Aberystwyth. *Signs work:* "David Wilson Bridell." *Address:* Treleddyn Isaf, Bridell, Cardigan SA43 3DQ. *Second Address:* The Studio, 3 Cambrian Quay, Cardigan SA43 1EZ.

WILSON, Douglas, R.C.A., D.F.A., F.R.S.A.; painter in oil and water-colour; *b* 1936. *m* Heather Hildersley Brown. one *s*. *Studied:* Oxford University (1959-62, Percy Horton, Richard Naish, Geoffrey Rhodes). *Exhib:* R.A., R.B.A., R.O.I., R.Cam.A., Vis Art I (prizewinner), Edinburgh Festival, National Library of Wales, New Grafton Gallery, Piccadilly Gallery, Thackeray Gallery, Jablonski Gallery, Waterman Fine Art, St. James's, London; one-man shows: Bluecoat Gallery, Williamson A.G. (1981, 1983), King St. Galleries, St. James's (1983, 1986, 1991), Metropolis International Galerie d'Art Geneva (1985), Phoenix Gallery, Lavenham (1987, 1989), Phoenix Gallery, Kingston upon Thames (1987), Anthony Dawson Artists at the Barbican (1987, 1990), Outwood Gallery (1987), Newburgh St. Gallery (1988), Highgate Fine Art, London (2001). *Work in collections:* Lord Wandsworth College, Williamson A.G. *Publications:* author, Wirral Visions. *Signs work:* "Douglas Wilson." *Address:* 123 Masons Pl., Newport, Salop. TF10 7JX.

WILSON, Eleanor Mavis: see GRÜNEWALD, Eleanor Mavis.

WILSON, Helen, B.A. (F.A.) 1995 (Uni.S.A.); painter in oils; administrator at Somerset Art Week Ltd.; *b* Surrey, 1 Sept., 1948. *m* Mua Wilson. two *s*. *Studied:* City and Guilds of London Art School (1987-88), University of South Africa (1990-95). *Exhib:* solo show at National Art Gallery of Namibia (1996), S.B.A. (1997), Brewhouse Theatre and Arts Centre, Taunton (1999). *Work in collections:* Telecoms Namibia. *Publications:* article in "De Arte" (1994). *Clubs:* Greenpeace. *Signs work:* "HW" joined. *Address:* Orchard Cottage, Hare Lane, Buckland St Mary, Chard, Somerset TA20 3JS. *Email:* helen@orchardstudio.freeserve.co.uk

WILSON, Helen Frances, D.A. (1975), R.G.I. (1984), R.S.W. (1998); artist in oil, water-colour, mixed media; *b* Paisley, Scotland, 25 July, 1954. one *d*. *Educ:* John Neilson High School, Paisley. *Studied:* Glasgow School of Art (1971-76); Hospitalfield (1973). *Exhib:* R.G.I., R.S.A., R.S.W., etc. and various galleries in Britain and U.S.A. *Work in collections:* Glasgow A.G., Kelvingrove; Scottish Arts Council; Royal College of Physicians, Edinburgh; Paisley A.G. *Commissions:* portraits: Royal College of Ophthalmologists, Royal College of Physicians, etc. also private commissions. *Address:* 1 Partickhill Rd., Glasgow G11 5BL.

WILSON, Lorna Yvette, B.A. Hons. (1989), Dip.F.A.- R.A. Schools (1992); artist in oil and gouache; *b* Jamaica, 6 July, 1967. *Studied:* Kingston University (1986-89, Derek Hirst), R.A. Schools (1989-92, Prof. Norman Adams, R.A.). *Exhib:* many mixed exhbns. in London. Currently doing series of prints for C.C.A. Galleries. *Address:* 8 Petherick House, 79 Stanley Rd., Hounslow, Middx. TW3 1YU.

WILSON, Peter Reid, D.A.; artist in oil paint on canvas; *b* Glasgow, 4 Sept., 1940. one *s*. one *d*. *Studied:* Glasgow School of Art (1960-64). *Work in collections:*

Contemporary Arts Soc., A.C.G.B., S.A.C., Sheffield City A.G., Ferens A.G. Hull, Nottingham Castle Museum and A.G., Leicester Museum and A.G., Glasgow A.G., Kelvingrove, Stoke-on-Trent Museum and A.G., Kettles Yard, Cambridge, Museum of Modern Art, Glasgow, Loyola Marymount University, Los Angeles. *Publications:* Peter Wilson - Paintings 1979-1985 (Third Eye, Glasgow, 1985), Dacapo - Drawings (Arc Publications, 1989). *Clubs:* Chelsea Arts. *Signs work:* c within a circle "Peter Wilson" and date. *Address:* 1 The Square, South Luffenham, Oakham, Rutland LE15 8NS.

WILSON, Susan Ahipara, B.F.A., Dip.R.A. Schools; artist in oil on canvas; *b* Dunedin, N.Z. *m* E.W. Gretton. *Studied:* Camberwell School of Art (1978-82), R.A. Schools (1982-85). *Work in collections:* National Trust, H.R.H. The Prince of Wales, Usher Gallery, Rochdale A.G., Auckland Museum, Contemporary Art Soc., etc. *Commissions:* portrait of Baroness Helena Kennedy Q.C. for Oxford Brookes Univ. *Publications:* illustrated: Katherine Mansfield's Short Stories (Folio Soc., 2000), Balancing Acts (Virago), Gillett: The Mind and Its Discontents (O.U.P., 1999), Catalogues to Touring Shows (co-curator), Reclaiming the Madonna (1993) and In the Looking Glass (1997 - Usher Gallery Publications). *Address:* 16 Balliol Rd., London W10 6LX.

WILSON, Timothy Hugh, M.A., M.Phil., F.S.A. (1989), Hon.R.E. (1991), Fellow of Balliol (1990); Keeper of Western Art, Ashmolean Museum, Oxford (since 1990); *b* Godalming, 8 Apr., 1950. *m* Jane Lott. two *s.* one *d. Educ:* Winchester College; Mercersburg Academy, U.S.A.; Corpus Christi College, Oxford; Warburg Inst. (London University); Dept. of Museum Studies (University of Leicester). *Publications:* books and articles chiefly on Italian maiolica and Renaissance applied arts. *Address:* Balliol College, Oxford OX1 3BJ.

WILSON, Vincent John, A.T.D., Mem. Penwith Soc. of Arts, Devon Guild of Craftsmen (prints); painter and etcher; *b* Mold, Flintshire, 24 Nov., 1933. *m* Sheila Richards. one *d. Educ:* Alun Grammar School, Mold. *Studied:* Chester School of Art (1950-54), Liverpool College of Art (1954-55). *Exhib:* R.A., R.W.A., R.C.A., Piccadilly, Thackeray, Gagliardi, Penwith Galleries, Celle, W. Germany, Welsh Arts Council (1958, 1974, 1981), Cornwall Now (Sussex 1986), Cornwall in the Eighties (Chichester 1987); one-man shows: Exeter University (1966), Newlyn (1971, 1972, 1980), Plymouth (1979), Taunton (1981), Guernsey (1990), St. Ives (1992), St. Ives Artists (Dublin, 1998). *Work in collections:* Plymouth A.G., Devon C.C., Surrey Educ. Com., Royal Cambrian Academy, Celle, British Foreign and Commonwealth Office (etchings). *Signs work:* "V. Wilson." *Address:* 3 Drakefield Drive, Saltash, Cornwall PL12 6BU.

WILTON, Andrew, M.A., F.R.S.A., Hon.R.W.S.; museum curator; Keeper of British Art, Tate Gallery (1989-); Curator, Turner Collection, Clore Gallery (1985-89), Curator of Prints and Drawings, Yale Center for British Art (1976-80), Asst. Keeper, Dept. of Prints and Drawings, British Museum (1967-76, 1981-84); *b* Farnham, Surrey, 7 Feb., 1942. *Educ:* Dulwich College; Trinity College, Cambridge. *Publications:* British Watercolours 1750-1850 (1977); The Life and Work of J.M.W. Turner (1979); Turner and the Sublime (1980); Turner in his Time (1987) and numerous exhbn. catalogues, articles and reviews. *Clubs:* Athenaeum. *Address:* Tate

Gallery, London SW1P 4RG.

WINDSOR, Alan, B.A. (Lond.), Dip.F.A. (Lond.), N.D.D., D.A.(Manc.); artist and writer; art historian; Senior Lecturer, Reading University; *b* Fleetwood, Lancs., 10 July, 1931. *m* Elfriede Windsor. one *s.* two *d. Educ:* Audenshaw Grammar School. *Studied:* Regional College of Art, Manchester (1949-54); Slade School, University College (1954-56); Universities of Paris and Aix (1956-57); Courtauld Institute, London University (1967-69). *Exhib:* Young Contemporaries, London Group, Gimpel Fils, Roland, Browse & Delbanco, Pollock, Toronto, New Ashgate, Farnham. *Publications:* Peter Behrens, 1868-1940, Architect and Designer (Architectural Press, 1981); Handbook of Modern British Painting, 1900-1980 (Scolar Press, 1992). *Clubs:* Architectural Association. *Signs work:* "A. Windsor." *Address:* 2 Wykeham Rd., Farnham, Surrey GU9 7JR.

WINER, Zalmon, R.B.A. (1984); painter in oil, pastel, acrylic, water-colour; designer, etcher and lithographer; *b* Gateshead, Co. Durham, 21 Nov., 1934. married. one *s.* two *d. Educ:* Gateshead Grammar School. *Studied:* art and architecture at Durham University; etching at Central School of Art and Design. *Exhib:* R.A., R.B.A., P.S., U.A., N.S., Ben Uri Gallery, C.P.S., Safrai Gallery, Jerusalem, Discerning Eye Exhbn. at Mall Galleries (1990), etc. *Work in collections:* Shipley A.G., Oundle Public School Gallery. *Publications:* illustrated Haggadah for the Exilarchs Foundation. *Signs work:* see appendix. *Address:* 53 Shirehall Park, London NW4 2QN.

WINKELMAN, Joseph William, B.A. (1964), C.F.A. (1971), R.E. (1982), R.W.A. (1989), Hon. R.W.S. (1996); artist and printmaker; Past President, Royal Soc. of Painter-Printmakers; *b* Keokuk, Iowa, U.S.A., 20 Sept., 1941. *m* Harriet Lowell Belin. two *d. Educ:* University of the South, University of Pennsylvania. *Studied:* University of Oxford, Ruskin School of Drawing (1968-71). *Exhib:* New Grafton Gallery, R.A., Bohun Gallery, Lumley Cazalet Gallery, Graffiti Gallery, Anthony Dawson, Oxford Gallery, M.O.M.A. Oxford, Matsuya Ginza, Tokyo, Space Gallery, Seoul, Connecticut Graphic Arts Centre, Taller Galeria Fort, Barcelona. *Work in collections:* Ashmolean Museum, Hereford Museum, Usher Gallery, Victoria A.G., Graves A.G., Bowes Museum, The Museum of London, The Royal Collection, Fitzwilliam Museum, National Museum of Wales, Science Museum London. *Commissions:* Balliol College, Oxford, St. Anthony's College, Oxford. Prizes: International Print Shows: Spain '82, Korea '82, New York '98, Connecticut 2001. *Signs work:* "J. W. Winkelman." *Address:* The Hermitage, 69 Old High St., Headington, Oxford OX3 9HT. *Email:* winkelman@ukgateway.net

WINSTANLEY, Roy, Cert. Ed. (Hons.) 1961, B.A. (Hons.) 1973, Dip. (1986); painter in water-colour, acrylic, oil, mixed media; *b* Wakefield, 31 Mar., 1940. *m* Jean. two *s. Studied:* Westminster College, Oxford (1959-61), University of Leek (1970-73), Goldsmiths' College (1986). *Exhib:* R.I., R.W.S., John Laing Landscape, Images of Dorset, Poole, Honiton Festival, Thomas Hardy Conference Dorchester, Twin Tracks Bridport, Modern British Painting Exeter, Battersea Contemporary Art Fair. *Work in collections:* Sheffield City A.G. *Commissions:* series of paintings: Capital Interiors, London for a Royal Villa in Rabat, Morocco (1998); water-colours: The Constable Wing of Colchester General Hospital (1998). *Signs work:*

"Winstanley." *Address:* Fig Tree Cottage, Preston, Weymouth, Dorset DT3 6DD.

WINTER, Faith, F.R.B.S., Feodora Gleichen Sculpture Award, F.R.B.S., Silver Medal Open Award (1984), Bronze, William Crabtree Memorial Award (1993), Bronze; sculptor in stone, wood, and bronze; *b* Richmond, Surrey, 1927. *m* Col. F. M. S. Winter, M.B.E., F.R.S.A. two *s.* one *d. Educ:* Oak Hall. *Studied:* Guildford and Chelsea Schools of Art. *Exhib:* R.A., R.B.A., R.W.S., Glasgow Academy of Fine Art, Covent Garden and elsewhere in the U.K.; International Centre of Contemporary Art, Paris; Malaysia and Singapore. *Commissions:* include: "The Soldiers" Catterick Camp; "Compassion" Hambro Foundation; Falklands Islands Memorial relief; The Mysteries of the Rosary, Church of Our Lady Queen of Peace, East Sheen; John Ray statue, Braintree; Air Chief Marshal Lord Dowding and Marshal of the Royal Air Force Sir Arthur "Bomber" Harris statues, The Strand, London; Lennard standing figure 'The Spirit of Youth', Ontario, Canada; Salters' Hall Coat-of-arms, London; Archbishop George Abbot, Guildford; H.R.H. The Princess Royal, The President of Kenya, Jeffrey Archer, Maria Callas and the late Kamal Jumblatt; David Devant, Magic Circle; memorial relief Mulberry Harbour, Arromanches, Normandy; General Sikorski, Portland Place, London. *Signs work:* "Faith Winter" (formerly "Faith Ashe.") *Address:* Venzers Studio, Venzers Yard, The Street, Puttenham, Guildford, Surrey GU3 1AU. *Website:* www.FaithWinter.co.uk *Email:* Faith@FaithWinter.co.uk

WINTERINGHAM, Claude Richard Graham, Dip. Arch., F.R.I.B.A., R.B.S.A.; Architect; chairman, Sir Barry Jackson Trust (1982-96); R.N.V.R. Fleet Air Arm Lt. (1941-46), chairman, Solihull Round Table (1956-57), founder mem. and vice chairman, Solihull Civic Soc. (1958-62), president, B'ham Architecture Assoc. (1971-72); *b* Louth, Lincs., 2 Mar., 1923. *m* Lesley Patricia. two *s.* one *d.* Awards: Mason Court Civic Trust (1969), Lichfield City Hall, Civic Soc. Commendation (1976), Lench's Close, Moseley, D.O.E. Housing Design (1983), B'ham Repertory Theatre Architecture (1972). *Clubs:* R.I.B.A. Sailing, Edgbaston Priory. *Address:* 7 Sir Harry's Rd., Edgbaston, Birmingham B15 2UY.

WISE, Gillian, artist, architectonic reliefs and paintings; *b* London, 1936. one *s. Educ:* Wimbledon School of Art (1953-57); post-graduate, Repin Inst., Leningrad (1969-70); Unesco Fellowship, Prague (1968); Fellow, C.A.V.S (M.I.T.) 1981-82; Research Fellow, Open University, U.K. (1983). Awards: A.C.G.B. (1976); Research Grant, International Communication Agency (1981); Graham Foundation, Chicago (1983). *Exhib:* London, Paris, Chicago, Liverpool, Japan, Germany, Finland. *Work in collections:* Tate Gallery (London and Liverpool), V. & A., British Council, Contemporary Arts Society, University of E. Anglia, D.O.E., Amos Andersonin Taidemuseo (Helsinki), Unilever, Gulbenkian Foundation (Lisbon), Henry Moore Foundation. *Commissions:* Steel wall relief: Nottingham University Hospital (1975); Relief panel in wood: Unilever House (1982); painting/relief: Barbican Centre (1983); three wall relief: Open University (1984). *Publications:* currently: transcriptions of life-story for British Library National Sound Archives: "Artists' Lives". *Clubs:* M.I.T. Club of France. *Signs work:* "Gillian Wise." *Address:* 3 Passage Rauch, Paris 75011. *Email:* alexwise@noos.fr

WISHART, Michael, painter, writer; Knight of St. Lazarus; nominated

Academician of Italy with gold medal (1980); *b* London, 12 June, 1928. *m* 1950, Anne, d of Sir James Dunn, Bt. one *s. Studied:* Academie Julian, Paris (1948). *Exhib:* one-man shows: Archer Gallery (1944), Redfern Gallery (1956, 1958, 1960), Leicester Galleries (1963, 1967, 1969, 1973), portrait of Rudolf Nureyev, Royal Academy (1968), Arts Council "Six Young Painters" (1957), Contemporary Art Society "Recent Acquisitions" Whitechapel Gallery (1968), Morley Gallery (1969); retrospective exhbn., "Paintings 1964-76" David Paul Gallery, Chichester (1976); Parkin Gallery (1985); R.A. Summer Exbhn. (1980, 1985, 1988, 1989, 1990); group shows: Parkin Gallery (1985-95). *Work in collections:* Arts Council, C.A.S., Garman Ryan Collection, Walsall. *Publications:* work repro.: Apollo, Burlington Magazine, Studio International, The Book of Joy, The Observer, Arts Review, Dance and Dancers, La Revue Moderne, Art and Literature, "High Diver" (autobiography), 1977. *Clubs:* Travellers', Chelsea Arts. *Signs work:* "Michael Wishart." *Address:* 34 Brunswick Sq., Hove, E. Sussex BN3 1ED.

WISHART, Sylvia, D.A. Aberdeen, A.R.S.A.; painter in oil; lecturer in Fine Art, Gray's School of Art, Robert Gordon University, Aberdeen; *b* Stromness, Orkney, 11 Feb., 1936. *Educ:* Stromness Academy, Orkney. *Studied:* Gray's School of Art. *Exhib:* R.A., R. Scot. Academy, various solo exhibs. *Signs work:* late work unsigned. *Address:* Heathery Braes, Stromness, Orkney KW16 3JP.

WISZNIEWSKI, Adrian, painter, sculptor, interior designer; *b* Glasgow, 31 Mar., 1958. *m* Diane. two *s.* one *d. Studied:* Mackintosh School of Architecture, Glasgow School of Art. *Work in collections:* Tate, M.O.M.A., New York, Setegaya, Tokyo. *Commissions:* Liverpool Cathedral. *Publications:* exhib. catalogues and historical books. *Signs work:* "A. Wiszniewski." *Address:* Calder House, Main St., Lochwinnoch, Renfrewshire PA12 4AH. *Email:* awiszniewski@btclick.com

WITHINGTON, Roger, Dip.A.D. (Graphics) (1966), A.T.D. (1967), A.R.E. (hon. retd.); artist in pencil and water-colour; artist/designer at Bank of England (1983-93), designed new series of banknotes known as Series E; *b* Prestwich, 4 Oct., 1943. *m* Rose-Marie Edna Cobley. one *s.* one *d. Educ:* Barry Grammar/Technical School, S. Glam. *Studied:* Cardiff College of Art (1962-63, etching: Philip Jennings, A.R.E.), Newport (Gwent) College of Art (1963-66, illustration: John Wright). *Exhib:* R.E. Galleries, Bankside Galleries. *Publications:* designed/part author series of booklets to accompany new banknotes. *Signs work:* "R. Withington" or "R.W." *Address:* Hedge-Rose, Goodleigh, Barnstaple, N.Devon EX32 7NP.

WITHROW, William John, Honour B.A., Art and Archaeology (1950), Art Specialist, O.C.E. (1951), B.Ed. (1955), M.Ed. (1958), M.A. (1965); Director Emeritus, Art Gallery of Ontario; Member: Order of Canada (1980), Fellow, Canadian Museums Assoc. (1985), Canadian Art Museums Directors Organisation, American Assoc. of Museums, Assoc. of Art Museum Directors, Canadian National Com. for I.C.O.M., Art Advisory Com., University Club of Toronto; *b* Toronto, 30 Sept., 1926. *m* June Roselea Van Ostrom. three *s.* one *d. Educ:* University of Toronto. *Studied:* University of Toronto (1946-65, Professor Peter Brieger, Professor Stephen Vickers). *Commissions:* Ricard/Withrow report on National Museums, Canada. *Publications:* Sorel Etrog Sculpture, Contemporary Canadian Painting. *Clubs:* University Club of Toronto, Highland Yacht. *Address:* 7 Malabar Pl., Don Mills, Ontario M3B 1A4.

WNEK-WEBB, Ewa, N.D.D.; artist; *b* Przemysl, Poland, 7 Jan., 1940. *m* Michael Robert Webb. two *s*. one *d. Studied:* St. Martin's School of Art (1958-61), Regent St. Polytechnic School of Art, and Chelsea College of Art (1961-63), London College of Printing. *Exhib:* R.O.I., U.A., S.W.A. Mall Galleries, R.A. Summer Show; solo shows: Gallery 47 London, Terrace Gallery Worthing, Ropner Gallery London, Heifer Gallery London, St. Rafael Gallery London. *Clubs:* Assoc. of Polish Artists in G.B. *Address:* 8 King Edward's Gr., Teddington, Middx. TW11 9LU.

WOLKERS, Joan Elizabeth Margaret, N.D.D. (Painting, 1948), Abbey Scholarship (1949), R.A. Silver Medals (1951, 52, 53); retd. teacher; *b* Tunbridge Wells, 28 Aug., 1928. *m* G.L. Wolkers (decd.). one *s. Educ:* Lawnside, Malvern. *Studied:* Malvern School of Art under Victor Hume Moody (1945-50) and R.A. Schools under Henry Rushbury, Fleetwood Walker and William Dring (1950-54); Royal Academy, Amsterdam (1954-58). *Exhib:* R.A., R.B.S.A., R.P., N.E.A.C., Brighton A.G., Worcester A.G., Malvern Art Club, Kenn Group, Exeter. Specialises in portraiture. *Commissions:* portraits. *Signs work:* "J.E.M. Wolkers." *Address:* 37 Powderham Cres., Exeter EX4 6BZ.

WOLSTENHOLME, Jonathan, artist/illustrator in water-colour, oil, pen and ink; *b* London, 22 Nov., 1950. *m* Margaret. one *s*. one *d. Educ:* Purley Grammar School. *Studied:* Croydon College of Art (1969-72). *Exhib:* several one-man shows in London, others in Paris, Brussels and New York. *Work in collections:* private and corporate collections internationally. *Commissions:* many. Gallery affiliation: Campbell's of Walton St. Ltd., 164 Walton St., London SW3 2JL. *Signs work:* "Jonathan Wolstenholme." *Address:* c/o Campbell's of Walton St. Ltd., 164 Walton St., London SW3 2JL.

WOLVERSON, Margaret Elizabeth, N.D.D., A.T.D., elected A.R.M.S. (1977); painter of living landscape, portraits etc.; formerly lectured Hornsea Inst. of Further Education and Stourbridge College of Art; *b* 1937. *m* 1961. one *s*. (div. 1985); *m* 1987, S. Jones-Robinson. *Studied:* Dudley School of Art, Wolverhampton College of Art, Leicester College of Art. *Exhib:* R.M.S., Mall Galleries, Cheltenham Group, Britain's Painters; one-man show Dean Heritage Centre, Workshop Gallery, Chepstow, Taurus Gallery (1999). *Work in collections:* East Riding Collection for Schools, Ferens A.G.; private collections in U.K., U.S.A. *Commissions:* numerous. *Clubs:* Forest Artists Network. *Signs work:* see appendix. *Address:* Sunny Bank, Pope's Hill, Newnham-on-Severn, Glos. GL14 1JX.

WOLVERSON, Martin, F.R.B.S. (1971), F.R.S.A. (1976); R.B.S. Silver medal (1971), Trident Television Fine Art Fellow (1977-78), Fulbright Prof. Kansas City Art Inst. (1985); sculptor in wood, stone, metal, lecturer; *b* Wolverhampton, 26 May, 1939. *m* (1) Margaret Smith; one *s*. (2) Sandra Tipper. *Educ:* Wednesbury Boys High School. *Studied:* Wolverhampton School of Art (1956-60, Tom Wright, John Paddison), Goldsmiths' College (1960-61). *Exhib:* widely in the North, London and in the U.S.A. *Work in collections:* Ferens A.G., Hull, Usher A.G., Lincoln, Yorkshire Television, N.C.B., Ecclesiastic Insurance Co. Ltd., Lincolnshire and Humberside Arts, Humberside C.C., Leeds City A.G., and private collections. *Signs work:* "M. Wolverson." *Address:* The Holbrooks, Mount Pleasant East, Robin Hoods Bay, Whitby, N. Yorks. YO22 4RF.

WONNACOTT, John Henry, Slade Dip. (1962); Hon. R.P.; *b* London, 1940. *m* Anne Rozalie Wesolowska, B.Sc. one *s.* two *d. Educ:* University College School. *Studied:* Slade School (1958-63). *Exhib:* Hayward (1974), R.A. Jubilee (1952-77), Marlborough (1981), Marlborough, N.Y. (1983), Tate Gallery (1984), The Foudation Veranneman (1986-87), The Pursuit of the Real, Barbican (1990); one-man shows, Minories, Colchester (1972), Rochdale (1978); touring, Marlborough (1980-81), 1985, 1988), Scottish National Portrait Gallery (1986-87), A.G. News (93, 97, 2000), Hirschl & Alder, N.Y. (2000), N.P.G. (2000), N.M.M. (2001). *Work in collections:* Nat. Art Collection, Arts Council, Rochdale A.G., Norwich Castle Museum, Tate Gallery, Scottish National Portrait Gallery, N.M.M., I.W.M., Met. Mus. York, Brit. Council. *Commissions:* Sir Adam Thomson (N.P.G.), Rt. Hon. John Major (N.P.G.), Lord Lewin (Nat. Mar. Mus.). *Signs work:* "C.B.E." *Address:* 5 Cliff Gdns., Leigh-on-Sea, Essex.

WOOD, Andy, Dip.A.D. (1970), A.R.B.A. (1980), R.I. (1981); painter in acrylic, oil and water-colour; *b* Porlock, Som., 1947. *m* Katrina Wood. two *s.* two *d. Educ:* schools in Walton-on-Thames, Hersham and Dorking. *Studied:* Croydon and Newport Colleges of Art (1965-70). *Exhib:* R.I., R.B.A., Thackeray Gallery, etc. *Work in collections:* Sultan of Oman; Duke University, N.C., U.S.A.; Central Carolina Bank, N.C., U.S.A.; Lyme Regis Museum. *Commissions:* Sultan of Oman; British Telecom; Southern Gas. *Publications:* Dictionary of 20th Century British Painters, Sculptors and other artists (Antique Collectors Club Ltd). *Clubs:* Chelsea Arts. *Signs work:* "Andy Wood" or "A. Wood." *Address:* Woodside, Hill Rd., Lyme Regis, Dorset DT7 3PG.

WOOD, Annette (Mrs.): see GARDNER, Annette.

WOOD, Christopher Paul, B.A.Hons. (1984), M.A. (1986); painter in oil on canvas; *b* Leeds, 10 June, 1961. *m* Simone Abel. two *d. Educ:* Leeds. *Studied:* Jacob Kramer School of Art (1980-81), Leeds Polytechnic (1981-84), Chelsea School of Art (1985-86). *Exhib:* one-man shows: Oldham City A.G. (1986), Sue Williams Gallery, London (1989, 1990, 1992, 1994), Rebecca Hossack Gallery, London (1996, 1997, 1999), Newark Park, Glos. (1998); retrospective exhibition Mercer Gallery Harrogate (1999), Michael Carr Gallery, Sydney Australia (2000); mixed shows include Festival Hall (1986), New Contemporaries (1986), New Generation (1991), Hunting Prize (2000) R.C.A. *Publications:* 'Echo Moment' Mercer Gallery (1999). *Signs work:* full signature on back of canvas; initialled on front of paintings - "C.P.W." and date. *Address:* 1 Norfok Pl., Chapel Allerton, Leeds LS7 4PT.

WOOD, Duncan, B.A. Hons. Fine Art, Sheffield Hallam University, P.G.C.E., London University, M.A. Fine Art, University of Central England (2001-); oil, water-colour, charcoal/chalk; *b* London, 14 Nov., 1960. *Educ:* Brockhurst Preparatory School, Berks., Kingham Hill School, Oxfordshire. *Studied:* Gloucestershire College of Art (1980-81), Sheffield College of Art (1981-84), City & Guilds of London Art School, London University. *Exhib:* R.C.A., R.A., City art galleries: Sheffield, Glasgow, Nottingham; galleries: Cardiff, Edinburgh, Birkenhead, London, Fosse Gallery, Stow-on-the-Wold; also exhib. at 'Discerning Eye Exhbns.' (work chosen by Glynn Williams, Prof. of Fine Art at R.C.A. 1992, and by Sir Brinsley Ford former Chairman of National Art Collections Fund 1991, William Packer, art critic Financial

Times, and Martin Gayford, writer and art critic of the Daily Telegraph and Modern Painters 1996), National Trust (1997-99). *Work in collections:* London, throughout the U.K. and in the U.S.A., Germany and Japan; public collections: The Finnish Embassy, Sheffield University, Chatsworth House, Derbyshire. Established "The New English School of Drawing" at Nottingham City Art Galleries (1993). Artist in Residence: National Trust (1997-99). *Clubs:* N.E.A.C. (1991), mem. Com., N.E.A.C. School of Drawing (1995). *Signs work:* "Duncan Wood." *Address:* 1 Church St., Baslow, Derbyshire DE45 1RY.

WOOD, Gerald Stanley Kent, M.B.I.A.T. (1968), M.S.A.I. (1977), F.E.T.C. (1978); artist and architectural illustrator in pencil, ink, water-colour, gouache and tempera, perspectivist, architectural technologist, tutor, lecturer; *b* Cambridge, 29 Oct., 1923. *Educ:* Perse Preparatory School, Cambridge, Elmers Grammar School, Old Bletchley, Bucks. *Studied:* under H. J. Sylvester Stannard, R.B.A. (1934-39). *Exhib:* R.A., R.B.A., R.I., R.M.S., N.E.A.C., U.A., N.S., S.B.A., S.G.A., P.S., Contemporary British Watercolours, Pictures for Schools, Britain in Water-colours, Britain's Painters, Lord Mayor's Art Award, Hesketh Hubbard Art Soc., Chelsea Art Soc., Open Salon, Luton Museum. *Work in collections:* Theatre Royal, Haymarket, National Westminster Bank Theatre Museum; private collections: England, Wales, Australia, Canada, Germany, Saudi Arabia. *Signs work:* see appendix. *Address:* 21 Salisbury Rd., Luton, Beds. LU1 5AP.

WOOD, Nigel, Dip. (wildlife illustration) 1984; painter in oil and pastel; *b* Reading, 26 Dec., 1960. one *s.* one *d. Studied:* Dyfed College of Art (1980-84). *Exhib:* solo and group shows including N.P.G., R.C.A., Aberdeen A.G., Glyn Vivian Gallery, Ceri Richards Gallery, Mall Galleries, Martin Tinney Gallery, Oriel Myrddin, Fountain Fine Art and Edith Grove Gallery. *Work in collections:* Carmarthenshire County Collection. *Signs work:* "NIGEL WOOD." *Address:* Ty Dderwen, Maesycrugiau, Pencader, Carms. SA39 9LY.

WOOD, Tom, painter in oil, printmaker, lecturer; Hon. Fellow, Sheffield Hallam University (1989); *b* Dar es Salaam, Tanzania, 1955. *m* Elaine Barraclough. three *d. Studied:* Batley School of Art (1975), Sheffield School of Art (1976-78). *Exhib:* solo shows: Huddersfield A.G., Leeds City A.G., Schloss Cappengberg, Kreissunna, Germany, Hart Gallery London and Nottingham. *Work in collections:* H.R.H. The Prince of Wales, N.P.G., Yale University, Provident Financial Group. *Commissions:* portraits: Arthur Haigh and W.T. Oliver (1984); H.R.H. The Prince of Wales (1987); Alan Bennett (1990); Prof. Lord Winston for the National Gallery (1999). *Publications:* Man and Measure - The Painting of Tom Wood by Duncan Robinson (Hart Gallery Pub.). Studio: Dean Clough, Halifax. *Signs work:* "TOM WOOD." *Address:* 4 Westfield Ave., Lightcliffe, Halifax, W. Yorks HX3 8AP.

WOODFORD, David, N.D.D., A.T.C. with distinction, Cert. R.A.S.; painter in oil and water-colour; Royal Cambrian Academician; *b* Rawmarsh, Yorks., 1 May, 1938. *m* June. two *s. Educ:* Lancing College. *Studied:* West Sussex College of Art (1955-59), Leeds College of Art (1959-60), Royal Academy Schools (1965-68). He lives by his painting. *Signs work:* "David Woodford." *Address:* Ffrancon House, Ty'n-Y-Maes, Bethesda, Bangor, Gwynedd LL57 3LX.

WOODINGTON, Walter, R.P., R.B.A., N.E.A.C.; painter in oil and water-colour; part-time teacher, Woolwich Polytechnic Art School (1946-60); appointed Curator, Royal Academy Schools (1961-84); *b* London, June, 1916. *m* Jacqueline Murray. *Studied:* Woolwich Polytechnic Art School and City and Guilds Art School under A. R. Middleton-Todd, R.A. *Exhib:* R.A., R.P., R.B.A., N.E.A.C., etc. *Publications:* work repro.: for Hutchinson's and Odhams Press. *Signs work:* "WOODINGTON." *Address:* 5 Kenver Ave., Finchley, London N12 0PG.

WOODS, Grace Mary, A.R.C.A.; artist in black and white and pastel, and weaving; *b* Ilford, Essex, 25 Feb., 1909. *m* Sidney W. Woods, A.R.C.A. (decd.). two *s.* three *d. Educ:* Ursuline Convent, Forest Gate, E7. *Studied:* West Ham Art School and Royal College of Art in Design and Engraving Schools. *Exhib:* R.A. and other London galleries. Work purchased by private collectors. *Signs work:* "Mary Woods." *Address:* 157 Warren Rd., Chelsfield, Orpington, Kent BR6 6ES.

WOODSIDE, Christine A., D.A. (1968), Post Dip. (1969), R.S.W. (1993), R.G.I. (1999); artist in water-colour and mixed media; *b* Aberdeen, 24 Apr., 1946. partner: Charles T.K. Macqueen, R.S.W., R.G.I. one *s.* one *d. Educ:* Aberdeen High School for Girls. *Studied:* Gray's School of Art, Aberdeen (1964-69, Ian Fleming, Robert Henderson Blythe). *Exhib:* numerous including R.S.A., R.S.W., R.G.I. *Work in collections:* Saltire Soc., R.S.A., Perth Museum. *Clubs:* The Scottish Arts Club. *Signs work:* "Woodside" and year. *Address:* Tower View, 1 Back Dykes, Auchtermuchty, Fife KY14 7AB.

WOODWARD, Justine, H.S. (1998); artist in water-colour and oil; *b* 23 Feb., 1943. divorced. one *s.* one *d. Exhib:* Sunningdale, Virginia Water, H.S., Wells, Som. *Signs work:* see appendix. *Address:* Fauns Glen, The Friary, Old Windsor, Berks. SL4 2NR.

WOOLF-NELLIST, Meg, B.A., A.T.D., F.S.D.C; awarded Exhibition, R.C.A. (1949); formerly lecturer in art, Rachel McMillan College of Educ., Director, Bermuda Art Assoc. School (1950-52); artist in stone, wood, calligrapher; *b* Isle of Thanet, 10 Dec., 1923. *m* Anthony Nellist (decd.). one *s.* three *d. Educ:* Couvent des Oiseaux. *Studied:* Ravensbourne College of Art, Brighton College of Art (1939-42). *Exhib:* Roland, Browse and Delbanco, A.I.A., R.B.A., R.A., V. & A., Russell Cotes, Hove A.G. (one-man, 1948); with Designer Craftsmen (1968-69), Hornchurch A.G. (1986, 1987, 1989, 1991, 1993, 1994, 1998, 1999), Oxford Scribes (2000). *Work in collections:* Canada, U.S.A., Germany, Australia. *Publications:* work repro.: Studio. *Signs work:* see appendix. *Address:* 84 Front Lane, Cranham, Essex RM14 1XW.

WORSDALE, John Dennis, painter in water-colour, oil; tutor and art soc. demonstrator; *b* Southend, Essex, 18 Apr., 1930. *m* Ann. one *s.* two *d. Educ:* Southend High School for Boys. *Studied:* Southend Art School and privately. *Exhib:* R.I., R.O.I., R.S.M.A., Britain in Watercolours, galleries in London and elsewhere; four solo exhibs. *Work in collections:* private collections in Europe, U.S.A., Australia, S.Korea, Morocco. *Publications:* greetings cards and calendars. *Clubs:* Wapping Group of Artists. *Signs work:* "JOHN WORSDALE." *Address:* 11 Central Close, Benfleet, Essex SS7 2NU.

WORTH, Leslie Charles, A.R.C.A. (Lond.) (1946), R.B.A. (1951), R.W.S. (1967), N.E.A.C. (2001); prizewinner Hallmark International Art Award, New York

(1955); painter in water-colour and oil; Past President, R.W.S.; *b* Bideford, Devon, 6 June, 1923. *m* Jane Taylor. one *s*. three *d*. *Educ:* St. Budeaux School, Plymouth. *Studied:* Plymouth School of Art (1938-39, 1942-43), Bideford School of Art (1940-42), Royal College of Art (1943-46). *Exhib:* Agnews, Mercury Gallery, Wildenstein, W.H. Patterson Fine Art. Several mural commissions, National Trust Commissions. *Work in collections:* R.A., National Gallery of New Zealand, Aberdeen, Birmingham, Brighton, Burton (Bideford), Rochdale, Southport and Wakefield Art Galleries, Whitworth A.G. (Manchester University), Eton College, West Riding of Yorks. Educ. Authority, G.L.C., Admiralty; private collections: H.M. Queen Elizabeth, Queen Mother, H.R.H. The Prince of Wales and several private collections. *Publications:* The Practice of Watercolour Painting (Pitmans and Watson Guptil, 1977, Search Press 1980); magazine articles. *Signs work:* "Leslie Worth." *Address:* 11 Burgh Heath Rd., Epsom, Surrey KT17 4LW.

WORTH, Philip, M.A., LL.B., Hon. Sec. F.P.S.; self taught artist in acrylic; *b* Gillingham, 23 June, 1933. *m* Jennifer Louise. two *d*. *Educ:* Royal High School, Edinburgh, Edinburgh University. *Exhib:* many one-man and group shows throughout U.K. since 1984. *Signs work:* "P. WORTH." *Address:* The White House, 282 St. John's Rd., Boxmoor, Hemel Hempstead, Herts. HP1 1QG.

WOUDA, Marjan Petra, A.R.B.S., B.A. (Hons.) Fine Art (1987), M.A. Fine Art/Sculpture (1988); sculptor in clay/bronze; *b* Aduard, The Netherlands, 20 Feb., 1960. *m* Immy Deshmukh. two *s*. *Studied:* N.E. London Polytechnic, Manchester Polytechnic. *Exhib:* Curwen Gallery, London; Kunsthandel Pieter Breughel, Amsterdam, Art Fair, Islington, London (1997, 1998). *Work in collections:* Provident Financial Head Office, Bradford, Bury Art Gallery and Museum, Blackburn Museum and Art Gallery. *Commissions:* London Dockland Development Corp.; Groundwork Trust, Wigan; Arcades Shopping Centre, Ashton-under-Lyne: major bronze sculpture at centre of development; drawings for British Consulate, Hong Kong, River Lane Millenium Park, Lancashire. *Clubs:* R.B.S., M.A.F.A., R.Cam.A. *Signs work:* "Marjan" or "M.W." joined. *Address:* Whitehall, Queen's Rd., Darwen, Lancashire BB3 2LN. *Website:* www.marjanwouda.co.uk *Email:* marjan.wouda@lineone.net

WRAGG, John, R.A., A.R.C.A., R.I.B.S.; sculptor in wood; *b* York, 20 Oct., 1937. one *s*. *Studied:* York School of Art (1954-56), Royal College of Art (1956-60). Awards: Sainsbury Award (1960), Winner of Sainsbury Sculpture Competition (1966), Arts Council (1977), Chantrey Bequest (1981). *Exhib:* solo shows: (1963-97), include; Hanover Gallery, Gallerie Alexandre Iolas Paris, York Festival, Devizes Museum Gallery, L'Art Abstrait London, Monumental '96 Belguim; Courcoux, etc.; group shows (1959-93): Bradford A.G., Gimpel Hanover Galerie Zurich, L'Art Vivant, Bath Festival Gallery, Quinton Green Fine Art London, Connaught Brown, etc. *Work in collections:* Sainsbury Centre, University of E. Anglia; Israel Museum, Jerusalem; Tate Gallery, London; A.C.G.B.; Arts Council of N.I.; Contemporary Art Soc.; Wellington A.G., N.Z.; National Gallery of Modern Art, Edinburgh. *Publications:* Neue Dimensionen der Plastic (Undo Kutterman), British Sculpture in the 20th Century (1981), etc. *Address:* 6 Castle Lane, Devizes, Wilts. SN10 1HJ.

WRAITH, Robert, R.P.; painter in oil, water-colour, drawing, etching; *b* London, 11 Dec., 1952. *m* Tina. one *s*. two *d*. *Educ:* Stowe. *Studied:* Florence (Pietro

Annigoni). *Exhib:* fourteen one-man shows, also N.P.G., R.A., R.P., etc. *Work in collections:* H.M. The Queen, H.R.H. The Prince of Wales, Chatsworth, The Vatican, M.C.C., National Trust, Oxford University, fresco in the Church of Ponte Buggianese, Italy, etc. *Commissions:* Many portrait commissions, including H.M. The Queen, The Duke and Duchess of Devonshire. Invited by H.R.H. The Prince of Wales to accompany him on his state visit to South Africa as travelling artist, 1997. *Signs work:* "WRAITH" or "Robbie Wraith." *Address:* The Old School House, The Green, Holton, Oxon. OX33 1PS.

WRAY, Peter, R.E. (1991), M.A. (1992), P.G.Dip.A.D. (1984), Cert.Ed. (1972); artist in printmaking/painting; Senior lecturer in Printmaking, University College of Ripon and York St. John (1987-2001); *b* Sedgefield, Co. Durham, 27 Oct., 1950. two *d. Educ:* St. Mary's School, Darlington. *Studied:* St. Mary's College, Strawberry Hill, Twickenham (1969-72), Goldsmiths' College (1983-84, John Rogers, Peter Mackarrell), Leeds Polytechnic (1990-92, Geoff Teasdale). *Exhib:* R.E., International Print Biennale, New Academy Gallery, Curwen Gallery, etc. *Work in collections:* Price-Waterhouse, Sainsbury, Intel U.K., St. Thomas's Hospital, Bank of England. *Clubs:* Royal Society of Painter/Printmakers (R.E.). *Signs work:* "P. Wray." *Address:* The Old School, 62 York Rd., Acomb, York YO24 4NW.

WRIGHT, Anne, N.D.D., R.A.Dip. ; portrait painter in oil and pastel; Mem. Chelsea Art Soc., and The Small Paintings Group; *b* Nottingham, 28 Mar., 1935. *m* Henry Brett. two *d. Studied:* Nottingham College of Art (1952-54), R.A. Schools (1954-59, Peter Greenham). *Work in collections:* Candie Museum, Guernsey. *Commissions:* murals: McAlpine and General Dental Council. *Clubs:* Chelsea Arts. *Signs work:* "A" above"W". *Address:* 55 Englewood Rd., London SW12 9PB.

WRIGHT, Bert, P.R.S.M.A., F.R.S.A.; President, Royal Society of Marine Artists, Governor, Federation of British Artists; marine painter of contemporary subjects, plein air painter on location worldwide, also paints landscape and architectural subjects in both oil and water-colour; *b* 1930. *Studied:* Nottingham College of Art. *Exhib:* R.A., and regularly at major galleries in the London area and in the U.S.A. *Work in collections:* U.K., U.S.A., Far East and the Middle East. *Commissions:* New York Yacht Club, Sultan of Oman, Daily Express, Standard Chartered Bank, British American Tobacco, Mullard Electronics, Beecham Group, Lloyds, Allied Dunbar, P. & O. *Publications:* listed in '20th Century Marine Art', articles for 'Artist' magazine. Prizewinner Sunday Times/Singer Friedlander Water-colour competition. *Address:* 19 Carew Rd., Ealing, London W13 9QL.

WRIGHT, Bill, R.S.W. (1974), R.G.I. (1990), P.A.I. (1996); painter in water-colour and acrylic; President, Scottish Artists' Benevolent Soc.; *b* Glasgow, 1931. *m* Annie. three *d. Studied:* Glasgow School of Art. *Exhib:* many solo and national exhbns. *Work in collections:* several public collections including H.R.H. The Duke of Edinburgh. *Clubs:* Glasgow Art. *Address:* Old Lagalgarve Cottage, Bellochantuy, Argyll PA28 6QE.

WRIGHT, Gordon Butler, F.B.S. Comm., F.Inst.C., Mem. International Association of Artists; professional artist in oils; *b* Darlington, Co. Durham, 2 Apr., 1925. *m* Joan. *Educ:* Gladstone School, Darlington and Kings College, Newcastle. *Studied:* Chichester College of Art (1943-44) followed by two periods of study in

Amsterdam and The Hague. Influenced by the Dutch Romantic School. *Exhib:* Galerie Montmartre, Paris, Grosvenor Gallery and Portal Gallery, London, Trinity Art Gallery, Wareham, Whitgift Galleries, London, Recorded in the National Maritime Museum, Greenwich. *Publications:* The Collector's Guide to Paintings as an Investment. *Signs work:* "G. B. Wright." *Address:* 123 Wetherby Rd., Harrogate, Yorks.

WRIGHT, Lisa, B.A. Hons 1st Class (1987), M.A. Fine Art (1993); painter in oil; part-time lecturer, Falmouth College of Art; *b* Kent, 3 Jan.,1965. *m* Mark Surridge. two *s. Studied:* Maidstone College of Art (1983-1987), R.A. Schools (1990-1993). *Exhib:* Beardsmore Gallery, London, solo exhibs. (1999, 2001), regularly at R.A. Summer exhibs. and Newlyn Gallery, Hunting Art Prizes (1998, 2000), Royal Overseas League (1993, 1994, 1996), Cheltenham Drawing Open (2000), Contemporary Arts Soc., N.E.A.C. (prizes 1994, 1996), Merriscourt Gallery, Oxon., national and international group exhibs. *Work in collections:* Unilever, Guiness, B.U.P.A., Zeneca, etc. *Publications:* catalogues for solo exhibs. (1999, 2001). *Clubs:* Newlyn Soc. of Artists. *Signs work:* "Lisa Wright." *Address:* Chapel House, Crelly, Helston, Cornwall TR13 0EY.

WRIGHT, Sally Diane, S.B.A.; artist in water-colour and pencil; *b* London, 21 Oct., 1952. *m* Robert Wright. one *s.* one *d. Exhib:* Westminster Gallery, Brighton Festival. *Publications:* work published by Medici. *Address:* 21 Elven Lane, East Dean, E. Sussex BN20 0LG.

WRIGHT, Stuart Pearson R., B.A. Fine Art (1999); painter in oil; *b* Northampton, 11 Oct., 1975. *Studied:* Slade School of Fine Art (1995-1999). *Exhib:* B.P. Portrait Award (1998-Travel Award Winner, 1999, 2000, 2001-First Prize Winner), Hunting Art Prizes (1998, 2000, 2001), Garrick Prize (2000-Third Prize), Winsor and Newton Millenium Comp. (2000), Singer and Friedlander Sunday Times, Watercolour Comp. (1998, 1999-Third Prize). *Work in collections:* National Portrait Gallery, Royal Academy. *Commissions:* John Hurt, Adam Cooper, The Six Presidents of the Royal Academy. *Signs work:* "SPW" see appendix. *Address:* 3 Carlisle Buildings, Carlisle Rd., Eastbourne, E. Sussex BN21 4DB. *Email:* stuart-pearson@wright.bpenet.net

WRIGHT, Valerie Margaret, B.Ed.Hons. (1977), S.W.A. (1986), S.B.A. (1987); landscape, botanical and wildlife painter in water-colour; *b* Manchester, 6 Jan., 1934. *m* Norman Wright. one *s.* two *d. Educ:* Peterborough High School, Hendon Polytechnic, Coloma College of Educ. London University. *Studied:* Coloma College (Constance Stubbs, Norma Jameson). *Exhib:* R.I., S.W.A., S.B.A., Portico Gallery, Manchester, Manchester Academy, B.W.S., Gorstella Gallery; one-man shows: Chester, Warrington, Bolton Octagon Theatre, Frodsham Arts Centre, Norton Priory. *Signs work:* "Valerie Wright." *Address:* Appletree Cottage, 55 Rushgreen Rd., Lymm, Ches. WA13 9PS.

WROUGHTON, Julia, N.D.D. (1957), A.R.C.A. (1960), R.W.A. (1963); painter in oil and water-colour; Principal, Inniemore School of Painting (1967-1999); *b* Bridge of Allan, Stirlingshire, 24 Oct., 1934. *m* Alastair Macdonald (decd.). Bruce Killeen M.A., R.W.A. one *s.* three *d. Educ:* Beacon School, Bridge of Allan. *Studied:* Colchester School of Art (1953-57) under John O'Connor, Hugh Cronyn, Royal

College of Art (1957-60) under Carel Weight, R.A., Colin Hayes, R.A. and Roger de Grey. *Exhib:* R.A., one-man show: Torrance Gallery, Edinburgh, Glengorm Castle, Isle of Mull, R.W.A., Malcolm Innes Gallery, Edinburgh, Alpha House Gallery, Sherborne. *Work in collections:* Royal West of England Academy, Nuffield Foundation, Mrs. Nelson, Glengorm Castle, Marquess of Bath, Longleat. *Signs work:* "Julia Wroughton," "J. W." *Address:* Balmeanach, By Tiroran, Isle of Mull PA68 6EH.

WU, Ching-Hsia, artist; paintress in water-colour and poetess; Prof. Shanghai Academy of Fine Arts, Prof. Shanghai Normal University; Vancouver Golden Jubilee Chinese Carnival Honorary Prize, Canada (1936); *b* Changchow, China, 11 Feb., 1910. *Educ:* at home and studied art under father. *Exhib:* Shanghai, Nanking, Peking, Rome, Jakarta, Surabaya, Singapore, Helsinki, Tokyo, Hong Kong, Osaka, Paris, Stockholm, Canton, etc. *Work in collections:* Shanghai Art Gallery; Katesan House, Jakarta; etc. *Publications:* Select Work of Wu Qing-Xia. *Clubs:* China Art Society, Shanghai, Accademico d'Europa. *Signs work:* "WU Ching-Hsia," (Wu Qing-Xia). *Address:* 301/3, Lane 785, Ju Lu Road, Shanghai (China).

WUNDERLICH, Paul, painter in oil, gouache, lithography; sculptor; *b* Eberswalde, 10 Mar., 1927. *m* Karin Székessy, photographer. two *d. Educ:* Berlin High School. *Studied:* Academy Hamburg. *Exhib:* all over Europe, United States, Japan, S. Africa and Australia. *Work in collections:* museums in Europe, U.S.A. and Japan. *Publications:* Paul Wunderlich (Denoel, Paris 1972), Lithografien 1959-73 (Office du Livre, Fribourg Suisse), Monographie 1978 (Filipacchi Paris), Monographie (1955-80), Huber, Offenbach, Homo Sum 1978 (Piper, Munich), Bilder zu Manet (Cotta, Germany 1978), Skulpturen and Objecte I and II, Huber, Offenbach, Germany. *Signs work:* "Paul Wunderlich." *Address:* Haynstr. 2. D-20249, Hamburg. *Email:* paul@wunderlich.org

WYATT, Arthur Leonard, T.D. (art pottery), F.F.P.S.; artist in acrylics, mixed media; art teacher (1950-82); *b* London, 6 Dec., 1922. *m* Margaret Sybil Lucy. two *s. Educ:* West Ham Grammar School. *Studied:* Hornsey School of Art (1950's). *Exhib:* 22 one-man shows in U.K., America, Germany, Norway, S. Africa; numerous group shows with F.P.S.; invited exhibitor (11 works) 49th World Sci-Fi Convention, Brighton (1987); Astro-Physics Dept., Queen Mary College, London; F.P.S. Fellows exhbn. at Loggia Gallery (1996), F.P.S. group exhbn. '5 Decades' at Loggia Gallery (1996), F.P.S. Selected at R.B.S.A. (1996). *Work in collections:* Pennsylvania Museum of Modern Art, City A.G. Lichfield, Gateshead Municipal Collection, Save and Prosper, Head Office. *Publications:* Illustrated five rambling books (Essex, Herts.). *Clubs:* F.P.S. *Signs work:* "WYATT." *Address:* 1 Kenwood Gdns., Gants Hill, Ilford, Essex IG2 6YH.

WYATT, Joyce (Mrs Derek Wraith), R.M.S., V.P.S.W.A., Hon. U.A., F.R.S.A.; Prix Rowland and Mention Honorable (Paris Salon, 1963); Médaille D'Argent (Paris Salon, 1965); Médaille D'Or (Paris Salon, 1969); Member of La Société des Artistes Français (1969); portrait painter in oil, water-colour, etc.; *b* London. *m* Dr. Derek Greenway Wraith. one *s.* one *d. Exhib:* R.A., R.P., R.M.S., R.B.A., Société des Artistes Français, U.A., S.W.A., etc.; one-man shows: Federation British Artists, Edinburgh Festival Exhbn., Rutland Sq., Edinburgh, La Galerie Mouffe, Paris. *Work* *in collections:* Fresco (Christ Consoling the Women) Italy; St. Andrew's Church, Totteridge (The Nativity). *Commissions:* include portraits for H.R.H Prince Michael of Kent. *Signs work:* "WYATT." *Address:* Archgate, North Stoke, nr. Wallingford, OX10 6BL.

WYER, Annraoi, B.A. Hons. Fine Art (1986), Dip. Design Hons. (1985); Greenshield Foundation award, Montreal (1988), President's Gold medal (1987); Prof. of Art, Blackrock College; painter, printmaker, illustrator; *b* Dublin, 7 Sept., 1963. *m* Sheila. *Educ:* Blackrock College. *Studied:* National College of Art and Design, Dublin, Dublin Inst. of Technology (1981-84, Alice Hanratty, Patrick Graham). *Exhib:* Ljubljana (1987, 1989), Varna (1989, 1991), Taipei (1988), various national exhbns. Work in corporate and private collections. *Publications:* Blackrock College 1860-1995. *Clubs:* Assoc. of Artists in Ireland, Black Church Print Studio. *Signs work:* "Annraoi Wyer." *Address:* 3 Ardmore Wood, Herbert Rd., Bray Co., Wicklow, Eire.

WYLES, June, B.A. (Hons.) Fine Art, M.A. Printmaking; painter/printmaker in oil, charcoal - landscape and the human form; lecturer of art, Berkshire College of Art and Design; *b* Berks., 1955. *Studied:* St. Martin's School of Art. *Exhib:* one-man shows: Dusseldörf, London. *Signs work:* "June Wyles." *Address:* 14a Eldon Rd., Reading, Berks. RG1 4DL.

WYLIE, Rose Forrest, M.A., R.C.A.; painter; *b* 1934. *Studied:* Folkestone and Dover School of Art, R.C.A. *Exhib:* Hayward Annual (1982), Cleveland International Drawing Biennale (1985), Scottish Drawing Competition (1988), Pomeroy Purdy Gallery (1988), Odette Gilbert Gallery 'Women and Water' (1988), Towner Gallery (1991), John Moores (1991), R.A. Summer Exhbn. (1992, 1993, 1997, 1998, 1999, 2000 & 2001), Towner Gallery 'Interiors' (1993), Norwich Gallery EAST (1994), Seattle Art Fair (1996), Cheltenham Open Drawing (1996, 1998 & 2000), Jerwood Painting Prize (1997), Velan, Turin (2000); two person shows: Odette Gilbert Gallery (1988), Towner Gallery (1994); one person shows: Reed's Wharf Gallery, London (1995), Abbotsbury Studio (1998), Stephen Lacey Gallery, London (1999). *Work in collections:* Deal Collection, Dallas, Railtrack, London, Arts Council of England, Contemporary Art Soc., University College, Oxford J.C.R., York City Art Gallery. Dupree Award (R.A. 1999). *Address:* Forge Cottage, Newnham, Sittingbourne, ME9 0LQ.

WYLLIE, George Ralston, A.R.S.A., R.G.I., D.Litt.; Fellow, Hand Hollow, N.Y.; sculptor; writer; performer; *b* Glasgow, 1921. *m* Daphne Winifred Watts. two *d. Educ:* Allan Glen's and Bellahouston, Glasgow. *Exhib:* (selected): Demarco Gallery, Third Eye, Serpentine, Watermans, Worcester Art Museum, U.S.A., World Finance Center, N.Y. *Work in collections:* (selected): A.C.G.B.; S.A.C.; Glasgow, Whitworth Manchester, Worcester (U.S.A.) museums; U.F.A. Fabrik, Berlin; Getty Foundation. Events: 'A Day Down A Goldmine', Edinburgh Festival, I.C.A., London; 'Tramway', Glasgow; 'Straw Locomotive', Glasgow; 'Paper Boat', Glasgow, London, New York, Antwerp. *Signs work:* "G.R.W." *Address:* 9 McPherson Drive, Gourock, Renfrewshire PA19 1LJ.

WYLLIE, Gordon Hope, D.A. (Glas. 1953), R.S.W. (1967); artist in water-colour, acrylic and oil; *b* Greenock, 12 Feb., 1930. *m* Helen Wyllie. two *s. Educ:*

Greenock High School. *Studied:* Glasgow School of Art (1949-53) under Wm. Armour, R.S.A., R.S.W.; Hospitalfield College of Art (1953) under Ian Fleming, R.S.A., R.S.W. and Mary Armour, R.S.A., R.S.W. *Exhib:* R.S.A., R.G.I., R.S.W., Compass Gallery, Glasgow; one-man shows in Gateway, Edinburgh, Douglas & Foulis, Edinburgh, Citizens Theatre, Glasgow, Blythswood Gallery, 208 Gallery, Glasgow, Strathclyde University Staff Club, Lillie A.G., Compass Gallery, regular exhibitor Open Eye Gallery, Edinburgh. *Work in collections:* of Argyll, Fife, Renfrewshire, Ross and Cromarty Authorities, Paisley A.G., Lillie A.G., Milngavie and many private collections in U.K., U.S.A., Israel, Germany, etc. *Publications:* at one time part-time illustrator for the Glasgow Bulletin. *Signs work:* "Wyllie." *Address:* 17 Fox St., Greenock.

WYNNE, Althea, A.R.C.A. (1960), F.R.B.S. (1994); sculptor in clay and plaster; *b* Bedford, 6 Oct., 1936. *m* Antony Barrington-Brown. one *s.* two *d. Educ:* North Foreland Lodge School. *Studied:* Farnham Art School, Hammersmith College, R.C.A. *Exhib:* Henley Arts Festival (1994), Margam Sculpture Pk. (1991), Tower Bridge Plaza (1995), Winchester Cathedral (1997), Shape of the Century (1999). *Work in collections:* 3 horses 1.5 x L/size, bronze, Mincing Lane EC1; Family of goats L/size bronze, Barnard's Wharf Rotherhithe; "The Family" group L/size, Walsall Maternity Hospital; "White Horses" L/size resin, QE2 liner; "Chalk Columns" 9m obelisk, Bluewater. *Address:* Mizmaze, 26c Upton Lovell, Warminster, Wilts. BA12 0JW.

Y

YALLUP, Pat, Dip.Ad.S.A. (1956), S.I.A.D., A.T.D. (1963); artist in water-colour (landscapes and abstracts), oil (portraits); Pat Yallup Studio/Gallery, Llandogo, Gwent, (teacher own School); *b* Johannesburg, S. Africa, 29 Sept., 1929. *m* R. W. Yallup. three *s. Studied:* Witwatersrand, Johannesburg; Byam Shaw School (portraiture). *Exhib:* 35 one-man shows, six in London (1984-94). *Work in collections:* S. Africa, Canada, Germany, America, Australia and New Zealand. *Commissions:* many portraits, landscapes and places. *Publications:* work repro.: Calendars, Limited Prints. *Signs work:* "Pat Yallup" (water-colours and abstracts), see appendix. *Address:* Gallery House, Llandogo, nr. Monmouth, Monmouthshire NP25 4TJ.

YARDLEY, Bruce Christopher, A.R.O.I. (2000); painter in oil; *b* Reigate, Surrey, 18 Jul., 1962. *m* Caroline Rosier. *Educ:* Reigate Grammar School, Bristol University, Worcester College, Oxford. *Exhib:* R.O.I., biannual solo exhibs. at various galleries in U.K. *Signs work:* "Bruce Yardley." *Address:* 22 Somers Rd., Reigate, Surrey RH2 9DZ.

YARDLEY, John Keith, R.I.(1990); painter, particularly interior and street subjects, in oil and water-colour; *b* Beverley, Yorks., 11 Mar., 1933. *m* Brenda. two *s.* one *d. Educ:* Hastings Grammar School. *Exhib:* R.I., R.W.S., N.E.A.C., numerous one-man shows; awarded Water-colour Foundation prize R.I. (1990). *Work in* *collections:* Merrill Lynch, C.T. Bowring, A.P.V., and private collections. *Publications:* Water-colour - A Personal View; The Art of John Yardley by R. Ranson; Water-colour Impressionists by R. Ranson; John Yardley by Susanne Haines; videos: 'Sunlight in Water-colour' and 'Water-colour in Venice'. *Clubs:* Arts. *Signs work:* "John Yardley" in script. *Address:* 5 Evesham Rd., Reigate, Surrey RH2 9DF.

YATES, Alan, A.R.B.S. (1976), M.S.D.C. (1973), Cert.Ed. (1969), F.R.S.A. (1973); sculptor in cast bronze and aluminium, art teacher; *b* Bishop Auckland, 30 Nov., 1947. *Educ:* Leeholme School; Bishop Auckland Grammar School. *Studied:* Bede College, Durham University (1966-69). *Exhib:* R.A., R.S.A., R.W.A., Paris, Durham University, York, Grantham, Darlington, Perth, Newcastle Polytechnic, Edinburgh, S. Shields, Swansea University, Stratford, Northern Open Touring Exhbn., Chelsea Harbour, Manchester Academy. *Work in collections:* St. James' Youth Centre, Coundon; Grey College, Durham University. *Signs work:* "A. YATES." *Address:* Leaside, Frosterley, Bishop Auckland, Co. Durham DL13 2RH.

YATES, Marie, B.A.Hons (1971); artist; *b* Lancashire, 9 Aug., 1940. *Studied:* Manchester and Hornsey. *Exhib:* Arts Council, British Council, Arnolfini. *Work in collections:* Arts Council, Arnolfini Trust, Cornwall Educ. Com., Plymouth City A.G. *Publications:* A Re-Evaluation of a Proposed Publication (1978). *Signs work:* "Marie Yates." *Address:* 17 Victoria Rd., London N22.

YEOMAN, Martin, R.P., N.E.A.C.; artist in oil, pencil, pen and ink, silver point, pastel, etching, clay; *b* Egham Hythe, 21 July, 1953. *m* Anne Louise. one *s*. *Studied:* R.A. Schools (Peter Greenham). *Exhib:* Agnews, New Grafton Gallery, R.A., N.P.G., Mallett, Waterman Fine Art, Hampton Court Palace, National Gallery, Yemen. *Work in collections:* H.M The Queen, H.R.H. The Prince of Wales, N.P.G., Sir Brinsley Ford, National Trust, Barings Bank. *Commissions:* The Queen's Grandchildren; The Royal Household. *Publications:* National Trust Foundation for Art, catalogue; British Council, catalogue; Ford Collection (The Walpole Soc.); illustrated: Yemen Travels in Dictionary Land by T. MacIntosh Smith. *Clubs:* R.P., N.E.A.C. *Signs work:* "Yeoman." *Address:* 152 Boreham Rd., Warminster, Wilts.

YHAP, Laetitia, D.F.A.(Lond.) (1965); artist; *b* St. Albans, 1 May, 1941. partner: Michael Rycroft. one *s*. *Educ:* Fulham County Grammar School. *Studied:* Camberwell School of Art (1958-62, Euan Uglow, Frank Auerbach), Slade School of Fine Art (1963-65, Harold Cohen, Anthony Green). *Exhib:* solo shows, Piccadilly Gallery (1968-73), Serpentine Gallery (1979), Air Gallery (1984), 'Life at the Edge' Charleston Farmhouse (1993); 'The Business of the Beach' 1988-89 Touring show organised by Laing A.G., Newcastle-upon-Tyne, 'Bound by the Sea', The Berwick Gymnasium (1994), Maritime Counterpoint (1996), Boundary Gallery, London. *Work in collections:* Tate Gallery, Unilever House, Hove A.G., Hastings Museum, Rugby Museum, Portsmouth City A.G., British Council, Contemporary Art Soc., New Hall Cambridge, S. East Arts Coll., University College London, Walker A.G., Liverpool, Nuffield Foundation, D.O.E., Arthur Anderson Coll., Yorkshire, Leicestershire Educ. *Signs work:* "Laetitia Yhap." *Address:* 12 The Croft, Hastings, Sussex TN34 3HH.

YOSHIMOTO, Eiko, P.S., S.W.A., S.B.A., S.P.F.; artist in pastel, conte, charcoal, oil; *b* Japan, 5 July, 1937. *Educ:* Notre Dame Sacred Heart School, Japan; Diploma from Drama School of Toho Film Company, Tokyo. *Studied:* City & Guilds of London Art School (part-time, 1994-96, Eric Morby), École de Société des Pastellistes de France (Jean Pierre Merat). *Exhib:* P.S. (1986-), S.B.A. (1986-), S.W.A. (1987-), Glyndebourne Opera House (1989, 1991), R.A. (1993, 1994, 1997), N.E.A.C. (1986-), Royal Opera House (1992); solo shows: S.P.F. Paris (1992, 1993, 1995, 1996, 1997). *Signs work:* "Eiko Yoshimoto." *Address:* "Hermitage Lodge", The Hermitage, Richmond, Surrey TW10 6SH.

YOUNG, Florence, R.M.S., S.W.A., Associe, Société des Artistes Français; Hon. Mention, Paris Salon (1968), Prix Marie Louise Jules Richard, Paris Salon (1971), Diplôme d'honneur, Biarritz (1971), silver medal, Paris Salon (1981); self taught artist in oil, pastel and water-colour, miniaturist; *b* Preston, Lancs., 19 Nov., 1919. *m* Kenneth Young. one *s.* one *d.* (decd.). *Educ:* Farnworth Grammar School, Lancs. *Exhib:* P.S., R.I., S.W.A., R.M.S., R.W.S. Flower Painting, R.I. Galleries Summer and Winter Salons, Paris Salon, S.M., U.A., Medici, and Llewellyn Alexander Gallery, London. *Work in collections:* Swedish Tool Mfrs., Kingston, Diaform Ltd. Uxbridge, Public Address Engineers Assoc., Harrow, Barclays Bank, Uxbridge. *Commissions:* Swedish Tool Mfrs., Kingston, Diaform Ltd. Uxbridge, Public Address Engineers Assoc., Harrow, Barclays Bank, Uxbridge. *Signs work:* "F. Young." *Address:* 1a Maylands Drive, Uxbridge, Middx. UB8 1BH.

YOUNG, Dr. Joseph L., F.I.A.L.; pioneer of reintegration of art in architecture; creator of over 50 cultural landmarks for civic, educational and religious structures throughout America, including works in mosaic, metal, wood, stained glass, concrete, granite, etc.; author of 2 books on mosaics published by Reinhold, N.Y. (1957-63); guest lecturer and artist-in-residence at numerous institutions of higher learning in U.S.A. and Europe; *b* Pittsburgh, Pa., 27 Nov., 1919. *m* Millicent E. Young. two children. *Educ:* Westminster College, New Wilmington, Pa. *Studied:* Boston Museum School of Fine Arts; American Academy of Art, Rome. *Signs work:* "J. Young." *Address:* Art in Architecture, 7917¹/₂ W. Norton Ave., Los Angeles, Ca. 90046, U.S.A.

YOUNGER, Alan Christopher Wyrill, F.M.G.P.; stained glass designer and maker; part-time lecturer, Richmond University; *b* London, 13 Mar., 1933. *m* Zoë Birchmore. two *d. Educ:* Alleyn's School. *Studied:* Central School of Art (1954-57), and in the Studios of Carl Edwards and Lawrence Lee. First prize Worshipful Company of Glaziers (1960), Sir Arthur Evans travelling scholarship (1961). *Exhib:* Centre International du Vitrial, Chartres (1982). *Work in collections:* Westminster Abbey, Durham, St. Alban's, Southwark, Gloucester and Chester Cathedrals, numerous parish churches in Britain including Luton, Tamworth, Boldre, Haselbech and Monea. *Publications:* The Laporte Rose Window (1989). *Signs work:* overlapping A and Y - see appendix. *Address:* 44 Belvedere Rd., London SE19 2HW.

YOUNGER, Elspeth Chalmers, D.A. (1957), Post Dip. (1958); embroiderer, painter in inks, water-colour, gouache; *b* Paisley. *m* John Gardiner Crawford. one *s.* one *d. Educ:* Camphill Secondary School, Paisley. *Studied:* Glasgow School of Art (1953-58, Kathleen Whyte); National Wool Textile Award (1957), Travelling Scholarship, Paris (1958). *Exhib:* solo shows: 57 Gallery, Edinburgh (1965), Lane

Gallery, Bradford (1965), Civic Arts Centre, Aberdeen (1969, 1971), University of Aberdeen (1971), Cornerstone Gallery, Dunblane (1983, 1984, 1988, 1989), Haddo House, Aberdeen (1988), McEwan & Ritchie Fine Art, Dundee (1990), Tolquhon Gallery, Tarves (1992), Cottage Gallery, Newtyle (1993, 1995, 1997, 1999); group shows include Glasgow School of Art, S.A.C., S.S.A., Scottish Gallery, R.S.W., etc. *Work in collections:* Aberdeenshire Educ. Authority, Tayside Educ. Authority, North British Hotel, Dundee A.G., and private collections throughout Britain, and Norway, Holland, Germany, France, Australia, Canada, U.S.A. *Publications:* in various publications, and in "20th Century Embroidery in Gt. Britain", Vols. 2, 3, 4, by Constance Howard. *Signs work:* "ELSPETH YOUNGER" and date, embroidery unsigned, label on reverse. *Address:* 34 Strachan St., Arbroath, Angus DD11 1UA, Scotland.

YULE, (Duncan) Ainslie, D.A. (1963); sculptor/teacher; Head of Sculpture, Kingston University 1982- (Reader 1987-); *b* North Berwick, 1941. *m* (1) Patricia Carlos (m dissolved). one *d*. (2) 1982, Mary Johnson. *Educ:* Edinburgh College of Art. *Exhib:* regular solo and group exhbns. including Whitechapel A.G. (1973), Gubbio Biennale (1973), Silver Jubilee Exhbn. Battersea Park (1977), Fruitmarket Gallery and travelling (1977-79), Angela Flowers (1986-99), Scottish Gallery (1989-91), Talbot Rice (1999). *Work in collections:* include Aberdeen A.G., A.C.G.B., Dundee A.G., Leeds City A.G., S.A.C. University of Leeds, Gregory Fellow (1974-75). *Clubs:* Chelsea Arts. *Signs work:* "Ainslie Yule." *Address:* 11 Chiswick Staithe, Hartington Rd., London W4 3TP.

Z

ZALMON: see WINER, Zalmon.

ZAO, Wou Ki, Commandeur de la Légion d'Honneur; Commandeur de Mérite National; painter; *b* Pekin, 13 Feb., 1921. *m* Francoise Marquet. *Studied:* Ecole Nationale de Beaux Arts at Hang Tcheou (1935-41). Professor of Drawing, Ecole Nationale de Beaux Arts at Hang Tcheou (1941-47). *Work in collections:* in Germany, England, Austria, Belgium, Brazil, Canada, Switzerland, U.S.A., France, China, Taiwan, Hong Kong, Israel, Italy, Japan, Luxembourg, etc. Praemium Imperiale Lauréat (peinture) 1994, Japan. *Address:* 19 bis, Rue Jonquoy, 75014, Paris, France.

ZEVI, Bruno B., Doctor in Architecture; Academician of San Luca; critic and architect; Prof. of History of Architecture, Rome University; President, International Committee of Architectural Critics; Mem. of the Italian Parliament; *b* Rome, 22 Jan., 1918. *m* Tullia Calabi. one *s*. one *d*. *Educ:* Rome and Harvard University. *Studied:* architecture: Cambridge, Mass., U.S.A. *Publications:* Towards an Organic Architecture, Architecture as Space, Storia dell'Architettura Moderna, Biagio Rossetti, Architectura in nuce, Michelangiolo Architetto, Erich Mendelsohn, Saper vedere la cittá, The modern language of architecture; author of the Voice

"Architecture" in Universal Encyclopedia of the Arts; editor of L'architettura-cronache e storia (Rome and Milan), architectural columnist of the weekly L'Espresso. *Address:* Via Nomentana 150, 00162 Rome.

ZIAR, Elizabeth Rosemary, painter; *b* St. Ives, Cornwall. *m* Ian Ziar, L.D.S., R.C.S. one *s. Educ:* West Cornwall School for Girls (art mistress Miss M.E. Parkins of "Newlyn School"); Penzance School of Art (1936-41 James Lias, 1945 Bouverie Hoyton); Leonard Fuller (1945). *Exhib:* over 30 solo shows in Britain, France and Italy with usual complement of mixed international expositions, e.g. Paris Salon, Monaco, Biarritz (Dip. d'Honneur 1973), Juan-les-Pins (premier award Coupe d'Antibes 1979), R.I., R.B.S.A., S.W.A., U.A., Hesketh Hubbard, etc. *Publications:* 'Good Morrow, Brother.'. *Signs work:* "ZIAR" or with monogram (see appendix); occasionally: "E. R. ZIAR" or "E.R.Z." *Address:* Trevidren, Penzance TR18 2AY.

ZYW, Aleksander, painter; *b* Lida, Poland, 29 Aug., 1905. *m* Leslie Goddard. two *s. Studied:* in Warsaw, Athens, Rome and Paris. *Exhib:* Warsaw, Paris, Basle, Milan, London, Edinburgh. *Work in collections:* State Collection of Poland, National Gallery of Poland, Union of Polish Painters, Tate Gallery, Glasgow Art Gallery, Arts Council of Scotland, University of Edinburgh, Scottish National Gallery of Modern Art, Rhodes National Gallery, Salisbury, Carnegie Trust. *Signs work:* "Zyw." *Address:* Bell's Brae House, Dean Village, Edinburgh EH4 3BJ. *Second Address:* Poggio Lamentano, 57022 Castagneto-Carducci (Livorno), Italy.

APPENDIX I

MONOGRAMS AND SIGNATURES

Ackroyd,
Norman

Adams,
(Dorothea Christina) Margaret

Arnold,
Phyllis Anne

Atkin, Ann

Auld, J.L.M

Backhouse,
David John

Bailey, Caroline

Baines, Richard
John Manwaring

Barber Kennedy,
Mat

Barlow, Gillain

Baumforth,
David John

Baynes,
Pauline Diana

Beilby,
Pauline Margaret

Beltrán, Félix

Benjamin,
Anthony

Bennett,
William

Benton, Graham

Bewick, Pauline

Blackwood, Brian

Blaker, Michael

Blandino, Betty

Blik, Maurice

Bond, Jane

Bransbury, Allan
Harry

Brasier, Jenny

Brazier, Connie

CMB   (water-colours)

CMB   (engraved glass)

Brent, Isabelle

Bridgeman,
John

Brindley,
Donald

Brown, Neil
Dallas

Brown, Ralph

(drawings)   (stamped)

Bruce, George
J.D.

or

Buck, Jon

raised letters
on indented
stamp in
bronze

Budd, Rachel

Bumphrey, Nigel

Butler, Vincent — *Vincent Butler* or **V.B.**

Butt, Anna Theresa — *AA*

Byrom, Gillie Hoyte — *GB*

Caine, O. — *Osmund Caine a Cloine*

Campbell, Huw Phillip —

Camp, Jeffery — *Jeffery Camp*

Carlton, Cedric Charles — *©C*

Carrick, Desmond — *CARRAIS*

CARRAIS (Up to and including 1979)

CARRICK (After 1979)

Carrington-Kerslake,
Lynette

Carter, Joan
Patricia

Cavaciuti, Peter

Chang,
Chien-Ying

Chao, Shao-An

Chatterton,
George Edward

Chauvin, E.

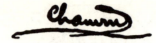

Cheyne, Anna

Clark,
Kenneth Inman
Carr

Clark, Thomas
Humphrey

Clarke, Granville
Daniel

Clements, Jeff

(paintings)

Clyne, Henry Horne

Cobley, David
Hugh

Cochran, Margi

Collins, Michael

Conner, Angela

Conway, Jennifer Anne  (miniatures)

Cooke, S.

Cooper, Emmanuel

Coote, Michael Arnold

Corbett, Peter George

Cornwell, Arthur Bruce

Coutu, Jack 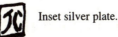 Inset silver plate.

Carvings

Cox, Stephen B.
 or

(on art work)   (on designs/interiors etc.)

Cramp,
Jonathan David

Crawshaw, June

(ceramic signature)

Creber, Frank

Croft, Richard
John

Crossley, Gordon

Crow,
Kathleen Mary

Crowther,
Hugh M.

Crowther,
Stephen

Cummings, Albert
Arratoon Runciman

Curtis,
Anthony Ewart

Czimbalmos,
Magdolna Paal

Czimbalmos,
Szabo Kalman

Dack, Tom

Dakeyne, Gabriel

Dalby, Claire

Danvers, Joan

d'Arbeloff, Natalie or

Darbishire,
Stephen John

Davidson Davis,
Philomena

Davis, Michael
Robert

Day, Jane

de Francia, Peter

Demel, Richard

Dennis,
Christopher John

Dickens, Alison
Margaret

Dickson,
Evangeline Mary
Lambart   small paintings

Di Girolamo,
Megan Ann

Dmoch, Paul

Dowling, Jane

Duffy, Stephen
James

Duffy, Terry

        or

Dunne, Berthold

Durrant, Roy
Turner

        or

Eastop, Geoffrey
Frank

Edwards, Benjamin
Ralph

Elstein, Cecile

Emery, Edwina

Emmerich, Anita
Jane

Evans, Margaret
Fleming

Evans, Ray

Fakhoury, Bushra

Farrell,
Alan Richard

and dated on
reverse of painting

Faulds. James
Alexander

Feeny, P.A.

Fei, Cheng-Wu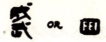

Fellows,
Elaine Helen

Ffyffe, Terrance
Michael

Finch, Michael

Fisher, Don
Mulready

Fisher,
Reginald Stanley

Fleming,
James Hugh

on illustrations
and prints

Forrest, Martin
Andrew

Foster,
Sir Norman Robert

Francyn
(Dehn Fuller)

Frankenthaler,
Helen

Franklin, Annette
Winifred

(paintings and own
design Pottery and
wooden plaques)

(Poole Pottery - painting
a scraffito, 1945-1950)

(mark on bottom of
pots)

Fraser, D.H.

Friers, R.B.

Gamlen, Mary

Gatteaux, Marcel

Giardelli, Arthur

Gibson, Veronica

Gili, Katherine   some works signed:

Gillick, James Balthazar Patrick

Gilmour, Judith   (ceramic Pieces)

Goaman, Michael

Goodwin, Leslie Albert

Gow, Neil

Granger, Margaret I.   or

Granville

Gray, Jane Campbell

Gunn, James Thomson

Grice, David

Hackney, Arthur

Haines Nick

(with finger print and year)

Hallowes, Veda Nanette

Hammick, To Henry St. Vincent

Hampton, Michael

('M' & 'H' WITH GREBES HEAD)

Harris, Alfred

A HARRIS , AH or A Harris

Harrison (née Roberts), Marguerite Hazel

Harvey, Jake

Haughton, Wilfred James

Hawkins, Diana

DIANA HAWKINS. (and date)

(on minitures)

Heron, Susanna

illustrations

Herriot, Alan B. and dated

Hickey, Michael 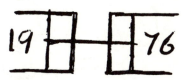 or

Hill, Anthony

Hinchcliffe, Michael

Hind, Margaret Madeleine

Hitchcock, Harold Raymond

Hoare, Diana C.

Hoflehner, Rudolf

Holland, Frances

Homes, R.T.J.

Hooke, Robert
Lowe, Jr.

Horwitz, Angela

House, Ceri
Charles

Hoyland, John

Huckvale, Iris

Hudson, Thomas
Roger Jackson

Hughes, Jim

Hurn, J. Bruce

(oils and acrylic paintings)

(drawings and gouache paintings)

Huston, John I.

Ibbett, Vera

Irvin, Albert

Isom, Graham Michael

Jackson, Ashley

Jefferson, Annelise

(potters stamp)

Jellicoe, Colin

Jenkins, Christopher

Jennings,
Walter Robin

Jobson, Patrick

Jones, Barry Owen

Jones, Heather
Edith

Jones,
Stanley Robert

Jukes, E.E.

Kalashnikov, Anatoly
Ivanovich

Kanidinç,
Salahattin

Kendall, Kay
Thetford

Kennedy, C.

Kern, Doreen

Key, Geoffrey

Portraits and landscapes

Kianush - Wallace,
Katty

Japanese and Chinese
miniatures

Persian miniatures

King, Gordon
Tomas

King, Phillip

Klein, Anita

Kolakowski,
Matthew Edmund

Kuo, Nancy

Lackner, Suzanne O.

Lago, Darren

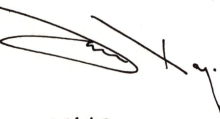

Lake,
C. Elizabeth Matheson

Lambert,
Colin Joseph

Landers,
Linda Anne

Lang, Wharton

Larmont, Eric

Lauder,
Kenneth Scott

Lawrence,
Gordon Robert

Leach, D.

 or seal in foot of pots.

Leach, Mark Alan

Lee, Sidney
Edward

Leech, Raymond

Leyden, J.M.

Lilley, Geoffrey
Ivan

Lillford, Ralph

Littlejohn,
William Hunter

Lockhart, David

Logan, Andrew

Loudon, Irvine

Lucas, Suzanne

Luckas, Joy
Heather

Macarrón, Ricardo

McCarter, Keith   (on small works)

McCullough,
George

MacDonald,
Alastair James
Henderson   or

McEwan Reid,
Marjorie

McEwan Reid,
Robert

Macey, Leo

McFall, David

McGookin, Colin
Trevoe

McIntyre, Donald

Macmiadhachain,
Padraig

Madgwick, Clive

Magis, Pascal

Maklouf, Raphael

Malcles, Jean-Denis

Mapp, John Ernest

Margrie, Victor

Marr, Leslie

Marriott, Michael

Martin, Marie-Louise

Master, Jean

Matania, Franco

Matheson, Andrew
Kenneth Mackenzie

Mendoza, Edwin

Mendoza, June

Micah, Lisa

Middleton, Renée

(or appropriate date)

Miller, David T.

Millner, Etienne
Henry, de la Fargue

Miners, Neil

Moncher - Dunkley,
Anthea

Montané, Roger

Moodie, Stuart

Moreton, Nicolas (sculpture)

Munslow, Angela E.

Muszynski,
Leszek Tadeusz

Nalecz, Halima

Neal, Trevor

Nellens, Roger

Ng, Kiow Ngor

Noad, Julie Ann

Norland
(Neuschul), Khalil

Ohl, Gabrielle

Paes, Rui

Parsons,
Denis Alva

Initials
Banker mark based on
hobby of unicycling

Pass, Donald James

Pavitt, Diane

Peace, David

Pearson, James E.

Penketh-Simpson,
Barbara   miniatures

Perrin, Sally Jane

Piché, Roland

Pike, Mark Walter

Pincus,
Helen Frances

Pitfield,
Thomas Baron

Plowman,
Christopher Charles

Polaine, Peter

Pollard, Michael
Vincent

or

Pullan, Margaret
Ida Elizabeth

Pullan, Tessa

Purnell, John

stamped on sculpture

Pye, William

or

Quigley, Vlad

Rank-Broadley, Ian

Roberts,
Phyllis Kathleen

P. K. ROBERTS

Robertson,
Sheila Macleod

(on still life and flower paintings)

Robinson, Barbara

Rogers, Joseph
Shepperd (Nevia)

Roper,
Geoffrey John

Roseman, Stanley

Ross, Alastair
Robertson

Roy, Michael

Sahai, Viréndra

Saltzman, William

Sanderson, Roger

Sapieha, Christine

Schmook, Berhard

Schwarz, Hans

Seal, Norman

Searle, Ronald

See-Paynton,
Colin Frank

Senft, Nadin  (signature on bronzes etc.)

Shackleton,
Keith Hope

Shaw,
Barbara Nancy

Shipsides, Frank

Shorthouse,
G. Sydney

Simpson, Cathy

Simpson, Noelle

Sitwell, Pauline

Sloan, Bob   and/or

Smith, Basil

Smith, Edward
John Milton

Snelling, John

Snowden,
Hilda Mary

Soulages, Pierre

Souza, F.N.

Spencer, Claire

Stevens, Margaret
Cecilie

Stokes, Vincent

Storey, Terence

Stuart, Kiel

Sullivan, Jason

Sullivan, Wendy

Summers,
Leslie John

Tajiri, Shinkichi

Tate, Barbara

Tate,
Barbara and James

Tavener, Robert

Taylor, Alan

Taylor,
Michael John

⬤ ⬅ red

Taylor, Pamela   *Taylor*   or   *T*   or   Pam Taylor

Taylor, Wendy Ann

Wendy Taylor. (prints and work)

Thelwell, Norman   ·thelwell·

Thomas, M.   Margaret Thomas

Till, Michael John   Michael Till.

Tisdall, H.

Tolley, Sheila

Tuckwell,
George Arthur

Turnbull, William

Turner,
William Ralph

Underwood,
Keith Alfred

Vango, David

Verdijk, Gerard

Vogel, Suzi

Walker, Richard
Ian Bentham

Wasim, L.

Watson,
Arthur James

Watson, Heather

Watson Stewart,
Avril Veronica

 (Owl followed by maiden name,
Avril V. Gibb)

Watts, Dorothy

Watts,
Michael Gorse

 (Generally)   (As Septimus
Pike)

Watts, Peter

Wattson Dean, Meg (miniatures)

Wauters, Jef

Webb, Elizabeth

Weeks, John
Lawrence Macdonald

Wells, Peter *PETER WELLS* or

Weltman, Boris

Werge-Hartley, Alan

Werge-Hartley,
Jeanne

White, Mary

Whitten,
B. Janice E.

Williams-Ellis,
Bronwen Mary

Stamp

Written

Willies, Joan

Winer, Zalmon

Wolverson,
Margaret Elizabeth

Wood,
Gerald Stanley Kent

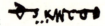

Monogram Stamp

Woodward, Justine

Woolf-Nellist,
Meg

Wright, Stuart
Pearson R.

Yallup, Pat

Younger, Alan
Christopher Wyrill

Ziar, Elizabeth
Rosemary

OBITUARY

ADAM-TESSIER, Maxime
ARMOUR, Mary, A.R.S.A., R.S.W., R.S.A., R.G.I., LL.D.
BARRETT, Roderic, D.U.
BENJAMIN, Anthony, N.D.D., R.E., F.R.S.A.
BLAKE, Jane, R.M.S., M.A.A.
BLESKY, Wiltold John
BOWETT, Druie
BRAYER, Yves
BRUCE, Matt, D.A., R.I.
BURROUGH, Thomas Hedley Bruce, T.D., R.W.A., F.R.I.B.A.
CHILD, Josephine Heather, M.B.E.
CLARK, Jean Manson, R.W.S.
CLARKE, Richard Cambridge, B.A.
COLE, Sibylle, R.B.S.A., F.R.S.A., L.F.A.C.
COLLET, Ruth Isabelle
DEAN, Beryl, M.B.E., A.R.C.A., F.S.D.C.
de MERIC, Rosalie, F.F.P.S., B.A.
DICKER, Molly, S.W.A.
EARDLEY, Enid Mary, N.S.
FOLLAND, Ronald Norman
FOOT, Victorine, D.A.
FRENKIEL, Stanislaw, R.W.A.
FRIERS, Rowel Boyd, M.B.E., Hon. M.A., R.U.A., U.W.S.
GAGE, Edward, M.B.E., R.S.W., D.A., P.P.S.S.A.
GIFFORD, Denis
GILES, Phyllis Margaret, M.A.
GILL, Stanley Herbert, A.R.C.A., A.T.D.
GOMBRICH, Sir Ernest Hans, O.M., Kt., C.B.E., Ph.D., F.B.A., F.S.A.
GOODCHILD, Francis Philip, A.R.C.A., F.S.A.E.
GRANGER, Margaret I, S.B.A.
GREENWOOD, Sydney, A.T.D., R.I., R.W.A., F.R.S.A.
HAINARD, Robert
HALE, Elsie, H.S.
HANKEY, Christopher Alers, O.B.E., M.A., B.Sc.
HAUGHTON, Wilfred James, U.W.S., F.R.S.A., R.U.A., W.C.S.I.
HILL, Derek, C.B.E.

HITCHCOCK, Malcolm John, R.W.A.
HOFFER, Francis Peter Bernard, Dip. Arch., F.C.S.D., F.F.B.
HOGARTH, Arthur Paul
HUTCHISON, Sidney Charles, C.V.O., F.S.A., F.M.A., F.A.A.H., F.R.S.A.
JEFFERSON, Alan, A.R.C.A.
JOHNSTON, Duncan
JOHNSTONE, JOHN, D.A., A.R.S.A.
KIFF, Ken
LAIRD, Michael Donald, O.B.E., F.R.S.A., F.C.S.D., F.R.I.A.S., R.I.B.A.
LASDUN, Sir Denys, C.H., Kt., C.B.E.
LEE, Rosie, D.F.A.
LINDLEY, Brian
LINDSAY, Rosemary, S.B.A.
MACCABE, Max, F.R.S.A., W.C.S.I., Hon. R.U.A.
McKENZIE, Winifred
MESSELET, Jean
MOORE, Leslie Lancelot Hardy, R.I.
MULLARKEY, Audrey Eunice, E.A.C., C&G.
PAINE, Ula, R.D.S.
PARRY, Sheila Harwood, R.M.S., F.R.S.A.
POMERANCE, Fay
RENNIE, Neil, M.C. B.Sc., F.F.P.S
ROBERTS, Will, R.C.A.
ROSSITER, Anthony, M.C.S.D., R.W.A.
SANCHA, Carlos, R.P.
SAYCE, Harry H, F.I.A.L., N.D.D.
SHIELD, George William, B.Sc.
STEPHENSON, Prof. Ian, B.A., D.Litt., R.A.
SWANN, Peter C., M.A., LL.D.
SWEET, George
TAMBLYN-WATTS, Harold William
TRIBE, Barbara, F.R.B.S., R.W.A.
TUCKWELL, George Arthur, D.F.M., A.T.D., N.D.D.
VIGG, Bob, B.Ed.
WARD, Thomas William, A.R.C.A., R.E., R.W.S.
WOOLFORD, Harry Russell Halkerston, O.B.E., Hon. M.A.
WORSLEY, John Godfrey Bernard, P.P.R.S.M.A.

QUALIFICATIONS AND GENERAL ABBREVIATIONS

In using this list of abbreviations care should be taken to split up any compound abbreviation into its constituent parts, e.g., "F.R.S." should be broken into "F." and "R.S.," the equivalents of these letters being found under "F." and "R.S." respectively.

A.	Associate; Associate-Engraver (of Royal Academy).
A.A.	Architectural Association; Automobile Association.
A.A.A.	Allied Artists of America; Australian Academy of Art.
A.A.D.W.	Association of Artists/Designers in Wales (disbanded).
A.A.E.A.	American Academy of Equine Art.
A.A.H.	Association of Art Historians.
A.A.I.	Association of Art Institutions.
A.A.L.	Academy of Art and Literature.
A.A.P.L.	American Artists Professional League.
A.A.S.	Aberdeen Art Society.
A.B.	Art's Bachelor (American).
A.B.I.R.A.	American Biographical Institute Research Association.
A.B.P.R.	Association of British Picture Restorers.
A.C.A.	Association of Consultant Architects; Atlanta College of Art.
A.C.G.B.	Arts Council of Great Britain.
A.C.T.C.	Art Class Teacher's Certificate.
A.C.W.	Art Council of Wales (formerly W.A.C.).
A.D.	Anno Domini.
A.D.A.E.	Advanced Diploma in Art Education.
A.D.B.	Associate of the Drama Board.
A.D.C.	Aide-de-camp.
A.D.G.	Architect Diplome par le Gouvernement.
A.D.M.S.	Assistant Director of Medical Services.
A.E.C.	Adult Education Centre.
A.F.I.A.P.	Artiste, Fédération Internationale de l'Art Photographique.
A.G.	Art Gallery.
A.G.B.I.	Artists' General Benevolent Institution.
A.G.I.	Artistes Graphiques Internationales.
A.G.M.S.	Art Gallery and Museum Services.

A.G.P.A.	Artes Graficas de Pan America.
A.G.P.P.	Academia Gentium Pro Pace.
A.I.	Auctioneers' Institute.
A.I.A.	Academy of Irish Art; American Institute of Architecture.
A.I.A.L.	Association of International Institute of Art and Letters.
A.I. Archts.(Scot.).	Association of the Incorporation of Architects in Scotland.
A.I.C.A.	Association Internationale des Critiques d'Art.
A.I.D.	American Institute of Decorators.
A.I.I.D.	American Institute of Interior Design.
A.K.C.	Associate, King's College.
A.M.	Air Ministry; Member of Order of Australia.
A.M.A.	Associate of the Museums Association.
A.M.C.	Art Masters' Certificate.
A.M.I.P.	Associate Member, Institute of Plumbing.
A.M.T.C.	Art Masters' Teaching Certificate.
A.N.A.	American National Academy.
A.O.C.	Artists of Chelsea.
A.O.I.	Association of Illustrators.
A.O.S.D.A.N.A.	Aosdana is an affiliation of artists engaged in literature, music and visual arts in Ireland.
A.P.A.	Association of Polish Artists.
A.P.S.	American Portrait Society.
A.R.C.A.	Associate of the Royal College of Art.
Ariz.	Arizona.
A.R.W.A.	Associate of the Royal West of England Academy.
A.S.A.	American Society of Artists Inc.
A.S.B.A.	American Society of Botanical Artists.
A.S.G.	Air Services Grants.
A.S.L.A.	American Society of Landscape Architects.
A.S.M.A.(Q).	Australian Society for Miniature Art (Queensland).
Assoc.	Association.
Asst.	Assistant.
A.S.T.M.S.	Association of Scientific, Technical and Managerial Staff.
A.T.C.	Art Teachers' Certificate.
A.T.D.	Art Teachers' Diploma.
A.U.C.	Anno Urbis Conditæ (from the foundation of the city).
A.V.A.W.	Association of Visual Artists in Wales.
Ave.	Avenue.
A.W.G.	Art Workers' Guild.
A.W.I.	Australian Water-colour Institute.
b.	born.

B.A.	Bachelor of Arts; British Airways.
B.A.A.T.	British Association of Art Therapists.
B.A.C.	British Aircraft Corporation.
B.A.D.A.	British Antique Dealers' Association.
B.Ae.	British Aerospace.
B-A.S.	Britain-Australia Society.
Batt.	Battalion.
B.B.C.	British Broadcasting Corporation.
B.C.	Before Christ.
B.C.C.	British Craft Centre.
B.Chrom.	Bachelor of Chromatics.
B.C.L.	Bachlor of Civil Law.
B.D.	Bachelor of Divinity.
B.E.A.	British European Airways.
B.Ed.	Bachlor of Education; Board of Education.
B.E.D.A.	Bureau of European Designers' Association.
Beds.	Bedfordshire.
B.E.F.	British Expeditionary Force.
B.E.N.A.	British Empire Naturalist Association.
Berks.	Berkshire.
B.F.A.	Batchelor of Fine Arts.
B'ham.	Birmingham.
B.H.P.	Broken Hill Priority Ltd.
B.H.S.A.I.	British Horse Society Assistant Instructor.
B.I.A.T.	British Institute of Architectural Technicians.
B.I.F.	British Industries Fair.
B.I.I.A.	British Institute of Industrial Art.
B.I.I.D.	British Institute of Interior Design.
B.I.M.	(see I.Mgt.).
B.I.P.P.	British Institute of Professional Photography.
B.I.S.	British Interplanetary Society.
B.L.	Barrister-at-Law.
Bldg.	Building.
B.Litt.	Bachelor of Letters.
Blvd.	Boulevard.
B.M.	British Museum.
B.O.A.C.	British Overseas Airways Corporation.
B.of E.	Board of Education.
B.O.U.	British Ornithologists' Union.
B.P.D.	British Society of Posters Designers.
B.P.S.	British Psychological Society; Birmingham Pastel Society.
B.R.C.	British Refugee Council.
Bros.	Brothers.
B.S.C.	British Society of Cinematographers.
B.Sc.	Bachelor of Science.
B.S.I.	British Standards Institution.

B.S.M.G.P.	British Society of Master Glass Painters.
B.Soc.Sc.	Bachelor of Social Science.
Bt.	Baronet.
B.T.A.	British Travel Association.
Bucks.	Buckinghamshire.
B.W.S.	British Water-colour Society.
C.	Central.
c.	century.
C.A.C.	Chertsey Art Club.
Caerns.	Caernarvonshire.
Calif.	California.
Cambs.	Cambridge; Cambridgeshire.
Capt.	Captain.
C.A.S.	Cathcart Art Society.
C.A.S.T.	Centre for Art, Science and Technology.
C.A.S.W.	Contemporary Art Society for Wales.
Cav.	Cavalière (Knight).
C.A.V.S.	Center for Advanced Visual Studies.
C.B.	Companion of the Bath.
C.B.E.	Commander Order of the British Empire.
C.C.	County Council; County Councillor.
C.C.H.	Cacique Crown of Honour.
C.D.S.	Cambridge Drawing Society.
C.E.M.A.	Council for the Encouragement of Music and Arts.
C.E.R.N.	Centre for European Nuclear Research.
Cert.	Certificate.
Cert.A.D.	Certificate in Art and Design.
Cert. F.A.	Certificate in Fine Art.
Certs.	Certificates.
C.F.E.	College of Further Education.
C.G.A.	Cheltenham Group of Artists.
Chas.	Chambers.
Ch.B.	Bachelor of Surgery.
C.H.E.	College of Higher Education.
C.I.	Channel Isles.
C.I.A.D.	Central Institute for Art and Design.
C.I.E.	Companion of the Order of the Indian Empire.
C.I.H.A.	Comité Internationale de l'Histoire de l'Art.
C.I.S.	Institute of Chartered Secretaries and Administrators.
Cl.	Close.
C.L.A.S.	Calligraphy and Lettering Art Society.
C.M.	Master of Surgery.
C.M.G.	Companion of St. Michael and St. George.
C.N.A.A.	Council for National Academic Awards

	(disbanded).
Co.	Company; County.
c/o	care of.
C.O.I.D.	Council of Industrial Design.
Col.	Colonel.
Com.	Committee; Common.
Comdr.	Commander.
Conn.	Connecticut.
Corp.	Corporation.
Cos.	Companies.
C.P.	College of Preceptors.
C.P.A.	Craft Potters Association.
C.P.R.	Canadian Pacific Railway.
C.P.S.	Contemporary Portrait Society.
Cres.	Crescent.
C.S.	Chemical Society; Conchological Society of Great Britain and Ireland.
C.S.D.	The Chartered Society of Designers (formerly Society of Industrial Artists and Designers).
C.S.I.	Companion of the Order of the Star of India.
C.S.M.A.	Cornish Society of Marine Artists.
C.S.P.	Chartered Society of Physiotherapists.
C.T.	Connecticut.
Ct.	Court.
Cttee.	Committee.
C.U.P.	Cambridge University Press.
C.V.O.	Commander of the Royal Victorian Order.
C.W.A.C.	City of Westminster Arts Council.
d.	daughter.
D.A.	Diploma of Art; Diploma of Edinburgh College of Art; Doctor of Arts.
D.A.E.	Diploma in Art Education.
D.B.E.	Dame Grand Cross Order of the British Empire.
D.C.	District of Columbia.
D.C.L.	Doctor of Civil Law.
D.C.M.	Distinguished Conduct Medal.
D.D.	Doctor of Divinity.
decd.	deceased.
Dept.	Department.
Des. R.C.A.	Designer of the Royal College of Art.
D.F.A.	Diploma of Fine Art.
D.F.Astrol.S.	Diploma of the Faculty of Astrological Studies.
D.I.A.	Design and Industries Association.
Dip.A.D.	Diploma in Art and Design.
Dip.F.A.	Diploma in Fine Art.
Dip.H.E.	Diploma in Higher Education.

D.L.	Deputy Lieutenant.
D.Litt.	Doctor of Letters.
D.N.B.	Dictionary of National Biography.
D.O.E.	Department of the Environment.
D.P.M.	Diploma in Psychological Medicine.
Dr.	Doctor.
D.R.C.O.G.	Diploma of Royal College of Obstetricians and Gynaecologists.
D.S.	Dental Surgery; Dental Surgeon.
D.Sc.	Doctor of Science.
D.S.L.U.	Association of the Slovene plastic artists.
D.S.O.	Companion of the Distinguished Service Order.
D.St.J.	Dame of Honour, Order of St. John of Jerusalem.
E.	East.
E.A.G.M.A.	East Anglian Group of Marine Artists.
E.C.I.A.	European Committee of Interior Architects.
Educ.	Educated; Education.
E.E.C.	European Economic Community.
E.I.S.	Educational Institute of Scotland.
E.M.F.	European Management Foundation.
E.S.	Entomological Society.
Esq.	Esquire.
etc.	etcetera.
Exam.	Examination.
Exhbn.	Exhibition.
Exhib.	Exhibited.
F.	Fellow; Foreign Member.
F.A.T.G.	Fine Art Trade Guild.
F.B.A.	Fellow of the British Academy.
F.B.S.Comm.	Fellow of the British Society of Commerce.
F.C.A.	Federation of Canadian Artists.
F.C.B.S.I.	Fellow of the Chartered Building Societies Institute.
F.E.T.C.	Further Education Teacher's Certificate.
F.F.S.	Fellow of the Franklin Society.
F.G.A.	Fellow of the Gemmological Association.
F.G.C.L.	Fellow, Goldsmiths' College, London.
F.G.E.	Fellow of the Guild of Glass Engravers.
F.I.A.L.	Fellow of the International Institute of Arts and Letters.
F.Inst.C.	Fellow of the Institute of Commerce.
F.I.S.A.	International Federation of Works of Art.
Fla.	Florida.
F.L.S.	Fellow, Linnean Society of London.
F.M.A.	Fellow, Museums Association.
F.N.C.F.	Federation Nationale de la Culture Française.

F.P.E.	Fellow, Philosophical Enquiry.
F.P.S.	Free Painters and Sculptors.
F.S.I.	Fellow of the Surveyors' Institute.
F.S.P.	Fellow of Sheffield Polytechnic.
F.S.S.	Federation of Scottish Sculptors.
Ft.	Feet; Foot.
F.T.D.A.	Fellow of the Theatrical Designers and Craftsmen's Association.
Ga.	Georgia.
G.B.E.	Knight Grand Cross Order of the British Empire.
G.C.B.	Knight Grand Cross of the Bath.
G.C.M.G	Knight Grand Cross of St. Michael and St. George.
G.C.S.I.	Knight Grand Commander of the Star of India.
g-d.	grand-daughter.
Gdn.	Garden.
Gdns.	Gardens.
G.E.S.M.	Group for Educational Services in Museums.
G.I.	Royal Glasgow Institute of Fine Arts.
G.L.C.	Guild of Lettering Craftsmen; Greater London Council.
Glos.	Gloucestershire.
G.M.A.S.	Miniature Art Society of Georgia.
G.M.C.	Guild of Memorial Craftsmen.
Govt.	Government.
G.P.D.S.T.	Girls' Public Day School Trust.
G.P.Fire E.	Graduate Institution of Fire Engineers.
G.P.O.	General Post Office.
G.P.S.	Glasgow Printmaking Society.
Gr.	Grove.
G.R.A.	Guild of Railway Artists.
g-s.	grandson.
G.S.	Geological Society.
G.S.A.	Glasgow School of Art.
G.S.W.A.	Glasgow Society of Women Artists.
Gt.	Great.
H.	Hon. Member.
H.A.C.	Hampstead Artists Council.
Hants.	Hampshire.
H.D.F.A.	Higher Diploma in Fine Art.
H.Dip.A.D.	Higher Diploma in Art and Design.
Herts.	Hertfordshire.
H.F.R.A.	Hon. Foreign Academician.
H.L.I.	Highland Light Infantry.
H.M.	His Majesty; Her Majesty.
H.M.I.	H.M. Inspector of Schools.

H.M.S.O.	Her Majesty's Stationery Office.
H.R.H.	His Royal Highness; Her Royal Highness.
H.S.	Hilliard Society.
H.S.A.	Hampstead Society of Artists.
H.S.S.	History of Science Society (American).
Hunts.	Huntingdonshire.
I.A.A.	International Association of Art.
I.A.A.S.	Incorporated Association of Architects and Surveyors.
I.A.A.S.B.A.	International Associate, American Society of Botanical Artists.
I.Ae.E.	Institute of Aeronautical Engineers.
I.A.L.	International Institute of Arts and Letters.
I.Arb.	Institute of Arbitrators.
I.A.S.	Incorporated Association of Surveyors; Irish Art Society.
I.B.A.	International Biographical Association.
I.B.D.	Institute of British Decorators and Interior Designers.
I.B.I.A.	Insititute of British Industrial Art.
I.C.	Institute of Chemistry.
I.C.A.	Institute of Contemporary Arts.
I.C.E.	Institute of Civil Engineers.
I.C.O.GRA.D.A.	International Council of Graphic Design Association.
I.C.O.M.	International Council of Museums.
I.C.O.M.O.S.	International Council of Monuments and Sites.
I.C.S.	Indian Civil Service.
I.C.S.I.D.	International Council of Societies of Industrial Design.
I.D.	Institute of Directors; Institute of Decorators.
I.E.D.	Institution of Engineer Designers.
I.E.E.	Institute of Electrical Engineers.
I.E.L.A.	Irish Exhibition of Living Art.
I.F.A.	Incorporated Faculty of Arts.
I.F.A.W.	International Fund for Animal Welfare.
I.F.I.	International Federation of Interior Artchitects/Designers.
I.F.S.	Irish Free State.
I.G.A.	International Guild of Artists.
I.G.B.	Brazilian Institute of Genealogy.
I.I.C.	Internatioanl Institute for Conservation of Paintings.
I.L.E.A.	Inner London Education Authority.
I.L.G.A.	Institute of Local Government Administration.
Ill.	Illinois.
I.M.B.I.	Institute of Medical and Biological Illustration.

I.M.C.E.	Institute of Mechanical and Civil Engineers.
I.M.E.	Institute of Mechanical Engineers; Institute of Engineers.
I.Mgt.	Institute of Management (formerly British Institute of Management.
I.M.M.	Institute of Mining and Metallurgy.
Imp.	Printer (Imprimerie, Imp).
I.N.A.	Institute of Naval Architects.
Inst.	Institute; Institution.
I.O.M.	Isle of Man.
I.O.W.	Isle of Wight.
I.P.A.	Portuguese Institute of Archaeology.
I.P.A.T.	International Porcelain Artist Teachers.
I.P.D.	Institute of Professional Designers.
I.P.G.	Independent Painters Group; Industrial Painters Group.
I.P.I.	Institute of Patentees and Inventors.
I.P.M.	Institute of Personnel Management.
I.S.	International Society of Sculptors, Painters and Gravers.
I.S.C.A.	International Society of Catholic Artists.
I.S.L.F.D.	Incorporated Society of London Fashion Designers.
I.S.M.P.	International Society of Marine Painters.
I.S.O.	Imperial Service Order.
I.S.T.D.	Imperial Society of Teachers of Dancing.
I.T.A.C.	Imperial Three Arts Club.
I.T.D.	Institute of Training and Development.
I.W.S.	International Wool Secretariat.
I.W.S.P.	Institute of Work Study Practitioners.
J.H.A.M.I.	Johns Hopkins University Association of Medical Illustrations.
J.I.	Institute of Journalists.
J.P.	Justice of the Peace.
Junr.	Junior.
K.A.A.G.	Kirkles Art Action Group.
K.B.E.	Knight Commander Order of the British Empire.
K.C.	King's Counsel.
K.C.B.	Knight Commander of the Bath.
K.C.C.	Kent County Council.
K.C.M.G.	Knight Commander of St. Michael and St. George.
K.C.S.G.	Knight Commander of St. Gregory the Great.
K.C.S.I.	Knight Commander of the Star of India.
K.C.V.O.	Knight Commander of the Royal Victorian Order.
K.G.	Knight of the Order of the Garter.
K.I.A.D.	Kent Institute of Art and Design.

Kt.	Knight.
L.	Licentiate.
La.	Louisiana; Lane.
L.A.	Library Association; Los Angeles.
L.A.A.	Liverpool Academy of Arts.
L.A.M.D.A.	London Academy of Music and Dramatic Art.
Lancs.	Lancashire.
L.A.W.	Liverpool Artists Workshop.
L.C.	Legislative Council.
L.C.A.D	London Certificate in Art and Design.
L.C.C.	London County Council.
L.D.A.D.	London Diploma of Art and Design.
L.D.S.	Licentiate in Dental Surgery.
Leics.	Leicestershire.
L.G.	Life Guards.
L.G.S.M.	Licentiate, Guildhall School of Music and Drama.
L.I.	Landscape Institute.
Lieut.	Lieutenant.
L.I.F.A.	Licentiate of International Faculty of Arts.
Lincs.	Lincolnshire.
L.I.S.T.D.	Licentiate of the Imperial Society of Teachers of Dancing.
L.L.A.	Lady Literate in Arts.
LL.B.	Bachelor of Laws.
LL.D.	Doctor of Laws.
LL.M.	Master of Laws.
L.P.T.B.	London Passenger Transport Board.
L.S.	Linnean Society.
L.S.A.	Licentiate of the Society of Apothecaries.
L.S.I.A.	Licentiate of the Society of Industrial Artists.
L.S.U.	Louisiana State University.
Ltd.	Limited.
M.	Member; Ministry; Monsieur.
m.	married; metre.
M.A.	Master of Arts.
MA.	Massachusetts.
M.A.A.	Medical Artists' Association; Miniature Artists of America.
M.A.F.A.	Manchester Academy of Fine Arts.
M.A.I.	Master of Fine Arts International.
Mans.	Mansions.
M.A.S.-F.	Miniature Art Society/Florida.
M.A.S.-N.J.	Miniature Art Society/New Jersey.
M.A.S.-W.	Miniature Art Society/Washington.
Mass.	Massachusetts.

M.B.	Bachelor of Medicine.
M.B.E.	Member of the Order of the British Empire.
M.C.	Military Cross.
M.Chrom.	Master of Chromatics.
M.D.	Doctor of Medicine; Managing Director.
M.D.E.	Mitglieder - Meister der Einbandkunst.
Mem.	Member.
men.	mention.
Messrs.	Messieurs.
M.F.A.	Master of Fine Art.
M.G.P.	Master Glass Painters.
Mich.	Michigan.
Middx.	Middlesex.
Minn.	Minnesota.
M.Inst.M.	Member, Institute of Marketing.
M.Inst.Pkg.	Member, Institute of Packaging.
M.I.T.	Massachusetts Institute of Technology.
M.L.	Licentiate in Medicine.
M.Litt.	Master of Letters.
Mme.	Madame.
Mo.	Missouri.
M.of D.	Ministry of Defence.
M.of E.	Ministry of Education.
M.of H.	Ministry of Health.
M.O.I.	Ministry of Information.
M.of S.	Ministry of Suppl.y
M.of W.	Ministry of Works.
M.O.M.A.	Museum of Modern Art.
Mon.	Monmouthshire.
M.P.S.G.	Miniature Painters, Sculptors and Gravers Society of Washington D.C.
M.S.	Society of Miniaturists; Motor Ship.
MS.	Manuscript.
M.Sc.	Master of Science.
M.S.M.	Meritorious Service Medal.
M.Soc.Sc.	Master of Social Science.
MSS.	Manuscripts.
M-S.S.E.	Multi-Sensory Sculpture Exhibitions.
M.V.O.	Member of the Royal Victorian Order.
N.	North.
N.A.	National Academy of Design (New York).
N.A.A.	National Artists Association.
N.A.C.F.	National Art Collection Fund.
N.A.D.F.A.S.	National Association of Decorative and Fine Arts Societies.
N.A.M.M.	National Association of Master Masons.

N.A.P.A.	National Acrylic Painters' Association.
N.B.	North Britain.
N.B.A.	North British Academy.
N.B.L.	National Book League.
N.C.	North Carolina.
N.C.A.C.	New Chertsey Art Club.
N.C.B.	National Coal Board.
N.C.D.A.D.	National Council for Diplomas in Art and Design.
N.C.R.	National Cash Register.
N.D.D.	National Diploma in Design.
N.E.A.C.	New English Art Club.
N.E.C.	National Executive Committee.
N.E.C.A.	National Exhibition of Children's Art.
N.F.T.	National Film Theatre.
N.F.U.	National Froebel Union.
N.G.A.	National Gallery of Australia.
N.H.	New Hampshire.
N.I.	Northern Ireland.
N.J.	New Jersey.
N.M.	New Mexico.
N.M.G.M.	National Museums and Galleries on Merseyside.
No.	Number.
Notts.	Nottinghamshire.
Notts. S.A.	Nottingham Society of Artists.
N.P.	Notary Public.
N.P.G.	National Portrait Gallery.
N.P.S.	National Portrait Society.
nr.	near
N.R.D.	National Registered Designer.
N.S.	National Society.
N.S.A.	New Society of Artists; Natal Society of Artists; Newlyn Society of Artists.
N.S.A.E.	National Society for Art Education.
N.S.M.P.	National Society of Mural Painters.
N.S.P.S.	National Society of Painters, Sculptors and Printmakers.
N.S.W.	New South Wales.
N.U.M.	National Union of Mineworkers.
N.U.M.A.S.T.	National Union of Marine, Aviation and Shipping Transport Officers.
N.U.T.	National Union of Teachers.
N.W.A.B.	North West Art Board.
N.Y.	New York.
N.Y.S.	New York State.
N.Z.	New Zealand.
O.	Ohio.

O.A.S.	Oxford Society of Artists.
O.B.E.	Officer Order of the British Empire.
O.C.	Order of Canada (Officer).
O.C.R.	Officer of the Crown of Roumania.
O.C.S.	Oriental Ceramic Society.
O.D.A.C.A.	Original Doll Artist Council of America.
O.H.M.S.	On Her Majesty's Service.
Okla.	Oklahoma.
O.L.J.	Officer Companion of Order of St. Lazarus of Jerusalem.
O.Ont.	Order of Ontario.
O.S.	Optical Society.
O.S.A.	Ontario Society of Arts.
O.S.B.	Order of St. Benedict.
O.St.J.	Officer of the Most Venerable Order of the Hospital of St. John of Jerusalem.
O.U.D.S.	Oxford University Dramatic Society.
O.U.P.	Oxford University Press.
O.W.S.	Old Water-colour Society (defunct).
Oxon.	Oxford.
P.	President.
P.A.I.	Paisley Art Institute.
P.A.S.I.	Professor Associate of the Surveyor's Institution.
P.C.	Privy Councillor.
P.C.F.C.	Polytechnics and Colleges Funding Council.
P.E.N.	Poets, Playwrights, Editors, Essayists, Novelists Club.
Penn.	Pennsylvania.
P.G.C.E.	Post Graduate Certificate of Education.
Ph.B.	Bachelor of Philosophy.
Ph.D.	Doctor of Philosophy.
Phil.	Philosophy.
P.I.	Portrait Institute.
P.I.H.	Pictures in Hospitals.
Pk.	Park.
Pl.	Place.
P.M.C.	Personnel Management Centre.
P. & O.	Peninsular and Oriental Steam Navigation Co., Ltd.
Pres.	President.
Princ.	Principal; Principle.
Prof.	Professor.
P.S.	Pastel Society.
Q.C.	Queen's Counsel.
Q.E.H.	Queen Elizabeth's Hospital School.
Q.M.W.	Queen Mary and Westfield College, London.

R.A.	Royal Academician; Royal Academy.
R.A.A.	Runnymede Association of Arts.
R.A.A.S.	Royal Amateur Art Society.
R.A.C.	Royal Automobile Club.
R.A.E.	Royal Aircraft Establishment.
R.A.F.	Royal Air Force.
R.A.I.	Royal Anthropological Institute.
R.A.M.	Royal Academy of Music.
R.A.M.C.	Royal Army Medical Corps.
R.A.S.	Royal Astronomical Society; Royal Asiatic Society; Richmond Art Society; Ridley Art Society.
R.B.A.	Royal Society of British Artists.
R.B.C.	Royal British Colonial Society of Artists.
R.B.G.	Royal Botanic Gardens.
R.B.S.	Royal Society of British Sculptors.
R.B.S.A.	Royal Birmingham Society of Artists.
R.C.A.	Royal College of Art; Royal Canadian Academy; Royal Cambrian Academician.
R.Cam.A.	Royal Cambrian Academy.
R.C.G.P.	Royal College of General Practitioners.
R.C.I.	Royal Colonial Institute.
R.C.M.	Royal College of Music.
R.C.N.	Royal College of Nursing.
R.C.O.	Royal College of Organists.
R.C.O.G.	Royal College of Obstetricians and Gynaecologists.
R.C.P.	Royal College of Physicians.
R.C.S.	Royal College of Surgeons.
R.C.S.E.	Royal College of Surgeons, Edinburgh.
R.D.I.	Royal Designer of Industry.
R.D.S.	Royal Drawing Society.
R.E.	Royal Society of Painter-Printmakers (formerly Royal Society of Painter-Etchers and Engravers); Royal Engineers.
Regt.	Regiment.
Retd.	Retired.
Rev.	Reverend.
R.F.A.	Royal Field Artillery.
R.G.A.	Royal Garrison Artillery.
R.G.I.	Royal Glasgow Institute.
R.G.I.F.A.	Royal Glasgow Insitute of Fine Art.
R.G.S.	Royal Geographical Society; Royal Graphic Society.
R.H.A.	Royal Hibernian Academy.
R.H.S.	Royal Horticultural Society.
R.Hist.S.	Royal Historical Society.
R.I.	Royal Institute of Painters in Water-colours.

R.I.A.	Royal Irish Academy.
R.I.A.I.	Royal Institute of Architects in Ireland.
R.I.A.S.	Royal Institute of Architects in Scotland.
R.I.B.A.	Royal Institute of British Architects.
R.I.C.	Royal Institute of Chemistry.
R.I.C.S.	Royal Institution of Chartered Surveyors.
Rly.	Railway.
Rlys.	Railways.
R.M.	Royal Marines.
R.M.A.	Royal Military Academy.
R.M.I.T.	Royal Melbourne Institute of Technology.
R.M.S.	Royal Society of Miniature Painters.
R.N.	Royal Navy.
R.N.C.M.	Royal Northern College of Music.
R.N.I.B.	Royal National Institute for the Blind.
R.N.L.I.	Royal National Lifeboat Institution.
R.N.R.	Royal Naval Reserve.
R.N.V.R.	Royal Naval Volunteer Reserve.
R.O.I.	Royal Institute of Oil Painters.
R.P.	Royal Society of Portrait Painters and Member.
R.P.S.	Royal Photographic Society.
R.S.	Royal Society.
R.S.A.	Royal Scottish Academy; Royal Society of Arts.
R.S.A.I.	Royal Society of Antiquaries of Ireland.
R.S.E.	Royal Society of Edinburgh.
R.S.F.S.R.	Russian Soviet Federative Socialist Republic.
R.S.G.S.	Royal Scottish Geographical Society.
R.S.L.	Royal Society of Literature.
R.S.M.A.	Royal Society of Marine Arts.
R.S.P.A.	Royal Society for the Prevention of Accidents.
R.S.P.B.	Royal Society for the Protection of Birds.
R.S.T.	Royal Society of Teachers.
R.S.W.	Royal Scottish Water-colour Society or Royal Scottish Society of Painters in Water-colours.
Rt.	Right.
R.T.P.I.	Royal Town Planning Institute.
R.T.Y.C.	Royal Thames Yachting Club.
R.U.A.	Royal Ulster Academy of Painting, Sculpture and Architecture; Royal Ulster Academician.
R.W.A.	Royal West of England Academician; Royal West of England Academy.
R.W.S.	Royal Water-Colour Society (formerly Royal Society of Painters in Water-colours).
S.	South.
s.	son; sons.
S.A.	Society of Antiquaries; Society of Apothecaries.

S.A.A.	Society of Aviation Artists.
S.A.A.C.	Society of Scottish Artists and Artist Craftsmen (renamed 'Visual Arts Scotland').
S.A.B.A.	Scottish Artists' Benevolent Association.
S.A.C.	Scottish Arts Council.
S.A.E.	Society of American Etchers; Society of Automobile Engineers (American).
S.A.F.	Société des Artistes Français.
S.A.G.A.	Society of American Graphic Artists.
S.A.I.	Scottish Arts Institute; Society of Architectural Illustrators.
S.A.I.I.	Society of Architectural and Industrial Illustrators.
Salop.	Shropshire.
S.A.M.	National Society of Art Masters.
S.A.P.	Society of Artist Printmakers.
S.B.A.	Society of Botanical Artists.
S.B.St.J.	Serving Brothers of the Order of St. John of Jerusalem.
S.C.	Senefelder Club; South Carolina.
Sc.	Sculptor.
s-d.	step daughter.
S.D.C.	Society of Designer Craftsmen and Craft Centre (formerly Arts and Crafts Exhibition Society).
S.E.A.	Society for Education in Art; Society of Equestrian Artists (see S.Eq.A.).
Sec.	Secretary.
S.E.F.A.S.	South Eastern Federation of Art Societies.
S.Eq.A.	Society of Equestrian Artists (formerly S.E.A.).
S.F.P.	Society of Floral Painters.
S.G.A.	Society of Graphic Art.
S.G.E.	Society of Glass Engravers.
S.G.F.A.	Society of Graphic Fine Art (formerly Society of Graphic Art).
S.G.P.	Society of Graver Printers.
S.G.T.	Society of Glass Technology.
S.I.	Surveyros' Institute.
S.I.A.C.	Société Internationale des Artistes Chretiens.
S.I.A.D.	(see C.S.D.)
S.I.D.	Society of Industrial Designers of U.S.A.; Mem. Swedish Industrial Designers.
S.I.P.E.	Societe Internationale de Psychopathologie de l'Expression, Paris.
S.K.M.	South Kensington Museum.
S.Lm.	Society of Limners.
S.M.	Society of Miniaturists.
S.M.O.M.	Knight of Magistral Grace of the Sovereign Military

	Order of Malta.
S.M.P.	Society of Mural Painters.
S.N.A.D.	Society of Numismatic Artists and Designers.
S.N.G.M.A.	Scottish National Gallery of Modern Art.
S.N.P.G.	Scottish National Portrait Gallery.
Soc.	Société; Society.
Socs.	Societies.
S.O.F.A.	Society of Feline Artists.
Som.	Somerset.
South. S.A.	Southern Society of Artists.
S.P.	Société Internationale de Philogie, Sciences et Beaux Arts.
S.P.A.B.	Society for the Protection of Ancient Buildings.
S.P.C.K.	Society for the Promotion of Christian Knowledge.
S.P.D.A.	Society of Present-Day Artists.
S.P.E.	International Society of Philosophical Enquiry.
S.P.F.	Société des Pastellistes de France.
S.P.S.	Society of Portrait Sculptors.
S.P.S.A.S.	Swiss Society of Painters, Sculptors and Architects.
Sq.	Square.
s-s.	step son.
S.S.	Royal Statistical Society.
S.S.A.	Society of Scottish Artists.
S.S.C.	Solicitor to the Supreme Court (in Scotland).
S.S.I.	Society of Scribes and Illuminators.
S.S.M.C.E.	Society of Sculptors Medal and Coin Engravers.
S.S.N.	Societaire de la Société Nationale des Beaux Arts.
S.S.S.	Surrey Sculpture Society.
S.S.S.A.	Society of Sussex Sporting Artists.
S.S.W.A.	Scottish Society of Women Artists.
St.	Saint; Street.
Staffs.	Staffordshire.
S.T.C.	Sydney Technical College.
S.T.D.	Society of Typographical Designers.
S.W.A.	Society of Women Artists.
S.W.A.N.	Society for Wildlife Art of the Nations.
S.W.A.S.	Society of Women Artists of Scotland.
S.W.E.	Society of Wood Engravers.
S.WL.A.	Society of Wildlife Artists.
T. & T.	Trinidad and Tobago.
T.C.D.	Trinity College, Dublin.
T.C.M.	Trinity College of Music.
T.C.T.A.	Teaching Certificate for Teachers of Art.
T.D.	Territorial Decoration; Teacher's Diploma.
Terr.	Terrace.
T.E.S.	Times Educational Supplement.

Tex.	Texas.
T.G.C.	Teacher's General Certificate.
T.L.S.	Times Literary Supplement.
TN.	Tennessee.
T.P.I.	Town Planning Institute.
T.R.H.	Their Royal Highnesses.
T.S.B.	Trustee Savings Bank.
U.	Unionist.
U.A.	United Society of Artists.
U.A.E.	United Arab Emirates.
U.C.H.	University College Hospital.
U.C.L.	University College, London.
U.L.U.J.	Union of the plastic artists of Yugoslavia.
U.S.A.	United States of America.
U.S.M.	Ulster Society of Miniaturists.
U.S.S.R.	Union of Soviet Socialist Republics.
U.S.W.A.	Ulster Society of Women Artists.
U.W.A.	Ulster Women Artists.
U.W.P.	University of Wales Press.
U.W.S.	Ulster Water-colour Society.
V.	Vice.
v.	versus.
V. & A.	Victoria and Albert Museum.
Va.	Virginia.
V.A.D.	Voluntary Aid Detachment.
V.C.	Victoria Cross.
V.D.	Volunteer Officers' Decoration; Victorian Decoration.
Vol.	Volume.
V.P.	Vice-President.
V.R.D.	Volunteer Reserve Decoration.
W.	West.
W.A.	Western Australia.
WA.	Washington.
W.A.C.	Welsh Arts Council (see A.C.W.).
W.A.G.	Walker Art Gallery.
W.A.S.C.E.	World Art Science and Cultural Exchanges.
W.C.C.	World Crafts Council.
W.C.S.I.	Water-colour Society of Ireland.
W.S.W.	Water-colour Society of Wales.
W.E.A.	Workers' Educational Association.
W.E.R.P.	Wood Engravers and Relief Printers.
W.G.A.	Wapping Group of Artists
W.G.I.H.E.	West Glamorgan Institute of Higher Education.

W.I.A.A.	Women's International Arts Association.
W.I.A.C.	Women's International Art Club.
W.I.A.S.	Women's International Art Society.
Wilts.	Wiltshire.
Wis.	Wisconsin.
Worcs.	Worcestershire.
W.P.W.	Women Painters of Washington.
W.S. of V.	Water-colour Society of Victoria.
W.W.F.	World Wildlife Fund.
Xmas	Christmas.
Y.A.E.	Yorkshire Artists' Exhibition.
Y.M.(W.)C.A.	Young Men's (Women's) Christian Association.
Yorks.	Yorkshire.
Y.W.D.A.	Yiewsley and West Drayton Arts Council.
Y.W.S.	Yorkshire Water-colour Society.
Z.S.	Zoological Society.